FROMMER'S

BUDGET TRAVEL GUIDE

HAWAII '95
ON $75 A DAY

by Faye Hammel and Sylvan Levey
Assisted by Alexandra Horn

GW00597220

MACMILLAN • USA

Macmillan Travel
A Prentice Hall Macmillan Company
15 Columbus Circle
New York, NY 10023

ISBN 0-671-88471-9
ISSN 1059-7603

Design by Robert Bull Design
Maps by Geografix Inc.

SPECIAL SALES

Bulk purchases (10+ copies) of Frommer's Travel Guides are available to corporations at special discounts. The Special Sales Department can produce custom editions to be used as premiums and/or for sales promotion to suit individual needs. Existing editions can be produced with custom cover imprints such as corporate logos. For more information write to: Special Sales, Prentice Hall, 15 Columbus Circle, New York, NY 10023.

Manufactured in the United States of America

CONTENTS

LIST OF MAPS

INVITATION TO THE READER

In researching this book, we have come across many wonderful establishments, the best of which we have included here. We are sure that many of you will also come across appealing hotels, inns, restaurants, guesthouses, shops, and attractions. Please don't keep them to yourself. Share your experiences, especially if you want to comment on places that have been included in this edition that have changed for the worse. You can address your letters to:

Faye Hammel and Sylvan Levey
Frommer's Hawaii '95 on $75 a Day
c/o Macmillan Travel
15 Columbus Circle
New York, NY 10023

A DISCLAIMER

Readers are advised that prices fluctuate in the course of time and travel information changes under the impact of the varied and volatile factors that affect the travel industry. Neither the author nor the publisher can be held responsible for the experiences of readers while traveling. Readers are invited to write to the publisher with ideas, comments, and suggestions for future editions.

SAFETY ADVISORY

Whenever you're traveling in an unfamiliar city or country, stay alert. Be aware of your immediate surroundings. Wear a moneybelt and keep a close eye on your possessions. Be particularly careful with cameras, purses, and wallets, all favorite targets of thieves and pickpockets

CHAPTER 1
GETTING TO KNOW HAWAII

This book is written for the express purpose of disposing of a couple of myths. The first is that a South Seas idyll—that longed-for journey to enchanted islands that everyone dreams of at one time or another—is beyond the means of the budget traveler. We're here to tell you that all that is ancient history. Less than 5 jet hours and less than $200 away from the West Coast lie the islands of Hawaii, a name to conjure dreams, a place to explore on a shoestring budget.

People will tell you, of course, that the 50th American state is one of the most expensive areas on earth to visit. It is—and it isn't—depending on which Hawaii you care to see. If you choose prepackaged and preconceived Hawaii, you'll undoubtedly stay at plush hotels, dine at expensive restaurants, be herded around in sightseeing limousines with people just like the folks you left back home—and pay a pretty penny for it. But if you agree with us that travel is a do-it-yourself activity, if you'd rather leave the plush and nonsense to others and strike out on your own to find out how the islanders really live, youll find that a vacation in Hawaii is one of the best travel bargains anywhere. For, contrary to legend, Hawaii has dozens of comfortable, clean, and reasonable hotels; scores of restaurants where the food is exotic and inexpensive; and most important, an almost endless list of free and low-cost entertainment—from beaches to bon dances, from museum browsing to mountain climbing, from hiking to dancing the hula. Add to that an incredibly low airfare, and you've got the ideal place for a budget vacation—even in these costly times.

MYTHS & PARADOXES

The second myth was neatly put by a friend of ours, a sophisticated woman who travels regularly to Europe. "Why go all the way to Hawaii," she asks, "just to find yourself at a beach?" Now no one in his or her right mind would dispute the glory of Hawaii's beaches, some of the best in the world. But anyone who looks on Hawaii as merely a seaside resort is missing some of the most profound, exciting, and exotic travel experiences available anywhere.

The essence of Hawaii, its special mystery, lies in its startling and subtle paradoxes. Take its people, as fascinating a mixture of humanity as youll find on this planet. The children and grandchildren of Stone Age warriors, New England missionaries, and Asian plantation workers mingled and intermarried to create nothing less than a new race. Scratch an islander and youll find a Hawaiian-Chinese-Portuguese, a Japanese-American-Tahitian, or perhaps an English-Filipino-Korean. The typical islander—if such a creature exits—long ago gave up counting the racial

DID YOU KNOW . . . ?

- In Hawaii, pineapples are planted to stunt their growth: They must grow to a uniform size in order to fit into cans!
- Charlie Chan's real-life counterpart was Chang Apana, a flamboyant member of the Honolulu Police Department in the early years of the century.
- Hawaii has the longest life expectancy of any of the states, 77 years, for someone born in 1979–81.
- All fish in Hawaii are line-caught, so no dolphins are endangered.
- Hawaii consumes more Spam than all other states combined!
- For political and administrative purposes, Honolulu County is the largest in the United States—it goes all the way to Midway Island, encompassing over 1,000 miles.
- Hawaii is the only state with an active volcanic eruption (since 1983).
- Two of the four major Hawaii counties are governed by women mayors: Linda Crockett Lingle on Maui and Joanne Yukimura on Kauai.
- There are 10,000 species of insect in the Hawaiian Islands, and of these, 98% are found nowhere else on earth.
- In 1989, the median age in Hawaii was 32.3.
- Waialeale, on the island of Kauai, is one of the wettest spots on earth: average annual precipitation is 444 inches.
- The highest sea cliffs in the world—3,200 feet—are found on the northern coast of Molokai.

strains in his or her background; it got too complicated. Hawaii's people, American in ideals, optimism, and drive, still retain the serenity of Polynesia and Asia. They avidly follow the scores of baseball games played by fellow citizens 6,000 miles away in Boston or Philadelphia, yet many of them dream of going to visit the "old country"—Japan, China, the Philippines. And as if in answer to the bigots who cringe at "mongrelization," the interracial mingling has produced some of the most attractive Americans. Hawaii's children are exquisite, a mixture of the best the races can give to each other.

But the paradoxes don't stop here. They are even more astonishing on a sheer topographical level; Hawaii has the kind of scenery that all but overwhelms the senses. Steep cliffs tumbling down to coral beaches, tropical rain forests and woods that run a hundred shades of green, black-sand beaches and pounding blue surf, scores of tropical blossoms, vying for attention at every turn—this is the landscape. Even more awe-inspiring, the volcanoes that created these islands from the vast nothingness of ocean are still alive. The land is still being born. Drive mile after mile on the Big Island of Hawaii and see where the lava flows have scalded their way to the sea and how slowly life renews itself over the years. Then go to Kauai and see what the centuries and the forces of erosion have done to a much older and extinct volcano. You'll have a sense of the youth—and age—of the earth that you can get nowhere else.

The paradox of Hawaii continues on a third level as well. In less than 200 years it has gone from Stone Age to Space Age, from a primitive island kingdom ruled by stern gods of nature to one of the fastest growing states in the country, ruled by equally stern laws of economics. For the past number of years, industry has thrived, hotel and apartment construction has grown astronomically, population and tourism have increased to record levels. Now there is some pulling back: Hawaii is rethinking its dependency on tourism now that plantation agriculture and military spending have decreased. It is concerned about its fragile ecosystem and the siphoning off of profits to foreign inventors. A movement for Hawaiian sovereignty, small but vocal, is growing. And yet Hawaii still remains one of the most popular visitor destinations on earth: almost seven million travelers per year. For despite the complications of changing times, the spirit of aloha remains untouched, the tranquil eye of the hurricane of progress. Perhaps this is why so many people who have been everywhere and back can't seem to get enough of Hawaii.

THE ALOHA SPIRIT

The warm, welcoming hospitality of the islanders is perhaps what impresses the visitor most. One celebrated visitor expressed it very well. Mrs. Jacqueline Kennedy Onassis, returning home after a visit to Hawaii with her family some years back, wrote to the editors of the *Honolulu Star-Bulletin and Advertiser* (who had asked the public to give the Kennedys privacy and assigned no reporters or photographers to follow them around): "In this strange land everyone constantly goes out of his way to be kind to the other. From Governor Burns, who so kindly watched over us and asked people to help make our visit private, to the driver of a vegetable truck who went out of his way to lead us several miles, when we merely asked for directions, everyone in Hawaii has been the same. Now I know what the Aloha spirit means. I hope it is contagious—for it could change the world."

1. GEOGRAPHY, HISTORY & POLITICS

GEOGRAPHY

Most people think of Hawaii as synonymous with Honolulu and Waikiki Beach (and probably know that both are on the island of Oahu), but they're a bit vague about the names of the other islands. Actually, there are 122 islands in the Hawaiian chain, a great volcanic mountain range spreading 1,500 miles across the floor of the Pacific, from Hawaii on the southeast to Midway and Kure islands in the northwest. Many of these are just jagged rocks or sand shoals, however, and the term "Hawaiian Islands" usually refers only to eight: Oahu (on which you find Honolulu), Hawaii or the Big Island, Maui, Kauai, Molokai, Lanai, Kahoolawe, and Niihau. The first five are the ones of greatest interest to the visitor, and the ones we'll describe in this book. Of the last three, Lanai, formerly a pineapple plantation island, owned almost completely by Castle & Cooke, the parent company of the Dole Pineapple Company, began resort development a few years ago with the opening of two new luxury Rockresorts, The Lodge at Koele and the Manele Bay Hotel. Kahoolawe, uninhabited, is a target range for American planes and ships; and Niihau, where an ancient Hawaiian community survives, is private property, not open to the general public.

DATELINE

- **A.D. 400–790** First Polynesian settlers arrive from the Marquesas and Tahitian islands.
- **1778** Capt. James Cook discovers the islands, naming them the Sandwich Islands after his patron, the Earl of Sandwich. *(continues)*

HISTORY

The Hawaiian Islands were settled between 1,200 and 1,500 years ago by Polynesians who most likely came from the Marquesas and Tahitian islands, a feat of navigation undreamed of by their European contemporaries. They crossed thousands of miles of ocean in double-hulled sailing vessels, connected by long bamboo poles that supported a tiny hut between the canoes. They brought with them their animals and plants, introducing such new foods as the sweet potato.

They settled primarily on the largest islands of the Hawaiian archipelago—Hawaii, Kauai, Maui, Molokai, and Oahu. The islands were fragmented into little kingdoms, each ruled by its own chief, with its own *kapus* and particular customs. Power belonged to the strongest, and the bloody overthrow of leaders was quite common. But life was stable, and very probably even comfortable. None of the settlers ever made any attempt to return to the tribes

DATELINE

• **1779** Cook is slain on the island of Hawaii.

• **1790** Kamehameha the Great controls all the islands, establishing the Kingdom of Hawaii.

• **1820** New England missionaries of the Congregational church arrive.

• **1824** Kamehameha II (Liholiho) dies; his brother, Kauikeaouli, becomes Kamehameha III and transforms a semifeudal state into a constitutional monarchy.

• **1831** Lahainaluna School, the oldest high school west of the Rockies, is opened.

• **1840** A Hawaiian constitution is proclaimed.

• **1843** Great Britain cedes the Hawaiian Kingdom, and Hawaii's independence is officially recognized.

• **1850** Kamehameha III officially declares Honolulu the capital of the Hawaiian Kingdom.

• **1852** Chinese arrive under contract to work the sugar plantations. The Japanese begin
(continues)

from which they had come. In the warmth of the sun, these Stone Age people remained undisturbed and untouched by outsiders until the 18th century.

In 1777 Capt. James Cook, looking for the Northwest Passage, stumbled on the island of Kauai. The natives, who had long believed that their great god Lono would one day return to them, mistook Cook and his crew for the god and a full entourage of lesser deities. At first Cook received a god's reception, but soon fighting broke out between the natives and the sailors, and 8 months later, on another voyage, Cook was clubbed to death by natives and drowned off the Kona shore of the island of Hawaii. But from that time on, the Sandwich Islands, as he had named them in honor of the Earl of Sandwich when he claimed them for Great Britain, became part of the modern world. By 1790 King Kamehameha the Great, based on the island of Hawaii, conquered the other islands in the chain in a series of bloody forays (except for Kauai, which surrendered) and united them under his rule. Hawaii was already one nation when the first emissaries from the Western world—merchants, fur traders, whaling men—started their invasion of the islands.

19TH CENTURY In 1820 a band of New England missionaries arrived in Hawaii, determined to save the heathen islanders from the devil. They brought piety, industry, and Congregationalism to the natives; their arrival speeded the end of the old Hawaiian life. (Their story is eloquently told in James Micheners *Hawaii*, in both the novel and the film.) They smashed the idols and continued the destruction of the rigid *kapus* (already weakened by the king prior to their arrival), taught the people to read and write, and "civilized" the natives. And although they undoubtedly did an enormous amount of good, many of the natives here have never forgiven them, as the island saying goes, for doing so well. Some of the missionaries' children turned into businesspeople, bought up the land, and started industries; it is their descendants who are still among the ruling forces of Hawaii's great corporate empires.

The native Hawaiians never really adjusted to the *haole's* (white man's) world, refused to work the plantations, and died from diseases in horrendous epidemics. Today, just a few thousand pure-blooded Hawaiians remain. The rest have disappeared or become intermingled with the other races—mostly Japanese and Chinese—who came to work the plantations.

The Asians began to arrive around 1852, when the whaling trade was dropping off and the sugar plantations were becoming big business. The Chinese came first to work the plantations, then the Japanese, last the Filipinos. The Hawaiian melting pot began to simmer.

Meanwhile, the reign of the second Kamehameha, Kamehameha II, had been short. He and his queen died of measles in London in 1824. Kamehameha III reigned for 30 years, during which time the independence of the island kingdom was recognized by France, Great Britain, and the United States. An English-language newspaper was started and a public school opened at that time, both in the islands' capital, Lahaina, on the island of Maui. But the capital remained there only until 1845, when the king and his court moved to Honolulu. Commerce was picking up in the harbors, and in 1850 that city was declared the capital of the 19th-century kingdom.

The line of the Kamehameha descent ended by 1872, after Kamehameha IV and V. The legislature elected William Lunalilo as successor, but he died within a year; David Kalakaua succeeded him. Queen Emma, the widow of Kamehameha IV, appeared to have a rightful claim to the throne, and it was to this end that many riots were staged. American and British marines were called in.

In the latter part of the 19th century, industry continued to boom, with sugar the leading crop and coffee a close second. (Rice, now of small importance in the state, was once the number-two crop.) Finally, in 1875, the Hawaiian sugar planters worked out a reciprocal agreement with the U.S. government by which Hawaiian sugar companies were assured an American market; when it was renewed in 1887 the Americans were given the freedom to use Pearl Harbor as a coaling station for American ships. The American Age was beginning in Hawaii; the annexation of the Republic of Hawaii took place in 1898, but statehood would not be achieved until more than half a century late, in 1959.

King Kalakaua, "The Merrie Monarch," was followed by Queen Liliuokalani, the last reigning monarch of the islands. When her plans for a new constitution were violently opposed, she was removed from office in the bloodless uprising of 1893 and replaced by Sanford B. Dole, a haole representing American commercial interests. While she was under house arrest, the queen wrote the poignant "Aloha Oe," now a song of farewell to those leaving the islands. But it was also a lament, a farewell to the days of the past when kings and queens, and even an occasional god, walked the earth.

20TH CENTURY The 20th century saw the booming of the pineapple industry in Hawaii. The U.S. Armed Forces moved into the area and made Hawaii an independent army department in 1913. Although Hawaii was not directly involved in World War I, many islanders had volunteered for the French and German armies before the United States entered the conflict. The Depression of the 1930s blew through the islands with the relative calm of a trade wind, compared with the hurricane devastation on the mainland. Big business was not yet too big, industry not yet well developed.

But Hawaii felt the impact of World War II more than any American state. Because the United States had developed the harbors and military installations on the islands, they were a prime target area for the enemy. After the dreadful bombing attack of December 7, 1941, Hawaii entered a period of martial law. Liquor consumption was regulated, curfews were imposed, and blackouts were common. Fortunately, the islands' Japanese population was not herded off into concentration camps as it was in California. In fact, a group of Nisei volunteers became one of the great heroic regiments of the U.S. Army, fighting in southern Eu-

DATELINE

arriving in 1868; the Filipinos, Koreans, Portuguese, Puerto Ricans at a much later date.

• **1872** King Kamehameha the Great's line of descent ends after the death of Kamehameha V.

• **1874** David Kalakaua elected king; Queen Emma, widow of Kamehameha IV, loses her claim to the throne.

• **1875** Sugar planters work out an agreement with the U.S. government assuring them of an American market; when it is renewed in 1887, the U.S. is given exclusive rights to use Pearl Harbor as a coaling station for its ships. The American Age in Hawaii begins.

• **1891** Kalakaua's sister Liliuokalani becomes queen upon his death.

• **1893** When her plans to strengthen the monarchy are violently opposed, Liliuokalani is deposed and put under house arrest; Sanford B. Dole, an American businessman, becomes head of a provisional government.

• **1894** The

(continues)

DATELINE

Provisional
Government
converts Hawaii
into a republic, and
Sanford P. Dole
becomes its first
president.

1898 Hawaii is
annexed by
President
McKinley; Dole is
appointed
governor.

1903 James Dole
produces the first
canned pineapple.

1936 Pan
American Airways
inaugurates
commercial
passenger flights
to Hawaii.

1941 Pearl Harbor
bombed.
December 7, by
Japan. Martial law
declared. Nisei vol-
unteers in the U.S.
Army in southern
Europe are noted
for extraordinary
valor.

1959 Hawaii
achieves statehood
on August 21,
1959, now known
as Admission Day.

rope. The 442nd Regimental Combat Team has been called "probably the most decorated unit in United States military history," and one of its members, Daniel K. Inouye, is the senator of Watergate fame. This participation in the war did a great deal to break down race lines in Hawaii. Today, the Japanese are the largest single ethnic group, and one of the most powerful, in the state.

After the war, increasing lines of transportation developed between the American mainland and Hawaii. Tourism became a major industry and the already existing industries grew at phenomenal rates. Years of labor disputes in the 1940s, spearheaded by the militant ILWU, raised the standard of living for the Hawaiian worker to an all-time high. Finally, in 1959, after a 30-year struggle for statehood that began with Hawaii's first representative to Congress, Prince Jonah Kuhio Kalanianaole, delegate John A. Burns (later Hawaii's governor) affected passage of the bill that made Hawaii the 50th American state. Dancing in the streets celebrated a goal long promised and arduously won.

Since statehood, Hawaii has blossomed and boomed and burst forth into a new era. Now largely Democratic in politics, with a mostly Japanese/American legislature, it is liberal in its outlook, proud of its ability to blend the races, to let the newcomer "do his own thing." Garment industries, steel mills, and cement factories are growing. Agriculture uses the most advanced techniques, and pineapple and sugar are still big business, although on the island of Lanai, pineapple is being phased out. Technology has moved in and made Hawaii the mid-Pacific outpost of Americas space efforts and oceanography research. The University of Hawaii and the East-West Center for Cultural and Technical Interchange have raised the level of education in the state remarkably, bringing in scholars from all over the world. Population is up to 1.1 million; more than six million tourists are expected annually. Despite economic uncertainty here as everywhere, it looks as if Hawaii is still going strong.

POLITICS

A Republican stronghold for many years, in the days when the Big Five ruled the islands, Hawaii, with the rise of labor unions and ethnic groups to positions of political and financial power, has become strongly Democratic in its politics. Up until 1954, there had never been a Democratic majority in either house of the legislature; in 1962, the Democrats captured both branches of the legislature and the governorship as well. Both of its senators in the U.S. Congress, Daniel K. Inouye and Daniel Akaka, are Democrats, as are its representatives in Congress, Patsy Mink and Neil Abercrombie. Both Inouye and Mink are of Japanese-American backgrounds; Akaka is pure Hawaiian; and Abercrombie is 100% haole.

In the state legislature, there are 51 representatives (only 3 are Republicans), and 25 senators (3 are Republicans). Most are of mixed backgrounds; 7 are Hawaiian. John Waihee, the current governor, is about 75% Hawaiian; Lt. Gov. Benjamin Cayetano is pure Filipino.

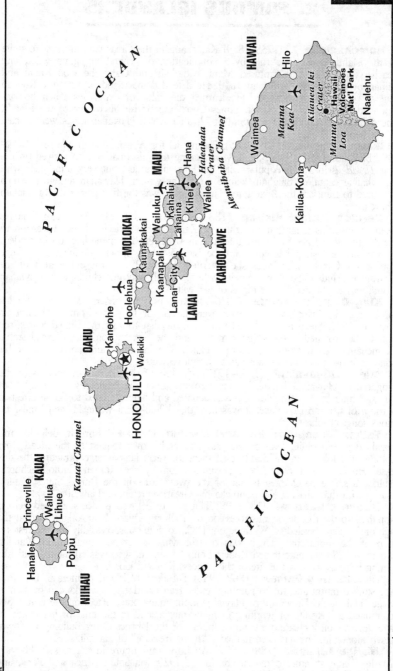

HAWAII

N 0 50 km.
       31 mi

PACIFIC OCEAN

HAWAII
Hilo
Kilauea Iki Crater
Mauna Kea △
Hawaii Volcanoes Nat'l Park
Mauna Loa △
Naalehu
Waimea
Kailua-Kona

MAUI
Hana
Haleakala Crater
Wailuku
Kahului
Lahaina
Kihei
Wailea
Alenuihaha Channel

MOLOKAI
Kaunakakai
Hoolehua

KAHOOLAWE

LANAI
Kaanapali
Lanai City

OAHU
Kaneohe
Waikiki
HONOLULU

PACIFIC OCEAN

KAUAI
Princeville
Wailua
Lihue
Hanalei
Poipu
Kauai Channel

NIIHAU

PACIFIC OCEAN

Airport ✈   Mountain △

6782

2. FAMOUS ISLANDERS

Kamehameha I (1758–1819) Kamehameha the Great was the first to unite all the islands under one rule by a combination of generalship, gunpowder, and treachery. After he had captured Maui, Molokai, and Oahu, he won Kauai and Niihau by treaty negotiations in 1810. He defended the islands against the Russian general Georg Anton Scheffer. He learned the value of explosives when he was wounded in a battle with Capt. James Cook, the British discoverer of the islands. The dynasty he founded lasted until 1872, after which Hawaiian kings were elected by the people.

Hiram Bingham (1789–1869) The model for Abner Hale in Michener's *Hawaii*, Bingham and his wife, Sybil, were among the missionaries who arrived on the brig *Thaddeus* in 1820. Popular with the Hawaiian rulers but very unpopular with the whaling captains, Bingham helped create the written Hawaiian alphabet, which was used to translate the Bible into Hawaiian. He was the first pastor of Kawaiahao Church.

Bernice Pauahi Bishop (1831–84) Married to the American Charles Reed Bishop, this great-granddaughter of Kamehameha I declined the succession to the throne offered her by Kamehameha V in 1872. But her name lives on in modern Hawaii in the Bishop Museum and the Bishop Estate, which administers the huge portion of Kamehameha lands she inherited, almost 9% of the entire area of the Hawaiian islands. The Kamehameha School, which educates children of Hawaiian blood, was established by the terms of her will.

King David Kalakaua (1836–91) Known as the "Merry Monarch" for his fun-loving, high-living ways, he ruled over Hawaii for 17 years, from 1874 until his death in 1891. He was the elected monarch, the first to visit the United States, the first to be crowned publicly (by himself), and the first to construct a royal statue (Kamehameha's, in front of Aliiolani Hale). The ineptness and corruption of his reign gave rise to numerous antimonarchy movements.

Queen Liliuokalani (1839–1917) The last of the reigning monarchs of the kingdom of Hawaii, Liliuokalani sought to strengthen the monarchy by means both fair and foul; for her troubles, she was deposed and later confined to house arrest in a room of her former palace. It was here that Liliuokalani wrote Hawaii's most famous song: "Aloha Oe."

Father [Joseph de Veuster] Damien (1840–69) Born in Belgium and ordained in Honolulu, Damien was assigned at his own request to the dread leper colony on Molokai in 1873. He died there 16 years later after contracting the disease. He is now a candidate for canonization by the Roman Catholic church. Marisol's statue of Damien is one of the two statues in the United States Capitol (along with that of King Kamehameha the Great) representing Hawaii.

Princess Kaiulani (1875–99) The widely beloved princess, named heiress apparent to the throne on the accession of her aunt, Queen Liliuokalani, died at the age of 24. She traveled to Washington, D.C., to argue unsuccessfully for the restoration of the monarchy after it was overthrown. Her estate, Ainahau, in Waikiki, where in 1889 she entertained Robert Louis Stevenson, who was enchanted with the young princess, is now the site of the Princess Kaiulani Hotel.

Juliette May Fraser (1887–1983) The dean of island painters in her time, she studied mural and fresco painting under Jean Charlot. Her works can be seen at Bilger Hall at the University of Hawaii, among many other places on the island. She continued a busy life of working in many media, and at the time of her death, at age 96, was busy creating a ceramic mural for the District Court Building in downtown Honolulu. She has been named a "living treasure" of Hawaii.

Madge Tennent (1889–1972) An important figure in the arts in Hawaii, Madge Tennent came to the islands in the 1920s via South Africa and Paris, and broke away from the academy and its conventions to record on canvas her massive portraits of the Hawaiian people. The Tennent Art Foundation, still open, was a showplace for the work of island artists.

Duke Kahanamoku (1890–1968) Hawaii's most famous athlete, Kahanamoku won Olympic swimming medals in 1912, 1920, 1924, and 1928. He has been honored by the Swimming Hall of Fame and the Surfing Hall of Fame. The Invitational Surfing Championships of Hawaii are named in his honor. His trophies and mementos are on display at the Parker Ranch Visitor Center on the Big Island.

Jean Charlot (1898–1979) Born in Paris, he worked with the great Mexican muralists Rivera and Siqueros. His work in that medium can be seen in Hawaii, Fiji, Mexico, and mainland United States. He came to Hawaii in 1946, published plays in both English and Hawaiian, and taught at the University of Hawaii until 1967, where the Hamilton Library houses the remarkable Jean Charlot Collection.

John Anthony Burns (1909–75) Elected governor in 1962, Burns was instrumental in devising the strategy that led to Hawaiian statehood in 1959. During his three terms in office he spearheaded the movement that led the state from the Republican to the Democratic camp. The John A. Burns School of Medicine at the University of Hawaii bears his name.

Rev. Abraham Akaka (1917–) Since 1957 the pastor of Hawaii's oldest and most prestigious church, Kawaiahao in Honolulu, Akaka, whom the islanders affectionately call "Kahu," delivered the keynote address at the Statehood Service of Dedication, linking the spirit of aloha with the spirit of Christianity in a sermon that has since become a classic in the writings of Hawaii.

Daniel Inouye (1924–) Hawaii's senior senator in the U.S. Congress, Daniel Inouye won national fame in 1974 as a member of the Watergate committee, and again in 1987 as chairman of the committee to investigate the Iran-Contra affair. He continues to hold major positions among Senate Democrats. Inouye has been reelected to the Senate four times. The grandson of Japanese immigrants who came to Hawaii to work the sugar plantations, Inouye was born in Honolulu, graduated from the University of Hawaii and the George Washington University Law School. During World War II, he was a member of the distinguished 442nd Regimental Combat Team, perhaps the most decorated unit in U.S. Military history.

Wally Amos (1936–) This unofficial ambassador of Hawaii is an adopted son: He has lived in the islands since 1977 and claims he'd "rather be a beggar in Hawaii than a king anywhere else." King of the designer cookie market, Uncle Amos promotes his cookies when he's not busy traveling around the country as a motivational speaker. For more than a decade, hes been national spokesman for Literacy Volunteers of America. Amos and his wife and daughter live in Lanikai, on the island of Oahu.

Bette Midler (1945–) Hawaii's gift to show business was born and raised in Hawaii (and named after Bette Davis by her mother, a movie buff). Active in local community theater, she was chosen to play a missionary wife in the movie *Hawaii* when she was 18; she saved her movie money, moved to New York, got a job as understudy in *Fiddler on the Roof*, appeared on "The Tonight Show," started making records—and the rest is history.

Lt. Col. Ellison S. Onizuka, USAF (1946–86) The first Asian-American in manned space flight, astronaut Onizuka died with his six fellow crew members 74 seconds into the flight of the *Challenger* space shuttle on January 28, 1986. A Big Island boy, he was an outstanding athlete and scholar, and flew his first mission on the space shuttle *Discovery* in 1978.

3. HAWAIIAN CULTURE

Traditional Hawaiian culture centers around a worldview best summarized in the term "Aloha Aina"—love for the land. To the Hawaiian, the world and everything in it—minerals, plants, animals, humans, gods—is alive and conscious, sentient. Matter is not something mechanical, a view that dominates Western thinking. It is something that humans can communicate with directly, which nourishes and protects them, and which they, in turn, must nourish and protect. To the Hawaiians, the world is peopled with gods; they may take the forms of mountains, or trees, or the sun or the ocean; they may inhabit the taro root or the breadfruit. Nature is not only conscious, it is often divine.

Out of this understanding of the cooperative relationship between humans and nature grew a system of ethical rules designed to keep this harmony. For example, one was never to take anything from nature—even a flower or a rock—without first asking permission, lest the spirits be displeased. It was also good to leave something of value as a replacement. (It's interesting to note how this ancient prohibition still seems valid. Numerous visitors who have taken lava rocks from Kilauea Volcano on the Big Island, the domain of the volcano goddess, Pele, have sent them back to the park rangers, telling of all sorts of misfortunes that had befallen them afterward.) Because the Hawaiians took care of nature, it took care of them: Thus many plants, stones, etc., were thought to have helpful and healing powers.

Although the traditional religion went underground with the growth of Christianity in the islands, many of its ideas still bubble beneath the surface; they are still in the consciousness of the Hawaiian people. Today something extremely interesting is taking place. There is a drive afoot for a sovereign Hawaiian nation, for establishing places on each island where Hawaiians can live in harmony with nature in the old ways. Unless this happens, they fear, more and more lands will be given away for foreign investment, more and more concrete will cover the once sacred earth, and the old ways—of people and gods and nature living in community the way they did in ancient Hawaii—will be irrevocably lost.

4. HUNA—THE ANCIENT RELIGION

The ancient religion of Hawaii—Huna—remained a mystery to Westerners for many years, as the old teachings were forced underground with the coming of the Christian missionaries and the outlawing of the *kahunas*, the native priests. The tradition had been strictly an oral one, passed on from one generation of kahunas to another. It was not until Max Freedom Long, a teacher who lived and worked in Honolulu in the early years of the century, broke the code after almost 50 years of research into Huna lore and began publishing his works (especially *The Secret Science Behind Miracles* and *The Secret Science at Work*) in the late 1940s and early '50s, that this knowledge became available.

Long and writers who came after him believe that Huna religious beliefs can be traced back to ancient Egypt, and that its followers have left traces in the languages and teachings of many peoples as they brought their philosophy across the world to its last stop in the Polynesian islands.

Although Huna (which means "secret") does not include the concept of a supreme being, the kahunas ("keepers of the secrets") may have included that teaching among those that were never given out except under threat of death. The highest gods of the Hawaiians—Kāne, Kū, Lono, Kanaloa, and Hina—each possessed enormous power, or *mana*, of different qualities, which gave each of them different abilities, such as creation, manifestation, fertility. Similar ideas have been found throughout Polynesia.

But the Hawaiians made a unique contribution to Huna—namely, the belief that lesser gods can be created by the kahunas through special ritual ceremonies in which sufficient mana is given to the bones of deceased chiefs so they take on various degrees of *akua*, or spirit consciousness. (Chiefs go to different heavens than commoners.) This is done to keep the departed spirits bound to their descendants for purposes of protection. The practice of imparting mana—*ho'omanana*—was central to the deification process.

Huna includes the belief that humankind has evolved from the animal kingdom and we are each allied to some specific animal, or totem, which can be called on for help. Unlike Westerners, the Polynesians believe that humans live communally with all forms of life, not just with other humans. This requires attention to all lesser forms of nature. Every aspect of life is made sacred, and there is constant praying for every activity in life—planting and harvesting, relating to people, sailing, swimming, etc.

All life forms operate in pairs: Each sea animal has its land counterpart, night has day, directions are paired with their opposites, the rising sun has the setting sun, male has female—such is the world of polarity.

It is claimed that "all the souls of the departed went to *pō*, place of night, and were . . . eaten by the gods there." Eventually, all human souls are reincarnated, to learn additional lessons on their evolutionary path to godhood. This is called *hou-ola* (ola = life, hou = new) or "preceding life."

In addition to this process of spiritual evolution, God is brought down to the level of humans in the form of the *aumakua* or High Self, which is the guiding spirit of each human, which also possesses a low self or animal self (the *unihipili*) and a middle self or intellect (*uhane*). There is an allowance for higher beings in the cosmos, but for the purpose of daily living, the practical Polynesians consider it sufficient to know that there is a divine soul in humans that is an intimate part of our total being and is ever ready to aid us when we call to it.

The process by which humans enlist the aid of the High Self or aumakua is known as *ho'oponopono*. This process requires the cooperation of the middle and low selves. The middle self or uhane asks the low self or unihipili to carry a message to the aumakua on the medium of desire (which is lacking to the intellect). First one charges the unihipili by a special breathing technique, and if one is on good terms with his low self the low self is perfectly willing to carry the prayer to the High Self, which responds by meeting the request. Many unanswered prayers are thus explained as a lack of a friendly relation between the intellect and ones emotional nature, or subconscious mind, as it is called in Western psychology.

When one's male and female humans are united after a life of living in love, the uhane graduates to the status of aumakua upon death and is eventually reincarnated as a guiding spirit for a new uhane and unihipili for a new round of incarnation.

It has been speculated that corrupt kahunas had the ability to extract mana from human sacrifices, which they absorbed into their beings for malignant uses. These dark kahunas often used departed spirits to murder their enemies. Women were considered less advanced than men and were discriminated against in many ways, including the prohibition from eating many kinds of food and from participating in religious ceremonies. The tabu system was not broken until the widow of Kamehameha I, Kaahamanu, confronted the old gods and smashed their powers in the 1820s.

5. PERFORMING ARTS & EVENING ENTERTAINMENT

Hawaii has a rich artistic life, ranging from chamber music concerts to Broadway revivals, from performances of ancient hulas to nightclub Polynesian spectaculars. Visi-

IMPRESSIONS

The loveliest fleet of islands that lies anchored in any ocean.
—MARK TWAIN, 1872

"See Naples and die"—They spell it differently here: See Hawaii and live.
—JACK LONDON, 1916

tors can go to concerts by the Honolulu Symphony and the Hawaii Opera Theater or hear Chamber Music Hawaii; they can choose from a variety of theaters including the 43-year-old Diamond Head Theater, the always-innovative Manoa Valley Theater, the Starving Artists Theatre Company, and the John F. Kennedy Theatre at the University of Hawaii, known for performances of everything from Kabuki to Shakespeare. And Waikiki at night is a continuous festival of music, dance, and entertainment. For details, see Chapter 7, "Honolulu Attractions," as well as the chapters on the individual Hawaiian islands.

6. SPORTS & RECREATION

The opportunities are endless; swimming, snorkeling, sailing, scuba diving, hiking, tennis, golf, parasailing, windsurfing—even ice skating and snow skiing! Hawaii's got them all, and more. For details, see Chapter 7, "Honolulu Attractions," as well as the chapters on the individual Hawaiian islands.

7. FOOD & DRINK

THE CUISINE

The food of Hawaii, like its people, reflects a cultural diversity—a lot of American, quite a bit of Japanese, a little less of Chinese, a smattering of Hawaiian, Korean, Filipino, and you-name-it thrown in for good measure. You quickly get used to the fact that a delicatessen can be Japanese and to the fact that saimin (a Japanese-type noodle soup with a seaweed base) is just as popular as a hamburger and is often served at the same counter.

You soon learn that the exotic-sounding *mahimahi* is Hawaiian for dolphin, a pleasant-tasting fish—not to be confused with the intelligent mammal of the same name, the porpoise. You'll be introduced to poi (crushed taro root), the staff of life of the early Hawaiians, at your very first luau—you may develop a liking for this purple-gray goo thats one of the most nutritious foods known, so high in vitamin B and calcium that its fed to babies and invalids. Just ignore the old joke that it tastes like library paste; the Hawaiians, and quite a few malihinis, think it's delicious.

Hawaii's fruits are among the islands special glories. Pineapple, while not exactly invented here, might just as well have been. It's well priced in the markets, served everywhere, and as good as you'd imagine. Pineapple juice is a kind of national drink, something like tea for the English. If you hit the mango season in summer, when the local trees are bursting with this succulent fruit, you're in for a great treat. Guavas, coconuts, and papayas (one of the most common breakfast foods) are all superb, as are guava juice and passion-fruit juice, which you'll often see listed under its Hawaiian name, *lilikoi* (lilikoi sherbet is wonderful). In the supermarkets, you'll see a very popular drink called POG—that's short for passion-fruit juice, orange juice, and guava juice—very popular and very good. Macadamia-nut pancakes, as well as coconut ice cream and syrup, are special treats that taste better in Hawaii than anywhere else. We should warn you coffee addicts right here and now—the kind of coffee you'll get everywhere is Kona coffee, grown on the Big Island of Hawaii, and it's so good that you may find yourself drinking innumerable cups a day.

Don't miss the chance to try Hawaii's game fish, caught fresh in local waters and served up in fish houses under "catch of the day." If you're lucky, the catch that day will be ahi (a kind of tuna and a personal favorite), aki (another tuna), marlin, ulua, opakapaka, rock cod, or a special island delicacy called ono. That word has, in fact, slipped into local parlance as meaning "delicious"—or even "great"—as in "ono ono." At this writing, "catch of the day" was selling for about $16 to $20 in most restaurants.

LUAUS Youll probably first experience Hawaiian food at a luau, and then you'll find the same dishes in Hawaiian restaurants. You're already on speaking terms with poi. Other basic dishes are kalua pig (pig steamed in an underground oven, or *imu*), laulau (ti leaves stuffed with pork, salt fish, bananas, sweet potatoes, and taro shoots, and steamed), chicken luau (chicken cooked with coconut milk and taro or spinach leaves), sweet potatoes, pipikaula (jerked beef), and lomi-lomi salmon. The last is a triumph of linguistics: Lomi-lomi means massage, and this is salmon massaged with tomatoes and chopped onions, then marinated. Haupia (coconut pudding) and a piece of coconut cake are the usual desserts, along with fresh pineapple.

Most luaus are serve-yourself buffet affairs; food is usually eaten from paper plates, with plastic cutlery. The correct way to eat poi, by the way, is to dip one or two fingers in it (in the old days, you could actually order "one-" or "two-finger" poi, scoop it up quickly, and attack). But nobody expects that of a malihini.

LOCAL FOOD Local food does not really have deep roots in Hawaiian culture. What most people refer to as local food—and it's eaten in "plate lunches" popular everywhere in Hawaii—consists of dishes such as fried chicken, beef stew, teriyaki pork, breaded mahimahi, and the like; much of it is deep-fried. This is invariably accompanied by *two* carbohydrates, usually rice and a macaroni or potato-macaroni salad. A very popular local dish is called the loco moco—thats a hamburger patty over rice topped with a fried egg and brown gravy. Warning: Don't go local if you're counting calories or looking for "heart-healthy" food!

HAWAII REGIONAL CUISINE A style called Hawaii Regional or sometimes Pacific Rim cuisine is served more and more in better restaurants. This cuisine marries the remarkable fresh local produce of the islands, the freshly caught fish, the locally grown beef, and the like, with the best of European and Asian cooking traditions. Prime examples: Avalon Restaurant in Maui, A Pacific Café in Kauai, and Roy's in Honolulu and Maui.

KOREAN CUISINE The islands contain quite a few Korean restaurants, and they're good to know about for the budget traveler because of their modest price and delicious food. Although Koreans make up a small part of the population, their culinary tradition has left its mark, especially in the ubiquitous kimchee—pickled cabbage seasoned with red-hot peppers. You'll find it in grocery stores, on menus everywhere in Honolulu, and even at beach stands along Waikiki serving kimchee dogs. Korean cuisine has much more to offer, including barbecued meat and chicken, hearty noodle soups, tasty meat dumplings, fish filets sautéed in spicy sauces, and daintily shredded vegetables. Some but not all dishes are served with fiery hot sauces; if you're not accustomed to that sort of thing, check with the serving staff before you order.

SHAVE ICE A unique treat thats loved by just about all islanders is a phenomenon called shave ice. That's not "shaved" ice, or a snow cone or a slush. It's just wonderful Hawaiian shave ice. You can have a "plain" shave ice—that's just the incredibly fine ice particles bathed in syrup—and there are all kinds of syrups. Strawberry is the most popular, but there's also vanilla, guava, lemon, cherry, orange, root beer, coconut, and combinations of the above, known as "rainbow." Or you can have ice cream or adzuki beans (a sweet Japanese bean used in desserts) on the bottom, or throw caution to the winds and order ice cream *and* beans on the bottom. Shave ice is served in a cone-shaped paper cup, with both a straw and a spoon.

DRINK

Generally, you need not worry about drinking tap water, except, alas, in some areas on Maui and upcountry on the Big Island. Because of acid rain pollution, it's best to drink bottled spring water here. Soft drinks and mineral waters are the same as you find back home. As for beer, the favorite local brew is called Primo. There's a potent local liquor called okolehao, distilled from the ti root. Wine is now produced on Maui: Tedeschi Vineyards offers a pineapple wine, a champagne, a blush, and a red table wine in the Beaujolais Nouveau tradition. Wine and liquor are sold in supermarkets.

8. RECOMMENDED BOOKS, FILMS & RECORDINGS

BOOKS

HISTORY, POLITICS & SOCIOLOGY   The definitive book on Hawaii is Gavan Daws's *A Shoal of Time* (University Press of Hawaii), a history of Hawaii from 1778 until statehood (1959). It reads like a novel. Collaborating with George Cooper, Daws has also written *Land and Power in Hawaii* (University of Hawaii Press), a controversial, much-talked-about book on politics and personal financial interests in the state.

Frederick Simpich, Jr.'s book *Anatomy of Hawaii* (Coward, McCann & Geoghegan) is considered one of the most comprehensive historical and sociological studies. Also of note is *Hawaii, an Uncommon History* by Edward Joesting (Norton). *Hawaii* by Gerrit P. Judd (Macmillan) is another worthwhile study, from the point of view of the missionaries. Kristin Zambucka's book on Princess Kaiulani is considered a classic: *Kaiulani, The Last Hope of the Monarchy* (Mana Publishing Co.). *The Betrayal of Liliuokalani* (Mutual Publishing) is a definitive account of the overthrow of the queen. Liliuokalani's story is told in her own words in her autobiography, written in 1896 and recently republished: *Hawaii's Story by Hawaii's Queen* (Mutual Publishing). *The Real Hawaii, Its History and Present Condition, Including the True Story of the Revolution* (reprint edition published by Arno Press) by Lucien Young, USN, covers the author's personal observations of the political situation in 1892 and 1893 and later years.

FICTION   James Michener's *Hawaii* (Random House) is required reading before a trip to Hawaii. Michener has taken a leading figure from each of the groups who settled the islands—the Polynesians, the American missionaries, the Chinese, the Japanese—and through their stories, told the story of Hawaii. Reading it will illuminate your trip as nothing else will. Also illuminating, beautifully written, and tremendously informative are the five historical novels written by O. A. Bushnell, a ka-maaina with a touch of Hawaiian blood, and a reverence for Hawaii and his heritage. They are: *Molokai*, which tells the story of the leper colony (University Press of Hawaii); *The Return of Lono* (University of Hawaii Press), dealing with Captain Cook; *Kaawa* (University Press of Hawaii), set in Hawaii in the 1850s; and his last two, *The Stones of Kannon* (University Press of Hawaii) and *The Water of Kane* (University Press of Hawaii), both of which are about the Japanese who came to the islands to work the sugar plantations. For another fictional account of the Japanese in Hawaii, read Kazuro Miyamoto's *Hawaii, End of the Rainbow* (Tuttle).

James Jones's *From Here to Eternity* (Scribner's), set at Schofield Barracks, was a big best-seller of the 1950s and is still worth reading for its portrayal of army life in Hawaii in the early 1940s. There is also a noted film adaptation.

IMPRESSIONS

Midway across the North Pacific, space, time and life uniquely interlace a chain of islands named "Hawaiian." . . . These small fragments of land appear offered to the sky by water and pressed to earth by stars.
—CHARLES A. LINDBERGH

Several collections of short stories make for absorbing reading. Among these are *A Hawaiian Reader*, edited by A. Grove Day (Appleton), and its companion volume, *The Spell of Hawaii* (Meredith), which include, among others, stories by Jack London, Robert Louis Stevenson, W. Somerset Maugham, Mark Twain, and James Michener. Jack London's *Stories of Hawaii* (Appleton) and Gerrit P. Judd's *A Hawaiian Anthology* (Macmillan) are also engaging.

NATURE Sherwin Carlquist's *Hawaii: A Natural History* (Doubleday) is comprehensive and authoritative. George Munroe's *Birds of Hawaii* (Tuttle) is well illustrated and very helpful for bird-watchers. For a well-illustrated guide to Hawaii's seashells, with 380 full-color illustrations, read *Seashells of Hawaii* by Stephen Quirk and Charles Wolfe (W. W. Distributors). *Stars Over Hawaii*, originally written by E. H. Bryan, Jr., of the Bishop Museum and published by the Petroglyph Press, is an illustrated paperback with monthly star charts of the Hawaiian skies. Robert Decker's *Volcano Watching* (Hawaii Natural History Association and U.S. Natural Park Service), features colorful photos of volcanic eruptions. For more book suggestions, see "Hiking" under "Sports and Recreation" in Chapter 7.

PHOTOGRAPHY Scores of photographers were given 1-day assignments in Hawaii and the result was a fascinating tome: *A Day in the Life of Hawaii* (Workman Publishing). Robert Wenkham has produced five superb pictorial books with magnificent full-color photographs, all published by Rand McNally. They are *Honolulu Is an Island*; *Hawaii*; *Maui: The Last Hawaiian Place*; *Kauai*; and *The Park Country of Hawaii*. A wonderful remembrance of the Big Island is *Hawaii: The Big Island, a Visit to a Realm of Beauty, History and Fire* (Mutual Publishing), with text by Glen Grant and breathtaking photos by principal photographers Peter French and Greg Vaughan. Jocelyn Fujii's *Under the Hula Moon* (Crown Publishers) contains beautiful photographs of Hawaiian homes and environments.

FOLKLORE, LEGEND & PHILOSOPHY Martha Beckwith's *Hawaiian Mythology* (University of Hawaii Press) is a reprint of a valuable scholarly text. David Kalakaua's *The Legends and Myths of Hawaii: The Fables and Folklore of a Strange People* (Tuttle) is an early source of folklore recorded by King Kalakaua. *Man, Gods and Nature*, by Michael Keone Dudley (Na Kane Oka Malo Press), outlines traditional Hawaiian spiritual practices.

The classic books on Huna, the ancient philosophy of Hawaiians passed down by secret oral tradition, were written by Max Freedom Long, beginning with *The Secret Science Behind Miracles* (Huna Research Publications). Leilani Melville's *Children of the Rainbow* (DeVorss Publishers) is another classic on Huna. A modern-day Hawaiian shaman, Serge Kahili King, has also written books on Huna, including *Kahuna Healing, Mastering Your Hidden Self* and *Imagineering for Health* (both published by Quest) and *Urban Shaman* (Simon & Schuster). All these books are available at Kauai Village Museum, 4-831 Kuhio Hwy. in Kauai (tel. 808/822-9272).

RECREATION Craig Chisholm's *Hawaiian Hiking Trails* (Touchstone Press) is considered one of the best hiking guides. As for surfing, read Fred Hemming's *Surfing, Hawaii's Gift to the World of Sport* (Zokeisha Publications), which covers everything from history to surfboards to wave formation. Tony Rizzuto's *Modern Hawaiian Gamefishing* (University of Hawaii Press) tells all about fish, alive and cooked, including some fish stories. *Hawaii Parklands* gives the would-be camper complete information about national, state, and county parks on all six major islands, as well as 97 full-color photographs of wild and scenic places (available from

---

IMPRESSIONS

You'll never know Hawaii 'til you've felt the foaming surf about your knees; 'til you've plunged into the breakers with a cry of pagan glee.
—DON BLANDING, 1928

Hawaii Geographic Maps & Books, 49 S. Hotel St., Suite 218, Honolulu, HI 96813; tel. 808/538-3952). For more book suggestions, see "Hiking" under "Sports and Recreation" in Chapter 7.

TRAVEL For an understanding of travel in Hawaii over a century ago, read Isabella Bird Bishop's *Six Months in the Sandwich Islands*, an engaging account of Hawaiian life in 1873. Robert Wallace's *Hawaii*, part of the Time-Life American Wilderness series, focuses on the wilderness areas of the state.

VIDEOS/FILMS

Popular videos at World of Music at Ala Moana Center include *You Can Do the Hula, The Polynesian Cultural Center, Portrait of Elegance*, and—not to be missed—*The 1990 Merrie Monarch Hula Festival*, highlights from the annual world Olympics of hula.

Hawaiian Paradise is the only video sold by the Bishop Museum. Its a breathtaking travelogue, showing volcanic eruptions, underwater scenes, and many other scenic wonders.

Tropical Visions Video (62 Halaulani Place, Hilo, HI 96720) puts out *Volcano Scapes I* and *Volcano Scenes II*, which documents the current 9-year-long eruption of Kilauea with some extraordinary footage.

Forever Hawaii (P.O. Box 26147, honolulu, HI 96825) presents four exciting videos: *Forever Hawaii, Forever Maui, The Volcanoes of Hawaii*, and, on the unusual side, *Whalesong, Whales and Dolphins of the Pacific*; profits support cetacean research and conservation.

RECORDINGS

Here are some of Hawaii's favorite recording artists. For music of the Monarchy period, listen to anything by Palani Vaughan. Emma Veary features many lovely Monarchy songs on her albums. The late Aunty Edith Kanakaole is known for wonderful Hawaiian music and chants. For lyrical old Hawaiian songs, the best are recordings by Aunty Genoa Keawe and the Brothers Cazimero. For authentic, spirited Hawaiian music, it's the Makaha Sons of Niihau. And for true Hawaiian falsetto singing, nobody can beat Tony Conjugación.

For mostly contemporary Hawaiian and hapa-haole music, our favorite group is Olomana, starring a wonderful singer named Jerry Santos. Santos's mentor, the renowned kumu hula (hula master) Frank Hewett, also has a few excellent recordings. Also rating way up there are two sets of brothers—the Cazimeros, Roland and Robert, and the Beamers, Keola and Kapono, who have made albums together and separately—and a delightful group of three hefty local gentlemen called the Pandanus Club. Willie K., a new talent, took top honors recently at the Horu awards. Alfred Apaka's works are classics, and Ho'okena is a new group to look for. Women vocalists offering mostly contemporary music are Nohelani Cypriano, Karen Keawehawaii, and Melveen Leed. (Leed is leaning toward a sort of "country" sound these days.) For awesome slack-key guitar: the Beamer brothers again, and the late Gabby Pahiniu. Also, the Peter Moon band, featuring two of Gabby's sons, Cyril and Martin. These three brothers Pahiniu—Cyril, Martin, and rascally Bla—are also highly successful recording artists.

Regarding comedy albums, we'd recommend anything by the incredibly funny Frank DeLima or by impressionist Billy Sage, who does devastating takeoffs on local and national politicos. Albums of the late, lamented Rap Reiplinger, who wrote his own material and did all the voices, are also hysterically funny. Two new "Best of Rap Reiplinger" albums have been issued recently. Theres a new album by the Japanese comedienne Tamayo Otskua, who was featured on the TV show "Coach" and performs in Hawaii frequently. Anything by Booga Booga or Andy Bumati can be counted on for good fun.

CHAPTER 2

PLANNING A TRIP TO HAWAII

In this chapter, the where, when, and how of your trip to Hawaii is discussed—the advance planning that gets your trip together and takes it on the road.

After deciding where to go, most people have two fundamental questions: What will it cost? and How do I get there? This chapter not only helps answer those questions, but addresses such important issues as when to travel, whether to take a tour, what kind of health precautions to take, what kind of insurance to carry, where to obtain additional information, and much more.

WHICH ISLANDS TO VISIT?

Too many tourists start and end their Hawaiian holidays in Honolulu on Oahu—and think they've seen Hawaii. Yes—and no. They've seen the largest city and the principal resort area, but far more awaits: a Hawaii at once more gentle and more savage, where the old gods still have powers. To see the desolate moonscapes of the volcanoes and Hawaiian cowboys riding the range, to see beaches so remote and pristine as to make Waikiki seem like Times Square, and to visit South Seas villages just coming into the modern age, plan to venture to the three other important Hawaiian Islands: the Garden Island of Kauai, the Big Island of Hawaii, and the Valley Isle of Maui. If you have more time, you may also want to visit Molokai and Lanai.

Following is an overview of the individual Hawaiian islands. Much more information on each appears later in this guide.

OAHU Known as the Gathering Place, the island of Oahu contains Honolulu, Hawaii's capital and main cultural center, in the southeast, and great ocean surfing locations in the northwest and west. Among Oahu's many other attractions are the USS Arizona Memorial at Pearl Harbor, Waimea Falls Park, and Nuuanu Pali, scene of a bloody battle in 1795.

KAUAI Kauai is not as well known as it should be. It's refreshingly rural, small, beautiful, and easily assimilated. Waimea Canyon, a smaller version of the Grand Canyon, is it's principal natural attraction. It also has a string of unforgettable beaches (you've seen them as Bali H'ai in the movie version of *South Pacific* and as Matlock Island in the television production of *The Thorn Birds*). Most of the devastation wrought by Hurricane Iniki in 1992 is now history.

HAWAII The Big Island of Hawaii encompasses the most varied geography of the islands, and is like a small continent in miniature. It has few beaches (except in the Kona area), but contains the islands' second-biggest city (Hilo), the volcanic wonderlands of Mauna Kea and Mauna Loa (Volcanoes National Park is a must on any itinerary), and a cattle ranch big enough for Texas.

MAUI Maui has become the most popular of the neighbor islands and appeals especially to an affluent condo crowd; it has some of the best golf courses in the state of Hawaii. Maui's great natural wonder is Haleakala, the largest dormant volcano in the world, with a moonlike crater that you can explore on foot or horseback. Also alluring are the popular, picturesque old whaling town of Lahaina, remote and lovely Hana, and a succession of golden beaches.

MOLOKAI & LANAI Next to largely inaccessible Niihau, Molokai is the most Hawaiian of the Hawaiian Islands, with the largest number of native Hawaiians. A festival celebrating the birth of the hula takes place there every year. The island of Lanai, once nothing more than a gigantic pineapple plantation, has entered the world of modern tourism with two posh Rockresorts—Manele Bay and Keole Lodge. You may want to splurge about $139 on one of the sailing-ship cruises out of Lahaina, Maui, and spend a day on Lanai.

1. INFORMATION, ENTRY REQUIREMENTS & MONEY

SOURCES OF INFORMATION

For further information on traveling and living in Hawaii, you can contact the **Hawaii Visitors Bureau (HVB)**, which has offices in the following cities:

On the Mainland Suite 1031, 180 N. Michigan Ave., **Chicago,** IL 60601 (tel. 312/236-0632); Room 610, Central Plaza, 3440 Wilshire Blvd., **Los Angeles,** CA 90010 (tel. 213/385-5301; Suite 808, 350 Fifth Ave., **New York,** NY 10018 (tel. 212/947-0717; and Suite 450, 50 California St., **San Francisco,** CA 94111 (tel. 415/392-8173.

In Hawaii *On Oahu:* Suite 801, Waikiki Business Plaza, 2270 Kalakaua Ave., Honolulu, HI 96815 (tel. 808/923-1811). *On the Big Island:* 75-5719 W. Alii Dr., Kailua-Kona, HI 96740 (tel. 808/329-7787); 250 Keawe St., Hilo, HI 96720 (tel. 808/961-5717). *On Maui:* Maui Visitors Bureau, 1727 Wili Pa Loop (Wailuku Millyard), P.O. Box 580, Wailuku, HI 96793 (tel. 808/244-3530). *On Kauai:* Suite 207, Lihue Plaza Building, 3016 Umi St., Lihue, Kauai, HI 96766 (tel. 808/245-3971).

ENTRY REQUIREMENTS/MONEY

If you're a U.S. citizen or permanent resident, one of the nicest things about going to Hawaii is that you don't have to fiddle with passports or visas. Nor do you have to worry about currency exchange. Despite it's exotic flavor, Hawaii is still part of the U.S.A. Entry requirements for foreigners are discussed in Chapter 3.

WHAT THINGS COST IN HAWAII	**U.S. $**
Taxi from Honolulu International Airport to Waikiki	$20–$25
Van from Honolulu International Airport to Waikiki	$5.00
Local telephone call	.25
Double room at the Westin Maui (deluxe)	$210–$345
Double room at the Maui Islander (moderate)	$69.00
Double room at the Royal Grove, Honolulu (budget)	$36.00
Lunch for one at Lahaina Coolers, Maui (moderate)	$7.00
Lunch for one at Ocean View Inn, Big Island (budget)	$5.00
Dinner for one, without wine, at Cascada, Honolulu (expensive)	$25.00
Dinner for one, without wine, at the Café Pesto, Big Island (moderate)	$12.00
Dinner for one, without wine, at the Old Spaghetti Factory, Honolulu (budget)	$7
Bottle of beer	$2.50
Cup of coffee	$1.00–$2.50
Coca-Cola	$1.15
Roll of ASA 100 Kodacolor film, 36 exposures	$4.69
Admission to Bishop Museum, Honolulu	$7.95
Movie ticket	$5.50
Theater ticket to Manoa Valley Theater, Honolulu	$14–$25
The Brothers Cazimero Show, Monarch Room, Royal Hawaiian Hotel, Honolulu	
dinner show	$56.00
cocktail show	$22.50

2. WHEN TO GO—CLIMATE, HOLIDAYS & EVENTS

CLIMATE

The Hawaiian "season" has little to do with the weather in the islands. Rather, it's tied to the weather back home. In the islands, the weather is usually good year round. Hawaii's climate is tropical, with springlike temperatures averaging about 75°F and seldom ranging more than 6° or 7° above or below this point. In midwinter, you can occasionally get some "raw" days in the low- to-mid-60s, and in midsummer, you can experience some humid ones in the 80s. (August is probably the most humid month of the year; if your room does not have cross-ventilation to allow the trade winds to come through, air conditioning is essential at that time). Cool waters drifting down from the Bering Sea make the islands 10° cooler than other places in the same latitude—and the trade winds provide balmy breezes. As for rain, we have experienced some dreary, rainy days here, especially in winter—

anytime from November to March. But most of the time, showers are brief and seldom heavy enough to spoil the pleasures of a vacation.

HOLIDAYS

Just about all businesses and banks will be closed on the major holidays: Christmas, New Year's, Easter Sunday, and Thanksgiving Day. In addition to the legal holidays observed throughout the United States—Memorial Day, July 4th, Labor Day, Martin Luther King, Jr., Day, Election Day, and Veterans Day—there are specific Hawaiian holidays on which many business close: Prince Kuhio Day (March 26), Kamehameha Day (June 11), and Admission Day (the third Friday in August).

HAWAII
CALENDAR OF EVENTS

JANUARY

☐ **Molokai Makahiki.** The annual Hawaiian "time of peace" celebration takes place on the island of Molokai, usually on the second and third Saturdays of January. In addition to a skin-diving tournament and competitions in Hawaiian games, several of Hawaii's most popular music groups perform. For information, phone Walter Ritte at 808/553-3688.

FEBRUARY

☐ **Cherry Blossom Festival.** A Japanese cultural and trade show, complete with a Queen Pageant, crafts fairs, and the Red and White Song Festival. For information, telephone 808/955-2778. From early February through April.

☐ **Narcissus Festival.** For 3 weeks before and 5 days after the Chinese New Year (which usually falls at the end of January), a series of lantern parades, fashion and flower shows, banquets, house-and-garden tours, the crowning of the Narcissus Queen, and dancing in the streets. For information, call the Chinese Chamber of Commerce at 808/533-3181.

✪ **PUNAHOU SCHOOL CARNIVAL** *One of the most popular family events in Honolulu, this yearly carnival features 23 rides, including a Ferris wheel and a merry-go-round, and 60 booths offering plants, foods, arts and crafts, and so forth. Best of all is the White Elephant tent at the end of the carnival, when leftovers—often clothing in good condition—sell for ridiculously low prices.*
> ***Where:*** *Punahou School, 1601 Punahou St., Honolulu.* ***When:*** *First week in February.* ***How:*** *Free admission. Call 808/944-5753 for information.*

MARCH

☐ **Prince Kuhio Day.** Hawaii's beloved "people's prince" and first delegate to the U.S. Congress is honored with impressive ceremonies at Prince Kuhio Federal Building. At Kuhio Beach in Waikiki, the site of his home, a memorial tablet is decorated with leis. Hawaiian societies hold special programs and events. March 26.

MARCH/APRIL

☐ **Easter Sunrise Service** at Punchbowl Cemetery is a moving Honolulu tradition.

APRIL

⊙ *MERRIE MONARCH FESTIVAL COMPETITIONS   Workshops, performances and more hula than you can shake a hip at. The statewide olympics of hula and one of the most popular events in the islands. Nightly television broadcasts are watched by just about everyone.*
Where*: Edith Kanakaole Multi-Purpose Center, Hilo, HI.* **When:** *April 16–22.*
How: *On January 1 send order to Merrie Monarch Festival, Dorothy Thompson, Executive Director, Hawaii Naniloa Hotel, 93 Banyan Dr., Hilo, HI 96720 (tel. 808//935-9168). Send cashier's check or money order only.* **Prices:** *$20 to $25 for three nights.*

MAY

⊙ *LEI DAY   May Day is Lei Day in Hawaii. Lei competitions are held throughout the state. Everybody wears a lei, a Lei Queen is crowned, and there's a Lei Day concert at the Waikiki Shell, usually with the beloved Brothers Cazimero in the evening.*
Where: *Oahu events are held in Kapiolani Park.* **When:** *May 1.* **How:** *Tickets are on sale at Waikiki Shell after 5pm (before that at Blaisdell Center and Sears outlets). The price is around $15 for general admission. Come early, bring a picnic supper and a blanket, and join Hawaii's people for a joyous event. Some visitors plan their entire trip around this event.*

- ☐ **Buddha Day.** Flower festival pageants at island temples throughout the state celebrate the birth of Buddha. May 7.
- ☐ **Molokai Ka Hula Piko.** A celebration of the birth of the hula takes place on Molokai and features performances by Molokai hula halau, musicians, and singers, along with demonstrations of traditional Hawaiian crafts. Crafts, Hawaiian foods, and Molokai specialties can be purchased throughout the day-long celebration. For information, telephone Molokai Visitors Association at 808/553-3876, or toll free 800/800-6367. Third weekend in May.

JUNE

- ☐ **Kamehameha Day.** A state holiday (many offices closed), honoring Kamehameha the Great, Hawaii's first monarch. It's one of the biggest celebrations of all; there are parades and festivities all over the islands. In Honolulu, the annual King Kamehameha Celebrations Floral Parade includes floral floats, pageantry, Pa'u mounted riders, bands, and more, concluding with a cultural and arts festival at Kapiolani Park. June 11, with festivities starting a few days earlier.

JULY

- ☐ **Hale'iwa Bon Odori Festival.** This is one of the happiest and most colorful events in the islands, and includes traditional dances to welcome the arrival of departed souls in paradise. The dances are sponsored by Japanese Buddhist temples whose members practice their steps for months. Usually mid-July.
- ☐ **Prince Lot Hula Festival.** Local hula halaus perform ancient and modern hulas in a festival that honors King Kamehameha V. At Moanalua Gardens in Honolulu. Usually the third week in July.

AUGUST

○ **36th ANNUAL HAWAIIAN INTERNATIONAL BILLFISH TOURNAMENT** *This is the leading international marlin fishing tournament in the world, and it draws fishers and fans from everywhere.*
Where: *Kailua-Kona, Big Island.* **When:** *August 8–12, with a parade on August 9.* **How:** *Book rooms in Kailua-Kona well in advance; the place is mobbed. Telephone 808/329-1148 for information.*

SEPTEMBER

☐ **Aloha Festivals.** Take the celebrations of all the ethnic groups, roll them into one, and you'll get some idea of Aloha Festivals, which are held on the different islands in a more-or-less progressive order. The Asian, Polynesian, and Western groups all get together for this *hoolaulea* (gathering for a celebration), each vying to demonstrate the warmth and beauty of the wonderful Hawaiian aloha. Music and dance events, demonstrations of ancient arts and crafts, a beautiful orchid show, water sports, an enormous flower parade, pageants, the crowning of both a king and a queen, are featured. Check with the Hawaii Visitors Bureau for the exact dates of the Aloha Festivals. They usually begin on Oahu at the end of August, then move to Hawaii, Molokai, and Lanai, before ending in late October on Kauai and Maui. Telephone 808/944-8857 for information.

☐ **Molokai-to-Oahu Canoe Race.** This is the most important event in the sport of outrigger canoeing. Participants paddle from Molokai to Fort DeRussy Beach in Honolulu in traditional Hawaiian canoes, going over some very choppy water. The women's race takes place in September, the men's race in October.

☐ **Parade of Homes.** Here's a chance to see what's behind the closed doors of Hawaii's homes, town houses, and high-rise apartments. The major annual event of Hawaii's building and real estate industries, the Parade of Homes showcases the latest trends in homebuilding, remodeling, interior design, and landscaping, with entrants competing for a variety of awards. Realtors host open houses from 10am to 5pm on the third and fourth weekends in September. For information, telephone 808/847-4666.

OCTOBER

○ **WAIMEA FALLS PARK MAKAHIKI FESTIVAL** *Hawaiian games, music, and food are featured in this festival, whose highlight is the Hula Kahiko Competition, in which ancient dances of Hawaii are performed.*
Where: *Waimea Falls Park, Oahu.* **When:** *Usually the first week in October.*
How: *Events are included in general admission to the park. For information, telephone 808/638-8511.*

○ **GATORADE IRONMAN WORLD TRIATHLON CHAMPIONSHIPS** *Only world-class athletes need apply. This internationally acclaimed event includes a 2.4 mile swim, a 112-mile bicycle ride, and a 26.2 mile run, with no resting between events.*
Where: *Kailua-Kona, Big Island.* **When:** *October 15.* **How:** *Make reservations at least 6 months in advance. For information, telephone 808/329-0063.*

NOVEMBER

☐ **Kamahameha School Ho'olaulea.** This old-time Hawaiian festival features continuous hula, Hawaiian and contemporary entertainment, arts and crafts, Hawaiian children's games, and food. Festivities are held on all five islands; on Oahu, at Kamehameha Schools. Usually mid-November. For information, telephone 808/832-4104.

☐ **International Hula Festival.** Moanalua Gardens Foundation sponsors an annual international hula festival called "E Ho'i Mai I Piko Hula," which usually takes place at the Blaisdell arena the second week in November. Competing hula halua have come from many mainland states, Europe, and Japan to compete. For information, telephone 839-5334.

☐ **Mission Houses Museum Christmas Fair.** This popular Honolulu event features many specialty gift items for Christmas and food. Craftspeople from all over the islands show their wares. Free admission. Thanksgiving weekend. For information, telephone 808/531-0481.

DECEMBER

☐ **Bodhi Day.** The enlightenment of Buddha is commemorated with religious observances in the Buddhist temples and with Japanese dance programs and ceremonies elsewhere. Nearest Sunday to December 7.

○ **HONOLULU MARATHON**   this is one of the most popular—and scenic—U.S. marathons. It draws some 15,000 entrants, about 10,000 from Japan, but many from the U.S. mainland, Europe, and Canada.

Where: The marathon starts at Ala Moana Beach Park and ends at Kapiolani Park. **When:** December 10. **How:** Spectators line the route: no admission fees. For runners: To obtain entry forms, send a stamped, self-addressed business-size envelope to Honolulu Marathon Association, 3435 Waialae Ave., Honolulu, HI 96816.

☐ **Princess Bernice Pauahi Bishop's Birthday.** Throughout the islands, societies and schools remember the beloved princess at the Royal Mausoleum. December 19.

☐ **Christmas.** What could be nicer than a Polynesian Christmas? There aren't any chimneys, so Santa might arrive in an outrigger canoe or on a surfboard. He might—it's not as bad as it sounds—be wearing a hula skirt. Carols are sung to ukulele accompaniment. Christmas lights are hung on everything from evergreens to bamboo; the decorations in downtown Honolulu are enchanting. There are special programs for children at the Honolulu Academy of Arts. The stores are jammed, just as they are on the mainland—a view of the bustling crowds (thronging the mall at Ala Moana Center, for example) is one of the prettiest of holiday pictures. The Christmas greeting: "Mele Kalikimaka!"

☐ **New Year's Eve.** "First Night," a moveable feast of theater, music and dance performances, art exhibits, and cultural demonstrations is held on sidewalks, streetcorners, and in lobbies and store windows all over town. Otherwise, celebrations are much like those on the mainland, except that the firecrackers are noisier (Asian style), costume balls are held at the leading hotels, and purification ceremonies are performed at the Buddhist temples (visitors welcome). January 1 is open house among island Japanese families.

3. HEALTH & INSURANCE

HEALTH   You don't have to worry about unsanitary food or polluted drinking water in Hawaii. Standards of sanitation are very high, and the islands have an excellent supply of pure water (except in some parts of Maui and some mountain areas on the Big Island where there is a problem with acid rain). As far as health goes, Hawaii is way ahead of the rest of the United States: Males have a life expectancy of 74 years compared to 66.5 on the mainland; females have a life expectancy of 78.1 years compared to 73 for women in the other 49 states.

INSURANCE   It probably won't be necessary for you to take out any insurance for your trip to Hawaii if you already have adequate coverage at home. Take a look at your current insurance policies first. Many plans cover doctor and hospital visits you may need while traveling. Your homeowner's insurance policy may cover stolen luggage. Your automobile insurance may be sufficient for Hawaii. Should you not be adequately covered, you might contact the following organizations to get supplemental insurance:

Access America, 6600 W. Broad St., Richmond, VA 23230 (tel. 804/285-3300, or toll free 800/284-8300), offers a comprehensive travel insurance and assistance package, including medical expenses, on-the-spot hospital payments, medical transportation, baggage insurance, trip-cancellation insurance and collision-damage insurance for a car rental. Their 24-hour hotline connects you to multilingual coordinators who can offer advice and help on medical, legal, and travel problems.

Carefree Travel Insurance, P.O. Box 310, Mineola, NY 11501 (tel. toll free 800/323-3149), offers two comprehensive plans that include trip cancellation, interruption, and delay; accident and sickness medical expense; accidental death and dismemberment; emergency evacuation; and baggage loss and baggage delay. A 24-hour telephone hotline offers worldwide medical, travel, and legal assistance.

Travel Guard International, 1145 Clark St., Stevens Point, WI 54481 (tel. toll free 800/826-1300), has been endorsed by the American Society of Travel Agents as it's preferred supplier of travel insurance. Included in it's comprehensive coverage are medical and accident insurance, medical transportation evacuations, on-the-spot hospital payment, baggage insurance, trip-cancellation insurance with penalty waiver, and collision-damage insurance for a car rental. Travel Guard Assistance, included in all policies, provides the multilingual 24-hour Worldwide Emergency Service Network. They can coordinate help, interpret, and provide advice, as well as perform medical assistance and evacuations.

4. WHAT TO PACK

An important way to save money on your Hawaiian trip is to give careful thought to the clothes you take and the way you pack. First rule is not to go on a big shopping spree in advance—the Hawaiian stores are packed with colorful island resort clothes at prices lower than those you'll probably pay at home.

Second important rule: Try to limit yourself to one suitcase (you can also carry a small travel bag for reading matter on the plane, then use it later as a beach bag). If you can carry your own bag, you are not dependent on porters, bellhops, and expensive taxis. Having a light bag, or a bag with wheels (or at least one of those

wheeled luggage carriers), is practically essential, since it's sometimes difficult to locate porters at the airports, and in small hotels and condos you are usually expected
to carry your own luggage.

If you plan to shop, you may want to leave some space for bringing back the
things you'll buy. Its best to buy your luggage before you go; it will generally be
more expensive in Hawaii, although we've been able to purchase reasonably priced,
lightweight luggage at many of the Woolworth's stores in Hawaii. If, however, despite your best intentions, you find you've got just too much to carry home, head
for one of the inexpensive gift stores (like ABC in Honolulu), and buy yourself one
of those soft, stand-up bags (usually under $30).

CLOTHING   You need only spring or summer clothes of the simplest kind. There
are no extremes in temperature between day and night, so you don't need the usual
all-purpose travel coat or overcoat you'd take to Europe or Mexico—unless you're
coming from the eastern United States and plan to spend a few days in San Francisco on the way back; then you'll have good use for it. A light raincoat or poncho
with a hood is helpful, and so is a folding umbrella—and let's hope you won't need
them! Women will find a shawl or light jacket useful at night. The only heavy garment that you will require is a warm sweater or hooded parka for exploring the
volcano regions on the islands of Hawaii and Maui. Good canvas or other heavy-
soled hiking shoe and socks are a must for hiking or for trekking over recent lava
flows on Hawaii.

For Men   Island dress is extremely casual, and many of our readers say they've
never worn a suit in the islands! Some of the fancier places do require a jacket for
dinner, however. The islands are dotted with quick-service launderettes (many apartment-hotels have their own), so you can have a stack of clothes washed and ready
to wear in a few hours. Think about buying a colorful aloha shirt when you're in
Hawaii (it's worn outside the trousers and cut a little fuller than the usual sports
shirt). You can use it back home for beach or country wear.

For Women   Before you pack, you'll want to know a little bit about what
women wear in Hawaii. Allow us to introduce you to the muumuu, the most comfortable garment known to woman. Try one and see. They're loose enough to provide their own inner air conditioning, require a minimum of underwear underneath,
and look pretty enough to flatter almost everybody—especially large women, who
look positively graceful in them. (You'll see more than a few hefty Polynesian
women, by the way, a carryover from the days when the *alii*, the nobility, cultivated
fat as a royal status symbol.)

The thing we love most about Hawaiian fashion is that many women wear muumuus or other long dresses outdoors, especially at night. Even though many island
women are extremely fashion-conscious and favor the same kinds of spring-summer
fashions that might be seen in New York or Paris or San Francisco, the muumuu is
still seen, especially on "Aloha Fridays," when many women wear them to work.
You'll see full-flowing muumuus (the colorful Hawaiian version of the Mother
Hubbards the missionaries forced on the native population); long, slim adaptations
of classic Chinese tunics; or, prettiest of all, holomuus, long muumuus, slightly fitted
at the waist. We strongly urge you to buy a long dress while you're on the islands.
You can use it later for an at-home gown, and you'll have a great time walking
through the streets with it swishing gracefully at your ankles. Be sure that the muumuu at least touches the instep if you want to look like a kamaaina. You may also
want to buy a short muumuu or island-style sundress; the selection is tremendous,
and the prices suit everybody. Of course, many women visitors live in pants and
shorts in Hawaii, and there's no reason why you shouldn't. It's just that muumuus
are so much more a part of the island scene.

We should warn you: Matching aloha shirts and muumuus for couples are considered definitely "tourist tacky" by the local people.

So pack your bathing suit (or get a bikini in Hawaii), a sturdy pair of sandals or
sneakers (maybe some hiking boots if you're going to go out on the trails), a

lightweight woolen sweater, stole, or throw to wear in the evenings, a warm jacket if you're going up into the mountains. Leave your tights at home. You'll live in sandals or Japanese zoris, or go barefoot the way many islanders do. (Island kids, by the way, wear shoes as little as possible, usually not even to school, with resulting household crises when they need to find their shoes to go to a movie or restaurant.) The idea, in summer, is to fortify yourself against the heat by wearing open shoes and sleeveless dresses. Leave all your city cottons and little dark dresses at home. In the winter months, when Hawaiian weather can be springlike, pants and tops are practically a uniform. And T-shirts are worn everywhere, year-around. Wash-and-dry clothes are helpful but not crucial, since launderettes are so handy. As for jewelry, the kind most people wear is island craft, shell or coral necklaces, and the like, which can be picked up in any gift shop. The most beautiful jewelry of island women is the natural kind: blossoms in the hair, flower leis around the neck.

A final word on Hawaiian clothing: We don't want to give you the impression that the islanders never get dressed up. They do, especially for fancy social events. In downtown Honolulu, businesswomen wear more conservative summer clothing, and many men wear regular business suits with tuck-in shirts. But that's for work—not fun.

OTHER ITEMS It's not necessary to bring a travel iron from home: Most hotels have boards and irons for guests. Get plastic bottles for your liquid toilet articles; they won't break and they take up less space. Seal perfume bottles with wax or masking tape for plane flights. Get little packets of cold-water soap and scatter them in odd corners of your suitcase. The plastic clotheslines, complete with miniature clothespins and soap, sold in most department stores, are very, very handy. Those inflatable or plastic hangers are good to have too, since you can't always count on finding wooden hangers on which to drip-dry your clothes in an inexpensive hotel. Disposable wash-up tissues are nice to carry with you, particularly on long plane or auto trips.

SOME PRECAUTIONS Let's hope your suitcase won't be stolen, lost, or misdirected onto the airlines to Australia. But it doesn't hurt to take a few sensible precautions, especially if you're flying in a huge group where bags often get shipped to the wrong hotels and you may have to go without them for several hours. Always tag your bags, inside and out, with your name and home address. Inside each bag, put a note that gives your address in Hawaii—so that, if your bag should arrive at somebody else's hotel, it can easily be sent to yours. Carry with you your valuables, medicines, prescriptions, cameras, and so on—anything that you can't easily replace if your bag is among the missing.

5. TIPS FOR THE DISABLED, SENIORS & FAMILIES

FOR THE DISABLED Disabled people are made very welcome in Hawaii. There are more than 2,000 ramped curbs on Oahu alone, hotels provide special facilities, and tour companies offer many services. In fact, the Society for the Advancement of Travel for the Handicapped considers Oahu the country's most accessible place. Helpful brochures are available for each island. Each brochure lists accessibility features of Hawaii's major hotels, shopping malls, beach parks, and sightseeing and visitor attractions. Write to the **Commission of Persons with Disabilities,** 5 Waterfront Plaza, Suite 210, 500 Ala Moana Blvd., Honolulu, HI 96813 (tel. 808/586-8121), or to **Hawaii Centers for Independent Living,** 677 Ala Moana Blvd., Suite 118, Honolulu, HI 96813 (tel. 808/537-1941; TTY/TDD, 521-4400). Enclose a check or money order for $3 payable to *Aloha Guide to Accessibility.*

Handicaps of the Pacific, P.O. Box 22428, Honolulu, HI 96823 (tel. 808/ 524-3866), provides special transportation facilities for the disabled: wheelchair taxi service and a variety of tours, including luaus, cruises, and sightseeing journeys.

FOR SENIORS See "Educational/Alternative Travel," below, for information on educational tours for seniors.

For information on activities for senior citizens, contact the Department of Parks and Recreation at either 973-7262 or 973-7258; they can give you up-to-the minute information. Also, be sure to check local newspapers for special events, sightseeing tours, picnics, etc.

Discounts for seniors are available at almost all major attractions in the islands, and occasionally at hotels and restaurants. When making a hotel reservation, always ask. Members of the American Association of Retired Persons (AARP), 601 E. St. NW, Washington, DC 20049 (tel. 202/434-2277), are usually eligible for discounts.

In Honolulu, seniors can ride MTL buses at a reduced rate after obtaining a bus pass at 811 Middle St. (tel. 808/848-4444).

If you're visiting some of the national parks on the neighboring islands, like Hawaii Volcanoes National Park on the Big Island, you may get a **Golden Age Passport** free. It can be picked up at the park, and is available to anyone over age 62 who can show proof of age.

FOR FAMILIES Hawaii is a very easy place to travel with children (we did it with our own daughter for many years). Airlines provide a discount for children under 12, and most hotels allow children to stay free in their parents' rooms providing they use existing bedding (there is usually a fee for a crib or a rollaway bed). Strollers can be easily rented. Many restaurants offer special menus for the *keikis*, as they're called here. And you'll have no trouble amusing children—in addition to numerous attractions suitable for them, they have the best playground in the world right at their doorstep—the beach.

6. EDUCATIONAL/ALTERNATIVE TRAVEL

Everybody has a different idea of what travel should be like. If your ideas include some hands-on participatory tours as opposed to the "just looking" variety; or if you wish to learn something new while you're on vacation; or if you're interested in going to a spa or to a New Age center where you can cultivate body, mind, and spirit—all against a background of the natural beauty of the Hawaiian Islands—read on.

You'll see that for these tours and trips, you'll need to break our usual $75-a-day budget. But while these may be considered "big splurges," all of them represent excellent value.

Note: Other active adventures—snorkeling, horseback riding, helicopter trips and the like—are listed in their appropriate chapters.

EDUCATIONAL/STUDY TRAVEL

You've had enough of sightseeing, swimming, shopping, and the usual tourist pleasures. Want to learn something new, stimulate your imagination and curiosity? The following will provide some suggestions.

FOR SENIORS If you're 60 or older, or the spouse or companion of someone of that age, you are eligible to participate in one of the splendid Elderhostel educational programs, held all over the world, including Hawaii. Rates are reasonable. Write or call for their latest catalog: **Elderhostel,** 75 Federal St., Boston, MA 02110-1941 (tel. 617/426-7788).

FOR ALL AGES University Research Expeditions Program, Desk M05, University of California, Berkeley, CA 94720 (tel. 510/642-6586), offers a number of unique adventures in which interested members of the public team up with University of California scholars on research expeditions around the world. The financial contribution qualifies as a tax-deductible charitable contribution. Excursions to Hawaii are scheduled every year. In the past, these have included a 3-week expedition to the island of Lanai to study the social patterns and behavioral interaction of spinner dolphins, an expedition to study endangered plants on Mauna Kea on the Big Island, and an expedition to Volcanoes National Park on the Big Island to locate, map, photograph, and draw newly found petroglyphs. The cost of most 2-week trips is $1,000 to $1,500.

Nature Conservancy of Hawaii, 1116 Smith St., Honolulu, HI 96817 (tel. 808/537-4508), a local affiliate of the Nature Conservancy, a national nonprofit conservation organization, offers regular hikes on Maui, Molokai, and Oahu.

Oceanic Society Expeditions, Fort Mason Center, Building E, San Francisco, CA 94123 (tel. 415/441-1106, or toll free 800/326-7491), is a nonprofit environmental education and research organization providing specially designed natural history expeditions. Since 1972, Oceanic's expert naturalists have led small groups to destinations such as Hawaii, Micronesia, Indonesia, Africa, the Arctic, the Antarctic, and the Americas. Oceanic is the travel affiliate of Friends of the Earth, a global environmental advocacy organization. Planned for winter 1995 are several week-long excursions on the Kona Coast of the Big Island and in Maui for sailing, whale watching, and snorkeling, and an excursion to Kauai and Ni'ihau to identify and photograph monk seals, among the most endangered of all seals. Costs of these trips run from $1,390 to $1,790. Write or call for schedules and itineraries.

Want to take a summer course? The **University of Hawaii** enrolls more than 17,000 summer students in some 500 courses. Get into Hawaii's social and cultural mix with, perhaps, some Asian Studies courses in history, languages, literature, etc. For a physical view of the islands, try ethnobotany, geography of the islands, or oceanography. For a catalog and details, write in advance to the Summer Session office, 101 Krauss Hall, 2500 Dole St., Honolulu, HI 96822. The university's summer noncredit courses are also intriguing. How about sailing, stained-glass craft, ikebana (Japanese flower arranging), hula, and meditation—for starters?

READERS RECOMMEND

"I have a suggestion for vacationers who would like to make a very reasonable trip. My mother took two very interesting but not difficult courses at the University of Hawaii, one on the geography of Hawaii, the other on the botany of Hawaii. Both courses enhanced our trip very much. My mother is a teacher, and with these credits she moved up one notch in her income bracket, about $1,000! Also, for the time she was in school (about 2 months), the trip was deductible from her taxes!"
—Bonny Warner, Mt. Baldy, Calif.

NEW AGE TRAVEL

Palm Hawaiian Adventures, P.O. Box 752, Madison, NJ 07940; P.O. Box 811, Makawao, HI 96768 (tel. 800/654-0021 or 201/377-6142 or 808/243-0110), offers personalized journeys, for individuals or groups, geared to Hawaiian mysticism. The journeys can include ecologically oriented and mystical adventures, natural healing, Hawaiiana, and holistic retreats. Participants can partake in seminars at sacred sites (on the Big Island at an ancient City of Refuge and at Volcanoes National Park; on Maui at Haleakala Crater), guided by individuals who have lived and worked with native teachers.

One of these is Pila of Hawaii, "Seer," a decorated Vietnam veteran whose vision in heavy combat led him home to the Big Island and an unusual gathering of healers. Pila's teachings are usually given at "a place of healing and forgiveness that some call the center of the universe."

Individual sessions of Hawaiian lomi-lomi massage, esoteric teachings and readings, Kahuna teachings, earth attunement and the like, can be booked in advance. Full travel arrangements are available, including air travel: A typical 7-night/8-day package from Los Angeles to the Big Island runs from $818 to $1423 (depending on hotel choice); a 7-night/8-day package to Maui is $878 to $1651. Call for details.

NEW AGE CENTERS & ACTIVITIES

Several programs and retreats in the serene Hawaiian environment are listed below.

ON OAHU The **Foundation of I, Inc.** (Freedom of the Cosmos), P.O. Box 10861, Honolulu, HI 96816-0861 (tel. 808/395-9278), presents lectures and classes on Ho'oponopono, an ancient Hawaiian process of problem solving and stress release that was updated for today's world by the late Morrnah Simeona, a native Hawaiian. Classes are presented in Honolulu, throughout the islands, and in many other parts of the world.

Science of Mind Center of Hawaii, 2909 Waialae Ave., Honolulu (tel. 808/735-6832), is a nondenominational organization that offers classes, workshops, and seminars. Sunday services are at 11am.

Silva Mind Control Training, P.O. Box 4466, Kaneohe, HI 96744 (tel. 808/247-5458), welcomes graduates and others seeking training to the seminars and workshops offered.

Unity Church of Hawaii, 3608 Diamond Head Circle, Honolulu, HI 96815 (tel. 808/735-4436), not far from Waikiki, warmly welcomes visitors to services held every Sunday at 7:30, 9, and 11am. Minister John Strickland is an outstanding inspirational speaker; music and singers are some of the islands' best. After the program, meet the people and browse in the excellent New Age bookstore. Classes and workshops are held on such subjects as relationships, yoga, tai chi, nutrition, and holistic healing.

ON THE BIG ISLAND (HAWAII) The **Dragonfly Ranch,** P.O. Box 675, Honaunau, HI 96726 (tel. 808/328-2159, or toll free 800/487-2159), is a private retreat on the Kona coast, a 2-minute drive from Honaunau Bay, an ancient Place of Sanctuary, with beaches and snorkeling. Hosts Barbara Moore-Link and David Link, will work out arrangements to provide guests with either total privacy or total attention: The Royal Treatment can include lomo-lomi (Hawaiian massage), health-oriented meals, fasting, flower essences, exercise program, and references to many healers.

One week of the month, around the time of the full moon, Barbara and David offer "The Hawaiian Experience," work/playshops with authentic kahunas and native Hawaiian guides. Amenities of the Dragonfly Ranch include private sun decks, an outdoor canopied waterbed, cable TV, fireplace, organic garden, and beautiful landscaping. Also available for B&B rentals. Rates range from $70 to $140 a day and $400 to $600 a week.

Kalani Honua, P.O. Box 4500, Pahoa, HI 96778 (tel. 808/965-7828, or toll free 800/800-6886), is Hawaii's prime intercultural retreat and conference center and offers a varied program of workshops and seminars in everything from dance and the arts to sports, health, and personal growth. Kalani Honua itself sponsors a limited number of programs, including summer and winter dance festivals. The cost of programs varies with each group. Kalani Honua is located in a spectacularly beautiful spot on the Kalapana coast, near a black-sand beach, and consists of four two-story wood lodges, each with an ocean-view meeting room/studio space on the upper level and a shared kitchen on the ground floor. There are accommodations for individuals, couples, families, and groups (see Chapter 12, "The Big Island," for specifics). Meals are largely vegetarian, with fish or fowl option. There's a pool, a spa, a sauna, and a hot tub. Guests are welcome to attend conferences, schedule their own, or use the facilities for their own personal vacations or retreats.

ON MAUI The **Akahi Farm and Bamboo Mountain Sanctuary,** 915 Kapakalua Rd., Haiku, Maui, HI 96708 (tel. 808/572-8795 for the farm or 808/527-5106 for the sanctuary), is a unique spot, a combination retreat center and bed-and-breakfast establishment situated on 55 magnificent acres on the slopes of Haleakala, overlooking the ocean far below. The place is rented to groups for workshops and seminars—in meditation, or yoga, or aikido, or rebirthing—and New Age teachers of the caliber of Ram Dass, Brook Medicine Eagle, Paul Horn, and Robert Masters, to name a few, are frequent presenters. You can write to the farm for a brochure about forthcoming workshops, or, if you're already in Maui, simply call the owner, Rick Smith, and he may be able to find an opening for you.

Adjoining the farm is the Bamboo Mountain Sanctuary, until recently known as the Old Maui Zendo. This wonderful old plantation house, with a huge deck overlooking the ocean, really was a Zen monastery for 17 years. Now it's a B&B but still given over to those who favor quiet pursuits; arrangements can be made for guests who wish to work with alternative health-care practitioners (Hellerwork, rebirthing, etc.), some of whom reside on the grounds. Rooms are nicely furnished with queen-size or double futons on frames, and have Japanese artwork on the walls and a lovely spare—but not monastic—aesthetic. Some of the rooms have private baths, but the shower is shared. Rates are $55 for one, $75 for two, seventh day free. Breakfast, served on the deck, features papayas from their own trees and bananas from their own banana plantation. A wonderful spot for a healing retreat, solitary or communal.

Island Adventures (tel. 808/874-9228) is a service that offers "magical journeys in nature." Romy Leah custom-tailors programs for small groups or individuals. Programs include hiking in Hana and in Haleakala Crater, a hike to birthing pools used by ancient Hawaiian women, a trip to bamboo forests and waterfalls, canyons, and ocean-fed pools, and more. Romy provides a safe, easy, and loving environment for people of all ages. Hikes are provided on a donation basis ($40 to $70 per day is suggested), of which 10% will be sent to a nonprofit environmental organization. Stop in at Alaya Unlimited, 52 Central Ave. in Wailuku, to get a copy of their free *Mauian* magazine and find out who's lecturing, giving a meditation workshop, or having a class on alternative lifestyles and healing techniques. *Mauian* magazine is the only voice of vegetarianism, alternative health practices, and hemp education on Maui. You can also call publisher Suzie O at 244-7400 to find out when the next Ohana Luncheon and Trade Fair, featuring noted New Age speakers and musicians, will be held.

Dr. Elaine Willis, a psychologist and nutritionist who has found her own Shangri-la in the lush Wailea area of Maui, makes her tropical ocean-view hideaway available to guests as a private bed-and-breakfast health retreat. **Hale Leini,** Box 1919, Kihei, Maui, HI 96753 (tel. 808/874-1490), is a perfect spot for those seeking rejuvenation and personal transformation. Three elegant ocean-view rooms overlook tranquil gardens; the house is a short drive down the hill to the Stouffer Wailea Beach Resort and the ocean. A beautiful breakfast of fresh living foods is served on the deck each morning; sunsets are special. For an extra fee, Dr. Willis will assist guests in creating individual Wellness Lifestyle programs. Sessions with bodyworkers and healers can be arranged. Rates go from $50 to $85 single, $110 double; a minimum stay of 3 days to 1 week is advised. Call for details.

Natalie and John Tyler, 3270 Kehala Dr., Kihei, HI 96753 (tel. 808/879-0097), who describe themselves as "fun-loving and spirited psychotherapists," have opened their lovely home in the Kihei area as a B&B accommodation for "non-smoking, conscious people." Their house is a mile from the beach and is filled with books, artwork, and classical music. Guests can watch the sunset over the ocean with cool drinks and pupus on the deck and enjoy morning breakfast on the screened porch to the sound of birds. They offer a separate two-bedroom wing with private bath, the oceanside room with it's own entrance deck. Rates are $75 per night for one room, $125 per night for both. Optional extras include a daily "Course in Miracles" meditation, gourmet dinners with wine on the lanai, massage, and couples and family therapy. Snorkeling, scuba lessons, and special trips are also available. Contact the Tylers for details and reservations.

ON KAUAI Dr. Serge Kahili King, who was adopted and trained by a Hawaiian family in the ancient traditions of Polynesian Huna, is in charge of **Hawaiian Shaman Training,** c/o Aloha International, P.O. Box 599, Kapaa, HI 96746 (tel/fax 808/822-9272), which presents frequent workshops in the islands. His organization also operates the Kauai Village Museum & Gift Shop in Kapaa.

Pick up a copy of *The Source,* P.O. Box 1259, Koloa, HI 96756 (tel. 808/246-9535), a free bimonthly newspaper, for listings and notices of New Age activities on Kauai, and on the Big Island and Maui as well. You'll find information on retreats, workshops, classes—everything from crystals and channeling to rebirthing, self-transformation, and yoga.

HOLISTIC HOLIDAYS

SPA & FITNESS CENTERS A magnificent Hawaiian spa experience awaits lucky guests at the fabulous new **Ihilani Resort & Spa,** centerpiece of the Ko Olina Resort, 92-1001 Olani St., West Oahu, HI 96707 (tel. 808/679-0079 or toll free 800/626-4446, fax 808/679-0080). Just opened a year ago, Ihilani is the first manor resort development outside of Waikiki, 17 miles west of Honolulu and a 25-minute drive from Honolulu International Airport, in a secluded 640-acre oceanfront setting of white sand beaches and abundant marine life. The world-class spa offers just about everything to enhance one's health, fitness, and well-being, including hydro therapies such as Thalasso treatments with seawater and seaweeds, Swiss showers, Grand Jets, Vivhy showers, and Roman pools. Shiatsu, Swedish, and Hawaiian lomi-lomi massages are offered, as well as herbal body wraps. Complete fitness and relaxation programs can be designed for each guest. Undoubtedly, this will be a celebrity magnet.

On Maui, extraordinary spa facilities are offered at the beachfront Spa Grande at the $600-million **Grand Wailea Resort & Spa,** 3850 Wailea Alaniu, Wailea, HI 96753 (tel. 808/875-1234, or toll free 800/233-1234), which combines the philosophies and practices of European, Japanese, and American spas. It offers such unique services as a soni relaxation room, a cascading waterfall massage, and green- and black-sand body treatments. lomi-lomi massage, Hawaii ti-leaf wraps, and limu (seaweed) baths are some of the special only-in-Hawaii services.

On the Big Island of Hawaii, there's ANARA (*A New Age Restorative Approach*) Spa at the **Hilton Waikoloa,** 1 Waikoloa Beach Dr., Kohala Coast, HI 96743 (tel. 808/885-1234, or toll free 800/233-1234). Eastern and Western philosophies are blended to offer guests at the fantasy resort spa options like oceanfront taichni, yoga and meditation classes, morning power walks, five kinds of facials, seven kinds of massage (including lomi-lomi), and body treatments utilizing products from the sea.

On Kauai, there's another ANARA Spa at the **Hyatt Regency Kauai,** 1571 Poipu Rd., Koloa, Kauai, HI 96756 (tel.808/742-1234, or toll free 800/233-1234), a tropical sanctuary whose design alone helps guests unwind. Each massage room has it's own private garden and open-air lava-rock shower. In keeping with the resorts authentic island theme, services include an ancient Hawaiian clay treatment and a ti-leaf body pack which alleviates the effects of sunburn.

Most spas offer services to nonguests as well as guests and have facilities for both men and women. A great way to give yourself a holiday treat.

7. ADVENTURE/WILDERNESS TRIPS

The spectacular beauty of the Hawaiian Islands is made to order for exciting eco-adventure travel opportunities. Here's a sampling.

Beginner and experienced outdoors people alike can enjoy the 13-day, three-island adventure trips offered by **Pacific Quest,** 59-603 Kawoa Place, Haleiwa, HI 96712 (tel. toll free 800/776-2518), Hawaii's oldest and most experienced eco-adventure company.

Treks are led by highly trained naturalist guides and explore the most spectacular cultural and natural areas of the islands. There is plenty of opportunity for snorkeling, swimming, body surfing, hiking, sea kayaking, and more through the islands of Kauai, Maui, and the Big Island. Two nights of mountain or beach camping alternate with 2 nights of housing in rustic cabins or "local" hotels. Participants range in age from young families to active seniors. The cost of $1,875 includes all expenses— meals, group camping equipment, guides, all ground transportation, entrance fees, boat charters, interisland transportation, and Hawaii state taxes. The trip starts in Kauai and ends on the Big Island.

Trips that are sensitive to environmental and cultural issues are offered by the **Sierra Club,** 730 Polk St., San Francisco, CA 94109 (tel. 415/923-5630), an organization that has set the standard for wilderness travel. Most trips are of 7 to 10 days' duration and are held from spring through Christmas. They are currently offering a family trip, a bicycling adventure, and a backpacking trip to the Big Island, a kayaking excursion to Kauai, and a service trip—in which participants will count whales—to Maui. There's often a choice of activities: hiking a trail or lazing on a beach. Price range is $705 to $1,145 per week, including all ground costs. For the current catalog, write to the above address and enclose a $3 check made out to the Sierra Club. Proceeds from these trips help support the conservation efforts of the Sierra Club.

BICYCLING TOURS

Backroads Bicycle Touring, 1516 Fifth St., Suite Q422, Berkeley, CA 94710 (tel. toll free 800/BIKE-TRIP from U.S. and Canada), is a well-known outfit that runs bicycling and walking tours in Europe, the U.S. and Canada, and the Pacific. From November through April, they take a number of tours to Hawaii. Couples, singles, families and seniors of all levels of ability are welcome. Tours, which average $140 a day, include all meals and accommodations at campsites and inns. Write for their free catalog.

BACKPACKING/HIKING

Crane Tours, c/o Bill Crane, 15101 Magnolia Blvd., Suite H10, Sherman Oaks, CA 91403 (tel. 818/784-2213 or 800/653-2545, or Milt McAuley at 818/347-6433), offers moderate to moderately strenuous trips for experienced backpackers. Planned for 1995 are two series. A backpacking/kayak series includes backpacking in Haleakala Crater in Maui and in Waimea Canyon on Kauai ($750 each trip) and backpacking ($750) or kayaking ($925) on the Na Pali coast of Kauai. A second series explores the Big Island., Maui, and Kauai in week-long trips at similar prices. Bring your own tents and backpacks. There is also a non-camping Christmas trip to the Big Island. One of 2 nights are spent in mountain cabins, and the last night is usually spent in a hotel. Prices include ground transportation, breakfast, and dinner; participants make their own lunches. Discounts are available for early sign-ups, groups, and repeat clients. Groups are usually 10 to 15 people. Day hikes are also offered. Summer only.

ON OAHU The **Hawaiian Trail and Mountain Club,** P.O. Box 2238, Honolulu, HI 96804 (tel. 808/534-5515 or 488-1161), welcomes visitors to join weekend and holiday hikes with an avid group of outdoor enthusiasts. Check the schedule in Thursday's "Today" section of the *Honolulu Star-Bulletin,* or, several weeks before your visit, send a stamped, self-addressed legal-size envelope for their current schedule. Add $1.25 and you will receive a packet of valuable information about hiking and camping in Hawaii.

Contact the **Sierra Club,** Hawaii Chapter, P.O. Box 2577, Honolulu, HI 96803 (tel. 808/538-6616), for hiking information. They also have groups on Maui, Kauai, and the Big Island.

ON THE BIG ISLAND Shena W. Sandler of **Wilderness Hawaii,** P.O. Box 61692, Honolulu, HI 96839, leads a unique wilderness experience. An accomplished outdoorswoman and former instructor for the Hawaii Bound School, Sandler leads backpacking trips in Hawaii Volcanoes National Park that are designed to be adventurous and challenging, to take people beyond their set limitations. Although most of her work is with Hawaii's teenagers, she will put together 4- to 14-day trips for groups of at least six people of any age. Cost of the 4-day trip is $300; the 14-day trip is $950.

On **Hawaiian Walkways,** P.O. Box 2193, Kamuela, HI 96743 (tel. 808/885-7759), psychologist Dr. Hugh Montgomery, a longtime Hawaii resident, leads day-long and half-day hikes at costs of $60 to $100 per person, respectively (see Chapter 13, "What to See and Do on the Big Island," for more information). For minimum groups of four he will also lead 3-day/2-night camping trips, with stops for swimming, sunning, exploring historical sites, and visiting petroglyph fields. At night, around the campfire, the groups learn the history and legends of old Hawaii. All camping equipment is provided; no backpacking is necessary. The trip is for those who are reasonably fit and can handle about 6 hours a day of hiking. No children under 12. Costs $425 for the Thursday-to-Saturday trips.

ON MAUI Ken Schmitt is everybody's favorite naturalist and tour leader (see Chapter 15, "What to See and Do on Maui"), and in addition to his regular day hikes, he designs special itineraries with lodging in country inns for groups of four to eight people. Prices start below $700 per person for 5 days of trekking and 6 nights of lodging, including lunches and some breakfasts. Contact **Hike Maui,** P.O. Box 330969, Kahului, HI 96733 (tel. 808/879-5270).

WATER SPORTS

Hawaii holds out myriad opportunities for snorkeling, scuba diving, underwater photography, windsurfing, and more.

KAYAKING TRIPS In addition to simple half-day kayaking trips for beginners ($48) and 1-day sea-kayaking adventures along Kauai's southeast coast in the shadow of 2,000-foot cliffs ($105 for a full-day excursion), **Outfitters Kauai,** P.O. Box 1149, Koloa, HI 96756 (tel. 808/742-9667), also offers an escorted Kayak Experience along the Na Pali cliffs, either as a 1-day-trip from Haena to Polihale following trade winds and currents, or as a 2-or-more day expedition featuring camping at Kalalau and Miloli'i, some of the most breathtakingly beautiful spots on the islands. Two-person kayaks may also be rented for self-guided tours to jungle rivers. Each boat comes with racks/straps to secure it to your car, maps, and personal information to help you select the ideal river. The cost is $30 or $45 for one- or two-person kayaks. Their store is located at Poipu Plaza, 2827A Poipu Rd.

Kayak Kauai—Na Pali Outfitters, 1340 Kuhio Hwy., Kapaa (tel. 808/822-9179) or on the main street in Hanalei (P.O. Box 508, Hanalei, HI 96714; tel. 808/826-9844 or toll free 800/437-3507, fax 808/822-0577), offers summer (May to September) journeys along 15 miles of Kauai's dramatic Na Pali coastline that involve some of the most challenging wilderness paddling to be found in Hawaii. Fully catered 6-day packages cost $1,050 per person. The company offers guided 1-day sea-kayak trips along the Na Pali coast, including lunch on an isolated beach ($125), and a 3-hour soft adventure Hanalei Wildlife Refuge and Bay Snorkel tour ($45). Their private canoe/kayak rentals, beginning at $48 for two persons, are very popular with families. Winter, from October to April, you can sea kayak Kipu Kai, the "little Na Pali" on Kauai's south shore; lunch, snorkeling, and whale watching are included ($100). Also available are: fully catered 6-day sea kayaking along the south shore from Lihue to Waimea, with hiking in the highlands of Kokee ($1,050); 6-day backpacking tours along the Na Pali coast trail ($900); 1-day guided hiking tours all over Kauai and/or guided Fern Grotto paddle and hike to a waterfall, lunch included ($75). New addition: Mountain Bike rentals ($20) and 3-hour bike tours in Hanalei and Kapaa ($45).

SAILING CRUISES With **Honolulu Sailing Company,** 47-335 Lulani St., Kaneohe, HI 96744 (tel. 808/239-3900, or toll free 800/829-0114), you can sail away aboard a sleek, modern yacht to the islands of Oahu, Maui, Lanai, and Molokai. This company runs day, overnight, and 1-week cruises out of Honolulu Harbor and Kaneohe Bay, combining sailing and snorkeling, at rates of about $60 for a half day, $130 overnight. Nautical weddings and whale-watching cruises are specialties. Boats sleep 4 to 10 passengers. Private state rooms are available for couples. One-day sailing, snorkeling, and Zodiac trips on Oahu are also available for about $85 per person. Private bareboat and skippered charters are also available.

Sailing, skin diving, fishing, exploring the environment and culture of Hawaii, or relaxing—or any combination thereof that suits the group—are offered aboard the 50-foot-luxury yacht *Maile* (P.O. Box 44335, Kamuela, HI 96743; tel. 808/326-5174, or toll free 800/726-SAIL; fax 808/885-6514), moored in Kawaihai Harbor on the Big Island. Capt. Ralph Blancato, an amazingly talented sailor and excellent host, knows the marine life of Hawaii, where to find the best, most secluded snorkeling spots, and lots more. He encourages passengers to participate as much as they wish in sailing the ship; groups are limited to six. Accommodations are luxurious (hot showers included), and the meals are gourmet—depending on the catch, they might include fresh sashimi Cajun-style and barbecue catch. Two regular excursions are scheduled each month: one a 5-day Big Island sail at $950 per passenger, the other a 7-day interisland sail with calls at Molokai and Lanai, at $1,125 per passenger. Charter sails for any duration are also available upon request.

SAILING/HIKING ECOTOURS ON HAWAII The goal of **Eye of the Whale,** Marine/Wilderness Adventures, P.O. Box 1269, Kapaau, HI 96755 (tel. 808/889-0227, or toll free 800/659-3544), is to promote understanding of Hawaii's delicate ecosystem through firsthand experience. Owner/operators Beth and Mark Goodoni lead 6- to 10-day hiking or hiking/sailing adventures for groups of no more than 6 to 10 people. Days are spent outdoors—hiking through mountain valleys and jungles or sailing the Big Island's Kona coast—but nights are spent either on boats (for sailing trips) or in B&Bs. There is no backpacking or camping. Beth, a marine biologist and naturalist, introduces participants to the natural history of Hawaii and emphasizes the origin and identification of tropical flora, the development and exploration of coral-reef ecosystems, and the biology and observation of marine mammals. On the boat, she's the crew; husband Mark is the licensed USCG captain. Costs are about $140 to $165 per day, including meals, accommodations, transportation, and interisland fares. A highlight of the trip is a private luau, where guests learn to dig the imu, string their own leis, and dance the old-time hulas.

SCUBA-DIVING PACKAGES On Oahu At **Aaron's Dive Shop** (tel. 808/262-2333) you'll get custom-designed package tours to suit a variety of needs. Four-day certification courses are offered. They also offer some neighbor-island trips. Call for details.

On the Big Island You can get dive packages at **Jack's Diving Locker** (tel. 808/329-7585, or toll free 800/345-4807) for trips within the Big Island and, possibly, to some exotic foreign locales as well. Prices range from $45 and up. **Kohala Divers** (tel. 808/882-7774) charges for only 4 days if you take a 5-day package.

Packages offered by **Kona Coast Divers** (tel. 808/329-8802, or toll free 800/KOA-DIVE) include lodging at Kona Billfish Condos and transportation to dive sites. Rates for 3 nights/2 days and four dives are $361 single and $261 per person double. Rates for 5 nights and six dives are $576 single, $407 per person double. **Sea Paradise Scuba** (tel. 808/322-2500, or toll free 800/322-KONA) offers

lodgings at Kona Surf Resort and Keahou Beach Hotel, plus a rental car. Packages are available.
On Maui You'll get custom packages at **Dive Maui** (tel. 808/667-2080), and **Lahaina Divers** (tel. 808/667-7497, or toll free 800/657-7885) offers 7 nights at Maui Islander Hotel, a Dollar Rent A Car, and three dives for $609.50 to $620.50 per person, based on double occupancy.
WINDSURFING PACKAGES Maui Windsurfari, P.O. Box 330254, Kahului, Maui, HI 96733 (tel. 808/871-7766, or toll free 800/736-MAUI), is the ticket for an ideal windsurfing vacation and is especially designed for the windsurfing enthusiast who can stay in Maui for a week or longer. Custom packages include choice of accommodations (ranging from quiet North Shore studios to deluxe oceanfront condos near prime sailing spots), rental cars with unlimited mileage, and Hi-Tech sailboard equipment. Also available are windsurfing lessons using Hawaiian Sailboard Techniques (HST) by world-famous sailor Alan Cadiz. Complete 7-day land packages for $496 to $580 in Kihie; $515 to $525 on the North Shore, per person in a double.

8. HAWAIIAN WEDDINGS

What could be nicer than marrying in Hawaii? You can marry and honeymoon in the same place, and the cost need not be exorbitant. The idea has become so appealing that thousands of visitors are now seeking out Hawaiian weddings in offbeat settings: on the beach, on top of a mountain, aboard a catamaran, in a helicopter—even in a church. For help in planning a Hawaiian wedding, you can contact several private organizations suggested by the Hawaii Visitors Bureau:
   Aloha Wedding Planners offers a variety of picturesque locations and takes care of every detail, from the ministers to the photographers. Susan and Sheryl, the wedding coordinators in charge, are both incurably romantic and decidedly practical; they promise that their service is always first class, even if your budget is strictly economy. Contact them at 1860 Ala Moana Blvd. no. 115, Honolulu, HI 96815 (tel. 808/943-2711; fax 808/949-1128).
   Waimea Falls Park is one of Hawaii's most popular locations for weddings. The experienced staff can make all the necessary arrangements for the perfect ceremony and reception, including minister, flowers, music, limousine, champagne, and more. Custom wedding packages are available with a wide range of prices suitable for any budget. Contact the Wedding Department, Waimea Falls Park, 59-864 Kamehameha Hwy., Haleiwa, HI 96712 (tel. 808/638-8511; or fax 808/638-7900).
   Planning to marry in Maui? We can't think of a more romantic or lovely spot than **The Westin Maui** at Kaanapali Beach, where couples can exchange vows in a variety of idyllic natural settings and even have their ceremony blessed with Hawaiian prayers. A wedding coordinator arranges everything from minister to musicians, flowers and photographers—the works. A variety of honeymoon packages are available at the same hotel. It's also an ideal spot for renewing vows or celebrating anniversaries. Contact The Westin Maui, 2365 Kaanapali Pkwy., Lahaina, HI 96761 (tel. toll free 800/228-3000).
   The **Hyatt Regency Maui,** also on Kaanapali Beach in West Maui, offers several dream wedding packages for ceremonies on it's lovely grounds, all including clergy, leis for the bride and groom, musicians, cake, and champagne. Packages range from the relatively simple "Maui Enchantment" to an air-land-and-sea nuptial adventure called "Journey into Paradise." Phone 808/228-9000 for details. In East Maui, the spectacular **Grand Wailea Resort** has it's own wedding chapel, surrounded by flower-filled gardens and overlooking the ocean. The hotel's wedding specialist handles all the details, including ordering flowers and cake, planning the reception, and even coordinating wedding attire. Wedding packages include the

Plumeria Package, which adds a couples' lomi-lomi massage and other beauty treatments at it's Spa Grande. Phone 808/875-1234 for information.
Aloha! Hawaiian Weddings! began by specializing in West Maui weddings, but it became so popular that it has expanded it's services to the other major islands as well. They've been pioneers in planning romantic weddings for islanders as well as visitors for many years, offering everything from sunrise ceremonies on the slopes of Haleakala to sunset weddings at the beach, weddings at a breathtaking waterfall in Hana as you fly there by a private sightseeing helicopter, or lavish Royal Hawaiian Wedding Luaus. Contact Kalani Kinimaka, who runs this family operation, at Aloha! Hawaiian Weddings!, Central Reservations, P.O. Box 8670, Honolulu, HI 96830-8670 (tel. 808/926-6688 or 926-6689, fax 808/926-6677), for wedding information on Maui, Kona, Kauai, and Waikiki.

On the Big Island, **Paradise Weddings Hawaii** is an all-inclusive wedding coordination service specializing in sunset ceremonies. Their motto, "Intimate to Outrageous," sums up the broad range of offerings, from simple, barefoot beach ceremonies to weddings on horseback. Owner Debbie Cravatta has a reputation for creating exactly the kind of wedding the couple envisions to match their budget. Prices start at $295. Contact Debbie at **Paradise Weddings Hawaii**, P.O. Box 383433, Waikoloas, HI 96738 (tel. 808/883-9067, or toll free 800/428-5844, fax 808/883-9067).

Also on the Big Island, a sunset wedding at the lush **Kona Village Resort** would be pure heaven: P.O. Box 1299, Kaupulehua-Kona, HI 96745 (tel. toll free 800/367-5290). Guests of the glamorous **Kona Surf Resort** on the Big Island can be married at the hotel's Kona Royal Chapel. For information on wedding and honeymoon packages, contact Kona Surf Resort & Country Club, 78-128 Ehukai St., Kailua-Kona, HI 96740 (tel. toll free 800/367-8011).

If you'd like to be married in Kauai, the people at **Weddings on the Beach** can help you. Not only do they arrange weddings on beautiful beach locations, but they can also arrange mountain-top and oceanfront settings, as well as adventure weddings aboard sailing ships and cabin cruises, even helicopters. They claim Hawaii is a spiritual island, and there's plenty of *mana* (power) here to get a marriage off to a good start. Contact them at P.O. Box 1377, Koloa, Kauai, HI 96756 (telfax 808/335-3327).

Hopefully, **Coco Palms Resort,** a favorite wedding and honeymoon spot for many years on Kauai, will have reopened by the time you read this. They have a private wedding chapel nestled amid a lush, 45-acre coconut grove. They'll do everything from selecting the minister, music, and flowers, to providing a Hawaiian conch-shell blower: 4-241 Kuhio Hwy., Wailua, Kauai, HI 96746 (tel. toll free 800/42-MARRY). Traditional weddings are the order of the day at the **Hyatt Regency Kauai.** The bride can arrange for a replica of an authentic Hawaiian wedding gown, featuring a Hawaiian quilt pattern on the train of the satin and lace gown. A variety of wedding packages are available, including the "Maile and Mokihana Wedding Package," complete with a Hawaiian conch-shell blower getting things off to an auspicious start. Call 808/742-1234 for information.

Kauai's restored-plantation estate of the 1930s, **Kilohana,** is also the site of numerous weddings; they can be held indoors in an elegant living room overlooking the gardens, in the gardens themselves, or even in a turn-of-the-century carriage riding through the plantations grounds. Write to Wedding Coordinator Kilohana, P.O. Box 3121, Lihue, Kauai, HI 96766.

Wedding Tips: If you're planning the details yourself, you should contact the State Health Department, 1250 Punchbowl St., Honolulu, HI 96813 (tel. 808/548-5862), for rules and regulations. You will need a permit to be married in a state park. Contact State Parks Division, P.O. Box 621, Honolulu, HI 96809 (tel. 808/548-7455). If you plan to be married in one of Hawaii's national parks, contact the Superintendent, Haleakala National Park, P.O. Box 369, Makawao, HI 96768 (tel. 808/572-9306); or the Superintendent, Hawaii Volcanoes National Park, HI 96718 (tel. 808/967-7311). Of course, if you use the services of a wedding planner, these details will be handled for you.

9. GETTING THERE

What will it cost you to travel to Hawaii? We wish we could tell you precisely, but our crystal ball is cloudy. Ever since the federal government deregulated the airline industry, competition—and massive confusion— has set in. Fares can vary from airline to airline, and even within one airline, depending on when you're going, how long you're staying, whether you make land arrangements through the airlines, and how far in advance you book your ticket. Fares can also vary depending on what new, low-cost gimmick one airline might introduce to beat the competition. But you can rely on this: The airlines want your business, and the 2,400 mile route from California to the Hawaiian Islands is a highly competitive one. A little smart shopping on your part and that of your trusted travel agent will usually turn up a good deal.

A *tip*: Try not to arrive in Hawaii on a weekend, when Honolulu is crowded with visitors from the outer islands. Everything is easier and less crowded on weekdays, especially checking into hotels; plus, airfares are lower during the week.

BY PLANE

To get the very best deal on a ticket to Hawaii you have to do some intensive shopping. Either you or your travel agent should get on the phone to the airlines that serve Honolulu and your area (see below), and find out what the lowest possible prices are. Ask for the lowest economy-class fare. On a specific date last summer, for example, Continental Airlines offered a round-trip ticket from Los Angeles to Honolulu for $349! Remember that you'll secure lower fares if you're willing to pay in advance, travel in the middle of the week rather than on weekends, and also in the fall or off-season rather than during holidays or peak winter vacation months.

THE AIRLINES The largest carrier with the most frequent service to Hawaii is United Airlines. Continental Airlines is the second-largest U.S. carrier serving Hawaii, with over 160 flights weekly. Its major connecting hubs are Denver, Newark, Cleveland, Los Angeles, Boston, and New Orleans; Honolulu is it's main Pacific hub. Nonstop flights depart daily from Houston to Honolulu and then travel on to Tokyo nonstop, with a daily reverse flight. Continental has also recently expanded it's service from Honolulu to Cairns and Brisbane, Queensland, and to Guam. As for fares, Continental frequently offers low-cost promotional fares, and you can also save a bundle by booking one of their package deals: In 1994, for example, a 7-night stay in Waikiki was available for $626, including round-trip airfare from Los Angeles! Packages to Maui, Kauai, and the Big Island are also available. Note that fares vary and restrictions apply, but, overall, this is one of the best travel bargains we know. For information, phone Continental Grand Destinations at 800/634-5555.

Airlines that fly into Honolulu include **American Airlines** (tel. 808/526-0044, or toll free 800/433-7300), **Canadian Airlines International** (tel. 808/922-0533, or toll free 800/426-7000), **China Airlines** (tel. 808/536-6951, or toll free 800/227-5118), **Continental Airlines** (tel. 808/523-0000, or toll free 800/231-0856), **Delta Air Lines** (tel. toll free 800/221-1212), **Garuda Indonesian** (tel. 808/945-3791, or toll free 800/826-2829), **Hawaiian Airlines** (tel. 808/537-5100, or toll free 800/367-5320), **Japan Airlines** (tel. 808/521-1441, or toll free 800/525-3663), **Korean Air** (tel. 808/923-7302, or toll free 800/223-1155 on the East Coast, 800/421-8200 on the West Coast), **Northwest Airlines** (tel. 808/955-2255, or toll free 800/225-2525), **Phillipine Airlines** (tel. 808/536-1928, or toll free 800/435-9725), **Qantas** (tel. 808/836-2461, or toll free 800/227-4500), **Singapore Airlines** (tel. 808/524-6063, or toll free 800/742-3333), **Trans World Airlines** (tel. toll free 800/221-2000), and **United Airlines** (tel. 808/547-2211, or toll free 800/241-6523).

BEST-FOR-THE-BUDGET FARES Super-APEX/APEX Although it carries restrictions and cancellation penalties, this fare is decidedly the best for the budget. APEX stands for Advance Purchase Excursion and typically you are required to reserve and pay for the ticket 14 days in advance, stay for a minimum and maximum number of days, and possibly fulfill some other requirements like flying before a specific date.

Continentals APEX fares for Los Angeles to Honolulu range from $349 to $488 round-trip, depending on which days of the week you travel and how far in advance you purchase your ticket. They are invariably the cheapest way to fly. These fares are known interchangeably as economy or APEX fares.

Regular Airfares Here's a price breakdown on how economy-class tickets compare with business and first class. Continental's fares for a first-class or business-class ticket from Los Angeles to Honolulu in summer 1994 were $690 to $1,180 one way, as compared to $349 to $488 for economy round-trip.

Special Promotional Fares You never know when an airline—or airlines—is going to offer promotional fares. Sometimes there's a price war, and then the consumer really benefits. Keep watching the newspapers for announcements of special deals. A few years ago, one airline was flying from Los Angeles to Honolulu for $99 for a very short period of time. Always ask your travel agent to inquire about promotional fares, too.

Bucket Shops These discount travel agencies purchase blocks of tickets direct from the airlines at wholesale prices, which they then discount. We found two agencies on the West Coast that offer flights to Hawaii at discounts ranging anywhere from 20% to 40%—depending on the season you fly and availability. You may do as well on your own or with your regular travel agent, but it wouldn't hurt to give these people a call and see what they have for you. Remember that it's very difficult to return these tickets, and many restrictions apply: So once you've bought them, they're all yours.

The following agencies offer discount flights to Hawaii: **Community Travel Service,** 5299 College Ave., Oakland, CA 94618 (tel. 510/653-0990), and **All Unique Travel,** 1030 Georgia St., Vallejo, CA 94590 (tel. 707/648-0237). The latter will also discount any package tour advertised in a current travel brochure, newspaper, or magazine.

JET LAG If you're going all the way through from the East Coast to Honolulu or the neighbor islands in one stretch—about 10 air hours—you'll be crossing at least six time zones, and your normal body rhythms are going to be thrown out of sync. Here are some tips for avoiding jet lag. First, several days before your departure, gradually accommodate your eating and sleeping times to be closer to those of your destination. You'll be heading west, so go to bed a little later each night and sleep a little later in the morning. When you come home, reverse that pattern. Second, avoid smoking, drinking, and heavy eating on the flight—another reason to bring your own picnic lunch! You may have heard of the Argonne Anti-Jet-Lag Diet, which alternates feasting and fasting for several days before departure, and is effective for many people. To get a free copy of the program (more than 500,000 cards have been sent out to date), send a stamped, self-addressed envelope to Office of Public Affairs, Argonne National Laboratory, 9700 S. Cass Ave., Argonne, IL 60439.

You may also want to look into an excellent book called *Jet Smart* by Diana Fairechild, a former international flight attendant, that is chock-full of tips on flying comfortably and avoiding jet lag—from what to eat on the plane to how to antidote radiation exposure. If it's not at your local bookstore, contact Flyana Rhyme, Inc., P.O. Box 300, Makawao, Maui, HI 96768; the cost is $12.95, plus $2 postage in the United States, $2.50 in Canada and Mexico. There is a toll-free ordering line: 1-800-LAG TIPS (524-8477).

Our personal prescription for avoiding jet lag is to stop off at one of the airport hotels in either Los Angeles or San Francisco en route. For years we've enjoyed staying at the Los Angeles Airport Marriott, which has a pool set in a magnificent garden and a variety of restaurants, including the very reasonable Fairfield and Lobby Bistro. If you call far enough in advance (tel. toll free 800/228-9290), you may be able to get a Family Plan rate (for at least two people) during the week; weekend rates are always available, and both of these are approximately $79, about half the regular price. After a swim in the pool (or a workout in the exercise room), and a good night's sleep, we board our plane the next morning and arrive in Hawaii refreshed.

BY SHIP

Forget about it. Only luxury cruise ships now call at Honolulu Harbor.

PACKAGE TOURS

We usually prefer the do-it-yourself brand of travel, but some excellent values are available on group tours, which usually involve short periods of 1 or 2 weeks. Many package options are available: The most expensive ones park you at the luxury hotels and take you sightseeing in private limousines; the cheapest put you up in standard hotels, take you sightseeing in motor coaches and may not provide meals. Do some careful studying and comparing before you sign up for one. Often you can find inexpensive restaurants that charge much less than what the tour companies figure on as the cost of three meals.

To help you get started, some of the major travel companies that offer tours to the outer islands are listed below. You can also consult your travel agent or airline for a variety of choices.

American Express, 2222 Kalakaua Ave., Honolulu, HI 96815 (tel. 808/946-7741, or toll free 800/241-1700).

Pleasant Hawaiin Holidays, 270 Lewers St., Honolulu, HI 96815 (tel. 808/922-1515).

Roberts Hawaii Tours, 680 Iwilei Rd., 7th floor, Honolulu, HI 96817 (tel. 808/523-7750).

10. GETTING AROUND

INTERISLAND TRAVEL

BY PLANE

Hawaii's two major interisland carriers are Hawaiian Airlines and Aloha Airlines; both have been around for many years and offer similar fares, give or take a few dollars. Because fares change often, and because both offer periodic promotional fares and tie-ins with hotel and car-rental packages, it pays to do some personal shopping either by calling the airlines directly or by consulting your travel agent. Expect fares to be highest during peak winter and summer travel periods. Standby tickets are no longer offered.

Hawaiian Airlines (tel. toll free 800/367-5320) operates one of the most exciting concepts in interisland travel in many years. Similar to a Eurail train pass, the

---

Ⓕ FROMMER'S SMART TRAVELER: AIRFARES

1. Use a travel agent only if you know he or she will really put in time and effort to get you the cheapest fare. Otherwise, do your own homework; it pays off!
2. Shop all the airlines that fly to your destination.
3. Always ask for the lowest fare, not just a discounted fare.
4. Keep calling: Airlines sometimes open up additional low-cost seats as departure date nears.
5. Make sure you purchase your tickets in advance to take advantage of the very cheapest APEX (advance purchase) fares.
6. Check "bucket shops."
7. Ask for air/land packages. Land arrangements are cheaper when booked with an airline ticket, although your choice of hotels is then limited.

Hawaiian Airpass allows visitors to take an unlimited number of interisland flights for a flat fee. Considering that a regular flight costs $74, the bargains are substantial: A 5-day Airpass costs $159; a 1-week pass $179; a 10-day pass $219; and a 2-week pass, $259. With prices like these, you can island-hop at will, or use one island as your base and make day trips to see the others. For those with limited vacation time, it's ideal. In addition, users of the Hawaiian Airpass receive special prices on car rentals with Alamo Rent A Car, beginning at $19.99 per day on availability. A phone call to the airline or to your travel agent can give you the details.

Special fares of $10 less are available for children 2 to 11. Hawaiian's mileage program, known as "Gold Plus," offers many advantages, including credits on American Airlines mileage plan, and "Gold Plus" members may also join Hawaiian's Premier Club and enjoy such extra niceties as free interterminal transportation, special check-in and boarding privileges, use of club lounges and free telephones, and priority baggage handling (membership is around $125 for one, $180 for a member and a spouse).

Aloha Airlines (tel. toll free 800/367-5250; TFD toll free 800/544-4833) provides scheduled interisland service between all major airports in Hawaii with a fleet of modern Boeing 737 jet aircraft. The regular Coach fare is $74; and children 2 to 11 are charged $62. Aloha also offers First Class service for $103. Aloha mileage counts toward United Airlines Mileage Plus or Canadian International Airlines Canadian Plus programs. Aloha's sister company, Island Air, provides daily service to all of Hawaii's smaller resort airports. Aloha is highly regarded by frequent business travelers, and rates very favorably in the area of passenger complaints, according to U.S. Department of Transportation surveys.

Empire Airlines dba Mahalo Air (tel. toll free 800/277-8333) is the latest upstart airline to challenge the Big Two with budget fares. Unfortunately, their rock-bottom fares of $25 on Tuesday, Wednesday, and Thursday, $35 on other days, are for kamaainas (local residents) only. Nonresidents pay $54 each way, still a savings. They fly only from Honolulu to Lihue, Kahului, and Kona and back on propeller aircraft, which seat 48 people; there are about five flights a day to each destination.

SAVING MONEY ON TRAVEL TO THE NEIGHBOR ISLANDS

- Take advantage of the Hawaiian Airpass if you have a limited stay.
- Fly Mahalo Air if it fits into your schedule.
- Note the special prices for the first and last flights of the day, as well as senior, military and other discounts.

- Check the special fly/drive deals that Aloha and Hawaiian frequently make with the leading car-rental companies. If the airlines are sold out on any of these special programs, try a local travel agency; they'll often be able to help you.
- See the neighbor islands on your own. While many people do it the easy way, taking a package tour in which one flat fee, paid in advance, covers plane fares, hotels, meals and sightseeing, we find it's usually cheaper to do it on your own, using the hotels and restaurants we suggest.
- Unless you have money to spare, don't "flightsee" the islands from the air, landing briefly for meals and hurried sightseeing and returning the same night; this is about as satisfying as those European jaunts that take you to seven countries in 6 days. And the 1 day costs about $175 to boot!

ON THE ISLANDS

Your major expense on the outer islands will be transportation. Only one city on one island—Hilo, on the island of Hawaii—has anything resembling a public transportation system, and even that is not very extensive. (Buses do cross the island of Hawaii east to west and back.) There is also bus service in the Lahaina-Kaanapali area of Maui, but none of the buses run for any great distance. So unless you want to stay put, you have only two choices: taking expensive sightseeing tours or renting your own car. The latter is not cheap either, especially on days when you must pile on a lot of mileage, driving from one end of an island to another. Plus, the high-season markup on hotels extends to car rentals and other visitors' services. The motto seems to be, alas: "Get what the traffic will bear."

BY RENTAL CAR

The quoted price for a car rental is not always what it appears to be. There have, in fact, been a great many complaints from consumer groups who are hoping to force the industry to include all mandatory charges in their basic advertised fees; many car-rental companies oppose the plan. Thus, the budget-wise car renter must be on the alert for hidden charges (delivery, drop-off, extra charges for drivers under 25, for example, and most especially for insurance coverage).

It's a good idea to have a major credit card if you're going to rent a car in Hawaii. Otherwise, you'll have to pay cash in advance, or leave a deposit or a blank check with a personal signature.

Be sure to check your self-drive carefully before going on a long trip, and get a phone number where you can reach the agency at night in case of problems. Remember, too, to ask the agency for some good road maps indicating distances, and don't hesitate to ask questions and directions before you leave.

If you're under 21, you're out of luck here when it comes to renting a car. Hawaii state law prohibits anyone under 18 from driving with an out-of-state license (even though islanders can get licenses at 15!). There used to be one or two agencies that would rent to drivers 18 to 20, but at press time, there are none that we know of. There may be special stipulations for 21-to-24-year-olds, like paying a surcharge and having a major credit card. When you reach 25, you can just show your license, fill out the papers, and drive away.

A *further tip*: In general, it's cheaper to pick up a car at the airport than to have it delivered to your hotel and picked up when you're finished with it. And airport pickup, of course, avoids the costs of cabs or bus coming into town.

If you're going to visit several of the major islands, the easiest way to rent your cars is to make one telephone call to a company that provides service on all of them. We've had excellent cars and service from **Alamo Rent A Car.** Give them a call and find out if they're offering one of their specials if you're traveling in the winter. Regular rates are about $32 per day, $173 per week for an air-conditioned, automatic, economy car, all with unlimited free mileage, and often less. Alamo is in

Honolulu, Waikiki, Maui, Hilo, Kona, and Lihue (cars at airport terminals on neighbor islands, courtesy bus in Honolulu). Call Alamo toll free at 800/327-9633, 24 hours a day. Certain restrictions apply, including age and credit-card requirements. Rates do not include gas, tax, or a nominal under-25 surcharge.

With a fleet of nearly 10,000 cars, **Budget Rent A Car of Hawaii,** the well-known mainland and international car-rental agency, offers a vehicle for every taste and pocketbook. Since rates fluctuate so much, Budget does not care to quote them, but they're always competitive. Their exclusive gift program—given to all renters—includes many free admissions, meals, and gifts. There are 9 offices in Waikiki (tel. 922-3600) and 31 others throughout the state, with airport locations on Oahu, Maui, Molokai, Kauai, and the Big Island. For reservations, call toll free 800/527-0700, or write Budget Rent A Car of Hawaii, Central Reservations, P.O. Box 15188, Honolulu, HI 96830-0188.

Friendly service and good deals are available at **Tropical Rent-A-Car Systems,** 765 Amana St. (tel. 957-0800), which offers flat rates only (no mileage charges). Automatic compacts with air conditioning begin at $23 daily and $117 weekly. Tropical features such GM cars as Geos and Pontiac Grand Ams and a few Geo Trackers. Convertibles are available. Tropical has offices on all the major islands and rents to drivers 21 years of age (with a major credit card) and to older drivers up to age 70. They have two offices in Waikiki (tel. 942-4293), or call toll free 800/678-6000.

National Interrent has nine convenient airport and downtown locations on Oahu, Hawaii, Kauai, and Maui and offers competitive unlimited-mileage rates on it's fleet of GM cars. Inquire about special daily and weekly rates, during the summer; for the rest of the year, subcompacts begin at $40 daily. They're known for excellent service. The toll-free number is 800/CAR-RENT.

Thrifty Car Rental has locations on Oahu, Maui, and Kauai (not on Hawaii). They have direct-line courtesy phones at all baggage-claim areas. Usually, standard compacts rent for $26.95 daily, $165 weekly. There's no mileage charge. Call 833-0046 in Honolulu or 800/367-2277 toll free for reservations, or write to them at 3039 Ualena St., Honolulu, HI 96819.

Avis Rent A Car, Honolulu International Airport (tel. 834-5536, or toll free 800/331-1221) serves all five major islands, and offers a special for 7 days of driving an automatic Dodge or similar car on a combination of two or more islands—about $149 a week. For toll-free reservations, call 800/831-8000.

Hertz Rent A Car, 233 Keawe St., Room, 625, features an All-Island touring rate that covers 7 days or more on any combination of the four major islands. Days do not have to be consecutive and there is no mileage charge. The 7-day rate starts at $209 for a compact car, or $44 for one day. Daily rates offer free unlimited mileage. For toll-free reservations and information, call 800/654-3131. Hertz has offices at airports and hotels on all the major islands. You are advised to reserve at least a day in advance. A major credit card is required.

Dollar Rent A Car has locations on the six major islands—including Molokai and Lanai. Rates average $34 a day, $185 a week. They will rent to drivers under 25 at an extra charge of $5 per day, with a major credit card. For toll-free reservations from the U.S. call 800/367-7006.

AUTO INSURANCE Since Hawaii is a no-fault state, if you don't have insurance you are required to handle any damages before you leave the state. However, you may be able to avoid the cost of collision-damage waivers (anywhere from $10 to $12 per day), which the car-rental companies are eager to sell you, if your can insurance back home provides rental-car coverage. Your policy should include personal liability, property damage, fire, theft, and collision. Your insurance company should also be able to provide fast claim service in the islands. It would be a good idea to obtain the name of your company's local claim representative in Hawaii before you leave home; bring along your policy or identification card if you plan to do that. And check with your credit card company to see if it provides rental-car coverage.

DRIVING TIPS In general, Hawaiian drivers seem more courteous than those in big cities on the mainland— and they often drive more slowly. You should be aware of some special rules:

- The state has a mandatory seat-belt law. Be sure to buckle up.
- You may make a right turn in the right lane at a stoplight after coming to a full stop, unless noted otherwise.
- You may make a left turn at the stoplight from the left lane on a one-way street onto another one-way street after coming to a full stop.
- The pedestrian is usually right.
- Remember that driving distances on the neighbor islands can be great, particularly on the Big Island, and you may have trouble finding gas stations open, especially on Sunday. Keep the tank full.
- Should you have a breakdown, call your car-rental agency for emergency service.
- Current mainland driving licenses may be used until their expiration date. After that, you'll need a Hawaiian license, obtainable from the Department of Motor Vehicles, for those 15 and older.

ROAD MAPS For most driving, the road maps printed in the various "Drive Guides" to the neighbor islands, and given free with your car rental, are excellent. Should you wish to have topographic maps, they can be ordered by mail from the Hawaii Geographic Society, P.O. Box 1698, Honolulu, HI 96808 (tel. 808/538-3952), or the Map Information Center, Federal Center, Denver, CO 80225.

SAVING MONEY ON TRANSPORTATION

- Shop around for the best car-rental deals: Be persistent.
- Inquire as to whether your hotel has a car-rental package. On the neighbor islands, car rental packages are usually available from Sand & Seas hotels, among others. If you're staying in a small hotel or guesthouse, they may also be able to get you attractive rates; inquire when you make reservations.
- Remember that prices fluctuate according to the season; a car will always be a few dollars cheaper in the summer than in the Winter, and when business is slow.

SUGGESTED ITINERARIES

Since it's easy enough to get to a neighbor island right after you land in Honolulu, you can be flexible with your itinerary. You might, for example, start in Honolulu, travel from there to Kauai, then to Maui, from there to Molokai, and on to Kona, where you pick up your plane for your return flight to Los Angeles or San Francisco. Another route that we have found very pleasant is to fly directly to Kona from the West Coast, then on to Maui, Molokai, and Kauai, making the last stop Honolulu, and departing from there for home. (Plan it this way if you want peace and quiet first, excitement later.)

IF YOU HAVE 1 WEEK Spend at least 2 or 3 days in Honolulu, then visit the neighbor island that appeals to you most.

IF YOU HAVE 2 WEEKS Spend 4 days in Honolulu, then 5 days each on two neighbor islands that appeal to you.

IF YOU HAVE 3 WEEKS Twenty-one days is enough time to see the three major neighbor islands—Maui, the Big Island, Kauai—plus Honolulu, and maybe a visit to

Molokai too. We'd spend 5 days each in Honolulu, Maui, and the Big Island, 4 days on Kauai, and 2 on Molokai.

READERS RECOMMEND

"If you wait until you get to Hawaii to book your trips to the other islands, you can take advantage of the overnighter packages available, which include round-trip airfare for two and a room and rental car for 2 nights, for low fees, from Roberts of Hawaii. You ought to be in the islands to make these reservations."—Kenneth Kendall, Omaha, Neb. [*Authors Note:* There are many deals like this that can only be booked from Hawaii, since the companies are usually forbidden from advertising them outside the islands; they are mainly for kamaainas. It's wise to check these out when you are in the islands.]

11. ENJOYING HAWAII ON A BUDGET

THE $75-A-DAY BUDGET

Our aim is to show you how to keep your basic living costs—*room and three meals only*—down to somewhere around $75 a day. The costs of transportation, shopping, sightseeing, and entertainment are all in addition to that figure.

By keeping room and meal expenses low, you can make a substantial dent in the overall cost of your trip. But more important, we believe you'll have more fun—and enjoy a more meaningful vacation—by relying on your brains rather than your pocketbook. Hawaii is one of the few places where you can still live comfortably on a limited budget. In fact, many people who used to travel abroad for their holidays are finding Hawaii one of the best bargain areas anywhere. And considering that this is an enormously popular resort area, $75 a day per person is very little to pay.

WHERE TO STAY

Hotel rates in Hawaii usually vary according to season and demand. The hotel industry is highly competitive, and room prices go up or down as conditions dictate. We've attempted in this book to tell you about the very best lodging values in Hawaii, whether in hostels, moderately priced hotels, or condos. If the B&B alternative appeals to you, check out the reservations services listed below. Remember that B&B accommodations are no longer necessarily the cheapest; that they are best for couples, since there is usually only one double (or queen-size) bed; and that they do not provide cooking facilities. For a family or several people traveling together, an apartment with kitchenette usually works out more economically. Also, most B&Bs are in residential areas rather than tourist areas, so a car is essential.

BED & BREAKFAST RESERVATIONS SERVICES Evelyn Warner and Al Davis started **Bed & Breakfast Hawaii**, P.O. Box 449, Kapaa, HI 96746 (tel. 808/822-7771, or toll free 800/733-1632; fax 808/822-2723) years ago, "not as a big business operation, but as a low-key, intimate way for people to visit Hawaii." They offer accommodations in private homes and apartments on all the islands, for rates ranging from $35 to $50 single, $40 to $125 double, including continental breakfast. They can often pass on substantial savings on car rentals to their guests. Write or phone for a free brochure. For $12.95 you receive a directory of homes and apartments with rooms for rent called *Bed & Breakfast Goes Hawaiian.*

Mary Lee, the woman who runs **Bed & Breakfast Honolulu** (statewide), 3242 Kaohinani Dr., Honolulu, HI 96817 (tel. 808/595-7533, or toll free 800/288-4666;

fax 808/595-2030), doesn't believe directories do the trick; in almost 11 years of operating her business she's found that almost any place a guest picks from a directory will probably be unavailable at the time the request comes in. So Mrs. Lee installed an 800 number and she, or one of her family, will engage you in a personal conversation and help you find accommodations—either a room in a home or a studio in an apartment building. She charges a $10 reservation fee for each unit she reserves. She currently offers more than 400 "homestays" and studios on all the major islands, even including Lanai! Prices range from about $45 to $150 single, $50 to $155 double. Mrs. Lee also handles car rentals and inter-island flights, and she can get you good discounts on each.

Doris Reichert of **Pacific-Hawaii Bed & Breakfast,** 99-442 Kekoa Place, Aiea, Oahu, HI 96701 (tel. 808/487-1228 or toll free 800/999-6026, fax 808/487-1228 or 808/261-6573), has many rentals in the lovely suburb of Kailua, not far from Waikiki. It's one of our favorite areas, since both Kailua and Lanikai beaches are superb—and it's also one of the new meccas for windsurfers. She also has about 200 listings on all the Hawaiian Islands, ranging from $45 a day for two guests. She requests 20% of the cost of the stay for confirmation, but she promises a complete refund if the room does not meet your expectations or you do not take occupancy because of a serious emergency; she's serious when she says "satisfaction guaranteed."

Upscale B&B lodgings throughout the state are the province of **Hawaii's Bed & Breakfasts,** hand-picked by Barbara Campbell from her headquarters on the Big Island. Each home, private cottage, or country inn is selected for it's distinctive personality, attention to details, and the warm hospitality of it's hosts. Daily rates go from $75 to $175. For a brochure describing these hidden gems, contact Barbara Campbell, P.O. Box 563, Kamuela, HI 96743 (tel. 808/855-4550, or toll free 800/ 262-9912 for reservations).

Go Native . . . Hawaii, 65 Halaulani Place (P.O. Box 11418), Hilo, HI 96721 (tel. 808/935-4178, or toll free 800/662-8483), has been matching guests with Hawaiian hosts for more than a decade. Coordinator Fred Diamond has 250 locations on all islands except Lanai, ranging from oceanfront to mountain sites, from traditional B&B rooms in private homes to unhosted studios and cottages. Rates begin around $40 single, around $65 double.

My Island, P.O. Box 100, Volcano, HI 96785 (tel. 808/967-7110; fax 808/ 967-7719) is a Hawaii-island-only reservation service run by Gordon and Joann Morse; they have rentals all over the Big Island, and encourage people to move around to explore the different atmospheres and climates of the various districts. Prices start at $30 to $45 single, $45 to $85 double, and go up.

Focusing on Maui, but with accommodations on the Big Island and Kauai as well, **B&B Maui Style,** P.O. Box 198, Puunene, HI 96784 (tel. 808/879-7865, or toll free 800/848-5567), has charming accommodations all over the Valley Island, from oceanside to mountain slopes. They handle rooms in private houses from $45 to $60 double, and vacation rentals in condos, cottages, studios, and homes, which go for $65 to $100. They're happy to offer advice on out-of-the-way places and activities.

A CONDO & HOUSE-RENTAL SERVICE Savings of up to 50% on condo rentals can be realized by working through **HALE** (Hawaiian Apartment Leasing Enterprises), 479 Ocean Ave., Suite B, Laguna Beach, CA 92651 (tel. 714/497-4253, or toll free 800/854-8843, from the U.S. mainland and Canada), which handles rentals on all the major islands (including Molokai) with a wide range of prices, sizes, and locations. Most of the condos are custom-decorated and of high quality. Rates run roughly between $60 and $95 per night double. HALE also has some 200 private homes available, beginning with a two-bedroom house in Kauai for $445 a week. Cleaning services, cooks, chauffeurs, day care, and additional custom services can be arranged.

CAMPING Camping is popular with families on all the islands, but, unfortunately, tent camping is no longer as safe as it used to be, and there is no place where one can rent a camper or RV. Should you decide to camp, note that advance permits are required. Check with the offices of the Hawaii Visitors Bureau (see "Information, Entry Requirements, and Money," above in this chapter) to find out where to obtain permits for each island.

SAVING MONEY ON ACCOMMODATIONS

- To stay within the $75-a-day budget, you should be part of a twosome, which means that you will have a total of $150 per day to spend on room and meals. Unless otherwise noted, the rates do no include Hawaii's hefty hotel tax—9.43%. Also, all rooms include baths, unless otherwise noted.
- Stay at a small apartment-hotel or condominium complex, complete with a built-in money-saving device: a kitchenette. This doesn't mean, however, that you'll spend your vacation slaving away at a hot stove. It means only that you'll fix breakfast, maybe pack a sandwich or some marvelous fresh fruit for a picnic or a light supper, and dine out once a day (preferably at lunchtime, when prices are always low and values best). We've scoured the state looking for budget apartment-hotels and have come up with a surprisingly large number of them.
- Find bed-and-breakfasts with the help of the organizations mentioned above.
- Avoid the winter season—mid-December to mid-April. That's when everybody seems to want to go to Hawaii, and many visitors-especially those from cold areas like western Canada and Alaska—often stay a few months at the budget apartment-hotels. Many hotels routinely impose a surcharge of as much as $10 to $20 per room during that period. The summer months of June, July, and August are also busy, but many hotels maintain "low-season" rates in those months, and during the months of October, November, and May all kinds of choice rooms are yours for the picking. If you think you'd like to spend the Christmas–New Year's season in the islands, make reservations as far in advance as you possibly can; many hotels accept reservations as much as 6 months to a year in advance for this insanely popular period. The months of January and February are also extremely popular.
- Contact the **Hotel Exchange,** 1946 Ala Moana Blvd., Honolulu, HI 96815 (tel. 808/942-8544, or toll free 800/548-0330; fax 808/955-2627), which offers discounted hotel rooms. It works with 180 hotels on Oahu and all the neighbor islands, and will take advance reservations over the phone with an approved credit card, or you can simply walk in and see them if you're already in town and not happy where you're staying. Savings could be as little as $5 or as much as $100 per day at many leading hotels.

READERS RECOMMEND

"Some hotels will give a 25% to 50% discount off published room rates for military personnel and their families. We stayed at three- and four-star hotels at half the normal rate. I believe that many of your readers are in the U.S. military and would be happy to know about this benefit."—Joe and Robin Gruender, Wright-Patterson AFB, Ohio.

HOME EXCHANGES

If you'd like to exchange your own home or apartment for a place to stay in Honolulu, contact the **Vacation Exchange Club,** P.O. Box 650, Key West, FL 33041 (tel. toll free 800/638-3841), a worldwide home-swapping group. You can be listed in their directory for $60 a year and find out what's available in Hawaii. (A recent listing, for example, offered a three-bedroom/two-bath house, along with two cars and two bikes, in the posh Kahala region, for a 3-month exchange.) Rentals are also available. Vacation Exchange Club provides information only (it is not a travel agency); the actual arrangements are all up to you.

Another organization that provides a similar service is Intervac U.S. International Home Exchange, P.O. Box 590504, San Francisco CA 94159 (tel. 415/435-3497, or 800/756-HOME; fax 415/386-6853). It publishes three catalogs a year, containing over 8,800 homes in more than 36 countries, with about 100 in the Hawaiian Islands. Members contact each other directly. The $62 cost includes your own listing in one catalog and receiving all three catalogs. Seniors over 62 pay $55. Photos cost $11. Postage is extra. Hospitality and youth exchanges, as well as rentals, are also offered. This is the largest worldwide home-exchange network.

Trading Home International, P.O. Box 787, Hermosa Beach, CA 90254 (tel. toll free 800/877-TRADE; fax 310/798-3865), provides worldwide home-exchange listings and a goodly number in Hawaii. Membership, which includes your home listing (including photograph) and receipt of three directories per year, is $65. They also distribute *Trading Places,* a useful handbook of home trading for $12, and are the headquarters of the International Home Exchange Association, with member agencies throughout the world.

Teachers have more time for vacations than most of us, so it was inevitable that a service like **Teacher Swap Directory of Homes** would come about. They have an excellent list of international locations, as well as quite a few in Hawaii. The price is $42 for both a listing and the director, $50 for the directory only. Contact Teacher Swap, P.O. Box 454, Oakdale, NY 11769-0454 (tel. 516/244-2845).

READERS RECOMMEND

"We spent five weeks in Oahu, having previously arranged to exchange homes with a couple who lived in a delightful home in Manoa Valley. Surprisingly, many island people do like to have excursions to the mainland, and home exchange is an ideal way of providing the basis for a really inexpensive vacation. A government employees' bulletin circulates in Honolulu and elsewhere, and at the University of Hawaii; this provides a good place to advertise."—David Brokenshaw, Santa Barbara, Calif.

WHERE TO EAT

We'll show you how to eat inexpensively and well, figuring about $18 for dinner, about $5 or $6 for lunch, roughly $4 to $6 for breakfast. Of course, whatever you save by eating in means that much more in the kitty for other pleasures.

Also, even though it's easier than it used to be to find inexpensive places to eat as you scoot around the islands because of the rise of fast-food outlets, it can be a long drive between meals. It's always a good idea to throw a few sandwiches and some fruit in your beach bag, along with the suntan lotion and the road maps.

SAVING MONEY ON MEALS

If you really want to save money, plan to eat breakfast and at least one meal a day at home; that's when your kitchenette apartment more than pays for itself. Remember that lunch is always cheaper than dinner—often for much the same meal. Early Bird specials offer excellent dinner bargains all over town.

OTHER BUDGET TIPS

SAVING MONEY ON SIGHTSEEING & ENTERTAINMENT

- Check local tourist publications for discount coupons.
- Consider renting a car from a company that gives out free coupons.
- Check numerous sources of free and low-cost entertainment in Chapter 7, "Honolulu Attractions."

SAVING MONEY ON SHOPPING

- Patronize the ABC stores for best prices on sundries and souvenirs.
- Check our listings of discount and outlet stores in Chapter 8, "Savvy Shopping in Honolulu."

SAVING MONEY ON SERVICES & OTHER TRANSACTIONS

TIPPING As in other mainland cities, standard restaurant tips are 15%. Baggage handlers and porters should receive 50¢ to $1 for each large piece of luggage. To save money—carry your own. Cleaning service should get $1 per night.

TELEPHONE CALLS Check with your hotel to find out if there is a surcharge on calls. (There almost always is.) If so, use pay phones in the lobby.

MATTERS OF USAGE

It's preferable to refer to the residents of the 50th state as "islanders," rather than as natives or Hawaiians—unless they happen to be of Hawaiian descent. You are from the mainland, not the States; islanders are very sensitive about this. And don't make the dreadful mistake of calling Americans of Japanese ancestry "Japs." They're as proud of being Americans as any descendants of *Mayflower* passengers. During World War II, in fact, the Nisei volunteers so distinguished themselves in the bloody battles of southern Europe that their unit—the 442nd Regimental Combat Team— was designated probably the most decorated unit in United States military history. One of it's veterans is Daniel K. Inouye (of Watergate and "Irangate" fame), chosen as Hawaii's first representative in Congress, now it's senior senator. The late Spark M. Matsunaga, formerly it's junior senator, was also a veteran of the 442nd. Recent state leaders of Japanese ancestry have included the house leader, the past president of the University of Hawaii, the chairman of the Senate's powerful Ways and Means committee, and a number of judges. Remember, too, that although statehood was achieved only in 1959, residents of Hawaii have been American citizens since 1898, when, 5 years after the Hawaiian monarchy was overthrown in a bloodless coup with U.S. Marines standing by (a triumph for the haole sugar and other commercial interests), the Republic of Hawaii was annexed by the administration of President McKinley.

 HAWAII

Area Code All the Hawaiian Islands share one area code: 808.

Business Hours Most office workers in Hawaii are at their desks by 8am, sometimes even earlier, and it's *pau hana* (finish work) at 4 or 5pm, the better to get in an afternoon swim or a round of golf. Hawaii may be the only place where even executives can be reached by 8:30am! Normal bank hours Monday through Thursday are 8:30am to 3 or 3:30pm, until 6pm on Friday. Most shopping malls are open Monday through Friday from 9 or 10am to 9pm, on Saturday until 5:30pm, and for a shorter period on Sunday, usually until 4pm. Individual establishments at these malls will vary their hours, and some will close earlier than others.

Cigarettes Noncitizens over 21 are allowed to bring in 200 cigarettes or 50 cigars or two kilograms of tobacco.

Climate See "When To Go," in this chapter.

Crime See "Safety," below.

Driving Rules See "Getting Around," in this chapter.

Drug Laws Strictly enforced.

Electricity Hawaii uses standard North American current, 110 volts AC, 60 cycles.

Emergencies   Dial 911 for an ambulance, a fire, or the police.

Holidays   See "When to Go," in this chapter.

Information   See "Information, Entry Requirements, and Money" in this chapter.

Language   You don't have to learn a new language, since everyone speaks English. But the islanders do pepper their vocabulary with lots of Hawaiian words, and almost all place names are Hawaiian. So it's a good idea to bone up on a few pronunciation rules and learn a few words. The original Hawaiians spoke a Polynesian dialect, but they had no written language. Missionaries transcribed it in order to teach Hawaiians to read the Bible, and made it as easy as possible. There are only 12 letters in the Hawaiian alphabet: 5 vowels and 7 consonants: *h, k, l, m, n, p, w.* Every syllable ends in a vowel; every vowel is pronounced, no matter how many there are in the word (these have a frightening way of piling up one after another); and the accent is almost always on the penultimate syllable (the next to the last), as it is in Spanish. Consonants receive their English sounds, but vowels get the Latin pronunciation: *a* as in farm, *e* as in they, *i* as in machine, *o* as in cold, and *u* as in tutor.

Lists of Hawaiian words can be obtained in most tourist offices, but check out our Appendix—"Hawaiian Vocabulary"—first. Do bear in mind that the name of the state is pronounced Ha-WYE-ee (it does not rhyme with how-are-yuh). You are a newcomer, a *malihini* (mah-lee-HEE-nee), and longtime residents of the islands are *kamaainas* kama-EYE-nahs). The *haoles* (properly pronounced ha-o-lays, but more commonly HOW-lays) are the whites, originally foreigners.

The mysterious *lanai* (lah-*neye*) that landlords are always boasting about is nothing but a balcony or porch. *Kau kau* (*cow*-cow) means food; you'll go to a lot of *luaus* (*loo*-ows), Hawaiian feasts; and people will say thank you—rather, *mahalo* (mah-*hah*-low)—for you *kokua* (ko-*koo*-ah), your help. It's *kanes* (*kah*-nays) for men, *wahines* (wah-*hee*-nays) for women. You probably already know that a *lei* (lay) is a necklace of flowers. And just as you expected, everyone says *aloha* (ah-*low* hah)—one of the most beautiful words in any language—meaning hello, good-bye, good luck, and *salud!* It also means love, as in "I send you my aloha."

Laundry   Most hotels have washing machines and dryers for the use of guests; if not, self-service laundries can be found everywhere.

Legal Aid   The main office of the Legal Aid Society of Hawaii is at 1108 Nuuanu Ave. (tel. 536-4302).

Liquor Laws   The legal drinking age in Hawaii is 21.

Maps   Island maps suitable for driving tours are supplied by car-rental companies; more detailed ones are available at most bookstores and newsstands. An excellent source is Hawaii Geographic Maps and Books, 49 S. Hotel St., Suite 218 (P.O. Box 1698), Honolulu, HI 96808 (tel. 808/538-3952). Write or call to request lists of suggested books and maps. They have USGS topographic maps of Hawaii, plus various other road maps. You can visit their small store at the above address when in Honolulu. On the Big Island of Hawaii, Basically Books, 45 Waianuenue Ave. (tel. 961-0144), in downtown Hilo, has a complete selection of maps of Hawaii, including USCG topographic maps, NOAA nautical charts, road and street maps.

Newspapers   In Honolulu, it's the *Honolulu Advertiser* and the *Honolulu Star-Bulletin;* in Maui, it's the *Maui News;* in Kauai, the *Garden Island News.*

Radio and TV   See "Fast Facts: Honolulu," in Chapter 4, for a comprehensive listing of Honolulu radio and TV stations. All the major islands are equipped with cable TV and get all major mainland television channels.

Restrooms   Since this is the U.S.A., signs usually read MEN and WOMEN, although sometimes it will be KANES and WAHINES.

Safety   Yes, it's true; there is crime and violence in Hawaii, as there is everywhere else in the world. And because Hawaii was indeed a trouble-free paradise for so many years, people tend to ignore basic safety precautions. Our advice is: Don't! Never carry large sums of cash; traveler's checks are much safer. Don't go hiking on deserted trails except in a group; don't go wandering on isolated beaches alone; and don't go jogging in the cane fields alone at the crack of dawn, as one crime victim did (there are many marijuana farms in secluded areas, and the owners do not take kindly to strangers). Stay in well-lighted areas at night, travel with a friend if possible, lock your car and remove valuables from your trunk, and use your common sense—just as you would at home. Follow these precautions, and you should find a visit to Hawaii no more dangerous than one to your own hometown.

It's always advisable to put your valuables into your hotel's safe or an in-room safe. If you don't want to use a safe, then at least take you valuables with you. Never leave them unprotected in a hotel room, to which any number of people—staff, service personnel, guests past or present, and others—could have access.

Taxes   The hotel occupancy tax is 9.17%. Sales tax is 4%.

Telephone and Fax   The cost of a local call (from any one part of an island to another) at a pay phone is 25¢. Interisland calls cost more. Be aware that most hotels impose a surcharge on all calls.

Fax services are available at many copy centers around the islands, and at all Phone Mart locations (see separate chapters for listings).

Time   There are five time zones between the East Coast of the United States and Hawaii. That means that when it's noon Hawaiian standard time, it's 5pm eastern standard time, 4pm central, 3pm mountain, and 2pm Pacific. Hawaii does not do daylight saving time as the rest of the nation does, so from May through October, noon in Hawaii would mean 6pm eastern, 5pm central, and so on.

Tipping   See "Enjoying Hawaii on a Budget," in this chapter.

Tourist Offices See "Information, Entry Requirements, and Money," in this chapter.

CHAPTER 3

FOR FOREIGN VISITORS

1. PREPARING FOR YOUR TRIP

2. GETTING TO & AROUND THE U.S.

- **FAST FACTS: FOR THE FOREIGN TRAVELER**

- **AMERICAN SYSTEM OF MEASUREMENTS**

Although American fads and fashions have spread across Europe and other parts of the world so that America may seem like familiar territory before your arrival, there are still many peculiarities and uniquely American situations that any foreign visitor will encounter.

---

1. PREPARING FOR YOUR TRIP

ENTRY REQUIREMENTS

DOCUMENT REGULATIONS   Canadian citizens may enter the U.S. without visas; they need only proof of residence.

Citizens of the U.K., New Zealand, Japan, and most Western European countries traveling on valid passports may not need a visa for fewer than 90 days of holiday or business travel to the U.S., providing that they hold a round-trip or return ticket and enter the U.S. on an airline or cruise line participating in the visa waiver program.

(Note that citizens of these visa-exempt countries who first enter the U.S. may then visit Mexico, Canada, Bermuda, and/or the Caribbean islands and then reenter the U.S., by any mode of transportation, without needing a visa. Further information is available from any U.S. embassy or consulate.)

Citizens of countries other than those stipulated above, including citizens of Australia, must have two documents:

- a valid **passport,** with an expiration date of at least 6 months later than the scheduled end of the visit to the U.S.; and
- a **tourist visa,** available without charge from the nearest U.S. consulate. To obtain a visa, the traveler must submit a completed application form (either in person or by mail) 1½-inch square photo and demonstrate binding ties to a residence abroad.

Usually you can obtain a visa at once or within 24 hours, but it may take longer during the summer rush from June to August. If you cannot go in person, contact the nearest U.S. embassy or consulate for directions on applying by mail. Your travel agent or airline office may also be able to provide you with visa applications and instructions. The U.S. consulate or embassy that issues your visa will determine whether you will be issued a multiple- or single-entry visa and any restrictions regarding the length of your stay.

MEDICAL REQUIREMENTS No inoculations are needed to enter the United States unless you are coming from, or have stopped over in, areas known to be suffering from epidemics, particularly cholera or yellow fever.

If you have a disease requiring treatment with medications containing narcotics or drugs requiring a syringe, carry a valid signed prescription from your physician to allay any suspicions that you are smuggling drugs.

CUSTOMS REQUIREMENTS Every adult visitor may bring in free of duty: one liter of wine or hard liquor; 200 cigarettes or 100 cigars (but no cigars from Cuba) or three pounds of smoking tobacco; $100 worth of gifts. These exemptions are offered to travelers who spend at least 72 hours in the United States and who have not claimed them within the preceding 6 months. It is altogether forbidden to bring into the country foodstuffs (particularly cheese, fruit, cooked meats, and canned goods) and plants (vegetables, seeds, tropical plants, and so on). Foreign tourists may bring in or take out up to $10,000 in U.S. or foreign currency with no formalities; larger sums must be declared to Customs on entering or leaving.

INSURANCE

There is no national health system in the United States. Because the cost of medical care is extremely high, we strongly advise every traveler to secure health coverage before setting out.

You may want to take out a comprehensive travel policy that covers (for a relatively low premium) sickness or injury costs (medical, surgical, and hospital); loss or theft of your baggage; trip-cancellation costs; guarantee of bail in case you are arrested; costs of accident, repatriation, or death. Such packages (for example, "Europe Assistance" in Europe) are sold by automobile clubs at attractive rates, as well as by insurance companies and travel agencies.

MONEY

CURRENCY & EXCHANGE The U.S. monetary system has a decimal base: one American **dollar ($1)** = 100 **cents** (100¢).

Dollar bills commonly come in $1 (a "buck"), $5, $10, $20, $50, and $100 denominations (the last two are not welcome when paying for small purchases and not accepted in taxis or at subway ticket booths). There are also $2 bills (seldom encountered).

There are six denominations of coins: 1¢ (one cent or "penny"), 5¢ (five cents or a "nickel"), 10¢ (ten cents or a "dime"), 25¢ (twenty-five cents or a "quarter"), 50¢ (fifty cents or a "half dollar"), and the rare $1 piece.

TRAVELER'S CHECKS Traveler's checks denominated in U.S. dollars are readily accepted at most hotels, motels, restaurants, and large stores. But the best place to change traveler's checks is at a bank. Do not bring traveler's checks denominated in other currencies.

CREDIT CARDS The method payment most widely used is the credit card: VISA (BarclayCard in Britain), MasterCard (EuroCard in Europe, Access in Britain, Chargex in Canada), American Express, Diners Club, Discover, and Carte Blanche. You can save yourself trouble by using "plastic money" rather than cash or traveler's checks in most hotels, motels, restaurants, and retail stores (a growing number of food and liquor stores now accept credit cards). You must have a credit card to rent a car. It can also be used as proof of identity (often carrying more weight than a passport), or as a "cash card," enabling you to draw money from banks that accept them.

Note: The "foreign-exchange bureaus" so common in Europe are rare even at airports in the United States, and nonexistent outside major cities. Try to avoid having to change foreign money, or traveler's checks denominated other than in U.S. dollars, at a small-town bank, or even a branch in a big city; in fact, leave any currency other than U.S. dollars at home—it may prove more nuisance to you than its worth.

SAFETY

GENERAL While tourist areas are generally safe, crime is on the increase everywhere, and U.S. urban areas tend to be less safe than those in Europe or Japan. Visitors should always stay alert. This is particularly true of large U.S. cities. It is wise to ask the city's or area's tourist office if you're in doubt about which neighborhoods are safe. Avoid deserted areas, especially at night. Don't go into any city park at night unless there is an event that attracts crowds—for example, the Waikiki Shell concerts in Kapiolani Park. Generally speaking, you can feel safe in areas where there are many people, and many open establishments.

Avoid carrying valuables with you on the street, and don't display expensive cameras or electronic equipment. Hold on to your pocketbook, and place your billfold in an inside pocket. In theaters, restaurants, and other public places, keep your possessions in sight.

Remember also that hotels are open to the public, and in a large hotel, security may not be able to screen everyone entering. Always lock your room door—don't assume that once inside your hotel you are automatically safe and no longer need be aware of your surroundings.

DRIVING Safety while driving is particularly important. Question your rental agency about personal safety, or ask for a brochure of traveler safety tips when you pick up your car. Obtain written directions, or a map with the route marked in red, from the agency showing how to get to your destination. And, if possible, arrive and depart during daylight hours.

Recently more and more crime has involved cars and drivers. If you drive off a highway into a doubtful neighborhood, leave the area as quickly as possible. If you have an accident, even on the highway, stay in your car with the doors locked until you assess the situation or until the police arrive. If you are bumped from behind on the street or are involved in a minor accident with no injuries and the situation appears to be suspicious, motion to the other driver to follow you. *Never* get out of your car in such situations. You can also keep a pre-made sign in your car which reads: PLEASE FOLLOW THIS VEHICLE TO REPORT THE ACCIDENT. Show the sign to the other driver and go directly to the nearest police precinct, well-lighted service station, or all-night store.

If you see someone on the road who indicates a need for help, do *not* stop. Take note of the location, drive on to a well-lighted area, and telephone the police by dialing 911.

Park in well-lighted, well-traveled areas if possible. Always keep your car doors locked, whether attended or unattended. Look around you before you get out of your car, and never leave any packages or valuables in sight. If someone attempts to rob you or steal your car, do *not* try to resist the thief/carjacker—report the incident to the police department immediately.

2. GETTING TO & AROUND THE U.S.

Travelers from overseas can take advantage of the **APEX (Advance Purchase Excursion) fares** offered by all the major U.S. and European carriers. Aside from these, attractive values are offered by **Icelander** on flights from Luxembourg to New York and by **Virgin Atlantic Airways** from London to New York/Newark.

Some large American airlines (for example, TWA, American Airlines, Northwest, United, and Delta) offer travelers on their transatlantic or transpacific flights special discount tickets under the name **Visit USA**, allowing travel between any U.S. destinations at minimum rates. They are not on sale in the United States, and must, therefore, be purchased before you leave your foreign point of departure. This system is the best, easiest, and fastest way to see the United States at low cost. You should obtain information well in advance from your travel agent or the office of the airline concerned, since the conditions attached to these discount tickets can be changed without advance notice.

The visitor arriving by air, no matter what the port of entry, should cultivate patience and resignation before setting foot on U.S. soil. Getting through Immigration control may take as long as two hours on some days, especially summer weekends. Add the time it takes to clear Customs and you'll see that you should make very generous allowance for delay in planning connections between international and domestic flights—an average of 2 to 3 hours at least.

In contrast, travelers arriving by car or by rail from Canada will find border-crossing formalities streamlined to the vanishing point. And air travelers from Canada, Bermuda, and some places in the Caribbean can sometimes go through Customs and Immigration at the point of departure, which is much quicker and less painful.

For further information about travel to Hawaii, see "Getting There" in Chapter 2.

FAST FACTS FOR THE FOREIGN TRAVELER

Automobile Organizations Auto clubs will supply maps, suggested routes, guidebooks, accident and bail-bond insurance, and emergency road service. The major auto club in the United States, with 955 offices nationwide, is the **American Automobile Association (AAA).** Members of some foreign auto clubs have reciprocal arrangements with the AAA and enjoy its services at no charge. If you belong to an auto club, inquire about AAA reciprocity before you leave. The AAA can provide you with an **International Driving Permit** validating your foreign license. You may be able to join the AAA even if you are not a member of a reciprocal club. To inquire, call toll free 800/336-4357. In addition, some automobile rental agencies now provide these services, so you should inquire about their availability when you rent your car.

Automobile Rentals To rent a car you need a major credit card. A valid driver's license is required, and you usually need to be at least 25. Some companies do rent to younger people but add a daily surcharge.

Business Hours Banks are open weekdays from 9am to 3 or 4pm, although there's a 24-hour access to the automatic tellers (ATMs) at most banks and other outlets. Generally, **offices** are open weekdays from 8am to 4 or 5pm. **Stores** are open 6 days week, with many open on Sunday, too; department stores usually stay open until 9pm at least 1 day a week.

Climate See "When to Go" in Chapter 2.

Currency See "Money" in "Preparing for Your Trip" above.

Currency Exchange You will find currency services in major airports with international service. Most major banks on the four largest islands of Hawaii provide currency exchange. In addition, in Honolulu, the capital city, you can get reliable currency service at **Thomas Cook Currency,** 830 Fort Street Mall (tel. 808/523-1321); **A1 Foreign Exchange,** Royal Hawaiian Shopping Center (tel. 808/922-3327); and **Monyx International,** 307 Royal Hawaiian Ave. (808/923-6626).

Drinking Laws See "Liquor Laws" in "Fast Facts: Hawaii" in Chapter 2.

Electricity The United States uses 110–120 volts, 60 cycles, compared to 220–240 volts, 50 cycles, as in most of Europe. In addition to a 100-volt converter, small appliances of non-American manufacture, such as hairdryers or shavers, will require a plug adapter, with two flat, parallel pins.

Embassies & Consulates All embassies are located in the national capital, Washington, D.C.; some consulates are located in major cities, and most nations have a mission to the United Nations in New York City. Foreign visitors can obtain telephone numbers for their embassies and consulates by calling "Information" in Washington, D.C. (tel. 202/555-1212).

The consulate general of **Australia** is located at 1000 Bishop St. in Honolulu, HI 96813 (tel. 808/524-5050): the consulate general of **Japan** is located at 1742 Nuuanu Ave. in Honolulu, HI 96817 (tel. 808/536-2226).

Emergencies Call **911** to report a fire, call the police, or get an ambulance. If you encounter traveler's problems, check the local directory to find an office of the **Traveler's Aid Society,** a nationwide, nonprofit, social-service organization geared to helping travelers in difficult straits. Their services might include reuniting families separated while traveling, providing food, and/or shelter to people stranded without cash, or even emotional counseling. If youre in trouble, seek them out.

Gasoline One U.S. gallon equals 3.75 liters, while 1.2 U.S. gallons equals one Imperial gallon. You'll notice there are several grades (and price levels) of gasoline available at most gas stations. And you'll also notice that their names change from company to company. The unleaded ones with the highest octane are the most expensive (most rental cars take the least expensive "regular" unleaded) and leaded gas is the least expensive, but only older cars can take this any more, so check if you're not sure.

Holidays On the following legal national holidays, banks, government offices, post offices, and many stores, restaurants, and museums are closed:

New Year's Day January 1
Martin Luther King Day Third Monday in January
Presidents Day Third Monday in February
Memorial Day Last Monday in May
Independence Day July 4
Labor Day First Monday in September
Columbus Day Second Monday in October
Veterans (Armistice) Day November 11
Thanksgiving Day Last Thursday in November
Christmas Day December 25

Election Day, which falls on the Tuesday following the first Monday in November, is a national holiday during presidential-election years.

Languages Major hotels may have multilingual employees. Unless your language is very obscure, they can usually supply a translator on request.

Legal Aid The foreign tourist, unless positively identified as a member of the Mafia or of a drug ring, will probably never become involved with the American legal system. If you are pulled up for a minor infraction (for example, of the highway code, such as speeding), never attempt to pay the fine directly to a police officer; you may wind up arrested on the much more serious charge of attempted bribery. Pay fines by mail, or directly into the hands of the clerk of the court. If accused of a more serious offense, its wise to say and do nothing before consulting a lawyer. Under U.S. law, an arrested person is allowed one telephone call to a party of his or her choice. Call your embassy or consulate.

Mail If you want your mail to follow you on your vacation and you aren't sure of your address, your mail can be sent to you, in your name, **c/o General Delivery** at the main post office of the city or region where you expect to be. The addressee must pick it up in person and produce proof of identity (driver's license, credit card, passport, etc.).

Generally to be found at intersections, mailboxes are blue with a red-and-white stripe and carry the inscription U.S. MAIL. If your mail is addressed to a U.S. destination, don't forget to add the five-figure postal code, or ZIP (Zone Improvement Plan) Code, after the two-letter abbreviation of the state to which the mail is addressed (HI for Hawaii, FL for Florida, NY for New York, and so on).

Newspapers/Magazines National newspapers include the *New York Times, USA Today,* and the *Wall Street Journal.* National news weeklies include *Newsweek, Time,* and *U.S. News & World Report.* The *Honolulu Advertiser* and the *Honolulu Star-Bulletin* are the major local newspapers.

Radio and Television Audiovisual media, with four coast-to-coast networks—on ABC, CBS, NBC, and Fox—joined by the Public Broadcasting System

(PBS) and the cable network CNN, play a major part in American life. In big cities, televiewers have a choice of about a dozen channels (including the UHF channels), most of them transmitting 24 hours a day, without counting the pay-TV channels showing recent movies or sports events. All options are usually indicated on your hotel TV set. You'll find a wide choice of local radio stations, each broadcasting particular kinds of talk shows and/or music—classical, country, jazz, pop, gospel—punctuated by news broadcasts and frequent commercials.

Safety See "Safety in Preparing for Your Trip," above.

Taxes In the United States there is no VAT (Value-Added Tax) or other indirect tax at a national level. Every state, and each city in it, has the right to levy its own local tax on all purchases, including hotel and restaurant checks, airline tickets, and so on. In Hawaii, sales tax is 4%.

Petrol See "Gasoline," above.

Telephone, Telegraph, Telex The telephone system in the U.S. is run by private corporations, so rates, especially for long distance service, can vary widely—even on calls made from public telephones. Local calls in the U.S. usually cost 25¢.

Generally, hotel surcharges on long-distance and local calls are astronomical. You are usually better off using a **public pay telephone,** which you will find clearly marked in most public buildings and private establishments as well as on the street. Outside metropolitan areas, public telephones are more difficult to find. Stores and gas stations are your best bet.

Most **long-distance** and **international** calls can be dialed directly from any phone. For calls to Canada and other parts of the U.S., dial 1 followed by the area code and the seven-digit number. For international calls, dial 011 followed by the country code, city code, and the telephone number of the person you wish to call.

For **reversed-charge or collect calls,** and for **person-to-person** calls, dial 0 (zero, not the letter "O") followed by the area code and number you want; an operator will then come on the line, and you should specify that you are calling collect, or person-to-person, or both. If your operator-assisted call is international, ask for the overseas operator.

For local **directory assistance** ("information"), dial 411; for **long-distance information,** dial 1, then the appropriate area code and 555-1212.

Like the telephone system, **telegraph** and **telex** services are provided by private corporations like ITT, MCI, and above all, Western Union, the most important. You can bring your telegram in to the nearest Western Union office (there are hundreds across the country), or dictate it over the phone (a toll-free call, 800/325-6000). You can also telegraph money, or have it telegraphed to you, very quickly over the Western Union system.

Telephone Directory There are two kinds of telephone directories available to you. The general directory is the so-called **White Pages,** in which private and business subscribers are listed in alphabetical order. The inside front cover lists the emergency number for police, fire, and ambulance, and other vital numbers (like the Coast Guard, poison-control center, crime-victims hotline, and so on). The first few pages are devoted to community-service numbers, including a guide to long-distance and international calling, complete with country codes, and area codes.

The second directory, printed on yellow paper (hence its name, *Yellow Pages*), lists all local services, businesses, and industries by type of activity, with an index either in the front or in the back. The listings cover not only such obvious items as automobile repairs by make of car, or drugstores (pharmacies), often by geographical location, but also restaurants by type of cuisine and geographical location, bookstores by special subject and/or language, places of worship by religious denomination, and other information that the tourist might otherwise not readily find. The *Yellow Pages* also include city plans or detailed area maps, often showing postal ZIP Codes and public transportation routes.

Time The United States is divided into four **time zones** (six, if Alaska and Hawaii are included). From east to west, these are: eastern standard time (EST), central standard time (CST), mountain standard time (MST), Pacific standard time

(PST), Alaska standard time (AST), and Hawaii standard time (HST). Always keep changing time zones in mind if you are traveling (or even telephoning) long distances in the United States. For example, noon in New York City (EST) is 11am in Chicago (CST), 10am in Denver (MST), 9am in Los Angeles (PST), 8am in Anchorage (AST), and 7am in Honolulu (HST).

Daylight saving time is in effect from the last Sunday in April through the last Saturday in October (actually, the change is made at 2am on Sunday) except in Arizona, Hawaii, part of Indiana, and Puerto Rico. Daylight saving time moves the clock one hour ahead of standard time.

Tipping This is part of the American way of life, on the principle that you must expect to pay for any service you get. Here are some rules of thumb:

Bartenders: 10%–15%.
Bellhops: at least 50¢ per piece; $2–$3 for a lot of baggage.
Cab drivers: 15% of the fare.
Cafeterias, fast-food restaurants: no tip.
Chambermaids: $1 a day.
Checkroom attendants (restaurants, theaters): $1 per garment.
Cinema, movies, theaters: no tip.
Doormen (hotels or restaurants): not obligatory.
Gas-station attendants: no tip.
Hairdressers: 15%–20%.
Redcaps (airport and railroad station): at least 50¢ per piece, $2–$3 for a lot of baggage.
Restaurants, nightclubs: 15%–20% of the check.
Sleeping-car porters: $2–$3 per night to your attendant.
Valet parking attendants: $1.

Toilets Foreign visitors often complain that public toilets are hard to find in most U.S. cities. True, there are none on the streets, but the visitor can usually find one in a bar, restaurant, hotel, museum, department store, or service station—and it will probably be clean (although the last-mentioned sometimes leaves much to be desired). Note, however, a growing practice in some restaurants and bars of displaying a notice that "toilets are for the use of patrons only." You can ignore this sign, or better yet, avoid arguments by paying for a cup of coffee or soft drink, which will qualify you as a patron. The cleanliness of toilets at railroad stations and bus depots may be more open to question, and some public places are equipped with pay toilets, which require you to insert one or more coins into a slot on the door before it will open.

AMERICAN SYSTEM OF MEASUREMENTS
LENGTH

1 inch (in).	=	2.54 cm				
1 foot (ft)	=	12 in.	=	30.48cm	=	.305m
1 yard	=	3ft.	=	.915m		
1 mile (mi.)	=	5,280ft.	=	1.609km.		

To convert miles to kilometers, multiply the number of miles by 1.61 (for example, 50 mi. × 1.61 = 80.5km). Note that this conversion can be used to convert speeds from miles per hour (m.p.h.) to kilometers per hour (km/h).

To convert kilometers to miles, multiply the number of kilometers by .62 (for example, 25km × 15.5mi.). Note that this same conversion can be used to convert speeds from kilometers per hour to miles per hour.

CAPACITY

1 fluid ounce (fl.oz.)	=	.03 liter		
1 pint	=	16 fl. oz.	=	.47 liter
1 quart	=	2 pints	=	.94 liter
1 gallon (gal.)	=	4 quarts	=	3.79 liter
	=	.83 Imperial gal.		

To convert U.S. gallons to liters, multiply the number of gallons by 3.79 (example, 12 gal. × 3.79 = 45.58 liters).

To convert U.S. gallons to Imperial gallons, multiple the number of U.S. gallons by .83 (example, 12 U.S. gal. × .83 = 9.95 Imperial gal.).

To convert liters to U.S. gallons, multiply the number of liters by .26 (example, 50 liters × .26 = 13 U.S. gal.).

To convert Imperial gallons to U.S. gallons, multiply the number of Imperial gallons by 1.2 (example, 8 Imperial gal. × 1.2 = 9.6 U.S. gal.).

WEIGHT

1 ounce (oz.)	=	28.35 grams				
1 pound (lb.)	=	16 oz.	= 453.6 grams	=	.45 kilograms
1 ton	=	2,000 lb.	= 907 kilograms	=	.91 metric ton

To convert pounds to kilograms, multiply the number of pounds by .45 (example, 90 lb. × .45 = 40.5kg).

To convert kilograms to pounds, multiple the number of kilos by 2.2 (example, 75kg × 2.2 = 165 lb.).

AREA

1 acre	=	.41 hectare		
1 square mile (sq. mi.)	=	640 acres	=	2.59 hectares
	=	2.6km		

To convert acres to hectares, multiply the number of acres by .41 (example, 40 acres × 41 = 16.4ha).

To convert square miles to square kilometers, multiply the number of square miles by 2.6 (example, 80 sq. mi. × 2.6 = 208km^2).

To convert hectares to acres, multiple the number of hectares by 2.47 (example, 20ha × 2.47 = 49.4 acres).

To convert square kilometers to square miles, multiply the number of square kilometers by .39 (example, 150km^2 × .39 = 58.5 sq. mi.)

TEMPERATURE

°C	-18°	-10	0	10	20	30	40
°F	0°	10 20	32 40	50	60 70	80	90 100

To convert degrees Fahrenheit to degrees Celsius, subtract 32 from °F, multiply by 5, then divide by 9 (example, 85°F − 32 × 5/9 = 29.4°C).

To convert degrees Celsius to degrees Fahrenheit, multiple °C by 9, divide by 5, and add 32 (example, 20°C × 9/5 + 32 = 68°F).

INTRODUCING HONOLULU

Oahu means "the gathering place" in Hawaiian, and no other name could be so apt. Although it's merely the third largest of the islands in size (40 miles long, 26 miles wide), it is the most populous (850,000, and more arriving all the time). It also has the most skyscrapers, schools, hospitals, radio and television stations—and the most tourists.

Honolulu, the bustling capital city plunked in the middle of the Pacific, is the center of island life, the metropolis youngsters from the other islands dream of. It is also a tremendous military stronghold where approximately one-tenth of the island is owned by the military; defense is a major industry.

Just 10 minutes away from Honolulu is **Waikiki Beach,** a favorite resort of Hawaiian royalty long before the word "tourist" was invented. For the visitor, this is an ideal situation; it's as if Mexico City were just 10 minutes away from Acapulco, Paris a short bus ride from the Riviera. You can, with such geography, have the best of both worlds—as much beach or city, laziness or excitement, as you choose.

The island is dominated by two mountain ranges: the Waianae, along the west coast, and the Koolaus, which form the spectacular backdrop to the city of Honolulu. On the other side of the Koolaus is **Windward Oahu,** which is what islanders are referring to when they talk of going to the "country." Commuters tunnel through the mountains to pretty little suburbs that are developing here as the population booms. For the visitor, it's the closest thing you'll see—if you don't visit the neighbor islands—to rural Hawaii: tiny plantation villages, miles of red earth planted with pineapple and sugarcane, a breathtaking succession of emerald beaches, and gorgeous trails for riding and hiking.

1. FROM A BUDGET TRAVELER'S POINT OF VIEW

BUDGET BESTS & DISCOUNTS
[FOR EVERYONE]

- Try to travel to Hawaii during the "low season"—from April 1 through mid-December, when rates on air travel, hotel rooms, and rental cars can be significantly lower.
- Try to secure fly-drive packages from the interisland airlines.

WHAT'S SPECIAL ABOUT HONOLULU & OAHU

Natural Wonders

Diamond Head Crater, the sleeping volcano that has become the symbol of Honolulu.

Hanauma Bay, an idyllic beach cove created centuries ago when one side of Koko Head Crater washed into the sea. It is a marine reserve popular with snorkelers.

The Blow Hole, a natural geyser where water surges up through an underwater vent in the lava rock, sometimes as high as 60 feet.

Beaches

World-famous Waikiki Beach, great for swimming, surfing, people-watching.

Lanikai Beach in Kailua on Windward Oahu—gentle surf, no crowds—like Waikiki before the world discovered it.

Superb sandy swimming beaches all over the island of Oahu, especially Sunset Beach and Waimea Bay in the mild summer months when there are no waves.

Sports and Recreation

Great snorkeling, notably at Hanauma Bay.

Surfing, all over Oahu. Mighty winter waves at Sunset Beach and Waimea Bay on the North Shore.

Hiking the mountains and valleys, with many opportunities to go out with local groups.

Sailing, day and night. Recreational and dinner cruises out of Honolulu Harbor.

Golf and tennis at many public and private facilities.

Museums and Historic Houses

Bishop Museum, a prime resource center and a lively showcase for Pacific culture.

Hawaii Maritime Center, tracing Hawaiian maritime history from ancient times to the present.

Mission Houses Museum, for a look back at the days of the New England missionaries in Hawaii.

Major Historical Attractions

Pearl Harbor, where history was made on December 7, 1941.

National Memorial Cemetery of the Pacific at Punchbowl Crater, final resting place for thousands of American war dead.

Iolani Palace, the only royal palace on U.S. soil, where Hawaii's embattled monarchy made it's last stand.

Botanical Gardens

Foster Botanical Gardens, 15 splendid acres of rare trees, flowers, and plants.

Lyon Arboretum, a research and educational center prized as a beautiful nature spot.

Shopping

Ala Moana Center, one of the world's best malls, with products ranging from downhome to upscale.

International Market Place and Kuhio Mall, giant outdoor bazaars.

- Travel with someone else; savings on hotel rooms are great. If a third person is in the party, per-person rates go down even more.
- If youre making long driving tours, try teaming up with friends and splitting the costs.

FOR STUDENTS

- Investigate the hostels and inexpensive hotels mentioned in this book.
- Consider taking some courses and staying at the University of Hawaii; participate in their student activities whether or not you take courses.

FOR SENIORS

* Inquire about senior discounts—on airlines, in hotels, some restaurants, all sightseeing attractions.
* Contact the **Department of Parks and Recreation** (tel. 973-7262 or 973-7258) for news of many activities of interest to seniors.
* In Honolulu, ride TheBUS at a discount: For information on getting a bus pass, phone 848-4144.

WORTH THE EXTRA MONEY

* Meals at some of Hawaii's fabulous restaurants, like Alfred's European Restaurant or Sunset Grill (see Chapter 6, "Honolulu Dining").
* An evening at the Royal Hawaiian's Monarch Room, to see Hawaii's most beloved entertainers, the Brothers Cazimero.
* Sunset cocktails to the strains of Hawaiian music at the House Without a Key, an open-to-the sea lounge at the Halekulani Hotel—a Honolulu tradition.
* An evening at the Polynesian Palace of the Outrigger Reef Towers Hotel to see Hawaii's funniest funny man, Frank DeLima.
* A submarine dive on the *Atlantis*, to see the life of the coral reef, far below Waikiki's waters (see Chapter 7, "Honolulu Attractions").

2. ORIENTATION

ARRIVING

BY PLANE The **Honolulu International Airport,** about 5 miles out of town, is one of the world's largest and busiest airports. If you're traveling light, with one small bag that you can hold in your lap, you can hop right on **public bus** no. 19 (Hickam-Waikiki) or no. 20 (Pearlridge-Waikiki) that goes from the terminal to the beach area for 60¢. (The bus has no special section for luggage; your bag must not take up any extra space.) If you are traveling with luggage, you have two budget choices: **Airport Motorcoach** (tel. 946-4747), which makes pickups outside the airline baggage-claim areas every 20 to 25 minutes and operates 24 hours a day; or **Airport Express Transportation Services** (tel. 949-5249 or 941-4208), which operates from 6am to 10pm. Both charge the same fare: $6 adults, $3 children. A taxi into Waikiki should cost between $18 and $22.

If you've rented a car in advance, you can pick it up right at the airport.

BY SHIP Forget about it. Only luxury cruise ships now call at Honolulu Harbor.

TOURIST INFORMATION

The **Hawaii Visitors Bureau,** 2270 Kalakaua Ave., 7th floor (tel. 923-1811), in the heart of Waikiki, has a helpful staff. Stop in to pick up leaflets and brochures on all kinds of activities and on neighbor-island hotels. The bureau also has a booth at the Royal Hawaiian Shopping Center.

For daily news of what's going on, consult the *Guide to Oahu, This Week on Oahu, Spotlight Oahu, Paradise News,* or *Key,* **free publications** found in most hotel lobbies, on Kalakaua Avenue, and elsewhere. (These papers also carry many bargain discount coupons, which can add up to considerable savings on shopping, restaurants, car rentals, and the like.) The "Aloha" section of the *Sunday Star-Bulletin & Advertiser* lists events for the coming week. *Oahu Drive Guide,* available at the offices of rental-car companies, has plenty of information, plus excellent driving maps.

Kamehameha IV Rd. ↗

School St. 63

Alewa Dr.

Wyllie St.

Pali Hwy.

Nuuanu stream

78 Kaua St.

Fort Shafter Military Res.

H1 Lunalilo Frwy.

Houghtailing St.

2

Halona St.

Liliha St.

9

61

Booth Rd

Middle St.

92

Puuhale Rd.

Kalihi St.

Waiakamilo Rd.

N. King St.

Palama St.

Vineyard Blvd.

Lusitana St.

Auwaiolimu St.

Iolani Ave. Prospect St.

Sand Island Access Rd.

Nimitz Hwy.

Dillingham Blvd.

Iwilei Rd.

4

Kapalama Military Res.

3

Nuuanu Ave.
Bishop St.

Queen Emma St.

8

N. Beretania St.

10

1 ←✈

Kapalama Basin

U.S. Coast Guard Res.

Honolulu Harbor

5

Punchbowl St.

6 7

S. King St.

Mokauea Island

Sand Island

Sand Island State Rec. Area

Ala Moana Blvd.

South St.

Queen St.

Ward St.

11

12

92

Kakaako Waterfront State Rec. Area

Kewalo Basin

Ala Moana Park

M a m a l a   *B a y*

6783

HONOLULU ORIENTATION

CITY LAYOUT

GETTING YOUR DIRECTIONAL SIGNALS

In order to get your bearings, you should know that one seldom refers to directions in the standard north-south, east-west layout here. Since the islands sit in a kind of slanted direction on the map, those terms wouldn't make much sense.

This is how it's done in Hawaii. Everything toward the sea is **makai,** (MAH-kye); everything toward the mountains is **mauka** (MOW-kah). The other directions are **Diamond Head** (roughly eastward) and **Ewa** (roughly westward), named after two of the major landmarks of the city. Once you move out beyond Diamond Head, roughly eastward directions are referred to as **Koko Head** (Aina Haina is Koko Head of Kalani Valley, for example). Once you learn to use these simple terms, you'll be well on the way to becoming a kamaaina yourself.

NEIGHBORHOODS IN BRIEF

The Honolulu neighborhoods most tourists will be concerned with are:

Waikiki The Waikiki area runs from Ala Moana Boulevard in an Ewa direction, up to Kapahulu Avenue in a Diamond Head direction, and from the Ala Wai Canal on the mountain side to the ocean. Within Waikiki, Kalakaua Avenue is the main thoroughfare, bordering the ocean; parallel to it is Kuhio Avenue; and parallel to that is the Ala Wai Boulevard. Along these avenues and their side streets are the main hotels, restaurants, shops, and sights of the tourist area.

Kapahulu This is the area centered around Kapahulu Avenue, going one or 2 blocks on either side of the H1 Highway, otherwise known as the Expressway. Many stores, businesses, and restaurants are located here.

University This district runs from McCully to South King Street, until South King becomes Waialae Avenue, then mauka (toward the mountains) up into Manoa Valley. It includes the University of Hawaii.

McCully-Moiliili The area of McCully-Moiliili runs from Kapiolani Boulevard to South King Street. There are stores, businesses, and Asian restaurants.

Ala Moana The Ala Moana area extends mauka of Ala Moana Boulevard, between Waikiki and Restaurant Row. The Ala Moana Shopping Center is here.

Downtown Honolulu This includes everything from Restaurant Row to the Historical Chinatown District. The latter is bordered by Beretania Street on the mountain side, Nuuanu Avenue on the Diamond Head side, Nimitz Highway, harbor side, and River Street on the Ewa/airport side. Downtown contains the citys major business and financial district.

MAIN STREETS & HIGHWAYS

Your first introduction to the thoroughfares of Honolulu will probably be **Nimitz Highway/Ala Moana Boulevard,** a two-way divided highway that runs between the airport and Waikiki. **King Street** goes one way from downtown Honolulu to the University of Hawaii, passing Iolani Palace and the downtown historical sights. **Beretania Street** is one way going in the opposite direction; it starts at University Avenue and runs through Chinatown. The **H1 Freeway** runs from Pearl Harbor Airport to Kahala Mall, then continues as a divided express highway, Kalanianaole, which goes around the island.

STREET MAPS

Locals consider the best Oahu maps to be Bryan's *Sectional Maps of Oahu* and the *Oahu Reference Maps,* by James A. Bier, Cartographer. Both can be obtained in many bookstores, or from Hawaii Geographic Maps and Books, 49 S. Hotel St., Suite 218, (P.O. Box 1698), Honolulu, HI 96808 (tel. 808/532-3952). Maps in free tourist publications are acceptable for most ordinary touring.

3. GETTING AROUND

Many people think it's difficult to get around the islands and succumb to package deals that wrap up the vacation in advance: transportation, hotels, sightseeing from the limousine window, all for one flat—and unnecessarily high—fee. And even if they've already discovered the do-it-yourself trick of staying at budget hotels and eating at low-cost restaurants, panic strikes when it comes to sightseeing—and how else to "do" Honolulu unless someone takes you by the hand on a guided tour?

Tours are pleasant and useful, of course, if you have only a day or two and want to pack in as many sights as you can. And you may want to take one (or else rent a car) when you circle the island of Oahu. But for sightseeing in Honolulu, at your own pace, there are options that are much cheaper, and much more fun.

BY BUS/TROLLEY

TheBUS TheBUS is owned by the city and county of Honolulu and has routes all over the island. It operates daily from 5am to 12:30am on main routes. Adults pay 60¢ for a ride on TheBUS; children pay 25¢ (children under 6 free). Exact fare in coins is required. Free transfers, which can extend your ride considerably in one direction, must be requested when you board and pay your fare. Senior citizens can use the buses at a savings by showing a bus pass. A $15 pass is good for 4 years. (Call 848-4444 for information on the E & H Bus Pass program.)

Bus schedules are not, unfortunately, available on the buses themselves, but if you have any questions about how to get where, simply call **TheBUS information number** (tel. 848-5555) between 5:30am and 10pm. Keep in mind that the buses you will take from Waikiki to Ala Moana Shopping Center or to downtown Honolulu must be boarded on Kuhio Avenue.

If you're at Ala Moana Center, you can use the no-cost direct telephones to TheBUS information, located at the bus stops on the north and south sides of the center. You should also note that traffic on Kalakaua Avenue, Waikiki's main thoroughfare, goes Diamond Head most of the way. All buses running from Waikiki either uptown or downtown should be boarded on Kuhio Avenue.

THE WAIKIKI TROLLEY A way to make your sightseeing a bit more comfortable without breaking the bank: Hop aboard the Waikiki Trolley. All-day passes cost $15 for adults, $5 for children, and you can travel from 8am to 4:30pm between the Royal Hawaiian Shopping Center and Dole Cannery Square, making stops en route at Ala Moana Center, the Hilton Hawaiian Village, the Honolulu Academy of Arts, Ward Warehouse and Fishermans Wharf, Ward Centre, the state capitol and Iolani Palace, the Mission Houses Museum and the King Kamehameha Statue, Chinatown, the Hawaii Maritime Center, Restaurant Row, and the Hilo Hattie Factory. You can stay on for the entire 2-hour, narrated trip or hop on and off whenever you like and continue on another trolley. Recalling Honolulu's turn-of-century streetcars, these jaunty red motorized trolleys with an old-fashioned look (etched-glass windows, polished brass rails, hand-carved oak interiors) stop each hour at the locations listed above. As you study the trips outlined below, you'll be able to see when and where the trolley can take you to some destinations. Call 526-0112 or check local papers for exact routes and schedules. Tours operate daily between 8am and 4pm.

MONTHLY PASSES If youre staying in Honolulu and doing extensive bus riding for any length of time, it may pay to buy a monthly pass. They cost $15 for adults, $7.50 for youths up to high-school age (generally considered 19 or younger). Bus passes may be purchased anytime during the month. They are available at 811 Middle St. (tel. 848-4444). Fares are subject to change.

BY TAXI

It's easy to get a cab in Waikiki. Simply step to the edge of any major thoroughfare, lift your hand to signal, and within 5 minutes you'll undoubtedly be on your way. Although not cheap (the first flip of the meter is usually $1.50), taxis are useful for emergencies and for short trips, and can be practical if you are traveling in a group. If you want to call a cab in advance, your hotel desk can usually get one for you, or you can call any of the numerous companies listed in the telephone book. Here are a few: **Charley's Taxi** (tel. 531-1333), **Aloha State Cab** (tel. 847-3566), and **Sida of Hawaii** (tel. 836-0011).

BY BICYCLE

Honolulu, like big cities everywhere, has become very bicycle conscious. Bicycles used to be available for rental at a number of locations, but lately most hotels and car-rental agencies (like Hertz) have stopped renting them because of the high equipment-mortality rate. "We kept finding them in the ocean," said one supplier. But we did find *one* place where they can still be rented: **Blue Sky Rentals,** 1920 Ala Moana Blvd. (tel. 947-0101), at rates of $15 for 24 hours.

BY RENTAL CAR

If you're going to stay mostly in Waikiki and only venture forth to downtown Honolulu, the convenience of renting a car will not justify the expense. On top of that, street parking is very difficult to find, and most lots are very expensive. Most hotels charge parking fees. If, however, you want to spend time on the windward side of Oahu, or tour the entire island, then a car is a must.

If you decide to rent, you'll have your choice of just about any type of vehicle, foreign or domestic, from the numerous car-rental agencies in town. The most inexpensive cars are usually those with manual shifts. Prices are also higher for mid-size cars. And rates are always higher—by as much as $5 or $10—in the busy winter season than in summer. As for the car-rental agencies themselves, they are very much in competition for your business, and since rates are constantly changing and new attractive deals are offered all the time, a little comparison shopping at the time of your arrival will pay big dividends. However, we'll pass on the warning they gave to us: "Rates are subject to change at any time without notice." Most companies offer flat rates with unlimited free mileage.

See "Getting Around," in Chapter 2, for details on the car-rental agencies that operate throughout Hawaii and for some general tips on renting a car.

PARKING Parking for the night can be a problem in the Waikiki area. *Tip:* Ala Wai Boulevard, along the canal, is less crowded than other main thoroughfares. In the downtown area, there are both municipal and private parking lots. Most street meters charge 1¢ per minute; in some busy locations the meters allow no more than 12 to 24 minutes. Read each meter carefully.

DRIVING RULES A few words about driving in Honolulu. Many major thoroughfares are now one-way streets, which helps the flow of traffic, but often makes it seem that you are driving miles out of your way to reach a specific destination. Downtown Honolulu is an especially confusing place to drive in. You may want to keep in mind that in this area Beretania Street is Ewa, King Street is Diamond Head, Pensacola traffic now heads makai (to the sea), and Piikoi cars go in a mauka (to the mountains) direction. In Waikiki, Kalakaua traffic is Diamond Head most of the way, with a short stretch downtown running in both directions; Kuhio Avenue is two-way and the Ala Wai Boulevard is Ewa.

Those painted white arrows on the various lanes are not to be ignored. They indicate in which directions you are permitted to drive from each lane: right only, left only, left and straight ahead, or right and straight ahead. It's legal to make right turns when the light is red at most—but not all—intersections, so read the signs first. And if you come across a sign reading WE APPRECIATE YOUR KOKUA, it's not an invitation to pay a toll. *Kokua* means cooperation in Hawaiian.

FAST HONOLULU

AAA Hawaii The local office of the American Automobile Association is at 590 Queen St. (tel. 528-2600, or 537-5544 for road service).

Animal Hospital Your pet can get 24-hour emergency care at the Care Animal Hospital, 1135 Kapahulu Ave. (tel. 737-7910), and at the Kaneohe Veterinary Clinic, 45-480 Kaneohe Bay Dr. (tel. 235-3634).

Area Code The entire state of Hawaii has one telephone area code: 808.

Babysitters Check first at your hotel desk. You can also try Aloha Babysitting Service (tel. 732-2029), Available Sitters (tel. 951-6118), and Sitters Unlimited (tel. 262-5728).

Bookstores Waldenbooks has several bookstores on Oahu, including branches at the Royal Hawaiian Shopping Center, Waikiki Shopping Plaza, Waikiki Trade Center, and Ward Warehouse. Honolulu Bookshops has four locations, including one at the Ala Moana Center and another downtown at 1001 Bishop St.

Business Hours See "Fast Facts: Hawaii," in Chapter 2.

Camping Permits For information about camping permit's for city/county parks, call 523-4525; for state parks, call 548-7455.

Car Rentals Major car-rental companies, which rent automobiles on all four major islands, include Alamo Rent A Car, 2055 N. Nimitz Hwy. (tel. 808/833-4585) or 924-4444, or toll free 800/327-9633); Avis Rent A Car System, at Honolulu International Airport (tel. 808/834-5536, or toll free 800/831-8000); Budget Rent A Car, with many locations in Honolulu (tel. 808/922-3600, or toll free 800/527-0700); Dollar Rent A Car of Hawaii, 1600 Kapiolani Blvd. (tel. 808/944-1544, or toll free 800/367-7006); Hertz Rent A Car (tel. toll free 800/654-3131); and Tropical Rent-A-Car Systems, 765 Amana St. (tel. 808/957-0800, or toll free 800/678-6000). See "Getting Around," in this chapter and in Chapter 2, for details.

Climate See "When to Go," in Chapter 2.

Crime See "Safety" in "Fast Facts: Hawaii," in Chapter 2.

Dentists Dental Care Centers of Hawaii offers 24-hour emergency service. It has many locations around the island; addresses can be found in the telephone book. The after-hours number is 488-5200. Hawaii Family Dental Center (tel. 944-0011) is conveniently located at Sears at the Ala Moana Shopping Center (1450 Ala Moana Blvd.), and has a number of dentists on hand who can provide speedy treatment at reasonable cost.

Doctors We hope it won't happen, but should you need medical assistance while youre in Honolulu, it is readily at hand. Prominent Queens Medical Center has a Waikiki affiliate: **Queens Health Care Center**, 1860 Ala Moana Blvd. (tel. 943-1111). The clinic is open daily from 8am to 10pm, and no appointment is needed. If you are staying in Waikiki, your taxi fare to the Waikiki clinic and back to your hotel will be deducted from your bill; see any hotel desk for a taxi slip.

Doctors on Call [DOC] has several excellent clinics at Waikiki hotels; phone their central number—971-8000—and you will be directed to the one closest to you. Should you require a house call—or hotel call—call DOC at 926-4777 and a physician will arrive at your hotel room promptly. The charge is a hefty $96.

Of course, in a medical emergency, you can always call 911 and ask for an ambulance, or go to the emergency department of the Queens Medical Center, 1301 Punchbowl St. (tel. 547-4311).

Drugstores In Waikiki, try the Kuhio Pharmacy in the Outrigger West Hotel, 2330 Kuhio Ave. (tel. 923-4466); at Ala Moana Shopping Center, Long's Drug Store, 1450 Ala Moana Blvd. (tel. 941-4433) The Pillbox Pharmacy, 1133 11th Ave. (tel. 737-1777), is open Monday through Saturday from 9am to 11pm and on

Sunday from 7 to 11pm, and provides 24-hour emergency service (for prescriptions only).

Emergencies Dial **911** for fire, ambulance, or police; if you cannot reach 911, dial 0 (zero, not the letter "O") and the operator will assist you. For **poisoning** emergencies, call the Poison Center (tel. 941-4411).

Eyeglasses Elite Eyes, 2255 Kuhio Ave. (tel. 922-4884), in the Waikiki Trade Center, and Iris Optical, in the Moana Hotel, 2371 Kalakaua Ave. (tel. 923-5217), can help with emergency repairs or provide new glasses. Lenscrafters (tel. 947-3805), on the mall level mauka at Ala Moana Center, can prepare eyeglasses in about an hour.

Hairdressers and Barbers Both J.C. Penney and Liberty House at Ala Moana Center have good hairdressing salons. Theres an inexpensive barber at Hemenway Hall at the University of Hawaii.

Holidays See "When to Go," in Chapter 2.

Hospitals For emergency medical service, Queens Medical Center, 1301 Punchbowl (tel. 547-4311), has 24-hour emergency-room service and offers outstanding trauma care. On the windward side, it's Castle Medical Center, 640 Ulukahiki in Kailua (tel. 263-5500).

Information See "Tourist Information," in this chapter.

Laundry and Dry Cleaning Should your hotel not provide washers and dryers (most do), try Waikiki Laundromats, which also provide irons, ironing boards, and hairdryers, with four central locations: 2335 Kalakaua Ave., across from the International Market Place; in the Outrigger West Hotel, 2330 Kuhio Ave.; in the Outrigger East Hotel, 150 Kaiulani Ave.; and in the Edgewater Hotel, 2168 Kalia Rd. These are open daily from 7am to 10pm. The location at the Coral Seas Hotel, 250 Lewers St. (tel. 923-2057), is open around the clock. Quick dry-cleaning service is available from Al Phillips the Cleaner in the Waikiki Market Place, 2310 Kuhio Ave. (tel. 923-1971), open Monday through Saturday from 7am to 6pm and on Sunday from 10am to 4pm.

Libraries Hawaii has an excellent statewide public library system. Books borrowed at one library may be returned to any other public library. Obtaining a library card is quick and easy; $25 for nonresidents and visitors, free for residents. Close to Waikiki, the Hawaii State Library at 478 S. King St. has an excellent Hawaii and Pacific collection, as well as a large newspaper collection with newspapers from most major cities around the world. The Waikiki-Kapahulu Public Library at 400 Kapahulu Ave. (tel. 732-2777) also has an impressive newspaper collection, as well as a charming courtyard for the leisure reader.

General information, 586-3500; telephone reference, 586-3621.

Newspapers and Magazines There are two daily newspapers, both published by the Hawaii Newspaper Agency. The *Honolulu Advertiser* is the morning paper; the *Honolulu Star-Bulletin* is the evening paper with the bigger circulation. The Sunday paper is produced exclusively by the *Advertiser*.

Aloha magazine, published bi-monthly, and *Honolulu* magazine, published monthly, make for interesting reading.

Photographic Needs Best sources at the most reasonable prices are the ABC discount stores and Long's Drug Store at Ala Moana Shopping Center.

Police Dial 911; if that doesn't work, dial 0 for the operator.

Post Office In Waikiki, it's at 330 Saratoga Rd., next to Fort DeRussy (tel. 941-1062), open Monday, Tuesday, Thursday, Friday from 8am to 6pm and on Saturday from 9am to 1pm.

Radio and TV For all-Hawaiian music, tune in KCNN (1420 AM); for island music, contemporary Hawaiian to reggae, it's KCCN (1003 FM). KHPR (88.1 FM) is Hawaii Public Radio for classical music and news; KIPO (1380 AM and 89.3 FM) is Hawaii Public Radio for news and jazz, classical, and folk music. Station KTUH (90.3 FM) presents jazz, classical, rock, and Hawaiian music. Try KHVH (990 AM) for news, sports, and talk.

Most hotels have cable TV, as cable is necessary virtually everywhere on Oahu;

95% of the island is served by Oceanic Cablevision, whose major channels are: Channel 3, KHON (NBC); Channel 6, KITV (ABC); Channel 7, KGMB (CBS); Channel 10, PBS; Channel 14, CNN; Channel 24, HBO; Channel 25, Cinemax; Channel 28, A&E; Channel 29, TNT; Channel 31, MTV; Channel 32, TMC; Channel 33, Showtime; Channel 34, Disney. Channel 12 is the Oceanic Cable listing channel; it runs continual lists of what is running on the 32 free channels.

Religious Services Among Honolulu's many churches and temples, the following are easily accessible by public transportation: **Baptist:** Oliver Baptist Church, 1775 S. Beretania St. (tel. 946-6505), holds services every Sunday at 10:45am and 7pm. **Buddhist:** Honpa Hongwanji Buddist Temple, 1727 Pali Hwy. (tel. 536-7044), has an English service Sunday morning. **Roman Catholic:** The historic Cathedral of Our Lady of Peace, 1184 Bishop St. (tel. 536-7036), with daily masses. The church where Father Damien was ordained celebrated it's 150th anniversary in 1993. **Episcopalian:** St. Andrew's Cathedral, Queen Emma Sq. (tel. 524-2822), has a Sunday Hawaiian Eucharist at 8am; other services are at 7 and 10am. **Presbyterian:** First Presbyterian Church of Honolulu, 1822 Keeaumoku at Nehoa (tel. 537-3321), has Sunday services at 8 and 10am. **Methodist:** First United Methodist Church, 1020 S. Beretania St. (tel. 522-9555), begins morning worship at 10:30am. **United Church of Christ Congregational:** Kawaiaiahao Church, Punchbowl at King (tel. 522-1333), known as "The Westminster Abbey of Hawaii," offers a Hawaiian-English service at 10:30am on Sunday. **Jewish:** Temple Emanu-El, 2550 Pali Hwy. (tel. 595-7521), a Reform congregation, holds regular services on Friday night, Saturday morning, and on all Jewish holidays. Orthodox Jewish services are held Friday night and Saturday morning at 1956 Ala Moana Blvd., in the Park Plaza Waikiki Hotel, under the auspices of Chabad of Hawaii; call Rabbi Itchel Krasnjansky (tel. 635-8161) for details.

Rentals If you need to rent something while you're in Honolulu—maybe a TV set, a radio, a stroller, even wheelchairs or crutches, we have a terrific place to recommend: Dyan's Rental (tel. 531-5207). Their rates are low, and they deliver to your hotel cheerfully and promptly. Rent-A-Center (tel. 947-9933) is good for VCRs, video cameras, fax machines, typewriters, word processors, and other electronic paraphernalia.

Sears Hawaii Activity Center, Ala Moana Shopping Center, 1450 Ala Moana Blvd. (tel. 944-3222), offers a variety of neighbor-island overnighters at good prices.

Shoe Repair There are very few shoe-repair shops in town. Two good ones are Biltrite, 1145 S. King St., near Pensacola (tel. 533-2766), and Joe Pacific, 1680 Kapiolani Blvd., Shop 7F (tel. 946-2998).

Sundries ABC Discount Stores offer a little bit of everything one might need under one roof, from suntan lotion to sandwiches, from groceries to gifts, from liquor to laundry detergent, from postcards to photo processing and film, and much more, all at bargain prices. There are 30 ABCs in town, and most are open from 7am to midnight daily. Walk a block or two from where you are and you'll probably find one.

The 7-Eleven Food Stores now have almost 50 shops on Oahu; two convenient locations are 1901 Kalakaua Ave. and 707 Kapahulu Ave. They carry everything from grocery and toiletry items to pantyhose, hot food, soft drinks, etc. Open 24 hours daily.

Taxis See "Getting Around," in this chapter.

Telegrams, Telex, and Fax Telex services are available 24 hours a day from Business Center Services (tel. 955-9555) and Western Union (tel. toll free 800/227-5099). Fax services are available at many copy centers and at all Phone Mart locations. The ones closest to Waikiki are at Ward Warehouse (tel. 521-3373; fax 538-0361) and downtown Honolulu (tel. 521-2722); fax 523-6418).

Telephone Calls Five dollars doesn't buy a great deal in Hawaii these days, but it can buy you an 8-minute phone call back to the mainland, or a series of phone calls for up to 8 minutes. Here's how it works: You go to one of Phone

Line Hawaii's Waikiki telecom centers at either the International Market Place, 2330 Kalakaua Ave., or the Discovery Bay Center, 1778 Ala Moana Blvd., where the cards are on sale, every day from 8:30am to 11pm. Then you use your card from any telephone, either in a phone booth or your hotel room, and you eliminate the charges that hotels levy on operator-assisted calls. Cards for calling Canada cost $15 and cards for other countries are also available at $10 and $20.

Transit Information   For information on TheBUS, call 848-5555.

Travel Services   Roberts Hawaii, 680 Iwilei Rd. (tel. 523-7750), is known for excellent overnight tours to the major islands.

Useful Telephone Numbers   For time, call 983-3211. For a surf report, call 836-1952.

Visitors Bureau   The **Hawaii Visitors Bureau** (tel. 923-1811) is at 2270 Kalakaua Ave., 7th floor.

Weather   In the Honolulu area, call 833-2849; for the rest of Oahu, call 836-0121; for the Hawaiian waters, call 836-3921.

READERS RECOMMEND

"During a recent trip to Honolulu I located two establishments that sold newspapers from the United Kingdom (a rare item in the middle of the Pacific). The Financial Times *is available at the King Fort Magazine Store, 1122 Fort Street Mall. The store, one of my favorite magazine places, is just up the mall from Tay Do's Restaurant. And the* London Sunday Times *can be purchased from the Honolulu Book Shop at Ala Moana Center on the following Tuesday if it catches the air transport."*—M. G. Roach, Angaston, South Australia, Australia.

---

4. NETWORKS & RESOURCES

FOR STUDENTS   The **University of Hawaii at Manoa** sponsors a number of low-cost activities for the benefit of its students; nonstudents may also join in the fun and savings simply by paying an activity fee that covers a 6-week summer session. Inquire at the Campus Center, Room 212, on the Manoa Campus of the University of Hawaii.

FOR GAY MEN & LESBIANS   The gay-and-lesbian information line can be reached at 536-6000.

FOR SENIORS   Contact the Department of Parks and Recreation at 973-7262 or 973-7258 for news of senior citizen activities.

FOR THE DISABLED   Handicabs of the Pacific, P.O. Box 22428, Honolulu, HI 96823 (tel. 524-3866), provides special transportation for the disabled: wheelchair taxi service and a variety of tours, including luaus, cruises, and sightseeing journeys.

CHAPTER 5

HONOLULU ACCOMMODATIONS

1. **DOUBLES FOR ABOUT $40 TO $70**
2. **DOUBLES FOR ABOUT $70 TO $100**
3. **HOSTELS, Y'S & A MILITARY HOTEL**
4. **AT THE AIRPORT**
5. **BED & BREAKFASTS**

Most planes and ships to the Hawaiian Is lands land first on the island of Oahu, near the capital city of Honolulu. For those on a budget, Oahu is a good choice; it's the cheapest of all the Hawaiian Islands—and one of the most fascinating to boot.

However, inflation—as it is elsewhere—has been rampant in Hawaii. Many of the cozy little guesthouses that used to enable budget tourists to live comfortably very cheaply some years ago have been torn down and new, more expensive structures have been built. Because of the tremendous number of accommodations in Waikiki, though, it's still possible to find plenty of good rooms that are reasonably priced.

Prices Remember that prices fluctuate, so they may vary slightly from the figures quoted below. Even so, these establishments will be your best hotel buys on the island. Almost all hotels up their rates—by as much as $10 to $20 per unit—during the busy winter months. In slow seasons, however, rates are often discounted, and you can do especially well on weekly rentals. The hotel may eliminate cleaning service (which is costly), but you may be able to book a decent apartment for a low price.

Unless otherwise stated by us, all rooms listed below have private bath.

Note that Hawaii's hotel tax is a hefty 9.17%. The tax is not included in rates given in this book.

Reservations If you plan to arrive in Hawaii during the summer season—June through Labor Day—advance reservations are a good idea. They are essential during the peak winter season—roughly from December 20 to April 15. During the winter, reservations up to a year in advance at some of the most desirable places are not unheard of. But last-minute reservations are always possible.

How the Listings Are Organized The hotels are listed first by price and then by geographic location. The Waikiki hotels are split into the following areas: Diamond Head Waikiki, that part of town closest to Kuhio Beach and Kapiolani Park; Central Waikiki, the area centering, roughly, around the International Market Place; and Ewa Waikiki, the section near the Hilton Hawaiian Village Hotel and Ilikai Hotel and the closest area to downtown Honolulu; Near the Ala Wai, that area closest to the Ali Wai Boulevard; and Near Ala Moana, the area close to the Ala Moana Canal. Remember that all these areas are close to each other and all are comparable in terms of comfort and convenience. And they're all near the beach. The other geographic areas we've used are Downtown Honolulu and Windward Oahu.

HOTELS IN WAIKIKI Most tourists stay in Waikiki, mecca of the malihinis. This is a relatively small area of Honolulu, but within it are concentrated most of the town's best beaches, and therefore most of the hotels and entertainment facilities. Downtown Honolulu is only a short bus ride away.

Whether you choose to spend $70 or $100 a night, you'll be living sensibly and pleasantly—and far more inexpensively than most tourists, who are led to believe that a hotel in Waikiki under $100 a day doesn't exist. It certainly does exist, particularly at the Hawaiian wonder of wonders: the **apartment-hotel with kitchenette.** Many of them are individually owned condominium units, and they're almost always cheaper than the rooms in large seaside hotels.

They are a good choice for a number of reasons: They have excellent locations near the beach and mountains; they are fully available to transients; they permit you to reduce expenses by cooking at least one meal in (dishes and utensils are always provided); and, most important, they offer what many consider the most relaxing and enjoyable type of accommodation in Hawaii. We offer names, addresses, and descriptions of several dozen of these establishments below.

As a point of orientation, remember that most fancy hotels are located right on the beach and on Kalakaua Avenue, the main drag. Between Kalakaua and Ala Wai Boulevard (which marks most of the makai and mauka boundaries of Waikiki) are dozens of tree-lined pretty streets containing the bulk of the smaller and less expensive hotels. Waikiki itself is small enough that you can easily walk from any of these hotels to the beach; they are also near each other, so you should have no trouble in getting from one to another if you have to do some hotel hunting.

You can save money on hotels through **Hotel Exchange,** 1946 Ala Moana Blvd., Honolulu, HI 96815 (tel. 808/942-8544; fax 808/955-2627), an organization that makes deals with hotels at substantial discounts and passes on some of the savings to guests. They will take advance reservations with an approved credit card, or you can simply walk in if you're already in town and not happy where you're staying. Savings could be as little as $5 or as much as $100 a day at many leading hotels. Hotel Exchange works with some 180 hotels on Oahu and the neighbor islands.

Note: A number of hotels listed in this chapter bear the name "Outrigger." While all are now under the Outrigger Hotels Hawaii umbrella, they are not standardized chain hotels; each offers the traveler something a little different.

Also note: Since most tourists spend far less than a month in Waikiki, we have not covered apartment buildings that take only monthly or seasonal rentals; if you plan to stay for at least a month, it may be worth your while to investigate them, too. And, of course, many of the apartment-hotels listed here will accept guests for several months or more.

A CONDO- & HOUSE-RENTAL SPECIALIST If you're thinking of staying in a condo or a house on any of the Hawaiian islands, you should know about **HALE** (Hawaiian Apartment Leasing Enterprises), 479 Ocean Ave., Suite B, Laguna Beach, CA 92651 (tel. 714/497-4253, or toll free 800/854-8843). Hale means "home" in Hawaiian, and this outfit aims to provide visitors with a "home away from home" either in a privately managed condominium or a private house.

Daily rates in condominiums can be up to 50% less than the regular rate, and weekly and monthly rates are even lower. Most condos are custom decorated, and high quality. And they're often available when a property seems sold out, since this is a separate inventory within the property. HALE's condos offer a wide range of price, size, and location. For example, a studio at the Island Colony on Oahu starts at $60 a night for two in the low season, with Foster Towers studios at $75 a night for two in the high season. On Maui, rates range from $350 a week for two in Kihei at Kihei Bay Surf in low season and $455 a week for two in high season. Just north of Kaanapali, an oceanfront studio for two at Papakea is $65 a night in low season and $95 a night in high season. Condos are also available on Kauai, the Big Island, and Molokai.

As for private houses, there are some 200 of them available on all the islands; cleaning staff, cooks, chauffeurs, day care, and additional custom services can be arranged. Possibilities include a two-bedroom/two-bath, ocean-front house on the Kona Coast of the Big Island at $1,200 a week for six, and a two-bedroom/two-bath house in Princeville on Kauai for $800 a week in low season.

WAIKIKI ACCOMMODATIONS

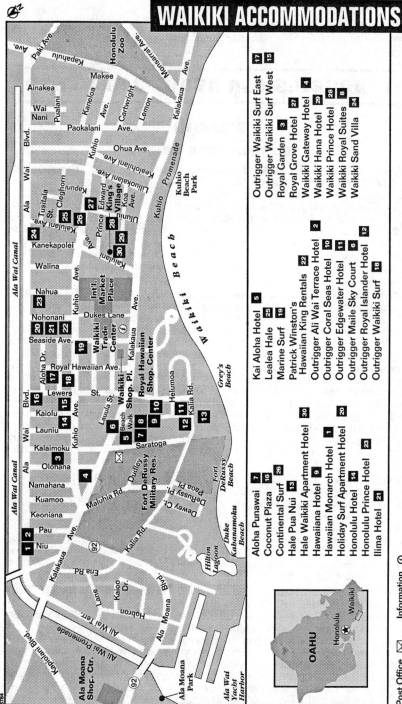

Outrigger Waikiki Surf East **17**
Outrigger Waikiki Surf West **15**
Royal Garden **3**
Royal Grove Hotel **27**
Waikiki Gateway Hotel **4**
Waikiki Hana Hotel **29**
Waikiki Prince Hotel **28**
Waikiki Royal Suites **8**
Waikiki Sand Villa **24**

Kai Aloha Hotel **5**
Lealea Hale **25**
Marine Surf **19**
Patrick Winston's
  Hawaiian King Rentals **22**
Outrigger Ali Wai Terrace Hotel **2**
Outrigger Coral Seas Hotel **10**
Outrigger Edgewater Hotel **11**
Outrigger Maile Sky Court **6**
Outrigger Royal Islander Hotel **12**
Outrigger Waikiki Surf **18**

Aloha Punawai **7**
Coconut Plaza **16**
Continental Surf **26**
Hale Pua Nui **13**
Hale Waikiki Apartment Hotel **30**
Hawaiiana Hotel **9**
Hawaiian Monarch Hotel **1**
Holiday Surf Apartment Hotel **20**
Honolulu Hotel **14**
Honolulu Prince Hotel **23**
Ilima Hotel **21**

Post Office ⌧   Information ⓘ

For information write HALE, requesting their brochure, which describes the properties and also shows proximity to golf, tennis, restaurants, and shopping.

1. DOUBLES FOR ABOUT $40 TO $70

WAIKIKI

DIAMOND HEAD WAIKIKI

HALE WAIKIKI APARTMENT HOTEL, 2410 Koa Ave., Honolulu, HI 96815. Tel. 808/923-9012. 15 apts. TV
$ **Rates:** Summer, $38.50–$45 apt. Winter, $50–$65 apt. No credit cards.

⭐ This is an old-but-livable building. Outside, an iron gate is kept locked most of the time. Inside, a long walkway lined with greenery fronts the low-rise building. Each unit accommodates two people comfortably, with a kitchenette and a bath with shower. There is no phone, but you can install your own (the room is wired for a phone). There is cleaning service twice a week on request and laundry facilities on the premises. You might have to scurry to find parking, but the central location, just 1 block from the beach and big hotels, makes up for it.

HONOLULU PRINCE, 415 Nahua St., Honolulu HI 96815. Tel. 808/922-1616, or toll free 800/922-7866 on the mainland U.S., 800/445-6633 in Canada. Fax 808/922-8785. Telex 634479 ASHIUW. 103 rms, 22 apts. A/C TV TEL
$ **Rates:** Apr–Dec 22, $63–$73 double; $99 one-bedroom apt; $125 two-bedroom apt. Dec 23–Mar, $77–$87 double; $120 one-bedroom apt; $140 two-bedroom apt for four. CB, DC, DISC, JCB, MC, V. **Parking:** $9 per day.
This is one of Waikiki's older apartment hotels that has seen many years of comfortable, casual living. Our favorite units here are the spacious, nicely furnished one-bedroom apartments which have full kitchens and separate bedrooms and can accommodate four. Four to six people can be accommodated in the two-bedroom kitchen apartments, which have two double beds, a sofa bed, and plenty of room for puttering around. The studios are furnished with either two doubles or a king-size bed plus a sofa bed. Most units have lanais. Cleaning service is provided every day. The hotel is managed by Aston Hotels & Resorts, 2255 Kuhio Ave., Honolulu, HI 96815.

LEALEA HALE APARTMENT HOTEL, 2423 Cleghorn St., Honolulu, HI 96815. Tel. 808/922-1726. 20 rms. A/C TV
$ **Rates:** Apr–Dec 20, $45–$65 twin or double. Dec 21–Mar, $85–$95 twin or double. Discounted weekly rates available. DISC, JCB, MC, V. **Parking:** $7 per day.
On a quite, narrow, one-way road in the center of Waikiki, this three-story hotel is in well-preserved condition and boasts bedrooms with double or twin beds, full kitchen, lanai, and bath with shower. Weekly rates offer good bargains. There is no pool, and few amenities. Parking is limited. One of the better budget bets in Waikiki during the summer months.

ROYAL GROVE HOTEL, 151 Uluniu Ave., Honolulu, HI 96815. Tel. 808/923-7691. 87 rms. A/C TV TEL
$ **Rates:** $36–$52 single or double; $70–$75 one-bedroom suite; $75–$85 condo. Each additional person $10. AE, DC, MC, V. **Parking:** $4–$6.50 per day.

⭐ An old standby in this part of town, this is one of the prettiest of Waikiki's small hotels. The six-story pink concrete building is about 3 minutes from Kuhio Beach, but if you're really lazy you can dunk in the tiny pool right on the grounds. Some studios have kitchenettes while efficiencies have private lanais. The accommodations become fancier as prices go up, and all are nicely furnished and comfortable and have tub/shower facilities; the kitchens are all electric. Discounted weekly rates available on request. Amenities and dining facilities include round-the-clock desk service; twice-weekly or weekly cleaning service; Ruffage Natural Foods and Sushi Bar for health-food supplies, sandwiches, and sushi; and Na's B-B-Que, with Korean plate-lunch specials. Both restaurants are open daily.

Over the years, readers have continued to write to comment on the friendliness of the owners, the Fong family, who frequently have potluck dinners and parties so that everyone can get acquainted. Lots of aloha for a small price at this one.

The Fongs also rent a number of units at the lovely **Pacific Monarch Hotel and Condominium,** just across the street. These are comfortable, spacious quarters wonderfully set up for family living. Inquire about these when you make your reservations.

WAIKIKI HANA, 2424 Koa Ave., Honolulu, HI 96815. Tel. 808/926-8841, or toll free 800/367-5004 in the continental U.S. and Canada. Fax toll free 800/477-2329. 73 rms. A/C TV TEL

$ Rates: Apr–Dec 17, $65–$97 double; $160 one-bedroom suite. Dec 18–Mar, $75–$110 double; $170 one-bedroom suite. AE, DC, MC, V. **Parking:** $7 per day.

Tucked away behind the posh Hyatt Regency Hotel and just a short block from Kuhio Beach is the Waikiki Hana. A new management took over several years ago and totally renovated and refurbished an older hotel. The sparkling lobby is filled with wicker chairs, while the smartly decorated rooms have light woods, rose walls, and blue quilted bedspreads; each is entered from the outside. Only the top-of-the-line rooms have a kitchenette, which consists of a combination sink, refrigerator, and electric hotplate. All rates include the use of a car. The reasonably priced Super Chef Restaurant is located in the lobby. Considering that this is a full-service hotel with an excellent location, this is one of the better values on the beach. **Reservations:** Hawaiian Pacific Resorts, 1150 S. King St., Honolulu, HI 96814.

WAIKIKI PRINCE HOTEL, 2431 Prince Edward St., Honolulu, HI 96815. Tel. 808/922-1544. 30 rms. A/C TV

$ Rates: Apr–Dec 19, $40–$50 per day. Dec 20–Mar, $43–$53 per day. Weekly rates on request. MC, V. **Parking:** $3 per day.

Some of the most reasonable prices in this close-to-the-beach area are offered by this modest little hotel, which is mostly for undemanding types. But there is cable TV in all the rooms, and the 20 rooms with kitchenettes have new drapes, bedspreads, and pots and pans. The location needs no improvement: It's right behind the Hyatt Regency Hotel, just 2 short blocks from Kuhio Beach. The Waikiki Prince is very popular with foreigners (they make up about 75% of the clientele). And many students stay here when school is out. There are no phones, but a buzzer system alerts you to your messages. Rooms are cleaned every 3 or 4 days, and towels are changed every day.

CENTRAL WAIKIKI

OUTRIGGER CORAL SEAS HOTEL, 250 Lewers St., Honolulu, HI 96815. Tel. 808/923-3881, or toll free 800/462-6262 in the U.S. and Canada, 0014/800/124-171 from Australia. Fax toll free 800/622-4852. Telex MCI 650-502-8960. 109 rms, 7 suites. A/C TV TEL

$ Rates: Apr–June and Sept–Dec 18, $75 double; $85 kitchenette; $120 one-bedroom suite. Dec 19–Mar and July–Aug, $75 double; $85 kitchenette studio; $120 one-bedroom suite. Each additional person $15. Children under 18 stay free in parent's room. AE, CB, DC, DISC, JCB, MC, V. **Parking:** $7 per day.

Conveniently located a block from the beach and a block from the main drag in Waikiki, the Outrigger Coral Seas is one of the original hotels in the empire of Outrigger Hotels Hawaii. The rooms and lobby were recently renovated and are more comfortable than ever. Spacious rooms have either two queen-size or three twin beds, in-room safes, showers, and colorful decor; all have private lanais. Most rooms have small kitchenettes (with microwave oven, utensils, and refrigerator). No-smoking rooms are available, and the suites for four are a real family find. The beach is down the street, and right in the hotel are three restaurants: Pieces of Eight, House of Hong, and Perry's Smorgy, which offers good buffet bargains.

Note: If here are no rooms here, the Outrigger management can probably place you in an equivalent room elsewhere in one of the 21 Waikiki hotels. At last count, they were handling more than 7,500 rooms! Below you will find listings for many of their budget and medium-priced properties.

OUTRIGGER EDGEWATER HOTEL, 2168 Kalia Rd., Honolulu, HI 96815. Tel. 808/922-6424, or toll free 800/462-6262 in the U.S. and Canada, 0014/800/124-171 from Australia. Fax toll free 800/622-4852. Telex MCI 650-502-8960. 176 rms, 8 suites. A/C TV TEL

$ Rates: Apr–Jun and Sept–Dec 18, $65–$70 double; $80 efficiency with kitchenette; $145–$175 suite. Dec 19–Mar and July–Aug, $75–$80 double; $80–$90 efficiency with kitchenette; $145–$175 suite. Each additional person $15. AE, CB, DC, DISC, JCB, MC, V. **Parking:** $7 per day.

Situated right on the corner of Lewers, this hotel has long enjoyed one of the best locations in Waikiki. Halfway between the ocean and Kalakaua Avenue, the Outrigger Edgewater is a 2-minute walk to either the peace of sun and surf or the bustle of restaurants, shops, and nightspots. Rooms are pleasantly furnished, the color TV includes in-room movies, and the bathrooms have stall showers. Your lanai will be furnished, but nothing will separate you from your neighbor's porch. This is a homey place, with lots of space to stroll around the building, plenty of lobby area and public rooms. The Trattoria Restaurant, right on the grounds, is a Waikiki favorite for northern Italian food. Chuck's Original Steakhouse is another popular old-timer, and the Pâtisserie is a favorite French bakery.

OUTRIGGER SURF HOTEL, 2280 Kuhio Ave., Honolulu, HI 96815. Tel. 808/922-5777, or toll free 800/462-6262 in the U.S. and Canada, 0014/800/124-171 from Australia. Fax toll free 800/622-4852. Telex MCI 650-502-8960. 251 rms. A/C TV TEL

$ Rates: Apr–June and Sept–Dec 18, $65–$75 kitchenette studio for up to three people; $120 studio suite for four. Dec–Mar and July–Aug, $85–$95 kitchenette studio for up to three; $120 studio suite for four. AE, CB, DC, DISC, JCB, MC, V. **Parking:** $7 per day.

For those watching their dollars, this hotel on the corner of Nohonani Street and a short walk from the beach is one of the most suitable. It has the greatest number of standard units, with kitchenettes throughout. No-smoking rooms are available.

The tall, modern building has 16 floors of comfortable studios, each with a lanai, carpeting, in-room safe, and beds in a studio arrangement providing a living-room look. There's a stall shower in the bathroom, two closets for storage, a two-burner range, and small refrigerator. The lobby is small but comfortable, and there's a pool on the lobby level. The Waikiki Pasta Company is right at hand.

OUTRIGGER WAIKIKI SURF EAST HOTEL, 422 Royal Hawaiian Ave., Honolulu, HI 96815. Tel. 808/923-7671, or toll free 800/462-6262 in the U.S. and Canada, 0014/800/124-171 from Australia. Fax toll free 800/622-4852. Telex MCI 650-502-8960. 102 rms. A/C TV TEL

$ Rates: $75–$80 double/kitchenette; $110 one-bedroom suite/kitchenette. Each additional person $15. AE, DB, DISC, JCB, MC, V. **Parking:** $7 per day.

This is one of the lower priced of the Outrigger hotels, but there's no obvious reason why. It's quiet, rooms are tastefully and newly appointed, and there are many amenities. Perhaps it's the size; there's no wasted space here—when you register at the desk, be careful not to fall into the pool! All rooms have a refrigerator, cooking top or microwave, toaster and dining ware, stall shower in the bathroom, and a sliding glass door leading to a lanai large enough for dining or sunbathing. The corner rooms have two lanais. It's a 5-minute walk to the beach, the International Market Place, and the heart of the Waikiki action.

OUTRIGGER WAIKIKI SURF HOTEL, 2200 Kuhio Ave., Honolulu, HI 96815. Tel. 808/923-7671, or toll free 800/462-6262 in the U.S. and Canada,

0014/800/124-171 from Australia. Fax toll free 800/622-4852. Telex MCI 650-502-8960. 303 rms. A/C TV TEL
$ Rates: $70–$75 double, $75–$80 double with kitchenette; $110 one-bedroom suite, $200 two-bedroom suite. Each additional person $15. AE, CB, DC, DISC, JCB, MC, V. **Parking:** $7 per day.
Like all the Outrigger properties, this hotel is well set up for comfortable living. The spacious rooms usually have twin beds (a few double and queen-size beds are available) and a long, narrow lanai that is shared with the next room. Doubles with complete kitchenettes are available, and suites have kitchens. No-smoking and handicapped rooms are also available. The comfortable chairs in the lobby afford a view of passersby on the sidewalk, while the bustle of Kalakaua is just 1 long block away; the Pacific, 2. There's a pleasant pool for at-home swimming.

OUTRIGGER WAIKIKI SURF WEST, 412 Lewers St., Honolulu, HI 96815. Tel. 808/923-7671, or toll free 800/462-6262 in the U.S. and Canada, 0014/800/124-171 from Australia. Fax toll free 800/622-4852. Telex MCI 650-502-8960. 38 rms, 77 suites. A/C TV TEL
$ Rates: $75–$80 double/kitchenette; $100 one-bedroom suite/kitchenette. Each additional person $15. AE, CB, DC, DISC, JCB, MC, V. **Parking:** $7 per day.
This hotel shares the lobby and front desk with the main Waikiki Surf across the street, but it has its own large pool area. All the recently renovated rooms have kitchenettes, a bath with shower, and lanais. Suites can accommodate up to four. No-smoking and handicapped rooms available.

EWA WAIKIKI

ALOHA PUNAWAI, 305 Saratoga Rd., Honolulu, HI 96815. Tel. 808/923-5211. 19 apts. A/C TV
$ Rates: $47–$52 studio for one without air conditioning; $52–$57 studio for one with air conditioning; $57–$62 bedroom for one with air conditioning; $62–$67 large bedroom for one with air conditioning. Add $8 each additional person; children under 12 free. Minimum stay 3 days; weekly and monthly discounts available. No credit cards. **Parking:** $4 per day.
The owners of this place try hard to keep a low profile, but we are revealing their secret: There are not many places in Waikiki that are this cheap. Here you get a clean, comfortable apartment with a furnished kitchen, bath with shower, and a lanai. There are no telephones, although phones can be installed for those on long stays. Stay a month and the rate goes down to $32 and $52 a day. There are also both small and large one-bedroom apartments available. Towels and linens are provided and there is cleaning service twice a week. Aloha Punawai has been family-owned and -operated since 1959. Saratoga Road is near Fort DeRussy, and the hotel is only a block from the beach.

HALE PUA NUI, 228 Beach Walk, Honolulu, HI 96815. Tel. 808/923-9693. 22 studio apts. TV TEL
$ Rates: Mar 16–June 15 and Sept 16–Dec 15, $40 single or double. June 16–Sept 15 and Dec 16–Mar 15, $55 single or double. Each additional person $5. MC, V. **Parking:** $6–$10 per day at nearby garage.
⭐ One of our favorite streets in Honolulu is Beach Walk, a tiny street running from Kalakaua smack into the ocean, and relatively—for Waikiki—quiet. Here you'll find this lovely little complex of large studio apartments, many of whose guests come back year after year. The location is tops—just half a block to the beach at the Outrigger Reef Hotel and just around the bend from Fort DeRussy, where the swimming is excellent. The studio apartments have either twin or double beds and are tastefully outfitted with new carpets, drapes, bedspreads, and artistic touches. They all have cross-ventilation, soundproofing, and ceilings. Kitchenettes are thoroughly equipped (even to ironing boards). A maximum of three people can stay in a room. An excellent value!

KAI ALOHA HOTEL, 235 Saratoga Rd., Honolulu, HI 96815. Tel. 808/923-6723. Fax 808/922-7592. 18 apts. A/C TV TEL

$ Rates: $60–$65 studio apt with lanai; $68–$73 one-bedroom apt for two people, $80–$85 for three, $90–$95 for four. Each additional person $10. AE, DC, DISC, JCB, MC, V. **Parking:** $7 per day.

Faithful fans return year after year to this simple little hotel. They prefer the homey atmosphere, the friendliness of the management, and the feeling of intimacy, rare at the more impersonal concrete high-rise hotels. The location, very close to the beach and shopping area, is convenient, and the lush tropical plantings add an island flavor. Every unit has either a modern kitchen or kitchenette. Apartments have full-size refrigerators; the studios, half-size ones. All units have a garbage disposal, toaster, and ironing board. There are coin-operated laundry facilities available on the premises. One-bedroom apartments can comfortably accommodate families of four or five; children are welcome.

OUTRIGGER MAILE SKY COURT HOTEL, 2058 Kuhio Ave., Honolulu, HI 96815. Tel. 808/947-2828, or toll free 800/462-6262 in the U.S. and Canada, 0014/800/124-171 from Australia. Fax toll free 800/622-4852. Telex MCI 650-502-8960. 554 rms, 42 studios and suites. A/C TV TEL

$ Rates: $70–$80 double; $80–$90 double/kitchenette; $110 studio/kitchenette; $150–$180 suite/kitchenette. Maximum two in doubles, three people in studios. Each additional person $15. AE, CB, DC, DISC, JCB, MC, V. **Parking:** $7 per day.

Designed for the easy life, this hotel is located across the road from the well-known Nick's Fishmarket Restaurant, at the "Gateway to Waikiki," within easy walking distance of the beach and all the attractions of Kalakaua Avenue. There's a very pleasant ambiance here, evident as soon as you walk into the pretty open-air lobby, with its maroon-and-beige rugs and dusty-rose and rattan sofas. This 44-story resort offers a variety of accommodations. Rooms are of modest size, but most have views (some, from the higher floors, are spectacular) and all have attractive furnishings and cable TV. There are clocks, radios, and tub/showers, but no lanais. Even the hotel rooms boast small refrigerators; studios and suites add a two-burner electric range for light cooking. There's a pool and a Jacuzzi on the large, 360° sun deck and a poolside snack bar. No-smoking and handicapped rooms are available.

OUTRIGGER ROYAL ISLANDER HOTEL, 2164 Kalia Rd., Honolulu, HI 96815. Tel. 808/922-1961, or toll free 800/462-6262 in the U.S. and Canada, 0014/800/124-171 from Australia. Fax toll free 800/622-4852. Telex MCI 650-502-8960. 94 rms, 7 apts. TV TEL

$ Rates: Apr–June and Sept–Dec 18, $65–$85 double; $125–$130 suite. Dec 19–Mar and July–Aug, $75–$95 double; $125–$130 suite. Each additional person $15. AE, CB, DC, DISC, JCB, MC, V. **Parking:** $7 per day.

Rooms here are not large, but they are tastefully decorated. Each room has a private lanai, refrigerator, and a modern bathroom with shower. Families will do well in the one-bedroom apartments and suites. This hotel has a superb location, right near the Halekulani and Outrigger Reef hotels, across the road from a very good beach. The lobby is small and quite to the street. Complimentary coffee is available in the mornings. There's a McDonald's right in the hotel. No-smoking rooms are available.

WAIKIKI GATEWAY HOTEL, 2070 Kalakaua Ave., Honolulu, HI 96815. Tel. 808/955-3741, or toll free 800/633-8799 in the mainland U.S. and Canada, 0014/800/125-921 from Australia. Fax 808/955-1313. 190 rms. A/C TV TEL

$ Rates: Apr–Dec 20, $55–$100 double; $110 penthouse suite. Dec 21–Mar $80–$125 double. AE, DC, JCB, MC, V. **Parking:** $7 per day.

This hotel is well known as the home of Nick's Fishmarket, one of Honolulu's favorite restaurants. It's also well known as a good-value hotel. It offers rooms with a private lanai, cable TV, an under-the-counter refrigerator, an in-room safe, and a luxurious bath with tub and shower. There's daily cleaning service and a guest laundry. The beach is less than a 10-minute walk, but if you'd rather swim at home, try the beautiful pool backed by a volcanic rock wall and a spacious sun deck.

NEAR THE ALA WAI

HOLIDAY SURF APARTMENT HOTEL, 2303 Ala Wai Blvd., Honolulu, HI 96815. Tel. 808/923-8488. 34 rms. TV
$ Rates: Mid-Apr to Dec 14, $36–$57 studio; $39–$66 one-bedroom. Dec 15 to mid-Apr, $54–$69 studio; $60–$78 one-bedroom. Each additional person $3. AE, CB, DC, DISC, JCB, MC, V. **Parking:** Free.

A clean, white six-story building stands at the corner of Ala Wai Boulevard and Nohonani Street, anything but imposing, but well worth considering because it offers delightfully appointed accommodations at low rates. Most of the units have small lanais that accommodate two chairs. Most of the bathrooms have stall showers, but some have tub/shower combinations. There are no telephones in the rooms, but guests may make free local calls at the lobby office phone. Kitchens are fully equipped. From here to the beach it's 2 long blocks, about a 7-minute walk.

OUTRIGGER ALA WAI TERRACE HOTEL, 1547 Ala Wai Blvd., Honolulu HI 96815. Tel. 808/949-7384, or toll free 800/462-6262 in the U.S. and Canada, 0014/800/124-171 from Australia. Fax toll free 800/622-4852. Telex MCI 650-502-8960. 196 rms, 43 apts. A/C TV TEL
$ Rates: $55 studio; $60–$110 one-bedroom. Each additional person $15. AE, CB, DC, DISC, JCB, MC, V. **Parking:** $3.50 per day.

Some of the lowest rates in Waikiki are being offered at this hotel, which is located at the very beginning of Ala Wai Boulevard, not far from Ala Moana. This 47-year-old apartment building was converted into a hotel a few years ago, and while there's nothing at all fancy about it (don't expect tourist amenities like a pool or restaurant), it does offer clean and comfortable units all with full kitchens and all the necessities. There are two buildings: the renovated, 16-story Tower Building; and the low-rise, walk-up Garden Building.

WAIKIKI SAND VILLA HOTEL, 2375 Ala Wai Blvd., Honolulu, HI 96815. Tel. 808/922-4744, or toll free 800/247-1903 in the U.S. Fax 808/923-2541. 211 rms. A/C TV TEL
$ Rates: Off season, $60–$95 double; $130 one-bedroom suite. Winter, $75–$120 double; $160 one-bedroom suite. Each additional person $10. Children under 8 stay free in parent's room using existing bedding. AE, DC, DISC, JCB, MC, V. **Parking:** $4 per day.

The Waikiki Sand Villa Hotel is looking better than ever these days, thanks to a $3-million top-to-bottom renovation. The lobby now has a Hawaiian plantation-style ambiance accented with a Chinese pink slate floor. The best views are of the Ala Wai Canal, the golf course across it, and the Koolau mountains, but even the opposite views are not obscured by neighboring buildings. Rooms are adequate in size, and the decor is handsome; two tables—one inside and one out on the cozy lanai—afford a choice of breakfast spots. The rooms include a refrigerator and an in-room safe for valuables, and the bathrooms have both tub and shower.

Opening off the lobby is the Lobster Hut Restaurant, serving lunch and dinner and featuring 1½-pound stuffed lobsters.

NEAR ALA MOANA

BIG SURF HOTEL, 1690 Ala Moana Blvd., Honolulu, HI 96815. Tel. 808/ 946-6525. 10 small rms, 18 mountain-view studios, 20 ocean-view one-bedroom suites. TV
$ Rates: $33–$42 single small rooms; $37–$49 single or double mountain-view studios; $50–$75 one-bedroom ocean-view suites. MC, V. **Parking:** $3 per day.

Located 1½ blocks from Ala Moana Beach and a block from the Ala Moana Shopping Center, this one has some of the lowest rates in Waikiki. There is no pool, no restaurant, and the only telephone is one for local calls only in the small lobby. The small single rooms have one bed and a private bath with shower. A couple would require one of the larger studios, which come with twin beds and lanais. For parties of up to five people, there are one-bedroom suites with full kitchens. Color TV is available in the larger studios and some of the singles.

Most of the accommodations have been renovated and, though simple, are adequately furnished. Don't expect spaciousness at this price. The hotel is a few minutes stroll around the Ilikai lagoon to the beach, and just a few minutes in the other direction to the Ala Moana Shopping Center.

COLONY'S HAWAII POLO INN, 1696 Ala Moana Blvd., Honolulu, HI 96815. Tel. 808/949-0061, or toll free 800/777-1700. Fax 808/949-4906. 65 rms. TV TEL

$ Rates: $45–$75 single or double; $85–$95 minisuite with kitchenette. Each additional person $10. AE, DB, DC, DISC, MC, V. **Parking:** $5 per day.

This small boutique hotel is across the road from the luxury Hawaii Prince Hotel; it's also at the other end of the price spectrum. All rooms have been attractively renovated, and offer refrigerators, in-room coffee service, and daily cleaning service. There is a swimming pool, launderette, and parking on the premises. The hotel is less than 2 blocks from the Ala Moana Shopping Center and Ala Moana Beach Park, an excellent swimming beach and a local family favorite.

A stay at the Hawaii Polo Inn also entitles you to two tickets to the Hawaii Polo Club's Sunday polo matches from March through August; off-season, you can get a 10% discount on a polo lesson or beach ride.

OUTRIGGER HOBRON, 343 Hobron Lane, Honolulu, HI 96815. Tel. 808/ 942-7777, or toll free 800/462-6262 in the U.S. and Canada, 0014/800/124-171 from Australia. Fax toll free 800/622-4852. Telex MCI 650-502-8960. 550 rms, 46 suites. A/C TV TEL

$ Rates: $70–$75 double, $110 double/kitchenette; $150 two-bedroom suite/kitchenette; $180 three-bedroom suite/kitchenette. Each additional person $15. AE, DB, DISC, JCB, MC, V. **Parking:** $6 per day.

A skyscraper for this area, this 44-story condominium has attractive accommodations to its credit; it's very popular with tour groups. Most rooms look similar, the major difference being in height. All rooms have attractive blond-wood furniture (desk, vanity, chair), multicolored drapes and bedspreads, and in-room safes; they are small but well appointed, and many offer very good views of ocean, city, mountains, and the nearby Ala Wai Yacht Harbor. Most rooms have twin beds; only four on each floor have queen-size beds, which must be requested in advance. There are also differences in housekeeping facilities: The hotel rooms have refrigerators only; the studios have mini-kitchenettes. There's a pool on the mezzanine level, a sun deck plus Jacuzzi whirlpool and sauna on the fifth floor. Steens Bar & Grill offers continental breakfast and sandwiches, big-screen TV, and karaoke. No-smoking and handicapped rooms are available. All the excitement of the Ilikai and Hilton Hawaiian Village complexes is about 5 minutes away. Cars from Dollar Rent A Car are available for $5 a day.

DOWNTOWN HONOLULU

Tourists who prefer to stay in downtown Honolulu (an easy bus ride from Waikiki) rather than in the beach area will have somewhat tougher sledding. There are so few hotels outside Waikiki that most tourists never hear about them at all. They are primarily occupied by businesspeople. But there are a few in our budget category, and because this area is ideal for serious sightseeing, you may want to consider them.

NAKAMURA HOTEL, 1140 S. King St., Honolulu, HI 96814. Tel. 808/537- 1951. 41 rms, TEL

$ Rates: $40 single; $45 double; $47 twin. Each additional person $5. No credit cards. **Parking:** Free.

Though this isnt a large hotel, you may be lucky enough to find a room on the spur of the moment since this small, family-run establishment is out of the tourist mainstream. Just off Piikoi Street, this clean and quite comfortably appointed building offers rooms with wall-to-wall carpeting, a large tiled bathroom with a tub/shower combo, good drawer and closet space, and even a telephone. We prefer the rooms facing the mountains; even though they do not have air conditioning, they do have those refreshing trade winds. In the air-conditioned rooms, the machine also drowns out the traffic on King Street (so keep those jalousied windows closed). Some of the rooms are too small for a third person. TVs can be rented. Mrs. Winifred Hakoda, the personable desk clerk and day manager, advises that no late arrivals (after 9pm Monday through Saturday, after 8pm Sunday and holidays) are accepted.

TOWN INN, 250 N. Beretania St., Honolulu, HI 96817. Tel. 808/536-2377. 26 rms. TEL

$ Rates: $41 and $42 single or double; $53.41 one-bedroom air-conditioned suite. MC, V. **Parking:** Free.

This tastefully modern Japanese establishment is where you'll mingle, so the management promises, "with important personages and travelers of every race." And all this cosmopolitanism is very reasonable, too! Lower-priced singles and doubles do not have air conditioning; the higher-priced do. Don't expect to sleep on the floor Japanese style; the bedrooms are as Western as the air conditioning. There's a Japanese restaurant, Miyajima, on the premises.

WINDWARD OAHU

Windward Oahu is on the other side of the mighty Koolau mountain range, which serves as a backdrop to Honolulu. The scenery is comparable to what you'll find on the neighboring islands. This is "the country," where many local people spend their vacations, and it's far off the usual tourist track. Although this is a good jumping-off spot from which to visit many of the attractions of the windward side, it's essentially a place where you sit on the gorgeous beach surrounded by sea, sky, and fragrant blossoms and do absolutely nothing at all.

Dreaming of a cottage right on the beach? They're not easy to come by in modern Hawaii, but Pat O'Malley of **Pat's Kailua Beach Properties,** 204 S. Kalaheo Ave., Kailua, HI 96734 (tel. 808/261-1653 or 808/262-4128; fax 808/262-8275 or 808/261-0893), may be able to help you out. Pat offers more than 40 fully furnished houses and cottages along Kailua Beach, from a million-dollar beachfront estate to "beachy" cottages on or close to the water. About half of these fall within our budget, costing $65 to $95 a day. Each is different, but all are fully furnished and provide cooking and dining utensils, bedding and towels, telephone, and television. Some are duplex. The interiors of the cottages we saw were well maintained; some have been recently renovated. The exteriors of some are weather-beaten, which gives them a rustic look. Settings and views are lovely, and many have delightful yards and gardens.

A one-bedroom/one-bath beachfront cottage once owned by a prominent Hawaiian family is priced at $90 a day and can sleep two adults and two children. Overlooking Kailua Beach Park, less than 100 yards from the surf, are one-bedroom/one-bath units for $65 to $85 that can sleep three to four people, and two-bedroom units for $100 to $110 that can sleep five people.

Call Pat O'Malley for information and reservations, and ask about the deposit requirements.

Marilyn and Lucky Cole, who run **North Shore Vacation Homes,** 59-229 C Ke Nui Rd., Haleiwa, HI 96712 (tel. 808/638-7289, or toll free 800/678-5263; fax 808/638-8736), have four lovely vacation homes for rent on the North Shore, just 1½ miles west of the Turtle Bay Hilton Resort. All oceanfront, these are two- and three-bedroom beachfront cottages and homes with large, covered redwood decks, plentiful indoor space, and a sleeping capacity of from 4 to 10 persons. During the off-season, after Labor Day to Thanksgiving and after Easter to the first of June, the rates are $105, $150, and $160 per day; from Thanksgiving through Easter and from June 1 through Labor Day weekend, rates are $125, $165, and $175 per day; during the week before and after Christmas, rates are $150, $185, and $200. A minimum stay of 1 week is required, except during Christmas, when the minimum stay is 2 weeks.

BACKPACKERS, VACATION INN/PLANTATION VILLAGE, 59-788 Kamehameha Hwy., Haleiwa, HI 96712. Tel. 808/638-7838. Hostel bunks, rms, apts, cabins.

$ Rates: At Vacation Inn, $14 hostel bunk across from the beach, $16 hostel bunk oceanfront, $35–$45 room across from the beach; $70–$85 oceanfront studio apt. At Plantation Village, $16 hostel bunk; $95–$105 cabin for four to six, $105–$115 large cabin for six, $110–$120 deluxe ocean-view cabin for six, $135–$155 large ocean-view cabin for eight. Weekly rates available. MC, V. **Parking:** Free.

This place is definitely not for the perfectionist, as buildings and furniture have seen wear and tear, but management is always fixing and upgrading as much as possible. Backpackers caters to young and young-at-heart travelers from around the world. There are several possibilities here for casual country living. At Vacation Inn, one can find basic accommodations overlooking Waimea Bay. Backpackers like the inexpensive hostel facilities, which consist of several rooms furnished with four bunks each. There's a common living room with TV, a bathroom, and a kitchen. The quarters are cleaned each morning. Moving one step up, you can rent a single or double room with a common bath, kitchen, and TV room. Studio apartments can sleep four to six and are comfortably furnished, with TV and kitchenette; all have good views of surf and beach. Some of these units are right on Three Tables Beach, which is next to Waimea Bay; others are higher up in a building on the mountain side of the road and command great ocean vistas.

Plantation Village consists of nine restored plantation cabins located across from Three Tables Beach Park, on an acre of gardens; bananas, papayas, ginger, and mangoes grow in the yard. Each cabin has its own kitchen and bath, cable TV, linens and dishes; a common area offers pay telephone, picnic and barbecue areas, and laundry facilities. The Circle Island bus no. 52 stops out front every half hour; all facilities are a short walk to Waimea Bay, Waimea Falls Park, and a good supermarket, so one could conceivably get by without a car here. A protected area is safe for children's swimming. Boogie boards and snorkels are part of the North Shore lifestyle, so they are supplied free to guests, as are tennis racquets and balls. Chaz Wagner and Sharlyn Foo are warm hosts, who provide inexpensive sailboat and hiking trips and island tours. Scuba-diving instruction is available in summer. They also rent many vacation homes and condos "in all shapes, sizes, and locations" (rates on request). Again, remember that Waimea Bay is perfect for summer swimming and snorkeling, but the water is extremely rough in winter; it's the scene of world-famous surfing events.

2. DOUBLES FOR ABOUT $70 TO $100

WAIKIKI

DIAMOND HEAD WAIKIKI

EWA [EAST-WEST ADVENTURE] HOTEL WAIKIKI, 2555 Cartwright St., Honolulu, HI 96815. Tel. 808/922-1677, toll free 800/359-8639. Fax 808/923-8538. 90 studios, 12 suites. A/C TV TEL

$ Rates: $88 studio; $133 one-bedroom suite; $173 two-bedroom suite. AE, MC, V. **Parking:** $4 per day.

Up near the Honolulu Zoo, this old hotel has a new name and look thanks to a $3-million renovation. Italian-marble floors and counters, grass cloth on the walls, sand-colored carpets, and pastel color schemes in the lobby and the rooms make this hotel very attractive. The higher-priced studios have kitchenettes; all units have in-room safes, and tub-shower combos. Most have twin beds; some have queen-size beds. Studios are for one to three people, and suites, one to four people. There is no swimming pool or dining facility, but with the ocean and restaurants 2 short blocks away, this is no problem.

KAIMANA VILLA CONDOMINIUMS, 2550 Kuhio Ave., Honolulu, HI 96815. Tel. 808/922-3833, or toll free 800/367-6060. Fax 808/922-8061. 113 apts. A/C TV TEL

$ Rates: $110–$125 one-bedroom apt; $175–$190 two-bedroom apt. Each additional person $15. Senior rates available on request. AE, DC, DISC, JCB, MC, V. **Parking:** $3 per day.

Every room here has a private lanai facing Diamond Head: From the higher floors, you'll feel as if you can almost touch it. Located 2 blocks from the beach and from shopping and nightlife, this is the place for those who like space: Each tastefully appointed unit has over 600 square feet. Amenities include your own washer and dryer, dishwasher, clock radio, a full kitchen, a daily housekeeping services. There is also 24-hour front-desk service. The two-bedroom apartments can accommodate up to six guests.

Reservations: HTH Corp., 2490 Kalakaua Ave., Honolulu, HI 96815 (tel. 808/922-3833, or toll free 800/367-6060 in the U.S. and Canada; fax 808/922-8061; telex 633101).

KAULANA KAI, 2425 Kuhio Ave., Honolulu, HI 96815. Tel. 808/922-7777, or toll free 800/367-5666 in the U.S. and Canada, 0014/800-125-434 from Australia. Fax 808/946-8777. 69 rms, 21 suites. A/C TV TEL

$ Rates (Including continental breakfast): $85–$95 studio; $130 one-bedroom suite; $150–$200 suite for four with kitchen. AE, DC, JCB, MC, V. **Parking:** $5 (limited).

Located in a great spot 3 minutes from Kuhio Beach, this tall pyramidlike building designed by Scandinavian architect Jo Paul Rognstad has been taken over and transformed by a new Japanese management. The hotel is a little jewel, its lobby and guest rooms all done in shades of mauve and pink, with gold fixtures. Rooms are not large but they are attractive, with twin beds, small lanais, and a tidy two-burner kitchenette with a refrigerator underneath the range. Bathrooms are marble, and the kitchen and bathroom floors are tiled, as are the lanais. And it's fun to relax in the pool, whirlpool, and sauna. The lobby is beautiful, with its marble floors, indented Japanese-style ceiling, and gorgeous flower arrangements.

KUHIO VILLAGE RESORT, 2463 Kuhio Ave., Honolulu, HI 96815. Tel. 808/926-0641, or toll free 800/367-5004 in the U.S. and Canada. Fax 808/533-0472, or toll free 800/477-2329. 138 rms, 12 suites. A/C TV TEL

$ Rates (including free rent-a-car or 6th night free): Apr–Dec 24, $80–90 double; $120 family suite with kitchenette; $130 one-bedroom suite with kitchenette. Dec 24–Mar 31, $90–$115 double; $135 family suite with kitchenette; $150 one-bedroom suite with kitchenette. AE, DC, JCB, MC, V. **Parking:** $4 per day.

Just 1½ blocks from the beach, this renovated Hawaiian Pacific Resorts hotel enjoys a convenient central location. The 21-story two-tower structure has its own restaurant, a round-the-clock minimart, a launderette, and lots of big-hotel amenities. The rooms are furnished in soft pastels, with white furniture, in-room safes, and a refrigerator in every room. The rooms and suites with kitchenettes have microwaves and dining areas, and cooking and dining utensils. The junior suites have a sitting room with a sofa bed, and all bedrooms have queen-size beds. The handsomely renovated lobby is paneled in natural koa wood and has sections that are open to the sky, with planter boxes filled with palms and ferns.

OCEAN RESORT HOTEL WAIKIKI, 175 Paoakalani Ave., Honolulu, HI 96815. Tel. 808/922-3861, or toll free 800/367-2317. 800/999-6640 in Canada.

Fax 808/924-1982. 450 rms, 7 suites. A/C TV TEL

$ Rates: Diamond Head Tower, Apr–Dec 22, $69–$137 single or double; Dec 23–Mar, $75–$120 single or double. Pali Tower, Apr–Dec 22, $79–$147 single or double; Dec 23–Mar, $95–$140 single or double. Each additional person $15; $170–$280 suite. AE, DC, DISC, ER, JCB, MC, V. **Parking:** $4 per day.

A very welcome find in this area close to Kapiolani Park, this is a cheerful, sparkling hotel with a waterfall at the entrance, a golden lobby, and friendly people behind the desk. It has every hotel amenity, including two small swimming pools on the third floor, a tour desk, laundry room, and daily maid service. Prices are lowest in the Diamond Head Tower; rooms here do not have kitchenettes, but there are compact refrigerators, and you'll enjoy your lanai and the view. All rooms in the Pali Tower have kitchenettes. Rooms in both buildings are of standard size, and have dressing areas, and stall showers large enough and deep enough for a bath. The Mala Restaurant, adjacent to the lobby, serves three Japanese/American meals a day.

ROYAL KUHIO, 2240 Kuhio Ave., Honolulu, HI 96815. Tel. 808/538-7145 or 808/538-7145, or toll free 800/367-5205. Fax 808/533-4621. 385 apts. A/C TV TEL

$ Rates: Apr 16–Dec 15, $80 one-bedroom apt. Dec 16–Apr 15, $110 one-bedroom apt. AE, DC, DISC, MC, V. **Parking:** Free.

Apartments at this towering condominium building are quite attractive and nicely decorated, with a bedroom with twin beds that can be closed off from the sitting room or opened to make one big area. The sitting room has sofa beds, and rollaways are available for additional people. The kitchens are all-electric (with dishwashers), the closet space is ample, and every apartment has its own lanai. A pool and sun-deck area, billiard room, Ping-Pong, a shuffleboard court, and a huge laundry room and recreation area all make for easy living—not to mention that the Royal Kuhio is close to the beach. There is weekly chamber service.

Reservations: Paradise Management Corporation, Suite C-207, 50 S. Beretania St., Honolulu, HI 96813; or phone the toll-free number above.

WAIKIKI GRAND, 134 Kapahulu Ave., Honolulu, HI 96815. Tel. 808/923-1511, or toll free 800/535-0085. Fax 808/922-2421. 105 rms. A/C TV TEL

$ Rates: $80–$95 double; $95–$105 studio with kitchenette. Each additional person $15. Children under 18 stay free in parent's room (using existing bedding). AE, MC, V. **Parking:** $5 per day.

Now a member of the MarcResorts Hawaii group, this older hotel has recently been upgraded and remodeled. And what a pleasant location this one has, just across the street from Kapiolani Park and all its activities, and just around the bend from Kuhio Beach. From the lower-priced rooms, views are of the center of Waikiki, but go a little higher and you'll be rewarded with breathtaking views of Diamond Head. Super views or not, the rooms are pleasant if small (very little closet space), and have tub/showers. There's a pleasant swimming pool on the 10th floor sundeck. Many Japanese guests favor this one.

READERS RECOMMEND

Colony's Pacific Monarch Hotel, 142 Uluniu Ave., Honolulu, HI 96815 (tel. 808/ 923-9805, or toll free 800/777-1700). "I would like to strongly recommend Colony's Pacific Monarch Hotel, where we have vacationed for many years. It is ideally located 1 block from the beach and King's Village and close to many fine restaurants. The skytop pool, Jacuzzi, and sauna with weatherproofed picnic activity area add to the many pleasures available. Lanais are equipped with table and chairs so that you can have a relaxing meal while watching the beautiful views (many of them ocean view) and the sunset. Rooms have kitchenettes and include a welcome kit of coffee, tea, etc. Rates are structured by season. The studios with kitchenettes and walk-out lanais are $99 to $119. One-bedroom apartments with full kitchens and large lanais are $130 and $150.*

Maid service is included."—Dr. John Lopresti, Jr., Bricktown, N.J. [Author's Note: Check for dramatic "Managers Specials" as low as $55 for a studio, $75 for a one-bedroom during the off-season.]

CENTRAL WAIKIKI

CORAL REEF, 2299 Kuhio Ave., Honolulu, HI 96815. Tel. 808/922-1262, or toll free 800/922-7866 in the mainland U.S. and in Canada, 800/321-2558 in Hawaii. Fax 808/922-8785. Telex 634479. 247 rms, 45 suites. A/C TV TEL
$ Rates: Apr–Dec 20, $70–$80 double; $85–$95 junior suite; $95–$105 one-bedroom suite. Dec 21–Mar, $90–$100 double; $105–$115 junior suite; $115–$125 one-bedroom suite. Each additional person $12. AE, DC, MC, V. **Parking:** $7.
You get a really large room at this modern high-rise hotel directly behind the International Market Place and a short walk from Waikiki Beach. The hotel boasts every facility—swimming pool, garage, restaurants, shops—and nicely furnished rooms that have either one or two double beds (or a double and a single), private lanai, and cable TV. The hotel is managed by Aston Hotels & Resorts, 2255 Kuhio Ave., Honolulu, HI 96815.

HOTEL HONOLULU, 376 Kaiolu St., Honolulu, HI 96815. Tel. 808/926-2766, or toll free 800/426-2766. Fax 808/922-3326. 15 studios, 9 one-bedroom suites. A/C TV TEL
$ Rates: $66–$77 studio; $99 one-bedroom suite. Each additional person $9. AE, DISC, JCB, MC, V. **Parking:** Free, covered off-street.
A beautiful orchid collection, tropical birds, and hundreds of potted plants give a garden atmosphere to Hawaii's only gay hotel. They call it a "deco–post modern" building, but we call it a reminder of the plantation days. Whatever you call it, the Hotel Honolulu is an oasis in time and space. Located 2 blocks from the beach, the two buildings of the hotel compound are isolated from traffic. There's a rooftop garden sun deck, very popular for evening barbecues and drinks, and a variety of clubs, restaurants, and shops just around the corner.
Best choice for budgeteers here is the smaller, two-story building called the Bamboo Lanai, where small, nicely furnished studios go for $70. They have a small, fully equipped kitchenette, a bathroom with a tile-enclosed shower, and a closet. Larger studios and one-bedroom suites in the three-story main building, which is air-conditioned, are more elaborate and more expensive. The studios have a sitting area, queen-size bed, complete kitchen, full bathroom, ceiling fans and cross-ventilation, and a lanai. The one-bedroom suites are quite large, with king-size bed, lanai, complete kitchen, and full bath, and each one is distinctively decorated in various styles: Japanese, Chinese, bamboo, safari, Chippendale, deco, and so on. TVs (free) are available on request. There's free coffee all day in the lobby, and a laundry room as well.

ILIMA HOTEL, 445 Nohonani St., Honolulu, HI 96815. Tel. 808/923-1877, or toll free 800/367-5172 in the mainland U.S. and Canada. Fax 808/924-8371. 74 studios, 18 one-bedroom suites. 6 two-bedroom suites. A/C TV TEL
$ Rates: Apr–Dec 14, $65–$80 single; $70–$90 double; $99 executive suite; $119 large one-bedroom suite; $149–$159 two-bedroom suite; $175–$199 two- or three-bedroom penthouse. Dec 15–Mar, add $15 to all rates. Each additional person $8. AE, DC, DISC, JCB, MC, V. **Parking:** Free.
Still going strong after 25 years, the Ilima is eminently comfortable and offers many facilities and services, and a $1.2-million renovation has not upped the rates unreasonably. A walk of less than 10 minutes will take you to the beach. You can really kick off your shoes and feel at home here; floors are carpeted, rooms are condominium-size spacious, and the studios include two double beds, a fully equipped kitchen with microwave, TV, radio, full tub and shower, plenty of storage space, and a private lanai. There's a swimming pool at ground level and two sun decks on the 10th floor, as well as an exercise room and sauna. Generosities not

usually found in most Waikiki hotels include free parking and free local phone calls—not to mention those fully equipped kitchens in every unit. Sergio's Italian Restaurant is right at hand.

MARINE SURF, 364 Seaside Ave., Honolulu, HI 96815. Tel. 808/923-0277, or toll free 800/367-5176 in the mainland U.S., 800/663-1118 in Canada. Fax 808/926-5915. 115 studios, 1 one-bedroom suite. A/C TV TEL

$ Rates: Apr–Dec 20, $74–$84 studio single or double; $125 one-bedroom penthouse suite. Dec 21–Mar, $88–$98 studio single or double; $140 one-bedroom penthouse suite. Each additional person $14. Children under 18 stay free in parent's room. Cribs $10 a day. CB, DC, MC, V. **Parking:** $4 a day.

⭐ The Marine Surf has just about everything going for it. Located about 1½ blocks from the beach, this 23-story condominium hotel features smartly decorated studio apartments, each one with two extra-length double beds, lots of drawer space, a dressing room, a safe, and a bath with tub and shower. Best of all, each studio has a full electric kitchen, just in case you choose not to eat every night at Matteos Italian Restaurant, one of the finest in town, right in the lobby. Rooms, which have been completely renovated, are serviced daily. Those too lazy to walk on the beach can swim and sun at the lovely outdoor pool on the fourth floor. Studios accommodate up to four, and penthouse suites, six. There's on-site parking.

OUTRIGGER EAST HOTEL, 150 Kaiulani Ave., Honolulu, HI 96815. Tel. 808/922-5353, or toll free 800/462-6262 in the U.S. and Canada, 0014/800/124-171 from Australia. Fax toll free 800/456-4329. Telex MCI 650-502-8960. 407 rms, 38 suites. A/C TV TEL

$ Rates: Apr–Jun and Sept–Dec 18, $85–$105 double; $105 studio; $165–$250 suite. Dec 19–Mar and July–Aug, $95–$110 double; $120 studio; $165–$250 suite. Each additional person $15. AE, CB, DC, DISC, JCB, MC, V. **Parking:** $7 per day.

Outrigger Hotels Hawaii has a number of establishments in central Waikiki, and this renovated (to the tune of $5 million) hotel is the top of the line in the chain's mid-priced category. The 18-floor building is a short block from Waikiki Beach and has just about everything a visitor needs, from four restaurants (Pepper's, Islander Coffee Shop, Chuck's Cellar, and Jolly Roger) to a beauty shop, travel and tour desks, and laundry facilities. Rooms have been smartly furnished, each with either two double beds, a king-size bed, or a queen-size bed; all have TVs with pay movies, in-room safes, and refrigerators; studios have kitchenettes. Studios can accommodate up to three guests and suites can accommodate up to four. No-smoking rooms and handicap facilities are available.

OUTRIGGER MALIA HOTEL, 2211 Kuhio Ave., Honolulu, HI 96815. Tel. 808/923-7621, or toll free 800/462-6262 in the U.S. and Canada, 0014/800/124-171 from Australia. Fax toll free 800/622-4852. Telex MCI 650-502-8960. 280 rms, 47 suites. A/C TV TEL

$ Rates: $80–$90 double; $100 suite. Each additional person $15. AE, CB, DC, DISC, JCB, MC, V. **Parking:** $7 per day.

This bright and beautiful place features two wings. The rooms in the Malia wing, the taller of the hotel's two sections, have two double beds with Polynesian-print bedspreads in soft, muted colors and wall-to-wall carpeting. All rooms in the hotel have a lanai, both tub and shower in the bathroom, a small refrigerator, and an ironing board. Disabled people will be glad to know that there are 16 rooms in this wing specially designed for them, with wider doorways, grab bars in the bathrooms, and twin-size rather than double beds for greater wheelchair mobility.

The Luana wing has junior suites which can accommodate four guests comfortably; all contain a sitting room with two couches and a bedroom with two beds. The lanais in the suites are much larger than those in the bedrooms of the Malia wing. Pluses for guests at both wings include a Jacuzzi whirlpool, a rooftop tennis court, and the excellent Wailana Coffeeshop, open 24 hours a day. And, of course, the beach is just 3 blocks away.

OUTRIGGER VILLAGE HOTEL, 240 Lewers St., Honolulu, HI 96815. Tel. 808/923-3881, or toll free 800/462-6262 in the U.S. and Canada, 0014/800/ 124-171 from Australia. Fax toll free 800/622-4852. Telex MCI 650-502-8960. 399 rms, 41 kitchenettes. A/C TV TEL
$ Rates: Apr–June and Sept–Dec 18, $80–$90 double; $85–$120 kitchenette. Dec 19– Mar and July–Aug, $90–$105 double; $95–$120 kitchenette. Each additional person $15. AE, CB, DC, DISC, JCB, MC, V. **Parking:** $7 per day.

This is the first hotel we've ever seen with a swimming pool in the center of the lobby! The lobby is a quadrangle built around the pool, and there's no ceiling in the center, so you can swim and sunbathe while checking out the new arrivals. The hotel is decorated from lobby to rooms in a bright blending of contemporary and Polynesian styles. Each of the units has an in-room safe, and most have lanais. Rooms are all similar, although those on the lower floors are cheaper. No-smoking rooms are available. Steens Villager, a family-style restaurant, is at hand, as is the Red Lion Dance Palace. The location is superb, right in the middle of everything and close to the beach.

OUTRIGGER WAIKIKI TOWER HOTEL (A BEST WESTERN), 200 Lewers St., Honolulu, HI 96815. Tel. 808/922-6424, or toll free 800/462-6262 in the U.S. and Canada, 0014/800/124-171 from Australia. Fax toll free 800/622-4852. Telex MCI 650-502-8960. 439 rms. A/C TV TEL
$ Rates: Apr–June and Sept–Dec 18, $80–$90 double; $85–$120 studio; $130 kitchenette studio. Dec 19–Mar and July–Aug, $90–$100 double; $95–$120 studio; $130 kitchenette studio. Each additional person $15. AE, CB, DC, DISC, JCB, MC, V. **Parking:** $7 per day.

This renovated hotel is next to the Outrigger Edgewater Hotel, which means that it shares a prime, close-to-the-beach location. Access to restaurants is just as easy as to the beach; the Waikiki Broiler is downstairs, Trattoria and Original Chuck's Original Steakhouse at the Edgewater and popular Denny's are across Lewers Street. The open-air lobby is chock full of convenience desks and shops. The pleasantly decorated rooms have a lanai, an in-room safe, a shower, and a king-size or queen-size bed or two twin beds. Studios have kitchenettes, but whether or not you get a kitchenette, you will get a refrigerator, and that goes a long way to cutting costs on food. Kitchenette units include a microwave oven, refrigerator, and utensils. No-smoking rooms are available.

PATRICK WINSTON'S HAWAIIAN KING RENTALS, 417 Nohonani St., Honolulu, HI 96815. Tel. 808/924-3332, or toll free 800/545-1948. 11 units in 66-unit hotel/condominium. A/C TV TEL
$ Rates: Apr 15–Dec 15, $59–$89. Dec 16–Apr 14, $75–$109. Each additional person $10. Airline discounts. Minimum stay 4 days. AE, MC, V. **Parking:** $5 per day.

⭐ You could call Patrick Winston's units here a hotel-within-a-hotel—they're really something special. Winston, a delightful young man who takes a caring, personal interest in his guests, many of whom return year after year, purchased his first unit in the Hawaiian King when it became a condominium hotel back in 1981. He was the interior designer-contractor who furnished the entire project. All his units have gone through complete $20,000-and-more renovations. One unit is called the Blue Hawaiian Suite, since it is furnished with blue rattan and blue carpeting along with an accent color. Two large units (788 sq. ft.) are called the Corporate Suites; they contain a separate room with a complete work station including a typewriter, calculator, and other business supplies, along with a large living room with VCR, electronic safe, and a conference area. The Mount Fuji Suite has white and black accents along with Oriental furniture, futons, and shoji screens. His other one-bedroom units have new carpeting and furniture, ceramic tiles, floor-to-ceiling mirrors, stereos and cable remote televisions, kitchens with microwave and convection ovens, and washer/dryers. A rowing machine and bicycle are available in certain units. Winston states: "I am dedicated to concepts that ring out time and again in your literature and that is quality lodging at a price, with the aloha spirit ringing in loudly."

The Hawaiian King is a five-story building built around a lovely pool and garden area, about 2 blocks from the beach. There's a laundry on the premises, a cocktail lounge, a minimart, and 24-hour front-desk and telephone switchboard service.

WHITE SANDS WAIKIKI RESORT, 431 Nohonani St., Honolulu, HI 96815. Tel. 808/923-7336. 80 rms. A/C TV TEL

$ Rates: $62–$88 single; $69–$95 double. AE, DC, DISC, MC, V. **Parking:** Free, but very limited, in the hotel; public lot across the street.

On pleasant Nohonani Street, about halfway between Kuhio Avenue and Ala Wai Boulevard, this low-rise garden hotel is a longtime favorite. It's a time-sharing establishment, so it's not always easy to get an opening here, and reservations cannot be confirmed until 2 weeks before your arrival date. However, when you consider that rooms are nicely furnished and that you get a kitchenette and a private lanai with even a standard room, it's worth a try. Each apartment is furnished differently, but nicely, in a Polynesian decor, and the beds are large and comfortable. Rooms have every-other-day cleaning service. The deluxe swimming pool, in an inner court, is surrounded by gardens, shady nooks, and pathways for exploring this tranquil acre in the heart of Waikiki. Coffee is served free in the lobby in the morning.

EWA WAIKIKI

AMBASSADOR HOTEL OF WAIKIKI, 2040 Kuhio Ave., Honolulu, HI 96815. Tel. 808/941-7777. Fax 808/922-4579. 315 rms. A/C TV TEL

$ Rates: $72–$96 single; $80–$104 double; $140–$170 one-bedroom suite. AE, CB, DC, JCB, MC, V. **Parking:** $4 per day.

An old-timer in Waikiki, the Ambassador still gives good value for the dollar. It's a comfortable hotel with all the conveniences. No wonder you always find airline personnel staying here! All the rooms in this high-rise building are approached from outside walkways. Even the lower-priced studios, from the second through seventh floors, boast private lanais, contemporary furniture, and deep furo-type shower tubs. You can relax at the big pool and sun deck on the second floor and eat at the Café Ambassador; you're also fairly close to all the attractions of Waikiki. The deluxe one-bedroom suites are equipped with full electric kitchens. Studios with kitchens are available on request.

HAWAIIANA HOTEL, 260 Beach Walk, Honolulu, HI 96815. Tel. 808/923-3811, or toll free 800/367-5122 in the mainland U.S. and Canada. Fax 808/926-5728. 95 studios, 7 one-bedroom suites. A/C TV TEL

$ Rates: $80–$90 single; $85–$95 double; $135–$143 one-bedroom suite; $165–$190 Alii Studio. Each additional person $8. Packages available. AE, MC, V. **Parking:** $6 per day (limited).

⭐ A favorite old-timer in Hawaii, this place gets more mellow every year. One of the few low-rise garden hotels left in Waikiki, the Hawaiiana is wonderfully located just half a block from a good swimming beach in front of the Outrigger Reef Hotel and Fort DeRussy. Rooms are situated around a gorgeous tropical garden and two swimming pools in the two- and three-story buildings, so you can step out your door for a swim in the pool or a complimentary breakfast of juice and coffee out on the patio. Comfortable chairs at poolside are occupied most of the day by guests too content to move. All rooms have been remodeled and furnished with rattan furniture; each has an electronic safe and an electric kitchen; most have a lanai. One-bedroom suites can accommodate up to four guests. Niceties include free newspapers in the morning or afternoon, Hawaiian shows twice a week, and free use of washers and dryers.

HAWAII DYNASTY HOTEL, 1830 Ala Moana Blvd., Honolulu, HI 96815. Tel. 808/955-1111, or toll free 800/421-6662 in the U.S. and Canada. Fax 808/947-1799. 199 rms, 2 suites. A/C TV TEL

$ Rates: Apr–Dec 20, $86–$98 double; $230 suite. Dec 21–Mar, $98–$109 double; $240 suite. Each additional person $14. AE, CB, DC, MC. **Parking:** $3.50 per day.

A good medium-price choice in the Ilikai and Hilton Hawaiian Village complex of hotels, stores, and restaurants is this high-rise hotel with an inn atmosphere. A complete refurbishment has made it nicer than ever. The accent is on comfort, with medium-size rooms and oversize beds; twin beds are as big as most doubles, and the doubles are enormous. Suites can accommodate up to four guests. Rooms are tastefully furnished and have combination tub/showers in the bathrooms. A laundry room is available. The pool on the second floor is one of the largest in Waikiki.

OUTRIGGER REEF LANAIS, 225 Saratoga Rd., Honolulu, HI 96815. Tel. 808/923-3881, or toll free 800/462-6262 in the U.S. and Canada, 0014/800/124-171 from Australia. Fax toll free 800/622-4852. Telex MCI 650-502-8960. 62 rms. A/C TV TEL

$ Rates: $85–$95 double, $90–$125 double with kitchenette; $160 suite. AE, CB, DC, DISC, JCB, MC, V. **Parking:** $7 per day.

This hotel is yet another member of the popular Outrigger hotel chain. It's tops in location, with the beach just a hop-skip-and-a-jump away; there's a public right-of-way to the ocean just across Kalia Road. Although it lacks some of the frills of the other Outrigger hotels, this spot is still a good value for the price. The lobby and rooms have all been renovated. Guest rooms are nicely decorated and have either double or queen-size beds, an in-room safe, and a shower (no tub); some rooms have kitchenettes, which include a microwave oven, refrigerator, and utensils. No-smoking rooms available. There is no pool on the premises, but guests may use the one at Outrigger Village, right around the corner on Lewers Street. The ever-popular Buzz's Steak & Lobster is located on the premises.

THE ROYAL GARDEN AT WAIKIKI, 440 Olohana St., Honolulu, HI 96815. Tel. 808/943-0202 or toll free 800/367-5666 from U.S. and Canada; fax 808/946-8177. 235 rms, 17 deluxe suites, 2 royal suites. A/C TV TEL

$ Rates: $95–$180 double; $295–$500 suites. Each additional person $15; children 17 and under free accompanied by an adult and using existing beds. AE, CB, DC, JCB, MC, V. Valet **Parking:** $7.

While many of the rooms in this stunning new $45-million luxury hotel are above our budget, there are still some 75 standard rooms for just $95. Considering the charm of this place, they're well worth the tab. The lobby is right out of a movie set: marble in every imaginable color, crystal chandeliers, ornate gilded mirrors—smashing! There are two swimming pools in the huge garden at the rear of the lobby; the larger one is a vision in marble with huge Romanesque bathhouse in the middle and a waterfall crashing from the inside and cascading into the pool. Upstairs are the guest accommodations, which are also very special. Every room has a lanai, attractive off-white rattan furniture, a coffeemaker, in-room safe, refrigerator, pay-per-view in-room movies on the TV. Many of the rooms are wheelchair accessible. The only difference between the standard rooms at $95 and the moderate rooms at $120 is the height of the floor; they all are 365 square feet in size and have either a queen-size bed or twins. The beach is about a 10-minute walk away, but right at home guests can use the two swimming pools, two whirlpools, sauna, and fitness center with state-of-the-art equipment. There's a business center, and concierge service is available. Also at hand are two splendid and very popular restaurants: Cascada for Euro-Island cuisine and Shizu for classic Japanese cookery.

WAIKIKI ROYAL SUITES, 255 Beach Walk, Honolulu, HI 96815. Tel. 808/ 926-5641, or toll free 800/535-0085. Fax 808/922-2421. 47 suites. TV TEL

$ Rates (including continental breakfast): $139–$179 one-bedroom suite for up to four; $219–$299 two-bedroom suite for up to six; cheaper on a weekly basis. Crib $5, rollaway $15. AE, JCB, MC, V. **Parking:** $6 per day.

Enjoying a superb location half a block from the ocean, this is Waikiki's first all-suite hotel. You'll be able to stretch out and relax here, since the suites are all of good size, and the lanais, many of which have ocean views, are extra large. There's a queen-size sofa bed in the living room, large mirrored closets, and in-room safes, and each suite has its own fully equipped kitchen, with microwave oven, coffee makers, and fresh ground coffee. There is no pool. There's a warm feeling of hospitality here, and there's a sunset evening cocktail party daily. Rates include daily maid service. Laundry facilities are available.

WAIKIKI TERRACE HOTEL, 2045 Kalakaua Ave., Honolulu, HI 96815. Tel. 808/955-6000, or toll free 800/445-8811 in the mainland U.S. and Canada. Fax 808/943-8555. 250 rms and 3 suites. A/C TV TEL

$ Rates: Apr–Dec 19, $115–$145 double; $295 suite. Dec 20–Mar, $125–$155 double; $295 suite. Each additional person $15. Children 17 and under stay free in parent's room when using existing bedding. Additional person 18 and older, $18. AE, CB, DC, DISC, JCB, MC, V. **Parking:** $7 per day.

"Affordably elegant" is the operative term here. A $10.5-million renovation has transformed an older hotel into a sparkling new property, with four-star service and amenities not usually found in hotels in this price category. Completely refurbished guest rooms are handsome, with light furniture and splendid marble and granite bathrooms with grooming products, and Berber carpeting. Each room has its own safe, a refrigerator, and a dry bar with an instant hot-water dispenser and a complimentary basket of coffees and teas. Views from your private lanais—of the ocean or mountains—are special. Rooms for the disabled and non-smokers are available on request. A great stretch of Waikiki Beach (fronting Fort DeRussy and the Hilton Hawaiian Village) is about a 7-minute walk away (through Fort DeRussy Park), but there's also a sun deck with pool and spa at home, as well as a fitness center. And there's room service too, from the hotel's outstanding restaurant, the Mezzanine, which has become one of the hottest spots in Waikiki.

NEAR THE ALA WAI

COCONUT PLAZA, 450 Lewers St., Honolulu, HI 96815. Tel. 808/923-8828, or toll free 800/367-7040 in the mainland U.S. Fax 808/537-3701. 80 rms, 10 suites. A/C TV TEL

$ Rates (including continental breakfast): Apr–Dec 19, $85–$110 single or double. Dec 20–Mar, $95–$120 single or double. Suites from $140–$150 for up to four persons. Inquire about special senior rates. AE, DISC, JCB, MC, V. **Parking:** $7 per day.

A smashing $2.3-million renovation has made this charming boutique hotel lovelier than ever, from its open-air plantation-style lobby with French doors and wooden louvers admitting the trade winds to the lobby bar where guests gather for breakfast, to the tropical guest rooms with whitewashed rattan furniture and Mexican floor tiles. As comfortable as they are beautiful, all rooms have either a wet bar or a kitchenette with microwave oven, bathrooms with tub/shower combinations, and a private lanai. The complimentary continental breakfast includes fruits, juices, breakfast rolls, and tea or Kona coffee, but if you're up for more, there's a nifty $2.95 breakfast buffet, including eggs, hash browns, and other island favorites. Enjoying this at the outdoor patio is a nice way to start a Hawaiian day! Coconut Plaza also has a weekly manager's reception every Monday evening with complimentary appetizers and beverages. The hotel's delightful Coconut Café is known for its Friday and Saturday evening buffets and reasonably priced lunch and dinners.

Coconut Plaza is across from the Ala Wai Golf Course and 3½ blocks from Waikiki Beach. Coconut Plaza is now under the aegis of Hawaiiana Resorts, 1270 Ala Moana Blvd., Honolulu, HI 96814.

HAWAIIAN MONARCH, 444 Niu St., Honolulu, HI 96815. Tel. 808/949-3911, or toll free 800/535-0085 in the mainland U.S. Fax 808/922-2421. 293 rms, 73 suites. A/C TV TEL

$ Rates: Apr–Dec 22, $70–$89 double. Dec 23–Mar, $85–$99 double. Suites $84. Each additional person $15. Children under 18 stay free in parent's room. AE, MC, V. **Parking:** $6 per day.

The skyscraper hotel is very close to the Ala Wai Canal and halfway between Ala Moana Shopping Center and the beaches of Waikiki. It's a well-run establishment with a mixed international clientele, and complete with all the amenities of tourist life: a huge sun deck and regular pool, plus plenty of shops in the arcade. There's also the excellent Tandoor Restaurant.

The Hawaiian Monarch is part hotel, part condo, and the hotel rooms, which occupy the 7th through 24th floors, all have refrigerators, coffee bars, in-room safes, and bathrooms with full tubs and showers. They are done in modern tropical decor with whitewashed rattan furniture, pastel island-style pictures, and new bedspreads and chairs with color-coordinated fabric. The nicest views are those overlooking the Ala Wai Canal. Studio suites are available with kitchenette or kitchens.

NEAR ALA MOANA

INN ON THE PARK, 1920 Ala Moana Blvd., Honolulu, HI 96815. Tel. 808/946-8355, or toll free 800/922-7866 in the mainland U.S., 800/445-6633 in Canada. Fax 808/922-8785. Telex 634479 ASTHIUW. 134 units. A/C TV TEL
$ Rates: Apr–Dec 21, $67–$100 double; $89–$104 studio. Dec 22–Mar, $82–$100 double; $104 studio. Each additional person $12 per day. AE, CB, DC, MC, V. **Parking:** Limited, $6 per day.

Not far from the Hilton Hawaiian Village and a block from the popular Fort DeRussy Beach, this is a completely renovated hotel/condominium. The smallish but pretty rooms are decorated with floral spreads setting off the modern furnishings and decor. Very helpful for those wishing to fix breakfast or a light lunch are the refrigerators and wet bars in most of the units; kitchenette units are also available. This place would be most suitable for two, or perhaps three, people in a room, but families might find it a bit tight. There's a modern lobby with a convenience store and a nice pool and sun deck on the fifth floor. Castagnola's Restaurant, a favorite, is right on the premises.

Accommodations here are in three classes: standard (city or mountain view); superior (ocean view); and deluxe kitchenette (city view or ocean view), the latter on request only. In standard or superior accommodations, refrigerators and lanais are available on request only.

PAGODA HOTEL, 1525 Rycroft St., Honolulu, HI 96814. Tel. 808/941-6611, or toll free 800/367-6060 in the mainland U.S. and Canada. Fax 808/922-8061. Telex 633101. 361 rms. A/C TV TEL
$ Rates: Pagoda Hotel, $82–$92 single or double. Pagoda Terrace, $76 studio apt; $97 one-bedroom apt; $115 two-bedroom apt. Each additional person $15. AE, CB, DC, DISC, JCB, MC, V. **Parking:** $2 per day.

Although this hotel is about a 10-minute drive from Waikiki, you won't be isolated here: Not only are you near the Ala Moana Shopping Center, but right on the grounds is one of Honolulu's most spectacular restaurants, the Pagoda, with its colorful displays of flashing carp. Two buildings flank Rycroft Street—Pagoda Terrace and the Pagoda Hotel. All rooms at the Pagoda Hotel have been refurbished and are cheery and bright. Rooms at the Pagoda Terrace offer studio apartments nicely set up for housekeeping, with a full-size refrigerator, four-burner range, and all the necessary equipment. One- and two-bedroom apartments also offer plenty of comfort. There are full baths. Two swimming pools are here for dunking.

WAIKIKI PARKSIDE, 1850 Ala Moana Blvd., Honolulu, HI 96815. Tel. 808/955-1567, or toll free 800/237-9666. Fax 808/955-1564. 250 rms, 5 suites. A/C TV TEL
$ Rates: Apr–Dec 19, $99–$130 single or double; $175–$375 suite. Dec 20–Mar, $99–$130 single or double; $175–$375 suite. Children 17 and under stay free in parent's room when using existing bedding. Each additional person 18 and over, $15. AE, CB, DC, DISC, JCB, MC, V. **Parking:** $4 per day.

Located close to Ala Moana Shopping Center and Ala Moana Beach Park, this older hotel has completed a multi-million-dollar renovation and offers cozy, comfortable lodgings at reasonable prices. Newly refurbished guest rooms have rattan furniture, double or queen-size beds, mini-refrigerators, private safes, and tile bathrooms. Guests enjoy the outdoor pool deck with its snack bar and the convenience of having a branch of the popular Denny's chain on hand for meals or snacks 24 hours a day—and for room service too, from 7am to 9pm. Rooms for the disabled and non-smokers are available on request.

WINDWARD OAHU

KE IKI HALE, 59-579 Ke Iki Rd., Haleiwa, HI 96712. Tel. 808/638-8229. 12 units.

$ Rates: $85–$125 one-bedroom unit; $145 one-bedroom cottage; $150–$165 two-bedroom cottage. AE, MC, V. **Parking:** Free.

Here's a place for those who long to be right on the beach, or just a few steps away from it. Alice Tracy's rental cottages on the North Shore are on 1½ acres of palm-fringed land near Waimea Bay. They are nicely furnished, with full kitchens; some have large picture windows overlooking the ocean. Guests can enjoy the barbecue facilities, the picnic tables at water's edge, and a small volleyball court. There's a public telephone on the premises, but not a TV in sight. Remember that Waimea Bay is ideal for swimming in the summer months, but during the winter its sky-high waves are for experienced surfers only.

RODEWAY INN HUKILAU RESORT, 55-109 Laniloa St., Laie, HI 96762. Tel. 808/293-9282, or toll free 800/LANILOA (526-4562). 48 rms. A/C TV TEL

$ Rates: $79 single or double; $89 triple or quad. Children under 8 stay free in parent's room. Weekly packages available. AE, DC, DISC, MC, V. **Parking:** Free.

Located right next door the Polynesian Cultural Center, this modern, motellike building offers lots of comfort and a good location not far from many of the attractions of the North Shore. Right at your feet is a sandy ocean beach and pool; a short drive away is all the swimming surfing, windsurfing, diving, horseback riding, championship golfing, and the like available in the Sunset Beach and Haleiwa area. Waimea Bay offers some of the world's best swimming (in summer) and best surfing (in winter). Waimea Falls Park is delightful, and Haleiwa has many shops and restaurants and an artsy-craftsy atmosphere. Rooms at Rodeway Inn overlook the pool and courtyard and boast refrigerators, microwave ovens (on request), private lanais, and cable TV. The inn is within walking distance of the Brigham Young University Hawaii Campus and the Mormon Temple. Temple-patron rates are available upon request.

SCHRADER'S WINDWARD MARINE RESORT, 47-039 Lihikai Dr., Kaneohe, HI 96744. Tel. 808/239-5711, or toll free 800/735-5711. Fax 808/239-6658. 53 units. A/C TV TEL

$ Rates: $49–$146 one-bedroom; $110–$190 two-bedroom, $170–$320 two-bedroom with den (for up to six persons). Each additional person $7.50. AE, CB, DC, DISC, JCB, MC, V. **Parking:** Free.

On the shores of Kaneohe Bay, this older, rural hotel, about a half-hour drive from both Waikiki and downtown Honolulu, is something special for those who like a country setting. It's a world unto itself, dedicated to introducing the field of marine recreation to its guests. Its own pier services the North Bay Boat Club and Sailing School; daily boat trips are available and a variety of sailboats, Windsurfers, kayaks, and jet boats are also on hand. Beginners can learn how, and experts can just take off.

Five buildings here share a compound bordered by a stream on one side and Kaneohe Bay on the other. There's a swimming pool and a therapy pool (a Jacuzzi with unheated water). Picnic tables and barbecues abound.

Each unit has a living room, bathroom, lanais, and full-size refrigerator; some have kitchen facilities as well. Furnishings are modest but comfortable in this older establishment; you might have an old-fashioned tub instead of a shower. Rooms with waterfront views are more expensive. Daily cleaning service is provided. Three-bedroom suites are also available.

3. HOSTELS, Y'S & A MILITARY HOTEL

HOSTELS

HOSTELLING INTERNATIONAL-WAIKIKI, 2417 Prince Edward St., Hono-lulu, HI 96815. Tel. 808/926-8313. Fax 808/946-5904. 50 beds, 4 studios.
$ Rates: $15 bed; $32 studio. MC, V. **Parking:** $2 per day.
This hostel is just the ticket for beach buffs, since it's 2 short blocks from Waikiki Beach. It's for AYH or IYHF members only (you can purchase a $25 membership at the hostel in Manoa Valley—see below), and offers dormitory accommodations for 20 women and 30 men. Two common rooms provide kitchens, patios, TV, and the relaxed camaraderie for which youth hostels are famous. Dorms are closed and locked from noon to 2pm daily in accordance with the hostel tradition of promoting outdoor life. Couples might consider renting one of the four studios here which feature private bath and shower, mini-refrigerators, private entrance, and 24-hour access to the rooms; some have TV. The staff is helpful with information on low-cost vacationing and travel. Stays are guaranteed for 3 days; they'll let you stay longer if they're not busy.

INTERCLUB HOSTEL WAIKIKI, 2413 Kuhio Ave., Honolulu, HI 96815. Tel. 808/924-2636. 140 beds in shared rms (3-night minimum stay), 11 private rms.
$ Rates: $15 bed; $45 private rm. Each additional person $10. JCB, MC, V. **Parking:** Free but limited, mostly on street.
This hostel, just 2 blocks from the beach at Waikiki, is for international travelers only: You must show a passport and a ticket to a foreign destination. (Foreigners need only show tickets to the United States; Americans must be going beyond Hawaii.) According to one guest we met, "it's the looser of the hostels" in Waikiki, since it's open 24 hours and has no curfew, and there are no chores to be done. Each dorm room, with four or seven bunks, has its own private bath and shower. Private rooms are nicely set up with a couch out front, a bed in the back, and these, too, have their own private baths. There are common rooms, a game room with pool and Ping-Pong tables, a bar with an adjacent TV lounge, laundry facilities, and a friendly atmosphere. Movies on Wednesday and barbecues on Saturday are among the many special events.

NEAR THE UNIVERSITY OF HAWAII

HOSTELLING INTERNATIONAL HONOLULU, 2323A Seaview Ave., Hono-lulu, HI 96822. Tel. 808/946-0591. Fax 808/946-5904. 38 beds.
$ Rates: $12 members; $15 nonmembers. JCB, MC, V. **Parking:** Free.
In lovely Manoa Valley, this hostel facility has developed a reputation over the past 24 years as a safe, clean, friendly environment for world travelers. Nonmembers are accepted. There are beds for 18 women and 20 men. Common rooms, a kitchen, a Ping-Pong table, games, and a patio under the stars create a relaxed mood here. House parents Thelma and Susan Akau are helpful sources of information. Waikiki is a 10-minute bus ride away. Walking, hiking, and restaurant tours are available. Many restaurants are available within a quarter mile. Facilities are locked between 10am and 5pm daily.

Note: Hostels are for "the young at heart, regardless of age," although students—Australian, European, Canadian, Japanese, as well as American—do predominate. Simple chores are expected of all guests.

THREE Y'S

WAIKIKI

CENTRAL BRANCH YMCA, 401 Atkinson Dr., Honolulu, HI 96814. Tel. 808/941-3344. Fax 808/941-8821. 114 rms. TEL

$ Rates: $30 single without bath, $36.50 single with bath; $43 double without bath, $51.50 double with bath. Weekly rates available. AE, MC, V. **Parking:** Free 6pm–6am.

Located across the street from Ala Moana Beach Park and the Ala Moana Shopping Center, just a five-minute bus ride to the heart of Waikiki, this is a good choice for the single male tourist as well as couples (women are allowed only in those rooms with a private bath). It's a beautiful place, complete with an outdoor swimming pool and lovely grounds. The "Y-style" rooms are small but adequate, and you can add a rollaway bed to create a double. The Y has a reasonably priced coffee shop, a large-screen TV in the residents' lounge, and no end of recreational activities; guests are welcome to use all athletic facilities, including the weight-training center and racquetball courts. Reservations are accepted and welcomed.

DOWNTOWN HONOLULU

FERNHURST YWCA, 1566 Wilder Ave., Honolulu, HI 96822. Tel. 808/941-2231. 60 rms (all with adjoining bath). TEL

$ Rates (including two meals Mon–Fri): $28 single for YWCA members, $33 for non-members; $20 per person double for YWCA members, $25 per person for nonmembers. No credit cards. **Parking:** Limited parking at daily, weekly, and monthly rates.

For women tourists who'd like to stay at a Y, Honolulu has a terrific answer. Women can stay for up to 6 months at this pleasant tropical residence about halfway between downtown Honolulu and Waikiki. The residence accepts both short- and long-term visitors, many of the latter from afar. So staying here is a good way to get to know people from many countries and backgrounds. The accommodations consist of nicely furnished double rooms, each joined to another room by a common bath. Sometimes single rooms are available. Y membership ($30) is required for stays longer than 3 nights. Rates include two meals a day on weekdays—surely one of the best buys in town! Linens may be rented for a nominal fee if you don't provide your own. Pluses include a swimming pool, garden, laundry room, and a lounge area. Also available for use: typewriters, piano, TV, sewing machine. Advance reservations are accepted with a 1-night deposit. Fernhurst recommends that you write first to inquire about future accommodations.

NUUANU YMCA, 1441 Pali Hwy., Honolulu, HI 96813. Tel. 808/536-3556. 70 rms.

$ Rates: $28–$30 single. Weekly rates available. AE, MC, V.

For men only, this modern, $1.3-million facility downtown, convenient to bus lines, is a good bet. Advance reservations are accepted. There's a cafeteria here, excellent athletic facilities are made available to residents, and local phone calls are free.

READERS RECOMMEND

University of Hawaii at Manoa. *"Might I suggest to your readers that they visit Hawaii as I did? I spent 6 weeks in Honolulu as a student at the University of Hawaii at Manoa. The cost of dorm room and board was very economical. Many tours, at special prices, were provided through the university. Our summer student-identity*

cards even got us 'kamaaina' rates at various clubs and attractions. We were often roomed with local students and were thus able to share our different cultures. This is not just meant for single students; there were some dorm facilities for couples. The course selection is wide, ranging from golf and tennis to more academic studies. By the end of 6 weeks, I was referring to the dorm as 'home.'"
—Susan McEwin, Stratford, Ontario, Canada.

HOTEL FOR THE MILITARY

HALE KOA HOTEL, Armed Forces Recreation Center, Fort DeRussy, 2055 Kalia Rd., Honolulu, HI 96815-1998. Tel. 808/955-0555, or toll free 800/ 367-6027. Fax 800/943-0707. 419 rms. A/C TV TEL
$ Rates (depending on rank): $47–$75 standard, $56–$87 superior, $62–$89 park view, $70–$106 ocean view, $82–$114 oceanfront. Single occupancy deduct $2; more than two persons, add $10 per person. Children under 12 stay free in parent's room using existing bedding. Cribs $4. AE, CB, DC, MC, V. **Parking:** Free.
This hotel has a select guest list: It's available only to active-duty and retired military of all services, including Reserve and National Guard members, and their families. What a deal! Fronting a superb stretch of Waikiki Beach next door to the posh Hilton Hawaiian Village, it's comparable to many first-class beachfront hotels in Waikiki, and prices, depending on one's rank, are far less than what one pays in regular hotels. Reservations can be hard to come by; they can be made up to a year in advance, and are often honored within a much shorter time period. Rooms are of good size and nicely furnished, and most have two double beds. There's a pool, fitness center with sauna, volleyball and racquetball courts, and many services on the premises, including a Post Exchange, a military discount travel office, laundry facilities, and car-rental desk.

One needn't, however, be a guest at Hale Koa to use many of its facilities. In addition, military club members and DOD civilian employees are also welcome to enjoy many of the dining and recreational facilities, including a Sunday Champagne Brunch at the Hale Koa Room, and shows that include a delicious dinner or buffet: Tama's Polynesian Revue on Wednesday, Hale Koa Luau on Monday and Friday, and a Tuesday-night Magic Show.

4. AT THE AIRPORT

HONOLULU AIRPORT MINI HOTEL, Main Terminal Central Lobby, Honolulu International Airport. Tel. 808/836-3044. Fax 808/834-8985. 17 rms.
$ Rates (per person, single occupancy only): $30 sleep and shower (8 hr.), $17.50 nap and shower (2 hr.), $7.50 for shower only, including towels and toiletries. MC, V.

★ Here's something every airline traveler should know about—just in case. In case your plane departure is delayed, in case you have to wait several hours to make a connecting flight, in case you arrive late at night and there's no interisland plane service until the next morning—or in case you simply need a place to go if you've checked out of your hotel early and have a late-night flight. That's where the Honolulu Airport Mini Hotel comes in. This clean and pleasant facility offers private rooms and resting facilities and the opportunity to take a shower. "Travelers travel under stress," says owner Mona Dunn. "When they walk in this door, the stress ends." Each guest receives personal attention and a real feeling of aloha. There's a coffee pot perpetually brewing, plus a kitchen where flowers or medication can be refrigerated. The Honolulu Airport Mini Hotel is open 24 hours a day. Reservations are advised for sleeping space; they are usually booked after 10pm.

5. BED & BREAKFASTS

Hawaii Kai, Kailua, and Kaneuhe are suburban, easygoing, and just a few miles but seemingly worlds away from the hustle-bustle of Waikiki. We've picked a handful of B&Bs in this area, where you can enjoy rural charm, but be in town in a half hour or less when you crave excitement.

In addition to the following, see "Enjoying Hawaii on a Budget" in Chapter 2 for information on several organizations that will hook you up with the perfect bed and breakfast.

HAWAII KAI

JOAN WEBB AND BARBARA ABE, P.O. Box 25907, Honolulu, HI 96825. Tel. 808/396-9462. 2 rms (1 with bath). TV
$ Rates (including breakfast): $55–$65 double. No credit cards. **Parking:** Free.
If you'd like a bed-and-breakfast accommodation close to Hanauma Bay and Sea Life Park (and about a 25-minute drive from Waikiki), contact Mrs. Joan Webb, or her daughter, Barbara Abe—two Englishwomen who have a beautiful home, with garden and swimming pool, in Hawaii Kai. The larger room, with access to the pool area, has a queen-size bed, a small refrigerator, and a private bath. The smaller room, also cozy, has a double bed and shares a bath with the hosts. Joan and Barbara prepare full island breakfasts for their guests, who join them for fresh fruits, juices, homemade breads, English muffins, cereals, and beverages. They are generous with sightseeing advice and tips and also provide beach mats and towels.

KAILUA

AKAMAI BED AND BREAKFAST, 172 Kuumele Place, Kailua, HI 96734. Tel. 808/261-2227, or toll free 800/642-5366. 2 studios (with bath). TV
$ Rates: $60 double. Each additional person $10, to a maximum of four. Minimum stay 3 nights. No credit cards. **Parking:** Free.
Three blocks and an 8-minute walk from the beautiful white sand beaches of Kailua is this charming home. A separate wing from the main house has two spacious studios, each with its own kitchen, including a refrigerator and microwave oven. The refrigerator is stocked with some breakfast foods, and guests are free to do light cooking. Guests enjoy the convenience of the pool and lanai in a lovely tropical setting. Diane Van Ryzin and her husband, Joe, are cordial hosts.

Kailua is about a half-hour drive from Waikiki; its beaches are what Waikiki's used to be like, before the crowds.

LANIKAI BED & BREAKFAST, 1277 Mokulua Dr., Kailua, HI 96734. Tel. 808/261-1059. 1 studio, 1 apt (with bath). TV TEL
$ Rates: $55 garden studio, $85 one-bedroom apt, single or double. No credit cards. **Parking:** Free.

If you love being right on the beach, you can't beat this one. Mahina and Homer Maxey's large, comfortable home is just across the street from idyllic Lanikai Beach with its soft white sand and inviting, always-calm water. There's a large covered lanai in front, with banana trees, lawa'e ferns, and plentyof tables and chairs. The studio, which has a private entrance, is at the back of the house overlooking the garden with a stunning view of what many consider the most beautiful mountains in the islands—the Windward Koolaus. There's a queen-size bed, a sitting room/TV area, and a kitchen/dining area, complete with microwave, refrigerator and coffee maker. Upstairs is a spacious apartment with a living room/dining area, a den, one bedroom with a queen-size bed, refrigerator, coffee maker, toaster, and a small appliances for light meal preparation. Every few days

Mahina will bring homemade bread, muffins, juice, and coffee for your continental breakfast. There are ceiling fans, lots of beautiful plants, and, of course, that heavenly beach just across the street. By the way, both Maxeys are from old kamaaina families; ask Mahina about the family photos.

SHARON'S SERENITY, 127 Kakahiaka St., Kailua, HI 96734. Tel. 808/ 263-3834. 2 rms with private baths. TV TEL

$ Rates: $50–$55 single; $55–$60 double.

Sharon and Bob Price's lovely home is located on a quiet residential street a short walk from Kailua Beach. The house is decorated in an elegant Oriental and contemporary style enhanced by Sharon's striking floral arrangements. The two-room suite has a sitting room with a comfortable daybed, ceiling fans, small refrigerator, a queen-size bed, and a full bath with tub and shower and a door opening to the pool area. The Blue Room also has a queen-size bed, ceiling fans, and a small refrigerator. The Yellow Room, with twin beds and TV, can be used as an extra room if three people are traveling together; it shares the bath with the Blue Room. Each room has its own color TV, but guests are welcome to join the Prices in their spacious living room, with its three huge comfy couches, big TV, many plants, and plenty of books. The setting is gorgeous, with a pool, beautiful flowers, Kaelepulu Stream running by, and views of a private golf course and mountains. A cuddly Bichon Frise named Trouble (a misnomer if we've ever heard one) completes the Price ménage. A good breakfast is served; a washer/dryer is available at a small fee.

SHEFFIELD HOUSE BED & BREAKFAST, 131 Kuulei Rd., Kailua, HI 96734. Tel. 808/262-0721. 1 rm, 1 one-bedroom suite (both with bath).

$ Rates: $40 double; $60 one-bedroom suite; $95 two-bedroom suite. Minimum stay 3 days; monthly rates on request. No credit cards. **Parking:** Free.

Architects Paul and Rachel Sheffield and three bouncy little Sheffield children comprise the household here. Their house is in an ongoing process of renovation, but the cozy guest accommodations are all finished. Each has a private entrance, Mexican tile floors, bright tropical-print bedspread and accessories, and a kitchen area with a refrigerator, microwave, toaster oven, and coffee maker. The suite has its own sitting room, a small dining area, a queen-size bed in the bedroom, and a view of its own private garden. The room, which is wheelchair-accessible, has a queen-size bed. The two units may be combined as a two-bedroom/two-bath suite. There's no pool, but who needs one when you're just a hop, skip and a jump from beautiful Kailua beach. *Note:* Complimentary continental breakfast is provided on the first day only.

KANEOHE

A 5-STAR BED AND BREAKFAST—BJG'S, 44-491 Kaneohe Bay Dr., Kaneohe, HI 96744. Tel. 808/235-8235 or toll free 800/235-5214. 3 rms (1 with private bath).

$ Rates: $65 and $75 single or double. No credit cards. **Parking:** Free.

Next door to the posh Kaneohe Bay Yacht Club is the movie set–style home of Bonnie and Richard Green. We were entranced by the magnificent Italian tile pool nestled in a tropical garden and guarded by two stone lions; at night the area is illuminated by tiki torches. The house is decorated in an Asian motif with some extraordinary antiques and pictures. The living room has a great collection of books and magazines, which guests are invited to peruse. Two rooms share a bathroom; one has twin beds and the other has a queen-size bed. The master bedroom, which has a king-size bed, overlooks the pool area. Both bathrooms are gracefully appointed, with makeup lights and private garden views. Breakfast is served in the dining room or by the pool. The entire home, which comfortably sleeps six adults and four children, can be rented for $250 daily, with a 7-day minimum. There's a 20% discount for 1 month or more.

ALI'I BLUFF'S BED & BREAKFAST, 46-251 Ikiiki St., Kaneohe, HI 96744. Tel. 808/235-1124. 2 rms (with bath).

$ Rates: $50 Circus Room; $55 Victorian Room. No credit cards. **Parking:** Free.

⭐ Set in a lush tropical garden with a pool, this charming home is filled to the brim with Victorian antiques—toys, posters, teddy bears, ornaments—and fine paintings, reminders of the days when hosts L. De Chambs and Donald Munro ran an art gallery in New York. Now they're here in Hawaii, in a gracious home overlooking Kaneohe Bay. Their guest wing consists of the Victorian Room, with a wonderful old china doll on its double bed, and an attached private bath. The Circus Room has antique teddy bears on each of the twin beds, circus posters from all over the world on the walls, and a private bath across the corridor. The hosts are delightfully warm people who enjoy having their guests in for late-afternoon tea in the living room and library. And they serve breakfast—fruits, cereal, juices, toast, and coffee—out on the pool lanai whenever guests wish.

HULA KAI HALE, 44-002 Hulakai Place, Kaneohe, HI 96744. Tel. 808/ 236-6754. 2 rms (with bath).

$ Rates: King Room $60; with den for extra person, $25; Queen Room $50 single, $55 double.

⭐ Take an idyllic location right on Kaneohe Bay, a wonderful house with a swimming pool fronting the bay, and a pair of gracious hosts, and you have Hula Kai Hale, the House of the Dancing Water. Tom and Ditty Pico, long-time Hawaiian residents, thoroughly enjoy having guests and give them the run of the house. They serve an ample breakfast each morning poolside on the large lanai, just next door to the Kaneohe Yacht Club. There are two nicely decorated bedrooms, each with color TV, ceiling fans, cross ventilation, built-in dressers, rattan furniture, bar/refrigerator, coffeemaker, microwave, toaster oven and crock pot—it's easy to do your own cooking here. The King Room, which has an adjacent den with a king-size daybed, is perfect for a family; it has a garden view. The Queen Room has both garden and pool views; each room has its own spacious modern bathroom and an exit to the outdoors. Nearby you'll find a shopping center, restaurants, and movie theaters; about a 10-minute drive away are Kailua and Lanikai, two of the best beaches in Hawaii.

CHAPTER 6

HONOLULU DINING

1. WAIKIKI
2. BEYOND WAIKIKI
3. SPECIALTY DINING
4. IN NEARBY KAILUA & KANEOHE

Can the average tourist still find romance, happiness, and a good, inexpensive meal in Hawaii? Well, we won't make any promises on the first two counts (that's up to you), but on the third we can be quite positive. Despite inflation everywhere, Honolulu's restaurants still do very well for the tourist. Although the price for dinner at one of the really elegant restaurants can easily zoom into the stratosphere, there are still plenty of places where you can get a terrific meal for under $20. And there are also lots of places where you can eat well for under $12. To keep on a really tight budget, plan to eat breakfast and at least one meal a day at home; that's when your kitchenette apartment more than pays for itself. Remember that lunch is always cheaper than dinner—and often it's almost the same meal. Early Bird specials offer excellent dinner bargains all over town.

1. WAIKIKI

DIAMOND HEAD WAIKIKI

MEALS FOR LESS THAN $12

MONGOLIAN BAR-B-QUE, at Kuhio Mall, 2301 Kuhio Ave. Tel. 923-2445.
  Cuisine: MONGOLIAN. **Reservations:** Not accepted.
$ Prices: Appetizers $4–$5; main courses $7–$16. AE, MC, V.
  Open: Daily 10am–10pm.
The culinary adventurers among you will want to experience the cuisine here, which is indeed different. Seems that a very special dish in the northern part of China is strips of beef, barbecued with vegetables and spices, and this is one of the few restaurants we know of in Honolulu that serves it. You select your own meats, sauces, vegetables, and spices and pass them on to the chefs, who then cook them in an open fire pit. Complete dinners, from $10.95 for barbecued chicken to $12 for New York steak, come with crisp wun tun chips or an egg roll, chicken vegetable soup and salad, fresh vegetables, rice or fries, and dessert. For $16, adults ($8.95 for kids under 10) can have the full barbecue with seconds. Or have a "quick meal" or "mini meal"—the chefs make the selection—at $7 and $6. Also available: lunch plates, soups, salads, beers, wines, and cocktails. The barbecue has quite an unexpected taste, but many local people are addicted to it. It's one of those things you have to experience for yourself to judge.

NA'S BAR-B-QUE, in the Royal Grove Hotel, 151 Uluniu Ave. Tel. 926-9717 for take-out orders.
  Cuisine: KOREAN. **Reservations:** Not accepted.
$ Prices: Appetizers $5; main courses $3–$7.
  Open: Daily 6am–9pm.

If you like tasty Korean barbecue dishes, you'll be thrilled to discover Na's, where it's no trick at all to have a hearty meal for around $7. Each of the dishes, like our favorite, the barbecued chicken, or the barbecued beef, or fish jun, or the hot spicy chicken wings, comes with a choice of vegetables, plus two scoops of rice. The hot noodle and soup dishes are also delicious. This is a tiny place, with a counter inside (always seemingly jammed with Koreans, by the way), and just a few tables outside. Lots of condo dwellers nearby come here for take-out and go back home to feast.

RUFFAGE NATURAL FOODS, in the Royal Grove Hotel, 2443 Kuhio Ave. Tel. 922-2042.
   Cuisine: VEGETARIAN/SUSHI BAR. **Reservations:** Not accepted.
$ Prices: Main vegetarian courses $3.25–$6.75.
   Open: Mon–Sat 8:30am–7pm, Sun 10am–6pm; sushi bar, Mon–Sun 6pm–midnight.
What a treat to find a health-food store, restaurant, and juice bar right in the heart of the busy Waikiki scene and just a block from the beach. Ruffage specializes in organic foods and those that are as free as possible of processing, all modestly priced. They serve freshly squeezed juices; good fruit and vegetable salads; lunch and dinner dishes on the order of whole-wheat spaghetti with chili-and-cheese or veggie burritos; sandwiches like zucchini-cheese or tofu-tuna, on multigrain bread, stuffed with tomatoes and sprouts and practically a meal in themselves ($3.50 to $5.85), and yummy shakes and smoothies. At the front of the store is an authentic Japanese sushi bar, where you can order by the piece (yes, they have vegetable sushi). Take it out and go to the beach, or dine here at one of the several open-to-the-street tables. While you're here, pick up a few organically grown papayas to take back to your hotel for breakfast.

READERS RECOMMEND

Jack-in-the-Box, 134 Kapahulu Ave. (tel. 922-2235). "One of the few high-quality fast-food eateries in Waikiki is the Jack-in-the-Box restaurant next door to the Waikiki Grand Hotel. Here the customer can have h is choice of window-booth dining with views of the Honolulu Zoo across the street, sitting at one of the tables in back facing a pool and courtyard, or simply ordering "to go." Highly recommended, among the many fine budget offerings, which include hamburgers, chicken, steak sandwiches, and shrimp, are the various Breakfast Crescents stuffed with combinations of bacon, eggs, ham, and cheeses, from $1.99 to $3.49. This spot deserves recognition!"—Connie Tonken, Hartford, Conn.

W. C. Peacock Restaurant, in the Sheraton Moana Surfrider, 2365 Kalakaua Ave. (tel. 922-3111). "Granted, the normal prices here are heady, but they have a Sunset Special fixed-price meal from 5:30 to 6:30pm for $15.95. This is a gem! If you're celebrating a birthday or anniversary, let the maître d' know and voila! singing waiter, cake, and candle. The meal is served with decorum and elegance. We had two choices: teriyaki chicken or mahimahi, including an excellent salad bar and delicious soup served with fresh, warm buns. Our choice, teriyaki chicken, was succulent, served on a bed of tasty rice pilaf and veggies. The dessert was a large piece of scrumptious lemon cake with meringue and icing. Sipping a glass of house wine (red or white Mondavi, $5 a glass) was pure luxury, while we contemplated the setting sun and the passing parade on the beach from this luxurious patio restaurant . . . a must!"—J. A. Douin, Edmonton, Alberta, Canada.

CENTRAL WAIKIKI

MEALS FOR LESS THAN $16

CHILI'S GRILL AND BAR, 2350 Kuhio Ave. Tel. 922-9697.
   Cuisine: AMERICAN/SOUTHWESTERN. **Reservations:** Not accepted.
$ Prices: Appetizers $1.95–$7.95; main courses $6.45–$13.95. AE, DC, DISC, MC, V.

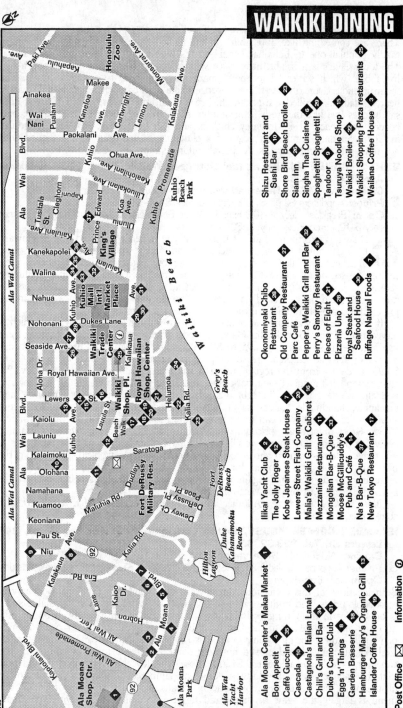

WAIKIKI DINING

Shizu Restaurant and Sushi Bar
Shore Bird Beach Broiler
Siam Inn
Singha Thai Cuisine
Spaghetti! Spaghetti!
Tandoor
Tsuruya Noodle Shop
Waikiki Broiler
Waikiki Shopping Plaza restaurants
Wailana Coffee House

Okonomiyaki Chibo Restaurant
Old Company Restaurant
Parc Café
Pepper's Waikiki Grill and Bar
Perry's Smorgy Restaurant
Pieces of Eight
Pizzeria Uno
Royal Steak and Seafood House
Ruffage Natural Foods

Ilikai Yacht Club
The Jolly Roger
Kobe Japanese Steak House
Lewers Street Fish Company
Malia's Waikiki Grill & Cabaret
Mezzanine Restaurant
Mongolian Bar-B-Que
Moose McGillicuddy's Pub and Café
Na's Bar-B-Que
New Tokyo Restaurant

Ala Moana Center's Makai Market
Bon Appetit
Caffè Guccini
Cascada
Castagnola's Italian Lanai
Chili's Grill and Bar
Duke's Canoe Club
Eggs 'n' Things
Garden Brasserie
Hamburger Mary's Organic Grill
Islander Coffee House

Post Office ⊠   Information ❶

Open: Breakfast daily 6:30–11am; lunch and dinner daily 11am–11pm.
There are something like 300 Chili's in the United States and Canada—including a madly popular one in Lahaina, Maui—so it's high time there was one in Waikiki! The local Chili's is a bright, busy place with booths, tables, many plants, and a big, lively bar, which serves "Top Shelf" margaritas (the best) to a happy crowd. The menu includes a bit of everything: appetizers like chicken nachos and buffalo wings; hearty salads like grilled Caribbean chicken and shrimp Caesar; burger platters; nifty sandwiches (we like the fresh fish); Southwestern grill specialties, such as fajitas; barbecued baby back ribs; Monterey chicken; and fish of the day. For dessert, indulge in Chili's Sundae—vanilla ice cream in a cinnamon-coated flour tortilla topped with hot fudge or cinnamon apples. A special children's menu is available.

DUKE'S CANOE CLUB, at the Outrigger Waikiki Hotel, 2335 Kalakaua Ave. Tel. 922-2268.
Cuisine: AMERICAN. **Reservations:** Recommended.
$ Prices: Appetizers $2.95–$7.95; main courses $7.95–$19.95.
Open: Breakfast daily 7–10:30am; Barefoot Bar Menu daily 11am–midnight; dinner daily 5–10pm; cocktails daily 11:30–1am.

Duke's is exactly the kind of restaurant you hoped you would find in Hawaii. It's right out there on the beach, romantic in the old Hawaiian style, with thatched umbrellas, teak chairs, and photographs and other memorabilia recalling the legend of Duke Kahanamoku, the great surfer and Olympic swimming champion, long known as Hawaii's "Ambassador of Aloha," to whom the restaurant is dedicated. Duke would have loved it; so do we—especially since you can enjoy all this atmosphere and still dine well for very little money.

If you're really watching the budget, order from the Barefoot Bar Menu, which is served from 11am to midnight. Hawaiian local plates—stir-fry chicken cashew, fresh fish and the like—go from $8.95 to $9.95. Sandwiches like roast beef and Cheddar *au jus* or teriyaki chicken breast, burgers, pizza, and pasta, range from $6.45 to $6.95. Ordering from the regular menu is still reasonable: fresh fish of the day, Pacific seafood fettuccine, Koloa pork ribs, and Polynesian chicken are all well priced, and all include a trip to the fabulous salad bar, which includes fresh papayas and pineapple, handmade Caesar salad, freshly baked muffins, sourdough rolls, and steamed rice. In fact, you can make your entire meal off the salad bar alone for just $7.95. Keiki dinners are priced from $4.50 to $5.95, so bring the whole family. Now for desserts: Of course you'll have to have Kimo's original hula pie ("this is what the sailors swam to shore for"), and some fabulous tropical drinks from the bar. And if you hang around for the local Hawaiian entertainment, which takes place from 4 to 6pm and again from 10pm to midnight, you could easily while away the better part of your vacation here.

Note to breakfast buffs: Another winner is the breakfast buffet, a full hot and cold buffet, for $9.95.

ISLANDER COFFEE HOUSE, in the Outrigger Reef Towers Hotel, 247 Lewers St. Tel. 923-3233.
Cuisine: AMERICAN. **Reservations:** Not accepted.
$ Prices: Appetizers (salads) $1.95–$5.45; main courses $7.25–$9.45. No credit cards.
Open: Daily 6am–11pm.

Both locations of this coffeehouse are always dependable for excellent food at very reasonable prices, and both are impeccably clean and attractive. The original Islander is oceanfront in the Outrigger Reef Tower Hotel; the newer, and much bigger one, at 150 Kaiulani Ave., is in the Outrigger East Hotel. Visit whichever one you happen to be closest to, and you won't go wrong. At both you can get their famous fresh-baked orange bread, served hot with dinner, as french toast, or as dessert; you can even take home a loaf for $1.75. Those who love breakfast food should note that the Islanders serve breakfast all day: the Jamboree Breakfast, a favorite, offers all the pancakes you can eat, plus bacon or sausage, and two eggs, for $4.95. The menu is largely the same at lunch and dinner. At dinner, along with your main course—perhaps mahimahi, teriyaki steak, or shrimp-fry platter—you get home-style soup or salad, potatoes or rice, plus hot orange bread. Don't miss one of their great pies from their Yum Yum Tree Bakery—maybe macadamia-nut cream, coconut cream, or the "pie of the month."

LEWERS STREET FISH COMPANY, in the Outrigger Reef Towers Hotel, 247 Lewers St. Tel. 971-1000.
Cuisine: SEAFOOD/PASTA. **Reservations:** Not required.
$ Prices: Appetizers 95¢–$3.95; main courses $5.95–$14.95. AE, MC, JCB, V.
Open: Dinner only, daily 5–11pm.
It doesn't surprise us a bit to see the lines in front of this restaurant at dinnertime. This place has just about everything a hungry tourist could want: great tasty food, an attractive ambience with sparkling tiled floors, a piano bar, a '40s decorative scheme, and prices that are downright appetizing. There are a number of main dishes under $10, such as mahimahi fish-and-chips, beer-batter mahimahi, teriyaki beef kebabs, garlic chicken, and fisherman's pasta Alfredo, a house specialty. Fresh fish from their own fishing boat is featured ("subject to season and condition of the weather and our captain"), and it is handsomely presented on an oversize, fish-shaped platter. All dinners come with a choice of rice, french fries, or fresh garlic pasta (we recommend the latter) and freshly baked bread. Start your meal with an excellent seafood chowder and end with one of their homemade cheesecakes, each only $2.95. There's entertainment at the piano bar nightly from 6 to 11pm.

MALIA'S WAIKIKI GRILL & CABARET, 311 Lewers St. Tel. 922-7808.
Cuisine: AMERICAN. **Reservations:** Not accepted.
$ Prices: Appetizers $2.50–$5.95; main courses $5.95–$13.95.
Open: Daily 11am–9:30pm; late night menu til 11:30pm; full bar til 4am.
Tasty American grill with an island flair, great prices, and a fun and friendly atmosphere are the big draws here. Pastas, seafood, salads, plate lunch specials (a local favorite), plus sizzling steaks and steak and lobster, bring in the crowds. A large bar covers one side of the restaurant, and there are paneled walls, wood floors, and a large photomural of Diamond Head, circa 1910. There's free live Hawaiian music Wednesday through Saturday. Monday and Tuesday is Karaoke Night, where you're encouraged to "sing the hits you want to hear!" Sunday is "Hot Country" Night with country music, dancing, and entertainment.

MOOSE McGILLYCUDDYS PUB AND CAFE, 310 Lewers St. Tel. 923-0751.
Cuisine: AMERICAN. **Reservations:** Not accepted.
$ Prices: Appetizers $4.95–$8.95; main courses $5.95–$10.95. AE, DC, MC, V.
Open: Daily 8am–2am.
Although it's primarily a night spot (see "Evening Entertainment," in Chapter 7), the Moose is well worth knowing about when the daytime hungries hit. It's very popular among the local folks, since portions are large and prices very reasonable. It opens for breakfast at 8am, when you can catch the Early Bird Breakfast Special—two eggs, bacon, toast or rice or potatoes, and orange juice—a great buy for $2.69. Three-egg omelets with various meats and vegetables, accompanied by rice and toast, are $5.50. Lunch and dinner feature such fare as gourmet hamburgers, several Mexican dishes, hot soups, sandwiches, good salads, and hot specials, like roast prime rib of beef, teriyaki chicken breast, and mahimahi. The Moose serves up great margaritas and daiquiris for $4—and to go with them, fried potato skins or nachos packed on the plate. There's a half-price happy hour from 4 to 8pm, and live rock 'n' roll bands with dancing to Top 40 hits from 9pm to 1:30am daily.
There's another Moose at 1035 University Ave. (tel. 944-5525), where the UH kids hang out, and it's a lot of fun, too.

PEPPER'S WAIKIKI GRILL AND BAR, 150 Kaiulani Ave. Tel. 926-4374.
Cuisine: TEX-MEX. **Reservations:** Not accepted.
$ Prices: Appetizers $3.75–$7.45; main courses $4.95–$15.25. AE, CB, DC, JCB, MC, V.
Open: Daily 11:30am–2am.

Here you are in the tropics, but you love the desert, too. What to do? Ride that lonesome trail to Pepper's, a hybrid of the islands and the Southwest, sprouting both cacti and palm trees, and serving some of the best Tex-Mex food in town. It's a casual, yet sophisticated spot in the very heart of Waikiki, dominated by a lively bar (watch out for those frosty margaritas!) but with well-spaced booths and tables conducive to good conversation. The secret ingredients here are the Kiawe woodsmoke oven that gives a true barbecue taste to the chicken and ribs, and the lava rock grill that turns out super burgers and steaks. In addition to the Mexican dishes, you can order smoke-oven baby back ribs and excellent salads, including the Cobb and the chicken-taco salad. Nachos, sandwiches, quesadillas, and yummy potato skins offer inexpensive and tempting possibilities for grazing. For dessert, try hula pie, a specialty of Hawaii, or fried ice cream, a specialty of Mexico (no, it's not really fried, but in such a simpatico spot, it's hard to quibble). There are no less than two Happy Hours here: from 2 to 6pm and from 10:30pm until closing. A full menu is served till 1:30am nightly.

PIZZERIA UNO, 2256 Kuhio Ave. Tel. 926-0646.
   Cuisine: ITALIAN. **Reservations:** Not accepted.
 $ Prices: Appetizers $1.95–$5.25; main courses $7.95–$11.95. MC, V.
   Open: Daily 11am–midnight.
This one's a great favorite with the younger crowd. Although it serves all sorts of good things—burgers, chili, salads (seafood, spinach, Caesar, and antipasto)—the specialty here is definitely the Chicago-style deep-dish pizza. We're especially fond of the Sea Delico, with the flavor of shrimp and crab; the steak and cheese; and the chicken fajita pizza, sizzling strips of marinated chicken breast, with a blend of cheeses, peppers, and onions. Pizzas come in two sizes: individual, priced from $6.75; and a larger size that serves two or three, priced from $13.45. Beer is at hand, by the glass or bottle. The full-service bar also dispenses some of the best piña coladas in town.
   There are two good lunch specials: pizza and salad or soup for $5.95, or spaghetti with garlic bread and salad for $6.45.

SHORE BIRD BEACH BROILER, in the Outrigger Reef Hotel, 2169 Kalia Rd. Tel. 922-2887.
   Cuisine: SEAFOOD/STEAK. **Reservations:** Not accepted.
 $ Prices: Main courses $6.95–$16.95. AE, JCB, MC, V.
   Open: Daily 7:30am–10pm.
It's not hard to figure out why this spot quickly became one of the most popular restaurants in Waikiki. First of all, you can't beat the location: The large, attractively decorated open dining room is right on Waikiki Beach. Second, the food is good; and third, the price is right because you're the chef, broiling your own portion of teriyaki chicken, ribs, fresh fish, seafood, New York steak, ground steak, or top sirloin. While the fire is doing its work, you can have a few drinks, then fill up on salad bar, chili, rice, and fresh pastas, all included in the price of your main course. Dessert (including their homemade cheesecake) is extra. This is the perfect place for sunset drinks and dinner. Early Bird specials are from 5 to 6:30pm. They also have an all-you-can-eat breakfast buffet at $6.95, served until 11am.

SIAM INN, 407 Seaside Ave. Tel. 926-8802.
   Cuisine: THAI. **Reservations:** Recommended at dinner.
 $ Prices: Appetizers $2.75–$7.25; main courses $7.95–$18.45. AE, MC, V.
   Open: Lunch Mon–Sat 11am–3pm; dinner daily 5–10:30pm.
A touch of Thai lives in Waikiki. This pretty, second-floor restaurant is the place to make, or renew, acquaintance with the subtle (and not-so-subtle) spiceries of Thai cuisine. Dine inside in a setting of white walls covered with colorful murals of Thai scenery, crisp green tablecloths, and tile floors; or outside on a little balcony under potted trees. When last we lunched here, the daily specials, $6.95, were Bangkok chicken, served with rice and the chefs special soup, and the chicken masaman curry—slices of tender chicken on a bed of avocado, peanuts, and coconut milk,

served with curried rice and cucumber sauce (mild or hot). Other luncheon possibilities are also very reasonable (there are 12 dishes at $7.50) and include a variety of noodle dishes featuring chicken, beef, port, or shrimp. Your waiter will ask if you wish your meal mild, hot, or very hot (for newcomers to Thai cooking, mild is the safest). Main dishes, which are also priced reasonably, include chicken, beef, pork, shrimp, and rice dishes, as well as fish specialties.

SPAGHETTI! SPAGHETTI!, in the Royal Hawaiian Shopping Center, 2201 Kalakaua Ave. Tel. 922-7724.
   Cuisine: ITALIAN. **Reservations:** Not Required.
$ Prices: Spaghetti buffet and salad bar $5.99 lunch, $6.99 dinner. AE, DC, JCB, MC, V.
   Open: Daily 11am–10pm.
Everybody seems to like spaghetti, so it's good to know that you can eat your fill—from a spaghetti buffet and salad bar—for small prices. This is a large multilevel restaurant with stylish furnishings, a huge and busy bar, and, on the buffet table, a choice of four different pastas, four freshly made sauces, and a variety of salad ingredients. Salad bar alone is $3.95; with soup, it's $4.95; and with the pastas, $6.99. A $2 slice of garlic bread rounds out the meal nicely. Also available are soups; hot meatloaf, mahimahi, and other sandwiches; chicken in a basket; and a giant burger. Top off a not-exactly-slimming meal here with cheesecake or a super Baskin-Robbins mud pie.

TSURUYA NOODLE SHOP, 325 Lewers St. Tel. 922-3434.
   Cuisine: JAPANESE. **Reservations:** Not accepted.
$ Prices: Main courses $4.75–$6.75. MC, JCB, V.
   Open: Mon–Sat 11am–10pm, Sun 11am–9pm.
We're great fans of Japanese noodle houses: They're just the ticket for those times you want a simple, tasty, nutritious, and extremely low-cost meal. So we were delighted to find this sparkling, clean little place with a horseshoe-shaped-counter in the middle, four tables with comfortable leather chairs, and some mirror-framed paintings on the walls. Try the hot soba broth called sansai, with vegetables and garnishes, or the teriyaki chicken teishoku—grilled marinated chicken and salad, which comes with miso soup and pickled vegetables—two hearty meals for $5.49 and $6.29, respectively. Cold soba (buckwheat) noodles are available, as are various other Japanese dishes, and side orders of shrimp tempura, cooked in "100% vegetable oil." Your food is served promptly, on a lacquered tray in a beautiful bowl. Take-out orders are available.

WAIKIKI BROILER, in the Outrigger Waikiki Tower, 200 Lewers St. Tel. 923-8836.
   Cuisine: AMERICAN. **Reservations:** Not accepted.
$ Prices: Appetizers $1.45–$6.25; main courses $5.45–$23.95. AE, CB, DC, JCB, MC, V.
   Open: Daily 6am–2am.
The budget crowd is kept well in mind at this cozy place, which is brightened by shell-shaped ceiling lights and modern paintings. The dining room overlooks the pool area of the Outrigger Edgewater Hotel; in fact, two of the tables are practically in the pool! The Broiler offers low-priced dinner main courses, like fried scallops, teriyaki chicken breasts, and mahimahi, in addition to such higher-priced offerings as steak, scampi, and prime rib, the specialty of the house. At lunch, there are special sandwiches served with soup or salad (around $6), plus daily specials like teriyaki chicken for $3.49. Breakfast is served all the way from 6am to 2pm, with a $2.49 special of pancakes, bacon, and egg. And there's always a "two for $15.95" dinner special—two teriyaki steak dinners served with soup or salad, rice or fries, and a croissant. There's a long happy hour from 6am to 9pm (when mai tais go for just $1.75), not to mention nightly lounge specials and entertainment, with karaoke on Sunday and Monday, and Billy Chapman and The Edge Tuesday through Sunday. Children have their own menu ($2.75 to $4.25).

WAIKIKI SEAFOOD AND PASTA COMPANY, in the Outrigger Surf Hotel, 2280 Kuhio Ave. Tel. 923-5949.

Cuisine: SEAFOOD/PASTA. **Reservations:** Not accepted.

$ Prices: Appetizers 95¢–$3.95; main courses $6.95–$14.95. AE, MC, JCB, V.

Open: Dinner daily 5–11pm.

The same management responsible for Lewers Street Fish Company runs this place, and it's an equally good bet. And it's so pretty, with its dining room ceiling totally covered by plants, and a smart New York–style deli and a bar up front. The food is inexpensive and delicious; gourmet pastas are made on the premises (you can ask to visit the "Pasta Factory"), so you know they're fresh. The fresh pasta comes along with house specialties, such as garlic basil chicken, chicken parmesan, and chicken Italiano. The chef whips up great specials nightly. Other popular menu items are fresh fish, seafood, mahimahi sauté, calamari steak, teriyaki beef kebab, and baby back ribs. Desserts? Just $3. Again, good food, good value, and a fun atmosphere. Piano bar from 6 to 11pm nightly.

READERS RECOMMEND

Waikiki Beachcomber Hotel, 2300 Kalakaua Ave. (tel. 922-4646.) "The Waikiki Beachcomber Hotel serves a very nice prime-rib buffet for only $12.95 before 6pm, in an attractive dining room. A chicken dish, mahimahi, and salad bar are also included . . . ."

Honolulu Elks Club, 2933 Kalakaua Ave. (tel. 923-5722). "Visiting Elks may enjoy good food in a very pleasant atmosphere at the Honolulu Elks Club on the no. 2 bus line. Their buffets are excellent and prices are reasonable. The atmosphere is great. Some of the 'Magnum P.I.' TV shows were filmed here."—both, Dr. John Lopresti, Jr., Bricktown, N.J.

MEALS FOR LESS THAN $20

CAFFÈ GUCCINNI, 2139 Kuhio Ave. Tel. 922-5287.

Cuisine: ITALIAN. **Reservations:** Recommended for more than four.

$ Prices: Appetizers $2.95–$6.50; main courses $8.95–$14.95. MC, V.

Open: Dinner only, daily 4–10:30pm.

Everyone likes Caffè Guccinni, both for the Italian meals and the delectable desserts. This is a modest place, with a counter inside, tables outside, and the menu posted beside the counter. Dinner specials include various pasta dishes on the regular menu (we're partial to the manicotti stuffed with five kinds of cheese), and two or three daily specials, such as veal, calamari, and Italian sausage. Homemade ravioli is a specialty. Main courses are accompanied by soup or salad, and homemade bread. As for desserts, we're always hard put to decide among a heavenly crème brûlée or chocolate torte, a Sicilian cannoli, or the amaretto cheesecake. The best solution is to bring a group of friends and share. Desserts are all $3.50. (If you've eaten elsewhere, come here just for dessert.) Along with your feast, have some of the best espresso and cappuccino in the islands, or an ice cream "shake with a shot." Mango daiquiris are also special. Everything is homemade in owner Jocelyn Battista's kitchen.

CAPPUCCINO'S, in the Waikiki Joy Hotel, 320 Lewers St. Tel. 921-1530.

Cuisine: CONTEMPORARY AMERICAN. **Reservations:** Recommended.

$ Prices: Appetizers $2.25–$9.75; main courses $11.95–$16.75. AE, MC, V.

Open: Lunch daily 11am–2pm; dinner daily 5–10pm; appetizers and cocktails til 12 midnight.

As pretty as the hotel that houses it, this tiny (10-table) place is charming, with its white walls and French windows with transom tops, its rosy-pink upholstered chairs and soft green tufted banquettes, and the beautiful round glass tables supported by ceramic tabourets. Plants hang everywhere, and there are soft pastel Italian street-scene pictures on the walls. It's an intimate, altogether charming place in which to dine or enjoy coffee and a light snack. Breast of chicken with mustard sauce is one of our favorites, as well as the island curry stew and the chicken tofu salad. Their pupu menu, in effect from 5pm until midnight, features steak fried potatoes, chicken strips, and sautéed New York steak. As its name suggests, coffee plays a big part here: How about Irish coffee or Kahlua coffee, Spanish coffee, Calypso coffee (with Tía Maria and Jamaican rum) all $3 to $4.75.

OKONOMIYAKI CHIBO RESTAURANT, in the Royal Hawaiian Shopping Center, 2201 Kalakaua Ave. Tel. 922-9722.
   Cuisine: JAPANESE. **Reservations:** Recommended.
$ Prices: Appetizers $3–$9.75; main courses $9–$29. AE, DC, MC, JCB, V.
   Open: Lunch Mon–Sat 11:30am–2pm; dinner daily 5–10:30pm.
There's a feeling of space and quiet elegance about this place, and an altogether new dining experience for Hawaii. The Chibo restaurants were founded in 1973 in Osaka, the city referred to as the "gourmet kitchen of Japan." Okonomiyake originated in the Edo period as a snack made of baked flour flavored with miso. Okonomiyake itself hasn't changed radically since the Edo period, but the Chibo restaurants have made it into something unique—a sort of Japanese pancake—by heaping it with all sorts of wonderful things. The Okonomiyaki "Chibo," the house specialty ($26 at dinner), is smothered in sirloin, prawns, squid, and scallops. On a smaller scale, you can build your own Okonomiyake for $13.75, choosing any two of the following: bacon, sirloin, pork, octopus, chicken, prawns, scallops, or Japanese mushrooms. Then there's Yoshoruyaki, which looks almost like a tortilla with lots of green onions, vegetables, and an egg on top—definitely something different. For big splurges, there are teppanyaki dinners ($34 to $48), cooked by your teppan chef at one of the teppan counters. At lunch, prices go down $3 to $4 for pretty much the same specialties: We like the special Okonomiyake lunch served with chef's salad, at $18. The restaurant is decorated with black lacquer and natural-wood furniture, gray carpeting and walls; it has soft track ceiling lights and abundant mirrors, a gracious setting for a special experience.

THE JOLLY ROGER, 2244 Kalakaua Ave. Tel. 923-1885.
   Cuisine: AMERICAN. **Reservations:** Not accepted.
$ Prices: Appetizers $3.75–$6.95; main courses $8.25–$13.75. AE, DC, JCB, MC, V.
   Open: Daily 6:30am–1am.
You can't go wrong at either branch of the popular Jolly Roger restaurants. The original one, in the center of Waikiki, gives you a choice of a sidewalk table right out on the busy avenue or, more peacefully, a table inside under an umbrella. The Crow's Nest, a lounge above the restaurant, has entertainment Tuesday through Saturday nights and a popular happy hour from 4 to 8pm. The newer Jolly Roger, at the corner of Kuhio and Kaiulani Avenues, is big and bright and has its own cocktail lounge, Blue Kangaroo, with a similar entertainment and happy-hour policy. As for the food, it's American coffeehouse style, quite tasty, and at good prices. Complete dinners—served with soup or salad, potatoes or rice, and dinner roll—include chicken Polynesian, mahimahi, barbecue beef ribs platter, and a vegetable stir-fry. There are daily specials like roast beef or steak or shrimp; burgers, salads, and sandwiches are also available. Breakfast is a special treat, since that's when you can get the MacWaple, a waffle covered in sliced, spiced hot apples topped with macadamia nuts. The cocktail lounges are open until 2am.
   There's a branch at 150 Kaiulani Ave. (tel. 923-2172).

NEW ORLEANS BISTRO, 2139 Kuhio Ave. Tel. 926-4444.
   Cuisine: CAJUN/CREOLE. **Reservations:** Recommended.
$ Prices: Appetizers $4.95–$9.95; main courses $14.95–$19.95. AE, DC, DISC, JCB, MC. V.
   Open: Dinner only, daily 5pm–1am (cocktails until 2am).
Like a boîte in one of those little streets in old New Orleans, the Bistro abounds in rococo black wrought iron, streamers hanging from the ceiling, white stucco walls, pink tablecloths, and prints of riverboats and characters reminiscent of Huck and Jim on the walls. The chef is from Louisiana, where he specialized in Cajun country cooking and Créole city cooking. Don't get blown away by a New Orleans

Hurricane or a Cajun martini from the bar before you have a chance to sample Louisiana red-hot prawns, the blackened prime rib, or the shelled crayfish étouffée or the mesquite-grilled lemon chicken. Appetizers, which are served until 1am, include Cajun popcorn (beer-battered and deep-fried shrimp), oysters Bienville, and blackened alligator, for those who dare. Betty Lou Taylor plays the piano, and late in the evening there's a jazz singer over by the bar. The staff is very friendly and attentive. On the way out you could get a T-shirt that says "I Ate Alligator"—or just a New Orleans Bistro logo shirt. Good fun here.

OLD COMPANY RESTAURANT, 2256 Kuhio Ave. Tel. 923-3373.
   Cuisine: AMERICAN. **Reservations:** Not accepted.
 $ Prices: Main courses $11.45–$14.95. AE, CB, DC, JCB, MC. V.
   Open: Breakfast daily 6am–4pm; lunch daily 11am–4pm; dinner daily 4pm–midnight.
When you step off Kuhio into this spot on the first level of a two-story building (there's another dining spot on the second floor) it's almost like entering someone's living room. Objets d'art fill the dividers while comfortable captain's chairs, polished wood tables, low rafters, plants, and carpeting contribute to the homey feel. Lunch is fun here, since it features an all-you-can-eat fruit and salad bar for $7.95. Sandwiches run the gamut from grilled cheese at $3.65 to chicken and avocado at $6.45. And dinner prices are modest, too: Barbecued ribs, for example, are $12.95; the seafood combination plate is $13.95. All regular dinners include a trip to the salad bar, plus vegetables and rice or potatoes (four choices). There's a bar with three television screens for viewing sports events, and live entertainment nightly, from 9pm. Arrive before noon and you can take advantage of the Sunrise Special: pancakes, egg, and bacon, for only $2.49.

PIECES OF EIGHT, in the Outrigger Coral Seas Hotel, 250 Lewers St.
   Tel. 923-6646.
   Cuisine: SEAFOOD/STEAK. **Reservations:** Not required.
 $ Prices: Main courses $6.95–$18.95. AE, MC, V.
   Open: Dinner only, daily 5–11pm.
One of Waikiki's oldest steak and seafood houses, Pieces of Eight has won many dining awards since it opened in 1967. The cannon located on the piano bar goes all the way back to the time of King Kamehameha II, and was presented to him by a Russian sea captain in 1822. This is the place for fresh fish of the day (market-priced), Pacific oysters, beer-battered shrimp, mahimahi amandine, top sirloin, and steak-and-seafood combos. Add $3.50 to your check if you take a turn at the salad bar; the salad bar alone is $6.95. In typical steak-house fashion, there's one major dessert: homemade cheesecake, $2.95. The bar is open from 4pm to midnight.

ROYAL STEAK AND SEAFOOD HOUSE, 2201 Kalakaua Ave., in the
   Royal Hawaiian Shopping Center. Tel. 922-6688.
   Cuisine: STEAK/SEAFOOD. **Reservations:** Recommended Sat–Sun.
 $ Prices: Appetizers $3.50–$9.95; main courses $12.95–$24.95. AE, MC, V.
   Open: Lunch daily 11:30am–2:30pm; dinner daily 5:30–10pm.
This is an attractive place, decorated in ocean colors, peacock-blue carpeting, blue and green upholstery, and a huge marine aquarium. The restaurant is divided into several small sections, separated by potted plants or natural-wood panels. The specialty here is seafood in combination with meat; main courses include rice or potatoes and vegetables. Among the many choices, some of our favorites are the steak and shrimp, the steak and salmon, steak and fresh oysters, and tournedos of beef and shrimp. Luncheon main dishes are similar fare: chicken or beef curry, teriyaki steak ($12.95 to $15.95), and a variety of salads and sandwiches.

EWA WAIKIKI

MEALS FOR LESS THAN $12

EGG'S 'N' THINGS, 1911B Kalakaua Ave. Tel. 949-0820.
   Cuisine: AMERICAN. **Reservations:** Not accepted.

$ Prices: Main courses $4.25–$8.50. No credit cards.
Open: Daily 11pm–2pm.
This longtime Waikiki favorite is near Ala Moana Boulevard. It's a spick-and-span white tile dining room with decorative wall plaques containing amusing sayings. Note the unusual hours. Various early- and late-riser specials are available. House specialty is the three buttermilk pancakes with eggs any style and a choice of meat (from $6 for Vienna sausage to $8 for steak). Also special are the nine kinds of crêpes suzette ($6 to $7.25), even more varieties of omelets ($7 to $8.50), 10 ways to enjoy pancakes ($4.25 to $7.25), and 9 different approaches to waffles ($4.50 to $7.25). Lots of side orders and fruit juices, too. Great for those who are truly devoted to breakfast.

HAMBURGER MARY'S ORGANIC GRILL, 2100 Kuhio Ave. Tel. 922-6722.

Cuisine: AMERICAN. **Reservations:** Not accepted.
$ Prices: Appetizers $3.50–$7; burgers and sandwiches $4.25–$7. No credit cards.
Open: Daily 7am–11pm.
Hamburger Mary's is known as one of Honolulu's most popular gay gathering places, but everyone is welcome here. The food is very good, the price is right, and the place itself looks like a bit of Old Hawaii with its beamed ceilings covered with lauhala mats and decorated with glass floats, photographs, and posters depicting a bygone era. Booths are upholstered with imitation leopard-skin fabric, and the lamps on each table sport shades made of aloha fabric decorated with fur and fringe (you really have to see this to believe it!). In the little front garden, there are umbrella tables and ice-cream chairs, and the bar's ceiling is decorated with photographs of Marilyn Monroe, Jean Harlow, and other departed luminaries. Breakfast is served all day and designed for the hearty eater: the Benedict Mary, served Saturday, Sunday, and holidays, is a favorite ($6.75 light load, $7.75 full load). Hamburger is king here, served in many varieties, on either multigrain or Hawaiian sweetbread, but you can also have good turkey and chicken sandwiches, and Mary's Mahi, a charbroiled fish sandwich served either teriyaki style or with mustard sauce. Several vegetarian items, including a garden burger, are popular. Charbroiled steak, mahimahi, breast of chicken, and a special of the day are also offered, from $9.25 to $11.75. Desserts are fresh and different every day.

WAILANA COFFEE HOUSE, 1860 Ala Moana Blvd. Tel. 955-3735.

Cuisine: AMERICAN. **Reservations:** Not required.
$ Prices: Main courses $7.25–$11.25. AE, DC, MC, V.
Open: Daily 24 hours.
Although this place looks imposing and expensive, its prices will surprise you. The nicest thing about the Wailana is that lunches and dinners are the same price—the tab does not go up after 5pm as it does in so many other places. So any time of the day you can have the homemade soup and sandwich lunch for $4.95, or the delicious "broasted" chicken, juicy and tender, served with a generous helping of french fries, coleslaw or salad, roll and honey, for $6.95. Other good buys are the old-fashioned beef stew at $7.75 and the New York steak at $10.75. All these are served with soup, salad bar, or fresh-fruit cup, as well as a choice of potato or rice. The salad bar is available from 11am to 11pm. Breakfast is served around the clock, so you can come by anytime to try their delicious classic french toast or all the pancakes you can eat, plus bacon and eggs at just $4.50.
There's another Wailana Coffee House in mid-Waikiki, with the same menu; it's called the **Wailana Malia** and it's located in the Outrigger Malia Hotel, 2211 Kuhio Ave. (tel. 922-4769). It's also open 24 hours a day. Another Wailana winner for Waikiki!

READERS RECOMMEND

Sizzler Steak House, *1945 Kalakaua Ave. (tel. 955-4069). "Sizzler Steak House offers senior citizens a 20% discount on meals with the exception of advertised specials* *on Monday nights. Senior ages start at 55. Their salad bar is bigger and better than it was last year—and the food, too.*"—Barbara and Ron LePage, Port Colborne, Ontario, Canada.

Chucks Cellar, *150 Kaiulani Ave. (tel. 923-4488). Chuck's Cellar in the Outrigger East Hotel has $5.95 Early Bird Specials from 5:30 to 6:30pm, which include very good thick soup, all-you-can-eat salad bar, and different main courses each night. A good variety salad bar and a good bargain.*"—Barbara and Ron LePage, Port Colborne, Ontario, Canada.

Kyo-Ya, *2057 Kalakaua Ave. (tel. 947-3911). "We discovered a 'Big Splurge' restaurant which is so good that we ate there three times. It is Kyo-Ya. Mostly Japanese eat there. The food is exquisite to look at and tastes wonderful. Portions are large, which is unusual for a Japanese restaurant.*"—Caryl Ritter, Dillon Beach, Calif.

MEALS FOR LESS THAN $20

CASTAGNOLA'S ITALIAN LANAI, in the Park Plaza Waikiki Hotel, 1956 Ala Moana Blvd. Tel. 949-6277.
   Cuisine: ITALIAN. **Reservations:** Recommended.
$ Prices: Appetizers $2.90–$7.90; main courses $7.90–$17.90. MC, JCB, V.
   Open: Mon 11:15am–3pm, Tues–Sat 11:15am–10pm.

Now that it's moved from Manoa Marketplace to a sparkling new location in Waikiki, this old favorite is more popular than ever. The new restaurant is a beauty, located on an open-air lanai, typical of trattorias found throughout Italy. The floor is flagstone, the decor is all green and white with touches of red (reminiscent of the Italian flag, which waves proudly from the wrought-iron railing). Tables are sheltered by green-and-white canvas-covered gazebos; the chair cushions are red, and green-and-white striped awnings flutter in the breeze. Castagnola's food, as always, is superb: Everything is fresh, and sausages, meatballs, desserts, and breads are all homemade. Complete meals, offered all day, can be ordered in regular-size portions or in smaller ones, for the light eater: For instance, rigatoni ricotta, linguine marinara or with white clam sauce, and eggplant parmigiana are all $10.90 regular, or $7.70 for the light eater. There are lunch sandwiches under $6, and an individual pizza is just $3.40. Castagnola's is one of the few places in Honolulu where you can find cannoli. Try it, or chocolate gelato, spumoni, or zabaglione for dessert. And have some wine: Top wines, usually sold by the bottle elsewhere, are available here by the glass.

THE GARDEN BRASSERIE, 255 Beach Walk. Tel. 923-1619.
   Cuisine: INTERNATIONAL. **Reservations:** Not required.
$ Prices: Appetizers $3.95–$8.95; main courses $11.95–$18.95. AE, CB, DC, MC, V.
   Open: Dinner daily 6–10pm.

This enchanting little place is actually an indoor "garden"; although it's entirely enclosed, it has an outdoorsy ambience, with its stone-tiled floor and myriad flourishing potted plants. The decor is semi–East Indian with some contemporary American touches. Green cast-iron chairs are covered with unique hand-embroidered seat, and back pillows. The staff is friendly without being at all intrusive, and Mr. Alexander Mendry, the charming Scottish gentleman who owns the Garden Brasserie, is much in evidence. Chef Ernesto Mera changes the menu every two days, always focusing on the freshest fish and produce available in the market. The results are quite special. Perhaps you'll begin with rigatoni with shrimp in a tomato-and-garlic sauce or with a chilled soup of the day. Then on to such main courses as fresh local fish poached with lemon and fine herbs and served with a light ginger and fresh tomato dressing or sliced breast of chicken slowly cooked with ginger and light eastern spices. Chef Mera is happy to oblige with vegetarian or other light dishes made to order. Fine wine and beers are available.

KOBE JAPANESE STEAK HOUSE, 1841 Ala Moana Blvd. Tel. 941-4444.
   Cuisine: JAPANESE. **Reservations:** Recommended.

$ Prices: Main courses $13.90–$32.90. AE, DC, JCB, MC, V.
Open: Dinner only, daily 5:30pm–10:30pm.
A meal here is a show in itself. First, there's the beautiful Japanese-country-inn sur-roundings and artifacts everywhere; second, the splendid sushi bar; and third, and most important, the communal tables where you and fellow diners can chat and watch your meal being prepared teppanyaki-hibachi style, by a master chef who stands at the grill in the center of it all. Order your teriyaki chicken, sukiyaki sirloin, or teppan shrimp; or a steak-and-teriyaki combo, and you have a complete meal. First, the chef sautés some teppan shrimp and serves you a delicate soup; then he stir-fries your order with mushrooms, onions, peppers, and bean sprouts. Vegetables, rice, and tea come with the meal, and you top it all off with delicate green-tea ice cream. Japanese beers and warmed saké make a perfect accompaniment to a fun meal.

MEZZANINE RESTAURANT, in the Waikiki Terrace Hotel, 2045 Kalakaua Ave. Tel. 955-6000.
Cuisine: CONTEMPORARY AMERICAN. **Reservations:** Recommended.
$ Prices: Appetizers $4.25–$8.50; main courses $8.50–$19.95; breakfast buffet 8.95; dinner buffet $16.95. AE, CB, DC, DISC, JCB, MC, V.
Open: Breakfast daily 6–10:30am; lunch Mon–Fri 11:30am–1:30pm; dinner Mon–Sat 5:30–9pm, Sun 6–9pm.

⭐ The raves keep coming in for this one, and it's not a bit surprising. Mezza-nine is on the mezzanine level of the sparkling Waikiki Terrace Hotel, and, like the hotel, it's handsome, with a sleek, contemporary look. Casual elegance is the keynote here. The indoor-outdoor setting showcases a kiawe-wood-burning oven and grill, from which come forth some extraordinary breads and pizza pies, with the chef concocting new and exciting combinations every evening ($10.75 to $15.25); try one for a special beginning to your meal. From the kiawe-wood broiler come seafood brochette and breast of chicken, and there are wonderful pasta platters, fresh salads big enough to share (Caesar, spinach, butter lettuce with plum tomatoes), and such tantalizing appetizers as beef-rolled scallion, baked Brie, and smoked salmon with Maui onions and capers. The chef dreams up extraordinary specials every day, including heavenly desserts. Premium wines can be had by the glass as well as the bottle.
Lunch features a similar but much smaller menu; breakfast offers granola and fresh fruit, waffles, french toast, and local favorites like eggs with Portuguese sau-sage. There's entertainment nightly.

NEW TOKYO RESTAURANT, 286 Beach Walk. Tel. 923-5411.
Cuisine: JAPANESE. **Reservations:** Recommended.
$ Prices: Appetizers $3.50–$11.95; main courses $10.95–$29.95. AE, DC, JCB, MC. V.
Open: Lunch Mon–Sat 11:30am–2pm; dinner daily 5:30–9:30pm.
This restaurant is getting to be an institution in Waikiki, attracting tourists, and lo-cals alike. The anteroom, with its Asian ambience and aquarium display of live sea-food, is both decorative and functional, and gets you in the mood for seafood. For lunch, you might have the grilled fish marinated in soy sauce for $4.95 or the as-sorted tempura vegetables with tempura fish at $6.25. Combination lunches run $5.50 to $8.25. At dinner, main courses range from noodle dishes to old favorites, such as sukiyaki and shabu-shabu.

SHIZU RESTAURANT AND SUSHI BAR, fourth floor, Royal Garden Hotel, 440 Olohana St. Tel. 943-0202.
Cuisine: JAPANESE. **Reservations:** Recommended.
$ Prices: Appetizers $3.50–$15; main courses $8–$14; complete dinner $32. AE, CB, DC, JCB, MC, V.
Open: Lunch daily 11:30am–2pm; dinner daily 5:30–10pm.
Classic Japanese cuisine in an elegant modern setting awaits at Shizu, named in honor of the wife of the owner of the exquisite new Royal Garden Hotel. An entryway decorated in green marble and shining brass leads to the dining room,

with its green-and-black marble floors and walls, blond wood furniture, and Japanese rock garden. The terrace, overlooking the hotel's gardens, is popular for alfresco dining. Waitresses wear elaborate kimonos and obi sashes. Master Chef Hideaki Moribe (formerly chef at Honolulu's Japanese consulate and most recently with the Westin Kauai) was trained in Osaka and is dedicated to classic Japanese cuisine. He creates many dishes not likely to be found outside of Japan. The best way to experience Shizu is to order the 10-course dinner at $32, but you can also enjoy such appetizers as assorted sashimi, seafood salad, and tempura zensai and such main courses as wafu beef steak, chicken amiyaki, and butter fish misozuke. For dessert, try the tempura ice cream—it's fried! Lunch has a variety of entrees priced under $10, like tomkatsu, tempura donburi, and various noodle dishes.

SINGHA THAI CUISINE, 1910 Ala Moana Blvd., corner of Ena Rd. (diagonally across from Hilton Hawaiian Village). Tel. 941-2898.
   Cuisine: THAI. **Reservations:** Recommended.
$ Prices: Appetizers $4.95–$11.95; main courses $7.95–$22.95. DC, JCB, MC, V.
   Open: Lunch Mon–Sat 11am–4pm; dinner daily 4–10pm.

Acclaimed as one of the top 20 restaurants in Honolulu by the readers of *Honolulu* magazine, Singha comes by its honors naturally: It is the only sister restaurant of the original in Bangkok, a four-time winner as best restaurant in that city. Since "singha" is the Thai word for lion, it is no wonder that its front door is guarded by two fearsome Thai lions. (Have no fear—they are metal sculptures.) Inside, the feeling is all soft lights and orchids of every description. There are handsome Thai artifacts everywhere, soft classical music in the background, dining room windows open to the courtyard and the balmy trade winds, and a delightful terrace for al fresco dining. And the food is wonderful, including all the classics—spring rolls, coconut chicken soup, pad thai, evil jungle princess, and the like—plus some only-in-Hawaii specialties featuring fresh Hawaiian seafood; try the scallops with Thai chili black-bean sauce, or the fresh local fish with curry sauce. The Royal Thai Dancers entertain at dinner on Sunday, Monday, and Tuesday evenings to music performed on authentic Thai instruments.

TANDOOR, in the Hawaiian Monarch Hotel, 444 Niu St. Tel. 949-3112.
   Cuisine: INDIAN. **Reservations:** Recommended on weekends.
$ Prices: Appetizers $3.95–$9.95; main courses $9.50–$22.95. AE, DC, MC, V.
   Open: Lunch daily 11am–2pm; dinner daily 5–10pm.

Indian food is relatively rare in Honolulu, so fans of this subtly spiced cuisine will be delighted to find Tandoor. It's a lovely looking place, decorated with woven Indian wall hangings, beautifully carved wooden screens at the windows, and round tables decked with green-and-gold tapestries. Lighting is soft, the ambience quiet and romantic. A discreet sign over the dark wood bar proclaims Tandoor the home of the Honolulu Cricket Club (shades of the Raj!). Tandoor specialties—baked in a traditional clay oven, which is charcoal-heated 24 hours a day—are featured. We like both the tandoor chicken and the shish kebab, and, as a side dish, the tasty masala kulcha, baked nan bread stuffed with minced vegetables and spices. Lamb, chicken, vegetarian, and seafood dishes are at the ready: Dal mutton, a savory dish of lamb and lentils, is a specialty. Lunch is similar to dinner.

2. BEYOND WAIKIKI

KAPAHULA

MEALS FOR LESS THAN $12

HEE HING, 449 Kapahulu Ave. Tel. 734-8474.
   Cuisine: CHINESE. **Reservations:** Not accepted.

$ Prices: Appetizers $3.95–$8.25; main courses $6.25–$18.75. MC, V.
Open: Daily 10:30am–9:30pm.

One of the most popular Chinese restaurants in Honolulu since 1963, Hee Hing is still going strong. There's good reason for its popularity: It's a handsome, spacious restaurant, with good-luck murals, paintings, and collages adorning the walls, and a superb Cantonese cuisine. And the prices for these delicious, authentic Chinese treats are always reasonable. The menu is voluminous, so take a little time to study it, or ask the waiter for advice. Don't miss the dim sum; they serve over 75 Hong Kong–style dim sum every day. The house specialty is drunken prawns—live prawns, marinated in white wine, cooked tableside, and priced seasonally. There's a vast variety of other live seafood dishes too, as well as fresh fish. Or you might decide to feast on one of the sizzling specialties, such as chicken with black-bean sauce, tenderloin of beef, or pork chops with onions, for $8.85 to $15.95. Earthen-pot casserole dishes ($7.25 to $15.75) are another way to go. Then there are taro-nest specialties and at least 16 vegetarian offerings. Everything we're tried here has been excellent. For dessert, forgo the fortune cookies in favor of a seasonal fruit pudding or fried apple fritters. A great find!

IRIFUNE, 563 Kapahulu Ave. Tel. 737-1141.
Cuisine: JAPANESE. **Reservations:** Not accepted.
$ Prices: Appetizers $3–$5; main courses $6.50–$9.50. MC, V.
Open: Lunch Tues–Fri 11:30am–1:30pm; dinner Tues–Sun 5–9:30pm.

For Japanese food with a local flavor, try Irifune. Short on decor, it's long on good food, large portions, and low prices, which are the same at lunch and dinner. For example, it's only $7.50 for the kushiyaki stick meal, which consists of miso soup, pickled vegetables, three skewers of barbecued chicken and veggies, a salad of lettuce, tomatoes, and chopped cabbage with a delicious house dressing, rice, and green tea. With seafood it's $8; with mixed seafood and chicken, $9. Irifune specialties include their barbecued chicken and beef teriyaki, and a variety of garlic creations, such as garlic tofu with veggies, and chicken or seafood with vegetables. Be sure to try their breaded tofu among the appetizers. Best of all, go with their fresh spicy garlic ahi, market-priced. Unlike most Japanese restaurants, Irifune does serve dessert, and a delicious one at that: ice-cream crêpes, filled with seasonal fruit, and just $3. No liquor but B.Y.O.B.

JO-NI OF HAWAII, 1017A Kapahulu Ave. Tel. 735-8575.
Cuisine: FILIPINO. **Reservations:** Not accepted.
$ Prices: Main courses $3.95–$9.75. MC, V.
Open: Lunch Tues–Sun 11am–2pm; dinner Tues–Sun 5–9pm.

Filipino food, it is said, originated with Malay settlers, was spread by Chinese traders, stewed for 300 years of Spanish rule, and was finally hamburger-ized by the Americans. What has arrived in Honolulu is delicious, especially so at Jo-ni of Hawaii. The windowed dining room is bright with a pink-and-cream decor and cane chairs made in the Philippines. Your first decision is whether to select a festive main dish or a regional specialty: You needn't worry about prices, since both are inexpensive; festive dishes range from $4.95 to $9.75, and regional specialties, mostly from $3.95 to $5.95. Festive items include langua—tender slices of ox tongue simmered in mushroom sauce (delicious!)—and beef flank rolled and stuffed with boiled eggs and sausage. Among the regional specialties, you might try adobo Manila, a stew with pork and/or chicken in a vinegar, garlic, and soy sauce; or the more delicate hipon sa gatong bicol, shrimps simmered in coconut milk, along with squash and long beans. Choose a few side dishes like pickled vegetables, to act as dipping sauces. There's a smaller version of Jo-ni at Makai Food Court at Ala Moana Center.

LA BAMBA, 847 Kapahula Ave. Tel. 737-1956.
Cuisine: MEXICAN. **Reservations:** Not necessary.
$ Prices: Appetizers $2.50–$6.75; main courses $6.50–$12.95. No credit cards.
Open: Lunch Sun–Fri 11am–2pm; dinner Sun–Fri 5–9:30pm. Closed Saturday.

There's nothing very unusual about the decor here—it's your standard Mexican budget eatery with tile floors, ceiling fans, white tablecloths, pictures of scenic Old Mexico on the walls. But the food is very good for the price, and you'll always get an enthusiastic welcome here, whether you come for lunch or dinner (the menu is the same all day). The taco salad appetizer is a favorite; and for something unusual, try the butaquito—that's large flour tortilla filled with chicken, lamb, beef or fresh mixed vegetables, deep-fried, then cut into small pieces and served with guacamole and sour cream. There are various Mexican plates for $6.50, a range of burritos from $6.95 to $8.95, and several Mexican style dinners from $11.95 to $12.95: carne asada (New York steak broiled and served with a green cheese enchilada), steak Jarocho (chunks of New York steak cooked with fresh veggies and herbs), and our favorite, the pollo entomatado (chicken in green sauce, served with rice, beans, salad and warm tortillas). Bring your own bottle and enjoy.

ONO HAWAIIAN FOODS, 726 Kapahulu Ave. Tel. 737-2275.
Cuisine: HAWAIIAN. **Reservations:** Not accepted.
$ Prices: Main courses $6.25–$8.25. No credit cards.
Open: Mon–Sat 11am–7:30pm.
Close to Waikiki, this very popular spot offers ono Hawaiian food. It's a little place with about 10 tables and walls covered with photos of popular local entertainers who are patrons. Try the kalua pig at $6.25, or the laulau plate at $6.50, or go mad and have the combination kalua pig *and* laulau at $8.25. These and other plates come with pipikaula (Hawaiian beef jerky), lomi-lomi salmon, poi or rice, and haupia. The atmosphere here is very friendly; the place may be short on size, but it's definitely long on aloha.

McCULLY/MOILIILI

MEALS FOR LESS THAN $12

CHIANG-MAI THAI RESTAURANT, 2239 S. King St. Tel. 941-1151 or 941-3777.
Cuisine: THAI. **Reservations:** Recommended.
$ Prices: Appetizers $2.25–$7.95; main courses $6.10–$12.55. AE, MC, V.
Open: Lunch Mon–Fri 11am–2pm; dinner daily 5:30–10pm.
Here's a small restaurant that the locals favor. With perhaps a dozen tables and simple decor, it specializes in the food of northern Thailand, and calls itself the "home of sticky rice and exotic food." Yes, you can order the sticky rice (really mochi rice in a bamboo container), and the exotic foods might include anything from golden-fried calamari with fresh lemongrass and spices among the appetizers and a creamy tofu soup to a shrimp pineapple curry, or hot-and-spicy clams, ginger beef, or cashew chicken. Vegetarians have a full menu—almost two dozen dishes—from which to choose.

DIÊM VIETNAMESE RESTAURANT, & COFFEE SHOP, in University **Square, 2633 S. King St. Tel. 941-8657.**
Cuisine: VIETNAMESE. **Reservations:** Recommended.
$ Prices: Appetizers $4.75–$5.95; main course $5–$13.95. CB, MC, V.
Open: Daily 10am–10pm.
To sample the exotic cuisine of Vietnam, you need only go to this little place, just a block Diamond Head of University Avenue, close to Waikiki. The small, family-run eatery is kept sparkling clean; its checkerboard floor is the dominant decorative theme. Nothing fancy here but the food. Spring rolls, roast shredded-pork roll, and beef grilled with lemongrass make good appetizers. There's a wide range of vermicelli (noodle) dishes—curry chicken vermicelli, seafood saimin, barbecued shrimp cake, chicken noodle soup—and none will set you back more than $6.50 for a filling meal. As for the house specialties, the Vietnamese shrimp crêpe, the coco-steamed chicken, and the seafood and vegetables are especially good. Desserts are cool and soothing—yellow mung-bean pudding, black-eye bean pudding, banana pudding—and just $1.25. The friendly management invites you to call ahead "for even faster service," and take-out orders are welcome.

DOWN TO EARTH DELI, 2525 S. King St. Tel. 949-8188.
Cuisine: VEGETARIAN. **Reservations:** Not accepted.
$ Prices: Main courses $3.25–$6.95. No credit cards.
Open: Daily 10am–9pm.
Enter Down to Earth Natural Foods, just west of University Avenue, go to the rear, and there you'll find this delightful spot where you can dine on "healthy, home-style vegetarian cooking at its best." Only natural ingredients are used (no sugar, white flour, eggs, lard, rennet, caffeine, MSG, or preservatives); there are many nondairy alternatives for vegans and those watching their cholesterol—and the food is delicious, as well! There's a changing parade of hot specials every day (you're invited to call and find out what's cooking for the day), that might include almond-vegetable tofu, chickpeas à la king, nondairy lasagne, or shepherd's pie, for $4.95. Always on hand are tofu or tempeh burgers, a variety of veggie sandwiches, like avocado or mock tuna ($3.65 each), hearty homemade soups, and a plentiful salad or pita-pocket sandwich bar that goes for $3.75 a pound. There are plenty of cold deli items, like tabbouleh, pesto pasta, burritos, and basmati salad to take out. Nearly a score of healthful desserts await your guilt-free enjoyment, none more than $2. There's a counter, a few tables right there, and more seating upstairs.

GRACE'S INN, 1296 S. Beretania St. Tel. 537-3302.
Cuisine: LOCAL. **Reservations:** Not accepted.
$ Prices: Main courses $4.45–$5.50. No credit cards.
Open: Mon–Sat 6am–10:30pm, Sun 7am–10pm.
Even before it was immortalized in song by Hawaii's favorite funny man, Frank DeLima, Grace's Inn and the staple food of Hawaii—the plate lunch—were all but synonymous. Grace caters more than her share of baby luaus—the Hawaiian tradition of celebrating the first birthday of a *keiki o ka aina* (child of the land)—weddings, office parties, and any other occasion you can think of. Her food isn't fancy or unique, but its popularity is mind-boggling. Chicken or beef katsu, teriyaki beef or pork, sweet-and-sour pork, seafood mix, and mixed beef curry, ribs, and teri pork plates, with the traditional two scoops of rice and salad, are the staples. Specialties include fried noodles, fish tempura, and big bowls of curry stew. There are a few tables inside, but the bulk of Grace's trade is take-out. The lady is definitely doing something right. Consult the telephone book for other locations around town.

JENNY'S, 2671D S. King St. Tel. 949-2679.
Cuisine: KOREAN. **Reservations:** Not accepted.
$ Prices: Main courses $4.50–$6. No credit cards.
Open: Mon–Sat 10am–9pm, Sun 11am–8pm.
Honolulu has only a handful of Korean restaurants, and this one in Moiliili, on the way to the university, is the oldest and best. This is the kind of family-style place that gives you a real experience in nontourist dining. Small and tidy with white walls and flower arrangements, it caters to local Korean and other Asian families (lots of cute keikis mill about), and a smattering of university students. There are a few booths and tables up front (at one, a man may be rolling dumplings for the soup), from which you can see the big open kitchen in the back. We love the combination of mon doo and kuk soo—hot noodle soup with Korean dumplings stuffed with beef, pork, and vegetables. The waitress once explained to us that this is "New Year's soup, but so popular we make it every day." The house specialty is kalbi, barbecued short ribs, and it's excellent. The plate lunch—barbecued meat, na mul (Korean-style vegetables and fish fried in an egg batter), and rice is a buy at $4.40. Kimchee and hot sauce come with all orders. While you're here, try the famed Korean ginseng tea.

KING TSIN, 1110 McCully St. Tel. 946-3273.
Cuisine: CHINESE. **Reservations:** Recommended.
$ Prices: Appetizers $2.95–$7.95; main courses $4.75–$8.95. DC, MC, V.
Open: Lunch daily 11am–2pm; dinner daily 5–9:30pm.
There are precious few northern Chinese restaurants in the islands, so praise be for this attractive, pleasantly decorated place popular with both visitors and local folk.

The food is reasonably priced, subtly flavored, and most fun to eat with a group, as we did the last time we were there. A Chinese friend had ordered for us over the phone, and our soup and appetizer were whisked to our table moments after we arrived. Our party of four began with potstickers, small dumplings stuffed with pork, and two orders of sizzling rice soup. For our main courses, we had moo shu pork; dry-fried beef—super hot; King Tsin chicken, a delicate combination of tender white meat of chicken and pea pods; braised bean curd; and sweet-and-sour fish, an entire rock cod, complete with tail and head, smothered in sauce. We all ate until we couldn't manage another bite—and still had a huge doggie bag to take home. Lunch prices are about 10% lower than dinner. With the exception of the aforementioned beef—about which the menu warns you—the food here is not overly spicy, as it can be at other northern Chinese restaurants.

KOZO SUSHI HAWAII, in Old Stadium Square, 2334 S. King St. Tel. 973-5666.
   Cuisine: SUSHI.
$ Prices: Sushi rolls 98¢–$5.50.
   Open: Most locations daily 9am–7pm; Sun 9am–6pm.
These little sushi-counter take-out places are insanely popular in Hawaii, just as they are in Japan. Everybody seems to love them. Sushi is fresh and delicious, the platters are artfully presented, and prices are remarkably low. Samples are displayed in sparkling glass cases. The $4.50 lunch box is generous, with a plentiful selection of roll sushi, nigiri, and shrimp. California maki (a blend of avocado, crab, and cucumber), at $3.50, is one of their biggest sellers. Would you believe the BLT maki—red lettuce, bacon, tomato, and rice! Almost all the Kozo Sushi Hawaii shops are strictly take-out, but the main one at 2334 S. King does have a few tables.
   Kozo Sushi Hawaii has shops at the Aiea Shopping Center (tel. 483-6800), Pearl Ridge Shopping Center, Phase II (tel. 483-6805), Kahala Mall (tel. 733-5733) and 1150 Bishop St. (tel. 522-9515). For other locations around the island, consult the telephone book; new Kozo Sushi Hawaii shops are opening all the time.

MAPLE GARDEN, 909 Isenberg St. Tel. 941-6641.
   Cuisine: CHINESE. **Reservations:** Recommended.
$ Prices: Appetizers $4.75–$9.50; main courses $4.95–$20.25. AE, MC, V
   Open: Lunch daily 11am–2pm; dinner daily 5:30–10pm.
Rating high with the local Chinese community is this small, attractive dining room with Chinese decorations on the walls, wood paneling, and soft lights. *Travel Holiday* magazine has named it one of the top 10 restaurants in Honolulu. The Szechuan dishes are so tasty and authentic that a doctor friend of ours from Taiwan brings all his visiting friends and relatives here. Mr. Robert Hsu, the owner, is constantly adding new delights to the menu. The house specialty is Szechuan smoky duck, crispy on the outside and tender on the inside, served with steamed buns—you tuck the meat into the buns. A very generous order (you'll probably need a doggie bag) is $6.95. If you really like the superhot Szechuan-style cooking, you'll love the eggplant with hot garlic sauce or the pork with hot garlic sauce; they're real eye-openers. (The eggplant recipe has received an award from the *Los Angeles Times*). There are more than 75 main dishes on the menu priced at $7 or less, including hard-to-find singing rice—actually it's more of a whistle—served either with pork and vegetables or with shrimp. There's ample parking space; and you can phone for easy bus or driving directions from Waikiki.

MEKONG RESTAURANT, 1295 S. Beretania St. Tel. 521-2025 or 523-0014.
   Cuisine: THAI. **Reservations:** Not required.
$ Prices: Appetizers $3.95–$8.95; main courses $6.95–$8.95. AE, DC, MC, V
   Open: Lunch Mon–Fri 11am–2pm; dinner daily 5:30–9:15pm.
Every now and then one discovers a place where the food is exotic and delicious, the staff cordial and attentive, the atmosphere warm and cozy, and the prices painless. Such a find is Mekong. The small dining room is outfitted with white linen tablecloths and blue linen napkins, posters on the wall, and a pretty

latticed ceiling. The voluminous menu will explain the basics of Thai cooking, but you'll do just as well to tell your waiter what you like and follow his or her suggestions. Thai cooking resembles both East Indian and Chinese, and while it can be highly spicy, almost every dish can be ordered either mild, medium, or hot. The hottest—and most popular—dishes are Thai green curry (beef, pork, or chicken sautéed in green chile and curry fresh coconut milk) and Evil Jungle Prince (beef, pork, or chicken sautéed with hot spices with either hot or sweet basil leaves). Mild dishes include not-to-be-missed spring rolls, a memorable chicken-ginger soup in a fresh coconut-milk base, a dish of thin, crisp noodles with tiny bits of chicken, water chestnuts fried rice, and shrimp curry. Bring your own bottle if you want wine. (Mekong II serves both beer and wine.) Dessert is another unforgettable treat: tapioca pudding unlike any you've ever tasted, in a warm coconut milk; and half-ripe Thai apple-bananas, again cooked in coconut milk. Thai teas are just a little bit different, brewed with vanilla beans and served with condensed milk to make them quite sweet.

A branch called **Mekong II** is located at 1726 S. King St. (tel. 941-6184).

Oswner Keo Sananikone has three more Thai restaurants; **Keo's Thai Cuisine,** 625 Kapahulu (tel. 737-8240 or 737-9250), **Keo's at Ward Centre** (tel. 533-0533), and **Keo's at King Street,** 1486 S. King St. (tel. 947-9989).

SALERNO, in the McCully Shopping Center, 1960 Kapiolani Blvd. Tel. 942-5273, or 946-3229.
  Cuisine: ITALIAN. **Reservations:** Recommended.
$ Prices: Appetizers $2.90–$6.90; main courses $8.90–$12.90 small, $9.90–$16.90 regular. AE, DC, MC. V.
  Open: Lunch Mon–Sat 11am–2:30pm; dinner daily 5–10pm.

Everybody raves about the authentic Italian food at Salerno, and no wonder. Only the freshest pastas, vegetables, seafoods, and the like are used in preparing the dishes; all the wonderful breads and pastries are baked right in their own kitchens; and they are happy to satisfy special dietary needs. On top of all that, the price is right! You have your choice of excellent antipasti, soups, salads, pizza pies, and a variety of pastas, like the popular linguine pesto or fettuccine carbonara, in small or regular portions. Among the notable main courses are veal marsala, shrimp scampi, chicken oregano, and such house specialties as calamari vegetable, stuffed eggplant, and pollo linguine. Beer, wine, drinks, and espressos are modestly priced, as are some filling Italian pastries. The setting is pretty, with soft lighting, plants, natural woods, lamps on the tables, and partitions affording a feeling of privacy. On the wayout, check out Slerno's Italian Grocery and maybe take home some homemade bread, pastas, sauces, or deli items for your hotel kitchenette.

SUEHIRO, 1914 King St. Tel. 949-4584.
  Cuisine: JAPANESE. **Reservations:** Recommended.
$ Prices: Main courses $7.95–$16.95. MC. V.
  Open: Lunch daily 11am–2pm; dinner Mon–Fri 5–9pm, Sat–Sun 5–9:30pm.

We've always liked Suehiro. Try to get one of their ozashiki or tatami rooms, where you sit on the floor and dine at a low lacquered table (take off your shoes before you enter); the setting will immediately put you in a tranquil mood, ready for a different kind of experience. You usually need a party of eight and a reservation for these rooms, but if a room happens to be open you may double up with other waiting guests. On one visit we teamed up with a big, charming family of Japanese-Americans and had a family-style dinner at $15.50 per person that included a tasty miso soup, namasu (pickled cucumber), sashimi, shrimp tempura, tenderloin filet, and mixed sushi, served with several side vegetables, sauces, rice, and plenty of tea. At the regular restaurant tables, you may order a similar dinner special for around $30 for two people, or order à la carte. There is an extensive sushi menu, and half a dozen special lunches for $7.95 to $8.50. *Note:* You can also get a tasty Japanese box lunch or bento for picnics and trips.

WOODLANDS POTSTICKER RESTAURANT, 1289 S. King St. Tel. 526-2239.

Cuisine: CHINESE. **Reservations:** Not required.
$ Prices: Appetizers $6.25–$16.50; main courses $6.25–$26. MC, V.
Open: Lunch Wed–Mon 11am–2pm; dinner Wed–Mon 5–9pm.

Do you like potstickers? That's one good reason for coming here, but not the only one. All the food is especially good, and this place is a local favorite. The Chinese-tiled ceiling and impressive Asian statuettes and art prepare you for a special experience. You may want to start with some of those Peking potstickers and gau-gee: We like the pan-fried dumplings, the chicken with chives, and the onion cake ($5.95 to $6.25). Bird's-nest soup—the real thing—with chicken is another impressive starter, or try the crabmeat tofu soup. Prawns, scallops, and steamed catch-of-the-day dominate the dozen seafood dishes. Best bargains are some 30 specialty chicken and duck choices (most $5.95 to $7.25), but watch out—some of these may be highly spiced. Parking is in the rear.

YUEN'S GARDEN SEAFOOD RESTAURANT, 2140 S. Beretania St. Tel. 944-9699.
  Cuisine: CHINESE. **Reservations:** Not required.
$ Prices: Appetizers $3.95–$7.95; main courses $5.50–$7.95. MC, V.
  Open: Daily 10:30am–10pm.

Of the many items on the menu, which includes Cantonese, Szechuan, and Mandarin dishes, it is the seafood that inspires most of the raves here. Prawns can be bought by the pound at $18; half a pound usually produces five large prawns. We like the fried prawns, served with radish and cilantro. Other good seafood choices, most in the $7.95 range, are scallops, clams with black-bean sauce, sweet-and-sour shrimp, and sea bass filet. Also great are the hot-pot courses served in casseroles. We vote for the seafood combo and the roast duck hot pot made with eggplant and plum sauce. An elegant Peking duck is $25.

NEAR WAIKIKI

MEALS FOR LESS THAN $12

HARD ROCK CAFE, 1837 Kapiolani Blvd. Tel. 955-7383.
  Cuisine: AMERICAN. **Reservations:** Not accepted.
$ Prices: Appetizers $3.25–$6.50; main courses $6.50–$13.95. AE, MC, V.
  Open: Sun–Thurs 11:30am–12:30am, Fri–Sat 11:30am–1am.

Honolulu is home to the world's ninth Hard Rock Café, which, like its sibling restaurants in Europe and on the mainland, is a restaurant-cum-museum of rock-music memorabilia and 1950s artifacts. Nonstop rock blares forth. The management prides itself on the fact that one can see and be seen by everyone in the place at all times, no matter where one is seated. Gold records and musical instruments—either donated by their famous owners or purchased at auctions—adorn the walls. A real '50s station wagon is suspended from the ceiling over the bar! Larger-than-life busts of Mick Jagger and Keith Richards dominate the foyer, where souvenirs such as T-shirts, lapel pins, baseball caps, and cigarette lighters bearing the HRC logo are for sale (daily 10am to 10pm). Like all the other Hard Rock Café's, this one will not accept dinner reservations; lines are common but seem to be part of the fun. The menu features house specials, such as watermelon barbecued ribs and lime barbecued chicken; burgers served with home-cut fries, green salad, and your choice of made-from-scratch dressing; sandwiches, including grilled chicken breast and avocado, Swiss cheese, and tomato; and thick, cold shakes. Hard Rock Café is proud of the fact that it uses absolutely no preservatives or additives.

ALA MOANA AREA

MEALS FOR LESS THAN $12

AUNTIE PASTO'S, 1099 S. Beretania St., at Pensacola. Tel. 523-8855.
  Cuisine: ITALIAN. **Reservations:** Not accepted.

$ Prices: Appetizers $2.95–$4.50; main courses $6.25–$11.95. MC, V.
Open: Mon–Thurs 11am–10:30pm, Fri 11am–11pm, Sat 4–11pm, Sun 4–10:30pm.
With its brick interior, café curtains, and checkered cloths, this place resembles a little trattoria in Florence or Rome. The food here is marvelous, and at lunchtime Auntie Pasto's attracts a lively crowd, many of whom work at the shops and medical clinics in the neighborhood. Special lunches, $3.95–$5.50, include frittata (an open-face omelet), a mortadella scramble, pan-fried sausage and vegetables, and a club sandwich served with pasta salad. Also very popular are Auntie's big sandwiches (meatball salami, subs) for $3.50 to $4.25, and her super pastas, especially those with clams and spinach, for $7.50 to $8.95. At dinnertime, there are also some flavorful specialties like stuffed calamari, veal parmigiana, and osso buco.

CHICKEN ALICE'S, 1470 Kapiolani Blvd., at the corner of Keeaumoku. Tel. 946-6117.
Cuisine: FRIED CHICKEN. **Reservations:** Not accepted.
$ Prices: Plate lunches $3.95–$5.95. No credit cards.
Open: Daily 9am–10:30pm.
One of our favorite places to pick up wonderful, portable food for a picnic or the beach—or just to take back to our hotel—is this spot. The stellar attraction here is Alice Gahinhin's flavorful fried chicken. It's ever-so-delicately spiced and definitely habit-forming. And you can't beat the price—$5.25 for a small box containing 12 pieces, $10.50 for the large box of 25 pieces, $25 for some 60 pieces (in case you're throwing a party or have a very large family to feed.) Chicken is also available by the piece. And plate lunches are king-size, to say the least. Our favorite is the combination Korean plate; kalbi (tender barbecued ribs), chicken, rice, and kimchee, for $5.75.

EMILIO'S PIZZA, 1423 Kalakaua, near the corner of King St. Tel. 946-4972.
Cuisine: ITALIAN. **Reservations:** Accepted only for parties of six or more Fri–Sat.
$ Prices: Appetizers $1.50–$6.25; main courses $6.95–$13.50. MC, CB, DC, V.
Open: Dinner only, Mon–Thurs 5–10pm, Fri–Sat 5–11pm.
One of Honolulu's favorite pizza parlors, Emilio's is a cozy spot, with interesting framed pictures and glass shelving lending a homey atmosphere. This is Sicilian-style pizza with a professional touch. There is a choice of 14 toppings, which are piled abundantly on the crusts, making a 10-inch pie a filling meal for two or three. Prices run from about $7.50 for the 10-inch cheese pie up to $19.50 for the mind-blowing combo with six toppings. Emilio's makes their own tasty dough every day, and their own sausages and sauces. They also make an excellent soup of the day—it might be seafood bisque or black bean—in addition to the regular homemade minestrone. There are also pasta specials every day, unusual appetizers like fresh pesto and cream cheese, and many vegetarian and low-fat specialties, all gourmet quality. Customers are welcome to bring their own beer or wine; there is no corkage charge. And yes, they will deliver to most hotels and condos in Waikiki.

HARBOR PUB AND PIZZERIA, 1765 Ala Moana Blvd. Tel. 941-0985.
Cuisine: ITALIAN/AMERICAN. **Reservations:** Not required.
$ Prices: Appetizers $1.95–$7.50; main courses $5.25–$17.50. AE, DC, MC, V.
Open: Daily 11am–1:30am.
In the evening, a "fun" crowd usually fills this cheerful little spot just below the Chart House. It's a favorite watering hole for people employed at nearby hotels and offices. The fare is not terribly varied here, but what there is, is just fine. Good sandwiches—roast beef, breast of turkey, vegetarian delight submarine, and tuna melt—go for $5.25 to $6.45. The specialty is pizza: Plain cheese pies are $8.95 small, and the Harbor combo, with everything, is $11.50 small. This is the sort of place where everyone talks with everyone else, and the atmosphere is friendly and fun.

ORIGINAL PANCAKE HOUSE, 1221 Kapiolani Blvd. Tel. 533-3005.
Cuisine: AMERICAN. **Reservations:** Not accepted.
$ Prices: Main courses $5.95–$7.95. AE, MC, V.

Open: Daily 6am–2pm.

This is a pleasant place to have breakfast or lunch on your way to or from Ala Moana Center. We like to sit out in the pretty little garden, where English sparrows, doves, Brazilian cardinals, and mynahs, all come looking for a handout. Pancakes and crêpes include blueberry pancakes at $4.95; cherry crêpes, made with liqueur, at $5.95; and the house special, apple pancakes (allow 30 minutes) at $7.50. Among the many omelets, all served with three buttermilk pancakes, our favorite is potato—made with green onions and bacon bits and served with a flavorful sour-cream sauce ($7.50). There are also hot sandwiches, such as teriyaki steak and French dip, in the $4.90 to $5.20 range, and daily specials, such as mahimahi, chicken-fried steak, spaghetti, and beef stew, are all priced at $4.75.

PENNEY'S RESTAURANT, 1450 Ala Moana Blvd., at Ala Moana Center. Tel. 946-8068.

　Cuisine: AMERICAN. **Reservations:** Not accepted.

$ Prices: Main courses, $3.95–9.50. AE, MC, V.

　Open: Mon–Sat 8am–8pm, Sun 9am–4pm.

Although J. C. Penney's, the huge department store at Ala Moana Center, is right up-to-date with its fashions, the prices they charge at Penney's Restaurant on the third floor went out of style years ago—which makes it a great place for us. It's a good deal for breakfast, lunch, or dinner. At lunch, for example, hot plates are all $4.75 or under. At 4pm, some dinner items are added to the menu, like grilled beef liver or choice sirloin steak. Main dishes are served with potatoes, vegetable, dessert, and beverage. Try to avoid the peak lunch hour unless you don't mind lining up for a few minutes. Early arrivals must use the special third-floor entrance.

QUINTERO'S CUISINE, 1102 Piikoi St. Tel. 593-1561.

　Cuisine: MEXICAN. **Reservations:** Not accepted.

$ Prices: Appetizers $3.50–$10.25; main courses $9.95–$13.95. MC, V.

　Open: Mon–Sat 11am–3pm and 4:30pm–10pm. Closed Wednesday.

Authentic Mexican dishes, cooked in the Aztec tradition would be baked in underground ovens. Thats not quite feasible in a city like Honolulu, but Mary and Louis Quintero do the next best thing in their restaurant, which is next to the Old Stadium Square shopping area. Tasty dishes include carne al arriero, steak cooked with garlic, onions, and peppers. Pollo a la mexicana, chicken fried with ranchero sauce, is also good. Among the appetizers and soups, we like the nachos and the fideo, a tomato-based broth with sautéed noodles and Mexican spices ($3.50). This is a small and plain little restaurant, but the service is personal and homey. The same menu is available all day.

SIAM ORCHID, 1514 Kona St. Tel. 955-6161.

　Cuisine: THAI. **Reservations:** Not required.

$ Prices: Appetizers $5.95–$8.95; main courses $6.50–$10.95. AE, MC, V.

　Open: Lunch Mon–Fri 11am–2pm; dinner daily 5:30–9:30pm.

Just across Kona Street from the Ala Moana Shopping Center is the Siam Orchid. The setting is charming: fans, Thai artwork on the wall, rattan chairs, white cloths under glass, orchids on the tables, banquettes. The menu is authentic, reflecting the different styles of the various regions of the country. And prices are modest at both lunch and dinner. There's a huge array of dishes, some hotter than others (ask your waiter), but you can't go wrong with such appetizers as stuffed chicken wings or squid salad. Or begin with a white tofu or Tom Yum soup and choose from such main dishes as fresh chile chicken, beef on a sizzling platter, pork with ginger-curry sauce, or Thai garlic shrimp. As in most Thai restaurants, there's a healthy list of vegetarian specialties. Lunch is always a good buy, with half a dozen noodle specials around $6. Everything is prepared to order, and no MSG is used.

VIM AND VIGOR FOODS, 1450 Ala Moana Blvd., at Ala Moana Center. Tel. 955-3600.

　Cuisine: VEGETARIAN/AMERICAN. **Reservations:** Not accepted.

$ Prices: Sandwiches $4.25 and $4.95; hot main courses $3.50 and $3.95. AE, DC, JCB, MC, V.

Open: Mon–Sat 9am–9pm, Sun 9am–5pm.

Need a healthful snack while you're shopping Ala Moana? Vim and Vigor, the big health-food store on the lower level, mountain side, has a tidy little take-out bar up front, which keeps huge lunch crowds happy with luscious sandwiches like avocado, tuna, or egg combinations on whole-grain breads with sprouts. Hot dishes, such as veggie burgers, chicken adobo, and teriyaki chicken, are also available. Fruit smoothies made with fresh Hawaiian fruits are especially good. There are a few tables where you can picnic in front of the store. While you're here, check out their selection of vitamins, teas, herbs, sports nutrition products, and natural cosmetics and beauty aids. This is one of the best health-food stores in Honolulu.

There's another Vim and Vigor in Kailua, right outside the Holiday Mart.

THE WISTERIA, 1206 S. King St. Tel. 531-5276.
Cuisine: JAPANESE/AMERICAN. **Reservations:** Not required.
$ Prices: Main courses $7.20–$11.50. MC, V.
Open: Sun–Thurs 6am–10:30pm, Fri–Sat 6am–11:15 pm.

When a restaurant has been going strong for over 40 years, it must be doing something right. Such a place is the Wisteria, a family restaurant very popular with the local crowd. The dining room is bright and airy, the atmosphere is pleasantly businesslike, the service swift and professional, and the deep booths comfortable. The menu is mostly Japanese, but there's a little bit of everything here: Daily specials often include Hawaiian plates, and such dishes as boiled corned beef brisket with cabbage, Hungarian beef goulash with egg noodles, and roast beef sirloin au jus, as well as a huge array of various sushi dishes, donburi, tempura, and sukiyaki specials. For a real local experience, try the chef's famous bowl of oxtail soup, served steaming hot with rice and grated ginger ($8.10). For dessert, go with the Portuguese doughnut—deep-fried and filled with ice cream—or have the peach Melba or strawberry sundae. The cocktail lounge, which always features daily bar specials, is open from 11am to 1am. A Saturday and Sunday brunch buffet is $5.25.

ZIPPY'S, 1450 Ala Moana Blvd., at Ala Moana Center. Tel. 942-7766.
Cuisine: LOCAL.
$ Prices: Main courses $3–$6. No credit cards.
Open: Mon–Fri 6:30am–9:30 pm, Sat–Sun 6:30am–9pm.

The kamaainas are mad about Zippy's and it's no wonder. The food is plentiful and the prices are as reasonable as you'll find anywhere in Hawaii. There are 17 Zippys restaurants on Oahu (theyre all listed in the phone book), including this convenient one at Ala Moana Center. Two of their most popular specialties are chili and fried chicken. In fact, many local clubs and children's athletic teams sell tickets for the chili to raise funds, and they sell like . . . Zippy's chili! A "barrel" of this taste treat is $16.25; a take-out for four people is $5. Fried chicken is $14.65 for a 12-piece bucket. And everyone seems to love Zippy's plate lunches: big platters of beef or pork, teriyaki, breaded beef cutlet, fried chicken, and the like. There's good news for the diet-conscious, too: Zippy's huge salads—we especially like the Italian chicken and chef's salads—are all $5.80 or less. Zippy's are self-service restaurants where you place your order at one window, pay, and collect it in very short order at the next windows. Eleven of them have table-service dining rooms as well, and all have a "Napoleon's Bakery," waiting to fatten you up with luscious cakes, pies, and freshly baked breads.

HACKFELD'S, ground level of Liberty House, 1450 Ala Moana Blvd., at Ala Moana Center. Tel. 945-5243.
Cuisine: FRENCH/CONTINENTAL. **Reservations:** Not accepted.
$ Prices: Appetizers $2.75–$5.50; main courses $10.25–$14.75. AE, CB, DC, JCB, MC, V.
Open: Lunch Mon–Sat 11am–2:30pm; dinner Mon–Fri 5–8:30 pm.

Call Hackfeld's an elegant bistro; the food has a French accent, and the artful presentations make continental dishes as pleasing to the eye as to the palate. Prices are the most reasonable at lunch, when main dishes run $7.95 to $12.50, and

Kamehameha IV Rd. ↗

School St.

Alewa Dr.

Wyllie St.

Pali Hwy.

Nuuanu Stream

63

78

Kaua St.

H1

Lunalilo Frwy.

Fort Shafter Military Res.

Houghtailing St.

Halona St.

Liliha St.

61

Booth Rd.

Middle St.

92

Puuhale Rd.

Kalihi St.

Waiakamilo Rd.

N. King St.

Palama St.

Vineyard Blvd.

Auwaiolimu S.

Sand Island Access Rd.

Nimitz Hwy.

Dillingham Blvd.

Iwilei Rd.

Lusitana St.

Iolani Ave. Prospe

Kapalama Military Res.

Nuuanu Ave.

Bishop St.

Queen Emma St.

2

Kapalama Basin

Punchbowl St.

N. Beretania St.

S. King St.

← ✈

U.S. Coast Guard Res.

Honolulu Harbor

1

South St.

Ward St.

5

Mokauea Island

Sand Island

Queen St.

3 4

Sand Island State Rec. Area

Ala Moana Blvd.

92

Kakaako Waterfront State Rec. Area

Kewalo Basin

Ala Moa Park

M a m a l a   *B a y*

6785

OAHU

Honolulu ★

Ala Moana area **5**
Ala Moana Center **6**
Contemporary Museum **10**
Honolulu Academy of Arts Garden Café **2**
Ilikai Marina **7**
Kapahulu Avenue **11**

McCully/Moiliili area **8**
Restaurant Row **1**
University area **9**
Ward Centre **3**
Ward Warehouse **4**

include such dishes as veal piccata, Thai curry, and New England crab cakes, all served with a choice of soup of the day or salad. The dinner menu is also intriguing: Try escargots maison or fettuccine Alfredo among the appetizers and the wonderful Burnt Crème (or any of the French pastries and tortes) for dessert. In between are dishes such as the fresh catch of the day, teriyaki steak, chicken fettuccine, veal Oscar and lamb chops, all served with soup of the day or salad, plus garlic pasta, fresh mashed potatoes, potato pancakes, or steamed rice.

LE GUIGNOL, 1614 Kalakaua Ave. Tel. 947-5525.
   Cuisine: FRENCH. **Reservations:** Recommended.
$ Prices: Appetizers $4.95–$7.95; main courses $14.95–$19.95. AE, MC, V.
   Open: Dinner only, Tues–Sun 5:30–10pm.

At last, a moderately priced French restaurant par excellence in Honolulu! This tiny place, reminiscent of a small dining room in a French boîte, is owned by French chef Marcel Trigue and his wife, Madeleine. It is most pleasant, with its crisp tablecloths and paintings of French scenery. Appetizers are typically Gallic: pâté, escargots, crevettes provençal; and some a bit different, like scampi flambe in Pernod with cream and garlic. The French onion soup is also flavorful. Main courses include Cornish game hen in a mustard sauce; rack of lamb béarnaise; sliced veal in a light, creamy mushroom sauce; shrimp with fresh basil sauce; and fresh fish of the day. These are served with bread and butter, vegetable, and potato. Finish your dinner with a light sherbet, caramel flan, or blueberries jubilee. Le Guignol is between King Street and Kapiolani Boulevard.

PAGODA FLOATING RESTAURANT, 1525 Rycroft St. Tel. 941-6611.
   Cuisine: SEAFOOD. **Reservations:** Recommended.
$ Prices: Appetizers $4.95–$6.75; main courses $11.95–$15.95. AE, DISC, MC. V.
   Open: Lunch daily 11am–2pm; dinner daily 4:30–9:30pm.

The Pagoda Floating Restaurant is one of those rare places where the scenery alone is worth the price of admission. The glass-enclosed Koi Room on the first floor, which specializes in seafood, and the more elegant La Salle overlook a lotus-blossom pond stocked with almost 3,000 brilliantly colored Japanese carp. Walkways lead to individual pagodas seemingly afloat in the pond. The pagodas are reserved for groups of eight or more, but don't despair! The view from the main dining rooms is also quite beautiful. Mahimahi is a favorite at $11.95. At lunch, you can order from the menu, or choose the local-style Kamaaina Lunch Buffet ($9.95 adults, $6.95 children 10 and under). There are also a variety of evening buffets: Monday and Tuesday it's a Family Night Prime Rib Buffet ($14.95 adults, $6.95 children); Wednesday and Thursday it's a gala Japanese Dinner Buffet ($16.95 adults, $8.95 children); and Friday, Saturday, and Sunday, it's the Prime Rib Weekend Buffet ($16.95 adults, $8.95 children). Try to plan your visit to catch the grand show at carp-feeding time—8am, noon, or 6pm. Bring the kids and the cameras.

TAHITIAN LANAI RESTAURANT, in the Waikikian Hotel, 1811 Ala Moana Blvd. Tel. 946-6541.
   Cuisine: AMERICAN/SEAFOOD. **Reservations:** Recommended.
$ Prices: Appetizers $3.95–$10.50; main courses $14.95–$28.95. AE, CB, DC, JCB, MC, V.
   Open: Breakfast daily 7am–11am; lunch daily 11am–2:30pm; dinner daily 5–10pm.

⭐ Just because you're saving money, it doesnt mean that you can't dine in style. To have breakfast at one of the most glamorous tropical settings in town, at coffeehouse prices, try this favorite old-timer, nestled beside a tranquil lagoon and surrounded by tikis, native carvings, Polynesian-style huts, and tapa designs. You can dine outdoors under striped umbrella tables or in the casual, open-air dining room. Recommended for breakfast: their renowned eggs Benedict or Florentine $7 for half order, $9.75 whole), served with hash browns, and a banana muffin or popover (weekends only). Coconut waffles or fresh banana griddle cakes ($4.75 each) are other winners.

Lunch and dinner are also good bets. You can still get those eggs Benedict or Florentine at lunch, plus specialties like chicken and shrimp curries ($8.50 to $10.25) and some very good salads—spinach, niçoise, and the Green Goddess Surprise: chicken or shrimp tossed with romaine lettuce ($7.25 to $8.50). There are complete dinners, with choice of soup or greens, potatoes or rice, garlic roll, and beverage accompanying such main courses as teriyaki steak, chicken curry, and seafood fettuccine, for $16.95 to $19.50. Higher-priced house specialties include jet-fresh seafood. (Maine lobster and Dungeness crabs are flown in fresh daily and displayed in live tanks), fresh catch of the day prepared in a variety of ways, and steak from the broiler. Don't miss the lively singing around the piano in the Papeete Bar nightly.

VANDA COURT CAFE, in the Ilikai Hotel, 1777 Ala Moana Blvd. Tel. 949-3811.
  Cuisine: AMERICAN. **Reservations:** Not accepted.
$ Prices: Appetizers $2.50–$9; main courses $7.25–$14.50. AE, CB, DC, DISC, JCB, MC, V.
  Open: Daily 6am–10pm.
To dine modestly at the Iliaki Hotel, try one of the most atmospheric "coffeehouses," in town, where all the booths and tables have a view of the ocean and of the passersby on the boardwalk. A window table gives you the added advantage of a bank of beautiful vanda orchids and the marina beyond. There, an early dinner provides a front-row seat for the sunset and the Ilikai's nightly torchlighting ceremony. There are a few dinnertime bargains, like the soup and salad bar at $10.50. Among the lower-priced dishes are the Oriental chicken salad at $8.50 and the chicken, Madras beef, or seafood curry for $12.75 to $13.50. Sandwiches and burgers are well worth the tab as they are robust and served with all the trimmings. A stylish spot.

READERS RECOMMEND

China House Restaurant, *1349 Kapiolani Blvd. (tel. 949-6602). "This restaurant near Ala Moana Center serves outstanding dumplings as well as the usual menu. Two of us feasted for lunch, and the bill came to just over $11. There's plenty of parking outside the mall-level entrance, mauka side of Sears."*—Pearl Ann Schwarts, Ardsley, N.Y.

RESTAURANT ROW

Restaurant Row, Honolulu's newest dining-shopping address, is alive and well and flourishing mightily at 500 Ala Moana Blvd., not far from downtown Honolulu. It's a high-tech, strikingly modern, neon environment, surely not your "old Hawaii," but an enjoyable contemporary urban playground.

In addition to those listed below, popular Restaurant Row establishments include Marie Callender, a popular family-style chain; Ruth's Chris Steak House, for top-of-the-line beef; and Studebaker's, a nightclub in the style of the '50s and '60s, where you "bop 'til you drop." From Waikiki, take any no. 19 or 20 bus from the Kuhio Avenue bus stop; it will take you directly to Restaurant Row.

MEALS FOR LESS THAN $12

CAFE ATHENA, One Waterfront Plaza, in Restaurant Row. Tel. 526-0071.
  Cuisine: GREEK. **Reservations:** Not required.
$ Prices: Appetizers $2.25–$7.50; main courses $8.25–$10.55. MC, V.
  Open: Mon–Sat 11am–11pm, Sun 5–10pm.
Authentic Mediterranean cuisine, low prices, and a cozy setting—just 10 tables with cane chairs, travel posters, soft lighting, and a tidy bar in the corner— make this new addition to Restaurant Row a winner. Only one menu is

S served all day, and everything on it is delicious: All dishes and sauces are made from "mom's authentic recipes." We like to start with the tasty taramosalata among the appetizers, then move on to one of the platters served with Greek salad and either rice or pita bread: perhaps the lamb kebab, the delicately spiced and marinated chicken Athena, or a beef-and-lamb gyros, right off the grill. Terrific sandwiches ($3.95 to $4.55) and salads ($4.50 to $5.85) are also good possibilities. Don't skip dessert—the Martinica, a blend of ice-cream cake and brandied rum chocolate, is nifty and just $2.95.

PIZZA BOB'S RESTAURANT, GAME ROOM & BAR, 500 Ala Moana Blvd., in Restaurant Row. Tel. 532-4600.
   Cuisine: ITALIAN. **Reservations:** Not accepted.
$ Prices: Pizzas $10.45–$15.95; pastas $6.95–$9.95. AE, DC, MC, V.
   Open: Mon–Thurs 11am–11pm, Fri–Sat 11am–2am, Sun 5–11pm.

S Voted "Hawaii's Best Pizza," this longtime favorite continues to pack in the crowds. It's a big, bustling place with a game room in back where you can try your hand at pinball or miniature basketball, and a lanai in front where you can eat, sip an espresso, and ogle the passing parade. In between is a large, rather high-tech–looking room done in black and gray, with a big and very popular bar. Despite its name, Pizza Bob's has lots more than just pies. There are beautiful salads, like a Caesar salad to which bay shrimp and avocado are added, and a green veggie salad topped with crunchy cashew nuts, which run $3.45 to $8.95. Then there are hot sandwiches like grilled mahimahi and cold ones like the garden burger, a treat for vegetarians, at $5.95 to $7.75. But to get back to those pizza pies: They are super-fresh and delicious, and range from traditional to innovative. We like the grilled chicken Milano, with mushrooms, artichoke hearts, fresh tomatoes, and sweet onions. You can get individual slices, too, for $2.85. A good place to pop into any-time—especially on Sunday night from 5 to 9pm, when "Pizzarama" is on—all the pizza you can eat for $5.99. The Pacific Street Band often plays in the evenings, too.

ROSE CITY DINER, 500 Ala Moana Blvd., in Restaurant Row. Tel. 524-ROSE.
   Cuisine: AMERICAN. **Reservations:** Not required.
$ Prices: Appetizers $2.50–$6.75; main courses $5.25–$9.25. AE, DC, MC, V.
   Open: Mon–Thurs 6:30am–11pm, Fri 6:30am–midnight, Sat 9am–midnight, Sun 9am–11:30pm.

★ The best bet for stylish budget dining here is this counterpart of the popular Los Angeles restaurant of the same name. This restaurant and soda fountain is pure '50s camp, complete with 1950s artifacts, including miniature juke-boxes at each table playing old Elvis records. There's turkey with gravy, salisbury steak, chicken breast, lots of great salads, malted-milk shakes, and hot dogs, and nothing on the menu is over $9.25. Dinner plates include sensational lumpy mashed potatoes! Rosie's "Sliders"—hamburger, tuna, or chicken breast on miniature rolls, served in a basket—are fun for lunch ($5.29 to $6.50).
   The Rose City Diner is also a great place to bring the family: There's a special menu for keikis which begins at $2.75, and includes such possibilities as a fresh roast-turkey sandwich, BLT sandwiches, burgers, burritos, griddle keiki cakes, and fabulous milk shakes and malts for only $1.75.

SALSA RITA'S, 500 Ala Moana Blvd., in Restaurant Row. Tel. 536-4826.
   Cuisine: MEXICAN. **Reservations:** Not required.
$ Prices: Main courses $5.55–$11.50. AE, CB, DC, MC, V.
   Open: Daily 11am.
There's good food and good fun here. The bar, outside on the mall, is always filled with a noisy, friendly crowd. The tiny dining room, done in brilliant yellow and hung with pictures of chili peppers and Mexican scenes, is the place for flavorful quesadillas, enchiladas, tacos, and the like. The light eater's and children's dishes—charbroiled chicken with tortillas ($4.95), quesadillas ($4.75) and vegetarian burrito ($5.50)—are good values. And huevos rancheros are a special treat.

MEALS FOR LESS THAN $20

SUNSET GRILL, 500 Ala Moana Blvd., in Restaurant Row. Tel. 521-4409.
Cuisine: CONTEMPORARY AMERICAN. **Reservations:** Recommended.
$ Prices: Appetizers $5.95–$9.95; main courses $7.95–$22.95. AE, DC, MC, V.
Open: Mon–Thurs 11:30am–10pm, Fri 11am–midnight, Sat 11am–11pm;
Sun 10am–10pm.

Our favorite Restaurant Row dining place—indeed, one of our favorites in all Honolulu—is this handsome 200-seat restaurant featuring grilled, rootisserie, wood-fire, and oven-roasted foods in a sophisticated indoor-outdoor setting. Blond woods, glass walls, and a large grill in the center of the restaurant set the mood for dining that's casual in style but elegant where it counts, in every detail of food preparation and service. Among the little touches that make a difference: parmesan cheese grated at the table for your pasta or Caesar salad, and wines poured tableside, even if all you order is a glass. Have a drink—they're known for terrific martinis—and doodle on the placemats (crayons are provided) while you're waiting for your meal; the best placemat art is displayed on the walls up front, along with autographs of famous visitors.

If you're watching the budget, come for just a sandwich. Their grilled marinated chicken breast, with honey Dijon glaze, American Cheddar, and grilled red peppers on a cracked whole wheat roll, is a wonder at $9.95. Or splurge a bit and try some of the appetizers, like the oven-roasted garlic and herbed goat cheese or the sweet-potato–battered shrimp with roasted red pepper rémoulade. Make your main course the smoke-infused marinated salmon with shiitake mushroom salsa, or perhaps the fettuccine with Florida rock shrimp; or choose one of the excellent rôtisserie dishes, which come with fresh vegetables. From the charcoal grill comes the nifty 16 oz. porterhouse steak served with Tuscan mashed potatoes and fresh seasonal vegetables; also tops are the fresh fish and marinated breast of chicken with salsa. Desserts are always splendid here, especially the bread pudding with fresh berries and whiskey sauce.

Sunset Grill is also a great spot for Sunday brunch (10am to 3pm); brunchgoers not only get complimentary muffins, but complimentary copies of the major weekend papers as well. Remember it, too, on a Friday or Saturday night after the theater or a concert for a late-night bite or just dessert.

TRATTORIA MANZO, 500 Ala Moana Blvd., in Restaurant Row. Tel. 522-1711.
Cuisine: ITALIAN. **Reservations:** Not required.
$ Prices: Appetizers $3.75–$10; main courses $8.25–$15.95. AE, DC, DISC, MC, V.
Open: Mon–Fri 11am–11pm, Sat–Sun 5–11pm.

Open to the court at Restaurant Row, with a beautiful fountain right outside the main entrance and ornate black iron gates to enclose it at night, this little trattoria might well be in Florence or Rome. Inside are graceful bentwood chairs and tables sporting bright-red cloths. The walls are lined with modern Italian oil paintings and numerous photographs of celebrities. Personable owner Signor Manzo greets passersby with a cheery "buono sera" and directs traffic within. Signor Manzo points out that, since they have 6 kinds of pasta and a huge variety of sauces to choose from, they offer 201 ways to eat pasta. Whichever one you choose—maybe fruitti di mare (seafood), pollo (sliced chicken and vegetables), vongole (clams with white or red sauce), or just a simple aglio olio (oil and garlic), it's going to be very good. And the antipasti, soups, salads, open-face sandwiches, and a few chicken and veal dishes, like the chicken parmigiana and the veal milanese, are also fine choices. Stylish and fun.

WARD WAREHOUSE

Just opposite Kewalo Basin is the delightful Ward Warehouse shopping complex, where there are several charming restaurants that match the appeal of the shops. Siam Orchid (see above) also has an attractive outpost here.

MEALS FOR LESS THAN $12

CHOWDER HOUSE, 1050 Ala Moana Blvd., in Ward Warehouse, Tel. 521-5681.

Cuisine: SEAFOOD. **Reservations:** Not accepted.

$ **Prices:** Appetizers $1.25–$8.50; main courses $4.05–$12.95. AE, DISC, JCB, MC, V.

Open: Mon–Sat 11am–9pm.

The Chowder House is a bright, bustling, and inexpensive seafood house, where you can watch the boats of Fisherman's Wharf through the glass wall behind the bar and have a light seafood lunch or dinner for under $10. At a recent meal, we enjoyed a good-size fresh salad, French bread, and a filet of red snapper with french fries for $9.95. Prices are the same all day. Fish sandwiches, also served with fries, are also inexpensive: $4.05 for mahimahi, $4.40 for calamari. There are also salads, seafood, cocktails, and three kinds of chowder, all reasonably priced.

OLD SPAGHETTI FACTORY, 1050 Ala Moana Blvd., in Ward Warehouse. Tel. 531-1513.

Cuisine: ITALIAN. **Reservations:** Not accepted.

$ **Prices:** Main courses $3.95–$8.95. DC, MC, V.

Open: Lunch Mon–Sat 11:30am–2pm; dinner Mon–Thurs 5–10pm, Fri–Sat 5–11pm, Sun 4–10pm.

This is perhaps the most stunning budget restaurant in town. It's worth a visit just to see the setting, which might be described as "fabulous Victorian," the rooms brimming with authentic European antiques and Oriental rugs, ornamental lamp shades, overstuffed chairs, many mirrors, and huge chandeliers. You may dine in an authentic trolley car, or more likely, at large, comfortable tables on plush velvet seats, some with backs made from giant headboards. So popular is this place that you can always anticipate a wait for lunch and dinner, even though the main dining rooms seat 350 and the bar upstairs about 125!

The menu is modest, concentrating mostly on spaghetti, and the food is not as dazzling as the surroundings but you'll eat heartily and well. Main courses include a good green salad with choice of dressing, and fresh-baked bread with marvelous garlic butter (a whole loaf is brought to your table with a knife, and seconds are available). It's fun to have either the Pot Pourri, a sample of the four most popular sauces, or the Manager's Favorite, which serves up two different sauces. Our favorite sauces are the clam and the browned butter with mizithra (a Greek cheese) Baked chicken Mediterranean style is tasty, and so is the homemade lasagne and spinach tortellini. Lunch offers smaller portions and slightly lower prices. Beer, wine, and cocktails are available.

ORSON'S RESTAURANT, 1050 Ala Moana Blvd., in Ward Warehouse. Tel. 521-5681.

Cuisine: SEAFOOD. **Reservations:** Recommended.

$ **Prices:** Appetizers $2.95–$13.95; main courses $9.25–$24.95. AE, DISC, JCB, MC, V.

Open: Mon–Sat 11am–10pm.

The people who run the Chowder House at Ward Warehouse also operate this much fancier restaurant, which is upstairs. It's a lovely dining room with spacious ocean and mountain views and a delightfully open and breezy feeling. Although there are a number of seafood specialties in the higher-priced ranges, you can get a good variety of fish and seafood sandwiches, served with salad and fries, for under $10; the smoked-salmon Reuben on sourdough bread is one of our favorites.

WARD CENTRE

The elegant Ward Centre shopping/dining complex at 1200 Ala Moana Blvd. and Auahi Street, a block from Ward Warehouse, boasts a number of first-rate restaurants. We could happily spend weeks eating here and nowhere else.

MEALS FOR LESS THAN $12

CREPE FEVER, 1200 Ala Moana Blvd., in Ward Centre. Tel. 521-9023.
Cuisine: GOURMET VEGETARIAN. **Reservations:** Not accepted.
$ Prices: Appetizers $1.75–$5.25; main courses $4.25–$8.25. MC, V.
Open: Mon–Thurs 8am–10pm, Fri–Sat 8am–11pm, Sun 8am–4pm.

⭐ 💲 The quality of food and the charm of the surroundings make this casual restaurant, on the street level and inside Le Pavillon shopping area, quite special. Red-tile floors, oak tables, pastel pennants overhead, plus tables in the pretty garden outdoors, set a sparkling background for a menu that's not limited to just crêpes. It has a lot to offer vegetarians, sophisticated "grazers," and those who just want to eat delicious, healthy food at very reasonable prices. Our favorite lunch here used to be the homemade soup served in a bowl of scooped-out cracked-wheat bread with salad; it's a satisfying meal for $4.25. But ever since owner Sandee Garcia came up with her Grain & Green salad bar (at lunch Monday through Friday only), it's been a toss-up. Here you build your own vegetarian meal from a selection of complementary protein combinations that changes every day; grains, legumes, greens, beans, and seeds are provided in a variety of ways that might have a Mexican or Italian or Indian accent. Have a medium-size bowl at $3.75 or a huge bowl for $5.25. Begin with a cup of that wonderful homemade soup and you've got a super meal. Now for those crêpes: They're filled with the likes of chicken and ham, tuna-salad melt, and lemon spinach (with cream cheese), as are croissants; either can be had with brown rice or salad or both for around $7. Desserts are yummy, too; cheese blintzes topped with sour cream, fresh strawberries and cream, and bananas-and-cream crêpes. Since Crêpe Fever serves the same menu continuously, you can have breakfast anytime: three-egg omelets, waffles, and (especially good) their french toast—thick slices of bakery wheat bread, garnished with bananas, at $4.25. From 4 to 9pm, evening specials are added: fresh mushroom fettuccine, spinach tortellini, vegetable burrito, and a chicken tostada salad, from $7.95 to $8.25.

Right next to Crêpe Fever and under the same management is **Mocha Java,** an espresso fountain bar with a variety of hot and iced gourmet coffees, cappuccino, plus real milkshakes (try the chocolate espresso), and homemade cakes and sundaes. Take anything here as a dessert for your Crêpe Fever meal. Wine, beer, and a full bar menu are available.

KEO'S, 1200 Ala Moana Blvd., in Ward Centre. Tel. 533-0533.
Cuisine: THAI. **Reservations:** Recommended.
$ Prices: Appetizers $3.95–$10.95; main courses $8.95–$11.95. AE, DC, MC, V.
Open: Lunch Mon–Sat 11am–5pm; dinner daily 5–10pm.

The most picturesque restaurant at Ward Centre must surely be Keo's, one of the many creations of Thai restaurateur Keo Sananikone. Keo runs six restaurants in town and this one is exquisite, with lovely plantings, flowers, a fountain splashing into a languid pool, pink tablecloths, black bentwood chairs, and seating indoors and out—just beautiful! Enjoy the European-Asian café ambience at either lunch or dinner for reasonable prices. While you're here, pick up a copy of *Keo's Thai Cuisine,* so you can try your hand at creating delicate wonders back home.

OINKS, 1200 Ala Moana Blvd., in Ward Centre. Tel. 591-0584.
Cuisine: BARBECUE RIBS. **Reservations:** Not required.
$ Prices: Appetizers $1.25–$7.50; main courses $6.25–$9.75. AE, DISC, JCB, MC, V.
Open: Mon–Thurs 11am–midnight, Fri–Sat 11am–1am.

💲 This is, literally, the place to pig out at Ward Centre. At a recent Taste of Honolulu competition, it won acclaim for the best pork dishes. It's a cheery spot, with its butcher-block tables, striped awnings, piggy posters, and photos; toy porkers abound as does old Coca-Cola memorabilia. One section is open to the street, so you can watch the passing parade. The shiny kitchen and busy chefs are visible from the inside dining room. They turn out nifty Hog Salads—pig, chicken, shrimp, or chicken skin—served on a bed of tossed greens with a jalapeño corn muffin, plus huge main platters of barbecued ribs and chicken. For an appetizer, don't miss their "atomic onion"—it's as luscious as it is enormous. Dessert is fun, too, especially the chocolate peanut-butter pie and the bread pudding with whiskey sauce. And don't miss a visit to the restrooms—you wont believe your ears. An engaging spot.

SCOOZEE'S, 1200 Ala Moana Blvd. Tel. 528-5400.
> **Cuisine:** ITALIAN. **Reservations:** Not accepted.
> **$ Prices:** Appetizers $5–$6; main courses $6.50–$10. AE, DC, MC, V.
> **Open:** Mon–Thurs 11am–10pm, Fri–Sat 11am–11pm.

★ If the prospect of great food served in generous portions, at reasonable prices, and in a fun and friendly atmosphere excites you as much as it does us, make tracks to ScooZee's. Everything is made from scratch, and the preparation and style belie the tiny prices: nothing on the menu is over $10. "Pizza, Pasta and Pizzaz" is the house motto. Standouts on the menu include the Italian pea soup with smoked ham and Italian sausage, the grilled chicken Caesar salad, the ahi with rigatoni, the eggplant parmigiana, and the mussels broiled in marsala wine and garlic. Watching your budget? For a mere $6.50, you can feast on a Peasant's Dinner, imported cheese, fresh fruit, Italian prosciutto, a chunk of peasant bread, and a glass of Chianti. And desserts are the best: the "Tita I Miss Su" (an original rendition—and spelling—of tiramisù), the ricotta cheesecake, and the Grand Marnier chocolate fudge cake are too good to pass up. Ice-cream and liquor smoothies, a nice selection of beers and wines, are the beverages of choice. ScooZee's is an altogether pleasant place to be at, whether seated indoors in the greenhouselike dining room or outdoors on the umbrellaed lanai. Service is fast and friendly. Neat!

YUM YUM TREE, 1200 Ala Moana Blvd., in Ward Centre. Tel. 523-9333.
> **Cuisine:** AMERICAN. **Reservations:** Not required.
> **$ Prices:** Main courses $7.95–$14.20. AE, CB, DC, JCB, MC, V.
> **Open:** Sun–Thurs 7am–midnight, Fri–Sat 7am–1am.

★ Fans of the delightful pie shop and restaurant at Kahala Mall (see below) are thrilled to find another branch at Ward Centre. That makes it all the easier to stop in whenever the urge for pie—maybe macadamia-nut, lemon-crunch or English-toffee—becomes overwhelming. Take home a whole pie or have a delicious slice here. All three meals are served: excellent breakfasts featuring omelets, waffles, and eggs Benedict; lunches and dinners with a wide variety of salads, sandwiches, burgers, pastas, and complete meals—all at low prices. The menu is the same as at Kahala, and the setting is charming, both inside and out, with the feel of a big country house with a large porch, shady and cool, thanks to the big blue umbrellas. Cocktails are served from 7am to 2am. As you travel around the island, you'll find Yum Yum Trees at Pali Palms, Mililani, and Pearlridge.

MEALS FOR LESS THAN $20

ANDREW'S, 1200 Ala Moana Blvd., in Ward Centre. Tel. 523-8677.
> **Cuisine:** ITALIAN. **Reservations:** Recommended.
> **$ Prices:** Appetizers $2.75–$9; main courses $10.75–$25.95. AE, CB, DC, JCB, MC, V.
> **Open:** Lunch Mon–Fri 11am–4pm. Sun 10am–4pm; dinner Mon–Sat, 4–11pm, Sun 4–10pm.

Another star at Ward Centre is this gourmet Italian restaurant. Muted rose and brown tones from floor to ceiling produce a sedate effect, reinforced by the upholstered banquettes with dropped lamps, fabric-covered walls, and flowers on the tables. You could have a complete dinner, including antipasto, mixed green salad, minestrone, ice cream, plus a beverage along with your main courses for $17.25 to $24.95. Or choose à la carte; pastas begin around $10.75, and include a tasty and filling cannelloni di mare (stuffed with seafood). There are also a few seafood and chicken dishes for under $14.

Lunch is à la carte, with a dozen pastas for $9.95 to $15.95. There are choices galore of fish and fowl in the same price range; beef and veal run a little higher. Daily specials, such as spaghetti putanesca, are $10.75. Drinks are moderately priced. Skilled service contributes to a memorable experience.

COMPADRES MEXICAN BAR & GRILL, 1200 Ala Moana Blvd., in Ward Centre. Tel. 523-1307.
Cuisine: MEXICAN. **Reservations:** Not required.
$ Prices: Appetizers $5.95–$9.95; main courses $7.45–$16.95. AE, DC, MC, V.
Open: Mon–Thurs 11:30am–11pm, Fri–Sat 11:30am–midnight, Sun 11:30am–10pm.

Mexico is represented at Ward Centre by Compadres, which gets a resounding *olé!* from us. We're not at all surprised that it has been voted "Best Mexican Restaurant" in Hawaii by the *Honolulu* magazine poll for several years in a row. It's a big, very attractive place with comfortable rattan basket chairs and soft lights, and a young and energetic staff. It's fun to sit on the lanai outdoors. The food is *muy bueno* and the prices won't damage your budget. The same menu and prices are in effect all day long. The sandwiches, like the chicken and avocado at $7.50, are all served with thick-cut deep-fried potatoes and Mexican salad, but you'll probably want to sample such Mexican specialties as the various combinaciones, which include refried beans, fiesta rice, and Mexican salad, $9.95 to $12.95. Arroz con pollo at $12.50 and mahimahi ala Vera Cruz at $14.50 are both good, and everybody loves the house specialty of fajitas—grilled, marinated beef or chicken, sliced thin and stuffed into warm tortillas with a great salsa. The new Quesadillas Internacionales menu offers such creative options as Greek, Thai, and Japanese quesadillas. Vegetarians have a number of good choices. As for the desserts, we can't resist the banana chimi—a whole banana wrapped in a flour tortilla, rolled in cinnamon, and topped with ice cream. And the "Compadres 400" Menu features dishes of 400 or fewer calories, including the grilled chicken breast and turkey enchiladas. On weekends only, Compadres serves breakfast, offering a wide assortment of omelets, plus chili rellenos, huevos dos Ricardos, and much more.

There's another nifty Compadres in Lahaina, Maui.

MONTEREY BAY CANNERS, 1200 Ala Moana Blvd., in Ward Centre. Tel. 536-6197.
Cuisine: SEAFOOD. **Reservations:** Not required.
$ Prices: Appetizers $3.75–$8.75; main courses $10.95–$34.95. AE, DC, JCB, MC, V.
Open: Lunch Mon–Fri 11am–4pm; dinner Sun–Thurs 4–11pm, Fri–Sat 4pm–midnight.

This is one of Honolulu's most popular restaurants, a big, bustling, nautical-type place which serves a tremendous variety of seafood specialties. If you're lucky enough to get a table by the window, you can overlook Kewalo Basin, where the commercial fishing charter boats are berthed. Fresh fish is the specialty of the house; in fact, several of the local radio stations carry MBC's "Fresh Catch" report several times a day. Fish is broiled over real kiawe-wood charcoal; choose from mahimahi, Hawaiian ono, Alaskan halibut, catfish, salmon steak, and seafood combination ($12.25 to $17.95). San Francisco–style sourdough bread, fresh steamed vegetables, and a choice of starch are included; add another $1 to $1.50 and you get chowder or salad as well. There are also pasta dishes from $10.95 (for chicken fettuccine). For dessert, try the watermelon sherbet. A similar lunch menu offers smaller portions ($7 to $16). There's music and live entertainment Tuesday through Saturday nights from 9pm to 1:30am.

RYAN'S AT WARD CENTRE, 1200 Ala Moana Blvd., in Ward Centre. Tel. 523-9132.
Cuisine: AMERICAN. **Reservations:** Recommended at dinner.
$ Prices: Appetizers $4.95–$6.95; main courses $8.95–$17.95. AE, MC, V.
Open: Lunch Mon–Fri 11am–5pm; dinner daily 5–11pm.

Ryan's is a big, rambling stunner of a room with highly polished wood floors, gleaming brass, lazily rotating ceiling fans, windows all around, myriad lush plants, and a shiny kitchen open to view. Ryan's is seriously committed to "foods for all moods"—and that means quality in everything from simple fare to gourmet dishes, from "heart-healthy" recipes to sinfully rich creations for sybarites. The menu includes meat, chicken, and fish broiled with mesquite-wood charcoal from Mexico; fish fresh from Hawaiian, mainland, and Alaskan waters; pasta made fresh daily; and desserts that range from low-cal Tofutti to Chocolate Suicide Cake. Special dietary needs will be given consideration. Prices, considering the high quality, are quite reasonable. Consider, for example, dishes like mesquite-grilled chicken with apricot-cilantro glaze ($9.95 at lunch, $10.95 at dinner) or lemon-pepper fettuccine with bay shrimp and fresh mushrooms ($8.95 to $10.95); or the Three-Salad Sampler, which includes Mediterranean chicken, pea salad, and pasta with pesto ($7.95 and $8.95). A good selection of California wines is available by the bottle or by the glass. There are also temperature-controlled beers and a moderately priced bar list. The bar also serves light meals—scaled-down portions of the regular fare—from $5.95 to $9.95. It stays open until 1:15am.

DOWNTOWN HONOLULU & ENVIRONS

MEALS FOR LESS THAN $12

A LITTLE BIT OF SAIGON, 1160 Maunakea St. Tel. 528-3663.
   Cuisine: VIETNAMESE. **Reservations:** Not required.
$ Prices: Appetizers $4–$11.95; main courses $5.95–$15. MC, V.
   Open: Daily 10am–10pm.

Because it's just around the corner from many of the Chinatown art galleries, you'll always find artists—as well as savvy businessfolk—frequenting this place. Changing art exhibits are the main decor. The food is artistic too, simple but sophisticated, and appealing to a wide variety of tastes. There's plenty for vegetarians. Only vegetable oils and coconut water (not the fat-rich coconut milk used in many Asian restaurants) are used in the food preparations, so cholesterol-watchers can rest easy. Many of the dishes—like the chicken brochettes, the catch of the day, or the shrimp on sugarcane—can be ordered as pupus, as meals in a bowl, or as rice-paper rollups. That last preparation is especially intriguing: You're presented with a large tray containing rice-paper wrappers, vegetables, sprouts, condiments, and your main course. You dip the wrappers in a finger bowl, stuff them like a burrito, then dip it all in a peanut or pineapple/anchovy sauce. Also recommended are the curries, the heart noodle soups, and the sweet and tender coconut chicken. Try the desserts—you may never again get a chance to taste azuki beans and tapioca strips in coconut milk. A treat!

THE BUDDHIST VEGETARIAN RESTAURANT, 100 N. Beretania St. Tel. 532-1868.
   Cuisine: CHINESE VEGETARIAN. **Reservations:** Not required.
$ Prices: Appetizers $4.95–$8.50; main courses $6.50–$15.95. MC, V.
   Open: Lunch daily 10:30am–2pm; dinner daily 5:30–9pm.

Devout vegetarians will have the best time ever here, because the entire menu is devoted to Chinese vegetarian cuisine, the kind favored by Buddhist monks. Mr. Anthony Tsui, the proprietor of this pretty little place—nicely decorated, brightly lit, and very modern—opened it in honor of his 82-year old mother, who has always been very fond of Chinese vegetarian cooking. And you will be, too, once you try some of these unique dishes—many using wheat gluten or bean curd to make them appear like meat. You could start your meal with a soup of bamboo pith with vegetarian slices or with an appetizer like deep-fried gluten in mashed taro. Then go on to a variety of tofu dishes or some of the entrees like braised elm fungus with bamboo shoots and mushrooms, satay kabobs on a sizzling platter, or even sweet-and-sour vegetarian "pork." There's a good selection of congee, noodles, and rice, too. It's hard to find meatless dim sum, but they're served here at lunchtime every day. For dessert, try something new: maybe steamed bamboo pith with coconut or green bean soup—sure beats fortune cookies and canned pineapple!

COLUMBIA INN, 645 Kapiolani Blvd. Tel. 531-3747.
   Cuisine: AMERICAN. **Reservations:** Not accepted.
$ Prices: Appetizers $1.55–$5.95; main courses $5.75–$13. MC, V.
   Open: Sun–Thurs 6am–11pm; Fri–Sat 6am–midnight.

News dominates the conversation at this old-timer favorite hangout for the staffs of Honolulu's two daily newspapers just a few doors away. The news about food is also good at this large, wood-paneled spot with its leather booths. At lunch you can choose from 26 complete lunches between $6.05 and $12.55, and that includes boiled brisket of corned beef and cabbage, choice rib-eye steak, and "award-winning" beef stew, all accompanied by fish chowder or fruit salad, dessert, and beverage. Order à la carte and the range is $5.50 to $11.30. At dinner there are some two dozen choices for $10.75 and under, beginning at $7 for a complete meal (higher-priced meals go up to $16). It's also a great spot for old-fashioned hearty breakfasts.

DONNA'S DINER, 1148 Bishop St. Tel. 531-8660.
   Cuisine: AMERICAN. **Reservations:** Not accepted.
$ Prices: Soups $4.25–$4.95; plate lunches $3–$5.25. No credit cards.
   Open: Mon–Fri 5:30am–2:45pm.

For a quick, inexpensive, and very good breakfast or lunch while shopping or sightseeing downtown, pop in at this tiny place. You can tell it's good because of its popularity with the office and shop workers. Breakfast begins at $1.75 and includes coffee. Soups are a specialty and a meal in themselves: Portuguese bean soup is $4.50; pig's feet or oxtail soup is $4.25; wonton min, $3.75; and saimin $3.25. And generous plate lunches start at $4.75, burgers at $1.85.

Donna has another diner at 2227 S. Beretania St., in the McCully-Moiliili area.

DOWNTOWN BISTRO by Heidi's, Grosvenor Center on Queen St. Tel. 536-5344.
   Cuisine: PASTA/VEGETARIAN/SEAFOOD. **Reservations:** Not required.
$ Prices: $4.95–$7.95; main courses $9.95–$13.95.
   Open: Mon–Fri 6:30am–9pm.

A great place to break a sightseeing tour of downtown Honolulu, Downtown Bistro is just half a block from Aloha Tower and the Fort Street Mall. At lunch it's jammed with business folk, but it's pleasantly relaxed for evening dining. The spot is intimate and casual, smartly appointed with candles on the brightly colored table-cloths, lots of greenery, and comfortable chairs. Everything is fresh, cooked from scratch, keeping in mind health-conscious folks who enjoy something special; serious dieters are given extra consideration. It's a creative menu with lots of pasta dishes, southwestern specialties like spinach and potato enchiladas or nacho supreme with fresh island chicken breast, vegetarian choices, big salads, and fresh island seafood (try the seafood Balinese). It's all done with a gourmet flair, and everything on the menu can be prepared for take-out.

The cozy lounge with full bar is a popular downtown hangout for Honolulu business people. A free pupu buffet is served from 5 to 6pm. There's entertainment and karaoke singing Tuesday through Friday.

FLAMINGO KAPIOLANI, 871 Kapiolani Blvd. Tel. 538-6931.
   Cuisine: AMERICAN. **Reservations:** Not required.
$ Prices: Main courses $7.20–$13.95. AE, MC, V.
   Open: Daily 6am–2am.

For years the Flamingo restaurants have been offering terrific quality for little money. Pink booths and paneled walls at this remodeled Flamingo provide a good background for the excellent food. They're well known for their oxtail soup ($7.90), roasts, and specials (brisket of beef, pot roast with noodles, and the like). Lunch offers half a dozen sandwich platters, including soup and fries for $6.15 to $6.95, as well as 12 lunch plates for $6.60 to $10.90. At dinner, you get a complete meal, with a choice of soup or salad, vegetable, starch, buns, and beverage. After 10pm, the crowd gathers at the bar for karaoke.

The same management also runs the Flamingo Chuck Wagon at 1015 Kapiolani Blvd. (tel. 538-1161). In the business district downtown, the Flamingo Coffee Shop, 841 Bishop St. (tel. 521-6616), and Arthur's Restaurant, at 841 Bishop St. (tel. 521-7133), are big local favorites. Flamingos at the Windward City Shopping Center in Kaneohe (tel. 235-5566) and at Pearl City, 803 Kamehameha Hwy. (tel. 456-5946), are very popular with local families.

FORUM, 100 N. Beretania St. Tel. 599-5022.
   Cuisine: CHINESE. **Reservations:** Not required.
$ Prices: Appetizers $4.50–$12; main courses $6.95–$19.50. DC, MC, V.
   Open: Lunch daily 11am–2pm; dinner daily 5–9pm; snacks, drinks, and karaoke daily 9pm–2am.

Despite its appearance of elegance, this spacious, attractive place in the Chinese Cultural Plaza manages very reasonable prices for its luscious Cantonese food, with an emphasis on unusual seafood dishes. Should you desire live Dungeness crab, scalded filet of king clam, or sautéed oysters, they're all available. So, too, are cold jelly fish and spiced cold chicken feet among the appetizers, as well as hard-to-find bird's-nest and shark's-fin soups. But even if you go with the more ordinary dishes, as we did at a recent meal, you'll be well satisfied. Deep-fried spring rolls ($5.95) are ample for two as starters. Both the fiery Szechuan-style shrimp and the stir-fried diced chicken are excellent. For dessert, the preserved, salty lemon cool drink is for exotic tastes, but the French iced coffee is easy to take.

GEE . . . A DELI!, downtown, in the Davies Pacific Center, 841 Bishop St. Tel. 528-3100.
   Cuisine: DELI. **Reservations:** Not accepted.
$ Prices: Appetizers $1.75–$4.95; sandwiches $4.25–$5.90; daily special $4.95.
   No credit cards.
   Open: Mon–Fri 6:30am–3pm, Sat 11am–2pm.

Kailua's favorite New York–style deli now has a second location in the heart of the downtown business district, and it's proving itself another winner. There's an array of homemade soups, hefty sandwiches like the triple decker club, sandwiches, salads, all-beef hot dogs, and lots more. The hot Reuben—hot corned beef, melted Swiss, and sauerkraut on an onion roll—will cure any wandering New Yorker's case of nostalgia. For dessert: New York–style cheesecake. What else?

HAWAIIAN BAGEL, 753B Halekauwila St. Tel. 523-8638.
   Cuisine: BAGELS/DELI. **Reservations:** Not accepted.
$ Prices: Main courses $2–$5.80. No credit cards.
   Open: Mon–Thurs and Sat 6am–3:30pm, Fri 6am–5:30pm.

Hawaiian Bagel—how's that for a marriage of concepts? This wholesale-retail delicatessen with a few tables for those who can't make it out the door is in a new, contemporary-style building located in the run-down but picturesque Kakaako section of Honolulu. The sights and scents are surpassed only by the tastes. Needless to say, proprietor Stephen Gelson is not a full-blooded Hawaiian. Nor are the bagels, blueberry muffins, and homemade rye bread. But the little restaurant and take-out bakery-deli is a hit with the local folk. And our readers love it, too.

They carry 10 varieties of bagels, including onion, sesame seed, and poppy seed, at 40¢ each. Muffins, bearclaws, and cinnamon rolls are 95¢. The sandwiches are typical deli variety: roast beef, lox or whitefish and cream cheese, corned beef, liverwurst, turkey, pastrami, and the like, for $4.50 to $5.50. In true deli tradition, they even serve celery tonic. You may want to take home a fragrant, round loaf of fresh-from-the-oven rye bread. There's parking on the premises.

LEGEND SEAFOOD RESTAURANT, 108 N. Beretania St., in the Chinese Cultural Plaza. Tel. 532-1868.
   Cuisine: CHINESE. **Reservations:** Not required.

$ Prices: Appetizers $4.50–$16.50; main courses $7.50–$15.95. AE, CB, DC, DISC, JCB, MC, V.
Open: Lunch daily 10:30am–2pm; dinner Mon–Sat 5:30pm–10pm.

This place has become something of a legend in these parts—for one of the best dim sum lunches in town and for some of the best Chinese seafood around. It's all served in a large, attractive space that looks expensive but isn't; there's an enormous, elegant crystal-bead chandelier (shades of *Phantom of the Opera*) in the middle of the room and some elaborate wall decorations. It seems to be a favorite among residents for birthday and anniversary parties, showers, and any other excuse to get the whole family together. The biggest crowds, though, are at lunchtime, because that's when the staff comes around with rolling carts, taking orders and offering the likes of sweet creambuns, egg tartletts, steamed shrimp dumplings, braised chicken feet with black peppers, barbecued pork pastry and more—all in small, delicious portions, most priced from $1.85 to $2.95. If you want a regular meal, you can have that, too: wonderful seafood specialties include baked live crab with ginger and green onion, skewered live prawns with spicy salt (both seasonal), and sautéed scallops Szechuan style. The friendly staff bustles about, making sure everyone is happy—and they are.

RAMSAY GALLERIES AND CAFE, 1128 Smith St. Tel. 537-ARTS.
Cuisine: INTERNATIONAL. **Reservations:** Not required.
$ Prices: $3.25–$6.95. AE, CB, DISC, MC, V.
Open: Mon–Sat 10am–10pm, Fri til midnight.

If you're browsing the Chinatown art galleries, there's no better place to stop in for sophisticated grazing than Ramsay's. First, see the latest exhibition next door, then settle into the pretty little café, which has a full bar, for drinks and pupus, dessert and coffee, or dishes that run the gamut from a bowl of saimin at $3.25 to bagel, lox, and cream cheese for $7.50, to a French pâté with truffles and toast, for two, at $9.75. In between: escargots in garlic butter, an assortment of fruit and Brie, quiche Lorraine with salad, chicken salad croissant, cheese blintzes with berries, and a yummy chocolate mousse pie. Lovely.

TGI FRIDAY'S, 950 Ward Ave., at King St. Tel. 523-5841.
Cuisine: AMERICAN. **Reservations:** Not accepted.
$ Prices: Appetizers $2.45–$6.95; main courses $6.95–$12.95. AE, CB, DC, DISC, MC, V.
Open: Sun–Thurs 11am–1am, Fri–Sat 11am–2am.

Everything about this place is delightfully different—from the *big* menu with some 160 items to the art nouveau leaded-glass hanging lamps and lovely antique furniture and accessories. It's obvious that no expense was spared. The food, too, is far from run-of-the-mill. Appetizers are super, including skewered and charbroiled Thai chicken, potstickers, and "loaded potato skins"—baked potatoes, scooped and fried to a delightful crispness, and slathered with cheese and crumbled bacon, plus a sour-cream dip ($6.95). Specialties include southwestern, Oriental, American, and pasta dishes. Among the main courses, which are accompanied by a fresh vegetable and cup of soup or salad and hot garlic bread, we especially like the lemon chicken and the blackened Cajun halibut. Save room for one of the sinful desserts, like the mocha mud pie. Fridays is insanely popular, and it's first-come, first-served. A super place to dine or have a drink.

YONG SING, 1055 Alakea St. Tel. 531-1366.
Cuisine: CHINESE. **Reservations:** Not required.
$ Prices: Appetizers $4.75–$7.25; main courses $5.75–$17.25. MC, V.
Open: Daily 9am–9pm.

One of the most popular Chinese restaurants in town, Yong Sing is a huge place that occupies all of a downtown building, and its vast dining room is nicely, if not elaborately, decorated in red and gold. There's a huge menu from which to choose, with many well-priced goodies. The last time we were here we had a succulent almond duck and chicken with oyster sauce, the house specialty. An excellent $23 dinner for two includes egg-flower soup, almond chicken, sweet-and-sour pork, beef broccoli, and fried rice. For something unusual, ask the waiter for a dim sum lunch. This consists of many different varieties of Chinese dumplings: either steamed, baked, or fried, some filled with sweetmeats and served as main dishes; others, dainty pastries for dessert. Have five or six of these and plenty of the free-flowing tea, and you've had a lovely, inexpensive treat. But be sure to get there between the hours of 9am and 2pm for the dumplings; they sell out fast. Yong Sing also has cocktails at reasonable prices, take-out orders anytime, and plenty of public parking in the area.

READERS RECOMMEND

Central Union Church, *1660 S. Beretania St. (tel. 941-0957). "Central Union Church has a nice lunch at their Union Station for seniors on Tuesday, Wednesday, and Thursday from 11am to 12:30pm, with a suggested donation of $3, for salad bar, main course, dessert, and beverage. And the second-floor cafeteria of the Kapiolani Women's and Childrens Medical Center, Punahou Street, near Wilder Street, also has good food."*—Mrs. Dorothy Astman, Northport, N.Y.

MEALS FOR LESS THAN $20

KABUKI RESTAURANT AT KAPIOLANI, 600 Kapiolani Blvd. Tel. 545-5995.
  Cuisine: JAPANESE. **Reservations:** Recommended.
$ **Prices:** Appetizers $1.50–$14; dinners $5.95–$17.45. AE, DC, MC, V.
  Open: Lunch Mon–Sat 11am–2pm; dinner Mon–Sat 5–9:30pm (sushi bar until midnight), Sun 5–9pm (sushi bar until 10pm).
Here's a very pretty restaurant—light-wood paneling, lots of mirrors, white stoneware dishes with blue flowers, an attractive little sushi bar—that offers a chance to sample many Japanese dishes at reasonable prices. Live Maine lobsters and live Dungeness crabs are available and prepared to your liking; also popular is the lobster sashimi. Hibachi dinners, cooked at your table for two or more people, include soup, rice, tsukemono, special sauces, and tea, along with main courses, such as beef or chicken yakiniku, and are mostly $10.75 to $15.95; tasty teishoki dinners might include a main course of salmon, sashimi, and assorted vegetables for $12.75. For lunch, the combination teishoku meal is $10.75.

UNIVERSITY AREA

MEALS FOR LESS THAN $12

ALOHA POI BOWL, 2671 S. King St., in University Sq. Tel. 944-0798.
  Cuisine: HAWAIIAN. **Reservations:** Not accepted.
$ **Prices:** Appetizers $2.15–$5; main courses $5.75–$8. No credit cards.
  Open: Sat 11am–8:30pm, Sun 3–8pm.
This is a good spot for Hawaiian food and it's close to Waikiki. There are only six booths and a few big, white plastic-topped tables in a plain, storelike room, but the food is the star here. In addition to those luau staples like laulau, lomi-lomi salmon, kalua pork, tripe or beef stew, and chicken long rice, which run $3 to $5.25, there's always a daily special; the day we were there it was fried akule fish at $7. Be sure to top off your meal with that coconut dessert called haupia.

CAMPUS CENTER, University of Hawaii. Tel. 956-7327.
  Cuisine: AMERICAN/LOCAL.
$ **Prices:** Snacks $1–$3.50; main courses $3–$5. No credit cards.
  Open: Mon–Fri 7am–2pm.
The best place to eat at the University of Hawaii is this spot close to University Avenue in the middle of the campus. It's huge, upstairs cafeteria serves both breakfast

and lunch. Depending on the day, you may get lemon chicken, tasty seafood items, veal cutlets, or barbecued ribs. They also have fresh saimin, pasta, grilled items, and a variety of salads and desserts. The lower level of the Campus Center is Campus Express (open 9:30am to 3pm), which features "local foods," such as loco moco, bentos, chili and rice, and plate lunches, for $2 to $4. Bakery items and gourmet Lion's coffee can be purchased at Kampus Konfections, located in the convenience store called Kampus Korner (open 9am to 6:30pm).

CHAN'S CHINESE RESTAURANT, 2600 S. King St. Tel. 949-1188.
Cuisine: CHINESE. **Reservations:** Not accepted.
$ Prices: Main courses $5.50–$10.95. AE, MC, V.
Open: Daily 10:30am–10:25pm.

⭐ We like everything about this restaurant, from the sparkling clean, modern de-cor (pale pink and gray walls, white cloths and red napkins, and Chinese art and artifacts) to the cheerful service and that delicious food—at very reason-able prices. Owner Jennifer Chan blends an array of Mandarin, Szechuan, Shanghai, Cantonese, and Peking dishes; Chef Kenneth travels widely each year and always bings back exciting new recipes. The Mandarin menu offers slightly spicier fare, such as the spicy stir-fried shrimp. If it's in season, go for the lusty crab with black-bean sauce, market-priced. Or feast on a meal of tasty dim sum; wagon service is offered from 10:30am to 2pm. If you'd like to try a Chinese breakfast, then join the locals who come here for their *jook*—that's rice soup, with a choice of chicken, seafood, meat, or fish; most jooks are $3 to $5.50. For lunch or dinner, there are dozens of dishes under $6—like a chicken with black-mushroom casserole, moo shu pork with pancakes, or roast duck. Parking in Pucks Alley is validated.

DETLEF'S HONOLULU, 2700 S. King St. Tel. 949-8889.
Cuisine: GERMAN/CONTINENTAL/ISLAND. **Reservations:** Recommended.
$ Prices: Appetizers $5.25–$7.25; main courses $6.25–$19.50. AE, CB, DC, MC, V.
Open: Tues–Sat 5:30–10pm, Sun 5:30–9pm.

⭐ It's hard to find a good German restaurant—in fact, any kind of German restaurant—in Honolulu, so if the thoughts of authentic beef goulash or Wiener Schnitzel, Bratwurst, and Apfelstrudel set your taste buds tingling, don't miss Detlef's. This is Old World food prepared with a nouvelle, gourmet touch by master chef Detlef Greiert, who left the prestigious Kahala Hilton to go out on his own. Detlef, his wife Cher, and friends Michael and Mary Wilson took over an old restaurant and turned it into a very pretty little place, with café curtains, tapestry chairs, three-walled booths topped by wrought-iron scrolls, and cheerful watercolors on the walls. The wait staff is enthusiastic and helpful. For starters, you could go with the Black Forest ham and Swiss air-dried beef with sun-ripened melon, or the escargots Florentine in an herb-and-butter sauce. Then try Detlef's classic onion soup or a new invention, The Sultan's Tomato Soup, with mushrooms, fresh tomatoes, cream, and a touch of gin. For the price of the main course, you get a complete meal, including soup of the day, house salad with celery-seed dressing, fresh veg-etables, and beverage, or order à la carte for $2 less. Highlights of the menu include the roast duck with orange confit in a poached pear, served with apple red cabbage and Spatzle; the Hungarian beef goulash and the Weiner Schnitzel, done in the tradi-tional style; or, in a more contemporary mode, the seafood potpourri in a light wine-cream sauce and the panfried filets of rainbow trout, on sautéed spinach greens with a bacon-lentil sauce. Lighter meals include bratwurst, frankfurters, and a veg-etarian pasta with crunchy vegetables. As for dessert, we wouldn't dream of missing the strudel with vanilla cream and strawberry coulis or, equally good, chocolate-chip ice cream piled with black cherries and a decadent hazelnut sauce. There are at least a dozen German beers, a good wine list, available by bottle or glass, and a variety of coffees and espressos to finish.

LITTLE CAESAR'S PIZZA, 2752 Woodlawn Dr., in Manoa Marketplace. Tel. 988-4998.
Cuisine: PIZZA/SPAGHETTI.

$ Prices: Pizzas $8.49–$23.48 for two. Spaghetti $1.59–$13.88. No credit cards.
Open: Sun–Thurs 11am–9pm, Fri–Sat 11am–10pm.

Three cheers for the Little Caesar's chain of pizza take-out shops, of which there are almost a dozen in Honolulu (see the phone book for other addresses): one cheer for their luscious pizza, deep-dish or regular; two for their speedy preparation; and three for their money-saving concept—two pies for the price of one! This is not a now-and-then coupon promotion, but an all-year-round pricing policy. You can phone ahead for pickup in 20 minutes or so (they don't deliver) or just go into one of their cheerful locations and have a soft drink while your pies are in the oven. For something unique and yummy, get an order of their home-baked "Crazy Bread," thin dough strips with cheese on top ($1.75 an order). Salads, antipasto, and a few sandwiches are also available.

MAMA MIA, 1015 University Ave., in Pucks Alley. Tel. 947-5233.
Cuisine: ITALIAN. **Reservations:** Not accepted.
$ Prices: Pizzas $7.80–$22.50; subs $4.65–$6.50; main courses $7.95–$9.95 AE, DC, MC, V.
Open: Daily 11am–2am.

The longtime mecca for pizza-lovers in this area is Mama Mia's, and real "New York pizza" it is, since the owner is a transplanted New Yorker. There's a pie for every taste (even a vegetarian pizza with whole-wheat crust—$9.90), terrific spaghetti and lasagne dinners for under $10, and some really lusty and crusty hero sandwiches. They have a full liquor license. The place stays open late, so it's fun to come here after the movies or a show—and fun to sit at the sidewalk café. Occasionally there's entertainment here, too—perhaps a grown-up puppet show, or just music.

MANOA GARDEN, Hemenway Hall, University of Hawaii. Tel. 956-6468.
Cuisine: DELI/STIR-FRY. **Reservations:** Not accepted.
$ Prices: Appetizers $2–$4.25; main courses $3.45–$5. No credit cards.
Open: Daily 8am–8pm.

Quite pleasant at HU is Manoa Garden, which features deli sandwiches to order, "Grab 'N' Go" sandwiches, and delicious stir-fry concoctions made before your eyes. The bar opens at 2:30pm daily. On most Fridays, a Manoa Garden Jam Session features live outdoor entertainment.

O-BOK, 2756 Woodlawn Dr., in Manoa Marketplace. Tel. 988-7702.
Cuisine: KOREAN. **Reservations:** Not accepted.
$ Prices: Main courses $4.90–$7.25. MC, V.
Open: Tues–Sun 10am–8pm.

Small, sparkly clean, and friendly sums up this little Korean place that serves wonderful food at very moderate prices. The menu is the same all day. All main dishes are served with na mul (vegetables), kimchee (a fiery coleslaw), and rice. The most popular Korean specialty in Hawaii seems to be kalbi, tender barbecued short ribs. They are particularly good here, and priced at $7.25. Other very good dishes are the barbecued chicken, the fish or meat jun (breaded with an egg batter), and the bi bim bap (mixed vegetables, beef, and fried egg on rice). Very tasty, too, are the mon doo (a kind of Korean wonton); try them in soup or fried, as a side dish. To explore several taste sensations, order one of the mixed plates. The special plate at $5.50 includes kalbi, barbecued chicken, mon doo, tae-ku (dried codfish) and na mul.

WAIOLI TEA ROOM, 2950 Manoa Rd. Tel. 988-9488.
Cuisine: AMERICAN. **Reservations:** Recommended.
$ Prices: Lunch $8–$11; Sun brunch $12.50–$15.50. MC, V.
Open: Lunch Mon–Fri 11am–2:30pm; brunch Sun 11am–2:30pm; evenings only for private banquets and special theme events (Spanish, Indonesian, Cajun, etc.). Phone for information.

Great news! The famous Waioli Tea Room, a Honolulu tradition for many years and shuttered for the past few, is open once again. The charming restaurant, done in historic "plantation style," is operated by Tad & Pat,

Hawaii's premier caterers, and their skill is apparent here. Lunch consists of a delicious soup, and salad bar, featuring hot crab dip with toasted pita chips, plus such dishes as baked Brie with apricots and almonds, Kalua turkey with manapua buns, chicken Key Biscayne (stuffed with prosciutto and mozzarella), and Caribbean beef ribs. The Sunday brunch menu features a salad bar, pastas, Waioli chicken, fresh grilled fish, fresh fruits, and homemade desserts.

The Waioli Tea Room is on the Historical Register; it is rumored that Robert Louis Stevenson courted the muse in the little grass shack now rebuilt as the Robert Louis Stevenson Memorial Grass House. The beautiful tropical grounds are yours for the strolling, and unless there's a wedding going on, you can visit the Little Chapel on the grounds, designed for the children of Waioli.

READERS RECOMMEND

Aloha Cafeteria. *"The Aloha Cafeteria at the University of Hawaii has good food. It is on the first floor of the Aloha dormitory, off Dole Street, almost opposite East/West Road. For nonstudents there's a flat rate, inexpensive, and all you can eat."*—Mrs. Dorothy Astman, Northport, N.Y.

MEALS FOR LESS THAN $20

CAFE BRIO, 2756 Woodlawn Dr., in Manoa Marketplace. Tel. 988-5555.
   Cuisine: CONTEMPORARY AMERICAN. **Reservations:** Recommended.
$ Prices: Appetizers $4–$8; main courses $8–$17. AE, DC, DISC, JCB, MC, V.
   Open: Lunch Mon–Fri 11:30am–2pm; dinner Mon–Sat 5:30–10pm.

An island friend of ours says that the only thing wrong with Café Brio is that you never want to leave. It's a veritable indoor garden—plants in boxes, plants hanging from the rafters, huge tropical leaf patterns on the carpeting, and smashing hand-painted leaves and flowers on the backs of the banquettes. There are whimsical murals on the natural-wood plank walls and fresh flowers on the tables. Outside there's Brio Garden, a "light-food" wine bar where a three-item snack costs $6 to $8.

Chef Richard Schimizu's menu is creative with a contemporary touch: Witness the julienne of zucchini, smoked salmon with lemon-zest crème fraîche, and tomato among the appetizers; and the grilled boneless chicken breast with tomatillo-corn salsa with grilled zucchini, squash, and creamy polenta among the main courses. Lunch is similar with dishes $1 or $2 lower, plus tostadas, crêpes, and sophisticated sandwiches. Desserts are spirited, too—there are different homemade ones, plus gelatos and sorbettos every day. And, of course, the music is sprightly—the last time we had dinner there, it was Offenbach providing the background.

INDIA HOUSE, 2632 S. King St. Tel. 955-7552.
   Cuisine: INDIAN. **Reservations:** Recommended.
$ Prices: Appetizers $7.50; main courses $9.95–$15.70. MC, V.
   Open: Lunch Mon–Fri 11am–2pm; dinner daily 5–9:30pm.

Ram Arora, formerly the specialty chef at the elegant (and super-expensive) Third Floor Restaurant at the Hawaiian Regent Hotel, owns this restaurant near Puck's Alley. His own place, besides being very much more within our budgetary reach, is attractive, cool, and relaxing. Brass lamps and lush plants abound in the small dining room that accommodates perhaps a dozen tables. A sari-clad hostess will greet you, make you welcome, and assist you in ordering. Should you wish to try tandoori (clay oven-cooking), have the boti kebab, the fish tikka, or tandoori chicken, served with pullao (rice pilaf) and a wonderful naan bread. Combination dinners are a good buy, and there are plentiful à la carte choices—curries, keema, chicken, shrimp, lamb, or vegetarian dishes. A particularly good dessert choice is the gulab jaman, a "dairy delicacy served in rosewater syrup." This is one thoroughly delightful dining experience.

PAESANO, 2752 Woodlawn Dr., in Manoa Marketplace. Tel. 988-5293.
  Cuisine: ITALIAN. **Reservations:** Recommended on weekends.
$ **Prices:** Appetizers $3.90–$6.90; main courses $8.90–$17.95. AE, MC, V.
  Open: Lunch Mon–Sat 11am–3pm; dinner daily 5–10pm.
At Paesano, you can watch the pastry chefs at work turning out lovely, chewy Italian bread and *bellissimo* pastries through the glass picture windows or from the dining room. Partitioned with wood panels for a feeling of privacy, the inviting dining room has white walls adorned with Hawaiian flower paintings and round tables or booths, all with spiffy white cloths and intricately folded crimson napkins. And, yes, there are portions of the room where you won't see the immense TV screen at the bar, usually tuned to some sports event. Start perhaps with a hearty bowl of pasta fagiolo or the delicate vichyssoise, then move on to one of the pastas, which come in both small ($8.90 to $10.90) and large ($10.90 to $12.90) portions. Veal saltimbocca, chicken Marsala, fish-of-the-day alla piccata and fish arregenata—with oregano, garlic, and oil—all are good. Homemade desserts are super, especially the zabaglione with imported Marsala and the New York cheesecake.

DESSERTS ONLY

BUBBIES, 1010 University Ave. Tel. 949-8984.
  Cuisine: ICE CREAM/DESSERTS. **Reservations.** Not accepted.
$ **Prices:** Desserts 96¢–$12.95. No credit cards.
  Open: Mon–Thurs noon–midnight, Fri–Sat noon–1am, Sun noon–11:30pm.
A popular destination in the Varsity Center is Bubbies, a favorite after-theater spot. Keith Robbins, who hails from the East Coast and named the shop after his grandmother, serves wonderful homemade ice cream and desserts. In addition to delectable ice cream ($2.26 per scoop), you can have cheesecake or apple pie, or chocolate-chip or macadamia-nut cookies along with your coffee. Curtains at the window, fans overhead, plants, an old-fashioned pendulum time clock, and a photograph of "Bubbie" complete the scene. Bubbie's ice cream is also served at some of Honolulu's finest restaurants.

WAIALAE-KAHALA

MEALS FOR LESS THAN $12

BERNARD'S NEW YORK DELI, in Kahala Mall Shopping Center. Tel. 732-DELI.
  Cuisine: DELI. **Reservations:** Not accepted.
$ **Prices:** Main courses $6.95–$9.99. DC, MC, V.
  Open: Mon–Sat 7am–9pm, Sun 7am–8pm.
Manhattan-style delicatessens may be catching on in Hawaii—this one is certainly getting kudos. Bernard's is kosher style from chicken soup to apple strudel. New Yorkers will get homesick just reading the menu: half a broiled chicken with matzoh balls and carrots, stuffed cabbage rolls with potato pancakes and salad, two kosher-beef knockwursts with baked beans and salad are all $8.99, as is gefilte fish with borscht and matzoh. You might want to start your meal with a bowl of homemade chicken soup or borscht with sour cream. Then perhaps on to a deli sandwich of corned beef or chopped liver, hot pastrami or kosher salami. Fancy a side dish, such as potato latkes, potato knishes, stuffed derma? They're all available. So are blueberry or cheese blintzes with sour cream, delicious old-fashioned creamy rice pudding, and cheesecake. Bernard's is a full-service restaurant with bentwood chairs and checkerboard floors. Deli breakfasts are served all day.

THE PATISSERIE, in the Kahala Mall Shopping Center. Tel. 735-4402.
  Cuisine: SANDWICHES/DESSERTS. **Reservations:** Not required.

$ Prices: Sandwiches $3.60–$4.75. MC, V.
Open: Mon–Fri 7am–9pm, Sat 7am–7pm, Sun 7am–5pm.
For a bit of Mittel Europa in Kahala Mall, stop in at the Pâtisserie, a bakery that also serves sandwiches and pastries at its sparkling counter and several little booths. Sandwiches, served on home-baked breads (we like the country Swiss), with sprouts or lettuce, include Black Forest ham, head cheese, roast beef, bratwurst, and pastrami. There's hot German potato salad, quiche Lorraine, and carrot salad, too. If you don't want anything quite so heavy, Black Forest cake, dobosh, and freshly baked pies should be just right.

Look for Pâtisserie shops at the Edgewater and Outrigger Westin hotels in Waikiki, and, downtown, at 33 S. King St. and 700 Bishop St.

KAIMUKI

VERBANO, 3571 Waialae Ave. Tel. 735-1777.
    Cuisine: ITALIAN. **Reservations:** Recommended on weekends.
$ Prices: Appetizers $5.90–$7.90; main courses $7.90–$14.90. AE, DC, MC, V.
    Open: Lunch Mon–Sat 11am–2:30pm; dinner daily 5–10pm.
The minimalist decor of this stunning restaurant makes for a warm, quiet elegance: the lights are low, the ceiling fans turn lazily, the wood partitions give a feeling of privacy. And the food is terrific and not at all overpriced, especially if you choose to go for one of the lighter portions offered on many dishes; we're always found them ample enough. After enjoying one of the appetizers, such as the deep-fried mozzarella and fresh garlic or the clams casino, you could have, for example: the stuffed Melba alla Sorentine (lightly breaded eggplant filled with several cheeses); the calimari verde (fried squid with vegetables and garlic sauce) for just $8.90 light portion or $12.90 regular; one of the veal specialties, such as the veal piccata or marsala, for just $12.90 or $14.90; or the seafood scampi for $10.90 or $13.90. All the meat, chicken, and seafood dishes come with a choice of vegetable, potato, or pasta; and the pastas are delicious—we like the unusual rigatoni with sautéed bacon, ham, and fresh garlic tomato sauce, just $7.90 or $9.90. There are plenty of vegetarian pastas, too: pesto, Alfredo, and primavera. If you have room for dessert, don't pass up the light, lovely zabaglione. Our local friends like this place so much they go back time and again.

YEN KING RESTAURANT, in the Kahala Mall Shopping Center. Tel. 732-5505.
    Cuisine: NORTHERN CHINESE/VEGETARIAN. **Reservations:** Recommended.
$ Prices: Appetizers $1.50–$9.50; main courses $6.50–$14.50. AE, MC, V.
    Open: Mon–Tues 11am–9:30pm, Wed–Sun 11am–2am.
Vegetarians who love Chinese food swear by this place near the Kahala Hilton. So do a lot of other folks who've discovered this attractive restaurant that specializes in the cuisines of Peking and Szechuan. There's a lot to choose from here—including at least 30 meatless dishes—but two dishes that we never miss are the famous Singing Rice Soup (it "sings" when the crispy rice is added to the hot broth), and Chinaman's Hat, which consists of very light "pancakes" that you stuff and wrap at the table with a luscious filling of pork and vegetables. From then on, choose what you like: crackling chicken, lemon beef, sautéed clams—they're all good. As for vegetarian dishes, we found the lo hom chai vegetable dish delectable. MSG is never used. Desserts at many Chinese restaurants are unimaginative, but not here. If they're not too busy, they might make you their unforgettable fried apple with honey: flaming apple cubes covered with a honey-maple syrup sauce and dipped in ice water right at your table. Everything on the regular menu is available for take-out, and take-outs during the dinner hours are charged lunchtime prices. Yen King has full bar service. There's karaoke music Wednesday through Sunday nights from 9:30pm to 2am.

YUM YUM TREE RESTAURANT AND PIE SHOP, in the Kahala Mall Shopping Center. Tel. 737-7938.

Cuisine: AMERICAN. **Reservations:** Not required.

$ Prices: Main courses $7.95–$14.25. AE, CB, DC, JCB, MC, V.

Open: Daily 7am–midnight.

Long a favorite in the lovely Kahala residential area, this pretty place has seating both on the lanai and in the wood-and-stone inside room. Service is fast and friendly, and the food is always good. We like their delectable chicken pot pie, a meal in itself for $8.95. Salads such as papaya stuffed with shrimp, and chicken salad Oriental, and sandwiches and burgers and pasta dishes are good, too. Dinners are served with soup or green salad, rice or potto, plus vegetables and fresh baked cornbread and honey butter. Selections include broiled chicken, mahimahi, shrimp fry, and broiled sirloin. Best of all are the yummy pies for dessert, baked in their own kitchens; the pie display at center stage makes it difficult to resist taking a whole one back to your hotel. It's rumored that folks who stay at the posh Kahala Hilton Hotel a few blocks away like to come here now and then for a quick and inexpensive change of pace. It's open for all three meals.

Also see the listing above for the newer Yum Yum Tree at Ward Centre. There's still another one by the beach in Kailua.

MEALS FOR LESS THAN $20

HALE VIETNAM, 1140 12th Ave., Kaimuki. Tel. 735-7581.

Cuisine: VIETNAMESE. **Reservations:** Recommended.

$ Prices: Main courses $7.25–$9.95. MC, V.

Open: Daily 11am–10pm.

Only a few restaurants in Honolulu offer Vietnamese cuisine, which combines a number of Asian and sometimes European influences. Chef Mark Fu, who is well known for his catering work, specializes in the cuisine of the Mekong Delta region, served in a casual setting of Southeast Asia art and tropical plants. Your main course is accompanied by an appetizer of imperial rolls, fried or nonfried Southeast Asian delights wrapped in rice paper and filled with seafood, pork, and fresh herbs. The complete dinner also includes a hearty Vietnamese beef-noodle soup. You may also order à la carte. Favorites include the chicken with ginger, the catfish in black pepper sauce, the sautéed tofu and vegetables in a peanut-curry sauce, and the Vietnamese fondue, cooked at your table.

KEEHI LAGOON

MEALS FOR LESS THAN $20

LA MARIANA RESAURANT & BAR, 50 Sand Island Rd. Tel. 841-2173.

Cuisine: SEAFOOD/STEAK. **Reservations:** Not required.

$ Prices: Appetizers $8.95–$15.95; main courses $7.75–$19.95. AE, DC, V.

Open: Lunch Mon–Fri 11am–2pm, Sat–Sun noon–5pm; dinner Mon–Fri 6–9pm, Sat–Sun 5–9pm.

Few Honolulu residents and practically no tourists know about Keehi Lagoon. This restaurant, too, is a well-kept secret, a hideaway for the boat owners of the La Mariana Sailing Club at Keehi Lagoon. The restaurant and the marina itself are owned by a feisty lady named Annette La Mariana Nahinu, who has been fighting to keep the area alive for over 40 years. The restaurant is ramshackle romantic, its furnishings—wooden tables, rattan chairs, glass balls, and fishing nets—reputedly salvaged from the old Don the Beachcomber restaurant. Dine either indoors or on the shaded lanai, in full view of the boats. Nothing formal, nothing fancy here—just the way Hawaii used to be before the big money took over. The restaurant's chef is excellent, specializing mostly in steak, seafood, and freshly caught fish. Prices are reasonable, and island favorites, including ahi, marlin, ulua, and red snapper, are all available. The price of a main course includes french fries, mashed potatoes, or rice, salad, hot rolls, and coffee or tea. Lunch is reasonable too, with the emphasis on meaty sandwiches (burgers from $4.50, a steak sizzler on a bun at $7.50). You'll need to drive here (it's not far from the airport); it's best to call for precise directions.

NEAR THE PINEAPPLE CANNERY

ANGELICA'S CAFE, at Gentry Pacific Center, 560 N. Nimitz Hwy. Tel. 537-6619.
   Cuisine: CONTEMPORARY AMERICAN. **Reservations:** Recommended.
$ Prices: Appetizers $6.95–$7.95; main courses $8.75–$15.50. AE, JCB, MC, V.
   Open: Breakfast Mon–Fri 8–10:30am; lunch Mon–Fri 11am–3pm; dinner Thurs–Sat 5:30–10pm.

★ Scarcely known to tourists but very much "in" with the local cognoscenti, Angelica's is a find. You'll find it just a few blocks from the Dole Pineapple Cannery, so it can easily be tied in with a drive there; it's also an easy stop if you're going to or from the airport. It's an uncommonly pretty place, with a bit of the feel of an English garden: pastel-flowered tablecloths, peach-and-white striped or green-flowered chairs, and soft peach umbrellas covering the tables out in the mall. And the food is marvelous—fresh, wonderfully imaginative, beautifully prepared. Only a few items are on each week's dinner menu, but they are distinctly different, and most appealing. For example, among the appetizers there are seared scallops with a roasted three-pepper sauce, or chopped lamb in radicchio, cups with fresh plum sauce; among the main courses, osso bucco with twice-roasted potatoes, or a roasted half-chicken stuffed with goat cheese and shiitake mushrooms, served with garlic mashed potatoes. Lunch provides a variety of gourmet treats at refreshingly low prices: Among our favorites on the sandwich menu ($7.95 to $9.25) are the scallops on homemade focaccia bread with herb-caper mayonnaise and the Szechuan shrimp with oven-dried tomatoes and won bok on a French roll. People rave about their salads, too ($7.95 to $13.95), especially the Oriental spicy chicken salad and the pasta salad with chicken, tarragon, apples, and capers. As for their scones made fresh daily, they are just not to be missed. Especially good with a bracing cup of cappuccino or espresso.

PEARL HARBOR

THE MARINA, Naval Station, Pearl Harbor. Tel. 471-0593.
   Cuisine: SEAFOOD/STEAK. **Reservations:** Recommended.
$ Prices: Appetizers, $4.95–$7.50; main courses $9.95–$15.95. DC, JCB, MC, V.
   Open: Lunch daily 11am–3pm; dinner Tues–Sat 5:30–9pm.
If you're driving out to Pearl Harbor, here's a good place for lunch. The Marina really is situated on a marina, a small boat harbor not far from the Pearl Harbor museum. One enters the Pearl Harbor Arizona Memorial complex and follows the simple directions. The restaurant is situated on the second floor of a building that overlooks the harbor and the Arizona Memorial in one direction and the Waianae Mountains in the other. Ships' lanterns provide pleasant, soft lighting in the big wood-paneled room with its high ceilings and ceiling fans. Lunch focuses on hearty meat and fish sandwiches ($3.50 to $6.95) and a daily hot plate, like the top sirloin at $6.25. Best time for an evening meal is Thursday, when there's a terrific prime rib and crab-leg buffet at $17.95 adults, $8.95 kids. On the regular dinner menu, such specialties as lobster tail, seafood platter, pepper steak, and deep-fried chicken all come with salad bar, soup, vegetables, hot rolls with butter, and a starch. "Smart Heart" selections include broiled or poached salmon, broiled mahimahi, oven-baked skinless chicken, and broiled Pacific prawns ($9.95 to $14.95). And there's a neat little menu for kids, too ($3.75 to $6.95). Sunday evenings, 6 to 10pm, they feature top local entertainers; no cover charge. A nice choice off our usual beaten path.

3. SPECIALTY DINING

BUFFETS

DYNASTY II, 1050 Ala Moana Blvd., in Ward Warehouse. Tel. 531-0208.
Cuisine: CHINESE. **Reservations:** Not required.
$ Prices: Weekday buffet lunch $8.45; weekend brunch buffet $11.45; appetizers $3.75–$14.75; main courses $7.75–$15.75. AE, CB, DC, DISC, JCB, MC, V.
Open: Lunch daily 11am–2pm; dinner daily 5:30–10pm.

This elegant Chinese restaurant offers two popular lunch buffets: during the week, you can eat all you want for $8.45; on Saturday and Sunday, when there's an expanded menu, the price goes up to $11.45. For a splurge, you might want to come back here for an à la carte dinner. Appetizers such as stuffed crab claw, and main courses like whole Peking duck and king prawns sautéed with honey-glazed walnuts, have earned this restaurant many awards. Impressive Oriental carpets and fixtures and beautiful ocean/sunset views are pluses.

HARE KRISHNA TEMPLE, 5, Coelho Way, in Nuuanu (call for directions). Tel. 595-4913.
Cuisine: ETHNIC VEGETARIAN. **Reservations:** Not accepted.
$ Prices: Lunch buffet $6.50; dinner buffet $7.50. No credit cards.
Open: Lunch Mon–Sat 11:30am–2pm; dinner Mon–Sat 5–8:30pm.

At this lovely old house, which is not only the temple but also the residence for the Hare Krishna followers on Oahu, you can get a great vegetarian lunch or dinner for a pittance. And be assured that is all you'll get—there is absolutely no proselytizing when you go there to eat. The little dining room seats 33 people; there are plain tables and chairs and paintings illustrating the Vedic scriptures on the walls. Lunch is either the wonderful East Indian style veggie buffet or the very well-stocked salad bar, for $4.50. You may also have soup, salad, and freshly baked bread for $5.50. At dinner, there's the usual salad bar; but on Monday evenings the buffet is Italian style, Wednesday is East Asian night, and Friday is Mexican. On Tuesday, Thursday, and Saturday the buffet is East Indian, like the one at lunch. On Sunday, no regular meals are served, but you may want to check out the Transcendental Love Feast, complete with group chanting and an East Indian meal. Adjoining the dining room is a book shop which sells a variety of Vedic literature as well as some pretty jewelry. Don't forget to look out at the backyard and see one of the largest banyan trees in the state—amazing!

KENGO'S ROYAL BUFFET, 1529 Kapiolani Blvd. Tel. 941-2241.
Cuisine: JAPANESE/AMERICAN. **Reservations:** Accepted only for groups of six or more.
$ Prices: Buffet breakfast $5.99; buffet lunch $9.95, Mon–Fri, $11.95 Sat–Sun buffet dinner $20.95 (all including beverage, tax, and tip). MC, V.
Open: Breakfast Sat–Sun 6–10am; lunch daily 11am–2pm; dinner daily 5–9:30pm.

This spot is immensely popular with local people, who keep it packed day and night. Although the atmosphere is plain, the combination of hearty food and low prices makes it a winner. The dinner buffet is especially good, with many luscious seafood dishes, such as shrimp tempura and lobster in black-bean sauce, as well as roast beef carved to order. There are two buffet tables, one laden with Japanese specialties such as sushi and salads; the other, haole favorites such as fried fish and lamb chops. Lunch offers a continental buffet. There's a modest dessert bar. Soup (we sampled a tasty Portuguese bean soup) is served at your table, as is your beverage. There's karaoke singing in the bar and lounge from 6pm to 2am, and in the main dining room from 10pm to 2am, every night.

PARC CAFE, in the Waikiki Parc Hotel, 2233 Helumoa Rd. Tel. 921-7272.
Cuisine: AMERICAN/JAPANESE/HAWAIIAN. **Reservations:** Recommended.

$ Prices: Breakfast buffet $11.50; regular lunch buffet $12.50; Wed Hawaiian lunch buffet $14.50; dinner buffet $17.50; Sun brunch $17.50. AE, CB, DC, JCB, MC, V.
Open: Breakfast daily 7–10am; lunch daily 11:30am–2pm; dinner daily 5:30–9pm; brunch Sun 11am–2pm.

⭐ For a buffet meal that's also a fine dining experience, the Parc Café, across from the Halekulani Hotel, is just the ticket. The garden-terrace atmosphere is charming, the service attentive, and the food of a gourmet quality not usually found on buffet tables. The dinner buffet features the likes of Peking duck salad, celery rémoulade, fresh fish of the day, pastas, and Asian favorites. The carving station offers roast beef or pork, charbroiled top sirloin, plus poultry and lamb. For dessert, you can have freshly baked pies and cakes or chocolate mousse, or make your own frozen yogurt sundaes with a lavish choice of toppings. Sunday brunch is another feast. One of our favorite things to do is to stop by on Wednesday for a spectacular Hawaiian lunch buffe;t the food is better than at many a luau. Lomi-lomi salmon, kalua pig, chicken long rice, lau lau, and the traditional haupia pudding are all featured, along with such treats as seafood chowders, soup, wild-bamboo-shoot salad, and mashed Molokai potatoes. The rest of the week, the luncheon buffet features a create-your-own sandwich bar, a Cobb salad station, a fresh taco salad station, pastas, chicken from the rôtisserie, a do-it-yourself frozen yogurt bar, and more. The breakfast buffet has a table full of goodies, including exotic fresh fruits, pastries, eggs, meats, cereals, pancakes, and delicious french toast. A great place to conduct quiet business or a morning tête-à-tête. Full à la carte service is also available.

PEACOCK ROOM AND GARDEN LANAI, in the Queen Kapiolani Hotel, 150 Kapahulu Ave. Tel. 922-1941.
Cuisine: INTERNATIONAL. **Reservations:** Recommended.
$ Prices: Buffets $10.95–$14.95. AE, CB, DC, JCB, MC.
Open: Breakfast daily 6:30–10:30am; lunch Mon–Sat 11am–2pm; dinner daily 5:30–9pm; brunch Sun 11am–2pm.

This restaurant provides a variety of intriguing buffets at lunch and dinner. The most popular is the crab leg and Hawaiian dinner buffet, with many traditional Hawaiian dishes, held every evening except Thursday, at $14.95. Thursday, there's a Japanese buffet dinner at $14.95. A Hawaiian luncheon buffet is held on Friday, Saturday, and Sunday, at $10.95 and a Japanese luncheon buffet on Thursday. Every day, there's a breakfast buffet at $7.98. Live entertainment is featured on Wednesday, Thursday, Friday, and Saturday nights. Prices, schedules, and types of buffets may change slightly, so be sure to check in advance.

PERRY'S SMORGY RESTAURANT, 2380 Kuhio Ave., at the corner of Kanekapolei. Tel. 926-0184.
Cuisine: AMERICAN. **Reservations:** Not accepted.
$ Prices: Breakfast buffet $5.16; lunch buffet $6.20; dinner buffet and Sun brunch $8.28, AE, MC, V.
Open: Breakfast daily 7–11am; lunch (Mon–Sat) 11:30am–2:30pm; dinner daily 5–9pm; brunch Sunday 11:30am–3pm.

⭐ Just about the best buffet values are offered at the two Perry's restaurants, which have been serving hearty American-style buffet meals for as long as we can remember. The food is really good, there's no limit to how much you can eat, and the prices are certainly right. Both restaurants are attractive, especially ⓢ the one on Kuhio, with its lush indoor-outdoor garden setting. At both, lunch and dinner feature a huge fruit and salad bar; hot vegetables; rice or potatoes; homemade corn muffins and dinner rolls; and lots of hot main dishes, including mahimahi, beef and vegetable stew, southern-style chicken, Italian spaghetti and garlic bread, and baked macaroni and cheese. Dinner adds a hand-carved round of roast beef au jus, golden fried shrimp, and sliced turkey. In addition to the generous dessert table, there's also a create-your-own sundae and dessert bar. Fresh island pineapple and local Kona coffee are served at each meal. Breakfast features carved smoked ham, french toast, pancakes, blueberry muffins, fresh doughnuts and

cinnamon rolls, an attractive fruit bar, and more. You can have as many refills as you like, but no doggie bags, please.
The second Perry's is at the Coral Seas Hotel, 240 Lewers St., oceanside of Kalakaua Avenue (tel. 922-8814).

PIKAKE TERRACE BUFFET & BROILER, in the Princess Kaiulani Hotel, 120 Kaiulani Ave. Tel. 922-5811.
Cuisine: AMERICAN. **Reservations:** Recommended for dinner.
$ Prices: Breakfast buffet $14.25 adults, $10.95 children 12–17, children 11 and under free; lunch buffet $15.25 adults, $12.95 children 12–17, free children 11 and under; dinner $21.95 adults, $14.95 children 12–17, free children 11 and under. AE, CB, DC, JCB, MC, V.
Open: Breakfast daily 6–11am; lunch daily 11am–2pm; dinner daily 5:30–10pm.
It all began with a few tables around the pool at the newly expanded Princess Kaiulani Hotel. But every year the tables increased, and now this restaurant is a dominant feature of the hotel's poolside and public areas. It lives up to its name with sumptuous buffets served morning, noon, and night in an open-air fantasia. All-you-can-eat breakfast buffets offer juices, fruits, cereal, crêpes, meats, and eggs. At lunch, choose from a huge salad table, a hot table with half a dozen choices, gourmet burgers, and a dessert table that tempts you to take one of each. The salad bar alone is $12.50; the chef's table alone, $13.50. At dinner, choose between an expanded buffet at $21.95, salad bar at $15.95, chef's table at $18.95, and an elaborate menu, featuring such dishes as herb-marinated jumbo shrimp en brochette and filet mignon.

PLANTATION CAFE, in the Ala Moana Hotel, 410 Atkinson. Tel. 955-4811.
Cuisine: INTERNATIONAL. **Reservations:** Not required.
$ Prices: Breakfast buffets $10.95; lunch soup-and-sandwich bar $8.50; weekend dinner buffets $14.95. AE, DC, JCB, MC, V.
Open: Breakfast daily 6–11am; lunch daily 11am–5pm; dinner daily 5pm–midnight.
Although this place serves more than just buffets, it's hard to resist the luscious treats at the smörgåsbord. The restaurant looks opulent, with a huge glass wall that opens onto a richly planted area, but prices are not out of line. The sumptuous breakfast buffet includes fruits, juices, eggs, meats, and pastries galore. Lunch features a soup-and-sandwich bar. The regular menu includes nasi goreng, Indonesian fried rice with chicken, shrimp, veggies, and eggs, and there are also Chinese, Indian, and other exotic dishes. Come dinnertime, the chef's talents are displayed with out-of-the-ordinary soups and tantalizing appetizers, such as the shrimp and vegetable tempura.
At this writing, buffet dinners were being held on weekends only; Friday, a Mediterranean one, Saturday, a southwestern barbecue spread; and Sunday, Pacific Rim buffets. Call to make sure of the schedule.

RESTAURANT BENKEI, 1050 Ala Moana Blvd., in Ward Warehouse. Tel. 523-8713.
Cuisine: JAPANESE. **Reservations:** Recommended.
$ Prices: Buffet lunch $7.95; buffet dinner $15.95. AE, MC, V.
Open: Lunch daily 11am–2pm; dinner Tues–Sun 5:30–9:30pm.
Japanese food can be expensive, so it's great to know that you can go to this delightful place and feast on a bountiful buffet table of Japanese delicacies for just $7.95 at lunchtime, $15.95 at dinner. The restaurant is decorated in Old World Japanese style, and pleasant tables look out over the street. (If there are 20 people in your party, you can command the upstairs teahouse-style room for a special $50 per-person kaiseki menu.) The buffet table always features miso soup, an array of chicken, beef, and seafood dishes, plus sashimi, noodle dishes, and a tasty array of Japanese salads. Tea comes with your meal; dessert is extra. If you opt for the à la carte menu (appetizers $5 to $10, main courses $10 to $20 at dinner), you can choose from a variety of seafood tempura, fried and broiled fish, sashimi, steak salad, and Japanese-style steak—all served with appetizer, rice, pickles, and soup.

READERS RECOMMEND

Trellisses Restaurant, *in the Outrigger Prince Kuhio Hotel, 2500 Kuhio Ave. (tel. 922-0811)* "...*Trellises Restaurant at the Outrigger Prince Kuhio Hotel charges around $18.95 for its Friday-night seafood buffet. It is excellent in every way, recommended for a 'Big Splurge' meal.*"—Lynda Lamb, Colo. S.C.

EXOTIC SNACK FOOD

Honolulu has myriad snack bars where you can sample exotic cuisines at penny-pinching prices. Right in Waikiki, for example, is the **Hung Yun Chinese Kitchen** in Kuhio Mall, where the luscious aromas wafting from the restaurant will lead you to Chinese dishes that start at $1 for pieces of chicken, beef, and pork. Top prices on other main courses: $3.60 to $4.25.

The **Oriental Snack Bars at Woolworth's** at Ala Moana Center is a great place to sample authentic Japanese dishes for just pennies. It's a big hit with the office workers and shoppers. After filling up your paper plate, you can go out and sit in the pretty mall watching islanders mill about. Incidentally, two cone sushis (cold, marinated rice cakes) tucked in your bag make a tasty lunch-on-the-run. (Many of the ubiquitous ABC Discount Stores also carry cone sushi to go.)

Ala Moana Center has another extraordinary source for sampling Japanese food: the gourmet food department on the second floor of **Shirokiya,** the large Japanese department store. There are many booths and counters where delicious food is cooked, baked, and/or sold. Booths offer freshly roasted chestnuts, tasty manapuas, and, of course, a vast array of wonderful sushi and other traditional Japanese fare. You can assemble a meal for yourself out of these offerings, and then take them home or to a little dining lanai to savor on the spot. Most days, from 3:30 to 8pm, there's an evening buffet and sushi bar, priced according to what you eat.

Rada's Peroscki, 1144-1146 Fort Street Mall (tel. 533-2388), is practically a Honolulu institution. This Russian snack bar specializes in piroshki—delicate, flaky buns stuffed with beef cheese, cabbage, mushrooms, or whatever combination suits your fancy. We simply can't resist the chicken, mushrooms, and cheese piroshki, but the other combinations are also delicious. One big pirog is $1.50. The Russian fried squid, $1.10 a bag are . . . different. Rada's is a family operation, and the people in charge make you feel welcome. Warning: Piroshki may be habit forming.

What, you've never had a Vietnamese sandwich? A stop at one of the numerous **Ba-Le Sandwich** shops will quickly take care of that. (There's one in Waikiki at 2330 Kuhio Ave. (tel. 926-4707), and another downtown at 1154 Fort St. Mall (tel. 521-4117); more shops are listed in the phone book.) In case you didn't know, a Vietnamese sandwich mingles both French and Asian influences. They use French bread or croissants, stuff them with ingredients like steamed pork or chicken or Chinese meatballs, then add Asian condiments like daikon, pickled carrots, onions, and soy sauce. Prices range from $1.75 for the vegetarian sandwich to $3.75 for the roast beef. Decor is nonexistent: vinyl floors, white walls, one or two tables, and a service counter. Take-out is the thing here. Closed Sundays.

For take-out barbecue—barbecued chicken, chicken cutlets, barbecued short ribs, deep-fried shrimp, and the like—the local people favor the chain of **L&L Drive-Inns;** the closest one for us is downtown at 100 N. Beretania St. (tel. 524-3313). Everything is grilled rather than fried. Plate lunches, including two scoops of rice and two scoops of potato or macaroni salad, are priced from $3 to $4.95.

MUSEUM DINING

CONTEMPORARY CAFE, in the Contemporary Museum, 2411 Makiki Heights Dr. Tel. 523-3362.
   Cuisine: INTERNATIONAL. **Reservations:** Recommended.
$ Prices: Appetizers $2.25–$8.25; main courses $7.25–$11.95. MC, V.

Open: Lunch Tues–Sat 11am–2pm (desserts and beverages to 3:30pm). Sun noon–2pm (desserts and beverages to 3:30pm).

⭐ If you visit the Contemporary Museum—and you should—you can also enjoy an artistic dining experience in its small and highly popular café. Done in old Hawaiian-style architecture, the Contemporary Cafe is set in a lush tropical garden. On the walls are some of Hawaii's finest contemporary art exhibits. The menu is sophisticated: You can graze on such appetizers as smoked salmon carpaccio or red curry mussel;, on pastas, quiches, and salads (the wilted spinach is a favorite); or on sandwiches ($7.95 to $8.50) such as the vegetarian favorite, grilled tempeh with tahini. And if all you want is an espresso or cappuccino and a rich dessert, like flourless chocolate roulade or amaretto crème caramel, you've come to the right place.

GARDEN CAFE, in the Honolulu Academy of Arts, 900 S. Beretania St. Tel. 532-8734.
Cuisine: INTERNATIONAL. **Reservations:** Recommended.
$ Prices: Sandwiches and main courses $6–$9.95. No credit cards.
Open: Lunch Tues–Sat 11:30am–2pm.
Closed: Aug and 2 weeks at Christmas.

⭐ At the Garden Cafe of the Honolulu Academy of Arts, the dining lanai is under the trees outside one of the world's great art collections. The serving staff, the cashier, and even the cooks are volunteers, and all profits from your meal go to further the work of the academy. Almost everything has a sophisticated touch: The menu changes every week and consists largely of gourmet sandwiches like the tea-smoked chicken sandwich, the grilled vegetable sandwich, and the smoked Gouda sandwich; there's usually a plate of fruit and cheese, and one or two vegetarian offerings, such as a vegetable casserole served with buckwheat walnut focaccia and chick pea spread and a tamale pie baked in a cornmeal crust. Desserts are under $4 and may include a lovely cherry plum crisp (plums and cherries baked with fresh ginger in an almond crust and served with green tea ice cream. Wine and beer are available.

A RESTAURANT FOR KIDS

CHUCK E. CHEESE PIZZA, 820 W. Hind Dr., in the Aina Haina Shopping Center. Tel. 373-2151.
Cuisine: PIZZA/SALAD BAR. **Reservations:** Not required.
$ Prices: Pizzas $7.95–$12.95 small. DISC, MC, V.
Open: Mon–Thurs 11am–9pm, Fri 11am–11pm. Sat 10am–11pm, Sun 10am–5pm.
Closed: Christmas, Thanksgiving.

So you're traveling with the kids? By all means, take any youngsters up to age 12 or so to this spot, which is on Kalanianaole Highway, not far from the Kahala Mall. There's a big stage at the front of the dining room, and every so often the curtains part to reveal cleverly designed, life-size mechanical-animal musicians and singers, such as Chuck E. Cheese, Jasper, and Pasqually. These ingenious creations appear most lifelike, and they "sing" and "play" instruments. There are also people in animal costumes who circulate in the dining room and visit with young diners. As if that weren't enough, there are myriad video games. This is a most popular place for local kids to celebrate birthdays. And the food isn't half bad. The pizzas include Super Combo (cheese, sausage, beef, pepperoni, etc.), Aloha Delight (cheese, ham, pineapple, toasted almonds), and Vegetarian Favorite. There's a salad bar with a good variety of fixings, $4.95 for all-you-can-eat, plus minipizzas, sandwiches, beer, and wine. You can even buy the kids a Showbiz Pizza T-shirt.

DINING COMPLEXES

INTERNATIONAL MARKET PLACE & KUHIO MALL

Few tourists who set foot in Waikiki leave without at least one visit to the **International Market Place,** in the heart of the beach area at 2330 Kalakaua

Ave., where throngs of merchants offer everything from grass skirts to wooden idols to T-shirts and pearls-in-the-shell. Immediately adjoining it, and fronting on Kuhio Avenue, is **Kuhio Mall,** another lively bazaar. Just about in the middle of the two of them is the attractive **International Food Court** (follow the yellow-brick line), where some 30 fast-food stands offer a variety of tempting foods that you eat at central tables. You can certainly make a meal here, lunch or dinner, for $5 or under: Some of our favorites include Peking Garden, Beef & Burger, The Mad Greek, Aloha Yakitori, Beaches and Cream, Choi's Kitchen, Bautista's Filipino Kitchen, Yummy Korean BBQ, and Mario's Pizza and Pasta. Cinn-a-Yums dispenses enormous, fattening, delicious cinnamon buns with various toppings. Open daily from 8:30am to 11pm.

WAIKIKI SHOPPING PLAZA

Shopping here (2250 Kalakaua Ave., at the corner of Seaside) can be expensive, and most of the upper-level restaurants are pricey, but the below-street level is a veritable bonanza for the budget-conscious diner who wants something a little bit different. Start in the Japanese sector at **Ramen** for freshly made Japanese noodles. You can have them seated at the open tables or at the Japanese counter flanked by Japanese lanterns. Prices start at $5.80 for shoyu ramen and go to $7.05 for gyoza—Japanese dumplings—and shrimp tempura. This is one of the few plaza spots that opens early, at 10am. There are no tables at the Japanese fast-food outlet **Okazu-Ya Bento** (*bento* means take-out). Here they custom-design your take-out lunch or dinner, filling the large plate with Japanese favorites: yaki soba, meatballs, chicken cutlet, and cone sushi, for 65¢ to $5.25. All items are in view in a glass showcase, Japanese style, so you can just point, or take their daily special at $5. To round off this Japanese trio, there's **Plaza Sushi,** a tidy little restaurant that serves a mostly Japanese crowd (prices run $6.50 to $11.50 during the day, $8.90 to $26.95 at night).

Want more variety? At the **Chinese Kitchen,** you get your choice of main dishes, plus noodles, chow fun, or steamed rice at the price of $5.30 for two main dishes, $6.30 for three, $7.30 for four. There's a familiar Taco Bell for Mexican goodies.

Your best all-around choice here is the huge **Plaza Coffee Shop,** where changing lunch specials go for $5.75 to $6.95 and include the likes of boneless barbecued chicken, corned beef and cabbage, and filets of mahimahi. Similar specials at dinner are mostly in the 8.95 to $12.95 range.

ALA MOANA CENTER'S MAKAI MARKET

Makai Market, occupying half an acre of space, has a score of self-service specialty kitchens where 13,000 meals a day are prepared. It employs more than 500 people—who obviously don't starve. Name your desire—Hawaiian, Italian, New York deli, seafood, Japanese, Chinese, health food—the food is here and you can put together a meal for around $4 to $5 at lunch, $6 to $7 at dinner. You serve yourself, then take your food to the pretty tables under the bright buntings overhead. There's karaoke singing every Saturday night from 6 to 8:30pm. You can start with a drink from the center bar with its LET'S MAKE A DAIQUIRI neon sign; daiquiris, piña coladas, and other favorites are about $3 to $4, and there are smoothies and nonalcoholic cocktails as well.

Take a look around and see what you might like. **Thirst Aid Station** has "Remedies and Prescriptions" that include sodas, smoothies, yogurt, and soup (72¢ to $2.50). **Tsuruya Noodle Soup** dishes up bowls of hot soba or udon, at $3.75 to $5.29. At **Sbarro Pizza,** folks line up for the calzone ($3.40), and for specials like baked ziti Sicilian style at $4.59.

Panda Express has both Mandarin and Szechuan dishes. Try the Mandarin spicy chicken with peanuts at $3.59, or go Szechuan with roast duck at $5.95. There's no way you can miss **Hawaiian Poi Bowl,** which dishes out food from a bright-red lunchwagon. There's a teri-chicken plate and a poi-bowl combo, for $5.20 to $6.70.

Yummy Korean BBQ has full-meal combo plates at $4.75 to $6.25, lunch or dinner. The **Aloha Grill Bar** is a '50s theme eatery, with '50s music on the juke-boxes; it has its own bar seats on which to enjoy the super burgers, at $3.89 to $5.99.

Looking for light food? Try the **Kitchen Garden,** which offers croissant sand-wiches and salads, plus baked potatoes, plain and fancy; both quiche and chili go for $3.59. For a cholesterol feast, however, we might suggest **La Rôtisserie,** which offers a fried-food buffet including seafood, beef burgundy and mahimahi in ginger butter for $3.75 to $5.50—as well as a delicious shrimp and crab salad for $7.50.

For years before Makai Market opened, **Patti's Chinese Kitchen** and **Lyn's Delicatessen** were bywords among visitors and locals alike. Now they've moved into the market and are still mighty crowd pleasers. Patti's is famous for its plate lunches; for a choice of any two items, the price is $4.30, $5.20 for three items, $6.20 for four. As for Lyn's, it has long been one of the best kosher-style delis in town, known for thick corned beef and pastrami sandwiches ($4.68), lox and bagels, fragrant and garlicky hotdogs, plus plate lunches, and very special buys on steak dinners.

Want more? **Orson's Chowderette** is a small version of the popular Orson's in Ward Warehouse. Finger foods like fish nuggets and clam strips, salads, and burgers of mahimahi, shrimp, or oysters, are all low-priced, $3.35 to $6.40. You can sample Thai food—plate lunches for $2.85 to $6.15, spring rolls at $2.99—at **Little Café Siam.** No MSG here! **Wingo** is fine when you crave fried chicken; it's served on a jumbo plate for $4.25 and up.

Mama's Italian Pastas is another good choice: they offer pastas from $4.75 to $6.50, and entrees such as shrimp marinara, garlic steak, and the like, from $5.95 to $7.50.

WORTH THE EXTRA MONEY

ALFRED'S EUROPEAN RESTAURANT, 1750 Kalakaua Ave. Tel. 955-5353.

Cuisine: EURO-CUISINE. **Reservations:** Recommended.

$ Prices: Appetizers $6.95–$12.50; main courses $17–$28. CB, DC, MC, V.

Open: Lunch Mon–Fri 11am–2pm; dinner Tues–Sat 6–10pm.

The dining critic of the *Honolulu Star-Bulletin* has called this "one of the top five restaurants in the city." We couldn't agree more. A visit to chef/owner Alfred Vollenweider's gracious dining room on the third floor of the Century Center, at the corner of Kapiolani Boulevard and Kalakaua Avenue, is like visiting a fine restaurant on the Continent where every detail is handled perfectly, from the china on the table to the attentive service by the waiters to the superb cuisine. Everything is prepared fresh, using only the best market ingredients. And nothing comes out of the kitchen until Alfred—who spends part of each evening walking around the restaurant in his tall chef's hat—makes sure that it's perfect. While a meal here is not inexpensive, neither is it overpriced and it offers top value for the dollar.

Dinner starts with four or five salad-relish dishes prepared according to the sea-son, plus Armenian flat bread (lavash). Homemade soup follows that, and then it's your choice of such dishes as a flavorful coquilles St-Jacques au beurre blanc, rack of lamb Provençale, filet mignon aux champignons, live Maine lobster, or fresh fish taken from local waters and sautéed, steamed, or poached in a light champagne sauce. Desserts are more than worth the price, especially for creations like the soufflé glacé Grand Marnier or the unforgettable strawberries Romanoff, fresh strawberries marinated in liqueur and topped with ice cream. Wines are decently priced. Irish, Swiss, and other specialty coffees, English and herbal teas, plus brandies and cordials top off the meal. Lunch is also pleasant and well priced, from about $9 to $16 for egg dishes, salads, fresh fish, sandwiches, plus a daily chef's special that includes soup or salad. Validated parking.

BON APPETIT, 1778 Ala Moana Blvd., in Discovery Bay. Tel. 942-3837.
Cuisine: FRENCH. **Reservations:** Recommended.
$ Prices: Appetizers (tapas) $2.95–$7.50; main courses $18.95–$27.95; 3-course dinners $21.95–$26.95. CB, DC, DISC, JCB, MC, V.
Open: Dinner daily 5:30–10:30pm; drinks and light fare 4:30–10pm.

★ Visitors to Honolulu and local residents can only be grateful that Guy Banal, the young chef/owner of Bon Appetit, decided to leave his native France some years ago and try his luck here on these far Pacific shores. For Banal is a true master, and his superb cuisine has won him a large and enthusiastic following, not to mention a *Travel/Holiday* award. A visit to his charming bistro, so pretty with its mirrors and red banquettes, potted palms and white curtains, is a must for those who are really serious about French food. Banal's style might be called light country nouvelle and classic cuisine with an island flair. Making good use of local produce and specialties, he also leans toward bistro fare and turns out a creditable three-course dinner, which changes every week, from $21.95 to $26.95. Banal has introduced a tapas meni—the only one in Honolulu—so it's fun to graze on these delectable morsels up front at the Cruvinet wine champagne bar, (35 French and California wines are served by the glass) or even make a full meal of them in the regular dining room. An ethereal lobster and scallop mousse, baked escargots and wild mushrooms, ceviche and steak tartare are just some of the tapas temptations.

On the regular à la carte menu, sample some of Banal's French Provincial specialties: a wonderful cassoulet, a hearty bouillabaisse Marseille, coq au vieux vin, and, from Normandy, tripe à la mode de Caen. The Spanish national dish, paella valenciana, is also well done here.

Guy Banal is also a master pastry chef, so try to save some strength for his marvelous homemade desserts: Our favorite is the clafoutis, a custard of peaches and black cherries sautéed in caramel and topped with a warm raspberry sauce. *Magnifique!*

Start your meal with a pitcher of Angel Sangria and end with Grandpa's Cappuccino (it's a secret recipe, made with a variety of liqueurs—and worth writing home about).

CASCADA, in the Royal Garden Hotel, 444 Olohana St. Tel. 943-0202.
Cuisine: CONTINENTAL–PACIFIC RIM. **Reservations:** Recommended.
$ Prices: Appetizers $5.95–$11; main courses $19.80–$28.95. AE, CB, DC, JCB, MC, V.
Open: Breakfast daily 6–10am; lunch daily 11:30–2pm; dinner daily 5:30–10pm.

A cascading waterfall is visible through the wall of windows at this enchanting new restaurant. Along with a hand-painted trompe-l'oeil ceiling and ceramic wall panels with a French country design, it makes for a striking background for Chef Toshiharu Koike's sophisticated menu. If you prefer dining alfresco, savor his creations out on the marble terrace, covered by its peach-and-white striped awning. Dinner here is rather pricey, so we like to come at lunchtime, when you can have a roast chicken Oriental salad or a yakinuku beef salad for $5.85–$6.25, seafood pasta or California-style linguine for $7.80 to $9.35, or crabmeat and avocado, roast chicken, smoked salmon, or a crabmeat sandwich for $6.50 to $7.95. Try one of the changing desserts, have a coffee or espresso, and you've dined like the rich—for just a little.

DUC'S BISTRO, 1188 Maunakea St. Tel. 531-6325.
Cuisine: FRENCH. **Reservations:** Recommended.
$ Prices: Appetizers, $4.50–$7.25; main courses $16.95–$19.95. AE, DISC, MC, V.
Open: Lunch Mon–Fri 11:30am–2pm; dinner daily 5:30–10pm.

★ Take a Vietnamese restaurateur, a Swiss chef, and a French menu and what do you get? The answer is Duc's Bistro, the latest creation of Dun Nguyen, the personable owner of A Little Bit of Saigon (see above). Duc's new place is exquisite to look at (white walls, hanging lamps providing soft lighting, fresh irises on every table, printed upholstery, and extraordinary black-and-white photographs by Anna Johnson) and exquisite to dine in, presenting the culinary masterpieces of

Escoffier-trained master chef Eduard Genhart. This is classic French cuisine, not easy to find these days. You might start with one of the soups, perhaps bisque of tomato and lobster, or a Caesar salad, or an appetizer like the prosciutto with papaya and gooseberries. Then on to a main course, such as one of the several seafood and fresh-fish presentations, or the boneless breast of chicken with crabmeat and mushrooms, or the steak aux poivres, flambéed with Armagnac. The lamb-rack cuts, served with potato crêpes and Bordeaux Chivy sauce, is an especially good choice. Pastry chef Benali dreams up special dessert creations every day, and they're almost too beautiful to disturb by eating. Lunch at Duc's features hot and cold sandwiches and burgers, pastas, meal salads (we like the Caesar with smoked chicken and the crab-cake salad), and several main courses from $9.25 to $11.95. A nice way to enjoy a wonderful scene at a lesser tab.

HAU TREE LANAI, in the New Otani Kaimara Beach Hotel, 2863 Kalakaua Ave. Tel. 923-1555.
   Cuisine: AMERICAN. **Reservations:** Recommended.
$ **Prices:** Appetizers $6.50–$8.95; main courses $18.50–$22.50. AE, CB, DC, JCB, MC, V.
   Open: Breakfast daily 6:30–11am; lunch daily 11:30am–2pm; dinner daily 5:30–9pm.

This is one of those sparkling, over-the water spots, where the atmosphere and food contend for the honors. It's so nice to dine here under the hau tree, watching the waves wash up to the shore at Sans Souci Beach, in the very setting that Robert Louis Stevenson once favored. Breakfast here is one of our favorite Honolulu experiences. The standard American breakfast, called the "Kamaaina," consists of two eggs and a choice of meat, potatoes or rice, and toast, for $9. Even more fun: the "Japanese Breakfast" at $15; thats a bowl of miso soup, rice, seaweed, grilled salmon, an egg, fresh fruit, pickled vegetables, and green tea—a meal big enough to last you for quite a while.

At lunch you can have many choices: refreshing salads like the Oriental chicken, the chicken seafood taco, and the crab-stuffed artichoke ($8.50 to $12.50); a variety of fitness selections including pastas and curries ($10.50 to $14.50); tasty sandwiches such as asparagus roll with turkey or mahi burger ($8.50 to $10.50); or main courses such as roasted garlic herb chicken, Kahuku shrimp rigatoni and seafood fettuccine, served with rice and vegetables ($10.50 to $13.50). The Aloha Friday lunch, with music by Arthur Lyman, is a special treat: There's a Hawaiian platter for $12.50, as well as a shrimp curry and a smoked fish salad at the same price. The dinner menu is even more extensive, including shrimp scampi, stuffed jumbo tiger prawns, veal medallion in wild-mushroom sauce, and broiled noisettes of lamb ($18.50 to $22.50). Complete dinners, which include soup or salad, sautéed fresh vegetables, and a selection from the dessert tray, plus beverage, are good buys at $29.50 and $32.50.

ILIKAI YACHT CLUB, RESTAURANT AND BAR, 1777 Ala Moana Blvd. Tel. 949-3811.
   Cuisine: CONTINENTAL. **Reservations:** Recommended.
$ **Prices:** Appetizers $4–$10; main courses $17.50–$36. AE, CB, DC, DISC, JCB, MC, V.
   Open: Dinner only, daily 5:30–10pm.

Save this one for a special night and enjoy every moment of it. This is a dining spot where eloquence and sophistication dominate the decor, music, and cuisine. The restaurant affords sheltered outdoor seating with views of the Ala Wai Yacht Harbor and, inside, a feeling of being served on a yacht. Large blue-glass columns are fish-filled aquariums. Upholstered chairs with a mahogany look seat you at the ample marble-top tables. Choose one of the superb appetizers to begin, like the kettle of steamed clams or the sugarcane shrimp, or maybe have the island seafood chowder, rich and hearty and made with Hawaiian sweet potatoes. On the lower-priced end of the dinner menu, you might have scallops and shrimp fettuccine for $22, tofu steak for $17.50 or stuffed breast of chicken South Pacific, stuffed with crab and served on a bed of spinach with lobster sauce. Even better, dine between 5:30 and

6:30 pm, when there are complete dinner specials, including dessert and beverage, for $15.95 to $18.95; entrees include sautéed breast of chicken, seafood linguine, and fresh catch of the day. Desserts are indescribable; the chef creates new wonders every day. There's live entertainment every night: From 4 to 7pm, it's Kawika and Friends, and then from 7 to 11pm, dancing to the music of Rudy Molina.

3660 ON THE RISE, 3660 Waiala Ave. Tel. 737-1177.
   Cuisine: EURO-ISLAND. **Reservations:** Recommended, especially on weekends.
$ Prices: Appetizers $6.75–$7.95; main courses $17.95–$21.
   Open: Lunch Tues–Fri 11:15am–2pm; dinner Tues–Sat 5:30–10pm, Sun 5:30–9pm.
The results of *Honolulu* magazine's 1994 reader's poll of their favorite restaurants surprised everybody. Newly opened 3660 on the Rise, an unpretentious restaurant in out-of-the-way Kaimuki, took two Hale Aina awards: one for Restaurant of the Year and another for Best Innovative Island Cuisine. If you have a car, it's no trouble at all to drive out there and see what people are talking about. The restaurant is located in the striking new Waialae Building, a vision in marble and granite. One side overlooks the all-marble lobby; another overlooks the pretty dining lanai. The immaculate kitchen is visible from the softly lit dining room, done in blond wood, with cozy booths to sink into. Chef Russell Siu takes island food—mostly Asian—and gives it a European flair. His menu changes monthly, but there are usually several of his signature dishes available: among the appetizers; the ahi katsu (ahi wrapped in nori, deep fried and served with a wasabe ginger sauce); and among the main courses, the New York steak Alaea (with Hawaiian rock salt) and the steamed fillet of opakapaka in a Chinese black-bean broth. The clam and corn chowder with roasted red pepper crème fraîche is a favorite soup. Lunch features at least 10 sandwiches, salads, pastas, and main dishes for under $10. Whenever you come, try one of the dessert creations of pastry chef Lisa Siu (Russell's wife)—maybe her warm chocolate soufflé cake or her unusual crème brûlee, she tops a vanilla bean custard with chocolate mousse and then tops it again, with caramel ice.

TOUCH THE EAST, JAPANESE BISTRO AND SUSHI BAR, 500 Ala Moana Blvd. in Restaurant Row. Tel. 521-5144.
   Cuisine: JAPANESE. **Reservations:** Not accepted.
$ Prices: Appetizers $4.95–$16.95; main courses $10.95–$22. AE, DC, DISC, JCB, MC, V.
   Open: Lunch daily 11:30am–2pm; dinner daily 5–10:30pm (sushi bar, Sun–Thurs to 11pm. Fri–Sat to 1am).
One of the most striking establishments in Restaurant Row, this popular bistro and sushi bar is a study in red and black, from the dramatic red-and-black facade out front to the black lacquer tables, bar, and sushi bar and the red walls, hung with pictures of Kabuki and Noh performers, within. The food is superb, from a wide variety of sushi and sashimi (platters are $5.95 to $16.95 at both lunch and dinner) to appetizers like braised tofu dumplings or fresh fried mozzarella, on to such main courses as chasoba (green tea pasta with Japanese eggplant, tomato sauce, and sausage), breast of chicken; sea scallops, and some very non-Japanese veal chops and hearty cioppino. Lunch features pleasant salads like the chicken salad with ginger-honey sauce ($4.95 to $10.95) and such dishes as butterfish, sea scallops, teriyaki chicken, and oyako-yaki (grilled salmon topped with salmon caviar). You could have chocolate mousse or cheesecake for dessert at either meal, but green-tea ice cream better suits the mood. Stay late and join the crowd for karaoke, every night from 9:30pm.

TRIPTON'S AMERICAN CAFE, 449 Kapahulu Ave. Tel. 737-3819.
   Cuisine: AMERICAN/CONTINENTAL. **Reservations:** Recommended.
$ Prices: Appetizers $6.50–$9.50; main courses $13.75–$22. AE, DC, MC, V.
   Open: Dinner only, Mon–Fri 5:30–10pm. Sat–Sun 5:30–10pm.
A modest splurge and a modest distance from Waikiki—2 blocks—is Tripton's, one flight above Hee Hing (there's parking in the basement garage). The owners, who ran restaurants in the Virgin Islands and, more recently, on Kauai, serve world-class cuisine at reasonable prices. Their liver pâté is more than just chopped liver: It is

carefully blended with nutmeg, mace, parsley, and garlic ($6.50). The salmon mousse is highlighted with dillweed and cucumber and blended with sour cream. Create your own salad at your table by choosing five condiments and the dressing; your server will toss it with romaine lettuce, tomatoes, cucumbers, and croutons. It comes with soup, is large enough to be a full meal, and costs $14.75; they call it "the biggest salad you've ever seen." Main dishes include daily chicken specials, fresh catch of the day—broiled or sautéed—New York steak, and prime ribs. The decor is lovely—peach and green tones accented by tropical greenery, and there are two levels, which add privacy. A well-equipped bar adds spirit. Check Susie's Dessert Board for marvelous desserts of the day, like the apple, cherry, and blueberry crisps with ice cream, lemon meringue pie, and much more.

4. IN NEARBY KAILUA & KANEOHE

MEALS FOR LESS THAN $12

CAFETERIA, in Castle Medical Center, 640 Ulukahiki St. Tel. 263-5500.
Cuisine: LACTO/OVO/VEGETARIAN. **Reservations:** Not accepted.
$ Prices: Main courses $1.50–$2. No credit cards.
Open: Mon–Fri 6:30am–6pm, Sat–Sun 4:30–6pm.
The most reasonable meals in Kailua can be found here at the cafeteria of the Castle Medical Center. The hospital is run by Seventh-Day Adventists, and, in keeping with their philosophy, everything served is vegetarian. The food is delicious, and at old-fashioned prices. All the hot dishes—like stir-fry veggies with tofu, or Créole patties—are $2 or under; a salad-and-sandwich bar is 25¢ an ounce, so you can easily put together a very reasonable meal. The à la carte breakfast menu features waffles, eggs, fresh fruit, and vegetables. Take the elevator or stairs down one flight as you enter the hospital.

GEE . . . A DELI!, 418-F Kuulei Rd. Tel. 261-4412.
Cuisine: DELI. **Reservations:** Not accepted.
$ Prices: Appetizers $1.50–$4; daily sandwich special $3.95. No credit cards.
Open: Mon–Fri 10am–7pm, Sat 10am–6pm, Sun 11am–5pm.
When we first saw this place, we exclaimed, "Gee, a deli!" and that turned out to be its name. You'll know this is a New York–style deli right away: Sandwiches can be served on onion roll or rye and are inches thick. There are all the usuals—hot pastrami, hot corned beef, Hebrew National salami—plus a terrific Italian sub at $4.95, a dozen or more clubs and subs, and bagels with cream cheese and lox. This is an extremely popular place, but service is fast and efficient. And there are five or six large tables, so you don't have to eat in the car. It's located directly behind McDonald's.

KIN WAH, 45-588 Kamehameha Hwy. Tel. 247-4812 or 247-5024.
Cuisine: CHINESE. **Reservations:** Not accepted.
$ Prices: Main courses $3.75–$12.50. MC, V.
Open: Daily 10am–9pm.
A friendly and bustling family-owned and -operated place off the tourist track in peaceful Kaneohe, Kin Wah is always full of local families gobbling up the terrific food. It's a spotless, attractive place, with its murals of swimming carp, maroon booths, wood paneling, and carved Chinese characters on the ceiling. You really can't go wrong with anything on the extensive menu, but the sizzling platters—such as chicken with black-bean sauce, combination seafood with vegetables, and scallops with vegetables ($5.50 to $7.50)—are definite winners. There are dozens of main courses priced at $5.50 or less.

YANI'S CAFE, 30 Aulike. Tel. 263-4601.
Cuisine: GREEK. **Reservations:** Not accepted.

$ Prices: Salads $3.95–$5.75; sandwiches and burgers $4.75–$6.50. No credit cards.
Open: Mon–Fri 7am–2pm, Sat–Sun 8am–2pm.

Right in the middle of the medical section of Kailua, this tiny, delightful café is full of doctors and nurses at lunchtime (don't worry, there'll be room for you), possibly because the food is healthful as well as delicious. Favorites include the gyros (grilled seasoned lamb in a warm pita bread), the traditional platter of Greek appetizers, the Greek burger (smothered with cheese), and a variety of omelets served at any hour. For a true Greek specialty, try the yummy loukoumades, tiny round doughnuts served piping hot and topped with a cinnamon-honey syrup.

MEALS FOR LESS THAN $20

ASSAGGIO ITALIAN RESTAURANT, 354 Uluniu St. Tel. 261-2772.

Cuisine: ITALIAN. **Reservations:** Recommended, especially on weekends.
$ Prices: Appetizers $1.90–$9.90; main courses $7.90–$16.90. AE, CB, DC, MC, V.
Open: Lunch Mon–Fri 11:30am–2:30pm; dinner daily 5–10pm.

A place that's won a big following for its wonderful food at oh-so-reasonable prices, Assaggio is something special. The service is special, too. The whole staff takes care of everyone; there's always someone watching to see if you're happy. At dinner the hot antipasto—which has *everything*—is exceptional. At dinner only, one may order a small or regular portion of pasta or any other main course. Our favorite pasta here—and one you don't see everywhere—is the baked ziti alla siciliano. Chicken, veal, seafood dishes—they're all good, especially the sauces. Lunch entrées are pretty much the same, and go down $1 or $2 in prices. Even if you have to get a take-out bag, don't leave Assaggio without sampling their liqueur-infused cheesecakes ($4); of course, you'd be perfectly safe with the tiramisu or the zabaglione with imported marsala, too, at $3.50. The restaurant is pleasant enough, with changing art work on the walls—but it's the food that shines here.

CINNAMON'S, 315 Uluniu St. Tel. 261-8724.

Cuisine: AMERICAN. **Reservations:** Recommended for parties of more than four.
$ Prices: Appetizers $2.25–$5.50; main courses $7.75–$17.95. CB, DC, MC, V.
Open: Breakfast daily 7am–2pm; lunch daily 11am–2pm; dinner Thurs–Sat 5–9pm.

Named after the bear in a French children's story, Cinnamon's is an immensely popular restaurant on the ground floor of a neighborhood shopping plaza. Its aim is to provide wholesome, natural, nutritious foods with no preservatives in a smoke-free atmosphere, and this it does—with style. The restaurant is small and cozy; four of the tables are under a pretty white gazebo. And the tab will be very reasonable. For lunch, we like the chicken-cashew salad ($6.50) and the grilled three-cheese deluxe sandwich ($3.95). Country quiches with salad, the garden vegetable platter, and burgers are all very popular, too. At dinnertime, pick one of the house specials, such as chicken fantasy, with "made from scratch" hollandaise; kebabs of chicken, beef, or mahimahi; or barbecued ribs. Meals come with soup or salad; rice, fries, or baked beans; vegetables; and hot dinner rolls. On the à la carte dinner menu, the fiesto taco grande salad and the chef's super salad ("a veritable salad bar brought to your table") are inexpensive and fun, as are the roast pork or roast turkey with apple dressing, chicken cutlet with country gravy and vegetables, seafood crêpes Florentine, seafood platter, and fresh fish. Breakfast has its own delights, including eggs Benedict, carrot pancakes, three-egg omelets, and freshly baked cinnamon rolls.

EL CHARRO AVITIA, 14 Oneawa St. Tel. 263-3943.

Cuisine: MEXICAN. **Reservations:** Recommended.
$ Prices: Appetizers $3.95–$7.95; main courses $7.50–$13.95. AE, DISC, MC, V.
Open: Daily 11am–9pm.

It's best come here on a weekday if you can, because this place is insanely popular and on weekends, even with a reservation, you'll probably still have to wait a little. But it will be worth it. This is some of the best Mexican food you'll find anywhere, prepared with love and care by the Avitia family (they have several successful restaurants in California and Nevada as well), and served in astounding portions; we always leave with doggie bags. The decor is beautiful indoors and out; you can dine outdoors on tables decorated with big clay lanterns and surrounded by ficus trees in mammoth clay pots, or indoors in a room laden with Mexican artifacts, with big, beautiful cutwater glass goblets, colorful Mexican pottery, and clay lanterns decorating your table. The chairs are carved in ornate Mexican style, and the music is pure south-of-the-border; you'll soon forget that you're in beautiful downtown Kailua and not in old Mexico. Anything you choose on the all-day menu will be good. Huevos Mexicanos—rancheros, colorados, revueltos—are served all day long. House specialties include shrimp enchiladas, ceviche tacos, sizzling shrimp fajitas, and a few specialties of Veracruz, like sautéed fresh fish smothered in a traditional Veracruz sauce. Start with a fresh fruit margarita; end with a simple flan or even fried ice cream. A treat.

HARRY'S CAFE & DELI, 629 Kailua Rd. Tel. 261-2120.
   Cuisine: MEDITERRANEAN. **Reservations:** Not required.
   $ Prices: Appetizers $4.50–$6.50; main courses $6.95–$11.95. CB, DC, MC, V.
   Open: Lunch Mon–Sat 11am–3pm; dinner daily 5:30–9pm.

Back in the 1930s and '40s, Harry Owens was one of the foremost composers of popular Hawaiian music: "Sweet Leilani" (which won him an Academy Award in 1939), "To You, Sweetheart, Aloha," and "Hawaii Calls" are standards of the hapa-haole repertoire. Now his son, Tim, has opened a charming restaurant that recalls the man and the era. Originals of the sheet music of many of his hits adorn the walls, as do superb Hawaiian quilts and changing art exhibits. The attractive young staff is impeccably trained: Servers are able to tell you exactly how each dish is prepared. And they know a good deal about wines, too (only wine and beer are served). The food lives up to the setting: We like to start with the pane formaggi (French bread stuffed with provolone cheese and baked with garlic-and-basil butter) or the rare carpaccio. Then we move on to such main courses as shrimp Provençale, pasta primavera, and chicken breast Medici. As for desserts, it's a hard choice. There are usually four kinds of cheesecakes made on the premises (strawberry, rum, amaretto, and chocolate are among the most popular), and there's always a sour-cream fudge cake with cream-cheese frosting, carrot or banana cake, and chocolate mousse. All are indubitably high in calories, but low in price ($3.75). Lunch is reasonable, especially the Beggar's Banquet—a bowl of soup with salad for $7.25. The Mediterranean shrimp salad, the Cobb salad, and the Reuben sandwich are all good bets, from $5.50 to $7.95. Relax over your meal as long as you like; no one is going to rush you. Harry's is a hit!

CHAPTER 7

HONOLULU ATTRACTIONS

The fantastic bargain of Honolulu is the enormous number of things to see and do that are inexpensive or free. Part of the reason for this, of course, is Hawaii's need to attract tourists—for tourism is one of its largest industries. But commercial motivations aside, there's enough genuine aloha to go a long way—and to give you so much to do that it becomes hard to decide what to sample and what to pass up!

There are three vital areas where the action takes place; they surround each other like concentric circles. First, there's Waikiki, the heart of the tourist scene. Some people never leave it and feel they've had a marvelous vacation. Just beyond that is the big, exciting world of Honolulu, one of the great cities (the 12th-largest in the United States, in fact). And beyond that, Windward Oahu and the joys of country life and rural beauty. We think you ought to try some of the doings in all three areas.

SUGGESTED ITINERARIES

IF YOU HAVE 1 DAY Get up early, drive, or take the bus to the USS *Arizona* Memorial at Pearl Harbor. Spend the rest of the day touring the Bishop Museum or loafing on Waikiki Beach.

IF YOU HAVE 2 DAYS Spend your first day as above. Spend the second day driving around the island of Oahu, seeing the Polynesian Cultural Center and the activities of the North Shore at Waimea and Haleiwa.

IF YOU HAVE 3 DAYS Spend your first two days as suggested above. On the third day take a walking tour of downtown Honolulu, stopping in at the Mission Houses Museum, Iolani Palace, and the Hawaii Maritime Center.

IF YOU HAVE 5 DAYS OR MORE Follow our suggestions above for the first three days. If you have more time, visit the National Memorial Cemetery of the Pacific at Punchbowl Crater, study the masterpieces at the Honolulu Academy of Arts, tour Chinatown or the University of Hawaii, or the Hawaii Children's Museum.

1. THE TOP ATTRACTIONS

Now we come to the serious center of any trip to a new place—seeing the basic sights. If you want to know what makes the 50th state tick, you must explore the city of Honolulu. Listed below are the major and minor attractions of the city—all of them worth your attention. Below that listing is a group of walking tours that will help you organize your sightseeing.

DOWNTOWN HONOLULU

HONOLULU ACADEMY OF ARTS, 900 S. Beretania St. Tel. 531-8865.

Don't leave Hawaii without a visit to the academy, one of the most beautiful small art museums in the world; it offers a look at the best of both Eastern and Western art. The physical plant is ideal for viewing art, divided as it is into a series of small galleries that open into tranquil courtyards; the Asian courtyard, in particular, is exquisite. There's a superb collection of Asian art—a magnificent sculpture of Kwan Yin, the Chinese goddess of mercy; Chinese scrolls and carvings; Korean ceramics; Japanese screens—as well as a good representation of Western masters, including Picasso, Braque, Monet, and van Gogh. Note also the Kress Collection of Italian Renaissance painting. Stop in the bookshop for prints and other distinctive gift items, and perhaps have a meal at the lovely Garden Café (see "Specialty Dining" in Chapter 6).

Admission: $4, $2 students, seniors, military.

Open: Tues–Sat 10am–4:30pm, Sun 1–5pm. **Bus:** 1 or 2; get off at the corner of Ward and Beretania, about a 15-minute ride from Waikiki. **Closed:** Major holidays.

MISSION HOUSES MUSEUM, 553 S. King St. Tel. 531-0481.

Three 19th century buildings offer tremendous insight into the lives of the missionaries in Hawaii—and the unlikely intermingling of New England and Polynesia. One of the houses, the home of missionary families, was built of ready-cut lumber that was shipped around Cape Horn from New England; a second, made of coral, houses a replica of the first printing press in the islands, which produced a Hawaiian spelling book in 1822; the third, also of coral, was the warehouse and home of the mission's first business agent.

An orientation exhibit and video introduces the Mission, its work with Hawaiians, and the controversy that still surrounds the role it played in Hawaii's history. Monthly "Living History" programs feature historical role-playing, hearth cooking, storytelling, work demonstrations, and candlelit evenings. Contact the museum for a current schedule of monthly events.

Be sure to visit the Museum Gift Shop, with an outstanding collection of Hawaiian and Pacific handcrafts, Hawaiian quilt patterns and kits, children's games and clothing, and many books. And try to take one of their morning walking tours of historic Honolulu, held Wednesday and Thursday at 9:30am; reservations are required. The cost of $7 includes museum admission.

Should you happen to be in town in June for the celebration of Kamehameha Day, don't miss their Fancy Fair; or if you're here on the weekend after Thanksgiving, join the festivities at their wonderful Christmas Fair, the opening of the holiday season in Honolulu.

Admission (including 45-minute tour): $5 adults, $4 seniors, military, $1 youths 6–15, free for children under 6.

Open: Tues–Sat 9am–4pm, Sun noon–4pm. **Bus:** 2 to the State Capitol; then walk 1 block down Punchbowl to King St., turn left, and walk half a block to the Mission Houses. The Waikiki Trolley also passes within a block.

KAWAIAHAO CHURCH, 957 Punchbowl. Tel. 522-1333.

⭐ The tall, feathered kahilis signify at once that this is royal ground. You're standing in the Westminster Abbey of Hawaii, the scene of pomp and ceremony, coronations, and celebrations since its dedication in 1841. On March 12, 1959, the day Hawaii achieved statehood, the old coral church was filled with ecstatic islanders ringing its bell noisily, giving thanks for the fulfillment of a dream long denied. The next day, the Rev. Abraham Akaka linked the spirit of aloha with the spirit of Christianity in a sermon that has since become a classic in the writings of Hawaii. Note the vestibule memorial plaques to Hawaiian royalty and to the Rev. Hiram Bingham, the missionary who designed the church. Note, too, the outstanding collection of portraits of the Hawaiian monarchy by artist Patric. If you have time, come back on Sunday morning at 8 or 10:30am to hear a Hawaiian-English service and some beautiful Hawaiian singing.

Admission: Free.

Open: Mon–Fri 9am–3pm, Sat 9am–noon, Sun services at 8 and 10:30am. Group tours Mon–Fri by appointment. **Bus:** 2 to Punchbowl and Beretania Sts.; then walk 1 block to King St.

IOLANI PALACE, S. King and Richards Sts. Tel. 522-0832.

⭐ Take a good look at the only state residence of royalty on American soil. Until 1969 the state capitol, it was built during the glittering golden era of Hawaii by King Kalakaua and his queen, Kapiolani. But it housed its royal tenants for only 11 years, from 1882 until the monarchy was overthrown in 1893 by a group of haoles linked to American sugar interests. Kalakaua's successor, his sister, Queen Liliuokalani, spent 9 months in the royal bedroom under house arrest after the abortive coup to restore the monarchy. (She is known for her song of farewell, "Aloha Oe.")

Now, after 9 years of work and at a total cost of $7 million, a massive restoration has been completed by the Friends of Iolani Palace, and the Hawaiian flag flies over it once again. Some of the furnishings are still being restored, but several rooms are ready for the public, and the American-Florentine building is eminently worth seeing. The crowns of King Kalakaua and Queen Kapiolani, as well as the royal scepter and sword of state, are on display in the throne room.

Tours are conducted by extremely knowledgeable docents who will fill you in on plenty of Hawaiian history as they show you the throne room with the king's tabu stick (made of narwhal tusk and topped by a gold sphere), the king's quarters, the entry hall, and the dining room with its royal portraits of European monarchs. Reservations are requested, and tickets not claimed 15 minutes before the start of a tour will be sold to anyone who happens to be waiting for a cancellation. You'll have to don enormous khaki "airplane slippers" over your shoes to protect the delicate wooden floors.

Also on the grounds are the Archives of Hawaii (open Monday through Friday from 8am to 4:30pm), the largest collection of Hawaiiana in existence.

Admission: Tours, $4 adults, $1 children 5–12; children under 5 not admitted.

Open: Tours, Wed–Sat every 15 minutes 9am–2:15pm. **Bus:** 2 to Punchbowl and Beretania Sts.

HAWAII MARITIME CENTER, Pier 7. Tel. 536-6373.

⭐ The Hawaii Maritime Center brings the stories of Hawaii's seas to life. The newest of the center's components—and its crowning glory—is the stunning, $6-million Kalakaua Boathouse, named after King Kalakaua (the "Merrie Monarch"). He was devoted to ocean sports, and his late 19th-century boathouse—of which the new structure is reminiscent in design—stood very close to this location. There's plenty to see here, so plan at least an hour to take it all in. William Conrad, the film and TV actor, narrates the museum's Sony Walkman Audio Tour.

Tastefully designed and brilliantly executed, the Center traces the maritime history of Hawaii from the first Polynesian settlers of the islands, and encompasses the arrival of the first Westerners, whalers, missionaries, plantation workers, and visitors. Suspended from the ceiling are giant canoes that once voyaged across the Pacific. On the second floor, you'll want to linger at such displays as the 1850s ship chandlery, a full-scale, walk-in diorama of H. Hackfeld & Co., the all-purpose whaler's store that later became Hawaii's leading department store, Liberty House! Dioramas and exhibits of the famed Matson Line luxury ships of the 1930s and '40s recall the languorous romanticism of early Hawaiian tourism. Audiovisual exhibits abound, such as the one showing scenes from the 1922 silent film on whaling, *Down to the Sea in Ships.*

Exhibits include "Polynesian Wayfinding," which highlights the revival of ancient Hawaiian navigation techniques and tracks the 1992 South Pacific voyages of the sailing canoe *Hokule'a.* The 45-foot humpback whale skeleton that hangs in the museum's atrium, named Leiiwi (garland of cherished bones), is one of the only two of its kind in the world.

At Pier 7 you can see the *Hokule'a,* a Hawaiian double-hulled canoe that is a replica of the one in which the islands' first settlers sailed from the Marquesas, using no instruments or charts—only stars, planets, and ocean signs. Also here is the National Historic Landmark *Falls of Clyde,* the only four-masted, full-rigged sailing ship in existence. Climb the nine (short) flights to the Observation Deck to see a glorious view of Honolulu Harbor. The gift shop has Boat Day posters, T-shirts decorated with old prints, *Falls of Clyde* aloha shirts, shark's-teeth pendants, antique bottles dug up in Honolulu, and the like.

Kids will enjoy everything here, and especially a visit to the *Cory Sause,* where they can steer a tot-size replica of a ship.

Note: From the Hawaii Maritime Center, you're just a short walk from the **Aloha Tower** at Pier 9. Long a symbol of Honolulu, it provides a good view of the harbor and the city in all directions, and it's also a fine spot for nighttime photography of harbor lights and the downtown area. Open daily from 8am to 7pm.

Admission (including boarding *Falls of Clyde*): $7 adults, $4 children 6–17, free for children under 6.

Open: Daily 9am–5pm. **Closed:** Christmas. **Bus:** 19 or 20 (Airport) to the Federal Building. There's a free shuttle to and from Waikiki via Hilo Hattie buses; the Waikiki Trolley also stops here.

PUNCHBOWL, LOWER TANTALUS & NUUANU

NATIONAL MEMORIAL CEMETERY OF THE PACIFIC, Punchbowl Crater. Tel. 541-1434.

⭐ Buried inside the crater of an extinct volcano (named, with prophetic irony, the Hill of Sacrifice by the ancient Hawaiians) are some 26,000 American service personnel who perished in the Pacific during World War II, the Korean War, and the Vietnam War. Astronaut Ellison Onizuka is also buried here (visit the administration office for information regarding grave locations). Also listed here are the names of all Pacific war service people who have been recorded missing or lost or buried at sea.

Parents from all over the mainland and from the islands come to Punchbowl on pilgrimages. The endless rows of gravestones of young people form a sobering sight, and awesome monument to the futility of war. When you've had enough, walk for another 10 minutes to the lookout at the crater's rim for a sweeping panorama of Honolulu just below.

Admission: Free.

Open: Daily 8am–5:30pm. *Note:* Possible federal budget cuts may necessitate closings on some days; call before coming out. **Directions:** Take bus no. 2 from Waikiki toward town (request a transfer). Get off at Alapai Street and walk half a block left and pick up bus no. 15 (Pacific Heights); this leaves every hour on the half hour, so time your trip carefully. Get off at Puowaina Drive and walk approximately 10 minutes.

QUEEN EMMA SUMMER PALACE, 2913 Pali Hwy. Tel. 595-3167.
Emma and her husband, King Kamehameha IV, called their Victorian country retreat Hanaiakamalama, and it is faithfully maintained as a museum by the Daughters of Hawaii. Hawaiiana mingles comfortably with the 19th-century European furnishings of which Hawaiian royalty was so fond. Note the superb collection of feather capes and kahili. There are conducted tours through the rooms for all visitors. Stop in at the gift shop for Hawaiian books, notepaper, postcards, and other items.
Admission: $4 adults, $1 children 12–18, 50¢ children under 12.
Open: Daily 9am–4pm. **Directions:** From Waikiki take bus no. 4 (Nuuanu/Dowsett from the mountain side of Kuhio Ave.); ask the driver to let you off near the palace.

ROYAL MAUSOLEUM, 2261 Nuuanu Ave.
Here's where the last of the Kamehameha and Kalakau dynasties and others of royal blood are buried. The curator gives a short orientation in the chapel; then you're free to pay your respects.
Admission: Free
Open: Mon–Fri 8am–4:30pm. **Closed:** Holidays, except Kuhio Day (March 26) and Kamehameha Day (June 11). **Directions:** See Queen Emma Summer Palace, above.

FOSTER BOTANICAL GARDEN, 180 N. Vineyard Blvd. Tel. 522-7060.
This is a marvelously cool oasis on a hot day, and one of the most impressive botanical collections to be found anywhere. There are 14 acres of rare trees, flowers, plants, and unusual species of vegetation, collected from the tropics and subtropics of the world. Orchids bloom throughout the year. Here you can measure your minuteness against a tree 20 times taller than you are, and ogle such rare specimens as the cannonball tree, the bombax, and the gold tree. On the grounds is a C-shaped granite monument, presented in 1960 to Honolulu by its cousin city of Hiroshima, from which most of the first Japanese immigrants came to work the island plantations. A free, self-guided-tour brochure is available at the reception area.
Note: Foster Botanical Garden is one component of the Honolulu Botanical Gardens, which also has four other splendid gardens to visit: the **Liliuokalani Botanical Garden** on N. Kuakini Street, a 7½-acre site, once part of Foster Botanical Garden but now separated from it by the HI Freeway, with native plants, a stream, and waterfalls; the Wahiawa Gardens, which has three other splendid gardens to visit; the **Wahiawa Botanical Garden** in Wahiawa, a 27-acre rain forest in central Oahu; **Hoomaluhia Botanical Gardens** in Kaneohe, 400 lush acres at the base of the Koolau mountains in Windward Oahu, and **Koko Crater Botanical Garden,** near Sandy Beach, still in the early stages of development. Free admission to these four gardens. For information on all of these gardens, phone 522-7060.
Admission (to Foster Garden): $1, free for children under 13 with an adult; guided tours free with admission.
Open: Daily 9am–4pm. Guided tours, Mon–Fri at 1pm (reservations suggested). **Closed:** New Year's Day, Christmas Day. **Directions:** From Waikiki take bus no. 2, 19, or 20 (Airport or Airport-Hickam) toward downtown (request a transfer); get off at the corner of Hotel and Bethel Sts. and change to bus no. 4 (Nuuanu/Dowsett); ask the driver to let you off at the garden, located at the corner of Nuuanu Ave. and Vineyard Blvd. The Waikiki Trolley also stops here.

UNIVERSITY OF HAWAII

UNIVERSITY OF HAWAII, Manoa Campus. Tel. 965-8855.
Although many of Hawaii's socially prominent families still send their children off to mainland colleges (in the old days it was the Punahou-Yale route), the island's own university is the goal of thousands of others. Established in 1907 as a small agricultural and mechanical arts college, the university has grown into an important center for the study of tropical agriculture, marine biology, geophysics, astronomy, linguistics, and other fields. Its student body of more than 21,000 reflects the multi-

Bishop Museum ❶
Damien Museum ⓬
Dole Pineapple Cannery ❷
Foster Botanical Garden ❹
Gandhi Statue ⓭
Hawaii Maritime Center ❸

Honolulu Academy of Arts ⓾
Honolulu Zoo ⓭
Iolani Palace ❺
Kapiolani Park ⓯
Kawaiahao Church ❻
Mission House Museum ❼

HONOLULU ATTRACTIONS

National Memorial Cemetery
 of the Pacific ⑨
University of Hawaii ⑩
U. S. Army Museum ⑪
Waikiki Aquarium ⑯

racial composition of the population of Hawaii. In addition, students come from the 49 other states and more than 60 foreign countries.

The **East-West Center** at the Manoa campus is particularly noteworthy. A meeting place of Eastern and Occidental cultures, it brings students, professionals, and research scholars here from Asia, the Pacific islands, and the United States for an exciting exchange of ideas. All students have been given awards that send them first to the University of Hawaii and later out on field work—in the mainland United States for the Asians, in Asia or the Pacific for the Americans. Later, most Asians return home to teach or work in government posts, and most Americans, too, will go to live and work in Asia.

The starkly simple East-West Center buildings are a masterful blend of Eastern and Western styles. Free tours leave Wednesday at 1:30pm from the Friends Lounge on the garden level of Thomas Jefferson Hall, but it's easy enough to walk around by yourself. The lounge area of Jefferson must certainly be one of the most interesting student centers in the world. Where else might you pick up copies of *Thailand Illustrated*, the *Wall Street Journal*, and *Social Casework*, all from one rack? Asian and other art exhibitions are frequently held in the lounge art gallery.

Walk now to the rear of Jefferson for a peaceful moment at the lyrical Japanese garden, with its waterfalls, stone ornaments, lanterns, and flashing carp. And be sure to see the **John Fitzgerald Kennedy Theater,** one of the best equipped in the world for staging both Western and Eastern dramas. It's the official home of the university's dance and drama department, and a technological center that draws theater people from both sides of the Pacific to study, teach, and produce plays. A typical season includes productions of a Japanese Kabuki classic, Shakespeare, and a contemporary Broadway comedy. An authentic Beijing opera was recently staged here—in English.

You'll want to tour the rest of the University of Hawaii campus, too. Stop in at the University Relations office in Bachman Annex 6 to obtain maps and directions for a self-guided tour. You'll find plenty to see, especially if you're interested in art: There are two art galleries, and frescoes, sculptures, and works in other media are seen everywhere.

Nature-lovers can have a treat here, too, trying to identify the 560 or so varieties of tropical plants and trees that bloom all over campus. The university's map shows names and locations. We'll give you a start: The tree on the side of Hawaii Hall, which looks as if it has large sausages dangling from it, is a native of West Africa, where the oddly shaped fruits are used for medicinal purposes.

GREATER HONOLULU

BISHOP MUSEUM, the State Museum of Natural and Cultural History, 1525 Bernice St. Tel. 847-3511.

Inside the museum's stone walls (which look more like those of a fortress than of a museum) is a world center for the study of the Pacific—its peoples, culture, history, artifacts. Most fascinating for visitors is the Hawaiian Hall, where special exhibits illustrate particular aspects of early Hawaiian culture. Note the collection of priceless feather cloaks; one uses half a million feathers from the rare mamo bird (each bird produced only a few feathers, so the kings built up feather treasuries—which were among the prime spoils of war). Other exhibits recreate the way of life of the Hawaiians, showing the outrigger canoes, a model heiau, weapons, wooden calabashes, or trace the history of the Hawaiian monarchy or explore the marine and plant life of the Pacific. A "please touch" gallery for children in the Hall of Discovery ties in with exhibits throughout the museum. All this, plus the fascinating exhibits of ethnographic art, makes for a rewarding visit, worth as much time as you can give it. You can have an inexpensive snack at the Museum Lanai Restaurant. Stop in, too, at Shop Pacifica for Hawaiian gifts, a cut above the usual, with books on Hawaiian and other Pacific cultures, handcrafted feather leis and native koa-wood boxes and bowls, reproductions of Polynesian artifacts, and rare and unique jewelry of the Pacific.

Note: If you're interested in studying **Hawaiian crafts,** you've come to the right place. Classes are held Monday through Saturday from 9am to 3pm, at a nominal charge (usually $5, plus a materials cost). It's quilting on Monday and Friday, fresh-flower lei-making on Tuesday, lauhala weaving and hula-implement making on Wednesday. Classes are held in the Atherton Halau (call 847-3511 for schedules), also the site of special events, which are usually held on weekends. Inquire, too, about field trips and special programs.

Admission (including a 1pm daily music-and-dance presentation and entrance to the Bishop Museum Planetarium, see below): $7.95 adults, $6.96 children 6-17, active military, and seniors; children under 6 free.

Open: Daily 9am–5pm. **Closed:** Christmas. **Directions:** Bus no2. to School and Kapalama Sts.; walk 1 block makai on Kapalama and then turn right on Bernice St.; the entrance is midblock.

BISHOP MUSEUM PLANETARIUM. Tel. 848-4136 for recorded program information.

Here's a great spot for anyone interested in space exploration and astronomy. Sky shows are held every day at 11am and 2pm, and also on Friday and Saturday at 7pm. After the evening shows, there's free observatory telescope viewing, weather permitting.

Admission: $3.50; or included with museum admission.

Directions: See Bishop Museum, above.

PEARL HARBOR

USS *ARIZONA* MEMORIAL. Tel. 422-0561.

⭐ Anyone who remembers—or has heard about—December 7, 1941, should not leave the Hawaiian Islands without seeing Pearl Harbor. As many as 5,000 visitors—many from Japan—come here every day. The handsome $4.2-million visitor center provides the starting point for your boat trip to the USS *Arizona* Memorial. Its museum contains exhibits related to the events surrounding the attack on Pearl Harbor by the Empire of Japan. Step up to the information desk, where you will be given a tour number, and find out approximately when your shuttle boat will leave. While you're waiting, you can study a detailed mural of the *Arizona* or check out the books in the bookshop. When your number is called, you enter the theater to see a 20-minute film, and then are ferried on a navy boat to the memorial.

Dedicated in 1962, the memorial is a white-concrete bridgelike structure rising starkly above the hull of the battleship *Arizona,* victim of several direct hits on the day that bombs fell on Hawaii, and the tomb of approximately 1,000 American service personnel (some 2,403 in all were killed that day). The outlines of the ship shimmer just below the water, and oil slicks still rise from the rusting hulk. Like Punchbowl Crater, it's an eloquent witness to the fury and folly of war. A big experience.

Note: If the weather is stormy, call the *Arizona* Memorial at 422-2771 to find out if the boats will be operating. Bathing suits and bare feet are taboo.

If you have time, you can take a short walk from the Arizona Memorial to visit **Bowfin Park** (tel. 423-1341 for information), where the USS *Bowfin,* a World War II submarine launched a year after the attack on Pearl Harbor, is moored. Next to the submarine is the **Bowfin Museum,** with fascinating submarine memorabilia and a gift shop. You can look through periscopes at a new structure built over the submarine's conning tower. A memorial honors submariners lost during World War II. Admission is $6 for adults ($1 for military personnel with ID), $1 for children 6 to 12. Open daily from 8am to 4:30pm.

Admission: Free

Open: Tours daily 8am–3pm. **Directions:** From Waikiki, bus no. 20 goes to Pearl City; from the Ala Moana Center, take bus no. 51 or 52. The trip should take about an hour. Ask the driver to let you off at the USS *Arizona* Memorial. Private bus service is $6 round-trip (tel. 926-4747).

PEARL HARBOR BY SEA

Another way to get to Pearl Harbor—and a moving and dramatic one—is by sea, aboard Paradise Cruise's sleek luxury vessel, *Star of Honolulu*. During the roughly 45-minute cruise to Pearl, '40s music plays on the loudspeaker, and a thoughtful narration, in both English and Japanese, sets the scene for the momentous events of December 7, 1941. At the *Arizona* Memorial, the ship stops for a few moments as the captain tosses a lei upon the waters in tribute to those still entombed there. Also clearly visible is the wreckage of the battleship *Omaha* nearby. The trip takes the better part of the morning (from about an 8am pickup at Waikiki hotels to a return around noon). Cost is $20 adults, $12.50 for children. Highly recommended. For reservations, call 536-3641, or toll free 800/334-6191 from the continental U.S.

2. MORE ATTRACTIONS

AROUND TOWN

DOLE PINEAPPLE CANNERY, at Cannery Square.
While it's no longer possible to tour the Dole Pineapple Cannery itself, you can still take a free bus out to Cannery Square to see a multi-media show on the role of Dole in Hawaiian history and to shop and browse at Cannery Square. Combine this with a trip to the Hawaii Children's Museum (see below) and the Hilo Hattie Fashion Center, and you have a worthwhile family excursion. For bus information (pickups are made every hour at 10 Waikiki hotels), see local tourist papers or call 537-2926. You can also take bus no. 19 (Airport Hickam) to Cannery Square.

LYON ARBORETUM, 3860 Manoa Rd. Tel. 988-7378.
Few tourists know about the arboretum, but Honolulu residents certainly do. It's prized as one of the most beautiful nature spots in Honolulu, an important research facility for the University of Hawaii, and an educational center where you can take short courses in such subjects as flower arrangement, bonsai, island cookery, orchid growing, and much more. You're welcome to visit on your own, admiring the beautiful gardens lush with orchids, camellias, gardenias, ginger, coffee, and many native plants; if you can manage to take a tour (see below), even better. Visit the gift and book store, which has high-quality items: haku leis, palm-seed and fungus jewelry, handmade cards, books on horticulture and Hawaiian history, kukui leaf T-shirts, and implements for use in Hawaiian crafts. Write for a class schedule.
Admission: Donation requested.
Open: Mon–Sat 9am–3pm. Tours given first Fri and third Wed at 1pm, third Sat at 10am; group tours by prior arrangement. **Closed:** Public holidays. **Directions:** Take TheBUS no. 8 from Waikiki to Ala Moana; transfer to no. 5 (Paradise Park); then walk approximately 15 minutes.

WAIKIKI

U.S. ARMY MUSEUM, Fort DeRussy Park. Tel. 438-2821.
Housed in Battery Randolph, built in 1909 as a key installation in defense of Honolulu and Pearl Harbor, this museum contains military memorabilia dating from ancient Hawaiian warfare to the present. On the upper deck, the Corps of Engineers Pacific Regional Visitors Center graphically shows how the corps works with the civilian community in managing water resources in an island environment.
Admission: Free.
Open: Tues–Sun 10am–4:30pm **Bus:** 8 (Ala Moana Center) from Kuhio Avenue, in an Ewa direction.

FROMMER'S FAVORITE
HONOLULU & OAHU EXPERIENCES

Annual Lei Day/May Day Concert at Waikiki Shell On May 1, everybody wears leis and there are contests for the most beautiful, with judging at Kapiolani Park. In the evening, the Brothers Cazimero present a fabulous show, and all Honolulu, in their aloha finery, turns out to attend. A joyous event.

Sunset Cocktails at Open-air House Without a Key At the Halekulani Hotel. As you watch the sun sink slowly into the Pacific, and a beautiful hula girl dances to melodious music, you know that picture-postcard Hawaii still exists.

A Walk Through Historic Chinatown Examine the open-air fish and vegetable stalls at the Oahu Market, peek in at herbalist's shops and noodle factories, stop for goodies at the Chinese bakeries, and end with a visit to some of the town's most sophisticated art galleries.

A Swim at Sans Souci Beach Across from Kapiolani Park, the ocean is gentle, the water temperature perfect, and the crowds far away.

Snorkeling at Hanauma Bay This idyllic beach cove, created centuries ago when one side of Koko Head Crater was washed into the sea, is now a marine reserve, and the fish are so gentle that they eat right out of your hand.

A Visit to Byodo-In Temple on Windward Oahu This exact replica of the venerable Byodo-In in Japan has a magnificent carving of Amida, the Buddha of the Western Paradise.

DAMIEN MUSEUM, 130 Ohua St. Tel. 923-2690.
In the Diamond Head area, behind St. Augustine's Catholic Church, this small museum presents a moving account of the work that Father Damien did with the victims of leprosy on the island of Molokai. The museum contains prayer books used by Father Damien in his ministry, as well as his personal items. A continuously running video, recounting Damien's story, is narrated by Terence Knapp, a local actor who has portrayed Father Damien in award-winning performances on stage and on TV. He fittingly honors one of Hawaii's heroes.
   Admission: Free, donations accepted.
   Open: Mon–Fri 9am–3pm, Sat 9am–noon. **Closed:** Holidays. **Directions:** Within walking distance of most major hotels, or take TheBUS no. 8, 19, or 20 running in a Diamond Head direction.

GANDHI STATUE, in front of the Honolulu Zoo.
   A new addition to the Hawaii scene is an impressive statue of Mahatma Gandhi, recently unveiled by the City and County of Honolulu and the Gandhi Memorial International Foundation. Created by the artist Zlatko Paunov of New York and a gift to the people of Hawaii from the Jhamanadas Watumull Fund, the statue is accompanied by a plaque quoting from Gandhi's philosophy: "It is possible to live in peace."
   Directions: See Honolulu Zoo, below.

HONOLULU ZOO, 151 Kapahulu Ave. Tel. 971-7171.

★ The big news at the Honolulu Zoo is the opening of the first phase of their multimillion-dollar African Savanna, 7½ acres that allow the visitor to see wild animals in settings approximating their native habitats. The Asiatic elephants are great favorites with the crowd; call for times of their public demonstrations. With Diamond Head providing the background, plenty of trees and flowers (including orchids, a giant banyan, and date palms), it's one of the most charming small zoos anywhere.

During the summer there's free entertainment on Wednesday starting at 6pm at the stage under the earpod tree, just behind the flamingos. Take a picnic supper and join the fun. Local artists hang their work on the fence outside on Tuesday, Saturday, and Sunday. Be sure to stop in at Zootique, the charming gift shop for imaginative animal gifts.

Admission: $3 adults, free for ages 12 and under.

Open: Daily 9am–4pm (June–Aug, also Wed to 7:30pm). **Closed:** New Year's Day and Christmas Day. **Directions:** You can walk from most major hotels or take TheBUS no. 8, 19, 20, 58, or 2 (Kapiolani Park), running in a Diamond Head direction.

KAPIOLANI PARK, Kalakaua and Monsarrat Aves.

The 99½ acres of the park have facilities for just about everything from tennis, soccer, and rugby to archery and picnicking. The Royal Hawaiian Band plays on Sundays in the bandstand, and major musical events take place in the Waikiki Shell. For a particularly beautiful view, note Diamond Head framed in the cascading waters of the splendid Louise C. Dillingham Fountain.

Bordering the ocean on the right is a stretch of wide, palm-dotted grass lawn with a fringe of sand to let you know you're still at the beach. Swimming here is excellent, since the surf is quite mild; it's a big favorite with local families. **Kapiolani Beach Park,** with restrooms, picnic tables, and snack bar, is just ahead.

Admission: Free.

Directions: Take TheBUS no. 2 (Waikiki-Kapiolani Park) from Kuhio Ave. in a Diamond Head direction.

WAIKIKI AQUARIUM, 2777 Kalakaua Ave. Tel. 923-9741.

Recent renovations have made the always entertaining Waikiki Aquarium more enthralling than ever. New exhibits include the Sea Visions Theater and accompanying jellyfish display, the outdoor Northwest Hawaiian Islands habitat with endangered Hawaiian monk seals, the Mahimahi Hatchery, and an expanded Hunters on the Reef shark exhibit. You can also see, among other sea creatures, the *lauwiliwilinukunukuoioi;* if you can't pronounce it, just ask for the long-nosed butterfish. An outdoor display, Edge of the Reef, is a simulated living-reef environment that includes hundreds of colorful fish, live coral, and a tidal surge. Stop in to see their attractive gift shop, the Natural Selection. Everything in it—T-shirts with fish designs, books, posters, cards, linens, home accessories—relates to the ocean and its life-forms. They have a good selection of children's toys and books, too.

Admission: $6 adults, $4 seniors, $2.50 youths 13–17; children 12 and under free.

Open: Daily 9am–5pm. **Closed:** Thanksgiving and Christmas. **Directions:** Take TheBUS no. 2 (Waikiki–Kapiolani Park) from Kuhio Ave. in a Diamond Head direction.

───────────────────────────────

READERS RECOMMEND

United Fishing Agency, 117 Ahui St. (tel. 536-2148). *"A fish auction is held every Monday through Saturday at 5:30am at United Fishing Agency. We went about 7am and saw fish we didn't know existed, such as a 114-pound moon fish. This auction was far bigger than others we've seen and the people were more than happy to answer our questions."*—Kenneth Kendall, Omaha, Neb.

THE ART SCENE

A lot of good artists are coming out of Hawaii—young people with a mixture of backgrounds whose work shows multiple influences. Perhaps because of the natural beauty that surrounds them, their paintings tend to be more representational here than in other art centers, but ways of seeing are as modern as they are in Paris or New York. Not a few have married Eastern atmosphere with Western techniques, another example of the fortuitous cross-fertilization that goes on in every area of Hawaiian life.

GALLERIES AROUND THE ISLAND

As you drive around the island, you'll have a chance to visit several worthwhile galleries. The ✪ **Ko'olau Gallery,** located on the second level of the Windward Mall Shopping Center in Kaneohe, is a co-op gallery, staffed by the artists themselves, showing a variety of locally produced artworks in many media. More than 40 artists from around the island are represented. You can say hello to the gallery artists daily from 9:30am to 9pm. Also in Kaneohe, serious lovers of art and beauty must not miss a visit to ✪ **Hart, Tagami & Powell Gallery and Gardens,** 45-754 Lamaula Rd., where painters Hiroshi Tagami and Michael Powell open their gallery and tranquil botanical garden to visitors on Saturday, Sunday, and Monday from around 10am to 3:30pm. An appointment is necessary: Call 239-8146. The **Fettig Art Studios,** 61-427A Kam Hwy. in Haleiwa shows work by artist Beverly Fettig, by appointment only (tel. 637-5340).

GALLERIES IN TOWN

Art is, in fact, everywhere in Honolulu; the builders of large public facilities are becoming more and more art-conscious, and you'll find monumental pieces of sculpture—some outstanding, such as a Henry Moore in Tamarind Park at Bishop and King Streets downtown, some less distinguished—in such places as the Ala Moana Shopping Center, Hemmeter Center, Royal Hawaiian Center, the Waikiki Shopping Plaza, the University of Hawaii, the state capitol, and at Sea Life Park in Windward Oahu. The fountain sculptures at Ala Moana are particularly worth a look.

To see some excellent works by Hawaii's talented craftspeople (and perhaps to pick up some distinctive small presents), pop into some of our favorite places. **Following Sea,** at Kahala Mall, is a visual experience. It presents the works of many American craftspeople in ceramics, glass, jewelry, fiber, and woodwork. Each piece is more glorious than the next. Many island artists are represented. A high level of taste and artistry is evident in the works found at **Nohea Gallery** at Ward Warehouse. With the work of more than 450 island artists and craftspeople in hand-crafted jewelry, paintings, koa boxes, chests and furniture, basketry, feather-work, quilts, pottery, glass, and sculpture, Nohea offers just about the widest selection of fine arts and crafts in the islands. **From Ed and Friends,** 2563 S. King St. (tel. 943-8680), is a mesmerizing hodgepodge of the work of 60 to 70 artists and craftspersons from Hawaii and the mainland. Owner Ed Higa is a master potter and his ceramic pieces are treasures. Also represented are a glassblower, several jewelry artisans, and woodworkers. Take note of the line of tie-dyed T-shirt animals—the shirts are tied and manipulated to resemble dragons, alligators, caterpillars, dinosaurs, and other fanciful critters. They are then dyed and allowed to remain in their tied state. Take your choice: untie it and wear it as a shirt, or keep the charming creature intact.

A great lady of the arts in Hawaii was Madge Tennent, who came to Hawaii at the turn of the century via South Africa and Paris and broke away from the academy and its conventions to record on canvas her massive portraits of the Hawaiian people. You can visit her gallery, the **Tennent Art Foundation,** on the slopes of Punchbowl at 203 Prospect St. (tel. 531-1987), from 10am to noon Tuesday through Saturday, 2 to 4pm on Sunday, or by special appointment.

Other fine galleries are all over town. You'll want to visit **Arts of Paradise** on the second floor of the International Market Place. Artist-owned, it features work in all mediums of Hawaii's top professional artists. Call about free demonstrations and talks by participating artists (tel. 924-2787). Then there's **Images International of Hawaii,** with galleries at Ala Moana Shopping Center (tel. 926-5081), featuring such internationally acclaimed artists as Hisashi Otsuka, Caroline Young, Tatsuo Ito, Raymond Page, Gary Hostallero, Robert Lyn Nelson, and the unique leather sculptor Liu Miao Chan. Worth your attention at Ward Centre is **Art A La Carte** (tel. 536-3351), an artists' co-op featuring ceramics as well as paintings.

Downtown, the impressive **Honolulu Advertiser Gallery** on the first floor of the News Building at 605 Kapiolani Blvd. (tel. 526-1322) continues to be a showcase for local and mainland artists despite its newer galleries at the Contemporary Museum (see below). The **Gallery at Pauahi Tower** in Bishop Square always has an outstanding show running. The **AMFAC Plaza Exhibition Room** at AMFAC Center, Fort Street Mall and Queen Street, has interesting group exhibitions of contemporary paintings, crafts, sculpture, and photography, as well as cultural and historical presentations. Exhibitions change monthly. It's open 9am to 5pm Monday through Friday. On Saturday and Sunday, local artists exhibit and sell their work on the zoo fence near Kapiolani Park.

The **Waimanu Street Gallery,** at 901 Waimanu St. (tel. 591-1126), features works of Jerry Kermode, whose bowls, made of Hawaiian woods (koa, milo, monkey pod, ironwood), are examples of the woodmaker's art par excellence. Each and every creation is different: sometimes two woods are combined into one piece. Potters Jermone Heck (raku) and Bob McWilliams are also represented, as is Janet Holaday, with her wonderful screenprinted shirts, cards, and bags. Open Tuesday through Friday from noon to 5pm, Saturday 11am to 3pm, or by appointment.

In Chinatown Something of an artistic renaissance is going on in Chinatown these days. Old buildings have been refurbished, there is new construction, and a small artistic colony continues to grow. At last count, there were a dozen galleries here: Take a little time to explore them. Pen-and-ink artist **Ramsay,** who has achieved national and international fame (an exhibition of her masterful architectural drawings appeared at the Senate Rotunda in Washington, D.C., in 1988), has her own gallery at 1128 Smith St. (tel. 537-2787), where she also shows works by prominent artists in other media. Next door is her café, with a sophisticated, medium-priced menu. **Pegge Hopper,** whose images of Polynesian women are seen everywhere in the islands, also has her own gallery here, at 1164 Nuuanu Ave. (tel. 524-1160). It features Hopper's original paintings, drawings, and collages, in addition to her posters, limited-edition prints, calendars, and gift items. At the corner, at 1050 Nuuanu, is an upbeat gallery, the **Gateway Gallery** (tel. 599-1559), featuring fine arts and unique gift items. They specialize in floral and tropical theme paintings and sculpture. Accessories start at $20.

THE CONTEMPORARY MUSEUM AT THE SPALDING ESTATE, 2411 Makiki Heights Dr. Tel. 526-1322.

With the opening of this museum, Honolulu has become the art center of the Pacific. The lovely old 1920s mansion in a magnificent garden setting overlooking the city and the sea has been transformed into a series of state-of-the-art galleries, housing temporary exhibits of works by artists of local, national, and international reputation. A permanent pavilion houses David Hockney's installation based on his stage set from the Metropolitan Opera production of *L'Enfant et les Sortilèges*, complete with a stereo sound system playing the Ravel opera that inspired this major work. Galleries, art, gardens—all vie for attention. The gardens alone, a series of exquisite terraces meandering down a hillside to a stream bed, falls, and pools, are worth the trip. They were designed by a Japanese landscape artist as a place to meditate and experience harmony, so each vista has its stone seat for contemplation. There's also an attractive gift shop with artist-designed T-shirts, jewelry, cards, and the like, and the Contemporary Café, an indoor-outdoor eating spot with sophisticated cuisine and moderate prices (see Chapter 6 for details).

Admission: $4 ages 15 and over; free for children under 15; free for everyone Thurs.

Open: Tues–Sat 10am–4pm. **Bus:** 15 to Makiki Heights Dr.

3. COOL FOR KIDS

In addition to the attractions listed below, your kids will also enjoy several of the attractions already described. At Pearl Harbor, U.S. history comes to life for children with a visit to the USS *Arizona* Memorial and *Bowfin* Park. At the Hawaii Maritime Center, kids can steer a child-size ship's replica. The Bishop Museum hosts regularly changing exhibitions for families on a wide range of topics, such as ecology and archaeology. Older children will be enthralled with the exhibits at the Bishop Museum Planetarium. And at the Kahala Hilton Hotel, kids can get close to porpoises at the daily feedings.

THE HAWAII CHILDREN'S MUSEUM, Dole Cannery Square. Tel. 522-0040.

If you've brought the kids with you, don't leave Cannery Square without a visit to this delightful museum, so enthralling, in fact, that it's worth an excursion in its own right. It's a state-of-the-art learning center, where everything is designed to give the child a hands-on experience. Five main galleries all revolve around "You . . . Wonderful You." Kids unzip a 7-foot-tall doll and take out its organs or actually walk through a huge mouth. They can ride a bike next to a kid-size skeleton (suitably attired in bike helmet and athletic shoes) also riding a bike and see what bones come into play in bike-riding. They can play with gigantic soap bubbles, work with pulleys and gears, or explore a bug zoo.

Admission: $5 adults, $3 children 2–17.

Open: Tues–Fri 9am–1pm, Sat–Sun 10am–4pm. **Directions:** See Dole Pineapple Cannery (above).

4. WALKING TOURS

If you really want to experience the sights and sounds and feel of Honolulu, the best way to do it is to get out and walk. Happily, it's also the cheapest way and the most fun.

Many commercial tours are expensive and touch only on the highlights. We think the city merits more attention. The local public buses, a good pair of walking shoes, and the instructions that follow will get you to all major places. And, more important, you can go at your own pace, devoting the most time to what most interests you—and you alone.

See also the walking tours described below, under "Organized Tours."

WALKING TOUR 1 — DOWNTOWN HONOLULU

Start: Honolulu Academy of Arts.
Finish: Kalanimoku (Ship of Heaven).
Time: Approximately 3 hours.
Best Times: Tuesday through Saturday.
Worst Times: Sunday and Monday, when the Art Academy and Mission Houses Museum are closed.

TheBUS no. 2 in Waikiki will take you right to the:

1. **Honolulu Academy of Arts,** at the corner of Ward and Beretania, a low, graceful building where magnificent art treasures await you.
   Retrace your steps across Thomas Square to King Street and you'll see the:

2. Neal S. Blaisdell Center, 777 Ward Ave., known as "NBC" to the locals. It's a giant $1.25-million complex with an arena, a concert theater (it's home to the Honolulu Symphony), and a convention hall. There are no official tours, but apply at the administration office if you're interested in seeing it; they will have someone show you around. Don't forget to ask for a schedule of upcoming events. Kids will enjoy feeding the tame ducks and geese that live in the ponds on the grounds.

Cross Ward Avenue on the Ewa side of the center, turn left onto King Street and walk Ewa 3 short blocks to King and Kawaiahao Streets. There you will come to the:

3. Mission Houses Museum, 553 S. King St. These three 19th-century buildings provide a glimpse of the historic encounter between the New England missionaries and the native Hawaiians in early 19th-century Honolulu. It was here that James Michener did much of his research for *Hawaii.*

Outside the Mission Houses Museum, turn left and cross Kawaiahao Street to the:

4. Kawaiahao Church, 957 Punchbowl. This is Hawaii's "Westminster Abbey," the church of the royal families of Hawaii and the scene of their coronations, weddings, and funerals. Explore the graveyard looking for missionary tombstones. Behind the church, and 7 or 8 years older than it, is an adobe schoolhouse, one of the oldest school buildings in the state.

On the sidewalk outside the Kawaiahao Church, walk across King Street to the Neo-Spanish City Hall to see some of the architectural highlights of the Civic Center, called Honolulu Hale, 530 S. King St. Just Diamond Head of Honolulu Hale are two very attractive New England–style red-brick buildings with white trim. These house such city and county departments as municipal reference and records.

Continuing in a Diamond Head direction, on the expanse of rolling lawn between these buildings and the towering gray-stone monolith beyond, you'll see:

5. Sky Gate, a highly controversial piece of art acquired by the city and county at a cost of $120,000. Created by famed sculptor Isamu Noguchi, it consists of four pieces of what is apparently a gigantic stove pipe, painted flat black and welded together. The aforementioned gray-stone monolith is the:

6. Honolulu Municipal Building, 650 S. King St. This is the home of the departments of transportation, buildings, and public works, and much more. Like *Sky Gate*, this building was greeted with something less than unmitigated joy by Honolulu's citizenry, many of whom feel that its architecture is out of keeping with the rest of the Civic Center.

When you stand in front of the municipal building by the flagpoles, the very attractive gray building with the terra-cotta roof that you see is the:

7. Hawaii Newspaper Agency, 618 Kapiolani Blvd., which houses the two daily newspapers. Many consider it one of the loveliest Monarchy-style buildings in the city.

Walk through the municipal building and out the other side, cross the little park area, and on the other side of Beretania Street you'll see the:

8. Board of Water Supply, 630 S. Beretania St., a lovely pale-green building with a beautiful lawn and fountain.

Now retrace your steps in an Ewa direction, this time along Beretania Street; the beautiful new building you see across from the rear of Honolulu Hale is:

9. Kalanimoku (Ship of Heaven), 1151 Punchbowl, a state office building at the Civic Center. It houses the state departments of land and natural resources, fish and game, and forestry, among others. The building has a cool, wonderfully open design, and at night, softly colored lights filter through the cutout designs at its top. It's gorgeously landscaped.

WALKING TOUR—DOWNTOWN HONOLULU

- 1 Honolulu Academy of Arts
- 2 Neal S. Blaisdell Center
- 3 Mission Houses Museum
- 4 Kawaiahao Church
- 5 *Sky Gate*
- 6 Honolulu Municipal Building
- 7 Hawaii Newspaper Agency
- 8 Board of Water Supply
- 9 Kalanimoku (Ship of Heaven)

Church ✝   Post Office ⊠   Ship ⬅

6788

start here

finish here

To Waikiki

To Airport

Ward Ave.
Kamani St.
Victoria St.
Ward Ave.
Osorio
Kapiolani Blvd.
Cooke St.
Kinau St.
Alapai St.
South St.
Mission Lane
Kawaiahao Cemetery
Halekauwila St.
Pohukaina St.
Auahi St.
State Office Building
City Hall
Punchbowl St.
Federal Bldg.
Ala Moana Blvd.
Falls of Clyde
State Capitol
Library
Iolani Palace
Kamehameha Statue
Queen St.
St. Andrew's Cathedral
Queen Emma St.
S. Beretania St.
Richards St.
Hotel St.
S. King St.
Alakea St.
Bishop St.
Vineyard Blvd.
Kukui St.
Fort Street Mall
Bethel St.
Nuuanu Ave.
S. Beretania St.
S. King St.
Merchant St.
Fish Market
CHINATOWN
Maunakea St.
Kekaulike St.
River St.
Aloha Tower
H1

WALKING TOUR 2 — HAWAII MARITIME CENTER
& HAWAII'S WALL STREET

Start: Aloha Tower.
Finish: Fort Street Mall.
Time: 2 or 3 hours.
Best Times: Any day before 5:30pm, when the Maritime Center closes.

From Waikiki take TheBUS no. 19 (Airport or Airport-Hickam) or no. 20 (Airport-Halawa Gate), and get off at the Federal Building on Ala Moana Boulevard. Then walk toward the water to the first component of the Hawaii Maritime Center:

1. **Aloha Tower,** at Pier 9, on the waterfront. Once the tallest building in Hawaii, it still provides a great view of the city in all directions. Then visit the:
2. **Kalakaua Boathouse,** an absorbing museum full of exhibits that highlight the maritime history of Hawaii. This is the centerpiece of the Hawaii Maritime Center. From Kalakaua Boathouse, you can step right onto the *Falls of Clyde*, the only four-masted, full-rigged sailing ship still in existence. If it's in port, you can also see the *Hokule'a*, an authentic replica of an ancient Hawaiian double-hulled canoe, similar to the ones that brought the first Hawaiians to these shores.

REFUELING STOP After your visit here, relax with a slightly splurgy meal or snack at lovely **Coaster's Restaurant,** behind the center and facing Honolulu Harbor. The food is sophisticated and upbeat, and the setting cannot be topped.

Leave the Maritime Center and walk across Ala Moana Boulevard to see some of the newer buildings of the State Civic Center Mall, including the:

3. **Prince Jonah Kuhio Kalanianaole Federal Building and the U.S. Courthouse,** two unusual low-lying structures with terraced roofs in the style of Nebuchadnezzar's Hanging Gardens of Babylon. (They are situated makai of the Civic Center; the state capitol is mauka, and Iolani Palace is in the middle.) Two outdoor sculptures here have also caused quite a stir. *Two Open Angles Eccentric* (and that's just what they are—two huge stainless-steel open and transparent frames that slice through the air but never collide as they frame buildings and sky) and *Barking Sands* (Peter Voulkos), composed of serpentine and geometric forms. Be your own art critic and give your verdict. Some lovely fiberworks by Ruthadell Anderson and Sharyn Amii Mills can be seen in the lobby and on the fourth floor of the courthouse.

Two blocks mauka of the federal building is Merchant Street, known as the:

4. **"Wall Street of Hawaii."** The "Big Five," the great financial powers of the islands, have their offices here. You'll see the handsome offices of Dole Inc., Davies Pacific Center, Dillingham Transportation, AMFAC Center (at Merchant and Bishop), and the almost-Asian decor of the Alexander and Baldwin, Ltd., building.

On Merchant Street, turn left until you come to the:

5. **Fort Street Mall,** a lively shopping thoroughfare lined with fast-food stands and throngs of local people. You'll find Liberty House here, one of Hawaii's leading department stores, as well as a big, fascinating Woolworth's, with plenty of souvenirs.

MORE WALKING TOURS
STATE CAPITOL & IOLANI PALACE

This tour, which begins at the State Capitol and winds up at Iolani Palace, will take you 2 to 3 hours. The best time to go is Wednesday through Saturday before 2:15pm. Don't forget to make a reservation for Iolani Palace.

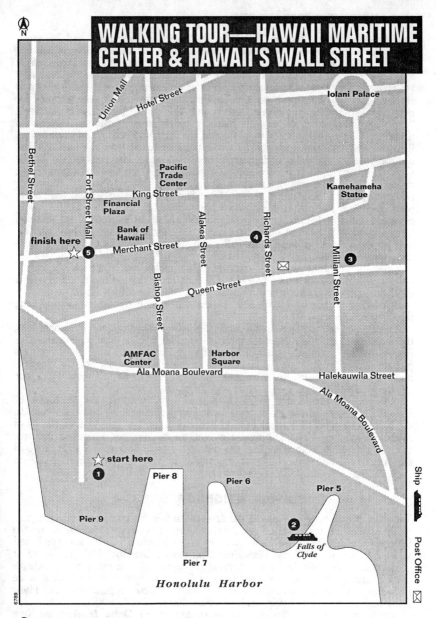

WALKING TOUR—HAWAII MARITIME CENTER & HAWAII'S WALL STREET

1 Aloha Tower
2 Kalakaua Boathouse
3 Prince Jonah Kuhio Kalanianaole
   Federal Buliding and the U.S. Courthouse
4 Wall Street of Hawaii
5 Fort Street Mall

Take TheBUS no. 2 from Waikiki to the corner of Punchbowl and Beretania. Across from you will be the **Hawaii State Capitol,** on Beretania Street between Punchbowl and Richards Streets. This magnificent structure, completed in 1969 at the cost of $25 million, has an open-air roof that sweeps skyward like the peak of a volcano, reflecting pools signifying an ocean environment, and Hawaiian materials and motifs throughout. Until sometime in 1995, the State Capitol will be closed for renovation, so one can no longer come in and see the state legislature in session or "experience" the offices of Hawaii's governor and lieutenant governor. However, a temporary Capitol District Visitor Center has been created on the corner of Beretania and Punchbowl, diagonally across the intersection from the Capitol. Here one can see an elaborate multimedia presentation about the construction of the Capitol, an accompanying videotape presentation about the interior appointments, statuary, and other works of art inside, and occasional touring exhibits. The visitor center is on the ground floor of the Mabel Smyth Building, 510 S. Beretania St.; open daily 8am to 4pm. In front of the Capitol building itself, note Marisol's controversial statue of Father Damien, and other works of art in front of the building, facing Beretania Street. Just outside the makai side of the building are two relatively new works: a replica of the Liberty Bell and a statue of Hawaii's last reigning monarch, Queen Liliuokalani.

Go back the same way you came in. Walk makai and you're at the central building of the **Hawaii State Library,** 478 King St., a Greco-Roman edifice with a delightful open-air garden court. Visit the Edna Allyn Children's Room to see Hawaiian legend murals by Juliette May Fraser, and take in the other paintings hung throughout the library.

Directly across King Street is the **State Judiciary Building,** and right outside it, the famous statue, **King Kamehameha,** dressed in a royal feathered cape and a helmet that look curiously Grecian. A symbol of Hawaii (you'll see it in countless pictures and on postcards), this larger-than-life statue of the unifier of the islands is not a great work of art, but it's appropriately heroic. On Kamehameha Day, June 11, the local citizenry decks the statue with huge leis.

Just Ewa of the library you'll see a streamlined building, the **Archives of Hawaii.** Inside are invaluable documents, journals, photographs, and other records, the largest collection of Hawaiiana in existence. The archives are on the grounds of **Iolani Palace,** which is Diamond Head of the building (at King and Richards Streets). This is the high point and the end of the tour: Plan your walking tour so that you'll arrive in time for your reservation to tour the only royal palace on American soil (tel. 522-0382 for reservations).

ASIAN NEIGHBORHOODS

Take this 2- to 3-hour tour during the day—the area is not considered safe at night.

From Waikiki, take TheBUS no. 2 or 19 (Airport or Airport-Hickam) or no. 20 (Airport) toward downtown Honolulu. Get off at Maunakea Street and you'll find yourself in the midst of the **Historical Chinatown District.** With its jumble of shops laden with crafts, herbs, and Chinese groceries, and with many new merchants from Vietnam, Thailand, and other parts of Southeast Asia here, the area is more fascinating and exotic than ever. There are several Chinese acupuncturists and Hong Kong herb doctors here (many locals swear by them).

Begin with a look at an old Chinatown fixture, the **Oahu Market,** on King Street near the waterfront. The open-air stalls contain all variety of fish, poultry, vegetables, in a dizzying array. A look at pre-supermarket Hawaii!

Next, walk over to one of the area's newer landmarks, the **Chinese Cultural Plaza,** in the block bounded by Beretania, Maunakea, Kukui, and River Streets. This is not one of our favorite shopping centers, since many of the goods seem overpriced. We do, however, like the Dragon Gate Bookstore, with dragon puppets, books, and calendars (in Chinese, of course), as well as Excellent Gems and Bin Ching, both of which carry pearls and jade and do jewelry repairing.

The biggest new development in Chinatown, however, is the **Maunakea Marketplace,** in the block bounded by Hotel, Puahi, and Maunakea Streets. There's a statue of Confucius, a clock tower, and thousands of bricks engraved with personal messages. The office of the Historical Hawaii Foundation is here, as is the Chinese Visitor Center, where you can pick up self-guided tour maps and tapes of Chinatown, and see a historical presentation on old Chinatown.

The Maunakea Marketplace Food Court has a truly international array of fast-food stands, with a central courtyard for dining. You can sample the foods of Thailand, Korea, the Philippines—even Puerto Rico—as well as China, of course. Directly behind the food court is a fresh seafood market, wholesale and retail; many restaurants shop here.

As you wander through Chinatown's little streets, you'll notice that Old Chinatown is giving way to several new buildings, a park, and continued upgrading of historic older buildings such as the **Hawaii Theatre,** 1130 Bethel St., which is in the process of being restored to its original '20s art deco architecture. It has hosted everything from beauty pageants and band concerts to the Hawaii International Film Festival and even political functions.

There are now about a dozen art galleries in the neighborhood, including **Pegge Hopper,** at 1164 Nuuanu St. (her works are seen all over the islands); accent; and **Ramsay,** 1128 Smith St., the renowned pen-and-ink artist, who has the charming Gallery Café adjacent, for light, sophisticated meals.

Before you leave Chinatown, be sure to check out the **lei sellers** on Maunakea Street, near Beretania. There are at least a dozen of them, and they offer the best prices and finest work in Honolulu.

You could end your tour here, or you may choose to walk another few blocks to climax your trip with an exotic sight: the Kuan Yin Buddhist Temple. Walk 3 blocks mauka from King Street to Beretania. Turn left and walk Ewa a block or two to the Nuuanu Stream, where the ambience is slightly Southeast Asian. Much of the old Japanese neighborhood that used to be here—scrubby little saimin stands and pool halls, fish and grocery stores under quaint Asian roofs—has been torn down to make way for new construction. You'll see the **Kukui Market,** with its distinctive blue roof. Now follow River Street toward the mountains—you're likely to see local people fishing for tiliapa, a nutritious fish that breeds rapidly in such brackish water—then cross Vineyard Boulevard and you'll be at the **Kuan Yin Buddhist Temple,** 170 N. Vineyard St. Slip off your shoes and walk inside. Joss sticks and incense burn at the altar, food offerings calm the ancestral spirits, and the USA seems far, far away. (There is another statue of Kuan Yin—far more splendid, we think—in the Honolulu Academy of Arts.)

PUNCHBOWL, LOWER TANTALUS & NUUANU

This adventure begins at Honolulu's number-one visitor attraction, the National Memorial Cemetery of the Pacific, covers some historic sites, and ends at a superb botanical garden. Begin early enough to have time to explore Foster Botanical Garden, which closes at 4pm. Plan on spending about half a day on this tour.

Start with TheBUS no. 2 on Kuhio Avenue heading for town (request a transfer). Get off at Alapai Street and walk a quarter of a block left, where you can pick up the TheBUS no. 15 (Pacific Heights). This leaves every hour on the half hour, so time your trip carefully. Get off at Puowaina Drive and walk for 10 minutes to the **National Memorial Cemetery of the Pacific,** in Punchbowl Crater. Buried inside the crater of an extinct volcano are some 26,000 American military personnel who perished in the Pacific during World War II, the Korean War, or the Vietnam War.

Walking back to the bus stop, get TheBUS no. 15 again and continue on it for a grand ride through **Pacific Heights,** a residential district. At the end of the line, another breathtaking view of the city and the Pacific awaits. When you pay for the return trip, get a transfer and leave the bus at Pauoa Road, along which you walk right two blocks to Nuuanu Avenue and The BUS no. 4R (Nuuanu-Dowsett). This bus will take you through **Nuuanu Valley,** damp, lush, glorious in scenery and island history (here Kamehameha won the battle that gave him control of Oahu). Unfortunately, there's no bus to the Nuuanu Pali with its magnificent view of Windward Oahu.

On the left side is the white-frame **Queen Emma Summer Palace,** 2913 Pali Hwy. Emma and her consort, King Kamehameha IV, called this Victorian country retreat of theirs Hanaiakamalama, and it is faithfully maintained as a museum by the Daughters of Hawaii.

Ride on the same bus farther down Nuuanu Avenue, past the brightly colored Chinese Consulate to the **Royal Mausoleum,** 2261 Nuuanu Ave., on the right. Here's where the last of the Hawaiian alii, the Kamehameha and Kalakaua dynasties, and others of royal blood are buried. Browse around.

Resuming your makai trip on TheBUS no. 4, ride down to the **Soto Mission of Hawaii,** at 1708 Nuuanu Ave. (between School and Kuakini Streets). This is a Zen Buddhist temple; just look for its severe central tower and eight smaller octagonal ones, which represent Buddha's Path of Life. Walk in and have a look. They'll be happy to answer any questions. Free.

Leaving the temple, walk mauka to Kuakini Street, then turn right one block to Pali Highway, and right again for half a block to the **Honpa Hongwanji Mission Temple,** on Pali Highway. This is the cathedral of the Jodo Shin Buddhist sect in Hawaii.

Now retrace your steps to Nuuanu Avenue and walk makai two blocks to Vineyard Boulevard. Turn right and about one block away you'll find the entrance to the **Foster Botanical Garden,** 180 N. Vineyard Blvd. Founded in the 1850s on royal lands, this superb botanical collection is one of Honolulu's favorite places.

For the return, walk back to Nuuanu Avenue below School Street, board TheBUS no. 4 to Hotel and Bethel Streets, where you will transfer to TheBUS no. 2 back to Waikiki.

UNIVERSITY OF HAWAII AT MANOA & MANOA VALLEY

Here's your chance to see what all those students are doing when they're not on the beach at Waikiki. Try to take this two- to three-hour tour during the week, when classes are in session.

Take TheBUS no. 4 (Nuuanu-Dowsett) from the corner of Kapahulu and Kalakaua to the **University of Hawaii at Manoa campus.** From here you can meander around the beautiful grounds of the university, one of the most relaxed institutions of higher learning we've seen anywhere. Nobody thinks it's unusual for that fellow in the library poring over the card catalog to be barefoot, so why should you?

After you've absorbed the ambience a bit, walk over to **Bachman Annex 6,** not far from the Founder's Gate. Here you can pick up maps and directions for a self-guided tour. The map will direct you to numerous examples of fine art on campus, and to some 560 varieties of tropical plants and blossoms that make the campus a garden.

Next make your way to the **East-West Center,** on East-West Road. Eastern and Western influences are reflected in the student composition and in the architecture. Visit **Thomas Jefferson Hall** and explore the student center. Tours leave every Wednesday at 1:30pm from the Friend's Lounge on the garden level. Walk to the rear of Jefferson for a peaceful moment at the lyrical **Japanese Garden,** and you'll find yourself face to face with the **John Fitzgerald Kennedy Theatre,** home of the university's Department of Theatre and Dance and the scene of fascinating productions, from Kabuki to Shakespeare.

If you're feeling hungry, head for the **Campus Center Cafeteria** close to University Avenue in the middle of campus, which offers excellent low-cost breakfasts and lunches. Or try **Manoa Garden** at Hemenway Hall, offering deli sandwiches and stir-fries all day.

Walk back to University Avenue, where you entered the campus, and board TheBUS no. 6. The ride up East Manoa Road to Woodlawn will take you past a **Chinese cemetery,** marked with a big Chinese gate at the intersection of Akaka Place, where there are often food offerings on the graves.

Taking the same bus back (on the opposite side of the road) toward the university, get off at the intersection of Manoa Road and Oahu Avenue. If you walk a little way to the right on Oahu Avenue, you'll discover the **Waioli Tea Room,** 3016 Oahu Ave., a charming place for lunch or Sunday brunch (see Chapter 6, "Honolulu Dining"). Even if you don't eat here, take a little time to explore the grounds, the Little Chapel, and the **Robert Louis Stevenson Memorial House** where it is said that the poet once lived.

WAIKIKI

There's more to Waikiki than just the beach. It's fun to explore the magnificent hotels, do some shopping, and stop in at a small museum or two (the Damien Museum, however, is closed on Sunday).

Take TheBUS no. 8 or walk to **Fort DeRussy Military Reservations,** a great, low-cost recreation area for the military, on a prime strip of Waikiki Beach. The beach is open to the public, and many claim it's the best in Waikiki. You may want to stop in for a quick visit to the **U.S. Army Museum in Fort DeRussy Park,** which contains military memorabilia dating from ancient Hawaiian warfare to the present.

From there it's a short walk to the **Hilton Hawaiian Village,** 2005 Kalia Rd., which has recently undergone a major, $80-million face-lift. It's a fascinating corn-ball beach city of its own, with 20 acres of tropical gardens, an artificial lagoon, a vast array of indoor and outdoor bars and restaurants, six pools, a beautiful beachfront (you're welcome to swim if you like), a dazzling array of shops, and even its own post office.

Leave the Hilton and walk (about 10 minutes), or take TheBUS no. 8 up Kuhio Avenue, which runs parallel to Kalakaua, to Royal Hawaiian Avenue. Walk one block toward the ocean to Kalakaua and the **Royal Hawaiian Shopping Center.** After you've browsed a bit, walk behind the shopping center to the magnificent **Royal Hawaiian Hotel,** the pink stucco Moorish-style hotel that is as much a landmark on the Waikiki skyline as Diamond Head. Explore the grounds and the magnificent interiors.

A few doors Diamond Head of the Royal Hawaiian, walk to the **Sheraton Moana Surfrider Hotel.** The $50-million restoration of the venerable Moana Hotel, for years the classic South Seas hostelry on the beach at Waikiki, is magnificent. Enter and step back into the elegant refinement of the 19th century, updated for sophisticated living today. Now cross Kalakaua, walk to the corner of Kalakaua and Uluniu, and stop in to explore the **Hyatt Regency Waikiki,** its inner courtyard dramatically landscaped with tropical foliage, trees and plantings, huge sculptures, many-storied waterfalls, flowing lagoons, picturesque kiosks, and Polynesian objets d'art.

On a more serious note, you may wish to visit the **Damien Museum,** 130 Ohua St. (corner of Kalakaua Avenue, behind St. Augustine's Catholic Church), which presents a moving account of the work that Father Damien de Veuster did with the victims of leprosy on the island of Molokai.

On the other side of Ohua Street, reward yourself with a visit to the **Hawaiian Regent Hotel,** where you'll enjoy one of the most beautiful daytime views in Waikiki. The hotel is tastefully done, with its open-air lobby surrounding a central court aglow with a fountain and two lagoons. Walk up two flights of stairs to the pool and the Ocean Terrace, which seemingly juts out right over the beach (even though it's across the street). The glorious colors of ocean and sky surround you wherever you look. From here, cross the street to **Kuhio Beach,** where you may want to have a look at the statue of **Duke Kahanamoku** with a surfboard.

(Incidental intelligence: Local people favored having the statue facing the sea instead of the traffic on Kalakaua Avenue, but it was placed this way so that tourists could take pictures with the ocean in the background.) Take a picture with Duke, then spend the rest of the day loafing in the sun.

DIAMOND HEAD WAIKIKI—ST. LOUIS HEIGHTS

There are more than a few things to see at the Diamond Head end of Waikiki, up near Kapiolani Park. This tour takes you from Honolulu Zoo to St. Louis Heights in about two hours. Be sure to go before 5pm, when the aquarium closes.

Past Kuhio Beach, at Kapahulu Avenue on your left is the **Honolulu Zoo,** 151 Kapahulu Ave. It's noted for its collection of native Hawaiian and other tropical birds, displayed in various bird-jungle habitats.

From here on, Kalakaua Avenue is a regal, although narrow, tree-lined drive. And a little farther on, where Kalakaua meets Monsarrat Avenue, begins **Kapiolani Park** (those are the Koolau Mountains in the background). The 220 acres of the park have facilities for just about everything from soccer to rugby to picnicking; also archery, a golf driving range, and tennis. Just ahead is **Kapiolani Beach Park,** with locker room, restrooms, picnic tables, and snack bar. Also up here, just past the beach, is the **Waikiki Aquarium,** 2777 Kalamaua Ave. Here's your chance to see, among other sea creatures like giant clams and sharks, the *lauwiliwilinukunukuoioi,* the long-nosed butterfly fish.

Now it's time to rest your feet—and see something new—by hopping aboard TheBUS no. 14 going Diamond Head on Kalakaua Avenue. The bus will take you through the suburbs of Waialae-Kahala and Kaimuki, and up the mountain to Maunalani Heights. From there, you can look straight down into **Diamond Head Crater.** Koko Head is on the left, Waikiki slightly to your right.

For your return trip, change to TheBUS no. 2, and you'll be back in Waikiki. Or if you prefer, stay on the no. 14 and ride up to **St. Louis Heights,** for a magnificent panorama of Honolulu. A forest of beautiful Norfolk pines with picnic tables and a splendid view of Manoa Valley awaits you here at **Waahila Ridge State Recreation Area.**

Note: If you're making this little trip by car, you can actually drive right inside Diamond Head Crater—the only drive-in crater on Oahu, except for Punchbowl. Here's how you do it. Follow Kalakaua until it circles left, just past the Colony Surf Hotel; then make your first right to Diamond Head Road. Come up Diamond Head Road, past the lighthouse on the right. Take your first left before the triangular park; you are now entering the Fort Ruger area. Watch for the DIAMOND HEAD CRATER sign on the left and follow the road to the left. Go through the tunnel, and you're in Diamond Head State Monument. Hiking trails go up to the rim of the crater. The area looks quite undramatic, but where else can you drive into a volcano!

5. ORGANIZED TOURS

WALKING TOURS The people at **Honolulu Time Walks,** 2634 S. King St., Suite 3 (tel. 943-0371), would like to take you for a walk. In the course of their popular 2½-hour walking tours, which leave from various points on Oahu, you can meet with the ghosts of Hawaii, relive the events of December 7, 1941, or follow in the footsteps of Mark Twain. Many of these tours are led by master storyteller Glen Grant. Costs range from $5 to $7. Call the number above for timely information and reservations.

Kapionai Community College presents a unique series of walking tours into Hawaii's past, including visits to Honolulu's famous cemeteries, to the almostvanished "Little Tokyo" neighborhood, to the old plantation community of Waialua, and much more. Tours cost $5; for information and reservations, call 734-9245.

The **Mission Houses Museum** presents a walking tour of "Historic Downtown Honolulu" Wednesday and Thursday at 9:30am. The cost of $7 also includes admission to the museum (tel. 531-0481 for reservations).

Aunty Malia Solomon, the well-known Hawaiiana expert, leads a free walk to places of historical interest in Waikiki, on Wednesday in summer at 10:30am, weather permitting, from Hyatt's Hawaii, a cultural and historical center on the second floor of the Hyatt Regency, behind the waterfall. Wear comfortable shoes, for it's about a two-mile, two-hour trek. For more information, call 923-1234, ext. 6410.

The **Hawaii Geographic Society** (tel. 538-3952) offers several unusual and highly worthwhile tours from April through September. One is "A Temple Tour," including Chinese, Japanese, Christian, and Jewish temples, cathedrals, and houses of worship; another is an archaeology tour in and near downtown Honolulu. Each is guided by an expert from the Hawaii Geographic Society. A brochure is available on request. Cost is $10 per person, a minimum of three persons required. Call for details and reservations.

The society's brochure, "Historic Downtown Honolulu Walking Tour," is a good self-guiding look at a fascinating part of Hawaii—the part that is 200 years old! It's $3, including postage, from Hawaii Geographic Maps and Books, 49 S. Hotel St., Suite 218 (P.O. Box 1698), Honolulu, HI 96808.

Three different organizations offer walking tours of Chinatown. Tours offered by the **Chinatown Historical Society,** a nonprofit organization, cost $2 and are very popular. They offer two different walking tours of Chinatown and Foster Botanical Garden. The morning tour departs Monday through Saturday at 10am, and covers shops and historical buildings. The afternoon tour departs Monday through Friday at 1pm.

This tour visits several Chinese and Japanese temples and the Foster Botanical Garden ($2 admission). The tours meet inside Asia Mall, 1250 Maunakea St. Reservations aren't necessary; for information, call 531-3045.

The 3-hour "Walk-A-Tour" run by the Chinese Chamber of Commerce only on Tuesday mornings at 9:30am is an old favorite. It includes visits to shops, markets, and historic sites. The price is $5, and lunch can be arranged. The tour leaves from **Chinese Chamber of Commerce** headquarters at 42 N. King St. (tel. 533-3181 for reservations).

The **Hawaii Heritage Center** at 1168 Smith St. (tel. 521-2749) focuses on the history and unique places of the area in its tour of Chinatown on Fridays from 9:30am to noon. The cost is $4 per person. Reservations required only for groups of 15 or more.

FREE & LOW-COST FACTORY TOURS Free refreshments and more than 40,000 fashions to select from at factory prices are available at **Hilo Hatti Fashion Center,** 700 Nimitz Hwy. (tel. 537-2926); call and they'll tell you where their free bus will pick you up in Waikiki. The **Hawaiian Heirloom Jewelry Factory** offers a free tour right in the heart of Waikiki—in the Royal Hawaiian Shopping Center, to be exact (tel. 924-7972). Free tours are conducted weekdays, every hour on the hour, from 10am to 4pm. You'll learn about the history of Hawaiian heirloom jewelry—it started back in the days of Queen Victoria—and see how these heavy gold handcrafted pieces are made today. The **Maui Divers Jewelry Design Center,** 1520 Liona St. (tel. 949-6729), is the home of Maui Divers of Hawaii, who were the first to mine black coral more than 30 years ago. Today their creations include a variety of corals, as well as other precious stones, in 14-karat-gold settings. The half-hour tour, given daily from 9am to 4pm, includes a film and a walk through the manufacturing center where you may watch artisans at work, followed by a visit to the showroom. Call for reservations and information. To see how many Hawaiian gift items—hula skirts, dolls, shell jewelry, ornaments, kitchen accessories, etc.— are made, you can take a free tour of **Lanakila Crafts** at 1809 Bachelor St., Monday through Friday (except holidays) from 8am to 3:30pm. Lanakila is a private nonprofit organization that provides vocational training and employment placement services for adults with disabilities. Their products are sold in the finest gift stores in Hawaii. They are also available in their Gift Shop. Call 531-0555 for information and to arrange tours.

TOURS FOR THE DISABLED Handicabs of the Pacific offers special tours for handicapped passengers, including luaus, cruises, and sightseeing tours in specially equipped vans that can handle six wheelchairs. Typical city tours cost $45 per person. For information, call 524-3866.

6. EDUCATIONAL/ALTERNATIVE ACTIVITIES

HAWAIIAN PHILOSOPHY The early Hawaiians were very practical psychologists, and some of their ancient practices are gaining the attention of psychologists and educators today. If you'd like to learn some of the secrets of that ancient wisdom, updated for today's world, try to catch one of the evening lectures on Ho'oponopono (the art of problem-solving and stress release), at the **Foundation of I (Freedom of the Cosmos)**, P.O. Box 10861, Honolulu, HI 96816-0861. The foundation was started by the late Morrnah Simeona, a native Hawaiian renowned throughout the islands as Kahuna Lapa'au, a healer, herbalist, and authority on the Hawaiian teachings. Among her colleagues is psychologist Stanley Hew Len, Ph.D. We attended one of these free lectures and a Ho'oponopono workshop (for which there is a fee) on a recent trip and found it fascinating. For information, call 395-9278.

CHANOYU: THE JAPANESE TEA CEREMONY As refreshing as a quick trip to Japan, the twice-weekly demonstrations of the Japanese tea ceremony held at 245 Saratoga Rd. (near Fort DeRussy) offers a fascinating look at the ancient "Way of Tea." Sponsored by the **Urasenke Foundation of Hawaii,** a nonprofit group whose goal is "to find peacefulness through a bowl of tea," the demonstrations are held every Wednesday and Friday (excluding holidays) from 10am to noon: Donations are welcomed. Seated in a formal Japanese tatami room in a garden setting, guests are introduced to the proper customs for the preparation and partaking of tea, and are served a sweet and powdered green tea from exquisite "tea bowls." You may ask questions and take pictures if you wish. A must for lovers of Asian culture. For information, call 923-3059.

MEDITATION Visitors are welcome at the **Siddha Yoga Meditation Center,** 1925 Makiki St. (tel. 942-8887). There is no charge for evening programs of chanting and meditation, held every Wednesday and Saturday at 7:30pm. Newcomers to Siddha meditation are invited to come at 7pm for a brief orientation. The center is up in the hills, in a beautiful residential area of Honolulu. Call for information.

7. SPORTS & RECREATION

Oahu has myriad facilities for riding, waterskiing, skin diving, plain and fancy fishing, even birdwatching (look for listings of Audubon Society programs in the daily papers). The Hawaii Visitors Bureau can direct you to the right places.

Kapiolani Park is certainly one of the world's most active recreational areas. It has archery and golf driving ranges; fields for soccer, rugby, and softball; courts for tennis and volleyball; a jogger's circuit training course; and lots more. For details, call the Department of Parks and Recreation headquarters (tel. 523-4631); they can also give you information on swimming lessons.

BEACHES The best place, of course, to get your basic training for a Hawaiian vacation is **Waikiki Beach,** that fabled stretch of sand that curves from the Ala Wai Canal to the shadow of Diamond Head. Stretched out among other bodies in various states of pose and repose, you can calmly watch the frantic traffic out in the breakers where the surfboard and outrigger-canoe crowds are busy trying to run each other down. The blue Pacific, the coconut palms, the trade winds—everything around you induces a lotusland lethargy that has caused more than one vacationer to tear up a return ticket home ($75-a-day-ers, naturally, should cash theirs in). The best part about all this is that it's absolutely free; there's no need to stay at any of the lush seaside caravansaries to use the beach. All the beach area is public property, up to the high-water mark, even though some of the big hotels do rope off special areas for their guests. Swim in front of the hotels if you like, but you'll have just as much fun at **Fort DeRussy Beach,** near the Ewa end of the beach (a good bet for families, but you can't buy anything at the snack bar unless you have a military card), and in the Diamond Head area, at **Kuhio Beach Park,** one of the best natural beaches in Waikiki and headquarters for the surfing and bikini crowd. It begins just past the Sheridan Moana Surfrider Hotel, at Uluniu Avenue. The beach has been considerably widened, and now it's better than ever. However, we should warn you that there is at least one 22-foot-deep hole in the midst of otherwise knee-high (for an adult) water, and there is no way such anomalies in the ocean floor can be corrected—fill them in one day and they'll be back the next. Parents of small children and nonswimmers should exercise caution here. In fact, the director of water safety for the city and county of Honolulu suggests that visitors always check with the lifeguard on duty at a beach before swimming.

Looking for a beach far from the madding crowd (well, as far as you can get)? **Queen's Surf,** just across from Kapiolani Park, a lovely beach area frequented mostly by local families and, at the Diamond Head end, the island's gay population. There's a snack bar here, plus locker rooms, showers, and picnic tables. **Ala Moana Park** is a popular family beach, almost surfless, but sometimes polluted. Magic Island here tends to be cleaner. If you drive out to the marina behind the Hotel Ilikai, all the way to the left, you'll find a delightful beach between the Hilton Hawaiian Village and the marina. It's kind of an "in" spot for kamaainas, but tourists don't seem to know about it. There's also plenty of space to park here.

FITNESS There's no need to let up on your fitness program just because you're on vacation. If you like to do your daily routines on the beach, join the free exercise class every day except Sunday from 9 to 10:30am at the beach at Fort DeRussy.

GLIDER RIDES [SOARING] You can take a glider ride at Dillingham Airfield on the North Shore, using the long-established services of the **Original Glider Rides** (a service of Honolulu Soaring Club since 1970). You can get instruction in doing it yourself or go for a piloted joy ride in a sailplane ($90 for two passengers, $60 for one). For an extra $20, they'll videotape your ride, using two cameras; one is pointed at the scenery below, the other at you, the passenger. They also have two aerobatic planes—one with a closed cockpit, the other with an open cockpit—that will take you on (gasp!) 20-minute aerobatic rides. One passenger only. Look ma, no engines! Phone "Mr. Bill" (tel. 677-3404) for information. Rates are subject to change. No reservations are required, and things glide along here seven days a week, 10:30am to 5:30pm. Bring your camera.

GOLF There are 14 public golf courses on Oahu, most with relatively low greens fees. The nearest one to Waikiki is the 18-hole **Ala Wai Golf Course** at 404 Kapahulu Ave. Reservations are taken by phone (tel. 296-4653) one week in advance starting at 6:30am. All reservations are usually given out by 7am. Huge lines of local people start to form before dawn to take advantage of any cancellations. Ala Wai is reputedly the busiest golf course in the world, with over 500 people playing daily. Visitor rates are $30. Cart rental is $12; club rental, $15. With a car, you can drive to the **Hawaii Kai Golf Course,** 8902 Kalanianaole Hwy., in about 20 minutes. It has an 18-hole par-3 course, an 18-hole championship course, and a driving range. Rates for the par-3 course are $35 with cart; for the championship, $80 with cart. There's a restaurant on the premises. Call 395-2358 for information and reservations.

If you're planning a drive out to the North Shore, you can take advantage of the little-known (to visitors) **Kahuku Municipal Golf Course,** which has the benefit of an ocean view and very low greens fees—for islanders. Out-of-state rates have recently been upped to $19 for 9 holes, $30 for 18 holes. The 2,725-yard course is seldom crowded except occasionally on weekends. Note that there is neither a pro shop nor a restaurant here. Tee times are required only on weekend mornings. For information, call 293-5842.

For a listing of golf courses elsewhere on Oahu, see "Golf and Tennis in Hawaii," available from the Hawaii Visitors Bureau.

HIKING If you'd like to discover what those mountains are actually like across the Ala Wai, the **Hawaiian Trail and Mountain Club** will take you on a hike along one of the numerous beautiful trails around Honolulu, where you'll feel far removed from both city and beach. You pack your own lunch and drinking water on these hikes, which usually start from the Iolani Palace grounds at 8am on Sunday and 9am on Saturday. The hiking fee is $1, plus a modest charge if you plan to carpool to the hiking site. Visitors are made welcome and usually make up about half the group. For a packet of valuable information about hiking and camping in Hawaii, as well as a schedule of upcoming hikes, send a legal-size stamped, self-addressed envelope plus $1.25 to P.O. Box 2238, Honolulu, HI 96804. If all you want is the schedule, just send the envelope (be sure to request the schedule!) and omit the $1.25. Or, you can check the schedule printed in the "Today" section of the *Honolulu Star-Bulletin.* For information, call 488-1161. If you'd like to go hiking with the local branch of the **Sierra Club,** contact the Sierra Club, Hawaii Chapter, P.O. Box 2577, Honolulu, HI (tel. 538-6616). The **Hawaii Nature Center** always has a hike or a class or a conversation project going on; it also has "Sunday Adventures" for kiddies. Some charge a small fee; some are free. Call 955-0100 for information.

For books, topographical and other maps, and information on camping, hiking, bicycling, and other outdoor activities in Hawaii, contact **Hawaii Geographic Maps & Books,** P.O. Box 1698, Honolulu, HI 96806, to request their free brochures and lists. In addition, their *Information Packets* are informal, revised regularly, and designed to provide a variety of useful things not found in one place. The Hiking/Camping Information Packet is $7, as is the Adventure Packet: Both are $12, including postage. Another worthwhile thing to have is their impressive publication *Hawaii Parklands,* with 100 color photographs. It sells for $25 hardcover, $15 softcover, plus $3 postage and handling. Also very helpful to hikers are the books by Robert Smith: *Best of Hawaiian Hiking, Hiking Oahu, Hiking Maui, Hiking Kauai, Hiking the Big Island,* each $9 and available from Hawaii Geographic Maps & Books. Two other excellent books are Craig Chisholm's *Hawaiian Hiking Trails,* $13, and *Kauai Hiking Trails,* $15, and also available from Hawaii Geographic Maps & Books or from the publisher, Fernglen Press, 473 Sixth St., Lake Oswego, OR 97034. *Road Guide to Hawaii Volcanoes National Park* and *Road Guide to Haleakala and The Hana Highway,* $5 each, are really helpful to hikers, bikers, *and* drivers, and, again, available from Hawaii Geographic Maps & Books.

HULA DANCING You, too, can do the hula! Hula-dancing lessons are given everywhere—at the Ys, at the university, and at any number of private dance studios. Free classes are sometimes given at hotels and shopping centers, but since the times of these lessons change with the seasons, it's best to consult the local tourist papers. The **Waikiki Community Center** (tel. 955-0100) has a wide variety of classes, including hula. And free hula classes are usually given Monday, Wednesday, and Friday at the **Royal Hawaiian Shopping Center,** Building C, third floor, at 10:30am. Call 922-0588 for further details.

ICE SKATING We realize that you probably didn't come to Hawaii to go ice skating, but if that's your pleasure, you'll love Honolulu's beautiful rink: the **Ice Palace.** Located in Stadium Mall, across from the rear of Aloha Stadium, this place has really caught on with the local folk. Admission is $5.75: children 6 and under, $5. All admissions include skate rental. Open daily, call 487-9921 for public skating hours. Don't fret if you forgot to pack warm hats, mittens, or gloves—there's a little shop here that will sell them to you. From Waikiki, bus no. 20 stops at Salt Lake Boulevard and Nimitz Highway, from which there is a 10-minute walk to the rink.

KAYAKING Visitors to Waimea Valley, Home of Waimea Falls Park, on the North Shore of Oahu (see Chapter 9, "Touring Oahu"), are invited to take a kayak ride along the Waimea River. They can paddle out to the white sands of Waimea Bay, where they can "park" their kayaks and take a dip in the crystal blue ocean. The $15 per person tours are offered daily at 10:30am, 12 noon, and 3pm and include paddling equipment, instructions, and a two-for-one all-day admission to the park. *Note:* We'd prefer this one for summer months only: during winter, waves at Waimea Bay are enormously high. For information, call 638-8511.

MASSAGE After all this exertion, you may be in need of a massage. Waikiki has many licensed massage therapists, but one we can personally and wholeheartedly recommend is Ed Hopai, whose studio is in the **Outrigger Village Hotel,** 250 Lewers St. (tel. 926-9045). Ed practices a combination of Swedish, Shiatsu, Hawaiian Lomilomi, acupressure, and deep-tissue work, and his rates are very affordable: $30 for half an hour and $45 for a full hour. You can also visit the **Honolulu School of Massage,** at 1123 11th Ave. in Kaimuki (right behind Diamond Head), a reputable, state-licensed organization that offers massages by advanced students at a cost of $25 an hour or by licensed massage therapists for $50 an hour. And, oh yes, massage helps relieve jet lag, too. Call 733-0000 for an appointment. The school is accessible by bus no. 1, 13, or 14. Fees subject to change.

MOUNTAIN BIKE TOURS Visitors to Waimea Valley, Home of Waimea Falls Park, on the North Shore of Oahu (see Chapter 9, "Touring Oahu") can participate in two-hour escorted mountain bike tours that start at the top of the North Valley summit and wind downhill on a scenic mountain bike trail. The cost of $60 includes all-day admission to the park. Participants must wear closed-toe shoes. For information, call 638-8511.

RUNNING Jogging is popular in Honolulu, as it is just about everywhere else. You can join those getting in shape for the **Honolulu Marathon** (it's held the first or second weekend in December) at a free Marathon Clinic, every Sunday at 7:30am at the bandstand in Kapiolani Park. If you're in town in mid-February, grab your sneakers and join some 32,000 other participants in the 8.25-mile **Great Aloha Run/Walk,** the largest running event in the islands, and the fifth-largest run in the United States. There's an entrance fee of $17 to $20; proceeds go to charity. Call 732-1-GAR or write to Great Aloha Run/Walk, 710 Palekaua St., Honolulu, HI 96816.

SAILING With **Honolulu Sailing Company,** 47-335 Lulani St., Kaneohe, HI 96744 (tel. 808/239-3900, or toll free 800/829-0114), you can sail away aboard a sleek, modern yacht to the islands of Oahu, Maui, Lanai, and Molokai. This company runs day, overnight, and one-week cruises out of Honolulu Harbor and Kaneohe Bay, combining sailing and snorkeling, at rates of about $55 for a half day, $150 overnight. Nautical weddings and whale-watching cruises are specialties. Boats sleep 4 to 10 passengers and there are private staterooms for couples. One-day sailing, snorkeling, and Zodiac raft trips on Oahu are also available for about $85 per person. Private bare-boats and skippered charters are also available.

SNORKELING Once you start traveling around the island, you have a choice of literally dozens of beaches, each one beautiful. One of the nearest of these beaches, and an ideal one for snorkeling, is **Hanauma Bay** (you can rent snorkeling equipment at many places in Waikiki, and other snorkelers are always willing to help beginners). And you don't need your own car to get to Hanauma Bay; simply board the Hanauma Bay Shuttle, operated by TheBUS. It runs from Waikiki to Hanauma Bay every half hour from 8:45am to 1pm, and can be boarded at the Ala Moana Hotel, the Ilikai Hotel, or at any city bus stop. It returns every hour on the hour from noon to 4:30pm.

Note: At press time the beach was closed on Wednesday; check the local papers when you arrive.

Serious snorkelers and scuba divers who will be touring the neighboring islands may wish to write for a copy of the *Dive Hawaii Guide,* by Dive Hawaii, a nonprofit association, and the University of Hawaii Sea Grant Extension Service. More than 44 locations are mapped and described. Send $2 (includes postage and handling), or $3 outside the U.S., to UH/SGES, 1000 Pope Rd., MSB 226, Honolulu, HI 96822, Attn: Dive Hawaii Guide.

SUBMARINE DIVING Even if you don't scuba dive, there's still a great way to see the world beneath the waters. We refer to a dive on the **Submarine Atlantis,** which descends to a depth of 100 feet in the waters off Waikiki, treating passengers to views of coral reef and brightly colored reef fish that normally only scuba divers can see. One of a growing fleet of such high-tech subs (theres another one in Kona on the Big Island, another on Maui, and several more in the Caribbean and Guam), the *Atlantis* is totally equipped for safety and comfort, is fully air-conditioned, and maintains normal atmospheric pressure—no chance of getting the bends. You will, however, get a thrill as you peer out the portholes and view the eerie world beneath the waves. The adventure begins at the Hilton Hawaiian Village where a catamaran takes you to the dive site, then back for an enjoyable sail along the Waikiki coast. Allow about two hours for the entire trip. Although the fee—$79 for adults, $38 for children—is high, this is such a special experience that we consider it a highly worthwhile splurge. For information, call 973-9800. *Note:* Children must be at least 3 feet tall to go on the sub.

SURFING If you'd like to learn to surf, try the concessions at Kuhio Beach, or in front of the Sheraton Waikiki, Sheraton Moana Surfrider, or Hilton Hawaiian Village hotels, or inquire at the recreation desk of any large hotel. Lessons are about $20 per hour. You must be a strong swimmer. According to the experts, you'll need three months to become a real surfer, but if you're reasonably well coordinated, you should be able to learn enough to have some fun in a day or two. If you're not, don't torture yourself. Take a ride in an outrigger canoe instead. With six or seven others in the canoe, you paddle out to deep water, wait for a good wave, and then, just as a surfer does, ride its crest back to shore. It's a thrilling experience, slightly strenuous, but with little possibility of broken bones.

For experienced surfers, the best surfing area in these parts is known as **The Cliffs,** at the base of Diamond Head. In surfers' language, the waves here are high-performance, nonhollow walls (no tube rides), and are usually 2 to 6 feet high. They can be some of the most beautiful peaks in Hawaiian waters. Combine them with the views of Diamond Head and you've got a surfer's paradise. The Cliffs is immediately past the lighthouse on Diamond Head Road, just past Waikiki. There is parking on the road and a paved trail to the beach below. Showers are available. We'd consider this one for serious surfers only, but the watching is also great.

Surfing, by the way, was the favorite sport of Hawaiian royalty and originally had religious connotations. In the early part of this century, Jack London, among others, helped revive the sport, and today it's an absolute passion with every able-bodied islander, far surpassing the interest of the mainlander in, say, baseball or skiing. Of course, many mainlanders move to Hawaii for the lure of the surf. (A T-shirt we saw on our last trip proclaimed, WORK IS FOR THOSE WHO CAN'T SURF.) Radio weather reports always include a report on the latest surfing conditions. A special phone (tel. 836-1952) also gives the latest reports. And the proudest possession of any island teenager is, naturally, his or her surfboard.

TENNIS Tennis in Honolulu? Certainly. It's free at 26 public courts. Pick up the brochure called "Golf and Tennis in Hawaii" at the Hawaii Visitors Bureau for complete listings. The **Ilikai Hotel** has a lot of tennis action: six specially surfaced courts, a ball machine, two full-time tennis pros, private lessons, twice-weekly clinics. Hours are 7am to 8pm daily, and the fee is $5 per hour singles or doubles. The pro shop rents racquets and does overnight stringing. They'll even help you find suitable partners (tel. 949-3811).

8. EVENING ENTERTAINMENT

Honolulu has a rich cultural life: Classical music, opera, theater, and dance are abundant, and of excellent quality. And ticket prices are often lower than in most other artistic centers. Check the local papers when you arrive, and also call the **Mayor's Performance Hotline** (tel. 527-5666) for a recording that describes activities planned for the current month at Honolulu Hale (City Hall), Iolani Palace, Kapiolani Park Bandstand, and Tamarind Park on Bishop Street. The service also announces any last-minute cancellations.

PERFORMING ARTS

OPERA & CLASSICAL MUSIC

Classical-music lovers have no cause for complaint in Honolulu. Western concert artists of the stature of Emanuel Ax stop here en route to the Far East or on round-the-world tours; Japanese soloists and orchestras pay frequent visits. You might even catch companies from China.

HONOLULU SYMPHONY, Neal Blaisdell Concert Hall, Ward & King Sts. Tel. 593-9391.
The Honolulu Symphony presents Great Performances and Light Side Pops concerts during the September to May season. These concerts feature internationally known guest artists and conductors and the presentation of a major ballet company. The music ranges from the great orchestral and choral masterpieces to swinging pops, Broadway, and Hawaiian. During the summer months, the symphony presents Starlight Festival Concerts in the beautiful Waikiki Shell as well as free community concerts in various beach parks.
Admission: Tickets, $10–$40.

CHAMBER MUSIC HAWAII. Tel. 947-1975.
If you enjoy chamber music, you'll want to hear this organization's excellent and highly professional ensembles. Some 20 concerts a year are given at various locations, including the Honolulu Academy of Arts.

HAWAII OPERA THEATER. Tel. 596-7372.
Try to attend a performance of this company, which holds a yearly Opera Festival in January, February, and March, featuring internationally acclaimed opera stars complemented by Hawaii's finest singers, a locally trained chorus, and the Honolulu Symphony. Recent performances have featured Verdi's La Traviata, Gounod's Faust, and Strauss's Der Rosenkavalier.
Admission: Tickets, $20–$65.

THEATER

Hawaiian theater is maturing and becoming more varied all the time. A number of professional and nonprofessional artists turn out some excellent productions.
The easiest way to find out what's playing when you're in town (and on neighbor islands, as well) is to call the **Theater Hotline** (tel. 988-3255) sponsored by the Hawaii State Theater Council. It's a 24-hour information line on all plays and musicals currently showing on Oahu, providing dates, places, and numbers to call for reservation information.

DIAMOND HEAD THEATER, 520 Makapuu Ave. Tel. 734-0274.
A year-round program of current Broadway shows, revivals, musicals, and classics are presented by this very popular group, which has been going strong since 1951 (it used to be known as the Honolulu Community Theater). Performances are held at the Diamond Head Theater, on the slopes of Diamond Head.
Admission: Tickets, $8–$40.

KUMU KAHUA, 16 Merchant St. Tel. 737-4161.
Now in its own theater in downtown Honolulu, in the restored Kamehameha V Post Office Building, this group performs only works by Hawaiian residents or plays about Hawaii.
Admission: Tickets, $8 adults, $6 seniors and groups, $5 students.

JOHN F. KENNEDY THEATRE, University of Hawaii at Manoa. Tel. 956-7655.
The beautiful 600-seat theater is the home of the university's Department of Theatre and Dance, known for its excellent programs in Asian as well as Western theater. Presentations may include Asian theater such as grand Kabuki, Noh, and Kyogen, or traditional Beijing Opera, performed in English by an all-student cast. Shakespeare, Western theater classics, contemporary plays, ethnic dance, classical ballet, and modern dance are also featured. Visiting troupes from around the world are presented occasionally.
Admission: Tickets, to $15.

MANOA VALLEY THEATER, 2833 E. Manoa Rd. Tel. 988-6131.
Now in its 25th season, this company provides an intimate setting for a broad spectrum of theatrical offerings. The 150-seat theater lights up 42 weeks of the year for a variety of productions ranging from the Bard to Broadway, from classics to musical comedy. Prices at "Honolulu's Off-Broadway Playhouse" depend on the production and the night of the week. Call for dates and availability of seats.
Admission: Tickets, $14–$25.

LOCAL CULTURAL ENTERTAINMENT

THEATER, SONG & DANCE There are quite a few opportunities to catch free Hawaiian entertainment. If you're in town on a Friday, don't miss the King's Jubilee, a tribute to King Kalakaua at the **Hilton Hawaiian Village;** it's an imaginative re-creation of the period of Hawaiian monarchy in the late 19th century. Things get underway at 6:30pm with a march to the hotel's porte cochère, where the Hawaiian anthem is sung; from then on it's a torchlight ceremony, Hawaiian music, and hula dancing at 7, fireworks at 8, plus more entertainment until 10pm (tel. 949-4321 for details.) There's a one-drink minimum ($3.50) for table seating; standing room is free.

The same Hilton Hawaiian Village is also the place to catch dances and musicians from the Polynesian Cultural Center who perform on the **Village Green** every Tuesday from 3 to 6pm. A different Polynesian culture is highlighted each month; phone 847-8200 for information. Every evening between 5:30 and 9:45, the lovely poolside terrace at the **Sheraton Princess Kaiulani Hotel** is the scene of a free show featuring songs and dances of Polynesia. Have a drink or not, as you like (tel. 922-5811).

Just as you expected, virtually everyone in Hawaii does the hula. Island youngsters learn it just as mainland children take ballet or tap lessons. Social directors and hotel instructors patiently instruct the malihinis, and wherever you look there's a hula show underway. All of this is fun, and some of it is good dancing, but much of it is a bastardization of a noble and beautiful dance, Hawaii's most visible contribution to the arts.

Happily, there has been a great revival of interest in serious hula lately, and if you're lucky you may get to see outstanding dancing at some of the better nightclub shows (the Brothers Cazimero at the Monarch Room of the Royal Hawaiian Hotel, for one) or at concert presentations. True devotees of hula should visit the islands during the month of April. That's when the ✪ **Merrie Monarch Festival** is held in Hilo, on the Big Island of Hawaii, a week-long virtual Olympics of hula, with dancers from all the various hula halaus (schools) of the islands competing in both ancient and modern hulas. You probably won't be able to get tickets to the events themselves (they're usually sold out by the preceding January), but they are fully covered on television and are a true joy to watch. On a recent trip, we sat enthralled viewing the competition and the judging—as did just about everyone else on the islands.

Not only hula shows but also ballet performances, choral and band concerts, martial arts demonstrations, and fashion shows are held frequently at **Centerstage** at Ala Moana Shopping Center. More than 500 free programs a year are presented, by island talent and international performing groups. Check tourist publications for exact times.

The **Kodak Hula Show,** a venerable Waikiki institution, showcases authentic music and dance by talented artists. Naturally, it's nirvana for photographers. There is special seating for the disabled. The show is held at the Waikiki Shell in Kapiolani Park, Tuesday through Thursday at 10am. Get here early for a good seat, because even with bleachers that seat 4,000 people, it's always crowded. (For free Hilo Hattie bus transportation, call 537-2926.)

Kuhio Mall presents a free hula show every night at 7pm and 8pm. Usually, there's a free show at the beach in front of the **Reef Hotel** every Sunday from 8pm to 9:30pm or 10pm. Lots of bright amateurs get into the act. Free concerts and cultural shows are given in the Great Hall of the **Hyatt Regency Waikiki,** often at noon or 5pm, but since the schedule varies greatly, you should check with the Hyatt Hostess Desk (tel. 922-9292) for exact times. The Pau Hana show, Friday at 5pm, featuring Aunty Malia Solomon, is a perennial favorite. Hawaiian music and dance performances are presented at the **Bishop Museum,** Monday through Friday at 1pm. There's free entertainment galore at the **Royal Hawaiian Shopping Center.** You can usually count on a minishow presented by the Polynesian Cultural Center, on Friday and Saturday between 6:30pm and 8pm and on Saturday between 10:30am and 12 noon, in the Fountain Courtyard. For exact times, and news of special programs check the local papers.

Look for notices in the papers of concerts presented by **Dances We Dance,** an educational and performing organization that sponsors both ethnic and modern dance concerts throughout the state. On one trip we were lucky enough to catch a concert by the Ladies of Na Pualei O Likolehua, as part of a special season of Hawaiian dance. Performances are usually held in the state-of-the-art Mamiya Theatre at the St. Louis Center for the Arts, on the St. Louis–Chaminade campus, 3140 Waialae Ave. To see a noncommercial dance presentation by a respected hula halau like this one is a very special experience.

Probably the best ethnic dancing of the Pacific Islands is done by the dance group at the **Polynesian Cultural Center.** They often do free minishows at the Royal Hawaiian Shopping Center. Watch for outstanding programs of Japanese, Korean, and other Asian dances at the University of Hawaii.

HAWAII IMAX THEATRE For a look at Hawaii that most tourists never get, a visit to the Hawaii IMAX Theatre, 325 Seaside Ave., just off Kalakaua (tel. 923-4629), is recommended. The gigantic screen is five stories tall and 70 feet wide, with wraparound stereo sound: The result is a feeling not of watching a film but of being *in* it. *Hidden Hawaii,* the theater's premiere attraction, shows some extraordinary footage of active volcanoes, of life beneath Hawaiian waters, and of an emerging new island, Loihi. By the time you read this, two more films will have been added to the agenda. Films are usually shown every hour on the hour, every day, from 11am to 9pm, but phone first for possible schedule changes. The cost is $7.50 for adults, $5 for children 3 to 11. After the film, you emerge into a tasteful shopping gallery, the Gathering Place Museum Shop. Many items by local artists and craftspeople are featured.

CONCERTS   Free concerts are generally held on Sunday at 2pm at the **Kapiolani Park Bandstand.** Entertainment includes Polynesian revues, ukulele clubs, visiting mainland troupes, jazz and rock musicians, and usually the famed Royal Hawaiian Band; call 926-4030 for more information. You can nearly always be sure to catch the Royal Hawaiian Band at its Friday noontime concerts at the **Iolani Palace bandstand.** These lunchtime concerts are very popular with the local people who work nearby; bring a lunch and have a listen. Also popular is the free concert at **Wilcox Park** (King Street next to Fort Street Mall) on the second and fourth Mondays of each month from noon to 1pm. On the fourth Thursday of each month, there's a free concert at 7pm in City Hall Courtyard. Or join the local crowd on Friday at noon for the **Mayor's Aloha Friday Music Break,** held at Tamarind Park, at the corner of Bishop and King Streets (tel. 527-5666). Tuesdays at noon it's the **Mayor's Chinatown Music Break,** at Gateway Park at the corner of Bethel and Hotel Streets (tel. 527-5666).

JAZZ   Jazz enthusiasts should note that there are frequent free jazz events at Ward Warehouse (check newspapers or call Victoria Ward, Limited at 531-6411). For jazz on the radio, tune in to Station KIPO (1380 AM and 89.3), Hawaii Public Radio for news and jazz, classical, and folk music. You can also phone Seth Markow at the station (tel. 955-8821) for information on jazz events throughout the state. Seth has a nightly show on KIPO at 6pm Monday to Friday.

LUAUS   Luaus are fun affairs—everyone arrives dressed in aloha shirts and muumuus, a great ceremony is made of taking the pig out of the imu (camera buffs have been known to go wild with joy at this part), there's lively Polynesian entertainment, and the mai tais flow freely.

Honolulu offers a number of luaus, but one that's most consistently praised is the **Paradise Cove Luau** (tel. 973-LUAU, or toll free 800/775-2683 in the mainland U.S.), held in a Hawaiian theme park 27 miles from Waikiki, on a 12-acre beachfront site of the town of Ewa. (Nearby is Oahu's newest resort development, Ko Olina, home to the exquisite Ihilani Resort & Spa.) Guest can wander through a village of thatched huts, learn ancient Hawaiian games and crafts, enjoy the spectacular sunset over the ocean, help pull in the fish in the nets during the hukilau, and watch a program of ancient and modern hula at the imu ceremony. Then it's a buffet meal and a Polynesian show: The fire dancer alone is worth the price of admission. Bus fare from Waikiki is included in the admission prices of $44.50 adults, $25 children 6 to 12. The luau is held every night of the week.

CLUB & MUSIC SCENE

NIGHTCLUBS, CABARET & COMEDY

Let's be perfectly honest: To see the top nightclub shows in Hawaii, you're going to break your budget—and then some. When a big name is entertaining, the local clubs usually impose a cover charge plus a minimum of two drinks, which can swiftly add up to more than you'd think. On top of that, many of them prefer to accommodate their dinner guests only—and dinner at these places is usually in the $50 or $60 bracket. Luckily, many of the clubs also have cocktail shows at about half the price, which usually include one drink and tax.

Here's the information on the top names and places. Check the local tourist papers when you're in town for exact details; a top star might just happen to be on the mainland when you're in the islands, but somebody new and unknown might be making a smashing debut.

THE BROTHERS CAZIMERO, the Monarch Room in the Royal Hawaiian Hotel, 2259 Kalakaua Ave. Tel. 923-7311.

⭐ We'd give up almost anything to catch a show by The Caz. They are beloved champions of authentic Hawaiian music and dance, and many of their songs, and the dances of their company, featuring the incredible Leina'ala, are truly from the heart of Hawaii. No need to splurge for the dinner show unless you want to, since cocktail shows are presented Tuesday through Saturday at 8:30pm and again on Friday and Saturday at 10:30pm. Local people say this late show is the best one of all, a time when Robert and Roland "let their hair down" for a mostly local crowd.

(*Note:* If you're in town on May 1, which is "Lei Day" in Hawaii, don't miss the Brothers Cazimero's annual concert at the Waikiki Shell. It's a fabulous production, and all of Honolulu comes dressed in their aloha finery. General admission is usually $15; reserved seats are around $20. Arrive early and bring a picnic supper.)

Admission: Cover charge, $22.50 cocktail show, $56 dinner show.

FRANK DeLIMA, at Polynesian Palace Showroom, Outrigger Reef Towers Hotel, 227 Lewers St. Tel. 923-SHOW.

⭐ Although a lot of his material is local—he loves poking fun at the various ethnic groups of Hawaii—Frank DeLima seems to be adored by both islanders and tourists alike. He's a musical comedian rather than a standup comic, and he uses the guys in his back-up group (who are also very funny) in his zany song parodies and skits. Frank is not smutty, just crazy, so you can feel perfectly comfortable bringing older children. Readers of *Honolulu* magazine have voted him "Best Local Celebrity/Entertainer." *Note:* Frank is highly visible these days—on TV, at benefit performances, at shopping-center promotions—so it's quite possible you may be able to see him for free. Watch for him. He's great! His show here is on Tuesday through Saturday at 9pm, with an early show on Saturday at 6:30pm.

Admission: Cover charge, cocktail show $7.50, plus two-drink minimum; dinner show $37.50.

HAWAII CALLS, in the Tropic Surf Club Showroom at the Hilton Hawaiian Village, 2005 Kalia Rd. Tel. 947-7993.

⭐ From 1935 to 1975, Hawaii Calls, a legendary show that introduced Hawaiian music to the world (Arthur Godfrey was one of its stars), became the most popular program in the history of radio, heard on some 750 stations around the globe. After a hiatus of almost 20 years, it's back, featuring five of its original performers, some of the children and grandchildren of the original artists, and host Bill Bigelow, a worthy successor to the show's creator, Webley Edwards. You can catch the show every Saturday morning beginning at 11:45am, with an hour or so of "warmup" music. Guest performers appear each week. A great way to become part of a legend.

Admission: $28 including a lavish buffet lunch; $12 cocktails only.

JOHN HIROKAWA, in the Hilton Hawaiian Village Dome Showroom, 2005 Kalia Rd. Tel. 949-4321, ext. 25.

The "early show" at the Hilton, and one that's especially suited for families with children, features Hawaiian-born illusionist John Hirokawa, a very talented fellow. Kids love it. The fun and games begin at 6:30pm.

Admission: Cover charge, cocktail show $20 adults, $17.50 children; dinner show $44.50 adults, $31 children.

DANNY KALEIKINI, in Hala Terrace of the Kahala Hilton Hotel, 5000 Kahala Ave. Tel. 734-2211.

⭐ Danny is undoubtedly one of the islands' top entertainers, a brilliant musician who dances, sings, plays a variety of instruments (including the nose flute), and watches over a talented company of Hawaiian entertainers. The show is deliberately low key and in excellent taste, suitable for a family evening. Show time is 9pm, with seatings at 7 and 7:30pm Monday through Saturday.

Admission: Cover charge, cocktail show $9, plus two-drink minimum, tax, and gratuity; dinner show $66, inclusive of cover charge, tax, and gratuity.

LEGENDS, Royal Hawaiian Shopping Center, 4th floor, Building B, 2201 Kalakaua Ave. Tel. 971-1400.

Talented impressionists take the audience back in time to some of the exciting moments of yesteryear. Jonathon von Brana steals the show as Elvis Presley; "Prince," "Madonna," "Marilyn Monroe," and "Michael Jackson" are some of the other featured artists.

Admission: Cover charge, cocktail show $28 adults, $25 children 8–18; dinner show $55 adults, $44 children.

PAU HANA SHOW, at the Hyatt Regency Waikiki, 2424 Kalakaua Ave. Tel. 923-1234.

On Friday at 5pm, when local people finish work, they like to head for this spot. So should you. Traditional Hawaiian music, dances, and songs are presented for the cost of a few drinks. You can also stand by the giant waterfall and just watch.
Admission: Free.

SHERATON'S SPECTACULAR POLYNESIAN REVUE, Ainahau Showroom, in the Princess Kaiulani Hotel, 120 Kaiulani Ave. Tel. 922-5811.

There are several good Polynesian shows on the beach, but if you're going to see just one, make it this stunning 1½-hour-long authentic Polynesian revue that pulls out all the stops (Fiji war chants, Samoan fire-knife dancers, Tahitian aparimas, and much more). You have a choice of a dinner show (consisting of an excellent prime rib buffet and one drink) or cocktail show.
Admission: Cover charge, dinner show 5:15pm seating $54, 8pm $47.50; cocktail show 6 and 8:30pm, $27.

SOCIETY OF SEVEN, Main Showroom, in the Outrigger Waikiki, 2335 Kalakaua Ave. Tel. 922-6408 or 923-0711.

For more than 20 years, the show put on by the seven talented entertainers who call themselves the Society of Seven has been an island favorite. These young men sing, act, play a variety of musical instruments, and even reprise Broadway musicals (we caught them once in their miniversion of *Phantom of the Opera*), and they know how to keep an audience cheering. Music, imitations, comedy routines, rock music, oldies, and island favorites are all part of the act. It's held at 7 and 9pm Monday through Saturday (on Wednesday at 9pm only). The cocktail show includes tax, tip and either one soft drink or one cocktail.
Admission: Cover charge, cocktail show $30 adults, $24 students 12–20, $20 children; dinner show $51 adults, $41 children under 12.

HONOLULU COMEDY CLUB, in the Ilikai Hotel, 1777 Ala Moana Blvd. Tel. 922-5998.

Comedy clubs are big everywhere these days, and Honolulu is no exception. This one features both local and mainland comedians in 90-minute performances held on Tuesday, Wednesday, and Thursday at 8:30pm, on Friday at 8 and 10pm, and on Saturday at 7, 9 and 11pm. Look for other Comedy Clubs at the Keauhou Beach Hotel on the Big Island, the Outrigger Kauai Beach Hotel, and the Maui Marriott.
Admission: Cover charge, $12.

COFFEEHOUSES

Coffeehouses are making a comeback all over the country, and Honolulu is no exception. None of them, however, has hit the major tourist areas yet. In the following cafés, you'll find local people relaxing, catching up with their friends, and enjoying some wonderful brews.

COFFEE TALK, 1152 Koko Head Ave., in Kaimuki. Tel. 737-7444.

A popular and fun place to go to after the movies or theater, Coffee Talk is full of charming eccentricities: chairs that don't match (one is "upholstered" in painted-on leopard skin), a mobile that looks like a bunch of petrified bagels, immense coffee cups that are more like soup bowls with handles, window lamps with bases made of brightly colored plastic toys. There are plenty of newspapers and magazines to peruse while you're drinking your giant cup of coffee. Any time of day, there will be happy people talking, reading, dining on light food, and generally having fun. There's the usual line-up of coffees, including espresso, all priced from $1 to $2.50, plus hot chocolate and a wonderful vanilla iced tea!
Admission: Free.

JAVA JAVA CAFE, 760 Kapahulu Ave. Tel. 732-2670.
Very popular with the college crowd, Java Java Café is also fun for people of all ages. The space is small, with little marble-topped tables and ice-cream chairs; there's always music playing in the background, either classical or jazz, depending upon who is on duty. There's a limited menu (salads, sandwiches), plus a variety of coffee and espresso drinks and an "eggnog smoothie" for $2.95. Entertainment is a sometime thing (call to find out if anything's happening), but you could catch poetry reading, a "work-in-progress," or a jazz and folk combo. (Sometimes there's a cover charge—inquire.)
Admission: Free.

DANCE CLUBS

The disco/rock scene is bigger, better, and noisier than ever in Honolulu. A recent look around revealed something like a dozen clubs packing them in, and more on the way (there's also a fairly high rate of turnover). Besides offering plenty of exercise, the local clubs are mostly inexpensive; usually, they have a modest cover charge or none at all, and just a few insist on a two-drink minimum and/or a fee. Live bands usually alternate with disco, and the action gets under way between 9 and 10pm in most clubs and only ends when everyone drops from exhaustion—anywhere between 2 and 4am.
In addition to the listings that follow, **Studebaker's,** in Restaurant Row (tel. 526-9888), is the best dancing spot outside Waikiki. Not only can you "bop till you drop," but you are given sustenance while doing so. See the listing under "Happy Hours," below, for more details.

HOFBRAU WAIKIKI, in the International Market Place, 2330 Kalakaua Ave. Tel. 923-8982.
This restaurant-cum-dance hall has been on the Waikiki scene a long time. There's a variety of entertainment. Food and drinks are inexpensive, and there is no minimum.
Admission: Free.

IRISH ROSE SALOON, in the Outrigger Towers Hotel, 227 Lewers St. Tel. 924-7711.
The 17th of every month is St. Patrick's Day at this jolly Irish pub, which boasts 200 kinds of beer. Everybody wears green, and Irish music is played. Dancing's every night (St. Paddy's day or not) from 9pm to 2am to a live band. There's also a free jukebox that plays old-time music, plus a giant TV for sports fans.
Admission: Free.

KENTO'S, in the Hyatt Regency Waikiki, 2424 Kalakaua Ave. Tel. 923-7400.
Jeff Burton and the Corvettes, "L.A.'s hottest band," are usually the featured artists and they draw the crowds for a lively evening of '50s to '70s "Oldies but Goodies." The rocking and rolling goes on from 7pm to 2am nightly.
Admission: $10.

MAHARAJA RESTAURANT AND DISCO, at the Waikiki Trade Center, 2255 Kuhio Ave. Tel. 922-3030.
The first Maharaja Club outside Japan (which has 100), this $5-million extravaganza is reputed to have the best sound-and-light system in the islands. The theme is East Indian, the mood is opulent (mirrored ceilings, Italian marble), and the crowd is an international mix, which perhaps accounts for the stiff dress code—no jeans, T-shirts, or sneakers (no formal wear, either). They play all types of music, including Top-40 hits. A restaurant serves a wide range of both Japanese and Western dishes at moderate prices. Open daily from 8pm to 4am.
Admission: $8.

RUMOURS, at the Ala Moana Hotel, 410 Atkinson Dr. Tel. 955-4811.
There's a fancy feeling and dress code to match at this completely redone spot, which has first-of-its-kind-in-Hawaii audio, video, and lighting gear. It features musical videos, a light show complete with special effects, laser karaoke, and four of the islands' best DJs. During the Friday happy hour, they play music from the early '60s through the late '70s, which they call "The Big Chill."

Admission: Free Mon–Thurs and before 9pm Fri–Sat, after 9pm Sun.

SCRUPLES, in the Waikiki Marketplace, 2310 Kuhio ave. Tel. 923-9530.
One of the town's hottest nightspots, Scruples has DJs spinning Top-40 hits every night from 8pm to 4am.

Admission: Cover charge, $5 after 9pm.

WAVE WAIKIKI, 1877 Kalakaua Ave. Tel. 941-0424.
Hawaii's biggest, brassiest live rock-and-roll nightclub features a live band and light show every night, cocktails and dancing from 9pm to 4am. You must be 21 or over.

Admission: Cover charge (beginning at 10pm), $5.

KARAOKE

KARAOKE GS STUDIO, at the Waikiki Joy Hotel, 320 Lewers St. Tel. 921-3534.
The Japanese karaoke craze is also very big in the islands—karaoke machines can be found in a number of clubs. In case you didn't know, karaoke means "empty orchestra"—an orchestra minus the singer. That's where you come in. A laser-disc video machine provides the words, and guests—which could mean you—take turns providing the singing. If you've been too shy to get up and do this in a big public place, private studio and, either solo or in the company of a few chosen friends, sing away to your heart's content. Prices begin at $10 per hour for two people, and there are also special package deals combining the rental of a studio with dinner at the hotel's charming and moderately priced Cappuccino's Restaurant (see Chapter 6, "Honolulu Dining"). There are even "happy singing hours" from 5 to 9pm, two hours for the price of one. To reserve a studio, call the number above.

BAR SCENE

BARS WITH LIVE MUSIC

BEACH BAR, in the Sheraton Moana Surfrider, 2365 Kalakaua Ave. Tel. 922-3111.
The music at this bar begins at 7am and continues—with some interruptions—until 11pm at night. Name artists such as Olomano and various steel guitar groups can be heard daily from 7am to 11am and 3 to 11pm. A neat place for a drink near the water's edge, the bar is tucked into one of Waikiki's classic oceanfront hotels, which has recently undergone a magnificent period restoration.

Admission: Free.

MAI TAI BAR, in the Royal Hawaiian Hotel, 2259 Kalakaua Ave. Tel. 923-7311.
Right on the sands of Waikiki, this is a glorious spot to hear Hawaiian music as the sun goes down. And who better to deliver it than Keith and Carmen Haugen, a highly admired local couple. They make their music from 5:30 to 8:30pm Tuesday and Wednesday evenings; the rest of the week, it's The Brothers. There's no drink minimum.

Admission: Free.

SOUTH SEAS VILLAGE, 2112 Kalakaua Ave. Tel. 923-8484.
This one is a big favorite with the Honolulu theater crowd, who come to hear John Saclausa at the piano bar Monday through Friday from 7pm until 12:30am. John plays, people get up and sing, and everybody has a good time. Saturday night, it's karaoke.

Admission: Free.

COCKTAILS WITH A VIEW

HALA TERRACE, in the Kahala Hilton Hotel, 5000 Kahala Ave. Tel. 734-2211.

A romantic spot we favor greatly is this beachside rendezvous a short drive from Waikiki. You can sip your drinks on the patio and watch the surf roll in. At 8:30pm, a cover descends for the Danny Kaleikini dinner show.

Admission: Free before 8:30pm.

HANOHANO ROOM OF THE SHERATON-WAIKIKI, 2255 Kalakaua Ave. Tel. 922-4422.

For one of the most majestic views in town, try this glorious spot where the panorama stretches all the way from Diamond Head to Pearl Harbor. There's entertainment and piano music nightly, from 6:30pm on. Beers will cost you around $4; gin and tonic, $5. Cocktails served from 4 to 11:30pm. No drink minimum.

Admission: Free.

HOUSE WITHOUT A KEY, in the Halekulani Hotel, 2199 Kalia Rd. Tel. 923-2311.

★ If ever you've dreamed of picture-perfect Hawaii, treat yourself to sunset cocktails in the oceanside lounge of this classic Honolulu resort. Here, under a century-old kiawe tree, you can watch the waves splash up on the breakfront, see the sun sink into the ocean, and hear the music of a top island group, The Islanders (Sunday, Monday, Tuesday, and Thursday from 5 to 8:30pm) and the Hiram Olsen Trio (Wednesday, Friday, and Saturday from 5 to 8:30pm). Kanoe Miller, a former Miss Hawaii, does some beautiful dancing. Don't miss this one. A sunset cocktail pupu (appetizers) and light dinner menu are served from 5 to 9pm daily. Bottled draft beers are $4.50; exotic drinks are $7.

Admission: Free.

PAPEETE BAR, in the Tahitian Lanai Restaurant at the Waikikian on the Beach Hotel, 1811 Ala Moana Blvd. Tel. 949-5311.

At some of the Waikiki hotels, the cocktail gardens overlook the lagoon—and one of our favorites of these is the Tahitian Lanai. In this delightfully "old Hawaii" hotel, a lively local crowd hangs out at the bar, known for its sing-alongs, from 5pm to 1am. During the afternoon happy hour, 2 to 6pm, beer and standard drinks are $1.50 to $2.50, exotic drinks $4.50.

TOP OF WAIKIKI, Waikiki Business Plaza Building, 2270 Kalakaua Ave. Tel. 923-3877.

At the center of Waikiki is a revolving restaurant that resembles a gigantic wedding cake. The top tier is the cocktail lounge, very glamorous by candlelight and starlight. Views of all of Waikiki are yours for the price of a drink. Beer begins at $3.50; a gin and tonic, $4.

Admission: Free.

HAPPY HOURS

Now we come to the more practical side of pub-crawling; how to drink at half the price and sometimes get enough free food for almost a meal at the same time. The trick here is to hit the bars during their happy hours (usually from 4 to 6pm, but sometimes greatly extended), when they serve free pupus or lower their prices, or both. Note that these hours and prices are apt to change often, but these places always offer a good deal of one sort or another.

CROW'S NEST, 2224 Kalakaua Ave. Tel. 923-2422.

There's a generously long happy hour (11am to 8pm) at this spot located above the Jolly Roger. Several readers have written to praise this place for being "the friendliest and cheapest bar in Waikiki." Entertainment is offered nightly from 8pm, along with plenty of free peanuts (their shells cover the floor). Beer is $1.50 and mai tais run $1.75; after 8pm they're $3.25 and $4.

Admission: Free.

HEIDI'S LOUNGE at the Downtown Bistro, Grosvenor Center on Queen St., near Alakea. Tel. 536-5344.

⭐ Part of the popular Downtown Bistro (see Chapter 6, "Honolulu Dining"), this is one of downtown's best deals. From 5 to 6pm, Monday through Friday, there are plentiful free pupus (they could be fried ravioli, barbecued wings, and fittata, plus salad, finger sandwiches, and more) served along with drink specials all night. As if this weren't enough, they offer free karaoke between 5:30 and 9pm, Tuesday through Friday.

MONTEREY BAY CANNERS LOUNGE, in the Outrigger Hotel, 2335 Kalakaua Ave. Tel. 922-5761.

There's nothing skimpy about the happy hour here. It runs from 7am to 7pm, and during all that time, mai tais are $1.95. As if that weren't enough, there's a second happy hour between 4 and 7pm, when well drinks and beer are $3.25. Oysters and clams on the half-shell are 85¢ each. And—you won't believe this—there's still a third happy hour, from 10pm to midnight. That's when drinks and beer are $2.75, and Irish coffee and chi chis are just $2.25.

Admission: Free.

RIGGER, in the Outrigger Hotel, 2325 Kalakaua Ave. Tel. 922-5544.

Here there's a big-screen TV for sports events and entertainment nightly beginning at 9pm. Snackmix is served free all day. The ever-popular mai tais are just $1.75 during the 6am to 6pm happy hour. From 6 to 10pm, Bloody Marys are $2.25.

ROSE AND CROWN, at King's Village, 131 Kaiulani Ave. Tel. 923-5833.

This jolly Old English pub offers brews from the mother country, of course, plus an assortment of beers and cocktails, sing-along piano (from 8pm to 1am Thursday through Sunday), darts, all sorts of special nights. Plus happy hours that run from 11am to 7pm; during that time, beer is $1 and a gin and tonic costs $1.75; other times, they're twice as much. On Sunday, mai tais are $3.75, $4.25 at other times.

STUDEBAKER'S, in Restaurant Row, 500 Ala Moana. Tel. 526-9888.

Ⓢ The all-out winner for free food has to be this lively, deafeningly noisy, 1950s time warp complete with a bright-red Studebaker, lots of neon, and a DJ spinning platters. A free buffet is served along with your drinks weekdays from 4 to 8pm and on Sunday from 6 to 8pm. There are always four hot main dishes—perhaps pepper steak, teriyaki chicken, or shrimp fettuccine, to name a few—plus four or five salads, brown breads, and raw veggies with dip. "Happy Hour" simply refers to the patrons' delight in the free buffet. (*Note:* No one under the age of 21 is allowed in after 4pm and IDs are checked.) Beer is $3.25 and $3.75; standard drinks, $3.50.

Admission: Cover charge, $1, plus one drink.

WAIKIKI BROILER, in the Waikiki Tower Hotel, 200 Lewers St. Tel. 923-8836.

All the way from 6am to 9pm the Waikiki Broiler serves up the mai tais and chi chis at low prices, $1.75 and $2.25. There's entertainment from 5 to 9pm daily in the outside garden patio.

Admission: Free.

CHAPTER 8
SAVVY SHOPPING IN HONOLULU

1. WAIKIKI
2. ALA MOANA CENTER
3. AROUND TOWN

Muumuus and macadamia nuts, koa woods and calabashes, tapas and tiki figures—these are some of the exotic items you can shop for in the islands. Although Hawaii is not one of the great bargain-shopping areas of the world (no free-port prices or favorable money exchange for dollar-bearing Americans), it does offer a fascinating assortment of things Polynesian, Asian, and American for the inveterate browser and souvenir hunter. We'll skip the expensive items—jewelry, objets d'art, Asian brocades and silk, elegant resort wear—and stick to the good buys for the shopper who wants quality and low prices. Although many stores have upgraded their merchandise and are concentrating on higher-ticket items with which to entice affluent Japanese tourists, there are still plenty of good buys left.

1. WAIKIKI

Much of your island shopping can be done right in Waikiki: along Kalakaua Avenue and in the hotel gift shops, and at the International Market Place, Kuhio Mall, King's Village, Royal Hawaiian Shopping Center, and the Waikiki Shopping Plaza.

SHOPPING CENTERS

INTERNATIONAL MARKET PLACE, 2330 Kalakaua Ave. Tel. 923-9871.
The oldest and most colorful shopping area in Waikiki, this place is still fun, despite the fact that there are now so many booths and tourists that it sometimes reminds us of rush hour in the New York subway. And prices are apt to be a mite higher than they are in the department stores or at Ala Moana Center, although they might come down considerably if you do a bit of bargaining. And do note that comparison shopping pays off here; one booth might be selling T-shirts for $12 that one around the corner sells for $8 or $9. Informal, semi-open shops set around a giant banyan tree and interspersed among tropical plantings allow for al fresco browsing. Directly behind it, with an entrance on Kuhio Avenue, is Kuhio Mall, with more of the same. An entertaining scene, especially in the cool of evening.

Unfortunately, few of the shops here now carry genuine Hawaiian and Polynesian craft items, such as lauhala hats, carvings from native woods, or tapa cloth. What you will find are scads of places selling jewelry (everything from plastic to shell, ivory, coral, and lapis), candles, T-shirts, beach cover-ups, and resort wear. Many stands called **The Pearl Factory** sell pearls in the oyster. Shops and kiosks turn over with great rapidity, so our best advice is simply to roam wherever fancy leads you. If you like lovely Balinese clothing, check out a well-stocked shop called **Bali Designs,** which imports clothing for men and women direct from Indonesia. **Fingernail Fashions** offers original artwork, painted right on your nails. The **All**

Elvis Gift Shop speaks for itself. Art lovers should pay a visit to **Arts of Paradise,** an attractive gallery featuring original art by artists residing in Hawaii. Frequent lecture and slide shows are presented.

The International Market Place is open daily from 9am to 11pm.

KUHIO MALL, 2301 Kuhio Ave. Tel. 922-2724.

Kuhio Mall is directly behind the International Market Place, and looks exactly like it. Here you'll find the **Rainbow Letter Artist,** the only artist in Hawaii who creates rainbow colored letters in the shape of local flora and fauna with a single stroke of his unique brushes. He works and sells his letter paintings on the ground level. **Pictures Plus,** also on the ground floor, features a display of posters and pictures by local artists at very affordable prices—and they can be shipped anywhere. Visitors can watch candle-making at **Island Candle, Sheila's Art Candle,** and **Young's Candles** on the ground level. The candles, in unusual scents and shapes, including current cartoon characters, can be purchased at reasonable prices.

Free Polynesian shows are held nightly at 7 and 8pm, featuring Faye "Aloha" Dalire, a noted hula artist, whose halau (hula troupe) features many talented keikis. It's a charming show.

Kuhio Mall is open daily from 9am to 11pm.

ROYAL HAWAIIAN SHOPPING CENTER, 2201 Kalakaua Ave. Tel. 922-0588.

Across Kalakaua from the International Market Place is one of Waikiki's newer shopping centers, and in many respects its most sophisticated. "An oasis of green in Waikiki" is what the builders promised when ground was broken, and despite the outcry against the lavish use of concrete, it's pretty much what they've delivered. Occupying three city blocks along Kalakaua Avenue and fronting the entrance to the Royal Hawaiian and Sheraton Waikiki hotels, this stunning 6½-acre, 150-store complex is indeed graced with flowers and trees, ferns and shrubbery, and hundreds of trailing vines and Hawaiian plants. A high level of taste is evident in the shops, restaurants, and a huge variety of daily programs—Polynesian minishows, classes in coconut-frond weaving, ukulele playing, hula dancing, lei stringing, and Hawaiian quilting—as well as special events—enough to keep the visitor busy and happy for a long time. Unfortunately for us budgeteers, the trend here is toward more and more upscale marketing. On the first level, wealthy visitors sometimes wait in line to get into the designer shops, such as Lancel, Chanel, and Cartier. **McInerny Galleria,** on the first and second levels, features a series of pricey boutiques—Armani, Hermès, Izod Lacoste, Polo by Ralph Lauren, and more of that ilk. However, the budget shopper can still do pretty well here at several discount stores, such as the **Sale Studio at Andrade's** or **McInerny's Sale Studio,** where sportswear can be found for up to 75% off the original prices. Other lower priced apparel shops include **Swim Suit Warehouse** on the third level, the ever-popular **Crazy Shirts** and **Sgt. Leisure,** the latter specializing in fun, colorful clothing perfect for the islands. **Allure** is a good spot to remember for exercise and swimwear—excellent selections and tops in value and quality. In addition, there are several unique spots where the merchandise is outstanding and prices are fair.

In this category, then, be sure to visit the ✪ **Little Hawaiian Craft Shop,** on the third level, where a fantastic assortment of unusual finished jewelry sits alongside buckets and barrels of raw materials, the same kinds that were used by the ancient Hawaiians. This is a workshop for craftspeople using natural island materials in both traditional and contemporary styles. Replicas of museum pieces sit among handcarved tikis and buckets of inexpensive shells. They have some wonderful hard-to-find sandalwood necklaces—fragrant, lovely, and well priced, from about $22. The hand-painted floral tote bags done by watercolor artist Terrie Marie are a special find at $26. This is also a good source for Hawaiian quilting and cross-stitch—patterns, books, kits, and some finished pieces. Almost everything here is handmade in Hawaii. Great ideas for presents include kukui-nut rings at $6 (many kukui rings, pendants, and necklaces), coconut soap at $3, Hawaiian exotic wood keychains at $4.50 each, and coconut shell necklaces at $10.

The shop also includes an outstanding wood gallery that shows local woodworkers, such as Pai Pai, known for his wood-carved replicas of Hawaiian and Pacific images, and Pat Colto, for traditional Hawaiian calabash bowls. Only island woods—among them koa, mango, Norfolk pine, milo, macadamia, ohia lehus, and keawe—are used. Prices range from $3.50 to $3,000. Collectors will want to see the traditional and contemporary handcrafts from the islands of the Pacific—Fiji, the Solomons, New Guinea, Tonga, and Micronesia—with an ever-changing kaleidoscope of spirit figures, tapas, weavings, war clubs, drums, masks, and spears. The owners make frequent trips to these areas to find these treasures. Well worth a look.

The ✪ **Hawaiian Heirloom Jewelry Factory,** located on the third level, deserves a stop. It conducts free factory tours every hour on the hour, from 10am to 4pm Monday through Friday. You'll learn something of the history of Hawaiian heirloom jewelry and see how these heavy gold handcrafted pieces are made today, each inscribed with the owner's name and accompanying floral designs. Have a look at the fine china and handblown glass at **Exquisite Collections.** Much of the merchandise here is pricey, but you could pick up some lovely floating candles for just $2 each. Also worth a stop for those who like Chinese crafts is the **China Marketplace,** which has an excellent selection of cloisonné vases and handmade cloisonné animals, at very good prices. They also have tongue scrapers with Chinese saying on an accompanying card, an amusing present for all of $1.25.

Ready to treat yourself to something special? Stop in and visit Marlo Shima who runs **Boutique Marlo**, on the third level of Building C. Using only silk, cotton, and other natural fabrics, and dying them in the subtlest and softest of colors, Marlo creates women's clothing of great beauty. Although dresses go for about $80 to $200, you can find many modestly priced scarves, necklaces, fabric bags, and the like, with the same high standards of quality and beauty. We also like the stylish women's clothing at **C&C, Accessory** on the third level, especially their handsome batik jackets for around $85. Treat your keikis to some cute clothing at **Sunshine Kids,** also on the third floor. **Van Brugge House** has a huge two-level store; the lower levels sells pricey Australian opal jewelry and watches, plus pink and champagne diamonds, but the upper level is more in our price range. It's got a smashing selection of Australian-designed sportswear, and is truly a surfer's paradise—you could even get yourself a Surfarang (a surfer's boomerang) here. Check out the lovely Victorian stuffed animals, potpourris, and more at **Extraordinaire.**

If you've bought a lot, and are wondering how to get it all home, visit **GBS** on the third floor. They'll do professional packing, wrapping, and shipping, or else sell you the materials—corrugated boxes, mailing tubes, sealing tapes, etc.—that you'll need to do it yourself. United Parcel Service is available here, and there's a U.S. post office inside the store.

Where can you eat here? We've already told you about **Spaghetti! Spaghetti!** and **Okono-Miyaki Chibo** in Chapter 6. There's also a lovely Chinese restaurant, **Beijing Garden; Naniwaya,** which has an old-fashioned Japanese-inn setting for popular Japanese food; and **Shilla Korean Restaurant** for authentic barbecue dishes. **Coffee Connection** is an enjoyable espresso bar on the second level.

Free entertainment, lectures, and demonstrations go on all the time; check the local papers for details. The Royal Hawaiian Shopping Center is open from 9am to 10pm Monday through Saturday, until 9pm on Sunday.

KING'S VILLAGE, 131 Kaiulani Ave. Tel. 944-6855.

It's supposed to look like a 19th-century European town, with its cobblestone streets and old-fashioned architecture, but King's Village is very much a part of modern Honolulu. Behind the gates at the corner of Koa and Kaiulani Avenues, across the street from the Hyatt Regency Waikiki, is a cozy bazaar that contains a variety of shops, several restaurants, and an open market—all done up in a style that recalls the 19th-century monarchy period of Hawaiian history, when royal palaces were built in Honolulu, and Hawaiian kings and queens journeyed to London to be presented at the court of Queen Victoria.

The shops, however, are not so much European as the typical Honolulu-international mix, with lots of Asian and Polynesian crafts, plus plenty of Hawaiian resort wear and souvenirs. All are small and in good taste; King's Village is a commercial venture, certainly, but there's no commercial ugliness about it. We think you'll enjoy browsing here.

Prices at King's Village go from just a little to quite a lot. For about $45, you can take home a good wooden tiki, courtesy of **Hime**, an intriguing wood-carving shop, which has many lower-priced items as well, like a collection of whaling figurines. The **Royal Peddler** can always be depended upon for quality brass gifts with a nautical theme. They also have Waikiki's largest selection of Coca-Cola collectibles.

Do Re Mi is a shop that smells wonderful; it has all manner of potpourri and sachets, plus wooden toys and jumping jacks from Australia, as well as music boxes from Germany, Taiwan, and the U.S. **Casa de Europa** features European men's and women's accessories and clothing.

There's a large branch of the ever-popular **Crazy Shirts** here. In addition to adorable T-shirts (we love the one of the exercising Kliban cats reading FELINE FITNESS CENTER HAWAII), they have wonderful stuffed Fat Cats for $29—a sumo cat or a hula cat. If you're going to colder climes, a coat from **Burberry's London Men's Shop** might be just the thing. **Young Generation,** an outdoor boutique, offers darling outfits for the kieikis.

Leather Hawaii has some outstanding carryalls, including hand-painted canvas ones that are quite lovely. **Island Thongs** has more than just thongs—hats, visors, shoes. There are many whimsical candles, including pineapple candles starting at $8, at **Candle Odyssey.** All kinds of inexpensive fun watches, from Mickey Mouse character watches beginning at $25, make up the wares at **Hawaii Watch Shop.** The **Royal Selection** features beautiful china and crystal gifts. And **Cubby's Gifts** is just the place if you want to bring home stuffed animals for the kids; they have a huge selection.

King's Village has a number of fast-food outlets and restaurants. It's always good fun to stop by for a drink or a meal (steak-and-mushroom pie, ploughman's plate) at a new Olde English pub, the **Rose & Crown.** Happy hour features neat munchies and continues from 11am to 6:30pm, and there are sing-alongs at the piano every night. **Caffè Presto** is a nice stop for espresso and specialty coffees. **Tanaka of Tokyo** and **Odoriki** are both popular for Japanese food. The Changing of the Guard ceremony plus a hula demonstration take place nightly at 6:15.

King's Village is open daily from 9am to 11 pm.

WAIKIKI SHOPPING PLAZA, 2250 Kalakaua Ave. Tel. 923-1191.

The first impression one gets on seeing the enclosed Waikiki Shopping Plaza, at the corner of Kalakaua and Seaside, is that it more properly belongs in New York or San Francisco or some sophisticated European city. Shops like **Paloma Picasso, Bally of Switzerland,** and **Hunting World** have little to do with the islands. But as you ascend the escalators to the four shopping floors, it gets better and more versatile, with more of an island flavor. The traffic-stopper here is the five-story fountain by island designer Bruce Hopper, a wondrous, half-million-dollar creation with lights that change colors, and fascinating Plexiglas spheres and bubbles that make the waters dance. There's a different point of interest at each level, creating new surprises as you ride the escalators.

If your Japanese isn't up to snuff, fully half the stores, their names, and merchandise descriptions will be unintelligible to you. Sticking to English, however, you can still browse around and find a few shops offering good bargains. Check the racks at **Villa Roma**, a high-fashion shop for women (they often run clearances on sports items). Stock up on some reading matter at **Waldenbooks,** which has a very large selection. Art lovers will enjoy the **Art Forum Gallery,** which also has branches in Tokyo, Osaka, and Los Angeles. **Island Casuals** is known for wide selections and good bargains. There's a nice array of swimsuits at **Beach Avenue,** and **Treasure**

Island is the place to find Hawaiian Heirloom Factory Jewelry. The owner of the **Hawaii Cloisonné Factory** makes some nice jewelry, fashion artifacts not available anywhere else in the United States, and not expensive. Check out **Betty's,** on the fifth floor, for very inexpensive wooden necklaces and matching earring sets, among other gift items. This is a wholesale import-export place open to the public.

Eelskin, in case you hadn't noticed, is that leather from the sea that is extremely popular in Hawaii, and "wholesale outlets" abound: One of the best of these, **Ali Baba Imports,** is right here. Among the huge display of merchandise, we saw well-made eelskin wallets for about $18 to $40, handbags for around $60. Note that Ali Baba has another store at the Waikiki Business Plaza, Suite 201, 2270 Kalakaua Ave., and a toll-free ordering number: 800/222-7785. You might also check and comparison-shop several other eelskin stores at the plaza, like **Leather from the Sea** and **Eelskin Elegance,** where we made some excellent purchases on our last trip.

While most of the shops at the Waikiki Shopping Plaza are not budget-oriented, the basement restaurants certainly are, with a bevy of fast-food counters offering varied ethnic foods. (See "Specialty Dining" in Chapter 6). Open daily from 9:30am to 9:30pm.

CLOTHING & GIFT SHOPS
CLOTHING

The manufacturers of Hawaiian clothing we like best include Malihini of Hawaii, Mamo Howell, Hawaiian Heritage, Bete, Sun Babies, Princess Kaiulani, Tori Richards, Shan-Yin, Carol Bennett, and Kahala and Cook Street (better men's apparel); you'll find these brands all over town. Note, too, that most of the specialty shops will make up muumuus for mother, aloha shirts for dad, and children's versions of either in matching fabrics, and will also make clothes for your special size. (We should tell you that locals consider this very "touristy.") Many will make bikinis to order, or at least allow you to match the top of one to the bottom of another. Made-to-measure work usually takes just a day or two and in most cases costs no more than ready-made garments.

Prices for Hawaiian clothes are pretty standard everywhere: Better muumuus average $60 to $70 (short), $80 to $90 or more (long). To realize substantial savings on aloha wear, your best bets are two places outside Waikiki that we'll tell you about later: Hilo Hattie's Fashion Center, and Muumuu Factory. For antique Hawaiian shirts, see "Vintage Aloha Shirts," below.

CASA D'BELLA II, 2352 Kalakaua Ave. Tel. 923-6426.
We like this store a lot. They carry some stylish designs from New York and California as well as local resort wear, and they have a good collection of fashion jewelry, too.

LIBERTY HOUSE, 2314 Kalakaua Ave. Tel. 941-2345.
⭐ The Waikiki branch of Hawaii's premier department store has an extremely attractive selection of clothing for men, women, and children, too, with a good collection of shoes and accessories for men, women, and juniors and an extensive selection of cosmetics and fragrances. Liberty House is not inexpensive, but it gives you an idea of the best of mainland and Hawaiian fashions.

PERIOD CLOTHING
REMINISCE, 2139-A Kuhio Ave. Tel. 921-9056.
⭐ This pretty little shop, one block from the Kuhio Theater, specializes in period clothing in mint condition for men and women, dating from the turn of the century through the 1950s. Evening and bridal fashions are the specialty here. We coveted the wonderfully outrageous beaded and sequined flapper dresses, the beaded cocktail gowns from the 1930s and 1940s, the Victorian and Edwardian ballgowns and bridal dresses, and the divine hats from all periods. We almost succumbed to a very Myrna Loy black taffeta dinner dress. There's a super collection

of costume jewelry, plus shoes, hats, and handbags. For gentlemen, there are authentic 1950s Aloha shirts, amazing cravats, and fascinating, one-of-a-kind cufflinks from more gracious days. Prices here are not, of course, of the bargain-basement variety—some of the Victorian bridals are priced well up into the thousands—but there were great retro earrings and brooches for as little as $5: something for everyone. The friendly staff treats each one like a treasured guest. Don't miss it if you love elegant things from days gone by.

VINTAGE ALOHA SHIRTS

You know, of course, that "antique" aloha shirts—those from the 1930s, '40s, and '50s—for some inexplicable reason have become high fashion on the mainland. Why show-biz celebrities and socialites are willing to pay $100 to $1,000 for rayon shirts that have been hanging in somebody's closet for 30 or 40 years is a mystery to us, but the demand is there. In addition to the shops listed below, see Reminisce above.

BAILEY'S ANTIQUE CLOTHES & ALOHA SHIRTS, 517 Kapahulu Ave. Tel. 734-7628.

The shirts that make their way into places like this are snatched up quickly by folks like Robin Williams, Tom Selleck, and Steven Spielberg, to drop just a few names. Bailey's is a fascinating store, however (it also stocks other early island wear from various cultures), and it's well worth a look; if you can't afford one of the pricey items, choose one of their more than 1,000 shirts in the $5 to $10 range, 1,500 shirts for $10 to $20, or something like 500 shirts from the 1950s, which range from $20 to $125. Approximately 300 "silky" rayon shirts from the 1940s command prices of $100 to $1,000. They have the world's largest inventory of aloha shirts. Have a look, too, at their nifty (albeit expensive) art deco and retro jewelry.

KULA BAY, in the Royal Hawaiian Hotel, 2259 Kalakaua Ave. Tel. 923-0042.

This store, which also has a branch at the Hilton Hawaiian Village (tel. 943-0771), has done some clever work taking authentic prints from shirts of the 1930s, 1940s, and early 1950s, having them painted on long-staple cotton in more muted colors, and turning out handsome, very well-tailored aloha shirts for about $50. For photos of the originals, and a history of the aloha shirt, read the book called *The Hawaiian Shirt*, by H. Thomas Steel (Abbeville Press), available at many local bookstores.

SOUVENIRS & GIFTS

ABC DISCOUNT STORES Scads of Honolulu tourists swear by the low prices at the ABC Discount Stores, and so do we! There are literally dozens of ABC stores in Waikiki, sometimes two to a block! You can usually expect to save 20% to 25% here on small items, sometimes more. Hawaiian perfumes and boxes of chocolate-covered macadamia nuts are always a bargain here, and very welcome presents back home. In addition to gift items (many packaged ready for mailing), ABC has just about everything you need for a vacation at the beach, including bathing caps, sunglasses, straw beach mats for under $1, beach cover-ups, cosmetics, drugs, not to mention inexpensive luggage, groceries, deli, fresh produce, and liquor, and usually the lowest prices anywhere on Hawaiian scenic postcards. Most are open daily, from 7:30am to midnight. Truly indispensable resources for the Hawaii visitor.

OTHER SHOPS A number of budget stores that sell perfumes, cosmetics, and souvenirs can be found on Kalakaua in the area just Diamond Head of Uluniu Avenue, up toward the Queen Kapiolani Hotel. You can also count on good buys at **Holiday Mart,** which you'll read about ahead. **Woolworth's,** in the Bank of Hawaii Building on Kalakaua, now charges more for some standard souvenir items than ABC and some of the other shops, but their discount on jade, coral, opal, and 14-karat gold items is good. They will also mail your gifts and souvenirs home for you. **Long's Drugstore** in Ala Moana is another excellent source for small items; their values are consistently tops.

What to buy? Hawaiian perfumes make delightful small presents. Royal Hawaiian is the leading brand name for island fragrances—pikake, ginger, orchid, plumeria—all of them sweetly floral and worlds away from the sophistication of Paris. Gift packages complete with artificial orchids begin around $5; higher-priced perfumes have a real orchid right in the bottle.

As for jewelry, black coral, mined from the waters off Maui, is handsome in small tree shapes and in numerous other pins and pendants. An exquisite pink coral called angelskin has also been found off Maui waters. Blue coral is the "look" with jeans and casual tops. Crystals are popular here, as they are everywhere. You'll see all of these, in abundance, at jewelry stores all over the islands.

Several island manufacturers turn out attractive, inexpensive wooden jewelry. **Elena,** for one, does colorful wooden composition fish, birds, and tropical flowers, in earrings, pins, necklaces, and such, beginning at $6 a pair for earrings. A firm called **"Oh My Gosh by Josh"** creates geckos and other delightful jewelry, with pins beginning under $10. And **Island Attitudes** has wonderful painted wooden jewelry with Polynesian themes. (The Hawaiian jewelry department at Liberty House—see above—usually has a good selection of these, often on sale.)

You can buy Hawaiian delicacies—such exotic tastes as guava jelly, coconut syrup, passion-fruit ambrosia, Kona coffee, macadamia nuts—at almost any grocery store, and should you want to send a package home, the best and most reasonably priced places are Long's Drugs, ABC Discount, and the **Waikiki A-1 Superette.** Pineapples ordered at Dole Pineapple's Cannery Square are also excellent value.

READERS RECOMMEND

Dole Pineapple Cannery, Cannery Sq. (tel. 523-3653). "We ordered our pineapples to bring home at the Dole Pineapple Cannery Square. They delivered it right to our airline check-in place. These were the best pineapples we have ever had. Plus, they made wonderful gifts to bring back for office coworkers."
—Julie Clark, Olean, N.Y.

The Endangered Species Store, 2335 Kalakau Ave., opposite the International Market Place, is a shop where you can gift yourself, your friends, and the planet. From T-shirts to artworks to squeezable dolphins at $5, everything here has to do with saving the environment. Our favorite is the Chilean Rain Stick: Seeds placed over cactus needles inserted into a pole travel over the needles as the pole is shaken, producing an oh-so-soothing musical sound. They cost $11, $18, and $38, depending on size.

T-shirts, practically a uniform in Hawaii, make fun presents for almost everybody on your list; they're in every store, at every price. **Crazy Shirts,** which, like the ABC Discount Stores, seems to be on almost every block in Waikiki, can be counted on for witty designs, good fabrics, and prices of around $18 for Ts, around $40 for sweatshirts. For information on Crazy Shirts' factory outlet stores, see "Discount Shops and Factory Outlets" in "Shopping A to Z," in "Around Town," below.

Eelskin is another very big item for presents. Almost every eelskin store claims that it sells "wholesale." Reputedly the country's largest wholesaler, **Leather of the Sea,** in the Waikiki Shopping Plaza, 2250 Kalakaua Ave., fourth floor, has many good buys. Also in the same shopping center, **Ali Baba** and **Eelskin Elegance** offer good values. *Just bear in mind that eelskin has been known to demagnetize credit cards and bank cards, rendering them useless.*

2. ALA MOANA CENTER

Honolulu's fabulous modern shopping center (the largest open-air mall in the world), the Ala Moana Center, 1450 Ala Moana Blvd. (tel. 946-2811), just across Ala Moana Beach Park, is an example of island architecture at its best. Landscaped with trees, flowers, fountains, and a meandering stream down its Central Mall, which is graced with large works of sculpture, the Ala Moana Center is always packed with enough island families to make it worth seeing for that reason alone. But the stores are, of course, the main attraction—more than 200 of them, an international bazaar full of intriguing wares. We'll mention just a few, but shopping buffs will come back here many, many times.

One of Hawaii's biggest department stores, **Sears Roebuck,** is here, with the usual mainland amenities and the unusual Hawaiian specialties—like orchid plants (Sears will ship to the mainland and guarantees live delivery), and a tremendous selection of muumuus and island clothing at very reasonable prices. **J.C. Penney** is known for fashion and for excellent value in all departments, as is **Watumull's.** The flagship store of **Liberty House** is here, and most striking it is, its eaves decorated with Hawaiian tapas. Count on top-quality goods in all departments. Their specialty boutiques can be quite pricey.

We always enjoy browsing around in the large Japanese-owned department store ✪ **Shirokiya,** which has everything from state-of-the-art stereo to kids' T-shirts that glow in the dark, with a wonderful array of fashion, cosmetics, china, housewares, furniture, and fine arts in between. Check out the first-floor section on shiatsu foot massagers, chairs, etc. Give your feet a rest. Shirokiya's gourmet-food department, on the second floor, is worth a trip in itself. A vast array of wonderful sushi and other traditional Japanese fare is offered at dozens of booths and counters. There's plenty of food to take home. Or you can create a meal for yourself out of these offerings and then devour them on the spot, in the dining lanai. Most days from 3 to 8pm there's an evening buffet and sushi bar, priced according to what you eat.

Shirokiya is also a good place to find unusual and inexpensive gift items. Check the luggage accessories counter in particular: Handsome coasters with designs of Ukiyoe prints or antique kimonos make marvelous small presents for around $5. Fashion note: Shirokiya also carries socks, with a space for the big toe. You wear these *tabis* with your *zories*, of course.

There are also dozens of small shops in the center, reflecting just about every interest and taste. One of our favorites is ✪ **Art Lines,** with a highly tasteful collection of jewelry, animal masks, carving, statuary, crystals, bells, Tiffany-type lamps, and the like, collected from all over the world—especially from Egypt, Morocco, India, Indonesia, Greece, and Africa. There's an exotic collection of sterling-silver earrings. Prices begin at $4.50 for a shark's tooth and could go as high as $3,500 for a superb Buddha. This is Ala Moana's "bestseller" shop. **The Nature Company** is a restful oasis "dedicated to providing products and experiences which encourage the joyous observation, understanding, and appreciation of the world of nature." To that end, they feature everything from yoyos to telescopes, including a good selection of minerals and fossils, books on natural history, field guides, natural jewelry—lots of things that kids can enjoy, like an inflatable *Tyrannosaurus rex* for $19.95. Ask about their calendar of free events: You might be able to go birding in Kapiolani Park, or let the kids participate in a scavenger hunt in Ala Moana Park (for ages 5 to 9).

Summer's Place is also ecologically oriented and sells a good deal of "unique" merchandise, as well as interesting and unusual T-shirts, the best selection of rubber stamps and accessories on the island, licensed merchandise, and novelties. Sportswear bearing exclusive designs such as "Royal Hawaiian Polo Club" and "Island Logo Palm Tree" can be found at **Island Logo,** which also carries nylon bags and wallets, visors, hats, earrings, and other accessories.

The **Warner Brothers Studio Store** is a big new hit at the center. It has fashion, one-of-a-kind art objects, and classic toys based on Warner Brothers film and TV characters. Looney Tunes sweatshirts are $52; a giant black duffel bag with the Warner Brothers logo, which could be very useful for shopping, is $52; and Bugs Bunny and Looney Tune coil keyrings are just $3.50. It's kid's heaven, and so is the **Disney Store,** which has a popular Mickey's Toy Shop.

Then there's **Best Friends,** with dog picture motifs—Beagles, Dalmations, Poodles, shih tzus and many more breeds—gracing mugs, T-shirts, and what-have-you. There are a few cat motifs, too. **Art Avenue** does custom framing and has lots of framed prints and posters, including holographic 3-D "Art Images." **Paniolo Trading** features clothes and accessories for the equestrian (*paniolo* means "cowboy" in Hawaiian). **Ethel's** has some stylish women's lines, including Liz Claiborne Petites). Popular chains such as **United Colors of Benneton** and **Banana Republic** have stores here.

Quality is the word at **Elephant Walk,** which has lovely hand-painted shirts, prints, Hawaiian dolls, jewelry, and wood chimes, among other treasures. The level of taste here is consistently high. Fashion is foremost at **Mosaic,** and **Chocolates for Breakfast,** which has the sort of elegant clothing for women that never goes out of fashion. Only linen, cotton, and other natural fabrics are used to create the stylish fashions at **Alexia.**

Need something neat for the beach, the boat, or the bar? **Island Snow** is the place. Lots of good trinkets and small presents can be found at both **Ala Moana Gifts** and **Products of Hawaii.** At the latter, we saw wind chimes, prints, pot holders, candy, coffee, and many gift items, all at good prices.

Women going into ✪ **Headshots** looking like Plain Janes come out looking like high-fashion models. Headshots is a "contemporary photographic studio specializing in women and beauty." A session includes complete makeup, hairstyling, the use of clothing, accessories, hats, flowers—whatever will turn Cinderella into the Princess. Or a sophisticated business look can be chosen. Men and kids, too, are welcome. After the photo session, you can see your pictures instantly on the Kodak computer viewing system (prints are sold separately), and the results are extraordinary. If you've got a few hours to spare, photos taken here might turn out to be one of your most unusual souvenirs of Hawaii.

Stop in at **Musashiya** for wonderful fabrics. They have Japanese kimono fabrics in polyester crepe, as well as Yukata prints, batiks from Holland (Dutch Java wax prints), silks from Paris, and calico prints for quilters—not to mention custom-made Japanese futons. **Tahiti Imports** takes Tahitian prints of their own design and makes them into muumuus, aloha shirts, bikinis, and pareus. They also sell their exquisite hand-printed fabrics by the yard.

The Sharper Image, the catalog store to end all catalog stores, is a fabulous playground for adults, so even if you have to push along the aisles with the crowds, don't miss it. Come in and try their exercise bikes, the self-massage table or massage chair (soothing after a hard day's shopping), and scads of other curiosities.

We often pick up gifts from the **Compleat Kitchen and More.** A company called What a Melon creates charming designs of Hawaiian flowers and fruits with a motto reading "Grown in Hawaii," and puts them on towels and more. We love their Manoa Lettuce Bag, with its pidgin commentary: "Mo bettah den da plastic from da supermarket." Agreed. We also like the handcrafted koa-wood paddles, chopsticks, and wine corks made at the Hilo Vocational Rehabilitation Center, $6.50, $10, and $12. Tutu Nene potholders, with Hawaiian quilt designs on one side and native Hawaiian animals on the other, would make nice gifts, as would the trays featuring designs from the menu covers of the Matson Line ships—pretty enough to hang as a wall decoration. **Island Shells** has lots of stunning jewelry, shell and wood chimes, shell roses, and the like, and prices are always fair. And their shell flower arrangements are beautiful. It's fun to go fly a kite in Honolulu, and the place to get your equipment is **High Performance Kites,** right near the center stage. Many of their kites come from one of our favorite places on Molokai, the Big Wind Kite Factory. Also near the center stage, and in a sense the "heart" of the shopping center, is the ✪ **Honolulu Book Store,** with superb selections in every category, especially Hawaiiana, and newspapers that may—or may not—make you nostalgic for home, like the *Los Angeles Times, San Francisco Chronicle, New York Times,* and *Wall Street Journal.*

Need some decorating ideas? Striking posters, many with an Eastern motif, begin around $30 at the **Art Board.** Many fine prints and posters can be found at **Art Avenue.** Otsuka Galleries specializes in Asian art. **Iida's** is crammed with colorful Japanese giftware and decorations.

For over 30 years, **Irene's Hawaiian Gifts** has been a favorite with residents and visitors alike for unique island gifts. Their specialty is unusual carvings from native woods and collector's items like porcelain dolls, handcrafted Christmas ornaments, quilt kits, lauhala purses, hula implements, and koa-wood outrigger canoes with tapa sails, made locally and sold at good prices.

Feet getting to you? The **Slipper House** is a good place to replace whatever worn-out sandals you're trudging around in. They claim to have the widest selection of casual footwear in the state, with over 400 styles of made-in-Hawaii sandals, plus popular Tevas, Birkenstock, Reefs and Fiojos, and a wide array of lightweight totes and carrying bags. Best known for traditional men's and boy's wear, beautifully made and well priced, **Reyn's** also features good-looking women's clothes, here and in many shops on Oahu and the neighbor islands. **Poi** is also known for distinctive menswear. Check in at the big **Vim and Vigor Health Food Store** for excellent selections of honey, nut butters, whole grains, organic foods, superb home-baked goods that should not be missed, and other healthies. Stop in, too, at the **Crackseed Center,** if you want to know what Hawaiian youngsters clamor for (crackseeds, originally a Chinese confection, are a cross between seed and candies— very sticky, very tasty).

Coffee-lovers should definitely pay a visit to **Gloria Jean's Coffee Bean,** where coffees from all over the world (not just Kona coffee) are featured. They're available by the cup and by the package. It's fun to stop at the little coffee bar for an espresso or the coffee of the day—perhaps a small Zimbabwe, or an iced decaf amaretto, for 75¢ to $1.50. And there are many wonderful decaf coffees to take home, like Irish Creme, Chocolate Raspberry, or Vanilla Nut Creme. The aromas are irresistible. Chocoholics, too, will find the temptations at Ala Moana hard to resist, like the chocolates at **Ed and Don's.**

The newest addition to Ala Moana is **Palm Boulevard,** which is being called the Rodeo Drive of Honolulu. Budgeteers won't find much to buy here, but it's always fun to browse at the likes of Chanel, Polo/Ralph Lauren, George Jensen Silver, Gucci, Jaeger, Emporio Armani, and Adrienne Vittadini, to drop just a few names. **Kenneth Jay Lane**—of London, Paris, and New York—has some marvelous costume jewelry that you'd swear was the real thing (society folks wear his creations because the real things are kept in a vault). **Carrera y Carrera of Madrid** features smashing jewelry by sculptor Manuel Carrera, whose specialty is beautifully sculpted 18-karat gold hands, with gems. While you're checking out these shops, you might want to stop at the tiny outdoor **Royal Cophenhagen Tea Lounge,** where you sip tea or coffee on fine Royal Copenhagen porcelain, enjoy freshly baked French pastries—for an elegant $7.50 price tab.

One of the most intriguing stores at Ala Moana is the **Foodland Supermarket.** It's like an international food fair, reflecting the cultures that make up Hawaii—and the rest of the world. You walk along seemingly endless aisles of exotic foods: fresh-frozen coconut milk, packages of weird-looking Japanese dried fish, health foods, tortillas, English biscuits, French cheese, you name it—if it's edible, this place has got it. The salad bar includes kimchee, lomi-lomi salmon, and fresh poi, so create your own lunch. You can, in addition, pick up some okolehao, Hawaii's potent ti-root drink, in the large liquor department. If life has become boring in that little kitchenette of yours, you shouldn't miss paying a visit here. You'll also find an inexpensive souvenir section.

For more bargains in souvenirs and small items at Ala Moana, it's trusty old **ABC Discount Stores, Long's,** and **Woolworth's** (check out Woolworth's weekly specials).

The best bargains at Ala Moana are available when the stores take to the sidewalks—the ground-floor level, that is—displaying racks and racks of clothing for very low prices.

Remember the center, too, for free shows Centerstage, on the main floor, features a variety of entertainment by some of the best island talent and international performing groups. Over 500 performances—from Hawaiian hula shows and ballet to martial arts demonstrations and fashion shows—are scheduled throughout the year. Check tourist publications for exact times.

Ala Moana Center has always been one of the best locales in town for inexpensive dining. And the 850-seat, glass-enclosed dining court called **Makai Market,** on the makai (ocean) side of the center, makes the possibilities for entertaining eating here better than ever. For a complete run-down of the possibilities here, see "Specialty Dining" in Chapter 6.

Most Ala Moana Center establishments stay open seven days a week: Monday through Friday from 9:30am to 9pm, on Saturday from 9:30am to 5:30pm (but restaurants at Makai Market close at 5pm), and on Sunday from 10am to 5pm.

From Kuhio Avenue in Waikiki, you can take TheBUS no. 8 and you'll be at Ala Moana (barring heavy traffic) in about 10 minutes. Parking areas are numerous—and they even have coconut palms coming through the concrete!

NEARBY SPECIAL SHOP There's a very special crafts shop located across the road and a block Ewa of Ala Moana Center, called ✪ **Creative Fibers,** 450 Piikoi St. (tel. 537-6374), just across Piikoi from Sears. It carries everything from needles and thread to glamorous batik jackets from Bali. Exotic cottons from Asia and Europe are stacked next to pareus, for about $6 a yard. There are molas from Central America, Indian spreads, and other unusual fabrics, as well as kilim carpets and pillows from Turkey and Iran. You'll find beads, trinkets and jewelry, Turkish handweaves, silk scarves, and marvelous indigo cotton fabric designed by Escher of Holland and inspired by themes from Java. Kits for making fabric nursery-rhyme books are $6, and a delight. Closed Sunday.

3. AROUND TOWN

SHOPPING CENTERS

WARD WAREHOUSE, 1050 Ala Moana Blvd. Tel. 531-6411.

One of the most eye-catching of Honolulu's shopping centers is Ward Warehouse, located on Ward Avenue between Auahi Street and Ala Moana, across from Fisherman's Wharf. More than 65 shops and restaurants occupy the handsome two-story structures fashioned out of great rough-hewn planks, and there seems to be a higher-than-usual level of taste and selectivity here. It's a favorite shopping destination for local people and visitors alike.

A dazzling showplace for handcrafts is **Nohea Gallery,** a gallery and outlet for many local craftspeople: You'll see beautiful ceramics, leaded glass, fine furniture made of local hardwoods, flower pillows, jewelry, modern and traditional metal sculpture, and soft sculpture. Note the Old Hawaiian prints (from $12) and lovely notepapers, too. Fine-art posters, art reproductions, and original prints may also be found at **Frame Shack.** There are nicely matted small prints. They also have art-related T-shirts. For American folk art, most of it collected on the mainland and all of it handcrafted, visit **Crescent Gallery.** Wood carvings, arks, building signs, weathervanes, checkerboard quilts, Steiff bears, boxes, glassware, and more are all impressive. So, too, is the collection of Oriental and European treasures—carvings, jade, Chinese vases, boxes, ceramics, hand-screened T-shirts, hand-painted bead necklaces, and more to be found at **Heavenly Lotus.** There are many small, surprisingly affordable items here, too.

Don't miss ✪ **Out of Africa,** an art gallery and shop with a smashing collection of African arts and artifacts. Most of the material that owners Marcus and Linda Gualter collect on their frequent buying trips to Kenya, Tanzania, Malawi, Zimbabwe, Ethiopia, and Swaziland are in the $20-to-$75 range, with some extremes at either end ($750 museum-quality masks, $10 Zulu bead bangles). Kiondo woven sisal bags from Kenya cost between $24 and $44; they're all handmade and will last a lifetime. African music plays on the sound system as you peruse the original batiks, sculptures, wood carvings, striking jewelry, and more. No products made from endangered species are carried in the store. (There's another Out of Africa at 55 N. Nimitz Hwy.)

The most striking women's clothing at Ward Warehouse might well be found at ✪ **Mamo Howell.** Mamo Howell was a well-known island hula dancer and later became a Christian Dior model in Paris. She's turned her artistic flair to designing, and the results are stunning muumuus long and short; their inspiration comes mostly from Hawaiian-quilt motifs. Her designs are unmistakable once you've seen them—and you'll see them on the best-dressed women in town. Dresses are out of our price range (they go upward of $135), but quite affordable and also lovely are an array of small items using similar patterns, especially the quilted tote bags, lined with nylon, $35. Mamo creates charming children's clothing, too.

In the few years that it's been here, ✪ **Pomegranates in the Sun** has established a loyal following of fashion-conscious women. It features local artists and designers inspired by the Hawaiian atmosphere. There are many one-of-a-kind items. Prices are not generally low, but there are some affordable items: We saw delightful cotton sundresses at $55, long T-shirts for around $25, designer umbrellas from Australia at $30. Look for the smashing Pomegranates in the Sun in Haleiwa when you journey around the island. **Cotton Cargo** is worth your attention, too: It carries women's fashions made entirely from natural fibers—cotton, silk, linen, and rayon—with an emphasis on patterns and prints having an Asian influence. Many of the items are Cotton Cargo exclusives.

There are tons of good buys—clothing, Balinese masks and carvings, paintings by Chinese artists, and more—at **Imports International.** Men can find good aloha shirts at $19; women can find many attractive items from Bali at delightfully low prices. (A good portion of our summer wardrobe comes from here!) For discounts on the popular Bebe line of women's sportswear, check the **Bebe Discount Outlet,** where savings can be as much as 40% to 75%.

Birkenstock Footprints deserves your attention: It's the place to get those clunky-looking, marvelous-feeling, naturally contoured sandals that give you a "barefoot on the beach" sensation even on hard surfaces. They're for men, women, and kids of all ages, and the average price is about $90 for adults, $60 for children.

You may want to pick up some Christmas ornaments from **Kris Kringle's Den,** or some gorgeous fans among the Chinese arts and crafts at **Heavenly Lotus.** They have charming inexpensive items—cinnabar necklaces at $10, Chinese cutout notepapers at $2.50, hand-painted T-shirts at $29—in addition to more costly treasures. Note the potpourris, sachets, and lacy and frilly things for bed and bath at **Private World.**

The **Executive Chef** is for the compulsive cook; we saw wineglasses, cookie molds, French copperware, and other kitchen joys at good prices. One of their niftiest items is the Vacu-Vin, a wine resealing system for home use, at $20. You'll also find natural-sandstone coasters, Matson Line menu trays, and a delightful selection of Hawaiian gourmet items—papaya salsa, macadamia nut oil, passion-fruit butter, and Hawaiian teas like guava, papaya, and passion fruit.

Close by the Executive Chef, the same management presents bath and travel accessories as well as unique personal-care items at **Bath and Butler.** We flipped for the Island Essence line of aromatherapy body oils. Check out their locally made backpacks, and their tote bags, too, in tropical and geometric prints.

Nora Estelle has terrific handbags and accessories, and a very large collection of Laurel Burch items, which we love—shirts, bags, cups, totes. Every kind of athletic shoe and then some is available at **Runners Route Plus,** and **Island Sunsport** is the place for swimwear for men and women. And the people at **L.A. Image** may change your life—they'll do your colors, suggest clothing, hairstyles, makeup—a complete makeover. And they have some clothing on hand, as well.

Candy fanatics will have to visit **Carousel Candyland,** like an old-fashioned candy store, with jellybeans in jars, rock candy, licorice drops, yummy chocolates made on the Big Island, and traditional Hawaiian treats such as crackseed and mocha crunch.

Honolulu mommies collect dollhouse miniatures in the gigantic dollhouse that is **My Favorite Things.** And moms-in-waiting, or those who've already delivered, find **In Bloom** just what they've been looking for: attractive maternity and baby clothes under one roof. As soon as baby gets older, they graduate to **The Next Generation,** which has charming clothing, furniture, and gifts for children from age 2 up. Children of all ages, and men and women too, love the line of hand-blocked batik fabric clothing at **Blue Ginger.**

Quality gift items—inlaid music boxes, scrimshaw, Italian porcelain antiques and collectibles—are easy to find at **Traditions.** Hawaiian quiltings, glass figurines, scrimshaw, and more can all be found at **The Royal Peddler.** Need a book or a tape, a newspaper or greeting card? **Waldenbooks** has a large branch here, and they'll order any book for you, at no extra charge.

End your excursion, perhaps, at the **Coffee Works,** a charming shop that purveys all manner of imported coffees, teas, and chocolates, as well as some very attractive vessels from which to sip them. Coffee makers, too. Happiness is a slice of carrot cake and a cup of café Vienna, at their coffee bar.

We've told you about the **Chowder House** for a quick seafood meal, the **Old Spaghetti Factory** for pasta in a fabulous setting, and **Restaurant Benkei** for some fabulous Japanese buffet meals. **Stuart Anderson's Cattle Company** is locally famous for well-priced prime ribs and chicken dinners, served in an upbeat setting with a great view of Kewalo Boat Basin. For light snacks, choose among the fast-food stands (seating in a central courtyard) at the **Food Express** (everything from burgers to saimin to health-food salads), or visit **Suzie's Korean Barb-B-Que** for delicious Korean dishes. There are outside tables on the lower level.

Ward Warehouse's **Amphitheatre** hosts a variety of events and entertainment, from jazz concerts to fashion shows to chili cookoffs and then some. Shopping hours are 10am to 9pm Monday through Friday, until 5pm on Saturday, and from 11am to 4pm on Sunday. Restaurants stay open until late in the evening. From Waikiki, take TheBUS no.8, marked WARD AVENUE, from Kuhio Avenue, or Kalia Road. It's about a 15-minute ride from Waikiki. And it's also located on the Waikiki Trolley route.

WARD CENTRE, 1200 Ala Moana Blvd. Tel. 531-6411.
Down the road a block from Ward Warehouse is Ward Centre, another sophisticated collection of boutiques and restaurants, all with a high level of charm and taste. The emphasis is on small, somewhat expensive boutiques, so we usually find ourselves coming here to eat at some of our favorite restaurants—**Compadres, Crêpe Fever, Mocha Java, Koe's at Ward Centre, Andrew's, Scoozy, Fresco, Monterey Bay Canners, Oinks,** and **Ryan's Grill** (see Chapter 6, "Honolulu Dining," for details) and browsing some of the more affordable shops.

It's fun to explore ✪ **Sedona,** "Your New Age Resource," a delightful store whose cactus in the window and crystals, jewelry, and such are reminiscent of that New Age town in Arizona. Check for news of the latest metaphysical happenings, and perhaps pick up some one-of-a-kind Native American handmade fans, pottery, drums, and dreamcatchers. Other unusual gift items include Egyptian genie bottles, hand blown and painted with real gold, from $20 to $50; animal energy stones; astrological calendars; and many kinds of angels. Minipsychic readings are available anytime.

Hand-carved chess sets, wind chimes, bells, furniture, textiles, quilts, and some lovely clothing, all from Indonesia, are shown in a handsome two-level store, **Indo Pacific Trading Company.** Collectors—of plates, dolls, miniature cottages, music boxes, paintings, and more—will have a field day at **Our House Collectibles.** Paintings by Thomas Kincade are featured.

Small women should definitely have a look at **Size Me Petite,** a shop with stylish collections for women 5'4" and under. There are swimsuits galore at **Allure,** lovely lingerie at **The Blush Collection,** unique fashions at **Summerhill.**

The name of **Craft Flair** says it all. All the craft items are made by local crafters. We love the darling children's dresses and T-shirts, the jewelry, dried flowers, and more. **Paper Roses** has an excellent variety of greeting cards and stationery, plus personalized children's gifts and many special-occasion and holiday gift items.

When we strike it rich, we're planning to furnish our home with all the beautiful handcrafted koa furniture at **Hawaiian Heritage** (*koa* is a native Hawaiian hardwood). Until then, it's fun to look; one could pick up a koa bracelet for as little as $15.

Art lovers will want to spend time at **Art A La Carte,** a cooperative venture featuring the work of a dozen local artists who take turns "sitting" the gallery and often work right here. Unframed works begin at $25, matted cards at $10.

Of course, you'll want to stop by **Mary Catherine's** for "an extraordinary bakery experience"; this European-style bakery uses only fresh and natural ingredients, avoids additives and imitation flavors, and produces divine breads, cakes, and pastries on the order of chocolate decadence or Biarritz cake—that's a European delicacy made with cream cheese, coconut, and macadamia nuts. They also do some multigrain breads and wonderful scones, like the English raisin tea scones, the chocolate scones, and the very berry scones—with raspberries, strawberries, blackberries, and blueberries. If you just can't wait to sample the goodies, repair to the tables a few steps up, in the rear, where you can enjoy them—as many local business people do—with an espresso or cappuccino. While your taste buds are thus activated, saunter over to **R. Field Wine Co.** at the opposite end of Ward Centre: In addition to fine wines, it stocks the likes of dried morels and foie gras imported from France, smoked butterfish, frozen pheasant, Cajun sausage, Beluga caviar, and top-of-the-line pastas and cheese flown in from Europe. Satisfying your sweet tooth, you can get the fabulous Crêpe Dentelle milk chocolate, Irish cream, strawberry, or cappuccino cordials, divine Kona coffee beans, or macadamia-nut popcorn among other goodies at **Honolulu Chocolate Company,** which also sells Valrhona—considered the world's finest chocolates. Watch out for the prices on this, however. We saw a chocolate bar for $5.75! Happily, there are also many items that are 30% to 50% off. This is a good place to get 100% Kona coffee whole beans.

To reach Ward Centre, again take TheBUS no. 8, 19, or 20 from Waikiki, a 15-minute ride.

KAHALA MALL, Waialae Kahala Shopping Complex. Tel. 732-7736.

Kahala Mall is an enclosed shopping center, with a main lobby like that of a hotel—carpeted and decorated with a beautiful fountain and plantings. Stretching out in various directions from the lobby are a bevy of interesting stores. Since the Kahala Mall has lately expanded from a popular neighborhood center into a "world-class shopping center," there's a great deal to see here. At some of the boutiques, it will be "just looking, thanks," but there are still many places of interest to the dollar-wise shopper.

Worth a special trip is ✪ **Following Sea,** a shop-gallery that represents the work of some 350 professional craft artists from 40 states, and sponsors outstanding monthly exhibitions. Everything is unique, and the inventory changes constantly. Prices range from a little to a lot, but there is a fine selection of ceramics, woodwork, and jewelry in the $30 to $60 range. Their most popular items are hand-blown oil lamps, from $20. On a recent visit we saw koa beautifully crafted into notebook covers, chimes, jewel chests, and unique boxes, for $25 to $300; plus exquisite leaded-glass boxes each with a beautiful seashell set into the top, for $53 to $75. Following Sea is working with local craftspeople to develop new and unique items. Keep this place in mind for a gift for a special person—or for yourself.

Cotton Cargo bursts at the seams with lovely, pricey clothes—mostly from Mexico and India. Both custom-made and ready-to-wear couture clothing, plus accessories and jewelry, draw the cognoscenti to **Jeffrey Barr. Cielo** also excels in the couture look for fashion-conscious women; **Altillo** has the tops in European men's clothing. In a more familiar, popular-priced range, there's **The Gap, Benetton, Banana Republic,** and the ubiquitous **Crazy Shirts.**

We like the beautiful ethnic jewelry and unique contemporary clothing at **Juma.** And **Corner Loft Kahala** is a good source for antiques, collectibles, jewelry, and gift items.

One of our favorite shops, **Something Special,** is here, with its beautiful gifts, cards, English toiletries, Cane Haul Road and Raj T-shirts (delightful), Hawaiian-designed silk-screened Ts, toys, and all sorts of enchanting pretties. **B.Cool** has zany novelties, gifts, and cards. We like the selection of beautiful stationery, cards, desk accessories, bookmarks, and calendars at **The Paperie.** You can choose upbeat houseware gifts at **The Compleat Kitchen.**

If you've brought the kids with you, there are four shops here just for them. **Kidding Around,** which specializes in infants to about seven years old, has wonderful hand-painted T-shirts and T-shirt dresses; **Bubble Gum** specializes in infants and preteens, with lots of good items in between; both of these are local stores. Mainland chains **Gymboree** and **Gap Kids** have branches here, too. All four carry toys.

Top off your shopping excursion with a snack or a meal at the **Yum Yum Tree,** a restaurant enormously popular with the neighborhood people for its well-priced food, deft service, and friendly atmosphere. Be sure to try a slice of their incredibly good pies—strawberry cheese and English toffee are among the choices; you'll want to take a whole pie home with you. Or enjoy a delicious northern Chinese meal at **Yen King,** one of the best such restaurants in these parts. **California Pizza Kitchen** is stylish with both table and counter seatings in a smart black-and-white room. Its pastas and pizzas—wood-fired with a variety of unusual toppings like Thai chicken or Cajun or vegetarian goat cheese—are light-years ahead of the ordinary. Other popular island restaurants represented here include **Bernard's New York Deli, Patti's Chinese Kitchen,** and **Randy's.**

To reach Kahala Mall, take TheBUS no. 58; or by car, take Kapahulu to the Lunalillo Freeway East to the Waialae exit. Open Monday to Saturday 10am to 9pm, Sunday 10am to 5pm.

PEARLRIDGE SHOPPING CENTER, Aiea. Tel. 488-0981.
Out in Aiea, about a half-hour drive from Waikiki, is the Pearlridge Shopping Center, a multimillion-dollar complex that's a big favorite with the local people. Pearlridge boasts 170 stores, 16 theaters, two food courts, and three "phases." It's built on opposite sides of an 11-acre watercress farm. Shoppers travel between Phase I and Phase II in Hawaii's only monorail train. From your perch in the monorail, you'll enjoy a panoramic view of Pearl Harbor. Across the street, Pearlridge Phase II houses several more shops, theaters, and an office complex. Kids will enjoy Pearlridge and so will grownups; it's a good place to keep in mind for a rainy-day family excursion.

As at most of the shopping centers catering to the local trade, familiar names such as **Liberty House, Sears, J.C. Penney, Long's Drugs,** and **Woolworth's** dominate the scene. **Shirokiya** shows the Japanese influence, with many captivating art objects from Asia. For those who must have the very latest in fashions, Pearlridge is an embarrassment of riches. For women, **Contempo Casuals, Pepperkorn, Casual Corner,** and **Ross Dress for Less** are just a few to tempt the shopper. For the latest in men's fashions, **Coda, Jeans West, Oak Tree,** and **Kramers** have it all. Other popular stores include **Taj Clubhouse, Boy London, Curious Porpoise,** and **Sam Goody.**

Point your kids in the direction of **Toy's 'R Us** and they'll be happy: It's jammed with just about every imaginable kind of toy. **Fernandez Fun Factory's Flagship** in Pearlridge Phase II must surely be one of the world's fanciest "penny arcades," featuring the newest and most elaborate electronic games.

Hungry? Pearlridge has two food courts that "bring the world to you": **Suzie's Korean Barb-B-Que, Bautista's Filipino Kitchen, Panda Express, Tsuruya Noodle Shop,** and **Sbarro's Italian Eatery** suggest the possibilities. Free-standing restaurants include **California Pizza Kitchen, Sizzler's Steakhouse, Denny's Bravo, Bandito's, Monterey Bay Canners,** and **Anna Miller's Coffee Shop.**

Official store hours at Pearlridge are 10am to 9pm Monday through Saturday and 10am to 5pm on Sunday. You can easily squeeze your visit to Pearlridge into your trip to Pearl Harbor. If you're driving to Pearl Harbor on Kam Highway, you see it on your right just after you reach Pearl Harbor's entrance to the USS *Arizona* Memorial. If you're driving out the H1 Freeway, take the Aiea exit. When driving out the Lunalilo Freeway from downtown, you'll see Pearlridge on the freeway directory signs. By bus, take TheBUS no. 20 from Waikiki to Pearlridge. *Note:* You can combine your visit to Pearlridge with one to the **Kam Super Swap Meet,** which is held at the Kam Drive-In, across from the shopping center, Wednesday and on weekends, beginning at 6am.

SHOPPING A TO Z

DISCOUNT SHOPS & FACTORY OUTLETS

BLAIR LTD, 404-A Ward Ave. Tel. 536-4907.

Visit this factory store for good buys in seconds of their fine monkeypod, koa, and other wood carvings. Blair has been known for excellent quality for many years. Some of these factory-store items may have small flaws, but they can be repaired, and the savings are huge. (Many of our readers have been happy with their purchases here.)

CRAZY SHIRTS FACTORY OUTLET, at Costeo Commercial Center, 4400 Lawehana St., in Aiea. Tel. 422-4522.

You'll see Crazy Shirt stores all over the Hawaiian Islands—everybody loves their clever designs and sayings. They make great presents too, so if you want to buy a lot of them, you can save a bundle by going to their factory outlet store, which offers factory seconds and display merchandise for 40% to 60% off retail prices.

The store is open every day. Phone for driving instructions.

HILO HATTIE FASHION CENTER, 700 Nimitz Hwy. Tel. 537-2926.

If garment factories appeal to you, here's one you can be bused to at no charge with extras thrown in. (They'll also take you to the Dole Pineapple Cannery.) This place offers something like 40,000 Hawaiian fashions to browse through, all for sale at factory prices, plus free refreshments, free hemming, and a lei greeting.

DAIEI/HOLIDAY MART, 801 Kaheka St. Tel. 946-1646.

A mecca for penny-pinchers, this huge discount store is in a residential neighborhood 2 blocks mauka of the Ala Moana Shopping Center. It's jammed with local people busy buying everything from groceries to books to toys to toasters, all at fat discounts. Buys are especially good if you watch for specials in Hawaiian wear for men, women, and keikis. While you're here, stock up on groceries and booze—the prices are excellent, much better than in the smaller stores at the beach. If it's time for lunch, you can join the crowd at the outside Chinese cafeteria deli, which has a good take-out department, as well as some 20 items on the steam table. Holiday Mart is open Monday through Saturday from 8am to midnight, until 10pm on Sunday.

KOMIL, 96-1185 Waihona St. (Pearl City Industrial Park, Bldg. Tel. 456-4272.

⭐ Advertised as "Hawaii's best kept secret," Komil is situated in a warehouse. There are no frills; the unique and lovely clothing (all made in India) hangs from iron-pipe racks, and there are small curtained fitting rooms. A well-dressed Honolulu friend of ours buys more than half of her clothes there and has never paid more than $40 for a dress. She's constantly asked how many Laura Ashleys she has; she has two, all the others are from Komil. Their clothes retail around the islands for up to $175. For women, there are dresses, jumpsuits, blouses, and skirts; for preteen girls, there are all four of the above plus playsuits; for men, there are often some great-looking aloha shirts for $10! The stock changes constantly, but the warehouse is a season behind the retail shops; yet at these prices, who can complain? *A word of caution:* Be sure to try everything on. Our friend has been a petite, a small, a medium, and a large all in the same day; the sizing leaves something to be desired by American standards. Open daily; call for driving directions.

LIBERTY HOUSE'S PENTHOUSE, 1 N. King St. Tel. 941-2345.

⑤ Downtown is where the local people do a lot of their shopping, and we'll let you in on a kamaaina secret known to very few tourists: Discounted merchandise from all Liberty House stores around town is brought here, and the initial reduction is a whopping 50%. On top of that, the price is automatically dropped another 30% on the first Monday of each succeeding month. Most of the items consist of women's, children's, and men's clothing and accessories. There are also terrific values on special-purchase items. On a recent shopping foray we found $100 handbags at $50, $150 dresses at $75, and $30 aloha shirts at $15. Enough said? At their clearing house, you can also get towels, sheets, pots and pans, and gift items at 50% off. This is one of those places where on some days you'll find nothing suitable, on other days you'll strike it rich!

The rest of Liberty House and the other Fort Street stores have merchandise similar to what you find in their Waikiki and Ala Moana branches, but perhaps a shade more citified, since they cater mostly to a local trade. It's fun to come here during the lunch hour, when local people are shopping, eating lunch on the many stone benches and seats that dot this fountained area, and watching their kids play in the sand. Traffic is closed off, creating one long window-shopping promenade. If you're hungry, stop at any of the restaurants or fast-food stands mentioned in Chapter 6.

PRINCESS KAIULANI, 1222 Kaumaulii St. Tel. 847-4806.

⑤ This manufacturer was the first to start using pretty, small-figured, calico prints in pastel colors. Their dresses are ultra-feminine, with eyelet or lace or ruffles; the fabrics are top-quality. This attractive factory showroom offers its own products and others at about 30% savings on most retail stores. Long muumuus, selling here in the $75 to $80 range, would be well over $100 at most stores. Open to the public Monday through Saturday from 8am to 5pm.

THE ULTIMATE YOU, 1112 Auahi St. Tel. 591-8388.

⭐ Just opposite Ward Centre is a shop known to few tourists; but the "Bergdorf Goodman of the consignment shops," as it might be called, is very well known indeed to Hawaii's most fashion-conscious women. This is where they come for new and next-to-new high fashion at surprisingly low prices. Owner ⑤ Kelsey Sears has contacts with socialites and celebrities in the islands, on the mainland, and in Europe; when they get slightly bored with their designer duds after a wearing or two (or when they've compulsively bought five-of-a-kind sweaters and never worn them), they send them to Sears, who resells them for anywhere from 50% to 90% off retail price. She insists that everything be in pristine condition. Half the store consists of brand-new merchandise, much of it from European designers, that is also heavily discounted. Obviously, the stock here changes daily, so you never can tell what you'll find, but it's worth a look-see. Some examples: A $3,000 Gucci alligator handbag sold for $495; a $600 Yves St. Laurent skirt for $90; and $300 garments worn once or twice for $80 or $90. A $100 dress could go for as little as $49, a $75 silk blouse for as little as $25. "Every day mini-miracles happen here," Sears says. The Ultimate You is open Monday through Saturday from 10am to 6pm.

READERS RECOMMEND

Thrift Shops. *"The seven Goodwill stores on Oahu are great places to find good, gently used muumuus from such stores as Liberty House, McInerny, Watumull, etc. They have a large selection, all dry-cleaned, for $7.95, sometimes less on sale . . . . I stopped in a Salvation Army store one day, and enjoyed it so much I went back. It was very clean and neat, and they had a big selection of muumuus, priced from $1.55 and up, about $10 for lovely Eastern brocades! I bought many, some just for the material, others to wear. One day, I got five long muumuus! They also have bathing suits for 98¢ and up, and monkeypod from 49¢. There are several Salvation Army stores on the island. I also like the Thrift Shop at the University of Hawaii for books, Hawaiian clothes, jewelry, household items. It was open only Tuesday, Wednesday, and Thursday, so check before going (also closed during the month of August). The thrift shop at Central Union Church on Beretania, near Kalakaua, is one of the best. It's large, bright, clean, and well stocked with nice items at reasonable prices. Open on Wednesday from 9am to 3pm and on Saturday from 9am to noon . . . . I found another thrift shop, the Laniolu Good Samaritan Thrift Shop, 333 Lewers St., open Monday, Wednesday, and Friday from 9am to noon. It is in the Lutheran Senior Retirement Center, and profits go to the center."*—Mrs. Dorothy Astman, Northport, N.Y. [Authors' Note: Another excellent thrift shop is St. Andrew's Economy Shop at St. Andrew's Cathedral, downtown at Beretania and Queen Emma Streets (tel. 536-5939), open Monday, Wednesday, and Friday from 9:30am to 4pm, Saturday until 1pm. The Punahou Thrift Shop, run by the famed Punahou School, also offers good values, and is open Monday, Wednesday, and Friday from 9am to 2pm. Should you happen to be in town for the Punahou Carnival (usually held in mid- or late January), be sure to check their Flea Market, especially at the close of the event, for sometimes extraordinary savings). The Iolani School Thrift Shop, 563 Kamoku St. (please enter through the Laau Street entrance off Date Street), has great bargains, new and used. Located only five minutes from Waikiki across the Ala Wai, its open on Wednesday from 10am to 3pm and on Monday and Saturday from 9am to noon. Hours can change at these shops, so be sure to call before you go.]

Kamaka Hawaii, Inc., *550 South St. (tel. 531-3165). "We purchased a lovely ukulele from Kamaka Hawaii, Inc., where factory seconds are priced $190 to $555, when available."*—William D. Devlin, San Francisco, Calif. [Authors' Note: Visitors are welcome to visit their small factory where they hire many disabled workers and train them as craftspeople.]

FASHIONS

NAKE'U AWAI, 1613 Houghtailing St. Tel. 841-1221.

⭐ This store is a bit out of the way—unless you combine it with a visit to the Bishop Museum—but it's worth a trip if you like unusual fabrics and designs. Joel Nake'u Awai is a young Hawaiian designer whose beautiful silk-screened fabrics are a blend of the traditional and the contemporary in Hawaiian art. After he designs and produces the textiles, he has them whipped up into long skirts, shirts, muumuus, bags, and sundresses. They're not cheap, but the prices are certainly competitive with those of the better department stores and specialty shops; and the designs are exclusive. We also saw some very good-looking T-shirts with Hawaiian designs and an interesting array of locally crafted items—lauhala fans, koa-bound books, gift cards, woven bags, and books of Hawaii—for $16 and up. Inquire about his fashion shows. If you can catch one of them you're in for a treat. They're as imaginative as the clothes and include appearances by guest luminaries. The shop is open only until 3:30pm Monday through Friday, until 2pm on Saturday. TheBUS no. 2 will take you there.

FLEA MARKETS

ALOHA SWAP MEET, Aloha Stadium. Tel. 486-1529.

Dauntless shoppers swear by this flea market, the biggest and best in Honolulu, with some 1,000 booths to browse through. This is definitely the place to get T-shirts: Hanes Beefy-Ts can usually be found here at a fraction of what they cost at Ala Moana or in Waikiki. University of Hawaii sweatshirts cost less here than at the university bookstore. Men can often get gecko Jams-style shorts at three pairs for $6 or $7. Seems the vendors here vie to undersell each other, and the shoppers get the benefit. Aloha Swap Meet is every Wednesday, Saturday, and Sunday (and daily for the three weeks before Christmas) from 6am to 3pm, and the really serious folks get there early. Take TheBUS no. 20 from Waikiki right to Aloha Stadium. Admission is 35¢ per person.

FOOD

If you're going to do any cooking in your kitchenette, you're going to be shocked when you do your first shopping for groceries. Food costs in Honolulu are substantially higher than in big cities on the mainland (almost one-third more, in some cases) and they are especially high in hotel shops. Hotel shops are a nice convenience, but if you're going to do any serious shopping, you're far better off taking your rented car and heading for the **supermarkets.**

The big Honolulu chains are Star, Times, Safeway, and Foodland (and Emjay's, a subsidiary of Foodland). There are several of each of these, with addresses, in the phonebook. Gem on Ward Avenue and Holiday Mart (801 Kaheka St., 2 blocks mauka of the Ala Moana Shopping Center), also offer low prices. In Waikiki, the best prices are found at Food Pantry, 2370 Kuhio Ave., an enormous supermarket located in central Waikiki, behind the International Market Place. Liquor prices are especially good here. There's another Food Pantry at 444 Hobron Lane, not far from the Ilikai Hotel. Prices are also good, although selection is limited, at the ABC Discount stores.

Natural foods are generally not inexpensive, so we were delighted to find "healthy food at prices that don't make you sick" at ✪ **Down to Earth Natural Foods,** 2525 S. King St. (tel. 947-7678), near University Avenue. *Honolulu* magazine has rated this friendly place as the best overall natural-food store in Honolulu. As big as a supermarket, Down to Earth has dozens of bins of grains and beans, a large refrigerator of organically grown fruits and vegetables, and a Natural Medicine Center that features, among other items, Chinese herbs, including ginseng and "dragon eggs." All products, including vitamin and mineral supplements, are totally vegetarian. Also on the premises is the Natural Deli for excellent vegetarian meals (see Chapter 6, "Honolulu Dining"). Open from 8am to 10pm every day.

Down to Earth is also associated with a stress-reduction center next door called the "Relaxation Station," which offers flotation tanks, massage, shiatsu, acupuncture—even brain-wave synchronization.

Just down the block, **Kokua Market, Natural Foods Co-Op,** 2357 S. Beretania St. (tel. 941-1922), offers a full line of natural foods and organic produce. They have fresh sandwiches, cold drinks, and a wide variety of snacks and gourmet vegetarian deli items. Open daily.

Terrific baked goods—freshly baked whole-grain breads (oatmeal, raisin, cinnamon, sprouted wheat), pies, and cakes—are the main reason for tracking down the popular **Vim and Vigor** store at Ala Moana Center. They also have good prices on an extensive selection of dried fruits, nut butters, fresh produce, and many other natural and organic items. Their snack bar is great, too.

If you'd like to shop for produce, fish, and meat with the locals, visit the **Ala Moana Farmer's Market** (a block from the Ala Moana–Ward intersection at Auahi Street), where the atmosphere is pungent and the prices low. It's a great place to get acquainted with local Hawaiian foods and taste sensations. The long, low building is lined with a number of stalls, some with ready-to-eat items. Here you can sample poi, raw fish, and other delicacies such as ogo, palu, and tako. In case you're not feeling all that adventurous, you can settle for a 12-ounce can of New Zealand corned beef or imu kalua pig, both cooked and ready for your own private luau. At **Haili's Hawaiian Foods,** in business since 1867, we saw one-day and two-day poi and even sour poi, all quite difficult to find.

It's also good fun—and good value—to attend one of the **People's Open Markets,** sponsored by the city of Honolulu. Farmers bring their produce to various spots on different days. The market closest to Waikiki takes place on Wednesday, from 9:45am to 10:45am, at Paki Playground; you'll find it on an outdoor basketball court behind the fire station on Kapahulu Avenue.

Get yourself downtown to **King's Bakery** at 1936 S. King St. (tel. 941-5211), which makes an incredibly delicious sweet bread; they will package and airmail this treat to the folks back home. A charge of $16 covers the shipping box, two loaves, and postage. Boxes of 6 and 12 are also available. You can sometimes find these breads sold at the airport, just before you reach the gate to board your plane.

GIFTS/NOVELTIES

MISSION HOUSES GIFT SHOP, Mission Houses Museum, 553 S. King St. Tel. 531-0481.

Here's an above-average selection of gift items, all of them reasonably priced. Some people find they can do almost all their gift shopping here. Consider for example, jugs and drinking glasses ($6.95) and appliqué pillow kits ($14 to $27) with Hawaiian quilt motifs. Or the tasteful T-shirts with Mission Houses or Hawaii quilt patterns or flowers ($14.95 and $17.95), the koa-wood bracelets ($16), Christmas ornaments made of lauhala and other local materials ($2 to $12.95), temple bells ($9), and—hard-to-find—tapas that can be framed ($8). The shop also has an excellent selection of Hawaiiana, plus soaps, potpourris, and adorable finger puppets for children, at just $1.75. Open Monday through Saturday from 9am to 4pm and on Sunday from noon to 4pm; closed Monday holidays.

THE ZOOTIQUE, at the Honolulu Zoo, 151 Kapahulu Ave. Tel. 923-7472.

This not-for-profit museum store operated by the Honolulu Zoological Society features educational and fun merchandise such as toys, books, posters, jewelry, apparel, and gift items with an animal theme. You'll find T-shirts signed exclusively for the Zootique, an array of exotic plush animals and souvenir items such as bumper stickers, pennants, and coffee mugs. The Zootique is open daily from 9am to 5:30pm (closed Christmas and New Year's). Shopping here is a great way to support the zoo and give yourself a nice treat.

READERS RECOMMEND

The Bishop Museum, 1525 Bernice St. (tel. 847-3511). "The Bishop Museum is always a 'must' on our list, but I want especially to recommend the museum bookstore and gift shop. It really is the only place to buy good books on Hawaii, beyond the picture books that have nice color pictures and price tags and little else, which one finds everywhere."—John and Anne Duffield, Costa Mesa, Calif.

University of Hawaii Bookstore, Manoa Campus (tel. 956-8252). "The University of Hawaii Bookstore is a delightful place to shop for take-home goodies: They have a wide variety of sweatshirts, jackets, caps, track bags, etc., all with the UH logo, plus lots of stationery, cards, etc."—Brenda English, Fox Creek, Alberta, Canada.

The Hawaiian Kukui Nut Co., *P.O. Box 685, Waialua, Oahu, HI 96791 (tel. 808/637-5620, or toll free 800/367-6010). "I have been a psoriasis sufferer off and on for 30 years. I bought some Kukui Nut Oil from the Hawaiian Kukui Nut Co., and it has been great for my skin. It's $9 for 4 ounces. Mail orders are available. This oil is used to soften dry skin, ease tiny lines, soothe sunburn, rashes, and windburn. Early Hawaiians first discovered that the plump, mellow nuts of their native kukui trees contained a pure, clear oil with amazing ability to protect their skin against the rigors of everyday life. For centuries, the Hawaiians kept this natural phenomenon a secret!"*—Judie Carbaugh, Sykesville, Md. [*Authors'* Note: Agreed. We, too, find kukui-nut oil extraordinary. It can be purchased at many shops in Waikiki and at the factory store in Waialua.]

JEWELRY & WATCHES

HAWAII TIME, 334 Seaside Ave., Suite 205. Tel. 922-7884.

Trust flight attendants to know the best places—they travel all over the world and love to bargain-hunt. One of them tipped us off that the prices here were better than in Bangkok, and so they are. Everything from Mickey Mouse watches to top name brands is available at wholesale prices; most watches, for both men and women, go for $10 to $100. If you need to have a watch repaired, try Patrick at Accurate Watch Repair, 1108 Fort Street Mall, Room 2C (tel. 521-3469).

KIM'S FASHION, 96 N. King St. Tel. 599-7721.

If you're looking for freshwater pearls, this little Chinatown shop is *the* place. Owner Kim Phung offers beautiful freshwater pearls at prices that are often lower than wholesale on the mainland; strands run $2 to $70, and beautiful they are. People come from all over for Kim's pearls, and once back home, they keep calling for reorders. She has a nice selection of handbags and cloisonné, as well.

LEIS

When local people need to buy leis, they usually head for Chinatown—and so should you. Although leis are sold all over town, especially at the airport and on the ocean side of Kalakaua Avenue, the best prices and finest quality can usually be found among the Chinatown lei sellers. There are several stores on Maunakea Street; some of our favorites are **Cindy's Lei Shoppe** at no. 1034, **Violet's** at no. 1165, **Jenny's Lei Stand** at no. 1151, and **Lin's** at no. 1107. A local friend advises us that **Aileen,** who has a little lei stand inside Aala's flower shop at 1104 Maunakea St., has done some extraordinary special-order work for her, always tries to give the fairest price possible, and feels it's rare that she is undersold. **Lita's Leis** is around the corner at 59 N. Beretania St., and **Aloha** is at the corner of Puuahi. Cindy and Lita both make beautiful haki-head leis that dry splendidly and can be worn for a long time. Cindy's carries the largest selection of flower leis in the state, and all six make up orchid, plumeria, double carnation, and other leis, at prices ranging from $5 to $10 and up, depending on the season and the availability of flowers. Should you want to send leis to your friends back home—a lovely but no longer inexpensive gift—expect to pay $27 and up by Express Mail. (And they may not be very chipper when they arrive. Near the University of Hawaii, good places to know about are **Rudy's** at 2122 S. King St. (tel. 944-8844), and **Flowers by Jr., Lou and T.** at 2652 S. King St. (tel. 947-5527). We also like the flowers—and the low prices—at **Chiyo's,** located inside and at the front of the Thrifty Drugstore at 3610 Waialae Ave. in the Waialae-Kahala area. You can shop by phone (tel. 734-6337 or 737-5055), and be assured that your order will be well and speedily taken care of. They'll bill you later.

If you'll see your friends within a day or two of your arrival, it's cheaper to carry flowers with you. Better still, give your friends the flower leis your Hawaiian friends will doubtless drape around your neck as they bid you aloha—if you can bear to part with them.

Buyers beware: The most expensive times to buy leis are May Day, the graduation season (end of May), and New Year's; that's when $5 vanda orchid leis can suddenly become $15 to $18!

MISCELLANEOUS

LOCAL MOTION, 1714 Kapiolani Blvd., near Ala Moana Shopping Center. Tel. 955-SURF.

If you're really serious about surfing, or learning to surf, you should know about this place. Any surfer will tell you that in order to learn to surf safely and joyously you need good instruction and a well-constructed board. Many of those for rent at beach stands are outdated, hence the need for a source like Local Motion. Here you can rent a board for $20 for the first day and $15 for every day thereafter. By the week, it's $75. And they also sell snappy sports and leisure clothes. Local Motion is also at the Windward Mall in Kaneohe, at Koko Marina in Hawaii Kai, and at the Walkele Shopping Center in the Pearl City area, as well as on Maui.

THE MILITARY SHOP OF HAWAII, 1921 Kalakaua Ave. Tel. 942-3414.

Once part of the Fort DeRussy Museum, this may well be the largest store of its kind in the country. Insignia, military patches from all the services, military models, camouflage clothing, and accessories are all for sale. And there's a large selection of military books as well. For those interested in such things, it's a fascinating spot. Open Monday through Saturday from 9am to 6pm; closed Christmas. A mail order catalog is available at no charge.

CHAPTER 9

TOURING OAHU

1. WAIKIKI TO HEEIA
2. HEEIA TO LAIE
3. LAIE TO HALEIWA
4. HALEIWA TO WAIKIKI

You haven't really seen Hawaii until you've left the urban sprawl of Waikiki and Honolulu and traveled to the other side of the mountains for a look at Windward Oahu. And what a look that is! There are jagged cliffs and coral beaches; Stone age ruins and tropical suburbs; a vast military concentration; backwoods country towns sleeping in the sun; endless stretches of breadfruit, banana, papaya, hibiscus, lauhala, coconut palms—the glorious vegetation of the tropics so ubiquitous as to be completely taken for granted. And best of all, some of the most intriguing sightseeing attractions in the 50th state are here: Sea Life Park, the Byodo-In-Temple, and the Polynesian Cultural Center.

Not one advertising billboard defaces the landscape; they're kapu in Hawaii. The only signs you will see are those of the Hawaii Visitors Bureau's red-and-yellow warrior pointing to the places of interest. There are dozens of spots for beachcombing and picnicking, so pack your bathing suit and lunch. If you get an early start, you can certainly make this trip in one day, but there's so much to see that two would be much more comfortable. We'll provide a basic itinerary around which you can plan your time.

TRANSPORTATION   You can see a good part of the island by sticking to public transportation. TheBUS no. 55, "Circle Island," which leaves Ala Moana Center daily at 5 and 35 minutes after the hour from 6:05am on, will enable you to see many island points of interest: the big surf at Haleiwa, Sunset Beach, and the North Shore, and the Polynesian Cultural Center, to name some. (The cost is $1.20, with no transfers; you'll have to pay 60¢ every time you reboard the bus.)

Many of our readers make the trip by public transportation and praise it highly, but we prefer to rent a car, since it's much more efficient time-wise and quite reasonable, especially for more than one person. *If you do drive, remember to lock your car doors and take your valuables with you when you get out to look at the sights. If you must lock things in your car trunk, do so before you arrive at your destination: You never know who may be watching.*

Alternatively, you could take one of the around-the-island sightseeing tours, such as those offered by **E Noa Tours** (tel. 599-2561).

MAPS   The maps in this book are for the purpose of general orientation. When doing any extensive driving, we suggest you follow a more detailed road map. We have personally found the maps in *Drive Guide to Oahu*, free from any car-rental company, to be excellent.

1. WAIKIKI TO HEEIA

From Waikiki, drive Diamond Head on Kalakaua Avenue past Kapiolani Park to Diamond Head Road, which runs into Kahala Avenue past the sumptuous residential area of Black Point. Sculptor Kate Kelly's monument to aviatrix Amelia Earhart is just past the Diamond Head Lighthouse. On your right, a paved trail leads to the cliffs, where you can watch some fancy surfing. At the end of Kahala Avenue, where it hits the Waialae Golf Course, turn left onto Kealaolu Avenue; follow this road to Kalanianaole Highway (Hi.72); the entrance will be on the right. Before you turn, you come to **Waialae Beach Park,** with modern facilities, covered pavilions, and wide, wide beaches, right next door to the prestigious Waialae Country Club. The swimming here is not too good, since there are many rocks in the water. Next door is the splendid Kahala Hilton Hotel; you might want to have a look at the lovely grounds.

Just before you reach Koko Head, you'll pass the entrance to Henry Kaiser's once-controversial **Hawaii Kai**—a 6,000-acre, $350-million housing development that's a small city in itself. You can drive in for your own tour of inspection. (A resident advises us that there's a beautiful view at the top of the hill past the Hawaii Kai Golf Course overlooking the ocean and the south end of Windward Oahu.) While you're in this area, you may want to stop in at **Waterfront Village,** a charming small shopping complex perched right out on the waters of Koko Marina, and tied in by walks and a shared parking lot with the much larger Hawaii Kai shopping center.

Koko Head and **Koko Crater,** now coming into view ahead, are reminders that Oahu, like all the Hawaiian Islands, is a volcanic mountain spewed out of the Pacific. During Oahu's last eruption (volcanologists say it was at least 10,000 years ago), these craters and the one that houses **Hanauma Bay** were born. One side of Koko Head has been washed away into the sea and the result is an idyllic beach, one of the most popular in the islands. Since the placid turquoise waters cover a cove in the purple coral reef, it's a perfect place for beginning and advanced snorkelers. (Rent snorkels in Waikiki or bring your own; none are available here.) Hanauma Bay is now a marine reserve, and so gentle have the fish become that parrot fish, bird wrasses, and others will eat bread from a swimmer's hand. There are dressing facilities, and camping, barbecue, and picnic areas. The beach is a very long walk from the parking area, but you can take a little bus from the parking lot to the beach for a small fee. *Be sure to lock your car and remove any valuables!* Needless to say, the islanders love this place, and the only problem is that you've almost always got to share it with quite a lot of them. The beach is now closed on Wednesday.

For the next few miles along Hi. 72, you drive along one of the most impressive stretches of rocky coastline in the islands. The black lava cliffs hurtle down to the sea to meet a surging purple Pacific, all set against a brilliant blue-green background of sky, trees, and flowers. Park the car at any of the designated areas or at the popular **Blow Hole,** where the water geysers up through an underwater vent. (The areas before the Blow Hole are just as pretty and much less crowded.) With the wind in your hair and the surf crashing below, you'll feel light-years away from civilization. Just beyond the Blow Hole is **Sandy Beach Park:** beyond that is **Makapuu Beach Park,** where people are actually surfing on those horrendous waves. These two beaches are strictly for the experts; beginners had better watch from the sand.

More important, this is the site of one of Hawaii's biggest sightseeing attractions—**Sea Life Park Hawaii,** where there's plenty of entertainment, education, and fun for the whole family. Descend 3 fathoms and see the thousands of colorful fish that inhabit Hawaiian waters at the 300,000 gallon Hawaiian Reef Tank; see whales and dancing dolphins at the Whaler's Cove Show as they tell the story of Hawaii's early whaling history around the 5/8-scale replica of the whaling ship *Essex;* attend a training session at the Hawaii Ocean Theater Show, where porpoises, penguins, and seals show off their agility, strength, and intelligence. And you won't want to miss their newest show, Kolohe Kai, which features some of the fun-loving antics of Sea Life Park's own seals and sea lions.

In addition, you'll want to visit the Bird Sanctuary, and see endangered marine birds such as the booby or iwa; the Penguin Habitat, with a colony of endangered

AN EXCURSION AROUND OAHU

0   5 mi
    8 km

6/90

PACIFIC OCEAN

Mokapu
Kailua Beach Park
Bellows Field Beach Park
Kailua Bay
Kaneohe Beach Park
Heeia
Kaneohe Bay
Kailua
Waimanalo Beach Park
Makapuu Beach Park
Koko Head Reg. Park
Sandy Beach
Hanauma Bay State Underwater Park
Waialae Beach Park
Diamond Head State Monument
Waimanalo
Waimanalo Beach
Kaaawa
Kaneohe
Ahuimanu
Kahaluu
Koolau Range
Mamalu Bay
Kaiwi Channel
Kalanianaole Hwy.
Watershed Forest Reserve
Honolulu
Pali Hwy.
Lunalilo
HONOLULU
Honolulu International Airport
Punaluu
Kamehameha Hwy.
Hauula
Laie
Kahuku
Sunset Beach
Pupukea Beach Park
Waimea
Waimea Bay
Waimea Falls Park
Haleiwa
Haleiwa Beach Park
Waialua Bay
Mokuleia
Mokuleia Beach Park
Ewa
Forest Reserve
Pacific Palisades
Pearl City
Ewa Forest Reserve
Wahiawa
Waipio Acres
Mililani Town
Waialua Kamehameha Hwy.
Leilehua Plateau
Honouliuli Forest Reserve
Makakilo City
Waipahu
Ewa
Pearl Harbor
Ewa Beach
Mamala Bay
Farrington Hwy.
Waianae Range
Makaha
Waianae
Maili
Nanakuli
Koolau Range
Kaena Channel
PACIFIC OCEAN
Airport

Legend

- Bellows Field Beach Park ⑦
- Beth Surdut Studio ⑫
- Byodo-In Temple ⑩
- Diamond Head State Monument ①
- Dole Pineapple Pavilion ㉒
- Haiku Gardens ⑨
- Haleiwa Beach Park ⑱
- Ho'omaluhia Botanical Garden ⑧
- Kahuku Sugar Mill ⑬
- Koko Head ③
- Nuuanu Pali State Wayside ㉕
- Pineapple Variety Garden ⑲
- Polynesian Cultural Center ⑬
- Puu O Mahuka Heaiu ⑯
- Sacred Birthstones—Kukaniloko ㉑
- Sandy Beach Park ④
- Schofield Museum ⑳
- Sea Life Park Hawaii ⑤
- Senator Fong's Plantation and Gardens ⑪
- Sunset Beach ⑮
- Tendai Mission of Hawaii ㉔
- Wahiawa Botanical Garden ㉓
- Waialae Beach Park ②
- Waimanalo Beach Park ⑥
- Waimea Falls Park ⑰

Humboldt penguins; and the 1,500-gallon Touch Pool, where you can touch a sea cucumber or a sea urchin. Observe endangered Hawaiian monk seals at the Hawaiian Monk Seal Care Center or endangered green sea turtles at the Turtle Lagoon. Visit the Pacific Whaling Museum, which houses the largest collection of whaling artifacts—scrimshaw, harpoons, rope work—in the Pacific. You can pick up T-shirts, ceramic art, stuffed animals, marine jewelry, and other souvenir items at the Sea Life Park General Store.

Admission to the park is $19.95 for adults, $8.95 for juniors (6 to 12), $3.95 for children (4 to 5), free for those under 4. (Prices are subject to change and are exclusive of tax.) The park is open daily from 9:30am to 5pm on Friday. On Friday nights, Hawaiian entertainment is included in the regular price of admission. For more information, call the park at 259-7933, or, for sales information, 942-3100. Note that Sea Life Park Hawaii provides free round-trip shuttle transportation from Waikiki. Public buses make hour runs to the park (call 848-5555 for information).

Continuing north on Hi. 72, you soon see **Rabbit Island,** where the water is turquoise. The inland view along this coast is also spectacular, thanks to the towering **Koolau Range;** its corrugated slopes (examples of erosion at work on volcanoes) provide a nice balance to the restless sea on your right.

Just past Sea Life Park, you'll find **Waimanalo Beach Park,** which many island families consider the best beach on Oahu: pleasant surf, grassy knolls, picnic tables, the works. You may want to come back here for a long stay. For now, drive on for a few more miles and, east off Hi. 72, you'll come upon what was long considered one of Oahu's most magnificent beaches by the few people lucky enough to enjoy it—the military. This is **Bellows Field Beach Park,** nestled against the mountains, a 46-acre strip of fine sand, lively but not dangerous surf, and wooded picnic groves of palm and pine. After long years, Bellows has been opened to the public, but on weekends only, from Friday noon to midnight Sunday; and on federal and state holidays. There are public bathhouses. (It's a favorite spot for tent and trailer camping; permits are available from the Recreation Department, City and County of Honolulu.) Bellows is a perfect place for a picnic lunch (bring your own, as there's nothing to buy), or a swim. The only danger (aside from an occasional Portuguese man-of-war) is that you may be tempted to spend the whole day and forget about your exploring. Keep going, for the best is yet to come.

At this point in the journey, make a brief side trip to **Kailua,** one of Honolulu's most pleasant suburbs. Stay on Hi. 72 until it intersects with Hi. 61, turn right (east) onto 61 and continue until you reach **Kailua,** a few miles down the road. The reason for this trip is the beach: **Kailua Beach Park,** and especially **Lanikai,** are absolutely beautiful, with gentle waves, white sand, and much smaller crowds than you see at Waikiki. We feel this is what Waikiki must have been like in the old, pretourist days.

If you have time for a bit of shopping after your swim, check out two distinctive shops on Kailua Road: **Elizabeth's Fancy,** 7678 Kailua Rd. (tel. 262-7513), and **The Creative Collection,** 761 Kailua Rd. (tel. 261-7080). Elizabeth Root's little shop, set back from the road, is filled with beautiful fancies. Elizabeth is the designer of the Hawaiian quilt-pattern bookmarks and Christmas-tree ornaments that you'll see around town, as well as all manner of quilt-patterned items, notably her pillow kits. There are wonderful imported and local jams and jellies, one-of-a-kind jewelry, stuffed animals, greeting cards, South American rain sticks, pretty china, and boxes; there's always something new and different. In front of Elizabeth's and just a few doors down is The Creative Collection, chock a block with fun things. There are unusual umbrellas printed with fish or flowers, about $35; great T-shirts, locally made ones as well as Sandra Boynton's whimsical-critter designs; cards; toys; jewelry (note the sterling silver earrings by Dian, handcrafted on Maui); bears; cookie jars; and so on. We never leave here without at least one irresistible bauble.

If it's the weekend and you're in the mood for a hike, you should know about **Ho'omaluhia Botanical Garden** in Kaneohe, at the end of Luluku Road. Here, at the foot of the Koolau mountains, are pleasant hiking trails, a Hawaiian garden, a lake, and much more. (Tent camping is available here.) At the center, you'll find a small art gallery and exhibit hall. Free guided nature walks are offered on Saturdays at 10am and Sundays at 1pm. Each walk is approximately two miles long and takes about two hours. Individuals and groups should call in advance to make reservations for these hikes (tel. 233-7323). Wear proper footwear and take an umbrella, since showers are common in any season. The garden is open daily from 9am to 4pm.

From Kaneohe, drive inland on Hi. 65 to Hi. 83, and go north. You might want to stop and stretch a bit at a lovely area called **Haiku Gardens,** just west of the Kahekili Highway. For years, Haiku Gardens Restaurant occupied this lovely kamaaina estate. Now it's a handsome Chart House Restaurant. The gardens are open to the public free, during daylight hours. A lily pond dominates all, and from it, trails lead off to, among other things, a lovely grove of golden bamboo from Java, Hawaiian grass huts, a palm grove, bird sanctuary, fragrant plantings of ginger and anthurium, and exotic fish ponds. To reach the gardens, turn left off the highway at Haiku Road and proceed mauka about a mile. It's open Tuesday through Sunday.

For devotees of Eastern culture, we know of no more rewarding spot in the islands than the **Byodo-In-Temple** in the Valley of the Temples, which should be your next destination. It's about two miles from Haiku Road, and you can reach it by driving back to Kahekili Highway from Haiku Gardens and proceeding north. (If you haven't stopped at Haiku Gardens, continue on Kamehameha Highway to the intersection on Pineapple Hill, then turn left the way you came onto Kahekili Highway; you'll come to the Valley of the Temples in about half a mile). An exact replica of the venerable Byodo-In, reputed to be the most beautiful temple in Uji, Japan, this temple was constructed at a cost of $2.6 million and dedicated on June 7, 1968, almost 100 years to the day after the first Japanese immigrants arrived in Hawaii. The temple sits in a magnificently landscaped classical Japanese garden fragrant with pine, plum, and bamboo. Inside, you can gaze at the intricately carved screens and panels, and pay obeisance to the magnificent gold carving of Amida, the Buddha of the Western Paradise. Many of the Buddhist faithful in the islands come here, of course, but a visit is every bit as much an aesthetic as a spiritual experience. While you're meditating, turn the kids loose in the gardens, supply them with a package of fish food (thoughtfully sold in a tiny teahouse gift store), and let them feed the flashing carp in the two-acre reflecting lake. The shop also imports religious items and other Japanese gifts from Kyoto. Have a look. Admission is $2 for adults, $1 for children under 12.

READERS RECOMMEND

Kahaluu Sportswear Garment Factory Outlet. "*Aloha wear bargains for those exploring Oahu can be found at Kahaluu Sportswear Garment Factory Outlet. The factory outlet is also the factory. Cotton Aloha shirts were $13.99. Sizes over XL were a dollar or two more. The quality and selection are as good as, or better than, everything in the Waikiki area. The outlet is located just past the Valley of the Temples on 83. The woman behind the counter dropped some key chains in with our purchases; 'In case you forgot to buy something for someone, here's a little extra.'*" —Thomas A. Marinello, Carson, Calif.

On Saturday, Sunday, and Monday from 10am to 3:30pm, art lovers who have made an appointment in advance by calling 239-8146 can stop to see the exquisite **Hart, Tagami & Powell Gallery and Gardens,** just a few miles from the Valley of the Temples. This combination art gallery, aviary, and botanical garden is the home and studio of two of Hawaii's leading painters, Hiroshi Tagami and Michael Powell. A visit here is a rare privilege, an extraordinary entry into a world of beauty. When you call for an appointment, ask for directions.

Just two miles past the Valley of the Temples, you'll come to one of Oahu's newer visitor's attractions: **Senator Fong's Plantation and Gardens.** Former

U. S. Sen. Hiram Fong has opened his magnificent 725-acre estate to the public; visitors are taken on guided tours in open-air trams through five gardens named for the various presidents under whom Fong served in his 17 years in Congress. After the tour stop at the Visitors Center, perhaps have lunch or take a class in lei making ($5 fee). Check out the Banana Patch gift shop, too. Plan on an hour or so for this delightful excursion. Admission is $8.50 for adults, $5 for children 5 to 12. Open daily from 10am to 4pm; the last tram tour departs at 3pm (tel. 239-6775).

For a change of pace, get back on Hi. 83 and head south to **Heeia,** on Kaneohe Bay. This is a good place to stop, stretch your legs, and switch to another mode of transportation. Glass-bottom boats at **Heeia Kea Pier** take you on a narrated excursion at a charge of $7.50 for adults, $3.50 for children under 12. Cruises depart at approximately 10 and 11am, and 12:30, 1:30, and 2:30pm daily. Make advance reservations by calling 235-2888. Also, check to see if the water is clear that day; if not, there's not much point in going out. The Deli Snack and Gift Shop, right on the pier, offers local-style plate lunches (around $4), as well as the usual snacks.

ALTERNATE ROUTE TO HEEIA You can begin your around-the-island trip via the **Pali and Makiki Heights** and pick up the route at Kaneohe on Hi. 83. This route takes you to a major attraction that our recommended route omits—the view from the **Nuuanu Pali,** a glorious panorama from the top of a jagged cliff. It's a historic spot, too, because it was here that Kamehameha the Great vanquished the Oahuans in a fierce battle in 1795. Thousands of the defeated fell to their deaths on the rocks below. The only drawback to this route is that you miss the scenery in the Koko Head area, which we find more appealing.

To see the Pali, turn left off Nimitz Highway (Hi. 92) in downtown Honolulu onto Nuuanu Avenue or Bishop Street. Follow it to Pali Highway (Hi. 61), which leads to the Pali.

Just before you reach the Pali, however, you might want to drive about a mile up the Pali and turn left at Jack Lane to reach the beautiful **Tendai Mission of Hawaii** and its enormously impressive 25-foot statue of Senju Kannon, the Thousand-Armed Goddess of Mercy. The Tendai sect of Mahayana Buddhism ended 1,200 years of confining its worship halls to Japan when it opened the Hawaii mission in 1973. You're welcome to inspect the grounds and building any day during regular activity hours. (There are no specific times of opening or closing.) Occasionally, you'll see local groups using the facilities for flower-arranging, tea ceremonies, and handcraft exhibits.

Another spectacular view that we think you shouldn't miss is the one from **Makiki Heights,** which you can see on your way to Nuuanu Pali. In a way, we like it better than the Pali, since this is a top-of-the-world view, completely unobstructed. Here's how to get there: From Waikiki, take Kalakaua Avenue until it ends at South Beretania Street. Go past Makiki to Keeaumoku Street, turn right, cross Interstate H1, and turn right onto Wilder. After one block, turn left onto Makiki, which runs into Round Top Drive, then Tantalus Drive, and continues up, up, and up. The road, which is excellent all the way, goes through the Round Top Forest Reserve. Stop at **Puu Ualakaa State Park** (open daily from 7am to 6:45pm) and have a look at the glorious view from Round Top. Back in the car, continue in the same direction you were going. When you reach H1 turn left and take it to the intersection with Hi. 61 (the Pali Highway), which leads to the Pali.

WHERE TO EAT

KANEOHE

Several shopping malls in Kaneohe offer a bonanza of inexpensive eateries. At the enclosed **Windward Mall,** for example, the standout restaurant is **Kin Wah,** a cozy family-style Chinese place (see Chapter 6). There is also a large food court, where you'll find many more places to choose from. **Cinnabon,** for example, is a singular experience. Customers start lining up before opening time (10am) to buy incredible cinnamon rolls, each measuring about five inches wide by about three inches high, topped with a cream-cheese frosting! You can watch the team of bakers turn them out. People have been known to make a meal out of them, if not exactly a balanced one. They're $1.39 small, $1.99 large.

Pizza fans have **Harpo's,** and brag of their fresh veggies on hand-rolled dough, secret-recipe sausage, and hand-rolled homemade pastas. Two slices of their gourmet deep-dish–style pizzas, plus green salad and soda, will set you back $5.75 for pepperoni, $6.10 for vegetarian. You've got to try the grilled eggplant pizza. If you've been to Ala Moana Center, you know that **Patti's Chinese Kitchen** is great. Now there's a Patti's here too, and it's inexpensive and filling.

Still hungry? The **Taco Shop** features tacos at $1.82 and enchiladas at $3.29; **Yunnie's Korean BBQ** offers barbecue chicken at $5.20, veggies and rice included. **Island Mixed Plate** creates a variety of sandwiches from $3.75 to $4.75, all with lettuce, tomatoes, and alfalfa sprouts. If you haven't tasted "luau food" yet, this is a good place at which to do so; get the Hawaiian plate of laulau, lomi salmon, kalua pig, chicken long rice, and poi. **Little Tokyo** displays a score of items in plastic replicas to help you decide, such as the teriyaki chicken or beef at $4.69 and $4.99. And don't forget the coffee shop on the second floor of **Liberty House,** where you can eat vegetarian sandwiches for $3.55 and roast beef for $4.95, as well as hot plates, such as a health plate or honey-dipped chicken, each at $4.75. Steak and seafood dinners, including soup and salad, run $11.95 to $20.95. Windward Mall's opening and closing times vary with holidays, seasons, and days of the week.

If you'd like an excellent Thai meal, drive to the intersection of Likelike and Kamehameha highways where you'll find **Thao Phya Thai** (tel. 253-3555). Here, in a garden atmosphere enlivened by Thai art, the staff radiates the Thai brand of warm aloha. We like to order their luscious vegetarian spring rolls as soon as we're seated, wrap them in lettuce, and dip them into a delicious sauce while we're making our menu decisions. Curries excel because they are made with fresh coconut milk. The same menu is in effect all day. Aroy!

READERS RECOMMEND

Smitty's, in the Kaneoha Bay Shopping Center (tel. 247-8533). "Don't forget Smitty's when you're in Kaneohe and you want to go to a really nice, comfortable, informal restaurant, but you don't want to spend much money. At Smitty's, most of your meals should be in the $4 to $7 range at lunch, in the $5 to $11 range at dinner. You'll sit there wondering how you can pay so little in such a nice restaurant. The menu has good variety for the whole family. And they sell pies to go. Smitty's is part of a very large Canadian chain."—Mark Terry, Maui, Hawaii.

2. HEEIA TO LAIE

Outside Heeia, it's one awesome view after another as you drive north on Hi. 83 along the coast, weaving along past acres of tropical flowers and trees whose branches frequently arch across the whole width of the road. You can't miss spotting **Pineapple Hut** on the right, which has a good selection of carved wood, shells, macrame planters, and the like at reasonable prices.

You're now coming to the end of Kaneohe Bay, and the next HVB marker you'll see will point to an island that looks like its name, **Mokoli'I** (little lizard), also called Chinaman's Hat. On the other side of the road, covered by weeds, are the ruins of a century-old sugar mill. Cane grown here was once shipped by boat to "distant" Honolulu.

Just over two miles past the large garment factory building on your left, look for a fruit stand on the right. The only indication is a sign reading COLD COCONUT JUICE.

Here you can purchase local fruits grown right in this area, at Waikane. In our opinion, they're the best.

In a short while you'll come to a rocky cliff that seems to resemble a crouching lion, hence its official name: **Crouching Lion.** The scenic **Crouching Lion Inn** is just in front. This area is fine for a picnic; **Kaaawa Beach Park** has good swimming, as does **Swanzy Beach State Park,** just south of Punaluu, and both are fully equipped with amenities. The next beach, at **Kahana Bay,** is safe for swimming inshore, but there are no dressing facilities, and the bottom is muddy.

There's a stop that art lovers should make in Punaluu, the town coming up next: the studio of silk artist Beth Surdut; it's in the garden of the **Punaluu Gallery,** at 53-352 Kamehameha Hwy. (tel. 237-8009). Walk through the garden with its castle sculpture and colorful twittering caged lovebirds and meet Beth, an artist as beautiful as her creations. Her lush paintings and fabrics are executed by painting on 100% silk with fiber-reactive dyes and traditional Japanese sumi-e brushes, which makes for a far softer product than fabric embellished with paint. Her colors are pure and beautiful, her subjects are from nature—flowers, birds, frogs, landscapes, undersea gardens. Surdut has achieved international recognition, and her works are represented in the Smithsonian Institution. In addition to painting, she does wall hangings, fabrics, and wearable art—dresses, fringed silk shawls, separates, men's aloha shirts, ties, and more. Surdut's works start at around $90 and go up to about $3,000. You may visit with her any day, except Sunday or Tuesday, between 11am and 6pm.

As you approach **Hauula,** you'll see the HVB marker pointing to a side road leading to the 87-foot **Sacred Falls (Kaliuwaa).** Even though the trail is lined with impressive trees and flowers, our advice is to pass this one up; in order to see the falls and the mountain pool below, you have to hike for about an hour on a rather rough path. Over the past few years there have been a number of drownings, robberies, and accidents here; locals definitely consider this place bad news. During the rainy season, killer flash floods can occur suddenly. Coming up now, the beach park at Hauula is well equipped with the usual bathing facilities, and the swimming is safe inshore. But keep going; you're about to reach the picturesque village of Laie, one of the high points of your Windward Oahu sojourn.

Laie is Salt Lake City with palm trees. No slouches at missionary work, the Mormons arrived in Hawaii not long after the first Protestants; more than 100 years ago they founded a large colony of Hawaiian and Samoan members of the Church of Jesus Christ of Latter-day Saints, whose descendants still live here.

In 1919 the Mormons established a Hawaiian Temple, the first Mormon house of worship outside the mainland; in 1955 the Brigham Young University–Hawaii Campus, a fully accredited liberal arts institution; and in 1963, the ✪ **Polynesian Cultural Center,** a loving re-creation of Polynesia. Built more than 30 years ago to provide work and scholarships for Polynesian students and to revitalize the ancient Polynesian cultures, it is the most popular paid-admission visitor attraction in Hawaii. Seven "authentic" Polynesian islands have been re-created: Hawaii, Tonga, Fiji, Samoa, Maori, Marquesas, and Tahiti, all staffed by Polynesians who came here just for this purpose.

The center offers families a full day of fun with a variety of activities for all ages. You could start with a guided canoe tour or a leisurely walking tour. Friendly villagers in each island greet and involve one in demonstrations: making *ngatu* or *tapa* cloth from the inner bark of the mulberry plant in Tonga; watching a villager climb a coconut tree with amazing agility and speed in Fiji; or pounding boiled taro roots into poi in Hawaii. In addition to the villages, demonstrations, and hands-on activities, the center also stages a variety of vibrant shows: "Mana! The Spirit of Our People," a 90-minute evening extravaganza with a cast of more than 100 islanders; the "Pageant of the Long Canoes," a colorful half-hour waterborne introduction to the young people of Polynesia; a brass band concert; an island farewell festival; even a "Keiki Polynesian Show" in which visiting keikis can see their own friends.

Since a visit here could take up to eight hours to enjoy it all, you may want to plan accordingly by arriving no later than 2pm. Admission to the villages and the afternoon highlights is $25 for adults, $13 for children. Add to this the buffet and admission to the evening production, "Mana!" and costs will be $42 adults, $25 children. For $54 adults and $35 children, you get a luau package, which also includes the IMAX presentation "Polynesian Odyssey"; this is considered the best value. Reservations can be made at the center's ticket office on the ground floor of the Royal Hawaiian Shopping Center in Waikiki: call 293-3333 or toll free from the mainland 800/367-7060.

The Polynesian Cultural Center is open Monday through Saturday; closed Thanksgiving and Christmas. If you're driving directly to Laie from Honolulu, take the Pali Highway (Hi. 61) and turn north on Kamehameha Highway (Hi. 83). Plan on at least an hour's drive.

While you're here, you'll also want to see the **Hawaiian Temple;** it stands back from the road on high ground, above a pond, an illuminated fountain, and at the head of a long avenue of royal palms. The best approach for a Taj Mahal–like vista is to leave the highway at Halelaa Boulevard. A complimentary Historical Laie Tour is available. You'll tour the Mormon Temple, Brigham Young University–Hawaii, and the Laie community on a re-created 1903 Hawaiian streetcar. By the way, not all the students here are Mormons; the school is open to others, provided they take the pledge not to smoke or drink, and "to live good Christian lives."

Laie-Maloo Beach used to be the scene of the Mormon hukilaus, once considered one of the island's top visitor attractions. The ocean at Laie-Maloo is safe for inshore swimming, although the beach is not a public park and has no dressing facilities.

You won't want to leave Laie without a drive out to **Laie Point** (the turnoff is just past the entrance to the cultural center), where you get a dramatic view of the rugged coastline. Walk out over the porous lava rock as far as you can go safely for the best view of all. Some old Hawaii hands swear it's the best view in the islands. Sunset devotees shouldn't miss this one.

READERS RECOMMEND

Polynesian Cultural Center. *"We highly recommend upgrading the Polynesian Cultural Center tour to an Ambassador tour. We paid extra for this, but we got a guided tour by one of the Brigham Young University students for the day, kukui-nut-leis, a video of the center, special seating for the evening buffet, seating within the first five rows for the evening show, plus the intermission dessert of mango sherbet. We wished that we had had even a few more hours to spend here. The evening show is thrilling, the buffet food was some of the best we had during our whole vacation, and the student performers are all eager to please."*—Margaret A. Pyzik, Napierville, Ill.

"Please let your readers know that at the PCC it is best to follow the crowds. We thought we'd be smart and avoid the crowds, but it turned out that we missed almost every exhibition because we arrived at the wrong times."—Carol Robinson, Lubbock, Tex.

WHERE TO EAT
PUNALUU

READERS RECOMMEND

The Crouching Lion Inn, *51-666 Kamehameha Hwy. (tel. 237-8511). "The Crouching Lion Inn, just about five miles from the Polynesian Cultural Center, is one of the best restaurants in Windward Oahu. An imposing structure, the inn was* *the actual residence of a Norwegian contractor and his large family who immigrated to Hawaii in 1912; the original hand-wrought iron fixtures add a charming quality to both the inside dining room (in which a fire blazes nightly in an enormous stone fireplace) and the outer dining room overlooking the bay. Among the menu specialties, I highly recommend the Slavonic steak continental and the luscious chicken macadamia (boneless breast of chicken, dipped in a brandy-and-egg batter, deep-fried, laced with a sweet-and-sour-sauce). Most main courses are $14.95 to $20.95. Lunch is pleasant too. And don't miss their 'mile high' coconut cream and other cream pies, each $3.50. Service is excellent, both pleasant and unobtrusive. I highly recommend the Crouching Lion as a first-class experience in leisurely dining in a beautiful setting, far removed from the hubbub of the city."—* Jane James, Pearl City, Hawaii.

---

3. LAIE TO HALEIWA

Highway 83 starts to run inland through sugar country at the village of Kahuku, the halfway point of your trip and the home of the **Kahuku Sugar Mill.** Alas, the color-coded walk-through tour that was so appealing to children is no longer available, but it's worthwhile to take a peek at the mill from the outside (sugar mills, a major part of Hawaii's agricultural history, are scarce these days), and perhaps stop here for lunch at a charming little restaurant called **The Old Plantation Cafe.** A number of local vendors also offer souvenir items.

Back in the car, keep an eye out for the roadside stands; in summer, you can get homegrown watermelon here—the best on the island. And you can also get fabulous shrimp here in Kahuku at **Amorient Aquafarm,** where we always stop off for a luscious snack. Amorient Aquafarm is a 175-acre diversified shrimp and fish farm; they grow a variety of prawns and other seafood in one-acre ponds that are visible from the highway. Their stand, open every day from 10am to 5:30pm, offers freshly cooked shrimp tempura ($7.25 for a dozen pieces), shrimp cocktail ($4), or cooked shrimp tails ($11.50 per lb). Feast at a roadside table or in your car. By the way, those beautiful white birds you see in this area are snowy egrets.

Just past Amorient Aquafarm, look for the Old Tanaka Plantation Store, newly restored, and now home to **The Only Show in Town** (tel. 293-1295), Paul Wroblewski's engaging antiques emporium, one of our favorites from Kauai in the pre–Hurricane Iniki days. Collectors and browsers can have a field day here: The selection of Hawaiiana, from stone artifacts to just about everything through the 1950s, is incredible. So, too, is the collection of old bottles (about which Paul is very knowledgeable) and multicolored insulators. Then there's a wonderful array of antique jewelry and ivory netsukes, as well as vintage political buttons and American trade memorabilia, particularly Coca-Cola items. We could get lost here for hours.

The road reaches the shore again at Kuilima, where you might want to have a look at the sumptuous Turtle Bay Hilton and Country Club, one of the most beautiful resorts in the islands. The scenery is spectacular here, especially the view from the swimming pool, perched atop a cliff overlooking the ocean on two sides as the waves pound in. (If it's time for lunch, you might want to try the 11am-to-2:30pm "minideli" buffet in the scenic Bay View Lounge. There's a charge for parking here, but your parking ticket can be validated at lunch.)

Back to the car again for a drive down the coast a bit to **Sunset Beach,** with its huge breakers crashing in at your right. It's safe for summer swimming, but in winter it's a wild, windy stretch, exciting to walk along; better still, you may be lucky enough to see some spectacular surfing here, for this is Oahu's North Shore, currently *the* place for the surfing set. Traffic may be jammed for miles from here south to Haleiwa if there's an important surfing contest going on. If you're wondering whether you should try it yourself, be advised that the surfing areas range from pretty dangerous to very dangerous to one that's called "Banzai Pipeline." (Remember the wartime suicide cry of the Japanese?) **Waimea Bay,** just below Sunset, has the distinction of having Hawaii's biggest waves, sometimes crashing in as high as 30 feet. However, in the summer months Waimea Bay is tranquil, the waves are gentle, and swimming here is close to perfection. **Pupukea Beach Park,** for instance, has good swimming and outstanding snorkeling in the summer months.

While the surfers on Waimea Bay are tempting fate, you can survey a more primitive form of human sacrifice (and this time we're serious) by turning left onto Pupukea Road, one of the few paved roads here, opposite a fire station and next to a marker. As soon as the road begins its ascent up the hill, take your first right and continue up to **Puu O Mahuka Heiau.** Here, on a bluff overlooking Waimea Bay (another view-collector's spot), are the ruins of a temple where human sacrifice was practiced. When Captain Vancouver put in at Waimea Bay in 1792, three of his men were captured and offered to the bloodthirsty gods. Today all is tranquil here, and the faithful still come, offering bundles of leaves in homage. Sadly, the road leading up to this national historic landmark is littered with trash and abandoned automobiles.

For a refreshing change of pace, head back to nature now at **Waimea Valley, home of Waimea Falls Park,** off Hi. 83 a little south of Pupukea Road, opposite Waimea Bay Beach Park. There's a lot to do at this botanical Eden nestled in a lush, 1,800-acre historic Hawaiian valley. You can watch world-class cliff divers plunge 60 feet into the waterfall pool, or see the park's resident hula troupe, dressed in authentic costumes, perform beautiful ancient (*kahiko*) hula. At the Hawaiian Games Site, you can play the sports of old Hawaii, such as *ulu maika* (lawn bowling), *o'o ihe* (spear throwing), or *konane* (Hawaiian checkers). You can wander through more than 30 botanical gardens that showcase some of the world's most exotic and rare plants, or explore numerous trails that wind their way through the park. Hop onto the narrated minibus to the waterfall, then join knowledgeable park guides for walking tours through the gardens and historical sites. At the *kauhale kahiko* (ancient Hawaiian living site), step into old Hawaii and experience the way Hawaiians were thought to have once lived.

Adventure seekers will enjoy the park's newest attraction, called **Waimea Adventure Tours,** a series of activities allowing guests to explore "never seen before" areas of Waimea Valley. They include guided all-terrain vehicle rides along 10 miles of wilderness trails; downhill mountain bike tours through the North Valley; kayak rides along Waimea River and out to Waimea Bay; and Waimea Nature Quest, a three-hour narrated van tour through untouched lands beyond the North and South valleys, including a nature hike and a visit to Pu'u O Mahuka, Oahu's largest heiau. (Extra fees are charged for these tours.)

You can also enjoy a relaxed picnic in the grassy meadow or a sumptuous lunch at the **Pikake Pavillion,** a spacious open-air dining center overlooking the mouth of the valley. Grab a quick island snack or cold drink at one of several snack bars in the valley, or browse through **Charlie's Country Store** for island gifts and mementos.

Twice each month the park offers romantic evening strolls to the waterfall and back by the light of the full moon. A donation of $5 per family directly benefits the Waimea Arboretum Foundation, a nonprofit scientific and educational organization dedicated to protecting Hawaii's rare and endangered plants.

Waimea Falls Park is also one of Hawaii's most popular wedding locations; couples can exchange vows in a lush, secluded garden or next to a gorgeous waterfall. For more information on planning such a special event, contact the park's **Wedding Department** at 59-864 Kamehameha Hwy., Haleiwa, HI 96712.

Admission is $19.95 for adults, $8.95 for juniors ages six to twelve, $3.95 for children four to five, and free for children under three. Waimea Falls Park is open daily, including holidays, from 10am to 5:30pm. For more information, call 638-8511 or 923-8448.

A few miles farther along Hi. 83, at **Haleiwa Beach Park** on Waialua Bay, you'll find the last swimming spot before you strike into the heart of Oahu. It's a fine family-type place—lawns, play areas, pergolas, dressing rooms, showers, fishing, camping, and a picnicking area.

YOUTH SCENE AT SUNSET BEACH AND HALEIWA If you're seriously interested—or even slightly—in the youth culture, you'll be welcome among the inhabitants of Sunset Beach and Haleiwa, an area that attracts a number of young people who want to live close to nature and the big surf. They're not putting on a show for sightseers or tourists, just quietly doing their thing—and an attractive thing it is. Haleiwa is like a very tiny version of Cape Cod's Provincetown, with its distinctively artsy atmosphere, small gift shops, art galleries, and boutiques. **Outrigger Trading Company,** 62-540 Kam Hwy., in Jameson's By the Sea, has an outstanding collection of works by local artists: hand-thrown pottery, leaded glass and seashell boxes, Hawaiian quilt pattern pillows, unique pillows and toys—starfish and sea horses and mermaids—and much more. They share their space with **Jameson's Fudge Works,** where fudge is creamed on marble tables and sold through the shop: everyone enjoys seeing, smelling, *and* tasting. **Silver Moon Emporium** is tucked away behind a garden with picnic tables at 66-037 Kam Hwy. This is the place for knockout, very feminine clothes and for jewelry and accessories that you won't see elsewhere. Much of it is handmade and one-of-a-kind; we saw beaded Mexican circular skirts, clingy Uru Uru dresses, earrings beginning at just $10, and lots more.

Hand-painted dresses and original designs, most of them made in the area, are offered by Inge Jausel at **Oogenesis Boutique** at 66-249 Kam Hwy. Japanese-inspired designs grace tops, pants ensembles, and simple dresses that can be worn belted or unbelted. Prices are reasonable. Under the "Inge Hawaii" label, these garments are now being sold in mainland stores. Inge's other store, **Deeni's Boutique,** at 66-079 Kam Hwy. in Haleiwa, specializes in swimwear, T-shirts, and sportswear, with some of the lowest prices and best selections in town.

We always like to make at stop at the **North Shore Marketplace,** 66-250 Kam Hwy., especially to visit **Pomegranates in the Sun,** with a smashing collection of clothing by Hawaiian artists and designers, inspired by the sun-drenched colors of Hawaii. Be sure to shop the consignment rack where they "recycle" Pomegranate clothes; we've made some terrific buys here! Men should check out **Patagonia** for attractive sportswear and outerwear, parkas, windbreakers, and the like, bearing the Patagonia label. They also have some cute rugged clothes for small boys. Then there's **Jungle Gems,** where you can shop for jewelry, crystals, and a variety of arts and crafts at very good prices. "Stress bracelets" of various tension-relieving stones and gems are $20. Note, too, their collections of Venetian glass and African trading beads. A good place to do some gift shopping. Everything at **Twelve Tribes** comes from Africa. There are Rastafarian hats and posters and some lovely and very reasonably priced clothing bearing the Addis Ababa label. We especially like a wonderful cotton patchwork vest and pants outfit for $40. There's some great-looking jewelry, as well, in silver and wood. Also in the same North Shore Marketplace complex is **Kau'ala Tropical Farms,** which offers free samples and fair prices on macadamia nuts. **Coffee Gallery** is a must for coffee fanatics, since they offer an enormous selection of Hawaiian and other coffees, roast their own beans, and sell them at very good prices. Organic coffee is available. You can also have a meal here on their outdoor terrace (see below). Peek in at **Haleiwa Arts,** a local gallery.

Art lovers will want to browse the galleries in Haleiwa, especially places like **Wyland Gallery,** 66-150 Kam Hwy., which specializes in the work of noted marine artist Wyland (everything from originals to posters) and also shows photographs, wood sculptures, and much more. Have a look, too, at the **Fettig Art Studio,** which exhibits local paintings by Beverly Fettig. Several prints are available at $20 each. Call 637-4933 for an appointment.

Hungry? You've come to the right town. Some of our favorite North Shore restaurants are here (see below). Wherever you eat, skip dessert and drive over to

Matsumoto's Grocery at 66-087 Kam Hwy. in Haleiwa (across from the intersection of Emerson Street) for the ultimate shave-ice experience. Local people drive out from all over the island to line up here, while no fewer than four workers form an "assembly line" to shave and season the ice. We won't swear that you'll really love shave ice with ice cream and azuki beans on the bottom, but can you say you really know Hawaii unless you've tried it? Matsumoto's also sells nifty T-shirts, caps, and sweatshirts with their logo in pretty colors—great souvenirs. **Aoki's,** just down the road, is an alternative if the lines are just too long.

Since Sunset Beach is a spiritually attuned community, it abounds in centers for yoga, Zen, and other such disciplines; the people at any of the shops can give you information on any groups that may interest you. This area is a world apart from the urban crush of Honolulu, the tourist scene at Waikiki, and the rat race everywhere. Try to schedule your visit in time for the fantastic sunset, which turns the horizon to a brilliant blazing red.

WHERE TO EAT

HALEIWA

COFFEE GALLERY, in North Shore Marketplace, 66-250 Kam Hwy., Haleiwa. Tel. 637-5571.
  Cuisine: AMERICAN/VEGETARIAN. **Reservations:** Not accepted.
  $ Prices: Sandwiches $3.75–$4.75; main courses $3.95–$8.95. AE, MC, V.
  Open: Mon–Fri 6am–9pm. Sat–Sun 7am–9pm.
It's so pleasant to sit at the outdoor café here and have a very special cup of freshly roasted gourmet coffee or a light lunch or dinner at this informal place. The emphasis is on healthy, fresh foods; some of the pastries, baked right in the back, are made without eggs or sugar. Lunch features quiches, waffles, veggie burgers, salads, and chili and rice; dinner (Friday to Sunday only) always offers a vegetarian specialty like tortillas, pesto, fettuccine, pastas, crêpes, or lentil burgers, along with a house salad. The espresso bar has some delightful combinations, like vanilla ice cream topped with espresso. To go along with the coffee, try a "death by chocolate brownie"—if you dare.

JAMESON'S BY THE SEA, 62-540 Kam Hwy., Haleiwa. Tel. 637-4336.
  Cuisine: SEAFOOD. **Reservations:** Recommended.
  $ Prices: Appetizers $3.75–$9.50; main courses $15.95–$24.95. AE, DC, MC, V.
  Open: Daily 11am–11pm.
This is a wonderfully picturesque spot for lunch or dinner. Savor the harbor view, the sunset, and great food and drink. Lunch is served downstairs in the Pub, and features hearty fish, seafood, and meat sandwiches; some excellent shrimp, crab, and seafood Louie salads; and a variety of interesting pupus (prices range between $5.50 and $9.95). There are many well-priced daily lunch specials, including fresh fish. Dinner features seafood caught daily in local waters.

KUA'AINA SANDWICH, 66-214 Kam Hwy., Haleiwa. Tel. 637-6067.
  Cuisine: SANDWICHES.
  $ Prices: Sandwiches $3.15–$5.25. No credit cards.
  Open: Daily 11am–8pm.
Where can you get the best sandwich on the North Shore, maybe on all of Oahu? We cast our vote for Kua'Aina, a sparkling sandwichery across the street from the courthouse in Haleiwa. It's tiny, neat as a pin, with wooden tables, framed pictures of local scenes, a few tables on the porch. And the atmosphere is casual, with people coming in off the beach. We haven't stopped raving yet about the sandwiches we had on our last visit: mahimahi with melted cheese, Ortega pepper, lettuce, and tomato at $4.25; tuna and avocado ("the tastiest combo in the Pacific") at $4.50; and a great baconburger at $5.10. Sandwiches are hearty enough to be a whole meal and are served on either a kaiser roll, honey wheat-berry bread, or earthy rye. A recent Zagat survey voted them as no. 10 in the state for food and no. 2 for "Bang for the Buck."

ROSIE'S CANTINA, in the Haleiwa Shopping Plaza, 66-165 Kam Hwy., Haleiwa. Tel. 637-3538.
Cuisine: MEXICAN. **Reservations:** Not required.
$ Prices: Appetizers $1.65–$7.95; main courses $10.45–$12.95. AE, MC, V.
Open: Tues–Sat 7am–10pm. Sun–Mon 7am–9pm.

This attractive, high-tech–looking spot is a favorite for tasty Mexican food. Rosie's serves all three meals, features delicious tortas (hamburger or chicken with fries or beans on thick bread), and offers spectacular savings at its Wednesday-night Taco Fiesta Buffets; from 5 to 7 pm, it's all you can eat for $5 per person; the ante goes up to $7 per person between 7 and 9pm.

4. HALEIWA TO WAIKIKI

Follow Hi. 82 from Haleiwa and turn left onto Hi. 99 (Kamehameha Highway) as it climbs to **Leilehua Plateau.** Here the tall sugarcane gives way to seemingly endless miles of pineapple—dark green and golden against the red earth. It's the largest pineapple area in the world. Just as you're beginning to feel like the Ancient Mariner (you can't pick any), you'll find the **Dole Pineapple Pavillion,** just north of Wahiawa, where you can buy a whole "pine" or get half a dozen delicious spears, fresher than any you've ever tasted. The custom here is to sprinkle a little unrefined Hawaiian salt on the pineapple; it helps cut the acidity. A fountain spouts juice that you can drink, free. You can also shop for Hawaiian souvenirs here and order fresh pineapple packs delivered to the airport for your flight back home. Dole does not conduct tours through the fields, but many operations are visible from the highway. In case you're curious, the variety of pineapple grown here is called sweet cayenne.

In the midst of these Wahiawa pineapple fields, one mile past the pineapple hut, is the Del Monte Corporation's **Pineapple Variety Garden,** near where the Kamehameha Highway becomes Hi. 80 for a short time. It's small, but it's well worth a brief stop to see a huge variety of species and pineapple plants from all over the world—Asia, Africa, South America, and various small islands. Just ignore the tremendous spiders that build their webs among the plants; they're nonaggressive and totally harmless—to people and pineapples.

Next stop is for the history-anthropology buffs: a Stone Age spot where the royal chieftains of Hawaii were born. Just before Wahiawa on Hi. 80, watch on the right for an HVB warrior marker pointing to a dirt road leading off to the right to a clump of eucalyptus trees in a pineapple field—the Sacred Birthstones-Kukaniloko. These large stones and the village that once surrounded the spot afforded prenatal care and birthing support to high chiefly women in childbirth—thus ensuring healthy mothers and children to continue the lineages of the high chiefs, the alii.

Just before you reach Wahiawa, still in the pineapple fields, you may want to stop and stretch your legs at a five-acre, working vegetable and flower farm called **Helemano Plantation,** which serves a tasty and inexpensive buffet lunch at $8.25 between 11am and 2:30pm. If it's past lunchtime, you can still browse at the gift shop, get some fresh produce at the country store, visit the bakery, or even join a lei-making class. Helemano Plantation provides many retarded people with training and vocational opportunities, and supports programs of Opportunities for the Retarded, Inc.

Now take Kamehameha Highway to Wahiawa, a town that serves as a center for personnel stationed at **Schofield Barracks** (where James Jones met his muse) and **Wheeler's Field.** It's also a huge pineapple depot. The bright spot here is **Kemoo Farms,** a famous name in these parts since 1921. The old restaurant building overlooking Lake Wilson now houses a good Mexican restaurant. Next door is the Kemoo Farms Visitor Center, where owner Dick Rodby has lined the walls and shelves with antiques, old photos, and historic memorabilia of the area, some of it for sale. Also for sale are Kemoo Farms' Happy Cakes (a very rich holiday fruitcake made with pineapple, coconut, and macadamia nuts, a big favorite of Ronald Reagan's), homemade chocolates, macadamia-nut coffee, and other goodies. Visiting the Rodbys is a real treat, like seeing friends from home.

In this area you may also want to visit the **Schofield Museum,** with its military and historical documents (open daily from 9am to 4pm). Garden lovers will want to make a stop at the **Wahiawa Botanical Garden,** at 1396 California Ave. (three-quarters of a mile east of Kam Highway), 1,000 feet high, to wander through 27 lovely acres of rare trees, ferns, and shrubs, and a Hawaiian garden. Admission is free (open daily from 9am to 4pm except Christmas and New Year's Day).

You'll pass through more sugar fields as you drive along the now-four-lane Kamehameha Highway (Highway 99 once again) or the new Interstate H2. From here on, it's fast sailing home. At the intersection with Interstate H1, turn left and drive past Pearl Harbor (you might visit the USS Arizona Memorial if you have the time) and Honolulu International Airport. At Middle Street, turn right onto Highway 92 (Nimitz Highway), which will take you past the harbor. Take Ala Moana and Kalakaua into Waikiki.

WHERE TO EAT

WAHIAWA

HELEMANO PLANTATION, 64-1510 Kam Hwy., Wahiawa. Tel. 622-3929.
   Cuisine: CHINESE. **Reservations:** Not required.
$ Prices: Buffet or sandwich and salad bar $8.25. MC. V.
   Open: Breakfast daily 7:30–11am; lunch daily 11am–2:30pm.

You can get a substantial, reasonably priced lunch in the big, gardenlike dining rooms of this spot, located on a five-acre complex amid pineapple fields on the outskirts of Wahiawa. Helemano Plantation is not only an agricultural farm, growing fruits, vegetables, and flowers; it's also a vocational and educational center for many of Hawaii's retarded citizens. They work as trainees in the many areas of Helemano: in the farm, the restaurant, the gift shop, country store, or in the bakeshop. Its Country Inn restaurant is known for its excellent Chinese cuisine and reasonable prices. At least five hot main courses are available each day, which might include roast duck, teriyaki beef, Chinese spareribs, beef with broccoli, spicy eggplant, and many more. A mini-lunch plate will cost you $3.95, and your choice of either a full all-you-can-eat Chinese buffet including fruit bar or a sandwich with all-you-can-eat salad bar is $8.25. You can also browse through the tempting display of freshly baked treats at the bakeshop, which includes island-style manapuas (steamed or baked buns stuffed with pork or chicken) as well as pineapple and coconut danish, and chocolate chip, peanut butter, and coconut-drop cookies. Stop by for the free hula show and take time to browse through their "Best of the Best" collection of handcrafted gifts and souvenirs made by the handicapped and disadvantaged from all over the world.

CHAPTER 10

KAUAI

1. **GETTING THERE &**
   GETTING AROUND
- **WHAT'S SPECIAL**
  ABOUT KAUAI
- **FAST FACTS: KAUAI**
2. **WHERE TO STAY**
3. **WHERE TO EAT**

About 110 miles to the west of Honolulu, yet seemingly light-years away, lies a tropical Switzerland. This is Kauai, the northernmost of the major Hawaiian islands, and one of the lushest tropical spots on earth. Kauai (pronounced correctly Kah-*wah*-ee, lazily Kah-*why*) is a small island, about 32 miles in diameter. Its central mountain receives an average of 500 inches of rainfall a year, making it one of the wettest spots on earth, which acounts for the lushness of the surrounding landscape.

Kauai is the oldest Hawaiian island both geologically and historically. In island lore, Kauai was the original home of Pele, the goddess of fire and volcanoes, before she moved southward. It was also the homeland of a race of pre-Polynesians whose origins are unknown. Some believe they were the survivors of the lost continent of Lemuria. In legend they're called Menehunes, South Sea leprechauns who stood about two feet tall, worked only in darkness, and accomplished formidable engineering feats between dusk and dawn.

The first Polynesian settlers chose Kauai, too, and landed at the mouth of the Wailua River somewhere between A.D. 500 and 900. They crossed the Pacific in double-hulled sailing vessels in a voyage of many months, probably from the Society Islands. Other Polynesians came later, but time stood still on Kauai and the rest of the Hawaiian Islands until 1778, when Captain Cook arrived at Waimea and the modern history of Hawaii began.

You can see all the important things in Kauai in three days—but the longer you stay, the luckier you are.

HURRICANE INIKI

In September 1992, a devastating hurricane struck the island of Kauai, demolishing homes and buildings, sweeping roofs and even refrigerators out to sea, tearing up the vegetation, and altering the very shape of the land. Since then, however, Kauai has made an amazing recovery. The flowers and foliage have come back, some of the beaches are wider and better than ever, the golf courses are in fine condition, and most homes, hotels, and visitor attractions have been repaired or totally rebuilt. The beauty of the island and of the people of Kauai is a superb testament to the human spirit, which succeeds in overcoming adversity.

1. GETTING THERE & GETTING AROUND

GETTING THERE

BY PLANE About 15 minutes after your interisland plane takes off in Honolulu, it lands at the sleek $36-million Richard A. Kawakami Terminal, the third-busiest airport in the state. Rent a car or hail a cab to get to Lihue town or other destinations.

WHAT'S SPECIAL ABOUT KAUAI

Natural Wonders

Waimea Canyon, a 3,657-foot gorge dubbed the "Grand Canyon of the Pacific" by Mark Twain.

Mount Waialeale, "the wettest spot on earth," receiving 480 inches of rain a year—best seen from a helicopter.

Spouting Horn, a saltwater geyser where water spouts up through the lava rocks, to heights of 50 feet.

Beaches

Superb swimming year-round at Kalapaki Beach in Lihue and, on the southern and western shores, especially at Poipu Beach Park and Salt Pond Beach Park. In summer, along the north shore, at romantic Hanalei Bay (where *South Pacific* was filmed), Haena Beach Park, and Ke'e Beach.

Snorkeling

At many spots around the island, especially good at Poipu Beach on the southern shore and Tunnels Beach on the north shore.

Museums and Historic Homes

Kauai Museum, with changing art, heritage, and cultural exhibits of both Asia and Hawaii, as well as a permanent showcase of Hawaiiana.

Grove Farm Homestead, a look back into the plantation days of 19th-century Hawaii.

Hawaiian Art Museum and Bookstore, Kapaa and Kilauea, with large selections of Hawaiian arts, crafts, books, music.

Kilohana Plantation, a combination historical house, museum, restaurant and shopping bazaar.

Kokee Natural History Museum, a tiny museum devoted to the indigenous bird and plant life of the island.

Wailoli Mission House in Hanalei, full of fascinating furniture, books, and mementos of 19th-century missionary days.

Botanical Gardens

National Tropical Botanical Gardens in Lawai, Kauai's best, a 286-acre tropical garden filled with more than 5,000 varieties of tropical plants on exquisite grounds; guided tours.

Olu Pua Gardens in Kalakeho, a botan-ical showplace and historic home.

Hiking

Some of the best in the islands, with magnificent trails on the Na Pali Coast and into Waimea Canyon.

Movie and TV Locations

Some places on Kauai may seem familiar, if you've seen *Jurassic Park*, *Raiders of the Lost Ark*, *Indiana Jones and the Temple of Doom*, *The Thorn Birds*, or *South Pacific*—to mention just a few.

INFORMATION

The headquarters of the **Hawaii Visitors Bureau** is at 3016 Umi St., Suite 207 (tel. 808/245-3971), on the second floor of Lihue Plaza. Information is available on just about everything, including tips on where to play tennis and golf, deep-sea fishing charters, helicopter tours, boat tours, kayaking, and glider flights.

Kauai Vacation Helpers was set up after Hurricane Iniki to help visitors find their way to the best island activities. Call them at 808/246-0745 and they'll steer you right, giving you advice on which companies have the best safety and customer satisfaction records. They'll fill you in on the best places to swim, snorkel, and fish and, in general, will lend a helping hand. A phone call is all that's necessary. Eventually, they will have half-a-dozen offices on the island.

GETTING AROUND

BY RENTAL CAR For information on the major budget car-rental companies—offering excellent flat-rate packages on all the islands—see Chapter 2. If, however, you haven't done so, or prefer a time-plus-mileage deal, simply walk up to any of the car-rental agencies just across the road from the airport. We drove a car from **Sunshine of Hawaii** (tel. 808/245-9541, or toll free 800/367-2977) on our last trip and were pleased with both the car and the courteous service. And it's especially nice that the cars are right at the airport. Rates begin at $22.95 daily for a compact two-door automatic with air conditioning, $139 weekly. For an automatic four-door with air conditioning, the price is $28.95 and $159.

BY BUS & TAXI While a car is definitely the best way to go, there is some public transportation. The **Kauai Bus,** a new company, operates a fleet of 15 buses that serve the entire island. For scheduling and destinations, phone 246-4622. The bus costs $1.

Should you need a cab for a short trip, **Kauai Cab** (tel. 246-9554) is a reliable outfit.

FAST FACTS: KAUAI

Area Code The telephone area code is 808.

Babysitters Inquire at your hotel desk.

Business Hours See "Fast Facts: Hawaii," in Chapter 2.

Car Rentals See "Getting Around," above.

Climate See "When to Go," in Chapter 2.

Dentists Contact Dr. John R. Black, 4347 Rice St., Lihue (tel. 245-3582); or Dr. Mark Baird, 4-9768 Kuhio Hwy., Kapaa (tel. 822-9393).

Doctors Kauai Medical Group has clinics in Lihue (tel. 245-1500), Kapaa (tel. 822-3431), Koloa (tel. 742-1621), and Princeville (tel. 826-6300). Physicians are on call 24 hours (tel. 245-1831).

Emergencies Call 911.

Eyeglasses Try Jenkins Optical Service, 4491 Rice St., Lihue (tel. 245-7425).

Fax Services Phone Mart, Kukui Grove (tel. 245-9511), can assist you.

Holidays See "When to Go," in Chapter 2.

Hospitals Wilcox Memorial Hospital, 3420 Kuhio Hwy., Lihue (tel. 245-1100) has an emergency room open 24 hours.

Iniki Express This free daytime bus service, set up after the 1992 hurricane, may still be in operation by the time you read this. For details, call 241-6410.

Libraries Branches include Lihue Public Library, 4444 Hardy St., Lihue (tel. 245-3617); Kapaa Public Library (tel. 822-5041); and Koloa Public/School Library (tel. 742-1635).

Other Useful Numbers State Commission on Persons with Disabilities (tel. 245-4308; Voice/TDD); Helpline Kauai (tel. 245-3411); YWCA Sexual Assault Services (tel. 245-4144). On Call (tel. 246-1441) is a 24-hour free service offering news, sports, weather, community-service information, etc. See also the Aloha Pages of the Kauai telephone directory.

Photographic Needs The ABC Discount Store, in the Anchor Cove Shopping Center, and Long's offer the best prices.

Police Call 911 for emergencies, 245-9711 for all other matters.

Poison Control Center Call toll free 800/362-3585.

Post Office It's at 4441 Rice St., Lihue (tel. 245-4994).

Safety Exercise the same precautions you would elsewhere: Never leave valuables in your car, even in the trunk; leave personal valuables in hotel safes or in-room safes; don't flash cash conspicuously in public.

Taxis See "Getting Around," above.
Time of Day Call 245-0212.
Visitors' Information Program Call 246-1440.
Weather Information For current weather, call 245-6001; for a marine report, 245-3564; for a surf report, 335-3611.

2. WHERE TO STAY

Bed & Breakfast Hawaii, the largest reservation service in the islands, is headquartered right here in Kauai. Not only do they have a wide range of carefully inspected accommodations all over the state, but they also work with Avis Car Rental to provide lower prices on car rentals for their guests. For a free brochure, contact Bed & Breakfast Hawaii, P.O. Box 449, Kapaa, HI 96746 (tel. 808/822-7771, or toll free 800/733-1632; fax 808/822-2723). For $12.95, you receive a directory of homes and apartments with rooms for rent called *B&B Goes Hawaiian.*

IN & AROUND LIHUE

The town of Lihue and its adjacent Nawiliwili Harbor are the most centrally located places to stay in Kauai, since they're the starting points for your eastern and western tours of the island. Lihue is the county seat and the center of Kauai's government, commerce, and culture.

DOUBLES FOR ABOUT $30

MOTEL LANI, 4240 Rice St. (P.O. Box 1836), Lihu, Kauai, HI 96766. Tel. 808/245-2965. 10 rms. TEL
$ Rates: $30–$48 or double; from $48 triple. Each additional person $14 extra. Minimum stay 2 nights. No credit cards. **Parking:** Free.
The only budget accommodation in the center of town we think most visitors will find suitable. It's a pleasant place, patronized by both Islanders and tourists. Rooms are small, but modern, with a small refrigerator. Rollaway cots are provided. Owner Janet Naumu requires a 2-night deposit. Rates are subject to change without notice.

WORTH THE EXTRA MONEY

ASTON KAHA LANI, 4460 Nehe Rd., Lihue, Kauai, HI 96766. Tel. 808/822-9331, or toll free 800/922-7866. Fax 808/922-8785. Telex 634479 ASTHI UW. 65 condominium apts.
$ Rates: Apr–Dec 21, $117–$147 one-bedroom apt; $154–$185 two-bedroom apt; $250 three-bedroom apt. Dec 22–Mar, $147–$175 one-bedroom apt. AE, CB, DC, MC, V. **Parking:** Free.
Located behind the Kauai Resort Hotel, adjacent to the beautiful Wailua Golf Course, on the beach at Wailua Bay, this condominium complex is great for those who want to swim in the ocean or pool, snorkel, golf, or play tennis (there is one court, lit for night play). Across the road is the Coco Palms Resort with its three fine restaurants, and just down the road Coconut Plantation beckons.
    Kaha Lani means "Heavenly Place" in Hawaiian and the resort is aptly named. Each unit is privately owned, so the decor is different in each. We've seen several units and found them all—well, heavenly. Each condo includes a full kitchen with dishwasher, a lanai, ceiling fans, and a clock radio. Room prices depend on whether the view is garden, ocean, or oceanfront. One-bedroom units can accommodate up

to four people, the two-bedroom/two-bath apartments have room for six, and the three-bedroom/two-bath accommodations fit up to eight people. Some rooms are especially equipped for the disabled.

NAWILIWILI HARBOR

GARDEN ISLAND INN, 3445 Wilcox Rd., Lihue, Kauai, HI 96766. Tel. 808/245-7227, toll free 808/648-0154. 15 rms, 6 suites. MINIBAR TV TEL

$ Rates: $45–$60 double; $55–$65 family room; $65–$85 suite. MC, V. **Parking:** Free.

One of Kauai's top budget choices is two miles from the center of town, at Nawiliwili Harbor. The Garden Island Inn is an older hotel that has been taken over by new owners, renovated from top to bottom, and spruced up with white paint and green trim. Owners Steven and Susan Layne have done a terrific job in transforming the three-story hotel, which is surrounded by lovely gardens and miniature waterfalls cascading into several koi pools. You can help yourself to bananas and the fruit on the orange and papaya trees, and be at beautiful Kalapaki Beach, one of our favorites in the islands, in about a minute.

Rooms are light and sunny, with rattan furniture and floral spreads, ceiling fans, tropical flowers, and original watercolors. Most have ocean views, and some include private lanais. Each room features a wet bar with refrigerator, cable color TV, microwave oven, and coffee maker complete with complimentary chocolate macadamia nut Kona coffee. Bedding is either a queen-size bed or two twin beds; bathrooms have showers but no tubs. The cheapest doubles are on the ground floor, and the more expensive doubles are on the second floor with private lanais. A suite with a living room, four beds, a microwave oven, and a large refrigerator could house a family of four. Another suite has a three-sided private lanai, a daybed in the living room and a queen-size bed in the bedroom, a microwave oven and a large refrigerator. Steve and Susan will lend guests beach gear, golf clubs, snorkels, coolers, etc., at no charge.

THE EASTERN SHORE: COCONUT COAST

Nine miles out of Lihue, near where the Wailua River meets the ocean, begins Kauai's "Coconut Coast" stretching from here through the town of Kapoa. It's also know as Coconut Plantation. The area has beautiful scenery, lots of good, inexpensive restaurants, plus the Coconut Marketplace. The hotels here are more expensive than the ones in the Lihue area since they are situated directly on the ocean. Here on the windward side of the island the surf is rougher (and the weather apt to be rainier) than on the leeward side. If you have a car, it's no problem, since it's a short drive to the splendid beaches of leeward Poipu. If you don't have a car, however, and want to swim in the ocean, we recommend choosing a hotel in Poipu (see below).

DOUBLES FOR AROUND $50 TO $85

HOTEL CORAL REEF, 1516 Kuhio Hwy., Kapaa, Kauai, HI 96746. Tel 808/822-4481, or toll free 800/843-4659.

$ Rates (including continental breakfast): Oceanfront Building: $67–$85 double. Main Building: $50–$75 double, $60–$85 kitchenette suites. Each additional person $10 extra; crib or rollaway, $10. CB, DC, MC, V. **Parking:** Free.

This cute little hotel is right on the ocean and close to everything: public swimming beach, freshwater swimming pool, tennis court, library, launderette, and several great little budget restaurants. The hotel has a stretch of white, sandy beach, and there's good swimming and snorkeling in the deep water between the reefs. You could even make do without a car here.

There are two wings; the Oceanfront Building, prettier than ever since its renovation after the hurricane, is a winner. Spacious rooms overlook the beach, which is just 50 yards away, and boast private lanais, new rattan furniture, colorful floral bedspreads and drapes, new color cable TVs, small refrigerators, large glass sliding doors, louvered windows to catch the prevailing trade winds, and either double or twin beds. Bathrooms have been retiled in pastel colors and new showers have been installed. The Main Building, not yet completed at the time of this writing, will have nicely furnished rooms with color cable TV, and private bath with both shower and tub. Four suites will feature cooking facilities. A complimentary continental breakfast is served each morning. There's an activities center, barbecue grills, and snorkel rental. For reservations, contact Iron Mike & The Princess, Inc., at the above address.

KAPAA SANDS, 380 Papaloa Rd., Kapaa, Kauai, HI 96746. Tel. 808/882-4901, or toll free 800/222-4901. 21 rms. TV TEL
$ Rates: $75–$85 studio; $99–$109 two-bedroom apt. Minimum stay 3 days in summer, 7 days in winter. MC, V. **Parking:** Free.

★ One of our favorite places to stay on Kauai is the comfortable and very attractive Kapaa Sands. It's just a few minutes' walk from Coconut Plantation, yet it's secluded and right on the beach. The pretty, two-story green buildings house studios and two-bedroom apartments; choose between garden with ocean view or oceanfront. All units have ceiling fans. Studios have lanais and separate, fully-equipped kitchens. The two-bedroom units are charming duplex apartments (two bedrooms and full bath upstairs, sofa bed and half-bath downstairs), each with two lanais.

KAPAA SHORE, 4-0900 Kuhio Hwy., Kapaa, Kauai, HI 96746. Tel. 808/822-3055, or toll free 800/827-3922. Fax 808/822-1457. 81 condominiums (40 for rent). TV TEL
$ Rates: $65–$120 one-bedroom unit; $85–$140 two-bedroom unit. Weekly rates available. MC, V. **Parking:** Free.
For a touch of luxury in Kapaa, this condominium complex may be just the ticket. It's right at the beach, and each apartment has a view of the ocean, garden, or pool. All are beautifully furnished, many in avocado-and-white decorative schemes, with fully-equipped kitchens, and patio furniture to make dining on your lanai a treat. The one-bedroom units can accommodate up to four people, with a queen-size bed in the bedroom and a queen-size sofa in the living room. Six people can be cozy in the two-bedroom units, which are duplexes with vaulted ceilings, a queen-size bed in one of the bedrooms, two twins in the other, and a queen-size sleeper sofa in the living room. Facilities include a tennis court, 40-foot swimming pool, sunbathing decks, and barbecue area.

KAUAI SANDS HOTEL, 420 Papaloa Ave., Kapaa, Kauai, HI 96746 Tel. 808/822-4951, or toll free 800/367-7000 in U.S. Fax 922-0052. 200 rms, 2 suites. A/C TV TEL
$ Rates: Apr to Jan 31, $75–$80 single or double, $100 single or double with kitchenette, $105 suite; Feb–Mar, $85–$90 single or double, $110 single or double with kitchenette. AE, MC, V. **Parking:** Free.
This attractive and informal hotel is part of the hospitable, locally owned and operated chain of Sand & Seaside Motels. It faces green lawns and a mile of white sand beach, beautiful but often rough for swimming; there are two swimming pools as well. Rooms are of good size, decorated in ocean hues of greens and blues. All have refrigerators, private lanais, and either two double beds or a king-size bed. Save money by patronizing the hotel's dining room, Al and Don's, which serves dinner main courses between $5.95 and $12, and features fresh catch of the day nightly.
Reservations: Sand & Seaside Hotel, Suite 714, 222 Kalakaua Ave., Honolulu, HI 96815; or call the hotel directly.

MOKIHANA OF KAUAI, 796 Kuhio Hwy., Kapaa, Kauai, HI 96746. Tel. 808/822-3971. 80 studio apts.
$ Rates: $55 single or double. MC, V. **Parking:** Free.
It's not easy to get an apartment at this attractive condominium complex in the busy winter months; that's when it's usually chock-full of owners. The best time for rentals is from late April through late September. Apartments are nicely furnished with limited kitchen facilities (refrigerators, hotplate, and electric frying pan), bath, and/or shower.

The apartments are right on the oceanfront, and two miles away from a championship golf course. Mokihana also boasts an 18-hole, par-36 putting green, shuffleboard, a large swimming pool, and a barbecue area. The Bull Shed Restaurant, a superb steak house, is right on the waterfront. For information, contact Hawaii Kailani, 119 N. Commercial, Suite 1400, Belingham, WA 98225 (tel. 206/676-1434).

ROYAL DRIVE COTTAGES, 147 Royal Dr., Kapaa, Kauai, HI 96746. Tel. 808/822-2321. 2 cottages, 1 single in the main house.

$ Rates: $60 single; $80 double. Futon for a third person $10. 10% discount on stays of 1 week or longer. **Parking:** Free.

⭐ Up in the lush green hills of the Eden-like Wailua district, down a private road, you'll find Bob Levine's beautiful guest cottages. Bob refers to his little bit of paradise as a "cozy tropical hideaway," a most apt description. Each cottage has twin beds that make up as a king-size bed; a kitchen equipped with a small refrigerator, microwave oven, coffee maker, blender, and everything in the way of utensils for preparing and serving a meal; a private bath; ceiling fans; and views of the garden from every window. The first cottage has a huge screened lanai facing a part of the garden planted with palm trees, heliconia, ginger, and papaya trees. The second cottage is literally *in* the garden. It has a tiny porch with one chair; down the steps is an enormous kukui-nut tree with chairs under it; nearby is a fish pond filled with water hyacinths and inhabited by sparkling fish. The temptation to settle under the three and never move is strong. Guests are invited to pick pomelos, papayas, and bananas in season. They are welcome to use the hot tub in the main house. There are coolers, a big beachball, and a boogie board to tote to the beach. Bob's house is between the cottages and he is very available and happy to share his considerable knowledge of the islands and offer suggestions to help make your stay truly special.

DOUBLES FOR AROUND $90

ASTON KAUAI BEACHBOY HOTEL, 484 Kuhio Hwy., no. 100, Kapaa, Kauai, HI 96746. Tel. 808/822-3441, or toll free 800/922-7866. Fax 808/922-8785. Telex 634479 ASTHI UW, 243 rms. A/C TV TEL

$ Rates: $88–$118 single or double. Each additional person $12 extra. AE, CB, DC, MC, V. **Parking:** Free.

About a mile past the famed Coco Palms Resort, on the ocean side of the road, is this very pleasant, moderately priced hotel. A branch of Honolulu's terrific Perry's Smorgy Restaurant, which serves three hearty and reasonably priced buffet meals a day, is on the premises. Rooms are nicely decorated, face either the garden or the sea, and each has its own private lanai, a small refrigerator, and a large dressing room. You can swim in the ocean—the hotel is located on the white sand beach at Coconut Plantation—or in the almost Olympic-size swimming pool. Coconut Marketplace, a Hawaiian-style shopping village, is just across the street.

BED & BREAKFAST

FERN GROTTO INN, 4561 Kuamoo Rd., Wailua, Kauai, HI 96747. Tel. 808 /822-2560. 3 rms.

$ Rates (including breakfast): $70–$90 single; $80–$100 double. MC, V. **Parking:** Free.

This plantation home in the midst of Wailua River State Park offers a serene atmosphere, gracious charms, and a practical location, just off Hi. 56, close to all the attractions of Coco Palms Resort, and a short walk to Wailua Beach. The three rooms—the Serena, Isabella, and Tara—are priced according to size. All are furnished with fine pieces and feature queen-size beds with designer sheets and comforters, goose-down pillows, and European down-feather beds; each has a private bathroom with quality amenities. Manager Sharon Knott serves a continental tropical breakfast—fruits, croissants, bagels, muffins, cereals, Kona coffee, and herbal teas—on fine English china in the many-windowed Plantation Dining Room. Perfect for honeymooners and small wedding parties; the entire house may be rented.

HOUSE OF ALEVA, 5509 Kuamoo Rd., Kapaa, Kauai, HI 96746. Tel. 808/ 822-4606. 3 rms. 1 with private bath. TV
$ Rates: (including breakfast): $55 double, $40 single. No credit cards.

⭐ Ernie and Anita Perry, the retired couple from Oahu (she's a former nurse, he was in the Merchant Marine for many years), are the best kind of B&B hosts: they love having guests in their home and share it freely. Guests have
💲 the run of the house, which means they're more likely to be lolling out on the porch swing or in the comfortable living room, rather than in the guest rooms. There are two nicely furnished upstairs rooms—one done in pink, the other in blue—which boast their own TVs and queen-size orthopedic beds. They share a spacious bathroom. Downstairs is a small single room with its own bath and a nifty indoor/outdoor shower. Guests have use of beach towels, mats, picnic and snorkeling gear, a washer-dryer, even a full-size back massager. The Perrys are into health food and health teas, and will tailor breakfast to personal dietary needs. They serve papayas from their own garden. The house is situated two miles inland from the main highway, in the lush Wailua district, just across the road from Opaekaa Waterfall. Be sure to ask to see Anita's work; she's a talented sculptor of Hawaiiana. Many Europeans have discovered this place, so the conversation around the breakfast table and in front of the TV is apt to be multilingual. A delightful find.

KAY BARKER'S BED & BREAKFAST, P.O. Box 740, Kapaa, Kauai, HI 96746. Tel. 808/822-3073, or toll free 800/835-2845. 5 rms.
$ Rates (including breakfast): $35–$60 single; $45–$70 double. Direct booking special: 15% discount on stays over 6 days. MC, V. **Parking:** Free.

This very casual bed-and-breakfast inn is on the slopes of the Sleeping Giant mountain, a 10-minute drive from Hi. 56. The back deck runs the length of the house (80 ft.) and looks out over peaceful gardens and pastures. There is also a large living room and dining room, a separate TV room, a refrigerator for storing snacks, and a washer-dryer. Guests can also use ice chests, beach mats, and boogie boards.

The Lokelani Room, next to the kitchen, has a double bed and a private bath; it rents for $35 single, $45 double. The Plumeria Room (with a king-size bed or twin beds) and the Orchid Room (king-size bed) both have private bathrooms with showers and look out over the front garden; they rent for $40 single, $50 double. The Ginger Room, "the honeymooner's favorite," has its own entrance, wicker furniture, and a private bath with tub/shower, and overlooks the back garden and pasture lands of Mount Waialeale; rates are $50 single, $60 double. Hibiscus, a two-room cottage, is private, in the back garden; it has large rooms, a king-size bed, a sitting room with wet bar, refrigerator, and microwave, and a private lanai from which to catch the great views, and it rents for $60 single, $70 double.

Gordon Barker, who runs the place, whips up good breakfasts (they might include fresh fruits and juices, banana-nut muffins, macadamia-nut pancakes, and beverages). Families with children are welcome. Smoking and "social drinking" are acceptable. If this place is full, he may be able to put you in touch with other B&Bs in the area.

THE SOUTHERN SHORE

In the other direction from Lihue, 12 miles south, stretches the idyllic Poipu Beach area, dry and sunny, where the surf crashes a Mediterranean blue-green on palm-fringed, white-sand beaches. Of course, this area is more expensive than Lihue, but you're right at the beach, in our opinion the best on Kauai.

DOUBLES FOR AROUND $25

KAHILI MOUNTAIN PARK, P.O. **Box 298, Koloa, Kauai, HI 96756. Tel. 808/742-9921.** 10 cabins, 15 cabinettes.
$ Rates: $24 cabinettes for two people; $35 cabins with inside toilet and private outdoor shower for two people; $50 cabins with full bathroom facilities for two people. Each additional person $6 extra. Minimum stay of 2 days required. No credit cards. **Parking:** Free.

If you are really into the great outdoors—but not enough to backpack it and sleep under the stars—try this camp, located seven miles from Poipu Beach, off Ho. 50 west, just beyond the seven-mile marker. Mount Kahili rises majestically behind the little cabins and cabinettes nestled near a small lake where you can fish for bass and swim. The park is operated by the Seventh-day Adventist church, and their school is on the premises.

The cabinettes are grouped in a circle around the bathroom-and-shower buildings. Each has one room, with a small dining area where there's a small refrigerator, a two-burner hotplate, and a sink. Cookware is furnished. Cabins, consisting of either one large room or two small ones, have a bathroom with a sink and toilet; there's a private shower outside each cabin. They also have a full-size refrigerator, as well as the two-burner stove and sink. Six new cabins have private bathroom and shower, a stove, refrigerator, and hot water. All of the accommodations have screened windows with louvers. Linens are furnished. These facilities are very rustic, in a most beautiful setting. There is a laundry room on the premises. Prepayment in full is required for all reservations.

DOUBLES FOR AROUND $50 TO $70

CLASSIC VACATION COTTAGES, 2687 Onu Place (P.O. Box 901), Kalaheo, Kauai, HI 96741. Tel. 808/332-9201. Fax 808/332-9201. 3 cottages. TV
$ Rates: $58 studio; $60–$65 one-bedroom cottage; $64–$70 one-bedroom cottage with breakfast. Each additional person $10 extra. No credit cards. **Parking:** Free.
A stay in the tiny country town of Kalaheo is for those who prefer to be away from the tourist scene, yet close enough to enjoy its advantages. These three self-contained cottages on a hillside are set in a garden adjacent to the custom-built home of Richard and Wynnis Grow, in a residential neighborhood. The Grows have decorated them handsomely, with stained, leaded windows, well-equipped kitchens, a living room and porch, and a queen-size bed in the bedroom. The one-bedroom units have ocean or garden views for the same price, while the studio has a garden view. Each unit has its own barbecue; daily linen service is provided. Guests are welcome to use the hot tub, Jacuzzi, and outdoor barbecue. Snorkeling equipment and boogie boards are provided free, along with beach towels. The Kukuiolono Golf Course is a 5-minute drive away, and Poipu Beach about 10 minutes; tennis courts and a park for jogging are nearby.

GARDEN ISLE COTTAGES, 2666 Puuholu Rd., Koloa, Kauai, HI 96756. Tel. 808/742-6717. 10 studios and apts. TV
$ Rates: $76–$90 studio; $102–$113 one-bedroom apt. on ocean; $130–$140 one-bedroom deluxe; $160–$184 two-bedroom apt. for four persons. No credit cards. **Parking:** Free.

An old Poipu favorite, this group of private cottages set in Hawaiian flower gardens offers true island ambience. The hospitable owners, Sharon and Robert Flynn (Bob is an artist), work hard at preserving the feeling of old Hawaii by using batiks, ethnic fabrics and furniture, and Bob's paintings and sculpture. There are two separate locations, both picturesque. One block away from a sandy snorkeling and sunning beach are the Sea Cliff Cottages, whose unique location—perched on a cliff over Kaloa Landing, where the Waikamo Stream meets the ocean—gives them an idyllic ambience; you can watch the sun come up over the water from your lanai. There are four one-bedroom apartments for two people, plus another deluxe one-bedroom to which can be added a bedroom and bath, accommodating four. There are also two Sea Cliff studio apartments. Hale Waipahu, located on the highest point in Poipu at Poipu Crater, offers a 360° view of mountains, ocean, sunrises, and sunsets. Your own private "lap pool" overlooks the Poipu coast. There's a studio and a charming one-bedroom apartment with open-beamed ceilings, latticed dining lanai, full kitchen, and bath. A smaller bedroom/bath suite is also available.

The office of Garden Isle Cottages is located in Robert Flynn's gallery and is open only from 9am to noon. Good restaurants are nearby, but remember that you'll need a car to get around here.

KOLOA LANDING COTTAGES, 2704B **Hoonani Rd., Koloa, Kauai, HI 96756. Tel. 808/742-1470.** Fax 808/332-9584. 2 cottages, 2 studios, 1 house. TV TEL

$ Rates: $50 (plus $20 clean-out fee) studio single or double; $70 (plus $40 clean-out fee) two-bedroom/two-bath cottage for one or two, $85 for three or four; $100 (plus $60 clean-out fee) main house (two bedrooms, two baths) for one to four people, $10 each for up to two additional guests per day. No credit cards. **Parking:** Free.

Many people dream of moving to an island, having a lovely home of their own, and renting out a handful of cottages in their garden. Hans and Sylvia Zeevat (he is Dutch, she is Dutch-Indonesian), who came to Hawaii from Holland, have realized that dream on Kauai and the result is five wonderful, reasonably priced accommodations for those lucky enough to secure them. The Zeevats are exceptional hosts, and they delight in treating their guests like family: They ply them with fresh fruit from their own trees, and give them tips on where to snorkel and what to feed the fish. They have two cottages and two studios: Spacious and tastefully decorated, they have open-beamed ceilings, ceiling fans, cross-ventilation, well-equipped kitchens (blenders, dishwashers, microwave ovens, mixers, etc.), cable TVs, and—hard to find in Poipu—telephones with their own private numbers! Guests can have barbecues out in the garden; restaurants and good swimming beaches are a short walk or drive away. Each cottage has two bedrooms (queen-size beds), two baths, and a lovely living room. Studios accommodate one or two people, and one of them has no steps so it's very convenient for a disabled person. Since the Zeevats have moved to a nearby town, their own main house is also now available as a vacation rental. The two-bedroom/two-bath house has a large living room, dining area, and family room, a deck with private barbecue, and a carport. There's a full kitchen with microwave oven. Six could settle in comfortably here.

PRINCE KUKIO CONDOMINIUMS, 5160 **Lawai Rd., Koloa, Kauai, HI 96756. Tel. 808/742-1409,** or toll-free 800/722-1409. 48 rms. TV

$ Rates: Apr 15–Dec 15, $59 studio; $69–$79 one-bedroom apt; $115 two-bedroom penthouse. Dec 16–Apr 14 $69 studio; $79–$89 one-bedroom apt; $125 two-bedroom penthouse. No credit cards. **Parking:** Free.

This is a longtime Poipu favorite. It was badly damaged by Hurricane Iniki, but now it's in full swing again. The nicely furnished apartments overlook either Prince Kuhio Park and the ocean on one side or a lovely pool and a garden on the other; there's a beach known for good snorkeling right across the road, and there are good swimming beaches nearby (the one we like best is in front of the Hotel Sheraton). The famed Beach House Restaurant is a few steps away. A variety of studios for two and one-bedroom apartments for up to four are offered, all fully equipped for housekeeping with kitchen and comfortable living space and private lanai. Two handsome two-bedroom penthouses for four are also available. The central barbecue is a popular spot, and this is the kind of place where it's easy to make friends. For reservations contact Prince Kuhio Rentals, P.O. 1060, Koloa, Kauai. HI 96756, or call them at the above phone numbers.

POIPU PLANTATION, 1792 **Pe'e Rd., Koloa, Kauai, HI 96756. Tel. 808/ 742-7038** or 742-6757, or toll free 800/733-1632. Fax 808/822-2723. 12 units. TV TEL

$ Rates: $80, $85, and $90 one-bedroom unit for two; $105 two-bedroom unit for two; $80–$90 bed-and-breakfast room. Each additional person $10 extra. **Parking:** Free.

Evie Warner and Al Davis, the very nice people who run the statewide Bed &

Breakfast Hawaii (see above), have built some very attractive vacation-rental units behind their house on their own tropical acre of land, just up the road from Poipu Beach Park, one of the best places to swim in this area. All the units are of good size, attractively furnished, and have tropical decor, ceiling fans, and excellent modern kitchens. Washers and dryers are outside. The units have all been rebuilt and redecorated since the hurricane.

The cheaper one-bedroom units are on the garden level, and the more expensive ones have ocean views. There are also several luxury duplexes with two bedrooms, two baths, even marble floors in the bathrooms. Evie and Al also run the Poipu Plantation Bed & Breakfast Inn right on the premises, offering three attractive rooms, each with private bath and TV; continental breakfast is included. The twin and queen rooms are $80, the king room is $90. There's a gazebo with hot tub and barbecue out in the garden, which is quite lovely, with its apple trees, blossoming plumerias, bougainvilleas, and gardenias. Evie and Al are friendly hosts and see to it that everybody is well cared for.

BED & BREAKFAST

GLORIA'S SPOUTING HORN BED & BREAKFAST, 4464 Lawai Beach Rd., Koloa, Kauai, HI 96756. Tel. 808/742-6995. 3 rms. TV, TEL

$ Rates (including breakfast): $120 single; $125 double. Each additional person $25 extra: one-night stay $20 extra. $25 extra Dec 15–Jan 5. Add $5 to rates if payment is by credit card. MC, V.

If your idea of bliss is a hammock strung between two coconut palms overlooking the pounding surf, this is the place for you. Gloria's is located on an idyllic rocky coastline within sight and sound of the surf and the famed Spouting Horn saltwater geyser, and the hammock is right out there, behind the house. Good swimming beaches are a short drive away. Gloria's original house was swept out to sea by Hurricane Iniki, but her new, better-than-ever place has now reopened. It's charmingly furnished in country pine, English walnut, and American oak antiques. Each room is oceanfront—just 30 feet from the surf—and boasts panoramic views with three walls of glass. Each has a TV/VCR, a wet bar with sink, a refrigerator, a microwave, a queen-size bed, and lovely furnishings. All three rooms have Japanese-style deep soaking tubs, plus separate showers. The Punana Aloha Room ("Love Nest") is a favorite for honeymooners, with a four-poster willow bed with a full canopy. Speaking of honeymoons, Gloria and her husband, Bob, who's a minister (among other things), can help arrange weddings, either right on the premises or in other island locations. Breakfast, served in the lovely dining room on fine china or out on the oceanside lanai, consists of a papaya boat filled with fresh, locally grown fruit, juice and beverages, and home-baked pastry or muffin. No children under 14, no pets, and smoking only on the lanai.

POIPU BED & BREAKFAST INN AND VACATION RENTALS, 2720 Hoonani Rd., Koloa, Kauai, HI 96756. Tel. 808/742-1146, or toll free 800/552-0095. 8 rms and suites; 4 apts, cottages and homes; one oceanfront condo.

$ Rates (including breakfast at B&B only): $60–$175 double. Rooms can be combined into two- or three-bedroom suites, from $170–$300; single occupancy $10 less; each additional person $20 extra; $10 more for stays of 1 night. AE, CB, DC, DISC, MC, V.

⭐ We'd have to call this place one of the most beautiful bed-and-breakfast establishments in the islands. Dottie Cichon, an artist herself and a collector of art, has lovingly renovated and restored a 1933 plantation house, and filled it with carousel horses, pine antiques, ornate white Victorian wicker furniture, handcrafts, and tropical splashes of color everywhere. Rooms are luxury all the way: Each has its own private bath (with either a whirlpool tub and separate shower or a tub-shower combination), cable color TV and VCR, and clock radio. Some have wet bars and refrigerators. Continental breakfast—fruits, juices, muffins, pastries, beverages—is served in the morning out on the lanai or in the splendid "great room"; later on, the "great room" is the scene for afternoon tea and for evening popcorn-and-movie gatherings. (Incidentally, while most such places provide breakfast *and* bed, this is the only one we know that will provide breakfast *in* bed—if you ask.) Tennis and pool privileges at the nearby Kiahuna Tennis Club are included in the price of all rooms, and numerous beaches are just around the bend.

Four rooms are available in the new B&B annex, even closer to Poipu Beach. The beautiful cathedral-ceilinged great room and plantation-style white lattice breakfast lanai have a lovely ocean view overlooking a lush tropical garden. One of the loveliest of the rooms is fully handicapped accessible. Two oceanfront suites, each with giant whirlpool tubs for two.

Although some are beyond our budget, Dottie also has a number of cottages for rent nearby and in Kalaheo; these range from a $60-a-night spacious one-bedroom unit with kitchenette to a super-luxury oceanfront two-bedroom/two-bath condominium at nearby Whaler's Cove, from $225. All are furnished in exquisite taste; some are as large as a complete home and could comfortably suit a family for a long stay.

Space does not permit us to detail all the offerings in Dottie's little "B&B empire," so contact her for further information.

VICTORIA PLACE, P.O. Box 930, Lawai, Kauai, HI 96765. Tel. 808/332-9300. 4 rms with private baths.

$ Rates (including breakfast): $55 Raindrop Room; $65 Calla Lily Room; $75 Shell Room; $95 Victoria's Other Secret. No credit cards. **Parking:** Free.

An 8-minute drive from the beautiful beaches of Poipu, Edee Seymour's place is a gem—a gem enhanced by the gracious hospitality and wonderful cooking of the host. It's back-to-back with the National Botanical Garden, which is no more than a stone's throw from the poolside breakfast lanai. Three of the guest rooms are located in one wing of the spacious, skylit home, opening directly through glass doors to the gardenlike pool area. The Raindrop Room is for single travelers only. The Shell Room has twin beds that can be put together to form a king-size bed, and it can become barrier-free with a portable wheelchair ramp; its private bathroom has a wheelchair-accessible shower. The Calla Lily Room has a queen-size bed, a gorgeous view of the pool, and, like the others, plenty of closet and bureau space, bookcases liberally filled, and teddy bears on the bed. The fourth room, Victoria's Other Secret, has its own entrance, a kitchen, a daybed and a California king-size bed on a loft above the main studio, a library of cookbooks, a double coffee maker, a huge walk-in closet, laundry facilities—everything! Breakfasts are special, maybe ginger and banana breads fresh from the oven, arrangements of tropical fruits presented on exquisite table settings with flowers everywhere. When you finish your breakfast feast, you can feast your eyes on Edee's glorious collection of shells and antiques. There's a library filled with almost as many books as the local library, and a TV room. Edee is happy to share her collection of restaurant menus and steer you to off-the-beaten-track fun. She can also help with car rentals, including hand-operated vehicles for the physically handicapped.

WESTERN KAUAI: KOKEE & WAIMEA
KOKEE

Kokee Lodge, Kokee State Park, P.O. Box 819, Waimea, Kauai, HI 96796. Tel. 808/335-6061. 12 cabins.

$ Rates: $35 or $45 cabin. DC, DISC, MC, V. **Parking:** Free.

Forty-five miles from Lihue, in Kokee State Park (just beyond Waimea Canyon), you'll find Kokee Lodge, 3,600 feet up in bracing mountain air. The cabins are owned by the state but are operated by a private firm, and the prices are low—a practice we'd like to see imitated all over Hawaii. This is a place only for those who have enough time to really linger in Kauai (on a two- or three-day trip a stay would be impractical, since the time and cost of driving to the other sights of the island would outweigh the savings here). The cabins vary in size from one large room, which sleeps three, to two-bedroom units that will accommodate seven. The cabins are rustic, furnished with refrigerators, stoves, hot showers, basic eating and cooking utensils, blankets, linens, and pillows. You can buy a pile of wood and make a fire in the wood stove when the night air gets nippy in this cooler northern Kauai that seems a world away from beaches and coconut palms.

Daytime activities at Kokee include driving or hiking on gorgeous trails and swimming in hidden freshwater pools. You can hunt boar, wild goat, and game birds, fish for trout in the nearby mountain streams, or just laze in the sun.

Undoubtedly, you'll see the magnificent *moa* (chickens) of Kokee on the grounds of the lodge. These are jungle fowl, descendants of birds carried to Hawaii centuries ago by the Polynesians in their outrigger canoes. The brightly plumed chickens, protected by the state, survive only here, in the mountains of Kauai; those on the other islands were destroyed by mongeese, which, somehow, never got to Kauai.

Kokee Lodge Restaurant observes irregular hours at this writing (inquire when you're there), but it's known for such local specialties as Portuguese bean soup, lilikoi pie, and the popular Kokee Lodge Chili. It also provides take-out orders and snacks for outdoor picnics, and for those wishing to cook, there's a simple grocery store on the premises. Bring your own supplies, however, if you're planning on cooking anything fancy. There's also a cocktail lounge and a well-stocked gift shop. Management advises making early reservations, since holiday weekends are very popular here, and so is the trout-fishing season in August and September. Maximum stay is five days.

WAIMEA

A Bed-and-Breakfast

COOK'S LANDING BED & BATH, 9918 Waimea Rd. (P.O. Box 1113), Kauai HI 96796. Tel. 808/338-1451.

$ Rates: $60–$70 single or double with breakfast; $50–$60 single or double without breakfast. Minimum stay 3 nights. No credit cards.

Those who would like to experience small-town life in Hawaii far from the tourist scene might enjoy this one. Just across the street from the post office in Waimea town, and at the base of Waimea Canyon, this is a tiny, private first-floor "mother-in-law's bed and bath," located in the home of Maggie and Eddie Taniguchi. A guest entrance at the back of the house leads to a bedroom and private bath, with double bed, ceiling fan, cable color TV, and clock radio. Guests can use the backyard covered patio with shared refrigerator/freezer and hibachi for barbecuing; they can also do light cooking in the kitchenette area of the room, which has a toaster, coffee maker, microwave oven, some cookware, and utensils. A black-sand beach is within walking distance, and very good beaches are a short drive away. No smoking allowed.

Worth the Extra Money

WAIMEA PLANTATION COTTAGES, 9600 Kaumualii Hwy., Waimea, HI 96796. Tel. 808/338-1625, or toll free 800/9-WAIMEA. Fax 808/338-1619 or 808/338-2338. 52 cottages. TV TEL

$ Rates: $95–$200 double. Minimum stay 3 nights (8 nights during holiday periods). DC, DISC, MC, V.

About 45 minutes from Lihue Airport is a place where time literally seems to have stood still. The workers' cottages from the old Waimea Plantation have been restored or, in the case of the structures that were beyond restoration, rebuilt, adhering to the original 1919 blueprints. They're nestled in a grove of gigantic old coconut palms, just steps away from a black sand beach from which you can watch the sun set over Niihau. The cottages are furnished with updated versions of the furniture that was really in the house (although the workers surely did not have the luxury of private telephones and remote-control color TVs, blenders, coffee makers, rice cookers, toasters, ceiling fans, and state-of-the-art plumbing). Several of the units have four-poster beds, faithful reproductions of the ones that used to be here. There are multiple windows in each unit, from which to enjoy the views of the mountains, the waterfalls, and the abundant banyan and fruit trees on the grounds. Each cottage has a sign identifying the former occupant and his job. There's a large swimming pool and barbecue area, and a 1920 tennis court has been renovated. The Grove Dining Room, very pleasant with its oceanfront location, serves all three meals, with plenty of luncheons in the $6.95 to $7.95 range, and dinner selections from $14.95 and up. There's a Hawaiian plate every night for just $13.95.

If you're planning a family reunion (and many people are holding them in Hawaii these days), this could be a perfect spot. Because there are a number of large cottages with as many as three to five bedrooms, each room could be available for $50 to $75. The staff can assist in planning reunions that are highly structured or very informal. Call for details.

READERS RECOMMEND

Camping in State and Country Parks. *"We stayed at Polihale State Park and Kokee State Park. One needs permits to camp at any state park. On Kauai, the permits are issued at the state building in Lihue, or one can write to Division of State Parks, 3060 Eiwa St., Room 306, Lihue, HI 96766-1875 (tel. 241-3446). Rangers checked our permits. To stay at county campgrounds, go to the county building in Lihue (tel. 241-6600). If it's after 5pm, go to the police station. The county permits are $3 per person per night; the state permits are free, but the office is open only Monday through Friday from 8am to 4pm and identification must be presented for each adult."*—Rebecca Kurtz, Anchorage, Alaska.

THE NORTH SHORE: PRINCEVILLE, HANALEI, HAENA

PRINCEVILLE & HANALEI

Think of Princeville, on the north shore of Kauai, and you think of luxury living, of championship golf and tennis amid a green sweep of mountains and valleys. You don't think of budget accommodations here, but we did find a few needles in the haystack; some of the lowest prices in Princeville are at a B&B described below. Two low-priced condominium resorts in this area are currently closed, due to Hurricane Iniki. *Note:* If you want ocean swimming, choose this area only in summer. In winter, high surf and treacherous currents make the ocean dangerous.

HALE HO'O MAHA, P.O. Box 422, Kilauea, Kauai, HI 96754. Tel. 808/ 828-1341, or toll free 800/851-0291 in the U.S. mainland and Canada. 3 rms (1 with bath). TEL

$ Rates (including breakfast): $55–$70 single or double. MC, V. **Parking:** Free.

Toby and Kirby Guyer-Searles enjoy sharing their magnificent plantation-style home in its entirety with their guests. Set in the middle of five lush mountain acres, the house is minutes away from fine sand beaches, rivers, waterfalls, hiking trails, and just a minute from a world-class, 45-hole golf course. A short drive leads to a natural private swimming hole enclosed by lava rocks, where waves break over one side and create a Jacuzzi-like effect. The home has three bedrooms. The Pineapple Room has a seven-foot round bed, a full private marble bath, color TV, and a private entrance off the lanai. The Mango Room has two queen-size beds and color TV and shares a marble bath with the Papaya Room, which has a queen-size bed. Guests have full kitchen privileges and use of surf and boogie boards, beach mats, washer-dryer, and gas barbecue grill. A continental breakfast that always includes freshly baked breads and muffins is served in the dining room each morning. The handsome living room, with its wood-burning fireplace, Hawaiian and South Pacific artifacts, saltwater aquarium, and color cable TV, is a popular gathering spot. Smoking and social drinking are acceptable. Ask Kirby and Toby to show you the exquisite feather and satin leis they make. They sometimes take guests on trips to remote areas that require a four-wheel-drive vehicle, and Toby, a certified diver, often takes guests out to explore Kauai beneath the waters.

Worth the Extra Money

THE CLIFFS AT PRINCEVILLE, P.O. Box 1005, Hanalei, HI 96714. Tel. 808/826-6219, or toll free 800/367-7052. Fax 808/826-2140. 220 apts. TV TEL
$ Rates: $125–$155 one-bedroom apt; $155–$205 one-bedroom plus loft. AE, MC, V.
Parking: Free.

The largest condo complex in the area, The Cliffs is set amid graceful lawns and gardens and is perched atop cliffs overlooking the ocean far below. It offers as much peace, privacy, sports, or excitement as one would wish. Facilities include four tennis courts, a putting green, a large pool with Jacuzzi, and a recreation pavilion with a wet bar and a huge fireplace. All the suites are perfect little houses that have been decorated in excellent taste and are fully carpeted, beautifully and individually furnished in bamboo and oak, with oak doors, complete equipped kitchens, and cable TVs. These suites can be divided to provide the following possible combinations: a one-bedroom/two-bath unit for up to four, or a one-bedroom/two-bath unit with a loft for up to six. The Princeville Makai Golf Course, designed by Robert Trent Jones, is right at hand; the sandy beach at Hanalei is about a five-minute drive; and opportunities for horseback riding, surfing, windsurfing, scuba diving, and much more are all close by.

HANALEI BAY RESORT, 5380 Honoiki St. (P.O. Box 220), Hanalei, HI 96714. Tel. 808/826-6522, or toll free 800/827-4427. FAX 808/826-6680. 220 rms; 50 suites. A/C TV TEL
$ Rates: $130–$220 double; $240–$270 two-bedroom suite; $350–$460 two-bedroom suite with kitchen. CB, AE, DC, MC, V. **Parking:** Free.

This is the Hawaii of everyone's dreams: an oceanside resort surrounded by waterfalls and lush green mountains in a spectacular setting. Its lobby and outstanding Bali Hai Restaurant are on the top level, and low-slung buildings wind down 20 acres to the white sands of Hanalei Beach below. The center pond in the porte-cochère drops into a waterfall that cascades into a free-form, sandy-bottom swimming pool with a natural sand "shoreline." There is also good ocean swimming, a longish walk or a short jitney ride away. And there's fantastic hiking close by.

Buildings are named for flowers. Units are exquisitely furnished with island living in mind. Tropical bamboo and warm colors taken from the beautiful gardens have been used in the design of the interiors. Hotel rooms include coffee makers and refrigerators; large suites have full electric kitchens. There are eight tennis courts free for guests' use (three lighted for night play), plus a full pro shop and teaching programs; the 27-hole Princeville "Makai" golf course, rated number one in Hawaii, at which guests get a discount, is adjacent to the property. There are environmental lectures weekly, a Hawaiian choir performing Sunday nights, and jazz jam sessions Sunday afternoons in the Happy Talk lounge.

Bed-and-Breakfast in Hanalei

BED, BREAKFAST, AND BEACH, at Hanalei Bay, P.O. Box 748, Hanalei. HI 96714. Tel. 808/826-6111. 3 rms, 1 efficiency apt.
$ Rates (including breakfast): $60–$80 single or double. Each additional person $15 extra. No credit cards.

Carolyn Barne's stylish house is in a suburban neighborhood just 100 yards from Hanalei Bay, wonderful for summer swimming. The second-floor wraparound lanai is the perfect place for viewing sunsets over the ocean and sighting rainbows and waterfalls. The house is beautifully decorated with American oak antiques and Hawaiian memorabilia. Rooms, each with a queen-size bed, fan, and private bath, are romantically furnished with calico-print wallpapers and carefully selected linens and comforters. Honeymooners love this place! Also available is a large studio apartment with a private entrance and an efficiency kitchen. A continental breakfast, island style, is served each morning on the lanai; it consists of a smoothie or juice, fresh island fruit, pancakes with homemade coconut syrup, fresh-baked muffins or bread, and coffee or tea. No smoking. Well-behaved children only; crib available.

HAENA

CAMP NAUE, YMCA OF KAUAI, P.O. Box 1786, Lihue, Kauai, HI 96766.
Tel. 808/246-9090 or 246-4411. 42 bunks.
$ Rates: $12 bed; $10 tent space for one person, $7 each additional person. No credit
cards.
Hikers, backpackers, campers, take note: If you're about to hike the Na Pali trail
and need a place to relax and get a good night's sleep before or after, the YMCA of
Kauai has a perfect solution for you. The camp is 1½ miles from the trailhead at
Kalalau, right on the beach at Haena, in an idyllic setting under the ironwood and
kumani trees. Two bunkhouses situated on the crest of the beach are divided into
four separate areas, each with 10 to 12 bunk beds; the facilities are coed, but there
are separate baths for men and women, and hot showers. Bring your own sleeping
bag, as the camp does not provide linens or towels. There's a covered beachfront
pavilion, a campfire area with picnic tables, and one of the island's best beaches—in
summer—for swimming, snorkeling, and surfing (in winter, the ocean is very rough
here). There is no refrigeration (the kitchen is for group use only), and if you need
food supplies, it's best to stock up on them in Hanalei. You can also stop in at
Jungle Bob's in Ching Young Village for backpacking supplies.
   Camp Naue is usually filled with large groups, but often has space for walk-in
visitors. They don't take reservations, but if you call their Lihue office at 246-9090
not more than two weeks in advance, they'll advise you of the likelihood of getting
space here. On weekends, you can call the caretaker at the camp at 826-6419.

3. WHERE TO EAT

Dining on Kauai is always fun and can range from a bowl of saimin at a favorite local hangout, to spa cuisine at the top luxury resort—with many stops in between.

LIHUE & ENVIRONS

Lihue has some excellent budget restaurants frequented mostly by locals, and you'll
be glad you joined them.

LIHUE
Meals for Less Than $10

DAIRY QUEEN KAUAI, 4302 Rice St., Tel. 245-2141.
   Cuisine: AMERICAN/LOCAL. **Reservations:** Required for large groups only.
$ Prices: Appetizers $2–$4; main courses $4.35–$14.94. No credit cards.
   Open: Mon–Thurs 7am–9 or 10pm, Fri–Sat 7am–10 or 11pm. Closed Sun.
Locals, visitors, and condo dwellers have all discovered that the Dairy Queen hits
the spot for an inexpensive local-style meal. The menu is the same all day and lists
about 20 dishes under $6; served with rice, mashed potatoes, or fries, and a choice
of either soup or green salad, they include teriyaki steak, charbroiled teri butterfish,
pork chops with brown gravy, and beef stew. Dinner specials concentrate on seafood
and steak: mahimahi, seafood platter, shrimp scampi, and prime rib, for $7.50 to
$14.95. Also available are burritos, tacos, chili, saimin, salads, and several sub sand-
wiches, including a vegetarian one. Kids will love the soda-fountain desserts. Breakfasts are among the most reasonable in town: omelets $3 to $3.75 and local-style
breakfasts like the Local Boy—two eggs, four pieces of Portuguese sausage, two
scoops of rice, and coffee—all for $3.95.

HAMAMURA'S SAIMIN STAND, 2956 Kress St. Tel. 245-3271.
   Cuisine: LOCAL/JAPANESE.
$ Prices: Main courses $2.25–$5. No credit cards.

Open: Mon–Thurs 10am–2am. Fri–Sat 10am–4am. Sun 10am–midnight.

Locals have sung the praises of this beloved Kauai institution and gobbled up its saimim for as long as anybody can remember. It's a very simple spot, a trifle weather-beaten on the outside; inside are three rectangular counters with stools. Slide onto one, order anything on the small menu, and you're in for a great taste treat as well as one of the cheapest meals on Kauai. Our usual choice is the saimin special at $4—that's a large bowl of saimin topped with vegetables, eggs, and wontons—filling and delicious. Order a stick of tender barbecued chicken or beef, too (80¢), and finish up with their lilikoi chiffon pie at $1.10. All in all, quite a meal for $5.90. *Local color department:* Note the sign that reads, "Please do not stick gum under counter. Thank you."

KAUAI CHOP SUEY, in Pacific Ocean Plaza, 3051 Rice St., No. 107. Tel. 245-8790.
Cuisine: CANTONESE. **Reservations:** Not required.
$ Prices: Appetizers $3.75–$5.75; main courses $5.75–$8.75. No credit cards.
Open: Lunch Tues–Sat 11am–2pm; dinner Tues–Sun 4:30–9pm.

Despite the restaurant's unimaginative name, it serves superior food, all in the Cantonese style. There are about 75 items on the menu, at least 40 of them under $6. There's something for everyone: roast duck, egg foo yong, squid with vegetables, shrimp with broccoli, lemon chicken, stuffed tofu, sweet-and-sour pork, or char sui (an island favorite). And the soups—seaweed, scallop, abalone—are quite special. The place is large and comfortable, decorated in typical Chinese style. Large parties are seated at round tables with revolving lazy Susan centerpieces, the better to sample all the delicacies. The locals rave about this place—and so do we.

KUN-JA, 4252 Rice St., at the corner of Hardy. Tel. 245-8792.
Cuisine: KOREAN. **Reservations:** Not accepted.
$ Prices: Main courses $4.75–$6.25. No credit cards.
Open: Mon–Fri 10am–8pm. Sat 10:30am–2pm. Closed Sun.

Simple, tidy, with just a few decorations, Kun-Ja is another local eatery where you can eat a delicious meal for around $6. Owner Kun-Ja Woo greets you with a smile, takes your order, and prepares your meal. She does all the usual Korean dishes, such as mun doo kook so (dumpling and noodle soup), kalbi (broiled short ribs), and pul koko (barbecued beef), plus a few specialties of her own, including a hot-and-spicy kimchee soup. Kun-Ja's Special is barbecued beef and chicken and pork—a nice little meal in itself, since it's served with soup and several little dishes of mixed vegetables, sprouts, and rice. Should you want to have dinner here, remember that the restaurant closes early.

LIHUE BARBECUE INN, 2982 Kress St. Tel. 245-2921.
Cuisine: JAPANESE/AMERICAN. **Reservations:** Not required.
$ Prices: Main courses $7.95–$13.95. No credit cards.
Open: Breakfast and lunch Mon–Sat 7:30am–1:30pm; dinner Mon–Thurs 5–8pm; Fri–Sat 4:30–closing.

You'll know why the Barbecue Inn has been considered one of the best local restaurants in town for more than 50 years when you have a look at the low prices on the menu, which lists more than 20 complete dinners, most under $13, including soup or fresh fruit cup, tossed green salad, vegetable, beverages, and dessert. Typical main courses are shrimp tempura, baked mahimahi, broiled teriyaki pork chops, corned beef brisket with cabbage, and chow mein chicken with spareribs. Fresh fish is served when available. Complete lunches are also a good deal—there are about 20 choices, such as a seafood platter, Chinese chicken salad, a mahimahi sandwich, or teriyaki chicken, all for $6.95 to $8.95. The menu changes daily, but whatever you have here will most likely be good—especially the freshly made pies (can you believe $1)? and the homemade bread. Try their frozen chi chis—among the best on the island. One of the most appealing inexpensive restaurants in Lihue, the Barbecue is patronized mostly by local families.

RESTAURANT KIIBO, 2991 Umi St. Tel. 245-2650.
Cuisine: JAPANESE. **Reservations:** Recommended.

$ Prices: Main courses $4.25–$19. No credit cards.
Open: Lunch Mon–Fri 11am–1:30pm; dinner Mon–Sat 5:30–9pm. **Closed:** Holidays.

★ The food is outstanding at this tiny, comfortable, nicely furnished restaurant. The pretty sushi bar up front gives way to a small, spare dining room with 10 or so tables, and three tatami seating areas on a raised platform. Everything on the menu is à la carte, even the rice—that way, says the manager, you only order exactly what you wish to eat. We enjoyed our $7 chicken sukiyaki and $5.25 beef teriyaki to the accompaniment of soft Japanese music in the background. Other good choices include the tempura at $6.25, and the donburi, huge bowls of rice topped with sukiyaki or teriyaki or something equally interesting, for $5.50 to $10.50. A child's dinner is available at $6.25. Lunch offers similar dishes at lower prices. Chances are good that you'll be the only haoles at the Kiibo; it's a local favorite, off the usual tourist beat.

TIP TOP CAFE, 3173 Akahi St. Tel. 245-2343 or 245-2333.
Cuisine: CHINESE/AMERICAN. **Reservations:** Recommended.
$ Prices: Main courses $4.50–$6.95. No credit cards.
Open: Daily 6:30am–2pm.
Located just north of the Lihue Shopping Center, this air-conditioned family eatery is a local favorite. The prices are modest, and while the food is not of gourmet quality, it's dependable. We often have breakfast here (pancakes are served all day—macadamia-nut ones, at $5, are delicious). Lunch features local favorites like oxtail soup; beef stew, breaded mahimahi, and loco moco with two eggs, all served with vegetables and a choice of rice or fries. Bento lunches, for take-out, are $5.75. As of this writing, Tip Top was not serving dinner; inquire when you're there. Pick up some homemade jams from the gift department or some macadamia-nut cookies from the Tip Top Bakery. Upstairs, the Tip Top Inn offers modest motel rooms for around $50 a double.

READERS RECOMMEND

Dani's Restaurant, *4201 Rice St., Lihue (tel. 245-4991). "Dani's Restaurant in Lihue was a delight. Not the usual tourist fare. Rice was served with breakfast steak and eggs for $5.50. Coffee always there. Friendly, folksy people."*—Jon and Andy McCormick, Port Allen, British Columbia, Canada.

Meals for Around $25

CAFE PORTOFINO, 3501 Rice St., Nawiiwili. Tel. 245-2121.
Cuisine: ITALIAN. **Reservations:** Recommended.
$ Prices: Appetizers $5.75–$7.75; main courses $11.50–$18.75. AE, MC, V.
Open: Lunch Mon–Fri 11am–2pm; dinner daily 5–10pm.
One of the more stylish spots in town, Café Portofino is the place for an elegant and not overly priced Italian meal. Windows all around the dining room and a big lanai overlooking Kalapaki Beach and Nawiliwili Harbor also afford a splendid view of the surrounding luxuriant mountains. The ambiance is decidedly romantic: candles and flowers on the tables, opera music (Italian, of course!) on the stereo, sparkly glassware and silver, and abundant greenery hanging from the ceiling. We like the prosciutto and papaya (only in Hawaii) among the antipasti, the traditional Caesar among the salads, and, among the pastas, the linguine alla puttanesca. Rabbit in white wine, osso bucco in orange sauce, and sweetbreads in a white cream sauce are some of the signature specialty items. Desserts vary daily, but always include freshly made gelatin and sorbets.

KUKUI GROVE

Kauai's multimillion-dollar shopping center, Kukui Grove, just outside Lihue on Hi. 50 toward Poipu Beach, has several attractive budget eateries. In addition to the following restaurant, there are several good snack shops for everything from Chinese food at **Ho's Chinese Kitchen** to "local grinds" at **Joni Hana**. You can "take advantage of" Filipino dishes at Sidewalk Café. Or try **Sumo's Restaurant** for traditional Japanese food, including a sushi bar and karaoke on the weekends.

SI CISCO'S MEXICAN CANTINA & RESTAURANT, in Kukui Grove Shopping Center. Tel. 246-1563.
  Cuisine: MEXICAN. **Reservations:** Not required.
$ **Prices:** Appetizers $4.95–$7.95; main courses $9.95–$16.95. DISC, MC, V.
  Open: Mon–Sat 11am–10pm, Sun 11:30am–9pm.
Probably the most popular specialty restaurant at Kukui Grove is Si Cisco's, in an attractive indoor-outdoor setting; many plants, stained-glass lanterns, ceiling fans, stucco walls, cozy booths. You can dine leisurely here on Mexican and American favorites. Combination plates run $10.95 to $12.95. Don't pass up the margaritas; a 60-ounce pitcher is $15.

KILOHANA PLANTATION

GAYLORD'S, Hwy. 50, 1 mile southwest of Lihue. Tel. 245-9593.
  Cuisine: HAWAII REGIONAL. **Reservations:** Recommended for dinner.
$ **Prices:** Appetizers $4.95–$8.95; main courses $14.95–$23.95.
  Open: Lunch daily Mon–Sat 11am–3:30pm; dinner daily 5–9pm; brunch Sat–Sun 9am–3pm.
One of the nicest restaurants to open on Kauai in many a tropical moon is Gaylord's, at Kilohana, the legendary plantation estate of the 1930s that has been lovingly restored and is open to the public. Gaylord's is a courtyard restaurant facing a manicured green lawn around which tables are arranged on three sides. The restaurant is done in whites, pinks, and greens, with soft-cushioned chairs and fresh flowers on every table. Dinner at Gaylord's *is* pricey, but at lunchtime you can have a first-class dining experience for a modest tab—and many agree that the food is better at lunchtime. We like both Gaylord's Papaya Runneth Over, island papaya stuffed with delicate bay shrimp (or salmon or chicken) salad, at $8.95; and the bay-shrimp-and-avocado sandwich on homemade bread, also at $8.95. Baby back ribs with onion rings ($10.95) and the seafood quesadilla ($7.95) are signature lunch choices. At dinnertime, you can stay on the low side of the menu, with selections like angel-hair pasta with sautéed prawns, seafood linguine, and roasted chicken ($14.95 to $16.95), or come early, before 6:30pm, to enjoy the baby back ribs for $14.95 instead of $16.95. Homemade desserts, such as Kilohana mud pie, French silk, and double-chocolate mousse, all are chocoholic treats. The brunch menu offers cheese blintzes, eggs Benedict, Belgian waffles, and the like for $9.95 to $13.95. A lovely choice.

HANAMAULU

HANAMAULU RESTAURANT AND TEA HOUSE, Hi. 56. Tel. 245-2511.
  Cuisine: JAPANESE/CHINESE. **Reservations:** Recommended.
$ **Prices:** Main courses $11–$17. MC. V.
  Open: Lunch Tues–Fri 11am–1pm; dinner Tues–Sun 4:30–9pm.
  This old-time favorite is known for its Japanese garden, beautifully landscaped with stone pagodas, pebbled paths, and a pond filled with carp. We suggest that you call a day in advance and reserve one of the charming *ozashiki*, or teahouse rooms; you take off your shoes and sit on the floor at a long, low table, and the shoji screens are opened to face the lighted garden. (You may be able to get one of the rooms without reservations, but it's best to call ahead.) The food is excellent and inexpensive; the Chinese and Japanese plate lunches are a good value at $6.50. Special dinner platters are $12.50, and you can feast on a veritable Eastern banquet for about $15 per person. An excellent sushi bar and robatayaki are attractions here. The Miyaki family are cordial hosts.

THE EASTERN SHORE

This is the most populous part of the island, with many budget restaurants.

WAILUA & KAPAA

Meals for Less Than $15

ALOHA DINER, in Waipouli Complex, 4-971 Kuhio Hwy. Tel. 822-3851.
   Cuisine: HAWAIIAN. **Reservations:** Not accepted.
$ Prices: Main courses $5.50–$10.50. No credit cards.
   Open: Breakfast and lunch Tues–Sat 10:30am–pm; dinner Tues–Sat 5:30–9pm.
If you've developed a taste for real Hawaiian food, you can satisfy it here in plain surroundings. Best bets are the lunch specials for $5.50 to $7, including kalua pig or laulau, lomi-lomi salmon, rice or poi; and the more elaborate dinner specials for $8.50 to $10.50—including kalua pig or laulau, lomi-lomi salmon, chicken lau, poi or rice, and haupia (coconut pudding). Typical à la carte choices, at $3.75, include beef stew, squid lau, and other favorites.

BUBBA'S, 1384 Kuhio Hwy. Tel. 823-0069.
   Cuisine: SNACKS. **Reservations:** Not accepted.
$ Prices: $2.25–$5.50. No credit cards.
   Open: Sun–Thurs 10:30am–10pm, Fri–Sat 10:30am–2am.
Bubba's calls itself an old-fashioned hamburger stand that "cheats tourists and drunks and attorneys." Don't you believe it! The burgers, hot dogs, chicken burgers, fish-and-chips that you get here are really good and really cheap. You dine right on the sidewalk at polished wooden picnic tables with benches. The friendly proprietors know everyone who passes by, the food dispensed from their kitchen counter is plentiful and tasty, and the friendly spirit is contagious.

BULL SHED, 796 Kuhio Hwy. Tel. 822-3791.
   Cuisine: AMERICAN. **Reservations:** Not accepted.
$ Prices: Main courses $11.95–$18.50 ($25.50 for steak and lobster). AE, MC, V.
   Open: Dinner daily 5:30–10pm; cocktails from 4:30 pm.
A favorite of steak and seafood lovers, the Bull Shed, just north of Coconut Plantation, behind the Mokihana of Kauai condos, is a Kauai tradition. The atmosphere is great: a large airy, wooden-frame building overlooking the ocean, so close to it that waves wash up against the sea wall. If you're watching your budget or your waistline, you can make do with visits to the superb salad bar (salad bar alone is $6.95). Or splurge on some of the specialties, including prime rib, garlic tenderloin, yakitori, shrimp, scallops, and a variety of Hawaiian fish. The price of the main courses includes steamed rice and a trip to the salad bar. The restaurant is apt to be crowded, so get there early; prime rib, the house favorite for which many people make a special trip, can run out early on.

KING AND I, 4-901 Kuhio Hwy., in Waipouli Shopping Plaza. Tel. 822-1642.
   Cuisine: THAI/VEGETARIAN. **Reservations:** Recommended.
$ Prices: Appetizers $5.25–$8.95; main courses $5.95–$8.95. AE, DC, MC, V.
   Open: Dinner Mon–Thurs 4:30–9:30pm, Fri–Sat 4:30–10pm.
The King and I is a find. It's a small, family-run establishment, with crisp white tablecloths, nice paintings on the wall, greenery, orchids, Thai sculpture—a gentle atmosphere. The family grows all their own herbs and spices. The food is exceptionally good, and the prices are easy to take. Start with one of the appetizers, like the spring rolls or stuffed chicken wings, then have a soup (we like the Siam chicken-coconut soup) and a main dish, perhaps the garlic shrimp, the Siam eggplant with chicken, or one of the curries—like yellow curry with shrimp. (Watch out, though: Those curries can be hot, unless you tell

your server you'd like them mild.) Vegetarians have a choice of 13 good dishes. Now for dessert: How about banana with coconut milk, followed by Thai iced coffee with milk? Super!

KOUNTRY KITCHEN, 1485 Kuhio Hwy. Tel. 822-3511.
  Cuisine: AMERICAN/LOCAL. **Reservations:** Not required.
$ Prices: $4–$8.50.
  Open: Breakfast daily 5:30am–11pm; lunch daily 11am–1:30pm.

Kountry Kitchen is an old standby in Kapaa, with an atmosphere like that of an old-fashioned Midwest family restaurant. It's certainly one of the most popular places on this side of the island for breakfast: don't be surprised if you see a line at the door. However, service is fast, so you generally won't have to wait more than 5 or 10 minutes. Sumptuous build-your-own omelets complemented by fresh-baked cornbread and crispy golden hash browns are favorites, along with buttermilk and banana pancakes. These are accompanied by incredibly rich cups of coffee. Lunch is fun, too, with fresh local fish when available, super sandwiches, and burgers with steak-cut french fries. Kountry fried chicken and chef's salads are also favorites.

Note: The same management also runs Duane's Ono Charburgers in Anahola, a hamburger stand with a cult following all over the USA. You may see movie stars eating their "Gourmet Burgers."

MICHELLE'S CAFE & BAKERY, 1384 Kuhio Hwy. Tel. 823-6008.
  Cuisine: MEDITERRANEAN/VEGETARIAN/SOUTHWESTERN. **Reservations:** Not accepted.
$ Prices: Appetizers $3.75–$5.95; main courses $8.95–$12.95. No credit cards.
  Open: Breakfast and lunch Mon–Fri 7:30am–5pm, Sat 7:30am–3pm, dinner Fri–Sat 6–9:30pm.

Michelle O'Hearn, a talented California chef who apprenticed in Bay Area restaurants, moved to Kauai a few years back and along with husband, Nicholas Andersson, opened this nifty little place, small and cozy. Michelle is in the kitchen early in the morning, baking wonderful European breads (pumpkin seed, olive and basil, herb and cheese are a few specialties) and pastries that bring folks in early to shop and have a light breakfast: freshly squeezed juices, espresso, burritos ($3.95), and croissants with scrambled eggs and cheese ($2.95), sandwiches on homemade breads and focaccia are made fresh every morning. She does different lunch specials every day—usually vegetarian dishes like pesto fettuccine, polenta lasagne, calzones, perhaps a peanut-based West African stew—as well as chicken, turkey, and fish dishes; most are priced between $3.75 and $6.95. The ahi burger at $6.75 is very popular. Friday and Saturday evenings, magic happens at dinnertime, too, when Michelle whips up dishes like pasta primavera, New Orleans gumbo Sante Fe style, ahi with papaya salsa, and more, accompanied by tapenades, salads, and homemade desserts.

NORBERTO'S EL CAFE, 1375 Kuhio Hwy. Tel. 822-3362.
  Cuisine: MEXICAN/VEGETARIAN. **Reservations:** Not required.
$ Prices: Appetizers $2.50–$6.50; main courses $7–$12.95. AE, MC, V.
  Open: Dinner daily 5:30–9pm.

Norberto's has been a local favorite since 1977. The attractive, two-level dining room is decorated in Mexican style, and the food is as tasty as ever. Norberto's always cooks with fresh ingredients, does not use lard or any other animal fats (so vegetarians can feel comfortable here), and offers excellent value. Don't worry about breaking the budget, as complete dinners are reasonably priced and include soup, vegetables, refried beans, and Spanish rice; there's plenty of chips and hot salsa on the table to go with your margaritas or beer. The steak or chicken fajitas are just about our favorites, but olés, too, for the rellenos Tampico and the nifty Mex-Mix Plate: That's a chicken chimichanga, a chicken taquito, and an enchilada with Spanish rice and beans, all for $12.95. All dishes can be served vegetarian style if you ask. Be sure to try their taro-leaf enchiladas! If you have any room left, top your meal off with a piece of rum cake or chocolate-cream pie, both homemade and delicious. A good family choice.

ONO-FAMILY RESTAURANT, 4-1292 Kuhio Hwy. Tel. 822-1710.
Cuisine: AMERICAN. **Reservations:** Not required.
$ Prices: Main courses $3.65–$13. AE, MC, V.
Open: Breakfast and lunch daily 7am–2pm; dinner Mon–Sat 6–9pm.

Ono means "delicious" in Hawaiian, and this restaurant in the old Kapaa town lives up to its name. Pewter plates and fancy cookware hang on the wood-paneled walls, and European and Early American antiques and paintings add to the charm. This is a family-owned operation, and it shows in the care and attention that the owners lavish on their guests, especially senior citizens and children; many come back year after year because of that warm welcome. Omelets are featured at breakfast, and so are Canterbury eggs (grilled English muffins topped with turkey, ham, veggies, eggs, and cheese), at $6.25, and quite a way to start the day. Their $4.95 fish sandwich, with vegetables, sprouts, and Cheddar cheese on grilled Branola bread, is a meal in itself; super burgers cost $3.95 to $7.25; and for the health conscious, there is a variety of buffalo burgers, which have 70% less fat and 50% less cholesterol) than beef and taste just fine—they're $5.50 to $6.75. Be sure to try their Portuguese bean soup; it's an island classic. A variety of fresh fish meals are served daily, along with chicken and beef dishes. The price of a main course includes Portuguese bean soup or tossed salad, rice pilaf or fries, fresh sautéed vegetables, and Branola whole-wheat bread. There's a special menu for children. Note that the restaurant is closed between 2 and 6pm.

PAPAYA'S CAFE, 4-831 Kuhio Hwy., in Kauai Village, near Safeway. Tel. 823-0191.
Cuisine: NATURAL FOODS. **Reservations:** Not required.
$ Prices: Appetizers $2–$4; main courses $5–$9. MC, V.
Open: Daily 8am–10pm.

⭐ Lovers of natural foods need seek no further. They can find everything they need at this café adjacent to the huge Papaya's Natural Foods store. The food is absolutely delicious. At lunch you could have something from the burger bar (nutty burger, tempeh burger, grilled chicken teriyaki burger, or grilled fish burger, $4.75 to $5.95), or go with a simple soup and salad meal for $3.75, a combination plate (a choice of any three salads at $6.75), or a grilled fish plate at $8.50. From 4pm on, they offer three made-to-order dinner specials—a fish dish, a chicken dish, and a pasta—all cooked with Northern Italian flavors, and served with vegetarian Caesar salad and freshly baked garlic bread. Organically grown fruits and vegetables, mostly from local farms, are used whenever possible. Save room for some good desserts and for favorites from the espresso bar: cappuccino, lattes, mochas, and iced coffees. Call to find out if they're serving Sunday brunch: that's a special treat, offering strawberry-stuffed French toast and Belgian blue-corn waffles, just to mention a few possibilities. There's outdoor seating under umbrellaed tables, and more seats inside. They'll happily pack a picnic lunch to go.

PERRY'S SMORGY, in the Kauai Beach Boy Hotel, 4-484 Kuhio Hwy. Tel. 822-3111.
Cuisine: BUFFETS. **Reservations:** Not accepted.
$ Prices (including tax): Breakfast buffet $5.16; lunch buffet $6.20; dinner buffet $8.28; Sun brunch $8.28. AE, MC, V.
Open: Breakfast Mon–Sat 7–10:30am; lunch Mon–Sat 11am–2:30pm; dinner daily 5–9pm; brunch Sun 11am–2:30pm.

S If you've been to Honolulu, you know the great value and dining to be had at Perry's Smorgy restaurants. Perry's in Kauai has a glorious location overlooking the water. The dining room, which has both chairs and tables and booths, is enormous; the buffet tables are laden with goodies; and the price is always right. The breakfast bonanza features all you want of fresh fruits, juices, smoked ham and sausage, eggs, hotcakes, french toast, pastries, and wonderful Kona coffee. Lunch entitles you to unlimited fried chicken, mahimahi, beef stew, spaghetti, and garlic bread, plus plentiful helpings from the Orchid salad bar. Dinner includes a hand-carved round of beef, golden fried shrimp, mahimahi amandine, southern-style chicken, spaghetti, and garlic bread, plus the salad bar. Daily island specials—Hawaiian, Chinese, Japanese, American—are offered at lunch and dinner. All meals include beverage; lunch and dinner also include dessert. This is a super choice for families.

RESTAURANT KINTARO, 4-370 Kuhio Hwy., between Coco Palms and the Coconut Plantation. Tel. 822-3341.

Cuisine: JAPANESE. **Reservations:** Recommended.
$ Prices: Dinner $10.95–$26.95. AE, DC, JCB, MC, V.
Open: Dinner only, Mon–Sat 5:30–9:30pm.

Exquisite is the word for the dining experience at this sparkling bright restaurant, authentically Japanese down to the prettily wrapped chopsticks on the table. The rather bland exterior does not even suggest the harmonious Japanese scene inside: kites and kimonos on the walls, blond woods, shoji screens, a long sushi bar from which the chefs turn out tender marvels. Several complete dinners run $12.50 to $14.95 and include a variety of delicious small dishes. First you are served chilled buckwheat noodles in a flavorful sauce, presented on a *zora*, a wooden box with bamboo top. Next, also served on traditional wooden platters, is miso soup, rice, Japanese pickled vegetables, and your main course—it could be the delicious chicken yakitori (boneless broiled chicken, onion, bell pepper, and teriyaki sauce and salad) or salmon yaki. Or it could be a tasty tempura combination. Kintaro is justifiably proud of its teppan cuisine, including oysters, steak, lobster, and fresh island fish with scallops, for $13.95 to $26.95. Be sure to have the green-tea ice cream for dessert. A pot of green tea accompanies your meal. There are various sushi and sashimi combinations for appetizers or for those who wish to eat at the sushi bar.

SIZZLER STEAK, SEAFOOD, SALAD RESTAURANT, in Wailua Shopping Plaza, 4361 Kuhio Hwy. Tel. 822-7404.

Cuisine: AMERICAN. **Reservations:** Not required.
$ Prices: Main courses $6–$16.50. AE, CB, DC, MC, V.
Open: Daily 6am–10pm.

Located across from the Kinipopo Shopping Village, Sizzler is one of the most popular budget restaurants in Kauai. It's a semi–self-service operation. You place your order at the counter and pay for it as soon as you come in, then you sit back at your table while your server brings you your food and serves you coffee. The best feature is the fresh soup, salad, and fruit-salad bar combined with the pasta and tostada bar, with luscious papayas and avocados grown a few trees away, delicious pastas, protein salads, breads, rolls, and sweets. You could easily make a complete meal of this alone: It's $7.99 at lunch, $8.99 at dinner. However, most people opt for the meat and fish dishes; the steak, always excellent, starts at $6.99. Fresh local game fish is featured whenever it's available. Breakfast is another bargain meal: $6.99 for eggs Benedict, $2.99 for french toast. On Saturday, Sunday, and holidays, there's a terrific Breakfast Bar at $8.99, including breakfast specialties and the salad bar, all you want. And there are always great drink specialties, too, including mai tais, chichis, and daiquiris, for $1.99 to $3.70. Bring a big appetite. Perfect for families.

WAILUA MARINA RESTAURANT, in Wailua River State Park. Tel. 822-4311.
Cuisine: SEAFOOD/STEAK. **Reservations:** Recommended.
$ Prices: Appetizers $2.75–$6.95; main courses $9.50–$23. AE, MC, V.
Open: Breakfast daily 9–11am; lunch daily 11am–2pm; dinner daily 5–9pm.

Good food, good prices, and a very special setting have long made this place a favorite. You can dine riverside and catch the breezes on the open lanai, or indoors in the huge dining room with its slanted ceilings and murals, stuffed fish, and turtle shells on the wall. Although we wouldn't call the food gourmet, it is still a good deal for the price, especially since all dinners come with a tossed garden salad, vegetable of the day, a choice of starch, plus coffee or tea. "Special selections"—oxtail soup with ginger and parsley, baked stuffed pork chops, prime rib of beef au jus—are the most reasonable, from $8.75 to $15.25. Charbroiled specials, including fresh catch of the day and slipper lobster tail and New York steak, range from $13.25 up to around $25.

Our favorite luncheon choices here are the sandwiches—including a Monte Cristo with ham and turkey, mahimahi on a bun, and pastrami on rye—all from $5.75 to $8.50 (for tenderloin steak on toast). There's a special menu for children ages 3 to 9.

Worth the Extra Money

A PACIFIC CAFE, in Kauai Village, Kuhio Hwy. Tel. 822-0013.
Cuisine: PACIFIC RIM. **Reservations:** Recommended.
$ Prices: Appetizers $4.75–$9.25; main courses $14.95–$24.50. AE, DC, MC, V.
Open: Dinner Tues–Sun 5:30–9pm.

⭐ For a splurge meal worth every cent, indulge yourself with dinner at this restaurant that's created a stir in island food circles. A Pacific Café is the creation of executive chef/owner Jean-Marie Josselin, who's garnered awards for creative cooking in Paris, on the mainland, and here in Hawaii, where he was formerly executive chef at the Coco Palms Resort. Josselin has created a stylish restaurant that boasts Asian art and decor, native Hawaiian woods and plants, and an open kitchen with rôtisserie and a wood-burning grill and wok, so guests can watch the chefs create their magic. And magic it is—Josselin creates extraordinarily good ethnic dishes of the Pacific Rim, using a blend of Asian and European culinary techniques. The superb pottery on which you dine was created by Sophronioa, Jean-Marie's wife.

Since the menu changes constantly to take advantage of the freshest local fish, game, and locally grown vegetables, there's no telling what you may encounter on a specific night, but here are some samples of his signature dishes. Appetizers include smoked shrimp lumpia with a curried lime dip, or deep-fried sashimi, with a wana sauce, or potato skins with smoked marlin and sour cream. For salads and soups, $4.25 to $8.25, how about a Caesar salad with spicy ahi, or baked potato soup with smoked marlin, sour cream, and chives. It's easy to make a meal on two or three of the appetizers, soups, and salads. From the wood-burning grill come such main dishes as wok-seared mahimahi with garlic sesame crust, grilled rack of lamb with a plum-tamarind sauce, or grilled fish skewer with angel hair pasta and Chinese pesto. All main courses are served with vegetables and rice. Save room for dessert, preferably the platter of assorted miniature pastries baked fresh every day.

COCONUT PLANTATION MARKETPLACE

In addition to the restaurant listed below, Coconut Marketplace has a variety of eating establishments, including, for quick meals, Aunt Sophie's Grill, specializing in burgers, Big Mel's Deli, Fish Hut, Taco Dude, and Paradise Chicken-'n'-Ribs. For a more leisurely meal, it's Wild Palms Bistro, serving lunch and dinner every day, with palm trees at each table. For relaxing drinks in a picturesque setting, it's Tradewinds: A South Seas Bar.

Budget

JOLLY ROGER RESTAURANT, adjacent to Coconut Marketplace. Tel. 822-3451.
Cuisine: AMERICAN. **Reservations:** Not required.
$ Prices: Main courses $9.95–$12.95. AE, MC, V.
Open: Breakfast daily 6:30am–noon; lunch daily 11am–4pm; dinner daily 4–10pm.

Part of a family of island restaurants that offer consistently good food and service, this Jolly Roger is always busy, and with good reason. There's everything you ever wanted for breakfast, including the Mac-Waple, a golden-brown waffle smothered with spicy cinnamon apples and macadamia nuts, for about $4.25. Lunch features salads, sandwiches, burgers, and specialties like a stuffed quesadilla, fettuccine Alfredo, grilled mahimahi, or a Monte Cristo sandwich, for $6.25 to $8.45. And for dinner, choose from the complete meals, such as smothered chicken, mahimahi, a delightful seafood combination platter, or chicken Polynesian with a fragrant sweet-and-sour sauce, all accompanied by soup or salad, hot vegetables, and a starch.

Check the local tourist papers for discount coupons; you might be able to get the likes of two steak teriyaki dinners for $18.25. A prolonged happy hour goes from 11am to 7pm, and there's entertainment every night with cocktails served until 2am.

READERS RECOMMEND

***Al & Don's Oceanfront Restaurant,** in the Kauai Sands Hotel (tel. 822-4221). "Your best dinner bargain near Coconut Plantation is Al & Don's Oceanfront Restaurant. The menu features a surprisingly extensive variety of dishes for a budget hotel, including fresh island fish, steak, ham steak Hawaiian, hibachi chicken, and cheese lasagne, for $6.90 to $10.95, and the price includes a vegetable, whipped potatoes or rice, and biscuits.*—Connie Tonken, Hartford, Conn.

THE NORTH SHORE: KILAUEA/PRINCEVILLE-HANALEI

Meals for Less Than $20

THE BISTRO OF HANALEI, Ching Young Village. Tel. 826-9436.
   Cuisine: ITALIAN. **Reservations:** Recommended.
   $ Prices: Appetizers $3–$10; main courses $10–$16.50. AE, D, DC, MC, V.
   Open: Dinner Tues–Sun 5:30–10pm.
There's an air of casual elegance about this new place, which has all the local folks cheering. It's a sprightly scene, with mountain views from the windows, green-and-white tablecloths and napkins, rattan-backed chairs, and light jazz and blues on the grand piano, courtesy of pianist Jake Welsh, accompanying one's meal. And the food is terrific! Everything is done from scratch—all pastas, breads, and sausages are made on the premises, and salad greens are grown organically right in the neighborhood. Start with one of the tasty anipasti, like the prosciutto with ripe island fruit or the baked, stuffed sausage in a red pepper purée; maybe move on to a classic Caesar salad or the Gorgonzola and walnut spread of local greens and diced apples. The vegetable lasagne and the linguine whisky (shrimp and snow peas in a whisky cream sauce) are good pasta choices; or try the veal saltimbocca, the chicken Sorrentino, or the steak e marsala (New York steak coated with cracked pepper and garlic, grilled with marsala wine demiglaze). Imaginative pizzas like the grilled shrimp, papaya, and asiago pie are also fun. Relax with a glass of wine, finish off with an espresso and one of owner/chef Jeff Shepard's fabulous desserts—perhaps it will be the chocolate Amaretto cheesecake or the crunchy pecan lilikoi tart or the chocolate cinnamon torte the day you're there. A lovely way to spend an evening.

CHUCK'S STEAK HOUSE, at Princeville Center. Tel. 826-6211.
   Cuisine: SEAFOOD/STEAK/SALAD. **Reservations:** Recommended for dinner and for parties of six or more at lunch.
   $ Prices: Appetizers $5.35–$7.60; main courses $14.50–$21.50, to market price for fish and lobster. AE, CB, DC, MC, V.
   Open: Lunch Mon–Fri 11:30am–2:30pm; dinner daily 6–10pm.
This is rightfully one of the most popular places at Princeville Center. An attractive porch, plants, ceiling fans, dark walls, secluded booths, paintings, and antiques everywhere set a cozy scene. Lunch is fun here, with daily specials for $5.75–$8.50 and an array of salads, burgers, and sandwiches. Dinner features steaks and prime rib, seafood, and fresh fish specials. All meals include salad bar, hot bread and butter, and steamed rice or rice pilaf; the salad bar is available on its own for $8.50. For dessert, hesitate not: The mud pie is wonderful. Chuck's is also known for great tropical drinks and fine wines; cocktails are served Monday through Friday from 11:30am to 11pm and on Saturday and Sunday from 5 to 11pm.

HANALEI GOURMET, Old Hanalei School, Hanalei Center, 5-5161 Kuhio Hwy. Tel. 826-2524.
Cuisine: AMERICAN/DELI. **Reservations:** Not accepted.
$ Prices: Sandwiches and salads $3.95–$9.25; dinner specials $10–$15.95. MC, V.
Open: Mon–Thurs 8am–10:30pm, Fri–Sat 8am–midnight, Sun 8am–8pm.

⭐ Ever since it opened in the superbly restored Old Hanalei School, Hanalei Gourmet has been deservedly one of the most popular spots in Hanalei, with both locals and tourists. Half the operation is a bakery, cheese shop, and take-out deli, with a splendid wine cellar (almost 100 bottles). This is the place to get your picnic fixings if you're hiking the Na Pali coast or kayaking up a river. The other half of the operation is a cheery sit-down café that serves tropical drinks, breakfast, lunch, and dinner with a gourmet touch. Breakfast features their own muesli cereal, a croissant sandwich, bagel with lox and cream cheese, and a tangy huevos Santa Cruz, for $4.25 to $6.50. Lunch and dinner offer generous Italian sandwiches (the Oregon bay shrimp open-face, on Na Pali brown bread, with bay shrimp and melted Jack cheese, is one of the best, at $7.50); imaginative salads and antipasti; varied pupu plates of meats, cheeses, and smoked fish; and bountiful "Shrimp Boils"—that's unpeeled shrimp boiled in seasoned broth and served with melted garlic butter, from $7.50. Dinner specials on the chalkboard might include ahi fettuccine Alfredo or spinach lasagne. Desserts, fresh from the bakery, are on the delicious and decadent side. There's live entertainment in the evenings, Tuesday through Saturday, when local performers join ranks, on occasion, with jazz stars from Honolulu and the mainland. Sunday, from 5 to 8pm, there's a light Hawaiian jam session. A lively spot.

KILAUEA BAKERY & PAU HANA PIZZA, in the Kong Lung Center. Tel. 828-2020.
Cuisine: GOURMET PIZZA. **Reservations:** Not accepted.
$ Prices: Pizzas $6.75–$15.75; specialty pizzas $10.50–$24.50. No credit cards.
Open: Mon–Thurs 11:30am–9pm, Fri–Sat 11:30am–10 pm. Bakery open from 6:30am.

⭐ This tiny little café is much beloved by folks who live on Kauai's North Shore and by tourists heading for the Kilauea Lighthouse and the Princeville/Hanalei area. And with good reason. Tom and Katie Pickett, a young couple who live just around the corner, specialize in fabulous breads (chewy French sourdough, guava sourdough, Gorgonzola and olives, garlic and black pepper, and pumpkin walnut sweet bread, to mention just a few) and in fabulous pizzas, available by the slice or by the piece. You can build your pie to order with such ingredients as goat cheese, chipotle peppers, Kalamata olives, fresh pineapple, and smoked mahimahi (the latter most likely caught by Tom himself on one of his diving expeditions). Every day they do a few specialty pizzas like the Pesto Mystic (basil pesto, sun-dried tomatoes, mushrooms, and onions) and the Great Gonzo (roasted eggplant, red onion, goat cheese, and roasted garlic). Trust us, they're terrific. So are the cookies, the bagels, and the coffee, each cup made to order of organically grown, fresh-ground and dark-roasted beans, drip brewed with filtered water in unbleached filter paper. Once you know about this place, driving north without a stop here is a virtual impossibility.

ZELO'S CAFE, at Princeville Center. Tel. 826-9700.
Cuisine: AMERICAN. **Reservations:** Not accepted.
$ Prices: Appetizers $1.95–$5.95; main courses $7.95–$10.95 MC.V.
Open: Daily 9:30am–9pm.
Where can you find a goodly percentage of the employees of the Princeville Center come lunch or snack time? One of two places: either in Zelo's Café, a pretty tile-and-woody spot with a counter and tables out on a small lanai—or in their offices enjoying Zelo's take-out goodies. We're not surprised: Zelo's Café serves tasty food at modest prices. At both lunch and dinner, for example, you can have dishes like a super spinach lasagne at $9.95 or Cajun chicken for $10.95, or a tempeh burger for the vegetarians in the crowd for $6.95. More burgers (including chicken and mahimahi burgers), plus full-meal salads, are served up at both meals, and delicious pastas and fresh fish, market-priced, at dinner.

Ching Young Village Shopping Center

There are several budget eateries at this shopping center. The **Village Snack and Bakery Shop** has plate lunches, such as fried chicken and teriyaki beef, for $5.95, and is also a popular spot for breakfast, which runs $2.95 to $4.95. The best treats here are the home-baked pies: guava, lilikoi, chiffon, lemon-cream cheese, at $1.50 a slice. Box lunches are $5.75, with a salad and drink.

Or you can get your pizzas on a homemade whole-wheat crust with sesame seeds at **Pizza Hanalei,** which really works at making a good pie; they use fresh vegetable toppings and herbs picked from their own garden. It's $2.11 for a slice, $7.58 for a small pie, or try their unusual pizzaritto: That's cheese, vegetables, meats, and spices rolled up into a pizza shell and eaten like a burrito, $4.79.

Also at Hanalei, Tuesday through Sunday from 11am to 3pm, you'll find Roger Kennedy and his ✪ **Tropical Taco**—a green truck next to the Hanalei River at the parking lot of the Dolphin Restaurant, where he dishes up gourmet-quality, all-organic burritos, tacos, and the like, all including beans, meat, lettuce, salsa, cheese, and sour cream (vegetarian combos, too), a complete lunch for around $3 to $5. The menu is on a surfboard hooked to the front of the "Taco Wagon." Next door, Roger sells shave ice at the Hanalei Freeze, which can help you cool off from the hot sauce. Take your food to the shady riverbank just a few steps away and enjoy your picnic Mexicana.

THE SOUTHERN & WESTERN ROUTE

You should have no problem dining on your trip around the southern and western end of the island, for there are several excellent choices. Not all, however, are in the budget category.

OLD KOLOA TOWN

Meals for Less Than $10

KOLOA BROILER, Koloa Rd. Tel. 742-9122.
   Cuisine: AMERICAN. **Reservations:** Not required.
$ Prices: Appetizers $3.25–$3.75; main courses $7–$11.95. AE, CB, DC, DISC, JCB, MC, V.
   Open: Daily 11am–10pm.

✪ If you don't like the way your food is done at this restaurant in the heart of Old Koloa Town, a few miles from Poipu Beach, you have no one but yourself to blame. This cute little place is one of those broil-it-yourself affairs—and that way, they really manage to keep the prices down. You can choose from top sirloin, marinated beef kebab, barbecued baby back ribs, mahimahi, barbecued chicken, and beef burger; fresh fish is usually available at market price. The price of all main courses includes salad bar, baked beans, rice, and sourdough bread. Lunch offers the same choices, but the burger is $6. The Koloa Broiler is a lively, fun kind of place, simply decorated (try to get a seat out on the lanai), with a bar, a list of exotic drinks, and lots of local people enjoying their meals.

PANCHO & LEFTY'S CANTINA & RESTAURANTE, Koloa Rd., Old Koloa Town. Tel. 742-7377.
   Cuisine: MEXICAN. **Reservations:** Not required.
$ Prices: Appetizers $4.95–$6.95; main courses $5.25–$20.95. AE, MC, V.
   Open: Breakfast daily 8am–noon; lunch and dinner daily 11am–10pm.
Everything about Pancho & Lefty's bespeaks sunny Mexico; parrots in the windows, a fountain of greenery, baskets, wooden tables, sombreros on the walls—even the salt-and-pepper shakers are in the shape of red peppers! The restaurant, which got started in Maui a few years ago, has been so successful that it's opened branches here and on the Big Island, and the food is the same—spicy, delicious, inexpensive. You can start the day with a Mexican breakfast—Lefty's Mexican omelet with chorizo and jalapeño, or huevos rancheros or a breakfast burrito, $4.95 to $9.95, as well as the more usual American offerings. The menu is the same at lunch and

dinner. You can't go wrong with the huge seafood salad in a taco shell ($9.95), the steak or chicken fajitas to which you add your own amounts of guacamole, salsa, and sour cream ($12.95 to $15.95), or with specialty items like the enchiladas rancheros or pechuga pollo relleno (chicken breast stuffed with Jack cheese and chiles, batter-fried and topped with enchilada sauce). Begin your meal with a tropical drink from the lively bar, end with an ice-cream pie for dessert, and top it all off with a Café Siesta—maybe a Mexican coffee (tequila and Kahlúa) or a non-Mexican, but altogether satisfying, Irish coffee.

POIPU

Meals for Less Than $5

TAQUERIA NORTENOS, 2827-A Poipu Rd., Koloa. Tel. 742-7222.
   Cuisine: MEXICAN. **Reservations:** Not required.
$ Prices: $2.15–$5.
   Open: Thurs–Tues 11am–11pm. **Closed:** Weds.

   Next to the Kukuila Store in Koloa is a tiny taco bar that packs a mighty wallop. Owner Ed Sills, former chef at the prestigious Plantation Garden Restaurant, has been running his own place for several years now, turning out excellent food and keeping the prices low. You can get a meal here for under $5. Ed often does regional specialties, such as posole (pork-and-hominy stew) and enchiladas in the style of Sonora and Chalupa. Vegetarians can be accommodated nicely. When you want some good Mexican munchies, pop in for tacos, burritos, tostadas, or nachos. Pick up your food at the counter and eat in the tiny dining room or take it out. Call them in advance and they'll pack you a nice picnic for the beach.

Meals for Less Than $15

CAFE VENTURI, Poipu Shopping Village, Poipu Rd. Tel. 742-9168.
   Cuisine: CONTINENTAL. **Reservations:** Not required.
$ Prices: Appetizers $3.25–$6.50; main courses $6.75–$12.50 to market price for fresh fish.
   Open: Mon–Fri 6am–9pm, Sat–Sun 11am–9pm.

   Tim Venturi, the chef/owner of Café Venturi, claims that his is the only restaurant in Hawaii that guarantees its food. "If you don't like it, we buy it," he claims. Venturi has little to worry about in that area; people from all over the island love the food, and rightfully so: it's delicious, it's served in a charming setting, and the strain on the pocketbook is minimal. Café Venturi is small and pretty, looking a bit like a verandah, with open windows, tile floors, koa-wood tables, and many plants; there's also seating outside in good weather. Tim learned to cook at the Culinary Institute of America in Hyde Park, NY, worked in some of Kauai's finest restaurants, then set up a catering business and this new venture. His cooking, a mixture of European and Asian influences, uses the freshest of ingredients and a reverse osmosis water purifier which enhances the natural flavor of the foods. He does everything from quesadillas to fresh pastas to fresh fish of the day, the last prepared in appealing ways—perhaps with a citron or a Maui ginger sauce. To begin your meal, start with the homemade soup de jour, the fresh-fish tempura, or maybe the Caesar or Cobb salad. Grilled chicken with teriyaki sauce, top sirloin steak, vegetable platter, and scallops Dore are among the featured dinner entrées. Lunch offers fresh-fruit platters, fish and chips, a good grilled chicken or veggie sandwich, pasta of the day, and a fresh-fish sandwich. Have some zabaione or fresh-baked pie for dessert. You may want to linger: there's a full bar, a good wine selection, and local entertainers to provide Hawaiian and popular music every night.

PIZZA BELLA, in Poipu Shopping Village, Poipu Rd. Tel. 742-9571.
   Cuisine: ITALIAN. **Reservations:** Not required.
$ Prices: Main courses $6.25–$10.95. MC, V.
   Open: Breakfast daily 6–10:30am; lunch and dinner daily 11:30am–10pm.
This is much more than your average pizza parlor. It has an attractive layout—black-and-white tile floors, white wicker chairs, greenery, ceiling fans, even a few outside

tables. Nearby condo dwellers like to start the day here with an inexpensive breakfast. Eggs any style, blueberry pancakes, french toast, omelets, and the like are all $4.25 and under. The menu is the same the rest of the day: 10-inch, California-style gourmet pizzas—topped with homemade sauce and four cheeses; barbecued chicken and cilantro; a mélange of seafood, starting at $8.75. Less modern tastes might go for the old-fashioned pies, the hot and cold sandwiches, and several pastas, including a veggie lasagne. There's wine, beer, and a nice atmosphere. Keep Pizza Bella in mind for lunch or a light dinner if you're staying in the Poipu area. They also deliver.

Meals for $15 to $20

BRENNECKE'S BEACH BROILER, 2100 Hoone Rd., Poipu Beach. Tel. 742-7588.
   Cuisine: AMERICAN. **Reservations:** Recommended.
$ Prices: Appetizers $5.95–$12.95; main courses $5.95–$23.95. DC, MC, V.
   Open: Lunch daily 11am–4pm; dinner daily 4–10pm; brunch Sun 10am–2pm.
Located on the second-floor balcony directly across from Poipu Beach Park, Brennecke's likes to proclaim that it's "Right on the beach, right on the price." True. Cheerfully decorated with window boxes blossoming with bright flowers and an assortment of family photos and memorabilia, this popular restaurant/sports bar is a lively place—day and night.
   The menu offers plenty of possibilities, starting with a beautiful salad bar that's offered with most lunch and dinner entrées. Sandwiches and burgers are available at both lunch and dinner. On the low side of the dinner menu, try the creamy clam chowder, with sourdough bread and a little salad bar for $11.95; or the pasta primavera or Oriental chicken stir-fry, both with salad bar, for $13.95. Brennecke's is famous for its kiawe-broiled fresh-fish selections, which vary daily depending on what's biting; all are complete meals at $19.95. There's a keiki menu, too, from $3.95 to $6.95.
   Sunday Sports Brunch brings in the regulars to watch their favorite games on the satellite-dish video receiver. Customized omelets at $6.95 and prime rib 'n' eggs at $9.95 are featured. During Happy Hour, 2 to 5pm daily, most drinks are reduced in price, and mai tais are $3. Browse in their minideli for take-out sandwiches and snacks that you might want to take back to your apartment: it's open daily for coffee and pastry from 8am to 9pm.

Worth the Extra Money

KEOKI'S PARADISE, Poipu Shopping Village, Poipu Rd. Tel. 742-7534.
   Cuisine: SEAFOOD/STEAK/MEXICAN. **Reservations:** Recommended.
$ Prices: Taco Bar Menu: Appetizers $1–$5.95; main courses $6.95–$9.95. Regular Menu: Appetizers $3.95–$6.95; main courses $9.95–$19.95. AE, MC, V.
   Open: Dinner daily 5:30–10pm; cocktails 4pm–midnight.
⭐ We think you'll agree that this restaurant is aptly named. Open and airy, with beautiful vistas everywhere, it overlooks a gemlike lagoon with cascading waterfalls and luxuriant tropical trees and flowers. In such a setting, everything tastes good—and the kitchen is first-rate, too. If you're counting pennies, dine in the Taco Bar. Here you can have pupus, Hawaiian local plates, sandwiches and burgers, and Mexican dinners; nothing is more than $10. In the restaurant proper, there are several entrées on the low side of the menu: veggie brochettes and lasagne, and such island classics as Koloa pork ribs; with plum sauce; Balinese chicken breast marinated in garlic and lemongrass; chicken and ribs; and kushiyaki, a brochette of teriyaki chicken and top sirloin. Nothing is more than $15.95. Fresh fish, higher priced, is served in a variety of imaginative sauces, or just plain and healthy and very delicious. All items come with Caesar salad, a basket of freshly baked bread, and stir-fried rice. Hula pie is the dessert of choice; it's "what the sailors swam to shore for." The idyllic setting and the friendly ambience here are sure to make you want to linger. The restaurant is run by the same talented management that runs Duke's Canoe Club in Waikiki and, on Maui, Kimo's, the Kapalua Grill & Bar, Leilani's, and Chico's.

HANAPEPE

GREEN GARDEN, Hwy. 50. Tel. 335-5422.
  Cuisine: AMERICAN. **Reservations:** Recommended for dinner.
$ Prices: Main courses $6–$20. AE, MC, V.
  Open: Breakfast and lunch Mon, Wed–Fri 9am–2:15pm. Sat 8am–2:15pm. Sun 7:30am–2:15pm; dinner Wed–Mon 5–9pm.

The Green Garden is a Kauai tradition, a more than 40-year-old restaurant run by Sumika Hamabata and her family. You'll feel as if you're sitting in the middle of a greenhouse, with orchids on the tables, plants everywhere, an entire screened wall facing a garden, bamboo chairs, and white walls. For a real treat, do as the locals do: Call them at least half an hour in advance and order a family-style meal, with a variety of Chinese and local dishes. Or you can make a lunch on one of their sandwich specials, like the fresh fish on toast, for about $5.95 and under. Lunch selections for $5.50 to $7.35, include sweet-and-sour spareribs, a seafood special, and Korean-style boneless barbecued chicken. Dinner is a complete meal, featuring similar main courses, all accompanied by homemade soup or fruit cup, tossed salad, a starch, vegetables and rolls, and beverage. Fresh fish of the day is a mere $13.95, and kiawe broiler specials, such as filet mignon at $14.95, are also well priced.

Be sure to save room for Sue's homemade pies—macadamia nut, lilikoi, chocolate cream—absolute marvels, and only $2. Note that if a tour bus happens to disgorge its hungry passengers here, things can get a bit hectic. Better to come on the late side of the lunch hour.

KALAHEO

BRICK OVEN PIZZA, 2-2555 Kaumualii Hwy. Tel. 332-8561.
  Cuisine: PIZZA/SANDWICHES. **Reservations:** Not accepted.
$ Prices: Appetizers 60¢–$3.10; main courses $2.35–$10.95. MC, V.
  Open: Tues–Sun 4–10pm, Sun 4–9pm.

On the main road in Kalaheo is this family-run, family-style restaurant that's been making delicious "pizza with the homemade touch" for many years now. It's a cozy restaurant with red-and-white gingham tablecloths in true pizzeria fashion. Children are treated especially nicely here. Hearth-baked pies with delicious crust, either whole wheat or white brushed with garlic butter, start at $7.35 for a 10-inch plain cheese pie, and go all the way up to $22.85 for a 15-inch pizza with almost everything. In addition to pizza, there are hot sandwiches, including a vegetarian one, and a yummy seafood-style pizza bread. Green salads are available, and so are wine and beer. Call ahead for pizza to go.

KOKEE

KOKEE LODGE, in Kokee State Park. Tel. 335-6061.
  Cuisine: AMERICAN. **Reservations:** Recommended for dinner.
$ Prices: Main courses $13.95–$16.95. DC, DISC, MC, V.
  Open: Breakfast daily 8:30–11:30am; lunch daily 11:30am–3:30pm.

If you're going to Waimea Canyon—and, of course, you should—it's nice to know that you can tie your visit in with a meal at Kokee Lodge in Kokee State Park. The kitchen is presided over by Sherrie Orr, who adds her unique natural food specialties to the menu. The rustic dining room affords views of both mountain and meadow. At lunch you can get a variety of salads, sandwiches (some of the selections guava-smoked on the premises, $2.95 to $9.95), Portugese bean soup (the local soul food), chili, or a modestly priced daily special. Any time of the day, try their delicious homemade hot cornbread, served with Kauai honey. Desserts—like lilikoi chiffon and Alakai Swamp pie—are always delicious. They serve Lappert's coffee (the best), a variety of teas, and cocktails, beer, and wine, as well.

CHAPTER 11

WHAT TO SEE & DO ON KAUAI

1. ADVENTURE TOURS
2. LIHUE
 • **FROMMER'S FAVORITE KAUAI EXPERIENCES**
3. EXCURSION ALONG THE EASTERN & NORTHERN SHORES
4. SEEING THE NA PALI COAST
5. EXCURSION ALONG THE SOUTHERN & WESTERN SHORES

There are plenty of opportunities on Kauai for hiking, fishing, camping, golf, water sports, and such for those who have the time to stay and enjoy them. Check with the **Hawaii Visitors Bureau,** 3016 Umi St., Suite 207, on the second floor of Lihue Plaza (tel. 808/245-3971), or write to them at P.O. Box 507, Lihue, HI 96766. Information on hiking, camping, fishing, and hunting is available at the Department of Land & Natural Resources, in the state building in Lihue, 3060 Eiwa St. (tel. 808/245-4444). For State Forest Reserve trail information, write to the District Forester, Division of Forestry and Wildlife, P.O. Box 1671, Lihue, HI 96766; for state park information, write to the Park Superintendent, Division of State Parks, P.O. Box 1671, Lihue, HI 96766.

SUGGESTED ITINERARIES

Count on at least three days to see Kauai. After Lihue, the first 2 should be devoted to separate all-day trips, which between them circle the island; to skip either would be unthinkable.

IF YOU HAVE 1 DAY We recommend a trip to the eastern and northern parts of the island, all the way to Hanalei, Hanea, and the Na Pali cliffs. Begin this trip seeing the sights of Lihue.

IF YOU HAVE 2 DAYS Spend the first day as above. The second day we would go to the southern and western parts of the island, whose high points are Poipu Beach, Waimea Canyon, and the magnificent end-of-the-road climax, Kalalau Lookout.

IF YOU HAVE 3 DAYS After seeing the main sights, spend the third day on side excursions, swimming, and going back to all the idyllic little spots you discovered on the first two trips.

IF YOU HAVE 5 DAYS OR MORE If you're lucky enough to have this much time in Kauai, break up your round-the-island trips, spending more time at each attraction, giving yourself half a day for swimming, golf, hiking, kayaking. Take time for a river trip to the Fern Grotto, browse through the Kauai Museum, hike the Na Pali Coast, or tour the National Tropical Botanical Garden.

1. ADVENTURE TOURS

On **Kauai Mountain Tours,** P.O. Box 3069, Lihue, Kauai, HI 96766 (tel. 808/

245-7224), a knowledgeable guide will take you on a one-of-a-kind trip into the Na Pali Kona Forest Reserve in an air-conditioned four-wheel-drive vehicle that traverses the winding mountain roads around the back of Waimea Canyon. It's around $78 for a seven-hour tour, with lunch and a light continental breakfast included.

Crane Tours, c/o Bill Crane, 15101 Magnolia Blvd., H10, Sherman Oaks, CA 91403 (tel. 800/653-2545 or 818/724-2213, or Milt McAuley at 818/347-6433), offers both kayaking trips and moderately strenuous trips for experienced backpackers to the Na Pali Coast and Waimea Canyon. The cost is approximately $695 to $925. This company is known for excellent values, terrific meals, and thoughtful service. They also offer a variety of excursions to the Big Island.

Rick Haviland and his excellent crew at **Outfitters Kauai,** Poipu Plaza, 2827-A Poipu Rd. (P.O. Box 1149), Poipu Beach, Koloa, HI 96756 (tel. 808/742-9667), are known for a variety of enjoyable and well-run trips, via kayak or bicycle. In addition to simple half-day kayaking trips for beginners ($48) and one-day sea-kayaking adventures along Kauai's southeast coast in the shadow of 2,000-foot cliffs ($105 for a full-day excursion), this outfit also offers an escorted Kayak Experience along the Na Pali cliffs, either as a 1-day trip from Haena to Polihale, or a two-day (or more) expedition featuring camping at Kalalau and Milolii—some of the most breathtakingly beautiful spots in the islands. Two-person kayaks may also be rented for self-guided tours to jungle rivers. Each boat comes with racks/straps to secure it to your car, maps, and information to help you select the ideal river. Cost is $30 or $45 for one- or two-person kayaks.

Outfitters Kauai also offers adventure for the cyclist. For personal tours, they rent mountain bikes of high quality, which are well maintained and well suited for off-road riding through Kauai's backcountry. They provide helmets, water bottles, spare tubes with pumps, and extensive trail information based on years of riding and exploring on Kauai. Car racks are available to carry bikes to other locations. Bikes rent for $20 a day, $60 for 4 days, $100 for a week.

New and very exciting are Outfitters Kauai's Kokee Mountain Bike Tours. Participants ride the cool, high forest backroads above Waimea Canyon in an ecosystem that supports plants, trees, and birds, many of which are found only here. A skilled guide discusses the legends and natural history of Kokee. The cost is $58. Outfitters Kauai also operates guided mountain-bike tours in the state parks of Hawaii.

Kayak Kauai Outfitters, 1340 Kuhio Hwy. Kapaa (tel. 808/822-9179), or on main street in Hanalei (P.O. Box 508), Hanalei, HI 96714 (tel. 808/826-9844 or 800/437-3507; fax 808/822-0577), offers summer (May to September) sea-kayak voyages for adventurers along 15 miles of Kauai's dramatic Na Pali coastline that involve some of the most challenging wilderness paddling to be found in Hawaii. Fully catered, six-day packages cost $1,050 per person. The company offers guided one-day sea kayak trips along the Na Pali coast, including lunch on an isolated beach ($125) and a three-hour soft adventure Hanalei Wildlife Refuge and Bay Snorkel tour ($45). Their private canoe/kayak rentals, beginning at $48 for two persons, are very popular with families. Winter—that is, from October to April—you can sea kayak Kipu Kai, the "little Na Pali" on Kauai's south shore; lunch, snorkeling, and whale watching are included ($100). Fully catered, six-day sea-kayaking trips along the south shore from Lihue to Waimea, with hiking in the highlands of Kokee, are $1,050. Six-day backpacking tours along the Na Pali coast are $900. One-day guided hiking tours are available all over Kauai; there's also a guided Fern Grotto paddle and hike to a waterfall, lunch included, for $75. Mountain bike rentals ($20) and three-hour bike tours in Hanalei and Kapaa ($45) are new additions to the programs.

IMPRESSIONS

Kauai—Nowhere in the entire national park system is there scenic beauty like this.—STEWART UDALL, 1963

2. LIHUE

Once a sleepy plantation village, Lihue is beginning to look startlingly modern, with shopping centers, supermarkets, mega-resorts, and the like.

GROVE FARM HOMESTEAD, P.O. Box 1631, Lihue, Kauai, HI 96766. Tel. 245-3202.

A visit here takes a little advance planning, either by mail or by calling for reservations. But it's worth the effort, as this is a trip backward in time, to the days of the old Hawaiian sugar plantations. Grove Farm Homestead has been lovingly preserved and still has a lived-in look. The plantation was founded by George N. Wilcox, the son of teachers who arrived with the fifth company of the American Board of Missions sent to Hawaii in the 1830s. (Part of Wilcox's original sugar plantation is now the site of Kukui Grove Center; see below). His niece, Miss Mabel Wilcox, who was born and lived at the homestead all her life, left her estate as a living museum. The homestead tour is leisurely and informative. The old homes are lovely, furnished with antiques, Oriental rugs, and handsome koa-wood furniture; there is an abundance of books, and sheet music is open on the piano. You'll visit the very different servants' quarters, too.

Admission: $3.

Open: two-hour tours given Mon and Wed–Thurs at 10am and 1pm. Call at least a week in advance, or write (reservations are accepted up to three months in advance).

KILOHANA PLANTATION, Hi. 50, Tel. 245-5608.

Gaylord Parke Wilcox, the nephew of the founder of Grove Farm Plantation, built his dream house back in 1935 and called it Kilohana, which, in Hawaiian, means "not to be surpassed." The Wilcox family lived at the estate for 35 years, during which time it was the setting for much of the cultural and social life of upper-class Kauai. Restored to look just as it did in the 1930s, with many of its actual furnishings and artifacts, it's now a combination historical house-museum and shopping bazaar, with boutiques taking over the old children's nursery, the family bedrooms, the library, the cloakrooms, and the restored guest cottages on the estate grounds. None of the shops is inexpensive, but all offer quality in accordance with Kilohana's standard of excellence.

Before you begin your shopping, stop in to have a look at the foyer of the main house, where you'll see two enormous monkeypod calabashes—reputedly the largest in the state of Hawaii. In the olden days, Hawaiian kings stored their feather quilts in such calabashes: Later, missionary women used them as "trunks" for patchwork quilts. These, however, are replicas, made for the movie *Hawaii*. Be sure to visit Stones at Kilohana, which specializes in arts and crafts from all over the Pacific, including Tonga, Samoa, New Guinea, and Fiji. You'll see traditional handwork, wood bowls, hand-screened aloha shirts, ritual and ceremonial items, Hawaiian photographs by such artists as Boone Morrison, Pegge Hopper prints, jewelry, pottery, and sculpture. **Kilohana Galleries** is noted for its collection of work by Hawaiian artists. Check out its Artisan's Room, too, for fine crafts—and its Hawaiian Collection Room for rare Niihau shell leis, wood carvings, and a good sampling of scrimshaw. **Sea Reflections** is the place for rare and unusual shells, shell sculptures, and a handsome selection of gold, black, and bamboo coral, as well as freshwater pearls. **Kahn Galleries** showcases works by top Hawaiian artists. Tahitian black pearls and opals are featured at **Grande's Gems & Gallery.** Hawaiian food products, crafts, and goods can be found at **The Country Store;** you can even order pineapple here to ship home.

In addition to browsing and shopping at Kilohana, you can take a 20-minute, horse-drawn carriage ride, an hour's ride through sugarcane fields, a guided tour, or a walk through the extensive manicured lawns and gardens. There's a full schedule

FROMMER'S FAVORITE

KAUAI EXPERIENCES

A Visit to Spouting Horn Park See the geysers shoot up through holes in the lava rock as the sea pounds relentlessly against the black rocks.

A Trip to Waimea Canyon Visit the "Grand Canyon of the Pacific" to see one of the most spectacular views in all Hawaii, with a stop for lunch on the way down at Kokee Lodge, in the bracing mountain air.

Swimming and Snorkeling at Poipu Beach One of the island's best—great for family fun.

Driving the Northern Route, Hi. 56 Travel all the way to Hanalei to catch one of Hawaii's most spectacular sunsets.

Swimming at Kalapaki Beach Gentle, rolling surf affords the best swimming in central Kanai.

of cultural events: hula performances, craft demonstrations, and the like. When you get hungry, you can have an excellent meal at the charming courtyard restaurant, Gaylord's (see "Where to Eat" in Chapter 10).

The Kilohana Plantation is located on Hi. 50, two miles southwest of Lihue, headed toward Poipu. It's on the other side of the road and very close to the Kukui Grove Shopping Center. Open daily from 9:30am.

KAUAI MUSEUM, 4428 Rice St. Tel. 245-6931.

A visit to this museum, adjacent to the shopping center and across from the post office, is well worth your while. Stop in first at the Wilcox Building to examine the changing art, heritage, and cultural exhibits of both Asia and Hawaii. The Museum Shop here is one of our favorites, with its fine collections of South Pacific handcrafts, tapas, baskets, rare Niihaw shell leis, Hawaiian books, prints, koa calabashes, and other wooden ware. The Rice Building, entered through a covered paved walkway and courtyard, contains the permanent exhibit, "The Story of Kauai," an ecological and geological history complete with photographs, dioramas, and an exciting video. Be sure to see the Plantation Gallery, a permanent showcase for a collection of splendid Hawaiian quilts, plus koa furniture, china, etc.

Admission: $3 adults; free for children under 18 accompanied by an adult.

Open: Mon–Fri 9am–4:30 pm, Sat 9am–1pm.

LIHUE PUBLIC LIBRARY, 4344 Hardy St. Tel. 245-3617.

The latest audiovisual aids are available in this handsome contemporary building, located a few blocks away from Kauai Museum. Ask about their free programs, which include films, art shows, story hours, and ethnic programs.

Admission: Free.

Open: Hours vary with season but are usually Mon, Thurs, Fri, Sat 9am–5pm; Tues–Wed 10am–8pm.

SPORTS & RECREATION

THE BEACH To get to the town beach, follow Hi. 50 a mile toward the sea from Lihue up until its junction with Hi. 51. You'll come to the deep-water port of **Nawiliwili** (where the wiliwili trees once grew), Kauai's largest harbor and the site of a bulk-sugar plant that looks out on Kalapaki Beach across the bay. This is Kalapaki, the town beach, and you're welcome to use it. The surf, similar to that at Waikiki, is fairly gentle, with enough long rollers to make surfing or outrigger canoe rides great fun. There's easy access to the sand from the Anchor Cove Shopping Center.

FITNESS CENTERS Physical fitness buffs don't have to miss their daily workouts while on Kauai. Next door to the Kukui Grove Center, at 4370 Kukui Grove St. (tel. 245-5831), is the **Kauai Athletic Club,** where guests may indulge in aerobic classes, weightlifting, racquetball, lap swimming, etc., to their heart's content at fees of $12 per day. It's a beautiful, classy club, and the instructors are excellent. Massage is available. It has reciprocal privileges with many health clubs, maybe yours. There's a full deli for healthy snacks, protein drinks, sandwiches, and soups. Open Monday through Friday from 6am to 10pm and on Saturday and Sunday from 8am to 6pm.

SHOPPING

KUKUI GROVE CENTER, Hi. 50. Tel. 245-7784.
Pint-sized Lihue now has the largest of all neighbor-island shopping malls, the $25-million Kukui Grove Center. Since it's just four miles from the airport on Hi. 50 (headed toward Poipu), it makes a logical first stop in town to stock up on food and vacation needs.

Star Market has everything from boogie boards to gourmet take-out foods. At **Sears,** you can shop for the whole family, rent a car, survey a good selection of Hawaiian wear and island souvenirs. Such other trusty island familiars as **Long's, Woolworth's, Liberty House, Waldenbooks,** and **J. C. Penney** are here.

The outstanding shop here, the one that makes Kukui Grove worth a special trip, is ✪ **Indo Pacific Trading Company.** The store is crammed full with goods from Java and Bali, from striking dresses, pareus, accessories, and jewelry for women, up front, to furniture, textiles, and quilts, in back. In between: carvings, museum-quality tapa cloth, ceremonial masks from Papua, New Guinea, original paintings, antique gongs, and much more.

Indonesian music plays in the background, and everything they play is for sale. There's a wonderful Espresso Bar here, which serves a variety of coffees, cakes, and pastries, as well as delicious vegetarian specials, including vegetable potpie, homemade soup, and *Gado-Gado*, from $5.50 to $6.50. All in all, a very difficult place to tear oneself away from.

Another of our favorite stops here is the **Deli and Bread Connection.** In addition to the likes of plates and platters from Mexico, handblown glass from Spain, salsa dip plates, and sushi servers, they have some terrific food to take home and eat: deli sandwiches, cheeses, pâtés, wines, coffees, and teas, plus bread and rolls fresh from their own bakery (which smells wonderful). Try the fresh cinnamon rolls and the macadamia-nut rolls, baked daily. They also have delicious hot soups.

Of the clothing boutiques, we especially like the tasteful collection at **Alexandra-Christian.** Most of the other stores are of the kind you find everywhere, with the exception of **Rava,** which carries women's fashions in sizes 1, 3, and "extra small." Basic items galore can be found at **EZ** discount. And **General Nutrition Center** runs many specials and is a good place to replenish your vitamin supply—as well as get some fruit or vegetable juice.

Si Cisco's Mexican Restaurant for spicy south-of-the-border fare is the big restaurant draw here, but there are also several good snack shops (see "Where to Eat" in Chapter 10).

Free entertainment is often presented on the mall stage; check the local papers for details. The Kukui Grove Center is open Monday through Wednesday and on Saturday from 9:30am to 5:30pm, on Thursday and Friday from 9:30am to 9pm, and on Sunday from 10am to 4pm.

HILO HATTIE'S FASHION CENTER, 3252 Kuhio Hwy. Tel. 245-3404.

This is always a good budget stop for resort fashions. Call ahead and they'll take you to their factory outlet, where you can buy men's aloha shirts and women's short muumuus from $16 plus souvenirs, and macadamia-nut candies. There are always great specials here.

EVENING ENTERTAINMENT

Watch the papers for news of free shows put on at the **Kukui Grove Center**—these shows by local entertainers are sometimes every bit as good as those at the high-priced clubs. The shows often take place on Friday nights or Saturday mornings, right in the mall.

KAUAI COMEDY CLUB, in the Outrigger Kauai Beach Hotel, 4331 Kauai Beach Dr. Tel. 245-1955.

If it's Thursday, you can catch local and mainland comics doing their acts here. Show time is at 8:30pm.

Admission: $12.

HAP'S HIDEAWAY, 2975 Ewalu St. Tel. 245-3473.

Looking for the cheapest drinks on Kauai? Hap's claims to have them, starting with 12-ounce draft beer for $1.50. Hap's shows live sports events via satellite on four color monitors. They also have more than 750 songs on the jukebox including Top-40 and country-and-western music, a happy hour that stretches from 1pm to 2am, a Montana accent, and not even a trace of Polynesian atmosphere.

Admission: Free.

SI CISCO'S CANTINA, at the Kukui Grove Center. Tel. 245-8561.

This is a popular bar and lounge where you can admire the western paintings on the walls, listen to local entertainers every night except Monday and Tuesday, and take your choice of the largest collection of tequilas on Kauai. They also serve up a great margarita in a 16-ounce mason jar. "Siesta Hour" is on weekdays from 4 to 6pm.

Admission: Free.

3. EXCURSION ALONG THE EASTERN & NORTHERN SHORES

Now you're ready for one of the big trips, an excursion by automobile along the glorious eastern and northern shores of Kauai. Hawaii 56, which starts at Kuhio Highway in Lihue town, takes you the entire length of the tour. The distance is about 40 miles each way, and it will take you a full day.

KAPAIA & HANAMAULU

A few miles out of town on Kuhio Highway (Hi. 56), look for a quaint store called **The Kapaia Stitchery** (tel. 245-2281), which avid sewers and quilters seek out because it has the largest selection of fabrics on the island (Hawaiian-print fabrics start at about $6 per yard for cotton). It also has many handmade items, including the dresses, muumuus, pareus, and aloha shirts made by owner Julie Yukimura, which she sells at low prices. Julie also asks local craftspeople, especially senior citizens, to make things up for her. Most exciting of these are the patchwork coverlets made of Hawaiian fabrics by four local grandmothers: Prices are about $85 to $95 and would be at least twice as much anywhere else. Much-sought-after traditional Hawaiian quilts ($2,000 to $4,000) are also in good supply. Hawaiian quilting cushions can be made to order: $90 for an excellent piece of work. And do-it-yourselfers can find Hawaiian quilt pillow kits and hand-painted needlepoint designs of local flowers and themes. Exclusive to the shop and immensely popular are the handmade Hawaiian doll, mermaid, and angel ornaments made by a young local woman, from $9.95 to $12. There's always something new and interesting here; it's worth a stop.

Back on the road, look to your left for the turnoff to Wailua Falls, about four miles inland from Lihue. Watch for the white fence on the right of the road and listen for the sound of rushing water; soon you'll see the HVB marker. After you've seen the falls, don't be tempted to drive farther; turn around here and drive back.

WAILUA

Continuing on Hi. 56, you'll soon come to the mouth of the **Wailua River** and one of the most historic areas in Hawaii. Here, where the Polynesians first landed, were once seven *heiaus*, or temple sites, by the sacred (*wailua*) waters. Just before you get there, you'll come to **Lydgate Park** on the right, a grassy picnic area directly on the water, in which are the remains of an ancient "City of Refuge." You'll get a better idea of what a City of Refuge actually looked like when you see the restored one at Kona on the Big Island. But the concept here was precisely the same. In the days when the Hawaiians still carried on their polytheistic nature worship, life was bound by a rigid system of *kapus*, or taboos, violations that were punishable by death. But if an offender, or a prisoner of war, could run or swim to a City of Refuge, he could be purified and was then allowed to go free. Not too much of the City of Refuge remains, but if you wade out into the river you may discover some ancient carvings on the rocks, once part of the heiau. More practically, **Lydgate Park Beach** is one of the best beaches on Kauai for children. Two natural "pools," created by rocks, make it safe for them to swim and play in the ocean. The snorkeling is lovely, there are stripies and butterfly fish feeding on the rock, the water is clean and clear, and the sand is white. There are restrooms, showers, and barbecue pits near the beach. Recently, alas, there have been reports of vandalism here.

The Wailua, one of the two navigable rivers in Hawaii, is also the place where you can rent a tour boat for an idyllic three-mile trip to the fantastically beautiful **Fern Grotto**—an enormous fern-fronted cave under a gentle cascade of water, unapproachable any other way. Personally, we'd love to take this trip in our own private craft and, instead of being "entertained," spend the time contemplating the rare tropical trees and flowers that line the bank and pondering about the old Kauai alii whose bones still lie undiscovered in the secret burial caves of the cliffs above. But the tour boats are well run, the captains are entertaining, and the musicians' singing the "Hawaiian Wedding Song" in the natural amphitheater of the Fern Grotto is a unique experience.

The cost of the 1½-hour boat trip is $10 ($5 for children 3 to 12), and both **Waialeale Boat Tours** (tel. 822-4908) and **Smith Motor Boat Service** (tel. 822-3467) make the cruises. You should call in advance to make a reservation.

You may want to make a little excursion to visit **Smith's Tropical Paradise,** a 22½-acre botanical garden that features a Japanese garden, a replica of Easter Island, huge tiki heads, a tropical fruit garden, and a small Polynesian village. Adults pay $5; children, $2.50. Open 8:30am to 4pm. This is also the site of an excellent luau and Polynesian show; you can see the show alone for $10.50, or enjoy the whole shebang for about $45. For reservations, call 822-4654 or 822-9599.

At this point on Hi. 56, a side road called the **King's Highway** (named after the kings who had to be carried uphill in a litter lest their sacred feet touch the ground) leads to the restored heiau, **Holo-Holo-Ku.** It's so serene here now that it's hard to imagine that this was once a site for human sacrifice to calm the ancient gods.

Now you move on from Hawaiiana to observe some of the history of the Japanese settlers in Hawaii, recorded in a quaint cemetery just up the wooden stairs to the right of the heiau. If you continue driving along the King's Highway, you'll pass a rice field and soon, **Poliahu Heiau,** now a park that affords you a splendid view of the Wailua River. Next is **Opaekaa Falls,** plunging down from a high cliff (the name, quaintly, means rolling shrimp).

COCONUT MARKETPLACE Back on the highway now, continue toward the Coconut Plantation hotels and there, near the Islander on the Beach and the Kauai Beach Boy, you'll find Coconut Marketplace. It's a handsome setup, with concrete planked walkways, country decor, flowers and shrubs everywhere, and enough diverting shops (more than 70 at last count) to keep you busy for an hour or two.

Ye Olde Ship Store is the place for maritime art, antiques, and a fabulous collection of scrimshaw, the largest on Kauai. All the work is done on antique fossilized ivory, which is becoming rarer all the time, and some distinctive pieces have high investment potential. If you're looking for something simpler, you might pick up some antique brass ship keys (ca. 1875-1925) from Hawaiian and other Pacific ships, which would make inexpensive and unusual little gifts—under $5.

Be sure to visit the exquisite **Kahn Gallery,** where a consistently high level of taste is evident in the selection of original artwork and limited-edition graphics. Note the lyrical glasslike sculptures by Donjo (you'd never guess they were acrylic). Featured island and international artists include Roy Tabora, George Sumner, Jan Parker, David Lee, and Randy Puckett. Posters of the work of these artists, among those of other artists, can be found at **Island Images,** on the other side of the marketplace. Small paintings to carry home and limited-edition prints could start low, although most are in the several-hundred-dollar range. There are several more Kahn galleries around the island.

Kyle Vision Kites will not only sell you a terrific kite, they'll also teach you how to fly it. Prices range from $1.95 to $40, and include everything from Lotus Blossom windsocks to dinosaur kites. And it's all old-fashioned kite flying—no batteries.

If you'd like to learn some magic, check in at **Kauai Magic,** where Kauai-born magician Peter Badua and his staff offer free magic demonstrations; you can buy gifts, magic tricks, and various novelty items. The kids will like this one.

Plantation Stitchery specializes in needlepoints and patterns, and has a few dresses, too. The **Dragon Fly** has a unique look for Hawaiian clothing—women's casuals in beautiful pastel shades of 100% cotton, hand-embroidered. Prices start at $25 and styles include sundresses, jumpsuits, and baby wear in the same soft colors.

Tropic Casuals has one of the best selections of children's muumuus and aloha shirts, as well as the usual resort wear for men and women. Note their Bird of Paradise, Coral Reef, and Banana Leaves scalloped umbrellas; they're original, $30.

Parrot Jungle of Kauai is the place for the environmentally conscious. This unique natural-history store offers antique natural-history art, beautifully mounted butterflies and insects, books, figurines, Hawaiiana, educational toys, handcrafted items, and kitchenware with rain-forest and conservation themes. A store or two away, the same owners, Mary and Patrick Dunn, run **Parrot Jungle's Bird Shop:** here one can buy captive-bred baby macaws, cockatoos, conures, eclectus, and Amazon parrots. The hand-fed baby parrots can be shipped or actually taken home on the plane with you! The Dunns breed these birds, as well as antelope, pheasant, and llamas, at Parrot Jungle's Breeding Center, in the nearby Wailua Homesteads.

Elephant Walk can always be counted on for beautiful gift items: wind chimes, oil lamps, dolls, shell flowers, and the like. You can get scrimshaw, 14-karat-gold charms, and Niihau-shell necklaces, which begin at $35 (and go way up!) at **Kauai Gold;** nuts, candies, and beautiful inexpensive flower leis at **Nutcracker Sweet. Crazy Shirts** has T-shirts with great designs—the gecko Ts are taking Kauai by storm.

The Whalers' General Store is one of those very useful sundry shops, with everything from macadamia-nut brittle to liquor, sandals, shell souvenirs, and drugstore items. Many kinds of coffees are for sale at **Café Espresso,** including chocolate-macadamia nut and decaffeinated Hawaiian Kona. While you're here, have a cappuccino or espresso, or a homemade banana-macadamia Belgian waffle.

We saw some elegant muumuus for kids, as well as many other lovelies, at **Happy Kauaian,** which also has special selections for queen sizes and petites, and sells fabrics, too.

The kids will get a kick out of playing with the heavy equipment from the defunct **Kilauea Sugar Mill** that has been transformed into sculptural fountains they can control. When they tire of that, they may enjoy running to the top of the high wooden tower to see the beautiful view. And they'll be delighted with the hula show presented by the local hula schools every Monday, Wednesday, Friday, and Saturday at 4:30pm. Be sure to check the calendar of events posted at each entrance for additional free daily activities.

Hungry? No problem. The marketplace abounds in snack bars and restaurants offering inexpensive meals (see "Where to Eat" in Chapter 10). And if you want to catch a first-run movie, **Plantation Cinema I and II** are right here. The marketplace is open daily from 9am to 9pm, with free entertainment every day.

READERS RECOMMEND

A note of caution. "*Our camera bag with camera equipment was stolen from our car, even though it was locked, while we watched the free Polynesian show at the marketplace at Coconut Plantation, which is held on Monday, Wednesday, Friday, and Saturday afternoon between 4 and 5pm. Local police advise that all equipment—even in car trunks—can be a target for theft, since most people enjoy the show and thieves know they won't be returning to their car at that time.*"— Karolyn Fairbanks, Oroville, Calif.

KAPAA & KEALIA

From Hi. 56, back on the northern drive, you'll soon see a remarkable formation on the left as you enter Kapaa, the **Sleeping Giant**—the subject of another Menehune tall tale. The old fellow, so the story goes, was a kind of Gulliver whom the South Sea Lilliputians inadvertently killed.

On the opposite side of the road, opposite Foodland, look for a little store shaped like a Samoan house and called **Marta's Boat,** 770 Kuhio Hwy. (tel. 822-3926). Marta Curry, who has five young children of her own, understands the needs of mothers and children and has a stock of items both pretty and practical, much of it handmade. Her specialty is 100% cotton (or silk or rayon; she does not carry blends) aloha clothing for children. Cotton T-shirts and infant sets hand-painted by local artists are especially lovely. She also has a good selection of educational toys, many of which are good for the long plane ride home. Moms should have a look at the inviting adult clothing racks. Next door is an old Kauai favorite, a natural-foods store run by her husband, Ambrose Curry, where you might pick up a cooling bottled fruit drink or a snack, or stock up on supplies.

READERS RECOMMEND

The Sleeping Giant. "*During our stay on Kauai we met some really nice people who took us to the top of Sleeping Giant. Take a jug of water, a camera, and a snack and leave early in the morning. The site at the top is beautiful. You hike past waterfalls, through large pine forests that make you think of the North Woods. This is an easy hike; we were a party of all ages, 6 to 65. Go to the intersection at Coco Palms and ask for directions. Even some of the locals don't know about this.*"—The Quid Family, Schaumburg, Ill.

KAUAI VILLAGE SHOPPING CENTER   A stop at the Kauai Village Shopping Center, 4-831 Kuhio Hwy. (tel. 822-9272) on the mountain side of the road, is well worth your time: There's a Hawaiian museum and gift shop here, the largest natural-foods store in the islands, an excellent shop featuring hand-painted clothing, and one of the famous Wyland Galleries.

The **Kauai Village Museum & Gift Shop** is in the clock tower building of Kauai Village, a short stroll from the big Pay-N-Save store. It is a special project of Aloha International, a nonprofit group founded by Dr. Serge Kahili King, dedicated to "Peace Through Aloha." The museum/store is a major part of the fund-raising program for a world peace center being built on Kauai. Sunday morning meetings by the leaders of Aloha International are held here, as are classes and workshops on Hawaiian culture. The museum and its minitheater, showing videos, are free to the public. The gift shop is a delight, with many made-in-Hawaii arts and crafts, especially native-wood products; volcanic glass, native olivine, and kukui-nut jewelry; books on Hawaiian shamanism and Hawaiiana; Hawaiian music, videos, and maps; fine arts cards, prints, and posters; potted native trees and plants; and novel gift items. Children's Hawaiian story and activity books, toys, and games are also featured as part of the attempt to preserve and pass on the essence of Hawaiian culture. Prices are reasonable, and all profits go to foster these worthy goals. (If you would like more information on Aloha International, write to them at P.O. Box 599, Kapaa, HI 97646, or phone 822-9272.)

If you're into health foods, then a stop at **Papaya's Natural Foods,** in Kauai Village (tel. 823-0190), is a must. This is the largest health-food store on Kauai, and one of the nicest in the islands. Their stock is extensive, they carry the best products (doctors send their patients here for vitamins and supplements), and they have a good selection of organic, locally grown produce. They also have a great deli counter and a wonderful little café (see "Where to Eat" in Chapter 10) where you can have everything from a soup-and-salad lunch for under $4, to a full meal. Be sure to check the interesting gift items made on Kauai.

Art to Wear Silks, located directly under the clock tower at Kauai Village (tel. 823-0191), showcases the work of proprietor Jacqueline Sibthorpe. Her magnificent hand-painted garments, done in tropical colors on cotton and silk, are not inexpensive, but they are original works of art. Hand-painted cotton T-shirts start at $25; her signature silk "cocoons" are $230. She also carries a large collection of swimwear, men's silk and rayon Hawaiian vintage shirts ($60 and under), and many charming accessories and gift items. Try "Kauai Rain," among her line of Hawaiian perfumes.

Wyland, the artist whose studies of marine life are seen all over Hawaii, has a gallery here at Kauai Village (tel. 822-9855). Always worth a look.

KAPAA TRADE CENTER There's something of a renaissance going on in downtown Kapaa; unusual gift shops and restaurants are blossoming, and it's easy to park the car, get out, and browse. Three shops of interest are virtually side by side at the Kapaa Trade Center on the ocean side of the road. First, there's **Far Fetched,** 1390 Kuhio Hwy. (tel. 823-8135)—the artistic wares in this shop have been fetched from far and wide. All are in exquisite taste and cover a wide price range. Plateware from Italy, glass from Mexico, rainsticks from South America, ikat woven cloths from Indonesia, begin to suggest the possibilities. There's a good selection of native Hawaiian crafts: wooden bowls, baskets, decorative *ipu* gourds, hand-painted Hawaiian figures by well-known island artists—and, for good measure, Tiffany-type lamps, handblown glass, and handsome papier-mâché plates. A must stop.

Be Ku Ma Rue, at 1388 Kuhio Hwy. (tel. 822-1766), is a treasure trove of exotic women's clothing, much of it from Bali. Lots of adventurous looks can be put together here. **Earth Beads,** 1392-A Kuhio Hwy. (tel. 822-0766), is stocked with semiprecious stones, trade beads, femo beads, findings . . . everything one needs to create unusual jewelry. Finished pieces include handsome necklaces, bracelets, and earrings of semiprecious stones; crystals; coins; clays; glass; and more. Great fun.

MOVING NORTH Continuing on now, turn half a mile up the hill just before the bridge over Kealia Stream and you'll come to **St. Catherine's Catholic Church,** which boasts murals by leading Hawaiian artists: Jean Charlot, Juliette May Fraser, and Tseng Yu Ho.

Beyond Kealia, watch for the turnoff to **Anahola Beach** for a glimpse of one of those golden, jewellike beaches that ring the island.

EAST KAUAI EVENING ENTERTAINMENT

COCO PALMS RESORT, Wailua. Tel. 822-4921.

⭐ Closed since 1992's Hurricane Iniki, Coco Palms will hopefully be back in full swing by the time you read this. If so, make it a point to see the torchlighting ceremonies that are held each night at sundown. Five miles out of Lihue town on Wailua Bay, Coco Palms is the site of an ancient coconut grove and lagoon, where Hawaiian royalty once lived. Flaming torches cast eerie shadows on the water, and there's much blowing of conch shells and other ritualistic goings-on, with an effect that reassures the visiting movie stars here that they've never left the set.

As we went to press, plans were not yet finalized for evening entertainment, but most likely you'll be able to hear Hawaiian and contemporary music in the Lagoon Terrace Lounge or catch the Larry Rivera Polynesian show in the Lagoon Terrace dining room.

Admission: Torchlighting ceremonies, free.

JOLLY ROGER, Coconut Plantation. Tel. 822-3451.

Probably the longest happy hour—let's call it a "happy day"—takes place here daily from 11am to 7pm. Standard drinks are available at special prices. Karaoke begins every night at 8pm. No cover charge.

OUTRIGGER KAUAI BEACH HOTEL, 4331 Kauia Beach Dr. Tel. 245-1855.

Thirty minutes before the sun sets, on a Wednesday night, there's Polynesian entertainment at the hotel's Poolside Stage. You're expected to have a drink or two, but otherwise, there's no charge for this entertaining music-and-dance show.

Admission: Free.

KILAUEA

The first church you'll see as you drive into Kilauea town, **Christ Memorial Episcopal Church,** has only-in-Hawaii architecture. It's made of lava rock. Its windows, executed in England, are of the finest design and construction. On the other side of the road you'll soon see **St. Sylvester's Catholic Church** in Kilauea— something new in church architecture. This octagonal "church-in-the round," constructed of lava and wood, has a beautiful, open feeling. You'll recognize the work of Jean Charlot again, this time in the fresco paintings of the stations of the cross.

Now follow the road for two more miles to **Kilauea Lighthouse** (turn right into Kilauea to Lighthouse Road, which becomes Kilauea Point National Wildlife Refuge). Kilauea Lighthouse, high on a bluff that drops sharply to the sea on three sides, affords a magnificent view of the northern coastline of the island. Birds drift effortlessly in the wind like paper kites sent up by schoolchildren; below, the turquoise sea smashes against the black lava cliffs. The historic lighthouse was built in 1913, has an eight-foot-high clam-shaped lens, but is no longer operative (a small light, 30 feet north of the old structure, is the present Kilauea light). The old U.S. Coast Guard Lighthouse Station has been taken over by the U.S. Fish and Wildlife Service. Birdlovers will have a field day here, as the area is frequented by such exotic Pacific sea birds as the red-footed booby, the wedge-tailed shearwater, the white-tailed and red-tailed tropic bird, and the Laysan albatross. Whales, spinner dolphins, and Pacific sea-green turtles are also seen in the area. Docents at the visitor center next door to the lighthouse can answer questions and point out current wildlife activity. Check out the bookstore with its books on Hawaiian natural history. The Kilauea Point Refuge is open daily from 10am to 4pm.

On the way to Kilauea Lighthouse, the **Kong Lung Center** makes a good stop for shopping, stretching, and having a snack. The buildings are turn-of-the-century plantation, and the atmosphere is charming. The Kong Lung Company (tel. 828-1822) is Kauai's oldest plantation general store (1881) and it's very special, stocked with designer clothing, beautiful antiques, tasteful craft items (we spotted handsome African baskets and made-on-Kauai ceramics on our last visit), home accessories, and imaginative gift items. It has perhaps the best collection of muumuus on Kauai, elegant and expensive gowns for very special occasions.

Be sure to make a stop at **Kilauea Bakery & Pau Hana Pizza** in the Kong Lung Center to have pastry and coffee, or a wonderful slice of gourmet pizza pie and to pick up some specialty breads to take back home with you (see "Where to Eat," in Chapter 10).

Continue past **Kalihiwai Bay,** whose sleepy little village was twice destroyed by tidal waves, in 1946 and 1957, a reminder that the much-celebrated mildness of Hawaii is a sometime thing.

HANALEI

ATTRACTIONS

The glorious views continue. Keep watching for the lookout at **Hanalei Valley,** where you'll be treated to one of the special sights of the islands. The floor of Hanalei Valley, which you see below, is almost Asian, with neatly terraced taro patches and the silvery Hanalei River snaking through the dark greens of the mountains. (A sunset visit here is spectacular; plan it for a later trip if you have time). You may want to drive through the luxury resort development of **Princeville, at Hanalei** and perhaps have lunch here at **Chuck's Steak House** or **Zelo's Café.**

Back on the road, you'll soon come to **Hanalei Beach,** one of the most imposing beaches in the islands, but swimming is safe only in summer months and only at the old boat pier at the river mouth. In winter, beware of high surf and undertow. To get to the beach, turn right at St. William's Catholic Church (another Jean Charlot mural is inside). There's a public pavilion, dressing rooms, and picnic facilities; your fellow bathers will include many local families.

In Hanalei Valley itself, history buffs will want to note the old **Waioli Mission.** The original church, built in 1841, is now used as a community center. More interesting, we think, is the old **Mission House,** restored in 1921 and full of fascinating furniture, books, and mementos of 19th-century Hawaii. On Tuesday, Thursday, and Saturday between 9am and 3pm, you can take a guided tour here, for which there is no admission charge, although donations are welcomed. Plan on 30 to 40 minutes for this excellent tour. For groups of 10 or more people, however, advance reservations are required and can be made by calling Barnes Riznik (tel. 245-3202) or writing to P.O. Box 1631, Lihue, Kauai, HI 96766.

SHOPPING

We loved the funky old Ching Young General Store that had sat in the middle of Hanalei town forever, so we looked upon its demise and the construction of the **Ching Young Village Shopping Center** with mixed emotions. The old-time aura is gone, certainly, but this is a pleasant and practical place with a few shops that are worth your time. The center was in a post-Iniki transition process at the time of our visit, but you can count on **Spinning Dolphin** (tel. 826-7641) to be there. The people here create custom T-shirts, sweatshirts, and dresses, silk-screened while you watch, and claim to be the only shop in the entire state that does so. They have more than 75 exclusive designs, including some partly screened, mostly handpainted scenes of the Hanalei and Na Pali coast areas. They also have an extensive selection of children's and infant's wear.

Another popular shop here is **Hot Rocket Clothing.** Owner Jay Schneider stocks exclusive T-shirts (most are $15) and sweatshirts (most are $45) that are hand-painted and silk-screened here. Some of the most striking designs include "Marilyn Monroe," "Andy," and "Hot Gecko, Hawaii." Lots of hip clothing for men and women, jewelry, accessories, and more.

If you need some fresh produce, vitamins, or natural sandwiches, stop in at **Halalei Health & Natural Foods** (tel. 826-6990). **Hanalei Florist** can provide you with fresh flowers. Other practical resources at Ching Young Village include a **Big Save Market** and several fast-food operations.

Now visit one of Hanalei's newer attractions: the **Old Hanalei School** (tel. 826-7677). Built in 1926, this actually was an old school; it's on the National Register of Historic Places as architecturally significant, and its design became a standard throughout Hawaii for school buildings. Carol and Gaylord Wilcox, of the prominent Kauai family who also restored Kilohana Plantation, saved the old building, moved it four blocks from its original site, and have lovingly restored it, keeping its significant architectural details intact throughout.

Among the several shops here, **Tropical Tantrum** (tel. 822-7301) is one of the most popular, featuring hand-painted women's clothing by Lauri Johns and Parker Price, a brother-and-sister team from Texas. They also show works by other island artisans; prices start at around $60. There's a branch of **Kahn Gallery** (tel. 826-6677) here, with outstanding selections of original and limited-edition graphics by top artists. **Hanalei Surf** (tel. 826-9000) is for the big-waves set or just the casual beachgoer. They carry a full line of beach rentals and claim to have the lowest rental prices on the North Shore.

Stop in at **The Hanalei Gourmet** (tel. 826-2524) here to pick up some cheese, wines, delicious deli and bakery items, or to get a picnic basket. You can also have a tasty meal here (see "Where to Eat" in Chapter 10) and join the local crowd for evenings of live music Tuesday through Saturday or for a jam session on Sunday from 5 to 8pm. You could have a nifty burger at **Bubba's** (which claims that it "cheats tourists, drunks and attorneys," but don't believe it), or maybe some divine chocolate cheesecake (guaranteed to wreak havoc with any diet) at **Hanalei Coffee Company,** an espresso café that also offers breakfast, lunch, and light meals.

Note: The second phase of the **Old Hanalei School** was a building at the time of this writing. A bookstore, a jewelry store, a gallery called Vanishing Cultures (artifacts as well as more affordable items from Afghanistan, Tibet, Cambodia, and elsewhere), an upscale beach store called Sand People, and several more shops and restaurants should be open by the time you read this.

One of our favorite shops in this area is called **Ola's** (tel. 826-6937) and it's right on the main road next door to the Dolphin Restaurant in Hanalei. This is a serenely tasteful environment, a showcase for American crafts—in wood, glass, ceramic, metal, fiber, and mixed media. We love the whimsical hand-blown glass paperweights by Josh Simpson of Massachusetts, from $45; the wooden bowls by Jack Straka of the Big Island, from $80, and the many boxes by American craftsmen. Local artists are well represented. There are many boxes from all over the country. And many delights for children, too—toys, books, whimsy. A wonderful spot.

LUMAHAI BEACH

Lumahai Beach is next, and you'll recognize it immediately from pictures appearing in dozens of books, postcards, and magazines. It's probably the most widely photographed beach on the island, and deserves its fame: golden sand, a long tongue of black-lava rock stretching to the sea, a background of unearthly blue-green mountain. If the surf is not high, swimming will be safe here. It's a little difficult to find the entrance to the trail down to the beach (not indicated by any signs), but once you do, it's easy to get down. If the surf is up, admire the view and move on.

HAENA

Beyond Lumahai Beach stretches the Haena region, where the shoreline gets dreamier by the mile. You can swim anywhere along here, but be very careful of surf and undertow in the winter months. Many people consider **Haena Beach Park** one of the best beaches on the island (although we personally prefer to swim at Ke'e, described below), and you won't go wrong swimming, camping, or picnicking here. Haena is what you always imagined the South Seas would be like—golden curving beaches, coconut palms, lush foliage, and jagged cliffs tumbling down to the sea. Is it any surprise that this spot was chosen as Bali Ha'i for the movie *South Pacific?*

On this drive through the Haena region, watch on the left side of the road for the **Manimi-holo Dry Cave,** which was supposedly dug by the Menehunes to capture an evil spirit that had stolen some fish. This is the area from which the

Menehunes were also said to have left Hawaii. A short distance from here, up a small rise, is the first of two **Wet Caves,** the **Waikapalae;** about 200 yards farther is the second, the **Waikanaloa.** For once, the Menehunes were not responsible—the caves were reputedly dug by Pele in a search for fire. Finding fresh water instead, she left in disgust. It's reported that you can swim in these pools (the old Hawaiians used to jump off the ledges into them), but we think you'll do better to wait for the end of the road a few hundred yards ahead and an out-of-this-world beach. ❂ **Ke'e.** This is one of those gentle, perfect beaches that's almost impossible to tear yourself away from. As you loll on the sand under the towering mountains, listening to the Pacific, which has quieted down to a ripple beside you, it's not hard to picture this spot when it was the site of a most sacred temple of Laka, the goddess of the hula. Nearby are the remains of a heiau that guarded the sacred hula halau, to which novitiates came from all over the islands to study the dances, meles, and religious traditions of their people. From the cliffs above, specially trained men would throw burning torches into the sea (possibly in connection with temple rites). To your left are the cliffs of the **Na Pali Coast** (see below) and the end of your auto trip.

PRINCEVILLE/HANALEI
EVENING ENTERTAINMENT

Although most clubs levy no cover charge, that may change if there is a featured artist. And be sure to check local papers and/or call for information before you attend any of these: Performers and times change frequently.

HANALEI GOURMET, in the old Hanalei School Building, Hanalei Center. Tel. 826-2524.
This casual café is always jumping! There's live music Tuesday through Saturday, a jam session Sunday from 5 to 8pm. No cover charge.

HAPPY TALK LOUNGE, in the Hanalei Bay Resort at Princeville. Tel. 826-6522.
Check local sources for information on a variety of jazz and contemporary Hawaiian music performances.

PRINCEVILLE HOTEL, at Princeville Resort. Tel. 826-9644.
Again, check a local source for information on a variety of entertainment events.

TAHITI NUI, Hi. 56, Hanalei. Tel. 826-6277.
Tahiti Nui has been the place for local color for many years. Done up with pareu fabric, Tahitian wood carvings on the walls, bamboo, and a thatched ceiling, it's a superfriendly place. There's Hawaiian and contemporary music in the lounge most nights and jazz after the Friday night luau. But the best entertainment here is impromptu; local entertainers often come in to sing, and owner Auntie Louise Marston, a bubbly Tahitian, can usually be persuaded to sing herself and do the hula. The Friday night luau is a local tradition; be sure you reserve in advance.
Admission: Luau $38 adults, $15 children 6–11, free for children under 5.

4. SEEING THE NA PALI COAST

If you'd like to see the spectacularly beautiful Na Pali Coast, southwest of Haena, you have three travel alternatives: by foot, by boat, and by helicopter. For the first, you can get some excellent information in the book called *Hiking Kauai* by Robert Smith, available in local bookstores. Of the many boat trips offered, two are quite special. **Captain Zodiac Raft Expeditions,** P.O. Box 456, Hanalei, Kauai, HI

96714 (tel. 808/826-9371, or toll free 800/422-7824), takes small groups out in boats similar to those used for shooting the rapids on the Colorado River. The trip is usually smooth and gentle, but can be as wet and wild as the Colorado River on occasion; a licensed Coast Guard captain is in command. A full day's expedition costs $105 to $115 (depending on season), and includes a landing at a remote beach, a picnic lunch, snorkeling, and a hike back to an ancient Hawaiian fishing village. Morning and afternoon excursions are $75 to $85.

Helicopter trips are perhaps the most exciting way of all to see Kauai and to experience the grandeur of its remote and isolated areas. These are not inexpensive (figure roughly $2 a minute), with prices starting around $100 and going up to $200 per person for trips over Waimea Canyon and the Na Pali Coast, into the wilderness areas of Kauai, often swooping down the canyon walls to make stops at pristine beaches. Early-morning and sunset flights can be the most beautiful of all. A number are now offering tours, and competition can be fierce. **Will Squyres** (tel. 245-7541) is a veteran helicopter-tour operator with thousands of flying miles under his belt; his tours are highly thought of. **Jack Harter** (tel. 245-3774) was the first of the Kauai helicopter pilots and still rates very highly. **Papillon Helicopters** (tel. 826-6591) is the largest in the state; **Island Helicopters Kauai** (tel. 245-8588) and **South Seas Helicopters** (tel. 245-7781) are all highly reputable. **Ohana Helicopters** (tel. 245-3996), one of the newer companies, is doing a nice job, as are **Pacific Island Helicopters** (tel. 335-3115) and **Safari Helicopters** (tel. 246-0136). **Niihau Helicopters** (tel. 335-3500) is the only one with a license to fly over Niihau, the "forbidden island"; its inflight narration concerns that island's history. Photographers are advised to bring plenty of film and a wide-angle lens if possible.

5. EXCURSION ALONG THE SOUTHERN & WESTERN SHORES

This tour is about as long as the eastern and northern one and requires another full day. Since the high point is Waimea Canyon, you might check with the forest ranger on duty before leaving (tel. 335-5871) to find out if there's fog over the canyon; if so, it might be preferable to save this trip for another day, if you have one. You may want a sweater, for the slightly cooler (but still pleasant) 4,000-foot altitude of the Kokee region. Most of this drive is along Hi. 50.

Starting from Lihue, you'll pass through the town of Puhi and then you'll see a mountain formation called Queen Victoria's Profile on your left. Continue driving until you see Hi. 52 on your left, which leads you through a spectacular arch of towering eucalyptus trees (popularly called the Tree Tunnel) and into the little town of Koloa.

KOLOA

Hawaii's first sugar-plantation town, Koloa was established in 1835 and continued through most of the 19th century as a busy seaport and home to a thriving sugar mill. The old plantation town has been restored, and now **Old Koloa Town** is an attractive collection of shops and restaurants, plus a few historic sites, such as the **Koloa Hotel,** a five-room inn built in 1898 for traveling salesmen from Honolulu, and its authentically restored *ofuro,* or Japanese bathhouse. Note the huge monkeypod tree planted in 1925; it stretches halfway across the road.

Some of the most enjoyable shopping on Kauai takes place here in Koloa, at the Koloa Ball Park, every Monday at noon—and other days at other island locales. It's called the **Sunshine Market,** similar to the greenmarkets and farmer's markets in other states and cities. Local vegetables and fruit growers truck in their produce fresh from their farms, and so do local flower growers and other vendors: The result is a shopping bonanza for anybody who likes to eat! Come early, because everything is snatched up in about an hour, as prices are incredibly low. Island papayas, bananas, lettuce, tomatoes, sprouts, you-name-it, are sold at a fraction of supermarket prices. There are usually a few trucks selling coconuts; the vendors will husk and crack them for you right there; you can drink the milk and take the rest of the coconut home, or eat it all.

In addition to the Monday at noon market at Koloa Ball Park, there's one on Tuesday at 4:30pm at the Kalakeo Neighborhood Center, Papalina at Kaumauli Hwy; another on Wednesday at 3pm at the Kapaa Ball Park; on Thursday from 3:30 to 5:30pm at the First United Church of Christ in Hanapepe; on Friday at 3pm at the Vidinha Stadium in Lihue; and on Saturday at 9am at the Kekaha Neighborhood Center, and from 10am to noon at the Puu Lani Produce and fruit stand in Kilauea. For more information on Sunshine Markets, call 826-9288.

POIPU

With its glorious dry climate, golden sandy beaches, and breathtakingly beautiful surf, Poipu is one of the choice areas of Kauai. From Koloa, Poipu Road leads you right into the heart of the area.

ATTRACTIONS

Poipu Beach is one of the best swimming beaches on the island. Since the hurricane, it has more sand than ever. Youngsters can swim in a shallow little pool; there's rolling surf farther out, and a picnic area and pavilion here, too. But please be warned: It's very, very easy to cut your feet on the rocks and coral here; we've seen it happen innumerable times. Please wear foot coverings to be safe. Another word of advice: Don't spend the *entire* day here, as there's plenty to see coming up ahead.

READERS RECOMMEND

Snorkeling and Shopping at Poipu Beach. *"The best snorkeling we've ever seen—including the Caribbean—was in the little bay directly in front of the Poipu Beach Hotel. The water is a little wavy here, but if you go out in the morning, it is manageable. The fish are absolutely unbelievable . . . There is a little market of jewelry vendors by the Spouting Horn near Poipu Beach almost every day. We picked up some gorgeous coral and shell necklaces of good quality at three for $5!"—Susan and Terry Young, Crystal Lake, Ill.*

EVENING ENTERTAINMENT

There have been many changes since the hurricane so, again, check local sources for latest information.

BRENNECKE'S BEACH BROILER, 2100 Hoone Rd. Tel. 742-7588.
Visitors are welcome to join the lively bunch of regulars clustered around the satellite-dish video receiver watching their favorite sports events. No cover charge.

HYATT REGENCY KAUAI, 1571 Poipu Rd. Tel. 742-1234.
There are various possibilities for nighttime entertainment at this enchanting resort. Stevenson's Library, an elegant library bar with game tables, TVs, and a book collection, is open every night; the Captain's Bar at poolside serves snacks and tropical drinks until early evening; Tidepools Lounge offers drinks in a spectacular setting overlooking a freshwater lagoon. There's live entertainment on Fridays and Saturdays at the Seaview Terrace and at Kuhio's, which offers high-energy entertainment and late-night dancing in an art-nouveau setting (until 2am). Disc jockey, dress code. Cover charge varies at Kuhio's; others charge no admission.

SAMPAN HARBOR, LAWAI, & KALAHEO

Trace your way back now to the fork in the road and this time take the other branch, the one on the right. Continuing past Kuhio Park (on the site of the birthplace of Prince Kuhio), you come to Kukuiula Small Boat Harbor, more familiarly known as **Sampan Harbor.** Be sure to walk out on the wharf for an absolutely gorgeous view; about a mile ahead to the right is **Spouting Horn,** where the water spurts up through several holes in the lava rock, and to your left the blue-green Pacific crashes upon the black rocks. When you can tear yourself away, have a look at the vendors selling jewelry outside the parking lot; quality is high and the prices are consistently among the lowest in the islands. A great place to take care of a lot of gift shopping.

Which eelskin wholesale house is the most wholesale? Hard to say, because such outfits abound in the islands (especially in Honolulu). Certainly, one of the biggest and best is **Lee Sands' Wholesale Eelskin Warehouse** at the Hawaiian Trading Post, which you can find right outside Lawai, on Koloa Road, where Hi. 50 meets Hi. 530. Sands, who claims to be the original importer of eelskin from Asia, sells to major eelskin distributors throughout the country and to such prestigious stores as Bloomingdale's in New York, where you can be certain the prices are much higher than what you find here. We saw lovely handbags from about $60. It is said that eelskin is 150% stronger than leather and becomes softer and more supple with use. (It's the kind of bag you just can't wear out). As if eelskin weren't exotic enough, this warehouse also sells accessories made of lizard, sea snake (snakeskin sneakers were $67), and (ugh!) chicken feet. They have a large collection of Niihau-shell leis. Novelty items like wooden postcards and jewelry are also sold here.

Just outside Lee Sands' is a cute little hut called **Mustard's Last Stand,** where you're free to add not only mustard but also guacamole, sauerkraut, salsa, chili, fresh mushrooms, and three kinds of cheese to any hot dogs, sausages, or hamburgers you buy there. They also have Lappert's ice cream. If you've got the kids in tow, they may want to take time out from touring for a game of miniature golf at **Geckoland,** a course with a Kauai theme. Open daily from 9am to 7pm.

You'll have to make reservations and pay $20 to tour the **National Tropical Botanical Garden** in Lawai, but nature lovers and photographers will find it eminently worthwhile. The 186-acre garden adjoins 100 acres of Allerton Gardens, a private estate. Tours covering the National Tropical Botanical Garden and the entire Allerton Estate are given daily. To reserve an escorted tour, which is limited to 12 people, and for driving directions, phone the visitor center (tel. 332-7361) or write to Reservations Secretary, P.O. Box 340, Lawai, Kauai, HI 96765.

Just outside Kalaheo, watch for enchanting **Kukui-O-Lono Park.** The entrance is through a majestic stone gate, just south of Kalaheo. The name means light of the god Lono; at one time kukui-oil torches here provided a beacon for fishermen at sea. Now the place is a public nine-hole golf course (greens fees are very reasonable) and a small park, where you can see a Stone Age Hawaiian exhibit and a charming Japanese garden. There are birds everywhere.

READERS RECOMMEND

Olu Pua Gardens. *"We stopped to visit the very beautiful Olu Pua Gardens, a botanical showplace in Kalaheo. But there's more than just magnificent plants, trees, and flowers: The guesthouse served as a stopping-off place for U.S. presidents and dignitaries en route to and from the Far Pacific. The drafts for the peace treaty ending the war with Japan were crafted there before being carried to Tokyo. The charming guide told us that Olu Pua is now up for sale, and they are hoping someone interested in preserving the grounds as is will buy it. Up to now it's not on any historical preservation list, but it certainly should be."*—Helen Schwarz Robbins, Little Rock, Ark. [*Authors' Note:* Olu Pua is open Monday through Friday, for guided tours only, at 9:30 and 11:30am and 1:30 pm. It's located just past the town of Kalaheo, en route to Waimea Canyon.]

HANAPEPE

Another of the wondrous scenic views of Hawaii awaits you as you approach the town of Hanapepe. Stop at the overlook for a glorious vista of **Hanapepe Valley** below, where rice shoots, guava trees, and taro patches cover the fertile floor. Waimea Canyon is off in the distance to the left.

Hanapepe is quaint, with old wooden, balconied, tin-roofed buildings and an air not unlike that of an Old West town. A small artistic renaissance is happening here, as artists, attracted by the sun-drenched landscapes and the splendid light, move in. **James Hoyle Gallery**, 3900 Hanapepe Rd., is a must stop: Hoyle, who has been called a modern-day van Gogh, applies his brilliant brushstroke impressionist techniques to many Kauai scenes. While his hand-painted serigraphs are beyond our budget, posters start at $100. The **Lele Aka Gallery**, 3876 Hanapepe Rd., shows the striking mystical paintings of Ralph Adams. Have a look, too, at the **Andy Lopez Gallery**, 3878 Hanapepe Rd., and browse through the antique maps and prints and Hawaiian artifacts at **Kauai Fine Arts**, 3848 Hanapepe Rd. More galleries are opening here all the time.

Now, treat yourself to a lovely lunch at the **Green Garden** (see "Where to Eat" in Chapter 10), then drive a few miles farther on to the factory outlet store for **Lappert's Ice Cream**, that incredibly rich, incredibly delicious ice cream that uses fresh local ingredients: passion fruit, mango, and coconut–macadamia nut fudge are a few of the flavor possibilities. There are two reasons for getting your ice cream here: One, they have the best selection of flavors on the island; and two, since this is the factory outlet, they always have a scoop-of-the-day special for just 75¢ (as opposed to their regular price of $1.95 for a single scoop, $2.95 for a double). Even those who normally don't care much about ice cream become converts after the first swallow.

Art gallery, bookshop, coffee shop and restaurant, gift shop—the **Hanapepe Bookstore and Espresso Bar**, at 3830 Hanapepe Rd., is all these, as well as one of the most imaginative shops on Kauai. It started life long ago as a drugstore, and the counter from that store is now the coffee bar, where you can partake of some of the best espressos and desserts on the island. They also have plenty of gourmet vegetarian treats: multigrain waffles and pancakes, croissants, veggie burgers, appetizers, soups, and salads. Wednesday through Saturday nights, from 5:30 to 9pm, they serve delicious vegetarian Italian suppers, featuring locally made fresh pastas with a variety of sauces. There's a fine collection of Hawaiian reading material for such a small shop: plenty of Kristin Zambucka and Herb Kane, Hawaiian stories for children, and many books on Hawaiian crafts and language. Locally made gift items include Hawaiian potpourri, carved wooden candelabra, silver and wooden jewelry, and pillow covers and bib aprons made in the patterns of Hawaiian quilts. There's also a super selection of greeting cards, including most of the magnificent Kim Taylor Reece photographic cards. Hawaiian background music sets the mood for browsing.

Just past Hanapepe, turn left at the sign that says HANAPEPE REFUSE TRANSFER STATION. Go three-tenths of a mile and turn right at the HVB marker, and you'll find yourself at **Salt Pond**. It looks like a marsh dotted with strange, covered walls, and it's here that salt is mined and dried (some of the drying beds in operation date back to the 17th century) as the Hawaiians have been doing it for centuries. You may be lucky and arrive while they are working; members of a local *hui* collect the crystals during the summer months. Then you can head for **Salt Pond Pavilion**, a great swimming and picnicking beach, with safe, calm water. This beach is a good place to recoup your strength for the next big series of sensations coming up at Waimea Canyon.

WAIMEA

But first you arrive at the town of Waimea, which, like Wailua, is steeped in history. A favorite deep-water harbor in the olden days, it was the center of government before the coming of whites, and the place where Captain Cook decided to come ashore in 1778. Whalers and trading ships put in here for provisions on their long voyages in the Pacific. It was also here that the first missionaries landed on Kauai, in 1820. And it was on this site that an employee of the Russian Fur Company, Dr. Anton Scheffer, built a fort and equipped himself with a Hawaiian retinue, promising Chief Kaumuali help in defeating Kamehameha. The latter got wind of the scheme and gave Kaumuali orders to get his foreign ally out of Hawaii—which he did, pronto. But the **ruins of the old fort,** a stone wall mostly hidden by weeds, are still here; an HVB marker points the way on your left, before you come to the Waimea River. The fort may one day be restored—already restrooms and parking facilities have been built, and some of the old stonework is now visible. Until then, however, there's not much else to see here; the interest is mostly historical.

After you've passed the **Captain Cook Monument** and just before the police station, look for the turnoff to the **Menehune Ditch.** Follow the river about 1¼ miles, past some Japanese shops, a Buddhist temple, taro patches, rice paddies, and tiny houses; when you come to a narrow bridge swinging across the river, stop and look for a stone wall protruding above the road for a few feet on the left side. This is all that remains visible of the Menehune Ditch, a remarkable engineering accomplishment that brought water to the neighboring fields several miles down from the mountain. The curious stonecutting here has convinced anthropologists that some pre-Polynesian race created the aqueduct. Who else but the Menehunes? It is said that they did the whole thing in one night and were rewarded by the pleased citizens of Waimea with a fantastic feast of shrimp, their favorite food. They later made so much noise celebrating that they woke the birds on Oahu, 100 miles away. While you're busy creating some legends of your own, you might see some Hawaiian Huck Finns, placidly floating down the river on rafts made of logs tied together, little bothered by either Menehunes or tourists.

The main highway now continues beyond **Kekaha** to the arid countryside around **Mana,** and beyond that to some enormous sand dunes known as the **Barking Sands.** The Kauaians swear they say "woof" when you slide down the dunes, but that's pretty hard to prove. The U.S. Navy has now closed the area, so take the shorter drive to the canyon; you turn off the highway just past Waimea to Hi. 550. (A possible side trip at this point could be to **Polihale State Park;** just continue on Hi. 50, past Mana. Polihale Beach is surely one of the most spectacular beaches in Hawaii, with awesome cliffs and sparkling white sand, but swimming here is treacherous. (For sunbathing, walking, and a picnic, though, it's fine.)

WAIMEA CANYON

Now the road starts going up, through forests of eucalyptus, silver oak, and koa; soon you'll see the white ohia trees with their red blossoms of lehua (you'll see lehua again when you visit Volcanoes National Park in Hawaii). On you go to the first lookout, Waimea Canyon Lookout. Park your car and prepare yourself for one of the most spectacular views in all Hawaii. You're standing now at the top of a 3,657-foot gorge, about a mile wide and ten miles long. Millions of years ago this was the scene of a tremendous geologic fault, a great crack in the dome of the island; erosion, streams, and ocean waves cut the cliffs into jagged shapes whose colors change with the sun and the clouds—blue and green in the morning, melting into vermilion, copper, and gold as the sun moves across it and finally sets. The gorge is comparable to, though smaller than, the Grand Canyon, and sometimes outdoes it in colorfulness.

Now the road continues another eight miles, and you're at **Kokee State Park,** very different from anything else you've seen on Kauai. You're in the midst of bracing mountain country now, with wonderful hiking trails, freshwater streams for trout fishing (rainbow-trout season is each August and September) and swimming, wild fruit to pick in season, and wild pigs and goats to hunt. The forest ranger here will give you details on trails. You can relax for a few minutes at the **Kokee**

Museum, right next to the **Kokee Lodge Restaurant** and **Kokee Cabins** (see Chapter 10), where you could spend a long, blissful holiday.

From here, it's just four miles to a spectacular climax for this trip, the view from the **Kalalau Lookout.** Driving the winding road for these last few miles, you will pass the Kokee tracking station, now world famous for its part in the success of the *Apollo II* mission to the moon. It was from this site that a laser beam was flashed to reflectors that Neil Armstrong had set up on the lunar surface. Beyond, at Kalalau, the thick tropical forest suddenly drops 4,000 feet down to the breathtakingly blue sea. Below, on the knifelike ridges, are the remnants of irrigation ditches, tar patches, and signs of careful cultivation that have been long since abandoned to the elements. Read Jack London's story, "Koolau the Leper" (in *A Hawaiian Reader*), for a fictional rendering of the indomitable Koolau, who hid in the ridges here and single-handedly held off the Hawaii National Guard in its attempt to get him to the leper colony at Molokai. His heroic wife crossed the dizzyingly narrow ridges hundreds of times in five years to bring food to her husband and son until they both died of the fearful disease and left her to return to her people alone.

This marks the end of your trip. Depending on whether you want an early or late view of Waimea Canyon, you might schedule some of the other sights for the return trip. Another possibility is to drive directly to the canyon in the morning, to avoid having your view obstructed by clouds, which sometimes form in the afternoon. Then plan your other events—perhaps lunch at the Green Garden, a swim at Poipu Beach—for the return trip in the afternoon.

CHAPTER 12

THE BIG ISLAND

Ever hear of a tropical island with black beaches, snowcapped mountains, cedar forests, and one of the largest cattle ranches in the world? This is Hawaii, the orchid capital of America, about 200 miles southwest of Honolulu and twice as large as all the other Hawaiian Islands combined (4,030 square miles). Hawaii is also the residence of Pele, the ancient goddess of volcanoes, who stages some spectacular eruptions every couple of years. Islanders invariably refer to Hawaii as the Big Island, but it's also called the Orchid Island or the Volcano Island; all the names are appropriate, and all reflect the fascination many have with this astonishing continent in miniature. To know the 50th state, you must know the island of Hawaii.

You'll know why this is called the Orchid Island as soon as you arrive at Hilo's General Lyman Field. Rain may be helping those orchids to grow, but don't despair, it's just a "Hawaiian blessing" and it probably won't last long. Nobody in Hilo lets a little drizzle interfere with life. (In winter an occasional rainstorm will hit this part of the island harder than any other.) In fact, local residents feel that Hilo's sometimes soggy weather is the very thing that has kept it unspoiled and still charming.

Hilo, the only real city on the island and the second largest in the state, is the takeoff point for the imposing Hawaii Volcanoes National Park and the lava-scarred Puna area. Located on the east coast, Hilo has been experiencing a slump of late, but it still has its own gentle charm.

Most residents of Hilo are convinced that this is the world's greatest little city and they wouldn't consider living anywhere else. The fact that they live between the devil and the deep-blue sea bothers them not a bit. Huge mountains dominate the skyline: Mauna Kea is an extinct volcano, but Mauna Loa is still very much alive.

If you've read James Michener's *Hawaii*, you'll remember that the Alii Nui Noelani went to Hilo in 1832 to confront Pele and implore her to halt the fiery lava that came close to destroying the town. Pele has toyed with the idea more than a few times since, as recently as 1935, 1942, and 1984, but she has always spared the city—even without the intervention of priestesses. The citizens are convinced she always will.

The citizens are just as nonchalant about tidal waves—at least they were until 1960. On the May morning when seismic waves hurtled across the Pacific headed for Hawaii, the citizens of Hilo had mere hours to evacuate; instead, some of them actually went down to the bridge to watch the show. This time the gods were not so kind. Sixty-one people were swept into the waves, and a big chunk of waterfront area was wiped out. For several years after, one could see the devastation along the ocean side of Kamehameha Avenue; now there is grass and palm trees. Past Pauahi Street, however, look to your right and see the surprisingly modern architecture of the county and state office buildings. Despite much opposition, they were built to inspire confidence in the devastated bayside area, and so far there hasn't been further tsunami activity.

WHAT'S SPECIAL ABOUT THE BIG ISLAND

Natural Wonders

- ☐ Active volcanoes; especially Kilauea in Hawaii Volcanoes National Park, which has been spewing red-hot lava for the last 10 years.
- ☐ Mauna Kea, one of the world's great volcanoes, rising 13,796 feet above sea level.
- ☐ Rainbow Falls in Hilo, where rainbows form in the morning mist.

Sports and Recreation

- ☐ Hiking a diversity of trails, ranging from fern forests to black sand beaches, over lava fields, through desert scrubs, and along dramatic coastlines.
- ☐ Scuba diving and snorkeling on the Kona Coast with its fascinating natural rock and coral formations.

Museums

- ☐ Lyman House Memorial Museum Complex in Hilo, especially for a look at how the missionaries lived; many cultural and natural history exhibits as well.
- ☐ Puuopelu, a historic home at Parker Ranch in Waimea, with a superb collection of impressionist works.

- ☐ Kamuela Museum, in Waimea, a small museum full of curiosities including ancient and royal Hawaiian artifacts.
- ☐ Hulihee Palace, in Kailua-Kona, museum of Hawaiiana, once a vacation home for Hawaiian royalty.

Beaches

- ☐ The black sand beach at Punalu'u on the southern coast.
- ☐ Hapuna Beach and Samuel Spencer Beach Park, on the west coast, fine for swimming.

Arts and Crafts

- ☐ Volcano Art Center, at Hawaii Volcanoes National Park, for superb work by Big Island artists.
- ☐ Galleries islandwide, especially at Holualoa, above Kailua-Kona, an artists' colony.

Historic Sites

- ☐ Pu'uhonua o Honaunau National Historical Park, the remains, partially restored, of a place of sanctuary built more than 400 years ago.
- ☐ Petroglyphs along the Kohala coasts—stick figures drawn by the ancient Hawaiians.

This knowledge impresses itself strongly on the mind of the visitor, making Hilo far more than a make-believe world for tourists. It forms a curious backdrop to the beauty and gentleness of this city arching around a crescent bay (Hilo's name means new moon). Once a whaling port of the Pacific, Hilo is still a seaport, from which raw sugar (note the bulk-sugar plant on the waterfront) and cattle are shipped to the other islands and the mainland. Flowers are big business, too; 132 inches of rainfall a year (most of it at night—but there are plenty of misty mornings, too) make the orchids and anthuriums grow like crabgrass on a suburban lawn. Nearly a quarter of a million tropical blossoms are sent from Hilo all over the world.

The **Kona Coast**, in the west, is to the Big Island what Waikiki is to Oahu: the resort area. The little town of Kailua-Kona is the tourist center. Unlike Waikiki, though, it still has a small-town charm. Once the playground of the Hawaiian alii, Kona lures deep-sea fishermen (its marlin grounds are the best in the Pacific), families, and anyone looking for relaxed, tropical beauty. And the weather is almost always perfect.

SEEING THE ISLAND ON A BUDGET

Like all the neighbor islands, the Big Island is more expensive for the budget tourist than Oahu; nevertheless, you should be able to stay fairly close to your $75-a-day budget. Your car rental—unless it's split up three or four ways—is your biggest expense here, for driving distances are great, especially from one side of the island to the other (about 100 miles).

The island is large enough to have two airports, one on the east coast outside the small city of Hilo, the other at Kailua-Kona on the west coast. Which city should you choose as your first stop? We've done it both ways, and our considered opinion is that it doesn't make a particle of difference. Let your itinerary and the airline schedules—the ease with which you can make connections to the next island on your agenda—be the determining factor.

From either Hilo or Kailua-Kona, you can drive the 100 miles across the island and see all the sights. We prefer to visit each side of the island separately, but you can make one side your base if you don't mind long drives. (Please limit your driving to daytime hours for safety!) Read up on the sights, hotels, restaurants, and nightlife in each area, and you'll know just where you want to stay and for how long.

1. GETTING THERE & GETTING AROUND

GETTING THERE

BY PLANE Both Hawaiian and Aloha Airlines will take you from Honolulu to Hilo on the east or to Kailua-Kona on the west in roughly half an hour. You can also fly directly to or from Kona from the West Coast. Pick up your car at **General Lyman Field** in Hilo or at **Keahole Airport** in Kona, or take a cab, as there is no public transportation to take you to your hotel in either area. At Keahole, you can save money over regular cab fares by calling SpeediShuttle, which can take you from the airport to Kailua-Kona town, for example, for only $12 for one person, $14 for two, while a taxi would cost $20, plus baggage charge. There are courtesy phones located at the Aloha and Hawaiian baggage-claim areas, or phone 329-5433 in advance. They offer transportation to any location on the Big Island, as well as economical guided tours.

GETTING AROUND

The **Mass Transportation Agency (MTA)** provides islandwide public transportation bus service with buses operating Monday through Saturday, and fares ranging from 75¢ to $6 per ride. Bus routes connect Hilo with Kailua-Kona, Waimea, Honokaa, Pahoa, and Hawaii Volcanoes National Park, among others. Call MTA at 935-8241. Bus schedules are sometimes available at the **State Visitor Information booths** in the airport, and usually at the **Hawaii Visitors Bureau** at 250 Keawe St. (tel. 961-5797). Mrs. Lei Branco is the helpful woman to contact.

Hilo For all practical purposes, you're going to need a car in Hilo, even though there is a city bus system. It's limited; however, the **Hele-On** bus does make two trips a day around town, one early in the morning, one in midafternoon. You can ask for the bus schedule at your hotel or call the MTA (tel. 935-8241).

BY RENTAL CAR Most agencies on the Big Island offer a flat rate with unlimited mileage—you buy the gas. You have your choice of the trusty and popular inter-island outfits like **Alamo, Avis, Dollar, Budget,** and **Tropical,** whose main offices are all in Honolulu (see "Getting Around," in Chapter 4, for details). Remember that reservations are a good idea at any time and a must in peak seasons; other times, you may be able to get your best deal by careful on-the-spot shopping.

One of your biggest expenses if you're driving from Hilo to Kona or vice versa will be the drop-off charge; it's usually a hefty $45 from Hilo to Kona or $30 from Kona to Hilo. The cheapest way to avoid it is to take the county bus which crosses the island for a cost of $6 (see details, above), then rent a car in Kona if necessary. The only drawback is that you will miss the sightseeing en route.

READERS RECOMMEND

Car Rentals. *"Your advice was to call around. We did, and found that Avis had the best rates for one week on a special. We originally were to have a Geo Metro, unlimited mileage for one week, at $99 rate! When we went to pick up our car, we had a coupon for an upgrade: Avis was out of the upgrade for a Geo Metro, so we poor souls ended up with a double upgrade: an Oldsmobile 98! The service was excellent, and the car was in tip-top condition. The price was right. Call around!"*—Catherine and Mike Praisewater, Albuquerque, N.M.

 FAST FACTS — **THE BIG ISLAND**

Area Code The telephone area code is 808.

Babysitters Inquire at your hotel desk.

Car Rentals See "Getting Around," above.

Climate See "When to Go," in Chapter 2.

Dentists Contact Hilo Dental Associates, 475 Kinoole St., Hilo (tel. 935-1149); Dr. Frank Sayre/Dr. Daniel Walker, Frame 10 Center, Kailua-Kona (tel. 329-8067); or Dr. Craig Kimura, Kamuela Office Center (tel. 885-3300).

Doctors Contact the Hilo Medical Group, 1292 Waianuenue Ave., Hilo (tel. 969-1325); Kaiser Permanente, 75-184 Hualalalai Rd., Kona (tel. 329-3866); or Waimea Medical Associates, Kamuela (tel. 885-7351).

Emergencies Ambulance, fire, and rescue 961-6022.

Holidays See "When to Go," in Chapter 2.

Hospitals Major facilities are Hilo Hospital, 1190 Waianuenue Ave. (tel. 969-4111), and Kona Hospital, Keealekekua (tel. 322-9311).

Libraries Branches include the Hilo Public Library (tel. 933-4650), the Kona Public Library (tel. 329-2196), and the Kamuela Public Library (tel. 885-4651).

Other Useful Numbers To learn about services for the disabled, call the Commission on Persons with Disabilities (tel. 961-8211). Big Island Crisis & Help Line in Hilo (tel. 969-9111) and Kona (tel. 329-9111), and Sexual Assault Crisis Line (tel. 935-0677), can assist you. On Call (tel. 935-1666), a 24-hour free service available from any pushbutton phone, offers the latest news, sports, local and worldwide weather, community services, horoscopes, soap-opera updates, and more. Complete listings are given in the Aloha Pages of the Hawaii (Big Island) telephone book.

Photographic Needs Long's Drug Store, with branches at 555 Kilauea Ave., Hilo (tel. 935-6474), and 75-5595 Palani Rd., Kailua-Kona (tel. 329-8477), carries camera supplies.

Poison Control Center Call toll free 800/362-3585.

Police Call 935-3111 for assistance anywhere on the island.

Post Office In Hilo, the Post Office is at 1299 Kekuanaoa Ave. (tel. 935-2821); in Kona, there is a branch at 74-5577 Palani Rd. (tel. 329-1927); in Kamuela, the Post Office is on Lindsey Rd., off Hi. 19 (tel. 885-4026).

Safety Exercise the same precautions you would elsewhere: Never leave valuables in your car, even in the trunk; leave personal valuables in hotel safes or in-room safes; don't flash cash conspicuously in public.

Taxis Call A-1 Bob's Taxi in Hilo (tel. 959-4800), or Kona Airport Taxi (tel. 329-7779).

Weather Information For conditions on Hilo, call 935-8555; on the Big Island, 961-5582. For marine forecasts, call 935-9883.

2. WHERE TO STAY

The Big Island is rich in **bed-and-breakfast** accommodations, and more are cropping up all the time. We'll tell you about many of these as we cover specific locations, but first you should know about ✪ **Hawaii's Best Bed & Breakfasts,** run by Barbara Campbell, who was formerly director of sales and marketing at the prestigious Kona Village Resort. Barbara's standards are uncompromising: She handles only upscale B&B lodgings, each home selected for its distinctive personality, attention to details, and the warm hospitality of its hosts. Selections range from the most traditional host-home rooms to splendid private country cottages, some on the grounds of fabulous estates. Her service covers all the major islands. Daily rates run $75 to $175. Call or write for a brochure describing these hidden gems. P.O. Box 563, Kamuela, HI 96743 (tel. 808/885-4550, or toll free 800/262-9912 for reservations.

Then there's **My Island,** P.O. Box 100, Volcano, HI 96785, created by Gordon Morse and his wife Joann: they offer rentals in 28 houses, all on the Big Island. Call the Morses at 808/967-7110 or 808/967-7216—any time between 7am and 9pm Hawaiian time (fax 808/967-7719). They urge people to move around the Big Island, experiencing the different climates and atmospheres of the various districts, from Hilo to Puna to Volcano, from Kailua to Waimea to Honokaa, and then some. Accommodations are mostly in "nice mom-and-pop houses," with singles $35 and up, doubles $55 and up.

Volcano Reservations, P.O. Box 998, Volcano Village, HI 96785 (tel. 808/967-7244, or toll free 800/736-7140), is run by Brian and Lisha Crawford, whose charming Chalet Kilauea at Volcano is listed below. They have accommodations all over the island, ranging from budget to luxury, including B&Bs, inns, vacation homes, cottages, and condos, in a wide price range. Car rentals are also available.

Bed & Breakfast Hawaii, P.O. Box 449, Kapaa, Kauai, HI 96746 (tel. 808/822-7771, or toll free 800/733-1632; fax 808/822-2723), is an all-island reservation system. Rates start at $40 single, $45 double. Send them $12.95 for a copy of their directory of homes and apartments called *B&B Goes Hawaiian.*

Go Native . . . Hawaii, 65 Halualani Place (P.O. Box 11418), Hilo, HI 96721 (tel. 808/935-4178, or toll free 800/662-8483), has been matching guests with Hawaiian hosts for more than a decade. Coordinator Fred Diamond has 250 locations on all islands except Lanai, ranging from oceanfront to mountain sites, from traditional B&B rooms in private homes to unhosted studios and cottages. Rates begin at around $40 for a single and around $65 for a double.

Hawaii Island Bed and Breakfast Association, P.O. Box 726, Volcano, HI 96785, offers a free pamphlet listing their members. It is available at the airports or by mail, free. (*Note:* This is not a booking service.)

HILO

DOUBLES FOR AROUND $35 TO $45

ARNOTT'S LODGE AND HIKING ADVENTURES, 98 Apapane Rd., Hilo, HI 96720. Tel. 808/969-7097, or toll free 800/368-8752 from mainland U.S. 800/

953-7773 interisland. Fax 808/961-9638. 48 bunk beds in 2 apts, 5 additional apts, set up for singles, doubles, and suites.

$ Rates: $15 bunk, $26 single, $36 double (per night for two). $80 two-bedroom suite for up to 5 people; each additional person $5. CB, DC, MC, V. **Parking:** Free.

Here's your best budget buy in Hilo. Popular with everyone from European student backpackers to families and small groups, Arnott's Lodge is a converted two-story apartment building nestled in a lush tropical area, just a few minutes' walk to ocean beach parks and a short drive to the center of Hilo. Some of the rooms are hostel style with shared baths, but there are also singles, doubles, and suites. The suites are especially good for families or small groups; they have a living room with convertible sofa, two bedrooms (one with a double bed, one with two singles), a kitchen with a small refrigerator, and a private bath. All rooms have ceiling fans. Everything at Arnott's is simple, clean, casual—and very cozy. A resident manager is on hand to help plan activities. The Guest Pavilion is available 24 hours a day for "eating and drinking, partying, relaxing, gathering, late-night conversation." There's a treehouse deck in the lychee tree for communing with nature. Cooking facilities are available, and you can also have a $5 barbecue dinner here on Wednesday and Saturday nights. There's a TV lounge and laundry facilities.

Owner Doug Arnott claims there is no need to rent a car, since they offer a free shuttle to the airport and to town, as well as a series of five different hiking adventures, $20 to $25 each. These include excursions via a four-wheel-drive van to the high and wild places on the Big Island: to the top of Mauna Kea, to Kilauea Volcano to see night lava flowing and for daytime hikes, and to South Point and the extraordinary Green Sand Beach, through the rain forest of Waipio Valley and other "must see" spots. Arnott advises guests to save five days to do all the excursions and to be sure to pack hiking boots, as walking on lava is rough. There's a $5 surcharge for expeditions by nonhouseguests.

Look for another Arnott's Lodge on the Kona side of the island in the near future.

HILO HOTEL, 142 Kinoole St., Hilo, HI 96720. Tel. 808/961-3733. Fax 808/935-7836. 21 rms, 6 apts. A/C TV TEL

$ Rates: $39–$45 single or double; $85 two-bedroom apt. Each additional person $8. AE, DC, MC, V. **Parking;** Free.

Worlds away from the pleasantly hokey tourist world of Banyan Drive is the Hilo Hotel, a businessperson's hotel in the center of town. The outside is very pleasant, with lava-rock walls, a large swimming pool, spacious gardens, and the excellent Fuji Restaurant for Japanese food and drinks, where the locals like to gather. The hotel rooms are clean and adequate, and each one has a refrigerator. The higher-priced rooms also include a TV. Complimentary coffee is served every morning from 7 to 9am. The hotel is very proud of its newer Niolopa Wing, which offers extraordinary value for a family; there are six very large (800 to 900 sq.ft.) two-bedroom apartments, fully furnished, equipped with TV, all the utilities, and three telephones per unit, for up to four guests.

WILD GINGER INN, 100 Puueo St., Hilo, HI 96720. Tel. 808/935-5556, or toll free 800/882-1887. 30 rms.

$ Rates (including continental breakfast): $39 single or double, $59 deluxe room. Each additional person $10. Monthly rentals available. No credit cards. **Parking:** Free.

Here's something unique—a 30-room bed-and-breakfast inn! Robert and Sandra Woodword moved to Hilo from California a few years ago, took over an aging hotel, and are gradually converting it into a charming, old-fashioned inn. The setting is very pretty, a short walk from town, and the rooms look out on a large lawn and a garden lush with wild torch ginger, bamboo, papaya, and a private stream. Rooms (all nonsmoking) are small and plain but comfortable enough, and all have a small refrigerator and a private bath with shower but no tub. There's one deluxe room with a bathtub, wicker furniture, microwave oven, and ocean view. Phones are available in the spacious lobby, which is also the scene of a plentiful serve-yourself breakfast, with their own homemade muffins, granola, tropical fruits

HILO ACCOMMODATIONS & DINING

ACCOMMODATIONS:
Arnott's Lodge **33**
Dolphin Bay Hotel **4**
Hale Kai-Bjornen Bed & Breakfast **2**
Haili House **10**
Hilo Hotel **11**
Hilo Seaside Hotel **29**
Maureen's Bed and Breakfast **31**

Our Place–Papaikou's B & B **3**
Uncle Billy's Hilo Bay Hotel **24**
Wild Ginger Inn **1**

DINING:
Bears **9**
Café 100 **49**
Café Pesto Hilo Bay **16**

Dick's Coffee House **27**
Don's Grill **21**
Fiascos **26**
Harrington's **50**
Hukilau Restaurant **28**
Jasper's Espresso Café **12**
Jimmy's Drive Inn **47**
Karrot's Kitchen **6**

Kay's **10**
K. K. Tei Restaurant **22**
Lehua's Bay City Bar & Grill **7**
Nihon Restaurant & Cultural Center **23**
Pescatore **7**
Restaurant Fuji **9**
Restaurant Satsuki **42**

Reuben's Mexican Food **15**
Roussel's **43**
Royal Siam Thai Restaurant **44**
The Seaside **32**
Soontaree's **20**
Ting-Hao Mandarin Restaurant **28**

Airport ✈

from their own trees, eggs from their own bantam chickens, and Kona coffee. A hammock in the lobby invites serious relaxing. A coin-operated laundry is available. Improvements are being made here continually.

DOUBLES FOR $49 TO $69

DOLPHIN BAY HOTEL, 333 Iliahi St., Hilo, HI 96720. Tel. 808/935-1466. 18 units. TV
$ Rates: $45–$55 single; $55–$65 double; $75 one-bedroom apt; $85 two-bedroom apt. Each additional person $10. Discounted weekly rates available. MC, V.
Parking: Free.

Every now and then you come across a little hotel where you know you could comfortably settle down for a long, long time. Such a place is the Dolphin Bay Hotel, in a quiet residential neighborhood just a four-block walk from town. The building sits in the midst of a "small jungle," resplendent with papayas, breadfruits, bananas, and the like; you are invited to step right outside your room and pick your breakfast! The accommodations are modern, quite large, and nicely furnished with full kitchens and large tub/shower combinations in the bathrooms. The standard studios sleep one or two comfortably. The superior studios, usually with a rollaway and a queen-size bed (plus a built-in Roman-style tub!), are larger and can easily sleep three. There's also a marvelous honeymoon room with an open-beamed ceiling, and a large lanai for $61; and some really spacious one- and two-bedroom apartments, perfect for families. Since the hotel is near Hilo Bay, a cooling breeze keeps the units comfortable all year. Manager John Alexander dispenses the warmth and hospitality that have made this one of our best island finds over the years. He and his staff will map out tours, arrange trips, and advise on the best restaurants. Write or phone in advance, since the guests who come back each year—many from Canada and the Midwest—keep this place hopping. Lots of readers' hurrahs for this one continue to come in every year, even though there is no pool. Orchids are grown right on the grounds at the Iliahi Nursery.

HILO SEASIDE HOTEL, 126 Banyan Dr., Hilo, HI 96720. Tel. 808/935-0821. Fax 808/922-0052. 135 rms. A/C TV TEL
$ Rates: Single or double; $49 standard; $54 deluxe; $65 with kitchenette. Each additional person $12. Children 12 and under stay free in parents' room when using existing bedding. Rate increase expected. AE, DC, MC, V. **Parking:** Free.
The Hilo Seaside Hotel (formerly the Hilo Hukilau Hotel) near Hilo Bay has long been a pleasant place to stay. The local branch of the kamaaina-owned Sand & Seaside Hotels (there are others in Kona, Kauai, and Maui) has attractive rooms (most with air conditioning) with lanais—rooms that overlook either the freshwater swimming pool, a fish pond, or lush tropical gardens. The hotel has been attractively renovated, and the lobby is decorated with contemporary tiles and Oriental hardwood floors. Wood fenceposts, Polynesian murals, and tikis permit you to forget the mainland. The popular Hukilau Restaurant and Cocktail Lounge is a longtime favorite for well-priced meals.
Reservations: Sand & Seaside Hotels, 2222 Kalakaua Ave., Suite 714, Honolulu, HI 96815 (tel. toll free 800/367-7000 in the mainland U.S., fax 808/922-0052).

UNCLE BILLY'S HILO BAY HOTEL, 87 Banyan Dr., Hilo, HI 96720. Tel. 808/935-0861, or toll free 800/367-5102. Fax 808/935-7903. 145 rms. A/C TV TEL
$ Rates: Single or double; $54 moderate; $64 superior; $72 oceanfront; $69 with kitchenette. Room-car packages available. AE, DC, DISC, MC, V. **Parking:** Free.
Uncle Billy's, owned and operated by a Hawaiian family, is run on "Hawaiian time" and the pace is leisurely; you can feel that pleasant Polynesian paralysis setting in the moment you step into the South Seas lobby decorated with fish nets and tapa-covered walls. All rooms have a private lanai. The higher-priced rooms are huge: Two double beds look lost in the room. Most rooms face a tropical garden that leads to a path to the swimming pool, next to the ocean on Hilo Bay. Uncle Billy's Fish & Steak Restaurant, right in the hotel, is a fun place for food and entertainment (see "Big Island Evening Entertainment," in Chapter 13).

BED & BREAKFASTS

HAILI HOUSE, 239 Haili St., Hilo, HI 96720. Tel. 808/969-7378.
4 rooms with half-baths, one room with full bath.
$ Rates: $75 for rooms with half-bath, $90 for room with private bath. No credit cards.
This recently restored historic house offers visitors a bit of the past. Every room is decorated with mementos of "Old Hawaii" to make you feel as if you've stepped back in time. The five-bedroom house has four rooms with a toilet and basin (no shower or bathtub) and one room with a full bath. As much as we covet a private bath, we loved the rooms with half baths—they were quieter (located in the back of the house) and the decor and Hawaiiana artifacts were charming and inviting. The location of Haili House is another bonus—just half a block from the Lyman Museum and within walking distance of downtown Hilo.

HALE KAI-BJORNEN BED & BREAKFAST, 111 Honolii Pali, Hilo, HI 96720. Tel. 808/935-6330. Fax 808/935-8439. 4 rms (all with private bath), 1 cottage. TV TEL
$ Rates (including breakfast): $80–$90 double; $98 one-bedroom guest cottage with kitchen. Minimum stay 3 days. **Parking:** Free.

⭐ You'll be warmly welcomed and made to feel right at home at Evonne Bjornen's bed-and-breakfast. And what a home it is—a superb double-decker house with an entire wall of glass overlooking Hilo Bay and the island's best surfing spot, Honolii Surfing Beach. Guests have use of the magnificent living room looking out over the waterfront, and just beyond it, a pool with Jacuzzi and comfy lounge chairs. Downstairs are three bedrooms plus a family room, all beautifully furnished, with either a king- or queen-size bed. Mrs. Bjornen is a friendly woman who truly enjoys having guests in her home. Her husband, Paul Tallett, is a native Hawaiian, a well-known fisherman and hunter, ready to entertain you with songs on the ukulele and tell you about his island and the old tales of Hawaii. Mrs. Bjornen likes to whip up fabulous breakfasts, including such special treats as macadamia nut waffles and Portuguese sausages, and often puts her telescope out on the porch so that guests can watch the volcano when it's in action! Staying here is like being on a lovely retreat—you may forget to go out and explore Hilo. Hale Kai has been selected as one of the top 100 B&Bs in the U.S. and Canada."

MAUREEN'S BED AND BREAKFAST, 1896 Kalanianaole St., Hilo, HI 96720. Tel. 808/935-9018. 6 rms.
$ Rates (including breakfast): $40 single; $60 double. No credit cards.
Owner Maureen Small has restored a classic redwood house built in 1935 and lovingly decorated it with oak, mahogany, and koa-wood antiques. The living room is out of another era: a 30-foot vaulted ceiling with double staircases leading to a wraparound balcony. Rooms have semiprivate baths. The two upstairs rooms, with views of the mountains, are very large and have California (extra-large) king-size beds. The two downstairs rooms (one large, one small) have double beds and a garden view. Two single rooms also share a bath. The grounds are manicured Japanese gardens with koi ponds. James Kealoha Beach Park is just across the street (it has a sandy bottom, brackish water, and is okay for doing laps), and Richardson Ocean Beach Park (good for snorkeling) is a mile down the road. In addition to the usual fresh-fruit-and-main-course breakfast, Maureen likes to serve fresh fish whenever her fishing friends are lucky.

OUR PLACE–PAPAIKOU'S B&B, P.O. 469, Papaikou, HI 96781. Tel and fax 808/964-5250, or toll free 800/245-5250. 4 rms (1 with bath).
$ Rates (including breakfast and tax): $50 double; $60 loft tree-house room; $75 master bedroom. Each additional person $5. No credit cards. **Parking:** Free.

⭐ Four miles north of Hilo, on Hi. 919, Our Place–Papaikou's B&B is a charming place to stay close to Hilo town. Sharon Miller, a former Rolfer, and Ouida Taherne, M.D., both gave up busy lifestyles in California and Mississippi to move to Hilo and set up a guesthouse here. They've found a lovely cedar-paneled home overlooking a stream, set amid lush tropical vegetation. The "Great

Room," splendid with its cathedral ceiling, has a library, fireplace, and piano, and cable TV/VCR—all of which guests are invited to enjoy. Four rooms share a common lanai that looks out over Kupuu Stream. There are two doubles, a master bedroom with a private bath, and a loft "tree house." Miller and Taherne are excellent cooks (they do complete breakfasts) and are friendly, helpful hosts—and their prices are right.

THE NORTHERN ROUTE

HONOKAA

Doubles for About $45 to $55

HOTEL HONOKAA CLUB, Honokaa, HI 96727. Tel. 808/775-0678. 14 rms.
$ Rates: $32 single, $41 single with TV; $35 double, $44 double with TV. MC, V.
Parking: Free.

Forty miles north of Hilo on the northern, or Hamakaua coast, route, and not far from the cattle country of the Parker Ranch, is the venerable Hotel Honokaa Club, which has been serving local businesspeople and hunters for more than 50 years. Undemanding types will find the rooms acceptable. The hotel's inexpensive restaurant and bar are very popular with the local people.

WAIPIO WAYSIDE, P.O. Box 840, Honokaa, HI 96727. Tel. 808/775-0275, or toll free 800/833-8849. 5 rms (2 with bath).
$ Rates (including breakfast): $50–$80 single; $60–$90 double. DC, MC, V. **Parking:** Free.

Two miles from the center of Honokaa, on the ocean side, is Waipio Wayside, one of the most charming new B&Bs to open in this area. Jacqueline Horne, from California's Silicon Valley, settled in these peaceful parts, and renovated a 1938 sugar plantation home. It's now decorated to recall the charms of old Hawaii. Bordered by a white picket fence and set on 1½ acres of tropical fruit and vegetable gardens, the house overlooks sugarcane fields and the ocean far below. The outside deck with its double hammocks and the gazebo for sunset watching are popular spots; so, too, are the kitchen, where Jackie, a gourmet cook, often whips up special treats (she serves a full breakfast) and the living room with its 31-inch TV/VCR, where she might schedule a Japanese film festival complete with popcorn. The rooms are beautifully decorated with antique furniture, Chinese rugs, and silk drapes hand-painted by a local artist. Two rooms at the front of the house, the Moon Room with a full-size bed and the Plantation Room with twin beds, share a bath. At the back of the house is the Chinese Room, with its antique Chinese reclining barber's chairs; it overlooks the deck and gazebo, and has a half-bath. The Library Room upstairs is very special, with blond-wood paneling, an ocean view, skylights over the bed and shower, and something like 300 books on the shelves. The Bird's Eye Room at the back of the house is special, too—a spacious private bedroom suite with its own bath, blond-wood paneling, and a patchwork quilt on the bed. Double doors open onto the deck and a view of gardens, sugarcane fields, and ocean beyond. A great spot for a peaceful retreat.

KUKUIHAELE

Doubles for About $65 to $75

HALE KUKUI, Box 5044, Kukuihaele, HI 96726. Tel. 808/775-7130 or toll free 800/444-7130. Three units, each with private bath.
$ Rates: $75 studio for two to four; $96 two-bedroom apt for four to six; $150 three-bedroom apt for six to ten. Additional person $10 extra. For stays of less than 3 days add $10 per night. Discounts of 5% to members of Greenpeace, Sierra Club, and other national environmental organizations. MC, V.

Located on over four acres overlooking Waipio Valley, this guest cottage is nestled on beautifully landscaped grounds, complete with a recently planted two-acre organic orchard with 30 different species of tropical fruit (pick all you can eat!). A year-round stream sets a relaxing mood. Each modern, nicely furnished unit has its own living room, kitchenette, private full bath, and lanai; the studio unit and the two-bedroom unit can be combined to create a three-bedroom apartment. Television is available on request. Owners William and Sarah McCowatt are about 150 feet away, in the main house. Breakfast is provided the first day of your stay, but since each unit has a kitchen, you're on your own after that.

HAMAKUA HIDEAWAY, P.O. Box 5104, Kukuihaele, HI 96727. Tel. 808/ 775-7425. 2 units.

$ Rates: $65–$75 for two people for 2 or more days, $70–$80 for 1 night only. Discounted weekly and monthly rates available. No credit cards. **Parking:** Free.

Searching for the perfect romantic hideaway? Search no more. We've found it seven miles north of Honokaa, at Hamakua Hideaway, a charming home perched high on a cliff and affording magnificent views of breathtaking Waipio Valley and the dazzling ocean below. Kristan and Jim Hunt, a friendly couple who built the home themselves, have also created two separate guest accommodations, one connecting to the main house, the other down the way a bit, out on the cliff. The Tree House Suite, which connects to the main house, is nestled into a mango tree; has sunshine and windows on all sides, a private bath, and a kitchen; and is beautifully furnished. The Cliff House, nestled above a 50-foot waterfall, is more like a little house, with its own wood stove, a loft with a futon above, screened lanai and Jacuzzi tub, complete kitchen, and private bath. Both units have glorious views and as much privacy as one would wish. The Hunts' three tow-headed little boys add to the overall charm. Kukuihaele is midisland, about an hour from either Hilo or Kona Coast locations.

WAIPIO RIDGE VACATION RENTAL, P.O. Box 5039, Kukuihaele, HI 96727. Tel. 808/775-0603. 1 cottage.

$ Rates: $75 double for only 1 night; $65 double for more than 1 night. $385 double per week. Each additional person $15 extra. No credit cards. **Parking:** Free.

A thousand feet above the floor of Waipio Valley, Roger Lasko's little cottage commands a spectacular view; from this distance, the surf breaking below gently lulls one to sleep. The modestly furnished cottage contains a large living room, a bedroom, a well-equipped kitchen, a dining area, and bath. Lasko's friendly Dog, Bingo, is in residence. Lasko, a woodshop instructor in the Honokaa school system, lives next door; his phone is available for use.

WAIPIO VALLEY

A Super-Budget Choice

WAIPIO HOTEL, Waipio Valley, Tel. 808/775-0368 in Waipio or 808/935-7466 in Hilo; or write to Tom Araki, 25 Malama Place, Hilo. HI 96720. 5 rms (none with bath).

$ Rates: $15 single. No credit cards.

Remote and scarcely populated Waipio Valley, which can be reached only by a four-wheel-drive vehicle or by hiking down the steep cliffs, actually has two places where you might spend a night or two. It's like living in the jungle, with all its lush beauty—but also with the possibility of jungle rains. Tom Araki's Waipio Hotel has all of five rooms and one bath, and has absolutely no truck with such modern amenities as hot water, telephone, restaurants, or even electricity. A friend of ours, a very successful businesswoman in Honolulu, swears she'd rather spend her vacation here, at Tom Araki's $15-a-night hotel, than anywhere else. You no longer have to bring your own sleeping bag: Linens and blankets are furnished.

Worth the Extra Money

WAIPIO TREEHOUSE, THE HALE, and THE KAHU, Waipio Valley. Tel. 808/775-7160; or write to Linda Beech, P.O. Box 5086, Honokaa, HI 96727. 3 houses.

$ Rates: Waipio Treehouse and The Hale: $200 for two; $50 surcharge for 1-night stay; children under 12 free; children over 12 $25–$50 extra. The Kahu: $200 for two, plus $75 for each extra bedroom. AE, MC, V.

⭐ Waipio Valley also offers a possible haven for incurable romantics who don't mind splurging a bit for a home in the trees. The Treehouse, 30 feet up in a 60-foot monkeypod tree, faces a 1,000-foot waterfall, sleeps three, and even has a kitchen. A skylight offers moonlit views through the leaves. You can swim under the waterfall or in the ocean, about a 1½ mile-walk from here. Hot furo (deep hot tub) baths are available in an adjoining building. Fresh fruits can be picked on nearby paths. It could be paradise. For those who want more room to stretch out in, there's the Hale on the ground level. This is a private cottage with a living room, a loft, a full kitchen, and views of not one, but two waterfalls. Four to six people can be accommodated (there's a king-size bed, a queen-size bed, and a double futon). A massage therapist is on hand to help guests unwind totally.

For parties of up to 10 people, try the Kahu, a new addition on the property. This private residence comfortably sleeps 10, has three private bedrooms, each with separate bath, plus an upstairs sleeping loft with bathroom. Downstairs features a massive hikie'e (large Hawaiian sleeping couch), a living room, a kitchen, and an outdoor lanai that overlooks three waterfalls.

When you call to make reservations, they'll help you arrange transportation down into the valley: a four-wheel-drive is required.

KAMUELA

Doubles for About $55 to $105

KAMUELA INN, Kawaihae Rd. (P.O. Box 1994), Kamuela, HI 96743. Tel. 808/885-4243. Fax 808/885-8857. 19 rms, 12 suites.

$ Rates (including continental breakfast): $54–$67 single or double; $83–$93 kitchenette suites for three or four persons; $93 penthouse suite; $165 combination of two penthouse suites. Mauna Kea Wing: $72–$79 double; $165 executive suites. AE, DC, DISC, MC, V. **Parking:** Free.

From Honokaa, it's 15 miles on Hi. 19 to Kamuela or Waimea, heart of the Parker Ranch cattle kingdom. A good place to stay in this deliciously cool mountain town is the Kamuela Inn, an old standby that has been attractively renovated. Rooms in the older building are all nicely furnished, and kitchenettes are well equipped with all utensils, even including rice cookers. Two penthouse suites rented together are a nice arrangement for a large family or two couples traveling together: The front suite, which sleeps two on a queen-size bed, has an expansive mountain view, a full bath, and a private lanai with wet bar; the rear suite has a full kitchen and bath and generous-size bedroom, which sleeps three with a king-size and a single bed.

The recently completed Mauna Kea Wing offers rooms with either king-size or twin beds, as well as two luxury suites, each with two king-size beds, a full kitchen, a full bath, and a private lanai.

Continental breakfast is served in a cheery coffee lounge with broad windows admitting the morning sun. Scenic grounds (there's a bottlebrush tree with red flowers that really look like bottle brushes) just outside the hotel and a friendly management are pluses here. There are restaurants nearby and good swimming 12 miles away at Hapuna Beach Park. For reservations, contact manager Earnest Russell.

MORNINGSTAR MEADOW, P.O. Box 2396, Kamuela, HI 96743. Tel. 808/885-7674. 3 rooms.

$ Rates (including breakfast): $50–$60 single, $75–$85 double. Includes full gourmet breakfast. No credit cards.

BIG ISLAND ACCOMMODATIONS

PACIFIC OCEAN

PACIFIC OCEAN

Airport ✈ Mountain △

Aston's Kona Islander Inn 9
Champagne Cove 25
Carson's Volcano Cottage 27
Chalet Kilauea at Volcano 30
Colony's Kona Bali Kai 5
Country Goose 28
Dragonfly Ranch 1
Durkee's Coffeeland 6
Guesthouse at Volcano 29
H. Manago Hotel 2
Hale Kakui 20
Hale Ohio 37
Hamakua Hideaway 19
Holualoa Inn 5

Hotel Honokaa Club 21
Kalani Honua 26
Kilauea Lodge 31
Kona Magic Sands
  Condominium 8
Kona Riviera Villa 10
Kona Seaside Hotel 11
Kona Tiki Hotel 7
Lokahi Lodge 36
Merryman's B & B 3
Morningstar Meadow 16
Namakani Paio
  Campground 32
Paradise Place
  Bed & Breakfast 23

Parker Ranch Lodge 14
Rainforest Retreat 24
Sea Village 12
Uncle Billy's
  Kona Bay Hotel 13
Volcano Bed & Breakfast 33
Volcano Heart Chalet 34
Volcano House 35
Waimea Garden Cottages 15
Waipio Hotel 17
Waipio Treehouse
  and The Hale 18
Waipio Wayside 22

This beautiful country home is nestled at the 3,000-foot elevation in the rolling hills above Kamuela. Owner Dee Dickson is not only a gourmet cook, but also a creative interior decorator and travel-guide writer/local historian. Each of her rooms has a decor and a story to match its name. "Checkered Past" derives its name from the bricks that were taken from an old sugar mill. Inside are a pair of antique twin beds. An old koa rocker, lace curtains, Hawaiian art and artifacts grace the room. Next is "Heavy Metal Rose," decorated with an antique iron bedstead with overhead canopy and antique metal furniture. The third room, "Sunshine Corner," is entirely different, with brightly colored walls and a queen-size bed. The rooms are beautiful, but Dee's breakfasts are unbelievable. The meals are heavy on fresh fruit and produce, light on fat and cholesterol. Depending on the season, and where her guests are from, breakfast may begin with stuffed baked apples, followed by fresh spinach fritatta with grilled tomato or, if the ingredients are available, ask Dee to whip up her famous Scottish Coast breakfast: bangers, mashed potatoes with leeks, grilled tomatoes, fresh oatmeal scones, and just-picked Waimea strawberries.

THE PARKER RANCH LODGE, P.O. Box 458, Kamuela, HI 96743. Tel. 808/885-4100. Fax 808/885-6711. 21 units. TV TEL

$ Rates (including tax): $74.25 single or double, $85.15 single or double with kitchen. Additional person $10 extra. AE, MC, V. **Parking:** Free.

Also very pleasant in this area is the Parker Ranch Lodge, a modern motor hotel within walking distance of the Parker Ranch Center and all its sightseeing, shopping, and eating facilities. Horseback riding and golf are nearby, some excellent beaches a reasonable drive away. Each room boasts quality furnishings, attractive decor, and beamed ceiling. From this cool, 2,500-foot elevation you have a view of rolling green meadowlands and mountains. Singles have one king-size bed and doubles have two queen-size beds.

WAIMEA GARDEN COTTAGES, P.O. Box 563, Kamuela, HI 96743. Tel. 808/885-4550, or toll free 800/262-9912 for reservations. 2 cottages TV TEL

$ Rates (including breakfast): Cottages $100–$105 per night. Additional person $15 extra. No credit cards. Minimum stay 3 nights. **Parking:** Free.

Waimea Garden Cottages has to be one of our very favorite places on the Big Island. This is the perfect country retreat: two elegant private cottages where you can live in graceful surroundings, do your own cooking if you wish, spend your time riding or hiking in the mountains, or swimming at Hapuna Beach, just eight miles down the road. (The hosts provide beach towels, back rests, and coolers for the beach.) Barbara and Charlie Campbell, a charming local couple, have created the cottages adjacent to their own home. The newest Waimea cottage has a sitting room, gracious bedroom alcove with queen-size bed, hardwood floors, fireplace, TV, stereo, and French doors opening to a spacious brick patio. Your hosts welcome you with breakfast provisions and a tempting array of local fruits. You can even gather your own eggs from the family hens right on the grounds. The Waiaka Stream meanders right behind the property. If you're lucky enough to get into this place, you're in for a treat. If, however, the cottages are not available, Mrs. Campbell, who also runs Hawaii's Best Bed & Breakfasts, can assist you with equally charming accommodations elsewhere in Waimea and throughout the state.

READERS RECOMMEND

The Royal Waikoloan, 275-9763 Waikoloa Beach Resort Dr., Kohala Coast, HI 96743-9763 (tel. 808/885-6789 or toll free 800/462-6262). "We stayed at The Royal Waikoloan, a superb resort hotel, and paid $115 a night. Their excellent restaurants provide reasonably priced meals and buffet-type foods from their regular menu, thus allowing two to stay in a most beautiful resort and still be within the $150-a-day budget for two. I highly recommend this hotel."—Martin Model, British Columbia, Canada. [Authors' Note: Rates range from $115 to $200 double.]

THE SOUTHERN ROUTE
Driving the southern route (Hi. 11) between Hilo and Kona, there are a number of delightful places to spend a night or two. First, we'll tell you about a bed-and-breakfast choice in Keaau, about a 15-minute drive out of Hilo, and en route to Hawaii Volcanoes National Park; then we'll look at a cluster of guesthouses in the Volcano area itself. Finally, we'll stop at the most famous hotel in the area, perched right on the brink of Kilauea Crater, explore some nearby campgrounds, visit a house at the beach at Kapoho, and stop off at an international conference and retreat center which also takes travelers.

KEAAU
Doubles for About $65
PARADISE PLACE B&B, HCR 9558, Keaau, HI 96749-9318. Tel 808/ 966-4600. 2 rms. TV
$ Rates (including full continental breakfast)· $60 single; $65 double. 2 night minimum stay; seventh night free. No credit cards.
Paradise Park, six miles south of Keaau, is the home of Paradise Place, owned by Laura Richman and Steve Peyton. It's in a one-acre rural setting, just half a mile from the ocean. The view from the two rooms takes in the steaming volcano Mauna Kea in the distance and the tropical garden right outside the door. Each room has its own private entrance, bath, kitchenette with full refrigerator, washer and dryer, patio, and hammock. Those renting a double often get the entire apartment. A hot tub/spa and a ping-pong table are special pluses.

READERS RECOMMEND

Paradise Place Bed & Breakfast. *"This was the life! Large bedroom, TV, VCR, a large bathroom with everything you need and don't need—iron, shampoos, conditioners, razors, hand lotions, sunburn ointments, etc.—a wonderful kitchen with a dynamic view of Pu'uo'o, the smoking volcanic vent. The kitchen also had a microwave, toaster oven, a fully-stocked refrigerator, telephone, gorgeous paintings. The den was wonderful! Beautiful Hawaiian memorabilia, stereo, a second TV, beautiful wicker furniture. The backyard had a picnic table, swing, and a barbecue grill which we used for all of our meals. We went to the ocean a couple of times in the early morning. Each time we saw a whale and dolphins frolicking just 50 feet from shore. This was truly paradise. Steven and Laura checked on us to make sure we were comfortable and if we had enough food in the cabinets and the refrigerator. They lent us maps, snorkeling gear, ice chest, packs, and lawn chairs to use when we went out exploring and snorkeling. They gave us wonderful tips on where to go and the fastest way to get there. We had the most fantastic time with the best hospitality for an economical price. We enjoyed Steve and Laura's company very much."*—Catherine and Mike Praisewater, Albuquerque, N.M.

RAINFOREST RETREAT, HCR 1, Box 5655, Keaau, HI 96740. Tel. 808/ 982-9601. Fax 808/966-6898. 2 units.
$ Rates (including breakfast): Studio $49 single/$59 double. Ohia House $69 double/single. Additional person $10/night. Single night stay additional $10/night. No credit cards.
Tucked away in the rain forest of ohia trees and wild orchids, this is a very private, relaxing retreat. Lori Campbell, owner and operator, also has one of the largest orchid nurseries in Hawaii, specializing in cattleya and phalaenopsis. The Ohia House is on the grounds of the nursery with a second-story view of Mauna Kea and—if you're lucky—the glow from Kilauea's continuously erupting volcano. The real attraction here is the large hot tub to soak away your cares and contemplate the beauties of the rain forest. The house has a complete kitchen (which Lori fills with

everything you need for breakfast: Kona coffee, local teas, juice, milk, homemade muffins, waffles, french toast, island spreads, and fresh eggs). Also available is the comfortable, 400-square foot garden studio with a kitchenette, king-size bed, and full bath. Riding lessons ($20) are available on the property: riders must have appropriate attire (heeled shoes or boots and helmets).

VOLCANO AREA

The Volcano area is perfect for the guesthouse lifestyle. Country cottages are places where you can bring the kids, relax, drive off to the volcano or to the black sand beaches farther south, or just savor the simple charms of country life. But do bear in mind that the weather is highly changeable here, and in the mountains, rains come and go.

Doubles for About $50 to $60

CARSON'S VOLCANO COTTAGE, 501 Sixth St., Mauna Loa Estates (P.O. Box 503), Volcano, HI 96785. Tel. 808/967-7683, or toll free 800/845-LAVA. 3 rms. 1 private cottage, 1 suite, 2 vacation homes (all with bath).
$ Rates (including breakfast): $55 single; $75 double; $140 suite; from $85 vacation home. DISC, MC, V. **Parking:** Free.

Hosts Tom and Brenda Carson love meeting new people and aim to provide them with a welcome, peaceful—and romantic—environment. So romantic, in fact, that one recent guest wrote that he was so "overwhelmed by the enchanted, romantic atmosphere" that he was led to propose here! There is a private, cozy cottage that sleeps five, and a three-room cottage; all rooms have private baths and private entrances, and two have kitchenettes. Rooms are furnished in Victorian, Polynesian, Asian, country, and Hawaii 1940s style, with many unique pieces, homey touches, and fresh flowers indoors and out. The Carsons serve an elaborate breakfast, including the likes of Hawaiian french toast made from Portuguese sweet bread, bagels with cream cheese and lox, and cheese blintzes with strawberries. And there's a hot tub nestled among giant Hawaiian tree ferns. Vacation homes are affordable, and some sleep up to six.

THE COUNTRY GOOSE, Ruby Ave. and 8th St., Volcano, HI 96785. Tel. 808/967-7759. 2 rms, 2 vacation houses (all with bath).
$ Rates: $70 double (including breakfast); $85 two-bedroom/two-bath house for two; $100 three-bedroom/two bath house. Each additional person $20. D, MC, V. **Parking:** Free.
Joan Early's house is decorated with all kinds of country geese—wood, ceramic, cloth—sent to her by guests who've enjoyed her hospitality and her delicious breakfasts. She likes nothing better than to whip up some sour cream pancakes or quiches, or Hawaiian french toast made from Portuguese sweet bread, or waffles with fresh strawberries for her guests. The full breakfast comes with the King Room with king-size bed, bath, and private entrance, and the Queen Room with queen-size bed, double futon on a frame, bath, and private entrance. Each room has a TV and VCR with tapes and books of local interest. Around the corner are Joan's two vacation houses. The two-bedroom house can accommodate six people and the three-bedroom up to 12—so they're both very popular for small groups or family reunions. Joan has plenty of good tips on nearby attractions of the Volcano area.

THE GUESTHOUSE AT VOLCANO, 11-3733 Ala Ohia St. (P.O. Box 6), Volcano, HI 96785. Tel. 808/967-7775. Tel/fax 808/967-8295. 1 one-bedroom cottage.
$ Rates: $60 for two people. Additional person $10 extra. Minimum stay 2 days; seventh day free. No credit cards. **Parking:** Free.

Bonnie Goodell is in charge at the Guesthouse at Volcano, a perfect place for a family to settle into. Nestled in a tree fern forest, it consists of a living room downstairs with a double hideaway bed, a complete kitchen, and a nice bedroom upstairs with two twins and a queen-size bed. The apartment is fully furnished, including phone, black-and-white TV, books, magazines, games, electric heater, bikes for children, and even wool socks! The big outside porch has kids' toys and a big sink area for "cookouts, muddy boots, berries, etc." If Bonnie is booked, she will probably be able to help you find another similar place.

HALE OHIA COTTAGES, P.O. Box 758, Volcano, HI 96785. Tel. 808/967-7986. 4 units.

$ Rates (including continental breakfast): $60–$65 one bedroom; $75–$85 cottage. Additional person $15 extra. No credit cards.

Hale Ohia was once the historic Dillingham summer estate, located on beautifully landscaped grounds just a mile from Volcano National Park. Built in 1931, Hale Ohia consists of a main house, a guest cottage, a gardener's cottage, and other structures in a botanical garden. The gardener's cottage, now known as Hale Ohia Cottage, is a charming, two-story house with three bedrooms (sleeps five), a large living room, and a complete kitchen. For smaller groups or for travelers on a budget, the Hale Lehua Cottage (once a private study in the days of the Dillingham estate) is a one-bedroom house centered around a lava rock fireplace. The limited cooking facilities include a refrigerator, microwave, and hot plate.

Also available are the Iiwi and Camillia Suites, located on the first floor of the Hale Ohia Cottage. Each has a private entrance and private baths with gorgeous leaded-glass windows. The Camillia Suite, with parking right at the door, is easily accessible to disabled guests.

LOKAHI LODGE, Kalanikoa Rd. (P.O. Box 7), Volcano, HI 96785. Tel. 808/985-8647, or toll free 800/457-6924 from mainland U.S. 4 rms (all with bath). No credit cards.

$ Rates: $65–$70 single or double. Each additional person $15. MC, V. **Parking:** Free.

There's an old-fashioned country charm about this place, even though the house is new, built specifically as a bed and breakfast. There's a player piano and organ in the living room, lots of books and games, a wood-burning stove for those crisp Volcano nights. Framed leis line the hallway, leading to four rooms, each with its own entrance to the wraparound lanai overlooking a lush ohia forest. All rooms are nicely decorated and all have two extra-long double beds. Gracious hosts Judy and Graham offer a continental breakfast with fresh fruits and juice, coffee or tea, and fresh homemade bread.

VOLCANO BED & BREAKFAST, 19-3950 Keonelehua St. (P.O. Box 22), Volcano, HI 96785. Tel. 808/967-7779. Fax 808/967-7619. 3 rms (none with bath). TV.

$ Rates (including full breakfast): $45–$50 single; $50–$55 double; twin $65 for twin; $70 for three. Additional person $15 extra. Minimum stay 2 days. MC, V. **Parking:** Free.

This cozy little country house set in a pretty landscaped area is run by Jim and Sandy Pedersen. The entire house is turned over to the pleasure of their guests, who are free to enjoy the downstairs area, with its sun room, reading room, fireplace, piano, and cable TV—it would make an ideal spot for a small family reunion. There are two nicely decorated sleeping rooms with double beds upstairs, and one room done in bright yellow downstairs; baths are semiprivate. Breakfast features Sandy's french toast and homemade jams and jellies. The Pedersens describe themselves as "friendly, gracious Christian hosts with inside information about where to go and what to see."

VOLCANO HEART CHALET, Tel. 808/248-7725. 3 rms (1 with bath).

$ Rates: $50 single or double per night, $300 single or double per week. Minimum stay 2 nights. No credit cards. **Parking:** Free.

Although they reside in Maui most of the time, JoLoyce and John Kaia make their Volcano area home available to guests. The two-story cedar house, surrounded by trees, consists of three bedrooms (all with private locks), containing either queen-size or twin beds, warm comforters for cool nights, and either private or shared baths.

All guests can use the glass-enclosed porch for cooking and eating and the carpeted lounging and exercise room. It's a cute place: Each room has its own theme—hearts, cats, bears, and so on. Guests are provided with coffee, tea, cocoa, and fresh pastry. Adults only; no smoking or alcohol. **Reservations:** P.O. Box 404, Hana, Maui, HI 96713.

Doubles for $75 to $95

CHALET KILAUEA—THE INN AT VOLCANO, off Hi. 11 at the corner of Wright/Lauukapu Rd. (P.O. Box 998), Volcano Village, HI 96785. Tel. 808/967-7786, or toll free 800/937-7786. 3 rms, 1 suite, 4 vacation homes.

$ Rates: $75 single or double; $125 suite; from $75 vacation home. Additional person $15 extra. DISC, MC, V. **Parking:** Free.

After traveling around the world for nine years, Brian and Lisha Crawford settled down in Volcano Village, just a mile from Hawaii Volcanoes National Park, and opened an inn. They had plenty of art and unique furniture from their travels with which to decorate. The large living room, where afternoon tea is served, is filled with art from all over the world (it's a good place for small business meetings). The three guest rooms in the main house include: the Continental Lace room, with a queen-size bed, lace curtains, ballet slippers on the wall, straw hat on the hat rack, and daybed for reading; the Oriental Jade room, done in rose, black, and jade colors, complete with queen-size bed and antique Chinese screens; and the Out of Africa room, with treasures from Africa—masks, baskets, artwork. That's not all: Outside is a two-story "tree-house suite" with a master bedroom upstairs complete with a king-size bed, TV, and wraparound windows overlooking tree ferns, and a mini-kitchen and dayroom downstairs. The Jacuzzi on the lanai is available, a fire is lit every night, and breakfast consists of two gourmet courses.

Chalet Kilauea's vacation homes are spacious and graced with charming decor. All offer a full kitchen, complimentary afternoon tea, and use of the Jacuzzi. The Ohia Holiday Cottage at $75, the Hapuu Forest Cabin at $145, the Hoku Hawaiian House at $125, and Pele's Pavilion at $175 are the ultimate in Volcano comfort.

HYDRANGEA COTTAGE, P.O. Box 563, Kamuela, HI 96743. Tel. toll free 800/262-9912. 1 cottage.

$ Rates: $100 double. Minimum stay 2 days. No credit cards. **Parking:** Free.

Return visitors agree that Hydrangea Cottage, on a beautiful three-acre estate, is a rare jewel in this high-country mountain village. The cottage guest book overflows with praise from past guests with compliments on everything from the serene setting, luxurious furnishings, and beautiful fragrance of the redwood interior to the host's gracious hospitality and exquisite attention to every detail. The owner, who lives on Oahu, escapes as often as possible to her Big Island retreat, a stylish home located adjacent to the cottage. When the owner/hostess is not in residence, guests are left in the capable hands of her caretaker, who lives nearby. The cottage, with views of tall hapuu ferns and ohia trees from every window, has a separate bedroom with a queen-size bed, bath with full tub, a wood stove in a cozy living room, washer/dryer, and a full kitchen that has been stocked with breakfast provisions. The hostess's spacious home is also available for executive or family retreats on request. No smoking.

KILAUEA LODGE, Old Volcano Rd. (P.O. Box 116), Volcano Village, HI 96785. Tel. 808/967-7366. Fax 808/967-7367. 10 rms, 1 suite, 1 cottage (all with bath).

$ Rates (including full breakfast): $85–$125 single or double. Additional person $15 extra. MC, V. **Parking:** Free.

Perhaps the most beautiful rooms in this area are at Kilauea Lodge, one mile Hilo-side of Hawaii Volcanoes National Park, in Volcano Village. When you see the lodge—set on ten acres of greenery, bordered by magnificent ferns and towering pine trees—you'll know why everybody on the Big Island is excited about it. This former YMCA mountain retreat has now become a restaurant offering excellent meals (sorely needed in this area) and an inn offering exquisite rooms. Lorna and Albert Jeyte (she comes from Honolulu, he hails from Germany) are in charge here: He performs the magic in the kitchen; she's created the magic in the guest rooms. You'd never believe this used to be a YMCA dorm! Architects have opened up the top of the building to create a skylight, flooding the rooms with natural light. Hawaiian quilt patterns set the mostly soft pastel color schemes for the woodwork. Furniture is made of light oak, even down to the oak tissue box. Each room is decorated differently—most are in the country style; one is strikingly Japanese—some have working fireplaces. The one-bedroom cottage has a queen-size bed in the bedroom and a queen-size sofa in the living room; it can sleep up to four.

VOLCANO HOUSE, P.O. Box 53, Hawaii Volcanoes National Park, HI 96718. Tel. 808/967-7321. Fax 808/967-8429. 42 rms.

$ Rates: In Ohia Wing, $79 single or double. In the main building, $105 single or double without crater view. $131 single or double with crater view. Additional person $10 extra. AE, JCB, MC, V. **Parking:** Free.

The famed and venerable Volcano House is right on the brink of Kilauea Crater, where the ancient *kahunas* (priests) once gathered to make sacrifices to Pele. This hotel has changed hands several times in recent years, but the new management has things well in hand. All the guest rooms have been renovated and refurbished with koa furniture, including koa rockers in the rooms in the main building, and cheerful Hawaiian comforters. The least-expensive rooms are in the Ohia Wing, a separate building away from the main building. Better and more expensive rooms, in the main building, vary depending on their view of the crater. Even if you don't stay at Volcano House, at least come by to soak up the atmosphere (the floor-to-ceiling lava fireplace in the cozy living room lobby has been burning steadily for 119 years!), have a drink in Uncle George's Lounge, or a meal at the Ka Ohelo dining room. Enjoying a breakfast here in the early morning mountain air, seated at a table near the window where you can gaze right into the volcano as you savor your ono French toast and ohelo berry preserves, is one of the special treats of Hawaii.

A Campground

Any campers in the crowd? You might try one of the ten cabins at **Namakani Paio Campground**, in Hawaii Volcanoes National Park, three miles beyond Volcano House, at approximately 4,000 feet elevation. For those "who desire true outdoor living," the cabins, furnished with a double bed and two single bunk beds, have a Polynesian design and frame construction. Each cabin has its own lanai but shares a bathhouse. The cost is $32 for a double (each additional person $6 extra), and children under 12 stay free. This includes a linen bag (sheets, pillows, towel, soap, one blanket) for each bed. Extra blankets or sleeping bags are recommended; it gets cold at this elevation. Contact Volcano House (the concessionaires) at Hawaii Volcanoes National Park, HI 96718 (tel. 808/967-7321).

KAPOHO BEACH

Doubles for $70

CHAMPAGNE COVE, Kapoho Beach. Tel. 808/959-4487. 2 three-bedroom apts. TV

$ Rates: $70 for one or two readers of this book (mention when making reservations); $75 for one or two other guests. Extra charge for additional guests. Minimum stay 1 week, with some exceptions. No credit cards. **Parking:** Free.

Drs. Keith and Norma Godfrey, retired chiropractors from Alaska, live in Hilo, but they rent this vacation hideaway, built on a lava bed where the ocean meets the volcanic flows at Kapoho Beach in the Puna area. It's a stark setting, but the house is warm, cozy, and beautifully decorated. Each of the two stories is a complete apartment with a superb kitchen, all modern appliances, a living room, and three attractive bedrooms. The rates make this an extraordinary bargain. What a place for a family reunion! You can swim in a heated pool right in front of the house, or walk a short distance to a black sand beach and a warm tide pool in the ocean (good for snorkeling). The house is a half-hour drive from Hilo.

Reservations: Drs. Keith and Norma Godfrey, 1714 Lei Lehua St., Hilo, HI 96720.

KEHENA

Doubles for $62

KALANI HONUA INTERCULTURAL CONFERENCE AND RETREAT CENTER, Box 4500, Pahoa, HI 96778. Tel. 808/965-7828, or toll free 800/800-6886 for registration only. 30 rms, 3 cottages.

$ Rates: $52 single without bath, $65 single with bath; $62 double without bath, $75 double with bath; $28 each triple or quad with shared bath; $85 cottage, AE, MC, V. **Parking:** Free.

⭐ Although most guests come to Kalani Honua for conferences and retreats, there's no reason why other travelers cannot enjoy its lovely facilities close to the black sand beach at Kehena. Photographers, especially, enjoy the dawn-facing lava cliffs overlooking the sea, adjacent to the facility. Kalani Honua is situated five minutes from the former town of Kalapana, buried under a flood of molten lava in 1990.

Spacious grounds house rustic conference facilities, a dining hall with lanai seating, café, gift shop, sauna, 25-meter pool, and Jacuzzi (the pool area is clothing-optional after 7pm); massage is available. Nearby are natural warm springs and steam caves, and the beach at Kehena is famed for the dolphins, which frequently play with swimmers. Winter months bring humpback whales, which also come quite close to shore.

Rooms, in four cedar lodges and private cottages, are simply decorated and comfortable. Tent space (you bring the tent and linens) costs $15 per person. Meals are mostly vegetarian and skillfully prepared by a caring staff. Write or phone to receive a current list of workshops in yoga, holistic health, or the arts at Kalanai Honua.

KAILUA-KONA

DOUBLES FOR $25

H. MANAGO HOTEL, Hi. 11 (P.O. Box 145), Captain Cook, HI 96704. Tel. 808/323-2642. 64 rms.

$ Rates: Older building, $22 single without bath; $25 double without bath; $28 triple without bath. Newer wing, $35–$38 single with bath; $38–$41 double with bath; $41–$44 triple with bath. Japanese room with private furo, $52 single; $55 double. MC, V. **Parking:** Free.

⭐ Thirteen miles south of Kailua, on Hi. 11—and 1,400 feet high in coffee country—is the H. Manago Hotel, where you'll find some of the most reasonable accommodations in the Kona area. But staying here means more than getting a clean, comfortable room for rock-bottom prices; it's also a way to get to know nontourist Hawaii. The Manago Hotel is part of the history of the Kona coast, a favorite with island people since 1917, when two young Japanese immigrants, Kinzo and Osame Manago, started serving meals in their own house and gave the salesmen and truck drivers who wanted to stay overnight a futon to sleep on. The dining room and hotel grew over the years, and now a third generation of family management has taken over. The older rooms, with community bath, are strictly for nonfussy types. Rooms in the newer wing, with private baths and lanais, are modern and comfortable, and are nicely decorated with lovely brass-trimmed oak furniture, and fern-patterned quilted spreads in soft colors. The gardens that they overlook, incidentally, are tended by 95-year-old Osame Manago, who grows rare orchids and anthuriums in one garden, and fresh vegetables, which are served in the restaurant, in the other. She also creates the hand-knotted patchwork quilts found in many of the newer rooms. A deluxe Japanese-style room, with futons and its own furo (deep hot tub), is dedicated to Kinzo and Osame. It's delightfully quiet and cool here throughout the year. The hotel restaurant is a favorite with local people for its home-style Japanese and American cooking: breakfast starts at $4; lunch and dinner, about $6 to $10.75 (a typical meal is beef or fish with three kinds of vegetables, and beverage). They're known for their pork chops. And incidentally, the three-story frame building looks down the foot of the mountain to Kealakekua Bay, where Captain Cook met his end. Owner Dwight Manago advises reserving about three weeks ahead in season, two weeks other times.

ASTON'S KONA ISLANDER INN, 75-5776 Kuakini Hwy., Kailua-Kona, HI 96740. Tel. 808/329-3181, or toll free 800/922-7866 in the U.S. Fax 808/326-9339. 144 rms. A/C TV TEL

$ Rates: Apr–Dec 21, $76–$91 single or double. Dec 22–Mar $86–$101 single or double. Additional person $10 extra. AE, DC, JCB, MC, V. **Parking:** Free.

Newly refurbished and looking nicer than ever, this plantation-style complex boasts one of the most central locations in town, plus a pool set in a glorious garden and a barbecue pit out by the pool. All the rooms are identical, but the price is determined by location: garden, poolside, or with ocean view. Rooms all have either a queen-size bed or two twin beds, shower (no tub), and a private lanai furnished with a table and two director's chairs. There's a refrigerator in every unit.

DURKEE'S COFFEELAND B&B, P.O. Box 596, Holualoa, HI 96725. Tel. 808/322-9142. 2 rms, 1 garden apt.

$ Rates: $60 double, $5 surcharge for 1-night stay; $75 garden apt. for 1-night stay. No credit cards. **Parking:** Free.

This working family coffee farm enjoys a sylvan location: It's on the slope of the mountain, nestled among fern trees and palms, with papayas, mangoes, and guava—and, of course, coffee trees—growing everywhere. Marilyn and Chuck Durkee retired here, Chuck to grow coffee and rare varieties of orchids, Marilyn to take care of the guests who find their way to this modest retreat. Rooms are plainly furnished but comfortable enough. The two rooms in the house share a bath. The garden apartment is small, but does have its own private entrance, living room, kitchen, and TV. But the biggest draw here is the Sunset Lanai with its large rope hammock, spa, telescope, and barbecue grill. One could easily spend days in the hammock alone. Breakfast always includes fruit from their own trees, banana breads made from their own coconuts and bananas, and Kona coffee, grown right outside the door.

HALE MALUHIA, 76-770 Hualalai Rd., Kailua-Kona, HI 96740. Tel. 808/329-1123 or toll free 800/559-6627. Fax 808/326-5487. 5 rms, 1 studio, 1 two-bedroom apt. TEL

$ Rates (including breakfast): $45, $65, or $75 bedroom; $135 two-bedroom apt; $235 main two-bedroom house. Each additional person $15 extra. AE, MC, V. **Parking:** Free.

Just a 10-minute drive from the hustle and bustle of Kailua town is this peaceful country home at the cool 900-foot elevation of Holualoa Mountain. Ken and Ann Smith built their rambling home set on an acre of Kona coffee land more than 22 years ago and kept adding to it as their family grew; now the family is gone, and lucky visitors find their way here instead. The interiors are comfortably appointed with open-beam ceilings, natural woods, koa cabinets, Victorian and Hawaiian furnishings—not fancy, but cozy. There are two living areas which guests may use, two decks, a kitchen, an outdoor spa and massage table, and a fully equipped business office with fax, typewriter, and computer. Breakfast is continental-plus. The place is handicapped-accessible and wheelchair friendly. Hale Maluhia, the main house, with its two bedrooms, large lanai, and two double sofa beds, can sleep up to nine and can be rented in its entirety. The Gatehouse, the two-bedroom apartment with kitchenette and shared bath, can sleep up to seven and can also be rented in its entirety. The studio (called the Banyan Cottage) is a perfect nest for honeymooners, with its king-size bed, refrigerator, TV, Jacuzzi, and porch swing. Ken is an ordained minister and can help in making wedding arrangements.

KONA MAGIC SANDS CONDOMINIUM, 77-6452 Alii Dr., Kailua-Kona, HI 96740. Tel. 808/329-9177. Fax 808/329-5480. 37 studio apts. TV

$ Rates: $65–$75 studio apt for two. Additional person $10 extra. Minimum stay 3 days. AE, MC, V. **Parking:** Free.

Each and every apartment at the Kona Magic Sands Condominium overlooks the pounding ocean and the glorious sunsets of Kona. This is one of the older condos in the area, not as luxurious as some, but it's very beachy and cozy— the kind of place where it feels good to kick off your sandals and take life easy. The good-size studio apartments, furnished for two guests, have full kitchens; instead of a separate bedroom, they have a sleeping alcove off the living room, with a double, queen, or sofa bed. There are palm trees outside your window, a freshwater pool for swimming, and the convenience of having Jameson's by the Sea, a top restaurant, right downstairs. A few of the extra-large apartments have lanais overlooking the beach.

Reservations: Kona Vacation Resorts, P.O. Box 1071, Kailua-Kona, HI 96745 (tel. toll free 800/367-5168 in the mainland U.S., 800/800-KONA in Canada). Note that this company manages some 156 accommodations in the Kona area, all of them condos or private homes. The price range is wide, beginning at $75 per day. Of special interest to us budgeteers: Alii Villas, less than a mile from Kailua Town with an oceanfront setting and one-bedroom garden apartments at $70 for two; and Casa de Emdeko, also oceanfront, with saltwater and freshwater pools and one-bedroom garden apartments for two at $75.

KONA RIVIERA VILLA, 75-6124 Alii Dr., Kailua-Kona, HI 96740. Tel. 808/329-1996. 1-bedroom apts. TV TEL

$ Rates: Apr 15–Dec 14, $60 garden; $70–$80 oceanview; Dec 15–Apr 14, $70 gardenview; $80–$90 oceanview; $100 oceanfront. Additional person $10 extra. No credit cards. Minimum stay 3 nights. **Parking:** Free.

The Kona Riviera Villa is the kind of place we like best: charming, intimate, low-key, and affordable. It's an older condominium complex, set just far enough back from the water to bring in the cooling breezes—and not too much ocean noise. A freshwater swimming pool and patio with barbecue grill overlook the ocean, too rough here for swimming, but fine for snorkelers and surfers. Each apartment is comfortably furnished and nicely decorated. All units have one bedroom, and some of the living rooms have sofa beds, so that up to four people can be accommodated. Kitchens are electric, equipped with dishwashers and garbage disposals. This is a congenial place, so much so that many of the same guests come back year after year, and rates are very modest for this luxury area. Make reservations well in advance.

KONA SEASIDE HOTEL, 75-5646 Palani Rd., Kailua-Kona, HI 96740. Tel. 808/329-2455, or toll free 800/367-7000 from U.S. mainland, 800/654-7020 from Canada. Fax 808/922-0052. 225 rms, 14 kitchenette rms. A/C TV TEL

$ Rates: $54–$64 standard pool; $70–$80 superior; $75–$85 superior tower; $80–$90 deluxe; $85–$95 kitchenette. Cars available for $15 more per day. Additional person $12 extra. Children 12 and under stay free with parents when using existing bedding. AE, DC, MC, V. **Parking:** Free.

A good choice smack in the center of Kailua is the Kona Seaside Hotel and Kona Seaside Pool Wing, at the intersection of Kuakini Highway (Hi. 11) and Palani Road (Hi. 19)—just a parking lot away from the shopping and restaurant excitement of Alii Drive. Size is the byword—large rooms, spacious lanais, and an extra-large pool. Blue is the theme of the well-appointed rooms.

The rooms in the Kona Seaside Pool Wing (formerly the Hukilau Hotel), most of them overlooking another large lovely pool, are smartly furnished and have twin- or king-size beds; from many you can see the harbor across the road and a small public beach. Or you may just want to laze on the sun deck, which looks out on Alii Drive and the harbor, and watch the world go by below you. The pool wing leads directly into Stan's Restaurant, which serves three reasonably priced meals every day and has a popular cocktail lounge. The Calypso Restaurant specializes in seafood.

Kona Seaside is managed by Sand & Seaside Hotels, 2222 Kalakaua Ave., Suite 714, Honolulu, HI 96815.

KONA TIKI HOTEL, Alii Dr. (P.O. Box 1567), Kailua-Kona, HI 96745. Tel. 808/329-1425. 15 rms.

$ Rates: $54 single or double. $59 single or double with kitchenette. Additional person $6 extra (maximum of three people per room). Minimum stay 3 days. No credit cards. **Parking:** Free.

In a garden setting overlooking the ocean, away from the bustle of the center of town and very close to the Kona Hilton, is the petite Kona Tiki Hotel, a longtime budget stop in Kona. All the rooms have private oceanfront lanais looking out on the blue-green pounding surf (and it really does pound—noisily—against the sea wall). The ocean is great for fishing and snorkeling; there's a freshwater pool for gentler swimming. All rooms include queen-size beds, ceiling fans, and a small refrigerator. They have been redone in blue-and-green color schemes, with light furniture and new kitchenette units and refrigerators. Friendliness abounds at the Kona Tiki; it's the kind of small, family-owned hotel where guests usually get to know one another. Kona coffee and doughnuts are available in the morning. You can drive to the center of town in three minutes or walk in 15 minutes. Reserve a month in advance usually, two months in advance in busy seasons. Specify first and second choices on rooms with or without kitchenette (very few kitchenettes are available).

MERRYMAN'S BED & BREAKFAST, P.O. Box 474, Kealakekua, HI 96750. Tel. 808/323-2276, or toll free 800/545-4390. 4 rms. TV

$ Rates (including breakfast): $55 single with shared bath, $75 single with private bath; $65 double with shared bath, $85 double with private bath. MC, V. **Parking:** Free.

Don and Penny Merryman's pretty home 1,500 feet up on a hill in Kealakekua, about a half-hour drive from Kailua town, has plenty of charm: rooms filled with handsome antiques (the Victorian room has a four-poster bed), views of Kealakekua Bay far below or a lovely garden, and two large lanais (one with a refrigerator and microwave), where guests can relax and have breakfast. Don and Penny, a young couple from Alaska, are gracious hosts, and they usually put out something special for their guests: maybe quiche, or bagels and cream cheese, plus fruit, teas, and Kona coffee, of course—it's grown right down on the slopes of the mountain. Each room has its own TV and refrigerator.

PAPA CHANG'S HALE OHANA, 73-1026 Ahikawa St., Kailua-Kona, HI 96740. Tel. 808/325-5118. 8 rms.

$ Rates (including breakfast): $65 per day, $400 per week, with one double bed; $85 per day, $500 per week, with two double beds. Minimum stay three days. MC, V. **Parking:** Free.

A cross between a modern hotel and a homey B&B, Art Chang's place is one-of-a-kind. Chang, a retired airline maintenance supervisor, built it himself, not far from Keahole Airport (it attracts many airline people) and about a 20-minute drive into Kailua town, in a cool suburban area 1,000 feet above sea level. It was the dream of Chang and his late wife, Myrtle, to create a place where people on vacation could enjoy roomy areas. There's an enormous deck on each floor of the two-story polehouse, an equally enormous common room on each floor, with a television set, a dining room and kitchen, and a fully equipped laundry room. Guests have the run of all of them. Breakfast, which is put out in the common rooms, consists of fruit from the gardens—papayas, pineapple, bananas, grapefruit, limes—plus toast, crackers, juice, cereal, tea, and coffee. There's a good-sized pool out back. Larger rooms with two double beds boast 440 square feet of space, and each includes a small refrigerator and microwave oven, a double vanity, and a bidet. Smaller rooms, 300 square feet, are similarly equipped. Telephones and TVs are available on request. The grounds are beautifully landscaped with manilla palms and fruit trees, and from the decks where visitors like to relax, there's a fine view of the coastline and of Maui, off in the distance.

UNCLE BILLY'S KONA BAY HOTEL, 75-5739 Alii Dr., Kailua-Kona, HI 96740. Tel. 808/329-1398, or toll free 800/367-5102. Fax 808/935-7903. 145 rms. A/C TV TEL

$ Rates: Apr–Dec 15. $54 single or double; $74 double with car and breakfast. Feb 1–Mar 31, add $10 to all rates. Children under 18 stay free in parent's room. Additional person $10 extra. AE, DC, DISC, MC, V. **Parking:** Free.

Uncle Billy's Kona Bay Hotel, right in the center of town, is run by the same family that manages Uncle Billy's Hilo Bay Hotel. This newer hotel is landscaped with bridges and ponds, and a Polynesian longhouse restaurant surrounds a large circular swimming pool. The thatched roof over the registration desk and the koa-wood tables in the lobby create a warm Hawaiian feeling. The hotel's restaurant, Banana Bay, is popular for its low-priced breakfast and dinner buffets. The rooms, smartly decorated in gray, blue, and mauve, are of a comfortable size. Each room has a good-size lanai and a refrigerator; many have two double beds. Some rooms have an ocean view.

Reservations: Kona Bay Hotel, 87 Banyan Dr., Hilo, HI 96720.

WORTH THE EXTRA MONEY

COLONY'S KONA BALI KAI, 76-6246 Alii Dr., Kailua-Kona, HI 96740. Tel. 808/329-9381, or toll free 800/367-6046. Fax 808/526-2017. 155 apts. A/C TV TEL

$ Rates: $90–$115 studio; $110–$160 one-bedroom apt; $160–$190 two-bedroom apt. Children under 17 stay free in parents' room using existing bedding. AE, CB, DC, DISC, JCB, MC, V. **Parking:** Free.

The oceanfront Kona Bali Kai is another lovely condominium resort. The rooms are exquisitely and individually furnished, with every convenience—full kitchens, washer-dryers in oceanside units, daily maid service (unusual in most condominiums), and lanais from which those in the main building can watch the spectacular surf and tireless surfers (other buildings afford partial views of mighty Mount Hualalai or lush gardens). The surf is too strong here for casual swimmers, but there's a good swimming beach a mile away, and right at home is a sunning beach amid the coral-reef tidal pools, a swimming pool, Jacuzzi, and sauna. There are barbecue grills on the beach, and a Pupu Pantry in the lobby area for essentials, groceries, and sandwiches. Arrangements can be made at the activities desk in the lobby for golf (three miles south), tennis (two miles north), or for a variety of adventures nearby. One-bedroom apartments can sleep up to four people, and the spectacular two-bedroom/two-bath apartments can comfortably sleep up to six.

THE DRAGONFLY RANCH, P.O. Box 675, Honaunau, HI 96726. Tel. 808/328-2159, or toll free 800/487-2159. 2 rms, 4 suites.

$ Rates (including breakfast): $70 double per night; $420 per week in main house; Hale in the Trees $350 two nights, $700 per week; Redwood Cottage or the Writer's Studio $120 for one night, $300 for three nights, $600 per week; Outdoor Waterbed Honeymoon Suite $160 for one night, $400 for three nights, $700 per week. Rates based on double occupancy; each additional person $15 per night. MC, V. **Parking:** Free.

Barbara Moore-Link and David Link, the lovely couple who run the Dragonfly Ranch in Honaunau, 11 miles from Kalua-Kona, offer their place for families and small groups for weddings, reunions, workshops, and private retreats. They also have extraordinary accommodations for travelers and honeymooners, and you'll be happy if you luck into one of these unusual spaces. Our favorite is the Outdoor Waterbed Honeymoon Suite, in a jungle setting with private bathroom, outdoor shower with an old-fashioned bathtub, and a kitchenette. The king-size bed has a marvelous view of Honaunau Bay, while the adjoining redwood room (viewing the "pink garden") has a queen-size futon. This suite accommodates four people, but is ideally suited for two as a romantic getaway. The self-contained Redwood Cottage in the meadow is supercozy, with a hammock out on the deck, a double bed, kitchenette, toilet, and outdoor shower. The Writer's Studio is a spacious 20-by-22 foot apartment with its own kitchen, private bathroom, outdoor shower, king-size bed, and additional futons. Hale in the Trees, a rustic dwelling recommended for adventurous souls, has a sleeping loft with a queen-size bed overlooking the split-level 20-by-30-foot living area; there's also a queen-size sofa bed and a small room in back with a king-size bed. A large screen wall frames a dramatic view of the Kona coast. For music lovers, David has a vast selection of music, a piano, and a professional recording studio. All units have stereo cassette players; cable TV, VCR, and videotapes are available. For breakfast, there are baked goods and fresh homegrown fruits. Guests are welcome to harvest their own organic apple bananas and strawberry papayas, as well as the more exotic starfruit and soursop in season. And Barbara offers the use of a massage chair, aromatherapy, and flower essences; she's an expert at the ancient Hawaiian art of lomilomi massage.

The Dragonfly Ranch, itself a refuge, is just a two-minute drive from the ancient Place of Sanctuary (Pu'uhonua o Honaunau National Park), with some of the world's finest diving and snorkeling. An assortment of snorkeling gear is available for guests' use. If you're lucky, the dolphins might choose to swim with you. Barbara and David provide tips on secret, secluded beaches within a 20-minute drive of the ranch, and will even teach beginners to snorkel. For ocean lovers, their friend Keiko takes people out on his double-hulled Hawaiian canoe; exclusive moonlight cruises are available. One week of the month, around the full moon, Barbara and David offer "The Hawaiian Experience," work/playshops with authentic kahunas and native Hawaiian guides. Reservations are advised two months in advance. If they can't accommodate you, they'll gladly help you find a nearby place that will. The Dragonfly is 19 miles south of Kailua-Kona, and great for total escape.

HOLUALOA INN, P.O. Box 222, Holualoa, HI 96725. Tel. 808/324-1121, or toll free 800/392-1812. Fax 808/322-2472. 4 rms.

$ Rates (including continental breakfast): $100–$150 single or double. 15% discount on stays of 1 week or longer. Minimum stay 2 days. AE, MC, V. **Parking:** Free.

✪ Grander than most B&Bs and smaller than most hotels, the Holualoa Inn is in a class by itself: It's an exquisite small inn set high in the mountains in the farming community/art colony of Holualoa, about a 15-minute drive from the ocean at Kailua-Kona, which provides its magnificent views. The three-level mansion set in a 40-acre estate was originally built as a mountain hideaway for *Honolulu Advertiser* president Thurston Twigg-Smith. Now his nephew Desmond Twigg-Smith has taken it over and superbly decorated its guest bedrooms, which he rents out on a B&B basis to those lucky enough to find this serenely beautiful spot. The house is built of cedar wood, its floors of eucalyptus, its windows of spun glass. The handsome living room has a fireplace, reading areas, even a billiard table. The formal dining room is the scene of morning breakfasts of fresh fruits, juices, pancakes, sausages, pastries, and homemade muffins. The Kona coffee served is grown right here, as this is a working coffee farm. And the rooms are enchanting, each one done differently: one with an Asian theme, another in Balinese style, a third in Polynesian decor, a fourth with a Hawaiian-hibiscus motif. In addition to the use of the living and dining rooms upstairs, guests also have a common room on the lower level, where they can store food in the refrigerator. There's a large swimming pool outside, a tower from which to watch the sunset, and everywhere, the singing of birds.

KAILUA PLANTATION HOUSE, 75-5948 Alii Dr., Kailua-Kona, HI 96740. Tel. 808/329-3727. 5 rms. A/C TV TEL
$ Rates (including breakfast): $120, $125, $145, $150, or $175 double. AE, MC, V. **Parking:** Free.
This is Kona's only oceanfront bed-and-breakfast inn, elegant to the max. Exquisite rooms, each furnished differently and romantically (some with four-poster beds, one with a skylight above the platform whirlpool bath for two) are ideal for honeymooners. All have small refrigerators, hot-beverage equipment, and their own private lanais. There's an outdoor dipping pool and spa. Breakfast can be taken in the elegantly furnished living room or out on the oceanfront lanai, with a view of the water pounding the black boulders and surfers riding the waves. The staff is helpful with tips and information.

KALAHIKI COTTAGE AT HONAUNAU, P.O. Box 563, Kamue, HI 96743. Tel. 800/262-9912. 1 rm, 1 cottage.
$ Rates (including breakfast): $95 double, $125 cottage. Minimum stay 2 days.
This unusual bed-and-breakfast is on the grounds of a 15,000-acre working cattle ranch, run by the third generation of the same family. The superb ranch cottage is filled with heirloom furniture and other treasures representing the family's long and rich history in Hawaii. Its "living room" is a covered veranda open to a fully equipped kitchen and bedroom, and overlooking a 68-foot swimming pool and Jacuzzi. There's a barbecue grill poolside should you become too comfortable to drive out to a restaurant. Inside the owner's house, which is on the other side of the pool, is an attractive twin bedroom with private bath; breakfast is served out on their veranda, and guests are free to use the living room with its TV set. Owners Cynthia and Roy fill the refrigerator with breakfast provisions and provide warm hospitality.

THE SEA VILLAGE, 75-6002 Alii Dr., Kailua-Kona, HI 96740. Tel. 808/329-1000. 131 apts.
$ Rates: Apr 16–Dec 15, $90–$110 one-bedroom apt; $114–$134 two-bedroom apt. Dec. 16–Apr 15, $106–$126 one-bedroom apt; $130–$150 two-bedroom apt, less $10 per day on weekly rates. Minimum stay 3 nights. AE, DISC, MC, V. **Parking:** Free.
Condominiums are very big in Kona these days, and surely one of the nicest is the Sea Village, an idyllic spot overlooking the ocean just outside town. This is a large resort complex, with a tennis court, swimming pool, and Jacuzzi on the premises, as well as snorkeling off the rocks in front of the hotel for strong swimmers. Living quarters are outstanding: The apartments are beautifully furnished, ultraspacious and luxurious, with huge living rooms, one or two bedrooms, and shiny modern kitchens fitted with every appliance including dishwashers, washer-dryers, and refrigerators with automatic ice makers. Bathrooms are lovely, and there is ample closet and storage space, weekly chamber service, and private lanais. Views are of the garden or the ocean; the oceanfront apartments are the most expensive. Rates here are higher than our usual budget ones, but if you come during off-season, you might be able to manage it, keeping in mind that the one-bedroom apartments sleep four and the two-bedrooms sleep six.
Reservations: Paradise Management Corp., Kukui Plaza C-207, 50 S. Beretania St., Honolulu, HI 96813 (tel. toll free 800/367-5205; fax 808/533-4621).

WHITE SANDS VILLAGE, 77-6469 Alii Dr., Kailua-Kona, HI 96740. Tel. 808/329-6402, or toll free 800/345-2823. Fax 808/326-2401. 108 condominium units. A/C TV TEL
$ Rates: $85–$150 per day two-bedroom unit. Mar 16–Dec 14, $510–$700 per week; Dec. 15–Mar 15 $700–$1,050 per week. AE, MC, V. **Parking:** Free.
The thing we like about this place is that it's just across from Magic Sands Beach, one of the few remaining beaches in the area. It's a large condo complex, with many recreational facilities, including a pool, sauna, Jacuzzi, tennis courts, and barbecue area. Each of the two-bedroom units, large enough to sleep four, is individually owned, so furnishings and appointments vary.

As is usual with complexes of this type, several realtors handle apartments here; one with a good number of units is Jean Metz, of Triad Management Realtors, in the North Kona Shopping Center, 75-5629-P Kuahini Hwy., Kailua-Kona, HI 96740; you can reach her at the numbers listed above. Triad also handles many other vacation rentals—approximately 125 condominiums and houses—so see what she has to offer.

READERS RECOMMEND

Keauhou Beach Hotel, 78-6740 Alii Dr., Kailua-Kona (tel. 322-3441). "The Keauhou Beach Hotel was exceptional! It was lovely in every way. It had such a Hawaiian atmosphere, with its oceanside bar, torchlit gardens, pool with waterfall, and restaurant over the lagoon. Their weekend seafood buffet was exceptional. They even upgraded our partial ocean-view rooms to full ocean-view at no extra charge ($106 for partial ocean-view). I highly recommend this place."—Martha Farwell, Illinois City, Ill.

3. WHERE TO EAT

Big Island restaurants offer a marvelous variety of foods, in every price range, and to suit every taste. Hilo is especially good for the budget traveler, since its restaurants cater mostly to locals rather than tourists. Dine with them and you'll save a bundle.

HILO

MEALS FOR LESS THAN $12

BEARS, 106 Keawe St. Tel.. 935-0708.
    Cuisine: GOURMET DELI/VEGETARIAN/DESSERTS. **Reservations:** Not accepted.
$ Prices: $2.50–$7. No credit cards.
    Open: Mon–Fri 6:45am–5pm, Sat 8am–4pm.

Bears, a stylish little place (marble-top tables indoors and out, hand-stenciled walls) nextdoor to the Most Irresistible Shop in Hilo, is proving to be irresistible—so much so that its original menu of a variety of coffees and pastries keeps expanding: Now they start the day with breakfast items like "souffléd eggs" (steamed light and fluffy on the espresso machine) and "egg busters" (eggs, cheese, and ham on English muffin), and offer deli and vegetarian sandwiches ($3.60 to $3.95), organic salads, designer bagels (create your own toppings), hot and cold soups, in addition to the original coffee and pastry menu. What fun to indulge in coffee and espresso drinks like caffè latte or Mexican chocolate, and desserts like carrot cake or lilikoi cheesecake, plus their luscious chocolate brownies. You can also buy fresh-roasted coffee beans by the pound to take home. Pastries run $2.50 to $3.25. They pack neat picnic lunches to go—call two hours ahead. Bearvo!

CAFE 100, 969 Kilauea Ave. Tel. 935-8683.
    Cuisine: LOCAL. **Reservations:** Not accepted.
$ Prices: $3.25–$5.25.
    Open: Mon–Thurs 6:45am–8:30pm, Fri–Sat 6:45–9:30pm.

Whenever we used to drive by Cafe 100, we'd notice long lines of island people at the windows of this popular drive-in. We joined them one day and found out why: It's hard to spend more than $5 for a full hot meal. Breakfast, lunch, and dinner are served. Fried chicken, beef stew, breaded mahimahi, and teriyaki steak are all served with rice and potato-macaroni salad. Hiloans swear by the local favorite, which is reputed to have been invented here: LocoMoco, a hearty meal of a hamburger patty and fried egg on rice, topped with brown gravy; it's $1.50. They even have LocoMoco T-shirts! Chili, burgers, and sandwiches of all kinds start at $1. Try their specialties: yummy mahimahi sandwiches and Goody Goody sherbet. Cafe 100 is good to remember when you're in a hurry and the traveler's checks are running low.

CAFE PESTO HILO BAY, in the S. Hata Building, 308 Kamehameha Ave. Tel. 969-6640.
Cuisine: PACIFIC RIM/ITALIAN. **Reservations:** Not accepted.
$ Prices: Appetizers $2.95–$6.95; main courses $5.95–$12.95. MC, V.
Open: Sun–Thurs 11am–9pm, Fri–Sat 11am–11:30pm.

Great news for Hilo! The ever-popular Café Pesto in Kawaihae (see below) is now firmly ensconced in a second location on Hilo Bay, and its "pizza-pasta-provocative" menu is turning out to be a sensation here as well. A favorite spot among Hiloans for casual meals and after-theater drop-ins, the restaurant is located on the ground floor of the 1912 S. Hata Building, fully restored to its early charms under the auspices of the historic preservation society. An exhibition kitchen, the centerpiece of which is a six-foot Italian wood-fired pizza oven highlighted with brass detail and halogen lighting, allows diners to view the goodies issuing forth. To complement the pizzas nestled in among the coals, artwork and sculpture of the Volcano and Madame Pele are scattered throughout the art deco dining room. The menu focuses on those imaginative wood-fired pizzas (smoke-scented with ohia and guava woods), such as the scampi al pesto with steamer clams or the Greek pizza with feta cheese, and the flavorful pastas—smoked salmon, crab primavera, and pesto linguine marinara are favorites. There are also hot sandwiches, meal-size salads (the Thai curry pasta salad is special), calzones, and a good selection of wines and beers. There is often a daily special of local fish. Home-baked desserts are special, so even if you don't have a meal here, stop in for a drink from the espresso bar and, maybe, the fresh apple cake, the cookies and cream cheesecake with a macadamia-nut-crust, or the toasted coconut tart with crème anglaise (most desserts are $2.50).

DICK'S COFFEE HOUSE, at Prince Kuhio Plaza. Tel. 959-4401.
Cuisine: AMERICAN. **Reservations:** Not required.
$ Prices: Main courses $4.85–$7.50. MC, V.
Open: Mon–Fri 7am–9pm Sat–Sun 7am–5pm.

Dick's, a lively local place with sporting pennants on the walls, is one of the most popular coffee shops in town. On the à la carte dinner menu, you could choose chicken cutlet, grilled fish filet, teriyaki steak Oriental, or grilled pork chops; your main course comes with soup or salad, starch, rolls, and butter. Lunch features burgers from $3.20, gourmet sandwiches like pastrami on French bread or a steak sandwich for under $5—and homemade pies and cream pies for dessert for $1.30! Daily lunch specials go for $2.50 to $2.75, and there are also weekday lunch and dinner specials under $4. Breakfast is inexpensive, too: Three-egg omelets are just $3.30 to $4.15. A local friend raves about the fried chicken and the rhubarb pie, but advises that you come early, as one pie is baked each day.

DON'S GRILL, 485 Hinano St. Tel. 935-9099.
Cuisine: AMERICAN. **Reservations:** Not required.
$ Prices: Main courses $5.25–$11.25. AE, MC, V.
Open: Tues-Thurs 10:30am–9pm, Fri 10:30am–10pm, Sat–Sun 10am–9pm.

Don's Grill has everything a good family restaurant should have: It's large, comfortable, and inexpensive, and the food is fresh and good. Owner Don Hoota has won a large local following for this place. Tuck into one of the booths and treat yourself to courses like rotisseried chicken (the house specialty), or barbecued ribs, or filet of fish; soup or salad is included. They also have good sandwiches, burgers, plus local favorites like LocoMoco, saimin, and homemade chili; it's hard to go wrong.

DOTTY'S COFFEE SHOP AND RESTAURANT, Puainako Town Center. Tel. 959-6477.
Cuisine: AMERICAN. **Reservations:** Not required.
$ Prices: Main courses $5.25–$9.75. MC, V.
Open: Breakfast daily 7–11am; lunch daily 11:30am–2pm; dinner daily 5pm–closing.

If you love fresh fish *and* modest prices, this is a place to know about. Every evening, Dotty Frasco and her family do a fish-of-the-day special for under $10— and that might be ahi or mahimahi or ono—nicely grilled in garlic butter and white wine. What a deal! Everything else at Dotty's spiffy little coffee shop (green booths, nice photos on the wall) is a good deal too, since this is real home-cooking, with everything made from scratch ("We don't have a can opener," says Dotty). People come from all over just for her roast chicken and roast turkey, which she uses in her turkey plate. On Friday nights they come for the prime rib. Popular dishes include grilled pork chops, liver and bacon, sautéed shrimp, calamari, and shrimp scampi. Lunches, moderately priced, feature salads, sandwiches, and burgers. Dotty's pies are homemade, and at $1.70, we wouldn't think of resisting.

JASPERS ESPRESSO CAFE, 110 Kalakaua St. Tel. 969-6686.
   Cuisine: VEGETARIAN/AMERICAN. **Reservations:** Not accepted.
$ Prices: Main courses $3.75–$6.50. No credit cards.
   Open: Tues–Thurs 7am–8pm. Fri–Sat 7am–10pm. Sun 9am–2pm.

Here's a café that's not only charming but nutritionally, ecologically, and politically correct as well! As much a gathering place and a forum for addressing progressive political and social issues (the Green Party mayoral candidate recently spoke here) as a restaurant, it's a cute little place, with ceiling fans, prints on the wall, and a magazine rack for browsing. Owner/chef Jasper Moore uses only locally grown produce (much of it organic), even coffee beans that are chemical-free, in creating a wholesome, mostly vegetarian cuisine. Stuffed baked potato, nachos, chicken enchiladas, chicken cashew salad or sandwich, and lasagne with salad and bread are standbys on the day-long menu. Tuesday from 5:30 to 8pm is spaghetti night: all the spaghetti you can eat, plus garlic bread, $5. Breakfast features homemade granola, eggs Benedict and Florentine, and fresh island fruit salad. Coffee lovers must stop by for one of the specialty drinks, especially the Tsunami Shake—that's a double espresso frothed with two scoops of chocolate ice cream ($4). Jasper claims to sell "the strongest cup of coffee you can buy . . . without a prescription!"

JIMMY'S DRIVE INN, 362 Kinoole St. Tel. 935-5571.
   Cuisine: JAPANESE/AMERICAN/KOREAN. **Reservations:** Not required.
$ Prices: Complete dinners $5.75–$15.95. MC, V.
   Open: Mon–Thurs 10am–9:30pm; Fri–Sat 10am–10pm.

Jimmy's Drive Inn is a popular place with the local people, offering some of the best prices in town. The "drive inn" is misleading; you don't eat in your car, but at clean chrome tables or at the counter. The Japanese Ozen Special (steak, chicken katsu, shrimp, and sashimi) at $8.20, the Korean Combination Plate (kalbi, mundoo, and barbecue chicken) $5.25, and the Hawaiian Plate (laulau with pipikaula, lomi salmon, and poi or rice) at $6.50 are all big favorites. Eight complete American dinners and nine complete seafood dinners are offered, and these include such main courses as top sirloin steak, grilled island pork chops, ahi, butterfish, and shrimp tempura, all accompanied by soup or salad, fries or rice, vegetable, bread, and beverage.

KARROT'S KITCHEN, 197 Keawe St. Tel. 935-6191.
   Cuisine: HEALTH FOODS. **Reservations:** Not accepted.
$ Prices: Main courses $2.50–$4.50.
   Open: Mon–Fri 7am–6pm, Sat 8am–2pm.

This very attractive, modernistic restaurant, with its sleek black counter and about five tables, sits up front at the Spencer Health & Fitness Center. It's the kind of place you like to patronize when you want a quick and nutritious meal. Best choices here are the Holani special (a tasty broccoli, potato, and chicken dish cooked in a casserole), enchilada with beans and rice, and a few Thai dishes like Thai curry, Thai rice, and Pot Thai. The breakfast menu includes eggs, eggs, eggs—every way you like them: in an omelet, with enchiladas, with Thai rice. Not interested in eggs? Try the tofu scramble.

KAY'S, 684 Kilauea Ave. Tel. 969-1776.
 Cuisine: KOREAN. **Reservations:** Not required.
$ Prices: Appetizers $2.25; main courses $6–$9.25.
 Open: Breakfast/lunch Tues–Fri 6am–2pm, Sat–Sun 5am–2pm; dinner Tues–Sun 5–8:30pm.

One of our favorite Hilo eateries is Kay's, which serves just about the best barbecued chicken we've ever tasted, anywhere. Local friends put us on to this large, Korean-style family restaurant, full of local color: screaming babies, people reading the newspapers, Formica tables, orange-leather booths. Never mind. The atmosphere is friendly, the staff is charming, and the food is ridiculously inexpensive, and so good that you'll want to come back more than once. The house specialty is the Korean crispy fried chicken, which we found a bit heavy; instead, go with the barbecued chicken—it's boned, flattened, marinated in a very light shoyu sauce in the Korean manner, and simply delicious. All dinners include hot rice, miso soup, vegetable of the day, and four kinds of kimchee. You can order your meal either small or large (we found small to be adequate). One choice—Korean barbecued beef, kalbi, barbecued chicken, fried fish, shoyu pork, etc.—is $6 small, $7 for a full order, two choices are $8; three choices $9. Don't be misled by the sign reading KAY'S LUNCH CENTER; Kay now serves dinner too, thank heaven.

KEN'S HOUSE OF PANCAKES, 1730 Kamehameha Ave., at the intersection of Hi. 19 and Hi. 11. Tel. 935-8711.
 Cuisine: AMERICAN/LOCAL. **Reservations:** Not accepted.
$ Prices: Breakfast dishes $3.10–$8.95; dinner main courses $5.95–$9.50. AE, DC, DISC, MC, V.
 Open: Daily 24 hours.

The only place in town open 24 hours a day, Ken's is known for serving its entire menu around the clock. That means that at whatever time of day you're hungry for, say, macadamia nut or fresh banana pancakes, eggs Benedict, or eggs with Scottish bangers or Portuguese sausage, Ken's will dish them up and at very reasonable prices. They also feature local Hawaiian specialties at lunch and dinner. Good burgers, sandwiches, salads, delicious homemade pies and cakes, and fountain specialties are also available. Dinner selections—served with soup or salad, potato or rice, vegetable, and hot roll—include grilled mahimahi, broiled steak, and southern-style fried chicken. Everything is available anytime of the day or night.

K.K. TEI RESTAURANT, 1550 Kamehameha Hwy. Tel. 961-3791.
 Cuisine: JAPANESE/AMERICAN. **Reservations:** Recommended.
$ Prices: Appetizers $2.50–$6; main courses $8.75–$13.95. MC, V.
 Open: Lunch Mon–Sat 11am–2pm; dinner Mon–Sat 5–9pm.

You can relax in a very traditional Japanese setting at this place, a longtime Hilo favorite. Most selections are Japanese, with some American specialties. Plan on spending $5 to $11 for a complete lunch. Dinner choices include beef, chicken, pork, and seafood prepared in a variety of styles. Soups, salads, sandwiches, and noodle dishes are also available. If there are at least seven of you, call for reservations to sit in the authentic Tea House overlooking the Japanese rock garden and pond. Be sure to stroll through the garden to enjoy the beautiful plants and flowers. The Karaoke Lounge features free pupus from happy hour at 4pm until closing at 2 in the morning.

RESTAURANT SATSUKI, 168 Keawe St. Tel. 935-7880.
 Cuisine: JAPANESE. **Reservations:** Not required.
$ Prices: Main courses $4.75–$9.25. MC, V.
 Open: Lunch Wed–Mon 11am–1:45pm; dinner Wed–Mon 5–8:45pm.

Here's a place the locals like very much. It's small, plain, with partitions to give a little privacy; it's known for good food and large portions. The most popular meal is Satsuki's Special Teishokiu ($5.85 at lunch, $6.95 at dinner), which offers a choice of two main dishes, such as shrimp tempura, yakitori, beef teriyaki, butterfish, chicken katsu, and more, served with various side vegetables, soup, rice, and tea. Donburis, noodles, and bentos are also available ($4 to $9).

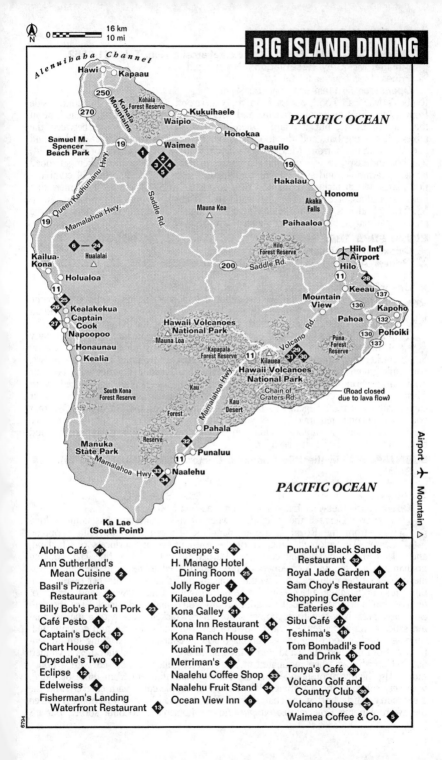

BIG ISLAND DINING

16 km / 10 mi

Alenuihaha Channel

PACIFIC OCEAN

PACIFIC OCEAN

Hawi — Kapaau
250
270
Kohala Forest Reserve
Kohala Mountains
Kukuihaele
Waipio
Honokaa
Samuel M. Spencer Beach Park
Waimea
Paauilo
19
19
Queen Kaahumanu Hwy.
Mamalahoa Hwy.
Saddle Rd.
Mauna Kea △
Hakalau
Honomu
Akaka Falls
Paihaaloa
Hilo Forest Reserve
Saddle Rd.
200
Hilo Int'l Airport
Hilo
11
Kailua-Kona
Hualalai △
Holualoa
11
Keeau
28
137
Mountain View
130
Kapoho
25
Pahoa
132
Kealakekua
Captain Cook
Napoopoo
Hawaii Volcanoes National Park
Mauna Loa
Puna Forest Reserve
130
Pohoiki
137
Honaunau
Kapapala Forest Reserve
11
Kilauea
29
31 30
Kealia
Hawaii Volcanoes National Park
Kau
Chain of Craters Rd.
(Road closed due to lava flow)
South Kona Forest Reserve
Kau Desert
Forest
Mamalahoa Hwy.
Pahala
Reserve
Manuka State Park
Punaluu
Mamalahoa Hwy.
11
Naalehu
Ka Lae (South Point)

Airport ✈ Mountain △

Aloha Café 26	Giuseppe's 20	Punalu'u Black Sands Restaurant 32
Ann Sutherland's Mean Cuisine 2	H. Manago Hotel Dining Room 25	Royal Jade Garden 8
Basil's Pizzeria Restaurant 22	Jolly Roger 7	Sam Choy's Restaurant 24
Billy Bob's Park 'n Pork 23	Kilauea Lodge 31	Shopping Center Eateries 6
Café Pesto 1	Kona Galley 21	Sibu Café 17
Captain's Deck 13	Kona Inn Restaurant 14	Teshima's 18
Chart House 10	Kona Ranch House 15	Tom Bombadil's Food and Drink 19
Drysdale's Two 11	Kuakini Terrace 16	Tonya's Café 28
Eclipse 12	Merriman's 3	Volcano Golf and Country Club 30
Edelweiss 4	Naalehu Coffee Shop 33	
Fisherman's Landing Waterfront Restaurant 13	Naalehu Fruit Stand 34	Volcano House 29
	Ocean View Inn 9	Waimea Coffee & Co. 5

6794

REUBEN'S MEXICAN FOOD, 336 Kamehameha Ave. Tel. 961-2552.
Cuisine: MEXICAN. **Reservations:** Not required.
$ Prices: Main courses $7–$9. MC, V.
Open: Mon–Fri 11am–9pm, Sat noon–9pm.

Reuben's Mexican Food, across from the waterfront, is a real local hangout. Aside from its shocking-pink color scheme and Mexican murals on the wall, it has little in the way of decor, but it's large (there's plenty of breathing room between the tables), has a big bar, and the food is good. Reuben's is run by chef Reuben and Sue Villanova (he's from Mexico, she's from Hilo). Our appetizer of nachos ($4) was hot and tasty, so was our chicken flautas (a flour tortilla with chicken, shredded lettuce, guacamole, and sour cream) combination plate for $8.50. Some 34 combination plates, which include beans and rice, go for $7 to $9. There are few interesting house specialties, like the gallina adovada (baked chicken), and a crab salad, $6 to $8. You'll find lots of local families here enjoying the food, the low prices, and the memorable margaritas. The same menu is available all day.

ROYAL SIAM THAI RESTAURANT, 68 Mamo St. Tel. 961-6100.
Cuisine: THAI. **Reservations:** Not required.
$ Prices: Appetizers $4.95–$7.95; main courses $5.95–$8.95. AE, CB, DC, JCB, MC, V.
Open: Lunch Mon–Sat 11am–2pm; dinner Mon–Sat 5–8:30pm.

This small (11-table) family restaurant has won a rousing reception from the local people. Thai paintings, flowers, planters, and white tablecloths provide a charming setting for the superb cooking typical of the Bangkok region. The family in charge insists that everything be superfresh; in fact, they grow many of the vegetables and spices in their own gardens to ensure that. Crispy chicken and spring rolls are terrific appetizers, and among the main courses, you can't go wrong with the cashew chicken, Thai broccoli noodles with beef, or Thai garlic shrimp. They do all the traditional curries—yellow, green, red—with chicken, beef, or vegetables; if you're lucky and they have fresh salmon, order your curry made with that. Vegetarians have a full menu of their own. *Warning:* Ask that your food be prepared mild, unless you *really* like it hot! Try the local coconut ice cream or the unusual tapioca pudding made with taro. Lunch is an especially good buy, since specials begin at just $4.95.

SOONTAREE'S, in the Hilo Shopping Center, 1261 Kilauea Ave. Tel. 934-SIAM.
Cuisine: THAI. **Reservations:** Not required.
$ Prices: Appetizers $2.95–$9.95; main courses $6.95–$9.95. MC, V.
Open: Lunch Tues–Fri 11am–2pm; dinner Tues–Sun 5:30–9pm.

Soontaree Gervais, the delightful owner of this restaurant, has come a long way—from the Royal Palace in Bangkok, Thailand, to the Hilo Shopping Center. The adopted daughter of the royal prince and princess of Thailand, and a lady in waiting at their court, she learned the subtleties of fine Thai cooking firsthand; when she and her American husband decided to move to Hawaii, it was inevitable that her culinary skills would someday find their way into her own restaurant. It's a charming place, simply decorated with Thai artwork and sprigs of orchids, but the food is special, as good as any you'd find in Bangkok. Try the delicate curry puffs served with cucumber sauce or the chicken satay with a macadamia-nut sauce as an appetizer. A hearty bowl of gai tom kha—chicken and coconut-milk soup—is another good beginning. Among the main courses, the gai yung (an authentic dish from northern Thailand and a favorite of Soontaree's childhood) is a winner: half a Cornish game hen marinated in Thai spices, grilled and served with a honey sauce. Also highly recommended are the curries (quite different from those of India), with very subtle exotic seasonings. We like the pineapple curry with chicken, and the green curry (fairly hot) with Thai shrimp. For dessert, it's hard to choose between the award-winning Kona coffee *haupia* and the homemade coconut sorbet. But it's difficult to go wrong no matter what you order; at prices like these, you'll find you've had a gourmet meal for a song.

TING-HAO MANDARIN RESTAURANT, Puainako town center. Tel. 959-6288.
   Cuisine: CHINESE. **Reservations:** Recommended.
$ Prices: Appetizers $3–$5.50; main courses $5.50–$10.
   Open: Lunch Mon–Sat 11am–2:30pm; dinner daily 4:30–9pm.

What brings the Mercedes and other fancy cars to the modest Puainako town center? Although not many tourists know of it, the Chinese population has discovered the Ting-Hao Mandarin Restaurant, and they come to enjoy the wizardry of master chef Ting Cheng, whose repertoire includes some 200 banquet dishes. He cooks Peking, Mandarin, Szechuan, and Cantonese style, so there is quite a variety on the menu. Everything we've tried—and we've dined here many times—has been special. And they never use MSG! Corn eggdrop soup is unusual and subtly flavored; potstickers, those tasty dumplings that are both steamed and fried (on one side), are a great beginning to your meal. Outstanding main courses in the Mandarin style include shredded pork with fungus and golden egg, shredded pork with garlic sauce (watch out, it's hot), and the eggplant with garlic sauce, each $6.50. Unusual and delicious, too, are the Kung Pao ika (cuttlefish) with spicy paprikas, $8.95, the Kung Pao shrimp with spicy paprikas, $9; the minced chicken with lettuce, $9.50; and the chicken with cashew nuts, $7.95. Most main dishes are inexpensive and hearty enough to fill you up for many hours. In fact, we find the portions here so generous that we usually wind up taking containers back to our kitchenette apartment for the next day's lunch. At lunch, there are four daily specials, served with spareribs or an egg roll, for under $5. Vegetarians can enjoy a number of good dishes. Ting-Hao is a large, very clean restaurant, simply decorated, with fans and prints on the wall. Service is helpful and friendly; there's a warm, family feeling here. Puainako town center is past the airport, and not far from Prince Kuhio Plaza; the restaurant is near the big Sack 'n' Save store.

MEALS FOR LESS THAN $20

FIASCOS, 200 Kanoelehua Ave., at Waiakea Square. Tel. 935-7666.
   Cuisine: AMERICAN. **Reservations:** Recommended on weekends.
$ Prices: Appetizers $2.50–$6.95; main courses $5.75–$16.95. AE, DISC, MC, V.
   Open: Sun–Thurs 11am–10pm, Fri–Sat 11am–11pm.

This is one of Hilo's most popular and enjoyable restaurants. It's done up attractively, with lots of plants and wood, and the atmosphere is lively and upbeat. The food (notwithstanding the rather precious menu descriptions depicting the journeys of one mythical Hans Fiasco) is consistently good, and there are enough possibilities to appeal to a variety of tastes and budgets. Appetizers include jumbo onion blossom (a deep-fried onion arranged like a beautiful flower), jalapeño popper (jalapeño peppers filled with cream cheese), and buffalo wings (deep-fried chicken wings served with a spicy-hot Cajun sauce). Many Hilo folks swear by the salad bar; it's a bountiful table of fruits and vegetables, served with homemade dressings, $6.50 as main course, $3.50 with any meal. If you come here on a weekday between 11:30am and 2pm, you can have a choice of four soups and salad bar for $5.95. There's a fresh fish sandwich every day. Hot dishes, served at both lunch and dinner, include many items for $5.95 to $10.95, like stir-fry chicken or shrimp, herb chicken, and country-fried steak. And there are good Mexican dishes and pizzas, including a shrimp-scampi-pesto pizza. Desserts? Try the cream-cheese brownie topped with ice cream and hot fudge for $3.95 or the lilikoi cheesecake at $3.50. Fiascos is good fun and good food for the price.

HARRINGTON'S, 135 Kalanianaole St. Tel. 961-4966.
   Cuisine: STEAK/SEAFOOD. **Reservations:** Recommended.
$ Prices: Appetizers $2.50–$7.95; main courses $12.25–$18.95. MC, V.
   Open: Dinner only, daily 5:30–10pm.

Overlooking the Ice Pond at Reed's Bay, near Banyan Drive, is Harrington's, one of Hilo's most upbeat restaurants. There's an atmosphere of casual elegance in the open-air dining room and lounge, a lively mood, and delicious food. Plan on this one for a splurge meal, since most main dishes—like seafood brochette, scallops Chardonnay, New York steak, chicken marsala, prime rib, and the like—are in the $13 to $20 range (they are accompanied by bread, choice of salads, and a starch). There is a way, however, to eat here inexpensively, if lightly. Ask to be seated in the lounge rather than the main dining room, and along with your beer or drink, you can order from the appetizer and side-dish menu, which means that items like deep-fried calamari strips, mushrooms tempura, etc., ranging from $4.75 to $8.50, will be served cut up, pupu style. You could even have a stuffed potato for $2.50 and a house salad (Caesar or pasta or tossed greens) for $2.95 or $4.25. There's entertainment Tuesday to Saturday, from 6 to 10pm.

HUKILAU RESTAURANT, in the Hilo Seaside Hotel, 126 Banyan Dr. Tel. 935-4222.

　　Cuisine: AMERICAN/SEAFOOD. **Reservations:** Not required.

$ Prices: Appetizers $5.50; main courses $8.50–$19.95. MC, V.

　　Open: Breakfast daily 7–10:30am; lunch Mon–Sat 10:30am–1pm; dinner daily 4–8:30pm.

This popular old-timer, the Hukilau Restaurant continues to be a Hilo favorite. Best buys here are at lunchtime: A daily lunch special at $5.50 includes a main dish, salad bar, rice or potato. And at least half a dozen à la carte dishes (including filet of mahimahi steak, calf's liver, and a Reuben sandwich) are also low-priced. At dinner, choose from either the seafood menu or the regular menu. Seafood dinners offer choices such as salmon steak, fresh fried oysters, rainbow trout, and fresh fish of the day, accompanied by soup of the day and salad bar. Favorites on the regular dinner menu include the prime rib roast, teriyaki steak, and steak and prawns, again with soup and the salad bar. Breakfast is fun here too, especially when you have pineapple hotcakes or french toast with macadamia nuts. The dining room is pleasant, and the staff has plenty of aloha.

LEHUA'S BAY CITY BAR & GRILL, 90 Kamehameha Ave. Tel. 935-8055.

　　Cuisine: PACIFIC. **Reservations:** Recommended for dinner only.

$ Prices: Appetizers $2–$9; main courses $6.75–$20. AE, DISC, MC, V.

　　Open: Lunch Mon–Sat 11am–4pm; dinner daily 5–9:30pm.

✪ This is the kind of sophisticated bistro that you'd expect to find in, say, San Francisco, rather than downtown in sleepy little Hilo. But there it is, attractively decorated in subdued shades of gray, with plants in the center of the room, mobiles hanging from the ceiling, a stage, a dance floor, and a big bar up front, from which flow some of the best margaritas in town. Owners Mark Himmel and Larry Johnson describe their reasonably priced cuisine as "East meets West with an island flair"—and that's just what it is. Almost everything is homemade; only the freshest ingredients are used, seasonings and sauces are imaginative, and since many dishes are marinated and charbroiled, it's possible to eat food that's light as well as delicious. There are some wonderful appetizers at dinner, like charbroiled prawns marinated in lime juice and served with a dill-cucumber sauce, the chicken yakitori on skewers, and the summer rolls—charbroiled chicken wrapped in lettuce and mint leaves, in the Thai style. Homemade soups are a good bet, as are the salads and burgers; charbroiled chicken burger is a house specialty at $6.75. All main courses are accompanied by delicious charbroiled garlic toast, a garden salad (the creamy garlic dressing is very good), a hot vegetable and a choice of fries, baked potato, or rice. They include barbecued ribs, charbroiled chicken, mixed grill, catch of the day, and porterhouse steak. Spinach lasagne, and the sauté medley of fresh vegetables will keep the vegetarians in the crowd contented.

　　Lunch offers similar dishes at lower prices, including soup-and-sandwich specials of the day, burgers, a very popular chicken with papaya, and the hearty Bay City saimin; it's the classic noodle dish, but topped with charbroiled chicken, shrimp, and fresh vegetables, $6.95. Desserts are homemade and super: Save some room for either the White Russian mousse or the chocolate banana cake. On Friday and Saturday nights, Lehua's turns into the place for live entertainment, which continues late, usually until about 2am.

NIHON RESTAURANT & CULTURAL CENTER, 123 Lihiwai St. Tel. 969-1133.
   Cuisine: JAPANESE. **Reservations:** Recommended.
$ **Prices:** Sushi $2.50–$14.95; main courses $6–$17. CB, DC, JCB, MC, V.
   Open: Lunch Mon–Sat 11am–1:30pm; dinner Mon–Sat 5–8pm.

For a true taste of Japan, the place to go is the Nihon Cultural Center, overlooking Hilo Bay and lovely Liliuokalani Gardens. The Nihon Restaurant houses an art gallery, a traditional tearoom, an auditorium for cultural events, and at the heart of it all, a restaurant where traditional Japanese chefs ply their art. Of course there is a sushi bar—the menu describes these dainty morsels of fish and rice as "health foods"—and a dining room for regular Japanese meals. Tempura and tonkatsu lunches are $10.95 and $9.95; sashimi is market-priced. Lunch specials, for $8.95, include a choice of two items and accompaniments, dinners include the traditional sukiyaki. Complete combination dinners feature tempura, sashimi, and beef teriyaki. Traditional Japanese soup, pickled vegetables, and rice accompany the meals. Of course there's saké or Japanese beer to wash down your meal, and homemade green-tea cream for dessert. The sushi bar is open at the same time as the dining room.

RESTAURANT FUJI, in the Hilo Hotel, 142 Kinoole St. Tel. 961-3733.
   Cuisine: JAPANESE. **Reservations:** Not accepted.
$ **Prices:** Appetizers $3.50–$12; main courses $8.25–$24. AE, DC, JCB, MC. V.
   Open: Lunch Tues–Sun 11am–2pm; dinner Tues–Sun 5–9pm.

For a traditional, authentic Japanese meal—and for an excellent bargain as well—count on Restaurant Fuji. This is one of those gracious, relaxed places where you can really relax and enjoy a meal at the comfortably spaced tables in the dining room. The bargains are best at lunchtime, when the "teishoku" meal includes appetizers, otsukemono, rice and soup or tea along with such main courses as grilled butterfish, salmon teriyaki, or a shrimp, fish, and vegetable tempura. Prices are only a dollar or two more at dinner for the same selections. If you wish to splurge, the house specialty, the teppanyaki teishoku—a melange of beef, seafood, fish, and vegetables prepared at your own table—will run you $24 per person. Menus for "ladies and children" are also served.

THE SEASIDE, 1790 Kalanianaole Ave. Tel. 935-8825.
   Cuisine: SEAFOOD. **Reservations:** Required.
$ **Prices:** Main courses $10.50–$19.95. MC, V.
   Open: Dinner only, Tues–Sun 5:30–8:30pm.

Want to eat the freshest fish in Hilo? Then head for the Seaside, a few miles out of Hilo town in the Kaukaha area, where the mullet or aholehole or rainbow trout on your plate will be taken out of the pond when you call to make your reservation! The Seaside, highly respected by Hilo people for years and virtually unknown to tourists, is actually a fish farm; the Japanese family in charge have been cultivating fish here for more than 50 years, in the same way that mullet was historically fattened in special fish ponds for the alii of old Hawaii. They catch fingerlings from the Waiola River, keep them in pens for six months, then release them into the pond for five years. Rainbow trout thrive in Hawaii's warm waters, and take less time to mature—just a year. The 30-acre pond, leased from the state, is set on 50 acres of land in a rural area. Susuma Nakagowa, a former research entomologist with the U.S. Department of Agriculture, took over the fish farm from his parents; now, he and his wife and son, Colin, the restaurant manager, are in charge.

If you come before dinner while it's still light, somebody will show you around and explain the operation to you. (The place is a favorite stop for school groups and those interested in acquaculture). Then on to the simple dining room where you can have your fish prepared in the traditional way, steamed in ti leaves, with onion slices and lemon juice, or fried. The menu is quite simple: For dinner, there's mullet or trout at $15.95; a combination of any fish with chicken, $14.95; fried chicken only, $10.50; a combination of one steamed fish and one fried fish (perhaps the best choice for first-timers), $18.95. Bottled wine is available. And for dessert—homemade apple pie. This place is not fancy, but the fish is the freshest, and coming here is a real experience in nontourist, old-time Hawaii. Be sure to call first, as they serve only when they have fish available. A nice adventure for the kids, too.

WORTH THE EXTRA BUCKS

PESCATORE, 235 Keawe St., at the corner of Haili. Tel. 969-9090.
   Cuisine: ITALIAN. **Reservations:** Recommended, especially at dinner.
$ Prices: Appetizers $6.95–$15.95; main courses $15.95–$24.95. CB, DC, MC, V.
   Open: Lunch daily 11am–2pm; dinner Sun–Thurs 5:30–9pm. Fri–Sat 5:30–10pm.

Gourmet Italian cuisine is a rarity anywhere on the Big Island, so it's nice to find this little place right here in Hilo. Attractively decorated with green tablecloths, red chairs, and shuttered windows with lace curtains, it's a homey and inviting spot. And the food is inviting too, all of it done with great style. Among the antipasti, the carpaccio di pesce—fresh raw ahi—gets kudos, as does the prosciutto with fresh cantaloupe. There are specialty pasta, meat, and fish dishes to choose from every night (they do wonderful fish preparations), but good regular menu choices include the agnello marinata (charbroiled lamb chops), the pollo alla piccatine (sautéed chicken breast in a lemon-caper sauce), a lusty cioppino (the Italian version of a bouillabaisse), and—when they can get it—fresh venison from Lanai. Desserts are wondrous, especially that double-chocolate–truffle cake made with espresso syrup—and the amaretto bread pudding, too.

ROUSSEL'S, 60 Keawe St. Tel. 935-5111.
   Cuisine: FRENCH CREOLE. **Reservations:** Recommended.
$ Prices: Appetizers $3.25–$8.50; main courses $12.85–$24.95. AE, DC, MC, V.
   Open: Dinner daily 5–10pm.

Believe it or not, *mes amis*, there's a bit of New Orleans right here in old Hilo town. The setting is one of Southern charm: potted palms, white curtains at the windows, bentwood chairs, white tablecloths, sparkling wooden floors. Bert Roussel and Spencer Oliver from New Orleans know their gumbo and their shrimp rémoulade and their blackened fish; their menu is authentic and delicious. You'll want to sample the hearty gumbo, thick with bits of shrimp, oyster, and okra, then proceed to such main dishes as shrimp Créole, shrimp étouffée or trout meunière amandine. This is the place for blackened fish: Chef Paul Prudhomme's Louisiana style of blackening the outside, keeping the inside moist and tender, is well carried out here, applied to the local catch of the day and market-priced. Blackened Cajun prime rib is another specialty of the house. A select assortment of Yvonne Oliver's cakes, pies, and mousses, which appear on the dessert tray every day, are quite special. French and California wines are available by the bottle and glass. Call Roussel's an experience in elegant dining.

BETWEEN HILO & KONA ON THE NORTHERN ROUTE

In Chapter 13, we'll describe the drive from Hilo to the resort center of Kona, a trip you should take. Here are some suggestions for meals as you drive the northern route, along the Hamakua Coast (Hi. 19). First stop: Waimea.

WAIMEA

Meals for Less Than $12

ANN SUTHERLAND'S MEAN CUISINE, in Opelo Plaza, Waimea. Tel. 885-6325.
Cuisine: AMERICAN "ECLECTIC."
$ Prices: Main courses $4–$7. MC, V.
Open: Mon–Sat 6am–8pm.

⭐🅢 We highly recommend this delightful eatery; as a local resident put it, "This is wickedly good food at wonderfully low prices." Chef Ann Sutherland (who was once the private chef for the Ethel Kennedy clan) whips up what she calls "casual eclectic American cuisine" at unbelievable budget prices. When this warm, homey restaurant opens at 6am, wonderful smells from the bakery invite you in. Grab a cup of freshly brewed Kona coffee and wander through the mouth-watering wonders in the bakery, a pastry and bread lover's dream come true—everything from an assortment of muffins and breads to tropical fruit turnovers and traditional pastries. Believe it or not, their just-made sushi (from vegetarian to classic Japanese) sell out within a few hours.

The real draw for this upcountry restaurant is Chef Ann's main entrées, a complete meal from $4 to $7 featuring 30 different types of dishes a day ranging from turkey, mashed potatoes with gravy, and all the trimmings to gourmet dishes like Hunan lamb and taro goat-cheese eggplant roulades or lilikoi-cilantro fish with basmati-curry rice and fresh asparagus. You can eat it right there, with classical music playing in the background and fresh tropical flowers at each table, or you can take it out in easy-to-microwave containers. Leave room for dessert—they have everything from a heart-healthy lilikoi cream tart to more decadent chocolate cake with a triple raspberry sauce.

CAFE PESTO, in the Kawaihae Shopping Center, Kawaihae. Tel. 882-1071.
Cuisine: ITALIAN/PIZZA/PASTA. **Reservations:** Not required.
$ Prices: Appetizers $2.95–$7.95; main courses $6.95–$16.95. AE, DISC, MC, V.
Open: Sun–Thurs 11am–9pm, Fri–Sat 11am–10pm.

⭐ If you're driving on Hi. 19 to Kona after leaving Waimea, it's no trouble at all to stop off first at the harbor town of Kawaihae, where you'll find the highly praised Café Pesto. So popular has this gourmet pizza-pasta restaurant become that it's regularly patronized by folks staying at the plush resorts of the Kohala coast, as well as by food fans from all over the island. Two noted Big Island chefs, Jim Williams and David Palmer have put their considerable talents into creating a "pizza-pasta-provocative menu"—which translates into exotic pizzas and pastas, gourmet hot sandwiches, and some satisfyingly rich desserts. It's all served in a sophisticated black-and-white café atmosphere with a single rose on every table. Fine Italian wines and cold beers are available, and paintings by local artists change every month. Have someone in your party order one of the pastas, someone else one of the pizzas; that way, you get a chance to sample. Of the pastas, the ceviche pasta salad with cilantro pesto is delicious, with its Tahitian lime-marinated scallops and shrimps; the Thai curry pasta salad, with shrimp, sun-dried tomatoes, red onions, and spinach, is another taste treat. As for those pizza pies, they begin with a base of handmade and baked-to-order crust (a blend of white, rye, and wheat flours, plus olive oil and honey); they're topped with gourmet cheeses, fresh herbs, sun-dried tomatoes, and the like. The house special, and our favorite, is the pizza Oriental al pesto—fresh basil pesto, roasted garlic, sun-dried tomatoes, and Japanese eggplant. Scampi al pesto is also quite special. Soups and desserts also have the gourmet touch. Call ahead and they'll have your orders ready for take-out if you wish.

WAIMEA COFFEE & COMPANY, Hwy. 19, Waimea. Tel. 885-4472.
   Cuisine: NATURAL FOODS. **Reservations:** Not accepted.
$ Prices: Main dishes $3.95–$5.50. MC, V.
   Open: Mon–Fri 7am–5pm, Sat 8am–4pm.

⭐ If you're driving across the island and want to stop for some light, healthful foods, or maybe just a cup of coffee or a yummy espresso drink, and a luscious pastry, Waimea Coffee & Company is a good choice. It's a plain little place with wooden chairs and tables and some local art on the walls. Homemade soups and quiches are very popular here, as are the Caesar salad, the tabbouleh salad, and the garden burger. Quiche and a salad is $5.50. As for those pastries, some come from the noted French Bakery in Kailua-Kona and some from Beverly, the pastry chef of nearby gourmet restaurant Merriman's. They're all delightful, especially the lemon poppy-seed cake and what a nearby customer proclaimed was "the best apple pie in any restaurant on the Big Island." It's $2.50; coffee of the day, the perfect accompaniment, is 96¢.

Meals for Less Than $25

EDELWEISS, Kawaihae Rd. Tel. 885-6800.
   Cuisine: GERMAN. **Reservations:** Not accepted.
$ Prices: Appetizers $4.95–$6.25; complete dinners $15.50–$19.75. MC, V.
   Open: Lunch Tues–Sat 11:30am–1:30pm; dinner Tues–Sat 5–9pm.

⭐ Long a favorite in Waimea, Edelweiss is a homey place with a European country feeling, seating only about 50 guests. So renowned has master chef-owner Hans Peter Hager's reputation become that there's usually a wait of an hour or so at dinnertime. But it's usually not too crowded at lunchtime; just be sure you get there before 1:30pm or you won't be seated. Hans Peter's cuisine does not disappoint. The luncheon specialty of bratwurst and sauerkraut is $5.95; also popular is the Puu Haloa ranch burger at $6.25, or in a more continental mood, the sautéed chicken breast with champignons and melted Monterey Jack cheese, $7.50. Complete dinners are served with soup of the day, salad, and beverage, and include such dishes as roast duck bigarade braised with a light orange sauce, wienerschnitzel, roast pork with sauerkraut, a wonderful roast rack of lamb for two, and the Edelweiss specialty—sautéed veal, lamb, beef, and bacon with pfifferling (European wild mushrooms—very tasty, indeed. Since Hans Peter is also a master pastry chef, you'd be well advised to save room for dessert, especially if the incredible Grand Marnier parfait is available that day. Black Forest cake, chocolate mousse, fresh peach pie, and Edelweiss specialty with raspberry sauce are also heavenly.

MERRIMAN'S, in Opelo Plaza, Hi. 19. Tel. 885-6822.
   Cuisine: HAWAII REGIONAL. **Reservations:** Recommended.
$ Price: Appetizers $3.75–$6.75; main courses $12.50–$22.50. AE, MC, V.
   Open: Lunch Mon–Fri 11:30am–1:30pm; dinner daily 5:30–9pm.

⭐ Ask local people about the best restaurants in Waimea and the first name you're likely to hear is Merriman's. In fact, ask anybody on the Big Island and you'll get the same answer. Merriman's is rated four stars by just about everybody, and Peter Merriman, the 39-year-old-owner, is rapidly gaining a reputation as one of the most innovative young chefs in the country. Stop by for a meal and see why. Merriman uses only the freshest and finest local products—10 different kinds of mangoes, for example, each with a subtly different flavor, or white pineapples, or shellfish he may have gone diving for himself—to produce an imaginative, contemporary, and highly sophisticated cuisine. The setting is lovely: A Hawaiian art deco room done in soft peach/green colors, with comfortable upholstered chairs, and many plants and flowers that create a light, airy feeling in the daytime. In the evening the atmosphere is more intimate, with flickering candles on the tables highlighting the original paintings on the walls and the island memorabilia of the 1920s, '30s, and '40s.

With such a creative chef as Merriman, the menu changes frequently—but you can be sure that whatever you eat will be outstanding. On the low side of the menu, you might go for the stir-fried vegetables with spicy curry at $12.50, or the roast chicken at $14.50. Among the memorable signature dishes, around $20 or market-priced, are the wok-charred ahi (seared on the outside, sashimi inside), the Kahua ranch lamb, and the locally raised filet steak with Gorgonzola and cabernet sauce. A salad of fresh Waimea greens, a vegetable, and starch accompany all dishes. To begin your meal, try Pahoa corn-and-shrimp fritters, goat cheese baked in phyllo dough, or a Caesar salad that's just a bit different—with sashimi.

Lunch is very reasonable and still of the same high gourmet quality. We could happily make an entire meal of the bouillabaisse, its fresh fish and shellfish piping hot in a saffron broth, $8.25. Or try the salade niçoise, again with the distinctive Merriman difference—made with artichokes, potatoes, and grilled fish on a bed of tossed greens, $6.75. Desserts, like the fabulous lilikoi mousse, are great at both meals. And the wine list is priced invitingly.

BETWEEN HILO & KONA ON THE SOUTHERN ROUTE

There are several interesting choices for meals on this trip listed below. One recommended stop is about halfway between Hilo and Kona, when you come upon an oasis in the lava flows. This is the beautiful town of Naalehu, the southernmost community in the United States. As you drive through town, keep your eyes peeled for the **Naalehu Fruit Stand**, next door to the library. Locals swear by this one! You get your food at the counter, then take it to eat at tables outside. Try one of their unique pizza sandwiches on homemade Italian bread, $8 to $10 for a whole sandwich. They also have the more usual kinds of pizzas, homemade pies, fruit breads, giant cookies, health foods, and deli sandwiches.

KEAAU

Meals for Less Than $10

TONYA'S CAFE, across from the U.S. Post Office and Keaau Town Center. Tel. 966-8091.
Cuisine: INTERNATIONAL VEGETARIAN. **Reservations:** Not accepted.
$ Prices: Appetizers $2–$5.50; main courses $3.50–$5.75. No credit cards.
Open: Mon–Fri 11am–7pm.

Natural-food types should look in on Tonya's Café, across from the shopping center and next door to Keaau Natural Foods. Tonya Miller spent 15 years cooking vegetarian foods "all over California," and now she's on the Big Island, offering international vegetarian cuisine, with many dishes of Thai, Italian, Mexican, and especially Jamaican inspiration (she learned many of her recipes in Jamaica). For about $5.75, you can get a complete meal with a hot dish, soup or salad, and bread. A large organic salad is $3.50; a bowl of soup, $3.50. There are also vegetable juices, fruit smoothies, homemade corn muffins, and some wonderful peanut butter macadamia cookies. This is a tidy little place, very small, with just a few tables inside and out: Eat here, or take food out.

IN & AROUND HAWAII VOLCANOES NATIONAL PARK

Meals for Less Than $15

VOLCANO GOLF AND COUNTRY CLUB, Volcano. Tel. 967-8228.
Cuisine: AMERICAN. **Reservations:** Not required.
$ Prices: Main courses $14–$20. AE, MC, V.
Open: Continental breakfast Mon–Fri 7–10am; full breakfast Sat–Sun and holidays 6:30–10am; lunch daily 10am–3pm; cocktails to 5pm. Dinner Fri–Sat 5:30–9pm.

Two miles south of the Hawaii Volcanoes National Park entrance, watch for the sign that reads GOLF COURSE, directly across the Kilauea Military Camp. It will lead you to the Volcano Golf and Country Club, where many local people take visitors to avoid the Volcano House crowds. The clubhouse, open to the public, has a rustic modern dining room with glass windows, huge ceiling, and wood-burning fireplace. From the windows, you can gaze at Mauna Loa and often sight the rare Hawaiian nene goose. Complete lunches, $5.75 to $11, including soup or salad, vegetable, rice or fries, offer such dishes as mahimahi, honey-stung chicken, chili, and many local favorites like saimin, and Hawaiian stew. Excellent burgers, including fish burgers, run $6.75 to $7.25. Weekend dinners feature prime rib, steak, and scampi.

Meals for Less Than $20

KILAUEA LODGE, Volcano. Tel. 967-7366.
   Cuisine: AMERICAN/CONTINENTAL. **Reservations:** Recommended.
$ Prices: Appetizers $4–$5.75; main courses $12.50–$26. MC, V.
   Open: Dinner only, daily 5:30–9pm.
One mile Hilo-side of Hawaii Volcanoes National Park is Kilauea Lodge, a current "hot" place for dining in the area. The huge room is dominated by the "Fireplace of Friendship," its rocks donated by civic and youth organizations from 32 countries around the Pacific during the years when this was a mountain retreat of the YMCA. The place is still warm and friendly, the dining room is spacious and attractive, and chef Albert Jeyte is known for excellent continental dinners with a touch of local flavor, everything made from the freshest of ingredients. Main courses come with tiny loaves of freshly baked bread and homemade soups. There are at least four specials every day—perhaps ahi, roast duck, lamb provençale, or Hasenpfeffer (that's rabbit in wine sauce); venison and game are often on the menu. Regular dishes include seafood, beef, chicken, fresh fish of the day, plus a few vegetarian dishes, like eggplant suprême and fettuccine primavera. For dessert try the macadamia-nut or ohelo-berry pie—quite special. (*Note:* A wheelchair-lift is available.)

VOLCANO HOUSE, in Hawaii Volcanoes National Park. Tel. 967-7321.
   Cuisine: AMERICAN. **Reservations:** Recommended for dinner.
$ Prices: Appetizers $3.50–$9.50; main courses $9.50–$27; buffet breakfast $7.50; buffet lunch $11. AE, DC, MC, V.
   Open: Breakfast daily 7–10:30am; lunch daily 11am–1:30pm; dinner daily 5–9pm.
The traditional lunch stop here has long been Volcano House, noted for its lovely buffet—a tempting array of salads, fruits, and main dishes, served with beverage and dessert, in a spectacular setting overlooking Halemaumau Crater. The dining room at Volcano House, named Ka Ohelo, in honor of the sister of Madame Pele, the fire goddess, has seating on two levels to provide views for up to 260 people. However, since lunch is a very busy time, what with all the tour buses disgorging hungry passengers, we prefer to come here for a quieter breakfast served late (until 10:30am). Just remember to offer some of the ohelo berry preserves to Madame Pele first, as a sign of respect. (Ohelo is sacred to Pele; you can also sample it in ohelo berry pie, served at Volcano House's snack shop.) The inviting dinner menu includes scampi, prime rib, New York steak, sauteed mahimahi, and Cornish game hen; main dishes are served with a dinner salad, rice or potatoes, and vegetables, plus homemade sweet breads and rolls. It's fun to start—or end—your meal with an only-in-Volcano-House drink: Ohelo Berry Smoothie. It's made with wild berry schnapps, tropical juices, and sacred-to-Pele ohelo berries.

IN NAALEHU

NAALEHU COFFEE SHOP, Naalehu. Tel. 929-7238.
   Cuisine: AMERICAN. **Reservations:** Not required.
$ Prices: Appetizers $3.95–$13.95; main courses $5.95–$13.95. No credit cards.
   Open: Mon–Sat 7:30am–8pm.

Here, in the southernmost town in the United States, the venerable Naalehu Coffee Shop has been doing business since 1941. Owners Roy and Arda Toguchi serve local dishes, fresh fish from South Point Kau, gold oranges, local bananas, and other local produce. The Hawaiian fishburger is a house specialty; other good sandwiches include the Farmer John Baked Ham and the oven-baked turkey sandwich, accompanied by relishes and salad, $4.95 to $6.95. Lunch and dinner main courses are served with salad, vegetable, bread, and rice or potatoes. After your meal, check out the art gallery and Menehune Treasure Chest and browse among the local handcrafts. If you approach from Hilo, make your third left when you pass the school; from Kona, turn right when you pass the theater.

KONA RESTAURANTS

There are three distinct areas on the Kona coast for dining: first, the Kailua-Kona area, home of the busiest tourist scene; second, Keauhou-Kona, just south of Kailua-Kona, and also a tourist area; and third, "Up Mauka" in the coffee-growing country in the mountains, where most of the local folks live.

IN KAILUA-KONA

Meals for Less Than $15

BASIL'S PIZZERIA RESTAURANT, 75-5705 Alii Dr. Tel. 326-7836.
   Cuisine: ITALIAN. **Reservations:** Not accepted.
$ Prices: Individual pizzas $4.85–$7.95; pasta $4.95–$6.95; main courses $5.95–$10.95. No credit cards.
   Open: Sun–Thurs 10am–midnight, Fri–Sat 10am–1pm.
Basil's is small and cozy, serves wonderful food, and is incredibly cheap—no wonder it's so popular! It's *the* place in Kailua town for pizza and pasta. A range of individual pizzas on fresh homemade dough can be ordered individually, everything from the very popular shrimp pesto pizza to the barbecued chicken pie (cilantro is the secret ingredient). For a crowd, their New York–style pizzas are design-it-yourself. Pasta dishes, served with either Caesar or house salad and wonderful garlic bread, are generous. And they also have Italian dinners (complete with salad, a side order of pasta, and garlic bread), featuring eggplant parmigiana, seafood specialties, chicken dishes, and even a New York steak with baked potato or fries for non-Italian-food eaters. There are wonderful coffees and espresso drinks and an array of daily dessert specials.

READERS RECOMMEND

Basil's. *"We liked Basil's so much that we went there twice for dinner and recommended it to everyone we could. It's very small but everything else is on a grand scale. The salad is romaine lettuce with either Caesar or vinaigrette dressing—both of which are flavorful but not overbearing. My favorite dish is the stuffed eggplant parmigiana: it's actually sliced eggplant (breaded and fried but not greasy) with the creamiest ricotta filling, baked with marinara sauce. The cheese ravioli taste homemade and the pizzas are also fantastic. Service is quick, efficient, yet you can linger over a cup of coffee and never be made to feel rushed to leave. Iced tea as well as soft drinks are refilled continuously for free. The owner is there at all times checking orders and dispensing free garlic-bread samples to waiting patrons. Best of all are the prices: our family of five could eat for under $40."—Karen P. Maggio, Glen Ellyn, Ill.*

THE CAPTAIN'S DECK AT SHIPWRECK POINT, in the Kona Inn Shopping Village, 75-5739 Alii Dr. Tel. 326-2555.
   Cuisine: SEAFOOD. **Reservations:** Not required.

$ Prices: Appetizers $2.25–$6.95; sandwiches $5.99–$6.95; main courses $5.95–$8.95. AE, DC, DISC, JCB, MC, V.

Open: Daily 11:30am–10pm.

Here's a nifty budget choice that shares a spectacular sunset-on-the-water location with the renowned seafood restaurant, Fisherman's Landing (see below). The lounge area of that restaurant has been turned into a restaurant of its own: Hearty fish and meat sandwiches, skewers of fish, meat, and seafood, substantial salads (crab and shrimp Louie, Cobb, and pasta salad with chicken and shrimp), and fishnet baskets all make this a fine spot for a light meal. A lively bar is the centerpiece of the room. There's entertainment nightly from 6 to 10pm.

ECLIPSE, 75-5771 Kuakini Hwy. Tel. 329-4686.

Cuisine: CONTINENTAL. **Reservations:** Recommended.

$ Prices: Appetizers $5.95–$7.50; main courses $6.95–$9.95. AE, MC, V.

Open: Lunch Mon–Fri 11am–2pm.

Established over a decade ago, the Eclipse is one of the "in" spots for Kona's business-lunch crowd because of its good food and fast, efficient service—qualities that we tourists enjoy, too. And with nothing on the regular menu over $9.95, it's a good bet for family dining as well. The lunch menu is quite extensive, featuring everything from crêpes to dieters' salads. We like the Greek salad, a meal in itself for $5.95. You might try the eggplant or prawns as an appetizer, and then move on to a pasta, a poultry dish, steak, or seafood as a main course. The fresh catch of the day is available at market prices. The chef offers daily specials with island fish and local produce. This fern-filled restaurant is a quiet retreat most of the time, but as one of Kona's few late dancing spots, the Eclipse is transformed into a foot-stomping disco after 10pm on Friday and Saturday. On Wednesday and Saturday nights it's country and western music from 6 to 10pm, and on Sunday nights 6 to 10pm you can swing to the sounds of the Big Bands.

GIUSEPPE'S ITALIAN CAFE, at Kailua Bay Inn, 75-5699 Alii Dr. Tel. 329-7888.

Cuisine: ITALIAN. **Reservations:** Not accepted.

$ Prices: Appetizers $4.25–$6.25; main courses $7.25–$15.25. MC, V.

Open: Lunch Mon–Sat 11am–9pm; dinner Mon–Sat 5–9pm.

It's just a little hole-in-the-wall place, but Giuseppe's Italian Café turns out lusty Italian fare in generous portions and at reasonable prices—no wonder it's quickly become a Kona favorite. The place is attractive with its red-checkered tablecloths and cozy booths. Owner/chef Joe Stiles learned everything from his mother, Anna Prizzi of Palermo, so you know this is real home cooking, with everything made from scratch. A bowl of slow-cooked minestrone, stuffed mushrooms, or fried calamari makes a good starter. There are a dozen pasta dishes to choose from, including a pleasantly light aglio e olio linguine, fettuccine al pesto, and a traditional lasagne bolognese, as well as a lighter version with spinach. Other favorites include chicken marsala, chicken parmigiana, seafood marinara, and scallops sautéed in sherry wine. All meals come with either fresh green salad or two slices of delicious garlic bread. Pastas are several dollars less at lunchtime, ranging from $4.95 to $6.95. Children's menus are available at $3.95. No liquor is served, but you are welcome to bring your own beer or wine.

THE JOLLY ROGER, Waterfront Row, 75-5776 Alii Dr. Tel. 329-1344.

Cuisine: AMERICAN. **Reservations:** Not accepted.

$ Prices: Appetizers $3.55–$6.75; main courses $8.75–$13.95. AE, DC, DISC, MC, V.

Open: Daily 6:30am–10pm.

Honolulu has its Restaurant Row, and Kailua-Kona has its Waterfront Row, a handsome on-the-ocean, multiple-level dining-shopping complex with a boardwalk and plenty of space from which to watch the pounding surf. One of the more reasonable dining establishments here is the Jolly Roger. The on-the-water location is superb and the food is the kind you remember from the popular Jolly Rogers in

Waikiki: good American fare with reasonable full-course meals, including teriyaki steak, barbecued beef ribs, fish-fry platter, and chicken Polynesian. (Watch the local papers for two-for-one dinner offers for about $18.) Jolly Roger also has lots of sandwiches and salads at lunch, plus hearty breakfasts, which many people consider the restaurant's best meal. Eggs Benedict, delicious Mac-Waples (waffles with cinnamon apples and macadamia nuts), and steak and eggs go for about $3.45 to $7.75. Jolly Roger serves food continuously every day from 6:30am to 10pm, with contemporary music and rock groups playing from 9:30pm to 1:30am. Nice for a drink at sunset, too, when happy hour prices prevail.

KONA RANCH HOUSE, Hi. 11, at the corner of Kuakini and Palani.
   Cuisine: AMERICAN. **Reservations:** Recommended for dinner.
$ Prices: Paniolo Room, complete meal $8.95–$14.95; Plantation Lanai, complete meal $10.95–$22.95. DISC, MC, V.
   Open: Breakfast and lunch 8am–2pm; dinner daily 5–9pm.

Take your choice of food and mood at the Kona Ranch House, really two restaurants in one. For a splurge, choose the lovely Plantation Lanai, so pretty in wicker and green: Dinner features steaks and seafood ranging from $10.95 to $21.95. For a meal that's right within our budget, choose the adjoining Paniolo Room or "family style" room. Here, one can indulge in such dishes as sliced roast pork, broiled or sautéed mahimahi, grilled liver and onions, paniolo stew, or vegetarian spaghetti with garlic bread, all served with soup or salad plus a choice of beans, rice, or potato. Feeling really famished? Go for the Ranch House Family Platter—these are "ranch-hand size dinners" with main courses like New York steak and deep-fried coconut shrimp, teriyaki steak and mahimahi, and barbecued pork ribs and chicken. With them comes cornbread, soup or salad, a choice of baked beans, rice pilaf, or mashed potatoes, plus beverages, all for $14.95. Children's menus, tasty tropical drinks, luscious homemade desserts—Kona Ranch House has all of this, and reasonably priced lunches (from $4.95) and breakfasts, too, from $2.95. Japanese menus are available.

OCEAN VIEW INN, Alii Dr. Tel. 329-9998.
   Cuisine: AMERICAN/CHINESE/VEGETARIAN. **Reservations:** Not required.
$ Prices: Main courses $2.75–$13.50. No credit cards.
   Open: Breakfast Tues–Sun 6:30–11am; lunch Tues–Sun 11am–2:45pm; dinner Tues–Sun 5:15–9pm.

Every time we dine at the Ocean View Inn, we realize why it has survived and thrived for so many years while other newer, flashier establishments come and go. This business has been owned by the same family for more than half a century. It's a big, comfy place, nothing fancy; the view across the road is ocean all the way, the tables are filled with local residents, and the waitresses are old-timers who know their trade. American and Chinese meals are inexpensive and generous. And there is a wide variety of Chinese vegetarian dishes that are surprisingly delicious. Vegetarians bored with yet another salad bar had best make tracks for this place. Dishes based on vegetarian beef (textured vegetable protein) and tofu run $3 to $5; the sweet-and-sour crisp vegetarian wontons rank with the tastiest Chinese food anywhere. Complete dinners ($7.50 to $14.50) offer good value: They include soup or fruit cup, rice or mashed potato or fries, green salad, tea, and coffee. Broiled ahi, broiled ono, breaded mahimahi, and butterfish are all good, and there are at least 24 other choices, including corned beef and cabbage, fried chicken, and roast pork with applesauce. And there are over 80 Chinese dishes beginning at $3.50. Lunch is also a good buy, with many hot plates to choose from, like shoyu chicken or teriyaki steak, for $6.50 to $9.25. These are served with rice or potato, salad, and beverage. Breakfast has everything from ham and eggs and french toast to beef stew, saimin, and poi. The bar is open from 6:30am to 9pm.

QUINN'S ALMOST BY THE SEA, 75-5655A Palani Rd. Tel. 329-3822.
   Cuisine: SEAFOOD/STEAK/VEGETARIAN. **Reservations:** Not accepted.

$ Prices: Appetizers $3.95–$7.75; main courses $6.25–$17.95. MC, V.
Open: Daily 11am–2am.

⭐ There's an informal, relaxed feeling about this place. A lively young crowd hangs out in the garden dining lanai, whose two open walls and one of lava rock give an outdoor feeling. Blue-canvas director's chairs and laminated wooden tables continue the same mood. Indoors, there's an attractive air-conditioned dining room for nonsmokers. There's food here for just about every taste, and all of it is good: fresh seafood and fish, caught and delivered from the pier across the street; juicy steaks; selections for vegetarians; lots of salads with homemade dressings. Main courses come with salad, vegetables, and potato or rice. Lunch is served all day, which means that you can come by at any time for their great fresh fish sandwich or perhaps the fish low-cal plate. French dip, burgers, and roast beef sandwiches are priced about $6.50 to $7.95. Lots of cheer inside at the bar. Local residents consider Quinn's a favorite.

SIBU CAFE, in Banyan Court, 75-5695 Alii Dr. Tel. 329-1112.
Cuisine: INDONESIAN. **Reservations:** Not required.
$ Prices: Appetizers $3.50–$5.50; main courses $8.95–$11.95. No credit cards.
Open: Daily 11:30am–9pm.

⭐ The exotic Sibu Café is a semi-open place where you can sample the mood and food of Indonesia. Balinese decorations, tables topped with sarongs covered with glass, and revolving fans overhead set the scene for wonderfully flavorful food. Every year, readers write to tell us that this was their favorite place! The house specialty is satay: skewers of marinated meats or vegetables broiled over an open flame. Far Eastern dishes like Balinese chicken, spicy pork, ginger beef, Indian curries, and vegetarian stir-fries are also delicious, and everything is accompanied by either brown or fried rice plus a marinated cucumber-and-onion salad. Combination plates are excellent, as is their special peanut sauce. Prices go up a few dollars at dinnertime. Daily Indonesian and international specials are also available, spiced to taste, and there are always several vegetarian dishes.

READERS RECOMMEND

A Piece of the Apple, New York Style Sandwiches, Alii Sunset Place (tel. 329-9321) and **Kona Seafood,** just north of Middle Keei Rd. in Honaunau (tel. 328-9777). "*In Kailua-Kona, one of our favorite spots is A Piece of the Apple: they do real New York–style deli sandwiches, which are so big we share and still have plenty. Prices run from $5.50 to $7. The lean pastrami with Swiss cheese and red onions is great, and so is the corned beef and Swiss with plenty of sauerkraut. In Honaunau, near the City of Refuge, local people love to stop at Kona Seafood, run by 'Stan the Man.' The freshest sashimi, with sauce, is served on plastic plates with chopsticks to go for about $5. Local dishes such as poki and other exotic Hawaiian tasties are available in small portions to go.*"— David Link, Honaunau, Hawaii.

Meals for Less Than $20

FISHERMAN'S LANDING AT SHIPWRECK POINT, in the Kona Inn Shopping Village. 75-5739 Alii Dr. Tel. 326-2555.
Cuisine: SEAFOOD. **Reservations:** Not required.
$ Prices: Appetizers $3.95–$7.95; main courses $10.95–$21.95. Early Sunset Special (5:30–7:30pm) $10.95–$13.95. AE, DC, DISC, JCB, MC, V.
Open: Dinner daily 5:30pm–10pm.

⭐ A seafood restaurant in a spectacular setting. Fisherman's Landing boasts splashing fountains, pools, and nautical decorations all setting the stage for the grand show put on by the pounding surf splashing up on the beach. Fresh island fish, featured daily, is done in a variety of styles. There are also such seafood specialties as lobster tail and shrimp scampi, a few steak offerings, and a variety of

Asian specialties on the order of shrimp tempura and beef teriyaki chicken. All main courses come with soup or salad (their Oriental salad is superb), starch, fresh vegetables, and freshly baked bread from the restaurant's own ovens. Save room for dessert, too, like the lava macadamia nut ice cream pie. There's music every night from 6 to 10pm.

KONA GALLEY, 75-5663 Palani Rd., across from King Kamehameha's Kona Beach Hotel. Tel. 329-5550.
Cuisine: SEAFOOD. **Reservations:** Recommended especially at dinner.
$ Prices: Appetizers $5.95–7.95; main courses $9.95–$17.95. AE, MC, V.
Open: Lunch Mon–Sat 11am–9:30pm; dinner daily 4–9:30pm.

It would be pretty hard to beat the location of Kona Galley: The one-flight up, open-air lanai dining room looks right out over Kailua Pier. The food is special, too. Only fresh, locally caught or grown ingredients are used in such ingenious dishes as the seafood baked in a Puna papaya and topped with a light curry sauce, the large shrimps sautéed in a lilikoi-basil sauce, and the skinless breast of chicken braised in coconut milk and presented on a bed of taro leaves. A baked vegetable lasagne, grilled shrimp linguine, and roast chicken served with a three-peppercorn sauce are other favorites. Start with an appetizer like the baked escargots (unusual in Hawaii) and top off your meal with a memorable dessert like the fresh apple strudel with strawberry-citrus sauce. Luncheon offers a similar menu at slightly lower prices, plus several sandwiches and meal-size salads.

KONA INN RESTAURANT, in the Kona Inn Shopping Village, 75-5744 Alii Dr. Tel. 329-4455.
Cuisine: AMERICAN/SEAFOOD. **Reservations:** Recommended at dinner.
$ Prices: Appetizers $2.95–$8.95; main courses $3.95–$9.95 on the Café Grill menu, $12.95–$18.95 and up on the regular dinner menu.
Open: Café Grill menu daily 11:30am–midnight; dinner menu daily 5:30–10pm.

The lovely Kona Inn Restaurant is a splurge for us at dinner, but it's such a special spot, with a spectacular view of the bay and some tables perched right at water's edge, that it's worth your while to have lunch here or choose from the Café Grill menu anytime. You can have Hawaiian chicken for $6.95, calamari for $5.95, pasta and chicken salad for $7.95, and a host of good sandwiches for $3.95 to $9.95. Having a cocktail out on the oceanfront lanai is lovely, too.

KUAKINI TERRACE, at the Keauhou Beach Hotel, 76-6740 Alii Dr. Tel. 322-3441.
Cuisine: BUFFETS/CHINESE/SEAFOOD. **Reservations:** Recommended.
$ Prices: Chinese buffet $12.95 adults, $6.95 children; seafood buffet, $19.95 adults, $9.95 children; Sun champagne brunch $16.95 adults, $8.95 children. AE, MC, V.
Open: Breakfast daily 6:30–11am; lunch daily 11am–5pm; dinner daily 5–9pm.

Keauhou is one of the loveliest areas of the Kona Coast, with its historic sites, glorious views of the bay and mountains, and grand resort hotels. It's well worth a short drive out here to enjoy the fabulous buffets for which the Kuakini Terrace has become known. Set in an open-air atmosphere, the restaurant affords views of the hotel's lush and beautifully landscaped grounds, as well as an enticing view of Kahaluu Bay. The buffet table is also enticing: Monday through Thursday evening it's a super Chinese feast, the tables laden with many unusual Far Eastern salads, greens, hot dishes like Chinese roast duck, steamed clams with black beans, sweet-and-sour shrimp, Chinese barbecued spareribs; there's a complete dim sum table, and a table of luscious desserts, as well. Considering the setting, the charm and the quality of the food, this is definitely one of the best buys in town. Also very popular is their seafood buffet, served Friday through Sunday. Sunday champagne brunch is another winner, with a wide selection of local favorites.

SAM CHOY'S RESTAURANT, 73-5576 Kauhola St., Koloko Industrial Area. Tel. 326-1545.
Cuisine: PACIFIC RIM. **Reservations:** Required for dinner.

$ Prices: Main courses $15.95–$18.95. No credit cards.
Open: Breakfast and lunch: Mon–Fri 5am–2pm and Sat 6:30am–2pm; dinner Wed–Sat 5pm–9pm.

Chef Sam Choy, born and raised in Kona, has been cooking his entire life; he started by helping his father prepare traditional Hawaiian luaus on weekends and grew into a world-renowned chef. Both local residents and visitors flock to Sam's, tucked away in the Koloko Industrial Area (call to get directions). This simple, high-ceilinged restaurant with an exhibition kitchen and Formica-topped tables serves some of the best food (at hard-to-beat prices) in all of Hawaii.

Breakfasttime is packed with construction workers, attorneys, secretaries, and visitors persistent enough to discover this find. Try the french toast, made from extra-thick slices of island sweet bread for only $2.75; or, if you're very hungry, try, for $7.95, the fresh island fish (Sam has the best fishing connections and always has fresh fish), complete with eggs, choice of rice, hash-brown potatoes or home fries, and toast (you can skip lunch, you will be so full).

Lunch has everything, from traditional burgers ($4.25) to such Asian favorites as bento, spam and egg musubi, and poki musubi, as well as Koloko noodle mania (chow mein noodles cooked with fresh vegetables and meats, and served in a crisp wonton bowl) for only $6, including rice and salad. Nothing at lunch is more than $7.50.

Dinners are our favorite: That's when the white tablecloths come out and flowers grace the tables, transforming the restaurant. Reservations are a must—word is out on the food and the prices, so book in advance. We recommend Sam Choy's award-winning seafood lau lau, made with fresh fish and assorted vegetables in the traditional ti-leaf wrapper ($18.95), or the Chinese honey duck with Kau orange sauce ($15.95), or the nightly specials. All entrées come with soup and salad. Children's menu includes fried chicken or hamburger steak served with rice or french fries for $7.50 and hamburger sandwiches with fries, $5.

SU'S THAI KITCHEN, 74-5588A Pawai Place. Tel. 326-7808.

Cuisine: THAI. **Reservations:** Recommended.
$ Prices: Appetizers $3.95–$10.95; main courses $6.95–$17.95. MC, V.
Open: Lunch Mon–Fri 11am–2:30pm; dinner daily 5–9pm.

Tucked away in the industrial area not far from town, this cute little indoor-outdoor restaurant with a pleasant garden draws fans from near and far: Everybody loves the exotic, authentic Thai dishes. Two people could have an exotic dinner here for under $25! Not only can you go with all the old standbys like pad thai or a variety of curries and coconut milk–based soups, but you can also try some rather unusual offerings: a whole fish in a sweet chili sauce, crab claws in a pot, or stir-fried chicken with macadamia nuts. Vegetarians have a dozen dishes of their own. Lunch specials are a good deal: Every dish is $5.95. Ask to be seated out on the lanai.

TOM BOMBADIL'S FOOD AND DRINK, 75-5864 Walua Rd., off Alii Rd. Tel. 329-1292 or 329-2173.

Cuisine: AMERICAN. **Reservations:** Not required.
$ Prices: Appetizers $2.50–$8.95; main courses $5.75–$14.95. MC, V.
Open: Daily 11am–10pm.

There's an outpost of Middle Earth right on Alii Drive, across from the Kona Hilton Hotel, known as Tom Bombadil's Food and Drink. And while murals and decor and names on the menu are mythic (Aragorn picca, Misty Mountain sandwiches, Elven King salads), the food is downright substantial and filling. Tom Bombadil's is known for its broasted chicken (the unique taste is a result of its being deep-fried under pressure), about $7.25 for a two-piece dinner; for pizzas (from $11.95); and for hot or cold sandwiches (like roast beef dip or turkey, bacon, and avocado). Sandwiches range from $5.45 up to $9.75 for the huge submarine. There are also tasty appetizers such as fried mozzarella, calamari, and pesto cheese bread, plus soups, salads, pastas, and flame-broiled specialties, which include fish of the day, chicken teriyaki, hamburgers, and combination dinners. You can enjoy ocean-view dining from the covered lanai, relax in the cozy pub area with a drink, or view live satellite coverage of sporting events on their cocktail patio. All food is available for take-out; you can call in your order first.

Worth the Extra Money

THE CANOEHOUSE, at the Mauna Lani Bay Hotel and Bungalows, Kohala Coast. Tel. 885-6622.
Cuisine: PACIFIC RIM. **Reservations:** Recommended.
$ Prices: Appetizers $10.50–$14.50; main courses $26–$32. AE, DC, DISC, MC, V.
Open: Dinner only, daily 6–9pm.

⭐ Well worth the half-hour drive from Kailua town, this is one of the most enjoyable restaurants in all Hawaii. The al fresco setting, overlooking the moonlit beach, is extraordinary, and so is chef Alan Wong's menu, full of taste surprises from the countries of the Pacific Basin. Wong uses only the freshest of ingredients and employs light and healthful low-fat methods of food preparation. There are so many wonderful things on the menu that it's hard to choose—nori-wrapped tempura ahi, with soy mustard sauce and tomato ginger relish, and hoisin barbecued baby back ribs make great starters. Seared peppered ahi, opakapaka with a ginger-scallion crust on a miso vinaigrette, grilled tenderloin beef médaillons in a coconut-chili sauce with shiitake mushrooms, and grilled chicken marinated in macadamia-nut oil begin to suggest the possibilities for main courses. Dessert is unforgettable: a quintet of regional specialties that include gratinée of bananas and macadamia nuts in Kahlùa and frozen passion-fruit cannolis with lilikoi sauce. Two of you can share, with great pleasure.

THE CHART HOUSE, at Waterfront Row, 75-5770 Alii Rd. Tel. 329-2451.
Cuisine: STEAK/SEAFOOD. **Reservations:** Recommended.
$ Prices: Appetizers $3.50–$8.95; main courses $12.95–$39.95. AE, DC, DISC, MC, V.
Open: Dinner only daily 5–10pm.

⭐ If you've ever dined at a Chart House restaurant (there are very popular ones on Maui and Oahu), you know you can expect nothing but the best from these restaurants in the way of food, service, and ambience. This Chart House is no exception. It's architecturally striking, with huge sails hanging from the tall ceilings, an upstairs open-air lounge, koa-wood booths, beautiful fabrics and decor within. Note the photographs of legendary Hawaiian athletes on the walls. The Chart House is a bit above our usual price range, but you can have an early evening dinner special (fish, chicken) for $14.95 from 5 to 6pm or one of their light-dining main courses—grilled chicken Caesar salad, grilled Sante Fe chicken salad, a Hawaiian chicken or Hawaiian beef skewer, for just $8.95 to $10.95 any time. Their fabulous soup-and-salad bar is a meal in itself for $12.95. Daily seafood and fresh food selections begin around $23. As for desserts, we wouldn't dream of passing up their mud pie, even at $5.95. An alternative is to come here simply for pupus and a drink in the outdoor cocktail lounge, and watch the sunset as you munch on the likes of garlic jalapeño cheese bread, New England clam chowder, or other tasty pupus ($4.95 to $9.25).

PALM CAFE, at the Coconut Grove Market Place, 75-5819 Alii Dr. Tel. 329-7765.
Cuisine: ASIAN/FRENCH. **Reservations:** Recommended.
$ Prices: Appetizers $5–$9.50; main courses $14–$25. AE, DISC, MC, V.
Open: Dinner only, daily 5–10pm.

Everything about Palm Café is special—from the great location overlooking Alii Drive and the waterfront (sunset-watchers, take note), the spacious cool interior with upholstered wicker chairs, and the arrangement of bonsai on every table, to the unique cuisine prepared by chef/owner Daniel Thiebaut, who describes his style as "French by way of Asia." Sauces are flavorful but not heavy; only the freshest natural ingredients are used; garnishes are edible. Fish preparations shine, especially the oven-baked ono, with an almond-sesame crust in a ginger-lime butter sauce, accompanied by papaya and Kono tomato relish, or the pepper Hawaiian snapper with tomato fondue and Thai salsa. Lamb chops are done Hunan style, with Puna goat cheese and eggplant-zucchini compote. Signature appetizers include the seared yellowfin tuna on a bed of spicy leek and jicama stir-fry and the ravioli stuffed with Chinese greens, with balsamic vinegar and ginger beurre blanc. There are specials and vegetarian dishes every night. Desserts are strictly for sybarites, like the chocolate croquant: two crunchy wafers filled with chocolate mousse and topped with a Tahitian vanilla ginger sauce. Once a month, visiting chefs prepare some outstanding meals here: If you catch one of these, you're in for a special treat.

KONA "UP MAUKA"

Meals for Less Than $8

BILLY BOB'S PARK 'N PORK, Keopuka Square, Captain Cook, just south of mile marker 111. Tel. 323-3371.
   Cuisine: CHICKEN/RIBS/VEGETARIAN. **Reservations:** Not required.
$ **Prices:** Appetizers $3.25; main courses $3.95–$9.95. No credit cards.
   Open: Lunch Mon–Fri 11am–2:30 pm; dinner daily 5–9pm or later.

This little mom-'n'-pop restaurant—cute as can be, with Old West decor and country and western music playing in the background—is a big local favorite. Neighbors keep coming back and bring their kids (there's a big toy box near the window). Owners John Koch and Kathleen Markwell do everything, from cooking the food to serving it up. John, a former rodeo rider (his nickname was "Billy Bob"), is also pretty skillful at turning out the barbecued chicken, beef, and pork ribs, as well as creating vegetarian pastas and enchiladas, fish sandwiches, homemade soups, and salads. His wife, Kathleen, does "Miss Kitty's Desserts," which could be peach cobbler or cherry crisp or cheesecake—a different one each day. Everything is homemade from scratch and prices are ridiculously low: $6.95 buys a full "Bodacious Meal Deal"—a serving of chicken or meat, plus a choice of two side dishes, such as campfire potatoes, chili, green salad and cornbread with honey butter. Beverages—including soda, Kona coffee, and iced or herbal tea—are included. For $9.95 you can have a complete prime-rib dinner. Vegetarian specials are $5.95 and $6.95. It's fun to start with hot and spicy hog fries (like nachos but with potatoes instead of corn chips). No liquor, but bring your own beer or wine and join the local people in a fun scene.

CAPTAIN COOK INN, Hi. 11, Captain Cook. Tel. 323-2080.
   Cuisine: AMERICAN/LOCAL. **Reservations:** Not accepted.
$ **Prices:** Plate lunches $2.80–$6; dinner specials from $5.95. No credit cards.
   Open: Daily 7am–8pm.

Friends of ours who live in this area never eat dinner at home on Sunday anymore; it doesn't pay to cook when Captain Cook Inn is dishing up its oven-roasted turkey dinner, complete with stuffing, mashed potatoes, cranberry jelly, green salad, and hot roll—for only $6.79! And that's not the only reason for giving thanks: This friendly, local-style restaurant has specials every day, which could be Filipino, Hawaiian, Chinese, Japanese, or American. On Friday it's likely to be pot roast, baked ham, or baked pork. There's always stew, chili, teriyaki and Korean chicken, seafood platters, burgers ($2.50 to $5.50). Everything is homemade, including the desserts—bread pudding and pies, mochi, and cheesecake ($1.25 to $2.50). They also offer some hearty bento box lunches and can do vegetarian or fruit-box lunches on request.

Meals for Less Than $14

THE ALOHA CAFE, Hi. 11, Kainaliu. Tel. 322-3383.
   Cuisine: NATURAL FOODS. **Reservations:** Not accepted.
$ Prices: Appetizers $2.95–$5.95; main courses $6.95–$14.95. MC, V.
   Open: Mon–Sat 8am–8pm; brunch Sun 9am–2pm.

⭐ On your way to City of Refuge at Honaunau (see Chapter 13, "What to See and Do on the Big Island"), try the Aloha Café. Located in the lobby of the Aloha Theater in Kainaliu, it has wonderful, healthful food and an unusual atmosphere. The artistically decorated counter-service café is in the lobby of the theater, but it's even more fun to sit out on the terraced lanai that borders the building, especially all the way down near the meadow. The menu features homemade vegetarian burritos, tostadas, nachos, and quesadillas, generous sandwiches (veggie, tofu/avocado, fresh fish), and charbroiled burgers. These items run about $5.25 to $6.75. Dinner adds filet mignon at $14.95, fresh fish (market-priced), and several vegetarian specials. Wines and beers are available. If you get here in time for breakfast, you'll be treated to three-egg omelets, pancakes, and whole-wheat french toast. Even if you don't have a meal here, stop in for some of the homemade fresh-baked goods. The last time we were there it was raspberry linzer tortes. Ono! The Aloha Café, by the way, seems to be local headquarters for transplanted mainlanders to hang out, so it's always a fun stop. Their adjoining health-food and gift store can provide picnic ingredients—cheese, organic fruits (we recently tried organic lychees!) and vegetables. They also offer a large selection of gifts and cards, specializing in children's gifts and books. The store is open Monday through Saturday from 8am to 8pm and on Sunday from 9am to 5pm.

DRYSDALE'S TWO, in the Keauhou Shopping Village. Tel. 322-0070.
   Cuisine: AMERICAN. **Reservations:** Not accepted.
$ Prices: Appetizers $3.50–$8.50; main courses $8.75–$13.50. AE, MC, V.
   Open: Daily 11am–midnight.

Drysdale's Two, in the graceful Keauhou Shopping Village, is a popular gathering spot, especially with sports fans who will be sitting in the huge, pennant-bedecked bar area, watching their favorite teams on the TV. There are several attractive dining areas here too, as well as very good food on a popular-priced menu that is served all day long. Possibilities include such specialties as barbecued pork back ribs, breast of chicken teriyaki, and a vegetable stir-fry, excellent hamburgers, including low-fat buffalo burgers (honest!), for $5 to $6.85; and hearty meat sandwiches, croissant sandwiches, homemade chili, and a good variety of salads, including a fresh Hawaiian fruit salad with sherbet at $7.95. Just about any taste can be accommodated here. Fabulous tropical drinks and ice-cream/liqueur drinks are great for sipping out on the lanai; Peggy's Peanut Butter Ice Cream Pie is a must for dessert, at $3.75.

H. MANAGO HOTEL DINING ROOM, in the H. Manago Hotel, Captain Cook. Tel. 323-2642.
   Cuisine: AMERICAN. **Reservations:** Not required.
$ Prices: Main courses $6–$10.75. MC, V. No credit cards.
   Open: Breakfast Tues–Sun 7–9am; lunch Tues–Sun 11am–2pm; dinner Tues–Thurs 5–7:30pm, Fri–Sun 5–7pm.

⭐ This old-fashioned family-style restaurant is the place to catch a slice of local life. It has enjoyed a good reputation for years among the local people, although very few tourists make their way here. Everything is served family style: big plates of rice, salad (the macaroni salad is especially good), vegetables, and whatever the cook has made that night are brought out and served to everyone at the table, along with such main dishes as pork chops, liver, ahi, opelo, ono, mahimahi, or steak. The menu is limited and the food is not fancy, but this is a good chance to experience the nontourist life of the Kona Coast. Very pleasant.

TESHIMA'S, Hi.11, Honalo. Tel. 322-9140.
  Cuisine: JAPANESE. **Reservations:** Not required.
$ Prices: Main courses $6–$11. No credit cards.
  Open: Breakfast and lunch daily 6:30am–1:45pm; dinner daily 5–9:45pm.

⭐ For a change of ambience from the tourist world of Kailua, drive out on Hi. 11 (one block mauka from the main street of Kailua), a few miles south to Teshima's, at Honalo in coffee-growing country, a very popular place for over 46 years with the local Japanese, Hawaiians, Filipinos, and haoles. You might spot Sen. Dan Inouye there—he always comes in for a meal when he's in Kona. Say hello to Mrs. Teshima—she's a great lady. On one visit she proudly showed us the report that Teshima's had won first prize—the Gold Plate Award—for best Japanese cuisine on the Big Island, from the *Gourmet Guide of Hawaii.* You can have a complete Teishoku lunch of miso soup, sashimi, sukiyaki, plus various side dishes, served on an attractive black-lacquered tray, for $6.50 to $8. At dinner, vegetable tempura and shrimp tempura run $7.50 and $10, and there are plenty of dishes like sashimi, beef, pork, or chicken tofu, for $6.75 to $9.50, all served with miso soup, tsukemono, rice, and tea. Sashimi is market-priced.

SPECIALTY DINING

Shopping Center Eateries

Kona Coast Shopping Center The lively Kona Coast Shopping Center, near the intersection of Hi. 11 and Hi. 19, offers you a chance to mingle with the local folk at some inexpensive restaurants. **Sizzler** is always busy, for they offer consistently good value in steaks, seafood, and salad bars. There's always a special on fresh fish of the day, plus prices like $8.99 for sirloin steak, and $11.59 for hibachi chicken or prime rib. The $7.99 salad bar lunch is a good deal, with fruit, tostadas, soup, hot pasta dishes, and beverage included. An all-you-can eat breakfast buffet is $8.99. A 20% senior citizen discount is offered and children's menus are available. The answer to a hungry family's prayer. For great Mexican food at affordable prices, try Poquito Mas, a tiny take-out restaurant located right next to the umbrella-covered tables in the middle of the shopping center. You can sit and rest as you munch on tacos ($1.75 to $2.10), burritos ($3.50 to $4.10 for meat), or tostadas ($4.25 to $4.85). We love their burrito mojada—that's a "wet burrito" with red sauce, which makes it more like an enchilada. There are also several different ent salsas, from mild to hot. **Kim's Place** is a small take-out shop, where traditional dishes like kalbi, bulgogi, Korean chicken, and the like, are all under $5—and all very good. **Betty's Chinese Kitchen,** small but sparkling, offers Chinese food in serve-yourself cafeteria style; most dishes are $4.10 for two portions, $4.80 for three, $5.75 for four. Betty also has an interesting selection of dim sum—pork manapua, brown sugar manapua, egg rolls, and Chinese doughnuts, for 35¢ to 95¢ each. You can't go wrong with the hearty sandwiches on cracked-wheat bread sold at the health-food store, **Kona Healthways.** It's around $3.95, hearty and delicious.

  Lanihau Center Across the road is a newer shopping plaza, Lanihau Center, which also has several restaurants and fast-food places. **Royal Jade Garden** is a cheerful, attractive Chinese restaurant, with large round tables, fans, and paintings on the walls, and a good menu with many reasonably priced main courses. Pork and beef dishes begin at $4.50 and there are almost two dozen seafood dishes— spicy shrimp, deep-fried oysters, abalone with black mushrooms—at higher prices. A meal at **Yuni's Special Korean BBQ** is a treat: It's neat and clean, and the food is very tasty and reasonably priced. You could have baked goods or a super deli-sandwich at **Buns in the Sun**, pick up some **Kentucky Fried Chicken**, or snack on natural, fat-free (and quite delicious!) frozen yogurt at **Penguin's Place**, the first local branch of the popular West Coast chain.

  Just below Lanihau Center, across from Hilo Hattie's, is Kopiko Plaza, home of ✪ **Kona Mix Plate**, which local friends put us on to—now it's one of our favorites. This is a bustling place with a busy counter, very popular with the local people.

The food is good and cheap, and the service is fast. Sautéed mahimahi and broiled mahimahi, each $5.25, are as good as dishes you'd pay more than twice as much for elsewhere. Also very good: the vegetable tempura and the Korean chicken. Open from 10am to 8pm; closed Sunday.

Three Bakeries Plus

The perfect place to relax and meditate on the beautiful Pacific Ocean is **Island Lava Java**, on Alii Drive at the Alii Sunset Plaza. Not only will you have a ringside seat on the ocean, but this is *the* coffee and bakery spot on the west side. You'll find a great assortment of coffees and espressos to complement the bakery specialties, such as biscotti (all types), scones and our personal favorite, macadamia-nut chocolate brownies. Lava Java offers an assortment of sandwiches (on a croissant) for $5.50 and a wonderful spanakopita (spinach-cheese pie) for $1.99. Drop by on a hot day for ice cream or sorbets ($1.85 for one scoop) or sit around for hours late at night drinking coffee and munching on fresh-baked pastries.

Although it's really not a restaurant, **Suzanne's Bake Shop**, at 74-5603 Pawai Place, in the industrial area, serves as a breakfast place and snack shop for many people. The doors are open at 4:30am every morning, and that's when fragrant and flavorful muffins, doughnuts, danish, iron bars and iron cookies, and other goodies start coming out of the ovens. Pastries are 50¢ to $1.75 each, and the caramel-macadamia-nut danish is a special treat. Snacks are available throughout the day.

Whenever we're in the industrial area, we make it a point to drive over to 74-5467 Kaiwi St. to check out **The French Bakery**, which supplies many top restaurants in the area and also sells directly to the public. Although the name and the pastry chef are French, it's actually an international bakery, with quite an array of interesting goodies, including French bread, whole-wheat croissants, blueberry brioches, rum balls, divine Irish whiskey bread pudding, and a selection of sandwiches, too. For something different, try the Tongan bread (some of the employees come from Tonga), and fill it with chicken or spinach or a sausage/bacon combo, $3.75 and quite good. There's a table for coffee and your selection.

CHAPTER 13

WHAT TO SEE & DO ON THE BIG ISLAND

- **BIG ISLAND CALENDAR OF EVENTS**
1. **ADVENTURE TOURS**
2. **HILO & ENVIRONS**
- **FROMMER'S FAVORITE BIG ISLAND EXPERIENCES**
3. **HAWAII VOLCANOES NATIONAL PARK**
4. **THE PUNA REGION**
5. **FROM HILO TO THE KONA COAST**
6. **THE KONA COAST**
7. **BIG ISLAND EVENING ENTERTAINMENT**

There's so much to see on the Big Island—active volcanoes, verdant tropical valleys, ancient historical sites, black-sand beaches, snowcapped mountains, lush rain forests, and funky old plantation towns where "Old Hawaii" still lives—that ideally you should spend a week or more exploring and enjoying this continent in miniature. However, even if you have only a few days there's much you can accomplish. You'll want to spend at least 1 or 2 nights in picturesque Hilo or perhaps in Volcano Village (where there are numerous guesthouses), then maybe a night or two on the dry and sunny Kona Coast. You could also arrive at Hilo, drive immediately to Hawaii Volcanoes National Park (about an hour's drive), spend a few hours there, then continue right across the island on the southern route to Kona, where you can relax in the sun for as long as you want. Or fly into Kona and reverse the trip, from west to east. The following itinerary will give you basic information with which you can do your own improvising.

SUGGESTED ITINERARIES

IF YOU HAVE 1 DAY Spend the day at Hawaii Volcanoes National Park, the premier sight of the Big Island.

IF YOU HAVE 2 DAYS Spend your first day as above. On the second day, explore Hilo and visit the Puna area.

IF YOU HAVE 3 DAYS Use your first 2 days as suggested above. Spend the third day driving across the island from Hilo to Kailua-Kona on the Hamakaua Coast (northern route), stopping off at the cowboy mountain town of Waimea, perhaps touring the Parker Ranch there.

IF YOU HAVE 4 DAYS Spend the first 3 days as recommended above. On the fourth day, tour the Kailua-Kona area and upcountry Kona Coast, driving to Pu'uhonua o Honaunau National Historical Park, an ancient "Place of Refuge."

IF YOU HAVE 5 DAYS After spending your first 4 days as suggested above, use the fifth day for an exciting excursion: Go diving in a submarine off the Kona coast; or descend 1,000 feet in a four-wheel-drive vehicle into remote, Eden-like Waipio Valley, site of an ancient Hawaiian settlement; or take a safari to the top of snowcapped Mauna Kea (13,796 ft.) to see an unforgettable sunset and night sky. Or just go swimming at lovely Hapuna Beach.

BIG ISLAND
CALENDAR OF EVENTS

APRIL

⊙ **MERRIE MONARCH FESTIVAL** *Competitions, workshops, performances, and more hula than you can shake a hip at. The statewide olympics of hula.*
    Where: *Edith Kanakaole Multi-Purpose Center.* **When:** *April 16–22.* **How:** *Send ticket order January 1 to Merrie Monarch Festival, Dorothy Thompson, Executive Director; Hawaii Naniloa Hotel, 93 Banyan Drive, Hilo, HI 96720 (tel. 808/935-9168). Send cashier's check or money order only. Prices: $20 and $25 for three nights. Write in for specifics any time.*

MAY

☐ **Lei Day.** There's lei-making in most of the hotel lobbies. May 1.
☐ **Big Island Spring Art Festival.** A major event for local artists and a wonderful chance to see the best of island arts. Wailoa Center, Hilo. For information, telephone 808/933-4360. Month of May.
☐ **Golden Goddess Fishing Tournament.** A ladies-only 2-day tournament in Kailua-Kona. End of May. For information, telephone 808/322-3832.

JUNE

☐ **Kamehameha Day Celebrations.** Complete with entertainment, crafts, demonstrations, food booths, and a Royal Court Procession. Coconut Island, Hilo. Free. Sponsored by Malia Puka O Ka Lani Church; for information, telephone 808/935-9338. June 11.
☐ **Hawaii State Horticultural Show.** Held yearly at Edith Kanakaole Multi-Purpose Stadium, Hilo. Displays of anthuriums and plants by members of the Hawaii Anthurium Industry. Usually held the third weekend in June. For information, telephone 808/965-9522.

JULY

☐ **Independence Day Celebrations.** Rodeos in Waimea and Naalehu, roughwater swimming in Hapuna, and an anniversary celebration for Pu'uhonua o Honaunau in Kona, showing off old Hawaiian crafts in a cultural festival. July 4.

AUGUST

⊙ **HAWAIIAN INTERNATIONAL BILLFISH TOURNAMENT** *This is the world's leading international marlin fishing tournament, and each year it draws fishers and fans from everywhere.*
    Where: *Kailua-Kona pier.* **When:** *August 8–12, parade August 7.* **How:** *Book rooms well in advance—the place will be mobbed. For information, telephone 808/329-1148.*

SEPTEMBER/OCTOBER

☐ **Aloha Festivals.** The opening ceremony is at Halemaumau, with dance performances and offerings to Pele. End of August to late October.

OCTOBER

✪ *GATORADE IRONMAN WORLD TRIATHLON CHAMPIONSHIPS* *Only world-class athletes need apply. This internationally acclaimed event includes a 2.4-mile swim, a 112-mile bicycle ride, and a 26.2-mile run, with no resting between events.*

Where: Kailua-Kona. When: Usually in mid-October. How: Make reservations at least 6 months in advance (tel. 329-0065). Every available room on the Big Island will be taken.

1. ADVENTURE TOURS

EYE OF THE WHALE, MARINE/WILDERNESS ADVENTURES, P. O. Box 1269, Kapaau, HI 96755. Tel. 808/889-0227, or toll free 800/659-3544.

With a goal of promoting understanding of Hawaii's delicate ecosystem through firsthand experience, Beth and Mark Goodoni lead 6- to 10-day hiking and hiking/sailing adventures for groups of no more than 10 people. Days are spent outdoors, hiking through mountain valleys and jungles or sailing the Big Island's Kona coast. Nights are spent either on boats (for sailing trips) or in B&Bs. There is no backpacking or camping. Beth, a marine biologist and seasoned naturalist, introduces participants to the natural history of Hawaii, emphasizing the origin and identification of tropical flora, the development and exploration of coral-reef ecosystems, and the biology and observation of marine mammals. On the boat, she's the crew; husband Mark is the licensed USCG captain. Cost is about $150 per day, including meals, accommodations, transportation, and inter-island fares. A highlight of the trip is a private luau, where guests learn to dig the imu, string their own leis, and dance the old-time hulas.

CRANE TOURS, c/o Bill Crane, 15101 Magnolia Blvd., H10 Sherman Oaks, CA 91403. Tel. 818/742-2213, or toll free 800/653-2545; or Hilt McCauley at 818/347-6433.

Crane Tours offers moderate to moderately strenuous week-long trips for experienced backpackers, at a cost of about $695. Participants bring their own tents and backpacks, although several nights are spent in mountain cabins, and the last night is usually spent in a hotel. There is also a noncamping Christmas trip. The company, known for excellent value and service, also offers trips to the islands of Maui and Kauai.

2. HILO & ENVIRONS

The best way to see Hilo and environs is on a driving tour. Below are two tours. It's possible to do both in 1 day if you're pressed for time.

DRIVING TOUR 1

Start: Hilo Tropical Gardens.
Finish: Reed's Bay Park.
Time: 2 to 4 hours, depending on how long you spend at major stops.
Best Time: Early mornings, to see as much as possible.
Worst Time: Late afternoon.

Our first tour of Hilo begins with a visit to:

1. **Hilo Tropical Gardens.** Follow Hi. 19 to the eastern strip of town; you'll find the gardens at 1477 Kalanianaole Ave., about 2 miles from the airport. Paved walkways (accessible to the disabled) lead you through a tiny jungle of tropical flowers, shrubs and trees, splendid orchids, native Hawaiian plants and herbs, past water lily pools, waterfalls, even a Japanese pond with a footbridge and statuary. After you've seen the gardens and used up a little bit of film, stop in at their gift shop for Hawaiian handcrafts, wood products, and, of course, flowers. Anything can be shipped home. Admission is $3. Open daily from 8:30am to sunset. Call 935-4957 for driving directions.

   Make your way back to town, now, toward Hilo Bay, where you'll soon spot the:
2. **Wailoa Center,** whose building resembles a volcano. Located just behind the state office building, it features free exhibits ranging from cultural to natural history, and a permanent exhibit on tsunamis (tidal waves). Services and admission are free. For information, phone 933-4360. The entrance is on Piopio Street, between the state office building and Kamehameha Avenue. Open Monday, Tuesday, Thursday, and Friday from 8am to 4:30pm, on Wednesday from noon to 8:30pm, and on Saturday from 9am to 3pm. From here it's not far to the:
3. **Suisan Fish Market,** where the freshest fish in town can be found. Weekdays at 8am the fishermen's catch is lined up and auctioned off to restaurants and grocery stores around the island. The public is invited. Don't miss the opportunity not only to experience this fast-paced auction, but also to see the magnificent bounty of Hawaii's waters: huge marlin, tunas weighing over 200 pounds, prehistoric-looking broadbill swordfish, and many other species. Coming up soon is the:
4. **Nihon Japanese Culture Center,** at 123 Lihiwai Street. In addition to serving authentic and excellent Japanese cuisine (see "Where to Eat," in Chapter 12), the center has an art gallery, a tearoom, and music, dancing, films, and other entertainment. Check to see if anything special is going on. Coming up on your right is:
5. **Liliuokalani Gardens** with its lovely Japanese bridges, ponds, plants, and stone lanterns. It's believed to be the largest such formal Japanese garden and park outside Japan. Look for the authentic Japanese tea ceremony house. On your left is:
6. **Coconut Island,** a favorite picnic spot for the local people. If you continue around the park, you'll find yourself on Banyan Drive, which takes you past many of the resort hotels in the city. The magnificent trees are labeled in honor of the celebrities who planted them: James A. Farley was one, Amelia Earhart another; Cecil B. DeMille has a tree, as does Mrs. De Mille. Continuing in the same direction you'll come to:
7. **Reed's Bay Park,** a cool picnic spot on the bay.

DRIVING TOUR 2

Start: Nani Mau Gardens.
Finish: Lyman House Memorial Museum Complex.
Time: 2 to 4 hours, depending on stops.
Best Time: Early morning, so that you can see Rainbow Falls at its best.
Worst Time: Late afternoon.

To see one of our favorite gardens, drive about three miles south of Hi. 11 (the road to the volcano) from Hilo Airport, then turn left onto Makalika Street just after Hi. 11 divides. Drive seven-tenths of a mile (look for the familiar Hawaiian warrior sign for the turnoff), and you'll soon find:

1. **Nani Mau Gardens,** a wonderland of 20 acres of the fruits and flowers of many lands; their orchid garden, with thousands of varieties, is the largest in Hawaii. A ginger/helicona garden, an anthurium garden, a tropical water-lily and carp pond, an enclosed nursery, and waterfall and stream are also featured. You can tour the gardens by foot, on a tram ($4 per person, seven-person minimum). Lunch, available from 11am to 1pm, features a buffet and made-to-order sandwiches. The gift shop is a good source for souvenir items, art posters by local artists, and USDA-certified plants and flowers to ship back home. You can stay in the gardens as long as you like, to picnic or just relax. Open daily from 8am to 5pm, with an admission charge of $6.50. Call 959-3541 for information. Drive back up Hi. 11 and pick up Hi. 19. About 7 miles north of Hilo on the 4-mile scenic route at Onomea Bay, near Hi. 19, is the:

2. **Hawaii Tropical Botanical Garden,** a spectacular garden in a valley on the ocean—acclaimed as one of the most beautiful areas in Hawaii. Nature trails meander through a true tropical rain forest, cross streams and pass by spectacular waterfalls, and provide ocean vistas along the rugged coast. The garden's collection of tropical plants includes more than 2,000 different species collected from tropical jungles throughout the world. The garden won the coveted Kahili award for 1993 as the "Best Attraction" in the state of Hawaii. For serious students of nature and lovers of natural beauty—not to mention photographers—it's a paradise. Admission is $12 (children under 16 free), which is tax-deductible because the garden is a nonprofit foundation. It's open every day (except New Year's Day, Thanksgiving, and Christmas Day), rain or shine (they furnish umbrellas), from 8:30am to 4pm. Call 946-5233 for exact driving directions. No food is sold and there are no picnicking facilities.
   On Hi. 11 just outside the city is the:

3. **Panaewa Rain Forest Zoo.** Turn right on the Stainback Highway and watch for signs on the right for the zoo. This is by no means the big time as zoos go; it's a small place, but with its own special Hawaiian charm. You'll see denizens of the South American rain forest, the rare Hawaiian nene (goose), the Hawaiian pueo (owl), many brightly plumaged birds, tigers wading through a jungle stream, and peacocks roaming the grounds; cutest of all are the monkeys, which seem to enjoy the funny humans walking about. Free admission. Open every day from 9am to 4:15pm.
   Now it's time for some Kamehameha lore, since the Big Island is where that doughty old warrior was born and where he first started dreaming his dreams of glory and conquest.
   Continue driving on Kamehameha Avenue, turn left onto Waianuenue Street, and drive 3 blocks to the modern county library on the right side. See the two stones out in front? The bigger one is the:

4. **Naha Stone,** Kamehameha's Excalibur. According to Naha legend, only a chief of the royal blood could even budge the gigantic boulder; any warrior strong enough to turn it over would have the strength to conquer and unify all the is-

BIG ISLAND ATTRACTIONS

0 ——— 16 km
      10 mi

Alenuihaha Channel

PACIFIC OCEAN

PACIFIC OCEAN

Hawi Kapaau

250

270

Kohala Forest Reserve

Kukuihaele

Kohala Mountains

10 Waipio **13**

Samuel M. Spencer Beach Park

9
8 **19**
7

11
12 Waimea

Honokaa

Paauilo

14

19

Hakalau

15 Honomu

Akaka Falls

Paihaaloa

17 **18** **20** **21**

Mauna Kea
16

Hilo Forest Reserve

19

22 Hilo Int'l Airport

23

24 Hilo **25**

11 **26**

Queen Kaahumanu Hwy.

Mamalahoa Hwy.

Saddle Rd.

19

Hualalai

Kailua-Kona

6 Holualoa

11

5

4 Kealakekua
3 Captain Cook
   Napoopoo

2 Honaunau
1 Kealia

200 Saddle Rd.

Mountain View

Keeau **137**

Kapoho **130**

Pahoa **132**

Pohoiki

27

Hawaii Volcanoes National Park

28
Mauna Loa

29 **30** **31** **32**

Volcano Rd.

Puna Forest Reserve

130 **137**

Kapapala Forest Reserve

11 Kilauea **33**

Hawaii Volcanoes National Park

Chain of Craters Rd.

(Road closed due to lava flow)

South Kona Forest Reserve

Kau

Kau Desert

Forest

Mamalahoa Hwy.

Pahala

Manuka State Park

Reserve

Mamalahoa Hwy.

11 Punaluu

Naalehu

Ka Lae (South Point)

Airport ✈ Mountain △

Akaka Falls **15**

Boiling Pots **23**

Captain Cook Monument **3**

Hapuna Beach **7**

Hawaiian Macadamia Plantation **13**

Hawaii Tropical Botanical Garden **18**

Hawaii Volcanoes National Park **27**

Hilo Tropical Gardens **21**

Huhilee Palace **6**

Kahaluu Beach Park **5**

Kalopa State Recreation Area **14**

Kaumana Cave **24**

Kilauea **33**

Kilauea Military Rest Camp **31**

Liliuokalani Gardens **20**

Lyman House Memorial Museum Complex **22**

Mauna Kea **16**

Mauna Loa **28**

Mauna Loa Macadamia Nut Mill **26**

Mokuaikaua Church **4**

Naha Stone **19**

Nani Mau Gardens **25**

The Painted Church **1**

Parker Ranch **11**

Pu'uhonua O Honaunau National Historic Park **2**

Puukohola Heiau National Historic Site **9**

Rainbow Falls **17**

Thurston Lava Tube **32**

Samuel Spencer Park **8**

Volcano Arts Center **29**

Volcano House **30**

Waimea Center **12**

Waipio Valley **10**

FROMMER'S FAVORITE
BIG ISLAND EXPERIENCES

A Visit to Hawaii Volcanoes National Park Start with break-fast at historic Volcano House, and end with a stop at the Volcano Art Center.

A Submarine Dive in the *Atlantis* Dive 80 to 100 feet below the surface into the clear waters of Kona Bay to explore the world of the coral reef.

A Walk Into the Tropical Rain Forest and Wild Jungle at Hawaii Tropical Botanical Garden Travel 7 miles north of Hilo to 17 acres of waterfalls, meandering streams, and more than 2,000 plant species, some bordering a wild stretch of ocean.

Doing Anything in the Picturesque Mountain Town of Waimea Shop the boutiques and galleries, sightsee, stroll, as long as it's not raining.

Taking Waipio Valley Wagon Tours Down into One of Hawaii's Few Remaining Shangri-las See almost-deserted Waipio Valley, where there's a black sand beach, an ancient fish pond, and the dramatic Hiilawe Falls.

Snorkeling at Kaahaluu Beach Park on the Kona Shore Snorkel in a pretty lagoon bordered by salt-and-pepper sand, thanks to an ancient lava flow. This is the best snorkeling on the Big Island.

lands of Hawaii. Kamehameha did the deed, but since the stone weighs at least a ton, no one has bothered, as yet, to repeat it. Off Waianuenue Avenue at Rainbow Drive is:
5. **Rainbow Falls.** The best time to see this sight is early in the morning: Try to come between 9:15 and 10am, when the sun gets up high enough over the mango trees so that you might see rainbows forming in the mist. It's pretty at any time, however, and so are the beautiful yellow flowers growing near the parking lot. Continue along Waianuenue about 2 miles to Peepee Street to the:
6. **Boiling Pots,** deep pools that appear to be boiling as turbulent water flows over the lava bed of the river. From the parking lot you can walk over to the edge and observe the show below. Both Rainbow Falls and the Boiling Pots are part of the Wailuku River State Park. Return to the fork at Hi. 20 and turn right onto the other branch of the fork, Kaumana Drive. About 3 miles out is:
7. **Kaumana Cave,** where you can see some of the work of Pele at close range. The cave is a lava tube, created in 1881, when Pele came closer to wiping out Hilo than at any other time. Lava tubes are sometimes formed when lava flows down a ravine or gully; the top and sides cool while the center keeps racing along. Millions of years of volcanic eruptions have left hollow tubes like this all over the islands; in many of them are hidden the bones of the alii, which were always buried in remote, secret places. Of the two tubes here, only the one on the right—whose entrance is an exquisite fern grotto—is safe for exploration.

The one on the left is treacherous, and who knows—perhaps the bones of Kamehameha, never discovered, are buried here.

Retrace your steps to Kamehameha Avenue, and turn onto Haili Street in a mauka direction (away from the bay and uphill); cross Keawe, Kinoole, and Ululani Streets, and on the left-hand side you'll see:

8. **Haili Church.** Its architecture is pure New England, but its fame stems from its great Hawaiian choir. Continuing up Haili Street from the Haili Church, cross Kapiolani Street, and on the right-hand side you'll find the:

9. **Lyman House Memorial Museum Complex,** at 276 Haili St. The original Lyman House is another of those old mission homes that the grandchildren and great-grandchildren turned into a museum; this one, originally built in 1839, has been fully restored and furnished as a home of the late 19th century. The white-frame building, Hilo's oldest structure, contains hand-molded New England glass windows, doors made of native koa wood, and the original wide koa floorboards. As you tour the rooms, you'll see how the missionary family lived: the clothes, old four-poster beds, and white marble-top table stands and dressers. The fascinating Hawaiian artifacts and worldwide curios that used to be displayed here have now been transferred to the recently built Lyman Museum building. In this very modern $1-million museum addition, you begin at the Island Heritage Gallery on the first floor, where a raised relief map shows routes taken by all the groups that came to Hawaii. Then you can see the artifacts of each group and study their cultures; the Hawaiian exhibit includes a full-size grass house, Stone Age implements, feather leis, etc. There are also Chinese, Japanese, Portuguese, Korean, and Filipino displays. The second floor also has fascinating exhibits, among them the Earth Heritage Gallery with its display of volcanic eruptions and worldwide gem mineral collections, one of the finest and most extensive collections in the country. The Chinese Art Gallery has pieces dating back as far as the Shang Dynasty, 13th century B.C., and the Artists of Hawaii Gallery features works by early Hawaiian artists. There's also an astronomy exhibit.

Lyman House is open Monday through Saturday from 9am to 5pm and on Sunday from 1 to 4pm. Admission is $4.50 for adults, $2.50 for children 6 to 17 and for seniors. For information, call 935-5021.

SHOPPING

Shopping is concentrated in three areas here: at the Kaiko'o Hilo Mall, just behind the county and state buildings; downtown, where stores and boutiques are housed in quaint wooden buildings; and out on Hi. 11, at the newer megabucks Prince Kuhio Plaza Shopping Center.

KAIKO'O HILO MALL

Kaiko'o Hilo Mall, with its supermarket, specialty shops, and drugstores, is of most interest to local people, but we always do very well at the **J. C. Penney's** here, where values and selections are excellent in every department. It's a good place to shop for muumuus, and luggage too.

DOWNTOWN

If you're in Hilo on a Wednesday or Saturday morning and you don't mind getting up early, go downtown to the bus terminal at the corner of Mamo Street and Kamehameha Highway at about 6am. This is the scene for Hilo's biggest **Farmer's Market,** where people come from all over to pick up produce, lots of flowers, some fish, and some arts and crafts, at low, low prices. Some 120 vendors show their wares. They sell out quickly—usually by 8am—so it's best to be there early.

ABUNDANT LIFE NATURAL FOODS STORE, 292 Kamehameha Ave. Tel. 935-7411.

Almost 19 years old and right on the bay front, this is Hilo's only complete natural-foods store. Along with the top major brands of supplements, quality skincare products, health-oriented groceries, and the like, Abundant Life carries a unique selection of local and imported items. Their deli section is great for a healthy and hearty meal on the run, and their produce section features organic, locally grown fruits and vegetables—strawberry-papayas, apple-bananas, mangoes, tangerines, avocados, and more. Their bulletin board lists just about all of Hilo's happenings.

BASICALLY BOOKS, 46 Waianuenue Ave. Tel. 961-0144.

Basically Books specializes in Hawaii and the Pacific, with videotapes and a complete selection of maps of Hawaii, including USGS topographic maps, NOAA nautical charts, and road and street maps. They also have a good selection of travel books, posters, and attractive souvenirs, as well as a selection of maps for destinations worldwide.

THE CRYSTAL GROTTO, 290 Kamehameha Ave. Tel. 935-2284.

Wendy Gilliam creates a wonderful atmosphere in her shop: There's New Age music to listen to and an eyeful of unique gift items—handcrafted custom jewelry, crystals, Hawaiiana, Native American arts and crafts, posters, books, and more—to look at. She has hard-to-find items like kukui-nut oil, and an extensive selection of beads for craftspeople. Check here for news of New Age and holistic workshops. Tapes and videos are available. A most inviting place, hard to tear yourself away from.

CUNNINGHAM GALLERY, 116 Keawe St. Tel. 935-7223.

Here you'll find prints and paintings by local artists, such as Pegge Hopper, John Thomas, Robert Nelson, Tom Rissacher, and Kim Taylor Reese. Attractive koawood–frame mirrors start at around $75. Cards by Herb Kane, Jane Chao, and others begin at just $1.50.

DAN DE LUZ'S WOODS, 760 Kilauea Ave. Tel. 935-5587.

Dan De Luz is considered Hawaii's master bowl-turner, and his creations, which may range from a tiny bowl for $25 to works going up into the hundreds of dollars, are as fine as they come. De Luz works mostly with koa, but there are also works in milo and sandalwood. He is known for his covered bowls and nested sets of bowls. Jewelry, bookmarks, letter openers, and the like sell for low prices. De Luz will gladly take you through his woodworking shop in the rear and show you how he produces his marvels. There's another Dan De Luz's Woods in Waimea, located at 64-1013 Hwy. 19.

DRAGON MAMA, 266 Kamehameha Ave. Tel. 934-9081.

This shop abounds with lovely wares: natural fiber futons, tatamis, kimonos, and zafus (meditation pillows), among others. Their wool sleeping pillows, at $28, are wonderfully cozy.

FUTON CONNECTION, 104 Keawe St. Tel. 935-8066.

A lot of the items here are too big for you to carry home but do have a look at their jewelry, chimes, porcelain nightlights, beautiful cotton pareaus from India ($21), and many other unique gifts.

GAMELAN GALLERY, 277 Keawe St. Tel. 969-7655.

One of Hilo's most distinctive shops, this is a showcase for the handcrafts of Indonesia, many of them personally collected by Marc Platt, whose wife, Eva, is in charge of the shop. And while you may not be able to afford the bronze masks or the wood sculpture or the rare textiles, there are quite a few very affordable items—batik T-shirts at $20 and $30, shirts and shorts made from used batik sarongs, hand-woven Ikat bags from $10, for example. Traditional shadow puppets, baskets made from rattan and straw grass, and lacquered boxes are among the many treasures here.

OLD TOWN PRINTERS & STATIONERS, 201 Kinoole St. Tel. 935-8927.
This is the retail store of the Petroglyph Press, which has been publishing books on Hawaiiana since 1962. Drop in to browse through their publications, notes, and postcards, including many with Hawaiian designs. In addition, walk a few blocks to their other store, Basically Books (see above).

SIG ZANE DESIGNS, 122 Kamehameha Ave. Tel. 935-7077.
Sig Zane Designs is known for its distinctive designs in Hawaiian sportswear. You'll see them sold at many places in Hawaii, but this is the source: muumuus, T-shirts, aloha shirts, pareaus, handsome quilted designer jackets, jewelry, accessories, all bearing Sig's signature touch. Everything is 100% cotton. Prices are not low, but this is top of the line. Hawaiian music cassettes are also available at the best prices in town.

THE MOST IRRESISTIBLE SHOP IN HILO, 110 Keawe St. Tel. 935-9644.
⭐ Housed with several other boutiques in the renovated and quite attractive 1922 Pacific Building is one of our favorite shops. It's always worth a look-see, since owner Sally Mermel is forever coming up with something new and exciting for her flocks of loyal customers. Examples: one-of-a-kind jewelry by local artisans (earrings made of Hawaiian woods, dolphin rings); Hawaiian quilt-design mugs in a variety of pastel colors; lovely pareaus from Tahiti, Hawaii, and Indonesia, some of them exclusive here; cassettes and CD's by Hawaiian artists; koa-wood mirrors, cutting boards, and rice paddles; island perfumes; T-shirts with designs of whales, sharks, volcanoes, and turtles—and lots more, the best selection in Hilo. Hawaiian jams, jellies, and fruit butters make great small take-home presents. Adjoining the shop is Bears' (see "Where to Eat," in Chapter 12), with wonderful coffees, light foods, and desserts, all with a bear theme—Bear Claws, Teddy Bear Pie—and more.

PRINCE KUHIO SHOPPING PLAZA

This mall, the largest enclosed regional shopping center on the Big Island, will remind you of Kaahumanu Center on Maui or Kukui Grove on Kauai; it's vast, it cost millions to build (in this case, $47.5 million), and it boasts the traditional big department stores like **Liberty House, Sears,** and **Woolworth's,** plus 65 other specialty stores ranging from the latest women's apparel fashion shops to charming little boutiques. **The Most Irresistible Shop in Hilo** (mentioned above) also has a shop here, this one with an emphasis on children. **Imagination Loves Toys** is an educational toy center, with all kinds of creative playthings. We always like to have a look at **Book Gallery,** especially to browse through their wide selection of island cookbooks. They carry all the local cookbooks of church groups, women's groups, and the like. They have a good selection of Hawaiiana books and videos, books for the keikis back home, and some unique Petroglyph Press paperbacks, printed right here in Hilo. The **Hilo Hattie Fashion Center** is well worth a visit. The company is the largest manufacturer of aloha wear in the state; the store carries gifts, candies, and jewelry in addition to clothing, all at less-than-usual prices. Everybody gets a complimentary shell lei and refreshments too. (In fact, you can even get free transportation here by calling 961-3077). **Contempo Casual, RAVE, Jay Jacobs,** and **Hartfields/Hartfields Plus** are all known for their trendy fashions and accessories. For beachwear and surfing attire, **Local Style** has everything. Accessorize anything and everything at **Afterthoughts Boutique. Tee's 'n' Togs** has lots of cute tops that can be imprinted with your choice of design, or personalized; and **Casual Corner** has good contemporary women's fashions. Throughout the center, you'll find various carts and kiosks selling their own brands of unique and/or flavorful merchandise—including espresso coffee, seeds and candies, jewelry, and blown glass.

There are some pleasant places to eat here, including **Dick's Coffee House** (see

"Where to Eat," in Chapter 12). But keep in mind that you're about a 2-minute drive from the Puainako town center, home to **Dotty's Coffee Shop,** a favorite local place, and the **Ting-Hao Mandarin Restaurant,** one of the best Chinese restaurants in town (see "Where to Eat," in Chapter 12).

READERS RECOMMEND

Tips on Buying Flowers. *"John Alexander, the delightful host at the Dolphin Bay in Hilo, gave us a helpful hint that we want to pass on. He told us to buy our flowers at an inexpensive place, such as a grocery store or small florist, obtain a carton, and pack them carefully with shredded, wet newspapers, covered with plastic, to keep them moist. We did this, and carried them on the plane with us. I am writing this over a week later and they are still in good shape. I have four dozen anthuriums and six birds of paradise to give to my friends, and all for just a little over $15."*—Mrs. Dean James, Celina, Ohio.

"A United Airlines employee at Kahului gave me this helpful tip. If your plane stops in Hilo en route home, buy flowers at the airport—fresher and cheaper. I bought a beautiful orchid, carnation, and plumeria lei, and orchid plants were $1 to $2 less than at other flower stands elsewhere. The saleswomen were extremely helpful and cordial."—Elizabeth C. Greer, El Cerrito, Calif.

SPORTS & RECREATION

Your ramblings have worn you out, your budget hotel doesn't have a pool, and you want a swim. Where do you go? We'd start out at Kalanianaole Avenue, drive 3 miles to **Onekahakaha Beach Park** or a mile farther to **James Kealoha Park,** where the swimming in the rocky bay is okay if not memorable. But it's pleasant to drive through this Keaukaha area, the most beautiful part of Hilo, to see the exquisite private homes, some with their own tranquil Oriental fish ponds. Picnic and swimming spots continue until the end of the paved road. Watch for the signs pointing to **Richardson's Ocean Park,** the home of an outdoor marine recreation and interpretive center. You can swim, snorkel, fish, and surf in waters that front the center; tour a coastal trail which features coastal plants and brackish water ponds; and picnic on the lawn areas. The center contains marine-life displays that interpret nearby ocean and coastal environments. Open Monday through Saturday from 8:30am to 4:30pm. Free admission. Call 935-3830 for details.

If you favor pool swimming, join the local people at the Olympic-size **Sparky Kawamoto Swim Stadium** at 799 Piilani St., near the civic auditorium (tel. 935-8907). Admission is free. Open Monday through Friday, from 11am to 1pm for adults, from 1 to 4pm and 6 to 8pm for everybody; on Saturday and Sunday, from 10am to noon for adults and 1 to 4pm for everybody.

3. HAWAII VOLCANOES NATIONAL PARK

You must not leave the Big Island without paying homage to the goddess Pele. Not to visit her residence at Halemaumau, the firepit crater of Kilauea (this is the smaller volcano nestled along the southeastern slope of Mauna Loa), would be unthinkable. If Pele is entertaining, you're in for one of the world's great natural spectacles; if not, just a look at a volcano and damage it has done in the past will be a big experience.

It's more exciting than ever to visit the volcano, because for several years there has been a great deal of activity in Mauna Ulu, Pauahi Crater, and others. These new eruptions on the flanks of Kilauea have been big enough to spurt enormous fountains of fire 1,800 feet up above the crater's rim. In 1984 both Kilauea and Mauna Loa were active at the same time, the first time this had happened since 1868. Lava flows came dangerously close to the city of Hilo. As of this writing 10 years later, Pele is still acting up. Call 967-7977 anytime for recorded information on eruptions, or try the park rangers at 967-7311 before you start, for news of the latest eruptions and viewing conditions. But whether or not anything is happening, the volcano trip is a must. Try to plan this for a morning trip, as clouds often appear in the afternoons.

EN ROUTE TO THE PARK

Take Hi. 11 out of Hilo for about 30 miles until you reach Hawaii Volcanoes National Park. Be sure to take a warm sweater and a raincoat; the air gets refreshingly cool 4,000 feet up at Kilauea Crater. The weather can change quickly and dramatically, as sunshine gives way to mist and fog.

There are several possible stops en route for flower fanciers. The first, at the 14-mile marker in the tiny town of Mountain View, is the **Hawaiian Flower Garden Nursery,** which specializes in anthuriums at very low prices. (While you're on the main street of Mountain View, look for the Mountain View Bakery and see if they have some of their "stone cookies.") At the 22-mile marker is **Akatsuku Orchid Gardens,** a lovely botanical-type garden with many varieties of orchids; you'll receive one free as a gift. Just before you get to the park, it's fun to stop in at tiny **Volcano Village and Volcano Store** (on Hi. 11, make a right at Haunani Road directly to the store). Half the porch is the home of a snack bar and small restaurant called Alii Bakery and Drive-in; the other half is the place where local people go to scoop up reasonably priced flowers: Just to give you an example, we saw birds of paradise for 50¢ a blossom, 10 calla lilies for $3, king protea for $4 and less. Prices of flowers vary every day. The store will pack and ship anywhere in the United States. Poke around inside a bit—it's great for local color. The bulletin board out front often has leads on cottages to rent and news of local events.

SEEING & TOURING THE PARK

Once you reach the park (entrance $5 per car, good for 7 days; free for those over 62), signs will direct you to the **Kilauea Visitor Center,** which should be your first stop. Check with the very helpful park rangers here for directions on the current eruption—if any. Be advised that if an eruption is going on, extreme caution must be exercised on the hiking trails, as there may be earth cracks anywhere, hundreds of feet deep, and a fall could be deadly. Those with heart and respiratory problems and pregnant women should beware of noxious fumes, children must be kept under control, and all visitors should protect themselves from the intense rays of the sun. Most visitors, however, simply drive to the important points on Crater Rim Drive (more about that ahead), which is much safer. If you can afford it, there is, of course, nothing to compare to the spectacular helicopter flights directly over the lava flows.

First, though, explore the visitor center a bit. You can get information here on self-guided walks, the Kipuka Puaulu Walk, which is a 1-mile loop, and the Halemaumau Trail, a 6½-mile round-trip hike. Trail guides for both are available at the visitor center. And try not to miss the terrific color films of the latest eruptions, shown every hour on the hour from 9am until 4pm. There used to be a display case here consisting of letters from people who had taken rocks from the volcano—despite being warned never to do so—and had spells of bad luck, and sent the rocks back. Many of the letters ask forgiveness of Madame Pele. For example: "My

IMPRESSIONS

I have seen Vesuvius since, but it was a mere toy, a child's volcano, a soup-kettle, compared to this [Kilauea].
—MARK TWAIN, 1872

---

friends are no longer in my life, I am divorced, I've lost my business, my property is being foreclosed. Pele is angry about something. . . I took the rock. . . Pele is a very busy woman and surely she would not miss a handful of stones from the firepit. Right? Wrong!" More letters and more rocks continue to make their way back to Hawaii.

VOLCANO ARTS CENTER & VOLCANO HOUSE

Now that you know not to break any Hawaiian kapus by taking lava rocks back home, walk a few doors from park headquarters to the **Volcano Art Center,** P.O. Box 104, Hawaii Volcanoes National Park, HI 96718 (tel. 967-7511) Here, in the 1877 original Volcano House Hotel, a nonprofit group shows the work of some 200 artists and craftspeople, most of them from the Big Island. Fine arts reflective of Hawaii, bowls and sculptures of native Hawaiian woods, and posters are for sale, as well as small distinctive gift items. Note the Jack Straka native-wood bowls, the Chiu Leong raku pottery, the Dietrich Varez block prints, and the "Trashface Jewelry" of wearable art made from found and recycled objects by Ira Ono, considered collector's items. There are concerts and special events as well as excellent arts programs for long-term visitors. During the month of December, Christmas is celebrated with a blazing fire, hot apple cider, holiday music, and Santa Claus too. Always a worthwhile stop.

Note: If Ira Ono's "Trashface Jewelry" excites you, as it does us, call the artist and make an appointment to visit his studio to see more (tel. 967-7621). His "Spirit Fans"—personal collages composed of one's mementos—are outstanding. Ono, a well-known performance artist, is a most engaging fellow. (And if you're staying in Volcano, and it rains—well, here's a way to make the best of a rainy day.)

Just across the road from the Volcano Art Center is **Volcano House** (see "Where to Stay," in Chapter 12). Situated on the rim of the crater, it's a magical spot. Eruption movies are shown in the lobby every evening. It's cozy just to sit here for a few minutes in front of the fireplace, where the fire, so it is said, has been burning continuously for 119 years. Burning ohia logs fill the air with a wonderful aroma. Or repair to Uncle George's Lounge, where the bartenders, volcanologists all, can whip up some unique drinks—Pele's Fire, or an Ohelo Berry Smoothie.

Some simple nature trails begin right in back of Volcano House, and we urge you to take at least one. The upland air is fragrant, the vegetation glorious, the views spectacular. The silvery trees that look something like gnarled birches are ohia, and their red-pompom blossoms are lehua, the flower of the Big Island, sacred to Pele. (It's rumored that if you pick one, it will rain before you arrive home.) That's the big bald dome of **Mauna Loa** towering 10,000 feet above you into the heavens; you're on **Kilauea,** which rises on its southeastern slopes. Pele hangs out in Halemaumau, the firepit of this enormous, 2½-mile-long crater.

There is trouble in this paradise, however, according to conservationists and local people who are launching a mighty protest to stop the industrialization of the Big Island. Geothermal drilling is already getting under way on the slopes of Kilauea Volcano, in the midst of a Hawaiian rain forest. Planned for the near future are geothermal wells, power lines crisscrossing the island, a metals-smelting plant, a "spaceport," and an underseas cable, all of which could produce huge quantities of toxic waste and severely harm Hawaii's unique and endangered environment. Native Hawaiians also consider the drilling a desecration of their religion and their respect for the goddess Pele and her sacred places. If you'd like to get more information, perhaps help them in their cause, contact the Pele Defense Fund, P.O. Box 404, Volcano, HI 96785 (tel. 808/935-1633).

AROUND CRATER RIM DRIVE

To see the important views, take Crater Rim Drive, the 11-mile circle road, in either direction around the rim of Kilauea Crater. The rangers' map is easy to follow. Begin your trip around this wonderland of rain forests and volcanic desert at the **Sulfur Banks,** just west of park headquarters. The banks have that familiar rotten-egg odor. Farther along the road you'll see eerie wisps of steam coming out of some fissures, but don't be alarmed—they've been puffing along for centuries. You can stop to enjoy a hot blast from the steam jets, a natural underground "sauna."

Just beyond the Kilauea Military Rest Camp is a road that swings off to the right and across the highway that brought you here; if you follow this side path, you'll come upon an interesting clump of tree molds, formed in the same freakish way as the ones at Puna. The 100-acre **bird park** (Kipuka Pualu) is here too, a sweet spot for a picnic or a nature ramble through many rare trees; but you'll have to be sharp to spot the birds chirping away above your head.

Driving back to the rim of the crater road, turn right and continue the journey into the weird world ahead. You'll get your first view of Halemaumau, that awesome firepit 3,000 feet wide and 300 to 400 feet deep, from the lookout at the **Thomas A. Jaggar Museum.** Stop inside, too, to learn something about the history and development of volcanoes, and to see the murals by artist Herb Kane on the legends of Pele. The museum is named in honor of Thomas A. Jaggar, the first person to understand the necessity of having trained observers on site before and after volcanic eruptions.

Continue along the well-marked Crater Rim Road now to **Halemaumau Overlook** itself, the home of Pele. When Pele decides to act up, everyone from there to the Philippines seems to descend on the area; whole families sit bundled in their cars all night long watching the awesome fireworks. Nobody can say when Pele will blow her top again. It is still local custom to appease her, but now that human sacrifice is out of fashion, she is reputed to accept bottles of gin! For a more intimate glimpse of Halemaumau, the 3-mile (one-way) hike through a hushed forest to the eerie heart of the volcano is recommended. The walk, a tough one, starts at Volcano House; be sure to get the descriptive pamphlet at park headquarters to guide you.

The drive now takes you to the area hit by the 1959 eruption of Kilauea Iki (Little Kilauea; all the volcanoes have little siblings here). A boardwalk has been set up over the cinder ash here; and a walk along this **Devastation Trail** will take you past the twisted ghosts of white trees felled by the lava. At the end of the trail you can look down into the **Kilauea Iki Crater.** (This walk takes about 15 minutes, so to conserve energy you might send one member of your party back to the parking lot to bring the car around to the lookout area at the end of the walk.) A favorite 4-mile hike around the crater's edge begins here.

The forest takes over at **Thurston Lava Tube,** a few miles farther, and a magnificent prehistoric fern forest it is. The lava tube shaded by this little grotto is another of those volcanic curiosities, even more spectacular than the one you saw in Hilo.

Now, if you're determined to see lava flowing into the ocean and you have more time to spend—at least two hours—continue around the **Crater Rim Drive** until you come to the Chain of Craters Road. It's a dramatic drive, the road descending 2,700 feet in 24 miles, all the way to the point where, if an eruption is going on, the lava flow enters the sea. The flow creates steam clouds that are white during the day and orange or red at night. You'll pass a jungle of ferns, an ohia forest, historic lava flows, and sea arches, as you go all the way down to the sea. But first, we repeat, you must check in with the rangers at the Mobile Visitor's Center for an update on the ever-changing conditions. They provide the latest information on where the flow is and how close you can get to it, what the weather conditions are, and everything else you'll need to know before heading out. The checklist of what to take with you includes the following: a minimum of one liter of water per person (it's unbelievably hot walking on black lava, because of the heat of the sun combined with the heat of the lava flow); good shoes (hiking boots preferred); and to protect against the sun, a hat, sunscreen, and sunglasses.

The Mobile Visitor's Center is constantly moving to keep up with the flow. Generally, it's about 20 miles down Chain of Craters Road. Park your car and walk about a quarter of a mile from where the road ends to the Mobile Visitor's Center. There's a half-mile loop trail off the paved road along the coast with good views of the flow into the ocean (be sure to carry a flashlight at night). Rangers conduct a lava exploration walk (conditions permitting) at 2:30pm (the Mobile Visitor's Center at the park entrance will know if lava-flow conditions will allow the exploration walk to take place).

Occasionally, the National History Association will be set up near the Mobile Visitor's Center, selling small bottles of water, film, and flashlights. Park rangers suggest supplying your own bottled water, as the National History Association is not present every day.

Note: Since a lava flow has covered part of Chain of Craters Road, blocking the park's eastern boundary, there is no longer any way to continue on Hi. 130, which once led to Kalapana and the black sand beach at Kaimu, destroyed by recent lava flows. You will have to return to park headquarters the same way you came, via the Chain of Craters Road. Note also that there is no food or gasoline available along this route, but both are available in Volcano Village, 1 mile Hilo-side of Hawaii Volcanoes National Park.

THE VOLCANO FROM THE AIR

★ There's no doubt about it: The most extraordinary way to see the volcano is by air. It's not inexpensive ($139 per person), but a flight over the steaming volcano on one of Big Island Air's Cessna 420s could well be the high point of your trip to Hawaii. Sunset flights fly directly over active surface lava flows and over the steaming Pu'u Oo Vent, where one can look down into a 2,000-degree river of molten lava flowing into the sea. The tour also takes in black and green sand beaches and the lava deserts. If you have a little more time, the complete 2-hour Circle Island Tour ($169 per person) is recommended: It covers all 266 miles of the Big Island's spectacular coastline and includes bird's-eye looks at remote Waipio Valley and waterfalls dotting the shores. All flights leave from Keahole Airport on the Kona Coast. Planes seat nine passengers; every seat is a window seat. For information and reservations, phone 808/329-4868.

HUNTING & CAMPING IN THE VOLCANO AREA

If you're brave enough to tackle Mauna Loa (the largest mountain in the world, more than 32,000 feet from sea floor to summit—18,000 of them below sea level), make your requests for information to the Superintendent, Hawaii Volcanoes National Park, HI 96718. The area is under the jurisdiction of the federal government and is administered by the National Park Service, U.S. Department of the Interior. There is an overnight camping area at the **Namakani Paio Campground,** 3 miles from Volcano House. Ten cabins, nicely furnished, with beds and cooking utensils, each sleep four people, at about $32 per night (for more details, see "Where to Stay," in Chapter 12).

In addition, Hawaii Volcanoes National Park manages two drive-in campgrounds on a first-come, first-served basis at no charge: These are the above-mentioned Namakani Paio on Hi. 11, 2½ miles west of park headquarters, with eating shelters, fireplaces, water, and restrooms; and **Kipuka Nene,** on Hilina Pali Road, 11½ miles south of park headquarters, with eating shelters, fireplaces, water, and pit toilets.

Wood is not provided at any site. You cannot reserve sites in these campgrounds in advance. There is no camping fee, and no permits are required. However, your stay is limited to no more than 7 days in any one campground.

Backpackers who wish to camp in the volcano area must register at the Kilauea Visitor Center before beginning their trip (shelters and cabins are managed on a first-come, first-served basis at no charge). They may use the two Mauna Loa Trail Cabins (one at Red Hill at an elevation of 10,000 feet, 7 miles from the end of the Mauna Loa Strip Road, and another on the southwest side of Mokuaweoweo, the summit caldera, at an elevation of 13,250 feet, each with bunks but no mattresses), or the Pepeiao Cabin, another patrol cabin on the Ka'u Desert Trail at Kipuka Pepeiao.

For additional information on camping around the Big Island, details on current conditions of parks, fees, and so on, contact the County Department of Parks and Recreation, 25 Aupuni St., Hilo, HI 96720. Summers and holidays should be booked far in advance.

4. THE PUNA REGION

Although everybody goes to Kilauea, many tourists miss one of the most fascinating places nearby—the Puna region east of the volcano. Here you can gain an understanding of what a volcanic eruption means, not as a geologic curiosity, but rather in terms of the farms, stores, orchards, graveyards, and cucumber patches that got in its way. From Hilo, make the volcano trip your first priority; if you have a little extra time, visit the fascinating Puna region too.

FROM HILO TO KEAAU

This outing begins on Volcano Highway (Hi. 11), which branches off from Kamehameha Avenue southward past the airport. About 6 miles out of Hilo, you'll come to a possible stop, the **Mauna Loa Macadamia Nut Mill and Orchard**, the world's leading grower, processor, and marketer of macadamia nuts. Luther Burbank called macadamias "the perfect nut." This major island crop tastes better than peanuts. On the drive from the highway to the visitor center (past roads with names like Butter Candy Trail and Macadamia Road), you'll see hundreds of thousands of macadamia trees. From an observation gallery you can see the processing and packing operation, and observe colorful displays about history and horticulture. You can also take a mini–nature walk through a macadamia-nut grove with papaya, monkeypod, and banana trees. Open daily from 8:30am to 5pm.

You may want to turn left off Volcano Highway and drive through town until you find Hi. 130 and **Keaau,** an old, rather run-down plantation town that is now home to many artists and craftspeople. To the mountainside of the Keaau Police Station is **Puna Tropical Buds** (in the historic Plantation Store), a good stop if you're planning to send flowers to anybody back home. Puna is the largest grower of cymbidium orchids on the island and sells them at very reasonable prices. They also sell interisland airline tickets at substantial discounts when available. And once you're back home, send the nice people here $35 (or $55 for a deluxe box) and they'll ship you, pronto, a gorgeous tropical bouquet. (Write to Jonna & Scotty, P.O. Box 1593, Keaau, HI 96749; tel. 808/966-8116.)

On the same street, across from the shopping center, is **Keaau Natural Foods,** one of the best-stocked health-food stores on the Big Island, with lots of organic produce, a nice selection of deli items (dips, tabbouleh, vegetarian sandwiches, carrot juice, etc.) to munch on. You can also stock up on guilt-free temptations like Russian tea cake and date bars, made only with unbleached flour and little or no sugar.

Also in stock: incense, candles, hammocks, sandals, T-shirts, and the like.

PAHOA

Back on Hi. 130 now, you'll find Pahoa about 10 miles farther south. Here you'll enter the area that bore the brunt of the 1955 eruption of Kilauea. This had been peaceful farm country for 100 years, dotted with papaya orchards, sugarcane fields, coffee farms, pasture lands. Then a rift in the mountain opened, and the lava fountains began to spout erratic caldrons that might turn a farm into ashes, but leave a gravestone or an old building untouched. You'll see cinder cones along the road and tiny craters still steaming. The most spectacular—and chilling—scenery comes later.

Downtown Pahoa is a funky little town you might want to explore a bit, a kind of unreconstructed hippie haven. Everything is on the main street, so wander at will along its wooden sidewalks in search of serendipity. If the ambience of the town speaks to you, make a note to come back some time and stay at the newly restored **Village Inn,** a remodeled 1910 hotel nicely done up with Victorian and turn-of-the-century antiques, its six rooms honoring historic figures like Mark Twain, Robert Louis Stevenson, Princess Kaiulani, and Don the Beachcomber—with decor to match their eras (P.O. Box 1987, Pahoa, HI 96778; tel. 808/965-6444; doubles from $40 to $80, weekly rates available). The Village Inn's lobby gift shop is a favorite stop for antique collectors, especially for 1930s and '40s glassware, plus a wide variety of local, Oriental, and occidental antiquities and collectibles. **Pahoa Emporium** has a good selection of clothing and antiques, and the **Hawaiian Hemp Company** has a name that speaks for itself (some interesting clothing here). **Huna ohana,** run by Dawn Hurwich, a retired dress designer from the Midwest, is our favorite spot here. It has a good selection of metaphysical books and music, crystals and such, plus excellent vegetarian food, most of it organic and locally grown. Breakfast, served until 11am, features yummy croissants, bagels, and muffins, plus soufflé eggs and Belgian waffles. At lunch there are pita pizzas, garden burgers, and quiche and salad combinations, all very reasonably priced. There's also a wonderful list of coffee specialties and smoothies. Another all-time breakfast favorite here is the **Paradise West Coffee Shop,** where the ahi Benedict, made with their own hollandaise sauce, is famous. **Naung Mai Thai Kitchen, The Godmother, Ristorante Italiana,** and **Luquin's Mexican Restaurant** all have their following; and many of the locals swear by the food—pork adobo, sesame and shoyu chicken, chow fun, and more—prepared by Kimo, a famous chef in these parts, at **Koho Okazuya.**

Pahoa Natural Groceries is the place to get natural deli sandwiches and fresh carrot juice. And keep your eyes open for the local vendors who can sometimes be found downtown selling anthuriums, puka products, papayas, and the like—all at very reasonable prices. Look for the one who sometimes sells six papayas for $1. Don't be lazy: Get out of your car and stock up! Nowhere can you beat these prices.

FROM PAHOA TO KAIMU

Continue along Hi. 130, and prepare yourself for a chilling sight: a look at the lava flow that destroyed the idyllic garden community of Kalapana in May 1990. Flows from the Pu'u o'o vent of Kilauea, which began erupting in 1983, finally reached the sea 7 years later, after destroying in its terrible path at least 123 houses, a church, local stores, and the idyllic Harry K. Brown Park. Also in its path was the Star of the Sea Painted Church, one of the two "painted churches" on the island, known for its colorful, indoor murals painted in 1931. The church was removed before the lava flow could consume it, and was to be relocated somewhere in this area (check local sources for its exact whereabouts).

Also destroyed by lava was the black sand beach at Kaimu and the junction connecting Hi. 130 and Hi. 137. Consequently, you'll have to retrace your path up Hi. 130 and look for the sign indicating the turnoff to **Opihikao.** The ride down to

Opihikao is like going through an enchanted forest: Huge ohia trees form a canopy across the top of the road, papaya farms dot the landscape, and a cornucopia of flowers grow wild along the roadside.

At the junction of Opihikao Road and Hi. 137, turn right; between the 17- and 18-mile markers on Hi. 137 you'll see a banner that reads KALANI HONUA. **Kalani Honua** is a unique conference and retreat center, on 20 secluded acres, hosting classes, workshops, performances, and special events year round promoting healing, the arts, and traditional Hawaiian culture. They also offer lodging, accommodations, and meals (see "Where to Stay," in Chapter 12). You may wish to stop and browse in the gift shop, which features clothing and craft items including colorful tropical pareaus. Dinner is served daily at 6:30pm. The cuisine is mostly gourmet vegetarian (quite delicious), and reservations are suggested (tel. 965-7828).

Four miles from Kalani Honua the road has been blocked by a lava flow. Again, the only thing to do is to retrace your steps on Hi. 137, this time bypassing Opihikao Road and continuing on Hi. 137 toward Kapoho. This fantastic 15-mile trip is one of the most exotic coastlines in Hawaii. From the red roller coaster of a road, you'll see where the tropical jungle alternates with black rivers of lava that laid waste miles of earth before they reached their violent end in the steaming Pacific. The sea pounds relentlessly on the black lava rocks, eventually grinding them into more black sand; on the land the jungle creeps back slowly, reclaiming the land for itself and breaking it down into what will once again be red earth. This is how the islands of Hawaii—and many of the earth's surfaces—were formed, and no textbook description will ever leave such a vivid picture in your mind.

Continuing toward Kapoho on Hi. 137, you'll find two good spots for picnicking, fishing, or hiking (no swimming); **MacKenzie State Park** near Opihikao and **Isaac Hale Park** at Pohoiki. Continue on Hi. 137 until you reach Kapoho, a Hawaiian Pompeii that was buried under spectacular lava flows in 1960. The day-by-day fight to keep the village from being overwhelmed by the lava flow and pumice cinders from the new cinder cone (which now overlooks the remains of Kapoho) was one of the most dramatic episodes in recent Hawaiian history. A cinder cone on the concrete floor is all that remains of Nakamura's Store, and nearby, a desolate lighthouse stands inland from the new coastline created by the lava flow. Come back from Kapoho on Hi. 132 and look for **Lava Tree State Park.** An old lava flow encircled the trees here, and they were eventually burned out, but the lava trunk molds remain, surrealistic witness to the whims of Pele.

You'll note that we've now described a triangle almost back to Pahoa; from here it's Hi. 130 back to Keaau, and then home to Hilo.

---

5. FROM HILO TO THE KONA COAST

THE THREE ROUTES There are three possible routes across the Big Island from Hilo to the Kona coast.

   (1) The Southern Route. If you're continuing on from the volcano, simply follow the excellent Hi. 11 another 90 miles. You'll pass through the Ka'u Lava Desert (where an explosion of Kilauea in 1790 routed an army of Kamehameha's chief enemy, Keoua); you might stop off at Punalu'u to see the black sand beach. You'll hit the pretty little village of Naalehu before encountering miles of lava flows, until you get to the other side of Mauna Loa and the welcoming Kona coast.

   (2) The Northern Route: The Hamakua Coast. If you're starting from Hilo, however, and have already been to the volcano, it's impractical to take the 126-mile southern route, when you can reach Kona directly in 96 miles, and sample in-between terrain so varied that Hawaii seems more like a small continent than a large island. We're referring to the drive along the majestic Hamakua coast, through the rolling pasture lands of the Parker Ranch, and then around Mauna Kea and Hualalai Volcano to Kona.

(3) The Saddle Road. An alternative route for the first 50 miles of this trip crosses over the saddle between Mauna Loa and Mauna Kea, giving you wild, unforgettable views of both—but also a not-so-comfortable ride. Car-rental companies prohibit driving on this Saddle Road—Hi. 200 out of Hilo—mostly because help is so far away. Should your car break down, the towing charge is enormous, not to mention your being stranded in the wilderness!

The drive in the opposite direction, from Kona to Hilo, is described briefly at the end of this section.

STARGAZING

For those interested in the stars, there are two programs available to the public. At the 9,000-foot elevation, the Ellison Onizuka Visitor's Center (named after the Hawaiian-born astronaut who died in the 1986 *Challenger* space shuttle tragedy), features displays and programs about Mauna Kea and the astronomical work taking place there. The center is open Friday from 1 to 5pm and Saturday and Sunday from 8am to noon, 1 to 2pm, and 4 to 5pm. Stargazing with a portable telescope takes place every Friday and Saturday at the Visitor's Center between 7 and 10pm.

The Mauna Kea Observatory at the summit has tours on Saturday and Sunday. The tours meet at the Visitor's Center at 1:30pm and proceed up to the observatory at the summit. Since the observatory is located at nearly 14,000 feet, in high-altitude, rarefied air, no one under 16 is allowed on the tour and anyone with a heart or respiratory condition, or who is pregnant, is advised not to make the trip to the summit. A four-wheel-drive vehicle is required to make the journey on the road from the Visitor's Center to the summit.

Before you venture up to either the Visitor's Center or the observatory, be advised that the weather at high altitude is changeable and can be quite dramatic. High winds and sudden drops in temperature, along with rain, hail, and snow, are common occurrences. Before you go, call the Visitor's Center for information, 961-2180; and call 969-3218 for road and weather conditions.

HAMAKUA COAST DRIVE
HILO TO HONOKAA

The drive we prefer—and the one that we'll explore in depth—starts from Hilo on Hi. 19, paralleling Kamehameha Avenue along the waterfront and heading for the northern shore of the island and the Hamakua coast. This is sugar-plantation country, miles of cane stretching inland to the valleys (the produce eventually goes to the bulk-sugar plant in Hilo and then to the mainland); the coastline is a jagged edge curving around the sea, broken up by gorges and streams tumbling down from the snowcapped heights of Mauna Kea. The views from the modern and speedy Hi. 19 are good, but if you really want to soak up the scenery, get off now and then on the old road that winds through the gullies and goes to the sea.

Ten miles out of Hilo, at Honomu, the HVB marker indicates the way to **Akaka Falls.** Four miles inland on a country road, you'll find not only the falls—perhaps the most beautiful in the islands, plunging dizzily 420 feet into a mountain pool—but also a breathtakingly beautiful bit of tropical forest turned into a park which is lush and fragrant with wild ginger, ancient ferns, and glorious tropical trees and flowers. It's a rhapsodic spot, very difficult to leave. Console yourself, then, with a bit of snacking and shopping in Honomu. At **Ishigo's General Store** you can pick up a hot cup of Kona coffee, as well as some scrumptious pastries at the bakery adjoining it. A few steps down the road is the **Akaka Falls Flea Market,** fun and inexpensive.

The little town of **Laupahoehoe**—you can drive down to it from the highway—is a "leaf of lava" jutting into the Pacific, its local park another idyllic spot for a picnic. But it's also a grim reminder of the savagery of nature that's always possible in Hawaii; it was in a school building here that 20 children and their teachers were swept away into the sea by the 1946 tidal wave.

If you have time for a little hiking and nature study, watch for the signs leading to **Kalopa,** a 100-acre Native Forest State Park containing trees, shrubs, and ferns indigenous to pre-Polynesian Hawaii, with trails through the ohia rain forest and many spectacular views—a nice spot for a picnic. Cabins are available for rental here through the County Department of Parks and Recreation.

Thirty miles past Akaka Falls is **Honokaa,** second-largest city of the Big Island and the site of the **Hawaiian Macadamia Nut Plantation.** You can view the plant and visit the retail store, which features, a mind-boggling array of 200 macadamia-nut products. A macadamia-nut festival is held here in late August. Follow the warrior signs to the MACADAMIA NUT CAPITAL OF THE WORLD, open daily from 9am to 6pm for self-guided tours. On your way down the hill to the factory, you might want to stop in at **Kamaaina Woods** on Lehua Street, a factory and gift shop that turns out distinctive carvings in koa, milo, and other local woods. Koa bowls are their specialty. A glass panel separates the visitors from the artisans who are busy transforming raw koa logs into finished products. Handcrafted items begin under $5. Open weekdays and most Saturdays from 9am to 5pm.

Seconds To Go, on the main street in Honoka Town, is always worth a stop. You never know what antiques, collectibles, or "quality used goods" owner Elaine Carlsmith may have dug up—maybe antique kimonos ($5 to $85) or aloha shirts ($2 to $500), or even hula-girl lamps. We spotted some superb obis that could be given a second life as table runners, from $15 to $400.

WAIPIO VALLEY

Honokaa is best known as the takeoff point to pastoral Waipio Valley. This side trip from your cross-island route takes you 8 miles from Honokaa, branching off to the right on Hi. 240. The best way to explore this spectacular valley (where 7,000 full-blooded Hawaiians lived less than 100 years ago; today there are fewer than 10, plus a few hippie families) is by the **Waipio Valley Shuttle,** a 1½-hour four-wheel-drive-vehicle tour starting and ending at the Waipio Valley Lookout. The tour takes you down into the valley, through taro fields, a $200,000 Ti House, the Lalakea fish pond, and the dramatic Hiilawe Falls (the water drops 1,200 feet here when it's running). Cost of the shuttle trip is $31 for adults, $15.60 for children under 11. Trips leave daily on the hour from 8am to 4pm. Make reservations by calling 775-7121 in Kukuihaele.

It costs more—$35—than the four-wheel-drive trip, but an excursion into Waipio Valley on a mule-driven wagon would surely be memorable. ✪ **Waipio Valley Wagon Tours** runs a 1½-hour tour five times a day (except Sunday) to explore the sights of the valley; mule power gets you across most of Waipio's streams and rivers, but there is one stop midpoint where passengers must walk across a stream to get to the view from the other side (appropriate footwear should be worn—passengers can borrow rubber slippers or use plastic boot covers). Reserve at least 24 hours in advance. Call 889-6850 or fax 889-0650.

Whether or not you go down into Waipio Valley, you should make a stop at **Waipio Valley Lookout** for one of the most spectacular views in the islands. From the steep pali, the waves below look like bits of foamy lace. In winter, you can often see whales frolicking offshore. There are picnic tables and restrooms; it could be an ideal spot to break your trip. And by all means, pay a visit to ✪ **Waipio Valley Artworks,** snuggled in the sleepy town of Kukuihaele, which overlooks the valley (turn at the sign that reads KUKUIHAELE 1 MILE). Waipio Valley Artworks showcases the works of island artists exclusively, with some incredible wood products (they have the largest selection of bowls and other practical wood items on the island), as well as ceramics, basketry, hand-painted silk scarves, and original art and prints. Prices begin at $3.75 and go up, with a large selection of items to choose from under $35. (*Note:* Mail orders are now available; tel. 800/492-4746.)

WAIMEA & PARKER RANCH

On the next leg of your trip you'll begin to see why Hawaii is so often called a continent in miniature. West of Honokaa, winding inland on Hi. 19, the sugar plantations of the tropics give way to mountain forests of cedar and eucalyptus as you climb up the slopes of Mauna Kea toward a vast prairie of rangelands and the plateau of Kamuela (also known as Waimea) and the 225,000-acre **Parker Ranch,** one of the largest cattle ranches in the United States under single ownership.

King Kamehameha started the whole thing, quite inadvertently, when he accepted a few longhorn cattle as a gift from the English explorer Capt. George Vancouver. The cattle multiplied and ran wild until John Parker, a young seaman from Newton, Massachusetts, tamed them and started his ranch. The Parker family still owns it today, and many of the current generation of paniolos are descendants of the original Hawaiian cowboys. The Parker Ranch is the biggest, but certainly not the only one—ranching is a way of life on the Big Island.

The Parker Ranch is headquartered in **Waimea,** a bright little mountain town that is one of the fastest-growing shopping areas on the Big Island, with delightful boutiques, galleries, and upscale restaurants opening all the time.

There are two visitor facilities at Parker Ranch that are well worth your time. The first is the **Parker Ranch Visitor Center,** where you'll see a historical museum and a video presentation of ranch history providing an insight into daily operations on the ranch. It's open daily from 9am to 5pm; admission is $5 for adults, $3.75 for children. The second is the **Historic Parker Ranch Homes** and their beautiful gardens. Mana, the 1847 home of the ranch founder, is built entirely of koa wood and is open for touring. Puuopelu, home of the last ranch owner, the late actor Richard Smart, houses a splendid art collection, with the works of many impressionist masters as well as objets d'art personally collected from around the world by Richard Smart. It's open daily from 10am to 5pm, and admission is $7.50 for adults, $3.75 for children. Better yet, buy a combined admission at $10 adults, $7.50 children, and see both.

Another stop in this area could well be the **Kamuela Museum** (tel. 885-4724), the largest private museum in Hawaii, founded and owned by Albert K. Solomon, Sr., and Harriet M. Solomon, great-great-granddaughter of John Palmer Parker, the founder of Parker Ranch. You'll see ancient and royal Hawaiian artifacts (many of which were formerly in Iolani Palace in Honolulu) alongside European and Asian objets d'art, plus cultural objects brought to the islands by various ethnic groups in the 19th century. The museum, a charmer, is at the junction of Hi. 19 and Hi. 250; open daily, including holidays, from 8am to 5pm; $5 admission for adults, $2 for children under 12.

Waimea is also something of a cultural center for the Big Island and during your visit, you may be lucky enough to catch performances by such groups as the Peking Acrobats, the Honolulu Symphony, or even the World Famous Glenn Miller Orchestra at the 500-seat **Kahilu Theatre,** just across from the Parker Ranch Visitor Center. For ticket information, call 885-6017.

Shopping in Waimea

PARKER SQUARE One of our favorite shopping complexes in town, Parker Square has a group of tasteful boutiques. The most exciting is **Gallery of Great Things,** which shows an extraordinary collection of works by local and Pacific island artists; we coveted the stunning appliquéd quilts from Tahiti and the handcrafted silver jewelry from Bali. Prices can go way up, but many things are surprisingly affordable: We saw koa-wood rice paddles at $7, koa-wood hair sticks at $9, Tutu Nene potholders at $10, and feather necklaces at $55. There are many prints and posters by local artists. The **Waimea General Store** is a tasteful bazaar with a highly sophisticated potpourri of merchandise: distinctive handcrafts, kitchen gadgets, toys and games, handmade baby quilts, men's clothing, pottery. There's an excellent collection of Hawaiian books. **Bentley's** is an exquisite store, like a French country home, with furniture, hand-painted wicker baskets, dried flower wreaths, and much more.

Almost directly across from Parker Square, you'll find **Waimea Coffee and Company,** known for 100% pure Kona coffee grown on family-run, local coffee farms. Coffee-making supplies, espresso machines, and a variety of snacks and light meals are available at this friendly spot. Hawaiian gourmet food items are a specialty. They also have a mail-order operation: toll free 800/854-4472 in Hawaii, or 800/854-5662 from the mainland.

DAN DE LUZ'S WOODS, 64-1013 Hwy. 19.

Look for the tikis out front and you'll find yourself at the shop of Dan De Luz, famed as Hawaii's master bowl-turner (for information on his Hilo factory, see above). While some of the superb bowls here could go up into the thousands, there are plenty of small koa-wood treasures to take home—like $15 bracelets, $10 earrings, or $1.95 bookmarkers.

PARKER RANCH SHOPPING CENTER This mall is given over mostly to local shopping, but there are a few interesting shops for the visitor. At the **Parker Ranch Store,** adjacent to the visitor center, you can buy many Parker Ranch logo items, including sweatshirts and jogging outfits. At **Topstick Fiber Arts Espresso Galleries,** everything—quilts, clothing, pillows—is handmade, usually by an island artisan. They have one of the best selections of pillow quilts on the island. **Reyn's** well-known island shops for men and women has an outpost here too. You'll find casual clothes at **Blue Sky Apparel** and **Malia Kamuela Pueo Bookshop.**

WAIMEA CENTER The newest shopping mall in town seems to be of interest mostly to local folks, but there's one place here not to be missed—**Cook's Discoveries** in the historic Spencer House in the middle of the center. For more than a century, the Spencer family's two-story home, built in 1850 (in what was then the heart of Waimea town), served as a general store. Big Island families came to Spencer House for the necessities of life, and also for the "luxuries"—sweets, hats, fine soaps, clothing, and dozens of other treasures. The Spencer House once again offers a treasury of goods. Owners Patti and Bill Cook have filled the shop with "Made in Hawaii" products that would make superb gifts for the people back home. Choose from toys, books, Nake'u and Sig Zane clothing, koa umbrellas, jewelry, music boxes, pens and bowls, and delicious edibles, even poi (taro) dog biscuits. The price range is enormous, from $6 koa key rings to $17 feather earrings, $24 and up koa bowls and $92 Hawaiian quilted pillows. Note to collectors of Hawaiian quilts: quilts that we've seen in Honolulu go from $6,000 to $8,000; here, they're $4,000. A wonderful place, not to be missed.

Also in Waimea Center, note the excellent **Pueo Bookshop. Princess Kaiulani Fashions** offers great muumuus, as well as long, lacy wedding dresses. Should you need to have packages wrapped and mailed home, a visit to **Postmark** is in order. **The Great Wall Chop Suey** is a family-style place where you can fill up on a "Big Lunch" for $6.95, or have an all-you-can-eat buffet, Monday to Saturday, 11am to 3pm, also for $6.95. Plate lunches run $3.95 to $5.95. The Country's Best Yogurt—for low-cal shakes, parfaits, fruit sundaes, crêpes, and Belgian Waffles.

C & S CYCLE AND SURF. Tel. 885-5005.

This store, madly popular with the local people, has just about everything needed for the active life. It's a full-service bike and surf shop, specializing in mountain bikes, boogie boards, and camping equipment. They also have a large selection of surf clothing and swimwear, sunglasses, T-shirts, sweatshirts, and the like. Look for it at the second stoplight in Waimea.

SIDE TRIP FROM WAIMEA TO HAWI

From the cool green oasis of Waimea you can make another side excursion, 22 miles to the little town of Hawi, on the northernmost tip of the Big Island. The drive is along Hi. 250, winding uphill through the slopes of the Kohala Mountains, and the sights are unforgettable—the Pacific on your left, looking like a blue-velvet lake lost in misty horizons; the shimmering, unearthly peaks of Mauna Kea, Mauna Loa, and Hualalai, their slopes a jumble of wildflowers, twisted fences of tree branches, and giant cactus. Your destination, **Hawi**, is an end-of-the-world spot, recommended for those who like to be far away from the nagging complexities of civilization.

Hawi's riches—and those of its neighboring **Kohala district**—are in its memories. The great Kamehameha was born in this area, and if you travel east a few miles to **Kapaau,** you'll see a statue of the local hero that looks amazingly like the one you saw in Honolulu. Actually, this one is the original; it was made in Florence, lost at sea, and then found after another just like it had been fashioned for the capital. The trip to this North Kohala area is thrilling, but remember that you've got to come down the road again (Hi. 270), which links up to Hi. 19 and the Kona coast, adding a total of 44 miles to your cross-island trip.

READERS RECOMMEND

Pololu Valley Lookout. *"We took a nice side trip to Pololu Valley Lookout on the northern tip in the Kohala district. After viewing the beautiful valley we stopped about 3 miles back down the road from the lookout on Hi. 27 at Keokea Park, which had a lovely view, picnic tables, outdoor showers, and a little sea pool. There is a sign off Hi. 27; you can drive in from the road about 1 mile."*—Mr. and Mrs. Donald Plumlee, Santa Clara, Calif.

WAIMEA TO KONA VIA THE KOHALA COAST

From Waimea, you could zip right along the coastal road, Hi. 19, and be in Kailua-Kona within an hour. However, it's fun to stop off along the way to have a look at some of the fabled Kohala coast resorts that dot these shores, and maybe have a meal or a swim. Anae'hoomalu Bay, a splendid crescent-shaped white sand beach with public facilities and picnic tables, is actually the beach fronting the glorious Royal Waikoloan Hotel. And very close to that is the megaresort that everyone in Hawaii seems to be talking about and wants to see: the **Hilton Waikoloa Village.** You should see it and plan an hour or two to enjoy it: If you can't squeeze the time in on your cross-island trip, then come back once you've settled in Kona. Guests of the fantasy resort pay $250 a day for their accommodations, but you can enjoy many of the resort's facilities as a visitor. For something organized, call the Hilton (tel. 885-1234, ext. 2715) and reserve a space on one of their guided tours: an art tour, a garden and wildlife tour, a petroglyph tour, a facilities tour, and a back-of-the-house tour. What we like to do is simply hop one of the canal boats or tubular trams that continually circle the property, and stop where fancy leads us. There are lush tropical gardens and a wildlife collection; a multimillion-dollar, mile-long museum walkway filled with superb examples of Pacific and Asian art; a shopping arcade with upscale boutiques; enormous swimming pools with slides, waterfalls, grottoes (one even has a "riverpool," and its currents float guests from level to level); and a million-gallon saltwater lagoon, teeming with tropical fish, which is the home of six trained dolphins. Definitely get off the boat here, for here's your chance to experience or watch a dolphin encounter. (Call the hotel for details.) And it's fun to have a drink or a bite at **Hang Ten,** the snack bar overlooking Dolphin Pond. You're also welcome to watch the daily training sessions at 12:30pm. Kids will adore this one.

Feeling hungry? Nothing could be better than lunch (11am to 5pm) at the out-door-indoor **Orchid Café,** near the main swimming pool, which features cuisine naturelle. Lunch need not cost you more than $12 to $16, and the food is remark-able—among the best of its kind we've had anywhere. When you're feeling flush, come back and have a fabulous dinner at **Donatoni's,** a formal dining room deco-rated with masterpiece paintings, which serves perhaps the best northern Italian cui-sine on the Big Island. A number of other restaurants, lounges, and entertainments are available here, including a traditional luau called **Legends of Polynesia;** you can see the show and have a cocktail for $29 (dinner show is $55).

If you can tear yourself away from the Hilton, and you still feel like seeing more playgrounds of the rich and famous, look for the entrance to the ✪ **Mauna Lani Bay Hotel,** 5 miles north on Hi. 19; to our way of thinking, it's one of the most purely beautiful resorts anywhere, especially in its landscaping and gardens and the massive indoor waterfall in the Grand Atrium. Golfers rave about the Francis Ii Brown golf course here, a 36-hole championship course carved out of barren lava. The hotel has won numerous awards for excellence, including the coveted Five-Dia-mond Award from AAA. If time permits (or if not, come back later once you're snugly ensconced in Kona), have a splurge meal at one of the most enchanting of its seven restaurants, the **Canoe House,** which features Pacific Rim cuisine by a master chef in an al fresco oceanfront setting—incomparable! (Call 885-6622 for reserva-tions.)

In the same Mauna Lani Resort which houses the Mauna Lani Bay Hotel is the newer **Ritz-Carlton Mauna Lani,** another exquisite gem nestled between the ocean and the lava desert. You're welcome to take a look around and admire the glamor-ous setting and the lovely beach.

You can then continue along the coastal road, Queen Kaahumanu Highway (Hi. 19), until you reach Kailua-Kona.

ALTERNATE ROUTE TO KONA

Alternatively, you can leave Waimea on Hi. 19 and drive about 12 miles to the deep-water port of **Kawaihae,** where you descend through prairie land, grazing cows, and ocean vistas all about you, until you're suddenly in sultry tropics.

On the road above the harbor is **Puukohola Heiau National Historic Site,** a well-preserved heiau and historical park that figures prominently in the history of the islands. Here Kaahumanu, the sweetheart-queen of the great Kamehameha, began af-ter his death the breakdown of the dread kapu (taboo) system by the startling act of eating in public with men (previously, such an act would have been punished by death). But the place is better remembered for a bloody deed. Remember Keoua, Kamehameha's biggest rival, the one who lost an army at K'au? Kamehameha had to decide to dedicate this heiau to the war god Kukailimoku, and invited Keoua to a peace parley in the new temple. Instead of offering peace, however, he had Keoua speared as he approached the land and sacrificed him to the god. Then Kamehameha was free to unify Hawaii and the other islands.

After digesting this gory bit of history, you deserve a change of pace. Return to Hi. 19 and turn right (south) for a mile to the turnoff for **Samuel Spencer Park.** This scenic ocean beach park has recently undergone renovations to the picnic and camping area. About three miles farther south is the more spacious **Hapuna Beach** (watch for signs warning about dangerous tides and rip currents). Continue on Hi. 19 through the lava desert, which on clear days will afford glorious views of all the volcanoes of Hawaii and perhaps of Haleakala on Maui, too. Lava flows from Mauna Loa and Hualalai mark the eerie landscape, punctuating the miles until you emerge at last into the verdant world of the Kona coast.

(*Note:* We're sorry to have to issue this caveat, but we've been told that rowdies sometimes hide in the bushes near these beaches, wait for tourists to dutifully put their valuables in the trunks of their cars, and then proceed to pick the locks while the tourists are out on the beach. If you're going to put anything in your trunk, do so a few miles before you reach your destination.)

SOUTHERN ROUTE FROM KONA TO HILO

If you've arrived at Kona first, you could drive across the island to Hilo on Hi. 11, through the K'au Desert and miles and miles of lava flows, desolate enough to be reminiscent of Doré's engravings. But before the landscape turns bleak, there's plenty of magnificent scenery. If you make the trip in November or December, you'll see unbelievably beautiful poinsettias.

For a swim, try **Hookena Beach Park,** 22 miles from Kailua. It's a long drive down the road to an almost-deserted, lovely sandy beach. **Manuka State Park,** farther on, with its arboretum of extraordinary plants and trees, is a good spot to stretch your legs and perhaps have a picnic lunch. The approach to the little village of **Waiohinu** is marvelously scenic, and the village itself, once a small farming center, is one of the quaintest on the Big Island. Have a look at the monkeypod tree planted by Mark Twain, and a few miles farther on you can make a side trip (about 1½ miles off the highway) to the black sand beach at **Punaluu.**

Another favorite jaunt is the 12-mile drive off the highway outside Naalehu down to **Ka Lae** (South Point). Local people fish there on this wild shore of cliffs and surf, the southernmost point in the United States.

Now you approach the desolate K'au region where Pele obligingly destroyed an army of Keoua, Kamehameha's archenemy, in 1790; the footprints of the victims can be seen under glass. The landscape is moonlike, and not only metaphorically; space scientists are studying the lava fields of the Big Island because they believe it's similar to conditions on the moon. The lava flows lead you to Kilauea, Hawaii Volcanoes National Park, and on to Hilo.

READERS RECOMMEND

Scenic Drives. *"It is interesting to drive up the 13-mile road on the slope of Mauna Loa for the view. From there the trail leads to the summit. On this ride in the morning at 7am, I saw plenty of wild pigs and wild goats. Before Waiohini, it is worthwhile to drive 9 miles down to the left to the South Point (Ka Lae), the southernmost point of the U.S. There is a lighthouse and steep cliffs. The fishermen have to tow the fish over the cliffs from their boats."*—Prof. Dr. W. K. Brauers, Berchem-Antwerp, Belgium.

---

6. THE KONA COAST

A man we know in Kona, a refugee from the Bronx, swears he will never go back home: "I've found my bit of paradise right here, and I'm staying!" A lot of other people have waxed ecstatic about Kona, the vacation resort of Hawaiian royalty ever since the word got out that the sun shines here about 344 days a year. (Kona winds, that nasty stuff they get in Honolulu, should properly be called southerly winds, say the Konaites.) It's such a deliciously lazy spot that you may be very content to do nothing at all. Of course, looking at the surf as it smashes along the black-lava coast, noting the brilliant varieties of bougainvillea, the plumeria, and the jasmine tumbling about everywhere, and lazing on the beach can keep you pretty busy. But we suggest that you take a day off from these labors and have a look at the sights. Kona is an important historic center; within the space of a few miles, Captain Cook met his end, the New England missionaries got their start, and Kamehameha enjoyed his golden age.

KAILUA-KONA This tiny village is the resort center, modern enough to be comfortable, but still unspoiled. The people at the Hawaii Visitors Bureau office, in the Kona Plaza Shopping Arcade, can help you with all sorts of practical information.

DRIVING TOUR — KAILUA-KONA TO PU'UHONUA O HONAUNAU NATIONAL HISTORICAL PARK

Start: King Kamehameha's Kona Beach Resort.
Finish: Kahaluu Beach Park.
Time: 2 to 4 hours.
Best Time: Begin early, so you can spend as long as you like.
Worst Time: Late in the day.

Your sightseeing tour begins with a stop at:

1. **King Kamehameha's Kona Beach Resort.** There's only one street, Alii Drive, running down the length of Kailua town, so you won't get lost. The hotel is in the northern end of town, at the site of the monarch's heiau, which has been restored. There are tasteful museum-caliber displays throughout the lobby highlighting Hawaiian history and various free activities: Ethnobotanical, historical, and "hula experience" tours are held several times a week (inquire at the hotel for a schedule). Just about 150 years ago, Kamehameha ruled the Hawaiian Islands from a grass-roofed palace on this very site. (Lahaina became the next capital; Honolulu did not become the capital until 1820.) The old king died here in 1819, only a year before the first missionaries arrived from Boston, bringing with them the purposeful Protestant ethic that would effectively end the Polynesian era in Hawaii. The missionaries were responsible for the:

2. **Mokuaikaua Church,** standing on the mauka (mountain) side of Alii Drive, a handsome coral-and-stone structure that's the oldest Christian church in Hawaii, built in 1838. Note the sanctuary inside; its architecture is New England, but it's made of two Hawaiian woods, koa and ohia. Across from it, on the ocean side of the street is:

3. **Hulihee Palace.** Until 1916 this was a vacation home for Hawaiian royalty. Now it's a museum, full of Hawaiian furniture and effects, as well as more primitive curiosities like Kamehameha's exercise stone (it weighs about 180 pounds, so maybe that story about the Naha Stone isn't so crazy after all). Check out the charming little gift shop; it has an especially nice selection of native wood plus books and jewelry. Profits go to the Daughters of Hawaii. The museum is open daily from 9am to 4pm; closed federal holidays. Admission is $4 for adults, $1 for students 12 to 18, 50¢ for children under 12.

 The shore road extends for about 6 more miles, but we're going to leave it temporarily, taking a left at Hualalai Street and heading out of town on Hi. 11 (the mauka road) to explore:

4. **Kona "Up Mauka."** Upcountry Kona is far removed from the tourist scene at Kailua-Kona. It is, for one thing, the place where Kona coffee, that dark, rich brew you've seen all over the islands, is grown. Hawaii is the only state in the union that has a commercial coffee crop. There are no big plantations, only small farms where everybody in the family pitches in to bring in the crop. Watch the road for the shiny green leaves of the coffee bushes with the little clusters of red betties at harvest time. There are small cattle ranches here too, although they're not visible from the road.

 The drive is a beautiful one, winding through the cool mountain slopes, with fruit trees and showers of blossoms all around. A possible stop for garden lovers is an unusual new bonsai center, located about 6 miles south of Kailua town. Between the 115- and 116-mile markers of Hi. 11, turn up at the junction of Hi. 180 (Mamaloa Highway) and follow the three Hawaii Visitors Bureau markers to the:

5. Fuku-Bonsai Center. Nine themed gardens and an indoor educational center explore the worlds of Japanese bonsai, Chinese penjing, and Hawaiian and indoor bonsais. The gardens, beautiful as they are, are still in their early stages and will not be completed for many years. While you're waiting, you may want to pick up some bonsais to send back home: A certified nursery is on the grounds. Open daily 8am to 5pm.

Now, for those in the mood for a little offbeat shopping, continue along the road until you come to:

6. Kainaliu Village and Kealakekua. In Kainaliu, **Kimura's** is a favorite old-timer. Some say Mrs. Kimura has the best collection of fabrics in the islands. Hawaiian and Japanese prints are specialties, and prices are reasonable. Look for the **Aloha Café** in Kainaliu now, and perhaps stop in for a tempting pastry or snack (see "Where to Eat," in Chapter 12). Next door is the **Aloha Village Store,** with cards, baskets, toys, and gourmet items, plus healthy snacks and vitamins. Across from it is **Blue Ginger Gallery,** a showcase for about 50 local artists. You'll find an enticing collection of stained glass, ceramics, jewelry, hand-painted silks, and more, plus many crafts from Bali. Close to that, **The BadAss Coffee Company,** named for the hardworking donkeys that used to haul heavy loads of coffee up and down the mountains, sells fragrant, locally grown coffee. Out in back is the semi-open **Coffee Pub,** with tables, a chessboard, cards for sale—a pleasant stop. **Paradise Found Boutique** is the place for unique clothing, like raw silk outfits designed here and made in China, a line of batik designer clothes, beautifully cut lacework garments from Indonesia, and men's silky aloha shirts. There are gift items by local artisans as well as Asian imports, too. They have another shop down in Kailua town and one at Lanihau Center.

A popular shop in Kealakekua is the **Grass Shack,** a real grass shack that has been here almost forever. The inside is laden with tasteful and authentic Hawaiian and South Pacific handcrafts. The nice people here will give you a native flower and some coffee beans for planting as you leave; within 3 to 4 weeks (the time it takes for the seed to germinate) you'll be on your way to having your own potted coffee plant.

After about 12 miles from the beginning, the road winds gently down the slopes of the mountain (watch for the HVB marker), past Royal Kona Coffee Mill and Museum, through the lush tropical village of Napoopoo on to Kealake-kua Bay. Visitors are welcome at the mill. Now, pause for a bit of history and a look at the:

7. Captain Cook Monument, visible across the bay, erected at a spot near where he was killed in 1779. It was here that Cook and his men pulled into the Kona coast a year after their first landing on Kauai, were again treated as gods, and then wore out their welcome. When their ship was damaged in a storm and they returned to Kealakekua a second time, the men got into a fight with the natives, and Cook was killed trying to break it up. You can't see the monument up close unless you approach it from the water or hike down a dirt trail (for hiking directions, see the reader's recommendation, below). There's a "Captain Cook Cruise" that leaves Kailua wharf daily (tel. 329-6411); it gives you a good look at the monument and lets you swim and snorkel in the bay. It's a good way to combine a suntan and a history lesson for $54 for adults, $27 for children 5 to 12. The cost includes a continental breakfast and a barbecue lunch.

There are two plaques you can see on the Napoopoo shore: One commemorates the first Christian funeral in the islands; the other is in honor of the remarkable young Hawaiian boy, Opukahaia, who swam out to a ship in 1808, got a job as a cabin boy, converted to Christianity, and convinced the missionaries that they were needed here in the pagan, ignorant Sandwich Islands. Right near the shrines are a few jewelry stands that offer good buys in clothing and necklaces of local seed and kukui-nut leis.

Continuing along the shore road now to Honaunau, you'll pass Keei Battlefield, a lava-scarred stretch where Kamehameha started winning wars. In the tiny fishing village of Keei, there's a beach with good swimming. But the best is yet to come: The high point of this little excursion is a visit to:

8. **Pu'uhonua o Honaunau National Historical Park.** This ancient, partially restored Pu'uhonua still has about it the air of sanctuary for which it was built over 400 years ago. In the days when many chieftains ruled in the islands, each district had a spot designated as a place of refuge to which kapu breakers, war refugees, and defeated warriors could escape; here they could be cleansed of their offenses and return, purified, to their villages. (There is another such place on the island of Kauai, near Lydgate Park, but this one is far better preserved.) The heiau, Hale-o-Keawe, the temple of the purifying priests, has been reconstructed (it was in such temples that the bones of the high chiefs of Kona— which had mana, or spiritual power—were kept), and so have the tall ki'i carved for the god Lono. After you've driven into the park and left your car in the parking lot (an improvement over the old days when the only way to get here was to run, or, if one came from the north, to swim, since the feet of commoners were not fit to tread on the Royal Grounds) on the north side of the place of refuge, we suggest you take in one of the orientation talks given daily at 10, 10:30, and 11am, and at 2:30, 3, and 3:30pm, in the spacious amphitheater staffed by the National Park Service, which administers this facility. Besides explaining the concept of refuge, the park ranger also talks about the plants and trees of the area. Then you're free to have a swim (but sunbathing is not allowed), a picnic, go snorkeling or fishing—or just absorb the peace on your own. Or you can tour the area by yourself with a self-guiding leaflet. "Cultural demonstrators" are usually on hand, carving woods, weaving, and performing other ancient Hawaiian tasks. Canoes, fishnets, and traps are on display, and are sometimes used outside the work sheds. Entrance fee is $2 per person, to a maximum of $4 per vehicle (children under 17 and seniors over 61 enter free).

There's one more curious sight in Honaunau, which you reach by turning north on a side road as you go back up the highway. This is:

9. **The Painted Church,** the name that everyone gives to St. Benedict's Church. The Catholic missionaries created biblical murals that gave a feeling of spaciousness to the tiny church, presumably so that the congregation would have more of a feeling of the outdoors—to which pagan nature worship had accustomed them. Between Pu'uhonua o Honaunau and the Painted Church, you might want to make a stop at:

10. **Wakefield Gardens and Restaurant** (tel. 328-9930). You can take a free, self-guided tour through this 5-acre botanical garden and macadamia-nut orchard, with some 1,000 varieties of plants and flowers. The gift shop sells those little macs very reasonably ($5 buys 2½ pounds in the shell), and also features small wood items made by local artisans. They also have a very pleasant restaurant that features real roasted turkey sandwiches, papaya boats, and vegetarian fare, with daily specials at $5.95. Homemade desserts—on the order of Mystery Macadamia Nut Pie, Hawaiian Spice Delight, and Lime Cream Pie—are a prizewinning specialty. And they have the best macadamia-nut brittle anywhere! They're on Hi. 160, open daily from 11am to 3pm.

Now go up Hi. 160 to Hi. 11 and make a left turn north toward Kailua. Just before Middle Keei Road, on the ocean side, look for a sign that reads "Healthy Food to Go" and you're at:

11. **Bong Brothers Coffee.** This is an authentic coffee mill and store dating back to the 1920s; a roaster in back turns out a complete line of Kona coffee in me-

dium, Vienna, and French roasts. Their country store features an espresso bar and snack bar, local fruits and vegetables, and a line of natural foods and Hawaiian food products. If you haven't eaten yet, pick up some of their delicious organic vegetarian food to go; tofu curry dips, pesto with macadamia nuts, fresh salads, and dishes like zucchini tofu lasagne make a complete meal for just a little. The gift shop sells their yummy chocolate-covered coffee beans.

Continue north on Hi. 11 headed toward Kailua. Another possible stop is 3 miles south of Captain Cook at the:

12. **Kona Coffee Emporium.** The meadow below is a good place to let kids run loose. Attractions include a 5,000-year-old lava tube to walk through and ornamental pheasants strolling the grounds. Upstairs, you can watch coffee being roasted. The company has the largest selection of Kona coffees in the area, and they sell and ship them at very good prices: Eight ounces of Pure Kona Chocolate Macadamia Nut Coffee sells for about $8. There's also a self-serve deli for light foods and picnic lunches, and **Summer Breeze,** which sells aloha attire and gifts and rents snorkeling equipment.

Now continue for about 11 miles until you come to a turnoff to the left that brings you back to the shore at Keauhou Bay. Before you descend, though, you might want to stop off to have a look at the handsome:

13. **Keauhou Shopping Village.** Here you could have a drink or a meal with the local sports fans gathered around the large-screen TVs at **Drysdale's Two** (see "Where to Eat," in Chapter 12), or an espresso or cappuccino at **Kona Kai Coffee Café.** Just about our favorite made-in-Hawaii arts shop here is **Alapaki,** a stunning showcase of arts and crafts. You enter through a lava arch flanked by 10-foot-tall royal kahilis on either side, containing 6,000 feathers and 500 feather flowers. Inside you'll find imposing sculptures by artists like Herb Kane, paintings and posters, handcrafted native wood carvings and bowls, feather leis, baskets, and much more. **Designer's Loft** shows some handsome interiors. The **Keahou Village Book Shop** has a vast array of books, including a strong collection of Hawaiiana, as well as some vintage postcards like the ones reading ALOHA FROM WAIKIKI, 1935. If your feet are getting tired, pop into **Accent on Bed and Bath** to get "Sole Salvation," a luxury foot-massage pillow. Check out **Wild Mango Fashions** for casual clothing, **Hot Pacific Casuals** for resort wear, and **Hawaii Floral** for fresh flowers. At the **Showcase Gallery,** you can find works by leading island painters and craftspeople, perhaps originals by Phan Barker and Leah Neimoth, posters by Robert Lyn Nelson. A collection of beautiful jewelry ranges from about $20 to $400.

Have a look at the **Liberty House Penthouse** here. No telling what you'll find at a place like this on any particular day, but we've seen $40 jeans for $10, $50 bathing suits for as low as $7, $50 leather bags for $25. Items are from various Liberty House shops on the islands; it's worth a look.

Note that there's a new U.S. Post Office substation at Keauhou Shopping Village.

Drive down the shore now to visit our next destination, the grounds and public areas of the fabulous:

14. **Kona Surf Resort.** The Asian and Polynesian art objects scattered about, the glorious use of natural materials, the 14½ acres and 30,000 plants on the property make it a sightseeing stop in its own right. Complimentary garden tours are given on Sunday, Tuesday, and Thursday at 2:30pm, but you're welcome to come on your own and have a look.

Continuing back to Kailua now, the old vies with the new for attention everywhere. To your left is Keauhou Bay, a naturally occurring small boat harbor, home to a small number of charter fishing, dive, and excursion boats; to your right, faintly visible on the mountain slopes, are the remains of a rocky royal slide, down which the alii of Hawaii once scooted into the water. Coming into sight soon is:

15. Kahaluu Beach Park, and your sightseeing labors are over. Now you can concentrate on the important business of Kona, sunworshiping. Kahaluu Beach Park is a fine place for swimming, snorkeling, and picnicking. Snorkelers claim it's the best place on the Big Island. There's a pretty lagoon, the swimming is safe, and the sand, once a fine white, is now salt-and-pepper, thanks to an ancient lava flow that came pounding across it. Even prettier is White Sands Beach (sometimes called Magic Sands or Disappearing Beach, since the high surf occasionally removes and then returns the sand), a gorgeous, if tiny, spot. Palm trees arch across the sand, the surf is a Mediterranean blue, and the brilliant reds, yellows, and purples of tropical blossoms are everywhere. It can be dangerous, though, when the surf is rough, especially if the sand is gone.

Back in Kailua, you can swim in front of the luxurious King Kamehameha's Kona Beach Resort; the beach here is a public one, something that old King Kam would probably have approved of. The water is very gentle, safe for kids.

READERS RECOMMEND

Hiking and Snorkeling at Kealakekua Bay. "*The Captain Cook Monument at Kealakekua Bay is a fabulous snorkeling spot. Seeing dolphins and whales is not uncommon. The bay is an undersea marine reserve, and the fish are very tame. Here are the directions for hiking to the monument. Turn off Hi. 11 onto Napoopoo Road and go down about 200 yards to the dirt road on the right. Park your car there, being careful not to block the gate. Walk down the road, staying toward the left. As the coast becomes visible, the trail veers to the left. Eventually you'll come to the water and the monument. The hike down takes 30 to 45 minutes. On the return, it's all uphill and mostly unshaded. Wear walking shoes (not sandals) and take water and food. Picnic lunches are available at the Galley Restaurant. Horseback rides and picnics are available to the monument with King's Trail Rides (tel. 323-2388) for a cost of $95.*"—Barbara Moore-Link, Honaunau, Hawaii.

Whale Watching. "*If you want to go whale watching on a small boat, with somebody who really knows about humpback whales, then you should sail with Capt. Dan McSweeney in Kona (tel. 322-0028). The boat only holds 32 passengers, so you don't have a problem walking around the boat taking pictures. What makes it so much fun is listening to Dan McSweeney talk about his stories researching the humpbacks, and hearing about the lives of humpbacks. It was like being on a Jacques Cousteau expedition. McSweeney even had hydrophones so we could hear the whales singing. We were fortunate to see breaching whales. The cost was $39.50 per person for 3 hours, including snacks and drinks. It was great.*"—Catherine and Mike Praisewaer, Albuquerque, N.M.

MORE ATTRACTIONS

Before you leave the Kailua-Kona area, drive out to Keahole Airport, especially if you have children with you, to visit the **Astronaut Ellison S. Onizuka Space Center** (tel. 329-3441), a living memorial to Hawaii's first astronaut. Interactive and audiovisual exhibits provide a lively educational experience of America's manned space program: Especially exciting for kids is the "Manned Maneuvering Unit" in which the visitor sits in an MMU and manipulates the hand controls to rendezvous with an object in space. Another unique and popular exhibit allows the visitor to launch a miniature space shuttle 20 feet into the air. Open daily from 8:30am to 4:30pm; admission is $2 for adults, 50¢ for children.

UNDERWATER ADVENTURES

A definitely "thrill-of-a-lifetime" experience is a dive aboard the submarine *Atlantis,* which takes passengers 80 to 100 feet down into the clear waters of Kona Bay to explore an exotic world usually seen only by scuba divers or research scientists. You'll feel as if you're in a Jacques Cousteau documentary, gazing out of the portholes as schools of brightly colored tropical fish—butterfly fish and saddle wrasses, moray eels and often a barracuda or two, all denizens of the coral reefs—surround the sub: It's something like an aquarium in reverse, with you inside the glass. Divers are sent down to feed the fish, so there's always something to see. (Bring cameras with high-speed film, 400 ASA, as flashbulbs will not work through the portholes.)

The 65-foot submarine, one of a growing fleet of such high-tech recreational subs (they also operate in Waikiki, from the Hilton Hawaiian Village; and in Maui, from the Pioneer Inn in Lahaina), is superbly equipped for safety and comfort; it is air-conditioned and maintains normal atmospheric pressure. Everyone from youngsters (over 4) to septuagenarians enjoy it. Although the cost of the "Odyssey" dive—$69 for adults, $29 for children—is high, this is a unique adventure, well worth a splurge. There are six dives daily, departing from the office of Atlantis Submarines in King Kamehameha's Kona Beach Resort; a launch takes you out to the boarding site in the bay. For reservations, phone 329-6626 in Kona, or toll free 800/548-6262 from the mainland.

To see the wonders of the coral reefs *without* diving, there's a new operation available in Kona: a cruise aboard the 32-passenger **Nautilus II,** a semi-submersible craft whose viewing area sits 5½ feet below the surface of the water. Thus you can enjoy shallow-water viewing (5 to 30 feet down) of turtles, dolphines, eagle rays, octopuses, and the like, while sitting in the hull. And since part of the boat is always above the surface of the water, you can go topside at any time out into the open air. The boat is air-conditioned, and accessible to people of any age. One-hour trips depart daily between 9:30am and 1:30pm from the Kailua Pier (the office is underneath the Kona Galley, just across from the pier). The cost is $34.95 for adults, $19.95 for those under 12. For reservations, phone 326-2003.

READERS RECOMMEND

Glass-Bottom Boat Tour. *"We found a great boat tour at the Kailua pier in Kona: Glass Bottom Boat Tours (tel. 987-8588), charging $14.95 for adults and $7.50 for children. It was very informative and interesting, and didn't have any distractions, such as hula lessons or a refreshment stand—big pluses, as far as we're concerned!"*—Jan Bell, St. Charles, Mo.

OTHER ADVENTURES & SPORTS

If you can afford a fee of about $105 to $110 for a roughly 7-hour trip, you can have a great adventure with **Paradise Safaris,** P. O. Box A-D, Kailua-Kona, HI 96745 (tel. 322-2366), an outfit that takes small groups in four-wheel-drive vans almost 14,000 feet up to the top of Mauna Kea to experience extraordinary sunsets (visibility is 100 miles) and have a look at the night sky through their large portable telescope. They pick up at West Hawaii hotels and, thankfully, even provide warm parkas and hot drinks against the chilly mountain air. Be sure you're in good physical condition and can handle high altitudes for this one (not recommended for scuba divers). Call 322-2366, or write in advance to Paradise Safaris.

DEEP-SEA FISHING Deep-sea fishers consider Kona their favorite place in the world. And it's also one of the least expensive "world class" fishing spots anywhere. "Share" charters are available at very reasonable prices (under $50), and many local fishing businesses will book one to six individuals on a share basis—sharing the otherwise high cost ($300 to $600 a day). Whether you go out fishing or not, you can view the catch of Kona's fisher folk. The morning weigh-in of the giants is from noon to 1pm, the afternoon one from 4 to 5pm, at the pier in front of King Kamehameha's Kona Beach Resort and at The Fuel Dock, in Honokohau Harbor. Either place is good for information about fishing charters.

GOLF   Golf? That's easy too. The place to play is at the beautiful **Keauhou Kona Course,** 6 miles south of Kona; make arrangements at your hotel.

HIKING   Those who would like to hike through the Big Island's beautiful trails are encouraged to visit the national and state parks, which maintain a number of scenic hiking trails. The state's **Na Ala Hele Trail and Access System** can provide information and maps on island trails, along with local hiking club contacts. (Division of Forestry & Wildlife, P.O. Box 4849, Hilo, HI 96720-0849. Hawaii Volcanoes National Park can be addressed at HVNP, Volcano, HI 96718.)

Another good possibility is to join one of the day-long or half-day hikes led by psychologist and longtime Hawaii resident Dr. Hugh Montgomery, of **Hawaiian Walkways,** P.O. Box 2193, Kamuela, HI 96743 (tel. 808/885-7759, or toll free 800/457-7759 in the mainland U.S. and Canada). One walk is along a traditional Hawaiian shoreline trail seeking ancient petroglyphs; another is a walk in the Kohala Mountains, following the jungle stream of the rain forest; and a third is a hike down Mauna Kea, beginning at 13,000 feet, near Lake Waiau, one of the highest lakes in the world. All-day hikes, which include lunch, cost $100; half-day hikes are $60.

RAFTING EXPEDITIONS   Here's a chance for an extraordinary adventure—a 4-hour raft excursion to remote sea grottoes, caves, and ancient ruins on a shallow-draft 23-foot Captain Zodiac inflatable craft. Well known for its expeditions along the Na Pali coast on Kauai, Captain Zodiac is now in Kona. Two tours a day sail out of Honokohau Harbor, with pickups at Kailua Pier and Keauhou Bay, sailing the Kona coast and stopping for spectacular snorkeling (instruction provided for first-timers) in the crystalline waters of Kealakekua Bay. Groups are small, the crew members are all knowledgeable naturalists, and a good time is had by all. Dolphins often accompany the rafts, and whales are usually visible in the winter months. Cost of the trip, including a light tropical lunch, is $60 for adults, $50 for children 2 to 12. Because the trip can get a mite bumpy, pregnant women or people with back problems are not accepted as passengers. For information and reservations, contact Captain Zodiac, P.O. Box 5612, Kailua-Kona, HI 96745 (tel. 808/329-3199).

SNORKELING   A number of our readers have written over the years to recommend an idyllic snorkeling adventure aboard the *Kamanu,* a 36-foot catamaran run by **Kamanu Charters** (tel. 329-2021, or toll free 800/348-3091 for reservations). The great thing about this trip is that it's just as simple for nonswimmers as it is for Red Cross lifeguards, since those who wish to may enter the water in an inner tube. Capt. Jay Lambert, the owner/operator of the tours, claims that snorkeling is even easier than swimming, requiring little exertion or water knowledge. Those who only want to sail without getting wet are welcome, too. And the *Kamanu* really sails (the only boat in Kona that does) to Pawai Bay, a protected **State Fisheries Management Area,** for a 3¼-hour adventure. Equipment, professional instruction, and even a complimentary tropical lunch, along with beer, wine, or juice, are provided, all at $39 for adults, $21 for children 12 and under (free for toddlers under 2). Prescription masks, to improve vision, are free; and underwater cameras are available.

READERS RECOMMEND

A Snorkeling Cruise. "*Allow yourself enough time when planning your vacation to be able to see and do everything you want, and some extra time for just relaxing and enjoying the Hawaiian way of life. We did the Big Island in 5 days and moved on to Kauai for 4 more days. It just wasn't enough time! We managed to see everything, but didn't have the time to stop and really enjoy the beauty of the areas . . . . The highlight of our trip was the snorkeling cruise on the* Fairwinds *(tel. 322-2788) in Kona. The crew was great and took us to Kealakekua Bay. I'm ready to go back just to snorkel and relax on the beaches, which I got to do only once!*"—Sandy and Dave Heinrich, Forks,

Wash. [*Authors' Note:* The cost of the 4½-hour *Fairwinds* trip is $56 adults, $31 children, which includes continental breakfast and a full barbecue lunch. Cheaper trips are available on Monday, Wednesday, Friday, and Sunday, from 1:45 to 4:45pm, because less time is spent on the ocean: costs are $37.33 adults, $23.47 children 5 to 12, children 4 and under free. The crew takes great pains with beginners, providing inner tubes for nonswimmers and view boxes for those who dislike masks. Kealakekua Bay is an outstanding place to snorkel: The water is always crystal clear, as many freshwater streams converge here.]

TENNIS If it's tennis you're after, try the free public court at the Kailua Playground near the Kona Sunset Hotel, or the four courts at the Old Airport Tennis Court. Courts are also available at nominal cost at King Kamehameha's Kona Beach Resort, the Keauhou Beach Hotel, the Royal Kona Resort, and the Kona Surf Hotel.

SHOPPING IN KAILUA-KONA

The shopping scene has blossomed like everything else in this bubbling resort town. At last count, there were something like 100 stores and shops, some in quaint arcades, some in small centers and hotels, others just there, all on or just off Alii Drive.

KONA SQUARE A good place to begin might be the Kona Square Mall, across from King Kamehameha's Kona Beach Resort. ✪ **Island Silversmiths,** a longtime favorite, has a sign on the door that reads WE ONLY LOOK EXPENSIVE, and they're right. We saw coral rings here for $6 that were $15 in hotel gift shops nearby. They're known for their sterling-silver charms: The most popular is the Humuhumunukunukuapua's (oh well, just ask for Hawaii's state fish), $34. Also nice is their Cleopatra silver perfume ring at $25.

ALONG ALII DRIVE Right across the road is another neat jewelry store called **Goldfish Jewelry and Gifts.** WE CATCH YOUR EYE is their motto. Their specialty is 14-karat-gold charms—pineapple, marlin, reef fish, whale's tails, and the like. Prices start at $10, average $40 to $50.

Whatever else you do, don't miss the ✪ **Kona Arts & Crafts Gallery,** across from the sea wall at 75-5699-0 Alii Dr. It's one of the few places that deals solely in genuine Hawaiian crafts: Their wood carvings, for example, are made only of native woods such as milo, ohia, and koa. Prices vary for the works of fine art here, but there are many small treasures: Hawaiian sand-art petroglyphs from $9.95, banana-bark art, notecards by local artists, bookmarks made from the flowers of Hawaii, opihi and sea urchin jewelry, limu art (limu is an edible seaweed). Note their chime collection: They bear the imprints of native ferns grown on volcanic soil, pressed and fired at the temperature of red-hot lava, and they have a worldwide reputation; they're priced from $16.95. The shop also carries genuine hula instruments (made of gourds with seeds), and much more. Owners Fred and Sally Nannestad are knowledgeable about their collection and take time to explain the intricacies of these native arts. It's a very worthwhile stop.

If you haven't brought the right walking shoes with you (doesn't it always happen), pay a visit to **Sandal Stop** in Seaside Mall, across from King Kamehameha's Kona Beach Resort. Their motto is BEST SELECTION/BEST PRICE—and they sincerely try to live up to it. Sandals by Birkenstock, S.A.S., Timberland, Clarks of England, Island Slipper, and much more.

KONA INN SHOPPING VILLAGE Cross the street now to the ocean side where you'll find the biggest cluster of shops in town at the rambling Kona Inn Shopping Village. With more than 40 shops and restaurants and a waterfront location, it's always pleasant for browsing about. Shops come and go, but you'll certainly find much to attract you. Women will come away with a different look from **Noa Noa.** Joan Simon's wild tropical designs on natural fabrics are stunning, and prices are not unreasonable. They also carry a selection of Indonesian artifacts which range from baskets at $39, on up to collectors' items such as masks at $100 to $350, as well as Ikat textiles, which make splendid wall hangings, starting around $175. Imagination runs wild at **Alleygecko's,** which boasts colorful gifts from all over the world. Balinese wooden "guardian" figures hang from the ceiling; there is all manner of stuffed geckos, an enormous collection of brightly colored magnets, Japanese prints, Indonesian shirts, and lots more. Don't miss. Hawaiian clothing for kids is well priced at **Kona Inn Children's Wear,** whose selections go from infants through young teens. Light cottons for women, and darling dresses for little girls, too, are featured at **Dragonfly Hawaii.** Like to sew? Check out **Fare Tahiti,** a fabric shop with Hawaiian and Tahitian prints, mostly cottons, from $8.50 per yard. Note, too, their hand-decorated pareaus, made on Maui, air-brushed in rainbow colors, at $21.50. They also sell men's tapa shirts, women's short and long dresses, and needlepoint and cross-stitch charts and kits.

    Tropical Touch is a delight, crammed full of colorful merchandise, most of it from Bali. There are wonderful tropical soft sculptures, bags, pillows, carvings, and more. **Crystal Visions of Hawaii** is charming, with crystals, jewelry, mystical gifts and cards, and even a "Visionary Art Gallery." We found stylish modern and vintage fashions and jewelry for women at **Flamingo's.** Need a hat to keep the sun off your head? **Big Island Hat Company** has plenty to choose from, including custom-blocked Panamas. They also have handcrafted Hawaiian feather-lei hatbands, and a good selection of men's and women's sandals. **Island Life Tee Shirts** sports some exclusive Kona designs on their Ts and sweats, plus some colorful gift items collected by owner Roberta Fair. (Fair's second shop, Island Salsa, is located in the Kona Marketplace, across the street.)

    Hula Heaven is one of those places collectors of vintage aloha shirts seek out, and it's one of the best in the islands. Do people actually wear these shirts? We know that celebrities love them, but with prices going from $100 to $1,000 for silk and rayon shirts of the 1940s and 1950s, our guess is that most of them wind up framed on somebody's walls. Also fun: the vintage aloha items that collectors snap up, like "nodders" (hula dolls with nodding heads) for $45 to $95, and menu covers from the Royal Hawaiian Hotel and cruise ships of the Matson Line of the 1930s and 1940s, for about $25 to $125. They also feature reproductions of most vintage items, at more affordable prices.

    Ready for a snack? **Deli and Yogurt** offers $3.95 sandwiches, pizzas, snacks; chairs and tables are vintage Formica, but those breezes coming off the oceanfront are the real thing. Another way to beat the Kona heat is to pick up a beverage and some chocolate-chip cookies from the **Kona Kai Farms** coffee espresso bar and head for the oceanfront patio. It's cool out there.

KONA PLAZA SHOPPING ARCADE Running out of things to read? Help is at hand at **Middle Earth Book Shoppe,** newly expanded in the Kona Plaza (across Alii Drive from the Kona Shopping Village), a shop not easy to find but well worth looking for. It's stocked with a good selection of maps as well as books. **Paradise Found Boutique** (across from Marty's Steak House), specializes in resort wear that is elegant and casual at the same time; prices are good. Note their hand-painted items on raw silk.

    Bill Traub's little shop called **B. T. Pottery,** 75-5707 "B" Alii Dr., is worth seeking out for collectors of ceramics. Traub uses Hawaiian black sand, materialized from disintegrated lava, as part of his clay bodies: The sand melts upon firing and produces a speckled pattern unique to each piece. Cups, bowls, and vases are all well priced.

KONA COAST SHOPPING CENTER Near the intersection of Hi. 11 and Hi. 190 is the Kona Coast Shopping Center. **KTA,** a big supermarket, is a good place to stock up on food for your kitchenette. It also might pay to join the local folks at places like **PayLess,** a huge drugstore with very low prices for film and other items, and **Kona Health Ways,** with a large selection of grains, nuts, teas, spices, and some fresh produce.

LANIHAU CENTER On the other side of the highway at 75-5595 Palani Rd. is the newer Lanihau Center. It's mostly of interest to local people, but you can shop for produce, baked goods, national brands, beers, and wines at low prices at the cavernous **Sack 'N Save** supermarket, which is open 24 hours a day, seven days a week; explore **Long's Drugs,** known for its excellent prices for film, macadamia nuts, and other gift items; pick up some reading matter at **Waldenbooks. Mail Boxes, Etc.,** is a good place to know about if you need to pack and ship things back home. Adjacent to Lanihau Center is the popular **Hilo Hattie Fashion Center,** where browsers are treated to a free shell lei and a free cup of coffee.

If candy is your passion, you may want to drive out to the **Kailua Candy Company** in the industrial area at the corner of Kaiwi Street and Kuakini Highway. It will be hard to resist buying some of these handmade and hand-packed candies, made with real butter, no preservatives, and a great deal of pride by the family that operates the business. Prices average $18 a pound for the likes of lemon macadamia nut and Kona café au lait tropical truffles. Tiny samples of chocolates and dry-roasted macadamia nuts are available. Mail-order is available: toll free 800/MAC-CHOC.

---

7. BIG ISLAND EVENING ENTERTAINMENT

HILO

Nightlife is quieter than it used to be in Hilo, what with the closing or conversion into condominium apartments of several major hotels. However, there's still enough to keep you busy making the rounds of some of the favorite places.

For an inexpensive, family-style evening in Hilo, try **Uncle Billy's Restaurant** at the Hilo Bay Hotel. The hotel and restaurant are owned and operated by Uncle Billy Kimi and his Hawaiian family, and each night from 6:30 to 8:30pm there's a free hula show, a totally nonslick warmhearted revue. Dinners feature fish just caught in Hilo waters, at $9.95 to $16.95; sandwiches are available for light eaters. Watch the local papers for news of entertainment at the posh **Hawaiian Naniloa Hotel,** 93 Banyan Dr.; name performers from Honolulu sometimes play the Crown Room. At the Karaoke Bar, which stays open from 11am until late at night, music to sing along to starts about 7pm, Thursday to Saturday only.

If it's just drinks and music you're after, there are several good spots around Hilo. **Harrington's,** 135 Kalanianaole St., has a scenic location overlooking the Ice Pond at Reed's Bay. You can enjoy live entertainment in the lounge Tuesday through Saturday nights, and have reasonably priced appetizers and drinks in a wonderfully romantic setting. They open at 4:30pm for the sunset cocktail hour. Sophisticated **Lehua Bay City Bar and Grill,** 90 Kamehameha Ave., has newer and bigger digs now, and more space for live music and dancing, Friday and Saturday from 9pm. One of the town's "in" spots.

KK Tei's Lounge, 1550 Kamehameha Ave., features karaoke sing-alongs, from 11am until closing Monday through Saturday nights. There's a vast selection of both Japanese and American songs.

The plush **Hilo Hawaiian Hotel,** 71 Banyan Dr., has the Waioli Lounge, overlooking Hilo Bay and majestic Mauna Kea volcano. Local friends rave about the authentic Hawaiian music presented Monday through Friday from 5 to 9pm by Alberta and Alvin Kalima. The Bobo Brown Trio performs contemporary music for dancing and listening on Thursdays from 8 to 11pm and Friday and Saturdays from 8pm to 1am. No cover, no minimum, and some of the best prices for beer and wine in town. In the historic downtown area, at 60 Keawe St., there's elegant **Roussels,** a French-Créole restaurant in a converted old bank. You can have cocktails there or after-dinner drinks nightly, perhaps treat yourself to New Orleans beignets and some dark French-roast coffee, brewed right at your table. The piano bar lounge at **Chapman's Land & Cattle Co., Ltd.** (760 Piilani St.), is a popular spot on Friday and Saturday from 9pm, when there's live entertainment. There's no entertainment and scarcely any atmosphere at the **Hilo Seaside Hotel bar** (126 Banyan Way), but always a local crowd full of fun, a big TV screen, and drinks at some of the lowest prices in town. When the bars close down, you can get some nourishment over at **Ken's House of Pancakes,** 1730 Kamehameha Ave. (see "Where to Eat," Chapter 12), where they serve not only pancakes and omelets, but everything on the menu around the clock.

KAILUA-KONA

There's plenty of nighttime entertainment in these parts, much of it centered around the big hotels. The **Keauhou Beach Hotel** is the place for fans of Hawaiian music, which can be heard Sunday mornings from 10am to 1pm and Friday evenings from 6 to 9pm at the Kuakini Terrace, during its buffet meals; and Sunday to Thursday from 6 to 10:30pm and Friday and Saturday from 5 to 11:30pm in the Makai Bar.

In the mood for a luau? Kona's only **beachfront luau,** and one of the best in town, is held every Sunday, Tuesday, Wednesday, and Thursday at King Kamehameha's Kona Beach Resort. The traditional rituals and feasting are followed by the Ports of Polynesia Revue, featuring traditional Pacific island dances. Cost is $49 for adults, $18 for children 6 to 12, free for children 5 and under. But you needn't pay anything to come and see the torchlighting ceremony. Just take yourself to the beach at 6pm and watch the beautiful ceremony, as torches are lit on land and sea in the shadow of an ancient heiau. Then you might proceed to the Billfish Bar, situated around the lovely pool, where there is a variety of musical entertainment every night from 5:30 to 10:30pm.

One of the most popular lounges in town is **Don Drysdale's Club 53** in the Kona Inn Shopping Village, on Kailua Bay, overlooking the waterfront. Exotic drinks—like Frozen Baboon, Fuzzy Willie, and Hawaiian Sunset—are unique, and the pupus—shrimp scampi, deep-fried spicy buffalo wings, and potato skins—are really special. There are burgers and sandwiches too, to go along with the drinks.

The terrace overlooking the ocean at **Fisherman's Landing** is a wonderfully romantic spot, great for sunset watching or star gazing. Hawaiian and contemporary music played every evening, from 6:30pm on. The cocktail lounges at **Jolly Roger, Kona Inn,** and **The Charthouse** are all seaside, offering super scenery along with the libations.

Keep the **Kona Surf Resort** in mind, especially on Tuesday and Friday nights, when you can watch a free Polynesian Paradise Revue from 5:30 to 7pm on the Nalu Terrace, on the cliffs overlooking Keauhou Bay. Have a tropical drink and enjoy the show.

If you're in a disco mood, go to romantic **Eclipse,** 75-5711 Kuakini Hwy., across from Foodland—candles, wooden beams, mirrors, and the disco sound on Friday and Saturday nights from 10pm to 1:30am. Sunday night it's big-band music; Wednesday and Saturday nights, the sounds of country and western music, from 6 to 10pm. Dinner from 5pm, dancing from 10pm Tuesday through Sunday.

The Windjammer Lounge of the Royal Kona Resort is one of the most scenic spots around, where you can listen to the sound of the surf smashing up against the rocks as you sit out on the patio and watch the Pacific perform. Walking around the big hotels like the Royal Kona, examining the gardens and lagoons by moonlight and floodlight, is a show in itself.

Have you experienced karaoke yet? It's been the rage in Japan for years, and it's big in Hawaii, too. Karaoke means "empty orchestra," an orchestra minus the singer. A laser-disc video machine provides the words, and guests—which could be you—take turns at providing the singing. One of the most popular places for karaoke is **Kona Bowl** (tel. 326-2695), mountainside of Lanihau Shopping Center, where a large local crowd loves to sing along every night, from 7pm to 2am. On Monday nights, there's football live on four big-screen TVs, with lots of live coverage of pro sports.

MAUI

Even though she lives two blocks away from highly celebrated Waikiki Beach, a woman we know in Honolulu regularly spends her vacations on Maui. The reason? To go to the beach! In addition, however, to possessing some of the world's most marvelous beaches, this second-largest island in the Hawaiian archipelago boasts one of the great natural wonders of the planet: Haleakala, the world's largest dormant volcano. Add to this a string of gorgeous little jungle valleys where the modern world seems incredibly remote, a picturesque whaling town kicking its heels after a long sleep in the South Seas sun, and a wonderfully hospitable local citizenry intent on convincing you that Maui *no ka oi*—Maui is the best! You just might end up agreeing.

INTRODUCING MAUI

The second-largest island in the Hawaiian chain, Maui is about 70 miles southeast of Oahu, and can be reached via plane in about 20 minutes. Geologically, the island is the result of the work of two volcanoes, Puu Kukui in the west and Haleakala in the east, which formed separate land masses as they grew and eventually created the valley in between which is now Central Maui—hence its nickname, the Valley Isle. But according to the legends of the ancient Hawaiians, their own special demigod, Maui, pulled up both ends of the island from the sea bottom with his fishhook. (There's an imposing statue of Maui doing just that on the grounds of the Stouffer Wailea Beach Resort.) The island is 729 square miles, 25 miles from north to south and 38.4 miles from east to west. Roads are excellent and it's very easy to explore.

Maui has been going through the throes of enormous expansion. But while new hotels and condominium apartments have been built at a formidable rate, the island still manages to retain a graceful, unhurried feeling. The laws here are stricter, and nowhere on Maui has there been such wanton destruction of natural beauty as there has been in Waikiki.

You'll find accommodations and restaurants in all price ranges, but generally Maui is more expensive than Waikiki. Again, your biggest expense will be car rentals or guided tours, your only alternative on an island with no public transportation.

IMPRESSIONS

It [Haleakala] was a scene of vast bleakness and desolation, stern, forbidding, fascinating . . . a place of fire and earthquake, a workshop of nature still cluttered with the raw beginnings of world-making. . . . It was all unreal and unbelievable.
— JACK LONDON, 1911

WHAT'S SPECIAL ABOUT MAUI

Natural Wonders

Haleakala Crater, 10,023 feet high, the world's largest dormant volcano with a crater big enough to swallow the island of Manhattan.

Hana, one of the most unspoiled places in all Hawaii, reached by a 52-mile road around the base of Haleakala, with 617 hairpin turns, 56 one-lane bridges, dozens of sparkling waterfalls, plus bamboo groves and gardens.

Sports and Recreation

Superb sandy swimming beaches all over the island, from Kapalua Beach in the west to Kamaole Beach Parks and Big Beach in the south to Hana Beach Park in the east.

Snorkeling spots in West Maui, Kapalua and Kaanapali Beaches; in East Maui, Wailea Beach; the off-shore island of Molokini, reachable by boat only.

Hookipa County Beach Park in Paia, Windsurfing Capital of the World, scene of many a competition; winter waves can be as high as 15 feet.

A chance to ride 10,000 feet down Haleakala Volcano on a guided bike tour; all you need is a cool head—and good brakes.

Alaskan humpback whales, wintering in Maui to mate and bear their young, visible from many coastal locations and on whale-watching cruises.

Fourth of July Rodeo in Makawao, erstwhile cowboy town.

Museums

Alexander & Baldwin Sugar Museum in Puunene, especially for its working model of sugar-factory machinery.

Bailey House Museum in Wailuku, with fascinating exhibits from Stone Age Hawaii to missionary days.

Whalers Village Museum, at Whalers Village Shopping Complex at Kaanapali Beach, with photos, artifacts, and an absorbing collection of whaling memorabilia.

Historic Lahaina

Baldwin Home, a missionary house museum, one of the projects of the Lahaina Restoration Foundation.

The *Carthaginian*, an authentic replica of a 19th-century sailing vessel, also run by the Lahaina Restoration Foundation.

Antiques

Good antique hunting on North Market Street in Wailuku.

Local Foods and Wines

Maui onions, the sweetest in the world (sometimes called Kula onions).

Maui potato chips, available in local stores—the best.

Maui wines, made from both local pineapples and grapes grown on the slopes of Haleakala by Tedeschi Vineyards.

Mountain Flowers

Proteas, grown on farms along the lower slopes of Haleakala.

Silverswords, rare botanical speci-mens which blossom only once, and only on lava rocks at the highest altitudes; found on the higher slopes of Haleakala.

Shopping

Lahaina, with numerous shopping complexes and hundreds of exciting individual stores.

Whaler's Shopping Village at Kaanapali Beach.

Kaahumanu Shopping Center and Maui Mall in Kahului.

Artistic boutiques and galleries in Paia and Makawao.

1. GETTING THERE & GETTING AROUND

GETTING THERE

BY PLANE Your plane will probably land at the very modern and airy **Kahului Airport.** The terminal is located in the 7-mile-wide valley that binds together the two great volcanic masses of Maui, the West Maui Mountains and Haleakala on the east. You're just a few miles here from modern Kahului and graceful old Wailuku, neighboring towns competing peacefully for the title of largest city. There is shuttle service from the airport to Kihei and Kaanapali. If you need assistance, stop by the state information kiosk at the airport.

If you're going to be staying in West Maui, you can save some driving time by flying directly to the newer **Kapalua–West Maui Airport** via either Hawaiian or Island Air (tel. 808/669-0255) on limited schedules.

ORIENTATION

Maui is small enough so that you can logically make your headquarters at one hotel and take off each day for various sightseeing and beach excursions: to Haleakala, to the historic old whaling town of Lahaina, and to remote, romantic Hana.

The **Wailuku-Kahului** area, closest to the main airport, is centrally located for sightseeing excursions but lacks a really good beach. The best beach area close to Kahului is **Kihei** (about a 15-minute drive) and this also enjoys a central location. The liveliest and most beautiful area, to our taste, is the **Lahaina-Kaanapali-Napili** region, about 40 miles from Kahului, generally more expensive than the Kihei area, which has a far greater number of condo accommodations. All of these places work as a base; the only place on the island that is inconvenient as a base if you want to move around is **Hana** in East Maui, a 3-hour drive from the airport; you might want to plan an overnight stay there as the drive each way is a long one, although most people do it on a 1-day trip.

TOURIST INFORMATION The **Maui Visitors Bureau** is at 1727 Wili Pa Loop (Wailuku Millyard), P.O. Box 580, Wailuku, HI 96793 (tel. 808/244-3530; fax 808/244-1337).

GETTING AROUND

Maui has no public transportation system, save for a few shuttles from resort areas to selected shopping centers.

TRAVEL ARRANGEMENTS FOR THE DISABLED Maui definitely need not be off-limits to the physically handicapped—even those who want to partake of the island's exhilarating outdoor activities. Jan and David McKown, the young couple who run **Over the Rainbow Disabled Travel Services,** 186 Mehani Circle, Kihei, Maui, HI 96753 (tel. 808/879-5521), can help out in a number of areas, from airline flights, airport arrangements, wheelchair-accessible vans, accommodations in hotels or condos equipped with roll-in showers or in private homes, and personal care service to arranging helicopter or kayak trips, snorkeling, or even scuba diving. After entertaining David's brother, a quadriplegic, on Maui, they realized that they had a great deal of resources and information they could share with others—which they do, with a great deal of care and aloha. They can act as a full-service travel, tour, and activity agency for the disabled. Write or call for a brochure and information.

BY RENTAL CAR   As in all the neighbor islands, the major low-cost, all-island car-rental companies—like **Alamo, National, Budget, Dollar**—are all represented on Maui. The best place to make your reservations with these companies is in Honolulu (see "Getting Around," in Chapter 4, for details).

Word of Mouth Rent-A-Used-Car, 607 Haleakala Hwy., Maui, HI 96732 (tel. 808/877-2436, or toll free 800/533-5929; fax 808/877-2439), can set you up in a subcompact for $89.95 per week, or $15.95 per day with a 3-day minimum (unlike most other car-rental companies, they prorate any additional days after a week's rental; for example, a 10-day rental on a subcompact would be 1 week at $85, and 3 days at $12.24 per day). These cars are 1986 and 1987 models. Their newer 1988 to 1990 Nissan Sentra four-door automatic, without air conditioning, rents for $109.95 per week, $10 more for air, prorated daily rates. Also available in the $119.95 price range are some Geo Prisms and Ford Tempo 4-door sedans. They also specialize in "windsurfer" station wagons with roof rack available, at rates ranging from $109.95 for a compact wagon to $125 for a full-size American wagon. They are two minutes from Kahului Airport, with free pickup and drop-off.

Atlas Rent A Car, P.O. Box 126, Puunene, Maui, HI 96784 (tel. 808/871-2860, or toll free 800/367-5238 in the U.S. and Canada), offers a late-model compact from $21.95 per day with "absolutely no hidden charges." All sizes of cars are available. They rent the Suzuki Samurai four-wheel-drive for as little as $29.95 per day. They will provide prompt and courteous airport service.

 MAUI

Area Code   The telephone area code is 808.

Babysitters   Inquire at your hotel desk.

Business Hours   See "Fast Facts: Hawaii," in Chapter 2.

Car Rentals   See "Getting Around," above.

Climate   See "When to Go," in Chapter 2.

Dentists   Emergency dental care is available from Maui Dental Center, 162 Alamaha St., Kahului (tel. 871-6283).

Doctors   Doctors on Call will make hotel visits (tel. 667-7676). You can also call West Maui Healthcare Center, Whalers Village, Suite H-7 (tel. 667-9721), until 10pm nightly.

Emergencies   Call 911 for police, fire, and ambulance.

Eyeglasses   International Optical, Maui Mall Shopping Center, in Kahului (tel. 871-0784), will fix glasses while you wait. At Lahaina Optical, 888 Wainee St., Lahaina (tel. 661-8926), most glasses can be made in 1 hour.

Fax Services   Contact Phone Mart Kahului (tel. 877-7345), Kaahumanu Shopping Center, 275 Kaahumanu Ave.

Holidays   See "When to Go," in Chapter 2.

Hospitals   Major hospitals are Maui Memorial Hospital, 221 Mahalani, Wailuku (tel. 244-9056); Hana Medical Center, Hana Highway, Hana (tel. 248-8924); and Kula Hospital, 204 Kula Hwy., Kula (tel. 878-1221).

Libraries   Branches include Kahului Public Library, 20 School St. (tel. 877-5048); Kihei Public Library, 131 S. Kihei Rd. (tel. 879-1141); Lahaina Public Library, 860 Wharf St. (tel. 661-0566); Makawao Public Library, 1159 Makawao Ave. (tel. 572-8094); and Wailuku Public Library, 251 High St. (tel. 244-3945).

Newspapers   The *Maui News* is the most important daily paper.

Other Useful Numbers   Help is available from the State Commission on Persons with Disabilities (tel. 244-4441; voice/TDD); Sexual Assault Crisis Center (tel. 242-4357); and Suicide and Crisis Center (tel. 244-7404). On Call (tel. 246-1441), a 24-hour free service available from any pushbutton phone, offers the latest

IMPRESSIONS

We are an island community gone mad, behaving like a limitless continent
on a world that has already turned into a crowded, strained island.
— HAWAIIAN HISTORIAN GAVAN DAWS, 1974, AT VISITORS CENTER, HALEAKALA NATIONAL PARK

---

news, local and worldwide weather, community services, sports, horoscopes, soap opera updates, and more. See also the Aloha Pages of the Maui telephone book.

Photographic Needs ABC Discount Stores and Long's Drug Store offer the best prices on supplies. There are now Fox Photo 1-hour labs in Lahaina Cannery Mall (tel. 667-7681), Whaler's Village (tel. 667-5490), 139 Lahainaluna Rd. (tel. 667-6255), 820 Front St. (tel. 661-8895), Pioneer Inn (tel. 667-0710), Azeka Place in Kihei (tel. 879-6351), and Wailea Shopping Village (tel. 879-7577).

Poison Control Center Call toll free 800/362-3585.

Post Office In Kihei, it's at 1254 S. Kihei Rd. (tel. 879-2403); in Kahului, 138 S. Puunene Ave. (tel. 871-4710); in Lahaina, 1870 Honoapiilani Hwy. (tel. 667-6611).

Safety Exercise the same precautions you would elsewhere: Never leave valuables in your car, even in the trunk; leave personal valuables in hotel safes or in-room safes; don't flash cash conspicuously in public.

Taxis Alii Taxi offers islandwide 24-hour service (tel. 661-3688, 661-0133, or 667-2605). Or try Kihei Taxi (tel. 879-3000), Wailea Taxi (tel. 874-5000), and Yellow Cab of Maui (tel. 877-7000).

Weather Reports For current weather, call 877-5111 from 4:30 to 8:30pm; for Haleakala weather, 572-7749; for surf and wave conditions, 877-3477.

2. WHERE TO STAY

Although most of the new condominium apartments are in the luxury category, some are fine for us. But even with these additions to the hotel scene, a room on Maui is probably going to be more expensive than one in Waikiki. Meals go from budget to luxury, but there are plenty of opportunities to do your own cooking.

BED & BREAKFAST Those of you looking for bed-and-breakfast homes should know about **B&B Maui Style,** P.O. Box 98, Puunene, HI 96784 (tel. 808/879-7865, or toll free 800/848-5567). Although headquartered in the Kihei area, where many of its accommodations are located, B&B Maui Style has discoveries all over the island, in Lahaina, Iao Valley, and upcountry in Kula, Haiku, and Olinda. They delight in being "matchmakers," finding just the right accommodation, the right host, and the right price for their clients. On their roster are rooms in private houses, which run from $45 to $60 for a single or double, and vacation rentals in condos, cottages, studios, and homes, which go for $65 to $100. A very popular car-and-condo package starts at $84. And they also have some secluded, romantic hideaways at higher prices, and even magnificent properties suitable for retreats or executive conferences. The staff is available for advice and assistance once you're on Maui. They now also have accommodations on the Big Island and Kauai.

Ann and Bob Babson, 3371 Keha Dr. in Maui Meadows, Kihei, Maui, HI 96753 (tel. 808/874-1166, or toll free 800/824-6409), the attractive young couple whose vacation rentals are described below, also have an all-island reservation service. If their own place is full, they can recommend others in Maui and on the other islands as well. They can also get you car rentals at a good price, recommend wedding planning services, and provide plenty of inside information on Maui. The people at **Maui Windsurfari,** P.O. Box 330254, Kahului, Maui, HI 96733 (tel. 808/871-7766, or toll free 800/736-MAUI), who specialize in complete windsurfing vacation packages, also service nonwindsurfers, with a good selection of North Shore and Kihei accommodations, ranging from simple studios and condos with full kitchens from $60 a night to luxurious oceanfront homes at $120 to $500 a night. Bed-and-breakfast accommodations are also available. There are good rates for car-and-accommodations packages as well.

READERS RECOMMEND

Renting condos reasonably. *"If you check want ads in large metropolitan newspapers, you may find condos for rent a lot cheaper than by going through a travel agency. We've done this many times, in many different areas, and we have always been pleased with the results. For example, on Maui we stayed at Napili Shores and saved over $30 a night by making the arrangements ourselves, after calling a listing we saw in the* San Francisco Chronicle.*"*—Deborah Shulman, Santa Cruz, Calif.

Camping on Maui. *"Camping is still inexpensive. On Maui, for Baldwin Park (a county park), you pay $3 per adult and 50¢ per child. State parks are free. For county park permits:* War Memorial Gym *(next to Baldwin High School), Kaahumanu Avenue, Wailuku, Maui, HI 96793. Office hours are Monday through Friday from 8am to 4pm. For state park permits:* State Office Building, *54 High St., Wailuku, Maui, HI 96793."*—Frank Bogard, Pasadena, Calif.

KAHULUI

Kahului has a string of four hotels within minutes of the main airport and across the road from three very attractive shopping centers dotted with inexpensive restaurants. The ocean, here, however, is rocky and can be fairly rough. With the development of a very good beach area in Kihei, just 15 minutes away, these hotels have become largely the place for local business travelers and for very large tour groups, rather than individual tourists, since Kahului does offer a central location for touring all of Maui.

EDY AND RAY ROBERTS B&B, 433 Nihoa St., Kahului, Maui, HI 96732. Tel. 808/244-4667. 2 rms (neither with bath).

$ Rates (including breakfast): $50 for one person, $60 for two. No credit cards. Minimum stay 2 nights. **Parking:** Free.

Mr. and Mrs. Roberts' home is located just a few minutes away from Kahului airport and thus enjoys a good, central location for touring Maui. One of the two rooms has twin beds, the other a queen-size bed; they share a common bath. Guests can relax in the quiet surroundings of the pool, ureka palms, and coconut trees. Continental breakfast is served out on the patio each morning. Adults only, no alcohol, and no smokers. Reservations should be made at least a month in advance.

MAUI SEASIDE HOTEL, 100 W. Kaahumanu Ave., Kahului, Maui, HI 96732. Tel. 808/877-3311, or toll free 800/367-7000 from the mainland U.S., 800/451-6754 interisland. Fax 808/922-0052. 190 rms, 10 kitchenette units, 6 suites. A/C TV TEL

$ Rates: Apr–Dec 14, $54–$78 single or double; $83 kitchenette unit; $88 junior suite. Dec 15–Mar, add $10 per room per night. Each additional person $12 extra. Children 17 and under stay free with parent using existing beds. Add $15 per night for rental car. AE, MC, V. **Parking:** Free.

Your best bet in Kahului is the Maui Seaside, which encompasses the old Maui

Hukilau Hotel (known as its pool wing). The entire complex has recently been renovated and is very attractive; there is also a new sand beach. Rooms are large, light,
and tastefully furnished, with two double beds. The standard rooms face the garden,
while the deluxe rooms are beside the pool. The superior tower rooms are the most
expensive and include a refrigerator by request. There's a coin-operated laundry on
the property.

You can save money by dining at Vi's, which offers a long menu of seafood,
American, Mexican, Italian, and Asian dishes—most for $8.50 to $12.50.

Reservations: Contact Sands and Seaside Resorts, 2222 Kalakaua Ave., Suite
714, Honolulu, HI 96815 (tel. toll free 800/367-7000).

WAILUKU

DOUBLES FOR $35 TO $43

**BANANA BUNGALOW TOO, 310 N. Market St., Wailuku, Maui, HI 96783.
Tel. 808/244-5090,** or toll free 800/8-HOSTEL. 27 rms (none with bath).
$ Rates: $31.95 single, $38.95 double; $15 per person in shared community rooms.
MC, V. **Parking:** Free on side street.

An international budget hotel and hostel with a casual atmosphere, Banana
Bungalow Too is well suited for backpackers, active travelers, and
windsurfers. It's virtual heaven for the last, since it's just 10 minutes from
Kanaha and Spreckelsville and 15 from Hookipa, three of Maui's best windsurfing
beaches. A dozen or more windsurfing shops carrying all the latest equipment are
within a 10-minute drive. Single rooms have a double bed, double rooms have either
a queen-size bed or twins, and community rooms house two or three people in either twin beds or cedar bunks. Bathrooms are shared. There's a large-screen cable
TV lounge that shows movies; free coffee and tea; a kitchen with refrigerators, microwaves, and a gas cooker; an activity center; a guest pay phone; laundry facilities;
a picnic area surrounded with tropical fruit tree; and a sand volleyball court. There
are beach parties and daily activities, plus a free airport and beach shuttle with a
free phone at the airport. Managers Mark and Janna Folger can help guests find the
cheapest car rental companies (some of which give special discounts) and will book
local activities, too.

**NORTHSHORE INN, 2080 Vineyard St., Wailuku, Maui, HI 96793. Tel.
808/242-8999.** Fax 808/244-5004. 60 beds (no rms with bath).
$ Rates: $33 single; $43 double or twin; $16.50 per person in community rooms.
MC, V. **Parking:** Free.

Here's more good news for the active budget crowd—travelers, hikers, scuba
divers, windsurfers, bikers, etc. This hotel right in the heart of historic
Wailuku town offers some of the most reasonable rates on Maui. After traveling around the world, owner Katie Moore looked for a way to settle on Maui and
create an inexpensive, comfortable, friendly lodging. She discovered the old Wailuku
Grand Hotel and has completely renovated and re$modeled the old building, so that
it's now quite pleasant. There's a common room with TV, VCR, coffeepot, and
games; a full kitchen where guests may cook; and a storage room for bicycles, surfboards, and other equipment.

The six double rooms are small but cozy, with white stucco walls, roll-up blinds,
a small refrigerator, and either double or twin beds. There are 12 dormitory-style
rooms, with two double-decker beds each, and a refrigerator. There are no private
bathrooms, but there are six shared bathrooms, all with showers. The Northshore
Inn attracts a lively international crowd and appears to be always full. It's convenient to many inexpensive restaurants, and good beaches are about a 15-minute
drive away.

KIHEI-WAILEA

The best beach area closest to Kahului (about 15 minutes away) is the Kihei-Wailea section of Maui—a windswept stretch of sea and sand, with miles and miles of unspoiled ocean beach, the waves lapping at your feet, air warm and dry, and the mighty volcano of Haleakala and its changing cloud colors to gaze at from the shore. It's blessed with the least rain and best weather on all of Maui. Full-scale tourist development began here not so long ago, and the area has blossomed mightily since then, with scores of condominiums, plus new restaurants and small shopping centers opening to keep pace. There are splendid luxury resorts in Wailea and Makena: the Maui Inter-Continental Wailea, the Stouffer Wailea Beach Resort, the Four Seasons, the Hyatt Regency Wailea, the Maui Prince, and the Makena Surf, with more coming up. Beaches here can be rather windy in the afternoon (swim in the morning and save sightseeing for later). Despite its beauty, the Kihei-Wailea region remains less glamorous and exciting, at least for us, than the Lahaina-Kaanapali region (see below), but if you like a quiet vacation, you'll do well at any of the places described below.

DOUBLES FOR $50 TO $65

KAMAOLE BEACH ROYALE RESORT, 2385 S. Kihei Rd., Kihei, Maui, HI 96753. Tel. 808/879-3131, or toll free 800/421-3661. Fax 808/879-9163. 63 condo units (44 for rental). TV TEL

$ Rates: Apr 15–Dec 14, $65 one-bedroom apt for two; $75–$80 two-bedroom/two-bath apt for two; $85 three-bedroom/two-bath apt with double lanai for two. Dec 15–Apr 14, $90 one-bedroom apt for two; $100–$105 two-bedroom/two-bath apt for two; $110 three-bedroom/two-bath apt with double lanai for two. Each additional person $10 extra. Minimum stay 5 days. No credit cards. **Parking:** Free.

This attractive condominium complex boasts tastefully furnished apartments, each with its own private lanai, ceiling fans, all-electric kitchen with dishwasher and washer-dryer. There's a roof garden for sunbathing and a swimming pool in a tropical garden. The complex is across the road and just a short walk from one of the lovely Kamaole beaches, with excellent swimming. Reserve well in advance as this is a popular place.

KAUHALE MAKAI RESORT, 978 S. Kihei Rd., Kihei, Maui, HI 96753. Tel. 808/879-8888, or toll free 800/822-4409. Fax 808/874-6144. 164 condo units. A/C TV TEL

$ Rates: Apr 15–Dec 15, $60 studio ($350 per week); $70 one-bedroom apt ($450 per week); $85 two-bedroom apt ($550 per week). Dec 16–Apr 14, $75 studio ($475 per week); $95 one-bedroom apt ($600 per week); $120 two-bedroom apt ($800 per week). No credit cards. **Parking:** Free.

We've always shied away from high-rise condominiums, but after we visited Kauhale Makai (Village by the Sea) we were convinced that, in this case at least, bigger also means better. Accommodations are in two five-story buildings, and some have been superbly decorated by their owners. All have full kitchen, laundry, central air conditioning, and color TV. The two buildings, right on the ocean, are separated by a well-tended lawn on which there is a pool and putting green, Jacuzzi, and barbecues. Also available are sauna and shuffleboard, tennis courts and golf. An in-house convenience shop makes housekeeping easy in case you've forgotten something at the supermarket in Kihei, or in Kahului, 15 minutes away.

KEALIA CONDOMINIUM RESORT, 191 N. Kihei Rd., Kihei, Maui, HI 96753. Tel. 808/879-0952, or toll free 800/367-5222. 30 condo units. A/C TV TEL

$ Rates: May–Nov $65 studio; $75 one-bedroom apt for two. Dec–Apr $80 studio; $90 one-bedroom apt. Each additional person $10 extra. Minimum stay 4 nights. No credit cards. **Parking:** Free.

Its beachfront location and sensible prices are pluses for this high-rise condominium with nicely furnished studios and apartments. All have cable TVs, full kitchens, washer-dryers, and lanais with ocean views. There's an attractive swimming pool and sunning area on the grounds, as well as the glorious beach.

KIHEI AKAHI, 2531 S. Kihei Rd., Kihei, Maui, HI 96753. Tel. 808/879-2778, or toll free 800/367-5242 on the U.S. mainland. Fax 808/879-7825. 70 studios and apts. TV TEL

$ Rates: Apr–Dec 14, $65 studio; $70 one-bedroom apt; $95 two-bedroom/two-bath apt. Dec 15–Mar, $85 studio; $100 one-bedroom apt; $135 two-bedroom/two-bath apt. Rates apply to stays of 4 (minimum) to 6 nights; less on longer stays. Inquire about possible car-rental packages with Alamo Rent A Car. No credit cards. **Parking:** Free.

Located across from a beautiful swimming beach, Kihei Akahi has the lowest rates of any of the many properties managed by Condominium Rentals Hawaii, a large vacation rental agency. Facilities include two swimming pools, barbecue grills, and a tennis court. Nicely furnished units have fully equipped kitchens, including washer-dryers, and private lanais.

Reservations: For reservations and information, contact Condominium Rentals Hawaii, 2439 S. Kihei Rd., Suite 205A, Kihei, Maui, HI 96753.

KIHEI ALII KAI, 2387 S. Kihei Rd., c/o Leisure Properties, P.O. Box 985, Kihei, Maui, HI 96753. Tel. 808/879-6770, or toll free 800/888-MAUI on the U.S. mainland. Fax 808/874-0840. 127 condo units (46 for rental). TV TEL

$ Rates: Apr 15–Dec 14, $65 one-bedroom apt for two; $80 two-bedroom apt for four; $90 two-bedroom/two-bath apt for four; $110 three-bedroom/two-bath apt for six. Dec 15–Apr 14, $90 one-bedroom apt for two; $105 two-bedroom apt for four; $115 two-bedroom/two-bath apt for four; $130 three-bedroom/two-bath apt for six. Each additional person $7 extra. Minimum stay 3 nights. MC, V. **Parking:** Free.

Although you'll have to walk a few steps and cross the road to get to beautiful Kamaole Beach, that effort will save you considerable dollars. It's much cheaper to stay here than at most beachfront condos. This is a well-kept and nicely run property. Each individually decorated apartment has its own private lanai and a full kitchen and washer-dryer. There are two tennis courts, a pool with spa, sauna, barbecue, and eating area.

KIHEI KAI, 61 N. Kihei Rd., Kihei, Maui, HI 96753. Tel. 808/879-2357, or toll free 800/735-2357. 24 one-bedroom apts. A/C TV

$ Rates: Apr 16–Dec 15, $65–$80 apt for two. Dec 16–Apr 15, $80–$95 apt for two. Minimum stay 4 days in summer, 7 days in winter. Each additional person $5 extra (maximum of four per apt). No credit cards. **Parking:** Free.

★ This one is a surprise: From the road, all one sees is a parking lot. But the front of this complex is sandy beach! These are very pleasant, breezy units, well suited for families. And the low price for on-the-beach accommodations has to make this one of the best bargains in Maui! All units are nicely furnished, and most have a view of the ocean from their private 16-foot lanais; rates depend on view and location. Self-service laundry facility, swimming pool, and barbecue area, too.

LEINAALA OCEANFRONT CONDOMINIUMS, 998 S. Kihei Rd., Kihei, Maui, HI 96753. Tel. 808/879-2235, or toll free 800/334-3305. Fax 808/879-8366. 24 apts. A/C TV

$ Rates: Apr 15–Dec 14, $65 studio for two; $75 one-bedroom apt for two; $100 two-bedroom apt for four. Dec 15–Apr 14, $85 one-bedroom apt for two; $110 two-bedroom apt for four. Each additional person $ 10 extra. Minimum stay 4 nights. 10% discount for 7 nights or more Apr 15–Dec 14. Monthly rates available. MC, V. **Parking:** Free.

Tennis buffs will be in heaven here, because this cozy little complex of apartments is sandwiched between public courts. After your game, you can cool off in the freshwater swimming pool, or snorkel or windsurf in the ocean right out front. The best swimming beaches in Kihei are about a mile away. The one- and two-bedroom apartments are nicely and individually furnished, with fully equipped kitchens. Each of them is oceanfront, with glorious ocean and sunset views, and the place is very quiet.

NANI KAI HALE, 73 N. Kihei Rd., Kihei, Maui, HI 96753. Tel./fax 808/ 875-0630, or toll free 800/367-6032. 46 condo units. TV TEL

$ Rates: Apr 16–Dec 14, $ 40 studio; $60–$90 one-bedroom apt for two; $95–$130 two-bedroom apt for four. Minimum stay 4 nights; 7-night stays discounted. Dec 15–Apr 15, $55 double; $65 studio; $80–$125 one-bedroom apt for two; $120–$150 two-bedroom apt for four. Each additional person $10 extra; children under 5 stay free in parents' unit. MC, V. **Parking:** Free.

Sitting on a 6½-mile walking and swimming beach at the entrance to the Kihei area, this old-timer is blessed with an ideal location. There's a barbecue and picnic area, and a congenial group around the pool or out on the sandy beach. Swimming is excellent, but snorkeling is limited. All units have an ocean view; some are oceanfront. These are condominium apartments, so decor varies with the individual owners, but all are attractively furnished and have either queen- or king-size beds, sofa beds in the living rooms, well-equipped modern kitchens with microwave ovens, and private lanais. And all apartments have two baths.

NONALANI, 455 S. Kihei Rd., Kihei, Maui, HI 96753. Tel. 808/879-2497, or toll free 800/733-2688. 8 cottages.

$ Rates: Apr 16–Nov, $65 cottage for two. Dec–Apr 15, $78 cottage for two. Minimum stay 4 nights in summer, 7 nights in winter. Weekly and monthly rates available. No credit cards. **Parking:** Free.

Each of the eight cottages that comprise Nonalani stands alone in a grassy tree-filled area, within sight of the ocean. There is a beach for swimming and walking 20 yards away. Each cottage has a living room, full bedroom (with a queen-size bed), kitchen, and an open lanai with dining table. Since there are two beds in the living room, a family of four could be comfortable here. For reservations, contact Dave and Nona Kong at the above address.

PUNAHOA BEACH APARTMENTS, 2142 Iliili Rd., Kihei, Maui, HI 96753. Tel. 808/879-2720. 15 units. TV TEL

$ Rates: Apr 15–Dec 14, $62 studio; $82–$84 one-bedroom apt; $87–$110 two-bedroom apt. Dec 15–Apr 14, $81 studio; $109–$111 one-bedroom apt; $120–$140 two-bedroom apt. Additional person $12 extra. Minimum stay 5 days. No credit cards. **Parking:** Free.

You'll be in good hands if you choose to stay at this little place. Each of the units has a private lanai, ocean views, a fully equipped kitchen, and smart, modern furnishings. It's surrounded by gardens, and it's right on the ocean. Sandy beaches, with good swimming and surfing, are adjacent; children love it around the rocks because of the fish. Punahoa gets booked way ahead with repeat visitors in winter, but accommodations are easier to come by in summer.

SHORES OF MAUI, 2075 S. Kihei Rd., Maui, HI 96753-8799. Tel. 808/ 879-9140, or toll free 800/367-8002. Fax 808/879-6221. 50 condo units. A/C TV TEL

$ Rates: Apr 15–Dec 19, $65 one-bedroom apt for two; $90 two-bedroom apt for four. Dec 20–Apr 14, $90 one-bedroom apt for two; $115 two-bedroom apt for four. Each additional person $8 extra. Minimum stay 3 days. MC, V. **Parking:** Free.

All units are oceanfront at this attractive, two-level condo complex across the street from the beach. Snorkeling is good, and there's a sandy swimming beach just a block away. You can relax in the good-size swimming pool, soak in the spa, play a little tennis, enjoy a barbecue here. Apartments are nicely and individually decorated, all with dishwasher and washer-dryer. The two-bedroom units also have two baths.

SUNSEEKER RESORT, 551 S. Kihei Rd. (P.O. Box 276), Kihei, Maui, HI 96753. Tel. 808/879-1261, or toll free 800/532-MAUI, Fax 808/874-3877. 8 units. TV TEL
$ Rates: $50–$55 studio with kitchen; $60–$65 one-bedroom apt; $80–$90 two-bedroom apt. Each additional person $6 extra. Minimum stay 3 days for studios and one-bedroom apts, 7 days for two-bedroom apts. No credit cards. **Parking:** Free.

Two former readers of this book, Milt and Eileen Preston, started traveling to the islands some years back and then decided to settle there. They've had their own place across the road from Kihei Beach for quite a while now, and will give you a warm welcome. All units have king-size beds, cheerful color schemes, original artwork, upholstered furniture on the lanais, cross-ventilation, and a full kitchen with microwave oven. Picture windows face the ocean. Hawaiian pitched roofs add a Polynesian touch. The two-bedroom apartments have two baths and a huge fenced, private Polynesian garden in back. The Prestons will provide you with free barbecue equipment. The Sunseeker Resort is near the beach at the spot where the 1792 arrival of Capt. George Vancouver is commemorated by an HVB marker and a Thunderbird totem carved by the Nootka people on Vancouver Island.

DOUBLES FOR $75 TO $95

ASTON MAUI LU RESORT, 575 S. Kihei Rd., Hihei, Maui, HI 96753. Tel. 808/321-2558, or toll free 800/922-7866 on the U.S. mainland, 800/445-6633 in Canada, 800/342-1551 interisland. Fax 808/922-8785. Telex 634479ASTHIUW. 170 rms. A/C TV TEL
$ Rates: Apr–Dec 21, $79–$140 double. Dec 22–Mar, $89–$150 double. Each additional person $12 extra. AE, DC, MC, V. **Parking:** Free.

The traditional big hotel in this area, this is a collection of low-rise, Polynesian-style buildings on 28 acres of tropical grounds, complete with a large Maui-shaped swimming pool, sandy beach, tennis courts, and a spirit of *ohana* or "family" reminiscent of an older, more gracious Hawaii. The rates here are much lower than at the fancier new resorts in Wailea, and good value, especially when you consider that they have many handy conveniences, including refrigerator and coffee maker. Furnishings are attractive. The Long House Restaurant serves excellent dinners.

Reservations: Aston Hotels and Resorts, 2255 Kuhio Ave., Honolulu, HI 96815; or call the above toll-free numbers.

HALE KAMAOLE, 2737 S. Kihei Rd., Kihei, Maui, HI 96753. Tel. 808/879-1221, or toll free 800/367-2970 in the U.S. and Canada. Fax 808/879-5576. 188 apts. TV TEL
$ Rates: Apr 1–Dec 15, $67 one-bedroom apt for two, extra person $5; $87 two-bedroom/two-bath apt for four, extra person $5. Dec 16–Mar 31, $99 one-bedroom apt for two, extra person $8; $129 two-bedroom/two-bath apt for four, extra person $8 per day. Minimum stay 3 nights. No credit cards. **Parking:** Free.

This low-rise apartment complex is across the street from a fine swimming beach. No studios, only lovely one-bedroom units and split-level two-bedroom/two-bath apartments. All units are nicely furnished and have complete kitchens. Facilities include a tennis court, two pools, and barbecue grills.

KAMAOLE NALU RESORT, 2450 S. Kihei Rd., Kihei, Maui, HI 96753-8694. Tel. 808/879-1006, or toll free 800/767-1497. Fax 808/879-8693. 36 two-bedroom apts. TV TEL
$ Rates: Apr 2–Dec 15, $95 oceanview apt for two, $115 oceanfront. Dec 15–Apr 2, $130 oceanview apt for two, $150 oceanfront. Each additional person $12 extra.

Special rates of $106 oceanfront, $80 oceanview, are offered June–Sept. Rates subject to change. Minimum stay 3 nights. No credit cards. **Parking:** Free.
Nestled between two lovely beach parks, Kamaole 1 and Kamaole 2, this one is for those who love the water. There's also a swimming pool and a barbecue grill. Apartments are all individually and nicely furnished, and good buys, considering that each has a living room, a fully equipped kitchen with dishwasher and laundry facilities, two baths, and a private lanai. A nice place for a family to spread out in.

KOA RESORT, 811 S. Kihei Rd., Kihei, Maui, HI 96753. Tel. 808/879-1161, or toll free 800/877-1314 on the U.S. mainland and Canada. 54 rms. A/C TV TEL

$ Rates: Apr–Nov 30, $85 one-bedroom apt for two (maximum four); $100 two-bedroom apt for four (maximum four); $110 two-bedroom/two-bath apt for four (maximum six); $135 three-bedroom/two-bath apt for six (maximum eight), $160 three-bedroom/three-bath apt for six (maximum eight). Each additional person over minimum pays $10. Dec 1–Mar 31, add $20 to all rates. Minimum stay 5 nights; 15% discount for monthly stays. No credit cards. **Parking:** Free.
It's so cozy and comfortable, you could easily spend a long time living here—and many people do. The five two-story wooden buildings are across the road from the ocean and surrounded by over 5½ acres of green gardens and lawns. There are two tennis courts, an 18-hole putting green, an oversize pool spanned by a bridge, a Jacuzzi, barbecues, and shuffleboard courts. Apartments are spacious and comfortable, with nice furnishings, cable TV, fully equipped kitchens, and large lanais. Rates are decent for Maui. The best buy is the two-bedroom unit at $100.

LUANA KAI RESORT, 940 S. Kihei Rd., Kihei, Maui, HI 96753. Tel. 808/879-1268, or toll free 800/669-1127. Fax 808/879-1455. 113 condo units. TV TEL
$ Rates (including car rental): Apr–Dec 19, $105–$120 one-bedroom apt; $125–$150 two-bedroom apt; $200 three-bedroom apt. Dec 20–Mar, $130–$145 one-bedroom apt; $150–$175 two-bedroom apt; $225 three-bedroom apt. AE, DC, MC, V. **Parking:** Free.
Gracefully situated on 8 acres of beautifully landscaped grounds, this is one of the nicest condos in the Kihei area. Step from your room—well, almost—to the ocean or swimming pool, heated whirlpool, saunas, tennis courts, putting green, barbecue area; everything is close at hand. Best of all, there's a peaceful feeling here. Inside, carved wooden doors lead to one-, two-, and three-bedroom apartments luxuriously furnished in light woods, all with full electric kitchens, lanais, and every comfort for vacation living.

MANA KAI MAUI CONDOMINIUM HOTEL, 2960 S. Kihei Rd., Kihei, Maui, HI 96753. Tel. 808/879-1561, or toll free 800/525-2025 on the mainland U.S. and in Canada. Fax 808/874-5042. 66 hotel rms, 66 condo apts. TV TEL
$ Rates (including car with unlimited mileage): Apr 17–Dec 16, $90 double (including breakfast); $155 one-bedroom apt; $175 two-bedroom apt for four. Dec 17–Apr 16, $95 double (including breakfast); $175 one-bedroom apt; $195 two-bedroom apt for four. Each additional person $10 extra. AE, CB, DC, MC, V. **Parking:** Free.
A unique resort in this area—or any other, for that matter—Mana Kai Maui offers a combination of condominium apartments and regular hotel rooms in a lively, upbeat setting. Situated on a mile-long, beautiful crescent of beach (it's known as one of the best snorkeling beaches around), with a pool, the open-air Ocean Terrace restaurant, and all sorts of activities going on, it offers a lot under one roof. The hotel rooms have the lowest rates; these are small bedrooms with either a king-size bed or twins, and an attractive bathroom with a large vanity sink. Beautifully furnished apartments include full kitchen with refrigerator, range, dishwasher, and dishes.

MAUI SUN, 175 E. Lipoa St., Kihei, Maui, HI 96753. Tel. 808/875-9000, or toll free 800/762-5348 from Hawaii, mainland U.S., and Canada. Fax 808/874-8446.

228 rms, 8 one-bedroom suites, 10 two-bedroom suites, 1 penthouse suite. A/C TV TEL
$ Rates: $79–$82 mountainview guest room, $89–$103 deluxe garden view, $99 partial ocean view; $135 one-bedroom suite, $150 two-bedroom deluxe garden view suite, $160 two-bedroom partial ocean view, $350 penthouse. AE, MC, V. **Parking:** Free.

The Kihei/Wailea area has modestly priced condos aplenty and expensive luxury hotels aplenty—what's been needed is a modestly priced luxury hotel. And that's why the local people are all excited about the Maui Sun, which has all the amenities one would expect to find in hotels costing two or three times as much. Situated on the mountain side of Kihei Road, the hotel is across from the Silversword Golf Course, and a short drive (or free shuttle-bus trip) to Kihei's splendid white sand beaches. An oversized freshwater swimming pool, whirlpool spa, waterfalls and koi ponds highlight the lush, landscaped grounds. The lobby is lovely, with a marble floor, etched-glass ceilings, and original artwork and sculpture. The rooms, in two six-story buildings, have wall-to-wall carpeting, well-appointed bathrooms, private lanais, and either one king- or two queen-size beds. Most have a connecting room, so the hotel is popular for family reunions and gatherings. Room-and-golf and room-and-car packages are available. The Frangipani Café, the main dining room and lounge, features local and international cuisine.

MENEHUNE SHORES, 760 S. Kihei Rd. (P.O. Box 556), Kihei, Maui, HI 96753. Tel. 808/879-5828, or toll free 800/558-9117 in the U.S. and Canada. Fax 808/879-5218. 70 condo units.
$ Rates: Apr 16–Dec 14, $75 one-bedroom apt for two; $88.50 one-bedroom/two-bath apt for two; $100 two-bedroom/two-bath apt for four; $120 three-bedroom/two-bath apt for four, $140 for six. Dec 15–Apr 15, $90 one-bedroom for two; $110 one-bedroom/two-bath apt for two; $120 two-bedroom/two-bath apt for four; $130 three-bedroom/two-bath apt for four, $150 for six. Each additional person $7.50 extra. Minimum stay 5 days. No credit cards. **Parking:** Free.

For family accommodations, try this big, beautiful condominium complex on the beach at Kihei. You could almost stay here and not want to leave the grounds—there's the ocean, a heated swimming pool, and the "Royal Fishpond," a swimming pond protected by a stone-and-reef formation built by the ancient Hawaiians, right on the premises. Akina's on the Beach offers steak and seafood, moderately priced lunches. There's even a whale-watching platform in the roof garden. All apartments face the ocean, are individually decorated, and have a full electric kitchen, with refrigerator/freezer and washer-dryer. The two- and three-bedroom apartments have two bathrooms each.

WAILEA OCEANFRONT HOTEL, 2980 S. Kihei Rd., Kihei, Maui, HI 96753. Tel. 808/879-7744, or toll free 800/367-5004 in the U.S. and Canada, 800/272-5275 interisland. Fax 808/533-0472. Telex 723-8582. 88 rms. A/C TV TEL
$ Rates (including car rental): $85–$100 double; $160 one-bedroom family unit. AE, MC, V.

An on-the-beach location and some of the more moderate prices in the Wailea area are pluses for this hotel, located at the entrance to the Wailea Beach Resort. Two championship golf courses and 14 tennis courts are within walking distance of the hotel, and right out front is a beautiful crescent of sandy beach, perfect for swimming and snorkeling. No need for a pool here. Corelli's on the Beach, a sophisticated spot for gourmet Italian dining, is right on the premises. Rooms are comfortable, nicely furnished, each with its own refrigerator. Complimentary coffee and doughnuts are available in the mornings. Most of the rooms are in the standard category, which means they have either double or twin beds and a garden view.

Reservations: Contact Hawaiian Pacific Resorts, 1150 S. King St., Honolulu, HI 96814; or call the toll-free numbers above.

BED & BREAKFAST

ANN AND BOB BABSON'S VACATION RENTALS, 3371 Keha Dr. in Maui Meadows, Hihei, Maui, HI 96753. Tel. **808/874-1166,** or toll free 800/824-6409. 2 rms., 1 apt, 1 cottage (all with bath). TV TEL
$ Rates: $65—$80 single or double guest rm. in main house (including breakfast); $80 double one-bedroom apt; $95 two-bedroom/two-bath cottage. Additional person $10 extra. Breakfast $5 extra outside of main house. No credit cards. **Parking:** Free.

⭐ Not only are Ann and Bob Babson just about the nicest hosts around, they also have one of the prettiest homes on the southwest side of Maui, 500 feet up the mountainside, just above the grand resort hotels of Wailea and within a 5-minute drive of sparkling swimming and snorkeling beaches. One-hundred-and-eighty-degree ocean views, spectacular sunsets, gorgeously landscaped grounds (bougainvillea, plumeria, papaya trees, rose bushes, night-blooming jasmine), and tastefully decorated interiors make this the kind of place you'd like to stay at for a long, long time. An entire family could settle into the cozy Sunset Cottage, completely separate from the main house, with living room, outside deck, cathedral ceilings, two bedrooms, and two baths; it can sleep up to six, with a sofa bed in the living room. The Hibiscus Hideaway apartment, on the ground floor of the main house, has its own private entrance and garden, living room, kitchen, separate bedroom and bath. There are also two bed-and-breakfast units in the main house: the Bougainvillea Suite, a one-bedroom, one-bath with queen-size bed and a small refrigerator; and the sunny Molokini Suite, a spacious master bedroom with spectacular views of the Pacific, a king-size bed, and a glamorous large bathroom. The Babson's breakfast table is a favorite place for guests to gather, since the hosts are not only generous with the food—tropical fruits, organic granola, waffles, french toast, fruit smoothies, homemade muffins, and bagels are all possibilities—but they are equally generous with insider's tips on favorite restaurants, hidden beaches and hiking trails, and quality attractions. And they even provide free laundry service. Plenty of that old-time aloha spirit here.

In addition, the hosts run their own reservation service: They can set you up with B&B accommodations and car rentals elsewhere in Maui or in any of the other islands.

BED, BREAKFAST, BOOKS & BEACH, 3270 Kehala Dr., Kihei, Maui, HI 96753. Tel. **808/879-0097.** 2 rms. TEL
$ Rates (including breakfast): $75 one rm; $125 two rooms; $5 less per rm for stays of 3–6 nights, $10 less per rm for a week or more. MC, V. **Parking:** Free.
A mile from the ocean in Maui Meadows, the home of spirited psychotherapists Natalie and John Tyler is filled with classical music, fine art, and books. Guests can enjoy breakfast ("natural high-energy gourmet") on a screened lanai with views of mountains and the songs of birds, plus sunsets over the ocean with cool drinks and pupus on the deck. A variety of options range from champagne breakfasts in bed for honeymooners to daily meditations to gourmet dinners and trips to "secret and isolated places." No smoking. Private bath.

HALE LEINI, P.O. Box 1919, Kihei, Maui, HI 96753. Tel. **808/874-1490.** 4 rms.
$ Rates (including breakfast): $50–$55 single, $110 double. No credit cards. **Parking:** Free.
Psychologist and nutritionist Dr. Elaine Willis makes this tropical hideaway on a hill overlooking the ocean and the resort hotels of Wailea available to guests as a private health retreat, perfect for those seeking personal transformation and rejuvenation. Three elegant ocean view rooms with bath overlook tranquil gardens; a fourth single room downstairs also has its own bath and garden view. A beautiful breakfast of fresh living food is served on the deck each morning; sunsets are special. For an extra fee, Dr. Willis will assist guests in creating individual Wellness Lifestyle programs. Sessions with bodyworkers and healers can be arranged.

MAALAEA BAY

Down by the small-boat harbor at Maalaea Bay, a few miles from Kihei, is a wonderful beach area, and perched here, at Maalaea Village, is a small group of condominiums.

DOUBLES FOR $65

HONO KAI RESORT, RR 1, Box 389, Maalaea Village, Maui, HI 96793. **Tel.** 808/244-7012, or toll free 800/367-6084. 40 condo units. TV TEL
$ Rates: Summer, $60, one-bedroom apt with garden view, $80 oceanfront. Winter, $75 one-bedroom apt with garden view, $95 oceanfront. Minimum stay 5 days. Inquire about summer specials. DISC, MC, V. **Parking:** Free.

Hono Kai is one of the most reasonably priced condominiums in the area, and would make an ideal place for a family vacation. You can swim in front of your door or at the public beach 50 yards away—or try your luck with surf at the harbor, which, according to some of the locals, is "the fastest surf in the world."

All units are on the ocean side of the street, and all are pleasantly furnished. Shoji doors separate the living room and bedroom. There are full kitchens, including microwave ovens, dishwashers, and cable TV. There's a swimming pool, washers and dryers on every floor, and two good restaurants—Buzz's Steak House and The Waterfront—nearby. We've had several good reports from our readers about this place and about rental agent Jeanne McJannet, who also represents two adjoining properties, Makani A Kai and Kanai A Nalu, as part of Maalaea Bay Rentals.

LAHAINA

The area surrounding the historic old whaling town of Lahaina, on Maui's west coast about 30 miles from Kahului, might be a good place to move on to after a day or two in the Kahului or Kihei area; or it could serve as a base for your entire stay in Maui.

A NEARBY CAMPGROUND

CAMP PECUSA, 800 Olowalu Village Rd., Lahaina, Maui, HI 96761. Tel. **808/661-4304.**
$ Rates: $5 per night.

Here's a chance to live on the beach, laze in a hammock on the shore, and sleep in your own tent under the stars. Camp Pecusa is an Episcopal Church Camp located on a secluded beach in Olowalu, 6½ miles southeast of Lahaina, 100 yards off the highway and behind a sugarcane field. From the campgrounds you have great views of Kahoolawe Island, Haleakala, and the West Maui Mountains, and from November through May, of humpback whales swimming just offshore. This is basic, no-frills camping. Campsites are scattered under sea grape and monkeypod trees, with fire pits and picnic tables. A central shower and portable toilets (kept very clean) are furnished. The parking area for the campsite is lighted at night, and security is provided by the managers, Linda and Norm Nelson, who live on the property. Snorkeling from the beach is excellent; there is a coral reef, and surge channels extend several hundred yards offshore. You must furnish all your own equipment, as there is none for rent.

For an information sheet on Camp Pecusa, send a stamped, self-addressed envelope to the address above.

DOUBLES FOR $30 TO $70

OLD LAHAINA HOUSE, P.O. Box 10355, Lahaina, Maui, HI 96761. Tel. **808/667-4663** or toll free 800/847-0761. Fax 808/667-5615. 5 rms. TV

$ Rates (including continental breakfast): $45–$95. AE, MC, V. **Parking:** Free.

⭐ John and Sherry Barbier, the hosts at Old Lahaina House, claim they're not aiming to run a "fantasy hotel"; what they're offering is a place where travelers can feel at home in a real Hawaiian setting. And the location couldn't be improved on: their lovely home is directly across the street from a serene beach perfect for swimming, snorkeling, and whale watching, and just a stone's throw from the heart of Lahaina's town action. You could conceivably get around here without a car. There are two rooms on the main floor: one is a small single in the owners' part of the house, which shares their bath; another is in a separate wing and has a private bath, a small refrigerator and microwave, and a lanai. There are three rooms upstairs in this wing: one with a private bath and small refrigerator; one with twin beds and a great view of the West Maui Mountains; and one small twin. All rooms have both air conditioning and ceiling fans, and all have TV. Breakfast (yummy pastries from a local French bakery, fruit, juices, beverages) is served each morning on the lanai/courtyard, and there's a beautiful swimming pool that guests are encouraged to use. John and Sherry know Lahaina well and are happy to help with activity, restaurant, and shopping recommendations. A couple of interesting notes: Sherry and her mother are the proprietors of a wonderful clothing boutique in Lahaina Center called Arabesque—*and* she's a former Mrs. Hawaii USA.

TONY'S PLACE, 13 Kauaula Rd., Lahaina, HI 96761. Tel. 808/661-8040. 3 rms.

$ Rates (including morning coffee): $50 single; $60 double. Continental breakfast $5. MC, V. **Parking:** Free.

⭐ After 17 years of adventuresome living in Alaska, journeyman electrician Tony Mamo decided to settle down in Maui, "to warm up" and run a small tourist home. Considering the high price—and relative scarcity—of accommodations in Lahaina town itself, Tony's Place is a great find for us budgeteers. There's nothing fancy here—it's just a clean, casual, comfortable home with three nice bedrooms (two share a bath with each other, one shares a bath with Tony's own room), and a communal kitchen/living/dining area, where guests can stock food in the refrigerator (they have kitchen privileges), make a phone call, watch TV, or socialize in the book-filled living room (like-minded people, many internationals, seem to find this place). What is special is the location: Access to Lahaina Beach is just across Tony's yard, and a short walk away is the center of Lahaina with all its myriad attractions. Tony himself sets the mood for easy, island-style living—which is, after all, what Hawaii should be all about.

DOUBLES FROM $70

LAHAINA HOTEL, 127 Lahainaluna Rd., Lahaina, Maui, HI 96791. Tel. 808/661-0577, or toll free 800/669-3444. Fax 808/667-9480. 12 rms. A/C

$ Rates (including breakfast): $89–$99 standard single or double; $129 large single or double (with queen- or king-size bed). AE, MC, V. **Parking:** $3 per day.

⭐ Anyone who remembers the shabby old Lahainaluna Hotel will be stunned to see the magical transformation it has undergone, emerging as the Lahaina Hotel, an intimate inn with all the grace and charm of turn-of-the-century Lahaina. The hotel was re-created from the ground up (the electrical wiring and plumbing were completely replaced), at a cost of $3 million, by Rick Ralston, of Crazy Shirts fame. Ralston, one of Hawaii's most avid preservationists, saw to it that every detail of the period restoration was complete, from the turn-of-the-century wood, brass, full-size iron beds, Oriental rugs, and wood wardrobe closets to the marble mantel clocks, leaded-glass lampshades, and even the lace runners on the dressers. All the antiques are from his personal collection. Modern conveniences include new private baths, ceiling "fly fans," and luxurious decorator fabrics and wall coverings. Guests are served a continental breakfast to enjoy either in bed or in the wicker rocking chairs on their balconies, which overlook busy Lahainaluna Street in the midst of Lahaina town. All rooms are one flight up, on the second floor; downstairs is a small, graceful lobby and, adjoining it, David Paul's Lahaina Grill, an upscale restaurant serving New American cuisine. If you can afford the tab, a stay here is clearly a special experience. Inquire about their special wedding packages.

LAHAINA ROADS CONDOMINIUMS, 1403 Front St., Lahaina, Maui, HI 96761. Tel. 808/661-3166, or toll free 800/624-8203. 21 condo units. TV
$ Rates: Apr 16–Dec 15, $95 one-bedroom apt for up to four; $130 two-bedroom apt for four to six; $150 penthouse apt for four. Dec 16–Apr 15, $115 one-bedroom apt for two; $150 two-bedroom apt for four; $200 penthouse apt for four. Minimum stay 3 nights. AE, MC, V. **Parking:** Free.

If you'd like to settle into your own little apartment right in Lahaina, this could be your place. The five-story elevator building at the Kaanapali end of Front Street sits in a cool and breezy spot right on a good snorkeling beach; you can look down at the ocean—and watch some spectacular sunsets—from your own lanai. A swimming beach is half a mile up the road, but there's a freshwater pool right at home. The attractively fully furnished apartments are soundproof, with wall-to-wall carpeting, fully equipped kitchens with washer and dryer, and large living rooms with convertible couches; local calls are free from your own telephone. Penthouse apartments have two baths. Cleaning service on request. A free shuttle to downtown Lahaina and Kaanapali is within 3 blocks.

LAHAINA SHORES BEACH RESORT, 475 Front St., Lahaina, Maui, HI 96761. Tel. 808/661-4835, or toll free 800/628-6699. Fax 808/661-4696. 199 condo units. A/C TV TEL
$ Rates: Apr–Dec 15, $95–$117 studio for two; $122–$172 one-bedroom apt for three; $162–$182 penthouse apt for four. Dec 16–Mar 31, $105–$137 studio for two; $147–$172 one-bedroom apt for three; $192–$227 penthouse apt for four. Cribs and rollaways $10 extra. Car/condo and special seasonal packages available. AE, MC, V. **Parking:** Free.

⭐ Considering that you can swim right in front of the hotel, this beachfront resort might be worth stretching your budget for a bit. All the units have complete electric kitchens, wall-to-wall carpeting, and lanais offering ocean or mountain views. The cheaper units face the mountains while the more expensive ones have ocean views or are oceanfront. The seven-story building, a charming example of Victorian architecture, is very much in keeping with the rest of old Lahaina—a welcome contrast to the burgeoning concrete high-rises flourishing all over the rest of the island. A swimming pool with adjacent heated therapeutic Jacuzzi sits on the ocean side, just off the huge, airy lobby. You can swim in Lahaina Harbor, right in front of the hotel, and play tennis across the street.
Reservations: Write to 50 Nohea Kai Dr., Lahaina, HI 96761; or call the toll-free number above.

MAUI ISLANDER, 660 Wainee St., Lahaina, Maui, HI 96761. Tel. 808/ 667-9766, or toll free 800/367-5226 from mainland U.S. and Canada. Fax 808/661-3733. 148 hotel rms, 90 studios with full kitchen, 134 suites. TV TEL
$ Rates: $69 hotel rm with refrigerator; $84 studio with full kitchen; $96 one-bedroom suite with full kitchen; $127 two-bedroom suite with full kitchen. Dec 20–Apr 1, add $8 to all rates. Room-and-car packages available. AE, DC, DISC, JCB, MC, V. **Parking:** Free.

⭐ Without a car, almost any vacation on Maui is difficult. But lack of wheels will not be a hindrance to anyone who chooses to stay at this hotel, which affords peace and privacy (its units are spread out over 9 acres on tropical grounds), while providing proximity to everything you could want in the area; it's a 3-block walk to a sandy beach, a 2-block stroll to the activities of Lahaina Harbor, a block away from the shops and restaurants of Front Street, 2 blocks to the supermarket, and a short free bus ride to the resort life at Kaanapali Beach. You can be picked up at the airport and taken to the Maui Islander at nominal cost. And the hotel-condo itself is lovely, its units simply but nicely decorated in island style with light woods, tile bathroom, tidy kitchen (hotel rooms have refrigerators only). Right at home is a swimming pool, three barbecue and picnic areas, and a tennis court lit for night play. Free continental breakfast is available at the daily briefing at the Activities Center. Good value in this pricey area.

PIONEER INN, 658 Wharf St., Lahaina, Maui, HI 96761-1295. Tel. 808/ 661-3636, or toll free 800/457-5457. Fax 808/667-5708. 48 rms. A/C TEL
$ Rates: $70–$90 estimated. AE, MC, V. **Parking:** $4.

At this writing, this landmark property was in the midst of an ambitious and total renovation. The public areas, restaurant, and lounge were the first to be completed; all the rooms are expected to be ready by the time you read this. They're simple yet very tasteful and still harbor their colorful histories. And you certainly won't find a location that's more in the middle of things in Lahaina town. Lots of special events like dinner dances are held in the courtyard; you'll want to check to see what's going on during your stay.

PLANTATION INN, 174 Lahainaluna Rd., Lahaina, Maui, HI 96761. Tel. 808/667-9225, or toll free 800/433-6815. Fax 808/667-9293. 14 rms, 4 suites. A/C TV TEL
$ Rates (including breakfast): $99–$149 double; $179 suite. Honeymoon and dive packages available. AE, DISC, MC, V. **Parking:** Free.

Just a block from the bustling waterfront and main street of Lahaina is this small, quiet, European-style country inn whose owners have come up with some terrific innovations in the art of making guests happy. Each of the soundproofed rooms is exquisitely decorated with antiques, stained glass, hardwood floors, brass and poster beds, ceiling fans, and floral wallpaper and bedspread. The TV (VCR on request) is tucked away in a graceful armoire; there are silk flower bouquets in every room; wall prints are charming. Some suites have cooking facilities. Guests have the use of a 12-foot-deep tiled pool with spa and sun deck out back, plus a club house for private meetings or dining. Guests receive a discount on dinner at Gerard's, one of Maui's best French restaurants, which occupies the front parlor and veranda of the Plantation Inn.

PUAMANA, Front St., P.O. Box 11108, Lahaina, Maui, HI 96761. Tel. 808/667-2551, or toll free 800/628-6731 in the U.S. and Canada. 40 condo units. A/C TV TEL
$ Rates: Apr 16–Dec 15, $95 one-bedroom gardenview apt for up to four; $120 center garden, $140 loft, $150 oceanfront; $135, $175, $200 two-bedroom house for up to six; $315 three-bedroom oceanfront house for up to six. Dec 16–Apr 15, $120 one-bedroom gardenview apt for up to four; $130 center garden, $160 loft, $175 oceanfront; $155, $225, $250 two-bedroom house for up to six; $350 three-bedroom oceanfront house for up to six. Minimum stay 3 nights. AE, MC, V. **Parking:** Free.

Not a commercial resort, a hotel, or a typical condo development, Puamana is the first planned residential development on Maui, a colony of privately owned town houses set on 28 acres of tropical gardens right on the beach. The place is secluded, private, and very peaceful, yet it's a short drive from all the shopping and restaurant excitement of downtown Lahaina. Puamana was a private estate in the 1920s, part of a large sugar plantation; the plantation manager's home is now the clubhouse, with a patio overlooking the ocean (the ideal place for sunset watching), a library, card rooms, sauna, and office. There are three swimming pools (one, for adults only, right on the beach), a Laykold tennis court, and table tennis, too. The town houses, built back in the 1960s, are all individually furnished, all comfortable, with complete kitchens, sofa beds in the living rooms; they can sleep four to six.

KAANAPALI TO KAPALUA

A few miles outside Lahaina, on Maui's exquisite west coast, you approach the Kaanapali-Napili-Kapalua region, one of Hawaii's most desirable vacation areas, blessed with miles of gorgeous beach and stunningly blue skies, with several world-famous championship golf courses thrown in for good measure. The road curves around a series of graceful bays, perhaps the most beautiful of which is Napili Bay, a gorgeous little stretch of sea and sand where not very long ago the breadfruit, papaya, and lichee trees ran helter-skelter to the sea. For us, this area is the end of the rainbow, and we don't mean the one likely to be arching across the sugarcane fields as you approach. The road reaches its end at the magnificent Kapalua Resort, one of Hawaii's most naturally beautiful playgrounds.

DOUBLES FOR $65 TO $90

HALE KAI, 3691 Lower Honoapiilani Rd., Lahaina, Maui, HI 96761. Tel. 808/669-6333, or toll free 800/446-7307. Fax 808/669-4747. 40 condo units. TV TEL
$ Rates: $90 one-bedroom apt for two; $120–$145 two-bedroom apt for four. Additional person $10 extra. Discounts available in summer. Minimum stay 3 nights. MC, V. **Parking:** Free.

These graceful apartments look out on flowering gardens, a park, and a good-size pool that fronts on the ocean beach. Each apartment is decorated differently and each has a different view: Some guests come back year after year for the ocean view, others for the quiet parkside units. Rooms on the upper levels have handsome cathedral ceilings. All are furnished nicely with electric kitchens and private lanais. All have VCRs, microwave ovens, and ceiling fans.

HALE MAUI APARTMENT HOTEL, 3711 Lower Honoapiilani Rd. (P.O. Box 516), Lahaina, Maui, HI 96767. Tel. 808/669-6312. Fax 808/669-1302. 12 suites. TV
$ Rates: Apr 15–Dec 15, $60–$85 one-bedroom suite for two. Dec 16–Apr 14, $75–$85 one-bedroom suite for two. Each additional person $10 extra. MC, V. **Parking:** Free.

Hans and Eva Zimmerman have been in charge at this small hotel right on the ocean for over 25 years now. The suites, each holding up to five guests, have been refurbished, and all have private lanais, radios, and good kitchens. There's a nice barbecue area out back. There's no pool, but steps from the lawn lead right into the water.

HONOKAWAI PALMS, 3666 Lower Honoapiilani Rd., Lahaina, Maui, HI 96761. Tel. 808/667-2712, or toll free 800/669-MAUI. Fax 808/661-5875. 30 apts. TV TEL
$ Rates: $65 daily, one-bedroom apt for up to four; $75 daily, two-bedroom apt for up to six. AE, MC, V. **Parking:** Free.

⑤ This is one of the older apartment complexes in this area, not as luxuriously furnished as some of the new condos, but good value for the money and just across the road from a small beach park. Apartments are spacious and comfortably furnished, with ample electric kitchens to make cooking easy. The more desirable one-bedroom apartments have ocean view and lanai. There's a large pool to dunk in plus a barbecue area. The management is friendly and helpful. Coffee is served mornings at the pool. Laundry facilities are available on premises.
Reservations: Write to 721 Wainee St., Suite 213, Lahaina, HI 96761; or call the toll-free number above.

HOYOCHI NIKKO, 3901 Lower Honoapiilani, Rd., Lahaina, Maui, HI 96761. Tel. 808/669-8343 or toll free 800/487-6002 from U.S. and Canada. 18

one-bedroom units, some with lofts. TV

$ Rates: May 1–Dec 14, $75, one-bedroom apt for two; Dec 15–Apr 30, $95, one-bedroom apt for two. Each additional person $10 extra. Minimum stay 7 days. No credit cards. **Parking:** Free.

You get the feeling of gracious retreat here at the "Resort of the Sunbeam," from the Asian architecture of the complex to the spacious oceanfront lawn and garden where you could easily laze away peaceful days. You can walk down the lawn stairs to the ocean and swim and snorkel inside the reef area, or swim in a freshwater pool in the garden. The units range in size from standard to large to "special." All have private lanais with full ocean views, "long boy" twin beds (a few queen-size), cable color TVs, and fully equipped kitchens with washer-dryers. There's a grill for barbecues, and sometimes pupu parties are held out in the garden. Despite the Japanese name, most of the guests here are North American, and many of them return each year.

THE KAHILI MAUI, 5500 Honoapiilani Rd., Lahaina, Maui, HI 96761. Tel. 808/669-5635, or toll free 800/786-7867 or 800/SUNSETS. Fax 808/669-2561. 30 condo units. TV

$ Rates: Apr–Dec 20, $79 studio for two; $110 one-bedroom/two-bath apt for up to four. Dec 21–Mar 31 $99 studio for two; $130 one-bedroom/two-bath apt for up to four. Children under 18 stay free with parents using existing beds. Rollaway bed $16 extra; crib, $5. AE, DC, MC, V. **Parking:** Free.

Kapalua is one of Hawaii's poshest resort areas, but at its gateway, adjacent to the world-famous Kapalua Bay Golf Course, is this moderately priced complex. Guest rooms, attractively furnished in tropical prints, all have complete kitchens and in-room washer-dryers. Napili Bay and Kapalua Bay, with their excellent swimming beaches, are just a short walk away, making this one cozy for serious swimmers and snorkelers as well as golfers. It's just across the road from the ocean, heading up toward the mountains. On the premises are a pool, Jacuzzi, and barbecue, and there are 10 tennis courts nearby.

KALEIALOHA, 3785 Lower Honoapiilani Rd., Lahaina, Maui, HI 96761. Tel. 808/669-8197, or toll free 800/222-8688. Fax 808/669-2502. 67 apts. TV TEL

$ Rates: $85–$95 one-bedroom oceanview apt for two. Each additional person (over age 2) $7.50 extra. MC, V. **Parking:** Free.

This lovely condo resort offers large, pleasantly furnished one-bedroom apartments, each with a queen-size bed and a double sofa bed in the living room that opens up to sleep two more. The well-equipped kitchens boast dishwashers and washer-dryers. The cheaper rooms have a mountain view, while the more expensive rooms face the ocean. As for swimming, you can relax around a pool sheltered from the parking area out front by an interior courtyard, or try the ocean out back; swimming isn't bad within the protective outer reef.

MAHINA SURF, 4057 Lower Honoapiilani Rd., Lahaina, Maui, HI 96761. Tel. 808/669-6068, or toll free 800/367-6086. 56 units. TV TEL

$ Rates: Apr 15–Dec 14, $95 one-bedroom apt; $115 two-bedroom/two-bath apt for up to four. Dec 15–Apr 14, $110 one-bedroom apt; $130 two-bedroom/two-bath apt for up to four. Each additional person (including children) $8 extra. Minimum stay 3 nights. Discounts on weekly and monthly rates. Inquire about excellent deals on car rentals. MC, V. **Parking:** Free.

This is a fine place to settle in for real at-home living. The units are not only charming and attractively furnished, but well priced for the area. Sizes of the apartments vary, but all are little "homes"; the cutest are those two-bedroom apartments with a loft area upstairs that serves as a second bedroom—these are big enough to sleep six. The one-bedroom apartment can accommodate up to four people. Mahina Surf is situated on a rocky strip of oceanfront, and snorkeling is fine, but there is no sandy beach. There is, however, a big pool as compensation.

MAUIAN HOTEL, 5441 Honoapiilani Rd., Lahaina, Maui, HI 96761. Tel. 808/669-6205, or toll free 800/367-5034. Fax 808/669-0129. 44 apts.
$ Rates: Apr 15–Dec 14, $70–$110 studio apt for two. Dec 15–Apr 14, $104–$124 studio apt for two. Rates flexible based on occupancy (call for details). Third person $9 extra; fourth person $6. Children under 12 free, special family rates. MC, V. **Parking:** Free.

The swimming here at Napili Bay, from a gentle, reef-protected beach, is among the best in the islands. These attractive studio apartments, big enough for four, each have private lanai, electric kitchen (including microwave oven), one queen-size and one trundle bed (that opens into two), and all the conveniences of home. For those capable of tearing themselves away from the idyllic beach, there's shuffleboard, a TV room, and a freshwater swimming pool. Facilities include a big laundry and ironing area. There's a weekly "Breakfast with the Manager," featuring a fresh-baked Hawaiian treat.

MAUI KAILANI, 4435 Lower Honoapiilani Rd., Lahaina, Maui, HI 96761. Tel. 808/669-6994. Fax 808/669-4046. 114 condo apts.
$ Rates: $65 studio with ocean view or two-bedroom apt with garden view. Minimum stay 3 nights. MC, V. **Parking:** Free.

This complex offers some of the most reasonable rates in West Maui. It's a time-share operation, very busy in the winter season, but in the slower summer months units are often available to the general public. Twenty-seven of the units are available for April to September rentals, 11 of these oceanside studios, the others two-bedroom duplex apartments on the mountainside. Two tennis courts, two pools, and other facilities are spread out over 8 acres—not to mention a stretch of sandy beach, perfect for gentle ocean swimming. Each of the seaside units is spacious, attractively furnished in studio style (with such touches as big, old-fashioned ceiling fans), and boasts a large kitchenette plus a lanai that's perfectly enormous. TVs can be rented.
Reservations: Maui Kailani, 119 N. Commercial St., Suite 1400, Bellingham, WA 98225 (tel. 206/676-1434).

MAUI PARK, 3626 Lower Honoapiilani Rd., Lahaina, Maui, HI 96761. Tel. 808/669-6622, or toll free 800/922-7866 on the U.S. mainland. 800/445-6633 in Canada, 800/342-1551 interisland. Fax 808/922-8785. 208 units. A/C TV TEL
$ Rates: Apr–Dec 21, $79–$89 studio for two; $99–$109 one-bedroom apt for four; $149 two-bedroom apt for six. Dec 22–Mar 31, $99–$109 studio for two; $119–$129 one-bedroom apt for four; $159 two-bedroom apt for six. AE, CB, DC, JCB, MC, V.
Parking: Free.

This economy hotel, just across the road from Honokawai Beach Park, is proving very popular. The Maui Park, under the management of Aston Hotels & Resorts, consists of six separate buildings surrounding a nearly Olympic-size swimming pool and sunning area. It features apartment-size studios and larger units attractively furnished, with full kitchens, cable TVs, clock radios, large closets, and daily cleaning service. The three-story buildings do not have elevators, but three rooms are accessible to the disabled. There's 24-hour service at the desk, and a grocery and sundry store right at hand, which makes cooking at home very easy.

MAUI SANDS, 3600 Honoapiilani Rd. (c/o Maui Resort Management, Suite C) Lahaina, Maui, HI 96761. Tel. 808/669-1902, or toll free 800/367-5037 on the U.S. mainland and Canada. Fax 808/669-8790. 76 condo apts. A/C TV TEL
$ Rates: $80 standard one-bedroom apartment for up to three, $105 garden, $135 oceanfront; $100 standard two-bedroom apt for up to five, $130 garden, $160 oceanfront. Each additional person $9 extra. Minimum stay varies from 2 to 10 nights (at Christmas). Ask about weekly rates and discounts on long stays and special "Off-Season" rates. MC, V. **Parking:** Free.

These apartments are ideal for families with lots of kids or for two couples traveling together. Imagine an enormous living room (about the size of two average hotel rooms put together), beautifully decorated, with two small but comfortable bedrooms, twin beds in one, a queen-size in the other; a full electric kitchen; tropical ceiling fans; a view of gardens or ocean from your private lanai; and enough space for six people to stretch out. You can get it all here at this attractive spot just past the Kaanapali gold coast area for about half the price of the luxury resorts. The apartments close to the road are for heavy sleepers.

Since the Maui Sands was built when it was feasible to buy large lots of land, there is plenty of it to spare; the grounds are abloom with lovely trees and plants. Facilities include a big laundry, a comfortable swimming pool and sunning area, and a narrow sliver of beach (it's been washed away by storms but, hopefully, will return). At sunset, it's pure enchantment as you watch the sun sink right between the islands of Molokai and Lanai off in the distance. The condo complex is completely refurbished, including new furniture. Kay and Adel Kunisawa are cordial hosts. Readers continue to praise this one. In fact, one of our readers, the Rev. Bob Waliszewski, wrote us about Maui Sands: "I called Maui Sands on their toll-free number because their rates were among the best in the Kaanapali area. And I thought I'd ask them if they had a discount rate for clergy. As it turned out, they gave me a 20% discount. Other clergy would, I'm sure, be glad to know this."

The same Maui Resort Management is in charge at some of the select units at Papakea, right next door, and these little homes are even more luxurious. Creature comforts include two pools, two Swedish saunas, two tennis courts, shuffleboard, barbecues, putting green, and picnic areas. Of course, it's all on the beach. Studio rooms for two start at $134. Discounts available on weekly stays. Call the same toll-free number—800/367-5037—anytime between 8am and 5pm to make reservations.

NOELANI CONDOMINIUM RESORT, 4095 Lower Honoapiilani Rd., Lahaina, Maui, HI 96761. Tel. 808/669-8374, or toll free 800/367-6030 in the U.S. and Canada. Fax 808/669-7904. 40 condo apts. TV TEL
$ Rates: $87 studio, $110 one-bedroom apt; $140 two-bedroom apt; $170 three-bedroom apt. Each additional person $7.50 extra. Minimum stay 3 days. Weekly and monthly rates available, as well as car/condo packages. AE, MC, V. **Parking:** Free.
Located in the Kahana area, these oceanfront condominiums are beautifully furnished, and the view from your oceanfront lanai—of Molokai and Lanai, blue seas, and tropical gardens—is even more beautiful. There are two freshwater swimming pools at seaside (heated for evening swimming), good snorkeling is right in front, and a wide sandy beach is adjacent to the property. Managers John and Donna Lorenz host mai tai parties in an oceanfront cabaña several times a month so that guests can get to know one another. And there's a concierge service, with orientation continental breakfasts at poolside. Readers have praised the warm, homey atmosphere here. Rooms are furnished in tropical decor, and have microwave ovens and in-room videos. Studios have a dressing room, bath, and kitchen. One-, two-, and three-bedroom units have their own washer-dryer and dishwasher. There is also a launderette for those staying in one of the studios.

DOUBLES FOR $95 TO ABOUT $120

HONOKEANA COVE RESORT CONDOMINIUMS, 5255 Lower Honoapiilani Rd., Lahaina, Maui, HI 96761. Tel. 808/669-6441, or toll free 800/237-4948 (call collect from Canada). 38 condo units. TV TEL
$ Rates: $95–$105 one-bedroom apt for two; $135 two-bedroom apt for four; $155 three-bedroom apt for six. $150 two-bedroom town house for four. Each additional person $10–$15 extra. MC, V. **Parking:** Free.

If snorkeling is your passion, you're going to be very happy at this lovely resort condominium directly on a private, rocky cove where the snorkeling is tops. Swimmers need walk only about 5 minutes to a gentle sandy beach. Each apartment is close to the water and the pool oceanside; the grounds are also ideal for whale-spotting. We were told that a whale once gave birth at the entrance to the cove! When you're not busy watching whales, snorkeling, or admiring the grounds with its beautiful trees—we spotted a 160-year-old kamani nut (or false almond) tree—you can be enjoying the view from your lanai and the comforts of your apartment, each individually owned and decorated. All have fully equipped kitchens with dishwashers. Outdoor barbecues are provided. The management is cordial, arranging a pupu party every Friday to bring the guests together.

NAPILI SURF BEACH RESORT, 50 Napili Place, Lahaina, Maui, Hi 96761. Tel. 808/669-8002, or toll free 800/541-0638 on the U.S. mainland and Canada. TV TEL

$ Rates: Apr 15–Dec 14, $99 gardenview studio; $115 oceanview studio; $155–$165 oceanview one-bedroom, all for two people. Dec 15–Apr 14, $99 gardenview studio; $115 oceanview studio; $165–$175 oceanview one-bedroom. Car packages available. Each additional adult $15 extra. Children 12 and under free. No credit cards. **Parking:** Free.

★ This complex, with its soundproof luxury units perched on the tip of Napili Bay, on a particularly lovely curve of beach, is one of the nicest places to stay in the area. Each of the units is well equipped for easy housekeeping, handsomely furnished, and with private lanais that overlook the garden or ocean. Even the lowest-priced accommodations, in the Puamala building, are superneat and functionally designed, with full kitchens, dishwashers, radios with digital clocks, the works. There may be discounts on these units in the summer months. Every Friday evening guests get together out on the lawn for an aloha party, when there may be special entertainment, or just some friends and guests who like to sit around with a guitar and sing the old songs. In such a gracious setting, the coconut palms swaying in the evening wind and the sea lapping gently at your feet, it's hard to remember what you were planning to worry about.

PAKI MAUI, 3615 Lower Honoapiilani Hwy., Lahaina, Maui, HI 96761. Tel. 808/669-8235, or toll free 800/535-0085 on the U.S. mainland and Canada. Fax 808/669-7987. 76 units. TV TEL

$ Rates: $119–$139 studio for two; $119–$159 one-bedroom for up to four; $179–$219 two-bedroom for up to six. AE, DISC, DC, MC, V. **Parking:** Free.

This lovely condominium suite resort is right on the oceanfront. The grounds are lush, with a waterfall, a swimming pool, and a pond with koi fish in the center of the property. Rooms are individually furnished with a great deal of charm, and all boast fully equipped kitchens and private lanais with splendid views of Molokai and Lanai out there across the waters. Free continental breakfasts, and a sunset manager's cocktail reception once a week.

Reservations: Write Marc Resorts, 2155 Kalakaua Ave., Suite 706, Honolulu, HI 96815; or call the toll-free number above.

POLYNESIAN SHORES, 3975 Lower Honoapiilani Rd., Labaina, Maul, HI 96761. Tel. 808/669-6065, or toll free 800/433-6284 on the U.S. mainland, 800/488-2179 in Canada. Fax 808/669-0909. 52 apts. TV TEL

$ Rates: $80–$100 one-bedroom apt for two; $90–$110 two-bedroom/two-bath loft apt for two, $155–$163 three-bedroom/three-bath apt for four. Minimum stay 3 nights. Each additional person $10. MC, V. **Parking:** Free.

It's ocean all the way at this one, the kind of small, relaxed place where everybody feels right at home—so much so that many of the same people come back year after year. Every apartment has an ocean view from its own private lanai, there's a deck on the oceanfront with barbecue facilities, and it's a great place to watch for whales. Snorkeling is good right out front; swimming is better at a nearby sandy beach, about a 5-minute walk away. The grounds are so lush that guests can pick bananas right off the trees. Once a week there's a pupu party on the Tiki Deck. Apartments are nicely furnished, with separate living rooms and private baths with tub and shower.

READERS RECOMMEND

The Napili Bay, 33 Hui Dr., Lahaina, Maui, HI 96761 (tel. 808/669-6044). "We highly recommend The Napili Bay, close to Kaanapali Beach and Lahaina. These are oceanfront studio apartments with one queen-size bed and two singles and kitchen; they are reasonably priced at around $75 to $95 per day. We had clean, fresh linens each day, including beach towels; the rooms are not air-conditioned, but have adjustable shutters so you can feel the incredibly refreshing trade winds and hear the ocean at night. Efficiencies are great! The owners were like grandparents to us, extremely friendly and accommodating." —Francine Schept, White Plains, N.Y.

WORTH THE EXTRA MONEY

KAANAPALI BEACH HOTEL, 2525 Kaanapali Pkwy., Lahaina, Maui, HI 96761-1987. Tel. 808/661-0011, or toll free 800/262-8450. Fax 808/667-5978. 442 rms. A/C TV TEL

$ Rates: $119 standard, $145 courtyard, $160 partial oceanview, $175 oceanview, $195 oceanfront, $180–$525 suite. Each additional person $20 extra. AE, DC, MC, V. **Parking:** Free.

The luxury resorts of Kaanapali are well beyond our budget, but just in case you're wondering which of the hotels has the lowest prices, it's this one. Even standard rooms here are large and well decorated, and have refrigerators, coffee makers, and private lanais facing into a garden. The Kaanapali Beach Hotel has a spacious, open feeling with its huge garden, a whale of a swimming pool (yes, it's in the shape of a whale), a beautiful ocean beach right next to the rock formation (which makes it good for snorkeling) on which the neighboring Sheraton Maui sits, and all the comforts of the luxury life. It's easy to save money dining here, since the Koffee Shop offers all-you-can eat buffets at every meal, starting at $6.95, including a prime rib buffet dinner for $11.95. The Tiki Terrace offers open air dining in a casual atmosphere, and the Tiki Grill boasts made-to-order sandwiches, hot dogs, and happy hour menus. Certainly worth a splurge—if your pocketbook is up to it. The Kaanapali Beach aims to be "the most Hawaiian of the hotels," and its gracious staff and unusually sensitive management live up to that ideal. All the Hawaiian activities here—from learning Hawaiian games to *real* hula lessons—reflect the beliefs of the old Hawaiians and the responsibility to live in harmony with one's surroundings. The hotel's Hawaiian education program for its employees is widely admired in Hawaii's hotel industry.

READERS RECOMMEND

Kahana Village, 4531 Honoapiilani Rd., Lahaina, Maui, HI 96761 (tel. toll free 800/ 824-3065). "We have stayed at Kahana Village five times. The units are very spacious and well appointed. When two couples share a two-bedroom unit, or if three couples share a three-bedroom unit, the rate is quite reasonable in today's world."—Bob Harrison, Provincetown, Mass. [Authors' Note: Kahana Village is a beautiful oceanfront resort located on a sandy beach. Off-season rates for two-bedroom apartments are $150 oceanview, $180 oceanfront; three-bedroom apartments are $190 oceanview, $230 oceanfront.]

Papakea Beach Resort, 3543 Lower Honoapiilani Rd., Lahaina, Maui, HI 96761
(tel. toll free 800/367-7052). "We had a one-bedroom unit with a huge sleeping loft
(really a two-bedroom). Papakea is a vision of loveliness everywhere you look. The
grounds are meticulously tended and filled with beautiful plantings. Other bonuses were
two putting greens, two pools, two Jacuzzis, 'swimmercize' classes each morning, tennis
clinics, and a rum-punch party by the pool with entertainment on Friday. This is a quiet,
family-oriented resort, yet very close to the abundant restaurants, supermarkets, and
shops of Kaanapali."—Frances S. Kielt, West Hartford, Conn. [Authors' Note: Current
rates would be about $135 for a studio room.]

MOUNTAINSIDE BED & BREAKFASTS

If you like mountains better than beach, charming private homes better than impersonal hotels or condos, and refreshingly old-fashioned prices best of all, we've got
some good news for you. We've discovered 17 delightful "up-country" guesthouses
and vacation rentals—8 in Kula, 1 in Makawao on the slopes of Haleakala volcano
(ideal locations if you want to drive to the summit to catch the sunrise), and 8 more
off the Hana road, in the tiny town of Haiku. You can't go wrong at any of these,
although each has a slightly different style and personality.

IN KULA

**AHINAHINA FARM COTTAGES, 210 Ahinahina Place, Kula, Maui, HI
96790. Tel. 808/878-6096,** or toll free 800/241-MAUI. 1 studio apt, 1 two-bedroom cottage. TV
$ Rates: $75 studio for two with a 3-night minimum ($85 for 2 nights), $10 for each
additional person; $90 cottage for two with a 3-night minimum ($110 for 2 nights),
$15 for each additional person. No children under 12. No credit cards. **Parking:**
Free.

★ Here's a chance to stay on a working upcountry citrus farm, at a 2,150-foot
elevation in the wind-shadow of Mount Haleakala—a location that means
sunny days, cool nights, and upcountry peace and quiet. Mike and Anette
Endres grow Bearrs Seedless limes commercially and have 2 acres of citrus and flowers (including orchids and protea) for guests to enjoy. Mike is the site manager of a
large observatory atop Mount Haleakala. Both are warm-hearted people who delight
in sharing their lovely home and cottage with guests. They provide special assistance
and information for hikers and walkers; honeymooners are given special attention
and amenities. A cozy studio apartment attached to their home, but with its own
private entrance and parking, has an efficiency kitchen, a queen-size bed with thick
comforters, color TV, and a spacious covered deck. It's best suited for two, but a
child or extra guest might sleep on a futon. A separate two-bedroom cottage, with
its own private drive and parking, is also a delight, also beautifully decorated with a
living room, dining area, a queen-size bed in one bedroom, twin beds in the other,
and a fully equipped kitchen with dishwasher and washer-dryer. From its large covered deck you have a view of ducks marching about in a neighbor's pond—she is
the only licensed breeder of endangered duck species on Maui. Smoking is not allowed. Coffee and tea are furnished, along with many extra amenities. Guests are
also welcome to pick from the pineapples, bananas, and grapefruits growing on the
grounds. Views abound: sunset over Maalea Bay, sunrise and moonrise over the
mountains. From Ahinahina Farm you're a 20- to 40-minute drive to good swimming beaches.

**BLOOM COTTAGE 229 Kula Hwy. (R.R.2, Box 229), Kula, Maui, HI 96790.
Tel. 808/878-1425.** 1 cottage. TV TEL
$ Rates (including breakfast): $90 per night. Minimum stay 2 nights. Each additional
person $15 extra. No credit cards. **Parking:** Free.
Wonderfully private and romantic, with sweeping views of pasturelands going down

to the sea, Bloom Cottage stands by itself behind a pretty house owned by Lynne and Herb Horner, a busy young couple who work for the *Maui News* and the Maui Oil Company, respectively. The charming 700-square-foot cottage is tastefully decorated in country style, and has a four-poster queen-size bed in the sleeping area plus a single bed in the second bedroom, plus a double foldout futon, which would be so nice by the living room fireplace (yes, they have them up here in the mountains). The fully equipped kitchen includes a microwave oven, and Lynne and Herb stock the refrigerator with coffees, teas, yogurt, fruit juices, and muffins. Guests can pick a wide variety of culinary herbs that grow in the garden. No smoking in the cottage; no pets; not suitable for small children.

ELAINE'S UPCOUNTRY GUEST ROOMS, 2112 Naalae Rd., Kula, Maui, HI 96790. Tel. 808/878-6623. 3 rms, 1 cottage.

$ Rates: $55 double (third person $10), 3-night minimum stay; $95 cottage for four (fifth and sixth adults $10 each, $7 for each child), 3-night minimum stay. No credit cards. **Parking:** Free.

We'd call Elaine and Murray Gildersleeve's splendid home in Kula probably the best value for the money. The Gildersleeves are a retired couple from Alaska: Murray devotes a lot of attention to his pineapple farm right on the premises and Elaine looks after the guests. Their Hawaiian pole house is designer-elegant, with three guest bedrooms on the ground floor sharing a separate kitchen and living room. Guests are welcome to use the refrigerator and to cook breakfast or whatever meals they like—a rare privilege in a guesthouse. Coffee, tea, and fruit from the garden are provided. The three bedrooms are beautifully furnished, and have private baths and either two twin beds or a king- or queen-size bed (third person sleeps on a futon). Rooms have a splendid view of the West Maui mountains and Haleakala.

Next to the main house is a delightful cottage made to order for a family. With a queen-size bed in the bedroom, twin beds in the loft, and two window seats in the living room that can also be used as extra beds—six people can sleep comfortably. There's a complete kitchen, windows on three sides, bougainvillea growing outside, and a charming decor within. The Gildersleeves ask that guests do not smoke or drink.

READERS RECOMMEND

Elaine's Upcountry Guest Rooms. "We stayed at Elaine's for 4 nights. Murray and Elaine are terrific people; their home is truly a dream home and a dream place to stay. The surroundings are beautiful and this is just one nice place to visit. They make you part of their family and even asked us to stay an extra day and have Thanksgiving dinner with them and their friends. Wish we had been there the entire 2 weeks."—Berta and Chuck Pettis, Roswell, Ga.

HALEMANU, 221 Kawehi Place, Kula, Maui, HI 96720. Tel. 808/878-2729. 1 rm.

$ Rates (including breakfast): $75 single or double. Minimum stay 2 nights. No credit cards. **Parking:** Free.

Halemanu ("Bird House" or "Perch") is a spectacular country home filled with fine arts and ethnic artifacts 2,500 feet up on the slopes of Haleakala, seemingly light-years away from the rest of civilization. Maui-raised owner Carol Austin, who delights in sharing her home, her intimate knowledge of the area, and often her time with visitors, provides a charming guest room with a queen-size bed and private bath, entered from a large deck with a nonpareil 180° view of the countryside below. Staying with Carol is like staying with a friend and becoming part of the family, although guests have as much privacy as they wish. They have the use of the entire house, including the kitchen and the loft area with its TV,

VCR, movie collection, typewriter, and fax. Carol, now a columnist for the *Maui News* is a former caterer and gourmet cook, so there's no telling what she may be inspired to serve for breakfast. Since she's single, she often takes people snorkeling or hiking, or sometimes asks them to join her for a pasta dinner.

KULA COTTAGE, 206 Puakea Place, Kula, Maui, HI 96790. Tel. 808/871-6230. Fax 808/871-9187. 1 cottage. TV TEL
$ Rates: $85. Minimum stay 2 nights. No credit cards. **Parking:** Free.

★ Three thousand feet up on the slopes of Haleakala, in a lush, half-acre mountain setting, is this exquisite little hideaway. Cecilia and Larry Gilbert, whose own lovely home is just up the hill from the cottage, have equipped it with just about everything one needs for a comfy vacation, from a wood-burning fireplace to a full kitchen, laundry, private driveway, gas barbecue, furniture out on the lanai, and much more. A black-and-white shoji screen leads to the bedroom, also tastefully done in black and white, with a queen-size bed; an additional futon is also available. There are graceful amenities in the bathroom. Cecilia delivers fresh flowers and freshly baked bread every morning and is helpful with hints and tips on enjoying the best of Maui.

Reservations and information: 380 Hoohana St., Kahului, HI 96732, or phone or fax the above numbers.

KULA VIEW BED & BREAKFAST, 140 Holopuni Rd. (P.O. Box 322), Kula, Maui, HI 96790. Tel. 808/878-6736. 1 suite. TV TEL
$ Rates (including breakfast): $85 single or double. No credit cards. **Parking:** Free
Susan Kauai, who comes from an old-time kamaaina family and knows Maui better than most people, is in charge here. Her luxuriously furnished suite is located on the upper level of her home with a private entrance and its own deck. There's a queen-size bed, a reading area, a wicker breakfast nook, a mini-refrigerator, and a private shower. Telephone and television are available on request. Susan is a gracious host who helps guests plan their holidays, fills their room with fresh flowers from her garden, and serves breakfasts in their room—Kona coffee or tea, lush island fruits, and home-baked breads and muffins. She has blankets and warm clothing on hand for those sunrise trips to Haleakala, whose summit is not far away.

RUSTY AND FRANK KUNZ, 513 Lower Kimo Dr., Kula, Maui, HI 96790. Tel. 808/878-2137. 1 apt, 1 house. TV
$ Rates: $65 two-bedroom apt; $95 owner's home for up to four people. Each additional person $10 extra. Minimum stay 3 nights. No credit cards. **Parking:** Free.
This lovely modern home is at an elevation of 3,000 feet, set on 8 acres of lawns and pastures, 20 miles from the summit of Haleakala Crater. The views are of the West Maui mountains and Kihei beach way below in the distance. Rusty and Frank Kunz divide their time between this home and one on Oahu. On Maui, they always have a two-bedroom vacation apartment available for rental—it's an excellent bargain and has its own private entrance, a deck (perfect for sunset watching), a kitchenette (refrigerator, toaster-oven, two-burner hot plate, sink), and a private bath.

From November to June, when they're not on Maui, the Kunzes will, on occasion, rent their own quarters, living room, master bedroom, full kitchen, and private bath. It's big enough for either one or two couples. Inquire also about their beautiful three-bedroom home, often available for rental, in Lanikai on the island of Oahu, a block from the beach.

Reservations: Contact Rusty and Frank Kunz, 1332 Mokolea Dr., Kailua, HI 96734; or phone the number above on Maui, or 808/263-4546 on Oahu.

SILVER CLOUD UPCOUNTRY RANCH, Old Thompson Rd., R.R. 2, Box 201, Kula, Maui, HI 96790. Tel. 808/878-6101. 8 rms and studios, 3 suites, 1 cottage.
$ Rates (including breakfast): $75–$95 rooms and studios for two; $125 suite; $135 cottage. No credit cards.

Bordered by a fragrant eucalyptus forest at an elevation of 2,800 feet in the historic Ulupalakua area, Silver Cloud Ranch is a 9-acre plantation (once part of Thompson Ranch, a working cattle ranch founded in 1902), born again as a bed-and-breakfast establishment with a turn-of-the-century charm and elegance. Each beautifully furnished accommodation has its own private bathroom; most have private lanais and entrances; and the Paniolo Bunkhouse's roomy studios all offer kitchenettes and lanais with views of either the Pacific or Haleakala Crater. The Haleakala Suite in the Paniolo Bunkhouse has both these views, its own bedroom and living room with fireplace, and a complete kitchen. For total privacy, there's the Lanai Cottage, with a complete kitchen, spacious bathroom with a clawfooted red bathtub, a main room with a wood-burning stove, and a private lanai surrounded by flower gardens. All guests have use of the main house and kitchen. Loverly.

Note: The entire property can be rented for groups and seminars.

OFF HANA ROAD

BAMBOO MOUNTAIN SANCTUARY, 911 Kaupakalua Rd., Haiku, Maui, HI 96708. Tel. 808/572-5106. 5 rms (3 with bath).

$ Rates (including breakfast): $55 single; $75 double; seventh day free. No credit cards. **Parking:** Free.

Once it was the old Maui Zendo, a Japanese monastery. Now this mountainside plantation house is a bed-and-breakfast establishment, but it still has an air of retreat about it. It's on the same grounds as Akahi Farms, one of the islands' primary New Age retreat and conference centers. If you're attending a workshop at Akahi Farms, you may want to stay here for a few days before or after. Or just come to the place itself, enjoy the peace and quiet, the wonderful grounds, with hiking trails, a natural swimming hole in the gulch, waterfalls. Built over 50 years ago, with huge octagonal windows that overlook the ocean, the house has five bedrooms, each with a queen-size or double futon on a frame, Japanese artwork on the walls. Some have private baths; all share the shower. There's a very large communal area and a deck where breakfast—including papayas from their own trees and bananas from their own banana plantation—is served.

HAIKULEANA, 555 Haiku Rd., Haiku, Maui, HI 96708-9607. Tel. 808/575-2890. 4 rms.

$ Rates (including breakfast): $65 single; $80 double. Discounts on stays of 5 days or more. No credit cards. **Parking:** Free.

This charming old house is set amid 1½ acres of garden with fruit trees and flowers. It was built around 1870 for a doctor from Scotland, but has been refurbished and tastefully decorated in country style with some antiques, tropical period pieces, and comforters on the beds. The house still has its original, 12-foot, open-beam ceilings. Owner Dr. Frederick Fox, Jr., has four nicely decorated guest rooms, two with queen-size beds, two with twin beds, each with its own private bath. Television is available. A full breakfast is served, with Hawaiian seasonal fruits and freshly baked breads. Not suitable for children under 6 or for pets; smoking is not allowed indoors. Haikuleana is 15 minutes from the airport and shopping centers, centrally located en route to Hana and Haleakala, and just 2 miles from Hookipa Beach, famous for windsurfing, as well as close to secluded coves for snorkeling and scuba diving.

READERS RECOMMEND

Haikuleana. "Dr. Fox was a charming and gracious host and did everything possible to make our stay a wonderful experience. His home was beautifully and comfortably decorated with large windows overlooking a wonderful yard. His breakfasts were elegantly served and delicious. The weather in Haiku was much nicer and cooler than on the Lahaina side of the island. When we woke at 4am to climb Haleakala Crater he located us jackets, gloves, and blankets to keep ourselves warm. He made sure we had fresh coffee and tea before we left and gave us some fruit and cans of juice to take with us on our early morning hike."—Cheri Sakai, no address given.

HALFWAY TO HANA HOUSE, 100 Waipio Rd. (P.O. Box 675). Haiku, Maui, HI 96708. Tel./fax 808/572-1176. 1 studio.
$ Rates (including breakfast): $55 single; $65 double. Minimum stay 2 nights. No credit cards. **Parking:** Free.
A 20-minute drive from Paia town on the Hana road, Gail Pickholz's cozy private studio has a spectacular location with a 180° wraparound ocean view. The studio has a double bed, a mini-kitchen, a private bath and entrance, and a breakfast patio that looks through a green valley to the ocean. There are bamboo groves, palm trees, citrus and papaya orchids, a pineapple field, tropical flowers, herb gardens, and a lily pond. Freshwater pools and waterfalls are a half mile away. Gail, who has lived on Maui for 26 years, delights in graceful touches like chocolate-covered macadamia nuts on the pillow and dazzling arrangements of tropical fruit at breakfast. She's helpful with restaurant and adventure tips, and may even invite you to go snorkeling with her on a Sunday morning.

HUELO POINT FLOWER FARM B&B, P.O. Box 1195, Paia, Maui, HI 96779. Tel. 808/572-1850. 1 cottage.
$ Rates: $85 single; $95 double. No credit cards. **Parking:** Free.
This is surely one of the most spectacular—and romantic—B&Bs in Hawaii, a great favorite with honeymoon couples. The glass-walled gazebo sits atop a 300-foot cliff overlooking Waipio Bay: From the patio where you have breakfast, you can often watch whales and dolphins at play. Close by are waterfalls and natural pools for swimming, and right on the property is a dramatic natural swimming pool with a waterfall, plus an oceanfront hot tub. The gazebo has a queen-size koa-wood captain's bed, two wicker chairs, a dining table and chairs, a CD player with stereo, and a private half-bath with a sheltered outside shower; cooking facilities include a hot plate, small refrigerator, microwave, toaster oven, and basic dishes. Guy and Doug, the hosts, live in a spectacular executive house on the property (also available for rental by the week at $1,850) and grow tropical flowers and organic fruits and vegetables on their 2-acre retreat; guests are welcome to pick whatever they like. Although this is an isolated, jungle valley, you can drive to restaurants and shops in Paia or Makawao in 20 minutes, to the airport in 35.

READERS RECOMMEND

Huelo Point Flower Farm B&B. *"You really outdid yourselves on this find. A more spectacular spot couldn't be found for this very unusual B&B. Guy and Doug couldn't have been nicer. Because it rains on this side of the island, one gets a very different perspective than one would staying in a condo on the southern part of the island. The gazebo has three walls of sliding glass doors and one wall of sliding mirror doors that hide the bathroom and kitchen stuff. Guy and Doug took us to some private pools that cascaded down the mountain to the sea—breathtaking. I kept saying, 'This can't be real!'"*—Beverly Carr, Toronto, Canada.

MALUHIA HALE, P.O. Box 687, Haiku, Maui, HI 96798. Tel. 808/572-2959. 2 one-bedroom units.
$ Rates: $60 single; $70 double; $80 triple. No credit cards. **Parking:** Free.
Here's a way to experience upcountry Maui in peace and privacy. The home of Diana Garrett and Robert Luyken sits on the crest of a sloping meadow looking up at the peaks of Haleakala and down to a sweeping view of the ocean; from it, one can walk to freshwater pools and waterfalls, or drive to Hookipa beach and Paia

town in 15 to 20 minutes. Diana and Robert have built a cottage on their grounds, which have been planted with flowers, tropical plants, banana and papaya trees. Each side of the cottage is a complete one-bedroom apartment, nicely furnished with antiques and found objects; each has its own living room, bedroom, and cozy private screened lanai for indoor-outdoor relaxation. Two or three people can be accommodated comfortably. Diana stocks the kitchenettes with coffee, tea, fruit, and muffins to start guests off for the first day or two.

PILIALOHA, 2512 Kaupakalua Rd., Haiku, Maui, HI 96708. Tel. 808/572-1440. Fax 808/572-4612. 1 cottage. TV TEL

$ Rates (including breakfast): $85 for two. Each additional person $10 extra. Minimum stay 2 nights. Seventh day free on weekly stay. No credit cards. **Parking:** Free.

A dollhouse of a bed-and-breakfast cottage sits in these cool upcountry lands, next door to the home of Bill and Machiko Heyde, a young couple who aim to treat their guests as friends (*pilialoha* means "friendship" in Hawaiian). Lovingly decorated, and with a little garden out front, it's a cozy retreat, ideal for two, but able to sleep up to six, what with its queen-size bed in the bedroom, a twin bed in an adjoining room, a queen-size sofa bed in the living room, and futons in the closet. There's a full kitchen in which to cook your own meals, and Machiko puts out teas and coffees, fresh tropical fruits, and home-baked pastries, breads, and muffins every morning. The cable TV has its own VCR. There's a washer-dryer, ironing board and iron, plus beach chairs, mats, snorkeling equipment to borrow—everything you need for easy vacation living.

TEA HOUSE COTTAGE BED AND BREAKFAST, P.O. Box 335, Haiku, Maui, HI 96708. Tel. 808/572-5610. 1 cottage.

$ Rates (including breakfast the first morning): $65 single; $75 double. No credit cards. **Parking:** Free.

You park your car and follow a tree-lined path to the front door. The cottage sits in the midst of a tropical garden filled with flowering plants, bananas, and palm trees. The picturesque screened lanai leads to a charming living room and bedroom filled with antiques and Oriental rugs; there's a small kitchen area, adequate for light cooking, in the living room. A deck leads to a private bathhouse. No electrical poles mar the landscape; an alternative energy system provides the utilities and phone. You can take long scenic walks by day, stroll along moonlit paths by night, and listen to the sounds of the surf pounding the cliffs. Does this sound like the ultimate retreat from civilization? It is, and it's located in Haiku, a mile off Hana Highway (18 miles east of Kahului), going toward the ocean. Ann DeWeese, an artist whose studio is on the premises, is the proprietor, and she makes the cottage available to guests who can appreciate the simple life. She provides fresh fruits, home-baked breads, and very good coffee and teas for breakfast the first morning. Smoking is permitted outdoors only.

WAIPIO BAY LOOKOUT LODGING, P.O. Box 1095, Haiku, Maui, HI 96708. Tel. 808/572-4530. 2 rms, 1 cottage.

$ Rates (including continental breakfast): $85 double, $125 cottage for up to four. No credit cards. **Parking:** Free.

The location's the thing at Waipio Bay Lookout. It's hard to believe that this secluded, 2-acre estate is just 30 minutes from Kahului Airport on the way to Hana. The setting—at the end of the road in Huelo—is truly spectacular. Set high on a 300-foot cliff on Maui's ruggedly magnificent north shore, the house often affords views of spinner dolphins "performing" right in Waipio Bay, according to host Jon Henderson.

The rooms in the main residence are on either end of the very large house, ensuring maximum privacy for guests as well as the owners. The rooms are pleasantly furnished with white wicker, have private baths, big closets, microwaves, toaster ovens, coffee makers, and small refrigerators. The separate 1,600-square-foot cottage has two bedrooms (one with a queen-size bed, the other with two twins), a full kitchen, bath, laundry facilities, television, VCR, and stereo system. Open beam ceilings, glass all the way around, and a big deck allow visitors to experience the magical views from just about anywhere. The landscaping is densely tropical. There's a wonderful swimming pool and Jacuzzi on a patio leading to the cliff's edge.

MAKAWAO & OLINDA

Makawao is Maui's own little cowboy town, fast turning into a mecca for city dwellers in search of the rural life. Beyond it, Olinda is even more peaceful, a true end-of-the-road retreat.

MCKAY COUNTRY COTTAGE, 536 Olinda Rd., Makawao, Maui, HI 96768. Tel. 808/572-1453. Fax 808/572-1453. 1 cottage. TV TEL
$ Rates (including breakfast): $95 cottage for two. Each additional person $15 extra. Minimum stay 2 days. No credit cards. **Parking:** Free.

⭐ Five miles up the hill from Makawao, on a country road that winds through a forest of 150-foot-tall blue-gum eucalyptus trees, lies the village of Olinda; and it's here, at the top of Olinda Road, at a 4,000-foot elevation, that lucky travelers will find one of the nicest cottages and B&Bs on Maui. McKay Country Cottage sits amid a 12-acre protea farm with its own driveway, a short distance from the home of Shaun and Stewart McKay. Shaun, a member of the noted Baldwin family, among Maui's missionary founders, and Stewart, a painter and decorator from Scotland, are very special hosts, indeed; their warmth and graciousness are evident everywhere on the property. They've furnished the cottage handsomely with original art by Maui artists, protea from their garden, lace curtains, a king-size bed in the bedroom, a queen-size pullout sofa in the living room (the beds sleep four adults, and futons are available for the kids), a full kitchen, and a working fireplace with enough wood for cool mountain nights. What fun to sit on the cushioned window seats, or out on the deck, and gaze at central Maui and the famed Hookipa windsurfing beach far below! First-day breakfast supplies are left in the refrigerator for you.

READERS RECOMMEND

Poli Poli Springs State Park. *"Your readers may be interested in hearing about the cabin at Poli Poli Springs State Park, on the slopes of Haleakala at 6,472 feet. The cabin is in a heavily wooded camping area—there are even redwoods—and the view, of central and western Maui, as well as Molokai and Lanai, is outstanding. The park is crisscrossed with miles of hiking trails, some of which lead to Haleakala Crater. The cabin has three bedrooms and will sleep up to 12. There is some furniture, a wood heating stove, a gas cooking range, complete cooking utensils, and bedding. There is no electricity. For information and reservations, write or call the State Department of Land and Natural Resources, Division of State Parks, 54 S. High St., Wailuku, Maui, HI 96793 (tel. 808/243-5354)."*—Roberta Rosen, Long Beach, Calif. [*Authors' Note:* Charges are $14 for two people, $19.50 for three, $24 for four; half-price for children under 12. A campground for tent camping is also available, free of charge; reservations are required.]

HANA

Since Hana is one of the more remote, untouched areas on all Maui (in all Hawaii, in fact), you might well want to spend a few days here just relaxing far away from civilization. Happily, the number of reasonably priced accommodations is growing.

RENTAL AGENCIES

Manager Stan Collins of **Hana Bay Vacation Rentals,** P.O. Box 318, Hana, Maui, HI 96713 (tel. 808/248-7727, or toll free 800/959-7727), rents a dozen properties scattered throughout the Hana area, with a wide variety of locations, including on the beach, in and out of town, plus some in very secluded and private places. He offers apartments, cabins, and homes, with either one, two, or three bedrooms, with ocean and mountain views. All are fully equipped with the essentials for comfortable vacation living. They can accommodate as few as 1, as many as 15 in a group, at prices ranging from $65 to $200 per night for two people, plus $10 to $25 for each additional person. Each cabin and home is private, and all have full kitchens, telephones, and cable TVs. A half-million-dollar home sleeps six, at rates of $200 per night, 3-day minimum. Stan can also arrange car rentals in Hana if you decide to fly direct; he will have you picked up at the airport.

Sina Fournier is the rental agent for **Hana Alii Holidays,** P.O. Box 536, Hana, Maui, HI 96713 (tel. 808/248-7742, or toll free 800/548-0478), and she has a number of options for Hana vacationers, starting at $60 a night for a studio with private bath, to oceanfront and other cottages ranging in price from $70 a night, all the way up to $225 for a large house with swimming pool and spa. Accommodations also include condominium apartments at the Hana Kai-Maui Resort (see below), which begin at $85 per night. Contact Sina Fournier or her son, Duke Walls, and they will try to find the right setup for you. Many accommodations are within walking distance of the beach: Some of the houses are directly on Hana Bay.

DOUBLES FOR UNDER $20

WAIANAPANAPA STATE PARK. 12 cabins.
$ Rates: $14 for two in a two-room cabin, $19.50 for three, $24 for four, half-price for children under 12; tent camping free. Maximum stay in cabins 5 nights. No credit cards. **Parking:** Free.

The most inexpensive accommodations in Hana are available courtesy of the Division of State Parks. These are the housekeeping cabins in this state park, a few trails away from a black sand beach. Local families like to come here to escape from civilization. The attractive bungalows are snuggled among the pandanus trees, some overlooking the ocean, and are supplied with bedding, towels, cooking utensils, dishes, electricity, and plenty of hot water. The only drawback may be mosquitoes; a reader who spent a hot August week here advised taking insect spray and repellent. Each two-room cabin has its own lanai and accommodates six people. Tent campers can use the campground free of charge, but reservations are required.

Reservations: Contact the Department of Land and Natural Resources, Division of State Parks, 54 S. High St., Wailuku, Maui, HI 96793 (tel. 808/243-5354), 6 months to a year in advance as this idyllic spot continues to grow in popularity.

DOUBLES FOR $55

ALOHA COTTAGES, 73 Keawa Place (P.O. Box 205), Hana, Maui, HI 96713. Tel. 808/248-8420. 5 cottages.
$ Rates: $55–$85 cottage for two. Each additional person $10–$20 extra. No credit cards. **Parking:** Free.

Located conveniently close to Hana Bay and the stores are these pleasant redwood cottages managed by Mrs. F. Nakamura. Each cottage has either two or three bedrooms (queen-size or twin beds), a living room, complete kitchen, and one or two bathrooms. And each has a view of Hana Bay or Kauiki Head. These older, plain cottages are clean, well ventilated, and comfortably furnished. All necessities are provided, including daily cleaning service. Three cottages have TVs.

DOUBLES FOR $80 TO $120

EKENA, P.O. Box 728, Hana, Maui, HI 96713. Tel. 808/248-7047. 2 self-contained units: downstairs rents as either a one- or two-bedroom/one-bath unit; upstairs rents as a two-bedroom/two and a half-bath unit.

$ Rates: Downstairs: $120 for two, $130 for three, one bedroom. $165 for up to four, $10 extra per person to a maximum of six, two bedrooms. Upstairs: $175 for two, $275 for three or four, $300 for five or six for two bedrooms. Both units: $400 for four bedrooms, four and one half baths, maximum of 10 people. Minimum stay three days (Dec 21–Dec 31, five days). No children under 14. No credit cards. **Parking:** Free.

If you're traveling as a family or group and looking for total relaxation in the peace and quiet of Hana, Ekena could be the place for you. This spacious, expansive home (more than 500 square feet) is beautifully decorated, completely furnished, and equipped right down to the cable TV, VCR, CD player, washer and dryer, place settings for 10 in each unit, beach mats, and coolers. The bedrooms are huge and so are the closets. The house and the grounds, with lots of fruit trees and tropical flowers, are impeccably maintained. It sits on nine acres, high on a hill, and it truly offers a 360° view of the ocean, coastline, and the green, green, green of the Hana district. There are wraparound decks from which to enjoy them.

These little extras make Ekena a special place: lots of fresh flowers, a chilled bottle of champagne for honeymooners. Hostess Robin Gaffney was born and raised in Hawaii and has lived in Hana for many years. She is as knowledgeable as she is helpful.

HANA KAI-MAUI RESORT CONDOMINIUMS, 1533 Uakea Rd. (P.O Box 38), Hana, Maui, HI 96713. Tel. 808/248-8426, or toll free 800/346-2772. Fax 808/248-7482. 12 apts.

$ Rates: $110 studio for two; $125 one-bedroom apt for two (third and fourth persons $10 each). 20% off on stay of 5 or more nights. Children under 8 stay free with parents; senior citizen discount 10%. MC, V. **Parking:** Free.

For first-class studio and one-bedroom apartments where you can prepare your own meals (almost a necessity in Hana, where there are very few eating places), this resort, right on Hana Bay, is a fine choice. The two low-rise condo units are located by the ocean on lush, tropical grounds. Studios include a bath with tub/shower combination, dressing vanity, well-equipped kitchen, and private lanai—a spacious open deck where you can enjoy the ocean just a few feet away. Pluses include a large patio area a few steps away from the beach, with gas barbecues, Ping-Pong, shuffleboard, horseshoes, daily maid service. The beach is better for surfers than swimmers, but good swimming beaches are within an easy drive. From December to May, you can watch great humpback whales from your private lanai.

ORIGINAL HANA PLANTATION HOUSES, P.O. Box 249, Hana, Maui, HI 96713. Tel. 808/248-7049, or 808/248-7365, or toll free 800/228-HANA. Fax 808/248-8240. 11 studios and houses.

$ Rates: From $80 for a small studio to $160 for a two-bedroom/two-bath black-sand beach house. AE, CB, DC, MC. V. **Parking:** Free.

Blair Shurtleff and Tom Nunn aim to provide their guests with "a vacation that will leave you feeling rejuvenated and thoroughly relaxed." "We're sure they succeed, for just contemplating the lovely custom homes they've created for visitors is relaxing in itself. The main compound, on five superbly landscaped acres abloom with ginger, heliconia, banana, and papaya (which guests are welcome to pick), includes a Japanese-style studio for two at $80, and a Japanese/Balinese-style two-bedroom cottage for four at $110.

A few miles away, near Hana Bay and picturesque beaches, is a two-story plantation house with two accommodations (upstairs, for four people, $140; downstairs, for two people, $100), and a superb solar-powered beach house for four, for $160 (with annex for two, $195). Amenities are plentiful. There are Jacuzzis indoors and out. Each house has its own kitchen and even its own coffee grinder. Hosts Blair and Tom are always on hand to advise guests on activities and to help them meet the people of Hana. They can set you up with anything from a hot tub spa to air tours to professional massage therapy. A 3-minute walk from the main compound is a secluded, natural spring- and ocean-fed pool, surrounded by lush, tropical plants. The ocean is a few steps away, and beautiful Hamoa Beach is less than a mile away. Waterfalls and jungle trails abound.

Note: Blair and Tom also have two lovely beachfront condominium units available in Molokai, at the Kaluakoi Resort (see "Where to Stay," in Chapter 16).

3. WHERE TO EAT

KAHULUI

Near the airport and around the big shopping centers across the way from the hotels—the Kahului Shopping Center, the Maui Mall, and the Kaahumanu Shopping Center—are almost a dozen places that are fine for a modest meal.

MARCO'S GRILL & BAR, 444 Hana Hwy., corner of Dairy Rd. Tel. 877-4446.

    Cuisine: ITALIAN. **Reservations:** Not required.

$ Prices: Appetizers $5.95–$7.95; main courses $10.50–$19.95. MC, V.

    Open: Breakfast Mon–Fri 7am–10:45am, Sat–Sun 7am–1pm; lunch/dinner 10:45am–10pm.

Whether you're shopping in Kahului, on your way to or from Hana, even going to or from the airport, Marco's is a convenient and tasty choice. Marco's became popular fast, especially with the local folks who work in town, which is always an endorsement of both food and service.

The authentic Italian flavors of this place are present even at breakfast in the form of specialties like the shrimp and eggplant omelet ($8.95). Marco DeSantis, who owns and operates the restaurant with his wife, Debbie, learned to cook at the elbow of an Italian grandmother in his native Philadelphia. He is also an experienced butcher, so if you enjoy meat, you won't go wrong here.

The salads are particularly excellent and many are available in half-orders which are as large as full orders in many other places. The Italian antipasto is a favorite and a half-order is just $5.95. Other salads and cold sandwiches range in price from $4.95 to $9.95. Hot sandwiches (the meatball is delicious) are priced from $5.95 to $10.95 for New York steak. We like the hot and tangy deep-fried mozzarella marinara among the appetizers and the pasta penne in spicy tomato sauce with ricotta cheese among the pastas—there are many to choose from, with a variety of sauces. Many of the desserts here are made by well-known Maui pastry chef Roy Stilwell (with the Kea Lani Hotel at this writing). Some think he's the best on the island, so save room for a slice of cheesecake or dense, rich chocolate cake.

MAUI BEACH HOTEL. Tel. 877-0051.

    Cuisine: ASIAN BUFFET. **Reservations:** Not required.

$ Prices: Buffet lunch $11 (including tax and tip) for all you can eat. AE, DC, MC, V.

    Open: Lunch only, daily 11am–2pm.

If you like buffet meals as much as we do, then you should know about the Rainbow buffet lunch served in the pretty Rainbow Dining Room and pool terrace. Locals like it because it includes many Asian dishes not usually seen on buffet meals: We ourselves are partial to the tsukemono (pickled-vegetable salad) and kamaboku (fish cakes). Also there for the taking—and still more taking—are those delicious Kula onions, Maui potato chips, lots of greens, rice, two hot main courses daily (fish, chicken, or a beef item, plus a noodle dish), soup, and cakes baked daily by the hotel's own bakery shop.

Now, if you're in this area in the evening, visit the Red Dragon Room of the same Maui Beach Hotel, which serves an All You Can Eat Chinese Buffet, 10 courses that include such favorites as shrimp Canton, ginger chicken, sweet and sour pork, priced very reasonably at $12.95. It is on Wednesday through Sunday, from 5:30 to 8pm. On Friday night only, from 5:30 to 8:30pm, the Rainbow Dining Room offers an all-you-can-eat prime rib, sautéed fish, and pasta buffet for $16.95. The Maui Palms hotel next door (under the same management) serves the Imperial Teppanyaki Dinner Buffet every night from 5:30 to 8pm, for $16.95. This is our favorite of the three: it's an incredible assortment of such delights as sweet potato tempura, yakitori chicken, teriyaki steak, local fish, salads, and much more. Reservations requested at all three evening buffets: 877-0051.

MING YUEN, 162 Alamaha St. Tel. 871-7787.
   Cuisine: CHINESE. **Reservations:** Recommended.
$ Prices: Appetizers $4.50–$7; main courses $5.95–$10.25. DISC, MC, V.
   Open: Lunch Mon–Sat 11am–5pm; dinner daily 5–9pm.

Attractive, moderately priced Chinese restaurants are hard to find on Maui, so praise be for Ming Yuen in the Kahului Light Industrial Park, off Hi. 380, recently chosen by readers of the *Maui News* as the best Chinese restaurant of the year. The food here just gets better all the time, and the service, by many longtime employees, provides a "family feeling." The specials here are authentic Cantonese and the spicier Szechuan cuisine. We always like to start off with crispy wonton and Chinese spring rolls. The menu offers a very wide choice—Mongolian beef, lemon chicken, moo shu pork (a personal favorite), and scallops with black-bean sauce. Vegetarians can have a field day here; there are at least 15 vegetarian specialties, including silken tofu with black bean sauce, mock sweet and sour pork with seitan, and minced mock squab with high fiber tofu. Desserts here are a little different; we like the Mandarin or chocolate mousse. Should you happen to be on Maui during Chinese New Year in February, don't miss their 10-course banquet, complete with firecrackers. Fabulous! Even if it's not New Year's, all you need is a party of eight people and you can enjoy a splendid banquet anytime, starting at about $13 a person.

MAUI MALL

Meals for Less Than $10

In addition to the restaurants listed below, you should know about the following. **Restaurant Matsu** serves fast and delicious Japanese-local-style food at very inexpensive prices. They're famous for their California rolls ($4.50); sushi starts at $1.20; and there's a plate-lunch special each day for just $5 (pork ginger teriyaki, miso pork, broiled akule [a local fish]). Right next door is **Siu's Chinese Kitchen**. Go through the cafeteria-style line for Chinese combination plates. Rice or noodles and one dish is just $4.10; two items are $4.49; three are $5.49. Beef broccoli, ginger chicken, lemon chicken are typical choices. The dry mein is good, too. And if your taste leans in a more "Western" direction, try **SW Barbecue** for local-style, barbecue plate lunches, hamburgers, and sandwiches. **Harvest House**, inside the Woolworth's store, has sandwiches, snacks, and plate lunches, too. **Classic Ice Cream & Cookies** serves sandwiches, soup, and snacks along with their assortment of cookies and ice creams. And if you're a real adventurer, you'll want to try **Tasaka Guri Guri**. There's no way to adequately describe the frozen dessert enjoyed by local folk of all ages, but the best way we've come up with is a cross between sherbet and tapioca. Here it comes in pineapple and strawberry flavors, it's made fresh every day, and sells out every day. Henry Tasaka now operates this business, which was started by his great-grandfather more than 70 years ago! There's also a big, bright **IHOP** at Maui Mall serving the same familiar breakfast, lunch, and dinner items as those on the mainland with the addition of little local touches such as sticky rice and Portuguese sausage

SIR WILFRED'S ESPRESSO CAFFE, Maui Mall, 355 Kamehameha Ave. Tel. 877-3711.

   Cuisine: GOURMET DELI/VEGETARIAN.

$ **Prices:** Main courses $2.95–$6.95. AE, DC, MC, V.

   Open: Mon–Thurs 9am–6pm; Fri 9am–9pm, Sat 9am–5:30pm, Sun 11am–5pm.

     The front area of Sir Wilfred's Coffee, Tea, Tobacco is the Espresso Caffè which serves breakfasts and light lunches, soups, home-baked croissants, and fine wines by the glass at good prices. Decorated with island woods and featuring paintings by local artists, it's a very attractive and inviting spot. Prices are low, and the quality of the food, atmosphere, and service is high. Try their breakfast special of "fluffy eggs" (which manage to be just that, with no fats or oils being used), served on a whole-wheat croissant. The talented chef also makes daily pasta specials, a flavorful pesto pasta salad, and unusual Boboli pizza. Cappuccino flavors include chocolate, coconut, almond, mint, and orange. Look for their pastry and coffee bar at the Cannery in Lahaina.

SIZZLER STEAK, SEAFOOD, SALAD RESTAURANT, Maui Mall, 355 Kamehameha Ave. Tel. 871-1120.

   Cuisine: AMERICAN. **Reservations:** Not accepted.

$ **Prices:** Soup/salad/fruit bar $9; main courses $6–$17. AE, DC, MC, V.

   Open: Sun–Thurs 6am–10pm, Fri–Sat 6am–midnight.

When you've seen one Sizzler, you've seen them all. And as far as we're concerned, the more there are in the islands, the better. This one is a beauty, with handsome decor and a large area for lanai dining. The menu has as much seafood and salad as it has steak, so take your choice. On Maui, seafood is an especially good choice; where else can one get the fresh catch of the day—mahimahi, swordfish, ulua—for $7 to $9 at lunch, $11 to $13 at dinner? Add the soup, salad, fresh fruit, pastas and tostada bar for $3.50 more ($4 at dinner) and you've got quite a meal. Lunches run from a fish sandwich at $4 to a steak lunch at $5.40. There are special menus for seniors and children, and great steaks for $8 to $10 for sirloin. Cocktails are available. The weekend Breakfast Bar at $8.99 is another great value.

KAAHUMANU SHOPPING CENTER

Here's a tip for lovers of sushi. Visit the bento (take-out) section at **Shirokiya's,** the Japanese department store at Kaahumanu Mall, order an assortment of sushi for about $4.50 to $6.75 and have yourself a picnic. The food is scrumptious (other Japanese dishes are also available), and the price is about half of what it would cost to have sushi in a restaurant.

Meals for Less Than $12

KOHO GRILL AND BAR, at Kaahumanu Shopping Center. Tel. 877-5588.

   Cuisine: AMERICAN. **Reservations:** Not required.

$ **Prices:** Appetizers $3.25–$5.75; main courses $8.65–$12.95. AE, MC, V.

   Open: Daily 8am–11pm.

     This one's a big local favorite, especially at lunch and before and after the movies. We like it anytime. It's attractively decorated in island style, with paintings by local artists on the walls, the menu is varied, the service excellent, the atmosphere friendly, and the prices certainly right. Burgers are great at lunchtime, and so are the sandwiches, the plate lunches ($4.95 to $5.65), and such international offerings as quiche, fajitas, tacos, and a blackened lemon chicken. Dinner offers pastas, stir-fries, more Cajun dishes, and steak and seafood offerings on the order of char-broiled fresh island catch of the day, pescado Veracruz, or top sirloin. Most main courses are served with salad or soup and a side dish. Come before 11am and treat yourself to one of their terrific omelets. Happy hour, 3 to 6pm, is very popular.

There's another Koho's at the Napili Plaza in Napili, and it's also proving to be a crowd pleaser, with the same menu (except no breakfast) and a casual and upbeat atmosphere. The Sports Bar, with its large screen TV with satellite dish, draws the fans.

SPECIALTY DINING

Lunch/Brunch

CLASS ACT, Maui Community College, 310 Kaahumanu Ave. Tel. 242-1210.
  Cuisine: AMERICAN. **Reservations:** Recommended, and accepted up to 2 weeks in advance.
$ **Prices:** 4-course lunch $9.50. No credit cards.
  Open: Lunch only, Wed and Fri 11am–12:30pm. **Closed:** Mid-May to mid-Sept.

The benefits of higher education can definitely be enjoyed at Class Act. Students in the college's food-service program get a chance to practice their skills; you get a chance to have a four-course gourmet meal for under $10. What a deal! The decor is pleasant enough, with new furniture and drapes, and the food can be excellent. Each week, the cuisine of a different country or region is featured: you may be treated to "A Taste of New Orleans," "A Taste of France," "A Taste of Vietnam," or "A Taste of New England," to mention a few possibilities. Each menu includes a "heart-healthy" selection low in sodium and cholesterol. Yes, there's a catch—lunch is the only meal served, except at the end of each semester, when a $35 gourmet dinner is presented. On Wednesday, half of the students cook and the other half serve; on Friday, they switch. High marks for this one.

Maui Community College also serves a cafeteria lunch from 11am to 12:30pm Monday through Thursday; plate lunch, including soup, is $4; salad and sandwich bar, 30¢ per ounce.

MAUI BAGEL, 201 Dairy Rd. Tel. 871-4825.
  Cuisine: BAGELS/DELI/SANDWICHES.
$ **Prices:** Bagels 50¢; main courses $3–$5.50. No credit cards.
  Open: Mon–Sat 6:30am–5:30pm.

Maui Bagel is an idea whose time has come. It's the only bagel bakery on Maui (there aren't so many bagel bakeries elsewhere in the islands, come to think of it), and it's been doing a thriving business ever since it opened 7 years ago. Since Maui Bagel is near the airport and on your route to Hana or Haleakala, it's a good first—or last—stop on the island, as well as a good spot to get a picnic lunch for your sightseeing trips. It's a cute little place, with blue-and-white café curtains and a warm, friendly atmosphere.

In addition to 11 varieties of bagels, warm from the oven, as well as delicious French, rye, and wheat bread baked daily, and challah on Friday, they also have yummy bakery items (brownies, macaroons, streudel, etc.), plus very good deli selections. So lunch might include a curried chicken salad or lox and bagel, as well as vegetarian items like pesto garlic calzone, or focaccia. There's an excellent selection of salads, meats, and cheese. Call ahead for take-out.

MAUI COFFEE ROASTERS, 444 Hana Hwy. Tel. 877-2877.
  Cuisine: HEALTHFUL AMERICAN. **Reservations:** Not required.

$ Prices: Fresh coffee menu 50¢–$3.90, bakery items $1–$1.95; breakfast $1.70–$7.25; sandwiches/salads $4.50–$7.95. AE, MC, V.
Open: Mon-Fri 7:30am to 6pm; Sat. 8am to 6pm. Sun 8am to 3pm.

You may hear it referred to as "Bean's World" or "Nicky Beans," or even just "Nicky's." It's all the same charming, fun place, serving some of the best coffee drinks you've ever tasted (the coffee is roasted on the premises), along with fresh and delicious fare. "Nicky," by the way, is Nick Matichyn, the proprietor, who's been roasting and selling coffee around these parts for years.

They're big on bagels here—the variety of stuffings include veggie, turkey, and, of course, lox ($1.75 to $7.25). There are turkey ($5.95), "Basmoto" (basil, mozzarella, tomato), and chicken salad ($4.50) sandwiches; Caesar ($5.95) and garden ($4.50) salads for lunch; as well as daily specials and soup of the day. Cake stands filled with goodies line the counter: scones, croissants, muffins, cookies, biscotti, cakes, and more. Three different coffees, five espressos, nine steamed espresso drinks, hot chocolate, iced specialty drinks, and all kinds of teas are served at the counter or at the funky, old tables—all with mismatched chairs that only add to the charm. Many of the beverages are served in whimsical, oversized vessels. We think the Caramel Cappuccino is incredible. Coffee by the pound, mugs, T-shirts, gift items are available for purchase.

If you have the time and the inclination, this is a good place to stop, sit a spell, read the newspaper, and people-watch. There are lots of interesting "regulars."

READERS ADVISE

Don't Drink the Water. *"You can't always be sure that the drinking water is good on Maui, so it's best to buy bottled water. Also, it's not wise to swim where a river mouth empties into the ocean, as sewage or chemicals from the cane fields may dump into the ocean."*—Katherine Flint, Lahaina, Maui.

WAILUKU

If you'd like to sample "local" food, there's no better place than Wailuku, which is a bit off the tourist track (it's the commercial and professional center of the island and the seat of Maui County). Prices are geared for the locals, which means that they're refreshingly low.

If you're in the mood for local color—and flavor—visit **Takamiya Market** on North Market Street. This old-time grocery store has a huge selection of prepared foods to go, like sushi or smoked salmon belly or mahi tempura or whatever, all at small prices. Our local spies tell us they are "outrageous." While you're there, throw in a piece or two of their equally outrageous "lemon booze cake" or "pistachio booze cake" for very good measure.

MEALS FOR LESS THAN $12

CHUMS, 1900 Main St. Tel. 244-1000.
   Cuisine: LOCAL. **Reservations:** Not accepted.
$ Prices: Main courses $4.50–$6.99. MC, V.
   Open: Breakfast Mon–Sat 6:30–10:30am, Sun 7–10am; lunch and dinner Mon–Sat 11am–10:30pm.

Local-style food served in hearty portions at old-fashioned prices, and in gracious surroundings—that's the combination that made Chums a favorite right from the start. The pretty dining room has koa-wood booths, many plants, and old, classic posters on the wall—a great place for "chums" to hang out. And the food is delicious, from the homemade oxtail soup with grated ginger, two scoops of rice and Chinese parsley, practically a meal in itself ($5.99); to the burgers and sandwiches ($4.50 to $5.50); to the island-style plate meals—mahimahi, hamburger steak, roast pork, and the like—all served with vegetables and macaroni salad plus a choice of rice or potatoes, for $5.10 to $5.99. Breakfast favorites include more island favorites, like fried rice with an egg or Loco Moco—that's a hamburger patty, an egg, rice, and gravy, at $4.65.

Note: There's also a Chums in Kihei, upstairs at Rainbow Mall, 2439 S. Kihei Rd. (tel. 874-9000), open daily and serving the same menu.

MAUI BAKE SHOP & DELI, 2092 Vineyard St. Tel. 242-0064.

   Cuisine: BAKERY/DELI/SANDWICHES. **Reservations:** Not accepted.

$ Prices: Sandwiches and light lunches $1.50–$5.25. No credit cards.

   Open: Mon–Fri 6am–6:30pm, Sat 7am–5pm, Sun 7am–1am.

This is a sophisticated little spot just fine for a lunch or a break while shopping the Wailuku antiques stores. It's nice just for coffee and some of their yummy pastries, but if you want more, try their salads, stuffed chicken, or one of the three soups made fresh every day. There's always a dish for vegetarians. A soup and sandwich lunch is a good deal at $5.50. As for sandwiches, choose turkey, pastrami, ham, or, our favorite, lox and bagel ($4.95).

MAUI BOY RESTAURANT, 2102 Vineyard St. Tel. 244-7243.

   Cuisine: LOCAL. **Reservations:** Not required.

$ Prices: Appetizers $3.75–$6.95; main courses $3.75–$8.95. MC, V.

   Open: Breakfast daily 7–11am; lunch and dinner daily.

Ramshackle outside, but coffeehouse cute inside, Maui Boy is a find. At lunchtime it's mobbed with local professionals and with county office workers. Breakfast is popular too, and filling: three-egg omelets ($3.50 to $5.25) come with a choice of rice or hash browns, plus two dollar-size hotcakes. And we love their french toast, made from Portuguese sweet bread with strawberry or blueberry filling, $3.50. A savvy local friend considers Maui Boy to have the best teriyaki on Maui; we tried their teri ono, potatoes, and macaroni salad, all for $6.95, and delicious. They also have the best Hawaiian plate in town: poi, laulau, lomi-lomi salmon, and kalua pig, all for $7.95 (get it early; they always sell out!). Plate lunches—including roast beef, chicken katsu, teri chicken, Korean short ribs, and mahimahi—all come with rice or whipped potatoes, vegetables, *and* potato macaroni salad, guaranteeing your carbohydrate fix for the day.

SAENG'S THAI CUISINE, 2119 Vineyard St. Tel. 244-1568.

   Cuisine: THAI. **Reservations:** Not required.

$ Prices: Appetizers $4.95–$8.50; main courses $7.50–$9.95. AE, MC, V.

   Open: Lunch Mon–Sat 11am–2:30pm; dinner daily 5–9:30pm.

Another very popular local spot, this is a gardenlike restaurant (one row of tables looks like a gazebo), with tiled floors and lush greenery. Hawaii provides aromatic herbs throughout the year, just as Thailand does, and these are used to advantage in the cooking here. Specialties of the house include kai yang (grilled Cornish hen, marinated with lemongrass and kaffir lime leaves), shrimp asparagus, and cashewnut chicken delight, each $7.25. Vegetarians are well taken care of, with a choice of 16 dishes, including a fairly mild garlic mixed vegetables and a sweet-basil tofu which, if you choose, can be very hot. A typical Thai tapioca pudding as well as an untypical coffee or macadamia-nut mud pie tops off a refreshing meal.

SAM SATO'S, The Mill Yard, 1750 Wili Pa Loop. Tel. 244-7142.

   Cuisine: LOCAL. **Reservations:** Not accepted.

$ Prices: Plates lunches $4.75–$5.

   Open: Mon–Sat 7am–2pm.

Now ensconced in a brand-new building with a dining room seating 50, this old favorite is still your totally local, down-home Wailuku restaurant. It's always filled with local families and office workers happily gobbling up chow tun, wonton soup, plate lunches, or sandwiches. Try their wonton special—it's hearty, delicious, and a complete meal at $4.15. This is the place where you should sample those filled pastries called manju, as Sam Sato's is reputed to have the best on Maui.

SIAM THAI, 123 N. Market St. Tel. 244-3817.

Cuisine: THAI. **Reservations:** Not required.

$ Prices: Appetizers $5.25–$7.50; main courses $5.95–$14.95. AE, MC, V.

Open: Lunch Mon–Fri 11am–2:30pm; dinner daily 5–9:30pm.

A big favorite among the residents of East Maui, this restaurant serves inexpensive, delicious Thai food. It's a pretty place too, typically Asian in decor, with travel posters, plants, a reclining Buddha near a small aquarium. You won't go wrong with the Evil Prince dishes (take your choice of beef, chicken, pork, or vegetables); the meat is sautéed in hot spices with fresh sweet basil and served on a bed of chopped cabbage. Even those who hate eggplant are converted by the eggplant tofu dish; it's sautéed with fresh basil and hot sauce, and available either hot, medium, or mild. Then there's Tofu Delight, tofu and other vegetables sautéed in a special sauce and served over steamed bean sprouts. Thai ginger shrimp sautéed with string beans and ginger, served on cabbage, is another winner.

TOKYO TEI, 1063 E. Lower Main St. Tel. 242-9630.

Cuisine: JAPANESE. **Reservations:** Recommended.

$ Prices: Appetizers $2.75–$12; main courses $5.50–$12. MC. V.

Open: Lunch Mon–Sat 11am–1:30pm; dinner Mon–Sat 5–8:30pm, Sun 5–8pm.

A local favorite: The atmosphere is simple and pleasant, the quality of the food high, and the prices easy to take. Lunch and dinner include rice, miso soup, and pickled vegetables along with such main courses as teriyaki pork, beef sukiyaki, and sashimi. You'll know why the restaurant is famous for its tempura dishes once you bite into the shrimp tempura—four large, flavorful shrimp, served with rice and soup, along with the traditional Japanese accompaniments. And their teishoko combination plates, $8.75 to $9.75, are very popular. This is a nice place for families, as children are treated graciously here.

IN & AROUND PAIA

Paia is one of our favorite little towns—full of seekers from everywhere who've found the natural lifestyle they were looking for in these Hawaiian uplands. Since the area is only a 15–minute drive from Kahului, at the beginning of the road to Hana and just past the cutoff to Hi. 37 (the Haleakala Highway), a visit to the restaurants here can be worked into almost any itinerary.

MEALS FOR LESS THAN $20

THE WUNDERBAR, 89 Hana Hwy. Tel. 579-8808.

Cuisine: EUROPEAN. **Reservations:** Recommended.

$ Prices: Appetizers $5–$10; main courses $12–$25. AE, MC, V.

Open: Breakfast daily 7:30–11:30am; lunch daily 11:30am–2:30pm; pupus and salads daily 2:30–6pm; dinner daily 5–10pm (bar open till 1am).

There's a lively feeling about the Wunderbar Restaurant and Bar. The place is attractive, with a handsome, huge wooden bar, tables made of monkeypod woods, a little garden patio out back. The chef, who has cooked in seven different European countries, brings traditional style plus an island flair to such dishes as wienerschnitzel, beef Stroganoff, Hungarian goulash, and Schweinebraten, the house special: a roast loin of pork with old-fashioned German-style braised red cabbage and parsley potatoes. The house pasta special is something a little different: seafood stewed in plum tomatoes, with garlic, white wine, and fresh dill. Start your meal with half an order of that, perhaps, or with one of the regular soups or appetizers, like the potato-leek soup or the calamari rings with aioli, or a Greek salad. Fresh fish and seafood, a nightly special, are prepared in a variety of styles. By all means, plan your meal with dessert in mind—it would be a shame to miss the likes of homemade Black Forest cherry cake, the ice-cream soufflé Grand Marnier or the Apfelkuechle, baked apple slices in cinnamon sugar, topped with vanilla sauce or ice cream.

There's live music and dancing after 10pm.

WORTH THE EXTRA MONEY

HALIIMAILE GENERAL STORE, 900 Haliimaile Rd., Haliimaile. Tel. 572-2666.

Cuisine: HAWAII REGIONAL. **Reservations:** Recommended for dinner.

$ **Prices:** Appetizers $4–$12; main courses $13–$24. MC, V.

Open: Lunch Mon–Sat 11am–2:30pm; dinner daily 5:30–10pm; brunch Sun 10am–2:30pm.

Folks who live in East Maui and are accustomed to driving long distances for a gourmet meal can't believe their luck, now that this place is firmly established right in their area, in the midst of 1,000 acres of pineapple fields. Owners Beverly and Joe Gannon (Bev also runs a highly successful catering business called Fresh Approach) have created a charming place with superhigh ceilings, walls covered with shelves of lovely pottery and china, great Hawaiian fabric tablecloths. The front dining room is the place in which "to be seen"; the back dining room is more romantic and quiet. A fantastic sushi bar in the back dining room draws crowds on Tuesday and Wednesday evening for the freshest of sushi, prepared by master sushi chefs.

The best time to check out the gourmet touch is at lunch (the restaurant is not far from the road to Haleakala or Hana, so it can fit into one of our excursions), when you can feast on Bev's Boboli (a six-inch pizza topped with her renowned crab dip) for $6. Fresh-from-the-field salads range in price from $4 to $12 for salad Niçoise, which is topped with grilled, fresh ahi. The vegetable torte in puff pastry is almost enough for two ($9); and there are specials every day.

Dinner is a bit pricier, but values are still good, and the food is extraordinary. Our favorite appetizers include the spicy, blackened ahi with cool, creamy potato salad; the grape quesadilla, served hot with a surprising secret pea guacamole, and the incredible sashimi Napoleon: crispy wontons layered with smoked salmon, ahi sashimi, and ahi tartar. Main courses are equally imaginative, among them rack of lamb Hunan style (the best in the islands!), fresh fish prepared three ways each evening, paniolo ribs with a homemade, not-your-usual, barbecue sauce served with fresh vegetables and mashed potatoes like mom used to make; all main courses are served with fresh vegetables, an appropriate starch, and delicious sourdough bread. The pastry chef is a master, so be sure to save room for dessert.

MAMA'S FISH HOUSE, 799 Poho Place at Kuau Cove. Tel. 579-8488.

Cuisine: FRESH FISH/SEAFOOD. **Reservations:** Recommended.

$ **Prices:** Appetizers $5.95–$13.95; main courses $9.95–$37.95. AE, DISC, MC, V.

Open: Lunch daily 11am–2:30pm; drinks and pupus daily 2:30–5pm; dinner daily 5–9:30pm.

Looking for the best fresh fish house on Maui? That one's easy. Mama's wins hands down. A converted beach house underneath the coconut palms leading to the ocean, Mama's has been garnering kudos ever since it opened back in 1973 (the readers of *Honolulu* magazine recently voted it the no. 1 seafood restaurant in Hawaii). "Mama" Doris Christiansen and husband Floyd serve fish fresh from their own boats in a thoroughly romantic setting—tapa ceilings, grass skirts on the wall, Maui memorabilia, vintage photographs—that bespeaks old Hawaii. No wonder it's a favorite with visiting celebrities—you might catch Frank Sinatra, Billy Crystal, or Willie Nelson here. Settle down with a mai tai—they use the original old recipe from Trader Vic's—and contemplate the menu. Choices are so appealing that it's good to come with a few other people and sample. The house salad, sprinkled with finely crumbled smoked fish, is not to be missed; nor is the delicate, wonderfully seasoned smoked fish mousse with capers. Incorporating touches of Pacific Rim cuisine, Mama's uses locally grown produce and herbs from their own garden out back, into a variety of styles of fish preparation. First choose your fish, then the style: It could be stuffed with champagne sauce or bouillabaisse (both on the winter menu), or fish sautéed in white wine and macadamia nuts. The tropically accented fish curry, or the Pua Me Hua Hana, a fish preparation in the style of old Hana, baked with banana and fruit in a fresh young coconut and served with Maui potatoes. Portions are huge, so two of you may want to share one dish; you will not be discouraged from doing so. After treats like this, it's hard to even contemplate dessert, but press on—the likes of key lime chiffon pie from freshly squeezed Kula limes, hot banana crisp à la mode, an award-winning macadamia-nut cheesecake, and homemade banana ice cream await you.

Lunch offers similar dishes with the addition of two terrific sandwiches: a fish salad sandwich of fresh and smoked fish, with Maui avocado and taro chips ($10.95), and a fresh fishburger, with cheese, tomato, and Maui onion ($12.95). A reasonably priced soup-and-salad combination is also offered at lunch.

SPECIALTY DINING

Picnic Fare

PIC-NICS, Baldwin Ave. Tel. 579-8021.
   Cuisine: SANDWICHES/BOX LUNCHES. **Reservations:** Not accepted.
$ **Prices:** Sandwiches $4.50–$5.15; box lunches $7.95–$15.95. No credit cards.
   Open: Daily 7:30am–3pm.

If you need a picnic lunch for your trip to Haleakala or Hana, this is the place to stock up in Paia. Pic-nics, a cheerful, clean Formica-tables-and-benches place, is known all over the area for its sandwiches: especially the spinach-nut burgers, served on whole-wheat sesame buns, and piled high with lettuce, tomato, sprouts, and dressing; they're $4.60 and terrific. They also serve a filet of mahimahi for just $5.15. Everything is delicious, since they use, as much as possible, freshly grown local produce and organically raised island beef. The very popular excursion lunches include sandwiches, Maui potato chips, salads, seasonal fruits, beverages, great muffins, and homemade cookies and desserts, plus many other basket stuffers, and begin at $7.95. No need to call ahead—your order will be prepared quickly. Pic-nics also features cappuccino, freshly baked breakfast pastries, scrambled eggs, and muffins for breakfast while you're waiting for your order.

VEGETARIAN

THE VEGAN RESTAURANT, 115 Baldwin Ave. Tel. 579-9144.
   Cuisine: GOURMET VEGETARIAN. **Reservations:** Not accepted.
$ **Prices:** Main courses $5.95–$8.95. MC, V.
   Open: Lunch and dinner Tues–Sun 11am–8:30pm.

This little place never advertises and has no need to do so; its popularity keeps growing by word of mouth. It's heaven for vegetarians (vegans eat no animal products, including dairy and eggs), since the cooks turn out some delicious dishes, like vegan burgers, organic carrot salads, avocado delights, and organic hummus. There's a fresh selection daily of $8.95 main courses that might include a Thai vegetarian special like pad Thai noodle or Thai curry vegetables, as well as lemon-broiled tempeh, vegetable kugel, enchilada pie, or seitan peppersteak. We like their desserts, too, especially the vanilla cake with cashew frosting and fruit topping and the strawberry shortcake.

PUKALANI, KULA & MAKAWAO

Since there is no food to be had in Haleakala National Park, you might want to eat on your way to or from the crater. We've often found that being at the 10,000–foot altitude of Haleakala can build up quite an appetite.

MEALS FOR LESS THAN $15

CASANOVA ITALIAN RESTAURANT AND DELI, 1188 Makawao Ave., Makawao. Tel. 572-0220.
   Cuisine: ITALIAN. **Reservations:** Recommended at dinner.
$ **Prices:** Restaurant, appetizers $4–$7; main courses $8–$22; pizzas $8.95–$14.50. Deli, most dishes around $5–$6. MC, V.
   Open: Deli, daily 8:30am–7:30pm. Restaurant, lunch Mon–Sat 11am–2pm; dinner Mon–Sat 5–9pm. Bar open to 1am.

⭐ An enjoyable place to eat is in nearby Makawao, a few miles off your route to Haleakala, but worth making a little detour for; turn right at Pukalani. Casanova looks as if it belongs more in Rome or Milan, Bologna or Naples, than it does in cowboy-town Makawao. These cities are, in fact, the homes of the four young partners, all professionals in other fields, whose restaurant has created quite a stir: People come from all over Maui for their fresh pastas and divine pastries; Casanova supplies them to some of the best hotels and restaurants on the island. Casanova has been voted "Best Italian restaurant in Maui" for the last two years by readers of the *Maui News*. There are two parts to the operation. One is the original deli, which serves breakfast, lunch, snacks, and classic Italian dishes in the $5 to $6 range. They have sandwiches with an international flair, such as Paris (Brie with artichoke hearts) and Parma (prosciutto and tomatoes), plus sensational pastries in the $2 to $3 range: lemon-brandy cheesecake and chocolate cheesecake are worthy of bravos, and people drive miles for their tiramisu.

For more relaxed dining, try the restaurant itself. Done in Hawaiian woods with works by local artists on the walls, it's divided into a café and bar on one side and a huge dance floor and stage area on the other, the scene for nightly entertainment and dancing Monday to Thursday, with live music on Friday and Saturday. From the café's huge, wood-fired Italian pizza oven emerge delicious crispy-crusted pizzas with a decidedly imaginative flair, like the Genova (pesto sauce, prawns, and fresh tomato) at $14.95 and the Romana (goat cheese, roasted peppers, thyme, and garlic), $12.95. The organic salads are wondrous, and a huge lunchtime favorite with the local crop of vegetarian and New Age types who live in the area. There are a variety of antipasti (try the carpaccio di salmone—natural smoked salmon topped with sweet onions and Italian capers) and pastas, from $7.50 to $15.50. There's a fresh catch of the day, a fresh veal preparation every day, a tasty chicken breast stuffed with prosciutto and fontina cheese. One of the best items on the menu is the Pesce Intero al Forno, a whole fresh opakapaka (red snapper) baked with fresh herbs and white wine, served on a large tray and enough for two or even three. Save some room, if you can, for the wonderful desserts. Stay around for the dancing and entertainment; some of Hawaii's major performers are featured, and an occasional jazz great from the mainland, too. The $5 cover is waived for dinner.

KULA LODGE, Hi. 377, Kula. Tel. 878-2517 or 800/233-1535.
   Cuisine: HAWAII REGIONAL. **Reservations:** Recommended at dinner.
$ **Prices:** Appetizers $6–$9; main courses $14–$20. MC, V.
   Open: Breakfast daily 6:30–11:30am; lunch daily 11:30am–5pm; dinner daily 5:30–8:30pm.

⭐ The most scenic spot for a meal in this area is on the slopes of Haleakala in the delightful mountain town of Kula. This charming country inn has a real fireplace and a nonpareil view of the West Maui mountains from its 3,200-

foot elevation. Now that the new Garden Terrace is open, offering al fresco dining in an exquisite setting, with specialty baked items from the outdoor wood-burning oven, the place is more attractive than ever. Go ahead, feast at breakfast on their eggs Benedict, served with cottage fries and a rich hollandaise; it's $7.50 and delicious. The "Afternoon Affair" menu, served from 11:30am until closing, represents a new departure for Kula lodge: "Hawaii regional cuisine," using fresh produce grown upcountry, plus homegrown herbs and spices. Start with a steamed, baked, and stuffed Kula artichoke or maybe the rich Kula onion soup, perhaps choose a hot or cold spinach salad or papaya and shrimp salad for a main luncheon course. You could go with sandwiches like the vegetarian macadamia-nut garden burger, the mahimahi, or even a hot pastrami sandwich. Main courses, which include a choice of soup or salad, freshly baked bread, rice or potatoes, and a vegetable, always feature a fresh catch from Maui waters, rack of New Zealand lamb, a boneless breast of chicken stuffed with ricotta cheese and broccoli, and a unique Thai soba noodle dish, with roasted eggplant and snow peas. Homemade desserts change daily.

POLLI'S CANTINA, 1202 Makawao Ave., at the corner of Olinda Rd., Makawao. Tel. 572-7808.

   Cuisine: MEXICAN. **Reservations:** Not accepted.

$ Prices: Appetizers $3–$6.50; main courses $6.50–$15. DC, MC, V.

   Open: Daily 11:30am–10pm; brunch Sun 10:30am–2pm.

This old standby is a cute little place that specializes in "cold beer and hot food." The decor is Mexican, the clientele is local, the music is lively, and the food is very tasty. Taco salad is $6.50; cheese enchiladas, $7.50 for two; a bowl of chili, $4.50. Many vegetarian dishes are available too. We love their desserts, especially the buñuelos: Mexican pastries topped with vanilla ice cream, drizzled hot pure maple syrup, and cinnamon, $3.50. ¡Muy bueno! Happy hour is from 2:30 to 5pm.

READERS RECOMMEND

Kitada's, in *Makawao (tel. 572-7241). "Makawao has our all-time-great cheap eats. At Kitada's, a place where the locals eat, you can get a clean, simple booth, a friendly proprietor, and really good Japanese-style food such as a $3 steak teriyaki lunch plate, including rice and a cucumberlike salad. Sandwiches are around $2. Two of us ate well one lunchtime for a total of $6."*—Loisellin Datta, Bethesda, Md.

SPECIALTY DINING

Breakfast/Lunch

GRANDMA'S COFFEE HOUSE, Hi. 37, Keokea. Tel. 878-2140.

   Cuisine: AMERICAN. **Reservations:** Not accepted.

$ Prices: Main dishes $2–$5.65. No credit cards.

   Open: Mon–Sat 7am–5pm.

This makes a nice stop if you're driving to Tedeschi Vineyards after you come down from the volcano (see Chapter 15). It's a green building right next to the gas station in the tiny town of Keokea. Alfred Franco, a young man whose family has been growing and roasting coffee on Maui since 1918 (you can buy a pound to take home), opened this little mom-and-pop café about 6 years ago. It's always busy, filled with neighborhood people who come for his wife's freshly baked breads, coffee cakes, cinnamon rolls, and such. Sit down, have a sandwich, a bowl of chili or saimin, a salad or a bread pudding or a pineapple coconut square, and some fragrant coffee—perhaps cappuccino or café au lait. Or try one of the changing daily hot plate lunch specials at $4.75. It could be chicken, spareribs, or maybe a Mexican dish. Photos on the wall, café curtains, and antique bottles make for a cozy scene.

UPCOUNTRY CAFE, 7-2 Aewa Place (just off Haleakala Hwy, in the Andrade Building in Pukalani). Tel. 572-2395.
 Cuisine: LOCAL STYLE AMERICAN. **Reservations:** Not taken.
$ Prices: Full breakfast $3.75–$6.25; lunch $4.95–$7.50. No credit cards.
 Open: Mon, Wed–Sat 6:30am–3pm; Sun 6:30am–12 noon. Closed Tues.

⭐ Food like mom made (especially if you grew up in Hawaii), friendly service, and a decor so cute you'll smile your way through your meal—all make the Upcountry Café a very popular little spot. Muffins fresh from the oven, steaming bowls of saimin, and plates piled high with another local favorite—loco moco—are just a sampling of the breakfast items available. Lunchtime brings simple, hearty homemade food: Cobb salad served with homebaked bread ($7.25), sandwiches, a plate lunch special, and fresh soup of the day are all available at very reasonable prices. The place literally teems with black-and-white cows: on T-shirts, aprons, menus, walls, and even salt and pepper shakers. So, it's no surprise that the café's signature dessert is . . . Cowpie—chocolate cream cheese with macadamia nuts in a chocolate cookie crust.

KIHEI

This area has a number of good eating spots for budget-watchers, some in centers or malls. By the time you read this, it should also have A Pacific Café Maui, a local counterpart of Chef Jean-Marie Josselin's famed restaurant on Kauai, a Pacific Café, known for extraordinary Hawaii regional cuisine. The Maui version, which will be located in the Azeka Shopping Center, will focus on a blend of Asian, Indian, and Mediterranean cuisine and will feature a Tandoori Oven. Appetizers will range from about $5.50 to $9.50, main courses from about $15 to $25.

MEALS FOR LESS THAN $10

ALEXANDER'S FISH & CHICKEN & CHIPS, 1913 S. Kihei Rd. Tel. 874-0788.
 Cuisine: AMERICAN. **Reservations:** Not required.
$ Prices: $4.95–$10.95. No credit cards.
 Open: Daily 11am–9pm.

One long-time Kihei resident we know says he eats here at least *five* times a week because he couldn't even prepare fish at home for the price he pays here. For $5.95 you get mahimahi, ono, or ahi—broiled or fried—plus french fries or rice and cole slaw. Or you can choose smoked ribs or chicken instead. "Baskets to go," a 13-piece fish basket, is just $14.95; and oodles of side orders, such as green salad, onion rings, deep-fried mixed veggies or mushrooms, corn bread, french fries and chicken wings, are the perfect answer for condo-dwellers, especially those traveling with their family or in a group. There's indoor and outdoor seating here.

KAI NANI VILLAGE

MEALS FOR LESS THAN $20

THE GREEK BISTRO, in Kai Nani Village. 2511 S. Kihei Rd. Tel. 879-9330.
 Cuisine: CONTINENTAL GRECIAN/MEDITERRANEAN. **Reservations:** Not accepted.
$ Prices: Appetizers $2.95–$6.95; main courses $9.95–$16.95. AE, JCB, MC, V.
 Open: Lunch daily 11am–5pm; dinner daily 5–9:30pm.

⭐ In the rear courtyard of Kai Nani Village, this cute little place has about 18 tables, some of them outside, so it's fun to sit under the blue-and-white striped umbrellas, listen to the Greek music, sip some wine, and pretend you're near the Mediterranean. A new cocktail lounge offers ouzo, Metaxa, cocktails, and tropical drinks. Dinner features "homemade Greek food" on the order of moussaka, lamb shish kebab, spanakopita, and pastitsio (Greek lasagne); it also offers such "bistro specialties" as a chicken-and-mushroom pasta, Mediterranean chicken, and the house specialty, fresh fish Greek style. Everything is nicely done. The lunch menu is similar, but smaller. A lamb gyro sandwich (spiced roast of lamb) served in pita bread makes a tasty dish at either meal for $7.95. For dessert, go with the homemade baklava or the white-chocolate raspberry cheesecake. Lots of readers' letters praise this one.

KIHEI PRIME RIB HOUSE, in Kai Nani Village, 2511 S. Kihei Rd. Tel. 879-1954.
   Cuisine: AMERICAN. **Reservations:** Recommended after 6:30pm.
$ **Prices:** Appetizers $6.95–$8.95; main courses $18.95 and up; Early Bird specials $11.95–$13.95. CB, DC, MC, V.
   Open: Dinner only, daily 5–10pm.
This has long been an island favorite. It's a bit high for our budget, but arrive early—between 5 and 6pm—and enjoy their Early Bird specials: prime rib dinner, Polynesian chicken, or fresh island fish—ahi is the best—for $11.95. Their salad bar, included with all dinners, uses only locally grown fruits and vegetables, and can be enjoyed alone at $11.95. All main courses include salad bar. Oceanview dining and the work of internationally known artists on the walls add to the warmth and charm.

LA BAHIA RESTAURANT & CANTINA, at Kai Nani Village, 2511 S. Kihei Rd. Tel. 875-1007.
   Cuisine: MEXICAN. **Reservations:** Not required.
$ **Prices:** Appetizers $3.95–$6.95; main courses $3.95–$20.95. MC, V.
   Open: Daily 11:30am–10pm. Bar and game room open till 1am.
There's nothing complicated about this place: It's big, noisy, and lively, dominated by a huge bar with live sports events on the giant TV screen. A game room is busy with darts, "football," and pinball machines. But there are a few spots away from the main action where one can dine in relative peace, on food that is good, filling, and inexpensive. Any time of the day one can get grilled fish, chicken, or hamburger sandwiches with special toppings, Caesar salad, a deep seafood basket, fajitas, quesadillas, poquito burritos. From 5 to 10pm daily one can, in addition, order any of the Mexican dinners—and that could include a chimichanga, enchiladas with a variety of stuffings, a Fiesta Bowl (tortilla salad plus grilled chicken, fish, ground or shredded beef), and more. Beans are all done vegetarian style, without lard. Everything is homemade, prepared fresh every day to satisfy those hungry crowds. And the margaritas, at just $1.50 a glass and $4 a liter, go a long way to making this one of the most popular nighttime spots in Kihei.

KEALIA BEACH PLAZA

MARGARITA'S BEACH CANTINA, in Kealia Beach Plaza, 101 N. Kihei Rd. Tel. 879-5275.
   Cuisine: MEXICAN. **Reservations:** Recommended.
$ **Prices:** Appetizers $4.95–$6.95; main courses $6.95–$13.45. AE, DC, MC, V.
   Open: Daily 11:30am–midnight.
Here's one restaurant that really lives up to its name: It's practically *on* the beach, with a huge dining lanai with umbrellaed tables overlooking the water. The inside is pleasant too, with tall, beamed ceilings, wooden tables, straw chairs, tile floors, plants, and piñatas. The lanai is quite a spot for sunset watching, whale watching, people watching, or just sitting in perfect contentment as you sip your margaritas and munch on delicious Mexican food with an island flair: Everything is made from scratch each day. Margarita's Munchies (appetizers) are first-rate, including buffalo wings, south-of-the-border nachos, and sombrero caliente. Combination plates are well priced at $8.95 to $13.95, and fresh fish, and Mexican specials are featured, at

higher prices. Remember the daily 2:30 to 5:30pm Happy Hour; margaritas are 96¢ per glass, $4 per liter.

SPECIALTY DINING

Lunch/Brunch/Buffet

THE NEW YORK DELI, in Dolphin Plaza, 2395 S. Kihei Rd. Tel. 879-1115.
   Cuisine: DELI.
$ Prices: Sandwiches $4.95–$5.95. MC, V.
   Open: Daily 8am–8pm.
Just across the courtyard from Pizza Fresh (see below) is the New York Deli, which should be a must for any homesick New Yorker—they even have a picture of former mayor Ed Koch on the wall. The wonderful bagels air-expressed from the homeland, the hot pastrami and corned-beef-on-rye sandwiches ($4.95), the hot and cold heros, and the pasta and potato salads, sold by the pound, will all soothe the pangs of Manhattan separation anxiety. This is a tiny but sparkly place, with brick floors, red-checkered cloths on all of three tables. Have an espresso or cappuccino and a slice of their New York cheesecake, or pick up your lunch and take off for the beach (you won't miss New York a bit).

PIKAKE BAKERY, 300 Ohukai Rd., in the Kihei Commercial Center (mountainside of Piilani Hwy.). Tel. 879-7295.
   Cuisine: EUROPEAN-STYLE PASTRIES AND UNIQUE BREADS. **Reservations:** Not accepted.
$ Prices: 65¢–$4.25. No credit cards.
   Open: Mon–Fri 7:30am–6pm; Sat 7:30am–5pm.
Although it's a great place to stop for pastry and coffee or a frothy, delicious cappuccino, it's the bread that has made Pikake Bakery famous. Peter Teimorabadi makes special breads worth driving for: Provolone and fresh garlic, red potato and rosemary, sun-dried tomato, kalamata olive, red onion and walnut, jalapeño, and Cheddar cheese and corn are truly memorable. Breads average $4. Peter was corporate pastry chef for Ritz Carlton before he moved to Maui, so you can be sure his assortment of pastries, breakfast Danish, cakes, and individual desserts is wonderful here, too.
   So enthusiastic was the response to Peter's goodies that he and his wife Tina have recently opened a second location at 505 Front St. in Lahaina. In addition to everything available in Kihei, they also offer light lunches of pasta salads or individual quiches, plus a variety of packaged gourmet foods and coffees (tel. 661-5616).

PIZZA FRESH, in Dolphin Plaza, 2395 S. Kihei Rd. Tel. 879-1525.
   Cuisine: PIZZA.
$ Prices: Appetizers $3.95–$4.95; pizzas $6.95–$26.95. No credit cards.
   Open: Daily 3–9pm.
Doug and Georgann Malone, the couple who run Pizza Fresh, came to Maui with a reputation to live up to; their pies had been voted "Best Pizza in Dallas." They may also be the best pizza on Maui. Their motto "We make it, you bake it" means that this is something to take back to your condo rather than eat there. We sampled their Garden Lite pizza—a whole-wheat vegetarian special with a variety of veggies, light on the cheeses, and with a thin crust—quite delicious. Other possibilities include Hawaiian-style (Canadian bacon, pineapple, mushrooms, etc.) and the traditional pies. On Tuesday all pizzas are 40% off (pickup only). They also have very good salads—veggie, Greek, and Caesar. Free delivery in the Kihei, Wailea, and Makena areas. Call-in orders for pickup or delivery are appreciated.
   There's another Pizza Fresh in Makawao, at 1043 Makawao Ave. (tel. 572-2000), and a newer one in Napili (tel. 661-6800).

SAND WITCH, at Sugar Beach, 145 N. Kihei Rd. Tel. 879-3262.
Cuisine: SANDWICHES/SNACKS/SALADS.
$ Prices: Appetizers, $3.95–$5.95; main courses $2.95–$6.95. AE. MC, V.
Open: Daily 11am–11pm.

In addition to turning out great tropical drinks, this cozy beach bar cooks up a variety of hot dogs, pupus, burritos, burgers, and "Sheer Witchery" sandwiches to go with them. Piled high with meats, cheeses, onions, tomatoes grown on Maui, sprouts, and romaine lettuce, they are a meal in themselves. Eat indoors or proceed directly to the beach.

SHAKA SANDWICH & PIZZA, 1295 S. Kihei Rd. (behind Jack in the Box). Tel. 874-0331.
Cuisine: PIZZA AND SUBS. **Reservations:** Not taken.
$ Prices: Pizza $1.50 & up/slice; $12.95 & up/pie. Sandwiches $3.50 & up/small; $7 & up/large. No credit cards.
Open: Mon–Sat 10:30am–9pm.

★ East Coasters in general and New Yorkers in particular seem to search, wherever they travel, for pizza that tastes like their favorite back home. Well, we have a well-traveled friend who moved to Maui from New York more than a decade ago, and who swears that this is the closest she's ever found. This is pretty much the real thing, the kind that droops and drips lots of olive oil onto the wax paper sheet on which it's served. You can add anything you like to your slice for just 25¢ per topping. An 18" cheese pie is $12.95 and you can add any topping to that for $1.75 each. Our friend also delights in the fact that this is the only pizza place on Maui that sets out *big* shakers of oregano, garlic salt, parmesan, and dried chile peppers—just like back home!

Visitors from the South Jersey–Philly area will want to try the Philly cheesesteak sandwich, served on homemade Italian bread. We think it'll bring tears to your eyes—and not just because you've topped it with sweet, luscious fried onions!

And yes, Shaka does deliver—on minimum orders of $10 for just $1 to anywhere in Kihei; $2 Wailea.

STELLA BLUES CAFE & DELI, in Long's Center, 1215 S. Kihei Rd. Tel. 874-3779.
Cuisine: AMERICAN. **Reservations:** Not required.
$ Prices: Complete dinners, $9.95–$14.95. MC, V.
Open: Breakfast Mon–Sat 8–11am, Sun 8am–2pm; lunch daily anytime after 11am; dinner daily 5–9pm.

★ On a hot Kihei day, this crisply air-conditioned place hits the spot. It's spacious, with cool white walls, plants aplenty, vibrant tablecloths under glass, white chairs, and several umbrellaed tables outside. The former owners of the Maui Bagel have created a flavorful menu here, and they make everything from scratch. Crab cakes served over rice pilaf with lemon-chive butter sauce, a quartet of chicken dishes (Cajun chicken, tarragon chicken, chicken parmigiana, and sweet Thai chili chicken), prime rib, baby back ribs, and fish specials are featured every night. And there are lots of imaginative vegetarian specialties on the order of Vegetarian Delight: tomato Provençal, grilled leeks, roasted eggplant, red peppers and garlic, steamed broccoli and snow peas, asparagus and shiitake mushrooms, served hot with sun-dried tomato dressing over a wild rice blend. Dinners come with salad, vegetable, French bread, and a choice of starch. The daytime menu features similarly sophisticated sandwiches, plus such hearty deli sandwiches as the traditional hot corned beef and pastrami. Homemade soups, generous salads (Cobb, Caesar, chicken), and fresh bagels and toppings are also popular. This is a good place to drop in for just coffee or espresso or cappuccino and some homemade pastries and desserts. The East Coast Scramble—two eggs scrambled with Nova Scotia lox and Maui onions, home fries, and a toasted bagel—is a breakfast treat at $7.50.

SUBWAY SALADS AND SANDWICHES, in Kukui Mall, 1819 S. Kihei Rd. Tel. 879-9955.
   Cuisine: SUBS.
$ Prices: 6-inch subs $1.89–$4.29; foot long subs $3.19–$5.99. No credit cards.
   Open: Sun–Thurs 9am–10pm; Fri–Sat 9am–midnight.
If you like to eat sandwiches at any and all hours of the day, you should also know about this branch of the popular Subway chain. At a Subway, you can get hot and cold subs—seafood and crab, roast beef, vegetarian, meatball, steak, and sirloin, to name a few—served on superfresh breads and rolls; you know they're fresh because you can watch them being baked right up front. Free fixings include cheese, onions, lettuce, tomatoes, pickles, peppers, and olives. A dining room has comfortable seating, but it's most fun to take your subs out to the beach. There are half a dozen other Subways on Maui.

WAILEA-MAKENA

Wailea-Makena, just beyond the Kihei area, is Maui's newest resort area and perhaps its most spectacular. The grand hotels here—Four Seasons, Stouffer Wailea Beach Resort, Maui Inter-Continental Wailea, Grand Wailea, and Makena Prince—are all top of the line and very pricey. We've chosen a few places here worth the extra money and a few with surprisingly good buys.

MEALS FOR LESS THAN $25

CAFE KIOWAIT, at the Maui Prince Hotel, 5400 Makena Alanui. Tel. 874-1111.
   Cuisine: HAWAII REGIONAL. **Reservations:** Recommended.
$ Prices: Appetizers $3.95–$8.95; main courses $10.95–$22.95.
   Open: Breakfast/lunch daily 6:30am–2pm; dinner daily 5–9:30pm.
Popular enough at breakfast and at lunchtime, this pleasant café downstairs at the Maui Prince is often overlooked and overshadowed at dinnertime by the Prince Court. But the food here is created by the same brilliant chef Roger Dikon, so it's a great alternative for those who prefer a much more casual atmosphere and a much smaller check—and that's where we come in.
   The Maui onion soup is served in a bread bowl and glazed with mozzarella cheese ($6.95). Add a ginger chicken salad with lychee, papaya pearls, and shrimp chips, and you've got a great dinner for just $14. Main courses include: Café house noodles with slipper lobster, shrimp, and scallops; 12 vegetables from the wok; roasted half chicken with farfalle pasta; and Napoleon of veal scaloppini with eggplant asiago, served with tomato basil garlic linguine. The menu changes often; trust us, everything is delicious.

WORTH THE EXTRA MONEY

CARELLI'S ON THE BEACH, next to the Wailea Oceanfront Hotel, 2890 S. Kihei Rd. Tel. 875–0001.
   Cuisine: ITALIAN. **Reservations:** Not accepted.
$ Prices: Appetizers $8–$14; main courses $15–$30. AE, MC, V.
   Open: Dinner daily 6–10pm; limited late menu daily 10–11pm.
Don't be surprised if you find Donald Trump or Harry Hamlin or Joni Mitchell or some other such luminary dining at Carelli's—it's the hottest spot in the Kihei-Wailea area. The reasons are not hard to find: a magnificent, on-beach location, a sophisticated European ambience, and a superb Italian fine-dining menu. Start with the antipasti—the staff will put together any combination from the seafood bar: The seared Hawaiian ahi is a favorite. Salads have a sophisticated touch: The Caesar is

prepared with Dungeness crab and avocado. Pizza of the day emerges from the Neapolitan wood-burning oven (the day we were there, it was prosciutto with pears and Gorgonzola cheese). Then on to pastas and such house specialties as grilled lamb, cioppino, grilled breast of chicken, and fish of the day, always done with a different and imaginative sauce. Desserts vary daily too, and can be quite special: We like the chocolate-peanut-butter gelato and the tiramisù. There's a $25 minimum at the tables, so if you just want to eat lightly, be seated at Rocco's Mangia Bar, where there is no minimum. And from here you also have a better view of those wonderful stern portraits of Italian family elders that watch over the entranceway.

RAFFLES, in the Stouffer Wailea Beach Resort, 3550 Wailea Alanui. Tel. 879-4900.
   Cuisine: PACIFIC RIM/HAWAII REGIONAL. **Reservations:** Required.
$ **Prices:** Appetizers $7–$15; main courses $22–$32; Sun champagne brunch $32 adults, $16 children 12 and under. AE, DC, DISC, JCB, MC, V.
   Open: Dinner Tues–Sat 6:30–10pm; brunch Sun 9am–2pm.

There's a new look and taste at Stouffer's signature restaurant these days. Named after the famed Raffles of Singapore (where the Singapore Sling was created), and long a bastion of traditional continental cuisine, Raffles, now so pretty with its elegant, airy rooms and verandas, has picked up on the two hottest trends in Hawaiian dining these days: Hawaii regional cuisine, featuring entrées locally grown, and Pacific Rim cuisine, including dishes from Alaska, the mainland West Coast, Australia, and East Asia. The menu changes daily, but there are always selections from both cuisines to mix and match as you choose. Pacific Rim specialties include Alaskan king crab, seafood, lamb from Australia and New Zealand, Seattle oysters, and scallops from Japan. Hawaii regional selections feature locally grown fresh prawns from Kauai and Oahu, venison from Molokai, goat cheese from the Big Island, beef and pasta from Oahu, and fresh fish, seafood, and greens from Maui. The restaurant also grows and uses fresh herbs from its own garden. Desserts, on the order of custard cream crêpes with fresh island fruits and rhubarb coulis, or chestnut and chocolate terrine with lady fingers and rum anglaise, change every day, and are always wonderful.

If you don't get to Raffles for dinner, at least come by for its bountiful Sunday brunch, a Maui classic. It features a sushi bar; seafood bar; roast beef carved to order; omelets made to order; lots of salads, fresh fish, lamb chops; and more. Desserts are sensational.

SEAWATCH RESTAURANT, One Wailea Golf Club Drive (at the Wailea Gold & Orange Courses Clubhouse). Tel. 875-8080.
   Cuisine: ISLAND REGIONAL. **Reservations:** Recommended.
$ **Prices:** Appetizers $4–$8; main courses $18–$24. AE, JCB, MC, V.
   Open: Breakfast/lunch daily 8am–3pm; dinner daily 5:30–10pm; pupus daily 3pm to closing.

The same savvy folks responsible for Koho Grill & Bar in Kahului (see above) and the Plantation House Restaurant in Kapalua (see below) have another winner to boast of. This big, beautiful restaurant on a hill has views of Ulupalakua, Makena, Molokini, Kahoolawe, and the West Maui mountains. You can sit in the main dining room, lovely with its whitewashed wood tables and the light pink and green colors, which are so often associated with Hawaii; in the lounge/grill area with its big-screen TV and stunning murals by Big Island artist Arthur Johnson; or out on the lanai with its teak chairs and tables—comfortable and a bit more casual than in the main dining room. Chef Richard Matsumoto, formerly the chef at the prestigious Raffles in the Stouffer Wailea Beach Resort, is one of the big reasons for SeaWatch's success. Matsumoto is a creative master. He changes the dinner menu regularly, but you will always find fresh fish prepared in interesting ways, perhaps wok-seared with spicy Thai lemongrass and black bean sauce, or kiawe-grilled with wasabe and soy butter sauce. Spicy Szechuan barbecued chicken breast served with macadamia nut–jasmine rice, and the SeaWatch filet mignon pan-seared with Japanese pepper spice and served with a red onion–Zinfandel jam, are just two examples of Chef Richard's culinary creativity. Chinese five-spice crab cakes and crab, avocado, and cucumber rolls are examples of the tempting appetizer selection.

The combined breakfast/lunch menu is extensive, and everything on it is served from 8am to 3pm every day. House specialties include: French toast made with Molokai sweet bread ($5); the Paniolo breakfast of three eggs, toast, two scoops of rice or breakfast potatoes and smoked ham, bacon, or Portuguese sausage ($6.95); the grilled fresh catch sandwich served with ginger-scallion mayonnaise (daily quote); and stir-fried veggies, Oriental style ($7 with chicken, $7.50 with beef tips).

SPECIALTY DINING

Lunch/Brunch/Snacks

MAUI ONION, in the Stouffer Wailea Beach Resort, 3550 Wailea Alanui. Tel. 879-4900.
Cuisine: American.
$ Prices: $7–$12. AE, DC, DISC, JCB, MC, V.
Open: Lunch daily 10am–6pm.

A delightful place to enjoy lunch or a snack, the Maui Onion sits both pool- and oceanside at this lush Wailea resort. Many of the seats are enveloped by a beautiful hanging gardens pavilion. The menu is small but varied, with salads, sandwiches, and light lunches from which to choose. We have a friend who drives from way upcountry just for the onion rings ($5.50) and for the incredible ice-cream smoothies, made with or without alcohol.

PRINCE COURT, at the Maui Prince Hotel, 5400 Makena Alanui. Tel. 874-1111, ext. 5460.
Cuisine: HAWAII REGIONAL. **Reservations:** Recommended.
$ Prices: Sun brunch 10am to 1pm, $29.95 includes champagne. AE, DC, JCB, MC, V.

"Awesome" is the only word we can use to describe this lavish brunch, which somehow gets better each time we visit. We do know it's due in large part to Executive Chef Roger Dikon, whose culinary imagination seems to know no bounds. He is proudest of his "80-square-foot antipasti table," which features vegetarian delights like Kula tomato, avocado and papaya salad, smoked duck with wild rice and grapes, Oriental bean sprout salad, soba noodles with shiitake mushrooms, black bean and corn salad, and more fresh breads and cheeses than you can imagine. But that's really just the beginning! Hawaiian macadamia-nut and banana pancakes with guava, strawberry, lilikoi, and maple syrups; baby lobster tail and caviar omelets; sashimi; smoked seafood; crab legs; shrimp; sliced tropical fruits; miso soup; crispy smoked duck on couscous with roasted peppers and olives, roasted fig sauce, and Ulupalakua oranges; shrimp, scallops, and fish in a coconut curry sauce with kafir lime leaf and basil; an entire table of *hot* and cold desserts; Kona coffee; loose herb teas. And that's just a sampling! What more can we say? Except "Make reservations". . . and bring your camera.

If you really want to splurge, try dinner here. It's expensive, but it's incredible.

LAHAINA

Lahaina is undoubtedly Maui's most enjoyable dining area. It's got everything, from French country bistros to barbecue houses to glamorous oceanside watering spots— and everywhere, the casual mood reflects its easy, relaxed approach to living.

MEALS FOR LESS THAN $10

CHEESEBURGER IN PARADISE, 811 Front St. Tel. 661-4855.
Cuisine: AMERICAN. **Reservations:** Not accepted.
$ Prices: $6–$10. AE, MC, V.
Open: Daily 11am–11pm.

S If it's a great big juicy, gooey burger you crave, this is the place to order it. And at Cheeseburger in Paradise it comes with a side order of ocean in both the downstairs and the upstairs dining rooms. No pretense here. We're talkin' all-American, five-napkin burgers, great onion rings ($4), and ice cold beer. There's also live tropical rock from 4:30 to 11pm, seven days a week. An interesting tidbit: In four short years, Cheeseburger in Paradise became the highest-grossing restaurant—per capita—on Maui. Partners Laren Gartner and Edna Bayliff and their staff serve an average of 1,200 people per day!

SUNRISE CAFE, 693A Front St., at the corner of Market St. Tel. 661-8558.
Cuisine: AMERICAN. **Reservations:** Not accepted.
$ Prices: Sandwiches $3.95; main courses $5–$6. No credit cards.
Open: Daily 6am–9pm.

S Home cooking, low prices, and a very casual atmosphere have made this little place, just across the road from the library (and next door to Lappert's), very popular very quickly. It's shaped like a half circle, with some tables inside and others out on the busy street. There are specials every day, including good vegetarian choices. If you're not feeling too hungry, you could have just a bowl of homemade soup with French bread for $2.95, or a croissant sandwich for $3.50; or quiches, or some luscious pastries from the Bakery, Lahaina's best. Gourmet coffees are featured at the full Espresso bar. Smoothies, freshly squeezed carrot juice, and healthy drinks like spirulina protein are also available for disciplined souls.

THAI CHEF, in the Lahaina Shopping Center. Tel. 667-2814.
Cuisine: THAI. **Reservations:** Recommended.
$ Prices: Appetizers, $2.50–$8; main courses $5.95–$13.95. DC, MC, V.
Open: Lunch Mon–Fri 11am–2:30pm; dinner daily 5–10pm.
The local people praise this cute little restaurant offering Thai specialties in a pleasant setting, with Thai decorations on the walls, lacy curtains, and mauve tablecloths under glass. Tell the waiter if you want your food mild, medium, or hot, so he can help you choose from among salads, soups (we like the chicken soup simmered in coconut milk with ginger at $8.50), a variety of curries, noodles, and such specialty dishes as stuffed chicken wings or sautéed seafood with bean sauce. Vegetarians have a complete menu of their own: appetizers, soups, noodles, and main dishes. Prices are reasonable. No liquor is served, so BYOB.

READERS RECOMMEND

Denny's, in Lahaina Square (tel. 667-7898). "The overall price increase was more obvious on Maui than elsewhere, but we found the Denny's in Lahaina Square to be a treat. The decor is like no other Denny's seen by us across the country; lovely fans in motion, live plants on each table, along with attractive, framed prints and a decorated, vaulted ceiling. And I found a delicious tropical fruit salad served with a choice of sherbet or cottage cheese. What a treat."—Elizabeth Greer, El Cerrito, Calif. [*Authors' Note:* Denny's is open 24 hours daily. There's another excellent Denny's in Kihei, at the Kamaole Shopping Center.]

MEALS FOR LESS THAN $20

ALOHA CANTINA, 839 Front St. Tel. 661-8788.
Cuisine: SOUTHERN CALIFORNIA/MEXICAN. **Reservations:** Not accepted.

$ Prices: $7–$20. AE, MC, V.
Open: Daily 11am–1am.

It looks as if the owners of Cheeseburger in Paradise (see above) have another big winner to their credit. Like the other restaurant, this one has both lower- and upper-deck dining; both locations jut out over the water. It's worth a margarita stop just to check out the incredible decor at Aloha Cantina. A light show dazzles and a simulated hurricane blows through every hour or so. Most popular dish is the Maui fish tacos, made with fresh ono. You get two tacos, rice, and great refried beans for $10.95. Or splurge on the lobster tacos for just $3 more. Fruit margaritas are the bartenders' calling cards; all margaritas are hand-shaken. There's sunset music daily; and you can dance to live bands on Thursday, Friday, and Saturday from 10pm to 1am.

CASA DE MATEO, upstairs at 505 Front St. Tel. 661-6700.
Cuisine: MEXICAN. **Reservations:** Recommended.
$ Prices: Appetizers $5.50–$12.95; main courses $12.50–$15.50. AE, MC, V.
Open: Daily 11:30am–11:30pm.

Maui's been hankering for "real" Mexican food for years and this is definitely it. Owner Mateo Madomi had already opened 13 restaurants around the world, and the moment he saw this location, right over the water, he knew it would be number 14. The restaurant is tastefully decorated: cacti on the tables, hand-carved chairs, hand-painted tables. But that wouldn't be enough to keep residents returning again and again; it's the food that does that.

Mateo is a fanatic about fresh and healthy foods—and you'll thank him for it as soon as you take your first bite. *Everything* is fresh and homemade, including the tortilla chips and the smoky salsa that start your meal (he smokes the jalapeños in his own smoker). Mateo says he doesn't even have a freezer in the restaurant. Guacamole ($5.50 for one person, $9.95 for two) and ceviche ($6.50) are prepared tableside in lava rock bowls. Pollo con chili pacilla (chicken legs topped with mole) and pato con mole verde (duck legs dipped in a sauce made with pumpkin seeds, sesame seeds, chili serrano, sunflower and peanut oils and small green tomatoes) are slow-cooked; the meat literally falls off the bone and melts in your mouth. The cactus for his signature hearts of cactus gratin appetizer comes from Kula; and if your order includes tortillas, you can watch them being made to order—masa, corn, and flour tortillas are all available. Even the margaritas are made with fresh-squeezed local limes only, no syrup. The menu here changes often. We've never been disappointed here, and neither has anyone we know.

CHILI'S GRILL & BAR, in Lahaina Center, 900 Front St. Tel. 661-3665.
Cuisine: AMERICAN/SOUTHWESTERN. **Reservations:** Not accepted.
$ Prices: Appetizers $1.95–$7.45; main courses $5.45–$13.95. AE, CB, DC, DISC, MC, V.
Open: Sun–Thurs 11:30am–10pm, Fri-Sat 11:30am–11pm.

A family restaurant with a dinner-house atmosphere, Chili's is done in southwestern motif, with lots of painted wood, tile floors and table tops, cactus plants, exposed wood ceilings and booths. Cocktails are served in a casual and fun atmosphere; lanai seating is available. The menu is eclectic, with everything from gourmet burgers, baby back ribs, quesadillas, and fajitas to a grilled tuna or shrimp Caesar salad. Among the starters, we like the "Awesome Blossom"—that's whole onion sliced to blossom, and then battered and deep-fried; and for dessert, the frozen Oreo yogurt pie is something a bit different. Kids have their own menu—grilled cheese, hot dogs, chicken, and burgers, served with fries, for $3.95.

COMPADRES MEXICAN BAR & GRILL, at the Lahaina Cannery, 1221 Honoapiilani Hwy. Tel. 661-7189.
Cuisine: MEXICAN. **Reservations:** Not required.
$ Prices: Appetizers $4–$7; main courses $10–$17. AE, MC, V.
Open: Daily 11:30am–10pm (bar open to 1am).

★ The first neighbor island location of Honolulu's popular Compadres Restaurant is a smash hit in Lahaina. And rightfully so, for the same formula—a combination of terrific food, respectable prices, wonderful setting, and an upbeat, fun atmosphere—that made the original Compadres one of Honolulu's "Top 20 Restaurants" is very much in evidence here. The setting is both casual and exotic, with a fountain, an aviary, a garden of greenery, pastel-colored terra-cotta pots, and an array of Mexican artifacts enhancing the indoor-outdoor dining setting. The chefs take their inspiration from the cooking of northern Mexico, Arizona, and California, and strive for food that is wholesome as well as flavorful. They use only the freshest of ingredients, make everything from scratch, and never use lard, so that many dishes are suitable for vegetarians. For the calorie-conscious, they've come up with a number of "Compadres 400" selections, dishes of 400 or fewer calories.

House specialties include chicken, shrimp, and beef fajitas, seafood tacos, mahimahi a la Vera Cruz, arroz con pollo, camarones al mojo de ajo (large gulf shrimp sautéed in fresh lime, white wine, garlic, and butter), and an array of fresh fish preparations. We love the nachos and the queso fundido among the appetizers, the taco split and mud pie among the desserts—not to mention those super margaritas!

Weekend breakfasts, served from 11am on, feature traditional favorites and are great fun.

HARD ROCK CAFE, at Lahaina Center, 900 Front St. Tel. 667-7400.

Cuisine: AMERICAN. **Reservations:** Not accepted.

$ Prices: Appetizers $2.75–$6.25; main courses $7.95–$13.95. AE, MC, V.

Open: Daily 11am–midnight.

If ever a restaurant was suited to the Lahaina night scene, this is certainly it. Like Lahaina itself, it's big, noisy, brash—and very endearing. Like its companion restaurants around the world, this Hard Rock is decorated with rock music memorabilia and 1950s artifacts; here they mingle with surfboards and ukuleles on the walls. Nonstop piped-in rock music makes it unlikely that you can indulge in much conversation with the waiter, but the choices are easy. Everything is made from scratch, using the freshest of ingredients, and "absolutely no preservatives or additives." We'll have to agree with the menu that "If you've been to the Hard Rock and haven't had our lime chicken or watermelon ribs, then you haven't been to the Hard Rock!" In addition to that lime barbecued chicken ($10.95) and those watermelon ribs ($12.50), other good choices might include fresh fish of the day (market-priced), grilled and served with a baked potato and green salad; a variety of burgers and sandwiches including grilled ahi; a top-notch grilled tostada salad; and, of course, a batch of Maui onion rings. Desserts are out of the '50s, too; root beer float, hot fudge sundaes, and our favorite, the fresh strawberries on homemade angelfood cake, topped with pure whipped cream.

You're likely to see lines at the door of Hard Rock, but don't be put off; they are usually for the HRC logo shop, which dispenses insanely popular T-shirts, baseball caps, cigarette lighters, and the like; the restaurant is so large that you're usually seated in a very short time.

KIMO'S, 845 Front St. Tel. 661-4811.

Cuisine: STEAK/SEAFOOD. **Reservations:** Recommended.

$ Prices: Appetizers $2.95–$9.95; main courses $8.95–$19.95. AE, MC, V.

Open: Lunch (downstairs bar) daily 11:30am–2:30pm; dinner (upstairs restaurant) daily 5–10:30pm. Bar open 11:30am–midnight.

Call Kimo's your quintessential Lahaina-style restaurant. It's been there forever right out on the waterfront, serves good fresh fish and steaks, and is a perfect place to nurse a drink, discuss the meaning of life, and/or watch a sunset from the upstairs oceanfront dining room. Fresh fish of the day, prepared in a variety of styles, is available from $16.95 to $19.95, but there are many tasty favorites priced much lower: veggie brochettes and a luscious upcountry vegetarian lasagne are each $9.95;

kushiyaki (marinated chicken breast and sirloin brochette) and Koloa pork ribs and Polynesian chicken are $13.95; a cheeseburger (available on the regular dinner menu) is $7.95. All main dishes come with tossed green salad with house dressing, a basket of freshly baked carrot muffins and sourdough rolls, and steamed herb rice. Don't forget to save room for the "original hula pie," reputed to be "what the sailors swam to shore for."

KOBE JAPANESE STEAK HOUSE, 136 Dickenson St. Tel. 667-5555.
    Cuisine: JAPANESE. **Reservations:** Recommended.
$ Prices: Sushi $7.25–$16.50; main courses $13.90–$32.90. AE, DC, DISC, JCB, MC, V.
    Open: Dinner only, daily 5:30–10pm.

What a surprise this place is! Just one block behind traditional Baldwin House is what could pass for an authentic Japanese country inn, magnificently decorated with traditional Japanese arts and artifacts, and serving delicious food in a most entertaining setting. You could eat at the enormous sushi bar (sushi assortments run $7.25 to $16.50), but we prefer to take our seats at one of the communal tables, and, along with other diners, spur the master chef on as he whips up our meal at the center grill, teppanyaki-hibachi style. In such a setting, people dining alone, friends dining together, even families with children can all feel comfortable. Every meal begins with grilled teppan shrimp pupus, followed by shabu-shabu soup. Then the chef takes whatever you've chosen—steak, chicken, shrimp—and sautés it with fresh vegetables and flavorful sauces. For dessert, wonderful green-tea ice cream and green tea itself, hearty because it's roasted with rice. Teriyaki chicken is $13.90; hibachi steak, $19.50; teppan shrimp, $18.90; and a steak-and-shrimp teriyaki combo is $21.90. Other steak, fish, and lobster choices go higher. We like to start the meal with warm sake; Japanese beer goes well with this food, and regular drinks and cocktails are also available. Special children's menus are available.
    Cocktail service begins at 5pm and continues to 2am. Plenty of free parking.

LAHAINA COOLERS RESTAURANT & BAR, 180 Dickenson St. Tel. 661-7082.
    Cuisine: NEW AMERICAN. **Reservations:** Not required.
$ Prices: Appetizers $3.50–$6.50; main courses $4.50–$15. AE, DC, MC, V.
    Open: Breakfast daily 7–11am; lunch daily noon–5pm; dinner daily 5pm–midnight. Bar open to 2am.

Located two blocks from busy Front Street, Lahaina Coolers is exactly the kind of place Lahaina needed—a place where you can get creative, upbeat food at almost any time of the day, in a relaxing setting and at a reasonable price. No wonder it became so popular so quickly! The restaurant looks like somebody's summer porch, with open windows on three sides (windsurfing sails provide shade), blue-and-white tiled floor, white chairs, whirling fans overhead, lots of potted plants—a very summery ambience. There are daily and nightly specials, and the menu changes frequently, but here are some ideas to get you going. For a snack or a starter, the spinach and feta cheese quesadilla and the tempura calamari rings are both great. Pastas ($9.50 to $12.90) are a specialty: The fettucine Diane—chicken and mushrooms in a brandy Dijon sauce—is a favorite. Or perhaps you'll want to try a tropical pizza: Evil Jungle pizza. Thai-style chicken in a spicy peanut sauce is a whimsical takeoff on the popular Thai dish ($10.50). There are also burgers from the grill, as well as fresh fish right off the boat, a Moroccan chicken spinach enchilada and a veggie stir-fry with ginger-shoyu sauce.
    Perhaps you'd better come here with a little group so you can sample a lot. But don't miss dessert—the chocolate taco filled with tropical fruit and berry "salsa" is worth a postcard home. The breakfast menu makes getting up in the morning something to look forward to, especially if you go for one of their eggs Benedicts. Try the Norwegian Benedict with smoked salmon and dill. The bar is popular, especially during the 4 to 6pm and 10pm to closing happy hours "8 days a week," when drinks and pupus are less. And don't miss their mango daiquiri!

LAHAINA FISH CO., 831 Front St. Tel. 661-3472.

Cuisine: SEAFOOD. **Reservations:** Not accepted.
$ Prices: Appetizers $3.50–$9.95; main courses $8.95–$21.95. AE, MC, JCB, V.
Open: Lunch daily 11:30am–2:30pm; dinner daily 4:30–10:30pm.

Take the combination of an oceanfront dining room jutting right out over the water, a Lahaina sunset, good fresh fish, and moderate prices and you know why Lahaina Fish Co. is always packed. Start with the chef's fresh fish chowder, thick and hearty and served with a cruet of sherry. Then proceed to one of the main courses, many of which are under $10, like the mahimahi fish-and-chips, the calamari, sautéed oysters, prime rib, grilled chicken, and vegetarian pasta. The sautéed scallops and the fresh fisherman's pasta are a treat. Fresh fish of the day and lobster are market priced. All main courses come with a choice of garlic-pesto pasta or french fries. Keikie dinners are available for $7.95. Lunch offers fresh-fish sandwiches and chicken sandwiches for $6.95 to $9.95. For desserts, take a pick of cheesecakes ($3.95).

LONGHI'S, 888 Front St. Tel. 667-2288.

Cuisine: ITALIAN. **Reservations:** Not required.
$ Prices: Appetizers $4–$7; main courses $12–$25. AE, DISC, MC, V.
Open: Daily 7:30am–10:30pm.

Everybody seems to like this across-from-the-ocean café, where Italian-accented specialties are fresh and hearty, the mood convivial (lots of plants, koa tables, a lively bar, and friendly service), and the desserts—and sunsets—superspecial. Sit upstairs or downstairs—the rooms are similar, but there's an even better ocean view upstairs. Owner Bob Longhi goes to great lengths (like to New York and Italy) to bring in the finest and freshest cheeses, produce, and Italian cold cuts, makes his own pastas, bakes his own breads and pastries, and maintains a high standard throughout. Our main problem here is that the menu is always verbal, and so long that you feel you need to take notes; it's also difficult to figure out just how much your meal is going to cost. It's easy for the bill to escalate, since main courses are served alone, and side dishes can add up (salads from $5, fresh vegetables for $5.50 to $8, etc.), so our recommendation is either go all out and consider this a big splurge, or tell the servers how much you want to spend and let them plan the menu for you. (You can also ask for a menu with prices before being seated.) The last time we dined at Longhi's, linguine with a delicious pesto sauce was $16; eggplant parmigiana was $12. It was $21 for shrimps, scallops, and pasta scampi, and $23 for fresh Maui fish.

It's wise to eat lightly and save your strength, in fact, because Longhi's otherworldly desserts have become something of a legend around town; there have been 1,000 different ones in the restaurant's 17-year history. You never know what they'll come up with, but you might sample, as five of us once did, an incredible strawberry shortcake, a superb macadamia-nut pie (better than any pecan pie we had ever tasted), an unusual chocolate-cake pie (chocolate cake between pie crusts with custard between the layers), a mouth-watering mango-topped cheesecake, and a cooling strawberry mousse. All desserts are priced at $6, and they are huge, so be sure to bring a friend to help you. There's an extensive wine list, including selections that you can order by the glass; Longhi's has won many awards from wine societies. The breakfast menu includes frittatas, omelets, homemade coffee cake, and strudel. On Friday and Saturday nights various bands provide music for dancing, from 10:30pm until 1:30am. Complimentary valet parking from 5pm.

MARIE CALLENDER'S, at the Lahaina Cannery, 1221 Honoapiilani Hwy. Tel. 667-7437.

Cuisine: AMERICAN. **Reservations:** Not required.
$ Prices: Appetizers $4.95–$6.75; main courses $6.25–$14.95. AE, DISC, JCB, MC, V.
Open: Daily 7am–9:30pm.

This restaurant is as American as apple—or chicken pot—pie. Both are served with gusto at this charming place, which has just about everything the cost-conscious diner could desire: a gracious, pink-and-pretty setting, comfortable seating that invites relaxing with friends, a wide variety of dishes, and wholesome American cooking—all at very realistic prices. As for that chicken pot pie, it's as good as we've tasted, with a flaky crust, lots of chicken chunks and vegetables, and a real bargain at $6.95.

Salads are also a specialty: Chicken Cobb, chicken curry, and Caesar salad are all delicious, as are the fresh pasta dishes, the quiches, omelets, and a variety of burgers and sandwiches. At dinner main courses like chicken teriyaki, mahimahi, and pot roast are added to the menu, and are served with salad, herb-roasted potato or rice or fries, plus cornbread with honey butter. Now for dessert: Marie Callender's is known for its home-baked pies, so have a slice here—of sour-cream blueberry, rhubarb, or macadamia-nut cream ($2.50 to $3.50), and see if you can resist taking a whole pie back to your hotel with you. Breakfast is very good too; we recommend the banana-macadamia-nut waffles.

MOOSE McGILLYCUDDY'S PUB/CAFE, 844 Front St. Tel. 667-7758.

Cuisine: AMERICAN. **Reservations:** Not accepted.
$ Prices: Appetizers $4.25–$8.50; main courses $5.75–$17.95. AE, DC, MC, V.
Open: Breakfast daily 8–11am; lunch daily 11am–4:30pm; dinner daily 4:30–10pm.

Like the Moose in Waikiki, this pub/café offers the same brand of good food, good drinks, and good fun here in Lahaina. It's one flight up, with a big bar, a lively atmosphere, and some tables set out on the lanai overlooking busy Front Street. The Moose is known as a "bargain" in pricey Lahaina; main courses include teriyaki chicken, stuffed mahimahi, porterhouse steak, and prime rib, and come with soup or salad, baked potato or rice or fries, and hot garlic bread. Early Bird dinners, served from 4:30 to 5:30pm, feature prime rib, mahimahi, and barbecued chicken for only $8.95 to $9.95. Then there are other favorites like the giant chicken taco salad at $7.95, Mexican specialties like chimichanga or giant burrito at $8.50, a variety of burgers like the University Burger ("highly ranked bacon and intelligent Cheddar") for $5.25 to $6.50. Margaritas and daiquiris are the big drink selections here, along with coffee drinks, Hawaiian exotics, and way-out house specialties.

The Moose's breakfast specials are considered the best deals in Lahaina: the Early Bird, served from 8 to 9am, $4 for egg, bacon, toast, and orange juice; and the Beggar's Banquet, $3.75 for three eggs any style, with potatoes or rice and Texas toast, $3.59.

OLD LAHAINA CAFE, 505 Front St. Tel. 661-3303.

Cuisine: SEAFOOD/AMERICAN. **Reservations:** Recommended for dinner.
$ Prices: Appetizers $4.95–$8.95; main courses $5.95–$19.95. AE, MC, V.
Open: Breakfast daily 7:30–11:30am; lunch daily noon–3:30pm; dinner daily 6–10pm; brunch Sun 7:30am–3pm.

What could be nicer than a beachside breakfast or lunch or a sunset dinner in this charming café overlooking the grounds of the Old Lahaina Luau? This is sophisticated cuisine, using fresh local ingredients and featuring just-caught fish with a variety of preparations—maybe kiawe broiled with shoyu lime chile, or poached with passionfruit cream—dreamed up by veteran chef Michael Ducheneau, who trained at the Culinary Institute of America. There are also vegetarian selections, broiled chicken and steak, and a luau dinner as well. The lunch menu—which can also be ordered in the evening—features hot and cold sandwiches (including kalua pig!) and some hearty salads, like the Upcountry Maui with grilled ahi. Breakfast offers many bargains, including $3.95 for a generous continental breakfast. Sunday brunch features their entire breakfast and lunch menu as well as brunch specials. What with the view and the sounds of the luau entertainment below, this is just the place to sit and linger over a fabulous tropical drink. Most Hawaiian!

PIONEER INN, 658 Wharf St. Tel. 661-3636.

Cuisine: FRONT STREET REGIONAL. **Reservations:** Recommended.
$ Prices: Appetizers $3.95–$11.95; main courses $8.95–$19.95. AE, MC, V.
Open: Breakfast daily 6:30–11am; lunch daily 11:30am–2:30pm; dinner daily 5–10pm.

Along with the renovation of the Pioneer Inn, there's a new look to its dining room, too, and it's much improved. Local art and harborside artifacts grace the walls. The food is imaginative and tasty. Specialties include: oatmeal brûlée ($3.25) and eggs à la Popeye ($6.95) on the breakfast menu; grilled ahi salad, pad Thai noodles, and shrimp Thai sticks at lunch ($4.95 to $11.95); and grilled sea scallops and prawns and island-spiced lamb chops on the dinner menu. The menus change often, including such yummy desserts as fried bananas and chocolate torte. There's live entertainment nightly, and you can hang out in the lounge and listen to the old-timers' stories until at least midnight.

SCAROLES VILLAGE PIZZERIA, 505 Front St. Tel. 661-8112.

Cuisine: ITALIAN. **Reservations:** Not required.
$ Prices: Appetizers $4–$12; pizzas $2.25–$24; pastas $6.50–$11.95 (all appetizers half-price after 8pm). AE, MC, V.
Open: Sun–Thurs 11am–11pm, Fri–Sat 11am–midnight.

There are so many great pizzas to choose from, you may just have to eat here more than once during your stay. Pizza by the slice and by the pie is offered in either Neapolitan (thin crust) or Sicilian (thick crust) versions. There are 12 toppings to choose from, among them house-made meatball and sausage, pepperoni, green peppers, ham, and pineapple. The clam-and-garlic house special is fantastic, priced from $16.50 to $23.50.

But there's more than just great pizza here. Choose from a full selection of appetizers like fried calamari and baked stuffed clams; have a sandwich like sausage and peppers or Italian cold cuts and cheese on homemade Italian bread with a side order of pasta ($5.95 to $6.95); or go for pastas like spaghetti marinara or sausage lasagne. They have rich Italian desserts, too, like tiramisù and ricotta cheesecake with chocolate chips.

If you want to splurge, the same folks own and operate two other full-on Italian restaurants: Scaroles Ristorante, at 930 Wainee St. (tel. 661-4466) in Lahaina, and Scaroles II, at 131 Eike Place in Wailea (tel. 875-7433). They're a bit pricey—$8.95 to $12.95 for appetizers and $13.95 to $24.95 for main courses—but the food is excellent.

WORTH THE EXTRA MONEY

AVALON, 844 Front St. Tel. 667-5559.

Cuisine: HAWAII REGIONAL. **Reservations:** Recommended.
$ Prices: Appetizers $5.95–$15.95; main courses $10.95–$26.95. AE, MC, V.
Open: Daily 11:30am–midnight.

Mark Ellman, one of the highly respected innovators of Hawaii regional cuisine, still continues to provide exuberant and imaginative cuisine at his pretty restaurant in the courtyard of Mariner's Alley. The dining room is decorated with old posters and antique Hawaiian shirts on the walls, oversize Fiestaware and flowered cloths on the tables. Using fresh local ingredients (some grown in a nearby farmyard), Chef Mark is always trying something new, so you can never tell what delights may be in store (at a recent meal, for example, we started with homemade shrimp ravioli with shiitake mushrooms and sun-dried tomatoes in a Szechuan cream sauce). Always on the menu, among the appetizers, there are such treats as summer rolls, Maui onion rings with a homemade tamarind catsup, and shrimp Thai style. Among the main courses, fresh fish of the day, fresh sea scallops, and large Asian prawns can be ordered with a variety of sauces. Vegetarians will love the Gado Gado salad, a classic Balinese dish of steamed vegetables on brown rice, with peanut sauce and condiments.

Still with us? How can we describe the caramel Miranda, the only dessert offered? Imagine a plate of fresh raspberries and strawberries, framed on one side by an incredibly delicious, thick, warm caramel sauce and on the other side by a giant scoop of Haägen-Daz macadamia-nut-brittle ice cream. Unforgettable! Depending on the season and the availability of exotic fruit, it might include, instead, coquitos (full-grown minicoconuts from Chile), or Kula blackberries and huckleberries. If you don't get to have dinner here, at least come by afterward for coffee and desserts (about $5). Lunch is well priced, at under $15.

Avalon holds many special events during the year—for example, wine-maker dinners and guest chef appearances by noted culinary artists from around the country. Call to see if something special is happening during your visit.

DAVID PAUL'S LAHAINA GRILL, 187 Lahainaluna Rd. Tel. 667-5117.
Cuisine: NEW AMERICAN. **Reservations:** Required.
$ Prices: Appetizers $6–$10.95; main courses $13.95–$24.95. AE, MC, V.
Open: Dinner daily 6pm–closing; wine tastings and complimentary cheese Mon–Fri 5pm.

David Paul Johnson is considered one of the rising young stars of Hawaii's culinary firmament; his charming restaurant, newly expanded and prettier than ever, is a must for those who seek out truly imaginative fare. Readers of *Honolulu Magazine* recently voted it "Best Restaurant on Maui." The soft tones of a desertscape are set off by simple black chairs; a pressed tin ceiling; Mikadasa dinnerware, flatware, and crystal; changing artwork; and spectacular floral displays created by David's wife and restaurant hostess, Michelle. The interior is a smoke-free environment: smokers can have a cocktail, after-dinner drink, coffee, or dessert in the tropical setting of the lanai. The menu is eclectic and ever changing, but you're likely to find such signature items as fried maki sushi with a sesame plum sauce and pan-fried Pacific oysters among the appetizers; tequila shrimp and firecracker rice (marinated tiger prawns with a blend of vanilla beans and chili rice), seafood painted desert, or an unusual Kona coffee–roasted lamb among the main courses. For dessert, it could be sweet red-chili carrot cake, chocolate pâté, or triple berry pie with créme fraîche and berry sauce. Children are welcome.

Wine is important here. There's an excellent wine list, and every evening at five David Paul's offers complimentary cheese and specially priced wines by the glass; these tastings give customers the chance to "judge" wines that are being considered for their list. There's nightly entertainment.

READERS RECOMMEND

The Chart House, *1450 Front St. (tel. 661-0937). "This place is not to be missed! It was simply wonderful—service excellent, food delicious, atmosphere tops!"—* Sue Tamny, Hersham, Penna. [*Authors' Note:* We agree. It's a great place, specializing in steak and seafood, and serving dinner daily from 5pm. Dinner should run about $25 or more. There are other Chart Houses in Kahului (tel. 877-2476) and Wailea (tel. 879-2875).]

SPECIALTY DINING

Dining Complexes

WHARF CINEMA CENTER Not only does the Wharf Cinema Center, a shopping complex at 658 Front St., have some of the most tasteful boutiques in the area, it also has a good supply of quick-service restaurants.

Lani's By Day—Alex's By Night is the name of a restaurant with a split personality. From 6am to 3pm, you can have breakfast and lunch at Lani's; from 5 to 9:30pm, you can have reasonably priced pasta dinners, the same that were served at Alex's Hole in the Wall for many years. Between 3 and 5pm, it's Happy Hour. All meals can be taken indoors, which is pleasant enough with its counters and booths, but more fun out on the large terrace, which is shared by several restaurants here. Lani's is known for its buttermilk pancakes, omelets, fish-and-chips, burgers, and sandwiches, all reasonably priced. At Alex's, pasta dinners will cost $9.95, $11.95, or $13.95, all served with salad, fresh-baked bread, and herb butter. Their lasagne verde, handmade pasta lathered with julienne vegetables and cheeses, is our favorite. Reservations are recommended for Alex's (tel. 661-3197).

Subway, one of our favorite sandwich shops, has a branch here (see "Specialty Dining," in Kihei, above). And for an Asian plate lunch, you'll do well at **Song's Kitchen,** in the rear of the Wharf. All is tidy and clean, and lunches run $4.95 to $5.95.

For a quick and tasty Mexican meal try **Taco Joe's:** They offer daily lunch specials like giant burritos with salad or mahimahi fish tacos, $6.95, or Mexican pizzas, $8.95. And if you like Korean barbecue—and who doesn't—seek out **Chun's Korean BBQ Restaurant,** where chicken, pork, and beef barbecues come with three kinds of rice and a variety of Korean salads, all from $5.50 to $6.50. They have some good and hearty noodle soups, too.

Up in the front area of the Wharf, the **Blue Lagoon Tropical Bar & Grill** is just the place to relax, indoors in the dining room or outdoors on the gardenlike lanai with a tropical drink (the Lahaina Sunrise was invented here), and maybe a charbroiled chicken sandwich or mahimahi Cajun style, the house specialty of hibachi chicken, or a steak-and-shrimp combo plate. Sandwiches run $5.95 to $8.50, main courses are $11.95 to $15.95, and there are daily lunch and dinner specials. They have some neat desserts too.

Should you be in the mood for a slight splurge, you can't do better than a teppanyaki-hibachi-style meal at the famed **Benihana of Tokyo,** which maintains stylish digs upstairs. An Asian treat. And if all you want is a brownie or a muffin or a divine macaroon to nibble on, and perhaps a cup of coffee to go with it, try the delicious homemade goodies (courtesy of the Bakery) at **Whaler's Book Shoppe and Coffee House,** a combination bookstore and European café, where you can sip and sit in un-Lahaina-like peace.

LAHAINA CENTER In addition to the **Hard Rock Café** and **Chili's** (see above) the handsome Lahaina Center at 900 Front St. is also home to Hawaii's first **Red Lobster,** which serves dinner only, nightly. Appetizers range from $3.99 for fried parmesan zucchini to $6.99 for a colossal shrimp cocktail. Entrées go from $9.99 for chicken teriyaki to $21.99 for the very popular Fisherman's Platter, with lobster, fresh fish, and seafood pasta. All entrées come with a tossed salad, baked potato, rice or vegetables, and as much cheese-garlic bread as you can eat. This chain loves families.

Also at Lahaina Center, **La Tasca Nouveau Bistro** is a charming Mediterranean tapas restaurant, a neat place to dine on wonderful hot and cold tapas—pan-fried oysters with chive mayonnaise, clams marinière, ratatouille, Greek salad, ceviche, dolmas, and the like. Tapas portions are small, but the prices are also low, from $3.25 to $6.95 each.

For real savings at Lahaina Center, try the take-out-oriented menu at **Arakawa's Chinese Food,** which reflects Mandarin, Szechuan, and Hunan styles of cookery. Every day there's a special for under $5; outdoor seating is available. Or have sandwiches, chili and rice, and local-style daily specials, along with ice cream, cookies, snacks, and sodas, at **Captain Snack Galley.**

LAHAINA CANNERY Lahaina Cannery is at 1221 Honoapiilani Hwy. on the Kaanapali side of town. **Compadres** and **Marie Callender's** (see above) are the big sit-down restaurants here. But don't ignore the restaurants in the food court: **Athens,** for one, turns out tasty traditional Greek specialties at modest prices. Then, of course, there are the standard fast-food outlets like **Yami Yogurt, Hamburger King, McConnel's Ice Cream,** and **Orange Julius.** But be imaginative and stop in for some flavored coffees and cappuccinos.

LAHAINA SQUARE Lahaina Square Shopping Center, 840 Wainee St., caters to the local people, not to the tourist trade, which means it's a good place for hungry budgeteers to note. In addition to **Thai Chef** (see above) and a good sandwich place, **Amilio's Delicatessen** (see below), there is a familiar **Jack in the Box,** as well as a large **Denny's.**

Natural Foods

JUICY'S TROPICAL FRUIT BAR, in the shopping arcade at 505 Front St. Tel. 667-5727.
Cuisine: NATURAL FOODS. **Reservations:** Not accepted.
$ Prices: Sandwiches $4–$5; main courses $2.95–$5.95. No credit cards.
Open: Mon–Sat 8:30am–9pm, Sun 11am–6pm.
With just one table in the window, two tables inside, a counter and several umbrellaed tables outside in the shopping arcade, Juicy's is hardly big in size but it is very big in popularity among Maui's natural-foods set. Every day there is a fresh vegan specialty: it could be shepherd's pie, chile rellenos, Mexican fiesta veggies, or coconut-curry soup. In addition, there are sandwiches, smoothies, baked potatoes, and freshly squeezed juices.

WESTSIDE NATURAL FOODS, 193 Lahainaluna Rd. Tel. 667-2855.
Cuisine: VEGETARIAN.
$ Prices: $1.50–$4.95. MC, V.
Open: Mon–Sat 7:30am–9pm, Sun 9am–7pm.
This local health-food store has salads, sandwiches, soup of the day, smoothies, and hot food to eat informally at outdoor tables or to go. Main courses include lasagne, chili, and enchiladas. Help yourself to goodies from the organic salad bar, $4.95 a pound. The shopping is good here too: You can get strawberry-papayas, unsprayed pineapples, and organic Maui mangoes.

Picnic/Take-Out Fare

AMILIO'S DELICATESSEN, at Lahaina Square Shopping Center, 840 Wainee St. Tel. 661-8551.
Cuisine: DELI.
$ Prices: Sandwiches $4.75–$5.95. No credit cards.
Open: Mon–Fri 8am–8pm, Sat 8am–6pm, Sun 10am–4pm.
This deli makes good sandwiches, some with an Italian flair, to take out or eat here. Buy one and you get another for only 99¢! Local-style plate lunches are also good buys at $3.95 to $5.95. You can pick up a box lunch or a full family picnic by calling ahead.

THE BAKERY, 991 Limahana Place. Tel. 667-9062.
Cuisine: BREADS/PASTRIES/SANDWICHES.
$ Prices: Pastries from 95¢; breads from $1.25; sandwiches $2.50–$4.50. No credit cards.
Open: Mon–Sat 6am–3pm, Sun 6am–noon.
Next to the train depot (the Lahaina-Kaanapali Railroad "Sugar-Cane Train") is a "Maui secret." Many of the fine restaurants in town get their bread and pastries here. The Bakery is a popular spot, crowded with locals who come early in the morning for the best croissants around, and brioches and pain au lait, hot from the oven. Chocolate–cream-cheese croissants and coconut macaroons are memorable. They've been known for years for their fabulous French bread in many shapes and sizes, but now they're doing a fantastic assortment of natural and whole-grain breads as well. These stay fresh much longer than conventional loaves, so you can buy one ($2.25 for a one-pound loaf) and have great sandwiches and morning toast for days. They also offer gourmet-quality deli items and sandwiches to go. It's worth stopping by just to inhale the aromas! (They have a full catering service, too, just in case you're planning on throwing a party while you're on the island.)

MR. SUB, 129 Lahainaluna Rd., near Front St. Tel. 667-5683.
Cuisine: SANDWICHES/SALADS.
$ Prices: Sandwiches $2.50–$6.50. No credit cards.
Open: Mon–Fri 7am–5pm, Sat 7am–4pm.

Long one of Honolulu's most popular submarine shops, Mr. Sub is repeating its quality act in Lahaina, with wonderfully fresh ingredients, seven varieties of breads and rolls, huge sandwiches, great salads, quick service, and low prices. You can eat right in their air-conditioned shop, but the best bet is to choose from the 31 combination sandwiches (or create your own combination) and head for your picnic. Special picnic packages, with coolers for the beach, include a sandwich, chips, fruit, and a drink, and run about $5 to $7. Call them the day before, and everything will be ready for pickup by 7am.

KAANAPALI BEACH

The strip of luxury hotels along Kaanapali Beach boasts a goodly share of luxury restaurants, but very few where the budget diner can relax. Some worthy exceptions:

MEALS FOR LESS THAN $15

KAANAPALI BEACH HOTEL KOFFEE SHOP, 2525 Kaanapali Pkwy. Tel. 661-0011.
Cuisine: BUFFETS. **Reservations:** Not required.
$ Prices: Breakfast buffet $6.95; lunch buffet $6.95; afternoon deli buffet $5.95; dinner buffet $11.95. Early Bird buffet 4–6pm $9.95.
Open: Breakfast daily 6–10:45am; lunch daily 11am–2pm; afternoon deli buffet daily 2–4pm; dinner buffet daily 4–9pm.

The Kaanapali Beach Hotel, one of the most Hawaiian of Maui's hotels, is always doing something nice for the visitor, and what could be nicer than this—quality food served buffet style all day long, and at very low prices. Plan to catch the dinner buffet and work it in with the free Sunset Hula Show, held nightly at 6:30pm. Authentic Hawaiian live entertainment continues until 9pm at the Tiki Terrace. Both lunch and dinner buffets feature a choice of six main courses (including fish, chicken, beef, pork), a salad-soup-and-fruit bar, rice, vegetables, desserts, and beverages; in addition, the dinner buffet offers prime rib. During the afternoon deli buffet, you can help yourself to soup, salad, and desserts, and fix your own sandwiches. Breakfast features fresh pineapple and papaya, eggs, pancakes, french toast, sausage, ham, muffins, and more.

MEALS FOR LESS THAN $25

COOK'S AT THE BEACH, in The Westin Maui Resort, 2365 Kaanapali Pkwy. Tel. 667-2525.
Cuisine: AMERICAN. **Reservations:** Not accepted.
$ Prices: Appetizers $4–$8.75; main courses $7.50–$14.75; breakfast brunch $13.75; prime rib buffet $21.75. AE, CB, DC, DISC, MC, V.
Open: Breakfast daily 6:30–11am; lunch daily 11:30am–2pm; dinner buffet daily 6–9pm; brunch Sun 9am–2pm.

It's worth the price of admission just to see the spectacular grounds of this hotel, with its waterfalls and islands and tropical lagoons, but it's also reasonable for the whole family to eat poolside at Cook's at the Beach, which even has a kid's menu, served "from 11:30am until bedtime," for $3.50 to $4.75. But the real knockout here is the prime rib buffet, a fabulous spread featuring unlimited roast beef carved to order, plus fresh local seafood, salads, and desserts, for $21.75. While you're feasting, enjoy a free hula show every night (except Sunday) at 7pm. True seafood lovers should opt for the seafood buffet at the Villa at the same hotel, a restaurant set on a tropical lagoon. The $22.75 meal features freshly cut sashimi, lomi-lomi salmon, steamed Alaskan snow crab legs, and catch of the day.

READERS RECOMMEND

The Swan Court, in the Hyatt Regency Maui, Kaanapali (tel. 661-1234, ext. 4420 until 5pm, ext. 4455 after 5pm). "The Swan Court is by far the most delightful place for 'the big splurge.' The restaurant is open to a pond/garden setting with black and white swans gliding by; service is very attentive and food is excellent. Most main courses are in the $20 to $35 range. Breakfast is also served here, buffet style. The Swan Court accepts reservations; however, hotel guests have first priority on reservations between 7 and 9pm, so it's easier for 'outsiders' to get reservations between 6 and 7 or after 9pm."—Bob Harrison, Provincetown, Mass.

WHALER'S VILLAGE

There's a salty but slick flavor to the handsome complex of shops and museums at Maui's Whaler's Village, and you can be sure that old-time seamen never had food as good as you'll find in the village's restaurants.

MEALS FOR LESS THAN $15

CHICO'S CANTINA & CAFE, in Whaler's Village. Tel. 667-2777.
   Cuisine: MEXICAN. **Reservations:** Recommended.
$ Prices: Appetizers $4–$6; main courses $7.95–$11.95. AE, MC, V.
   Open: Lunch daily 11:30am–2:30pm; dinner daily 5–10:30pm. Taco Bar 11:30am–11pm.
The atmosphere is tropical (white adobe walls, colorful Mexican hangings, heavy wooden furniture) and the menu is half-Mexican, half-American. On the Mexican side, there are combination plates for $9.50 to $10.95; fajitas, enchiladas, burritos, and all the rest; and such specialties as carnitas, carne asada, pollo asada, and mahimahi done in the style of Vera Cruz, each $10.95. American favorites feature mango fettuccine and smoked chicken, London broil, and Cajun shrimp, plus chicken and ribs barbecues, sandwiches, salads, burgers—in short, a menu to please many tastes. If you come by during their popular happy hour from 3 to 7pm, you can enjoy $2.50 margaritas, and a draft beer and a generous portion of nachos for only $2.90! There's Mexican music during lunch and dinner, then rock 'n' roll late night and during happy hour. A fun spot.

MEALS FOR LESS THAN $20

THE RUSTY HARPOON, in Whaler's Village. Tel. 661-3123.
   Cuisine: CONTEMPORARY AMERICAN. **Reservations:** Recommended for parties of six or more.
$ Prices: Appetizers $1.25–$9.95; main courses $14.75–$22.95. AE, DC, DISC, JCB, MC, V.
   Open: Breakfast daily 8–11am; lunch daily 11am–5pm; dinner daily 5–10pm.
This Whaler's Village standby for many years boasts a handsome interior (green colors, beautiful woods, a view of the ocean as well as the kitchen from every table), and a new menu concept: "nouvelle California–Maui cuisine." And it's still known for excellent value for the dollar. Come for the Early Bird specials, nightly between 5 and 6pm, and for $10.95 you can have dishes like pasta primavera, salsa chicken, prime rib, or fresh fish of the day, including fresh vegetables and rice pilaf or baked potato. Regular dinner main courses, accompanied by fresh vegetable and rice pilaf or baked potato, include pineapple teriyaki chicken, stir-fry beef, shrimp scampi, sea-

food brochette with fresh fish, and prime rib. Rusty's still has its famous half-pound burgers at $7.50 to $8.25, and there are some super salads—shrimp Louie, chicken walnut, fresh fruit—for $8.75 to $9.25. Appetizers have an international flavor, from fried mozzarella to kalbi ribs to nachos. Rusty's uses only fresh local produce and makes its own pastas and wonderful fresh island desserts. Of course those famous fresh-fruit daiquiris (how about banana or pineapple?) are still there and still make Rusty's the "Daiquiri Capital of the World." There's a full bar, a lively crowd, lots of fun. And, oh yes, that sunset over the ocean is terrific!

KAHANA

MEALS FOR LESS THAN $20

KAHANA KEYES RESTAURANT, 4327 Lower Honoapiilani Rd., at the Valley Isle Resort. Tel. 669-8071.
Cuisine: AMERICAN. **Reservations:** Recommended.
$ Prices: Appetizers $3.50–$5.95; main courses $9.95–$17.95. AE, DC, JCB, MC, V.
Open: Dinner only, daily 5–10pm.
Located 3 miles north of the Kaanapali Beach Resort, this has long been a favorite in the Kahana area. People like it because it has one of the best salad bars in the area (reputed to be Maui's largest), plus a variety of Early Bird dinners (from 5 to 7pm) from $9.95 for prime rib, as well as all-night specials, which include steak and lobster at $13.95. The regular menu features steak and seafood ($11.95 to $17.95), plus broiler items ($10.95 to $14.95). Salad bar alone is just $8.50. Every night local bands play contemporary Hawaiian music plus Top 40s and oldies, with dancing until 1:30am. Children's menus are also available.

ROY'S KAHANA BAR AND GRILL, 4405 Honoapiilani Hwy., at Kahana Gateway. Tel. 669-6999.
Cuisine: HAWAII REGIONAL. **Reservations:** Recommended.
$ Prices: Appetizers $5.75–$7.50; main courses $12.95–$23. AE, DC, JCB, MC, V.
Open: Dinner only, daily from 5:30pm.
Honolulu's most highly praised restaurant is also on Maui, and the mood and food are every bit as good—which means wonderful. *Wunderkind* chef Roy Yamaguchi blends the best of European and Asian cooking styles and techniques and uses the freshest of local ingredients to produce a new and exciting Hawaiian cuisine. And the setting is upbeat and exciting too—a large room with an open kitchen, wraparound picture windows giving onto views of rolling meadows, paintings by local artists on the walls, gorgeous flower arrangements everywhere. The menu changes very often, but just to give you some examples, Roy's innovations are apparent in such main courses as the mesquite-smoked Peking duck and the grilled chicken linguine with feta cheese and Mediterranean-style vegetables. Every night there's a long list of specials, including four or five imaginative fish presentations. And prices are surprisingly modest for food of this caliber; there are always individual pizzas on the menu, at an average price of $6.95. Pastas may be ordered in appetizer- or main-course-size portions and go from about $6 to $16.50. The restaurant is also known for its extremely creative and well-priced wine list; many wines are offered by the glass. Desserts change every night and are always memorable—consider the macadamia-nut tart or the mascarpone cheesecake, for starters. No wonder this is one of Maui's hottest new dineries.

And if you have a problem getting into Roy's Kahana Bar and Grill, fret not. You can try Nicolina's right next door. It's a virtual twin with its own creative kitchen staff and a slightly less expensive menu. Oh, yes, if you find yourself on Oahu, on Guam, or in Japan, there are Roy's restaurants there, too.

NAPILI

MAUI TACOS, Napili Plaza. Tel. 665-0222.
  Cuisine: MEXICAN. **Reservations:** Not required.
  $ Prices: $1–$6.50. No credit cards.
  Open: Mon–Sat, 10am–9pm; Sun 11am–7pm.
This is the first of what owner Mark Ellman says will be several high-quality Mexican fast-food locations he'll open around the island. (If his name sounds familiar, Mark's other restaurant is the immensely popular Avalon in Lahaina.) He has pledged to keep every menu item under $7. The menu is extensive, with all kinds of burritos ($3.50 for bean to $6.50 for beef, chicken, or chile verde), enchiladas ($2.75 for potato—our favorite—to $3.75 for cheese, beef, chicken or chile verde), tostadas, tacos, chimichangas, and quesadillas. His special hand-held burritos all have local names—like "Lahaina," "Napili," and "Paia"—and are stuffed with different combinations of rice, black beans, cheese, meats, and veggies. Top your selection with any one of the unusual and freshly made salsas at the salsa bar. You may bring your own beer or wine. There are a dozen or so seats at the restaurant—or grab a taco to go.

READERS RECOMMEND

Dollies, *4310 Lower Honoapiilani Hwy. (tel. 669-0266). "My husband and I both highly recommend Dollies, a pub and café which serves a good selection of sandwiches, salads, pizza, and more. The pizza is made on the premises and is absolutely delicious. The fettuccine Alfredo kept my 5-year-old niece quiet for an extended length of time. Their selection of beers is quite unmatched—even though the English beer is served quite a bit too cold!"* —Carole A. Greenwood, Angus, Ontario.

KAPALUA

MEALS FOR LESS THAN $25

THE MARKET CAFE, at Kapalua Shops, 115 Bay Dr. Tel. 669-4888.
  Cuisine: AMERICAN. **Reservations:** Recommended.
  $ Prices: Appetizers $4–$7; main courses $5–$15. AE, DC, MC, V.
  Open: Daily 8am–9pm.
You'd hardly expect to find any moderately priced eating places in the posh pastures of Kapalua Bay Resort, but here's one: The Market Café, half restaurant, half gourmet deli, a fun place for all-day dining. Breakfast offers such sophisticated choices as eggs Benedict or béarnaise, lox and bagel with cream cheese, and pancakes cooked with fresh fruit. The "All Day Dining" menu, available from 11am to 9pm, features a variety of deli sandwiches ($4.95 to $8.95), homemade soups, salads, burgers, and pastas. The "After Five" menu adds various Italian-style main selections, including chicken marsala, scampi bianco (in an herb cream sauce), and several pastas. Any time of the day is a good time to stop by for a fruit smoothie, a variety of wines and beers, tropical drinks, and flavorful coffees from the espresso bar.

PLANTATION HOUSE RESTAURANT, in the Plantation Golf Course Club-house, 2000 Plantation Club Dr. Tel. 669-6299.
  Cuisine: ISLAND REGIONAL. **Reservations:** Recommended.
  $ Prices: Appetizers $6–$8; main courses $16–$23.
  Open: Breakfast and lunch daily 8am–3pm; dinner daily 5:30–10pm.
There's a traditional, "old Hawaii" feeling about this handsome restaurant, reminiscent of the way things were back in the '40s—simple, comfortable, elegant. It sits high on a hill, affording extraordinary 360° views from various

parts of the dining room—of the mountains, the ocean, the golf course, and the most spectacular sunsets on Maui. Whitewashed mahogany, tables made of teak, upholstered chairs with pineapple carved back, original artworks gracing the walls, and a double-sided fireplace dominating the room create the feeling of a warm and cozy lodge. Dinnertime appetizers are great fun, especially the crab cakes with a green-peppercorn-lime mayonnaise and Hawaiian-style sashimi. House specialties among the main courses include fresh local fish in a variety of presentations (we like it charbroiled and served with a shiitake-soy sauce), chicken Mediterranean, breast of fresh duck, and double-cut lamb chops. The chef creates new specials every night. Lunch is very reasonable, with such dishes as chicken breast, steak, and wok-fried vegetables, going for $6.25 to $9.95, most accompanied by a choice of soup or salad, french fries, or sticky rice. Good sandwiches, salads, burgers, and pizzas too. As for desserts, fudge brownies with ice cream and chocolate sauce and the pot de crème au chocolate are delightful decadence personified.

HANA

Outside of the famed—and very expensive—Hotel Hana-Maui, there are very few public restaurants in Hana. The hotel restaurant is wonderful, but very pricey.

HANA GARDENLAND CAFE, corner of Kalo Rd. and Hana Hwy., before entering Hana town. Tel. 248-7340.
$ Prices: $2.25–$6.75. **Reservations:** Not taken.
   Open: Daily 9am–5pm, same menu all day.

There's such a paucity of restaurants in Hana that almost any new one would be welcome. But when the restaurant happens to be delightful and inexpensive to boot, cheers are in order. Dripping with baskets of flowering plants and herbs, the café has picnic tables, more plants, and even Miró puzzles to solve on every table. White Christmas lights are strung around the thatched, covered roof over the picnic tables, and crazy fruit and flower lights decorate the canopy at the café order window. After you've wandered around, meditated by the lily pond stocked with koi, and visited the tasteful art gallery and gift shop, stop in for something delicious. Hillary Rodham Clinton and Chelsea did.

The café serves delicious fresh food, much of it grown in the vegetable garden and on the fruit trees on the property. From avocados to starfruit and from herbs to eggplant, whatever is in season is featured on the menu. Breakfasts range from homemade banana bread, served warm with cream cheese and honey ($2.25), to steamed eggs and salsa served with Maui Crunch toast ($4.75). Lunch is luscious at Hana Gardenland: huge sandwiches of ahi tuna salad, veggies, and smoked turkey ($6.75) are served with sweet cherry peppers and a pickle spear. Or choose lasagne, salads, quiche, or a house specialty, hanamole and chips. Fresh-picked avocados are made into the café's own-style guacamole and served with taro chips ($4.95)—there's more than enough to satisfy at least two people. Yummy! Espresso Bar beverages are $2 to $3. A basketful of brightly colored cloth napkins invites patrons to "Help yourself and place in laundry basket when *pau* (done)." It's just one small indication of the environmental consciousness of all the folks here.

There's a special feel and fragrance to the Hana air. Hana Gardenland is an excellent way to experience it, especially for those unable to hike to more remote parts of this magical district.

SPECIALTY DINING

Breakfast/Lunch/Snacks

HANA RANCH RESTAURANT. Tel. 248-8255.
   Cuisine: AMERICAN. **Reservations:** Recommended.
$ Prices: Appetizers $5–$5.50; main courses $18.95–$37. AE, DC, MC, V.
   Open: Buffet lunch 11am–3pm; take-out counter 6:30am–4pm.

The Hana Ranch Restaurant is a bit away from the Hotel Hana-Maui, but still in the same Hana Ranch complex. It's a good choice, with an indoor dining room that features a nice buffet lunch for $12.95 (salad bar only, $7.95). Wednesday night is "Pizza Night": choose your own topping for a thick-crust pie; prices range from $7.50 to $17.50. A take-out counter serves up burgers, sandwiches, and hot dogs.

TUTU'S, at Hana Bay. Tel. 248-8224.
   Cuisine: LOCAL. **Reservations:** Not accepted.
$ Prices: Plate lunches $5.25–$5.50. No credit cards.
   Open: Daily 8:30am–4pm.

This longtime favorite is the best place for a reasonable lunch (or breakfast). Tutu's specializes in local-style plate lunches, plus very good fresh-fruit salads, green salads, sandwiches, ice cream (try the macadamia-nut), and such. The mahimahi sandwich at $3.50 is a popular choice.

CHAPTER 15

WHAT TO SEE & DO ON MAUI

It would be nice to have a week or more to spend on Maui. But if you have only a few days, you can still get to see and experience much of Maui's magic. *Note:* Excellent maps are in the *Maui Drive Guide,* free from your car-rental company.

SUGGESTED ITINERARIES

IF YOU HAVE 1 DAY Spend your day seeing mighty Haleakala Crater. On the way to or from Haleakala, explore the windsurfing mecca of Paia and the funky little cowboy town of Makawao, getting magnificent vistas of upcountry Maui all the way.

IF YOU HAVE 2 DAYS Spend your first day as suggested above. On your second day visit Lahaina, the old capital of the Hawaiian Islands, and enjoy its vibrant street life—shops, restaurants, galleries—and then drive north to the Kaanapali stretch of glamorous hotels and beaches, all the way to Kapalua.

IF YOU HAVE 3 DAYS Use the first two days as recommended above. On the third day, make the drive around the base of Haleakala to isolated and exquisitely beautiful Hana.

IF YOU HAVE 5 DAYS OR MORE To the above itineraries, add a trip to Wailuku to go antique hunting; stop in Kihei for a swim at one of its excellent beaches; then drive on to see the magnificent pleasure palaces of Wailea and Makena, and maybe have a swim there too. If you can, plan to stay overnight at Hana. As time permits, break up your sightseeing with swimming, riding, tennis, hiking, snorkeling trips—Maui offers endless opportunities for the outdoor life.

HIKING ON MAUI

So you want to get off the beaten path, away from the tourist routine, and explore the backcountry, the mountains, the jungles, and waterfalls and rain forests, perhaps even trek into the crater of mighty Haleakala, on foot? The best way we know to do all this is to team up with an amazing gentleman named ✪ **Ken Schmitt,** a professional nature guide and much more. Schmitt has lived on Maui for 17 years, three of them in the open—sleeping under the stars and living on wild fruits and vegetables on the jungle paths. He is a scholar and explorer—an expert in the natural history and geology of Maui, as well as in the ancient legends and wisdom of Hawaii. He leads very small groups, or individuals, on a variety of 50 different hikes, which range from easy walks to arduous treks, and cost anywhere from $75 per person for a half-day tropical-valley hike to $110 for an excursion into Haleakala (children under 16 are charged $50 to $75). Personalized trips concentrating on special interests can be arranged. We've had ecstatic reports on these hikes.

We asked Ken what he might suggest for our budget-conscious readers: "Take one or two of my day hikes to find out everything necessary to enjoy camping or backpacking on Maui. Then you can live for free, fishing and eating wild fruit, taro, and sweet potatoes. Of course, not everyone wants to live this way, but it can be done, and I will show you how. Each of my excursions is a workshop in natural history and environmental knowledge. In one day I can teach people as much as they could learn in weeks of research, including the following: locating safe and beautiful places to camp; selecting an itinerary appropriate to current weather conditions and personal interests and abilities; finding trailheads and following the trails; what fruit is in season and where to find it in the wilderness; where to rent equipment and what is needed; possible hazards in the environment and how to cope with them; how to get around without a car; where to buy inexpensive groceries, including farms that sell their own fresh fruit and vegetables. The emphasis of my programs is on enhancing our connection with our natural environment and teaching the skills that we need to feel comfortable in Hawaii."

Sounds great to us. You can contact Ken Schmitt in advance at **Hike Maui,** P. O. Box 330969, Kahului, HI 96733 (tel. 808/879-5270).

READERS RECOMMEND

Hiking on Maui. "*Maui has some 150-odd miles of coastline with some superb beaches. But if you're bored with sun and sand, try something different—say, a hike into Maui's backcountry, and enjoy some of the pristine beauty seldom seen by the average tourist. Pick up the book Hiking Maui, by Robert Smith (Wilderness Press); it's splendid reading. It also covers a large variety of hikes, complete with maps, difficulty ratings, where to obtain permission if needed, with a sensitive, no-nonsense approach to hiking. Our favorites: the Iao Stream (no. 16) or, for the more history minded, the King's Highway (no. 15) in La Perouse Bay.*"—J. A. Drouin, Edmonton, Alberta, Canada.

HELICOPTER TOURS

Should you want to indulge yourself and splurge on a helicopter trip, Kahului Airport is the place to do it. Although these tours are technically beyond our budget, they could provide your most memorable experiences of Maui. We should tell you that many residents do not love the helicopters because of their noise and their impact on a fragile environment. But if you decide to go, here are three of the most reliable companies. **Sunshine Helicopter,** Kahului Airport (tel. 808/871-0722, or toll free from the mainland 800/544-2520, toll free from other islands 800/469-3000), may well be the best budget choice, since they offer standby rates of 50%. They also offer a budget $59, 20-minute tour of the West Maui Mountains, including a look at the incredible "Wall of Tears," a spot where 17 waterfalls converge. Their deluxe tour, which circles the island and includes a "champagne stop" is $199 per person and includes 80 minutes of flying time as well as the 20-minute stop. Tours are provided in Japanese, German, and Spanish as well as English. Fares include a videotape of your adventure, and Sunshine boasts Maui's only four-camera video system; you can actually see yourself flying!

Papillon Helicopters, Kahului Airport (tel. 808/877-0022, or toll free from the mainland 800/367-7095, toll free from other islands 800/562-5641), has been operating for more than 15 years on Maui and is well recommended. Prices range from a low $49 for a 20-minute tour of the West Maui Mountains to $179 for a 65-minute tour of West Maui and the stunning shores of Molokai. All flights include a videotape of your trip.

At **Hawaii Helicopters,** Kahului Airport (tel. 808/877-3900, or toll free from the mainland 800/346-2403, toll free from other islands 800/994-9099), prices range from $89 for a half-hour tour of either the West Maui Mountains or Mt. Haleakala to $250 for a 2½-hour detailed tour of the island *and* a champagne picnic in Hana. If you can afford the splurge, you'll have an adventure to remember. Once again, a complimentary video is part of the deal.

1. KAHULUI-WAILUKU & KIHEI-WAILEA

KAHULUI AREA

SIGHTS & ATTRACTIONS

Kahului is too new to have any historic sights, but it's considered a good example by city planners of what a model city should be. Kahului boasts the only deep-water harbor on Maui, a bulk-sugar-loading plant, the cannery of the Maui Pineapple Company, and the Hawaiian Commercial and Sugar Company, the driving force behind the town's development (most of the homes belong to plantation workers). If you want to get a head start on seeing Maui's windsurfers do their stuff, drive to **Kanaha Beach Park,** next to the airport (go down the road from the Alamo Car Rental building heading towards the beach and turn right). Surfboard rentals and lessons are also available.

SAVVY SHOPPING

You can spend a pleasant hour or so browsing through Kahului's shopping centers.

KAAHUMANU SHOPPING CENTER A better name for Maui's biggest shopping complex, located at 275 Kaahumanu Ave., might be Ala Moana No. 2. Like its Honolulu counterpart, it has **Sears** at one end, Liberty House at the other, and that fascinating Japanese department store, Shirokiya, in between.

By the time you read this, Kaahumanu Shopping Center should have completed a major expansion and renovation, boasting a second level and even a state-of-the-art "roof" that allows air circulation and light in, but keeps inclement weather out. More than 100 stores—a mix of local businesses and national "brand names"—are represented. A food court seating up to 500 people provides a variety of ethnic foods—Japanese, Korean, Hawaiian, and Mexican, to name just a few. And there's a six-plex theater, just in case you want to take in the latest flick.

Among the old standbys here, we always check out the **Penthouse at Liberty House.** Like its Honolulu namesake, it features closeout merchandise—designer clothing, shoes, linens, towels, and the like—from various Liberty House stores. You never know what great bargains you might find here.

The Coffee Store is always fun, with a large roaster and sacks of coffee up front, every kind of coffee and coffee accessories to buy, and a neat little coffee bar and café area, with tables and bakery selections in back: café mocha, cappuccino, filled croissants, bagels, quiches, and lasagne, for $2 to $4.50. Among the attractive gift items here, huge Hawaiian quilted pot holders at $13.

You can get island prints by the yard, well priced, at **Sew Special,** which also has some wall hangings that would make neat gifts. Kids and hobbyists will enjoy **Kay-Bee Toys,** a very large shop with good values. You might find some saké cups to take home with you, or charming Hakata dolls, at **Shirokiya,** which also has those wonderful sushi take-out lunches we told you about in the preceding chapter. In case you haven't sampled crackseeds yet, **Camellia Imports** is the place.

MAUI MALL It's also fun to visit the Maui Mall, located at 52 Kaahumanu Ave., a community-style shopping center, more value oriented and with more local flavor

FROMMER'S FAVORITE MAUI EXPERIENCES

Getting Up Before the Sun Drive to Haleakala Crater to catch first light as the sun rises over Haleakala. Have hot coffee and a mango muffin at Sunrise Market and Protea Farm on the way down.

Sailing from Lahaina to Lanai Sail one of the sleek, multihulled yachts of Trilogy Excursions from Lahaina to Lanai, where you can go swimming, snorkeling, and exploring.

Antique Hunting and Browsing Wander through the intriguing array of antique and gift stores in historic Wailuku town.

Enjoying a Multimedia Spectacle Fly over an active volcano on the Big Island, scuba dive below the surface of the ocean on Maui, or swoop down into Kauai's Waimea Canyon—all vicariously at the Hawaii Experience Domed Theater in Lahaina.

Swimming and Snorkeling at Fleming Beach in West Maui Enjoy a perfect crescent of white sand and gentle surf—an ideal spot for the whole family.

Poking Through Paia's Shops and Arts-and-Crafts Galleries Have lunch at the Wunderbar, a local hangout, then watch windsurfers at nearby Hookipa Beach.

than its large competitor just up Kaahumanu Avenue. There are frequent sidewalk sales and free entertainment; check the local papers for details. Lovely umbrellaed tables and chairs are placed throughout the area.

Look for the kiosk called **Crystal Dreams,** which has lots more than crystals. We spotted some chimes made of crystal, brass, and copper that start at about $8.75 and go up to about $50, and lots of lovely jewelry, including beige shell nerite leis, very rare, mostly from the South China Seas, for about $30. Check out **Afterthoughts,** in a corner of Woolworth's, for fashion accessories and costume jewelry. **Roland's** has lots of neat shoes, including sandals. **Kahului Florist** has a very knowledgeable staff in terms of local flora and "lei etiquette."

Toys 'n' Joys, specializing in computer games, is a fun store for the kids. **Affordable Fashions** feature ladies' discount apparel at good prices, including large sizes. **JR's Music Shop** has some very good selections. **Long's Drugs** offers some of the best values for souvenirs and sundry items. And you can stock up on groceries at **Star Super Market,** where the locals shop; if you're going to be cooking in your kitchenette apartment, it pays to stop here after getting off the plane before driving on to the more expensive resort areas. You can pick up a T-shirt that reads JUST MAUIED at the **T-Shirt Factory.**

Roy's Photo Center probably has the most complete supply of camera accessories and films on Maui. **Sir Wilfred's Coffee, Tea, Tobacco Shop** has more than its name implies; in addition to a great selection of pipes, cigars, tobacco, and coffee beans, it also has gourmet gifts and gadgets, plus an espresso bar, a full bar, and a delightful menu of light foods at Sir Wilfred's Espresso Caffè. They always have tasteful handmade ceramic mugs, from about $10. Stop in at **Waldenbooks** if you've run out of reading material, and at **Maui Natural Foods** for anything and everything in the health-food line; it's the most complete store of its kind in the area.

Cost Less Imports is always worth a browse for straw baskets, wood carvings, and various and sundry craft imports. If you're in the market for Hawaiian Heirloom jewelry, check out **Kaneshige Jewelers,** which has been around since 1894; it is Hawaii's oldest fine jewelry store. They have an extensive selection of watches, some of which are exclusive to the island, as well as plenty of gold and sterling silver Hawaiian souvenir charms. Another fine selection of Hawaiian Heirloom jewelry awaits at **Hawaii Heirloom Jewelry,** which it sells exclusively. It's a good idea to comparison-shop these two.

After you've finished your shopping, pick up some bento (a box lunch to go) or perhaps some sushi at **Restaurant Matsu;** locals claim their California roll sushi is the best on the island.

DAIRY CENTER Our favorite store at Dairy Center, 395 Dairy Road., is **Baby's Choice,** which features lovely children's clothing and maternity wear, including fashionable swimwear for mothers-to-be.

SWAP MEET Flea-market fans will have a good time here. Every Saturday morning from 6:30am to noon, vendors gather next to the post office on Puunene Street to sell everything from vegetables and flowers to new and used clothing, jewelry, beautiful baskets and sculptures, exotic items from all over the world. Always worth a stop. Check with your hotel desk to make sure it's on.

KAHULUI EVENING ENTERTAINMENT

Nightlife is limited in this area. Your best bet is in the big hotels. Check the shopping centers for free Polynesian shows, presented several times a week. Maui Mall, for one, sometimes presents top revues from Honolulu clubs—free.

EAST WEST DINING ROOM, 170 Kaahumanu Ave., in Maui Palms Hotel. Tel. 877-0071.

On Thursday and Friday from 8:30pm to midnight, it's karaoke. On Saturday from 9:30pm to 1:30am, it's The Sakuras, a very popular musical group, playing Top 40, Hawaiiana, Japanese, country music, and more.

Admission: Free.

RED DRAGON ROOM, 170 Kaahumanu Ave., in Maui Beach Hotel. Tel. 877-0051.

The mood is more mod than Hawaiian; a DJ keeps the crowd happy on Saturday from 10:30pm to 2:30am.

Admission: Free.

LUIGI'S PASTA AND PIZZERIA, at Maui Mall, 52 Kaahumanu Ave. Tel. 877-3761.

This busy family eatery is always a popular place at night. There's women's disco dancing on Wednesday from 10pm to 1am. Karaoke is on Tuesday, Thursday, Friday, and Saturday.

WAILUKU AREA
SIGHTS & ATTRACTIONS

Historic old Wailuku, the commercial and professional center and the seat of Maui County (which also includes Molokai and Lanai), is quite different from Kahului—even though it's right next door. It's a bit ramshackle, strictly local. It's great fun for browsing and antiques shopping (see below), and for inexpensive dining at local greasy spoons (see Chapter 14, "Maui").

Wailuku

BAILEY HOUSE MUSEUM, 2375-A Main St. Tel. 244-3326.

MAUI

PACIFIC OCEAN

Pailolo Channel

Alenuihaha Channel

Alalakeiki Channel

Kealaikahiki Channel

Auau Channel

Kahoolawe (U.S. Navy Bombing Range)

Airport ✈

0796

Alexander & Baldwin Sugar Museum ⓫
Bailey House Museum ❿
Carthaginian Museum Ship ❻
Fleming Beach ⓲
Haleakala National Park ❶
Haleakala Visitor's Center ⓱
Hamoa Beach ㉔
Hana Cultural Center ㉓
Hana Gardenland ㉓
Hookipa Beach Park ⓭
Iao Valley ❽
Kaanapali Beach ❸
Kamaole Beaches ⓬
Kaumahina Park ⓳
Koolau Lookout ⓴
Lahaina Jodo Mission ❺
Lahaina-Kaanapali & Pacific Railroad ❷
Olowalu Petroglyphs ❼
Makawao ⓯
Maui Tropical Plantation ❾
Tedeschi Vineyards ⓮
Upcountry Protea Farm ⓰
Waianapanapa Cave ㉒
Wailua Falls ㉑
Waiola Church ❹

These buildings, on beautiful shaded grounds, once housed the Wailuku Female Seminary (where young females could be kept safely "away from the contaminating influences of heathen society") and the home of Edward Bailey, the seminary instructor. Today they are full of fascinating bits of Hawaiiana, from ancient petroglyphs and necklaces of human hair worn by the alii of Maui to missionary patchwork quilts and furnishings. Dating back to 1833–50, the building itself was completely restored in 1974–75, and is an excellent example of Hawaiian quality work and Yankee ingenuity. The smaller building, once the dining room of the school and later Bailey's studio, has been restored as a gift shop.

Admission: $3 adults, $2.50 seniors and students, $1 children.

Open: Mon–Fri 10am–4pm. **Directions:** Drive westward along Kaahumanu Avenue out of Kahului about 3 miles; you'll pass the Maui Professional Building at High Street on the right, and then, about a block farther, to the left on Iao Road, you'll reach the museum.

WAIKAPU

MAUI TROPICAL PLANTATION, Hi. 30, Waikapu. Tel. 244-7643.

Not far from Wailuku, in the sugar-plantation village of Waikapu, you can sightsee, shop, eat, and have an educational experience—all under one roof (or better yet, one sky)—at Maui Tropical Plantation. This showplace and marketplace for the tropical agriculture of the islands offers free admission to its agricultural pavilions and exhibits, but charges $8 for a 45-minute tour aboard the Tropical Tram, which traverses some 50 acres planted in bananas, papayas, coffee, pineapple, macadamia nuts, sugarcane, and other crops. What we like best about this place is the Tropical Market, where a huge variety of made-on-Maui products, plantation-grown fresh fruit, and gift items are available. And a mailing service makes it easy to send gifts back home. Mailing service is also available at their Tropical Nursery, where you can get orchids, hibiscus, or anthuriums.

There are dining and entertainment possibilities here as well. The Tropical Restaurant offers a buffet luncheon and à la carte service for light meals. A Hawaiian Country Barbecue, including a quick tram ride through the fields, takes place every Tuesday, Wednesday, and Thursday at 5pm, featuring Buddy Fo and his Hawaiian Country Band. Dinner is an all-you-can-eat Hawaiian tropical feast. Cost is $48.90 for adults, $20.80 for children. Inquire about transportation available from Lahaina/Kaanapali and Kihei/Wailea for the Hawaiian Country Barbecue.

Admission: Plantation, free; Tropical Express tour, $8 adults, $3 children.

Open: Daily 9am–5pm. The Tropical Express tour leaves every 45 minutes, 9:15am–4pm.

Iao Valley

Drive down Hi. 30 in the direction of Iao Valley, and about 2 miles from Wailuku, on the right, you'll note a sign reading BLACK GORGE PRESIDENT KENNEDY PROFILE. The jagged mountain cliff ahead of you, which does bear a resemblance to JFK's profile, has been there for centuries, but not until relatively recently, of course, did people begin to notice its timely significance.

In another mile you'll come to Iao Valley, a wildly beautiful gorge dominated by the **Iao Needle,** 2,250 feet of green-covered lava rock reaching straight up into the sky. In this dramatic setting, Kamehameha won the battle that was to give him the island of Maui; the local warriors, accustomed to spears and javelins, were no match for Kamehameha's forces supplied with a cannon by two English sailors. The carnage was so intense that the waters of Iao Stream were dammed up by the bodies of the conquered, giving the stream is present name: Kepaniwai, "damming of the waters." Now all is tranquil here, save for the shouts of happy keikis wading through the pools at **Kepaniwai Park,** where present-day Mauians love to go for a picnic or a swim. Beautifully landscaped gardens with Asian pagodas, swimming, and wading pools provide a palatial playground in this crisp mountain valley.

Puunene

THE ALEXANDER & BALDWIN SUGAR MUSEUM, 3957 Hansen Rd., Puunene. Tel. 871-8058.

This former residence of superintendents of the mill (still in operation next door) has been transformed into an award-winning museum with artifacts dating back to 1878, absorbing photo murals, and authentic scale models, which include a working model of sugar-factory machinery. Educational for the kids, entertaining for grown-ups too. Be sure to visit the museum shop, with unique items relating to the sugar industry and plantation life, including contributions of the various ethnic groups who came to the islands to work the plantations.

Admission: $3 adults, $1.50 students 6–17, free for children under 6.

Open: Mon–Sat 9:30am–4:30pm. **Directions:** From Kahului, take Hi. 350 to Hi 311 toward Kihei. The museum is at the Hansen Road intersection.

SAVVY SHOPPING

Shopping in Wailuku is offbeat. Shops are unpretentious, not a bit touristy. Antique lovers will be in heaven at **Antique Row,** a cluster of shops and galleries on North Market Street offering one-of-a-kind items from around the globe as well as from times gone by. Start at **Traders of the Lost Art,** at no. 62, where you might find owner Tye Hartall, unless he happens to be on one of his yearly journeys to New Guinea to collect ancestral carvings and primitive ritual art. His shop is reminiscent of a New Guinea spirit house, complete with split drums, crocodile tables, and a host of spirit masks and figures. Up front is more contemporary stuff: lovely new-Indonesian shirts for men, jackets and jewelry for women. **Himalayan Fine Arts,** a part of the same shop, deals in paintings, bronzes, and artifacts mostly from Nepal, plus rugs and carpet from Tibet. **Antiques Unique,** at no. 140, is the place for fine Oriental collectibles.

Memory Lane, at 158 N. Market St., is where Joe Ransberger shows the unusual and one-of-a-kind items he's collected from all over the world. Joe specializes in American artists—originals, lithos, stone engravings, woodblock prints—and also has a good collection of Hawaiiana too. He has those "silky" aloha shirts, starting at about $15 and going as high as $350. **Alii Antiques,** 139 N. Market St., is known for its fine collection of Asian art from the Ming and Ch'ing dynasties, as well as items from Europe and the mainland. A recent browse turned up antique guns from the Civil War, Persian rugs, paintings by local artists.

More antique and offbeat emporiums are in store for this neighborhood, so if antiques are your thing, be sure to save some time for exploring this area.

DOWN TO EARTH NATURAL FOODS, 1910 Vineyard St. Tel. 242-6821.

Now, if you need to stock up on certified organic produce, natural groceries, vitamins, herbs, and body-care products, this is the place to go. They also have homemade vegetarian food you can take with you. There's another Down to Earth at 1169 Makawao Ave. in Makawao.

GIMA BOUTIQUE, 21 Market St. Tel. 242-1839.

Elaine Gima is undoubtedly Maui's—perhaps Hawaii's—foremost silk artist, and her extraordinary hand-painted garments have won major crafts awards. Now she's opened her own shop in Wailuku, and while her pricier creations may not be within reach, there are, surprisingly, many affordable things here, like cotton T-shirts with hand-painted silk appliqués for $44. Any of her men's silk ties with Hawaiian motifs or her fanciful scarves would make fine presents, from $28 to $48. Well worth a visit.

JOVIAN GALLERY, 7 Market St. Tel. 244-3660.

Gallery owner Marcia Godindez not only shows some of Maui's best contemporary artists here, she also has a line of unusual jewelry, writing papers, art notecards, contemporary greeting cards, koa boxes, and much more, in every price range. You never know what bit of serendipity you might pick up here.

SHELL'S BAG'S HATS, in the Wailuku Industrial Park. Tel. 669-8439 (call first).

Have you always wanted a genuine Panama hat—not the imitation that passes for the real thing? Shell Hansson, who has been making hats in Maui for over 20 years, recently gave up his Lahaina retail store location and now invites customers to his warehouse, where they can see how genuine Panama straw handcrafts are made in the time-honored fashion. Hansson also has scads of other chapeaux—every known type of hat weave, including Maui lauhala, for men, women, and children. Claims Hansson: "If you've got the head, I've got the hat." Most hats run $3 to $40 and up; prices are very competitive and the value is excellent. He asks you to phone first, as he is not in the warehouse at all times.

NEW AGE RESOURCES

New Age types might want to stop in at **Alaya Unlimited,** at 52 Central Ave. in Wailuku, to get a copy of their free *Mauiana Magazine*, and find out who's lecturing, giving a meditation workshop, or having a class on alternative lifestyles and healing techniques. *Mauiana Magazine* is the only voice of vegetarianism, alternative health practices, and hemp education on Maui. You can also call publisher Suzie O at 244-7400 to find out when the next Ohana Luncheon and Trade Fair will be held, featuring noted New Age speakers and musicians.

KIHEI-WAILEA AREA

If you're staying in Kahului or Wailua, Kihei has a good nearby beach, about a 20-minute drive, via Hi. 350, and then Hi. 311 right to Kihei.

SIGHTS & ATTRACTIONS

Just past the end of Kihei, the road takes you into one of the most beautiful planned destination resorts in the islands. Should you like to see how the other half lives, by all means, visit some of the splendid, multimillion-dollar resorts here; they are examples of island indoor-outdoor architecture at its best. You definitely must make a stop at the **Grand Wailea Resort Hotel & Spa**, opened a few years ago to the tune of $800 million. Explore the spectacular grounds, note the Ferdinand Botero sculpture garden, stop in for a reasonably priced meal at Café Kula (spa cuisine with a special menu for children) or at the charming Bistro Molokini. Spa Grande is equal to the best in Europe and, surprisingly, many of their treatments are quite affordable. Should you happen to be in the area on a Tuesday or Friday at 10am, treat yourself to a complimentary tour of the resort's art collection. Led by a Maui artist schooled in art history, the tour highlights the collections of Picasso, Leger, Botero, and Warhol, while explaining the lore behind the many works depicting Hawaiian legend and history. Then you'll want to visit the **Maui Inter-Continental Wailea Resort**, newly redone to make it more Hawaiian in feeling and more gracious than ever: Its Hula Moons Restaurant, decorated with artwork and poetry of Don Blanding, is a delight. **Stouffer Wailea Beach Resort,** a AAA Five-Diamond winner for more than 10 years, has beautiful grounds, splendid artworks, the cute little Maui Onion for an inexpensive meal, Raffles and the Palm Court for superb Sunday brunches. **Four Seasons Resort Wailea** is exquisite, like a never-ending flower garden indoors and out. Its Pacific Grill is a wonderful choice for a medium-priced meal. Stop by, have a drink or a meal at any of these places, stroll the beach (all beaches are public in Hawaii), and enjoy a taste of *la dolce vita,* Hawaii style.

Drive a little farther and you can explore the **Makena Resort Maui Prince Hotel,** very modern and elegantly understated. Two waterfalls run down into the central courtyard and lead to the Japanese rock garden. You may want to stop in at the Café Kiowai on the garden level for an exotic dessert and a cup of coffee. Better yet, come back on a Sunday morning for one of the most elaborate and exquisite Sunday brunches in Maui ($29.95 including champagne).

SAVVY SHOPPING

While there's nothing remarkable about shopping in the Kihei-Wailea area, shopping malls are going up at a great rate, so you could easily spend an hour or two browsing, before—or after—the beach.

AZEKA PLACE & AZEKA PLACE II You'll find these twin malls, owned by an old Maui family, located in the heart of Kihei. **Azeka Place**, 1280 S. Kihei Rd. (oceanside), is where you'll find the gift boutique **Rainbow Connection.** Admire the handmade, hand-painted porcelain jewelry, the volcanic glass jewelry and the unique craft items created by Maui residents. Right next door is **Island Memories,** which specializes in quality Hawaiian-made products and collectibles. You can pick up swimwear and beach fashions at **Maui Waterworks** and casual aloha wear at **Leilani's.**

O'Rourke's Tourist Trap is a good place to get any necessities you forgot to pack, as well as postcards, monkeypod wood souvenirs, and the like. **Musicland** carries a wide selection of contemporary Hawaiian music on cassette tape or CD, and **Leathers of the Sea** offers eelskin items ranging from lipstick cases to briefcases, in a wide range of colors.

International House of Pancakes is a reliable breakfast stop. **Coffee & Confections** can pour you a quick hot cup of Kona coffee or cappuccino. If you're in the mood for something spicy, try Kihei's only Thai restaurant, **Royal Thai,** for lunch or dinner. Try **Azeka's Market Snack Shop** for an authentic local-style plate lunch—it's the only place on the island's south shore where you can get a laulau and poi plate. And if you have access to a grill, don't miss the legendary cook-your-own ribs from Azeka's Market.

Azeka Place II, 1279 S. Kihei Rd. (mountainside), is where you'll find **Maui's Best,** which features locally made crafts: handmade jewelry, potpourri oils and creams, koa-wood boxes, Christmas-tree ornaments, great hand-painted T-shirts—all reasonably priced. They also have coffees, teas, and delicious Island Princess candies. Texas customers swear the macadamia-nut popcorn and macadamia-nut brittle is even better than the kind at Neiman-Marcus! **Elephant Walk** is here with its usual tasteful array of gift items, and so is **The Coffee Store,** much like its bigger sister in Kaahumanu Center, with many kinds of coffees and coffee accessories. **Maui Dive Shop** offers scuba and snorkeling gear, beachwear, and even charter-boat dive trips. Discover rare and exotic shells, shell jewelry, and gift items right next door at **La Pre Shells and Gifts.** Check out **Liberty House** for its usual excellent selections, and Liberty House's bargain store, **Penthouse,** for special sale items. **Tradewind Treasures** offers family resort wear and a good selection of standard tourist fare.

The ever-popular **Panda Express** serves up a fast, fresh Chinese lunch or dinner for less than $5.

LONG'S CENTER Dominated by a huge Long's drugstore, this mall at 1215 S. Kihei Rd., also has a few smaller shops worthy of note. If you're ready to splurge on some jewelry, then consider **Topaz Goldsmith and Gallery.** They have Tahitian pearls, gold jewelry, and precious Niihau shell leis. **More or Less** is a good source of beachwear, and **Little Polynesians** has lots of good clothing for the keikis.

WAILEA SHOPPING VILLAGE This place at the Wailea Resort is always worth a stop. Many artistic and cultural events are held here, free, and the shops are of high quality. Yes, there sometimes is a herd of elephants at **Elephant Walk.** Last time we were there, the cute creatures were made of clay and priced from about $44 up. **Maui's Best,** which we told you about (above) at Azeka Place II, has a location here, with a more extensive clothing collection (beautiful, but expensive).

Other tasteful shops here include **Alexia Natural Fashions** (natural-fabric clothing from Greece, for women), and **Superwhale,** which has a large selection of children's clothing and gift items. Stop by on a Tuesday at 1:30pm and catch a free Polynesian show.

MARKETS If you're in Kihei on a Wednesday, Friday, or Saturday morning, visit the **Kihei Open Air Marketplace,** an enjoyable flea market held at 1945 S. Kihei Rd., next to McDonalds, from 8am to 3pm. You can find everything here from T-shirts to works by local artisans, all at great prices. We saw some beautiful hand-painted blouses here for $17; the next day, we spotted them in a gift shop for $25!

Pick up some Molokai watermelon, Hana sweet corn, or other locally grown produce at the **Maui Farmers Market,** on Tuesday and Friday from 2 to 5:30pm on the grounds of the Suda store. Cheeses, juices, and freshly baked breads are also available. (The farmer's market moves to Honokawai, in West Maui, on Monday and Thursday from 7:30am to 1:30pm.)

CRYSTALS Those who remember and miss the popular Miracles Unlimited store in Wailuku will be glad to know that much of its inventory—crystals, incense, jewelry, and crafts as well as art by Maui artists—is now safely ensconced in the Kihei area at **Treasure Cove,** 1945-D S. Kihei Rd. (tel. 875-0695). Owners Mary and Leon Overbay, metaphysical artists themselves, have created another wonderful, magical store.

SPORTS & RECREATION

SWIMMING Ready to call it a day and relax on the beach? This area has some of Maui's best swimming spots. ✪ **Kamaole Beaches I, II, and III** are fine, but the beach is public everywhere, and you can swim wherever you like. Look for the public-access sign pointing to **Ulua/Mokapu Beaches** near the Stouffer Wailea Beach Resort, park your car (there's a small paved area), and head for a lovely stretch of sand and ocean, with public restrooms and showers. Past Wailea you come to **Makena** and **Big Beach,** one of the prettiest beaches on Maui and a great favorite with the locals. Swimming and bodysurfing are excellent here.

KAYAKING **South Pacific Kayaks & Outfitters,** in the Rainbow Mall (tel. 875-4848) and also in Lahaina at 505 Front St. (tel. 661-8400), are good people to see if you want to do some kayaking. They rent six different styles of one-person kayaks, starting at $20 a day, with everything you need (no instruction), and two styles of two-person kayaks beginning at $40 a day, including everything except instruction. They also offer a variety of adventure tours, including the Turtle Reef Introductory Adventure (three hours, $55 per person) and the Marine Reserve Explorer (five hours, $85 per person). Their toll-free number from other islands, as well as from the U.S. mainland and Canada, is 800/776-2326.

RENTALS The same folks who run South Pacific Kayaks & Outfitters, Mike and Melissa McCoy, also rent snorkel gear, boogie boards, beach chairs, and the like at several shops that all bear the name **Auntie Snorkel and Uncle Boogie** (we hope this is politically correct). Their locations are at Rainbow Mall in Kihei (tel. 879-6263), in Honokowai (tel. 665-0804), and at 505 Front St. in Lahaina (tel. 667-6263). Rentals start at $3.95 a day, $9.95 a week, for basic snorkel sets or boogie boards.

Note: Their Lahaina store offers free use of bicycles for four hours to anyone who comes in; no purchase is necessary.

WHALE WATCHING From mid-December until the end of April, some 800 celebrities arrive at Maui, and everybody wants to see them. It's estimated that approximately 800 North Pacific humpback whales migrate 3,000 miles from their home in Alaska to mate and bear their young in the warm waters of Hawaii. You can probably spot a few whales from the beach or your lanai, but it's also fun to take one of the **whale-watching excursion boats** that leave daily from Maui harbors.

All the cruises are good, but we like to support the ones run by the **Pacific Whale Foundation.** When you travel with them, you're in the company of expert research scientists, and proceeds benefit the foundation's research and conservation efforts to save the endangered humpback whale. Cruises depart daily from Maalaea and Lahaina harbors, last 2½ hours, guarantee whales (or go again for free), and cost $27.50 for adults, $15 for children 3 to 12. Be sure to bring your camera for some spectacular shots. The same company also runs morning Snorkel/Whalewatches from Maalaea and Lahaina harbors every morning; cost of the 4-hour trip (with snorkeling instruction for beginners) is $44.25 for adults, $34.50 for children 3 to 12; again, whales are guaranteed.

Call the **Whale Hotline** (tel. 879-8811, or toll free 800/942-5311 from the mainland).

READERS RECOMMEND

Snorkeling at La Perouse Bay. *"We have our own snorkeling equipment and enjoy seeking the less-crowded spots. If you drive on the road that goes past Kihei and Wailea, south of Wailea the road continues to Makena. At the end of the road is a massive lava flow that forms La Perouse Bay, which is now an official sanctuary for over 90 species of exotic reef fish. We were the only ones snorkeling there. A word of caution: It's quite rocky, so be sure to wear something on your feet."*—Mrs. and Mrs. Dennis W. Randall, Seattle, Wash.

EVENING ENTERTAINMENT

Luaus

There are several luaus to choose from in this area, but check local listings when you arrive; prices, days, and entertainers change frequently.

Wailea's Finest Luau (tel. 879-1922 for reservations) takes place on Tuesday, Thursday, and Friday evenings at 5pm at the oceanfront Luau Gardens at the Maui Inter-Continental Wailea Resort. A lavish buffet meal precedes the colorful Polynesian Revue featuring Paradyse and Ka Poe O Hawaii. Adults pay $52; children 6 to 12, $26.

If it's a Monday or Thursday, it must be the luau at the **Stouffer Wailea Beach Resort** (tel. 879-4900 for reservations), a traditional Hawaiian party held in a beachfront garden setting. Luau time is 6pm. Adults pay $49, children under 12, $28.

Dancing and Listening

INU INU LOUNGE, in the Maui Inter-Continental Wailea, 3700 Wailea Alaniu. Tel. 879-1922.

The *Maui News* has called this "one of Maui's best places for dancing and listening to music." And so it is. Dance to Maui's hottest dance bands every Thursday, Friday, and Saturday night, from 9pm to 1am.

Admission: Free.

Free Polynesian Shows

MAUI PRINCE HOTEL, 5400 Makena Alanui. Tel. 874-1111.

A "Mini-Hula" show is performed poolside Monday, Wednesday, and Friday, 6 to 8pm.

Admission: Free.

SUNSET SPECTACULAR

GRAND WAILEA RESORT, 3850 Wailea Alaniu Dr. Tel. 875-1234.

The scenery here is so spectacular that you really don't need any other entertainment, but watching the sun go down in the Pacific from the lounge of Humu-

humunukunukukuapua's restaurant that "floats" on its own saltwater lagoon is one of the greatest shows on the islands. The price of one of Humuhumu's 32 custom-made tropical drinks is the only cost.

2. HALEAKALA, HOUSE OF THE SUN

Any schoolchild on Maui can tell you the story of the demigod Maui, the good-natured Polynesian Prometheus who gave human beings fire, lifted the Hawaiian Islands out of the sea on his fishhook, and trapped the sun in its lair until it agreed to move more slowly around the earth—so that his mother could have more time to dry her tapa before night came! And where did this last, most splendid achievement take place? Why, right at Haleakala, 10,023 feet up in the sky, just about the closest any Stone Age person—or god—ever got to the sun.

With or without benefit of legends, Haleakala is an awesome place. It's the world's largest dormant volcano (its last eruption occurred two centuries ago), whose 33-mile-long, 24-mile-wide, 10,000-foot-high dimensions make Vesuvius seem like a mud puddle. Even more spectacular is the size of the volcano's great cinder desert, 7½ miles long, 2½ miles wide—big enough to swallow a modern metropolis within its moonlike expanse. (Haleakala's summit has been carved away by erosion. The summit valleys have been partially filled in by later eruptions and are dotted with many small craters.) Haleakala is one of the great scenic wonders of Hawaii.

EXCURSION TO THE SUMMIT

Plan on at least 3 hours for the Haleakala excursion (37 miles from the airport each way) and bring a warm sweater or jacket with you (it gets surprisingly cold and windy almost 2 miles up). Note that anyone with a cardiac condition is advised not to make this trip because of the stress of the high altitude. We feel it's best to get an early start on this trip, since there's less likelihood of clouds early in the day. You might call the park headquarters (tel. 572-7749) to check on cloud, road, and weather conditions before you start out.

There's no place to eat once you enter **Haleakala National Park,** but you might pack a picnic lunch and stop at **Hosmer Grove** on the lower slopes. You can get sandwiches at **Subway,** in the Pukalani Terrace Shopping Center, in Pukalani, about halfway between Kahului and the park. You might also stop off at the **Pukalani Superette,** a real upcountry store, where you can get mangoes for about half of what they cost in town, plus delicious homemade sushi and lumpia, and local Japanese and Filipino delicacies.

The drive starts in Kahului on Hi. 32; head eastward to the Hana Highway (Hi. 36). Shortly after Hi. 36 swings left, it's intersected on the right by Hi. 37, which takes you to Hi. 377, where you head up into a cool forest of flowers, cactus, and eucalyptus.

Now watch for the turnoff to Hi. 378 to the left, Haleakala Crater Road, a serpentine two-lane highway curving through the clouds. You'll see cattle and horses on the pasturelands of Haleakala Ranch as you climb the slopes of the volcano. At 6,700 feet, you reach the entrance to Haleakala National Park. You'll then see Hosmer Grove on the left, a scenic place to picnic (or camp) among rare trees and plants. Temperate tree seedlings from around the world have been planted here, along a half-mile trail of native shrubs and trees that are home for a variety of birds; you may see a pueo (short-eared owl) or a ring-necked pheasant. Stop at **park headquarters** a mile ahead at 7,030 feet, where the friendly and knowledge-able rangers will give you maps, instructions, directions for hiking the trails, and camping permits. Admission to the park is $4 per car and $2 per bicycle. The choicest way to see Haleakala is to go into the crater on foot or horseback; it's best to check with the rangers before you do.

Now you're ready for the ascent on this South Seas Everest, to the **Haleakala Visitors Center,** almost 2 miles up, on the edge of the crater. Inside the observatory, you learn that the early Hawaiians used the crater as a highway across eastern Maui, camping in its caves and building rock shelters. The last eruption was just 200 years ago, and very likely the volcano will erupt again; it is *dormant,* not extinct. But the most thrilling show is what lies beyond the glass: a dark kaleidoscope of clouds and colors and light played against what might well be the deserts of the moon. On a clear day you can see over 100 miles to the horizon, your field of vision encompassing 30,000 square miles of the Pacific; from this altitude, the volcano's vast cones look like so many sand dunes. Their rustlike colors change as the day grows old. At sunrise the crater is in shadow; it seems to give birth to the sun. From midday to sunset the play of sun and shadow is more subtle, and sunset, according to some, is the most muted and lovely of all. One of the easiest ways to get a spirited debate going among Mauians is to ask whether sunset or sunrise is more superlative at Haleakala; suffice it to say that both are considered among the great natural sights of the world.

The summit of Haleakala is half a mile beyond, at **Red Hill,** atop a cinder cone 10,023 feet high. Nearby, there's a satellite-tracking station and the Haleakala Observatories (the clear air here in mid-Pacific permits research that could be done nowhere else).

On the way down from Haleakala, you should stop for some different—and spectacular—views at Kalahaku and Leleiwi lookouts. At **Kalahaku Lookout,** you view the vast cinder desert on one side; on the other you'll spot western Maui and your first silverswords. The silversword is a botanical rarity, a plant that grows at the highest altitudes. These curious, oversize cousins of the sunflower have swordlike leaves, and when they're ready to blossom (between June and October) they shoot up a stalk up to 6 feet high. The whole thing turns into a tower of pink and lavender flowers, blooms once, and dies, scattering its seeds into the cinders to begin the phenomenon all over again. At the next lookout, **Leleiwi Lookout,** you may, with great luck, get to see the rather spooky specter of the Brocken; the sun must be strong at your back with misty clouds in front of you in order for you to see your own shadow in the rainbow mist. It doesn't happen often, but when it does, it's unforgettable; a ranger told us that he has seen it many times, and with as many as seven rainbows!

Coming down from the heights of Haleakala, it's pleasant to stop on the lower slopes at **Sunrise Market and Protea Farm,** near the beginning of Crater Road. You can have a free sample of Maui pineapple, buy some sandwiches, homemade fudge, or local fruits, and get a cup of coffee and a muffin (maybe mango or banana or walnut) to go with it. If you like, take your picnic lunch out to the tables surrounding the protea fields outside. Sunrise Market has just about the best prices around on the operation; this is a good chance to walk around and see protea growing (several protea farms dot these Maui uplands; protea are becoming a big commercial crop). Their protea gift shop displays fresh protea bouquets, as well as dried arrangements, and crafts, which can be shipped home.

READERS RECOMMEND

Seeing Haleakala. *"It's becoming very popular to get up early to catch sunrise on Haleakala. The total experience of leaving the hotel at about 3am, driving up the mountain in pitch blackness, meeting other people with the same crazy idea, then slowly waiting for the sun to rise over the crater is absolutely breathtaking. At that hour, however, a sweater, jacket, and blanket may suffice for only some. It was cold! Bring breakfast/lunch and enjoy amid other sun/nature worshipers or on your own."*—Francine Schept, White Plains, N.Y.

"On the early-morning drive to Haleakala Crater for sunrise it took me an hour and 10 minutes from Kahului, and I am a cautious driver. It was freezing at the visitors center—about 45° in late August—so I would suggest gloves, especially for photogra-

phers; my "shutter finger" was stiff from the cold! First light—30 to 40 minutes before sunrise—is as lovely as the sunrise and should not be missed. On the way down, I was the only person to stop at Leleiwi Lookout, sharing it with a park ranger for 2 hours; I think the view from the lookout is superior to the one at the visitors center."—Martha F. Battenfeld, Brighton, Mass.

CAMPING

Strong hikers, take note: You can spend a magnificent 2 or 3 days in Haleakala for spectacularly low prices. At Haleakala National Park there are three primitive cabins, each sleeping 12, for overnight lodging. The cabins have wood-burning stoves and cooking and eating utensils. All you need bring is food, water, a sleeping bag, and matches! The three form a sort of triangle in the crater, and you can go from one to the other on your explorations. **Kapalaoa Cabin** is at the middle of the southern end of the crater, **Paliku Cabin** is northeast of Kapalaoa at the eastern tip, and **Holua Cabin** is northwest of Paliku across at the western tip of the crater. Write to the Superintendent, Haleakala National Park, P. O. Box 369, Makawao, Maui, HI 96768, to make reservations for use of the cabins. Give the details of your proposed trip, the number in your party, dates of the stay, and names of the specific cabins you wish to use each night. The price is minimal: under $10 per person per night. Cabins may be occupied for no more than three consecutive nights, with a maximum of 2 nights' stay in any one cabin. So popular are these cabins that assignments for each month are chosen by lottery three months before. In other words, if you want a reservation sometime in the month of July, be sure your request is received before May 1.

We should note that these cabins—and these trails—are for experienced hikers in good physical condition: The Park Service warns that "wilderness travel is arduous; the elevation and exertion required to return from the crater floor place excessive physical demands upon the body."

RIDING & BIKING

If you'd like to ride down into the crater, get in touch with the people at **Pony Express Tours,** P.O. Box 535, Kula, Maui, HI 96790 (tel. 808/667-2200), who offer half-day rides down to the crater floor and back up, lunch included, at $120 per person. A full-day ride explores the crater floor extensively, and costs $140 per person. Gentler 1- and 2-hour rides are also offered at Haleakala Ranch, on the beautiful lower slopes of the mountain, for $35 and $60. For all trips, you must wear long pants and closed-toe shoes. All levels of riding experience are accommodated, with well-trained horses and experienced guides. You must be at least 10 years of age and weigh no more than 230 pounds. Pony Express Tours can also be reached through any of the Activity Desks in Lahaina and Kaanapali.

Did you know that you can coast downhill on a bicycle, all the way from the 10,000-foot summit of Haleakala to sea level below? You must be a skilled rider and in good physical condition, and it helps if your nerves are in good shape. Several outfits offer these tours: Our local correspondent, who lived to tell the tale, claims that **Cruiser Bob's Haleakala Downhill** (tel. 579-8444 for reservations) offers the best experience. They have both sunrise and day trips. Riders of all ages are welcomed, but there is a 5-foot-minimum height requirement. The price is approximately $100 and may vary slightly from season to season. A neat family adventure.

Cruiser Bob also offers several nonmotoring travel packages. Call toll free 800/654-7717 for details.

READERS RECOMMEND

Biking Down Haleakala. *"I went biking down Haleakala in late November, the rainy season, and felt it was more a survival trip than a fun thing to do. Check on the* *weather first before booking. It rained the whole way down and the leader tried to make it fun, even though everyone was very cold and soaked to the bone."*—Jim and Deb Phillips, Hastings, Neb.

MAKAWAO

On your way back down from Haleakala, it's easy to visit Makawao, Maui's very own cowboy town, the scene every Fourth of July of the Famed Makawao Rodeo. Turn right at Pukalani and continue for just a few miles and you'll find yourself on the main street, whose clapboard storefronts make it look like something out of the Old West.

WHERE TO EAT

This is a good stop off for a snack: Local people swear by the fried doughnuts on a stick at **Komoda's General Store**—as well as by their great macadamia nut cookies and cream puffs. **Kitada's Kau Kau Korner** is known for the best saimin upcountry; many of the local people come here for home-cooked meals. **Casanova Italian Restaurant and Deli** and **Polli's Cantina** (see "Where to Eat," in Chapter 14) are both right here on Makawao Avenue. Voted number-one for several years by readers of the *Maui News*, **Courtyard Deli** is a charming indoor-outdoor spot, at 3620 Baldwin Ave., where you might enjoy an imaginative sandwich or salad (several vegetarian choices) or a coffee from the espresso bar, accompanied by wonderful, ever-changing desserts, like maple bread pudding with vanilla sauce. **Crossroads Caffè,** at the Crossroads Center, is a popular lunch spot with both residents and visitors. It has great salads and sandwiches, all fresh and homemade, as well as lunch specials each day and various regional cuisines (French country, Indian, Chinese, Japanese) every night. We've found the breakfasts and lunches absolutely delicious. You could pick up some sandwiches or California sushi at the **Rodeo General Store,** or have dinner at the **Makawao SteakHouse** at 3612 Baldwin Ave., which has long been popular in these parts.

SAVVY SHOPPING

As a sophisticated, upscale group moves into Makawao and other upcountry towns, the local shops are changing too, with blacksmith shops and barbershops and pool halls giving way to trendy boutiques and art galleries and New Age shops. Baldwin Avenue offers many enjoyable examples.

The restored **Makawao Theater Building** is worth a stop for several reasons. The first is **Viewpoints Gallery,** in the rear, Maui's only fine arts cooperative, showing the works of 30 of Maui's most respected artists, in a variety of media. The space invites serious looking. Across from that is **Hot Island Glass,** an actual glassblowing studio and gallery where you are invited to watch award-winning glassblowers Bill and Sally Worcester and their son Mike at work as they transform molten glass into exquisite pieces of art. The furnace is in operation from 10am to 5pm. Prices for these treasures can go up to about $1,000, but check out the unsigned seconds; some lovely things go for under $35, like their knobby "pickle glasses" at just $10. Also in the same building, **Upcountry Legends** has clothing, jewelry, and the like, as well as locally made quilts, pillows, and other fine handcrafts; and **Upcountry Kids,** with wonderfully unique children's clothing. **Maui Hands** shows the work of 66 artisans in basketry, prints, watercolors, jewelry, quilting, and more. The **Courtyard Deli** (see above) is just one more reason for a visit here.

Up and down Baldwin Avenue, the browsing and shopping continues. Handpainted handbags, hats, and silk-screened T-shirts by noted island artists await your inspection at **Gecko Trading Company.** Snazzy dresses, jewelry, pretty T-shirts, and lots more can be found at **Goodie's. Collections** concentrates on country items: quilts, teapots, aprons, even shoes. "Authentic Dry Goods" are purveyed at **The Mercantile**—dishes, quilts, kitchen gadgets, gourmet vinegars and mustards. Enamelware cups were just $3.50. **Encore!** is the setting for sophisticated women's clothing. It's a high-quality consignment boutique, popular with upcountry women. **Tropo** is the place for men's clothing and very nice locally made T-shirts.

If you've got the kids with you, they can sit and read while you shop at **Maui Child**. **The Rabbit Hole** is a charming children's bookstore, and **Children's Paradise** is a new and used children's clothing boutique.

New Age types will strike it rich at **Miracles Bookery, Too** (across from Casanova Restaurant), a madly popular New Age store. It's a lovely place to buy books, videos, maybe an engaging T-shirt reading EXPECT A MIRACLE. One can pick up health foods at **Down to Earth**, a well-stocked store, and find Chinese and herbal medicines, teas and teaware, and all manner of alternative and New Age remedies at **The Dragon's Den**. The shop also sells books, videos, crystals, and gifts, and frequently sponsors lectures and workshops. Check their bulletin board.

Art lovers should be sure to make a stop at **Hui No'eau Visual Arts Center** at 2841 Baldwin Ave. The historic Baldwin home, Kaluanui, now houses an exhibition gallery, art studios, and a gift shop on a superb 9-acre landscaped estate, worth a visit in its own right. Open Tuesday to Sunday, from 10am to 4pm (tel. 572-6560).

EVENING ENTERTAINMENT

CASANOVA ITALIAN RESTAURANT, 1188 Makawao Ave. Tel. 572-0220.

⭐ Maui's cowboy town, Makawao, suddenly became an entertainment venue when Casanova opened a few years ago. Now they consistently bring in big talents—performers like jazz greats Mose Allison and Jon Hendricks, rock-and-roll artists Mick Taylor and Billy Preston, zydeco musician C. J. Chenier and his Red Hot Louisiana Band, to name just a few. Willie Nelson, Kris Kristofferson, Thomas Mapfumo, Los Lobos, and Richie Havens have performed here recently. Readers of the *Zagat Survey* recently voted Casanova's as the "Best Food and Entertainment Combo in Maui" (see "Where to Eat," in Chapter 14, for our review). There's disco dancing Monday, Wednesday, and Thursday nights; country dancing Tuesdays; live music Fridays and Saturdays.

Admission: Usually $12–$20 for name entertainment, $5 on disco nights. The cover charge is waived for diners on weekdays and when local bands are featured.

A STOP AT PAIA

Unless you're planning to stop at Paia on the way to Hana (see "Road to Hana," below), we recommend that you do so now. Instead of taking the road back to Pukalani, just take Baldwin Avenue a few miles into Paia, where you can shop for gifts and antiques and hobnob with the local people before heading back home.

UNUSUAL SIDE TRIP

An unusual side trip you might want to take on your way back from an early trip to Haleakala is to the **Tedeschi Vineyards,** on Hi. 37 in beautiful upcountry Maui at the Ulupalakua Ranch. It's about 10 miles from Kula. Hawaii's only winery, Tedeschi cultivates 22 acres of grapes on the slopes of Haleakala to produce a champagne, a blush, and a red table wine in the Beaujolais nouveau tradition. It also produces a pleasant light, dry pineapple wine. You're welcome to take a free guided tour daily, from 9:30am to 2:30pm, to observe various phases of the bottling operation. After the tour, stop in at the tasting room in one of the early 18th-century buildings, sample the wines, perhaps purchase some. If you've brought your picnic lunch, there are tables outside the tasting room, amid beautiful scenery (including a splendid, huge camphor tree planted in the late 1800's) and spectacular views.

3. ROAD TO HANA

Some 10,000 feet down from the moon canyons of Haleakala, curving around the base of the old volcano, is a world light-years away, a place of such tropical lushness and splendor that it conjures up the word "primeval." This is remote Hana and the curving road leading to it—a road carved under the fringe of the lava cliffs, plunging down on one side to the sea, emerging on the other from overhanging jungle watered by the thousand streams of Haleakala.

In all of Hana, there are just a few dozen modestly priced accommodations. (The town's chief industry is the exquisite Hana Kai–Maui Resort, which caters to wealthy travelers only.) If you can reserve one of these (see "Where to Stay," in Chapter 14), it would be worth your while to stay overnight; otherwise, you'll have to do Hana in a 1-day trip. Count on 2 to 3 hours each way, more if you want to savor the magnificent scenery. And be sure to check with the Highway Department about road conditions before you take off. If the weather has been wet, you could get stuck in landslides or mud. If it's raining heavily, forget the Hana trip altogether. Parts of the road are easily washed away, and it may take hours for you to be rescued (which happened one year to friends of ours). There's always tomorrow, or the next visit to Maui.

Even though extensive highway repaving has made it much easier to drive the Hana road, it is still rugged and winding. There are plenty who love it as well as some who think that, despite the glory of the scenery, it's just not worth the effort. A picnic lunch is essential, unless you want to eat at the expensive Hana Kai–Maui or one of the little snack shops on the road or in Hana. Besides, you'll be traveling through the kind of country for which picnics surely were originally invented.

Hana glories in its remoteness. Rumor has it that a road is not being built because the local people like to keep Hana the way it is—difficult to get to. The current road was not completed until 1927, and by that time the Hasegawa General Store had already been in business 15 years and a hotel was already operating there. Hana's lush isolation attracted the late aviator and environmentalist Charles Lindbergh, who spent his vacations in Hana and is now buried there (the Lindbergh family has requested that his gravesite be kept private).

Because of its remoteness, Hana has been slow in accepting change. Throughout its history it has assimilated new cultures, new religions, and new institutions, but Hana has not become part of them; rather, they have become a part of Hana.

One thing we strongly recommend you do before you set out on your trip to Hana is to rent a cassette tour; it's like having your own guide in the back seat. Try either of the following: they're both terrific.

Best of Maui Cassette Tours, 333 Dairy Rd., Kahului (tel. 871-1555 for reservations, 871-6339 for information). Scott Golladay's entertaining tours to Hana and also to Haleakala have been widely praised. Included in the cost of $25 is a $10 discount on the second tour, plus a 30-minute video called "Visions of Maui" (a tour of Maui by helicopter). You also get a guidebook, a huge full-color map, flower/bird ID cards, a picnic lunch coupon, and Scott's Tip Sheet. Tapes are also available at locations in Kihei, Kahului, and Paia, as well as at the main office.

Hana Cassette Guide, on Dairy Road at the Shell service station (tel. 572-0550 for reservations). This tour is the creation of Craig Henderson, a local photographer who narrates the trip himself and is well versed in the lore and legends of the Hana Road. Craig no longer rents tapes; he *sells* them. Included in the $20 fee is a Hana Coast map and flower guide; a video of the Hana Coast drive is available for only $5 at the time of the tape/map purchase. Craig also narrates an excellent tour of Haleakala—$10 when you buy the "Hana Package." Readers continue to praise this one.

READERS ADVISE

A Reader's Warning. *"I'd like to pass on some information I learned the hard way. I mentioned to a clerk in a market that I was planning to drive to Hana the next day. He said, 'If it's raining when you get halfway, turn back, or you can get stuck out there.' I assumed he was being overly cautious. It sprinkled off and on as we drove to Hana, but it's a long trip and we didn't want to waste our day. The sun was shining as we visited the Seven Sacred Pools, and water rushed from the very top pool to the ocean. On our way back, cloudy but no rain, we were stopped in a line of about 30 cars, trapped by a landslide on a narrow, cliff-hugging road. Rescue crews had been called, but it took 2 hours with men, shovels, and a bulldozer to clear the road so we could get by. It could have been a tragedy, and we learned to take seriously what the Hawaiians say. They know best!"—*Mrs. Donald B. Newton, Saratoga, Calif.

FIRST STOP: PAIA

Start eastward on Hi. 32 in Kahului or Wailuku and switch (right) to Hi. 36. You may want to stop at **Pic-nics** on Baldwin Avenue in Paia to pick up a picnic lunch (see "Where to Eat," Chapter 14).

SAVVY SHOPPING

Take some time now, or on the return trip, to browse in some of the antiques, decorator, and gift shops that have sprung up in this unspoiled, upcountry community. The nice thing about shopping in Paia is that it's a local, not a tourist, area. Rents are not as high as in Lahaina or Kihei, so shopkeepers can afford to sell lovely things at good prices.

Be sure to visit the ✪ **Maui Crafts Guild,** at 43 Hana Hwy., a cooperative gallery showing outstanding work by local craftspeople. The two-story gallery carries a variety of crafts, ranging from bamboo (directly from the bamboo groves of Maui) to wooden bowls and boxes made of exotic local woods, baskets woven from native plants, jewelry, ceramics, hand-painted silk and cotton clothing, Hawaiian fish prints (gyotaku), and stone carvings. Prices are practically wholesale: Artist/members, who run the business themselves and wait on visitors, take only a 10% markup. Prices can go way up for some of the prints, collages, and sculptures, but there are many items at low prices too: We recently spotted black bamboo calligraphy brushes at $14, raku lava eggs at $20, and banana bark paintings at $17.50. Most prices range from $10 to $70.

One of the nicest of the local shops is **The Boutique II** at 104 Hana Hwy., which specializes in natural fabrics—cotton, silk, rayon. Owner/designers Patti and Dyan create many of their exclusive designs here and have them made up in Bali. Prices are surprisingly affordable. Another popular shop in this little cluster (they're all on either side of the road, across from the Wunderbar Restaurant on Hana Highway) is **Jagger,** 100 Hana Hwy., which sports a neat collection of men's shirts and ladies' fashions, lots of accessories to choose from, and a friendly staff.

Nuage Bleu, 76 Hana Hwy., has high-style women's wear and accessories, as well as a line of aromatherapy oils, and some unique gift items, too. We like the adorable kiddy clothes—especially the slippers with animal faces for $10—at **Just You and Me, Kid,** 90 Hana Hwy. Original artwork by Maui artists is featured at **Hana Hou Gallery,** which also has an impressive collection of Hawaiiana. **Summerhouse** is an old favorite here. Their specialties are casual island wear in natural fibers, Asian imports, and a swimsuit collection extraordinaire.

Around the corner from these shops at 12 Baldwin Ave. is **Maui Girl Co.,** a spot that has been sought out by such customers as Billy Joel, Cindy Lauper, and Ringo Starr for its collection of vintage rayon and silk aloha shirts. The collection, from the '30s, '40s, and '50s, comes from Canada, the mainland, and Japan. If you can't afford the prices ($50 to $500), just browse and have a look at some of their other fashionable sportswear; they do their own line of bikinis and clothing under the "Maui Girl" label and sell many suits at wholesale prices of $28. Then cross the street and check out **Creative Culture,** an import store featuring weavings and clothes from Bali. **Yoki's Boutique,** at 21 Baldwin Ave., has exotic clothing, jewelry, fashion items, and sensual lingerie. There's an elegant, Victorian, very feminine feeling at **The Silk Gallery,** 19 Baldwin Ave., which shows outstanding hand-painted women's clothing, plus lingerie, massage oils, and lotions; they will custom-scent anything you want. The place abounds in decorative angels and angel motifs, dried roses, Victorian baskets, and other whimsies.

SIGHTS & ATTRACTIONS

Before you get back on the road to Hana, you might want to make a short detour in Paia to **Hookipa County Beach Park,** otherwise known as the "Windsurfing Capital of the World." Windsurfing, or sailboarding, as it is also known, is an enormously popular sport, and nowhere are conditions better for it than right here on the northern shore of Maui. It's fun to watch the windsurfers anytime, and if there happens to be a competition going on (make local inquiries), you're in for a special treat. The park is right on the road. Get out your cameras—the views are incredible.

BACK ON THE ROAD

Now it's back on the road to Hana. The highway runs straight and easy, through cane fields, until you get to Pauwela. Here's where the road becomes an Amalfi Drive of the Pacific; the view is spectacular, but keep your eye on the curves. The variety of vegetation is enough to drive a botanist—or photographer—wild. Waterfalls, pools, green gulches beckon at every turn. You'll be tempted to stop and explore a hundred times, but keep going, at least until you get to **Kaumahina Park,** where you might consider picnicking high on the cliff, looking down at the black sand beach of Honomanu Bay below, watching the local folk fish and swim.

Believe it or not, from here on the scenery gets even better. From the road, you can look down on the wet taro patches and the peaceful villages of **Keanae** and **Wailua,** to which a short side trip, to see the old Catholic church built of lava rock and cemented with coral, is eminently worthwhile. It seems that this coral was strewn ashore after an unusual storm in the 1860s, providing the villagers with the necessary material to construct their church. To commemorate this miracle, they constructed the **Miracle of Fatima Shrine,** which you will see on the Wailua Bay Road, at the 18-mile marker (turn left at the road sign).

In a little while, you get another vista of Keanae from **Koolau Lookout.** In the other direction you look through a gap in the cliff over into Haleakala. A little farther on is **Puaa Kaa Park,** another made-in-heaven picnic spot. The flowers are gorgeous here, and so are the two natural pools, each with its own waterfall. You might have a swim here before you continue.

On you go, past grazing lands and tiny villages, to **Waianapanapa Cave,** another possible side excursion. This lava tube filled with water is the place where a jealous Stone Age Othello was said to have slain his Desdemona. Every April the water is supposed to turn blood-red in remembrance. Near the cave is a black sand beach (not always safe for swimming), another great place for a picnic.

A wonderful garden awaits you when you enter Hana. ✪ **Hana Gardenland,** at the corner of Kalo and Hana Roads, has 5 acres of splendid botanical gardens, plus a gallery, plants, gifts, and Hawaiian crafts for sale. There is also a delightful café in operation, with fresh salads, sandwiches, smoothies, many kinds of coffees, and herbal teas. Restrooms available. Admission free. (*Note:* The same people who run Hana Plantation Houses, described in Chapter 14, are the new owners, bringing their imagination and flair to this place.)

A wonderful garden awaits you when you enter Hana. Blair Shurtleff and Tom Nunn (the people who own and operate Hana Plantation Houses—see preceding chapter) have transformed this 5½-acre property from a place where one would quickly stop and buy an orchid plant into an experience so wonderful you'll want to spend an hour or more if you can afford the time. Stroll through the botanical gardens and jungle trails or just sit beside the lily pond stocked with koi (Japanese carp) and you'll know the meaning of tranquility. A small, tastefully arranged gallery is filled with the work of local artists, both those well known on Maui (Vijay and Piero Resta, for example) and those on their way to being known (such as oil-and-acrylic painter Rik Fitch and Vadra & Zolt, who create one-of-a-kind silver jewelry). There are also Hawaiian crafts. The gift shop offers hard-to-find classic Hawaiian T-shirts, books, postcards, and some unique gift items, such as beautiful koa-wood hairbrushes. And, of course, you can still buy all manner of plants and tropical flowers to send home, carry home with you, or to adorn your hotel room and condo. Restrooms available. Admission free.

The **Café** at Hana Gardenland (see preceding chapter) is a special delight; you sit at picnic tables dining on fresh salads, smoothies, sandwiches, and many kinds of coffees.

HANA

Not a little history was made at Hana. The Big Three—Captain Cook, the Protestant missionaries, and vacationing Hawaiian royalty—were all here. You can even follow the road to a historic Stone Age delivery room near the cinder cone of **Kauiki Head,** where Kamehameha's favorite wife, Kaahumanu, was born (there's a plaque near the lighthouse). Or you can just walk around the town for a while and soak up the atmosphere. A must on your list of sights should be the **Hasegawa General Store** where, it is reported, you can get anything and everything your heart desires (just like at Alice's Restaurant) in one place. (The old Hasegawa's burned down, but a new store has been constructed at the Old Hana Theater, on Hana Road, opposite the Chevron Station.) A song was written about this place some years ago, and its spirit has not changed in spite of all the hullabaloo. As for practical matters, the store has everything from soup to nuts and bolts, from gasoline to muumuus, but because of the scarcity of restaurants in Hana, the food department—plenty of local fruit, some vegetables, mostly sausage meats, and some staples—will be of most interest to you. And you may not be able to resist—as we couldn't—the bumper stickers that read: FIGHT SMOG—BUY HORSES, HASEGAWA GENERAL STORE.

A visit to the ✪ **Hana Cultural Center** (tel. 248-8622), in the middle of town, will fill you in on a bit of the history and background of this quaint town. Opened in 1983, the cultural center gets most of its collection from local residents, and it's full of wonderful old photographs, Hawaiian quilts (note the unusual Hawaiian-flag quilt dating from the 1920s), plenty of memorabilia from the '30s and '40s, as well as artifacts and tools, and rare shells. Admission is free, but donations are welcome; the center is open daily from 10am to 4pm.

Hana's best beach, **Hamoa,** is at the Hana Kai–Maui Resort, but you can also swim at the public beach on Hana Bay, at the black sand beach at Waianapanapa State Park, and at the red sand beach (ask locals how to get there).

Most visitors drive about 10 miles past Hana on to Kipahulu, an unspoiled extension of Haleakala National Park and **Ohe'o Gulch** (formerly, but incorrectly, known as the Seven Sacred Pools), a gorgeous little spot for a swim. Here the pools drop into one another and then into the sea. But it's a roller-coaster ride on a rough, narrow road filled with potholes, and again, unless you enjoy this kind of driving, it may not be worth your nerves.

En route to Ohe'o Gulch, you'll pass **Wailua Gulch** and a splendid double fall cascading down the slopes of Haleakala. Nearby is a memorial to Helio, one of the island's first Catholics, a formidable proselytizer and converter. A tribute to his work stands nearby—the *Virgin of the Roadside,* a marble statue made in Italy and draped every day with the fragrant flower leis of the Hawaiians.

The good road runs out a little farther on at Kipahulu, so it's back along the northern route, retracing your way past jungle and sea to home base.

READERS RECOMMEND

Staying in Hana. *"Our 4 nights at Waianapanapa Park were at our no. 1 idyllic spot. Hana was having a week-long Aloha Week festival. We went to a real Hawaiian luau with great performers for $6; the previous night the ladies of the village gave a real hula show at the village soccer field—free. October is a great time to go to Hana, as there are very few guests. Try the red sand beach for snorkeling at Hana Park, near the old frame schoolhouse, now a library, and follow the trail down a meadow, around a cliff, to a secluded beach behind a natural lava breakwall. Caution: Young couples still swim in the buff here!"*—Richard Welse, Westfield Center, Ohio.

"When hiking to the red sand beach in Hana, wear strong shoes, as the track is very narrow, with a steep cliff face on one side in some parts. We found the snorkeling equal to the best on the island. Since it is a nudist beach, though, one often sees more than fish underwater!"—Mrs. Jane Beecham, Victoria, Australia.

4. LAHAINA, KAANAPALI & KAPALUA

If Haleakala and Hana are nature's showplaces on Maui, Lahaina is humanity's. It was there that some of the most dramatic and colorful history of Hawaii was made: 100 years ago Lahaina was the whaling capital of the Pacific, the cultural center of the Hawaiian Islands (and for a time its capital), and the scene of an often violent power struggle between missionaries and sailors for—quite literally—the bodies and souls of the Hawaiians.

Your trip to Lahaina and the western Maui coast happily combines history with some of the most beautiful scenery in the islands. Take your bathing suit and skip the picnic lunch, since there are plenty of places en route where you can eat. Since there's no paved road completely circling the western tip of Maui, we'll take the road as far as Honokahua, and return by driving back along the same road to Kahului—a route that is more interesting and comfortable than the drive on the unpaved portion between Honokahua and Waihee on the northern shore.

The trip begins on Hi. 32, which you follow through Wailuku to Hi. 30 (High Street), where you turn left. At Maalaea the road swings right at the sea and continues along the base of the West Maui Mountains, along a wild stretch of cliffs pounded by strong seas, until it reaches Lahaina, 22 miles from Kahului. During the winter months, whale sightings are frequent along this stretch of ocean.

LAHAINA

Lahaina today is a comfortable plantation town, with pretty little cottages, a cannery, a sugar mill, and acres of cane and pineapple stretching to the base of the misty western Maui hills. Thanks to its having been declared a National Historic Landmark property, it still retains its late 19th- and early 20th-century architectural charm. New buildings must fit in with this architectural scheme, so there's no danger that it will ever look like Waikiki.

SIGHTS & ATTRACTIONS

STROLLING AROUND TOWN For some years, Lahaina has been in the process of a restoration that will cover the 150 or so years during which Hawaii rose from the Stone Age to statehood—from the reign of King Kamehameha I to the annexation of Hawaii by the United States. Re-created will be the days when Lahaina was the capital of the Hawaiian monarchy (before the king, in 1843, moved the palace to Honolulu, where there was a better harbor); the coming of the missionaries; the whaling period; and the beginning of the sugar industry. The restoration is being lovingly and authentically carried out by the **Lahaina Restoration Foundation,** a devoted group of local citizens and county and state interests. You may visit their office in the Master's Reading Room at the corner of Front Street and Dickenson Street (tel. 661-3262), open Monday through Friday from 10am to 4:30pm, for further information.

As you tour Lahaina, you'll notice various signs reading LAHAINA HISTORIC SITE: those with a square at the bottom indicate buildings that are either original or restored; those with a circle indicate structures that no longer exist. A booklet called *Lahaina Historical Guide,* free at many Lahaina locations, provides useful maps and descriptions.

Begin your exploration out on the old pier in the center of town, where you can gaze at the famed **Lahaina Roads;** from the 1820s to the 1860s this was the favorite Pacific anchorage of the American whaling fleet. Over on your left are the soft greens of Lanai, to the north the peaks of Molokai, on the south the gentle slopes of Kahoolawe. During the winter and early spring, you may get to see some non-paying tourists sporting about in the water; these are the sperm whales that migrate from their Aleutian homes to spawn in the warmer waters off Lahaina.

For the whalers, this place was practical as well as beautiful: They were safe here in a protected harbor, they could come or go on any wind, and there was plenty of fresh water at the local spring, plenty of island fruits, fowl, and potatoes. And there were also Hawaiian women, who, in the old hospitable way of the South Seas, made the sailors feel welcome by swimming out to the ships and staying a while. To the missionaries, this was the abomination of abominations, and it was on this score that violent battles were fought. More than once, sailors ran through the streets setting houses on fire, rioting, beating up anyone who got in their way, even cannonading the mission house. You can see the evidence of those days at **Hale Paaho,** the old stone prison (on Prison Street, off Main), where sailors were frequent guests while the forays lasted.

Across the street from the waterfront you'll see the **Pioneer Inn,** which may look oddly familiar—it has been the set for many a South Seas movie saga. Back in 1901 (it has since been tastefully renovated and enlarged) it was quite the place, the scene of arrival and departure parties for the elegant passengers of the Inter-Island Steamship Company, whose vessels sailed out of Lahaina. And since it was too difficult to make the hot trek to central Maui immediately, arriving passengers usually spent the night here. Walk in and have a look around: Note the lovely stained-glass window one flight up from the entrance to the Harpooner's Lanai and the grandfather clock at the foot. The lanai itself is a wonderful place to waste a few years of your life while soaking up the atmosphere.

Across Wharf Street from the hotel, a little to the north of the lighthouse, is the site of a palace used by Kamehameha in 1801, when he was busy collecting taxes on Maui and the adjoining islands. And across from that, where the Lahaina Branch Library now stands, is another spot dear to the lovers of the Hawaiian monarchy, the **royal taro patch** where Kamehameha III betook his sacred person to demonstrate the dignity of labor.

The huge banyan tree just south of the Pioneer Inn covers two-thirds of an acre; it's the favorite hotel for the town's noisy mynah bird population. In the front of the tree is the **Court House,** a post office, and police station, the post office part of which has been functioning since 1859. Between the Court House and the Pioneer Inn, you'll see the first completed project of the Lahaina Restoration, the **Fort Wall.** It's built on the site of the original fort, but since rebuilding the whole fort would have destroyed the famed banyan tree, the authorities decided to reconstruct the wall instead, as a ruin—a ruin that never existed.

Now that you've seen how the whalers lived, let's see how their arch opponents, the missionaries, fared. Walk 1 block mauka of the waterfront to Front Street and the **Baldwin House**—so typical, with its upstairs and downstairs verandas, of New England in Polynesia. The old house, built in the late 1830s with walls of coral and stone, served as a home for the Rev. Dwight Baldwin, a physician and community leader as well as a missionary (and incidentally, the founder of a dynasty; the

Baldwins are still an important family in Maui). Thanks to the Lahaina Restoration Foundation, the house has been faithfully restored; you can examine Dr. Baldwin's medical kit (the instruments look like something out of a Frankenstein film), kitchen utensils, china closets, old photographs and books, the family's furniture and mementos—all the little touches of missionary life 100 and more years ago. Open daily. Admission is $5 for families, $3 for adults, $2 for seniors, and free for children accompanied by their parents for a personally guided tour.

After you've seen Baldwin House, stop next door to visit the **Master's Reading Room,** a former seamen's library and chapel that now houses the office of the Lahaina Restoration Foundation. The unique coral-block-and-fieldstone construction has been preserved exactly as originally built in 1847.

Next stop might be the **Wo Hing Temple,** on Front Street, near Mariner's Alley. The restored 1912 fraternal hall is now a museum, with a display on the history of the Chinese in Lahaina. Stop in at the **Cook House Theater,** adjacent, which shows movies of Hawaii taken by Thomas Edison in 1898 and 1903. Open daily from 10am to 4:30pm; admission donation requested.

The Restoration Foundation also operates the floating museum ship *Carthaginian,* moored opposite the Pioneer Inn. Its "World of the Whale" exhibit features a series of colorful multimedia displays on whaling, whales, and the sea life of Hawaii. Maui's own humpback whale, which comes to these waters each winter to mate and calve, gets special treatment through videotape presentations made on the spot by the National Geographic Society, the New York Zoological Society, and others. The ship is a replica of a 19th-century brig and is open daily from 9am to 4:30pm. Admission is $5 for families, $3 for adults, $2 for seniors, free for children with their parents.

Head now for Wainee Street (to the right of Lahainaluna Road); here, where the recently built **Waiola Church** now stands, is the site of Wainee, the first mission church in Lahaina, to which the Reverend Baldwin came as pastor in 1835. The old cemetery is fascinating. Buried among the graves of the missionary families are some of the most important members of the Kamehameha dynasty, including no fewer than two wives of Old King Kam: Queen Keoupuolani, his highest-born wife, and Queen Kalakaua.

On the grounds of Lahainaluna High School stands **Hale Pai,** the original printing house of Lahainaluna Seminary, which the missionaries built in 1813. From the hand press here came the school books and religious texts that spread the Word. The coral-and-lava structure has been turned into a charming museum by the Restoration Foundation. Open Monday through Saturday from 10am to 4pm.

For those interested in Asian culture, it would be unthinkable to leave Lahaina without a visit to the **Lahaina Jodo Mission Cultural Park**. In a beautiful spot perched above the water is a 3½-ton statue of Amitabha Buddha, erected to commemorate the centennial anniversary of Japanese immigration in Hawaii. It's the largest Buddha outside Japan. You can meditate here as long as you wish, strike the huge temple bell, and perhaps leave a small donation in the offertory (there is no admission charge). *Note:* It's easy to miss this place. As you drive along Front Street, look for the big sign that reads JESUS IS COMING SOON. Then turn makai on Ala Moana Street and you'll find the Buddha.

JUST OUTSIDE TOWN Opposite Wahikuli State Park is the **Lahaina Civic Center,** an auditorium and gym, with a dramatic mosaic by one of Maui's most famous artists, Tadashi Sato.

Five miles east of Lahaina, on the highway headed toward Kahului, are the well-preserved **Olowalu Petroglyphs.** Two to three hundred years old, these rock carvings depicted the occupations—fishing, canoe-paddling, weaving, etc.—of the early Hawaiians. Unfortunately, they are rather difficult to get to.

On the other side of Lahaina, on the road leading toward Kaanapali, is another historical spot, the **Royal Coconut Grove of Mala.** Mala, one of the wives of Kamehameha, brought the trees from Oahu over a century ago. They are now being replaced by local citizens as part of the restoration.

CULTURAL ENTERTAINMENT

Check the local papers for news of frequent entertainment at the malls and shopping centers. On one visit to the **Wharf Cinema Center,** for example, we saw a full Polynesian review, including Samoan knife dances done by women on the center stage. And **The Cannery** presents a vast amount of free entertainment, so be sure to see if anything is going on while you're there. You may be lucky enough to catch someone of the caliber of noted island funny man Frank DeLima, as we did on a recent visit. Fabulous!

HAWAII EXPERIENCE DOMED THEATER, 824 Front St. Tel. 661-8314.

If there's one entertainment experience in Lahaina not to be missed, it has to be the 45-minute movie *Hawaii: Islands of the Gods,* at the Hawaii Experience Domed Theater. To call it a movie is really an injustice, for the traditional boundaries between viewer and film are broken down here as the floor of the planetariumlike theater seems to give way under you, and off you go, soaring into space. Soon you're flying over a burning volcano on the Big Island or swooping down into Kauai's Waimea Canyon, bicycling at breakneck speed down the slopes of mighty Haleakala, or scuba diving far below the surface of the ocean to the breeding grounds of the humpback whale off the coast of Maui. It's all courtesy of state-of-the-art technology. The screen is 60 feet around and more than 25 feet from the center, and your vision is a full 180°, which makes you feel you're part of the picture. The Domed Theater was created here by the Dankworths, who originated the concept in Alaska. "Hawaii is like Alaska," says Jim Dankworth, "in that it has so many extraordinary areas that are largely inaccessible to the average visitor. We wanted to capture that—to show the natural beauty, the history, the culture of the islands in a way that has never been done before." They have succeeded to an astonishing degree. For its price, this has to be the best bargain in Maui. We can hardly wait to see it again.

Admission: $6.95 adults, $3.95 children.
Open: Daily, hourly 10am–10pm.

READERS RECOMMEND

Tom Barefoot's Cashback Tours, *834 Front St. (tel. 661-8889). "Your readers may want to know about Tom Barefoot's Cashback Tours. You can book any and all of your activities through them and get an immediate 10% cash back at time of purchase."*—Pat McCallum, Bethesda, Md.

Information Tourist Booth, *in front of the Wharf Cinema Center, 658 Front St. "Ask anyone at the Information Tourist Booth for specialized personal tourist trips. They are always coming up with new things to show tourists. One day they took us to a windsurfing competition at Hookipa Beach; another time they arranged for three of us to hike into the interior with a native Hawaiian guide."*—Rue Drew, New York, N.Y.

SAILING TO LANAI

If sailing, snorkeling, swimming, whale watching, and rustic sightseeing—or any combination of the above—appeal to you, splurge once and spend a perfect day sailing to the island of Lanai aboard one of the sleek, multihulled yachts of ✪ **Trilogy Excursions** (tel. 661-4743, or toll free 800/874-2666 from the mainland). Jim and Randy of "The Sailing Coon Family" pioneered these trips back in 1973, and they are recognized today as the best on the Maui docks. The all-day excursion begins at 6:45am; watching the morning light brighten as you sail out of Lahaina Harbor is magical. Hot coffee and Mom Coon's home-baked cinnamon buns are served on board, and within about 1½ hours you're at Lanai. Then it's superb snorkeling (lessons for beginners) at the Hulupo'e Bay Marine Preserve, swimming on a crystal beach, an excellent lunch of barbecued chicken prepared over kiawe wood by the captain and served in a comfortable dining lanai overlooking the water. Another highlight of the trip is the tour around Lanai in an air-conditioned van; the native guides are delightful and will fill you in on island lore. (Should you want to stop off here at the venerable Hotel Lanai for the night, you can arrange to do so in advance and pick up another Trilogy boat the next day.)

Then it's back to Lahaina, and, with luck, a sighting of whales in season, maybe dolphins. Whales and dolphins cannot be guaranteed, but a thoroughly enjoyable day—and a return to Lahaina around 4:30pm—certainly can be. Bring the kids and the cameras.

The Trilogy "Discover Lanai" excursion costs $139 for adults, $69.50 for children 3 to 12, plus tax. Another of their popular trips, "Discover Molokini," sails to Molokini for a half-day of snorkeling and costs $75 adults, $37.50 children. Both excursions now also offer scuba diving—both an introductory and a certified dive—at an extra fee. Reservations are essential, as space is limited.

READERS RECOMMEND

Watching the Weather. "*Beware of heading off on a snorkeling cruise if the sea is up at all. I had the most miserable 6 hours either being sick or feeling sick, along with about another 10 hapless souls on a trip to Molokini and Lanai. We had 9-foot swells and even when the boat was moored, snorkeling was difficult with the rough seas. Make sure of the weather forecast before you go!!!*"—Mrs. Jane Beecham, Victoria, Australia.

SAVVY SHOPPING

We must confess: The thing we love to do most in Lahaina is shop. While the reconstruction of the historical sights is proceeding slowly, Lahaina (and Whaler's Village at Kaanapali Beach; see below) is fast emerging as one of the best shopping areas in the islands, second only to Honolulu. On each one of our visits there are new and exciting shops, boutiques, galleries to visit. Perhaps it's the influence of the young people and other newcomers moving into the area; they keep everything constantly stimulating and alive.

First, let's get your car parked. Finding a spot on the street is not easy, although it's often possible on Front Street, on the ocean side. There are 800 parking spaces at the new Lahaina Center, a good walk to the center of town. Also try the Lahaina Shopping Center, the area behind the Wharf Shopping Center, at the corner of Front and Prison Streets, and at the corner of Front and Shaw Streets. If none of that works, however, drive to one of the commercial parking lots, such as the one behind Baldwin House, at the corner of Luakini and Dickenson Streets: Charges are reasonable. Across from the parking lot is a place where you can get fresh island produce to take home, and in front of that is a stand selling ice-cold coconut juice.

Cool and refreshed now, let's start our wanderings.

Malls and Shopping Centers

LAHAINA MARKETPLACE, Front St. just south of Lahainaluna Rd.

Walk all the way to the back of the Lahaina Marketplace and you'll find ✪ **Donna's Designs,** a little house where Donna Sorenson does some fanciful hand-painted T-shirts and coverups (100% cotton, machine washable), and sells them for the lowest prices around: $10 to $36. Bags are $38. Donna points out— and we agree—that since shops directly on Front Street come and go at a rapid rate because of the high rentals, you're apt to get better bargains if you go slightly "off Front Street."

LAHAINA CENTER, 900 Front St.

Maui's newest shopping center is at the Kaanapali end of town, between the ocean and Wainee Street. Everything about this place is big, including the biggest Hilo Hattie's Fashion Center in the neighbor islands, a large Liberty House, and—especially welcome in a town where parking spaces are scarcer than gold nuggets—an

800-car parking lot! It's also the home of the Hard Rock Café and Chili's.

Top-of-the-line women's boutiques include **Bebe Sport,** offering upscale clothing from famous designers, and **Fashion Link,** focusing on unique hand-painted clothing, mostly by Maui artists. Popular-priced sportswear stores include **Local Motion,** which sells mostly 100% cotton clothing along with their surfboards, and **Splash! Hawaii** for an extensive collection of women's swimwear, including a made-in-Hawaii line called "Out of the Blue." **Wet Seal** provides rock music, video screens, and high-tech decor as a background for its youthful women's fashions.

Got the kids with you? Take them to **Maui Kids & Company,** where they'll love the aloha wear and swimwear as well as the great selection of toys and accessories. Soft, stuffed geckos "dressed" in island fabrics and an assortment of Hawaiian dolls in traditional costumes make neat gifts. **Youth's International Wear** is another good spot, with major name brands in children's and young people's clothing.

For budget buys in aloha wear and island gifts, it's hard to beat **Hilo Hattie's Fashion Center.** Selections are enormous, prices are right, and the nice people here even give you free pineapple-orange juice and a shell lei when you walk in. If you're waiting for someone who's shopping, you can relax in the lounge, watching island videos or reading the local papers.

Other popular shops here include **Kite Factory,** with a nifty array of high-flyers; **Watch-N-See,** which features the largest collection of Swatch Watches in Hawaii, as well as sunglasses; and a very large **ABC** store. Of course you already know about **Liberty House,** Hawaii's premier department store, with its usual quality selection of nationally recognized brands as well as lovely made-in-Hawaii merchandise.

WHARF CINEMA CENTER, 658 Front St.

Central to the Lahaina shopping scene, this stunning three-story arcade is built around a giant tree, with a fountain and a stage on the lower level, a glass elevator, a triplex theater complex, a number of attractive eating places, and dozens of shops reflecting quality and taste, some more so than others. Shops stay open late, so a visit here can be a good evening's activity. (The free Lahaina Express trolley, a double-decker British bus, makes its last run to Kaanapali at 10pm; it runs daily from Kaanapali every 35 minutes, beginning at 9:30am.)

Here you'll find places like **Seegerpeople,** which offers three-dimensional photo sculptures—of you, your family, your kids, your group. Photo sessions last an hour, it takes another hour for proofs, and then (in about 4 weeks) you have a sculptural collage unlike any other. Prices begin at $40 for one person, one pose; each additional pose is $25. Have a look around and admire.

Everything at **☼Tropical Artware** is handmade—by 25 local artists and by craftspeople from around the world. This is one of the best sources for hard-to-find dichroic glass jewelry; metallic vapors fused into glass create a range of subtly changing colors. Dichroic glass rings begin at $14; earcuffs and ornaments start as low as $10. Baskets, wood carvings, ceramics, and toe rings are all available. Look for the GREENPEACE HAWAII signs; they'll lead you right to **Earth and Company,** which sponsors Greenpeace Hawaii, and sells "gifts of environmental consciousness"—artwork, posters, jewelry, T-shirts, and more—at moderate prices. **Hawaii Memories–Maui** is a source for small shops and for individual customers as well: It has vast quantities of beads, necklaces, corals, earrings, crystals, amber, and more. **Gigi's Fashion Boutique** boasts classic design clothing from the 1920s, 30s, and 40s. And children can be nicely outfitted with island clothes at **Little Polynesians.**

We never miss a visit to the **Whaler's Book Shoppe,** a combination bookstore and European café, where you can sip and sit on their peaceful patio. We often find stunning local books of art and photography and Hawaiiana here that are not readily available elsewhere: Especially lovely is a book called *Maui on My Mind,* a beautiful book for $36.

LAHAINA CANNERY, 1221 Honoapiilani Hwy.

Once it was a pineapple cannery. Now the heavy equipment and the factory workers are gone, and in their place are a supermarket, a drugstore, scads of boutiques and restaurants, and plenty of tourists. One of Lahaina's newer shopping centers and its first enclosed, air-conditioned one, the Cannery is a very pleasant place to shop. It's sunny but cool, with lots of light and space. It's a boon to people staying out this way, since the **Safeway Supermarket** stays open around the clock, and **Long's Drugs** fills a variety of needs. There is ample parking, as well as free shuttle service from the Honokawai and Kaanapali areas. There's often free entertainment, like a Polynesian revue featuring dancers from the Maui Marriott's luau, which we caught recently.

As for the smaller shops, there are many branches of popular island stores like **Sir Wilfred's Coffee, Tea, Tobacco Shop,** which has great selections of their own coffee beans (unique flavors like Kona Hula Pie and Kona Banana Nut, regular and decaf) and of gift items as well; we're especially partial to their collection of Laurel Birch bags, cups, jewelry, T-shirts, umbrellas, and the like. Then there's men's and women's clothiers **Reyns**, where you must check out their Artwear collections of T-shirts; they'd make wonderful gifts. Other favorites include **Blue Ginger Designs,** where everything is made of hand-blocked batik fabrics, and **Super Whale**, which always has wonderful children's clothing. We like the fanciful women's clothing at **Arabesque.** For collectors of maps and old prints, internationally renowned **Lahaina Printsellers** is a must stop. Hawaii's largest gallery specializing in antique maps and engravings, it also holds the largest collection of Captain Cook material in the Western hemisphere. Stop by, if you can, on a Monday, Wednesday, or Friday afternoon at 2 to see Stephen Strickland, Lahaina Printsellers' exclusive artist and one of the nation's few *intaglio* artist/engravers, give a free demonstration. We were fascinated by the process. Steve inks the engraved (reverse image) copper plate and then presses it through his traditional handpress, producing a sharp, clear print. He often offers a magnifying glass to his audience, allowing them to see his minute figures, which are invisible to the naked eye!

Maui on My Mind is one of the more tasteful shops around, with a variety of wearable crafts and handmade jewelry. They even have T-shirts with prints by some of Maui's favorite artists; we like Robert Lynn Nelson's underwater scenes, at $16. The stock at **Hats Galore and More** is fun, especially their authentic Greek fishermen's hats. Note **Escape to Maui** for ladies' fashions, **Benetton** for sportswear, and **Dolphin Galleries** for fine art and jewelry.

Rocky Mountain Chocolate Factory will dip frozen bananas in chocolate for you, and will mail their famous fudge, chocolate-covered macadamias, and what-not anywhere.

While you're thinking of food, you can check out the variety of fast-food outlets here, sit down and have a bite at one of the tables in the big central courtyard. For a more serious meal, try **Marie Callender's,** an outpost of the Oahu favorite known for its wonderful potpies, or **Compadres,** for Mexican food, drinks, and fun.

Attention chocoholics and/or potato-chip junkies, or any combination of the above: Before you leave the Cannery, stop in at **Long's Drugs** and treat yourself to a gourmet munchie craze: **Chocolate Chips of Maui.** Believe it or not, these are Maui potato chips, dipped by hand in either rich dark chocolate or milk chocolate, packed in an elegant box, and signed by the dipper. They can be gobbled as is or, if you can wait, frozen and served with ice cream or sherbet or brandied whipped cream! It's $3.69 for a 1/4-pound box.

READERS RECOMMEND

Take Home Maui, *Dickenson St., near Front St. "This place handles shipping fruit, but has a great sandwich deli with exotic fruits. Very inexpensive and only four outdoor tables."*—Robin Ritchee, Lahaina, Hawaii. [*Authors' Note:* This delightful spot also serves homemade soups, fruit smoothies, stuffed papayas, quiches, Tongan pies, gourmet coffees, pastas, and bagels and cream cheese. They've expanded their fruit-shipping department to include papayas, Sweet Maui onions, macadamia nuts, Kona coffee beans, Maui-made jams and jellies, chocolates, and lots more. A good place to know about.]

Pearl Factories. *"Be careful with any of the pearl factories dotted all over Front Street. While picking your own oyster and getting your own cultured pearl out of it is fun for $6 (the bait), having the pearl mounted on gold is very overpriced (the hook). Check the price on the whole package (which is not posted anywhere) before doing anything, or just insist on doing the pearl part only."*—K. L., New York, N.Y.

Special Shops

SOUTH SEAS TRADING POST, 780 Front St. Tel. 661-3168.

There aren't too many places like the South Seas Trading Post left in Lahaina, places where the owners still search out and find authentic South Seas and Asian treasures. Although there are many collector's items here—primitive art from New Guinea, bronzes and Buddhas from Thailand, precious jades from China—most of the items are surprisingly affordable: Consider, for example, one-of-a-kind jewelry designs using antique pieces ($25 to $75), freshwater pearl necklaces with precious gemstones (from $18), 100-year-old porcelain spoons from China (at $10), Christmas ornaments in the shape of Hawaiian tutus ($3.50)—and much more.

THE WHALER LTD., 866 Front St. Tel. 661-4592.

Here's a unique shop with a nautical flavor. One of the oldest establishments on Front Street, it features a great variety of American crafts, especially art glass from Hawaii and the mainland, each piece with a nautical theme—fish, dolphins, and whales. There's also an intriguing collection of jewelry, perfume bottles, paper weights, vases, sculptures, scrimshaw, prints, and watercolors.

THE ENDANGERED SPECIES STORE, 707 Front St. Tel. 661-0208.

Should you wish a T-shirt that reads PROTECT THE DOLPHINS or PRESERVE HAWAII'S RAIN FOREST or some such, this is the place. This imaginative shop devoted to protecting the environment also has framed posters by such marine artists as Christian Reese Lassen and Robert Lynn Nelson, all very handsome.

LAHAINA HAT COMPANY, 705 Front St. Tel. 661-8230

If you can't find a hat here, you're not really trying! The collection is enormous, and all are reasonably priced. They carry a good selection of tote bags too.

Swap Meet

Handmade Hawaiian dresses, baskets, hand-painted clothing and T-shirts, and handcrafted jewelry are just some of the items for sale at the Sunday-afternoon **Lahaina Crafts Fair.** It's held either once, twice, or three times a month at the Lahaina Civic Center, next to the main post office in Lahaina. Check with your hotel desk to see when it's scheduled.

READERS RECOMMEND

Salvation Army Thrift Shop, off Front St. *"Best bet for shopping in Lahaina: The Salvation Army Thrift Shop off Front Street, near the Lahaina Shores Hotel, had very reasonable used and new clothing selling a few blocks away for five times the amount. The best sales appear to be on Saturday."*—Michael and Arlene Gladstone, Merrick, N.Y.

EVENING ENTERTAINMENT

Lahaina at night is the place for the drinking set, with no shortage of swinging bars.

And for families, check the local papers to see what entertainment is being presented at the malls.

Luaus

Should you be in the mood for a luau, we can't think of a nicer one than the ✪ **Old Lahaina Luau,** right out on the beach behind the shopping arcade at 505 Front St. (tel. 667-1998). This is a smaller and more personal, old-time luau than many of the slick hotel presentations; *Maui Magazine* called it the "best on the island," and it recently won the Hawaii Visitors Bureau's "Five Kahili" award for enhancing Hawaiian culture and aloha spirit. And the setting, on the grounds of Kamehameha's royal compound, is picture perfect: You dine as the sun sets over the water, then watch the traditional hulas of Hawaii by starlight. Everyone receives a fresh flower lei greeting, and a duo plays ukuleles on the luau grounds as guests are seated. The open bar includes frozen tropicals like piña coladas, chi chis, and Blue Hawaiis. And the food is much better than the usual luau fare; they even barbecue sirloin steaks and chicken over an outside kiawe grill as guests are arriving. The luau is held Monday through Saturday evenings at 5:30pm at a cost of $58 for adults, $29 for children 12 and under. Make reservations at least several days in advance, as this luau is very, very popular.

Drinking, Dancing, and Listening

In addition to the places listed below, keep in mind the following: The **Pioneer Inn** on Front Street always attracts a lively crowd for moderately priced drinks. The **Hard Rock Café** at Lahaina Center, 900 Front St., has one of the biggest bars in town and one of the jolliest crowds. **Compadres Bar & Grill** at the Lahaina Cannery is the spot for Mexican munchies and great margaritas. Looking for a late, late happy hour? You'll find it at the **Kobe Japanese Steak House,** 136 Dickenson St., from 10pm to 2am. **Lahaina Coolers,** 180 Dickenson St., offers two popular happy hours, one from 4 to 6pm, the other from 10pm to closing (which could be 2am) every day.

ALOHA CANTINA, 839 Front St. Tel. 661-8788.
  Hand-shaken fruit margaritas, sunset music daily, and live bands to dance to on Thursday, Friday, and Saturday from 10pm to 1am make this one of the most popular stops on Front Street. All this, and Maui fish tacos, too.
  Admission: Free.

BLUE TROPIX, at Lahaina Center. Tel. 667-5309.
  You can have a medium-priced dinner here or just come for the disco dancing and entertainment. Mostly there's a DJ, but there's also plenty of live entertainment and special concerts.
  Admission: $5 after 9pm, more for special events.

MOOSE MCGILLICUDDY'S PUB & CAFE, 844 Front St. Tel. 667-7758.
  The young crowd comes here to listen to rock and roll. There's a 3 to 6pm happy hour every day, special prices on Tijuana Tuesdays, Ladies' Night on Thursday, videos every night, and on Thursday, Friday, and Saturday, live bands from 9:30pm until closing.
  Admission: $3 Thurs–Sat after 9pm.

STUDIO 505, 505 Front St., atop Pacific's. Tel. 661-1505.
  This is the "in" spot for the young crowd. There's a large dance floor and an advanced sound system that gives forth with hip-hop, reggae, rock, contemporary disco. Henry Kapono and Marty Dread are the featured artists. There's cabaret occasionally.
  Admission: $5; special events $10.

***NAVATEK II* SUNSET CRUISES. Tel. 661-8787 or toll free 800/852-4183.**
  Here's a unique way to enjoy the Maui night—on a cocktail or dinner cruise aboard the *Navatek II*, whose revolutionary SWATH design (Small Water Plane Twin Hull) makes sailing smooth as glass. It's $39 for a cocktail cruise, $78 for a dinner

cruise, with island music setting the background for a spectacular scenic sail from Maalaea Bay to Lahaina. A snorkeling trip to Molokini ($65) and a half-day cruise around the island of Lanai ($120) are also available on this unique vessel.

Art Night

Lahaina boasts numerous galleries, and the best time to visit them is on Friday night. Friday evening, from 7 to 9pm, is "Art Night" in Lahaina; galleries present special appearances by artists and offer free entertainment and refreshments. Great fun! Check the local papers for what's happening where. Among the numerous galleries involved are **South Seas Trading Post, Dolphin Galleries, Wyland Gallery, Metropolitan Galleries,** and the **Lahaina Arts Society.**

ON TO KAANAPALI

If you want to continue your sightseeing out in the Kaanapali resort area now, there are two ways to go, in addition to driving your own car. The first is free: It's the **Lahaina Express,** a quaint green trolley that provides shuttle service between Banyan Tree Square and the hotels in the Kaanapali Resort every 35 minutes from 9:30am on. The last trolley leaves the Wharf Cinema Center in Lahaina at 10pm (for information, phone the Wharf Shops at 661-8748).

It's more fun, however (and also more expensive: $12 round-trip, $8 one way, half fare for children), to hop the old-timey **Lahaina-Kaanapali & Pacific Railroad,** a reconstructed, turn-of-the-century sugarcane train, for the 12-mile round-trip between Lahaina and Kaanapali. You'll be entertained with songs and stories en route by a singing conductor, and kids will get a kick out of the hoot of the locomotive's whistle. The railroad terminal is on Honoapiilani Highway, one block north of Papalaua Street; there is free transportation via a double-decker bus from the harbor and Front Street. Before or after the trip, you might want to check out the **Depot Snack Shop,** which friendly and knowledgeable Brad Reith has been operating for years. There are goodies here you can't get anywhere else. Fresh sugarcane, sweet and juicy, is $2 per package. And Brad isn't called the "king of the coconuts" for nothing! You can buy coconut in different stages of development: drink the delicious "milk" or enjoy the gourmet form "spoonmeat." Spoonmeat coconuts are just $2.25. If you're really lucky, you'll visit on a day when Brad has homemade mango muffins, huge and unbelievably delicious, for just $1.50. Don't miss **Sugar Cane Gifts** (tel. 661-3325) right at the railroad depot. They have some of the most handsome T-shirts and sweatshirts we've seen on Maui, as well as a variety of other gift items. Manager Shellie Fletcher is willing to accept mail orders as well.

While you're in the industrial area near the sugarcane train, have a look around, too, at some of the outlet stores. These include **Posters Maui, Lahaina Printsellers,** and **J. R.'s Music Shop.** Be sure to check the clothing racks that **Maui Clothing Company** places outside their warehouse in the parking lot; we've found excellent buys here on men's and women's Hawaiian resortwear. Merchandise varies from day to day, but value at all these outlet stores can be excellent.

SIGHTS & ATTRACTIONS

Now for some sightseeing, shopping, and swimming at the glamorous hotels of the Kaanapali Beach Resort (signs from the road lead you directly down to the hotels). Your first stop should be at the splendid ✪ **Hyatt Regency Maui,** where you can have a look at the $80-million, 20-acre complex, lush with waterfalls, gardens, tropical birds, an acre-long swimming pool with its own bar in a lava cavern, an atrium lobby, and an elegant shopping arcade that rivals Rodeo Drive. A walk here is like touring a park and botanical garden and an indoor-outdoor museum of priceless Asian art. This aesthetic and architectural tour de force offers gorgeous vistas wherever you look. You might want to pause and have a drink at the Weeping Banyan Bar beside a lagoon—and please don't throw crumbs at the penguins! Note, too, the unusual ceilings in the shops—there is one in stained glass—and perhaps pick up a trinket at a place like Elephant Walk, where prices go way up for safari exotica, but are relatively down-to-earth for elephant-hair jewelry. If you—or your children—are interested in astronomy, make plans to come back some evening to take the Hyatt Regency Maui's "Tour of the Stars." Guided by the resort's director of astronomy, participants first learn to interpret the sky with the naked eye, then giant binoculars, and then view it through a revolutionary new deep-space telescope that yields brilliant images of stars, planets, galaxies, and nebulae. Sessions are held every night (except Sunday) at 8, 9, and 10pm; cost is $10 per person, $5 for children 12 and under. (Information: 661-1234.)

By all means, pay a visit to the **Maui Marriott Resort**, on Kaanapali Drive next to the Hyatt Regency. This is an example of modern hotel architecture and landscaping at its best, especially beautiful at night, when lights, flowers, and a tropical moon over the ocean create dazzling effects.

Your next stop should definitely be the **Westin Maui Resort,** a sensational $165-million remake of the old Maui Surf Hotel. It's a toss-up as to whether this or the Hyatt Regency Maui (both Christopher Hemmeter creations) is the more sumptuous—you decide. This gorgeous pleasure palace by the sea has $2½ million worth of artwork gracing the public areas and gardens, a spectacular, multilevel swimming pool complex fed by waterfalls and bridges (twice as big as the giant pool at the Hyatt Regency), and swans gliding just a few feet from the registration desk. Art tours are held on Tuesday and Thursday at 9am, botanical tours on Tuesday and Friday at 10am, and wildlife tours on Sunday, Monday, and Wednesday at 10am—a great chance to photograph the flamingos, swans, and macaws. You'll need reservations (tel. 667-2525).

As you continue driving, you may want to stop at the **Sheraton Maui Hotel,** which sits atop **Black Rock,** the perch from which the souls of the dead Hawaiians were said to leap into the spirit world beyond. The majestic hotel, not in the least bit haunted, is worth having a look at, especially for the 360° view from the top, a sweeping panorama of ocean, islands, and mountains. The tasteful Polynesian formal lobby is on the top floor; you've got to take the elevators down to everything else, including Kaanapali Beach.

SAVVY SHOPPING

WHALER'S VILLAGE The main shopping attraction out here is Whaler's Village, recently done over and now bigger and better than ever. The one- and two-story buildings are of uniform design and materials, authentic reproductions of the type of buildings that the New England missionaries constructed in Lahaina between 1830 and 1890. First, pay a visit to the **Whaler's Village Museum** (on the top floor of Building G), study its absorbing collection of whaling memorabilia, and perhaps see the whaling film shown every half hour in the museum's theater. Then visit **Hale Koholo, House of the Whale**, a newer museum focusing on the humpback whale. Admission to both museums is free. After you've boned up on history and soaked in some gorgeous views, you can concentrate on the serious business of shopping—and there's plenty to concentrate on.

The ✪ **Endangered Species Store** is the kind of place the whole family will like. Kids will find minerals and fossils for collecting, and books on the environment; adults will like the posters by Christian Reese Lassen and Robert Lynn Nelson, the Maui tote bags and animal prints, and the EXTINCTION IS FOREVER T-shirts. And everyone will like the pool and parrot up front: Toss a coin, make a wish; proceeds go to further environmental causes.

If you're ready to invest in some really fine jewelry, then pay a visit to the **Dolphin Gallery.** Everything is exclusive here, of the highest quality, and fairly priced: We love their selection of spinner rings, gray Tahitian pearls, and the blue stone called tanzanite. There's also internationally renowned art, sculpture, and collectible glass, all of the highest quality.

"One-of-a-kind", "rare", "unusual"—these are words to describe the very special offerings at ✪ **Sea & Shell.** Many of the employees do watercolors or create belts and hair jewelry; owners Michael and Madaline Abrams do all the beautiful mountings and mirrors, and offer unique jewelry by island artisans, like the Kroma Glass line.

The magical art of Laurel Burch has its own store at Whaler's Village, called ✪ **Laurel Burch The Secret Jungle.** In it one can find jewelry, sculpture, T-shirts, tote bags, umbrellas, coffee mugs, and notecards—many with the whimsical cat motifs that have become Laurel Burch's trademark. Enchanting.

The ✪ **Ka Honu Gift Gallery** is a delight, with lots of Hawaiian handmade works: dolls (note the Hawaiian mermaid dolls and the potpourri dolls), ceramics, bowls of milo and koa wood, and Christmas ornaments like Santa on a surfboard, at $14.95. They have a large collection of precious Niihau shell jewelry. **Outta the Blue** features the striking designs done by Australian Ken Done, which are becoming so popular in the islands.

If money were no object, we'd simply buy out all the fabulous designs by local Hawaiian artists at **Silks Kaanapali Ltd.** In addition to hand-painted and unusually designed clothing, the shop carries striking bags and other accessories, starting around $30. **Maui Water Wear** has a great selection of swimsuits.

You can have a great time at **The Sharper Image**—at no cost. Work out on the exercise bikes, then massage your back as you experience a Japanese shiatsu massage table or a luxury recliner. Oh yes, you could buy something here too, like an airplane lamp—it taxis for takeoff—at $89.95. Scrimshaw collectors should head straight for **Lahaina Scrimshaw,** where there's an impressive selection of quality scrimshaw (done on nonendangered fossil walrus ivory), as well as a prize antique collection, including some particularly fine Buddhas from Thailand. Do-it-yourself scrimshaw kits go for $8.95 to $21.

Lahaina Printsellers has some fascinating antique maps and prints that would look great on those walls back home. **Esprit, Canoe,** and **Waldenbooks,** island regulars, are all represented here.

Whaler's Village is open from 9:30am to 10pm daily, and can be reached by foot on the beachwalk or on Kaanapali Resort's free trolley. If you drive, you will, unfortunately, have to pay for parking.

SPORTS & RECREATION

One of the nicest things about the Hawaiian Islands is that all beaches—even those at the fanciest hotels—are open to the public. As you stroll by the beachfront hotels (the Sheraton Maui, the Royal Lahaina, the Kaanapali Beach, the Marriott, the Westin Maui, the Hyatt Regency), you can stop by for a snack or a drink and treat yourself to a swim. **Kaanapali Beach** is wider in some places than others (storms occasionally carry away some of the sand), and we prefer the areas in front of the Westin Maui, the Royal Lahaina, and Sheraton Maui; the last is known for fabulous snorkeling at **Black Rock,** right in front of the hotel. Unfortunately, there is very little public parking in this area, and hotel parking lots may be crowded. You may want to swim behind Whaler's Village, which has a good beach, but you'll have to pay for parking in their indoor lot.

READERS RECOMMEND

Black Rock Cove. "*While Maui has many scenic beaches, there aren't many easily accessible from hardtop roads that are consistently suitable for novice snorkelers. In calm conditions, several of the west-coast beaches are acceptable. But when swells or windy conditions exist, your choices rapidly dwindle. One very notable exception is Black Rock Cove at Kaanapali. This sheltered cove has clear water and scores of colorful, small fish. If you are staying outside this immediate area, just park in the Whaler's Village lot, walk to the beach, and head north about a quarter of a mile; the cove is just below the Sheraton Maui Hotel.*"—Dale Knutsen, Ridgecrest, Calif.

Snorkeling near Kaanapali Airport. *"The best snorkeling we found was at the southern edge of the old Kaanapali Airport, next to the Royal Lahaina resort. The water was clear and safe for children, the coral plentiful and well below the surface, and the variety of fish amazing. Even beginning snorkelers will enjoy this beach, which is reached by turning in at the last Kaanapali sign going north, then walking about 50 yards down to the beach."*—Nick Howell, Camp Springs, Md.

Aquatic Charters of Maui *(tel. 879-0976). "One of our most pleasant experiences was taking a private charter boat to Molokai for snorkeling. The cost was the same as for the large boats, and the individualized attention from the owners was terrific. We heartily recommend the Aquatic Charters of Maui with Jim and Robyn Friend."*—Lindsay and Jay Johnson, Columbus, Ohio.

Rainbow Ranch, *near Kaanapali Beach (tel. 669-4991). "We took advantage of riding, at the Rainbow Ranch, near Kaanapali Beach. A variety of riding tours is available at all levels of experience for reasonable prices. Good-quality horses and great guides."*—Patti Connor, Arlington, Mass.

EVENING ENTERTAINMENT

Fun and games await you at the big beach hotels at Kaanapali. One of the greatest shows in town takes place every night at the **Sheraton Maui,** and it costs absolutely nothing to be in the audience. As the sun begins to set over the water, torches are lit all the way to the point. A native Hawaiian boy stands atop Black Rock (that eerie perch from which the souls of the dead were supposed to depart to the other world), throws his leis into the water, and then looks down some 20 feet or so to the waiting ocean below. The crowd—on the beach, lining the lobby floors—holds its breath. He plunges in, surfaces, and the evening festivities are under way.

If you need something to steady your nerves after viewing the diving spectacle described above, make your way to the nautically decorated "On the Rocks" Bar. The ship models, volcanic rock floor-to-ceiling columns, and the tables with compass designs are all unusual and handsome, but somehow we never notice anything except the view; from the crest of this black-lava cliff overlooking the sea it's a spectacular one, a must for us collectors of Hawaiian sunsets.

Luaus and Dinner Shows

Choosing among all the luau and dinner shows in the Kaanapali area can be difficult: All of them are good, but none is inexpensive (most run close to $50).

The **Royal Lahaina Luau,** at the Royal Lahaina Resort (tel. 661-3611 for reservations), is considered one of the best; it's presented nightly, September through April at 5:30pm, May through August at 6pm. It costs $47 for adults, $23.50 for children 12 and under. Children under 5 are free. On Tuesday and Friday "Family Nights," children 12 and under are free with a paying adult.

Drums of the Pacific at the Hyatt Regency Maui (tel. 667-4420 for reservations) offers a spectacular production of Polynesian dancing (Samoan slap dances, Tahitian drum dances and shimmies, spear and knife dances, fire dances, etc.), along with a traditional Luau Buffet and an imu ceremony. Festivities are held in an outdoor amphitheater beneath the stars. The dinner show is $44 for adults, $36 for children 6 to 12, but you can see the same show and enjoy a cocktail for just $26.

Another top choice is the **Marriott Luau,** at the Maui Marriott on Kaanapali Beach (tel. 667-1200 for reservations), held at the hotel's beautiful oceanfront luau gardens Tuesday through Sunday at 5pm. Admission is $48 for adults, $28 for children 5 to 12.

Karaoke Sing-along

LOBBY BAR, at the Maui Marriott. Tel. 667-1200.

In case you've not yet experienced karaoke, here's your chance. On Thursday, Friday, and Saturday nights from 8:30 to 11pm, there's a show in which you could be the star. Just walk up to the mike, choose from more than 5,000 popular tunes (words on the video screen), and sing along. Drink specials and pupus too. No cover, no minimum.

Contemporary and Hawaiian Music

MAKAI BAR, at the Maui Marriott. Tel. 667-1200.
There's live music here every night—plus spectacular sunsets. Readers of the *Maui News* have voted this "Maui's Best Pupu Bar" for two years in a row.

A Comedy Club

LOBBY BAR, at the Maui Marriott. Tel. 667-1200 for reservations.
The Honolulu Comedy Club is one of the top nightclub attractions in Waikiki; on Monday night it moves to Maui. You never know who the talent will be, but be assured they are among the nation's hottest stand-up comedians; you've probably seen them on TV with Jay Leno or David Letterman or Arsenio Hall.
Admission: $12. No one under 21 admitted. Tickets are available in advance at the front desk.

TO KAPALUA & NEARBY BEACHES

As you drive north from Kaanapali on Honoapiilani Highway through Kahana and Napili and finally to Kapalua, you're seeing some of the most beautiful countryside in West Maui. Some of the best beaches are here too, as well as the Kapalua Bay Resort, a particularly lovely spot perched on a promontory and surrounded by blue sea.

Although you could conceivably swim at Honokawai Beach Park, it's not particularly desirable, so we suggest you drive farther along until you come to some better beaches. One is **Napili Bay,** which has a small sign showing the public right-of-way; look for it—and park—when you see the sign for the Napili Surf Beach Resort. Our favorite, still farther north on this road, is old **Fleming Beach** (also known as **Kapalua Beach**), a perfect crescent of white sand, gentle surf, the ideal spot for the whole family to swim, play, and snorkel. There's a public right-of-way sign past the Napili Kai Beach Club, which leads to a small parking lot for this very popular beach. If it's full, we'll let you in on a secret: The parking lot at the Shops at Kapalua, adjacent to the plush Kapalua Bay Hotel, usually has plenty of space and you can walk from it, through the hotel, and down through the lovely grounds to the ocean. The Kapalua Bay Hotel itself is exquisite, and well worth a look.

Note: Despite any information you may receive locally, nude sunbathing is definitely against the law in the state of Hawaii.

FREE SHOWS

Cook's at the Beach, at the Westin Maui Resort (tel. 667-2525), is a charming indoor-outdoor café that hosts a free hula show Monday through Saturday at 7pm.

One of Maui's best entertainments is free. It's the presentation of ✪**Hula Kahiko O Hawaii** at the Shops at Kapalua, at the Kapalua Bay Resort, every Thursday morning at 10am. Unlike most hulas done in commercial shows, these are the authentic ancient dances of Hawaii, presented by a local hula halau (school), with Kumu Hula Cliff Ahue relating enchanting stories of Hawaii's history and ancient religion. It's all done in the spirit of the late Tutu Inez Ashdown, a great lady who originated these programs and was Maui County's historian emeritus. Local friends call this one of the best-kept secrets on the island!

READERS RECOMMEND

Touring Napili Bay. *"We found the prettiest part of Maui to be that short section of Hi. 30 that goes past the Napili Bay area: towering cliffs, crashing waves, lush valleys. Few tourists seem to drive up here because they know the road ends. We*

*packed a picnic dinner and ate it in total isolation on a cliff overlooking the water.
It was one of the best moments of our honeymoon."*—Sue and Terry Young,
Crystal Lake, Ill.

SAVVY SHOPPING

THE SHOPS AT KAPALUA We always stop to visit the Shops at Kapalua, at
the Kapalua Bay Resort, one of the most serenely tasteful of island marketplaces.
Most of the shops here are way beyond our budget, but there are many affordable
items at places like **Kapalua Kids,** which can outfit teens as well as children, and
at the **Kapalua Logo Shop,** where you can pick up T-shirts, bags, and many accessories with the distinctive trademark logo: the Kapalua butterfly.

Like its other shop in Lahaina, the **South Seas Trading Post** showcases arts,
handcrafts, and jewelry from Bali, New Guinea, and Asian and South Pacific shores,
much of it of museum quality. But there are some charming low-priced items too.
We especially like the jewelry created from 350- to 600-year-old shards of Ming Dynasty Chinese porcelain: These are set in sterling-silver rings, pendants, and earrings,
and start at just $22.

Have a sandwich and an espresso, now, at the European-style **Market Café,**
which also purveys cookbooks, cheeses, wines, and deli items. Or walk through the
lobby of the adjoining Kapalua Bay Hotel and have lunch at the lovely **Pool Terrace.** Best of all, wander out to the **Bay Club.** Here you can have a fancier lunch,
a drink, or simply a walk outside to see the breathtaking views, with blue sea at every vista. Beautiful Kapalua Beach is right below you. Let the peace and beauty of
the beaches stay in your memory as you turn around and go back the way you
came—the road continuing around the island is a poor one, and usually off-limits to
drivers of rented cars.

READERS RECOMMEND

Honolua Bay. *"The best snorkeling beach on Maui (we discovered it ourselves
and it was later pointed out to us by islanders) is Honolua Bay on the north end of
the island near the end of Hi. 30. Overnight camping permits should be obtained
from the Maui Pineapple Company in Lahaina, but we did not have one and had
no problems."*—Sandra Johnson, Santa Paula, Calif.

CHAPTER 16

MOLOKAI

What's the most Hawaiian of the Hawaiian Islands? If you're thinking in terms of the Hawaii of 50 years ago—the Hawaii before high-rises and shopping centers, before billboards and commercialism, it might well be the little island of Molokai. The closest of the neighbor islands—only 20 minutes by plane from Oahu—261-square-mile Molokai is the least developed and most sparsely populated of the major Hawaiian Islands. Its resident population (about 6,000) has the highest percentage of people with native Hawaiian ancestry anywhere in the islands (with the exception, of course, of privately owned Niihau). The environment is rural and the lifestyle traditional. Imagine a place with no buildings over three stories high, no elevators, no traffic lights (let alone freeways!), no movie theaters, no fast-food or supermarket chains. Instead, think of great natural beauty, vast uncrowded spaces, and ideal conditions for golfing, hunting, riding, windsurfing, big-game fishing, boating (swimming is not ideal here, since the beaches can be beautiful but the water rough), and leading the lazy life in an unspoiled setting. If that's the kind of relaxed Hawaii you're thinking about, then you should definitely visit Molokai.

Molokai sometimes gets overflow visitors from better-known tourist destinations, people who didn't even know what or where Molokai was. Yet once they start to unwind here, they find they like it, and come back again. Kamaainas have been in the know about Molokai for a long time: It's a favorite weekend spot for family holidays. And it's rapidly becoming a popular destination for "eco-tourism" and "cultural tourism."

In the past, Molokai was known mostly as a pineapple plantation island and as a treatment center for Hansen's disease (leprosy) at Kalaupapa. It was here that Father Damien (now known as Blessed Damien since his beatification in 1994) did his magnificent work among the lepers. But somehow the tidal wave of progress that has swept the islands since statehood left Molokai behind; it appears, at first glance, like a midwestern town in the Depression '30s. Yet there's a downhomeness and a realness here that most people find appealing, and a genuine friendliness among the locals. Artists and craftspeople, seeking a last refuge from overpriced civilization, have settled here. In some parts of the island there is a sense of tranquility that's almost palpable. And Molokai is changing. Although the pineapple industry has been phased out and many of the local people are experiencing hard economic times, luxury facilities for visitors are on the rise. Before Molokai changes too much, come see what rural Hawaii is still like. A visit to Molokai can be a rewarding experience, especially since you won't have to break the bank to do it; prices here are still somewhat lower than elsewhere in the state.

Molokai, now "The Friendly Isle," was once known as "The Lonely Isle." The power of Molokai's kahuna priests was feared throughout the other islands. Warring island kings kept a respectable distance from Molokai until, in 1790, Kamehameha the Great came to negotiate for the hand of the queen, Keoupuolani. Five years later he returned with an army to conquer Molokai on his drive for Oahu and dominion over all of Hawaii.

WHAT'S SPECIAL ABOUT MOLOKAI

Natural Wonders

Halawa Valley, a once-populous valley decimated by the tidal wave of 1946, and its high point, spectacular Moaula Falls.

Palaau State Park, where trails lead to Phallic Rock and to Kalaupapa Lookout, from which one can see the world's tallest (3,330 feet high) sea cliffs, at Umilehi Point.

Historic Attractions

Kalaupapa Peninsula, where Father Damien performed his labor among the lepers; now a National Historic Park and treatment center for the few remaining Hansen's disease patients.

R. W. Meyer Sugar Mill, an authentic restoration of an 1878 sugar mill now in operating condition; listed on the National Register of Historic Places.

Special Adventures

Going on camera safari at Molokai Ranch Wildlife Park, where more than 1,000 Asian and African animals roam free on a 1,000-acre natural wildlife preserve.

Molokai Foods

Molokai French bread, famed throughout the islands; Kanemitsu Bakery is the source.

Sports and Recreation

Big-game fishing, hunting, golfing, horseback riding, windsurfing, and boating are all popular. Beaches are fine for sunbathing, but often rough for swimming.

Annual Events

Annual August statewide rodeo at Molokai Ranch.

The September/October Molokai-to-Oahu Canoe Race, the Olympics of outrigger canoeing. It's September for the women's race, October for the men's.

The celebration in May of the birth of the hula on Molokai: Molokai Ka Hula Piko. A joyful event.

January's Molokai Makahiki, a traditional Hawaiian "time of peace" celebration.

Today Molokai presents a tranquil scene, an island mostly given to rural pursuits. The only town really worthy of the name is Kaunakakai, on the southern shore, almost in the center of the island, and it has only one street. A thickly forested backcountry populated with axis deer, pheasant, turkey, and other wild game makes life exciting for the hunter. For those of you who just like to look and sightsee, there is magnificent Halawa Valley, on the southeastern coast, about 25 miles from Kaunakakai, with its healing pool at the foot of Moaula Falls; the less-rugged Palaau State Park, about 10 miles north of Kaunakakai, with its Phallic Rock and Kalaupapa Lookout; and Kalaupapa itself, an isolated peninsula, once an exile colony for the victims of leprosy, which today you can visit on a guided tour. But more about that later.

You won't have to rough it on Molokai. The few hotel facilities are excellent, the roads for the most part are quite good, and you'll be able to get whatever comforts and supplies you need—from rental cars to color movie film. The drinking water is as pure as you'll find anywhere in the world, and the restaurants, especially those in the three major hotels on the island, serve very good meals.

One word of advice: Go directly to your hotel from the airport and get comfortable and adjusted to Molokai before visiting its nearby principal town, Kaunakakai. This sleepy village, made famous by the song "Cock-eyed Mayor," is best appreciated once you're in the Molokai mood. Especially after Waikiki.

To get a little head start on your sightseeing, you might note that, between the airport and town, on the ocean side of the road is Kapuaiwa, one of the last surviving royal coconut groves in the Hawaiian Islands, planted in the latter part of the 19th century. It was planted in honor of Kamehameha V and given his pet name. Opposite the grove is Church Row, a lineup of tiny rustic churches.

MOLOKAI VISITORS ASSOCIATION Molokai is serious about putting out the welcome mat for visitors and, to that end, it has set up the Molokai Visitors Association to promote tourism. If you phone their toll-free number, they'll send you a comprehensive brochure listing hotels, resort condominiums, tour companies, auto-rental companies, restaurants, visitor activities, and airlines serving the island, as well as individual brochures put out by these firms. From Canada and the continental United States as well as Alaska, Puerto Rico, and the Virgin Islands, call toll free 800/800-6367. If you're already in the islands, call 800/553-0404. The local number is 533-3876. Their office is under the mango tree at the Pau Hana Inn.

1. GETTING THERE & GETTING AROUND

GETTING THERE

BY PLANE

Molokai is 20 air minutes from Honolulu, 15 minutes from Maui. It is easily reached via **Hawaiian Airlines**, which runs 50-seat DH-7 aircraft into Hoolehua Airport on a frequent schedule. Two commuter airlines, which run small planes (anywhere from 9- to 18-seaters), also fly to Molokai: These are **Air Molokai** and **Island Air**. **Paragon** flies to Molokai from Maui. Flying low on these small planes can be quite thrilling, as we discovered on a recent Air Molokai flight. Molokai lies between the islands of Oahu and Maui (it can easily be seen from western Maui) and is, in fact, part of Maui County. Route it on your way to or from either Maui or Honolulu. A 1-day trip is quite feasible.

READERS RECOMMEND

Flying via Kalaupapa. "*If possible, when flying from Maui to Molokai, take an Aloha Island Air Twin Otter flight via Kalaupapa. One flies on a level with the 3,000-foot-high cliffs on the northern shore of Molokai, and what a spectacular sight that is! In using this form of interisland transport, we got for free what most people would pay $75 to $100 for on a helicopter tour! This flight was the highlight of our trip.*"—Mrs. Jane Beecham, Victoria, Australia.

BY SHIP

A more leisurely—and scenic—way to get to Molokai is to take the interisland ferry, **The Maui Princess**, a 118-foot luxury vessel that plies the routes between Maui and Molokai every day. It's about a 1¼-hour trip. One-way fare is $25 for adults, $12.50 for children. The tour is narrated, there are plentiful opportunities for taking pictures, and if it's between December and May, you may spot a few humpback whales taking the same trip you are. For reservations, call 533-6899 on Oahu, 661-8397 on Maui, 553-5736 on Molokai. From the mainland, call toll free 800/833-5800. Note that a number of attractive packages are available, including rental cars and guided tours; both 1-day trips and overnights are available.

READERS RECOMMEND

Agriculture Inspection. *"If you're leaving Molokai to go back to the main-land, there is no agriculture inspector there. Consequently, you must check all your luggage to Honolulu, pick it up there and take it to the agriculture inspectors, then to your airline back to the mainland. This is a real chore as both Aloha Island Air and Hawaiian Airlines are miles from the main terminal and a porter costs $4 and a taxi about the same, to say nothing of the walk you have to put in! In other words, if you're doing Molokai, don't do it last before you return."*—Howard S. Walker, Sequim, Wash.

GETTING AROUND

BY RENTAL CAR

You're going to need a car if you want to explore Molokai on your own, and it won't be difficult to get one, since Molokai now has local outlets of three major all-island rental companies: Budget Rent A Car, Dollar Rent A Car, and Avis. (See Chapter 2 for details on all-island rentals.) They're all located at the airport. Rates vary according to the season and business, and can vary from day to day, so it's wise to shop around.

BY TAXI & TOUR SERVICE

Friendly Isle Tours (tel. 553-9046) offers full- and half-day island tours and trans-fers, using 15-passenger vans or 20-passenger minibuses.

    Kukui Tours & Limousines (tel. 553-5133), run by Vandale K. Dudoit, Jr. and Joyce Dudoit, prides itself on its personal service and attention. Their air-conditioned limos provide half-day and full-day tours of the island, plus airport-hotel shuttle service. They can also provide wedding packages.

    Thadd R. Camara's **Molokai Limousine Taxi Service** (tel. 553-3979; call col-lect from other Hawaiian islands) calls itself Molokai's "first VIP limousine taxi ser-vice." All standard taxi services are available, including airport and harbor pickup and hotel transfers, on a 24-hour basis. They also provide several half-day and full-day sightseeing tours in their luxury stretch Lincoln Town Car limo.

FAST FACTS Molokai is part of Maui County. For details, see "Fast Facts: Maui," in Chapter 14. For local emergencies on Molokai, call 553-5355 for **police,** 553-5401 for **fire,** 553-5911 for an **ambulance,** and 553-5331 for **Molokai General Hospital.**

2. WHERE TO STAY

Molokai now has a grand total of eight hotels and condos plus a few bed and breakfasts—and that's more than twice what it had a few years ago! Since there are so few, we'll give you the details on all of them; they're not all budget, but they all offer good quality for the money.

KAUNAKAKAI

Kaunakakai is Molokai's most central area, and the following hotels are just a mile or so down the road from the town's center, Ala Malama Street.

DOUBLES FROM $45

PAU HANA INN, Kamehameha Hwy. (P. O. Box 546), Kaunakakai,

Molokai, HI 96748. Tel. 808/553-5342, or toll free 800/423-MOLO. Fax 808/ 531-4004. 40 units.

$ Rates: $45–$90 single or double; $90 studio; $125 suite. Each additional person $10 extra. DC, MC, V. **Parking:** Free.

The drive from Hoolehua Airport to the town of Kaunakakai takes about 10 minutes, across what seems to be typical western grazing land. About a quarter of a mile from the town, following Hi. 45 along the beach, you'll see the Pau Hana Inn, the best choice in town for budgeteers, the most local and the most laid-back. Pau Hana is a relaxed, cottage-type hotel with some units in the garden, others facing the ocean or pool. All rooms and public areas have been refurbished recently. The lowest rates are for small, plain, but clean budget rooms, with two twin beds and a shower, in the longhouse. The more expensive rooms, by the pool or the ocean, accommodate up to four people with two double or queen-size beds. The superior rooms with kitchenettes and deluxe oceanfront suites sleep up to four people. The one-bedroom units have a kitchenette, sitting room, a queen-size bed and a couch, also for four. A swimming pool compensates for the rather poor ocean beach. The oceanfront Banyan Tree Terrace Restaurant is open for three reasonably priced meals a day. On weekends, it's the local hot spot for dancing.

DOUBLES FOR $55 TO $85

HOTEL MOLOKAI, Kamehameha Hwy. (P.O. Box 546), Kaunakakai, Molokai, HI 96748. Tel. 808/553-5347, or toll free 800/423-MOLO. Fax 808/ 531-4004. 51 rms.

$ Rates: $55–$115 single or double. Each additional person $10 extra. CB, DC, MC, V. **Parking:** Free.

The Hotel Molokai is a modern Polynesian village that maintains the aura of the gracious past. The separate, three-unit cottages have lovely rustic bedrooms with baths and all the modern-day comforts, including wall-to-wall carpeting and very comfortable basket swings out on the furnished lanais. There's a swimming pool (the waterfront here is a shallow lagoon behind the reef, popular for snorkeling but not good for swimming), a comfortable open lobby, and the Holo Kai Restaurant, where the "family" (staff) entertains their guests at dinner. Although this is an oceanfront hotel, the waves break a quarter mile out, leaving the lagoon tranquil and still, with only a lapping sound to lull you to sleep. (*Note:* Light sleepers may want to ask for a room away from the restaurant area.) The cheapest rooms are standard, superior rooms are on the garden floor, and deluxe rooms on the upper floor have a lanai or face the ocean. Only deluxe rooms can accommodate one or two extra people.

MOLOKAI SHORES, Kamehameha Hwy. (P.O. Box 1037), Kaunakakai, Molokai, HI 96748. Tel. 808/553-5954, or toll free 800/535-0085. 102 apts. TV

$ Rates: Apr–Dec 22, $85 one-bedroom apt; $115 two-bedroom apt. Dec 23–Mar, $95 one-bedroom apt; $125 two-bedroom apt. Discounted weekly and "no frills" rates available during low season. DC, MC, V. **Parking:** Free.

Molokai Shores is located just a mile from Kaunakakai, between the Pau Hana Inn and the Hotel Molokai. The three-story, oceanfront apartment building has very pleasant units, all with ocean views, well-equipped kitchens, and private lanais overlooking tropical lawns. The one-bedroom units accommodate up to four people; the two-bedroom units, which have two baths, accommodate up to six. Picnic tables, barbecue units, and a putting green make outdoor life pleasant, and there's a pool for swimming (the beach is not particularly good here).

Reservations: Marc Resorts Hawaii, 2155 Kalakaua Ave., Honolulu, HI 96810 or the toll-free number above.

EASTERN SHORE

The eastern shore of Molokai is a newer area for tourist development and it's quite lovely, a good base of operations for ocean swimming and excursions to Halawa Valley.

DOUBLES FOR $50 TO $66

KAMALO PLANTATION, HC 01, Box 300, Kaunakakai, Molokai, HI 96748. Tel. and fax 808/558-8236. 1 cottage, 2 rms in main house.
$ Rates (including breakfast): $75 cottage; $55 and $65 room. No credit cards. **Parking:** Free.
On the eastern end of Molokai, across from Father Damien's historic St. Joseph's Church, lies Kamalo Plantation, a 5-acre lime orchid and tropical garden at the foot of Mt. Kamakou. Hosts Akikio and Glenn Foster, who have lived and sailed in the island for years, offer two rooms in the main house with a shared bath, or a private country cottage with fully equipped kitchen, and a pleasant deck for lounging and watching the birds. Breakfast items are provided in the cottage; breakfast—including fresh tropical fruits and freshly baked bread—is served in the main house. Kamalo Plantation is a logical stopover on the way to or from Halawa Valley.

WAVECREST RESORT, HC 01, Box 541, Kaunakakai, Molokai, HI 96748. Tel. 808/558-8101, or toll free 800/367-2980. Fax 808/558-8206. 126 units. TV
$ Rates: $75–$95 garden/oceanview units; $85–$105 oceanfront units. Minimum stay 3 nights. Each additional person $5 extra. MC, V. **Parking:** Free.
Nestled against the eastern Molokai mountains, Wavecrest Resort has tennis courts, a swimming pool, and all the amenities necessary for at-home resort living. There's not much of a beach, but it's good for fishing. The one-bedroom apartments, recently upgraded, are all smartly furnished with fully equipped kitchens. From your private lanai, you can see Maui and Lanai across the water. You can pick up picnic supplies, groceries, and drinks at the store here.

DOUBLES FOR $85

HONOMUNI HOUSE, HC 01, Box 700, Kaunakakai, Molokai, HI 96748. Tel. 808/558-8383. 1 cottage. TV
$ Rates: $85 double per night, $510 per week. Each additional adult $10 extra; each additional child, $5. No credit cards. **Parking:** Free.
Surrounded by lush green tropical forest, Honomuni House is a country cottage that can accommodate up to four adults. There's a private enclosed sleeping area, a large living/dining area with color TV and a sofa bed, a nicely equipped kitchen, a full bath plus a hot-water shower outdoors, and a covered lanai. Hosts Jan and Keaho, who are educators in marine biology and Pacific studies, are available to answer questions, and they invite guests to enjoy the papayas and other tropical fruits fresh from their garden.

KALUAKOI RESORT

Molokai's loveliest resort area is on the western shore, about 15 miles from the airport, next to the glorious, 3-mile stretch of almost-deserted Kepuhi Beach. Kaluakoi Resort, a 6,700-acre development, includes the luxurious Kaluakoi Hotel & Golf Club, along with three very pleasant condominium colonies.

DOUBLES FOR $85 TO $105

COLONY'S KALUAKOI HOTEL & GOLF CLUB, P.O. Box 1977, Kepuhi Beach, Molokai, HI 96770. Tel. 808/552-2555, or toll free 800/777-1700. Fax 808/552-2821. 174 rms. TV TEL
$ Rates: $90–$110 double; $135–$140 studio; $155–$165 one-bedroom suite for four; $185 one-bedroom oceanview cottage for four. Each additional person $15 extra. AE, CB, DC, DISC, JCB, MC, V. **Parking:** Free.

⭐ This is the grandest of Molokai hotels. The rooms, which are in two-story buildings overlooking ocean or golf course, are beautifully appointed (some have high-beamed ceilings) with wood, rattan furnishings, and vibrant Polynesian colors. All rooms have refrigerators. Besides the beautiful ocean (often not safe for swimming), there's a handsome free-form swimming pool, bar service at poolside, the championship 18-hole Kaluakoi Golf Course (a golfing friend tells us that at night deer come out to drink at the water hazards), four lighted tennis courts and a tennis pro, and all sorts of shops and services. Ohia Lodge provides excellent meals. As we sipped a cool drink by the pool recently, one of the guests smiled at us and said: "I think I'll never leave." We could understand that feeling; it's like being at one of the beach hotels at Kaanapali on Maui, but with nothing else around. Inquire about golf packages.

KALUAKOI VILLAS, Kaluakoi Resort, P.O. Box 200, Maunaloa, Molokai, HI 96770. Tel. 808/552-2721, or toll free 800/525-1470. Fax 808/552-2201. 103 units. TV

$ Rates: $105–$135 studio; $135–$165 suite; $185 golf/ocean villa. AE, MC, V. **Parking:** Free.

Kaluakoi Villas is very luxurious and very lovely. All its units have private lanais affording some degree of ocean view, and are richly decorated in the island mode with rattan furnishings. They boast a refrigerator, a countertop range, microwave oven, cooking utensils, china, and glassware. The golf and ocean villas have a full range and a dishwasher. All the activities of Kaluakoi Resort—the restaurants, day-and-night tennis courts, and 18-hole championship golf course—are available to guests. On the property are a freshwater swimming pool and Jacuzzi. Special "Molokai Magic" packages are available.

KE NANI KAI, P.O. Box 126, Maunaloa, Molokai, HI 96770. Tel. 808/ 552-2761, or toll free 800/888-2791. Fax 808/552-0045. 120 apts. TV TEL

$ Rates: $105–$125 one-bedroom apt for up to four; $125–$150 two-bedroom apt for up to six. Crib $8 extra. Minimum stay 2 nights. AE, MC, V. **Parking:** Free.

There's an air of tranquility about Ke Nani Kai that makes you feel like you could stay for weeks and simply unwind, never missing civilization a bit. Located at the entrance to the Kaluakoi Hotel (actually, between the 8th and 17th fairways of the golf course), this is a superb condominium resort, with some 55 units available to the general public. The apartments, each with a view of garden or ocean, are handsomely furnished, with very large living rooms, bedrooms with sliding doors, lanais affording splendid views, superbly equipped kitchens, VCRs, and washers and dryers in every unit. On the grounds are an enormous swimming pool, a volleyball court, two horseshoe pits, two tennis courts, and a whirlpool spa; the beach is just a short walk away. Hanging flowers cover the trellises of the units. This is the most popular condo in the area for families because of the large pool and the large dining/barbecue facilities.

MOLOKAI BEACHFRONT CONDOS, P.O. Box 249, Hana, Maui, HI 96713. Tel. 808/248-7049 or 808/248-7365 or toll free 800/657-7723, fax 808/248-8240. 2 units. TV

$ Rates: May 2–Dec 19, $70 for two; Dec 20–May 1, $98 for two. Each additional person $10.

Here's a little Molokai secret: Blair Shurtleff and Tom Nunn, who run the superb Hana Plantation Houses in Maui (see "Where to Stay," in Chapter 14), also have two delightful second-story oceanfront units with perhaps the best views at the Kaluakoi Resort. These large studios with lanais have 20-foot-high ceilings and are custom-decorated in a modern Hawaiian motif, with Hawaiian quilts, color TV, VCR, a king-size bed in one unit and a queen-size bed in the other, both with sofa beds. One has a complete kitchen, the other a mini-kitchen. The studios can connect to house a group traveling together. Guests here have use of all the facilities of Colony's Kaluakoi Hotel & Golf Club (see above), including the free-form swimming pool, four lighted tennis courts, and the 18-hole Kaluakoi Golf Course (the

MOLOKAI

0 5 mi
   8 km

PACIFIC OCEAN

Halawa Beach Park
Cape Halawa
Molokōhoomiki Island
Waialua
Halawa Valley
Kikipua Point
Pukoo
Patilolo Channel
Pali Coast
Wailau Trail
Molokai Forest Reserve
Kamalo
Mokapo Is.
Kahiu Point
Kaunakakai
Kalaupapa National Historical Park
Kamehameha Hwy.
Kawela
Kamiloloa
Kalaupapa
Kualapuu
Kalobi Channel
Kalae
Hoolehua
Molokai Airport
Paualaia Point
Puu Limi St.
Kapele Ave.
Pali
Farrington Ave.
Moomomi Ave.
Maunaloa Rd.
Mokio Point
Ilio Point
Kepuhi Beach
Papohaku Beach
Wahilauhue
Maunaloa
Halena
Kolo
Laau Point
Hale o Lono
Kaiui Channel

Palaau State Park ⑤
Papohaku Beach ①
Phallic Rock ⑥
Purdy's All Natural Macadamia Nut Farm ③
Puu O Hoku Ranch ⑭
St. Joseph's Catholic Church ⑧

Halawa Valley ⑫
Kalaupapa Settlement ⑦
Mapulehu Glass House ⑪
Mapulehu Mango Grove ⑩
Meyer Sugar Mill ④
Moaula Falls ⑬
Molokai Ranch Wildlife Park ②
Our Lady of Sorrows Church ⑨

Molokai
HAWAII

Airport ✈

units are, in fact, on the first tee). When you call to make reservations, ask Blair or Tom to give you tips on safe, secret beaches unknown to most Molokai visitors; they may even be able to send you a map.

PANIOLO HALE, P.O. Box 190, Maunaloa, Molokai, HI 96770. Tel. 808/ 552-2731, or toll free 800/367-2984 (call collect from Canada and Hawaii). Fax 808/ 552-2280. 77 apts. TV TEL
$ Rates: $95–$135 studio for two; $115–$160 one-bedroom apt for up to four; $145 (garden view) and $195 (ocean view) two-bedroom apt for up to four. Fifth and sixth persons in two-bedroom apt $10 each. Minimum stay 3 nights. AE, MC, V. **Parking:** Free.

Next door to the Kaluakoi Hotel, on Kepuhi Beach, Paniolo Hale is adjacent to the golf course; in fact, one must cross the fairway to get to the beach. Wild deer and turkeys are frequently seen on the grounds. There is a swimming pool and a paddle-tennis court, and guests receive a reduced rate when golfing at Kaluakoi. The Kaluakoi Hotel also offers its four lighted tennis courts to Paniolo Hale guests for a nominal fee. This is a luxury condominium complex. The best buys are the one-bedroom units, which have two baths and sleep up to four; the two-bedroom units, also with two baths, sleep up to six. Hot tubs are available on the lanais of all two-bedroom units for an additional charge. There are also oceanview units. All the apartments have full kitchens, VCRs, and attractive island furnishings, and each unit has its own screened lanai (a touch of old Hawaii), which you walk right onto from your room, without going through a door. The nearest restaurant is at the Kaluakoi Hotel, about a block away along the sea wall, and the nearest grocery store is 7 miles away. We continue to receive good reports on this one. Inquire about room/ car packages or golf specials.

3. WHERE TO EAT

Molokai has only a smattering of restaurants, but you can eat well here.

KAUNAKAKAI

Let's start out on Ala Malama, the main street of Kaunakakai, where you can mingle with the locals for some down-home good food, at old-fashioned low prices.

MEALS FOR LESS THAN $10

KANEMITSU BAKERY AND COFFEE SHOP, Ala Malama St. Tel. 553-5855.
Cuisine: LOCAL.
$ Prices: Plate lunches $4.50–$5. No credit cards.
Open: Wed–Mon 5:30am–1pm.

When was the last time you had a hot dog for $1.50, a hamburger for $1.56, and club sandwiches that go up to all of $3.85? These are the kinds of prices that have made this place a local standby for years. There are reasonable breakfasts, too. Kanemitsu is primarily a bakery, and a famous one, known for its flavorful Molokai French bread (a great gift item, by the way, for friends in Honolulu). They also bake excellent cheese and onion breads, and all breads and pastries are baked without preservatives. This humble bakery actually turns out up to 1,500 loaves a day. The bakery is open until 6:30pm.

OUTPOST NATURAL FOODS, 70 Makaena Place. Tel. 553-3377.
Cuisine: VEGETARIAN.
$ Prices: Sandwiches $2.50–$4.50; main courses $4.25–$5.49. No credit cards.
Open: Sun–Fri 10am–3pm.

Outpost Natural Foods, at the west end of town (next to the civic center) is a natural-foods store and juice bar/restaurant with picnic tables outside that's quite pleasant for a light and healthful meal. In addition to freshly squeezed orange juice, carrot juice, and the like, they offer vegetarian sandwiches for $3.95 (the whole-grain bread is baked fresh in Hawaii; the organic lettuce and greens are grown on Molokai), salads, burritos, and a low-fat hot lunch every day. The hot lunch has to be one of the best buys in town, since it always includes a main course, such as a pasta or tofu dish or stir-fry veggies, plus salad, for $4.50. Everything is available for takeout. Very popular here is the soft-serve machine, which dispenses a luscious all-fruit ice cream.

OVIEDO'S LUNCH COUNTER, Ala Malama St. Tel. 553-5014.
Cuisine: FILIPINO.
$ Prices: Lunch or dinner plates $7.50. No credit cards.
Open: Daily 10am–6:30pm.
To sample Filipino food, sit down for lunch or get a take-out plate at Oviedo's, a simple, home-style restaurant on the main street in Kaunakakai. Oviedo's features such Filipino specialties as pork adobo (adobo is a kind of stew), tripe stew, pigs' feet, sweet-and-sour spareribs, and roast pork.

RABANG'S RESTAURANT, Ala Malama St. Tel. 553-5841.
Cuisine: FILIPINO.
$ Prices: Main dishes around $6. No credit cards.
Open: Breakfast daily 6–10am; lunch and dinner daily 10am–9pm.
Take-out Filipino food is also available at Rabang's, next door to Molokai Fish and Dive. One can get a good rice and adobo dish, a different one every weekday, for about $6, served "from 10am until food *pau*," according to the owner, Mrs. Rabang. Hawaiian food is served every Friday. She also suggests that you try the Filipino dessert called *halohalo*—ask her to explain what it is.

MEALS FOR LESS THAN $20

BANYAN TREE TERRACE, at the Pau Hana Inn. Tel. 553-5342.
Cuisine: AMERICAN. **Reservations:** Recommended at dinner.
$ Prices: Appetizers $4.50–$6.50; main courses $10.75–$17.50.
Open: Breakfast Mon–Fri 6–11am, Sat–Sun 6am–1pm; lunch daily 11am–2pm; dinner daily 6–9pm.
Whether you're seated indoors in a big, rustic dining room with a tremendous fireplace or outdoors under the enormous, spreading Bengalese banyan tree out on the beach (the scene of nighttime entertainment), you're going to find a meal here very pleasant. The banyan, also known as an East Indian fig tree, has been standing sentinel over the ocean here for almost 100 years. Dinner is well priced, with such main dishes as shrimp tempura, barbecued beef short ribs, seafood platter, and top sirloin. Specialty of the house is prime rib, a 10-ounce cut for $16.95. The price includes soup and salad bar, hot vegetables, a choice of starch, and Molokai French bread. Lunch features daily specials at $5.25; with soup and salad bar, $7.25. And they have homemade pizza on Monday.

HOLO HOLO KAI, at the Hotel Molokai. Tel. 553-5347.
Cuisine: AMERICAN. **Reservations:** Recommended at dinner.
$ Prices: Appetizers $4.25–$5.95; main courses $8.95–$18.95. DC, MC, V.
Open: Breakfast daily 7–10am; lunch daily noon–2pm; dinner daily 6–9:30pm.
Hotel Molokai's dining room enjoys an excellent location right on the edge of the ocean and open to its charms. And the food is very good, too. Dinner is well priced, since all main dishes—such as huli huli chicken, prime rib, roast pork, New York steak, and mahimahi—are accompanied by soup and salad bar, vegetables of the day, a choice of steamed rice or mashed potatoes, and Molokai French bread. People rave about their hearty beef stew, a local favorite. Lunch features salads, sandwiches, and burgers, plus hot main dishes like beef stew, fried chicken, and mahimahi, for $5.75 to $6.25. Local musicians entertain at dinner.
Here's a special tip for those of you who are going to be in Molokai for only 1

day. Take an early-morning flight out from Honolulu or Maui, and go directly from the airport to the Hotel Molokai. Treat yourself to one of their famous breakfast specialties—banana french toast (which is Molokai bread in a banana-egg batter) or our personal favorite, papaya pancakes topped with crushed macadamia nuts. Both of these treats are under $5. Now, after your coffee, you're set for a day of exploring Molokai.

MAUNALOA & KALUAKOI RESORT

Maunaloa, the sleepy little plantation town on the western shore, boasts one of the island's most enjoyable budget eateries and its most glamorous luxury restaurant.

MEALS FOR LESS THAN $15

JO JO'S CAFE, Maunaloa. Tel. 552-2803.
   Cuisine: AMERICAN. **Reservations:** Not accepted.
$ Prices: Appetizers $4; main courses $9–$15. MC, V.
   Open: Lunch Mon–Tues and Thurs–Sat noon–2pm; dinner Mon–Tues and Thurs–Sat 5–7:45pm.

For a budget meal in this otherwise pricey area, dine with the islanders at homey Jo Jo's Café, not far from the Kaluakoi Resort; it's in Maunaloa, in the tavern section of the old Pooh's Restaurant. All main courses are served with vegetables and a scoop of rice. Jo Jo's specialty is fish; they serve several different fish dishes every day, either frozen or fresh, whenever it's available, so you may be lucky enough to get ahi, mahimahi, ono, aku, or opakapaka. Fresh fish with curry sauce is also very popular, as are the shrimp or chicken or lamb curries (a different one each day) that the owner, who hails from India, whips up in authentic style (he suggests you call a day in advance for a curry request). Korean ribs is another specialty. Lunch is a good buy, with main dishes around $5 to $8. Hamburgers, surf-burgers (a fresh fish sandwich), and salad are available, too. For dessert, try one of their fresh island homemade toppings on an ice cream sundae, or have a piece of pie—all for $2.50. Beer and wine are available. Management suggests you come early for dinner, since they take no reservations, and sometimes it's standing room only. Funky and fun.

WORTH THE EXTRA MONEY

OHIA LODGE, at Colony's Kalaukoi Hotel & Golf Club, Kaluakoi Resort. Tel. 552-2555.
   Cuisine: AMERICAN. **Reservations:** Recommended.
$ Prices: Appetizers $3.75–$5.50; main courses $10.50–$18.95. AE, CB, DC, DISC, JCB, MC, V.
   Open: Breakfast daily 6:30–10:30am; dinner daily 6–9pm.

Many of the local people feel that the glamorous Ohia Lodge, a South Seas spot overlooking the water, is the best dining room on Molokai. There's music for dancing here every night. Reasonably priced island specialties include chicken stir-fry tossed with fresh vegetables and Indonesian spices at $10.50 and the orange-glazed almond duck at $11.95. There's a tasty seafood medley and pasta—mahimahi, shrimp, clams, scallops, and calimari—at $14.50, and a group of beef and lamb selections from $16.95 to $18.95. All entrées come with a choice of rice pilaf, white rice, or gratin potato, and fresh sautéed vegetables. Appetizers include Cajun angel-hair pasta and hibachi beef. Portuguese bean soup is a local favorite. For dessert, a key lime torte is just about perfect. Molokai Country Breakfasts are hearty ways to start the morning.

KUALAPUU

You'll probably be driving through the little town of Kualapuu at some point in your stay on Molokai, perhaps to visit the Kalaupapa Lookout, or the Mule Barn, or the Meyer Sugar Mill. Here's where you should eat.

MEALS FOR LESS THAN $10

KUALAPUU COOK HOUSE. Tel. 567-6185.

Cuisine: AMERICAN. **Reservations:** Not required.

$ Prices: Main courses $6.50–$15. No credit cards.

Open: Mon–Fri 7am–8pm, Sat 7am–4pm.

Look for Kualapuu Cook House, a welcome addition to restaurant-poor Molokai, as you head up Kalae Road and then take a left turn onto Farrington Road. It actually was a cook house, back in the days of the Del Monte Plantation. Owner Nanette Yamashita has turned it into a quality eating place, with seating either indoors or on an outdoor patio. Fresh foods are featured at reasonable prices, like $4.50 to $6.50 for a complete breakfast—eggs, meat, rice, and pancakes or french toast. At lunch, nothing on the regular à la carte menu is over $7.50; local favorites are served, as well as gourmet burgers, made from hamburger ground fresh every day. A daily plate special gives you a full meal for $5.50 to $7.50, including main course, salad, and rice. At dinner, chicken stir-fry ($7.50) and local-style teriyaki chicken or pork ($8.50) are huge favorites; so are the New York steak and shrimp and the fresh fish of the day when available. And even if you don't eat a full meal here, you'll have to come by for one of Nanette's homemade pies; she bakes 8 to 10 different pies every day, using fresh local fruits when in season: Molokai lime, guava cream cheese, and passion-orange cream cheese are all delectable. Nanette's chocolate macadamia-nut pie is world-famous; she ships whole pies overnight to New York or London or wherever people demand them. (Cost is $12.50; other whole pies begin at $6.50; a single slice is $2 to $3.)

4. WHAT TO SEE & DO

Sightseeing on Molokai requires a bit more determination than it does on the other islands. A visit to the island's most spectacular scenic spot, Halawa Valley, involves some rugged driving and an hour's hike. To reach Kalaupapa, the major point of interest on the island, you have to fly, hike, or ride a mule down a steep *pali*. But if you're willing to put up with a few obstacles, you might find sightseeing on Molokai among the most rewarding adventures of your trip to Hawaii. Sightseeing tours and local guides are especially helpful on this island. For things to do, consult the *Molokai News* or the *Molokai Dispatch*, both free at local stores.

SUGGESTED ITINERARIES

IF YOU HAVE 1 DAY Make the trip to Kalaupapa Settlement—either by plane or by muleback.

IF YOU HAVE 2 DAYS Spend your first day at the settlement. On the second day, drive to Halawa Valley and swim at the base of Moaula Falls. Or take a hike with Discover Molokai Guided Nature Tours (see below).

IF YOU HAVE 3 DAYS Use your first 2 days as suggested above. For your third day, book a safari at the Molokai Ranch Wildlife Park in the morning, and spend the afternoon at the plantation town of Maunaloa shopping for arts and crafts.

IF YOU HAVE 5 DAYS OR MORE After spending 3 days as suggested above, if you have more time, take the Molokai Wagon Ride, or visit Palaau State Park, Purdy's Nut Farm, and the Meyer Sugar Mill.

SPECIAL EVENTS

Molokai is usually a relatively quiet place, but there are two events that draw the crowds from all over the islands. The first is the famous **Molokai-to-Oahu Canoe Race,** the most important event in the sport of outrigger canoeing. Participants paddle from Molokai to Fort DeRussy Beach in Honolulu in traditional Hawaiian canoes, going over some very rough water. The women's race takes place in September, the men's race in October.

An expression of the island's commitment to the preservation of authentic Hawaiian culture, the annual **Molokai Ka Hula Piko**—A Celebration of the Birth of Hula on Molokai—is now in its fifth season. Local hula halaus (schools) are joined by leading vocal and instrumental groups. There are also demonstrations of traditional Hawaiian crafts, and food booths selling Molokai specialties. According to legend, Molokai was the birthplace of the hula and it was here, at Ka'ana, that the goddess Laka learned to dance from her sister Kapo, and then spread the art of hula throughout the Hawaiian islands. For information on exact dates, usually in May, call Molokai Visitors Association (tel. toll free 800/800-6367 in the U.S. and Canada).

A third event, always held in January, is the annual **Molokai Makahiki,** a traditional Hawaiian "time of peace" celebration. In addition to a competition in Hawaiian games and a skin-diving tournament, the festivities feature several of Hawaii's most popular music groups. The event is held at Kaunakakai Park and the Manae Canoe Club; there is no admission charge.

THE TOP ATTRACTIONS

HALAWA VALLEY & MOAULA FALLS

For a beautiful day on Molokai, get up early, have your hotel pack you a picnic box lunch (or put one together from the supermarkets in town), hop into your car, and head for Halawa Valley. The trip is just about 25 miles from Kaunakakai along Kamehameha IV Highway, but it will probably take you 2 hours to get there, since the last part of the driving is rough going. This is Molokai's southeastern coast, dotted with ancient heiaus, old fish ponds (some of which are used for scientific studies), and many coastal churches built by Father Damien and others. You won't be able to see the heiaus unless you get permission to go on private property, but you can stop in at **St. Joseph's Catholic Church** in Kamalo. The church, with a lovely statue of Father Damien beside it, was designed and built by Father Damien, who was a skilled carpenter. A little farther is Father Damien's **Our Lady of Sorrows Church,** where you'll see a statue of Damien in a pavilion near the church. As you drive by the Kamalo mountains, watch for rainbows and double rainbows—they're not uncommon here. When you get to Mapulehu at mile 15, you may want to make a stop at the **Mapulehu Glass House,** an enormous greenhouse which is the largest glass house in Hawaii. This tropical-flower farm offers free tours at 10:30am Monday to Friday, as well as bouquets of flowers to take with you or ship home. Just east of the 15-mile marker on the mountain side of the highway are a driveway and a sign. It's open Monday to Friday from 7am to noon, or by appointment (call or fax 808/558-8160). At mile 15½, look on the right for a sign to the **Mapulehu Mango Grove,** the largest mango patch in Hawaii, with more than 2,000 mango trees of many varieties, and a coconut grove. You can stop to pick up some tropical fruits here, as well as mango and other fruit juices at a little stand fronting the ocean. (Snorkeling tours and equipment are also available.) You'll begin seeing sandy beach again in the Pukoo area. There are many secluded little beach coves along this coast, but they're unmarked and difficult to find, so it's best to ask local people for directions. From the beach here, you can see Maui, only 9 miles across the water.

About 20 miles out, past Waialua, the broad country road begins to narrow, and soon you're on a one-lane road where the sharp turns force the car to practically creep along while the scenery becomes more beautiful every minute. Then you begin to climb up through the ranchlands of **Puu O Hoku Ranch,** from which a narrow road takes you into the Halawa Valley. We hope you do make it into the valley, because this is a veritable tropical paradise, a remote Shangri-la that one may find difficult to believe still exists. Once a populous area, it was swept by a tidal wave in 1946 and largely deserted. You can explore the valley (a few people still live here), have a swim in the bay, or make a roughly 2-hour hike to the valley's most spectacular point, **Moaula Falls.** (You'll probably need mosquito repellent.) The rewards are a picnic or a swim at the base of a waterfall that plunges relentlessly down from dizzying heights. The water is cold and delicious, but according to Molokai legend, it's only safe to swim here if the ti leaf that you throw in floats. If it sinks, you'll have to make your own decision. Remember to make this trip in the morning, since, after a hike back to your car, you'll have to drive another 2 hours or so back to your hotel.

READERS RECOMMEND

Moaula Falls. "*To get to Moaula Falls, go up the dirt road in front of the small green church on the left side of the river as you face the falls. The small parking lot across from the church is the best place to leave your car. As you go up the road, past several houses, stay on the main road until it ends and a trail begins. Go up the trail about 100 yards to a row of rocks across the trail. Turn to the right here and follow the trail down to the stream. You have to cross both forks of the stream here. When you get to the other side, find a trail that goes up the hill perpendicular to the stream. (When you cross a mud flat, you'll see an orange mark on a tree. Here, go right through some heavy grass. When you leave the grass, look behind you as you go up the trail. If you see some more orange marks, you know you're on the trail.) Shortly you come upon a major trail that has been blocked off to the right. Turn left and now follow the white plastic pipe and white arrows marking the trail to the falls for a spectacular hike and view of the falls and the pool below.*"—Mr. and Mrs. Wayne Ditmer, Mott, N. Dak. [*Authors' Note:* Watch for homemade signs directing you to the home of a valley resident who will watch your car for a small fee. Soft drinks and a restroom are available.]

KALAUPAPA SETTLEMENT

Many people who have never been to Hawaii have heard about Father Damien of Belgium and what he did for the destitute lepers on Molokai over a century ago. Volunteering for the post, he set up a church on the isolated peninsula where victims of the dread disease were unceremoniously dumped and left to die. Damien ministered to their physical and spiritual needs and made Kalaupapa livable for them for 16 years, until he himself succumbed to the disease. In 1989, on the 100th anniversary of his death, a Damien Centennial Year was declared by both the state of Hawaii and the government of Belgium. Representatives of the Roman Catholic church, government officials, and the faithful from throughout the world gathered on Molokai to honor him. On May 15, 1994, Pope John Paul II declared him to have attained the blessedness of heaven and he has since been known as Blessed Damien; his title is "Damien of Molokai, Servant of Humanity." He performed his labors here at Kalaupapa, where a center for the treatment of leprosy—now called Hansen's disease—is still operating. Fewer than 100 patients and former patients are still at Kalaupapa, and to visit their island home is a moving experience. It is not, however, a trip we advise everyone to make. It's not for those who get nervous just thinking about diseases (although leprosy has been arrested by modern drugs and is presumably not contagious), and it's definitely not for the idly curious. The residents of Kalaupapa do not wish to be regarded as a tourist attraction. Getting to their beautiful but tragically isolated home takes a bit of doing, and the emotions the trip can raise have been overwhelming to more than one visitor. We can promise only one thing: It is a special kind of experience, one not easily forgotten.

There are a couple of ways to get to Kalaupapa. Unfortunately, as we went to press, the famous **Molokai Mule Ride** had been discontinued, but hopefully, it will be back by the time you read this. Check with Destination Molokai at 553-3876 or toll-free 800/800-6367 to find out its current status. It's an unforgettable experience as the mule descends a spectacular, steep switchback trail 1,600 feet below the towering cliffs at Kalae into Kalaupapa. You are met at the peninsula, given a tour and a picnic lunch, and then returned to the trail for the ride to the top at 2pm. Cost should be around $120.

It's more economical, of course, to hike down the trail; it's a scenic 3¹/8-mile cliff walk that should take about 1¹/2 hours. But be advised that the hike both down and up the *pali* is arduous; many people hike down and fly back. (Make plane reservations in advance if that's what you want to do.) Be sure you call Richard Marks at Damien Molokai Tours (see below) to meet you for a ground tour of the settlement. You are not allowed in on your own.

There is, of course, an easier way to get to Kalaupapa, the one we personally favor, and that's by air both ways. Call Richard Marks's **Damien Molokai Tours** at 567-6171 (the only tour service operated by former patients, who know Kalaupapa from the inside out), and they will arrange for you to fly in from upper Molokai via Aloha Island Air for $42 round-trip (best time to call is between 7 and 9am and 5 and 8pm). Keep in mind that you cannot walk past the gate at the top of the cliff trail or around the peninsula without a permit, according to Health Department rules (Damien Molokai Tours will handle all permits). Minors under 16 are not allowed at Kalaupapa. Bring some lunch, as there are no stores or restaurants open to visitors at Kalaupapa. You may bring cameras and binoculars. Advance reservations for the tour are a must: Call 567-6171, or write Damien Molokai Tours, P.O. Box 1, Kalaupapa, Molokai, HI 96742. The full, 4-hour grand tour costs $30 per person; a special 8-hour tour is $40.

What you'll see on the tour—the early settlement of Kalawo where St. Philomena Church, built by Father Damien, still stands; the cemetery where he was buried before his remains were returned to Belgium; the grave of Mother Marianne (also a candidate for canonization by the Roman Catholic church); Siloama Church; and a glorious view of Molokai's towering mountains—is just the beginning. All the tour guides are ex-patients, people who can give you a look at Kalaupapa off the record. It's a magnificent sight—a testimony to the patients who took barren lands and turned them into Eden, and a testimony to the medical pioneers and missionaries who preserved so many lives. Kalaupapa is a paradoxical place; it seems domestic, with many cozy little houses where people garden and watch TV, but it is incredibly silent, partly because there are no children. Only a small minority of the residents live with their spouses; when pregnancy occurs, the expectant mother is usually flown from the island for the delivery, where she either remains to raise her child without its father or chooses to return to Kalaupapa alone.

Under legislation passed by Congress, Kalaupapa—now known as Kalaupapa National Historic Park—will be left as it is until the last of the residents has died. The remaining residents, most in their 50s and 60s, like to joke about themselves as an endangered species. But all of them now live here by choice. What was once a veritable prison has now become a sanctuary.

The newest addition to the tour is a visit to the Kalaupapa Visitors Center, which has an excellent bookshop dealing with the history of Kalaupapa and Molokai. If you're lucky, your tour might include Richard Marks's own collection of Kalaupapa memorabilia, including antique bottles and clocks.

Note: On a recent visit to Kalaupapa, flying direct from Honolulu, we met two women who were making the exact same trip that we were; however, because they had booked the entire trip as a tour via a well-known tour operator, their cost was almost double ours. Make your own air arrangements and contact Damien Tours as we suggested: No need to waste your money.

READERS RECOMMEND

Discover Molokai Guided Nature Tours. "*Both of us are appreciative of two residents and their willingness to share this island with visitors. Ken and Gayle*

Gibson are transplants from the mainland who have made Molokai their home. Ken has begun an informal, friendly service which includes guided nature walks and farm visits. We had the wonderful opportunity of going on many hikes with them—to a quiet beach (we were the only ones there!), and the Halawa Valley Waterfalls Hike. Ken's knowledge of the history of the Polynesians and the vegetation, and his friendliness and eagerness to share this island's rich history, added another dimension to our trip. His tours are highly personalized, for only two to four people. Prices range from $50 to $75 per person. Gayle provided delectable sandwiches and home-grown vegetables for our lunches."—Tom and Debbie Farynowski, Columbus, Ohio. [Authors' Note: Ken Gibson can be reached at Discover Molokai, P.O. Box 1066, Kaunakakai, Molokai, HI 96748 (tel. 808/553-5619 collect). His standard tours include an Old Hawaii excursion (ancient religious sites, a sacrificial temple from the 1300s, a walk to the top of Halawa Falls), a kayak trip (including snorkeling) for both beginners and experienced paddlers, the Kalaupapa Trail Hike and Father Damien Tour (a hike down the pali onto Kalaupapa Peninsula, a tour of the settlement, and an optional plane trip out), and the Secret Beach Hike-Snorkel (a hike or Jeep ride to a magnificent secluded beach, then a snorkel to see a shipwreck). All trips include Molokai history, Hawaiian lifestyle information, geology, and plant life. Hikes are moderate (easy walks can be arranged) and suitable for all ages. Ken also offers custom tours for individuals and small groups, which might include kayaking, outrigger canoes, Hawaiian fishing, and overnight excursions. Recommended!]

MORE ATTRACTIONS

A TRIP THROUGH PALAAU STATE PARK TO KUALAPUU

Even if you don't get to Kalaupapa itself, you should pay a visit to the Kalaupapa Overlook in Palaau State Park. It's an easy trip on very good roads, about 10 miles from Kaunakakai on Hi. 460. After you make your right on Hi. 470 and begin to climb to Upper Molokai, the air becomes fragrant with eucalyptus and pine. Park your car at **Palaau State Park**, a well-maintained and popular camping and picnicking spot for local residents. A short walk through towering cypress and pine and suddenly you're high, high up, looking down immense cliffs to the Kalaupapa Peninsula below. From the overlook, you can see the world's tallest sea cliffs, 3,300 feet high at Umilehi Point. A series of six informative plaques tell the Kalaupapa story, but official descriptions seem superfluous. Just standing here, gazing down at the peninsula below, you are caught up in some of the tremendous sorrow of those who lived their lives of exile at Kalaupapa.

There is another trail, this one a bit longer (and steeply uphill some of the way), that leads to the **Phallic Rock**. According to legend, barren women who made offerings to the rock and spent the night here would then become capable of bearing children. Supposedly, an unfaithful husband of one of the minor goddesses was transformed into this rock and his mana still remains here.

While you're pondering this story (wrongdoers were often turned into stone in Hawaiian mythology), get back into your car and drive down the hill. Two miles below the overlook, on Hi. 470, you may want to pay a visit to the **R. W. Meyer Sugar Mill** (tel. 567-6436), an authentic restoration of an 1878 sugar mill now in operating condition after almost a century of neglect. The only surviving 19th-century sugar mill in Hawaii, it is listed on the National Register of Historic Places. Local volunteer labor spent several years on its restoration. The original machinery, including the mule-drive cane crusher, is still in operating condition. Photos and memorabilia of the mill's original owner, and of his Hawaiian-born wife, Kalama Waha, provide a glimpse into early Molokai history. The mill is open Monday through Saturday from 10am to 2pm, for guided and self-guided tours. Admission is $2.50 for adults, $1 for children ages 5 to 18, under 5 free.

Continue down the road now to the little town of Kualapuu, where, now that the Del Monte pineapple plantation has been phased out, diversified agriculture is a growing industry (Molokai is now the state's leading producer of watermelon). Here you'll also find the pleasant little **Kualapuu Cook House Restaurant** (see "Where to Eat," above, in this chapter). Turn left on Puupeelua Avenue and you'll be back on the airport road.

If you're in the mood for traveling, continue west on Hi. 460 past the airport; you'll be on Maunaloa Road, which goes 10 miles to the old Dole pineapple village at Maunaloa, about 1,300 feet high, with its unusual little crafts shops (see "Shopping," below).

PURDY'S NUT FARM

We don't know of any other macadamia farm in Hawaii where either the owner or his mother will greet you personally and take you on a tour of the orchards. But Purdy's All Natural Macadamia Nut Farm is different. Tuddie Purdy and his mother guide you through the only working macadamia-nut grove on the island, and not only do they tell you all you ever wanted to know about macadamia nuts, but they also show you a variety of Hawaiian fruits and flowers. Most fun of all, you get to crack some macadamia nuts and try them raw. Then you'll be given some fruit and macadamia-blossom honey to taste, plus samples of their Ono Toasted Macadamia Nuts, which are remarkably light, surprisingly non-oily, and absolutely delicious. You can buy them on the spot (they'll also give you the recipe), as well as raw macadamia nuts out of the shell, and the honey. The farm is located on 1½ acres in Hoolehua Hawaiian Homesteads and is open weekdays from 9:30am to 3:30pm, weekends from 10am to 3:30pm, or by appointment (tel. 567-6601 daytime, 567-6495 in the evening). It's not far from the airport, but it's best to ask them for driving directions. If you're in Molokai for a 1-day trip, this could be a fun way to start the day. Admission is free.

MOLOKAI RANCH WILDLIFE PARK

Yes, you can go on a safari of sorts on Molokai, a camera safari, to see about 80 African and Asian animals that live on the grounds of this 350-acre natural wildlife preserve. The dry terrain of western Molokai is similar to that of the expansive savannah lands of East Africa. The animals, which include giraffe, zebra, Barbary sheep, Indian Blackbuck, eland, oryx, greater kudu, sika deer, East African crowned crane, rhea, and wild turkey, thrive here. Tour guides lead visitors on a 90-minute photographic and educational adventure in an air-conditioned van. After the tour of the park, visitors adjourn to the picnic area where they can feed the curious and friendly giraffes and other animals that gather around to see the funny people. A light refreshment is served. Cost of the tour is $35 for adults, $20 for children under 18 and $5 for children under 5; arrangements can be made at the Kaluakoi Hotel Travel Desk, or by calling 552-2555 or 552-2767. Readers really like this one.

WAGON RIDES

This Molokai adventure is very popular. Your horse-drawn (or horse- and mule-drawn) wagon stops first at the Ili Ili O Pae Heiau, one of Hawaii's largest and best-preserved temples, built in the 13th century, where a guide explains the historical background; then it's back down the trail to the Mapulehu Mango Grove, the largest mango grove in the world. Then it's on to the beach for a Molokai-style barbecue and a fabulous party, complete with Hawaiian music, traditional Hawaiian net throwing, fishing, coconut husking, and many surprises. Guests are invited to try their hand at all the activities. Cost is $37 for adults, $18.50 for children 5 to 12, free for those under 5. Guided horseback rides are also available. For reservations, call Larry Helm at **Molokai Wagon Ride** (tel. 567-6773 from 6 to 8am and after 6pm, or 558-8380, the wagon-ride site, from 9:30am to 12:30pm, daily).

FROMMER'S FAVORITE MOLOKAI EXPERIENCES

Taking the Molokai Wagon Ride Admire a 13th-century heiau (temple), then party on the beach with Hawaiian music, traditional Hawaiian net throwing, and lots of fun and games.

Driving to Maunaloa Town Visit Jonathan Socher's Big Wind Kite Factory and his Plantation Gallery, and see the work of local artists and craftspeople in one of the most laid-back shopping scenes in the islands.

Flying into Kalaupapa Peninsula Tour the settlement for the treatment of Hansen's disease with ex-patient Richard Marks of Damien Molokai Tours, the "mayor of Kalaupapa."

SPORTS & RECREATION

SAILING, SNORKELING, & FISHING

Satans Doll, a 42-foot sloop, takes passengers on 2-hour sunset sails ($30), half-day sailing and whale-watching trips ($40), and sailings to Lanai for a full day of swimming, snorkeling, and whale watching in season ($75). There's a minimum of four passengers per trip. Share parties are put together. Contact Molokai Charters, P.O. Box 1207, Kaunakakai, Molokai, HI 96748 (tel. 808/553-5852).

Those interested in sports fishing have two good choices: **Shon-a-lei Sports & Marine** (tel. 808/553-5242) for excursions aboard the *Shon-a-lei II,* and **Capt. Joe Reich,** of the *Alyce C.,* at 553-5242 or 800/998-FISH.

BIKES, KAYAKS & RENTALS

Mike and Maria Holmes, the couple who run **Fun Hogs** at the Kaluakoi Hotel & Golf Club's Beach Activities Center, define a fun hog as a "two-legged mammal with a healthy appetite for the enjoyment of outdoor recreational activities that are in harmony with nature." To that end, they offer guided mountain-bike and kayak excursions, as well as rentals of kayaks, bikes, bodyboards, and fishing and camping equipment. Their office doubles as a gallery shop: note the Hawaiian woodwork and art, along with the T-shirts, hats, bicycling and camping equipment, and kayaks.

GOLF

Golfing is pleasantly inexpensive at Molokai's newest course, the recently reconstructed **Ironwood Hills Golf Club**, on Kalae Highway (tel. 567-6000). It's just $8 for 9 holes, $12 for 18. All this and power golf carts, too. For information on Molokai's most spectacular course, the championship 6,618-yard **Kaluakoi Golf Course** at Maunaloa, phone 552-2739.

HORSEBACK RIDES

Horseback riding can be arranged on 53,000-acre **Molokai Ranch**. Contact Molokai Ranch Ltd., P.O. Box 259, Maunaloa, HI 96770 (tel. 808/552-2767, fax 808/552-2908). Reservations are required.

HUNTING & FISHING

Walter Naki's **Ma'a Hawaii Action Adventures** (tel. 558-8184) is for adventurous souls. It offers various combinations of hunting (axis deer, wild boar, Spanish goats), bow hunting, rifle hunting, spear fishing, skin diving, reef trolling, and snorkeling.

THE BEACH

Papohaku Beach, on Molokai's western shore, part of Kaluakoi Resort, is the largest white-sand beach in the Hawaiian Islands, almost 3 miles long. It's the ideal spot for a beach picnic, but not—alas—for ocean swimming, since the water here is usually quite rough in winter, and there may be undertows and rip tides in summer. There's access at Papohaku Beach Park, which has picnic grounds, barbecues, showers, a pavilion with restrooms and changing area, plus parking. Camping is also available.

SHOPPING

Molokai is perhaps the only place in the islands that is *not* heaven for shopping buffs. There is so little available here that many locals go off-island (they'll fly to Honolulu on one of the little commuter planes) to do their shopping—even their grocery shopping! The local supermarkets, grocery shops, and liquor stores on Ala Malama, the main street of Kaunakakai, a general store here and there in the country, and a handful of craft shops just about do it.

KAUNAKAKAI

MOLOKAI DRUGS, Ala Malama St. Tel. 553-5790.
For the best selection of books on the island, try Molokai Drugs, on Ala Malama. They have a particularly good selection of Hawaiiana, and also sell local crafts and gift items in addition to the usual drugs and sundries.

MOLOKAI FISH AND DIVE, Ala Malama St. Tel. 553-5926.
To learn where the fish are biting, and to get fishing, diving, snorkeling, and camping gear, plus boogie boards and golf balls, this is the place to go. But they're more than just a sporting-goods store; they have the largest collection of Molokai souvenirs on the island, including a huge selection of T-shirts, designed and printed for them and sold exclusively here. Next door is their boutique for island fashions, called Molokai Island Creations.

MOLOKAI ISLAND CREATIONS, Ala Malama St. Tel. 553-5926.
This friendly boutique has Hawaiian-made swimwear, muumuus, and children's clothing at surprisingly affordable prices, plus a unique collection of jewelry, including sea opal, coral, and sterling silver. They also have a good selection of books on Hawaii, cards, and much more. There's plenty to catch your eye here.

MOLOKAI WINES 'N' SPIRITS UNLIMITED. Tel. 553-5009.
You can shop late, until 10pm Sunday through Thursday, 10:30pm Friday and Saturday, at Molokai Wines.

OUTPOST NATURAL FOODS, 70 Makaena Place. Tel. 553-3377.
To stock up on organic local produce—papayas, bananas, avocados, sprouts, etc.—try Outpost Natural Foods (next door to the Civic Center), which sells the usual health-food fare plus other items at the lowest possible prices. They also have an excellent lunch bar (see "Where to Eat," above, in this chapter). Pick up a fruit smoothie, a sandwich, a burrito, or some Molokai Taro Chips, a local delicacy.

IMAMURA'S, Ala Malama St. Tel. 553-5615.
Like an old-fashioned general store, Imamura's has a little bit of everything, and is lots of fun to poke around in.

THE MOLOKAI GIFT SHOP, in the Hotel Molokai, Kaunakakai. Tel. 553-5801.
Hotel shopping is limited on Molokai, but do stop in at the Molokai Gift Shop,

where proprietors Jim and Maria Watanabe offer clothing, T-shirts, books, sundries, soft drinks, and crafts by Molokai artists. We've found some nice things here, and prices are usually lower than on the other islands.

MAUNALOA

Our favorite Molokai shopping is out in Maunaloa (not far from the Kaluakoi Resort). Once a thriving plantation town, Maunaloa has been declining since Dole closed shop in 1975; however, young artisans are seeking it out and showing their wares here. We should tell you at the start that this is the most laid-back "shopping area" we've ever come across, with only one street, and with shops staying open more or less as inspiration moves the owners, who often seem to be out fishing or surfing or visiting Honolulu.

BIG WIND KITE FACTORY. Tel. 552-2364.

Owner Jonathan Socher is always on hand and happy to greet visitors. He and his wife, Daphne, not only create beautiful, high-flying kites (which are sold in many island shops), but they even offer free flying lessons with modern 100-m.p.h. "aerobatic kites." It's also fun to take a tour of their minifactory, where they demonstrate the techniques of kite making. Their most popular items are pineapple windsox and minikites at $14.95, and rainbow-spinning windsox at $15 to $35. Their Hula Girl Kite—"She Dances in the Sky"—is also very popular at $35. They now make their own two-string rainbow stunt kites, from $35. Their son Zachariah, 11 years old, is also designing kites, and his gecko with sunglasses and shark with sunglasses are two of their most popular designs. They now have 28-foot-long dragon-tail kites, plus butterflies, dinosaurs, and sun-moon-star kites, all with rainbow tails. The Sochers recently participated in Bali's International Kite Festival and have a spectacular collection of Indonesian and Malaysian kites on display.

PLANTATION GALLERY. Tel. 552-2364.

Jonathan Socher's Plantation Gallery, which shows the work of dozens of island artisans, is adjacent to the kite factory. There are handsome wood bowls and boxes by local artists Bob Moore and Rune Pederson. Woodcarver Bill Decker travels around the world, sending back tribal art such as New Guinea shields and Borneo blowguns. Unless the surf is up, you'll probably find Butch Tabano and his deerhorn jewelry, hair combs (from $12), and cribbage boards (around $40) made from the axis deer of Molokai. There's pottery sculpture by Chuck Moore from $20, and Hawaiian pillowcase quilts by Ginger Lavoie at $25. Several local artists do hand-painted shirts at $25, long-sleeved tops at $42. On our last visit, Jonathan proudly showed us his new collection of personally chosen imports from Bali and Southeast Asia: He calls this the "Bali Hale Gift Shop." It's full of delightful surprises, such as colorful wooden bird mobiles and birds of paradise stalks, at $25 and $35; batik pillow covers; pareaus; wonderful Balinese masks called "guardians" or "crib angels"; magnificent batik quilts for $250; and colorful wooden bird and fish earrings at $9.50, and you get another pair free. Note, too, the collection of books (more than 300 titles), cards, and prints by leading island artists. The gallery/shop is decorated with orchid plants and there's a garden outside. For lovers of the unusual, this is a must stop. Open Monday through Saturday 8:30am to 5pm, Sunday 10am to 2pm.

QUILTING LESSONS

If you're interested in quilting, get in touch with **Ginger Lavoie**—Fiber Artist of Molokai, Star Route, Box 359, Kaunakakai, Molokai, HI 96748 (tel. 808/558-8227), one of the finest quilters in the islands. She gives classes on Hawaiian quilting Friday and Saturday mornings at the Kaluakoi Resort. Complimentary lessons are offered with the purchase of one of her kits. She also has available for sale original quilt designs, fully basted quilts, and easy kits, as well as silk-screened T-shirts. Lectures and slide shows are also available.

EVENING ENTERTAINMENT

Nightlife on Molokai, as we travelers know it, is almost all in the major hotels, and it's largely impromptu. It all depends on when local people feel like doing things (people here are not apt to let work interfere with their lives!). Every Friday and Saturday night, the **Pau Hana Inn** becomes the town's "hot spot." There's music and dancing under the 100-year-old spreading banyan tree, right at the ocean's edge. Locals turn out to kick up their heels. You'll be asked to dance. Music is provided by F.I.B.R.E., Friendly Isle Band Rhythmic Experience—and it is!

Live entertainment is also featured Thursday, Friday, and Saturday nights at the **Hotel Molokai.** The K'Kai Trio provides the entertainment, mostly Hawaiian and country-and-western music, over at the **Ohia Lodge** of the Kaluakoi Hotel. Check the local papers for news of special events, maybe even a luau at one of the hotels.

APPENDIX

A. HAWAIIAN VOCABULARY

There are just 12 letters in the Hawaiian alphabet: five vowels—*a, e, i, o, u*—and seven consonants—*h, k, l, m, n, p, w*. Every syllable ends in a vowel, every vowel is pronounced, and the accent is almost always on the next-to-the-last syllable, as it is in Spanish. Consonants receive their English sounds, but vowels get the Latin pronunciation: *a* as in farm, *e* as in they, *i* as in machine, *o* as in cold, and *u* as in tutor. Note, also, that when *w* comes before the final vowel in a word, it is given the "v" sound, as in Hawaii. Purists say Ha-VYE-ee for Hawaii, but most people call it Ha-WYE-ee.

The following glossary will give you an idea of what the Hawaiian language sounds like. No one, of course, expects you to go around spouting phrases like "Holo ehia keia?" to ask what time it is, but a familiarity with the most important words is what distinguishes the kamaainas from the milihinis.

WORDS

ENGLISH	HAWAIIAN	PRONUNCIATION
Rough lava	Aa	AH-ah
Eat	Ai	EYE
Friends as in "Aloha, aikane"	Aikane	eye-KAH-nay
Smart	Akamai	ah-kah-MY
Road, as in Ala Moana (Ocean Road)	Ala	AL-lah
Noblemen, the old royalty of Hawaii	Alii	ah-LEE-ee
Welcome, farewell, love	Aloha	ah-LOW-hah
No	Aole	Ah-OH-lay
Alas! woe!	Auwe	OW-way
In the direction of Ewa, a town on Oahu ("Drive Ewa 5 blocks.")	Ewa	EH-vah
The pandanus tree, the leaves of which are used for weaving	Hala	HAH-lah
Pineapple	Halakahiki	hah-lah-kah-HEE-kee
School (as in hula halau)	Halau	HAH-lau
House	Hale	HAH-lay
To work	Hana	HAH-nah
Caucasian, white	Haole	HOW-lay
White man	Haolekane	how-lay-KAY-nay
White woman	Haolewahine	how-lay-wah-HEE-nay
A small part, a half	Hapa	HAH-pah
Pregnant (originally "to carry")	Hapai	hah-PIE
Happiness	Hauoli	how-OH-lee
Ancient temple	Heiau	hey-EE-au

ENGLISH	HAWAIIAN	PRONUNCIATION
To sleep	**Haimoe**	hee-ah-MOW-ay
To go, to walk	**Hele**	HEY-lay
Ashamed	**Hilahila**	hee-lah-HEE-lah
To run	**Holo**	HO-low
To have fun, to relax	**Holoholo**	ho-low-HO-low
Formal dress with train	**Holoku**	ho-low-KOO
A cross between a holoku and a muumuu (long and without a train)	**Holomuu**	ho-low-MOO
To kiss, as in "Honikaua wikiwiki!" (Kiss me quick!)	**Honi**	HO-nee
To flatter	**Hoomalimali**	ho-oh-mah-lee-MAH-lee
Angry	**Huhu**	HOO-hoo
A club, an assembly	**Hui**	HOO-ee
A fishing festival	**Hukilau**	hoo-KEE-lau
A dance, to dance	**Hula**	HOO-lah
Underground oven lined with hot rocks, used for cooking the luau pig	**Imu**	EE-moo
Sweetheart	**Ipo**	EE-po
The	**Ka**	KAH
Ancient (as in hula kahiko)	**Kahiko**	kah-HEE-ko
Sea	**Kai**	KYE
Money	**Kala**	KAH-lah
To bake underground	**Kalua**	kah-loo-AH
Old-timer	**Kamaaina**	kah-mah-EYE-nah
Man	**Kane**	KAH-nay
Tapa, a bark cloth	**Kapa**	KAH-pah
Crooked	**Kapakahi**	kah-pah-KAH-hee
Forbidden, keep out	**Kapu**	kah-POO
Food	**Kaukau**	kow-KOW
Child	**Keiki**	kay-KEE
Help, cooperation	**Kokua**	ko-KOO-ah
South	**Kona**	KO-nah
Sun, light, day	**La**	LAH
Porch	**Lanai**	lah-NYE
Heaven, sky	**Lani**	lah-NEE
Leaf of the hala or pandanus tree	**Lauhala**	lau-HAH-lah
Garland	**Lei**	LAY
Stupid	**Lolo**	low-LOW
Massage	**Lomilomi**	low-mee-LOW-mee
Feast	**Luau**	LOO-au
Thank you	**Mahalo**	mah-HAH-low
Good, fine	**Ma'i ka'i**	mah-ee-KAH-ee
Toward the sea	**Makai**	mah-KEY
Stranger, newcomer	**Malihini**	mah-lee-HEE-nee
Free	**Manawahi**	mah-nah-WAH-hee
Toward the mountains	**Mauka**	MAU-kah
Song, chant	**Mele**	MAY-lay
A mysterious race who inhabited the islands before the Polynesians (mythology claims they were pygmies)	**Menehune**	may-nay-HOO-nay

ENGLISH	HAWAIIAN	PRONUNCIATION
Loose dress (Hawaiian version of missionaries "Mother Hubbards")	Muumuu	moo-oo-MOO-oo
Lovely	Nani	NAN-nee
Coconut	Niu	nee-OO
Big, as in "mahalo nui" ("big thanks")	Nui	NOO-ee
Sweet taste, delicious	Ono	OH-no
Belly	Opu	OH-poo
Stubborn	Paakiki	pah-ah-KEE-kee
Precipice	Pali	PAH-lee
Hawaiian cowboy	Panilolo	pah-nee-OH-low
Finished	Pau	POW
Trouble	Pilikia	pee-lee-KEE-ah
Crushed taro root	Poi	POY
Hole	Puka	POO-kah
Couch	Punee	poo-NAY-ay
Hors d'oeuvre	Pupu	POO-poo
Crazy	Pupule	poo-POO-lay
Rain	Ua	OO-ah
Speech, mouth	Waha	wah-HAH
Female, woman, girl	Wahine	wah-HEE-nay
Fresh water	Wai	WHY
To hurry	Wikiwiki	wee-kee-wee-kee

PHRASES

ENGLISH	HAWAIIAN	PRONUNCIATION
Be careful	Malama pono	mah-LAH-mah PO-no
Bottoms up	Okole maluna	oh-KO-lay mah-LOO-nah
Come and eat	Hele mai ai	HEY-lay MY-EYE
Come here	Hele mai	HEY-lay MY
Come in and sit down	Komo mai e noho iho	ko-MO my ay NO-ho EE-ho
For love	No ke aloha	no kay ah-LOW-hah
Go away	Hele aku oe	HEY-lay AH-koo OH-ay
Good evening	Aloha ahiahi	ah-LOW-hah AH-hee-AH-hee
Good morning	Aloha kakahiaka	ah-LOW-hah kah-kah-hee-AH-kah
Greatest love to you	Aloha nui oe	ah-LOW-hah NOO-ee OH-ay
Happy Birthday	Hauoli la hanau	hah-OO-oh-lee-lah hoh-NAH-oo
Happy New Year	Hauoli Makahiki Hou	hah-OO-oh-lee man-kah-HEE-kee HO-oo
Here's to your happiness	Hauoli Maoli oe	hah-OO-oh-lee mah-OH-lee OH-ay
How are you?	Pehea oe?	pay-HAY-ah OH-ay
I am fine	Ma'i ka'i	mah-EE-kah-EE
I am sorry	Ua kaumaha au	OO-ah cow-mah-HAH OW
I have enough	Ua lawa au	OO-ah LAH-wah OW
I love you	Aloha wauia oe	ah-LOW-hah vow-EE-ah OH-ay

ENGLISH	HAWAIIAN	PRONUNCIATION
It isn't so	**Aole pela**	**ah-OH-lay PAY-lah**
Let's go	**E hele kaua**	**au-HEY-lay COW-ah**
Many thanks	**Mahalo nui loa**	**mah-HAH-low NOO-ee LOW-ah**
Merry Christmas	**Mele Kalikimaka**	**may-LAY kah-lee-kee-MAH-kah**
Much love	**Aloha nui loa**	**ah-LOW-hah NOO-ee-LOW-ah**
No trouble	**Aole pilikia**	**ah-OH-lay pee-lee-KEE-ah**
What is your name?	**Owai kau inoa?**	**OH-why KAH-oo ee-NO-ah**

PIDGIN

Despite the efforts of educators to stamp it out, pidgin, that code language of the islands, continues its not-so-underground existence. The Chinese developed it in their first contacts with English-speaking people, but you'll hear it spoken today by all the racial groups, from haoles to Hawaiians. Beachboys, cab drivers, university students, a few who don't know better and a lot who do, all occasionally descend into pidgin. Although its subtleties are unintelligible to the newcomer (that's part of the idea), you'll be able to pick up a few words: *wasamala, wasetime, lesgo, da kine.*

You'll hear all kinds of theories about the indestructibility of pidgin. Some sociological types feel its a subtle form of rebellion by the dispossessed Hawaiian, not unlike the jargon of mainland African Americans. The psychological types call it more of an adolescent code, a desire for teenagers to have their own language. Others say it's just plain bad English. Take your choice, whatever *da kine* reason, pidgin is "in" in Hawaii.

Note: After you've been in the islands a bit, get yourself a copy of Peppo's *Pidgin to Da Max.* It's one of Hawaii's most popular humor-cartoon books (over 130,000 copies in print), available in any bookstore, and an absolute hoot! We reprint the "Word of Caution to the Non-local: If you don't already speak pidgin, you might need some help from local friends to understand this book. Remember: *Pidgin to Da Max* is not a tourist guide to pidgin. So don't try to speak after reading this book. You'll just get into trouble." We agree. Don't try to speak pidgin. Just read the book—maybe on the plane trip back home—and try to keep yourself from rolling in the aisles. It's $4.95, published by Bess Press, Honolulu. There is, in fact, a whole series of Peppo's Pidgin books now; one is *Fax to Da Max*, which lists "everything you never knew you wanted to know about Hawaii," plus lots of "useless fax," too. Another howler.

B. GLOSSARY OF ISLAND FOODS

Chinese, Japanese, Korean, Filipino, and Portuguese influences are all reflected on island menus—as well as American and Hawaiian, of course. Here are some helpful definitions:

Adobo Filipino dish made with pork or chicken.

Bento Japanese box lunch.

Chicken luau Chicken cooked with coconut milk and taro or spinach leaves.

Crackseed Chinese confection that's a cross between preserved fruit and candy. Kids go crazy for these sticky sweets.

Guava Slightly tart tree fruit made into jams and juice. They grow wild on the mountainsides, and are under cultivation on Kauai, at Guava Kai Plantation.

Haupia Coconut pudding, the traditional luau dessert.

Kimchee Korea's contribution, pickled cabbage and red-hot peppers.

Kona coffee The best! Grown on the Big Island in many small family plantations.

Laulau Ti leaves stuffed with pork, salt fish, bananas, sweet potatoes, and taro shoots, then steamed.

Lilikoi Passion fruit (named after the passion of Christ). A tart fruit that's turned into wonderful juice or sherbet.

Macadamia nuts Delicious nuts grown on plantations on the Big Island. Chocolate-covered macadamias are one of the most delicious gifts you can bring the folks back home.

Malasadas Deep-fried Portuguese doughnuts, served hot and sugared. They have no holes.

Manapuas Steamed dumplings filled with pork, meat, or bean paste. The Chinese call them dim sum.

Maui onions Mild, sweet onions, sometimes known as Kula onions.

Papayas Grown on the Big Island, available everywhere: one of the favorite breakfast fruits in the islands. Highly nutritious and rich in vitamin C.

Pipikaula Jerked beef.

Poha Wild berry, used in jams.

Poi Staple starch of the Hawaiian diet, made from cooked and mashed taro root. Very digestible and nutritious. To the ancient Hawaiians, the poi bowl had an almost spiritual significance.

Portuguese bean soup Savory soup made from Portuguese sausages, beans, and vegetables, a veritable meal in a bowl.

Portuguese sweet bread Very soft bread made with eggs, wonderful in french toast.

Saimin Most popular soup in the islands, a thin noodle broth topped with bits of fish, shrimp, chicken, or pork, and vegetables.

Sashimi Raw fish, a favorite Japanese delicacy.

Sushi Vinegared rice topped with either raw fish or other toppings, and then rolled in seaweed, another great Japanese delicacy.

Now Save Money on All Your Travels by Joining
FROMMER'S ™ TRAVEL BOOK CLUB
The World's Best Travel Guides at Membership Prices

FROMMER'S TRAVEL BOOK CLUB is your ticket to successful travel! Open up a world of travel information and simplify your travel planning when you join ranks with thousands of value-conscious travelers who are members of the FROMMER'S TRAVEL BOOK CLUB. Join today and you'll be entitled to all the privileges that come from belonging to the club that offers you travel guides for less to more than 100 destinations worldwide. Annual membership is only $25 (U.S.) or $35 (Canada and foreign).

The Advantages of Membership

1. Your choice of *three* free FROMMER'S TRAVEL GUIDES (any *two* FROMMER'S COMPREHENSIVE GUIDES, FROMMER'S $-A-DAY GUIDES, FROMMER'S WALKING TOURS *or* FROMMER'S FAMILY GUIDES—plus *one* FROMMER'S CITY GUIDE, FROMMER'S CITY $-A-DAY GUIDE *or* FROMMER'S TOURING GUIDE).
2. Your own subscription to **TRIPS AND TRAVEL** quarterly newsletter.
3. You're entitled to a **30% discount** on your order of any additional books offered by FROMMER'S TRAVEL BOOK CLUB.
4. You're offered (at a small additional fee) our **Domestic Trip-Routing Kits.**

Our quarterly newsletter **TRIPS AND TRAVEL** offers practical information on the best buys in travel, the "hottest" vacation spots, the latest travel trends, world-class events and much, much more.

Our **Domestic Trip-Routing Kits** are available for any North American destination. We'll send you a detailed map highlighting the best route to take to your destination—you can request direct or scenic routes.

Here's all you have to do to join:

Send in your membership fee of $25 ($35 Canada and foreign) with your name and address on the form below along with your selections as part of your membership package to **FROMMER'S TRAVEL BOOK CLUB, P.O. Box 473, Mt. Morris, IL 61054-0473.** Remember to check off your *three* free books.

If you would like to order additional books, please select the books you would like and send a check for the total amount (please add sales tax in the states noted below), plus $2 per book for shipping and handling ($3 per book for foreign orders) to:

FROMMER'S TRAVEL BOOK CLUB
P.O. Box 473
Mt. Morris, IL 61054-0473
(815) 734-1104

[ ] **YES.** I want to take advantage of this opportunity to join FROMMER'S TRAVEL BOOK CLUB.
[ ] **My check is enclosed.** Dollar amount enclosed_____ *
          (all payments in U.S. funds only)

Name_____
Address_____
City_____ State_____ Zip_____
          All orders must be prepaid.

To ensure that all orders are processed efficiently, please apply sales tax in the following areas: CA, CT, FL, IL, NJ, NY, TN, WA and CANADA.

*With membership, shipping and handling will be paid by FROMMER'S TRAVEL BOOK CLUB for the three free books you select as part of your membership. Please add $2 per book for shipping and handling for any additional books purchased ($3 per book for foreign orders).

Allow 4–6 weeks for delivery. Prices of books, membership fee, and publication dates are subject to change without notice. Prices are subject to acceptance and availability.

Please Send Me the Books Checked Below:

FROMMER'S COMPREHENSIVE GUIDES
(Guides listing facilities from budget to deluxe,
with emphasis on the medium-priced)

	Retail Price	Code		Retail Price	Code
☐ Acapulco/Ixtapa/Taxco 1993–94	$15.00	C120	☐ Japan 1994–95 (Avail. 3/94)	$19.00	C144
☐ Alaska 1994–95	$17.00	C131	☐ Morocco 1992–93	$18.00	C021
☐ Arizona 1993–94	$18.00	C101	☐ Nepal 1994–95	$18.00	C126
☐ Australia 1992–93	$18.00	C002	☐ New England 1994 (Avail. 1/94)	$16.00	C137
☐ Austria 1993–94	$19.00	C119	☐ New Mexico 1993–94	$15.00	C117
☐ Bahamas 1994–95	$17.00	C121	☐ New York State 1994–95	$19.00	C133
☐ Belgium/Holland/ Luxembourg 1993–94	$18.00	C106	☐ Northwest 1994–95 (Avail. 2/94)	$17.00	C140
☐ Bermuda 1994–95	$15.00	C122	☐ Portugal 1994–95 (Avail. 2/94)	$17.00	C141
☐ Brazil 1993–94	$20.00	C111	☐ Puerto Rico 1993–94	$15.00	C103
☐ California 1994	$15.00	C134	☐ Puerto Vallarta/Manzanillo/ Guadalajara 1994–95 (Avail. 1/94)	$14.00	C028
☐ Canada 1994–95 (Avail. 4/94)	$19.00	C145			
☐ Caribbean 1994	$18.00	C123	☐ Scandinavia 1993–94	$19.00	C135
☐ Carolinas/Georgia 1994–95	$17.00	C128	☐ Scotland 1994–95 (Avail. 4/94)	$17.00	C146
☐ Colorado 1994–95 (Avail. 3/94)	$16.00	C143	☐ South Pacific 1994–95 (Avail. 1/94)	$20.00	C138
☐ Cruises 1993–94	$19.00	C107	☐ Spain 1993–94	$19.00	C115
☐ Delaware/Maryland 1994–95 (Avail. 1/94)	$15.00	C136	☐ Switzerland/Liechtenstein 1994–95 (Avail. 1/94)	$19.00	C139
☐ England 1994	$18.00	C129	☐ Thailand 1992–93	$20.00	C033
☐ Florida 1994	$18.00	C124	☐ U.S.A. 1993–94	$19.00	C116
☐ France 1994–95	$20.00	C132	☐ Virgin Islands 1994–95	$13.00	C127
☐ Germany 1994	$19.00	C125	☐ Virginia 1994–95 (Avail. 2/94)	$14.00	C142
☐ Italy 1994	$19.00	C130	☐ Yucatán 1993–94	$18.00	C110
☐ Jamaica/Barbados 1993–94	$15.00	C105			

FROMMER'S $-A-DAY GUIDES
(Guides to low-cost tourist accommodations and facilities)

	Retail Price	Code		Retail Price	Code
☐ Australia on $45 1993–94	$18.00	D102	☐ Israel on $45 1993–94	$18.00	D101
☐ Costa Rica/Guatemala/ Belize on $35 1993–94	$17.00	D108	☐ Mexico on $45 1994	$19.00	D116
☐ Eastern Europe on $30 1993–94	$18.00	D110	☐ New York on $70 1994–95 (Avail. 4/94)	$16.00	D120
☐ England on $60 1994	$18.00	D112	☐ New Zealand on $45 1993–94	$18.00	D103
☐ Europe on $50 1994	$19.00	D115	☐ Scotland/Wales on $50 1992–93	$18.00	D019
☐ Greece on $45 1993–94	$19.00	D100			
☐ Hawaii on $75 1994	$19.00	D113	☐ South America on $40 1993–94	$19.00	D109
☐ India on $40 1992–93	$20.00	D010	☐ Turkey on $40 1992–93	$22.00	D023
☐ Ireland on $45 1994–95 (Avail. 1/94)	$17.00	D117	☐ Washington, D.C. on $40 1994–95 (Avail. 2/94)	$17.00	D119

FROMMER'S CITY $-A-DAY GUIDES
(Pocket-size guides to low-cost tourist accommodations
and facilities)

	Retail Price	Code		Retail Price	Code
☐ Berlin on $40 1994–95	$12.00	D111	☐ Madrid on $50 1994–95 (Avail. 1/94)	$13.00	D118
☐ Copenhagen on $50 1992–93	$12.00	D003	☐ Paris on $50 1994–95	$12.00	D117
☐ London on $45 1994–95	$12.00	D114	☐ Stockholm on $50 1992–93	$13.00	D022

FROMMER'S WALKING TOURS

(With routes and detailed maps, these companion guides point out
the places and pleasures that make a city unique)

	Retail Price	Code		Retail Price	Code
☐ Berlin	$12.00	W100	☐ Paris	$12.00	W103
☐ London	$12.00	W101	☐ San Francisco	$12.00	W104
☐ New York	$12.00	W102	☐ Washington, D.C.	$12.00	W105

FROMMER'S TOURING GUIDES

(Color-illustrated guides that include walking tours, cultural and historic
sights, and practical information)

	Retail Price	Code		Retail Price	Code
☐ Amsterdam	$11.00	T001	☐ New York	$11.00	T008
☐ Barcelona	$14.00	T015	☐ Rome	$11.00	T010
☐ Brazil	$11.00	T003	☐ Scotland	$10.00	T011
☐ Florence	$ 9.00	T005	☐ Sicily	$15.00	T017
☐ Hong Kong/Singapore/			☐ Tokyo	$15.00	T016
Macau	$11.00	T006	☐ Turkey	$11.00	T013
☐ Kenya	$14.00	T018	☐ Venice	$ 9.00	T014
☐ London	$13.00	T007			

FROMMER'S FAMILY GUIDES

	Retail Price	Code		Retail Price	Code
☐ California with Kids	$18.00	F100	☐ San Francisco with Kids		
☐ Los Angeles with Kids			(Avail. 4/94)	$17.00	F104
(Avail. 4/94)	$17.00	F103	☐ Washington, D.C. with Kids		
☐ New York City with Kids			(Avail. 2/94)	$17.00	F102
(Avail. 2/94)	$18.00	F101			

FROMMER'S CITY GUIDES

(Pocket-size guides to sightseeing and tourist accommodations and
facilities in all price ranges)

	Retail Price	Code		Retail Price	Code
☐ Amsterdam 1993–94	$13.00	S110	☐ Montréal/Québec		
☐ Athens 1993–94	$13.00	S114	City 1993–94	$13.00	S125
☐ Atlanta 1993–94	$13.00	S112	☐ Nashville/Memphis		
☐ Atlantic City/Cape			1994–95 (Avail. 4/94)	$13.00	S141
May 1993–94	$13.00	S130	☐ New Orleans 1993–94	$13.00	S103
☐ Bangkok 1992–93	$13.00	S005	☐ New York 1994 (Avail.		
☐ Barcelona/Majorca/Minorca/			1/94)	$13.00	S138
Ibiza 1993–94	$13.00	S115	☐ Orlando 1994	$13.00	S135
☐ Berlin 1993–94	$13.00	S116	☐ Paris 1993–94	$13.00	S109
☐ Boston 1993–94	$13.00	S117	☐ Philadelphia 1993–94	$13.00	S113
☐ Budapest 1994–95 (Avail.			☐ San Diego 1993–94	$13.00	S107
2/94)	$13.00	S139	☐ San Francisco 1994	$13.00	S133
☐ Chicago 1993–94	$13.00	S122	☐ Santa Fe/Taos/		
☐ Denver/Boulder/Colorado			Albuquerque 1993–94	$13.00	S108
Springs 1993–94	$13.00	S131	☐ Seattle/Portland 1994–95	$13.00	S137
☐ Dublin 1993–94	$13.00	S128	☐ St. Louis/Kansas		
☐ Hong Kong 1994–95			City 1993–94	$13.00	S127
(Avail. 4/94)	$13.00	S140	☐ Sydney 1993–94	$13.00	S129
☐ Honolulu/Oahu 1994	$13.00	S134	☐ Tampa/St.		
☐ Las Vegas 1993–94	$13.00	S121	Petersburg 1993–94	$13.00	S105
☐ London 1994	$13.00	S132	☐ Tokyo 1992–93	$13.00	S039
☐ Los Angeles 1993–94	$13.00	S123	☐ Toronto 1993–94	$13.00	S126
☐ Madrid/Costa del			☐ Vancouver/Victoria 1994–		
Sol 1993–94	$13.00	S124	95 (Avail. 1/94)	$13.00	S142
☐ Miami 1993–94	$13.00	S118	☐ Washington, D.C. 1994		
☐ Minneapolis/St.			(Avail. 1/94)	$13.00	S136
Paul 1993–94	$13.00	S119			

SPECIAL EDITIONS

	Retail Price	Code		Retail Price	Code
☐ Bed & Breakfast Southwest	$16.00	P100	☐ Caribbean Hideaways	$16.00	P103
☐ Bed & Breakfast Great American Cities (Avail. 1/94)	$16.00	P104	☐ National Park Guide 1994 (avail. 3/94)	$16.00	P105
			☐ Where to Stay U.S.A.	$15.00	P102

Please note: if the availability of a book is several months away, we may have back issues of guides to that particular destination. Call customer service at (815) 734-1104.